THE ENGLISH AND SCOTTISH
POPULAR BALLADS

THE

ENGLISH AND SCOTTISH

POPULAR BALLADS

EDITED BY

FRANCIS JAMES CHILD

IN FIVE VOLUMES

VOLUME III

DOVER PUBLICATIONS, INC.
MINEOLA, NEW YORK

Bibliographical Note

This Dover edition, first published in 1965 and republished in 2003, is an unabridged republication of the works first published by Houghton, Mifflin and Company as follows:

- Vol. I—Part I, 1882; Part II, 1884
- Vol. II—Part III, 1885; Part IV, 1886
- Vol. III—Part V, 1888; Part VI, 1889
- Vol. IV—Part VII, 1890; Part VIII, 1892
- Vol. V—Part IX, 1894; Part X, 1898

Volume V also contains, as an appendix to Part X, an essay by Walter Morris Hart entitled "Professor Child and the Ballad," reprinted from Vol. XXI, No. 4 [New Series Vol. XIV, No. 4] of *Publications of the Modern Language Association of America,* 1906.

Library of Congress Cataloging-in-Publication Data

The English and Scottish popular ballads / edited by Francis James Child.
    p. cm.
   ISBN 0-486-43145-2 (pbk. : v.1) — ISBN 0-486-43146-0 (pbk. : v.2) — ISBN 0-486-43147-9 (pbk. : v.3) — ISBN 0-486-43148-7 (pbk. : v.4) — ISBN 0-486-43149-5 (pbk. : v.5)
    1. Ballads, English—England—Texts. 2. Ballads, Scots—Scotland—Texts. I. Child, Francis James, 1825–1896.

PR1181.E47 2003
821'.04408—dc21

2003053052

Manufactured in the United States of America
Dover Publications, Inc., 31 East 2nd Street, Mineola, N.Y. 11501

ADVERTISEMENT TO PART V

NUMBERS 114–155

Rev. Professor Skeat has done me the great service of collating Wynken de Worde's text of The Gest of Robin Hood, the manuscript of Robin Hood and the Monk and of Robin Hood and the Potter, and all the Robin Hood broadsides in the Pepys collection. Mr Mac-math has collated the fragments of the earlier copy of The Gest which are preserved in the Advocates' Library, and, as always, has been most ready to respond to every call for aid. I would also gratefully acknowledge assistance received from Mr W. Aldis Wright, of Trinity College, Cambridge; the Rev. Edmund Venables, Precentor of Lincoln; Dr Furnivall; and, in America, from Mr W. W. Newell, Miss Perine and Mrs Dulany.

F. J. C.

February, 1888.

ADVERTISEMENT TO PART VI

NUMBERS 156–188

MR MACMATH has helped me in many ways in the preparation of this Sixth Part, and, as before, has been prodigal of time and pains. I am under particular obligations to Mr ROBERT BRUCE ARMSTRONG, of Edinburgh, for his communications concerning the ballad-folk of the Scottish border, and to Dr WILHELM WOLLNER, of the University of Leipsic, and Mr GEORGE LYMAN KITTREDGE, my colleague in Harvard College, for contributions (indicated by the initials of their names) which will be found in the Additions and Corrections. Dr WOLLNER will continue his services. Mr JOHN KARŁOWICZ, of Warsaw, purposes to review in 'Wisła' all the English ballads which have Polish affinities, and Professor ALEXANDER VESSELOFSKY has allowed me to hope for his assistance; so that there is a gratifying prospect that the points of contact between the English and the Slavic popular ballads will in the end be amply brought out. Thanks are due and are proffered, for favors of various kinds, to Lieutenant-Colonel LUMSDEN, of London, Lieutenant-Colonel PRIDEAUX, of Calcutta, Professor SKEAT, Miss ISABEL FLORENCE HAPGOOD, Professor VINOGRADOF, of Moscow, Professor GEORGE STEPHENS, Mr AXEL OLRIK, of Copenhagen (to whom the completion of SVEND GRUNDTVIG's great work has been entrusted), Mr JAMES BARCLAY MURDOCH, of Glasgow, Dr F. J. FURNIVALL, Professor C. R. LANMAN, Mr P. Z. ROUND. and Mr W. W. NEWELL.

F. J. C.

JULY, 1889.

CONTENTS OF VOLUME III

JOHNIE COCK

A. Percy Papers, Miss Fisher's MS., No 5, 1780.

B. 'Johnny Cock,' Pieces of Ancient Poetry from Un-published Manuscripts and Scarce Books, Bristol, 1814, [John Fry], p. 53.

C. 'Johnny Cock,' Pieces of Ancient Poetry, etc., p. 51.

D. 'Johnie of Cockerslee,' Kinloch's annotated copy of his Ancient Scottish Ballads, p. 38 *bis*.

E. 'Johnie o Cocklesmuir,' Kinloch MSS, VII, 29; Kinloch's Ancient Scottish Ballads, p. 36.

F. 'Johnie of Breadislee,' Scott's Minstrelsy, I, 59, 1802.

G. 'Johnnie Brad,' Harris MS., fol. 25.

H. 'Johnnie o Cocklesmuir,' Buchan's MSS, I, 82; Dixon, Scottish Traditional Versions of Ancient Ballads, p. 77, Percy Society, vol. xvii.

I. 'Johnie of Braidisbank,' Motherwell's Minstrelsy, p. 23.

J. Chambers, Scottish Ballads, p. 181.

K. Finlay's Scottish Ballads, I, xxxi: one stanza.

L. Harris MS., fol. 25 b: one stanza.

M. Froude, Thomas Carlyle, II, 335, New York, 1882, supplemented by Mrs Aitken : one stanza.

THE first notice in print of this precious specimen of the unspoiled traditional ballad is in Ritson's Scotish Song, 1794, I, xxxvi, note 25: the Rev. Mr Boyd, the translator of Dante, had a faint recollection of three ballads, one of which was called 'Johny Cox.' Before this, 1780, a lady of Carlisle had sent a copy to Doctor Percy, **A.** Scott, 1802, was the first to publish the ballad, selecting "the stanzas of greatest merit" from several copies which were in his hands. John Fry gave two valuable fragments, **C, B** (which he did not separate), in his Pieces of Ancient Poetry, 1814, from a manuscript "appearing to be the text-book of some illiterate drummer." * I have been able to add only three versions to those which were already before the world, **A, D, G**; and of these **D** is in part the same as **E**, previously printed by Kinloch.

Pinkerton, Select Scotish Ballads, II, xxxix, 1783, has preserved a stanza, which he assigns to a supposititious ballad of 'Bertram the Archer:' †

    ' My trusty bow of the tough yew,
      That I in London bought,
    And silken strings, if ye prove true,
      That my true-love has wrought.'

This stanza agrees with **J** 6, and with **A** 18, **H** 19 in part, and is very likely to belong here; but it might be a movable passage, or commonplace.

All the versions are in accord as to the primary points of the story. A gallant young fellow, who pays no regard to the game-laws, goes out, despite his mother's entreaties, to ding the dun deer down. He kills a deer, and feasts himself and his dogs so freely on it that

---

* This manuscript, which Fry bought in Glasgow in 1810, contained several other ballads, "but written so corruptly as to be of little or no authority." It did not occur to Fry that the illiteracy of the drummer gave his ballads the best of authority. I have done what I could to recover the manuscript, but in vain, though I had the kindest assistance in Bristol from the Rev. J. Percivall, Mr Francis Fry, and Mr J. F. Nicholls.

† See Motherwell's apt remarks, Minstrelsy, p. 1.

they all fall asleep. An old palmer, a silly auld, stane-auld carl, observes him, and carries word to seven foresters [fifteen B, three (?) C]. They beset Johnie and wound him; he kills all but one, and leaves that one, badly hurt, to carry tidings of the rest. Johnie sends a bird to his mother to bid her fetch him away, F 19, 20, cf. B 13; a bird warns his mother that Johnie tarries long, H 21 (one of Buchan's parrots). The *boy* in A 20, 21 is evidently a corruption of *bird*. Information is given the mother in a different way in L. B-G must be adjudged to be incomplete; I-M are mere fragments. H has a false and silly conclusion, 22–24, in imitation of Robin Hood and of Adam Bell. Mrs Harris had heard another version besides G (of which she gives only one stanza, L), in which " Johnie is slain and thrown owre a milk-white steed; news is sent to Johnie's mother, who flies to her son." It is the one forester who is not quite killed that is thrown over his steed to carry tidings home, F 18, G 11. D 19, E 17, and Mrs Harris's second version are, as to this point, evidently corrupted.

The hero's name is Johnny Cock, B 2, C 1; Johny Cox, Rev. Mr Boyd; John o Cockis (Johny Cockis?), H 17; Johny o Cockley's Well, A 14; o Cockerslee, D 14; of Cockielaw, in one of the versions used by Scott for F; o Cocklesmuir, E 13, H 15. Again, Johnie Brad, G 1, L; Johnie o Breadislee, F 14; Braidislee, J 2.

The hunting-ground, or the place where Johnie is discovered, is up in Braidhouplee, down in Bradyslee, A 6, high up in Bradyslee, low down in Bradyslee, A 12; Braidscaur Hill, D 6, Braidisbanks, D 12, I 1; Bride's Braidmuir, H 2, 5; Broadspear Hill, E 2, 5; Durrisdeer only in F 4. The seven foresters are of Pickeram Side, A 3, 19; of Hislinton, F 9. B 1[1] reads, Fifteen foresters in the braid alow; which seems to require emendation, per-

haps simply to Braid alow, perhaps to Braidi᷍ lee.

With regard to the localities in A, Percy notes that Pickeram Side is in Northumbria, and that there is a Cockley Tower in Erringside, near Brady's Cragg, and a Brady's Cragg near Chollerford Bridge. There is a Cockley, *alias* Cocklaw, in Erringside, near Chollerton, in the south division of Tynedale Ward, parish of St John Lee. The Erring is a small stream which enters the Tyne between Chollerton and Chollerford. Again, Cocklaw Walls appears in the map of the Ordnance Survey, a little to the north and east of Cockley in Erringside, and Cocklaw Walls may represent the Cockley's Well of the ballad. (Percy notes that Cockley's Well is said to be near Bewcastle, Cumberland.) I have not found Brady's Cragg or Pickeram Side in the Ordnance Survey maps, nor indeed any of the compounds of Braidy or Braid anywhere.

There is a Braid a little to the south of Edinburgh, Braid Hills and Braid Burn; and Motherwell, Minstrelsy, p. 17, says that there is tradition for this region having been the hunting-ground.

Scott's copy, F, lays the scene in Dumfriesshire, and there is other tradition to the same effect.*

Percy was struck with the occurrence of the wolf in A 17, found also in B 10, C 5. He considered, no doubt, that the mention of the wolf was a token of the high antiquity of the ballad. " Wolues that wyryeth men, women and children " are spoken of in Piers Plowman, C, Passus, X, v. 226, Skeat, 1886, I, 240, and the C text is assigned to about 1393. Holinshed (1577), I, 378, says that though the island is void of wolves south of the Tweed, yet the Scots cannot boast the like, since they have grievous wolves.

F is translated by Schubart, p. 187; Wolff,

---

* " It is sometimes said that this outlaw possessed the old Castle of Morton in Dumfriesshire, now ruinous. . . . The mention of Durisdeer, a neighboring parish, adds weight to the tradition." Minstrelsy of the Scottish Border, 1833, III, 114 f. Mr W. Bennett, writing in 1826 in The Dumfries Monthly Magazine, III, 250, of which he was editor, speaks of a field a little to the southwest of Lochmaben as still show-

ing the trace of a circular tower, which was " called Cockiesfield, from one John Cock, or O'Cock, who had there his residence, and who during his lifetime was one of the most renowned freebooters in Annandale." Mr Macmath, who pointed out the passage to me, observes that in Thomson's map of Dumfriesshire, 1828, the name is given " Cocketfield," and that there is also a Cocket Hill.

Halle der Völker, I, 41, Hausschatz, p. 224; Doenniges, p. 10; Gerhard, p. 51; R. von Bismarck, Deutsches Museum, 1858, I, 897; Cesare Cantù, Documenti alla Storia Universale, V, 806; in Le Magasin Pittoresque, 1838, p. 127 b; by Loève-Veimars, p. 296. Grundtvig, p. 269, No 41, translates a compound of F, I, E (Kinloch's Ancient Scottish Ballads, p. 36), and B; Knortz, Schottische Balladen, No 18, a mixture of F and others.

A

Communicated to Percy by Miss Fisher, of Carlisle, 1780, No 5 of MS.

1 JOHNY he has risen up i the morn,
   Calls for water to wash his hands;
   But little knew he that his bloody hounds
   Were bound in iron bands.   bands
   Were bound in iron bands

2 Johny's mother has gotten word o that,
   And care-bed she has taen:
   'O Johny, for my benison,
   I beg you 'l stay at hame;
   For the wine so red, and the well baken bread,
   My Johny shall want nane.

3 'There are seven forsters at Pickeram Side,
   At Pickeram where they dwell,
   And for a drop of thy heart's bluid
   They wad ride the fords of hell.'

4 Johny he 's gotten word of that,
   And he 's turnd wondrous keen;
   He 's put off the red scarlett,
   And he 's put on the Lincoln green.

5 With a sheaf of arrows by his side,
   And a bent bow in his hand,
   He 's mounted on a prancing steed,
   And he has ridden fast oer the strand.

6 He 's up i Braidhouplee, and down i Bradyslee,
   And under a buss o broom,
   And there he found a good dun deer,
   Feeding in a buss of ling.

7 Johny shot, and the dun deer lap,
   And she lap wondrous wide,
   Until they came to the wan water,
   And he stemd her of her pride.

8 He 'as taen out the little pen-knife,
   'T was full three quarters long,
   And he has taen out of that dun deer
   The liver bot and the tongue.

9 They eat of the flesh, and they drank of the blood,
   And the blood it was so sweet,
   Which caused Johny and his bloody hounds
   To fall in a deep sleep.

10 By then came an old palmer,
   And an ill death may he die!
   For he 's away to Pickram Side,
   As fast as he can drie.

11 'What news, what news?' says the Seven Forsters,
   'What news have ye brought to me?'
   'I have noe news,' the palmer said,
   'But what I saw with my eye.

12 'High up i Bradyslee, low down i Bradisslee,
   And under a buss of scroggs,
   O there I spied a well-wight man,
   Sleeping among his dogs.

13 'His coat it was of light Lincolm,
   And his breeches of the same,
   His shoes of the American leather,
   And gold buckles tying them.'

14 Up bespake the Seven Forsters,
   Up bespake they ane and a':
   O that is Johny o Cockleys Well,
   And near him we will draw.

15 O the first y stroke that they gae him,
   They struck him off by the knee;
   Then up bespake his sister's son:
   'O the next 'll gar him die!'

16 'O some they count ye well-wight men,
　　　But I do count ye nane ;
　　For you might well ha wakend me,
　　　And askd gin I wad be taen.

17 'The wildest wolf in aw this wood
　　　Wad not ha done so by me ;
　　She 'd ha wet her foot ith wan water,
　　　And sprinkled it oer my brae,
　　And if that wad not ha wakend me,
　　　She wad ha gone and let me be.

18 'O bows of yew, if ye be true,
　　　In London, where ye were bought,
　　Fingers five, get up belive,
　　　Manhuid shall fail me nought.'

19 He has killd the Seven Forsters,
　　　He has killd them all but ane,
　　And that wan scarce to Pickeram Side,
　　　To carry the bode-words hame.

20 'Is there never a boy in a' this wood
　　　That will tell what I can say ;
　　That will go to Cockleys Well,
　　　Tell my mither to fetch me away ? '

21 There was a boy into that wood,
　　　That carried the tidings away,
　　And many ae was the well-wight man
　　　At the fetching o Johny away.

B

Pieces of Ancient Poetry from Unpublished Manuscripts
and Scarce Books, Bristol, 1814, p. 53.

1 FIFTEEN foresters in the Braid alow,
　　　And they are wondrous fell ;
　　To get a drop of Johnny's heart-bluid,
　　　They would sink a' their souls to hell.

2 Johnny Cock has gotten word of this,
　　　And he is wondrous keen ;
　　He['s] custan off the red scarlet,
　　　And on the Linkum green.

3 And he is ridden oer muir and muss,
　　　And over mountains high,
　　Till he came to yon wan water,
　　　And there Johnny Cock did lie.

4 They have ridden oer muir and muss,
　　　And over mountains high,
　　Till they met wi' an old palmer,
　　　Was walking along the way.

5 'What news, what news, old palmer ?
　　　What news have you to me ? '
　　'Yonder is one of the proudest wed sons
　　　That ever my eyes did see.'

＊　　＊　　＊　　＊　　＊

6 He 's taen out a horn from his side,
　　　And he blew both loud and shrill,
　　Till a' the fifteen foresters
　　　Heard Johnny Cock blaw his horn.

7 They have sworn a bluidy oath,
　　　And they swore all in one,
　　That there was not a man among them a'
　　　Would blaw such a blast as yon.

8 And they have ridden oer muir and muss,
　　　And over mountains high,
　　Till they came to yon wan water,
　　　Where Johnny Cock did lie.

9 They have shotten little Johnny Cock,
　　　A little above the ee :
　　.　　.　　.　　.　　.
　　'For doing the like to me.

10 'There 's not a wolf in a' the wood
　　　Woud ' ha' done the like to me ;
　　'She 'd ha' dipped her foot in coll water,
　　　And strinkled above my ee,
　　And if I would not have waked for that,
　　　'She 'd ha' gane and let me be.

11 'But fingers five, come here, [come here,]
　　　And faint heart fail me nought,
　　And silver strings, value me sma things,
　　　Till I get all this vengeance rowght ! '

12 He ha[s] shot a' the fifteen foresters,
　　　Left never a one but one,
　　And he broke the ribs a that ane's side,
　　　And let him take tiding home.

13 '. . . a bird in a' the wood
　　　Could sing as I could say,
　　It would go in to my mother's bower,
　　　And bid her kiss me, and take me away.'

C

Pieces of Ancient Poetry from Unpublished Manuscripts and Scarce Books, Bristol, 1814, p. 51.

1 JOHNNY COCK, in a May morning,
  Sought water to wash his hands,
And he is awa to louse his dogs,
  That 's tied wi iron bans.
  That 's tied wi iron bans

2 His coat it is of the light Lincum green,
  And his breiks are of the same;
His shoes are of the American leather,
  Silver buckles tying them.

3 'He' hunted up, and so did 'he' down,
  Till 'he' came to yon bush of scrogs,
And then to yon wan water,
  Where he slept among his dogs.

*   *   *   *   *

4 Johnny Cock out-shot a' the foresters,
  And out-shot a the three;

Out shot a' the foresters,
  Wounded Johnny aboun the bree.

5 'Woe be to you, foresters,
  And an ill death may you die!
For there would not a wolf in a' the wood
  Have done the like to me.

6 'For ''t would ha' put its foot in the coll water
  And ha strinkled it on my bree,
And gin that would not have done,
  Would have gane and lett me be.

7 'I often took to my mother
  The dandoo and the roe,
But now I 'l take to my mother
  Much sorrow and much woe.

8 'I often took to my mother
  The dandoo and the hare,
But now I 'l take to my mother
  Much sorrow and much care.'

D

Kinloch's annotated copy of his Ancient Scottish Ballads, p. 38 *bis :* a West-Country version.

1 UP Johnie raise in a May morning,
  Calld for water to wash his hands,
And he has calld for his gude gray hunds,
  That lay bund in iron bands.   bands
  That lay bund in iron bands

2 'Ye 'll busk, ye 'll busk my noble dogs,
  Ye 'll busk and mak them boun,
For I 'm going to the Braidscaur hill,
  To ding the dun deer doun.'

3 Whan Johnie's mither gat word o that,
  On the very bed she lay,
Says, Johnie, for my malison,
  I pray ye at hame to stay.

4 Your meat sall be of the very, very best,
  Your drink sall be the same,
And ye will win your mither's benison,
  Gin ye wad stay at hame.

5 But Johnie has cast aff the black velvet,
  And put on the Lincoln twine,

And he is on to gude greenwud,
  As fast as he could gang.

6 His mither's counsel he wad na tak,
  He 's aff, and left the toun,
He 's aff unto the Braidscaur hill,
  To ding the dun deer doun.

7 Johnie lookit east, and Johnie lookit west,
  And he lookit aneath the sun,
And there he spied the dun deer sleeping,
  Aneath a buss o whun.

8 Johnie shot, and the dun deer lap,
  And he 's scaithed him in the side,
And atween the water and the wud
  He laid the dun deer's pride.

9 They ate sae meikle o the venison,
  And drank sae meikle o the blude,
That Johnie and his twa gray hunds
  Fell asleep in yonder wud.

10 By ther cam a silly auld man,
  And a silly auld man was he,
And he 's aff to the proud foresters,
  As fast as he could dree.

11 'What news, what news, my silly auld man?
    What news? come tell to me:'
'I heard na news, I speird na news
    But what my een did see.

12 'As I cam in by Braidisbanks,
    And doun amang the whuns,
The bonniest youngster eer I saw
    Lay sleepin amang his hunds.

13 'His cheeks war like the roses red,
    His neck was like the snaw;
His sark was o the holland fine,
    And his jerkin lac'd fu braw.'

14 Up bespak the first forester,
    The first forester of a':
O this is Johnie o Cockerslee;
    Come draw, lads, we maun draw.

15 Up bespak the niest forester,
    The niest forester of a':
An this be Johnie o Cockerslee,
    To him we winna draw.

16 The first shot that they did shoot,
    They woundit him on the bree;
Up bespak the uncle's son,
    'The niest will gar him die.'

17 The second shot that eer they shot,
    It scaithd him near the heart;
'I only wauken,' Johnie cried,
    'Whan first I find the smart.

18 'Stand stout, stand stout, my noble dogs,
    Stand stout, and dinna flee;
Stand fast, stand fast, my gude gray hunds,
    And we will gar them die.'

19 He has killed six o the proud foresters,
    And wounded the seventh sair:
He laid his leg out owre his steed,
    Says, I will kill na mair.

20 'Oh wae befa thee, silly auld man,
    An ill death may thee dee!
Upon thy head be a' this blude,
    For mine, I ween, is free.'

E

Kinloch's MSS, VII, 29: from recitation in the North Country.

1 JOHNIE rose up in a May morning,
    Calld for water to wash his hands,
And he has calld for his gud gray hunds,
    That lay bund in iron bands.   bands
    That lay bund in iron bands

2 'Ye'll busk, ye'll busk my noble dogs,
    Ye'll busk and mak them boun,
For I'm gaing to the Broadspear hill,
    To ding the dun deer doun.'

3 Whan Johnie's mither heard o this,
    She til her son has gane:
'Ye'll win your mither's benison,
    Gin ye wad stay at hame.

4 'Your meat sall be o the very, very best,
    And your drink o the finest wine;
And ye will win your mither's benison,
    Gin ye wad stay at hame.'

5 His mither's counsel he wad na tak,
    Nor wad he stay at hame;
But he's on to the Broadspear hill,
    To ding the dun deer doun.

6 Johnie lookit east, and Johnie lookit west,
    And a little below the sun,
And there he spied the dun deer lying sleeping
    Aneath a buss o brume.

7 Johnie shot, and the dun deer lap,
    And he has woundit him in the side,
And atween the water and the wud
    He laid the dun deer's pride.

8 They ate sae meikle o the venison,
    And drank sae meikle o the blude,
That Johnie and his twa gray hunds
    Fell asleep in yonder wud.

9 By there cam a silly auld man,
    A silly auld man was he,
And he's aff to the proud foresters,
    To tell what he did see.

10 'What news, what news, my silly auld man,
  What news? come tell to me:'
'Na news, na news,' said the silly auld man,
  'But what mine een did see.

11 'As I cam in by yon greenwud,
  And doun amang the scrogs,
The bonniest youth that ere I saw
  Lay sleeping atween twa dogs.

12 'The sark that he had on his back
  Was o the holland sma,
And the coat that he had on his back
  Was laced wi gowd fu braw.'

13 Up bespak the first forester,
  The first forester ava:
'An this be Johnie o Cocklesmuir,
  It's time we war awa.'

14 Up bespak the niest forester,
  The niest forester ava:
'An this be Johnie o Cocklesmuir,
  To him we winna draw.'

15 The first shot that they did shoot,
  They woundit him on the thie;
Up bespak the uncle's son,
  The niest will gar him die.

16 'Stand stout, stand stout, my noble dogs,
  Stand stout, and dinna flee;
Stand fast, stand fast, my gude gray hunds,
  And we will mak them dee.'

17 He has killed six o the proud foresters,
  And he has woundit the seventh sair;
He laid his leg out oure his steed,
  Says, I will kill na mair.

———◆———

F

Scott's Minstrelsy, I, 59, 1802; made up from several different copies. Nithsdale.

1 JOHNIE rose up in a May morning,
  Called for water to wash his hands:
'Gar loose to me the gude graie dogs,
  That are bound wi iron bands.'

2 When Johnie's mother gat word o that,
  Her hands for dule she wrang:
'O Johnie, for my bennison,
  To the grenewood dinna gang!

3 'Eneugh ye hae o the gude wheat-bread,
  And eneugh o the blude-red wine,
And therefore for nae vennison, Johnie,
  I pray ye, stir frae hame.'

4 But Johnie's buskt up his gude bend bow,
  His arrows, ane by ane,
And he has gane to Durrisdeer,
  To hunt the dun deer down.

5 As he came down by Merriemass,
  And in by the benty line,
There has he espied a deer lying,
  Aneath a bush of ling.

6 Johnie he shot, and the dun deer lap,
  And he wounded her on the side,

But atween the water and the brae,
  His hounds they laid her pride.

7 And Johnie has bryttled the deer sae weel
  That he's had out her liver and lungs,
And wi these he has feasted his bludey hounds
  As if they had been erl's sons.

8 They eat sae much o the vennison,
  And drank sae much o the blude,
That Johnie and a' his bludey hounds
  Fell asleep as they had been dead.

9 And by there came a silly auld carle,
  An ill death mote he die!
For he's awa to Hislinton,
  Where the Seven Foresters did lie.

10 'What news, what news, ye gray-headed carle?
  What news bring ye to me?'
'I bring nae news,' said the gray-headed carle,
  'Save what these eyes did see.

11 'As I came down by Merriemass,
  And down amang the scroggs,
The bonniest childe that ever I saw
  Lay sleeping amang his dogs.

12 'The shirt that was upon his back
  Was o the holland fine;

The doublet which was over that
    Was o the Lincome twine.

13 ' The buttons that were on his sleeve
    Were o the gowd sae gude ;
The gude graie hounds he lay amang,
    Their mouths were dyed wi blude.'

14 Then out and spak the first forester,
    The heid man ower them a' :
If this be Johnie o Breadislee,
    Nae nearer will we draw.

15 But up and spak the sixth forester,
    His sister's son was he :
If this be Johnie o Breadislee,
    We soon shall gar him die.

16 The first flight of arrows the foresters shot,
    They wounded him on the knee ;
And out and spak the seventh forester,
    The next will gar him die.

17 Johnie 's set his back against an aik,
    His fute against a stane,
And he has slain the Seven Foresters,
    He has slain them a' but ane.

18 He has broke three ribs in that ane's side,
    But and his collar bane ;
He 's laid him twa-fald ower his steed,
    Bade him carry the tidings hame.

19 ' O is there na a bonnie bird
    Can sing as I can say,

Could flee away to my mother's bower,
    And tell to fetch Johnie away ? '

20 The starling flew to his mother's window-
    stane,
    It whistled and it sang,
And aye the ower-word o the tune
    Was, Johnie tarries lang !

21 They made a rod o the hazel-bush,
    Another o the slae-thorn tree,
And mony, mony were the men
    At fetching our Johnie.

22 Then out and spake his auld mother,
    And fast her teirs did fa ;
Ye wad nae be warnd, my son Johnie,
    Frae the hunting to bide awa.

23 ' Aft hae I brought to Breadislee
    The less gear and the mair,
But I neer brought to Breadislee
    What grieved my heart sae sair.

24 ' But wae betyde that silly auld carle,
    An ill death shall he die ;
For the highest tree on Merriemass
    Shall be his morning's fee.'

25 Now Johnie's gude bend bow is broke,
    And his gude graie dogs are slain,
And his bodie lies dead in Durrisdeer,
    And his hunting it is done.

G

Harris MS., fol. 25 : from Mrs Harris's recitation.

1 JOHNNIE BRAD, on a May mornin,
    Called for water to wash his hands,
An there he spied his twa blude-hounds,
    Waur bound in iron bands.   bands
    Waur bound in iron bands

2 Johnnie 's taen his gude bent bow,
    Bot an his arrows kene,
An strippit himsel o the scarlet red,
    An put on the licht Lincoln green.

3 Up it spak Johnnie's mither,
    An' a wae, wae woman was she :

I beg you bide at hame, Johnnie,
    I pray be ruled by me.

4 Baken bread ye sall nae lack,
    An wine you sall lack nane ;
Oh Johnnie, for my benison,
    I beg you bide at hame !

5 He has made a solemn aith,
    Atween the sun an the mune,
That he wald gae to the gude green wood,
    The dun deer to ding doon.

6 He luiket east, he luiket wast,
    An in below the sun,
An there he spied the dun deer,
    Aneath a bush o brume.

7 The firsten shot that Johnnie shot,
   He wounded her in the side;
The nexten shot that Johnnie shot,
   I wat he laid her pride.

8 He 's eaten o the venison,
   An drunken o the blude,
Until he fell as sound asleep
   As though he had been dead.

9 Bye there cam a silly auld man,
   And a silly auld man was he,
An he 's on to the Seven Foresters,
   As fast as he can flee.

10 'As I cam in by yonder haugh,
   An in among the scroggs,
The bonniest boy that ere I saw
   Lay sleepin atween his dogs.'

    *   *   *   *   *

11 The firsten shot that Johnnie shot,
   He shot them a' but ane,
An he flang him owre a milk-white steed,
   Bade him bear tidings hame.

H

Buchan's MSS, I, 82; Dixon, Scottish Traditional Versions of Ancient Ballads, p. 77, Percy Society, vol. xvii.

1 JOHNNIE raise up in a May morning,
   Calld for water to wash his hands,
And he 's commant his bluidy dogs
   To be loosd frae their iron bands.   bands
   To be loosd frae their iron bands

2 'Win up, win up, my bluidy dogs,
   Win up, and be unbound,
And we will on to Bride's Braidmuir,
   And ding the dun deer down.'

3 When his mother got word o that,
   Then she took bed and lay;
Says, Johnnie, my son, for my blessing,
   Ye 'll stay at hame this day.

4 There 's baken bread and brown ale
   Shall be at your command;
Ye 'll win your mither's blythe blessing,
   To the Bride's Braidmuir nae gang.

5 Mony are my friends, mither,
   Though thousands were my foe;
Betide me life, betide me death,
   To the Bride's Braidmuir I 'll go.

6 The sark that was on Johnnie's back
   Was o the cambric fine;
The belt that was around his middle
   Wi pearlins it did shine.

7 The coat that was upon his back
   Was o the linsey brown;
And he 's awa to the Bride's Braidmuir,
   To ding the dun deer down.

8 Johnnie lookd east, Johnnie lookd west,
   And turnd him round and round,
And there he saw the king's dun deer,
   Was cowing the bush o brune.

9 Johnnie shot, and the dun deer lap,
   He wounded her in the side;
Between him and yon burnie-bank,
   Johnnie he laid her pride.

10 He ate sae muckle o the venison,
   He drank sae muckle bleed,
Till he lay down between his hounds,
   And slept as he 'd been dead.

11 But by there came a stane-auld man,
   An ill death mat he dee!
For he is on to the Seven Foresters,
   As fast as gang could he.

12 'What news, what news, ye stane-auld man?
   What news hae ye brought you wi?'
'Nae news, nae news, ye seven foresters,
   But what your eyes will see.

13 'As I gaed i yon rough thick hedge,
   Amang yon bramly scroggs,
The fairest youth that eer I saw
   Lay sleeping between his dogs.

14 'The sark that was upon his back
    Was o the cambric fine ;
The belt that was around his middle
    Wi pearlins it did shine.'

15 Then out it speaks the first forester :
    Whether this be true or no,
O if it 's Johnnie o Cocklesmuir,
    Nae forder need we go.

16 Out it spake the second forester,
    A fierce fellow was he :
Betide me life, betide me death,
    This youth we 'll go and see.

17 As they gaed in yon rough thick hedge,
    And down yon forest gay,
They came to that very same place
    Where John o Cockis he lay.

18 The first an shot they shot at him,
    They wounded him in the thigh ;
Out spake the first forester's son :
    By the next shot he maun die.

19 'O stand ye true, my trusty bow,
    And stout steel never fail !

Avenge me now on all my foes,
    Who have my life i bail.'

20 Then Johnnie killd six foresters,
    And wounded the seventh sair ;
Then drew a stroke at the stane-auld man,
    That words he neer spake mair.

21 His mother's parrot in window sat,
    She whistled and she sang,
And aye the owerturn o the note,
    'Young Johnnie 's biding lang.'

22 When this reached the king's own ears,
    It grievd him wondrous sair ;
Says, I 'd rather they 'd hurt my subjects all
    Than Johnnie o Cocklesmuir.

23 'But where are all my wall-wight men,
    That I pay meat and fee,
Will gang the morn to Johnnie's castle,
    See how the cause may be.'

24 Then he 's calld Johnnie up to court,
    Treated him handsomelie,
And now to hunt in the Bride's Braidmuir,
    For life has license free.

————◆————

I

Motherwell's Minstrelsy, p. 23.

1 JOHNIE rose up in a May morning,
    Called for water to wash his hands, hands
And he is awa to Braidisbanks,
    To ding the dun deer down.   down
    To ding the dun deer down

2 Johnie lookit east, and Johnie lookit west,
    And it 's lang before the sun,
And there he did spy the dun deer lie,
    Beneath a bush of brume.

3 Johnie shot, and the dun deer lap,
    And he 's woundit her in the side ;
Out then spake his sister's son,
    'And the neist will lay her pride.'

*   *   *   *   *

4 They 've eaten sae meikle o the gude venison,
    And they 've drunken sae muckle o the
        blude,
That they 've fallen into as sound a sleep
    As gif that they were dead.

*   *   *   *   *

5 'It 's doun, and it 's doun, and it 's doun, doun,
    And it 's doun amang the scrogs,
And there ye 'll espy twa bonnie boys lie,
    Asleep amang their dogs.'

*   *   *   *   *

6 They waukened Johnie out o his sleep,
    And he 's drawn to him his coat :
'My fingers five, save me alive,
    And a stout heart fail me not !'

*   *   *   *   *

J

Chambers's Scottish Ballads, p. 181, stanzas 13, 16, 17, 21, 22, 23, 26: from the recitation of a lady resident at Peebles.

1 His coat was o the scarlet red,
   His vest was o the same;
His stockings were o the worset lace,
   And buckles tied to the same.

2 Out then spoke one, out then spoke two,
   Out then spoke two or three;
Out spoke the master forester,
   'It 's Johnie o Braidislee.

3 'If this be true, thou silly auld man,
   Which you tell unto me,
Five hundred pounds of yearly rent
   It shall not pay your fee.'

*   *   *   *   *

4 'O wae be to you seven foresters!
   I wonder ye dinna think shame,
You being seven sturdy men,
   And I but a man my lane.

5 'Now fail me not, my ten fingers,
   That are both long and small!
Now fail me not, my noble heart!
   For in thee I trust for all.

6 'Now fail me not, my good bend bow,
   That was in London coft!
Now fail me not, my golden string,
   Which my true lover wrocht!'

*   *   *   *   *

7 He has tossed him up, he has tossed him doun,
   He has broken his collar-bone;
He has tied him to his bridle reins,
   Bade him carry the tidings home.

K

Finlay's Scottish Ballads, I, xxxi.

'There 's no a bird in a' this foreste
   Will do as meikle for me
As dip its wing in the wan water
   An straik it on my ee-bree.'

L

Harris MS., fol. 25 b.

But aye at ilka ae mile's end
   She fand a cat o clay,
An written upon the back o it
   'Tak your son Johnnie Brod away.'

M

Froude's Life of Carlyle, 1795–1875, II, 335, New York, 1882, completed by a communication of Mr Macmath: as sung by Carlyle's mother.

'O busk ye, O busk ye, my three bluidy hounds,
   O busk ye, and go with me,
For there 's seven foresters in yon forest,
   And them I want to see.' see
   And them I want to see

A. 'The Seven Forsters at Pickeram Side' is a title supplied by Percy.
  6². I wun is added by Percy, at the end.
  7³, 17³. one water.
  15¹. Oh. 19⁴. bord words, or bood words.
B follows C in Fry without a break. Words distinguished by ' ' in B, C are emendations or

additions of Fry. 4, 5 come between 12 and 13.
  1¹. braid alow. 10¹. the word. 10⁵. would have.
  11². hearted. 13³. bows.
  4³. Out-shot.
D. "There is a West-Country version of this ballad, under the title of Johnie of Cockerslee,

differing very little from the present. The variations in the reading I have marked at their respective places." *Kinloch. Assuming that Kinloch has given all the variations (which include six entire stanzas), the West-Country version is reproduced by combining these readings with so much of the other copy, Kinloch's Ancient Scottish Ballads, p. 38, as did not vary.* 15³. *Kinloch neglected to alter* Cocklesmuir *here.*

E.   6³. lying *is* struck through, *probably to improve the metre. Kinloch made two slight changes in printing.*

H.   5¹. Mony ane. (?)   9¹. Johnnie lap: *probably an error of the copyist.*
      9², 18². wound: *cf.* 20².
      21⁴. bidding.
      Dixon has changed stane-auld *to* silly-auld *in* 11¹, 12¹, 20³; Cockis *to* Cockl's *in* 17⁴; *and has Scotticised the spelling.*

I.   *Motherwell notes a stanza as wanting after* 3, *some stanzas as wanting after* 4, 5.

J.   " The version of the ballad here given is partly copied from those printed in the Border Minstrelsy and in the publications of Messrs Kinloch and Motherwell, and is partly taken from the recitation of a lady resident at Peebles and from a manuscript copy sub-mitted to me by Mr Kinloch. The twelfth, thirteenth, fourteenth, sixteenth, seventeenth, twenty-first, twenty-second, twenty-third, twenty-sixth, and twenty-seventh stanzas are here printed for the first time." *Chambers.* *The 14th stanza had been printed by Scott,* F 12; *the 23d, repeated here* (6), *by Pinkerton; the 27th is* D 20. *The first half of the 12th is* D 13¹˒², *and the remainder Chambers's own: compare his 11 and* F 11, *from which it seems to have been made.*

L.   " I have heard another version, where Johnnie is slain and thrown ' owre a milk-white steed.' News is sent to Johnnie's mother, who flies to her son; But aye at ilka ae mile's end, etc."

M.   " While she [Carlyle's mother] was at Craigenputtock, I made her train me to two song-tunes; and we often sang them together, and tried them often again in coming down into Annandale." *The last half of the stanza is cited. Letter of T. Carlyle, May* 18, 1834, *in Froude's Life,* 1795–1835, II, 335.
      " Mrs Aitken, sister of T. Carlyle, sent me [January 15, 1884] the first two lines to complete the stanza of this Johny Cock, but can call up no more of the ballad." *Letter of Mr Macmath.*

115

ROBYN AND GANDELEYN

Sloane MS., 2593, fol. 14 b, British Museum.

PRINTED by Ritson, Ancient Songs, 1790, p. 48, and by Thomas Wright, Songs and Carols (selected from the Sloane MS.), No X, London, 1836, and again in his edition of the whole MS. for the Warton Club, 1856, p. 42. The manuscript is put at about 1450.

Wright remarks on the similarity of the name Gandelyn to Gamelyn in the tale assigned to the Cook in some manuscripts of the Canterbury Tales, and on the resemblance of the tale of Gamelyn to Robin Hood story. But he could hardly have wished to give the impression that Robin in this ballad is Robin Hood. This he no more is than John in the ballad which precedes is Little John; though Gandelyn is as true to his master as Little

John is, and is pronounced to be by the king, in 'Robin Hood and the Monk.' Ritson gave the ballad the title of 'Robin Lyth,' looking on the 'lyth' of the burden as the hero's surname; derived perhaps from the village of Lythe, two or three miles to the north of Whitby. A cave on the north side of the promontory of Flamborough, called Robin Lyth's Hole (popularly regarded as the stronghold of a pirate), may have been, Ritson thinks, one of the skulking-places of the Robin who fell by the shaft of Wrennok. "Robin Hood," he adds, "had several such in those and other parts; and, indeed, it is not very improbable that our hero had been formerly in the suite of that gallant robber, and, on his master's death, had set up for himself." Thought is free.

Translated by Grundtvig, Engelske og skotske Folkeviser, page 44, No. 6.

———•———

1 I ʜᴇʀᴅᴇ a carpyng of a clerk,
    Al at ȝone wodes ende,
Of gode Robyn and Gandeleyn ;
    Was þer non oþer þynge.
Robynn lyth in grene wode bowndyn

2 Stronge theuys wern þo chylderin non,
    But bowmen gode and hende ;
He wentyn to wode to getyn hem fleych,
    If God wold it hem sende.

3 Al day wentyn þo chylderin too,
    And fleych fowndyn he non,
Til it were a-geyn euyn ;
    þe chylderin wold gon hom.

4 Half an honderid of fat falyf der
    He comyn a-ȝon,
And alle he wern fayr and fat i-now,
    But markyd was þer non :
' Be dere God,' seyde gode Robyn,
    ' Here of we xul haue on.'

5 Robyn bent his joly bowe,
    þer in he set a flo ;
þe fattest der of alle
    þe herte he clef a to.

6 He hadde not þe der i-flawe,
    Ne half out of þe hyde,
There cam a schrewde arwe out of þe west,
    þat felde Robertes pryde.

7 Gandeleyn lokyd hym est and west,
    Be euery syde :
' Hoo hat myn mayster slayin ?
    Ho hat don þis dede?
Xal I neuer out of grene wode go
    Til I se [his] sydis blede.'

8 Gandeleyn lokyd hym est and lokyd west,
    And sowt vnder þe sunne ;
He saw a lytil boy
    He clepyn Wrennok of Donne.

9 A good bowe in his hond,
    A brod arwe þer ine,
And fowre and twenti goode arwys,
    Trusyd in a þrumme :
' Be war þe, war þe, Gandeleyn,
    Her-of þu xalt han summe.

10 ' Be war þe, war þe, Gandeleyn,
    Her of þu gyst plente :'
' Euer on for an oþer,' seyde Gandeleyn ;
    ' Mysaunter haue he xal fle.

11 ' Qwer-at xal our marke be ?'
    Seyde Gandeleyn :
' Eueryche at oþeris herte,'
    Seyde Wrennok ageyn.

12 ' Ho xal ȝeue þe ferste schote ?'
    Seyde Gandeleyn :
' And I xul ȝeue þe on be-forn,'
    Seyde Wrennok ageyn.

13 Wrennok schette a ful good schote,
    And he schet not to hye ;
þrow þe sanchoþis of his bryk ;
    It towchyd neyþer thye.

14 ' Now hast þu ȝouyn me on be-forn,'
    Al þus to Wrennok seyde he,
' And þrow þe myȝt of our lady
    A bettere I xal ȝeue þe.'

15 Gandeleyn bent his goode bowe,
    And set þer in a flo ;

He schet þrow his grene certyl,
    His herte he clef on too.

16 'Now xalt þu neuer ȝelpe, Wrennok,
    At ale ne at wyn,
    þat þu hast slawe goode Robyn,
    And his knaue Gandeleyn.

17 'Now xalt þu neuer ȝelpe, Wrennok,
    At wyn ne at ale,
    þat þu hast slawe goode Robyn,
    And Gandeleyn his knaue.'

Robyn lyȝth in grene wode bowndyn

⁂

*Written continuously, without division of stanzas
or verses. The burden, put after 1, stands at
the head of the ballad.*
And *for & always.* 1⁴. gynge.

4³. I now.   4⁵. Robyn *wanting.*   5¹. went.
7⁶. Ti I.   9³. & xx.   10². hir.   12³. ȝewe.   12⁴. seyd.
14³. þᵘ myȝt.   17⁴. Gandelyyn: knawe.
Last line: bowdyn.

⸻

116

ADAM BELL, CLIM OF THE CLOUGH, AND WILLIAM OF CLOUDESLY

a. Two fragments, stanzas 113⁴–128², 161²–170, of an edition by John Byddell, London, 1536 : Library of the University of Cambridge.*

b. A fragment, stanzas 53³–111³, by a printer not identified: formerly in the possession of J. Payne Collier.†

c. 'Adambel, Clym of the cloughe, and Wyllyam of cloudesle,' William Copeland, London [1548–68] : British Museum, C. 21, c. 64.‡

d. 'Adam Bell, Clim of the Clough, and William of Cloudesle,' James Roberts, London, 1605 : Bodleian Library, C. 39, Art. Selden.

e. Another edition with the same title-page: Bodleian Library, Malone, 299.

f. 'Adam Bell, Clime of the Cloug[he], and William off Cloudeslee,' Percy MS., p. 390: British Museum. Hales and Furnivall, III, 76.

⸻

'ADAM BELL' is licensed to John Kynge in the Stationers' Registers, 19 July, 1557–9 July, 1558: Arber, I, 79. Again, among copies which were Sampson Awdeley's, to John Charlewood, 15 January, 1582; and, among copies which were John Charlwoode's, to James Robertes, 31 May, 1594: Arber, II, 405, 651. Seven reprints of the seventeenth century, later than d, are noted in Mr W. C. Hazlitt's Handbook, p. 35.

The larger part of a has been reprinted by Mr F. S. Ellis, in his catalogue of the library of Mr Henry Huth, I, 128 f, 1880.§   b was used by Mr W. C. Hazlitt for his edition of the ballad in Remains of the Early Popular Poetry of England, II, 131.∥   c was reprinted

* Colophon : [P]rynted at London, in Fletestrete, at [the si]gne of the Sonne, by me Iohn [By]ddell. In the yere of our lord god m.ccccc.xxxvj. The seconde daye of June. Iohn̄ Byddell.
    Eight lines wanting : 120³·⁴; 121; 168³·⁴. Mutilated at the beginning: 169; 170. Mutilated at the end: 164¹; 165³; 167¹.
    † Eleven lines wanting : 60²·³·⁴; 67⁴; 68¹·²; 100³; 104⁴;

105¹·²; 110⁴. Mutilated at the beginning: 61–64¹; 64³–67³; 75⁴–83¹; 90⁴·⁵·⁶; 96⁴; 105³–110³; 111¹·². Mutilated at the end: 60¹; 101³; 102³; 103¹; 104²·³. Elsewhere: 97²·³; 104¹.
    ‡ Colophon.   Imprinted at London, in Lothburye, by Wyllyam Copeland.
    § "Two leaves, discovered in the pasteboard or fly-leaves of a book received from abroad."
    ∥ b was kindly copied for me by Mr J. P. Collier in 1857.

by Percy in his Reliques, 1765, I, 129, with corrections from f; and by Ritson, Pieces of Ancient Popular Poetry, 1791, p. 5, with the necessary emendations of Copland's somewhat faulty text. d is followed by a Second Part, described by Ritson, in temperate terms, as "a very inferior and servile production." It is here given (with much reluctance) in an Appendix.

Adam Bell, Clim of the Clough, and William of Cloudesly, outlawed for breach of the game-laws, swear brotherhood, and betake themselves to Inglewood, a forest adjacent to Carlisle. William is a wedded man, and one day tells his brethren that he means to go to Carlisle to see his wife and children. Adam would not advise this, lest he should be taken by the justice. William goes to Carlisle, nevertheless, knocks at his window, and is admitted by Alice, his wife, who tells him with a sigh that the place has been beset for him a half year and more. While they make good cheer, an old woman, whom William had kept seven years for charity, slips out, and informs the justice that William is come to town.* The justice and the sheriff come presently with a great rout to take William. Man and wife defend the house till it is set on fire. William lets his wife and children down with sheets, and shoots on till his bowstring is burnt, then runs into the thick of his foes with sword and buckler, but is felled by doors and windows thrown on him, and so taken. The sheriff orders the gates of Carlisle to be shut close, and sets up a gallows to hang William. A boy, friendly to the family, gets out at a crevice in the wall, and carries word to Adam and Clim, who instantly set out for the rescue.

Adam and Clim find the gates shut so fast that there is no chance of getting in without a stratagem. Adam has a fair written letter in his pocket: they will make the porter think that they have the king's seal. They beat on the gate till the porter comes, and demand to be let in as messengers from the king to the justice. The porter demurs, but they browbeat him with the king's seal; he opens the gate; they wring his neck and take his keys. First bending their bows and looking to the strings, they make for the market-place, where they find Cloudesly lying in a cart, on the point to be hanged. William sees them, and takes hope. Adam makes the sheriff his mark, Clim the justice; both fall, deadly wounded; the citizens fly; the outlaws loose Cloudesly's ropes. William wrings an axe from the hand of an officer, and smites on every side; Adam and Clim shoot till their arrows are gone, then draw their swords. Horns are blown, and the bells rung backwards; the mayor of Carlisle comes with a large force, and the fight is hotter than ever. But all for naught, for the outlaws get to the gates, and are soon in Inglewood, under their trysty-tree.

Alice had come to Inglewood to make known to Adam and Clim what had befallen her husband, but naturally had not found them, since they were already gone to William's rescue. A woman is heard weeping, and Cloudesly, taking a turn to see what this may mean, comes upon his wife and three boys. Very sad she is, but the sight of her husband makes all well. Three harts are killed for supper, and William gives Alice the best for standing so boldly by him. The outlaws determine to go to the king to get a charter of peace. William takes his eldest son with him, leaving Alice and the two younger at a nunnery. The three brethren make their way to the king's presence, without leave of porter or announcement by usher, kneel down and hold up their hands, and ask grace for having slain the king's deer. The king inquires their names, and when he hears who they are says they shall all be hanged, and orders them into arrest. Adam Bell once more asks grace, since they have come to the king of their free will, or else that they may go, with such weapons as they have, when they

---

Mr Collier described his fragment as "a scrap which once formed the fly-leaf of a book." Hazlitt says that the type is clearly older than Copland's, and very like Wynkyn de Worde's.

* This old woman gives the title 'Auld Matrons' to a ballad in Buchan's larger collection, II, 238, in which kitchen-tradition has made over some of the incidents in the First Fit of Adam Bell.

will ask no grace in a hundred years. The king replies again that all three shall be hanged. Hereupon the queen reminds the king that when she was wedded he had promised to grant the first boon she should ask; she had hitherto asked nothing, but now begs the three yeomen's lives. The king must needs consent.

Immediately thereafter comes information that the outlaws had slain the justice and the sheriff, the mayor of Carlisle, all the constables and catchpolls, the sergeants of the law, forty foresters, and many more. This makes the king so sad that he can eat no more; but he wishes to see these fellows shoot that have wrought all this woe. The king's archers and the queen's go to the butts with the three yeomen, and the outlaws hit everything that is set up. Cloudesly holds the butts too wide for a good archer, and the three set up two hazel rods, twenty score paces apart; he is a good archer, says Cloudesly, that cleaves one of these. The king says no man can do it; but Cloudesly cleaves the wand. The king declares him the best archer he ever saw. William says he will do a greater mastery: he will lay an apple on his son's head (a boy of seven), and split it in two at six score paces. The king bids him make haste so to do: if he fail, he shall be hanged; and if he touch the boy, the outlaws shall be hanged, all three. Cloudesly ties the child to a stake, turning its face from him, sets an apple on its head, and, begging the people to remain quiet, cleaves the apple in two. The king gives Cloudesly eighteen pence a day as his bowman, and makes him chief rider over the North Country. The queen adds twelve pence, makes him a gentleman of cloth and fee and his two brothers yeomen of her chamber, gives the boy a place in her wine-cellar, and appoints Alice her chief gentlewoman and governess of her nursery. The yeomen express their thanks, go to Rome [to some bishop, in the later copy] to be absolved of their sins, live the rest of their lives with the king, and die good men, all three.

The rescue of Robin Hood by Little John and Much in No 117, sts 61–82, has a general resemblance to the rescue of Cloudesly by Adam and Clim in this ballad, st. 52 ff. The rescue of Will Stutly has also some slight similarity: cf. No 141, sts 26–33, and 70, 79–81, of 'Adam Bell.'

The shooting of an apple from a boy's head, sts 151–62, is, as is well known, a trait in several German and Norse traditions, and these particular feats, as well as everything resembling them, have been a subject of eager discussion in connection with the apocryphal history of William Tell.

The Icelandic saga of Dietrich of Bern, compiled, according to the prologue, from Low German tales and ballads, narrates that young Egil, a brother of Weland the Smith, came to Nidung's court with the fame of being the best bowman in the world. Nidung, to prove his skill, required Egil [on pain of death] to shoot an apple from the head of his son, a child of three years, only one trial being permitted. Egil split the apple in the middle. Though allowed but one chance, Egil had provided himself with three arrows. When asked why, he answered the king that the two others were meant for him, if he had hit the boy with the first. Saga Điðriks Konungs af Bern, ed. Unger, c. 75, p. 90 f; Peringskiöld, Wilkina Saga, c. 27, p. 63 f; Raszmann, Die Deutsche Heldensage, II, 247 f; the Swedish rifacimento, Sagan om Didrik af Bern, ed. Hyltén-Cavallius, c. 73, p. 54. The Icelandic saga was composed about 1250.

Saxo, writing about 1200, relates nearly the same incidents of Toko, a man in the service of King Harold Bluetooth († c. 985). Toko, while drinking with comrades, had bragged that he was good enough bowman to hit the smallest apple on top of a stick at the first shot. This boast was carried to the king, who exacted a fulfilment of it on pain of death; but the apple was to be set on the head of Toko's son. The father exhorted the boy to stand perfectly still, and, to make this easier, turned the child's face from the direction of the shot; then, laying out three arrows from his quiver, executed the required feat. When the king asked why he had taken three arrows, Toko replied, To wreak the miss of the first with the points of the others. Saxo Grammaticus, Gesta Danorum, Book x, ed. Holder, p. 329 f.

The White Book of Obwalden, written about 1470, informs us that Tell, a good archer, having refused to bow to Gesler's hat, was ordered by the landvogt to shoot an apple from the head of one of his children. Unable to resist, Tell laid-by a second arrow, shot the apple from the child's head, and being asked why he had reserved the other arrow, replied that if the first had missed he would have shot Gesler or one of his men with the second.*

This story is introduced into a piece of verse on the origin of the Swiss confederacy, of nearly the same date as the prose document. In this the landvogt says to Tell that if he does not hit with the first shot, it will cost him his life; the distance is one hundred and twenty paces, as in the English ballad, and Tell says simply that he would have shot the landvogt if he had hit his son.† (Tell uses a cross-bow, not the long-bow, as the English.)

Henning Wulf, a considerable person in Holstein, who had headed an unsuccessful outbreak against Christian the First of Denmark, was captured and brought before the king. The king, knowing Henning to be an incomparable archer, ordered him to shoot an apple from the head of his only son, a child: if he succeeded, he was to go free. The exploit was happily accomplished. But Henning had put a second arrow into his mouth, and the king asked the object. The second arrow was for the king, had the boy been hit. Henning Wulf was outlawed. The story, which

is put at 1472, is the subject of a painting preserved in a church.‡

The Norwegian king, Haraldr Harðráðr († 1066), who has a grudge against Hemingr, son of Áslákr, undertakes to put him to proof in shooting, swimming, and snow-shoe sliding. They go to a wood, and both execute extraordinary feats with bow and lance; but Hemingr is much superior to the king. The king orders Hemingr to shoot a nut from his brother Björn's head, on pain of death for missing. Hemingr would rather die than venture such a shot; but his brother offers himself freely, and undertakes to stand still. Then let the king stand by Björn, says Hemingr, and see whether I hit. But the king prefers to stand by Hemingr, and appoints somebody else to the other position. Hemingr crosses himself, calls God to witness that the king is responsible, throws his lance, and strikes the nut from his brother's head, doing him no harm. Hemings Þáttr, Flateyjarbók, III, 405 f (1370–80); Müller, Sagabibliothek, III, 356 ff. This story was probably derived from an old song, and is preserved in Norwegian and Färöe ballads: 'Harald kongin og Hemingen unge,' Landstad, Norske Folkeviser, No 15, A, B, pp. 177–188; 'Geyti Áslaksson,' Hammershaimb, Færöiske Kvæder, No 17, A–C, II, 149–163. In Norwegian A, 5–10, the shot is exacted under pain of imprisonment. Hemingen insists that the king shall take a place near his brother [son], whom he exhorts to stand erect and bold; one half of the nut falls, the other is left on the head; the king asks what was to have been done with a second arrow which Hemingen had secreted, and is answered as in the previous cases.§ The first and last

---

* Vischer, Die Sage von der Befreiung der Waldstädte, pp 33, 36 f; Rochholz, Germania, XIII, 56 f. " Wa er das nit hette gethan, so hette er selbs müssen darumb sterben: " Russ's Chronicle, 1482, Vischer, p. 50.

† Liliencron, Die historischen Volkslieder der Deutschen, II, 109, Nᵒ 147; Böhme, p. 47, No 10; Vischer, p. 46; Rochholz, Tell u. Gessler, p. 180; Tobler, p. 3. This or a like song was known to Russ, 1482. Tschudi, about a hundred years later, c. 1570, says that the child was five or six, not more than six, years old: Vischer, p. 122. There is another, but later and even worse, "song" about William Tell and the confederacy: Böhme, No 11, p. 49; Wunderhorn, 1808, II, 129; etc.

‡ Müllenhoff, Sagen, u. s. w., der Herzogthümer Schleswig

Holstein u. Lauenburg, p. 57, No 66. The story is localized at another place in Holstein, with the change of apple to pear: Lütolf, Germania, VIII, 213.

§ Torfæus, in his history of Norway, III, 371, speaks of a ballad about Heming sung in his time, c. 1700, which would seem to have been the same as this, only somewhat fuller. Landstad, p. 187.

These ballads represent the king as regarding himself as quite unapproachable in athletic exercises. The little boy of ballads, smádrengin, kongins lítil svein, Norwegian B, Färöe A, or, in a Färöe variation (Hammershaimb, p. 161), Harald's queen, intimates knowledge of an equal or superior. Harald answers, in true ballad style, in Färöe A 6, If he is not my better, you shall burn for it. In Norwe-

of these incidents are wanting in B (19–22). In the Färöe ballad, A, 53–62, the king tells Geyti (whom he also calls Hemingur) that he must shoot a nut from his brother's head. Geyti asks the king to go to the wood with him to see the result, invokes God and St Olav, hits the nut without touching his brother. It is not till the next day that the king asks Geyti why he had *two* arrows with him in the wood.

The same story, pleasingly varied for the occasion, is found in the saga of the Norwegian king Ólafr Tryggvason († 1000). The king hears that Eindriði, a handsome, rich, and amiable young man, is unconverted. Eindriði is a good swimmer, bowman, and dirk-thrower. Ólafr, a proficient in all such exercises, proposes to try masteries with him in the feats which he has repute for, on the terms that if Eindriði is beaten he shall be baptized, but if victor shall hold such faith as he will. The first trial is in swimming, and in this Ólafr shows unequivocal superiority. The next day they shoot at a target, and the advantage, after two essays, is rather with Eindriði. The king compliments Eindriði; but the issue between them is not yet decided. This fine young fellow's salvation is at stake, and expedients which one might otherwise scruple at are justifiable. Ólafr knows that Eindriði tenderly loves a pretty child, four or five years old, his sister's son. This boy shall be our target, says the king. A chessman (the king-piece) on his head shall be the mark, to be shot off without hurting the boy. Eindriði must needs submit, but means to have revenge if the child comes to harm. The king orders a cloth to be passed round the boy's head, each end of which is to be held firmly by a man, so as to prevent any stirring when the whiz of the arrow is heard. Ólafr signs both himself and the point of his arrow with the cross, and shoots; the arrow takes off

the chessman, passing between it and the head, grazing the crown and drawing some little blood. The king bids Eindriði take his turn; but Eindriði's mother and sister beg him with tears to desist, and he, though ready to take the risk, yields to their entreaties, and leaves the victory with Ólafr. On the third day there is a match at a game with dirks. For a time no one can say which does the better; but in the end Ólafr performs feats so marvellous as in Eindriði's conviction to demonstrate the assistance of a deity: wherefore he consents to be baptized. Saga Ólafs Tryggvasonar, Fornmanna Sögur, II, 259–74, c. 235; Flateyjarbók, I, 456–64, cc. 359–64.

Punker, a warlock of Rorbach (a town not far from Heidelberg), had obtained from the devil, as the regular recompense for his having thrice pierced the crucifix, the power of making three unerring shots daily, and had so been able to pick off in detail all but one of the garrison of a besieged town. To put his skill to proof, a certain nobleman ordered him to shoot a piece of money from his own son's head. Punker wished to be excused, for he feared that the devil might play him false; but being induced to make the trial, knocked the coin from the boy's cap, doing him no damage. Before shooting, he had stuck another arrow into his collar, and asked why, replied that if the devil had betrayed him, and he had killed the child, he would have sent the other bolt through the body of the person who had obliged him to undertake the performance. Malleus Maleficarum, Pars II, Quæstio I, c. xvi.* The date of the transaction is put at about 1420.

The last three forms of this tradition have the unimportant variations of brother and brother, or uncle and nephew, for father and son, and of nut, chessman, or coin for apple.

The story is German-Scandinavian, and not remarkably extended.† The seven versions

gian B, Färöe A, the king immediately sets out to find his rival. Cf. Charlemagne and King Arthur, I, 275, 279, and the beginning of 'King Estmere,' II, 51, and Landstad, p. 177, note 1.

* The Witches' Hammer was composéd in 1486, and Punker is there recorded to have exercised his devil's craft sixty years before. Elsewhere Punker [Pumper] is said to have

been torn to pieces by oppressed peasants in 1420. The name is spelled Puncler in the edition of 1620, pp 248 f, and Puncher in the edition followed by Grimm. See Rochholz in Germania, XIII, 48–51.

† The Tell story, complete, Apfelschuss, Felsensprung und Tyrannenmord, is said to occur among the Finns and the Lapps: E. Pabst, cited by Pfannenschmid, Germania,

agree in two points: the shot is compulsory; the archer meditates revenge in case he harms the person on whose head the mark is placed.* These features are wanting in the English ballad. William of Cloudesly offers of his own free motion to shoot an apple from his son's head, and this after the king had declared him the best archer he had ever seen, for splitting a hazel-rod at twenty score paces; so that the act was done purely for glory. To be sure, the king threatens him with death if he does not achieve what he has undertaken, as death is also threatened in four of the seven German-Scandinavian stories for refusal to try the shot or for missing; but the threats in sts 154 f of the English ballad are a revival of the vow in sts 119 f. Justice has been balked by the unconditional boon granted the queen; aggravating and exasperating circumstances have come to light since this unadvised grace was conceded, and a hope is presented for a pretext under which the king may still hang the outlaws, all three. The shooting of the apple from the boy's head, isolated from any particular connection, is perhaps all of the German-Scandinavian story that was known to the English ballad-maker, and all minor resemblances may well be fortuitous.†

If the shooting of an apple by somebody from somebody's head is to be regarded as the kernel of the story, its area may then be considerably extended.

Castrén heard the following story among the Finns in Russian Karelia. Robbers had carried a man off over a lake. The son of the captive, a boy of twelve, followed along the other side of the lake, threatening to shoot them if they did not let his father go. These threats, for a time, only procured worse treatment for the prisoner; but at last the boy was told that his father should be released if he could shoot an arrow across the water and split an apple laid on his father's head. This the boy did, and his father was liberated. Castrén's Reiseerinnerungen aus den Jahren 1838–44, ed. Schiefner, p. 89 f.

A Persian poet introduces into a work composed about 1175 this anecdote.‡ A distinguished king was very fond of a beautiful slave, so much so that he was never easy unless he was in some way engaged with him. When the king amused himself with shooting, this slave would tremble with fear, for the king would make his mark of an apple placed on his favorite's head, split the apple, and in so doing make the slave sick with alarm.

J. Grimm had seen a manuscript of travels in Turkey, in the Cassel library, with a picture of an archer aiming at an apple on a child's head. Deutsche Mythologie, I, 317, note, ed. 1875.

With regard to the Persian story, Benfey observes that it must be admitted as possible that the shooting of an apple from the head of a beloved person may have been pitched upon in various localities, independently, as the mark of supreme skill in archery, but that this is not likely, and that the history of tradition requires us rather to presume that the conception was original in one instance

---

IX, 5. Particulars, which are very desirable, are not given. This would not add much to the range of the story.

* In the prose Hemings Þáttr, the intent to take vengeance appears from Hemingr's wish that the king should stand close to the mark; in the ballads he reserves an arrow. In the Ólafs Saga, Eindriði openly announces his purpose; in all but this version (treating the prose Hemings Þáttr and the ballads as one), the archer provides himself with two arrows, or three.

† Such as the penalty for missing, as above said; or Tell's shooting at a hundred and twenty paces, and bearing Cloudesly's name, William. If the coincidence as to the distance should be held to be very important, I, for one, should have no objection to admitting that this part of the ballad may be derived from the Tell story.

J. Grimm remarked in 1813, Gedanken über Mythos, Epos und Geschichte (Kleinere Schriften, IV, 77), that the simi-

larity of the names Tell, Bell, Velent, Bellerophon (see a little further on, p. 21), could hardly fail to strike even a superficial observer, and also pointed to the identity of Tell's and Cloudesly's Christian name. In his Deutsche Mythologie, I, 317, ed. 1875, it is simply said that the surname Bell, as well as Cloudesly's Christian name, is suggestive of William Tell.

‡ The poet is Mohammed ben Ibrahim, 1119–c. 1230, and he bore the honorary title of Furîd Uddîn (Pearl of Religion), and the sobriquet of Attâr, perfumer. The title of the poem is The Language of Birds. Garcin de Tassy, La Poésie Philosophique et Religieuse chez les Persans, Extrait de la Revue Contemporaine, t. xxiv, pp. 4, 35. "Nur den Apfel treffen wir hier. . . . Es bleibt also weiter nichts übrig als anzunehmen dass die persische Sage . . . in die grauesten Urzeiten des arischen Alterthums hinaufreichen muss." (Pfannenschmid, in Germania, X, 26 f.) A rapid inference.

only, and borrowed in the remainder; in which case the borrowing would be by the West from the East, and not the other way. We can come to no decision, however, he adds, until the source of the Persian story, or some older form of it, shall have been discovered. (Göttinger Gelehrte Anzeigen, 1861, p. 680.) The cautiousness of the imperial scholar is worthy of all imitation. The Persian saga, as it is sometimes called, is, in the perhaps mutilated form in which we have it, an inconsistent and inept anecdote; the German - Scandinavian saga is a complete and rational story. In this story it is fundamental that the archer executes a successful shot under circumstances highly agitating to the nerves; he risks the life of a beloved object, and in the majority of versions his own life is at stake besides. That the act must be done under compulsion is the simplest corollary. If the archer is cool enough to volunteer the shot, then the chief difficulty in making it is removed. This is a fault in the English ballad, where the father is unconcerned, and all the feeling is shown by the spectators. Cloudesly had already split a hazel - rod at twenty score paces; what was it for him to hit an apple at six score? *

But we are still far from covering the range of stories which have been treated as having some significant relation to that of Egil. Any shot at an apple, any shot at an object on a child's person (provided the case be not a fact and recent), has been thought worth quoting, as a probable sprout from the same root. For examples: In an Esthonian popular tale, one Sharpeye hits an apple which a man a long way off is holding by his mouth. In a Servian poem, the hero, Milosch, sends an arrow through a ring, and hits a golden apple on the point of a lance. Bellerophon's sons, Hippolochus and Isandrus, disputing which should

be king of the Lycians, it was proposed that the question should be settled by seeing which could shoot through a ring placed on the breast of a child lying on his back. Laodamia, sister of the competitors, offered her son Sarpedon for the trial, and the uncles, to show their appreciation of such handsome behavior, resigned their claims in favor of Sarpedon. The shot, we may understand, did not come off.†

With regard to all this series of stories, and others which have been advanced as allied, more will be required to make out a substantial relationship than their having in common a shot at some object in contiguity with a living human body, be the object an apple, or whatever else. The idea of thus enhancing the merit or interest of a shot is not so ingenious that one instance must be held to be original, and all others derivative. The archer Alcon, according to Servius,‡ was wont to shoot through rings placed on men's heads. Sir John Malcolm (Kaye's Life, II, 400) was told that at Mocha, when the dates were ripe, a stone, standing up some three inches, would be put on the head of a child, at which two or three of the best marksmen would fire, with ball, at thirty-one yards distance. A case was reported, about fifty years ago, of a man in Pennsylvania shooting a very small apple from the head of another man.§ A linen-weaver was judicially punished at Spires, some thirty years ago, for shooting a sheet of paper from his son's hand, and afterwards a potato ("also einen Erdapfel," Rochholz!) from the boy's head.‖ The keel-boat men of the Mississippi, in their playfulness, would cut the pipe out of a companion's hat-band at a long distance. "If they quarreled among themselves, and then made friends, their test that they bore no malice was to shoot some small object from each other's heads," such as

---

* Eindriði also had accomplished a harder shot before he tried the chessman. But Hemingr, having done what was thought a masterly thing in cleaving a nut, is compelled to knock the same nut, shooting at the same distance, from his brother's head.

† Das Inland, No 39, p. 630, cited by Rochholz, Tell und Gessler, p. 40 f. Gerhard's Wila, I, 147 f, cited by Rochholz, p. 39 f. Eustathius to Iliad, xii, 101, first cited by

Grimm, Deutsche Mythologie (who says, "Es stimmt auch theilweise," p. 317, ed. 1875); by others later.

‡ To Virgil, Ecl. v, 11, cited by Ideler, Die Sage von dem Schuss des Tell, p. 59, note 3.

§ Hiselv, Recherches Critiques sur l'Histoire de Guillaume Tell, p. 590.

‖ Pfannenschmid, in Germania, X, 25; Rochholz, Tell und Gessler, p. 41 f.

an apple. Such feats have of late been common on the American stage.

Whatever may be thought of the linen-weaver at Spires, it will scarcely be maintained that the Mississippi keel-boat men shot at apples in imitation of William Tell. As to the selection of an apple, it seems enough to say that an apple makes a convenient mark, is familiar to temperate climates, and at hand at almost any part of the year.* But the chief point of all to be borne in mind is, that whether the Mississippi boatmen took their cue, directly or indirectly, from William Tell, they do not become mythical personages by virtue of their repeating his shot. None the more does William of Cloudesly. A story long current in Europe, a mythical story if you please, could certainly be taken up by an English ballad-maker without prejudice to the substantial and simply romantic character of his hero.†

The late Mr Joseph Hunter unhesitatingly declared Adam Bell "a genuine personage of history," and considered that he had had "the good fortune to recover from a very authentic source of information some particulars of this hero of our popular minstrelsy which show distinctly the time at which he lived."

"King Henry the Fourth, by letters enrolled in the Exchequer, in Trinity Term, in the seventh year of his reign [1406], and bearing date the 14th day of April, granted to one Adam Bell an annuity of 4*l.* 10*s.* issuing out of the fee-farm of Clipston, in the forest of Sherwood, together with the profits and advantages of the vesture and herbage of the garden called the Halgarth, in which the manor-house of Clipston is situated.

"Now, as Sherwood is noted for its connection with archery, and may be regarded also as the *patria* of much of the ballad poetry of England, and the name of Adam Bell is a peculiar one, this might be almost of itself sufficient to show that the ballad had a foundation in veritable history. But we further find that this Adam Bell violated his allegiance by adhering to the Scots, the king's enemies; whereupon this grant was virtually resumed, and the sheriff of Nottinghamshire accounted for the rents which would have been his. In the third year of King Henry the Fifth [1416], the account was rendered by Thomas Hercy, and in the fourth year by Simon Leak. The mention of his adhesion to the Scots leads us to the Scottish border, and will not leave a doubt in the mind of the most sceptical that we have here one of the persons, some of whose deeds (with some poetical license, perhaps) are come down to us in the words of one of our popular ballads." (New Illustrations of the Life, Studies, and Writings of Shakespeare, I, 245 f, 1845.)

Mr Hunter's points are, that an Adam Bell had a grant from the proceeds of a farm in the forest of Sherwood, that Adam Bell is a peculiar name, and that his Adam Bell adhered to the king's enemies. To be sure, Adam Bell's retreat in the ballad is not Sherwood, in Nottinghamshire, but Englishwood, or Inglewood, in Cumberland (an old hunting-ground of King Arthur's, according to several romances), a forest sixteen miles in length,

---

* T. B. Thorpe, Reminiscences of the Mississippi, in Harper's New Monthly Magazine, XII, 30. A story is there related of a famous Mike Fink's striking an apple from a man's head by shooting between it and the skull, like the Scandinavian marksmen. In Captain Mayne Reid's Scalp Hunters, or Romantic Adventures in Northern Mexico, ch. 22, we are told of an Indian's shooting a prairie-gourd from the head of his sister, which may or may not be an invention. The title of the chapter is A Feat à la Tell, and this may perhaps be the only foundation for an assertion that the Tell story had been found in Mexico; at least, inquiries have not brought to light any other.

† For the interpretation which has been put upon the Tell story, see, among many, Pfannenschmid, in Germania, X, 1–40; Rochholz, Tell und Gessler, in Sage und Geschichte.

The mildew of myth spreads, of course, from William to his comrades. J. Grimm, in his Gedanken über Mythos, etc., 1813, interprets Clim, Cloudesly, and Clough all in the sense of nail, sharp point, arrow; and as Bell is βέλος, Tell is telum, Toko τόξον, and Egil is igel, hedgehog, and therefore the spine of the hedgehog, and therefore dart, the names are all one as to meaning. But Grimm appears to have been less confident about these etymologies in later days. Sir G. W. Cox, on the other hand, says that Cloudesly's name marks him as an inhabitant of Cloudland. (Meanwhile, every likelihood favors the derivation of Cloudesly from clúd, rock, and leáh, lea, and the interpretation of Clim as Clem and of Clough as ravine.) Cloudesly and his mates are all the more mythical because they are three, and because, as it is asserted, Robin Hood is mythical, with whom they are, one and all, assumed to be identical.

reaching from Carlisle to Penrith.* But it would be captious to insist upon this. Robin Hood has no connection in extant ballads with the Cumberland forest, but Wyntoun's Scottish Chronicle, c. 1420, makes him to have frequented Inglewood as well as Barnsdale.† The historical Adam Bell was granted an annuity, and forfeited it for adhering to the king's enemies, the Scots ; the Adam Bell of the ballad was outlawed for breaking the game-laws, and in consequence came into conflict with the king's officers, but never adhered to the king's enemies, first or last, received the king's pardon, was made yeoman of the queen's chamber, dwelt with the king, and died a good man. Neither is there anything peculiar in the name Adam Bell. Bell was as well known a name on the borders ‡ as Armstrong or Graham. There is record of an Adam Armstrong and an Adam Graham ; there is a Yorkshire Adam Bell mentioned in the Parliamentary Writs (II, 508, 8 and 17 Edward II,) a hundred years before Hunter's annuitant; a contemporary Adam Bell, of Dunbar, is named in the Exchequer Rolls of Scotland under the years 1414, 1420 (IV, 198, 325) ; and the name occurs repeatedly at a later date in the Registers of the Great Seal of Scotland.

The placability of the king in this ballad is repeated in the Gest of Robin Hood, and is also exhibited in the Tale of Gamelyn, where Gamelyn is made justice of all the free forest, as William is here made chief rider over all the North Country. The king, besides, forgives all Gamelyn's eight young men, and puts them in good office. The king of the outlaws, in the tale, had previously made his peace without any difficulty. Vv 888–94, 687–89.

Translated, after Percy's Reliques, by Bodmer, II, 78 ; by Fouqué, Büsching, Erzählungen, u. s. w., des Mittelalters, I, 1 ; the third Fit, by Knortz, Lieder und Romanzen Altenglands, No 70.

———

c. 1 MERY it was in grene forest,
   Amonge the leues grene,
   Where that men walke both east and west,
   Wyth bowes and arrowes kene,

2 To ryse the dere out of theyr denne ;
   Suche sightes as hath ofte bene sene,
   As by th[r]e yemen of the north countrey,
   By them it is as I meane.

3 The one of them hight Adam Bel,
   The other Clym of the Clough,
   The thyrd was William of Cloudesly,
   An archer good ynough.

4 They were outlawed for venyson,
   These thre yemen euerechone ;

They swore them brethen vpon a day,
   To Englysshe-wood for to gone.

5 Now lith and lysten, gentylmen,
   And that of myrthes loueth to here :
   Two of them were single men,
   The third had a wedded fere.

6 Wyllyam was the wedded man,
   Muche more then was hys care :
   He sayde to hys brethen vpon a day,
   To Carelel he would fare,

7 For to speke with fayre Alse hys wife,
   And with hys chyldren thre :
   ' By my trouth,' sayde Adam Bel,
   ' Not by the counsell of me.

* Camden, Britannia, II, 175, ed. 1772. King Edward the First, when hunting in this forest, is said to have killed two hundred bucks in one day. For Arthur's hunting there, see Robson, Three Early English Metrical Romances, p. 26, LV⁷, p. 59, V¹ ; Madden's Syr Gawayne, p. 298, v. 16 ; this book, I, 294, st. 9, etc.
† Cronykil of Scotland, Book vii, v. 3523 f, ed. Laing, II, 263.

‡ John Bell robbed the Chamberlain's men of cattle, 1337 : Exchequer Rolls of Scotland, II, 437. The Bells are included with the Grahams, Armstrongs, and others, among the bad and more vagrant of the great surnames of the border, by the Lord Warden of the Marches of England, 1593 (Rymer's Fœdera, XVI, 183, ed. 1727, cited by Bishop Percy), and had no better estimation in Scotland.

8 'For if ye go to Caerlel, brother,
  And from thys wylde wode wende,
If the justice mai you take,
  Your lyfe were at an ende.'

9 'If that I come not to morowe, brother,
  By pryme to you agayne,
Truste not els but that I am take,
  Or else that I am slayne.'

10 He toke hys leaue of hys brethen two,
  And to Carlel he is gone;
There he knocked at hys owne wyndowe,
  Shortlye and anone.

11 'Wher be you, fayre Alyce, my wyfe,
  And my chyldren three?
Lyghtly let in thyne husbande,
  Wyllyam of Cloudesle.'

12 'Alas!' then sayde fayre Alyce,
  And syghed wonderous sore,
'Thys place hath ben besette for you
  Thys halfe yere and more.'

13 'Now am I here,' sayde Cloudesle,
  'I woulde that I in were;
Now feche vs meate and drynke ynoughe,
  And let vs make good chere.'

14 She feched him meat and drynke plenty,
  Lyke a true wedded wyfe,
And pleased hym with that she had,
  Whome she loued as her lyfe.

15 There lay an old wyfe in that place,
  A lytle besyde the fyre,
Whych Wyllyam had found, of cherytye,
  More then seuen yere.

16 Up she rose, and walked full styll,
  Euel mote she spede therefoore!
For she had not set no fote on ground
  In seuen yere before.

17 She went vnto the justice hall,
  As fast as she could hye:
'Thys nyght is come vn to thys town
  Wyllyam of Cloudesle.'

18 Thereof the iustice was full fayne,
  And so was the shirife also:

'Thou shalt not trauaile hether, dame, for
    nought;
  Thy meed thou shalt haue or thou go.'

19 They gaue to her a ryght good goune,
  Of scarlat it was, as I heard say[n]e;
She toke the gyft, and home she wente,
  And couched her doune agayne.

20 They rysed the towne of mery Carlel,
  In all the hast that they can,
And came thronging to Wyllyames house,
  As fast [as] they might gone.

21 Theyr they besette that good yeman,
  Round about on euery syde;
Wyllyam hearde great noyse of folkes,
  That heytherward they hyed.

22 Alyce opened a shot-wyndow,
  And loked all about;
She was ware of the justice and the shrife bothe,
  Wyth a full great route.

23 'Alas! treason,' cryed Alyce,
  'Euer wo may thou be!
Go into my chambre, my husband,' she sayd,
  'Swete Wyllyam of Cloudesle.'

24 He toke hys sweard and hys bucler,
  Hys bow and hy[s] chyldren thre,
And wente into hys strongest chamber,
  Where he thought surest to be.

25 Fayre Alice folowed him as a louer true,
  With a pollaxe in her hande:
'He shalbe deade that here cometh in
  Thys dore, whyle I may stand.'

26 Cloudesle bent a wel good bowe,
  That was of trusty tre,
He smot the justise on the brest,
  That hys arrowe brest in thre.

27 'God's curse on his hartt,' saide William,
  'Thys day thy cote dyd on;
If it had ben no better then myne,
  It had gone nere thy bone.'

28 'Yelde the, Cloudesle,' sayd the justise,
  'And thy bowe and thy arrowes the fro:'
'Gods curse on hys hart,' sayde fair Al[i]ce,
  'That my husband councelleth so.'

29 'Set fyre on the house,' saide the sherife,
    'Syth it wyll no better be,
And brenne we therin William,' he saide,
    'Hys wyfe and chyldren thre.'

30 They fyred the house in many a place,
    The fyre flew vpon hye;
'Alas!' than cryed fayr Alice,
    'I se we shall here dy.'

31 William openyd hys backe wyndow,
    That was in hys chambre on hye,
And wyth shetes let hys wyfe downe,
    And hys chyldren thre.

32 'Haue here my treasure,' sayde William,
    'My wyfe and my chyldren thre;
For Christes loue do them no harme,
    But wreke you all on me.'

33 Wyllyam shot so wonderous well,
    Tyll hys arrowes were all go,
And the fyre so fast vpon hym fell,
    That hys bo[w]stryng brent in two.

34 The spercles brent and fell hym on,
    Good Wyllyam of Cloudesle;
But than was he a wofull man, and sayde,
    Thys is a cowardes death to me.

35 'Leuer I had,' sayde Wyllyam,
    'With my sworde in the route to renne,
Then here among myne ennemyes wode
    Thus cruelly to bren.'

36 He toke hys sweard and hys buckler,
    And among them all he ran;
Where the people were most in prece,
    He smot downe many a man.

37 There myght no man stand hys stroke,
    So fersly on them he ran;
Then they threw wyndowes and dores on him,
    And so toke that good yeman.

38 There they hym bounde both hand and fote,
    And in depe dongeon hym cast;
'Now, Cloudesle,' sayde the hye justice,
    'Thou shalt be hanged in hast.'

39 'One vow shal I make,' sayde the sherife,
    'A payre of new galowes shall I for the
    make,

And al the gates of Caerlel shalbe shutte,
    There shall no man come in therat.

40 'Then shall not helpe Clim of the Cloughe,
    Nor yet Adam Bell,
Though they came with a thousand mo,
    Nor all the deuels in hell.'

41 Early in the mornyng the justice vprose,
    To the gates fast gan he gon,
And commaunded to be shut full cloce
    Lightile euerychone.

42 Then went he to the market-place,
    As fast as he coulde hye;
A payre of new gallous there dyd he vp set,
    Besyde the pyllory.

43 A lytle boy stod them amonge,
    And asked what meaned that gallow-tre;
They sayde, To hange a good yeaman,
    Called Wyllyam of Cloudesle.

44 That lytle boye was the towne swyne-heard,
    And kept fayre Alyce swyne;
Full oft he had sene Cloudesle in the wodde,
    And geuen hym there to dyne.

45 He went out of a creues in the wall,
    And lightly to the woode dyd gone;
There met he with these wyght yonge men,
    Shortly and anone.

46 'Alas!' then sayde that lytle boye,
    'Ye tary here all to longe;
Cloudesle is taken and dampned to death,
    All readye for to honge.'

47 'Alas!' then sayde good Adam Bell,
    'That euer we see thys daye!
He myght her with vs haue dwelled,
    So ofte as we dyd him praye.

48 'He myght haue taryed in grene foreste,
    Under the shadowes sheene,
And haue kepte both hym and vs in reaste,
    Out of trouble and teene.'

49 Adam bent a ryght good bow,
    A great hart sone had he slayne;
'Take that, chylde,' he sayde, 'to thy dynner,
    And bryng me myne arrowe agayne.'

50 'Now go we hence,' sayed these wight yong men,
     'Tary we no lenger here;
  We shall hym borowe, by Gods grace,
     Though we bye it full dere.'

51 To Caerlel went these good yemen,
     In a mery mornyng of Maye:
  Her is a fyt of Cloudesli,
     And another is for to saye.

52 And when they came to mery Caerlell,
     In a fayre mornyng-tyde,
  They founde the gates shut them vntyll,
     Round about on euery syde.

53 'Alas!' than sayd good Adam Bell,
     'That euer we were made men!
b. These gates be shyt so wonderly well,
     That we may not come here in.'

54 Than spake Clymme of the Cloughe:
     With a wyle we wyll vs in brynge;
  Let vs say we be messengers,
     Streyght comen from oure kynge.

55 Adam sayd, I haue a lettre wryten wele,
     Now let vs wysely werke;
  We wyll say we haue the kynges seale,
     I holde the porter no clerke.

56 Than Adam Bell bete on the gate,
     With strökes greate and stronge;
  The porter herde suche a noyse therate,
     And to the gate faste he thronge.

57 'Who is there nowe,' sayd the porter,
     'That maketh all this knockynge?
  'We be two messengers,' sayd Clymme of the
        Clo[ughe],
     'Be comen streyght frome oure kynge.'

58 'We haue a lettre,' sayd Adam Bell,
     'To the justyce we must it brynge;
  Let vs in, oure message to do,
     That we were agayne to our kynge.'

59 'Here cometh no man in,' sayd the porter,
     'By hym that dyed on a tre,
  Tyll a false thefe be hanged,
     Called Wyllyam of Clowdysle.'

60 Than spake that good [yeman Clym of the
        Cloughe,
     And swore by Mary fre,
  If that we stande long wythout,
     Lyke a thefe hanged shalt thou be.]

61 [Lo here] we haue got the kynges seale;
     [What! l]ordane, arte thou wode?
  [The p]orter had wende it had been so,
     [And l]yghtly dyd of his hode.

62 '[Welco]me be my lordes seale,' sayd he,
     '[For] that shall ye come in:'
  [He] opened the gate ryght shortly,
     [An] euyll openynge for hym!

63 '[N]owe we are in,' sayd Adam Bell,
     '[T]herof we are full fayne;
  [But] Cryst knoweth that herowed hell,
     [H]ow we shall come oute agayne.'

64 '[Had] we the keys,' sayd Clym of the Clowgh,
     'Ryght well than sholde we spede;
  [Than] myght we come out well ynough,
     [Whan] we se tyme and nede.'

65 [They] called the porter to a councell,
     [And] wronge hys necke in two,
  [And] kest hym in a depe dongeon,
     [And] toke the keys hym fro.

66 '[N]ow am I porter,' sayd Adam Bell;
     '[Se], broder, the keys haue we here;
  [The] worste porter to mery Carlell,
     [That ye] had this hondreth yere.

67 '[Now] wyll we oure bowës bende,
     [Into the t]owne wyll we go,
  [For to delyuer our dere] broder,
     [Where he lyeth in care and wo.'

68 Then they bent theyr good yew bowes,
     And loked theyr stringes were round;]
  The market-place of mery Carlyll,
     They beset in that stounde.

69 And as they loked them besyde,
     A payre of newe galowes there they se,
  And the iustyce, with a quest of swerers,
     That had iuged Clowdysle there hanged to be.

70 And Clowdysle hymselfe lay redy in a carte,
     Fast bounde bothe fote and hande,
  And a strong rope aboute his necke,
     All redy for to be hangde.

71 The iustyce called to hym a ladde;
     Clowdysles clothes sholde he haue,
  To take the mesure of that good yoman,
     And therafter to make his graue.

72 'I haue sene as greate a merueyll,' sayd
        Clowd[esle],
     'As bytwene this and pryme,
  He that maketh thys graue for me,
     Hymselfe may lye therin.'

73 'Thou spekest proudely,' sayd the iustyce ;
   'I shall hange the with my hande : '
Full well that herde his bretheren two,
   There styll as they dyd stande.

74 Than Clowdysle cast hys eyen asyde,
   And sawe hys bretheren stande,
At a corner of the market-place,
   With theyr good bowes bent in theyr hand,
Redy the iustyce for to chase.

75 'I se good comforte,' sayd Clowdysle,
   'Yet hope I well to fare ;
If I myght haue my handes at wyll,
   [Ryght l]ytell wolde I care.'

76 [Than b]espake good Adam Bell,
   [To Clym]me of the Clowgh so fre ;
[Broder], se ye marke the iustyce well ;
   [Lo yon]der ye may him se.

77 [And at] the sheryf shote I wyll,
   [Stron]gly with an arowe kene ;
[A better] shotte in mery Carlyll,
   [Thys se]uen yere was not sene.

78 [They lo]used theyr arowes bothe at ones,
   [Of no] man had they drede ;
[The one] hyt the iustyce, the other the sheryf,
   [That b]othe theyr sydes gan blede.

79 [All men] voyded, that them stode nye,
   [Whan] the iustyce fell to the grounde,
[And the] sheryf fell nyghe hym by ;
   [Eyther] had his dethës wounde.

80 [All the c]ytezeyns fast gan fle,
   [They du]rste no lenger abyde ;
[There ly]ghtly they loused Clowdysle,
   [Where he] with ropes lay tyde.

81 [Wyllyam] sterte to an offycer of the towne,
   [Hys axe] out his hande he wronge ;
[On eche] syde he smote them downe,
   [Hym tho]ught he had taryed to longe.

82 [Wyllyam] sayd to his bretheren two,
   [Thys daye] let vs togyder lyue and deye ;
[If euer you] haue nede as I haue nowe,
   [The same] shall ye fynde by me.

83 [They] shyt so well in that tyde,
   For theyr strynges were of sylke full sure,
That they kepte the stretes on euery syde ;
   That batayll dyd longe endure.

84 They fought togyder as bretheren true,
   Lyke hardy men and bolde ;
Many a man to the grounde they threwe,
   And made many an hertë colde.

85 But whan theyr arowes were all gone,
   Men presyd on them full fast ;
They drewe theyr swerdës than anone,
   And theyr bowës from them caste.

86 They wente lyghtly on theyr waye,
   With swerdes and buckelers rounde ;
By that it was the myddes of the daye,
   They had made many a wounde.

87 There was many a noute-horne in Carlyll
    blowen,
   And the belles backwarde dyd they rynge ;
Many a woman sayd alas,
   And many theyr handes dyd wrynge.

88 The mayre of Carlyll forth come was,
   And with hym a full grete route ;
These thre yomen dredde hym full sore,
   For theyr lyuës stode in doubte.

89 The mayre came armed, a full greate pace,
   With a polaxe in his hande ;
Many a stronge man with hym was,
   There in that stoure to stande.

90 The mayre smote at Clowdysle with his byll,
   His buckeler he brast in two ;
Full many a yoman with grete yll,
   '[Al]as, treason ! ' they cryed for wo.
'[Ke]pe we the gates fast,' they bad,
   '[T]hat these traytours theroute not go.'

91 But all for nought was that they wrought,
   For so fast they downe were layde
Tyll they all thre, that so manfully fought,
   Were goten without at a brayde.

92 'Haue here your keys,' sayd Adam Bell,
   'Myne offyce I here forsake ;
Yf ye do by my councell,
   A newë porter ye make.'

93 He threwe the keys there at theyr hedes,
   And bad them evyll to thryue,
And all that letteth ony good yoman
   To come and comforte his wyue.

94 Thus be these good yomen gone to the wode,
   As lyght as lefe on lynde ;
They laughe and be mery in theyr mode,
   Theyr enemyes were farre behynde.

95 Whan they came to Inglyswode,
   Under theyr trysty-tre,
There they founde bowës full gode,
   And arowës greate plentë.

96 'So helpe me God,' sayd Adam Bell,
   And Clymme of the Clowgh so fre,

' I wolde we were nowe in mery Carlell,
  [Be]fore that fayre meynë.'

97 They set them downe and made good chere,
   And eate an[d dr]anke full well :
   Here is a fytte [of] these wyght yongemen,
   And another I shall you tell.

98 As they sat in Inglyswode,
   Under theyr trysty-tre,
   Them thought they herde a woman [wepe],
   But her they myght not se.

99 Sore syghed there fayre Alyce, and sayd,
   Alas that euer I se this daye !
   For now is my dere husbonde slayne,
   Alas and welawaye !

100 Myght I haue spoken wyth hys dere breth-
    [eren],
    With eyther of them twayne,
    [To shew to them what him befell]
    My herte were out of payne.

101 Clowdysle walked a lytell besyde,
    And loked vnder the grene wodde lynde ;
    He was ware of his wyfe and his chyldre[n
    thre],
    Full wo in herte and mynde.

102 ' Welcome, wyfe,' than sayd Wyllyam,
    ' Unto this trysty-tre ;
    I had wende yesterdaye, by swete Sai[nt John],
    Thou sholde me neuer haue se.'

103 ' Now wele is me,' she sayd, ' that [ye be here],
    My herte is out of wo : '
    ' Dame,' he sayd, ' be mery and glad,
    And thanke my bretheren two.'

104 ' Here of to speke,' sayd Ad[am] Bell,
    ' I-wys it [is no bote] ;
    The me[at that we must supp withall,
    It runneth yet fast on fote.'

105 Then went they down into a launde,
    These noble archares all thre,
    Eche of the]m slewe a harte of grece,
    [The best t]hey coude there se.

106 ' [Haue here the] best, Alyce my wyfe,'
    [Sayde Wyllya]m of Clowdysle,
    ' [By cause ye so] boldely stode me by,
    [Whan I w]as slayne full nye.'

107 [Than they] wente to theyr souper,
    [Wyth suc]he mete as they had,

[And than]ked God of theyr fortune ;
[They we]re bothe mery and glad.

108 [And whan] they had souped well,
    [Certayne] withouten leace,
    [Clowdysle] sayde, We wyll to oure kynge,
    [To get v]s a chartre of peace.

109 [Alyce shal] be at soiournynge,
    [In a nunry] here besyde ;
    [My tow sonn]es shall with her go,
    [And ther the]y shall abyde.

110 [Myne eldest so]ne shall go with me,
    [For hym haue I] no care,
    [And he shall breng] you worde agayne
    [How that we do fare.

111 Thus be these wig]ht men to London gone,
    [As fast as they ma]ye hye,
    [Tyll they came to the kynges] palays,
c.   There they woulde nedës be.

112 And whan they came to the kyngës courte,
    Unto the pallace gate,
    Of no man wold they aske leue,
    But boldly went in therat.

113 They preced prestly into the hall,
    Of no man had they dreade ;
    The porter came after and dyd them call,
a.   And with them began to [chyde.]

114 The vssher sayd, Yemen, what wolde ye
    haue ?
    I praye you tell me ;
    Ye myght thus make offycers shent :
    Good syrs, of whens be ye ?

115 ' Syr, we be outlawes of the forest,
    Certayne withouten leace,
    And hyther we be come to our kynge,
    To get vs a charter of peace.'

116 And whan they came before our kynge,
    As it was the lawe of the lande,
    They kneled downe without lettynge,
    And eche helde vp his hande.

117 They sayd, Lorde, we beseche you here,
    That ye wyll graunte vs grace,
    For we haue slayne your fatte falowe dere,
    In many a sondry place.

118 ' What is your names ? ' than sayd our kynge,
    ' Anone that you tell me : '
    They sayd, Adam Bell, Clym of the Clough,
    And Wylliam of Clowdesle.

119 ' Be ye those theues,' than sayd our kynge,
    ' That men haue tolde of to me ?
  Here to God I make a vowe,
    Ye shall be hanged all thre.

120 ' Ye shall be dead without mercy,
    As I am kynge of this lande : '
  c. He commanded his officers euerichone
    Fast on them to lay hand.

121 There they toke these good yemen,
    And arested them all thre :
  ' So may I thryue,' sayd Adam Bell,
    ' Thys game lyketh not me.

a. 122 ' But, good lorde, we beseche you nowe,
    That ye wyll graunte vs grace,
  In so moche as we be to you commen ;
    Or elles that we may fro you passe,

123 ' With suche weapons as we haue here,
    Tyll we be out of your place ;
  And yf we lyue this hondred yere,
    We wyll aske you no grace.'

124 ' Ye speke proudly,' sayd the kynge,
    ' Ye shall be hanged all thre : '
  ' That were great pity,' sayd the quene,
    ' If any grace myght be.

125 ' My lorde, whan I came fyrst in to this lande,
    To be your wedded wyfe,
  The fyrst bone that I wolde aske,
    Ye wolde graunte me belyfe.

126 ' And I asked you neuer none tyll nowe,
    Therfore, good lorde, graunte it me : '
  ' Nowe aske it, madame,' sayd the kynge,
    ' And graunted shall it be.'

127 ' Than, good lorde, I you beseche,
    The yemen graunte you me : '
  ' Madame, ye myght haue asked a bone
    That sholde haue ben worthe them thre.

128 ' Ye myght haue asked towres and towne[s],
    Parkes and forestes plentie : '
  c. ' None so pleasaunt to mi pay,' she said,
    ' Nor none so lefe to me.'

129 ' Madame, sith it is your desyre,
    Your askyng graunted shalbe ;
  But I had leuer haue geuen you
    Good market-townës thre.'

130 The quene was a glad woman,
    And sayd, Lord, gramarcy ;
  I dare vndertake for them
    That true men shall they be.

131 But, good lord, speke som mery word,
    That comfort they may se :
  ' I graunt you grace,' then said our king,
    ' Wasshe, felos, and to meate go ye.'

132 They had not setten but a whyle,
    Certayne without lesynge,
  There came messengers out of the north,
    With letters to our kyng.

133 And whan the came before the kynge,
    The kneled downe vpon theyr kne,
  And sayd, Lord, your offycers grete you wel,
    Of Caerlel in the north cuntre.

134 ' How fare[th] my justice,' sayd the kyng,
    ' And my sherife also ? '
  ' Syr, they be slayne, without leasynge,
    And many an officer mo.'

135 ' Who hath them slayne ? ' sayd the kyng,
    ' Anone thou tell me : '
  ' Adam Bel, and Clime of the Clough,
    And Wyllyam of Cloudesle.'

136 ' Alas for rewth ! ' then sayd our kynge,
    ' My hart is wonderous sore ;
  I had leuer [th]an a thousand pounde
    I had knowne of thys before.

137 ' For I haue y-graunted them grace,
    And that forthynketh me ;
  But had I knowne all thys before,
    They had ben hanged all thre.'

138 The kyng opened the letter anone,
    Hym selfe he red it tho,
  And founde how these thre outlawes had slaine
    Thre hundred men and mo.

139 Fyrst the justice and the sheryfe,
    And the mayre of Caerlel towne ;
  Of all the constables and catchipolles
    Alyue were left not one.

140 The baylyes and the bedyls both,
    And the sergeauntes of the law,
  And forty fosters of the fe
    These outlawes had y-slaw ;

141 And broken his parks, and slaine his dere ;
    Ouer all they chose the best ;
  So perelous outlawes as they were
    Walked not by easte nor west.

142 When the kynge this letter had red,
 In hys harte he syghed sore;
'Take vp the table,' anone he bad,
 'For I may eate no more.'

143 The kyng called hys best archars,
 To the buttes with hym to go;
'I wyll se these felowes shote,' he sayd,
 'That in the north haue wrought this wo.'

144 The kynges bowmen buske them blyue,
 And the quenes archers also,
So dyd these thre wyght yemen,
 Wyth them they thought to go.

145 There twyse or thryse they shote about,
 For to assay theyr hande;
There was no shote these thre yemen shot
 That any prycke might them stand.

146 Then spake Wyllyam of Cloudesle;
 By God that for me dyed,
I hold hym neuer no good archar
 That shuteth at buttes so wyde.

147 'Wherat?' then sayd our kyng,
 'I pray thee tell me:'
'At suche a but, syr,' he sayd,
 'As men vse in my countree.'

148 Wyllyam wente into a fyeld,
 And his to brothren with him;
There they set vp to hasell roddes,
 Twenty score paces betwene.

149 'I hold him an archar,' said Cloudesle,
 'That yonder wande cleueth in two:'
'Here is none suche,' sayd the kyng,
 'Nor none that can so do.'

150 'I shall assaye, syr,' sayd Cloudesle,
 'Or that I farther go:'
Cloudesle, with a bearyng arow,
 Claue the wand in to.

151 'Thou art the best archer,' then said the king,
 'Forsothe that euer I se:'
'And yet for your loue,' sayd Wylliam,
 'I wyll do more maystry.

152 'I haue a sonne is seuen yere olde;
 He is to me full deare;
I wyll hym tye to a stake,
 All shall se that be here;

153 'And lay an apple vpon hys head,
 And go syxe score paces hym fro,
And I my selfe, with a brode arow,
 Shall cleue the apple in two.'

154 'Now hast the,' then sayd the kyng;
 'By him that dyed on a tre,
But yf thou do not as thou hest sayde,
 Hanged shalt thou be.

155 'And thou touche his head or gowne,
 In syght that men may se,
By all the sayntes that be in heaven,
 I shall hange you all thre.'

156 'That I haue promised,' said William,
 'I wyl it neuer forsake;'
And there euen before the kynge,
 In the earth he droue a stake;

157 And bound therto his eldest sonne,
 And bad hym stande styll therat,
And turned the childes face fro him,
 Because he shuld not sterte.

158 An apple vpon his head he set,
 And then his bowe he bent;
Syxe score paces they were outmet,
 And thether Cloudesle went.

159 There he drew out a fayr brode arrowe;
 Hys bowe was great and longe;
He set that arrowe in his bowe,
 That was both styffe and stronge.

160 He prayed the people that was there
 That they would styll stande;
'For he that shooteth for such a wager,
 Behoueth a stedfast hand.'

161 Muche people prayed for Cloudesle,
a. That hys lyfe saued myght be,
And whan he made hym redy to shote,
 There was many a wepynge eye.

162 Thus Clowdesle clefte the apple in two,
 That many a man it se;
'Ouer goddes forbode,' sayd the kynge,
 'That thou sholdest shote at me!

163 'I gyue the .xviii. pens a daye,
 And my bowe shalte thou bere,
And ouer all the north countree
 I make the chefe rydere.'

164 'And I gyue the .xii. pens a day,' sayd the
        que[ne],
    'By God and by my faye ;
    Come fetche thy payment whan thou wylt,
        No man shall say the naye.

165 'Wyllyam, I make the gentylman
        Of clothynge and of fee,
    And thy two brethren yemen of my chambr[e],
        For they are so semely to se.

166 'Your sone, for he is tendre of age,
        Of my wyne-seller shall he be,
    And whan he commeth to mannës state,
        Better auaunced shall he be.

167 'And, Wylliam, brynge me your wyfe,' sayd
        th[e quene] ;
    Me longeth sore here to se ;

She shall be my chefe gentylwoman,
    And gouerne my nursery.'

168 The yemen thanked them full courteysly,
        And sayd, To Rome streyght wyll we
        wende,
    [Of all the synnes that we haue done
        To be assoyled of his hand.

169 So forth]e be gone these good yemen,
        [As fast a]s they myght hye,
    [And aft]er came and dwelled with the kynge,
        [And dye]d good men all thre.

170 [Thus e]ndeth the lyues of these good ye-
        men,
    [God sen]de them eternall blysse,
    [And all] that with hande-bowe shoteth,
        [That of] heuen they may neuer mysse !

Deficiencies in a, b *are supplied from* c *unless
it is otherwise noted.*

a. 120¹. deed.
b. 87¹. an oute horne.   *The emendation is Prof.
        Skeat's.*
    99¹,². and sayd *begins the second line.*
    100³. *supplied from* d, e.
c. 5⁸. singele.   11¹. be your.   13². In woulde.
    16². spende.   17¹, 107¹. whent.   18⁸. fore.
    22¹. shop-wyndow.   22⁴. great full great.
    23⁸. Gy.   26¹. welgood.   30⁸. Alece.
    33². all gon.
    34⁸,⁴. and sayde *begins the fourth line.*
    44². there Alyce.   44⁴. geuend.
    46⁴. Allreadye.   48⁴. in reaffte [?].
    51¹. Cyerlel.   52¹. Carelell.
        Variations from b.
    53⁸. shut : wonderous.
    54¹, 56¹, 64⁸, 76¹, 85⁸, 102¹, 107¹. Then.
    54⁸. Lee.   54⁴. come nowe.   55⁸. seales.
    56⁸. a *wanting.*   56⁴. faste *wanting.*
    57⁴. come ryght.   58². me *for* we.
    59¹. commeth none.   59². Be : vpon.
    61⁸. went.   62¹. he saide.   62⁸. full shortlye.
    63¹. are we.   63⁸. know.
    64⁴, 79², 106⁴, 108¹. When.
    65¹. a *wanting.*   65⁴. hys keys.
    66², 67⁸, 76⁸. brother.   66⁴. hundred.
    68¹. They bent theyr bowes.   Then, good yew
        from e, f.
    68⁸. in mery.   68⁴. in *wanting.*
    69⁸. And they : squyers.

70². bounde *wanting.*   71². Cloudesle.
71⁸. good *wanting :* yeman, *and* ye *always,
        as,* 88⁸, 90⁸, 93⁸, 94¹.
72¹. Cloudesli.   73². the hange.
73⁸. that *wanting :* brtehren, *or,* breehren.
74², 82¹, 84¹, 100¹, 103⁴. brethen.
74². stande *wanting.*   74⁸. marked.
74⁵. to chaunce.   75¹. good *wanting.*
75². will.   76¹. Then spake.   76⁸. Brother.
77¹. shyrfe.   77². an *wanting.*
78¹. thre arrowes.   78⁴. there sedes.
79². fell downe.   81². out of.
81⁴. he taryed all to.   82². togyder *wanting.*
82⁴. shall you.   83¹. shot.   83⁸. sede.
84¹. The : together.   85². preced to.
86⁸. mas myd.   87². they *wanting.*
88⁴. For of theyr lyues they stode in great.
90². brust.   90⁸. euyll.   90⁶. That.
91¹. yᵗ yᵉ.   91². to fast.   91⁴. at *wanting.*
92²,⁸. *Transposed :* Yf you do, *etc.,* Myne offce.
92⁴. do we.   93¹. theyr keys.
94². lyghtly as left.   94⁸. The lough an.
94⁴. fere.   95¹, 98¹. Englyshe.
95². Under the : trusty, *and* 98².
95⁸. There *wanting.*   95⁴. full great.
96¹. God me help.   96⁸. nowe *wanting.*
97². drynke.   97⁸. fet of.
97⁴. And *wanting :* I wyll.
98⁸. They thaught : woman wepe.
98⁴. mought.
99¹. the fayre ; and sayde *begins the next line.*
99². I sawe.   100². Or with.   100⁸. *wanting.*
100⁴. put out.   102². Under thus trusti.

102^4. had se. $106^1, 109^1$. Alce.

106^3. by me. 107^1. theyr *wanting*.

$107^{2,3}$. *Transposed :* And thanked, etc., Wyth such.

108^2. without any. 109^1. Alce shalbe at our.

110^3. you breng. 111^1. these good yemen.

111^2. myght hye. 111^3. pallace.

　　Variations from a.

114^3. you. 115^2. without any. 115^3. become.

116^1. the kyng. $116^3, 117^1$. The.

117^1. beseche the.

118^1. be your nams : then, *and* 119^1.

122^2. you graunt. 123^3. hundreth.

124^3. then sayd. 126^1. you *wanting*.

127^2. These : ye. 127^4. all thre.

128^1. town. 137^1. hauy graunted. 153^1. apele.

　　Variations from a.

162^2. myght se. 162^4. sholdest *wanting*.

164^1. .xvii. 164^3. when. 165^1. the a.

166^3. estate. 167^2. her sore.

167^4. To gouerne. 168^1. thanketh.

168^2. To some bysshop wyl we wend.

169^1. begone : there good.

170^4. they *wanting*.

a bout, a gayne, a monge, a none, a byde, a lyue, ther at, *etc., are joined.*

d, e, f. *The readings of all three are the same unless divergence is noted.*

1^1. f. in the. 1^3. whereas men hunt east.

2^1. raise. 2^2. d. sights haue oft.

e. sights haue not oft. f. has oft.

2^3. three yeomen. 2^4. as *wanting*.

3^2. Another. 4^2. thre *wanting*.

d, e. euery chone. f. eueryeche one.

4^3. brethren on a. 4^4. English wood.

5^2. And *wanting :* mirth. 5^3. e. were *wanting*.

6^3. brethren, *and generally.* e. on a.

7^1. There to : Alice. 7^2. f. with *wanting*.

8^1. e, f. we go. d. Carlell, *and generally.*

e, f. Carlile, *and generally.*

8^3. If that : doe you. 8^4. life is.

9^3. Trust you then that. d, f. tane.

e. taken. 11^1. Alice he said.

11^2. My wife and children three.

11^3. owne husband. f. thy.

12^2. e, f. very sore.

12^4. d, f. halfe a. e. Full halfe a.

13^1. e. I am. 13^2. d, f. in I. e. in we.

14^1. d. fet. 14^2. d. true and.

14^3. e. what she. 15^1. d. in the.

15^2. little before. 16^1. rose and forth she goes.

16^2. e. might. 16^3. not *wanting*.

16^4. e. yeeres. f. not 7 yeere. 17^1. into.

17^3. night she said is come to towne.

18^1. e. Thereat.

18^2. e. was *wanting*. f. And *wanting*.

18^3. e. dame *wanting*. 18^4. ere.

19^2. d, e. as *wanting*. d, e, f. saine.

20^1. raised. 20^2. that *wanting*.

20^3. e. And thronging fast vnto the house.

20^4. As fast as. e. gan.

21^1. the good yeoman. 21^2. Round *wanting*.

21^3. d. of the folke. e. of folke.

f. of the folkes.

21^4. thetherward : fast *for* they.

22^1. back *for* shot. 22^3. e. bothe *wanting*.

e, f. *second* the *wanting*.

22^4. e, f. And with them. e. a great rout.

f. a full great.

23^1. then cryed. 23^3. e, f. *second* my *want-ing*. f. sweet husband.

24^2. e. *second* hys *wanting*. 24^3. the *for* hys.

f. He went. 24^4. f. the surest.

25^1. Alice like a louer true. 25^2. f. Tooke a.

25^3. d, f. Said he shall die that commeth.

e. Said he shall dye. 26^1. right good.

26^2. of a. 26^4. burst.

27^4. had beene neere the.

28^2. d. *second* thy *wanting*. e. thine arrowes.

f. the bow and arrowes.

29^2. d, e. Sith no better it will be.

29^3. burne : saith. f. burne there.

29^4. and his. 30^1. f. The *for* they : *and often.*

30^2. d, e. vp *wanting*. f. fledd on.

30^3. then, *and generally.* e, f. said faire.

30^4. e. we here shall. f. here wee shall.

31^1. a *for* hys.

31^2. *second* on *wanting*. d. was on.

31^3. And there : he did let downe.

31^4. His wife and children.

32^1. f. Haue you here.

32^2. d, f. *second* my *wanting*.

$32^{1,2}$. e. *wanting*. 32^3. f. Gods loue.

33^2. d, f. agoe. e. go.

33^3. the *wanting*. about *for* vpon.

33^4. f. burnt. 34^1. fell vppon.

$34^{3\,4}$. and sayde *begins the fourth line.*

35^1. e, f. had I. 35^2. runne.

35^3. e. amongst. d, f. my. 35^4. So : burne.

36^1. buckler then. 36^2. f. amongst.

36^3. people thickest were.

37^1. man abide. e, f. strokes. 37^2. e. run.

37^3. f. Then the : att him. e. doore.

37^4. that yeoman. f. And then the.

38^1. both *wanting*. 38^2. in a.

38^3. d, e. then said. d, f. hye *wanting*.

39². e. gallowes thou shalt haue.

39³. d. al *wanting*. 40¹. There. f. helpe yett.

40⁸. f. a 100ᵈ men. 41¹. arose.

41². f. can he. 41³. d. them to: full *wanting*.

e, f. to shut close. 42³. d, e. he set vp.

f. There he new a paire of gallowes he sett vpp.

42⁴. f. Hard by the. 43². meant.

44¹. the *wanting*. f. The litle.

44³. f. seene William. 44⁴. e. gaue.

45¹. at a creuice of.

45². wood he ran (ron, runn). f. And *wanting*.

45³. e. he met. e, f. wighty yeomen.

46¹. e, f. said the. 46². e, f. You.

46³. e, f. tane. e. doomd.

46⁴. d. Already. e, f. And ready to be hangd.

47². saw.

47³. d, e. might haue tarried heere with vs.

f. He had better haue tarryed with vs.

47⁴. e. as *wanting*. 48¹. haue dwelled.

48². these *for* the. f. shaddoowes greene.

48³. haue *wanting*: at rest. 48⁴. d, f. of all.

49². he had. 50¹. e. we go.

d. wighty yeomen. e, f. iolly yeomen.

50². longer. 51¹. f. bold yeomen.

51². f. All in a mor[n]inge of May.

51⁴. f. And *wanting*. 52¹. f. to *wanting*.

52². f. All in a morning. 52³. vnto.

53³. wonderous. d, f. be shut. e. are shut.

f. ffast *for* well. 53⁴. therein. 54⁴. come.

e. the king. 55¹. wryten *wanting*.

55². e. Now *wanting*. f. wiselye marke.

56¹. d, f. at the. f. gates. 56². f. hard and.

56³. d, e. a *wanting*.

f. marueiled who was theratt.

56⁴. faste *wanting*. e, f. gates.

57¹. nowe *wanting*. f. Who be.

57². f. makes. 57³. e. said they then.

f. quoth Clim. 57⁴. come right.

58⁴. the *for* our. 59¹. none in. 59². e. of a.

59³. Till that. f. a *wanting*.

60¹. d. the *for* that.

e. that good yeman *wanting*.

f. spake good Clim. 60⁴. d, f. thou shalt.

61¹. got *wanting*.

61³. d, e. porter wend (weend).

f. had went *wanting*. 62¹. is my: he said.

62². d. ye shall. e, f. you shall.

62³. e, f. gates. d, e. full shortly.

f. ryght *wanting*. 63¹. are we.

63². Whereof: are right. 63³. d. knowes.

e, f. Christ he knowes assuredly.

63⁴. e. come *wanting*. f. gett out.

64²,³,⁴. then, When, *and nearly always*.

65¹. a *wanting*. 65³. cast.

65⁴. d, f. his keyes. 66². e. we haue.

66³. in *for* to. 66⁴. d. huńdred.

e, f. That came this hundred. 67¹. we will.

67³. brother. 67⁴. That *for* Where he.

68¹. d. Then : their good.

e, f. Then : their good yew. 68³. in *for* of.

69³. d, f. of squiers. e. squirers.

69⁴. e, f. That iudged William hanged.

70¹. e, f. hymselfe *wanting*.

f. ready there in. 70⁴. d, e. Already.

f. to hange. 71², he should. e. Cloudesle.

71³. good *wanting*.

71⁴. e. thereby make him a. f. And *wanting*.

72¹. a *wanting*. 72³. a graue.

73². I will thee hang. 73³. heard this.

74¹. eye. e. William.

74². two (tow) brethren : stande *wanting*.

74³. e. the corner : place wel prepard.

74⁴. d. good *wanting* : bent *wanting*.

e, f. *wanting*. 74⁵. d, e. the justice to chase.

f. the iustice to slaine. 75¹. good *wanting*.

75³. e. hands let free. 75⁴. d, e. might I.

76¹. Then spake. 76³. Brother : you.

76⁴. you. 77¹. And *wanting*.

78². d, e. they had.

78³. f. the shirrfe, the other the iustice.

78⁴. d, f. can. 79¹. e. stood them.

79³. fell *wanting*. 79⁴. d, e. deaths.

80¹. f. flye. 80². d, f. longer. 80³. e. Then.

81¹. d, f. start. e. stept. 81². out of.

81⁴. had *wanting* : all too. f. Hee thought.

82¹. e. brethren. 82². togyder *wanting*.

83¹. shot. e, f. in *wanting*.

83². full *wanting*. 83⁴. e. The.

d, f. long did. 84¹. like *for* as.

85². d, f. pressed to. 85³. e. swords out anon.

86³. d, f. was mid. f. were mid.

86⁴. had *wanting*.

87¹. e. There was *wanting*. e, f. Carlile was.

87². they *wanting*. d. backwards.

88¹, 89¹, 90¹. mayor, maior.

88³. thre *wanting*. 88⁴. For of.

d, f. they stood in great.

e. they were in great.

89⁴. e. Within that stoure. 90². brast.

d, f. he *wanting*. 90³. euill.

90⁴. f. ffull woe. 90⁵. f. Keepe well.

90⁶. That. 91². d, e. downe they.

f. were downe. 91⁴. gotten out. e. of a.

92². heere I. e. My. 92³. d, f. you.

92⁴. doe you. 93¹. d, f. their keyes at.

d. head. 93³. any. 94¹. e, f. be the.

d. word. 94². lightly. 94³. f. wood.

95¹. d, e. English wood. f. merry greenwood.

95². the trustie. 95⁴. d. full great.

96¹. God me helpe. 96³. nowe *wanting*.

96⁴. d. manie. e. many. f. meanye.

97¹. d, f. sate. e. Then sat they.

97². d, e. drunke.

97³. fit of: yeomen *for* yonge men.

f. A 2ᵈ ffitt of the wightye.

97⁴. And *wanting* : I will.

98¹. English wood. d, f. sate.

98². d, e. trustie. f. the greenwoode.

98³. woman wepe. e, f. They.

98⁴. e, f. could act.

99¹. Sore then : there *wanting*.

d, f. and sayd *begins the next line*.

99¹,². e. And sayd Alas *wanting*.

99². saw. 99³. f. nowe *wanting*.

100¹. e. spoke. 100². Or with.

100³. d, e. To shew to them what him befell.

f. To show them, *etc*. 101¹. aside.

101². f. He looked.

101³. *second* his *wanting*. e. He saw his.

102². Under. d. this trustie. e. a trusty.

f. the trustye. 102⁴. d, f. shouldest had.

e. shouldst had. 103⁴. d, e. brethren.

104⁴. e. It resteth. 105¹. the lawnd.

105². noble men all.

105⁴. f. that they cold see. 106². f. saith.

106³. Because : by me.

107¹. they went : theyr *wanting*.

107³. for their.

108², 115². without any leace (lease).

109¹. at our. 109². f. Att a. 110¹. My.

110². I haue. 111¹. good yemen.

111². d, f. might hye. e. can hye.

111³. pallace. 111⁴. e, f. Where.

d. neede. e, f. needs.

112¹. kings. f. But when. 112². f. & to.

113¹. proceeded presently. 113². they had.

113⁴. e, f. gan. 114¹. e, f. you.

114². e, f. to me. 114³. You : thus *wanting*.

114⁴. from *for* of. 115². f. Certes.

115³. the *for* our. 116¹. the *for* our.

d, f. when. e. whan.

117¹. d, e. beseech thee.

f. beseeche yee sure. 118¹. What be.

e, f. the *for* our.

118³. e. They sayd *wanting*.

119¹. d, e. than *wanting*. f. then.

e. the *for* our. 119². of *wanting*.

119³. f. Here I make a vow to God.

119⁴. You. 120³. f. officer[s] euery one.

121¹. e. Therefore. 122³. doo *for* be : come.

122⁴. from. 123². d. your *wanting*.

123³. d, e. hundreth : f. 100ᵈ.

123⁴. d, e. of you.

f. Of you wee will aske noe. 125⁴. **You.**

126¹. ye. 126⁴. f. itt shalbe.

127¹. f. good my. 127². These : ye.

127⁴. them all. 128¹. f. You : townes.

130². e. garmarcie. f. god a mercye.

130⁴. they shall.

131². d. they may comfort see.

e. they might comfort see.

f. some comfort they might see.

131³. e, f. the *for* our.

132¹. e. sittin. f. sitten. 132³. came two.

133³. e. our *for* your. 134¹. fareth.

135¹. e. slaine them. f. then said.

135². Anone that you.

135³. and *wanting*. 136¹. f. ffor wrath.

136³. then. f. rather then. 136⁴. of *wanting*.

137¹. f. y- *wanting*. 137². d. forethinketh.

138¹. d, f. king he.

138³. And there : thre *wanting*.

139². mayor. 139³. catchpoles.

139⁴. f. but one. 140¹. bayliffes.

140³. forresters. 140⁴. haue.

f. haue the slawe.

141². e, f. Of all. f. coice the. 141³. d. Such.

142². hys *wanting*. 142³. d. table he said.

e. table then said he. f. tables then sayd hee.

142⁴. e, f. I can. 143¹. then called.

143³. e, f. said he. f. To see.

143⁴. e. hath. 144¹. d, e. buskt : blithe.

f. archers busket : blythe.

144². f. Soe did the queenes alsoe.

144³. d, e. thre *wanting*. f. weightye.

144⁴. f. They thought with them.

145³. thre *wanting*. 145⁴. them *wanting*.

146². e, f. By him. 146³. d, e. a good.

f. him not a good. 147¹. e. the *for* our.

f. then *wanting*. 147². to me.

148¹. into the. 148². brethren.

148⁴. f. 400 paces.

149⁴. For no man can so doo.

150¹. f. syr *wanting*. 150². further.

151. d, f. our king. e, f. then *wanting*.

152³. tie him. 152⁴. e, f. see him.

154¹. hast thee. f. then *wanting*.

154³. f. dost : has. 155⁴. you hang.

156². d, e. I neuer will forsake.

f. That I will neuer. 157³. him fro.

158³. out *wanting*. f. meaten.

159². e. were. 160¹. were there.

160⁴. had neede of a. e, f. steddy.
162¹. claue. 162². myght see. d, f. As.
162⁸. Now God forbid then said.
162⁴. d, e. shouldst. 163¹. f. gaue : 8 pence.
163⁴. e. chiefe ranger. 164¹. xiii. e, f. Ile.
165¹. thee a. 165⁸. f. bretheren.
165⁴. are louely to. 166². e, f. he shall be.
166⁸. mans estate. e, f. coms, comes.
166⁴. d. aduanced I will him see.
e, f. Better preferred. 167². d. sore for to.

e. I long full sore to see. f. I long her sore.
167⁴. To.
168². d. To some bishop will we wend.
e, f. To some bishop we will wend.
168⁴. at his. 169¹. e. the good.
169². they can. d. So fast. 169⁸. and liued.
169⁴. good yeomen. 170¹. f. liffe.
170⁸. f. with a. 170⁴. d, e. they *wanting*.
*Insignificant variations of spelling are not no-
ticed.*

APPENDIX

THE SECOND PART OF ADAM BELL

August 16, 1586, there was entered to Edward
White, in the Stationers' Registers, 'A ballad of
William Clowdisley neuer printed before :' Arber,
II, 455. This was in all probability the present
piece, afterwards printed with 'Adam Bell' as a
Second Part. The Second Part of Adam Bell was
entered to John Wright, September 24, 1608 : Ar-
ber, III, 390. The ballad is a pure manufacture,
with no root in tradition, and it is an absurd ex-
travaganza besides. The copy in the Percy Folio,
here collated with the earliest preserved printed
copy, has often the better readings, but may have
been corrected. **a** has such monstrosities as y-then,
y-so.

a. 'The Second Part of Adam Bell,' London, James Rob-
erts, 1605. **b.** 'Younge Cloudeslee,' Percy MS. p. 398 ;
Hales and Furnivall, III, 102.

1 LIST northerne laddes to blither things
    Then yet were brought to light,
Performed by our countriemen
    In many a fray and fight :

2 Of Adam Bell, Clim of the Clough,
    And William of Cloudisly,
Who were in fauour with the king,
    For all their misery.

3 Yong William of the wine-seller,
    When yeoman he was made,
Gan follow then his father's steps :
    He loued a bonny maide.

4 'God's crosse,' quoth William, 'if I misse,
    And may not of her speed,

I 'le make a thousand northern hearts
    For very wo to bleed.'

5 Gone he is a wooing now,
    Our Ladie well him guide !
To merry Mansfield, where I trow
    A time he will abide.

6 'Soone dop the dore, faire Cicelie bright,
    I come with all the hast :
I come a wooing thee for loue,
    Here am I come at last.'

7 'I know you not,' quoth Cicelie tho,
    'From whence that yee bee come ;
My loue you may not haue, I trow,
    I vow by this faire sonne.

8 'For why, my loue is fixt so sure
    Vpon another wight ;
I swere by sweet Saint Anne, I 'le neuer
    Abuse him, out of sight.

9 'This night I hope to see my loue,
    In all his pride and glee ;
If there were thousands, none but him
    My heart would ioy to see.'

10 'God's curse vpon him,' yong William said,
    'Before me that hath sped !
A foule ill on the carrion nurse
    That first did binde his head !'

11 Gan William tho for to prepare
    A medicine for that chaffe :
'His life,' quoth he, 'full hard may fare ;
    Hee 's best to keepe alaffe.'

12 He drew then out his bright brown sword,
    Which was so bright and keene ;
A stouter man and hardier
    Nere handled sword, I weene.

13 ' Browne tempered, strong, and worthy blade,
    Vnto thy maister show,
If now to triall thou bee put,
    How thou canst bide a blow.'

14 Yong William till an oake gan hie,
    Which was in compasse round
Well six and fifty inches nie,
    And feld it to the ground.

15 ' So mot he fare,' quoth William tho,
    ' That for her loue hath laid
Which I haue loued, and nere did know
    Him suter till that maide.

16 ' And now, deare father, stout and strong,
    William of Cloudesley,
How happie were thy troubled sonne
    If here I mot thee see.

17 ' And thy too brethren, Adam Bell
    And Clim of the Clough ;
Against a thousand men, and more,
    We foure would be enough.

18 ' Growne it is full foure a clocke,
    And night will come beliue ;
Come on, thou lurden, Cislei's loue,
    This night must I thee shriue.

19 ' Prepare thee strong, thou fow[l] black caufe !
    What ere thou be, I weene
I 'le giue thy coxcomb saick a gird
    In Mansfield as neuer was seene.'

20 William a yong faune had slaine,
    In Sherwood, merry forrest;
A fairer faune for man's meat
    In Sherwood was neuer drest.

21 Hee hied then till a northerne lasse,
    Not halfe a mile him fro ;
He said, Dop dore, thou good old nurse,
    That in to thee I goe.

22 ' I faint with being in the wood ;
    Lo heere I haue a kid,
Which I haue slo for thee and I ;
    Come dresse it then, I bid.

23 ' Fetch bread and other iolly fare,
    Whereof thou hast some store ;
A blither gest this hundred yeare
    Came neuer here before.'

24 The good old nant gan hie a pace
    To let yong William in ;
' A happie nurse,' quoth William then,
    ' As can be lightly seene.

25 ' Wend till that house hard by,' quoth he,
    ' That 's made of lime and stone,
Where is a lasse, faire Cisse,' hee said ;
    ' I loue her as my owne.

26 ' If thou can fetch her vnto me,
    That we may merry be,
I make a vow, in the forrest,
    Of deare thou shalt haue fee.'

27 ' Rest then, faire sir,' the woman said;
    ' I sweare by good Saint Iohn,
I will bring to you that same maide
    Full quickly and anon.'

28 ' Meane time,' quoth William, ' I 'le be cooke
    And see the faune i-drest;
A stouter eooke did neuer come
    Within the faire forrest.'

29 Thick blith old lasse had wit enow
    For to declare his minde ;
So fast she hi'd, and nere did stay,
    But left William behind.

30 Where William, like a nimble cooke,
    Is dressing of the fare,
And for this damsell doth he looke ;
    ' I would that she were here!'

31 ' Good speed, blithe Cisse,' quoth that old lasse;
    ' God dild yee,' quoth Cisley againe ;
' How done you, nant Ione?' she said,
    ' Tell me it, I am faine.'

32 The good old Ione said weele she was,
    ' And commen in an arrand till you;
For you must to my cottage gone,
    Full quick, I tell you true ;

33 ' Where we full merry meane to be,
    All with my elder lad :'
When Cissley heard of it, truely,
    She was exceeding glad.

34 ' God's curse light on me,' quoth Cissley tho,
    ' If with you I doe not hie ;
I neuer ioyed more forsooth
    Then in your company.'

35 Happy the good-wife thought her selfe
    That of her purpose she had sped,
And home with Cisley she doth come,
    So lightly did they tread.

36 And comming in, here William soone
    Had made ready his fare;
The good old wife did wonder much
    So soone as she came there.

37 Cisley to William now is come,
   God send her mickle glee !
Yet was she in a maze, God wot,
   When she saw it was hee.

38 ' Had I beene ware, good sir,' she said,
   ' Of that it had beene you,
I would haue staid at home in sooth,
   I tell you very true.'

39 ' Faire Cis'᷾,' then said William kind,
   ' Misdeeme thou not of mee ;
I sent not for thee to the end
   To do thee iniury.

40 ' Sit downe, that we may talke a while,
   And eate all of the best
And fattest kidde that euer was slaine
   In merry Sirwood forrest.'

41 His louing words wan Cisley then
   To keepe with him a while ;
But in the meane time Cislei's loue
   Of her was tho beguile.

42 A stout and sturdie man he was
   Of quality and kind,
And knowne through all the north country
   To beare a noble minde.

43 ' But what,' quoth William, ' do I care?
   If that he meane to weare,
First let him winne ; els neuer shall
   He haue the maide, I sweare.'

44 Full softly is her louer come,
   And knocked at the dore ;
But tho he mist of Cislei's roome,
   Whereat he stampt and swore.

45 ' A mischief on his heart,' quoth he,
   ' That hath enlured the maide
To be with him in company !'
   He car'd not what he sayd.

46 He was so with anger mooued
   He sware a well great oth,
' Deere should he pay, if I him knew,
   Forsooth and by my troth !'

47 Gone he is to finde her out,
   Not knowing where she is ;
Still wandring in the weary wood,
   His true-loue he doth misse.

48 William purchast hath the game,
   Which he doth meane to hold :
' Come rescew her, and if you can,
   And dare to be so bold !'

49 At length when he had wandred long
   About the forrest wide,
A candle-light a furlong off
   Full quickly he espied.

50 Then to the house he hied him fast,
   Where quickly he gan here
The voice of his owne deere true-loue,
   A making bonny cheere.

51 Then gan he say to Cisley tho,
   O Cisley, come a way !
I haue beene wandring thee to finde
   Since shutting in of day.

52 ' Who calls faire Cisse ? ' quoth William then;
   ' What carle dares bee so bold
Once to aduenture to her to speake
   Whom I haue now in hold ? '

53 ' List thee, faire sir,' quoth Cislei's loue,
   ' Let quickly her from you part ;
For all your lordly words, I sweare
   I 'le haue her, or make you smart.'

54 Yong William to his bright browne sword
   Gan quickly then to take :
' Because thou so dost challenge me,
   I 'le make thy kingdome quake.

55 ' Betake thee to thy weapon strong;
   Faire time I giue to thee ;
And for my loue as well as thine
   A combat fight will I.'

56 ' Neuer let sonne,' quoth Cislei's loue,
   ' Shine more vpon my head,
If I doe flie, by heauen aboue,
   Wert thou a giant bred.'

57 To bilbo-blade gat William tho,
   And buckler stiffe and strong ;
A stout battaile then they fought,
   Well nie two houres long.

58 Where many a grieuous wound was giue
   To each on either part ;
Till both the champions then were droue
   Almost quite out of heart.

59 Pitteous mone faire Cisley made,
   That all the forrest rong ;
The grieuous shrikes made such a noise,
   She had so shrill a tongue.

60 At last came in the keepers three,
   With bowes and arrowes keene,
Where they let flie among these two,
   An hundred as I weene.

61 William, stout and strong in heart,
    When he had them espied,
Set on corrage for his part ;
    Among the thickst he hied.

62 The chiefe ranger of the woods
    At first did William smite ;
Where, at on blow, he smot his head
    Fro off his shoulders quite.

63 And being in so furious teene,
    About him then he laid ;
He slew immediatly the wight
    Was sutor to the maide.

64 Great moane was then made ;
    The like was neuer heard ;
Which made the people all around
    To crie, they were so feard.

65 'Arme! arme!' the country cried,
    'For God's loue quickly hie !'
Neuer was such a slaughter seene
    In all the north country.

66 Will[iam] still, though wounded sore,
    Continued in his fight
Till he had slaine them all foure,
    That very winter-night.

67 All the country then was raisd,
    The traytor for to take
That for the loue of Cisley faire
    Had all this slaughter make.

68 To the woods hied William tho —
    'T was best of all his play —
Where in a caue with Cisley faire
    He liued many a day.

69 Proclamation then was sent
    The country all around,
The lord of Mansfield should he be
    That first the traytor found.

70 Till the court these tydings came,
    Where all men did bewaile
The yong and lusty William,
    Which so had made them quaile.

71 Hied vp then William Cloudesley,
    And lustie Adam Bell,
And famous Clim of the Clough,
    Which three then did excell.

72 To the king they hied them fast,
    Full quickly and anon ;
'Mercy I pray,' quoth old William,
    'For William my sonne.'

73 'No mercy, traitors,' quoth the king,
    'Hangd shall yee be all foure ;
Vnder my nose this plot haue you laid
    To bringe to passe before.'

74 'In sooth,' bespake then Adam Bell,
    'Ill signe Your Grace hath seene
Of any such comotion
    Since with you we haue beene.

75 'If then we can no mercy haue,
    But leese both life and goods,
Of your good grace we take our leaue
    And hie vs to the woods.'

76 'Arme, arme,' then quoth the king,
    'My merry men euerychone,
Full fast againe these rebbells now
    Vnto the woods are gone.

77 'A, wo is vs ! what shall we doo,
    Or which way shall we worke,
To hunt them forth out of the woods,
    So traytrouslie there that lurke ? '

78 'List you,' quoth a counsellor graue,
    A wise man he seemd ;
The[n] craued the king his pardon free
    Vnto them to haue deemd.

79 'God's forbod !' quoth the king,
    'I neuer it will do !
For they shall hang, each mother's sonne ;
    Faire sir, I tell you true.'

80 Fifty thousand men were charged
    After them for to take ;
Some of them, set in sundry townes,
    In companies did waite.

81 To the woods gan some to goe,
    In hope to find them out ;
And them perforce they thought to take,
    If they might find them out.

82 To the woods still as they came
    Dispatched still they were ;
Which made full many a trembling heart,
    And many a man in feare.

83 Still the outlawes, Adam Bell
    And Clim of the Clough,
Made iolly cheere with venison,
    Strong drinke and wine enough.

84 'Christ me blesse !' then said our king,
    'Such men were neuer knowne ;
They are the stoutest-hearted men
    That manhoode euer showne.

85 'Come, my secretary good,
    And cause to be declared
A generall pardone to them all,
    Which neuer shall be discared.

86 'Liuing plenty shall they haue,
    Of gold and eke of fee,
If they will, as they did before,
    Come liue in court with me.'

87 Sodenly went forth the newes,
    Declared by trumpets sound,
Whereof these three were well aduis'd,
    In caue as they were in ground.

88 'But list you, sirs,' quoth William yong,
    'I dare not trust the king ;
It is some fetch is in his head,
    Whereby to bring vs in.

89 'Nay, stay we here : or first let me
    A messenger be sent
Vnto the court, where I may know
    His Maiestie's intent.'

90 This pleased Adam Bell :
    'So may we liue in peace,
We are at his most high command,
    And neuer will we cease.

91 'But if that still we shall be vrged,
    And called by traitrous name,
And threated hanging for euery thing,
    His Highnesse is to blame.

92 'Neare had His Grace subiects more true,
    And sturdier then wee,
Which are at His Highnesse will ;
    God send him well to bee !'

93 So to the court is yong William gone,
    To parley with the king,
Where all men to the king's presence
    Did striue him for to bring.

94 When he before the king was come,
    He kneeled down full low ;
He shewed quickly to the king
    What duty they did owe ;

95 In such delightfull order blith,
    The king was quickly wonne
To comfort them in their request,
    As he before had done.

96 'Fetch bread and drinke,' then said His Grace,
    'And meat all of the best ;
And stay all night here at the court,
    And soundly take thy rest.'

97 'Gramercies to Your Grace,' said William,
    'For pardon graunted I see :'
'For signe thereof, here take my seale,
    And for more certainty.'

98 'God's curse vpon me,' sayd William,
    'For my part if I meane
Euer againe to stirre vp strife !'
    It neuer shall bee seene.'

99 The nobles all to William came,
    He was so stout and trimme,
And all the ladies, for very ioy,
    Did come to welcome him.

100 'Faire Cisley now I haue to wife,
    In field I haue her wonne ;'
'Bring her here, for God's loue,' said they all,
    'Full welcome shall she be [soone].'

101 Forth againe went William backe,
    To wood that he did hie,
And to his father there he shewd
    The king his pardone free.

102 'Health to His Grace,' quoth Adam Bell,
    'I beg it on my knee !'
The like said Clim of the Clough,
    And William of Cloudesley.

103 To the court they all prepare,
    Euen as fast as they can hie,
Where graciously they were receiud,
    With mirth and merry glee.

104 Cisley faire is wend alone
    Vpon a gelding faire ;
A proprer damsell neuer came
    In any courtly ayre.

105 'Welcome, Cisley,' said the queene,
    'A lady I thee make,
To wait vpon my owne person,
    In all my chiefest state.'

106 So quickly was this matter done,
    Which was so hardly doubted,
That all contentions after that
    From court were quickly rowted.

107 Fauourable was the king ;
    So good they did him finde,
The[y] neuer after sought againe
    To vex his royall minde.

108 Long time they liued in court,
    So neare vnto the king
That neuer after was attempt
    Offred for any thing.

109 God aboue giue all men grace
    In quiet for to liue,
    And not rebelliously abroad
    Their princes for to grieue.

110 Let not the hope of pardon mooue
    A subiect to attempt

His soueraigne's anger, or his loue
From him for to exempt.

111 But that all men may ready be
    With all their maine and might
    To serue the Lord, and loue the King,
    In honor, day and night !

---

a. 1[4]. In mickle.   6[1]. Some.
   13[4]. canst thou.   20[3]. man's y-meat.
   21[2]. he fro.   28[2]. I drest.
   35[2]. That her purpose he had of sped.
   35[4]. they read.   37[4]. amaze.
   46[1]. was yso.   64[1]. ythen.   76[2]. euery chone.
   92[1]. more subiects true.   93[3]. Which *for* Where.
b. 1[4]. In many.   5[2]. will *for* well.   6[1]. Soone.
   6[3]. to thee.   13[1]. sword *for* strong.
   13[4]. thou canst.   18[4]. I must.   19[1]. ffowle.
   19[4]. was neuer.   20[3]. man's meate.   21[2]. him ffroe.
   21[3]. dop the.   22[3]. slaine ffor thee & mee.
   28[2]. To see : well drest.
   31[1]. God speed.   31[3]. doe yee.
   32[1]. woman *for* Ione.   32[2]. in *wanting* : to you.

35[2]. of her purpose shee had sped.
35[4]. they did tread.   37[3]. a maze.
40[3]. The ffattest.   44[3]. mist Cisleys companye.
45[2]. allured this.   46[1]. soe.
52[4]. in my *for* now in.   57[2]. That was both stiffe.
57[4]. Weer neere.   61[1]. strong & stout.
66[1]. William.   68[2]. Itt was the best.
73[2]. You shall be hanged.   73[3]. plott yee have.
76[2]. euer-eche one.   78[3]. The craued.
79[4]. I tell you verry true.   86[1]. Liuings.
92[1]. subiects more true.   93[3]. Where.
97[1]. Gramercy.
100[4]. Welcome shee shall bee soone.   104[1]. is gone.
105[4]. cheefe estate.   106[4]. rooted.
107[3]. ffought *for* sought.

117

A GEST OF ROBYN HODE

a. 'A Gest of Robyn Hode,' without printer's name, date, or place ; the eleventh and last piece in a volume in the Advocates' Library, Edinburgh. Reprinted by David Laing, 1827, with nine pieces from the press of Walter Chepman and Androw Myllar, Edinburgh, 1508, and one other, by a printer unknown, under the title of The Knightly Tale of Golagrus and Gawane, and other Ancient Poems.

b. 'A Lytell Geste of Robyn Hode,' etc., London, Wynken de Worde, n. d.: Library of the University of Cambridge.

c. Douce Fragment, No 16: Bodleian Library.

d. Douce Fragment, No 17: Bodleian Library.

e. Douce Fragment, No 16: Bodleian Library.*

f. 'A Mery Geste of Robyn Hoode,' etc., London, Wyllyam Copland, n. d. : British Museum, C. 21. c.

g. 'A Merry Iest of Robin Hood,' etc., London, printed for Edward White, n. d.: Bodleian Library, Z. 3. Art. Seld., and Mr Henry Huth's library.

THE best qualified judges are not agreed as to the typographical origin of a: see Dickson, Introduction of the Art of Printing into

Scotland, Aberdeen, 1885, pp 51 ff, 82 ff, 86 f. Mr Laing had become convinced before his death that he had been wrong in assigning

* a preserves stanzas 1–83[4], 118[4]–208[3], 314[2]–349[3] ; with defects at 2[2,3], 7[1], 123[4]–127[3], 133–136[3]. It has therefore about 200 stanzas out of 456.

c preserves 26[4]–60[3] ; d, 280–350, very much mutilated ; e, 435[4]–450[1], very much mutilated. e, inserted among the Douce fragments, was presented by Mr Halliwell-Phillips.

this piece to the press of Chepman and Myllar. The date of b may be anywhere from 1492 to 1534, the year of W. de Worde's death. Of c Ritson says, in his corrected preface to the Gest, 1832, I, 2: By the favor of the Reverend Dr Farmer, the editor had in his hands, and gave to Mr Douce, a few leaves of an old 4to black letter impression by the above Wynken de Worde, probably in 1489, and totally unknown to Ames and Herbert. No reason is given for this date.* I am not aware that any opinion has been expressed as to the printer or the date of d, e. W. Copland's edition, f, if his dates are fully ascertained, is not earlier than 1548. Ritson says that g is entered to Edward White in the Stationers' books, 13 May, 1594. "A pastorall plesant commedie of Robin Hood & Little John, &c," is entered to White on the 14th of May of that year, Arber, II, 649: this is more likely to have been a play of Robin Hood.

a, b, f, g, are deficient at 7¹, 339¹, and misprinted at 49, 50, repeating, it may be, the faults of a prior impression. a appears, by internal evidence, to be an older text than b.†

Some obsolete words of the earlier copies have been modernized in f, g,‡, and deficient lines have been supplied. A considerable number of Middle-English forms remain § after those successive renovations of reciters and printers which are presumable in such cases. The Gest may have been compiled at a time when such forms had gone out of use, and these may be relics of the ballads from which this little epic was made up; or the whole poem may have been put together as early as 1400, or before. There are no firm grounds on which to base an opinion.

No notice of Robin Hood has been down to this time recovered earlier than that which was long ago pointed out by Percy as occurring in Piers Plowman, and this, according to Professor Skeat, cannot be older than about 1377.‖ Sloth, in that poem, says in his shrift that he knows "rymes of Robyn Hood and Randolf, erle of Chestre," ¶ though but imperfectly acquainted with his paternoster: B, passus v, 401 f, Skeat, ed. 1886, I, 166. References to Robin Hood, or to his story, are not infrequent in the following century.

---

* Dr Farmer considered these leaves to be of Rastell's printing, and older by some years than b; which is not quite intelligible, since Rastell's work is put at 1517–38. c is cited under Rastell's name in Ritson's second edition as well as his first.

† 9⁴, a, allther moste: b, all other moste. (f, g, of all other; b, 283³, all ther best; 284¹, all theyre best; f, g, al of the best.) 61⁴, a, Muche in fere: b, Much also. 68⁴, a, By xxviii (eight and twenty) score: b (f, g), By eyghtene score, which gives no meaning. 138³, a, frembde bested: b (f, g), frend. 173⁴, a, same nyght: b, same day. 176⁴, a, wode hore: b (f, g), wode tre. 333², a, on rode: b (f, g), on a tre. 343²,·a, The sherif: b (f, g), The knyght.

‡ 13³, a, b, husbonde: f, g, husbandeman. 256¹, b, in yonder other corser: f, on the other courser: g, in the other coffer. 274⁴, 286², 387⁴, 412², b, trystell-tre: f, g, trusty tre. 385¹, b, "tarpe": f, g, seale. 371⁴, b, blyve: f, g, blythe, etc.

§ 111², That all this worldë wrought; 163², The whilë that he wolde; 316¹, To metë can they gone; 72⁴, But his bowë tree; 29¹, They brought hym to the lodgë dore.

255⁴, To seke a monkës male; 360³, He shall haue the knyghtës londys; 369¹, And I wyll be your ledës man; 376¹, Robyn toke the kyngës hors; 366³, 367², 368⁴, etc. 336³, For our derë lady loue.

31¹, With wordës fayre and fre; 34⁴, Of all these wekÿs thre; 210², Or a man that myrthës can; 318⁴, The wallës all aboute; 60², 331⁴, 332², 371², etc. 433⁴, And all his mennës fe.

21², By a dernë strete; 25¹, Welcome be thou to grenë wode; 298¹, But had I the in grenë wode; 327³, 373³, 374³. 56⁴, Ouer the saltë see; 173⁴, That ylkë samë nyght; 213², By the hyë way; 235², Of all this longë day; 241¹, 292⁴, 303², 305¹, 393², 455⁴, etc. 25², Hendë knyght & fre; 113³, Out, he sayd, thou falsë knyght; 242³, Therfore I cun the morë thanke.

47², 100², By God that madë me; 80⁴, To walkë by his syde; 222², And that shall rewë me; 297⁴, Other wyse thou behotë me; 426¹, So God me helpë, sayd our kynge. d, 282², 317², herkeneth.

‖ Ritson had seen, among Peck's collections for the history of Premonstratensian monasteries, a Latin poem with the title Prioris Alnwicensis de bello Scotico apud Dunbar, tempore regis Edwardi I, dictamen, sive rithmus Latinus, quo de Willielmo Wallace, Scotico illo Robin Whood, plura sed invidiose canit, and in the margin the date 22 Julii, 1304; whence he concluded that Robin Hood was both mentioned, and compared with Wallace, in 1304. The date refers to matters in the poem. The MS. (Sloane, 4934, pars II, ff 103–106) is of the eighteenth century, Hardy, Descriptive Catalogue, etc., III, 279, No 503. The title was supplied by Peck, one of whose marks is the spelling Whood.

¶ Either Randle the second, earl from 1128 to 1153, or Randle the third, earl from 1181 and for fifty years, would be likely to be the subject of ballads, but especially the latter. He figures in the story of Fulk Fitz Warine: Wright, p. 149.

In Wyntoun's Chronicle of Scotland, put at about 1420, there is this passage, standing quite by itself, under the year 1283:

Lytill Ihon and Robyne Hude
Waythmen ware commendyd gude;
In Yngilwode and Barnysdale
Thai oysyd all this tyme thare trawale.

Laing, II, 263.

Disorderly persons undertook, it seems, to imitate Robin Hood and his men. In the year 1417, says Stowe, one, by his counterfeit name called Fryer Tucke, with many other malefactors, committed many robberies in the counties of Surrey and Sussex, whereupon the king sent out his writs for their apprehension: Annals, p. 352 b, ed. 1631.* A petition to Parliament, in the year 1439, represents that one Piers Venables, of Derbyshire, rescued a prisoner, "and after that tyme, the same Piers Venables, havynge no liflode ne sufficeante of goodes, gadered and assembled unto him many misdoers, beynge of his clothinge, . . . and, in manere of insurrection, wente into the wodes in that contré, like as it hadde be Robyn-hode and his meyné:" Rotuli Parliamentorum, V, 16.†

Bower, writing 1441–47, describes the lower orders of his time as entertaining themselves with ballads both merry and serious, about Robin Hood, Little John, and their mates, and preferring them to all others ; ‡ and Major, or Mair, who was born not long after 1450, says in his book, printed in 1521, that Robin Hood ballads were in vogue over all Britain.§

Sir John Paston, in 1473, writes of a servant whom he had kept to play Robin Hood and the Sheriff of Nottingham, and who was gone into Bernysdale: Fenn, Original Letters, etc., II, 134, cited by Ritson.

Gutch cites this allusion to Robin Hood ballads "from Mr Porkington, No 10, f. 152, written in the reign of Edward IV:"

Ther were tynkerris in tarlottus, the met was fulle goode,
The "sowe sat one him benche" (sic), and harppyd Robyn Hoode.

And again, the name simply, from "a song on Woman, from MS. Lambeth, 306, fol. 135, of the fifteenth century":

He that made this songe full good
Came of the northe and of the sothern blode,
And somewhat kyne to Robyn Hode.

Gutch, Robin Hood, I, 55 f.

These passages show the popularity of Robin Hood ballads for a century or more

---

* Cited by Ritson. I have not found the writs.

† Cited in the Edinburgh Review, 1847, LXXXVI, 134, note ; and by Hunter, 1852, The Ballad-Hero, Robin Hood, p. 58 (where the year is wrongly given as 1432). It appears from many cases that the name was very often pronounced Róbinhode.

‡ "Robertus Hode et Litill-Johanne, cum eorum complicibus, de quibus stolidum vulgus hianter in comœdiis et in tragœdiis prurienter festum faciunt, et præ ceteris romanciis mimos et bardanos cantitare delectantur."

"Of whom the foolish vulgar in comedies and tragedies make lewd entertainment, and are delighted to hear the jesters and minstrels sing them above all other ballads:" Ritson, whose translation may pass. Ritson rightly observes that comedies and tragedies here are not to be understood as plays. Then follows this abstract of one of the 'tragedies.'

"De quo etiam quædam commendabilia recitantur, sicut patuit in hoc, quod cum ipse quondam in Barnisdale, iram regis et fremitum principis declinans, missam, ut solitus erat, devotissime audiret, nec aliqua necessitate volebat interrumpere officium, quadam die, cum audiret missam, a quodam vicecomite et ministris regis, eum sæpius perprius infestantibus, in illo secretissimo loco nemorali ubi missæ interfuit exploratus, venientes ad eum qui hoc de suis per-

ceperunt ut omni annisu fugeret suggesserunt. Quod, ob reverentiam sacramenti, quod tunc devotissime venerabatur, omnino facere recusavit. Sed, ceteris suis ob metum mortis trepidantibus, Robertus, in tantum confisus in eum quem coluit, inveritus, cum paucis qui tunc forte ei affuerunt inimicos congressus eos de facili devicit, et, de eorum spoliis ac redemptione ditatus, ministros ecclesiæ et missas in majore veneratione semper et de post habere præelegit, attendens quod vulgariter dictum est:

Hunc deus exaudit qui missam sæpius audit."

Scotichronicon, ed. Goodall, II, 104.

§ Major was in extreme old age in 1524: see Moir's Wallace, I, iv. "Robertus Hudus Anglus et Paruus Ioannes, latrones famatissimi in nemoribus latuerunt, solum opulentorum virorum bona diripientes. Nullum nisi eos inuadentem, vel resistentem pro suarum rerum tuitione, occiderunt Centum sagittarios ad pugnam aptissimos Robertus latrociniis aluit, quos 400 viri fortissimi inuadere non audebant. Rebus huius Roberti gestis tota Britannia in cantibus utitur. Fœminam nullam opprimi permisit, nec pauperum bona surripuit, verum eos ex abbatum bonis ablatis opipare pauit." Historia Maioris Britanniæ, fol. 55 b.

It will be observed that Wyntoun, Bower, and Mair are Scots.

before the time when the Gest was printed, a popularity which was fully established at the beginning of this period, and unquestionably extended back to a much earlier day. Of these ballads, there have come down to us in a comparatively ancient form the following: those from which the Gest (printed, perhaps, before 1500) was composed, being at least four, Robin Hood, the Knight and the Monk, Robin Hood, Little John and the Sheriff, Robin Hood and the King, and Robin Hood's Death (a fragment); Robin Hood and the Monk, No 118, more properly Robin Hood rescued by Little John, MS. of about 1450, but not for that older than the ballads of the Gest; Robin Hood and Guy of Gisborn, No 119, Percy MS. c. 1650; Robin Hood's Death, No 120, Percy MS. and late garlands; Robin Hood and the Potter, No 121, MS. of about 1500, later, perhaps, than any other of the group.* Besides these there are thirty-two ballads, Nos 122–153. For twenty-two of these we have the texts of broadsides and garlands of the seventeenth century,† four of the same being also found in the Percy MS.; eight occur in garlands, etc., of the last century, one of these same in the Percy MS., and another in an eighteenth-century MS.; one is derived from a suspicious nineteenth-century MS., and one from nineteenth-century tradition. About half a dozen of these thirty-two have in them something of the old popular quality; as many more not the least smatch of it. Fully a dozen are variations, some-

times wearisome, sometimes sickening, upon the theme ' Robin Hood met with his match.' A considerable part of the Robin Hood poetry looks like char-work done for the petty press, and should be judged as such. The earliest of these ballads, on the other hand, are among the best of all ballads, and perhaps none in English please so many and please so long.

That a considerable number of fine ballads of this cycle have been lost will appear all but certain when we remember that three of the very best are found each in only one manuscript.‡

Robin Hood is absolutely a creation of the ballad-muse. The earliest mention we have of him is as the subject of ballads. The only two early historians who speak of him as a ballad-hero, pretend to have no information about him except what they derive from ballads, and show that they have none other by the description they give of him; this description being in entire conformity with ballads in our possession, one of which is found in a MS. as old as the older of these two writers.

Robin Hood is a yeoman, outlawed for reasons not given but easily surmised, "courteous and free," religious in sentiment, and above all reverent of the Virgin, for the love of whom he is respectful to all women. He lives by the king's deer (though he loves no man in the world so much as his king) and by levies on the superfluity of the higher orders, secular and spiritual, bishops and arch-

---

* Because comic and not heroic, and because Robin is put at a disadvantage. In the other ballads Robin Hood is "evermore the best." Though there is humor in the Gest, it is kept well under, and never lowers Robin's dignity.

† The only one of these ballads entered in the Stationers' Registers, or known to have been printed, at a date earlier than the seventeenth century is No 124, 'Of Wakefylde and a Grene,' 1557–58.

The earliest known copy of Robin Hood's Garland is one in the Bodleian Library, Wood, 79, printed for W. Gilbertson, 1663. This contains seventeen ballads. An edition of 1670, in the same library, Douce, H. 80, for Coles, Vere and Wright, omits the first of these, a version of Robin Hood and Queen Katherine which is found nowhere else. There is an edition, printed by J. M. for J. Clarke, W. Thackeray, and T. Passinger, among Pepys's Penny Merriments, vol. iii, and Gutch had a copy, printed for the same, to which he gives the date 1686. Garlands of the eighteenth century increase the number of ballads to twenty-seven.

‡ In the Stationers' Registers, 1562–63, Arber, I, 204, ' a ballett of Robyn Hod' is licensed to John Alde. The best one would expect of this would be a better copy of some later broadside. ' Robyn Hode in Barnysdale stode ' is the first line of a mock-song introduced into the Morality of the Four Elements (which alludes to the discovery of America " within this xx. yere "): Halliwell, Percy Society, vol. xxii, p. 51. It is mentioned (" As R. H.," etc.) in Udall's translation of Erasmi Apothegmata, 1542 : Hazlitt, Handbook, pp 513 f. This line, Ritson observes, has been repeatedly cited, singularly enough, in law-cases (and always misquoted: in Barnwood stood, in Barnwell stood, upon Greendale stood): Ritson's Robin Hood, 1832, I, lxxxix ff. We find " Robyn stode in Bernesdale," Gest, 3¹; also, " As Robin Hood in the forest stood," No 138, 2¹; " When Robin Hood in the greenwood stood," No 141, 1¹, both texts very much later than the interlude. It is not strictly necessary to assume, as Ritson does, that the line belongs to a lost ballad; it may be from some older text of one that we have.

bishops, abbots, bold barons, and knights,[*] but harms no husbandman or yeoman, and is friendly to poor men generally, imparting to them of what he takes from the rich. Courtesy, good temper, liberality, and manliness are his chief marks ; for courtesy and good temper he is a popular Gawain. Yeoman as he is, he has a kind of royal dignity, a princely grace, and a gentleman-like refinement of humor. This is the Robin Hood of the Gest especially ; the late ballads debase this primary conception in various ways and degrees.

This is what Robin Hood is, and it is equally important to observe what he is not. He has no sort of political character, in the Gest or any other ballad. This takes the ground from under the feet of those who seek to assign him a place in history. Wyntoun, who gives four lines to Robin Hood, is quite precise. He is likely to have known of the adventure of King Edward and the outlaw, and he puts Robin under Edward I, at the arbitrary date of 1283, a hundred and forty years before his own time. Bower, without any kind of ceremony, avouches our hero to have been one of the proscribed followers of Simon de Montfort, and this assertion of Bower is adopted and maintained by a writer in the London and Westminster Review, 1840, XXXIII, 424.[†] Major, who probably knew some ballad of Richard I and Robin Hood, offers a simple conjecture that Robin flourished about Richard's time, " circa hæc tempora, ut auguror," and this is the representation in Matthew Parker's ' True Tale,' which many have repeated, not always with ut auguror ; as Scott, with whom no one can quarrel, in the inexpressibly delightful Ivan-

hoe, and Thierry in his Conquête de l'Angleterre, Book xi, IV, 81 ff, ed. 1830, both of whom depict Robin Hood as the chief of a troop of Saxon bandits, Thierry making him an imitator of Hereward. Hunter, again, The Ballad-Hero, Robin Hood, p. 48, interprets the King Edward of the Gest as Edward II, and makes Robin Hood an adherent of the Earl of Lancaster in the fatal insurrection of 1322. No one of these theories has anything besides ballads for a basis except Hunter's. Hunter has an account-book in which the name Robin Hood occurs ; as to which see further on, under stanzas 414–450 of the Gest. Hereward the Saxon, Fulk Fitz Warine, Eustace the Monk, Wallace, all outlaws of one kind or another, are celebrated in romantic tales or poems, largely fabulous, which resemble in a general way, and sometimes in particulars, the traditional ballads about Robin Hood ;[‡] but these outlaws are recognized by contemporary history.

The chief comrades of Robin Hood are : Robin Hood and the Monk, Little John, Scathlok (Scarlok. Scarlet), and Much ; to these the Gest adds Gilbert of the White Hand and Reynold, 292 f. A friar is not a member of his company in the older ballads. A curtal, or cutted friar, called Friar Tuck in the title, but not in the ballad, has a fight with Robin Hood in No 123, and is perhaps to be regarded as having accepted Robin's invitation to join his company ; this, however, is not said. Friar Tuck is simply named as one of Robin's troop in two broadsides, No 145, No 147, but plays no part in them. These two broadsides also name Maid Marian, who appears elsewhere only in a late and entirely insignificant ballad, No 150.[§]

---

* Knights and squires are exempted in the Gest, 14, inconsistently with 7, and, as to knights, with the tenor of what follows.

† Bower, as above. The writer in the L. & W. Review does not distinguish Fordun and Bower.

‡ Lieut.-Col. Prideaux states the resemblances between the story of Fulk Fitz Warine and that of Robin Hood, in an interesting article in Notes and Queries, 7th series, II, 421 ff, and suggests that the latter has borrowed from the former. Undoubtedly this might be, but both may have borrowed from the common stock of tradition.

§ The Pinder of Wakefield became, according to his bal-

lad, one of Robin Hood's men, but is not heard of in any other. Will Stutly is also one in No 141 ; Clifton, No 145 ; David of Doncaster, No 152. Robin Hood assumes the name Locksley in No 145, and by a blunder Locksley is made one of his men in 147 and 153. Scarlet and Scathlock are made two in the Earl of Huntington plays. Grafton says that the name of William of Goldesborough was graven, among others, with that of Robin Hood on Robin's tombstone : Chronicle, I, 222, ed. 1809. Ritson says that Munday makes Right-hitting Brand one of the band : I have not observed this.

Friar Tuck is a character in each of two Robin Hood plays, both of which we have, unluckily, only in a fragmentary state. One of these plays, dating as far back as 1475, presents scenes from Robin Hood and Guy of Gisborn, followed, without any link, by others from some ballad of a rescue of Robin Hood from the sheriff; to which extracts from still other ballads may have been annexed. In this play the friar has no special mark; he simply makes good use of his bow. The other play, printed by Copland with the Gest, not much before 1550, treats more at length the story of Robin Hood and the Curtal Friar, and then that of Robin Hood and the Potter, again, and naturally, without connection. The conclusion is wanting, and the play may have embraced still other ballads. The Friar in this is a loose and jovial fellow, and gave the hint for Scott's Clerk of Copmanhurst.*

The second of the Robin Hood plays is described in the title as "very proper to be played in May-games." These games were in the sixteenth century, and, it would seem, before, often a medley of many things. They were not limited to the first day of May, or even to the month of May; they might occur in June as well. They were not uniform, and might include any kind of performance or spectacle which suited the popular taste. "I find," says Stow, "that in the moneth of May, the citizens of London, of all estates, lightlie in every parish, or sometimes two or three parishes joyning together, had their several Mayinges, and did fetch in Maypoles, with divers warlike shewes, with good archers, morrice-dancers, and other devices for pastime all the day long; and towards the evening they had stage-plays and bonefires in the streetes."† In the Diary of Henry Machyn we read that on the twenty-sixth of May, 1555, there was a goodly May-game at St Martins in the Field, with giant and hobby-horses, morris-dance and other minstrels; and on the third day of June following, a goodly May-game at Westminster, with giants and devils, and three morris-dancers, and many disguised, and the Lord and Lady of the May rode gorgeously, with divers minstrels playing. On the thirtieth of May, 1557, there was a goodly May-game in Fenchurch Street, in which the Nine Worthies rode, and they had speeches, and the morris-dance, and the Sowdan, and the Lord and Lady of the May, and more besides. And again, on the twenty-fourth of June, 1559, there was a May-game, with a giant, the Nine Worthies, with speeches, a goodly pageant with a queen, St George and the Dragon, the morris-dance, and afterwards Robin Hood and Little John, and Maid Marian and Friar Tuck, and they had speeches round about London. (Pp 89, 137, 201.)‡

In the rural districts the May-game was naturally a much simpler affair. The accounts of the chamberlains and churchwardens of Kingston upon Thames for Mayday, 23 Henry VII–28 Henry VIII, 1507–36, contain charges for the morris, the Lady, Little John, Robin Hood, and Maid Marian; the accounts for 21 Henry VII–1 Henry VIII relate to expenses for the Kyngham, and a king and queen are mentioned, presumably king and queen of May; under 24 Henry VII the "cost of the Kyngham and Robyn Hode are entered together." §

"A simple northern man" is made to say in Albion's England, 1586:

---

* Robin Hood presents the friar with a "lady free," not named, who may be meant for a degraded Maid Marian, such as Falstaff refers to in 1 Henry IV, III, iii, 129.

† Stow, Survay of London, 1598, p. 72, in Ritson's excellent note EE, Robin Hood, I, cix ff, ed. 1832, which contains almost all the important information relative to the subject. Stow adds that in consequence of a riot on Mayday, 1517, the great Mayings and May-games were not after that time "so freely used as afore."

‡ These are the people's sports. Hall, fol. lvi, b, cited by Ritson, gives an account of a Maying devised by the guards for the entertainment of Henry VIII and his queen, in 1516. The king and queen, while riding with a great company, come upon a troop of two hundred yeomen in green. One of these, calling himself Robin Hood, invites the king to see his men shoot, and then to an outlaws-breakfast of venison. The royal party, on their return home, were met by a chariot drawn by five horses, in which sat "the Lady May accompanied with Lady Flora," who saluted the king with divers songs.

§ Lysons, The Environs of London, I, 225–32.

At Paske began our Morris, and ere Penticost our
May;
Tho Robin Hood, Liell John, Frier Tucke and
Marian deftly play,
And Lard and Ladie gang till kirk, with lads and
lasses gay.*

Tollet's painted window (which is assigned
by Douce to about 1460–70, and, if rightly
dated, furnishes the oldest known representa-
tion of a May-game with the morris) has,
besides a fool, a piper and six dancers, a May-
pole, a hobby-horse, a friar, and a lady, and
the lady, being crowned, is to be taken as
Queen of May.

What concerns us is the part borne by
Robin Hood, John, and the Friar in these
games, and Robin's relation to Maid Marian.
In Ellis's edition of Brand's Antiquities, I,
214, note h, we are told that Robin Hood is
styled King of May in The Book of the Uni-
versal Kirk of Scotland. This is a mistake,
and an important mistake. In April, 1577,
the General Assembly requested the king to
" discharge [prohibit] playes of Robin Hood,
King of May, and sick others, on the Sabboth
day." In April, 1578, the fourth session, the
king and council were supplicated to discharge
" all kynd of insolent playis, as King of May,
Robin Hood, and sick others, in the moneth of
May, played either be bairnes at the schools,
or others "; and the subject was returned to
in the eighth session. We know from various
sources that plays, founded on the ballads,
were sometimes performed in the course of

the games. We know that archers sometimes
personated Robin Hood and his men in the
May-game.† The relation of Robin Hood,
John, and the Friar to the May-game morris
is obscure. "It plainly appears," says Rit-
son, "that Robin Hood, Little John, the
Friar, and Maid Marian were fitted out at
the same time with the morris-dancers, and
consequently, it would seem, united with
them in one and the same exhibition," mean-
ing the morris. But he adds, with entire
truth, in a note : " it must be confessed that
no other direct authority has been met with for
constituting Robin Hood and Little John in-
tegral characters of the morris-dance."‡ And
further, with less truth so far as the Friar is
concerned : " that Maid Marian and the Friar
were almost constantly such is proved beyond
the possibility of a doubt." The Friar is found
in Tollet's window, which Douce speaks of,
cautiously, as a representation of an English
May-game *and* morris-dance. The only " di-
rect authority," so far as I am aware, for the
Friar's being a party in the morris-dance (un-
connected with the May-game) is the late
authority of Ben Jonson's Masque of the
Metamorphosed Gipsies, 1621, cited by Tollet
in his Memoir ; where it is said that the ab-
sence of a Maid Marian and a friar is a surer
mark than the lack of a hobby-horse that a
certain company cannot be morris-dancers.§
The lady is an essential personage in the mor-
ris.‖ How and when she came to receive the
appellation of Maid Marian in the English

---

* The last two lines are to be understood, I apprehend,
exclusively of the May, and the lord and lady mean Lord
and Lady of the May. The Lord of Misrule, " with his
hobby-horses, dragons, and other ántiques," used to go to
church: Stubbes, Anatomy of Abuses, ed. Furnivall, p. 147.

† Myselfe remembreth of a childe, in contreye native
    mine,
  A Maygame was of Robyn Hood, and of his traine, that
    time,
  To traine up young men, stripplings, and eche other
    younger childe,
  In shooting; yearely this with solempne feast was by
    the guylde
  Or brotherhood of townsmen don, etc.
    Richard Robinson, 1553, in Ritson, p. cxii f, ed. 1832.

‡ A Christmas game of very modern date is described in
The Mirror, XXVI, 42, in which there was a troop of morris-
dancers with Robin Hood and Maid Marian ; and also Beel-

zebub and his wife. Cited by Kuhn, Haupt's Zeitschrift, V,
481.

§ The entries in the Kingston accounts for 28 and 29
Henry VIII, if they refer to the morris-dance only, would
show the morris to be constituted as follows :
  (28 Henry VIII.) Four dancers, fool, Maid Marian, friar,
and piper. A minstrel is also mentioned.
  (29 Henry VIII.) Friar, Maid Marian, Morian (Moor ?),
four dancers, fool. This entry refers to the costume of the
characters, which may account for the omission of the piper.
Lysons, Environs of London, I, 228 f.

‖ It need hardly be remarked that the morris was neither
an exclusively English dance nor exclusively a May-game
dance. A Flemish morris, delineated in an engraving dated
1460–70, has for personages a lady, fool, piper, and six
dancers : Douce, p. 446 f. In Robert Laneham's description
of a bride-ale at Kenilworth, 1575, there is a morris-dance,
" according to the ancient manner," in the which the parties

morris is unknown. The earliest occurrence of the name seems to be in Barclay's fourth Eclogue,* "subjoined to the last edition of The Ship of Foles, but originally printed soon after 1500 : " Ritson, I, lxxxvii, ed. 1832. Warton suggested a derivation from the French Marion, and the idea is extremely plausible. Robin and Marion were the subject of innumerable motets and pastourelles of the thirteenth century, and the hero and heroine of a very pretty and lively play, more properly comic opera, composed by Adam de la Halle not far from 1280. We know from a document of 1392 that this play was annually performed at Angers, at Whitsuntide, and we cannot doubt that it was a stock-piece in many places, as from its merits it deserved to be. There are as many proverbs about Robin and Marion as there are about Robin Hood, and the first verse of the play, derived from an earlier song, is still (or was fifty years ago) in the mouths of the peasant girls of Hainault.† In the May-game of June, 1559, described by Machyn, after many other things, they had " Robin Hood and Little John," and " Maid Marian and Friar Tuck," some dramatic scene, pantomime, or pageant, probably two; but there is nothing of Maid Marian in the two (fragmentary) Robin Hood plays which

are preserved, both of which, so far as they go, are based on ballads. Anthony Munday, towards the end of the sixteenth century, made a play, full of his own inventions, in which Robert, Earl of Huntington, being outlawed, takes refuge in Sherwood, with his chaste love Matilda, daughter of Lord Fitzwaters, and changes his name to Robin Hood, hers to Maid Marian.‡ One S. G., a good deal later, wrote a very bad ballad about the Earl of Huntington and his lass, the only ballad in which Maid Marian is more than a name. Neglecting these perversions, Maid Marian is a personage in the May-game and morris who is not infrequently paired with a friar, and sometimes with Robin Hood, under what relation, in either case, we cannot precisely say. Percy had no occasion to speak of her as Robin's concubine, and Douce none to call her Robin's paramour.

That ballads about Robin Hood were familiar throughout England and Scotland we know from early testimony. Additional evidence of his celebrity is afforded by the connection of his name with a variety of natural objects and archaic remains over a wide extent of country.

" Cairns on Blackdown in Somersetshire, and barrows near to Whitby in Yorkshire

---

are Maid Marian, the fool, and six dancers : Furnivall, Captain Cox, p. 22 f. A painting of about 1625 has a morris-dance of seven figures, a Maid Marian, fool, piper, hobby-horse, and three dancers. A tract, of Elizabeth's time, speaks of " a quintessence, beside the fool and the Maid Marian, of all the picked youth, footing the morris about a Maypole," to the pipe and tabor, and other music; and a poem of 1614 describes a country morris-dance of a fool, Maid Marian, hobby-horse, and piper : Ellis's Brand, p. 206 f.

* The well-to-do Codrus says to the starving Menalcas, who has been venting his spleen against " rascolde " rivals,

'Yet would I gladly heare some mery fit
Of Maide Marian, or els of Robin Hood.'

Codrus is here only suggesting themes which would be agreeable to him. We are not to deduce from his words that there were ballads about Maid Marian. But if there had been, they would have been distinct from ballads about Robin Hood.

† See Monmerqué et Michel, Théatre Français au Moyen Age, 1842, Notice sur Adam de la Halle, pp 27 ff, the songs, pp 31 ff, the play, pp 102 ff; Ducange, Robinetus. Henryson's Robin and Ma'kyne was undoubtedly suggested by the French pastorals.

‡ I must invoke the spirit of Ritson to pardon the taking of no very serious notice of Robin Hood's noble extraction.

The first mention of this seems to be in Grafton's Chronicle, 1569. Grafton says: In an olde and auncient pamphlet I finde this written of the sayd Robert Hood. This man, sayth he, discended of a noble parentage ; or rather, beyng of a base stocke and linage, was for his manhoode and chiualry aduaunced to the noble dignitie of an erle. . . . But afterwardes he so prodigally exceeded in charges and expences that he fell into great debt, by reason whereof so many actions and sutes were commenced against him, wherevnto he aunswered not, that by order of lawe he was outlawed, etc.: I, 221, ed. 1809. (Some such account furnished a starting-point for Munday.) Leland also, Ritson adds, has expressly termed him " nobilis " (Ro: Hood, nobilis ille exlex), Collectanea, I, 54, ed. 1770, and Warner, in Albion's England (1586), p. 132, ed. 1612, calls him a "county":

Those daies begot some mal-contents, the principall of whom
A countie was, that with a troop of yeomandry did roam.

Ritson also cites the Sloane MS., 715, " written, as it seems, toward the end of the sixteenth century;" and Harleian MS., 1233, which he does not date, but which is of the middle of the seventeenth century. Against the sixteenth-century testimony, so to call it, we put in that of the early ballads, all of which describe Robin as a yeoman, the Gest emphasizing the point.

and Ludlow in Shropshire, are termed Robin Hood's pricks or butts; lofty natural eminences in Gloucestershire and Derbyshire are Robin Hood's hills; a huge rock near Matlock is Robin Hood's Tor; an ancient boundary stone in Lincolnshire is Robin Hood's cross; a presumed loggan, or rocking-stone, in Yorkshire is Robin Hood's penny-stone; a fountain near Nottingham, another between Doncaster and Wakefield, and one in Lancashire are Robin Hood's wells; a cave in Nottinghamshire is his stable; a rude natural rock in Hope Dale is his chair; a chasm at Chatsworth is his leap; Blackstone Edge, in Lancashire, is his bed; ancient oaks, in various parts of the country, are his trees." * All sorts of traditions are fitted to the localities where they are known. It would be an exception to ordinary rules if we did not find Robin Hood trees and Robin Hood wells and Robin Hood hills. But, says Wright, in his essay on the Robin Hood ballads (p. 208), the connection of Robin Hood's name with mounds and stones is perhaps one of the strongest proofs of his mythic character, as

if Robin Hood were conceived of as a giant. The fact in question is rather a proof that those names were conferred at a time when the real character of Robin Hood was dimly remembered. In the oldest ballads Robin Hood is simply a stout yeoman, one of the best that ever bare bow; in the later ballads he is repeatedly foiled in contests with shepherds and beggars. Is it supposable that those who knew of him even at his best estate, could give him a loggan for a penny-stone? No one has as yet undertaken to prove that the ballads are later than the names.† Mounds and stones bear his name for the same idle reason that "so many others have that of King Arthur, King John, and, for want of a better, that of the devil." ‡

Kuhn, starting with the assumption that the mythical character of Robin Hood is fully established (by traditions posterior to the ballads and contradictory to their tenor), has sought to show that our courteous outlaw is in particular one of the manifestations of Woden. The hobby-horse, which, be it borne in mind, though now and then found in the May-game

---

* The Edinburgh Review, LXXXVI, 123 (with a slight correction in one instance), mostly from Ritson, I, cix, cxxvi ff, 1832, and from Wright's Essays, etc., II, 209 f, 1846. Of course the list might be extended: there are some additions in The Academy, XXIV, 231, 1883, and four Robin Hood's wells in Yorkshire alone are there noted.

† A Robin Hood's Stone, near Barnsdale, of what description we are not told, is mentioned in an account of a progress made by Henry VII, and Robin Hood's Well, in the same region, in an account of a tour made in 1634: Hunter's Robin Hood, p. 61. The well is also mentioned by Drunken Barnaby. A Robin Hood's Hill is referred to in Vicars' account of the siege of Gloucester in 1643: The Academy, XXIV, 231.

‡ Gough, in the Gentleman's Magazine, March 8, 1793, cited by Gutch. Wright has, somewhat naively, furnished his own refutation: "A large tumulus we know well in our own county, near Ludlow in Shropshire, which is also called Robin Hood's But, and which affords us a curious instance how new stories were often invented to account for a name whose original import was forgotten. The circumstances, too, in this case, prove that the story was of late invention. The barrow, as regarded superstitiously, had borne the name of Robin Hood. On the roof of one of the chancels of the church of Ludlow, which is called Fletchers' chancel, as having been, when 'the strength of England stood upon archery,' the place where the fletchers held their meetings, and which is distant from the aforesaid barrow two miles, or two miles and a half, there stands an iron arrow, as the sign of their craft. The imagination of the people of the place,

after archery and fletchers had been forgotten, and when Robin Hood was known only as an outlaw and a bowman, made a connection between the barrow (from its name) and the chancel (from the arrow on its roof), and a tale was invented how the outlaw once stood upon the former and took aim at the weathercock on the church steeple; but the distance being a little too great, the arrow fell short of its mark, and remained up to the present day on the roof of the chancel." (Essays, I, 209 f.)

A correspondent of The Academy, XXIV, 181, remarks that one of the Anglo-Saxon charters in Kemble's Codex Diplomaticus mentions a "place" in Worcestershire called Hódes ác (now Hodsoak), that there is a village in Nottinghamshire called Hodsock, that it is improbable that two men living in districts so widely apart should each have given his name to an oak-tree, and that therefore we may safely conclude Hód to be a mythical personage. Somebody's tree is given as a boundary mark more than thirty times in these charters, somebody's thorn at least ten times, somebody's oak at least five times. How often such a mark might occur in connection with any particular name would depend upon the frequency of the name. Hód or Hóde is cited thirteen times by Kemble, and few names occur oftener. The name, we may infer, was relatively as common then as it is in our century, which has seen three Admiral Hoods (who, by virtue of being three, may be adjudged as mythical by and by) and one poet Hood alive together. Why may not three retired wícings and one scóp, of the name, have been living in Berks, Hants, Wilts, and Worcestershire in the tenth century?

or morris-dance, was never intimately associated, perhaps we may say never at all associated, with Robin Hood, represents, it is maintained, Woden. The fundamental grounds are these. In a Christmas, New Year, or Twelfth Day sport at Paget's Bromley, Staffordshire, the rider of the hobby-horse held a bow and arrow in his hands, with which he made a snapping noise. In a modern Christmas festivity in Kent, the young people would affix the head of a horse to a pole about four feet in length, and tie a cloth round the head to conceal one of the party, who, by pulling a string attached to the horse's lower jaw, produced a snapping noise as he moved along. This ceremony, according to the reporter, was called a h o o d e n i n g, and the figure of the horse a h o o d e n, " a wooden horse." * The word hooden, according to Kuhn, we may unhesitatingly expound as Woden; Hood is a corruption of " Hooden," and this Hooden again conducts us to Woden.

Glosyng is a ful glorious thing certayn.

The sport referred to is explained in Pegge's Alphabet of Kenticisms (collected 1735–36), under the name h o o d i n g, as a country masquerade at Christmas time, which in Derbyshire they call guising, and in other places mumming; and to the same effect in the Rev. W. D. Parish's Dictionary of the Kentish Dialect (soon to be published) under h o o d e n i n g, which word is an obvious corruption, or secondary form, of hooding. The word

hooding, applied to the sport, means just what it does in the old English hooding-cloth, a curtain; that is, a covering, and so a disguise by covering. It is true that wooden is pronounced hooden,† or ooden, in Kent, and that the hobby-horse had a wooden head, but it is quite inconceivable that the sport should receive its name from a circumstance so subordinate as the material of which the horse was made. Such an interpretation would hardly be thought of had not hooding in its proper sense long been obsolete. That this is the case is plain from two facts : the hooding used to be accompanied with carol-singing, and the Rev. Mr Parish informs us that carol-singing on Christmas Eve is still called hoodening at Monckton, in East Kent. The form Hooden, from which Robin's name is asserted by Kuhn to be corrupted, is invented for the occasion. I suppose that no one will think that the hobby-horse-rider's carrying a bow and arrows, in the single instance of the Staffordshire sport, conduces at all to the identifying of Robin Hood with the hobby-horse. Whether the Hobby-Horse represents Woden is not material here. It is enough that the Hobby-Horse cannot be shown to represent Robin Hood.‡

I cannot admit that even the shadow of a case has been made out by those who would attach a mythical character either to Robin Hood or to the outlaws of Inglewood, Adam Bell, Clim of the Clough, and William of Cloudesly. §

---

* Plot's History of Staffordshire, p. 434, cited in Ellis's Brand, I, 383 ; The Mirror, XX, 419, cited by Kuhn, Haupt's Zeitschrift, V, 474 f. The Kentish sport is also described in the Rev. W. D. Parish's Dictionary of the Kentish Dialect, p. 77, under Hoodening.

† In West Worcestershire *h* is put for *w*, "by an emphatic speaker," in such words as wood, wool : Mrs Chamberlain's Glossary. Hood for wood occurs in East Sussex ; also in Somerset, according to Halliwell's Dictionary. The derivation of Hood from wood has often been suggested : as by Peele, in his Edward I, " Robin of the Wood, alias Robin Hood," Works, Dyce, I, 162. The inventive Peck was pleased always to write Robin Whood.

‡ The Hobby-Horse, Schimmel, Fastnachtspferd, Herbstpferd, Adventspferd, Chevalet, Cheval Mallet, is maintained by Mannhardt to be figurative of the Corn-Sprite, Korndämon ; nichts anderes als das Kornross, Vegetationsross, nicht aber eine Darstellung Wodans, wie man nach Kuhns Vor-

gang jetzt allgemein annimmt : Mannhardt, Mythologische Forschungen, in Quellen u. Forschungen, LI, p. 165. " Man sieht den Ungrund der bei deutschen Mythologen so beliebten Identifizierung von Robin Hood und Wodan :" Mannhardt, Wald- u. Feldkulte, I, 546, note 3.

§ The reasoning, in the instance of Robin Hood, has been signally loose and incautious ; still, the general conclusion finds ready acceptance with mythologists, on one ground or another, and deductions are made with the steadiness of a geometer. Robin Hood, being one of the "solar heroes," " has his faint reflection in Little John, who stands to him in the same relation as Patroclus to Achilles," etc. " Maid Marian will therefore be the dawn-maiden, to be identified with Briseis," etc. " Friar Tuck is one of the triumvirate who appear also in the Cloudesly and Tell legends," etc. And again, by an interpreter of somewhat different views : " though a considerable portion of this story is ultimately derived from the great Aryan sun-myth, there is the strong-

Ballads of other nations, relating to classes of men living in revolt against authority and society, may be expected to show some kind of likeness to the English outlaw-ballads, and such resemblances will be pointed out upon occasion. Spanish broadside ballads dating from the end of the sixteenth century commemorate the valientes and guapos of cities, robbers and murderers of the most flaunting and flagitious description: Duran, Romancero, Nos 1331–36, 1339–43, II, 367 ff.* These display towards corregidores, alcaides, customhouse officers, and all the ministers of government an hostility corresponding to that of Robin Hood against the sheriff; they empty the jails and deliver culprits from the gallows; reminding us very faintly of the Robin Hood broadsides, as of the rescues in Nos 140, 141, the Progress to Nottingham, No 139, in which Robin Hood, at the age of fifteen, kills fifteen foresters, or of Young Gamwell, in No 128, who begins his career by killing his father's steward.† But Robin Hood and his men, in the most degraded of the broadsides, are tame innocents and law-abiding citizens beside the guapos. The Klephts, whose songs are preserved in considerable numbers, mostly from the last century and the present, have the respectability of being engaged, at least in part, in a war against the Turks, and the romance of wild mountaineers. They, like Robin Hood, had a marked animosity against

monks, and they put beys to ransom as he would an abbot or a sheriff. There are Magyar robber-ballads in great number; ‡ some of these celebrate Shobri (a man of this century), who spares the poor, relieves beggars, pillages priests (but never burns or kills), and fears God: Erdélyi's collection, I, 194–98, Nos 237–39; Arany-Gyulai, II, 56, No 49; Kertbeny, Ausgewählte Ungarische Volkslieder, pp 246–251, Nos 136–38; Aigner, pp 198–201. Russian robber-songs are given by Sakharof, under the title Udaluiya, Skazaniya, 1841, I, iii, 224–32; Ralston, Songs of the Russian People, pp 44–50. There are a few Sicilian robber-ballads in Pitré, Canti pop. Siciliani, Nos 913–16, II, 125–37.

The Gest is a popular epic, composed from several ballads by a poet of a thoroughly congenial spirit. No one of the ballads from which it was made up is extant in a separate shape, and some portions of the story may have been of the compiler's own invention. The decoying of the sheriff into the wood, stanzas 181–204, is of the same derivation as the last part of Robin Hood and the Potter, No 121, Little John and Robin Hood exchanging parts; the conclusion, 451–56, is of the same source as Robin Hood's Death, No 120. Though the tale, as to all important considerations, is eminently original, absolutely so as to the conception of Robin Hood, some traits and incidents, as might be ex-

---

est reason for believing that the Anglian Hód was not originally a solar personage, but a degraded form of the God of the Wind, Hermes-Woden. The thievish character of this divinity explains at once why his name should have been chosen as the popular appellation of an outlaw chief." (The Academy, XXIV, 250, 384.)

The Potter in the later Play of Robin Hood (not in the corresponding ballad) wears a rose garland on his head. So does a messenger in the history of Fulk Fitz Warine, Wright, p. 78, not to mention other cases referred to by Ritson, Robin Hood, II, 200, ed. 1832. Fricke, Die Robin-Hood Balladen, p. 55, surmises that the rose garland worn by the Potter may be a relic of the strife between Summer and Winter; and this view, he suggests, would tend to confirm "the otherwise well-grounded hypothesis" that Robin Hood is a mythological personage.

* "Desde la última década del siglo xvi hasta pocos años hace, no eran ya los héroes del pueblo ni los Bernardos, ni los Cides, ni los Pulgares, ni los Garcilasos, ni los Céspedes, ni los Paredes, porque su pueblo estaba muerto ó trasformado en vulgo, y este habia sustituido á aquellos los guapos

Francisco Estéban, los Correas, los Merinos, los Salinas, los Pedrajas, los Montijos." (Duran, p. 389, note.)

† Bernardo del Montijo, Duran, No 1342, kills an alcalde at the age of eighteen, "con bastante causa:" upon which phrase Duran observes, "para el vulgo era bastante causa, sin duda, el ser alcalde." Beginning with so much promise of spirit, he afterwards, in carrying off his mistress, who was about to be wedded against her will, kills six constables, a corregidor, the bridegroom, and a captain of the guard. For differences, compare the English broadside R. H. and Allena-Dale, No 138.

‡ "Doch sind sie meist ohne grossen poetischen Werth, nur als Zeugniss für die Denkweise des Volkes über die ' armen Bursche,' die es lange nicht für so grosse Verbrecher hält als der Staat, und die es, ihre Vorurtheile theilend, im Gegentheile oft als kühne Freiheitshelden betrachtet, die gegen grössere oder kleinere Tyrannen sich zu erheben und denselben zu trotzen wagen, und als ungerecht verfolgte Söhne seines Stammes in Schutz nimmt gegen die fremden Gesetzvollstrecker." (Aigner, Ungarische Volksdichtungen, p. xxvi f.)

pected, are taken from what we may call the general stock of mediæval fiction.

The story is a three-ply web of the adventures of Robin Hood with a knight, with the sheriff of Nottingham, and with the king (the concluding stanzas, 451–56, being a mere epilogue), and may be decomposed accordingly. I. How Robin Hood relieved a knight, who had fallen into poverty, by lending him money on the security of Our Lady, the first fit, 1–81; how the knight recovered his lands, which had been pledged to Saint Mary Abbey, and set forth to repay the loan, the second fit, 82–143; how Robin Hood, having taken twice the sum lent from a monk of this abbey, declared that Our Lady had discharged the debt, and would receive nothing more from the knight, the fourth fit, 205–280. II. How Little John insidiously took service with Robin Hood's standing enemy, the sheriff of Nottingham, and put the sheriff into Robin Hood's hands, the third fit, 144–204; how the sheriff, who had sworn an oath to help and not to harm Robin Hood and his men, treacherously set upon the outlaws at a shooting-match, and they were fain to take refuge in the knight's castle; how, missing of Robin Hood, the sheriff made prisoner of the knight; and how Robin Hood slew the sheriff and rescued the knight, the fifth and sixth fit, 281–353. III. How the king, coming in person to apprehend Robin Hood and the knight, disguised himself as an abbot, was stopped by Robin Hood, feasted on his own deer, and entertained with an exhibition of archery, in the course of which he was recognized by Robin Hood, who asked his grace and received a promise thereof, on condition that he and his men should enter into the king's service; and how the king, for a jest, disguised himself and his company in the green of the outlaws, and going back to Nottingham caused a general flight of the people, which he stopped by making himself known; how he pardoned the knight; and

how Robin Hood, after fifteen months in the king's court, heart-sick and deserted by all his men but John and Scathlock, obtained a week's leave of the king to go on a pilgrimage to Saint Mary Magdalen of Barnsdale, and would never come back in two-and-twenty years, the seventh and eighth fit, 354–450. A particular analysis may be spared, seeing that many of the details will come out incidentally in what follows.

Barnsdale, Robin Hood's haunt in the Gest, 3, 21, 82, 134, 213, 262, 440, 442, is a woodland region in the West Riding of Yorkshire, a little to the south of Pontefract and somewhat further to the north of Doncaster. The river Went is its northern boundary. "The traveller enters upon it [from the south] a little beyond a well-known place called Robin Hood's Well [some ten miles north of Doncaster, near Skelbrook], and he leaves it when he has descended to Wentbridge." (For Wentbridge, see No 121, st. 6; the Gest, 135^1.) A little to the west is Wakefield, and beyond Wakefield, between that town and Halifax, was the priory of Kyrkesly or Kirklees. The Sayles, 18, was a very small tenancy of the manor of Pontefract. The great North Road, formerly so called, and here, 18, denominated Watling Street (as Roman roads often are), crosses Barnsdale between Doncaster and Ferrybridge.* Saint Mary Abbey, "here besyde," 54, was at York, and must have been a good twenty miles from Barnsdale. The knight, 126^4, is said to be "at home in Verysdale." Wyresdale (now Over and Nether Wyersdale) was an extensive tract of wild country, part of the old forest of Lancashire, a few miles to the southeast of Lancaster. The knight's son had slain a knight and a squire of Lancaster, a, Lancashire, b, f, g, 53. It is very likely, therefore, that the knight's castle, in the original ballad, was in Lancashire. However this may be, it is put in the Gest, 309 f, on the way between Nottingham and Robin Hood's

---

* J. Hunter (Critical and Historical Tracts, No IV), whom I follow here, shows that Barnsdale was peculiarly unsafe for travellers in Edward the First's time. Three ecclesiastics, conveyed from Scotland to Winchester, had a

guard, sometimes of eight archers, sometimes of twelve, or, further south, none at all; but when they passed from Pontefract to Tickhill, the number was increased to twenty, *propter Barnsdale:* p. 14.

retreat, which must be assumed to be Barnsdale. From it, again, Barnsdale is easily accessible to the knight's wife, 334 f.* Wherever it lay or lies, the distance from Nottingham or from Barnsdale, as also the distance from Nottingham to Barnsdale (actually some fifty miles), is made nothing of in the Gest.† The sheriff goes a-hunting; John, who is left behind, does not start from Nottingham till more than an hour after noon, takes the sheriff's silver to Barnsdale,‡ runs five miles in the forest, and finds the sheriff still at his sport: 155 f, 168, 176–82. We must not be nice. Robin Hood has made a vow to go from London to Barnsdale barefoot. The distance thither and back would not be much short of three hundred and fifty miles. King Edward allows him a seven-night, and no longer, 442 f. The compiler of the Gest did not concern himself to adjust these matters. There was evidently at one time a Barnsdale cycle and a Sherwood cycle of Robin Hood ballads. The sheriff of Nottingham would belong to the Sherwood series (to which Robin Hood and the Monk appertains). He is now a capital character in all the old Robin Hood ballads. If he was adopted from the Sherwood into the Barnsdale set, this was done without a rearrangement of the topography.

5–7. Robin Hood will not dine until he has some guest that can pay handsomely for his entertainment, 18, 19, 206, 209; dinner, accordingly, is sometimes delayed a long time, 25, 30, 143, 220; to Little John's impatience, 5, 16, 206, 211. This habit of Robin's seems to be a humorous imitation of King Arthur, who in numerous romances will not dine till some adventure presents itself; a custom

which, at least on one occasion, proves vexatious to his court. Cf. I, 257 f.§

8–10. Robin's general piety and his special devotion to the Virgin are again to be remarked in No 118. There is a tale of a knight who had a castle near a public road, and robbed everybody that went by, but said his Ave every day, and never allowed anything to interfere with his so doing, in Legenda Aurea, c. 51, Grässe, p. 221; Hagen, Gesammtabenteuer, III, 563, No 86; Morlini Novellæ, Paris, 1855, p. 269, No 17, etc.

13–15. Robin's practice corresponds closely with Gamelyn's:

Whil Gamelyn was outlawed hadde he no cors;
There was no man that for him ferde the wors
But abbotes and priours, monk and chanoun;
On hem left he no-thing, whan he mighte hem nom.
vv 779–82, ed. Skeat.

Fulk Fitz Warine, nor any of his, during the time of his outlawry would ever do hurt to any one except the king and his knights: Wright, p. 77 f.

45. " Distraint of knighthood," or the practice of requiring military tenants who held 20 *l.* per annum to receive knighthood, or pay a composition, began under Henry III, as early as 1224, and was continued by Edward I. This was regarded as a very serious oppression under James I and Charles I, and was abolished in 1642. Stubbs, Constitutional History, II, 281 f; Hallam, Constitutional History, ed. 1854, I, 338, note x, II, 9, 99.

62–66. The knight has no security to offer for a loan " but God that dyed on a tree," and such security, or that of the saints, is peremptorily rejected by Robin; but when the knight says that he can offer no other, unless

* Hunter suspects that the Nottinghamshire knight, Sir Richard at the Lee, in the latter half of the Gest, was originally a different person from the knight in the former half, " the knight of the Barnsdale ballads," p. 25. Fricke makes the same suggestion, Die Robin-Hood Balladen, p. 19. This may be, but the reasons offered are not quite conclusive.

† And so, as to Nottingham and Barnsdale, in No 118; and perhaps No 121, for the reference to Wentbridge, st. 6, would imply that Robin Hood is in Barnsdale rather than Sherwood.

‡ I say Barnsdale, though the place is not specified, and though Sherwood would remove or reduce the difficulty as

to distance. We have nothing to do with Sherwood in the Gest: a rational topography is out of the question. In the seventh fit the king starts from Nottingham, 365, walks " down by yon abbey," 368, and ere he comes to Nottingham, 370, falls in with Robin, 375.

§ This was a custom of Arthur's only upon certain holidays, according to the earlier representation, but in later accounts is made general. For romances, besides these mentioned at I, 257, in which this way of Arthur's is noted (Rigomer, Jaufré, etc.), see Gaston Paris, Les Romans en vers du Cycle de la Table Ronde, Histoire Litt. de la France, XXX, 49.

it be Our Lady, the Virgin is instantly ac-
cepted as entirely satisfactory. In a well-
known miracle of Mary, found in most of the
larger collections, a Christian, who resorts to
a Jew to borrow money, tenders Jesus as se-
curity, and the Jew, who regards Jesus as a
just man and a prophet, though not divine, is
willing to lend on the terms proposed. The
Christian, not being able, as he says, to pro-
duce Jesus Christ in person, takes the Jew
to a church, and, standing before an image of
the Virgin and Child, causes him to take the
hand of the Child, saying, Lord Jesus Christ,
whose image I have given as pledge for this
money, and whom I have offered this Jew as
my surety, I beg and entreat that, if I shall
by any chance be prevented from returning
the money to this man upon the day fixed,
but shall give it to thee, thou wilt return it
to him in such manner and form as may please
thee. In the sequel this miraculous interpo-
sition becomes necessary, and the money is
punctually restored, the act of grace being im-
plicitly or distinctly attributed to Mary rather
than her Son; distinctly in an English form
of the legend, where the Christian, especially
devoted to the Virgin, offers Saint Mary for
his borrow: Horstmann, Die altenglischen
Marienlegenden des MS. Vernon, in Archiv
für das Studium der neueren Sprachen, LVI,
232, No 6.*

107. The abbot had retained the chief jus-
tice "by robe and fee," to counsel and aid him
in the spoliation of the knight, 93. Taking
and giving of robes and fees for such purposes
is defined as conspiracy in a statute of Ed-
ward I, 1305–06; and by another statute, 20
Edward III, c. vi, 1346, justices are required
to swear that they will take robes and fees
from no man but the king: et que vos ne
prendrez fee, tant come vos serez justicz, ne

robes, de nul homme, graunt ne petit, sinoun
du roi meismes. Statutes of the Realm, I,
145, 305: cited by J. Lewelyn Curtis, in
Notes and Queries, S. I, VI, 479 f. All the
English judges, including the chief justice,
were convicted of bribery and were removed,
under Edward I, 1289.

121. The knight would have given some-
thing for the use of the four hundred pound
had the abbot been civil, though under no ob-
ligation to pay interest. In 270 the knight
proffers Robin twenty mark (3⅓ per cent) for
his courtesy, which seemingly small sum was
to be accompanied with the valuable gift of a
hundred bows and a hundred sheaf of peacock-
feathered, silver-nocked arrows. But though
the abbot had not lent for usury, still less had
he lent for charity. The knight's lands were to
be forfeited if the loan should not be punctu-
ally returned, 86 f, 94, 106; and of this the
knight was entirely aware, 85. "As for mort-
gaging or pawning," says Bacon, Of Usury,
"either men will not take pawns without use,
or, if they do, they will look precisely for the
forfeiture. I remember a cruel moneyed man
in the country that would say, The devil take
this usury; it keeps us from forfeitures of
mortgages and bonds." But troubles, legal
or other, might ensue upon this hard-dealing
unless the knight would give a quittance,
117 f.

135–37. A ram was the prize for an ordi-
nary wrestling-match; but this is an occa-
sion which brings together all the best yeo-
men of the West Country, and the victor is to
have a bull, a horse saddled and bridled, a
pair of gloves, a ring, and a pipe of wine. In
Gamelyn "there was set up a ram and a ring,"
v. 172.

181–204. The sheriff is decoyed into the
wood by Robin Hood in No 121, 56–69, No

---

* Pothouis Liber de Miraculis S. D. G. Mariæ, c. 33, p.
377; Vincentius B., Speculum Hist., vii. c. 82. Mussafia,
Sitzungsberichte der Wiener Akad., Phil.-Hist. Classe,
CXIII, 960–91, notes nine Latin copies, besides that attrib-
uted to Potho, in MSS mostly of the 13th century. Gautier
de Coincy, ed. Poquet, cols. 543–52; Adgar's Marienlegen-
den, Neuhaus, p. 176, No 29; Miracles de Nostre Dame par
Personnages, G. Paris et U. Robert, VI, 171–223, No 35;
Romania, VIII, 16, No 3 (Provençal). Berceo, in Sanchez,
II, 367, No 23. Unger, Mariu Saga, No 15, pp. 87–92, 1064–

67. Mone's Anzeiger, VIII, col. 355, No 8, as a broadside
ballad. Afanasief, Skazki, vii, No 49, as a popular tale,
the Jew changed to a Tartar, and the Cross taken as surety,
Ralston, Russian Folk-Tales, p. 27. "God-borg" in Al-
fred's Laws, c. 33, Schmid, Gesetze der Angelsachsen, p.
88 f., was perhaps only an asseveration with an invocation of
the Deity, like the Welsh "briduw." And so "Ich wil dir
got ze bürgen geben," "Got den wil ich ze bürgen han,"
in the Ritter v. Staufenberg, vv 403, 405, Jänicke, Alt-
deutsche Studien.

122, A, 18–25, B, 20–27, as here by Little John. Fulk Fitz Warine gets his enemy, King John, into his power by a like stratagem. Fulk, disguised as a collier, is asked by King John if he has seen a stag or doe pass. He has seen a horned beast; it had long horns. He offers to take the king to the place where he saw it, and begs the king to wait while he goes into the thicket to drive the beast that way. Fulk's men are in the forest: he tells them that he has brought the king with only three knights; they rush out and seize the king. Fulk says he will have John's life, but the king promises to restore Fulk's heritage and all that had been taken from him and his men, and to be his friend forever after. A pledge of faith is exacted and given, and very happy is the king so to escape. But the king keeps the forced oath no better than the sheriff. Wright, p. 145 ff. There is a passage which has the same source, though differing in details, in Eustace the Monk, Michel, pp. 36–39, vv 995–1070. The story is incomparably better here than elsewhere.

213–33. The black monks are Benedictines. There are two according to 213 f, 218, 225[4], but the high cellarer only (who in 91–93 is exultant over the knight's forfeiture) is of consequence, and the other is made no account of. Seven score of wight young men, 229[3], is the right number for a band of outlaws; so Gamelyn, v. 628. The sheriff has his seven score in Guy of Gisborn, 13.

243–47. "What is in your coffers?" So Eustace the monk to the merchant, v. 938, p. 34, Michel: "Di-moi combien tu as d'argent." The merchant tells the exact truth, and Eustace, having verified the answer by counting, returns all the money, saying, If you had lied in the least, you would not have carried off a penny. When Eustace asks the same question of the abbot, v. 1765, p. 64, the abbot answers, after the fashion of our cellarer, Four silver marks. Eustace finds thirty marks, and returns to the abbot the four which he had confessed.

213–272. Nothing was ever more felicitously told, even in the best *dit* or *fabliau*, than the " process " of Our Lady's repaying the money which had been lent on her security. Robin's slyly significant welcome to the monk upon learning that he is of Saint Mary Abbey, his professed anxiety that Our Lady is wroth with him because she has not sent him his pay, John's comfortable suggestion that perhaps the monk has brought it, Robin's incidental explanation of the little business in which the Virgin was a party, and request to see the silver in case the monk has come upon her affair, are beautiful touches of humor, and so delicate that it is all but brutal to point them out. The story, however, is an old one, and was known, perhaps, wherever monks were known. A complete parallel is afforded by Pauli's Schimpf und Ernst, No 59 (c. 1515). A nobleman took a burgess's son prisoner in war, carried him home to his castle, and shut him up in a tower. After lying there a considerable time, the prisoner asked and obtained an interview with his captor, and said: Dear lord, I am doing no good here to you or myself, since my friends will not send my ransom. If you would let me go home, I would come back in eight weeks and bring you the money. Whom will you give for surety? asked the nobleman. I have no one to offer, replied the prisoner, but the Lord God, and will swear you an oath by him to keep my word. The nobleman was satisfied, made his captive swear the oath, and let him go. The hero sold all that he owned, and raised the money, but was three weeks longer in so doing than the time agreed upon. The nobleman, one day, when he was riding out with a couple of servants, fell in with an abbot or friar who had two fine horses and a man. See here, my good fellows, said the young lord; that monk is travelling with two horses, as fine as any knight, when he ought to be riding on an ass. Look out now, we will play him a turn. So saying, he rode up to the monk, seized the bridle of his horse, and asked, Sir, who are you? Who is your lord? The monk answered, I am a servant of God, and he is my lord. You come in good time, said the nobleman. I had a prisoner, and set him free upon his leaving your lord with me as a surety. But I can get nothing from this

lord of yours; he is above my power; so I will
lay hands on his servant; and accordingly
made the monk go with him afoot to the castle,
where he took from him all that he had.
Shortly after, his prisoner appeared, fell at
his feet, and wished to pay the ransom, beg-
ging that he would not be angry, for the
money could not be got sooner. But the no-
bleman said, Stand up, my good man. Keep
your money, and go whither you will, for your
surety has paid your ransom. Ed. Oester-
ley, p. 49. The gist of the story is in Jacques
de Vitry, Sermones Vulgares, fol. 62, MS.
17,509, Bibliothèque Nationale, Paris; Scala
Celi (1480), 159 b, "De Restitucione," and
elsewhere: see Oesterly's note, p. 480. A
very amusing variety is the *fabliau* Du povre
Mercier, Barbazan et Méon, III, 17; Mon-
taiglon et Raynaud, II, 114; Legrand, III, 93,
ed. 1829.*

293³. Reynolde. Possibly Little John bor-
rows this Reynolde's name in 149, but there
is no apparent reason why he should. In
the following very strange, and to me utterly
unintelligible, piece in Ravenscroft's Deuter-
omelia, which may have been meant to have
only enough sense to sing, Renold, a miller's
son, mickle of might (was he rechristened
Much?), becomes one of Robin Hood's men.
(Deuteromelia, p. 4: London, for Tho. Ad-
ams, 1609.)

1 By Lands-dale hey ho,
    By mery Lands-dale hey ho,
  There dwelt a jolly miller,
    And a very good old man was he, hey ho.

2 He had, he had and a sonne a,
    Men called him Renold,
  And mickle of his might
    Was he, was he, hey ho.

3 And from his father a wode a,
    His fortune for to seeke,
  From mery Lands-dale
    Wode he, wode he, hey ho.

4 His father would him seeke a,
    And found him fast a sleepe;
  Among the leavës greene
    Was he, was he, hey ho.

5 He tooke, he tooke him up a,
    All by the lilly-white hand,
  And set him on his feet,
    And bad him stand, hey ho.

6 He gave to him a benbow,
    Made all of a trusty tree,
  And arrowës in his hand,
    And bad him let them flee.

7 And shoote was that that a did a,
    Some say he shot a mile,
  But halfe a mile and more
    Was it, was it, hey ho.

8 And at the halfe miles end,
    There stood an armed man;
  The childe he shot him through,
    And through and through, hey ho.†

9 His beard was all on a white a,
    As white as whale is bone,
  His eyes they were as cleare
    As christall stone, hey ho.

10 And there of him they made
    Good yeoman, Robin Rood,
  Scarlet, and Little John,
    And Little John, hey ho.

302–05. The Klepht Giphtakis, wounded
in knee and hand, exclaims: Where are you,
my brother, my friend? Come back and take
me off, or take off my head, lest the Turk
should do so, and carry it to that dog of an
Ali Pacha. (1790. Fauriel, I, 20; Zambelios,
p. 621, No 32; Passow, p. 52, No 61.)

357–59. The king traverses the whole
length of Lancashire and proceeds to Plump-
ton Park, missing many of his deer. Camden,
Britannia, II, 175, ed. 1772, places Plumpton
Park on the bank of the Petterel, in Cumber-

* Le Doctrinal de Sapience, fol. 67 b, cited by Legrand,
is not to the purpose. Scala Celi refers to a Speculum
Exemplorum.
In Peele's Edward I, the friar, having lost five nobles at
dice to St Francis, pays them to St Francis' receiver; but

presently wins a hundred marks of the saint, and makes the
receiver pay. (The story has in one point a touch of the
French *fabliau*.) Peele's Works, ed. Dyce, I, 157–61.
† hey hoy.

land, east of Inglewood. (Hunter, p. 30, citing no authority, says it was part of the forest of Knaresborough, in Yorkshire.) Since this survey makes the king wroth with Robin Hood, we must give a corresponding extent to Robin's operations. And we remember that Wyntoun says that he exercised his profession in Inglewood and Barnsdale.

371 ff. The story of the seventh fit has a general similitude to the extensive class of tales, mostly jocular, represented by 'The King and the Miller;' as to which, see further on.

403–09. The sport of "pluck-buffet" (424³) is a feature in the romance of Richard Cœur de Lion, 762–98, Weber, II, 33 f. Richard is betrayed to the king of Almayne by a minstrel to whom he had given a cold reception, and is put in prison. The king's son, held the strongest man of the land, visits the prisoner, and proposes to him an exchange of this sort. The prince gives Richard a clout which makes fire spring from his eyes, and goes off laughing, ordering Richard to be well fed, so that he may have no excuse for returning a feeble blow when he takes his turn. The next day, when the prince comes for his payment, Richard, who has waxed his hand by way of preparation, delivers a blow which breaks the young champion's cheek-bone and fells him dead. There is another instance in 'The Turke and Gowin,' Percy MS., Hales and Furnivall, I, 91 ff.

414–450. Robin Hood is pardoned by King Edward on condition of his leaving the greenwood with all his company, and taking service at court. In the course of a twelvemonth,* keeping up his old profusion, Robin has spent not only all his own money, but all his men's, in treating knights and squires, and at the end of the year all his band have deserted him save John and Scathlock. About this time, chancing to see young men shooting, the recollection of his life in the woods comes over him so powerfully that he feels that he shall die if he stays longer with the king. He therefore affects to have made a vow to go to Barnsdale "barefoot and woolward."

Upon this plea he obtains from the king leave of absence for a week, and, once more in the forest, never reports for duty in two and twenty years.

Hunter, who could have identified Pigrogromitus and Quinapalus, if he had given his mind to it, sees in this passage, and in what precedes it of King Edward's trip to Nottingham, a plausible semblance of historical reality.† Edward II, as may be shown from Rymer's Fœdera, made a progress in the counties of York, Lancaster, and Nottingham, in the latter part of the year 1323. He was in Yorkshire in August and September, in Lancashire in October, at Nottingham November 9–23, spending altogether five or six weeks in that neighborhood, and leaving it a little before Christmas. "Now it will scarcely be believed, but it is, nevertheless, the plain and simple truth, that in documents preserved in the Exchequer, containing accounts of expenses in the king's household, we find the name of Robyn Hode, not once, but several times occurring, receiving, with about eight and twenty others, the pay of 3d. a day, as one of the 'vadlets, porteurs de la chambre' of the king;" these entries running from March 24, 1324, to November 22 of the same year. There are entries of payments to vadlets during the year preceding, but unluckily the accountant has put down the sums in gross, without specifying the names of persons who received regular wages. This, as Hunter remarks, does not quite prove that Robyn Hode had not been among these persons before Christmas, 1323, but, on the other hand, account-book evidence is lacking to show that he had been. Hunter's interpretation of the data is that Robyn Hode entered the king's service at Nottingham a little before Christmas, 1323. If this was so, his career as porter was not only brief, but pitiably checkered. His pay is docked for five days' absence in May, again for eight days in August, then for fifteen days in October. "He was growing weary of his new mode of life." Seven days, once more, are deducted in November, and

---

* 435. The three in 433, as in 416, is for rhyme, and need not be taken strictly.

† Critical and Historical Tracts, No IV, Robin Hood, p. 28 ff.

under the 22d of that month we find this entry: Robyn Hode, jadys un des porteurs, poar cas qil ne poait pluis travailler, de donn par comandement, v. s.   After this his name no longer appears.

A simple way of reading the Exchequer documents is that one Robert Hood, some time (and, for aught we know, a long time) porter in the king's household, after repeatedly losing time, was finally discharged, with a present of five shillings, because he could not do his work.   To detect "a remarkable coincidence between the ballad and the record" requires not only a theoretical prepossession, but an uncommon insensibility to the ludicrous.*   But taking things with entire seriousness, there is no correspondence between the ballad and the record other than this: that Robin Hood, who is in the king's service, leaves it; in the one instance deserting, and in the other being displaced.   Hunter himself does not, as in the case of Adam Bell, insist that the name Robin Hood is "peculiar." He cites, p. 10, a Robert Hood, citizen of London, who supplied the king's household with beer, 28 Edward I, and a Robert Hood of Wakefield, twice mentioned, 9, 10 Edward II.†   Another Robert Hood at Throckelawe, Northumbria, is thrice mentioned in the Exchequer Rolls, Edward I, 19, 20, 30: Rot. Orig. in Cur. Scac. Abbrev., I, 69, 73, 124. A Robert Hood is manucaptor for a burgess returned from Lostwithiel, Cornwall, 7 Edward II, Parliamentary Writs, II, 1019, and another, of Howden, York, 10 Edward III, is noted in the Calendar of Patent Rolls, p. 125, No 31, cited by Ritson.   In all these we have six Robin Hoods between 30 Edward I and 10 Edward III, a period of less than forty years.

433, 435–50 are translated by A. Grün, p. 166.

---

a. 1   LYTHE and listin, gentilmen,
    That be of frebore blode;
  I shall you tel of a gode yeman,
    His name was Robyn Hode.

2   Robyn was a prude outlaw,
    [Whyles he walked on grounde;
  So curteyse an outlawe] as he was one
    Was never non founde.

3   Robyn stode in Bernesdale,
    And lenyd hym to a tre;
  And bi hym stode Litell Johnn,
    A gode yeman was he.

4   And alsoo dyd gode Scarlok,
    And Much, the miller's son;

There was none ynch of his bodi
    But it was worth a grome.

5   Than bespake Lytell Johnn
    All vntoo Robyn Hode:
  Maister, and ye wolde dyne betyme
    It wolde doo you moche gode.

6   Than bespake hym gode Robyn:
    To dyne haue I noo lust,
  Till that I haue som bolde baron,
    Or som vnkouth gest.

7 .   .   .   .   .   .
    That may pay for the best,
  Or som knyght or [som] squyer,
    That dwelleth here bi west.

* Think of Robin as light porter, — Robin who had been giving and taking buffets that might fell an ox.   Think of him as worn out with the work in eleven months, and dropped for disability.   Think of his being put on three-pence a day, after paying his yeomen at thrice the rate, 171, not to speak of such casual gratuities as we hear of in 382. "There is in all this, perhaps, as much correspondency as we can reasonably expect between the record and the ballad," says Hunter, p. 38.

† Hunter asks if it is not possible to find in this Robert Hood of Wakefield, near Barnsdale, "the identical person whose name has been so strangely perpetuated."   This Rob-

ert Hood would be a person of some consideration, and he would thus be qualified "for his station among the vadlets of the crown," — three-penny vadlets, Great Hob, Little Coll, Robert *Trash*, and their fellows.   The Wakefield Robert's wife was named Matilda, "and the ballad testimony is — not the Little Gest, but other ballads of uncertain antiquity, — that the outlaw's wife was named Matilda, which name she exchanged for Marian when she joined him in the green-wood." (Pp 46–48.)   Hunter has made a trivial mistake about Matilda: she belongs to Munday's play, and not to the ballads (ballad) he has in mind.

8 A gode maner than had Robyn;
   In londe where that he were,
   Euery day or he wold dyne
   Thre messis wolde he here.

9 The one in the worship of the Fader,
   And another of the Holy Gost,
   The thirde of Our derë Lady,
   That he loued allther moste.

10 Robyn loued Oure derë Lady;
   For dout of dydly synne,
   Wolde he neuer do compani harme
   That any woman was in.

11 'Maistar,' than sayde Lytil Johnn,
   'And we our borde shal sprede,
   Tell vs wheder that we shal go,
   And what life that we shall lede.

12 'Where we shall take, where we shall leue,
   Where we shall abide behynde;
   Where we shall robbe, where we shal reue,
   Where we shal bete and bynde.'

13 'Therof no force,' than sayde Robyn;
   'We shall do well inowe;
   But loke ye do no husbonde harme,
   That tilleth with his ploughe.

14 'No more ye shall no gode yeman
   That walketh by grenë-wode shawe;
   Ne no knyght ne no squyer
   That wol be a gode felawe.

15 'These bisshoppes and these archebishoppes,
   Ye shall them bete and bynde;
   The hyë sherif of Notyingham,
   Hym holde ye in your mynde.'

16 'This worde shalbe holde,' sayde Lytell Johnn,
   'And this lesson we shall lere;
   It is fer dayes; God sende vs a gest,
   That we were at oure dynere!'

17 'Take thy gode bowe in thy honde,' sayde
     Rob[yn];
   'Late Much wende with the;
   And so shal Willyam Scarlo[k],
   And no man abyde with me.

18 'And walke vp to the Saylis,
   And so to Watlinge Stret[e],

And wayte after some vnkuth gest,
   Vp chaunce ye may them mete.

19 'Be he erle, or ani baron,
   Abbot, or ani knyght,
   Bringhe hym to lodge to me;
   His dyner shall be dight.'

20 They wente vp to the Saylis,
   These yéman all thre;
   They loked est, they loke[d] weest;
   They myght no man see.

21 But as they loked in to Bernysdale,
   Bi a dernë strete,
   Than came a knyght ridinghe;
   Full sone they gan hym mete.

22 All dreri was his semblaunce,
   And lytell was his prydę;
   His one fote in the styrop stode,
   That othere wauyd beside.

23 His hode hanged in his iyn two;
   He rode in symple aray;
   A soriar man than he was one
   Rode neuer in somer day.

24 Litell Johnn was full curteyes,
   And sette hym on his kne:
   'Welcom be ye, gentyll knyght,
   Welcom ar ye to me.

25 'Welcom be thou to grenë wode,
   Hendë knyght and fre;
   My maister hath abiden you fastinge,
   Syr, al these ourës thre.'

26 'Who is thy maister?' sayde the knyght;
   Johnn sayde, Robyn Hode;
   'He is [a] gode yoman,' sayde the knyght,
   'Of hym I haue herde moche gode.

27 'I graunte,' he sayde, 'with you to wende,
   My bretherne, all in fere;
   My purpos was to haue dyned to day
   At Blith or Dancastere.'

28 Furth than went this gentyl knight,
   With a carefull chere;
   The teris oute of his iyen ran,
   And fell downe by his lere.

29 They brought hym to the lodgë-dore;
    Whan Robyn hym gan see,
    Full curtesly dyd of his hode
    And sette hym on his knee.

30 'Welcome, sir knight,' than sayde Robyn,
    'Welcome art thou to me;
    I haue abyden you fastinge, sir,
    All these ouris thre.'

31 Than answered the gentyll knight,
    With wordës fayre and fre;
    God the saue, goode Robyn,
    And all thy fayre meynë.

32 They wasshed togeder and wyped bothe,
    And sette to theyr dynere;
    Brede and wyne they had right ynoughe,
    And noumbles of the dere.

33 Swannes and fessauntes they had full gode,
    And foules of the ryuere;
    There fayled none so litell a birde
    That euer was bred on bryre.

34 'Do gladly, sir knight,' sayde Robyn;
    'Gramarcy, sir,' sayde he;
    'Suche a dinere had I nat
    Of all these wekys thre.

35 'If I come ageyne, Robyn,
    Here by thys contrë,
    As gode a dyner I shall the make
    As that thou haest made to me.'

36 'Gramarcy, knyght,' sayde Robyn;
    'My dyner whan that I it haue,
    I was neuer so gredy, bi dere worthy God,
    My dyner for to craue.

37 'But pay or ye wende,' sayde Robyn;
    'Me thynketh it is gode ryght;
    It was neuer the maner, by dere worthi God,
    A yoman to pay for a knyhht.'

38 'I haue nought in my coffers,' saide the
        knyght,
    'That I may profer for shame:'
    'Litell Johnn, go loke,' sayde Robyn,
    'Ne let nat for no blame.

39 'Tel me truth,' than saide Robyn,
    'So God haue parte of the:'

'I haue no more but ten shelynges,' sayde the
        knyght,
    'So God haue parte of me.'

40 If thou hast no more,' sayde Robyn,
    'I woll nat one peny;
    And yf thou haue nede of any more,
    More shall I lend the.

41 'Go nowe furth, Littell Johnn,
    The truth tell thou me;
    If there be no more but ten shelinges,
    No peny that I se.'

42 Lyttell Johnn sprede downe hys mantell
    Full fayre vpon the grounde,
    And there he fonde in the knyghtës cofer
    But euen halfe [a] pounde.

43 Littell Johnn let it lye full styll,
    And went to hys maysteer [full] lowe;
    'What tidyngës, Johnn?' sayde Robyn;
    'Sir, the knyght is true inowe.'

44 'Fyll of the best wine,' sayde Robyn,
    'The knyght shall begynne;
    Moche wonder thinketh me
    Thy clot[h]ynge is so thin[n]e.

45 'Tell me [one] worde,' sayde Robyn,
    'And counsel shal it be;
    I trowe thou warte made a knyght of force,
    Or ellys of yemanry.

46 'Or ellys thou hast bene a sori husbande,
    And lyued in stroke and stryfe;
    An okerer, or ellis a lechoure,' sayde Robyn,
    'Wyth wronge hast led thy lyfe.'

47 'I am none of those,' sayde the knyght,
    'By God that madë me;
    An hundred wynter here before
    Myn auncetres knyghtes haue be.

48 'But oft it hath befal, Robyn,
    A man hath be disgrate;
    But God that sitteth in heuen aboue
    May amende his state.

49 'Withyn this two yere, Robyne,' he sayde,
    'My neghbours well it knowe,
    Foure hundred pounde of gode money
    Ful well than myght I spende.

50 'Nowe haue I no gode,' saide the knyght,
   'God hath shaped such an ende,
   But my chyldren and my wyfe,
   Tyll God yt may amende.'

51 'In what maner,' than sayde Robyn,
   'Hast thou lorne thy rychesse?'
   'For my greatë foly,' he sayde,
   'And for my kynd[ë]nesse.

52 'I hade a sone, forsoth, Robyn,
   That shulde hau[e] ben myn ayre,
   Whanne he was twenty wynter olde,
   In felde wolde iust full fayre.

53 'He slewe a knyght of Lancaster,
   And a squyer bolde;
   For to saue hym in his ryght
   My godes both sette and solde.

54 'My londes both sette to wedde, Robyn,
   Vntyll a certayn day,
   To a ryche abbot here besyde
   Of Seynt Mari Abbey.'

55 'What is the som?' sayde Robyn;
   'Trouth than tell thou me;'
   'Sir,' he sayde, 'foure hundred pounde;
   The abbot told it to me.'

56 'Nowe and thou lese thy lond,' sayde Robyn,
   'What woll fall of the?'
   'Hastely I wol me buske,' sayd the knyght,
   'Ouer the saltë see,

57 'And se w[h]ere Criste was quyke and dede,
   On the mount of Caluerë;
   Fare wel, frende, and haue gode day;
   It may no better be.'

58 Teris fell out of hys iyen two;
   He wolde haue gone hys way:
   'Farewel, frende, and haue gode day;
   I ne haue no more to pay.'

59 'Where be thy frendës?' sayde Robyn:
   'Syr, neuer one wol me knowe;
   While I was ryche ynowe at home
   Great boste than wolde they blowe.

60 'And nowe they renne away fro me,
   As bestis on a rowe;

They take no more hede of me
   Thanne they had me neuer sawe.'

61 For ruthe thanne wept Litell Johnn,
   Scarlok and Muche in fere;
   'Fyl of the best wyne,' sayde Robyn,
   'For here is a symple chere.

62 'Hast thou any frende,' sayde Robyn,
   'Thy borowe that woldë be?'
   'I haue none,' than sayde the knyght,
   'But God that dyed on tree.'

63 'Do away thy iapis,' than sayde Robyn,
   'Thereof wol I right none;
   Wenest thou I wolde haue God to borowe,
   Peter, Poule, or Johnn?

64 'Nay, by hym that me made,
   And shope both sonne and mone,
   Fynde me a better borowe,' sayde Robyn,
   'Or money getest thou none.'

65 'I haue none other,' sayde the knyght,
   'The sothe for to say,
   But yf yt be Our derë Lady;
   She fayled me neuer or thys day.'

66 'By dere worthy God,' sayde Robyn,
   'To seche all Englonde thorowe,
   Yet fonde I neuer to my pay
   A moche better borowe.

67 'Come nowe furth, Litell Johnn,
   And go to my tresourë,
   And bringe me foure hundered pound,
   And loke well tolde it be.'

68 Furth than went Litell Johnn,
   And Scarlok went before;
   He tolde oute foure hundred pounde
   By eight and twenty score.

69 'Is thys well tolde?' sayde [litell] Much;
   Johnn sayde, 'What gre[ue]th the?
   It is almus to helpe a gentyll knyght,
   That is fal in pouertë.

70 'Master,' than sayde Lityll John,
   'His clothinge is full thynne;
   Ye must gyue the knight a lyueray,
   To lappe his body therin.

71 'For ye haue scarlet and grene, mayster,
       And man[y] a riche aray ;
   Ther is no marchaunt in mery Englond
       So ryche, I dare well say.'

72 'Take hym thre yerdes of euery colour,
       And loke well mete that it be ; '
   Lytell Johnn toke none other mesure
       But his bowë-tree.

73 And at euery handfull that he met
       He lepëd footës three ;
   'What deuyllës drapar,' sayid litell Muche,
       'Thynkest thou for to be ? '

74 Scarlok stode full stil and loughe,
       And sayd, By God Almyght,
   Johnn may gyue hym gode mesure,
       For it costeth hym but lyght.

75 'Mayster,' than said Litell Johnn
       To gentill Robyn Hode,
   'Ye must giue the knig[h]t a hors,
       To lede home this gode.'

76 'Take hym a gray coursar,' sayde Robyn,
       'And a saydle newe ;
   He is Oure Ladye's messangere ;
       God graunt that he be true.'

77 'And a gode palfray,' sayde lytell Much,
       'To mayntene hym in his right ; '
   'And a peyre of botës,' sayde Scarlock,
       'For he is a gentyll knight.'

78 'What shalt thou gyue hym, Litell John ? '
       said Robyn ;
   'Sir, a peyre of gilt sporis clene,
   To pray for all this company ;
       God bringe hym oute of tene.'

79 'Whan shal mi day be,' said the knight,
       'Sir, and your wyll be ? '
   'This day twelue moneth,' saide Robyn,
       'Vnder this grenë-wode tre.

80 'It were greate shamë,' sayde Robyn,
       'A knight alone to ryde,
   Withoutë squyre, yoman, or page,
       To walkë by his syde.

81 'I shall the lende Litell John, my man,
       For he shalbe thy knaue ;

In a yema[n]'s stede he may the stande,
       If thou greate nedë haue.'

THE SECONDE FYTTE.

82 Now is the knight gone on his way ;
       This game hym thought full gode ;
   Whanne he loked on Bernesdale
       He blessyd Robyn Hode.

83 And whanne he thought on Bernysdale,
       On Scarlok, Much, and Johnn,
   He blyssyd them for the best company
b.   That euer he in come.

84 Then spake that gentyll knyght,
       To Lytel Johan gan he saye,
   To-morrowe I must to Yorke toune,
       To Saynt Mary abbay.

85 And to the abbot of that place
       Foure hondred pounde I must pay ;
   And but I be there vpon this nyght
       My londe is lost for ay.

86 The abbot sayd to his couent,
       There he stode on grounde,
   This day twelfe moneth came there a knyght
       And borowed foure hondred pounde.

87 [He borowed foure hondred pounde,]
       Upon all his londë fre ;
   But he come this ylkë day
       Dysheryte shall he be.

88 'It is full erely,' sayd the pryoure,
       'The day is not yet ferre gone ;
   I had leuer to pay an hondred pounde,
       And lay downe anone.

89 'The knyght is ferre beyonde the see,
       In Englonde is his ryght,
   And suffreth honger and colde,
       And many a sory nyght.

90 'It were grete pytë,' said the pryoure,
       'So to haue his londe ;
   And ye be so lyght of your consyence,
       Ye do to hym moch wronge.'

91 'Thou arte euer in my berde,' sayd the abbot,
       'By God and Saynt Rycharde ; '

With that cam in a fat-heded monke,
    The heygh selerer.

92 'He is dede or hanged,' sayd the monke,
    'By God that bought me dere,
    And we shall haue to spende in this place
    Foure hondred pounde by yere.'

93 The abbot and the hy selerer
    Stertë forthe full bolde,
    The [hye] iustyce of Englonde
    The abbot there dyde holde.

94 The hyë iustyce and many mo
    Had take in to they[r] honde
    Holy all the knyghtës det,
    To put that knyght to wronge.

95 They demed the knyght wonder sore,
    The abbot and his meynë:
    'But he come this ylkë day
    Dysheryte shall he be.'

96 'He wyll not come yet,' sayd the iustyce,
    'I dare well vndertake;'
    But in sorowe tymë for them all
    The knyght came to the gate.

97 Than bespake that gentyll knyght
    Untyll his meynë:
    Now put on your symple wedes
    That ye brought fro the see.

98 [They put on their symple wedes,]
    They came to the gates anone;
    The porter was redy hymselfe,
    And welcomed them euerychone.

99 'Welcome, syr knyght,' sayd the porter;
    'My lorde to mete is he,
    And so is many a gentyll man,
    For the loue of the.'

100 The porter swore a full grete othe,
    'By God that madë me,
    Here be the best coresed hors
    That euer yet sawe I me.

101 'Lede them in to the stable,' he sayd,
    'That eased myght they be;'
    'They shall not come therin,' sayd the knyght,
    'By God that dyed on a tre.'

102 Lordës were to mete isette
    In that abbotes hall;
    The knyght went forth and kneled downe,
    And salued them grete and small.

103 'Do gladly, syr abbot,' sayd the knyght,
    'I am come to holde my day:'
    The fyrst word the abbot spake,
    'Hast thou brought my pay?'

104 'Not one peny,' sayd the knyght,
    'By God that maked me;'
    'Thou art a shrewed dettour,' sayd the abbot;
    'Syr iustyce, drynke to me.

105 'What doost thou here,' sayd the abbot,
    'But thou haddest brought thy pay?'
    'For God,' than sayd the knyght,
    'To pray of a lenger daye.'

106 'Thy daye is broke,' sayd the iustyce,
    'Londe getest thou none:'
    'Now, good syr iustyce, be my frende,
    And fende me of my fone!'

107 'I am holde with the abbot,' sayd the iustyce,
    'Both with cloth and fee:'
    'Now, good syr sheryf, be my frende!'
    'Nay, for God,' sayd he.

108 'Now, good syr abbot, be my frende,
    For thy curteysë,
    And holde my londës in thy honde
    Tyll I haue made the gree!

109 'And I wyll be thy true seruaunte,
    And trewely seruë the,
    Tyl ye haue foure hondred pounde
    Of money good and free.'

110 The abbot sware a full grete othe,
    'By God that dyed on a tree,
    Get the londe where thou may,
    For thou getest none of me.'

111 'By dere worthy God,' then sayd the knyght,
    'That all this worldë wrought,
    But I haue my londe agayne,
    Full dere it shall be bought.

112 'God, that was of a mayden borne,
    Leue vs well to spëde!

For it is good to assay a frende
    Or that a man haue nede.'

113 The abbot lothely on hym gan loke,
    And vylaynesly hym gan call ;
    'Out,' he sayd, 'thou falsë knyght,
    Spede the out of my hall !'

114 'Thou lyest,' then sayd the gentyll knyght,
    'Abbot, in thy hal ;
    False knyght was I neuer,
    By God that made vs all.'

115 Vp then stode that gentyll knyght,
    To the abbot sayd he,
    To suffre a knyght to knele so longe,
    Thou canst no curteysye.

116 In ioustës and in tournement
    Full ferre than haue I be,
    And put my selfe as ferre in prees
    As ony that euer I se.

117 'What wyll ye gyue more,' sayd the iustice,
    'And the knyght shall make a releyse ?
    And elles dare I safly swere
    Ye holde neuer your londe in pees.'

118 'An hondred pounde,' sayd the abbot ;
    The justice sayd, Gyue hym two ;
    'Nay, be God,' sayd the knyght,
a.   'Yit gete ye it not so.

119 'Though ye wolde gyue a thousand more,
    Yet were ye neuer the nere ;
    Shall there neuer be myn heyre
    Abbot, iustice, ne frere.'

120 He stert hym to a borde anone,
    Tyll a table rounde,
    And there he shoke oute of a bagge
    Euen four hundred pound.

121 'Haue here thi golde, sir abbot,' saide the
      knight,
    'Which that thou lentest me ;
    Had thou ben curtes at my comynge,
    Rewarded shuldest thou haue be.'

122 The abbot sat styll, and ete no more,
    For all his ryall fare ;
    He cast his hede on his shulder,
    And fast began to stare.

123 'Take me my golde agayne,' saide the
      abbot,
    'Sir iustice, that I toke the : '
    'Not a peni,' said the iustice,
    'Bi Go[d, that dy]ed on tree.'

124 'Sir [abbot, and ye me]n of lawe,
b.   Now haue I holde my daye ;
    Now shall I haue my londe agayne,
    For ought that you can saye.'

125 The knyght stert out of the dore,
    Awaye was all his care,
    And on he put his good clothynge,
    The other he lefte there.

126 He wente hym forth full mery syngynge,
    As men haue tolde in tale ;
    His lady met hym at the gate,
    At home in Verysdale.

127 'Welcome, my lorde,' sayd his lady ;
    'Syr, lost is all your good ?'
    'Be mery, dame,' sayd the knyght,
a.   'And pray for Robyn Hode,

128 'That euer his soulë be in blysse :
    He holpe me out of tene ;
    Ne had be his kyndënesse,
    Beggers had we bene.

129 'The abbot and I accorded ben,
    He is serued of his pay ;
    The god yoman lent it me,
    As I cam by the way.'

130 This knight than dwelled fayre at home,
    The sothe for to saye,
    Tyll he had gete four hundred pound,
    Al redy for to pay.

131 He purueyed him an hundred bowes,
    The stryngës well ydyght,
    An hundred shefe of arowës gode,
    The hedys burnesshed full bryght ;

132 And euery arowe an ellë longe,
    With pecok wel idyght,
    Inocked all with whyte siluer ;
    It was a semely syght.

133 He purueyed hym an [hondreth men],
    Well harness[ed in that stede],

b. And hym selfe in that same sete,
　And clothed in whyte and rede.

134 He bare a launsgay in his honde,
　And a man ledde his male,
　And reden with a lyght songe
　Vnto Bernysdale.

135 But as he went at a brydge ther was a wraste-
　　lyng,
　And there taryed was he,
　And there was all the best yemen
　Of all the west countree.

136 A full fayre game there was vp set,
　A whyte bulle vp i-pyght,
　A grete courser, with sadle and brydil,
a.　With golde burnyssht full bryght.

137 A payre of gloues, a rede golde rynge,
　A pype of wyne, in fay;
　What man that bereth hym best i-wys
　The pryce shall bere away.

138 There was a yoman in that place,
　And best worthy was he,
　And for he was ferre and frembde bested,
　Slayne he shulde haue be.

139 The knight had ruthe of this yoman,
　In placë where he stode;
　He sayde that yoman shulde haue no harme,
　For loue of Robyn Hode.

140 The knyght presed in to the place,
　An hundreth folowed hym [free],
　With bowës bent and arowës sharpe,
　For to shende that companye.

141 They shulderd all and made hym rome,
　To wete what he wolde say;
　He toke the yeman bi the hande,
　And gaue hym al the play.

142 He gaue hym fyue marke for his wyne,
　There it lay on the molde,
　And bad it shulde be set a broche,
　Drynkë who so wolde.

143 Thus longe taried this gentyll knyght,
　Tyll that play was done;
　So longe abode Robyn fastinge,
　Thre hourës after the none.

THE THIRDE FYTTE.

144 Lyth and lystyn, gentilmen,
　All that nowe be here;
　Of Litell Johnn, that was the knightës man,
　Goode myrth ye shall here.

145 It was vpon a mery day
　That yonge men wolde go shete;
　Lytell Johnn fet his bowe anone,
　And sayde he wolde them mete.

146 Thre tymes Litell Johnn shet aboute,
　And alwey he slet the wande;
　The proudë sherif of Notingham
　By the markës can stande.

147 The sherif swore a full greate othe:
　' By hym that dyede on a tre,
　This man is the best arschére
　That euer yet sawe I [me.]

148 ' Say me nowe, wight yonge man,
　What is nowe thy name?
　In what countre were thou borne,
　And where is thy wonynge wane?'

149 ' In Holdernes, sir, I was borne,
　I-wys al of my dame;
　Men cal me Reynolde Grenëlef
　Whan I am at home.'

150 ' Sey me, Reyno[l]de Grenëlefe,
　Wolde thou dwell with me?
　And euery yere I woll the gyue
　Twenty marke to thy fee.'

151 ' I haue a maister,' sayde Litell Johnn,
　' A curteys knight is he;
　May ye leuë gete of hym,
　The better may it be.'

152 The sherif gate Litell John
　Twelue monethës of the knight;
　Therfore he gaue him right anone
　A gode hors and a wight.

153 Nowe is Litell John the sherifës man,
　God lende vs well to spede!
　But alwey thought Lytell John
　To quyte hym wele his mede.

154 'Nowe so God me helpë,' sayde Litell John,
    'And by my true leutye,
  I shall be the worst seruaunt to hym
    That euer yet had he.'

155 It fell vpon a Wednesday
    The sherif on huntynge was gone,
  And Litel Iohn lay in his bed,
    And was foriete at home.

156 Therfore he was fastinge
    Til it was past the none ;
 'Gode sir stuarde, I pray to the,
    Gyue me my dynere,' saide Litell John.

157 'It is longe for Grenëlefe
    Fastinge thus for to be ;
  Therfor I pray the, sir stuarde,
    Mi dyner gif me.'

158 'Shalt thou neuer ete ne drynke,' saide the stuarde,
    'Tyll my lorde be come to towne : '
 'I make myn auowe to God,' saide Litell John,
    'I had leuer to crake thy crowne.'

159 The boteler was full vncurteys,
    There he stode on flore ;
  He start to the botery
    And shet fast the dore.

160 Lytell Johnn gaue the boteler suche a tap
    His backe went nere in two ;
  Though he liued an hundred ier,
    The wors shuld he go.

161 He sporned the dore with his fote ;
    It went open wel and fyne ;
  And there he made large lyueray,
    Bothe of ale and of wyne.

162 'Sith ye wol nat dyne,' sayde Litell John,
    'I shall gyue you to drinke ;
  And though ye lyue an hundred wynter,
    On Lytel Johnn ye shall thinke.'

163 Litell John ete, and Litel John drank,
    The whilë that he wolde ;
  The sherife had in his kechyn a coke,
    A stoute man and a bolde.

164 'I make myn auowe to God,' saide the coke,
    'Thou arte a shrewde hynde

In ani hous for to dwel,
    For to askë thus to dyne.'

165 And there he lent Litell John
    God[ë] strokis thre ;
 'I make myn auowe to God,' sayde Lytell John,
    'These strokis lyked well me.

166 'Thou arte a bolde man and hardy,
    And so thinketh me ;
  And or I pas fro this place
    Assayed better shalt thou be.'

167 Lytell Johnn drew a ful gode sworde,
    The coke toke another in hande ;
  They thought no thynge for to fle,
    But stifly for to stande.

168 There they faught sore togedere
    Two mylë way and well more ;
  Myght neyther other harme done,
    The mountnaunce of an owre.

169 'I make myn auowe to God,' sayde Litell Johnn,
    'And by my true lewtë,
  Thou art one of the best sworde-men
    That euer yit sawe I [me.]

170 'Cowdest thou shote as well in a bowe,
    To grenë wode thou shuldest with me,
  And two times in the yere thy clothinge
    Chaunged shuldë be ;

171 'And euery yere of Robyn Hode
    Twenty merke to thy fe : '
 'Put vp thy swerde,' saide the coke,
    'And felowës woll we be.'

172 Thanne he fet to Lytell Johnn
    The nowmbles of a do,
  Gode brede, and full gode wyne ;
    They ete and drank theretoo.

173 And when they had dronkyn well,
    Theyre trouthës togeder they plight
  That they wo[l]de be with Robyn
    That ylkë samë nyght.

174 They dyd them to the tresoure-hows,
    As fast as they myght gone ;

The lokkës, that were of full gode stele,
    They brake them euerichone.

175 They toke away the siluer vessell,
    And all that thei mig[h]t get ;
    Pecis, masars, ne sponis,
    Wolde thei not forget.

176 Also [they] toke the godë pens,
    Thre hundred pounde and more,
    And did them st[r]eyte to Robyn Hode,
    Under the grenë wode hore.

177 ' God the saue, my derë mayster,
    And Criste the saue and se ! '
    And thanne sayde Robyn to Litell John,
    Welcome myght thou be.

178 ' Also be that fayre yeman
    Thou bryngest there with the ;
    What tydyngës fro Noty[n]gham ?
    Lytill John, tell thou me.'

179 ' Well the gretith the proudë sheryf,
    And sende[th] the here by me
    His coke and his siluer vessell,
    And thre hundred pounde and thre.'

180 ' I make myne avowe to God,' sayde Robyn,
    ' And to the Trenytë,
    It was neuer by his gode wyll
    This gode is come to me.'

181 Lytyll John there hym bethought
    On a shrewde wyle ;
    Fyue myle in the forest he ran,
    Hym happed all his wyll.

182 Than he met the proudë sheref,
    Huntynge with houndes and horne ;
    Lytell John coude of curtesye,
    And knelyd hym beforne.

183 ' God the saue, my derë mayster,
    And Criste the saue and se ! '
    ' Reynolde Grenëlefe,' sayde the shryef,
    ' Where hast thou nowe be ? '

184 ' I haue be in this forest ;
    A fayre syght can I se ;
    It was one of the fayrest syghtes
    That euer yet sawe I me.

185 ' Yonder I sawe a ryght fayre harte,
    His coloure is of grene ;
    Seuen score of dere vpon a herde
    Be with hym all bydene.

186 ' Their tyndës are so sharpe, maister,
    Of sexty, and well mo,
    That I durst not shote for drede,
    Lest they wolde me slo.'

187 ' I make myn auowe to God,' sayde the shyref,
    ' That syght wolde I fayne se : '
    ' Buske you thyderwarde, mi derë mayster,
    Anone, and wende with me.'

188 The sherif rode, and Litell John
    Of fote he was full smerte,
    And whane they came before Robyn,
    ' Lo, sir, here is the mayster-herte.'

189 Still stode the proudë sherief,
    A sory man was he ;
    ' Wo the worthe, Raynolde Grenëlefe,
    Thou hast betrayed nowe me.'

190 ' I make myn auowe to God,' sayde Litell
    John,
    ' Mayster, ye be to blame ;
    I was mysserued of my dynere
    Whan I was with you at home.'

191 Sone he was to souper sette,
    And serued well with siluer white,
    And whan the sherif sawe his vessell,
    For sorowe he myght nat ete.

192 ' Make glad chere,' sayde Robyn Hode,
    ' Sherif, for charitë,
    And for the loue of Litill John
    Thy lyfe I graunt to the.'

193 Whan they had souped well,
    The day was al gone ;
    Robyn commaunde[d] Litell John
    To drawe of his hosen and his shone ;

194 His kirtell, and his cote of pie,
    That was fured well and fine,
    And to[ke] hym a grene mantel,
    To lap his body therin.

195 Robyn commaundyd his wight yonge men,
    Vnder the grenë-wode tree,

They shulde lye in that same sute,
  That the sherif myght them see.

196 All nyght lay the proudë sherif
    In his breche and in his [s]chert;
  No wonder it was, in grenë wode,
    Though his sydës gan to smerte.

197 'Make glade chere,' sayde Robyn Hode,
    'Sheref, for charitë;
  For this is our ordre i-wys,
    Vnder the grenë-wode tree.'

198 'This is harder order,' sayde the sherief,
    'Than any ankir or frere;
  For all the golde in mery Englonde
    I wolde nat longe dwell her.'

199 'All this twelue monthes,' sayde Robin,
    'Thou shalt dwell with me;
  I shall the techë, proudë sherif,
    An outlawë for to be.'

200 'Or I be here another nyght,' sayde the sherif,
    'Robyn, nowe pray I the,
  Smyte of mijn hede rather to-morowe,
    And I forgyue it the.

201 'Lat me go,' than sayde the sherif,
    'For sayntë charitë,
  And I woll be the best[ë] frende
    That euer yet had ye.'

202 'Thou shalt swere me an othe,' sayde Robyn,
    'On my bright bronde;
  Shalt thou neuer awayte me scathe,
    By water ne by lande.

203 'And if thou fynde any of my men,
    By nyght or [by] day,
  Vpon thyn othë thou shalt swere
    To helpe them tha[t] thou may.'

204 Nowe hathe the sherif sworne his othe,
    And home he began to gone;
  He was as full of grenë wode
    As euer was hepe of stone.

205 The sherif dwelled in Notingham;
    He was fayne he was agone;
  And Robyn and his mery men
    Went to wode anone.

206 'Go we to dyner,' sayde Littell Johnn;
    Robyn Hode sayde, Nay;
  For I drede Our Lady be wroth with me,
    For she sent me nat my pay.

207 'Haue no doute, maister,' sayde Litell Johnn;
    'Yet is nat the sonne at rest;
  For I dare say, and sauely swere,
    The knight is true and truste.'

208 'Take thy bowe in thy hande,' sayde Robyn,
    'Late Much wende with the,
  And so shal Wyllyam Scarlok,
  b.   And no man abyde with me.

209 'And walke vp vnder the Sayles,
    And to Watlynge-strete,
  And wayte after some vnketh gest;
    Vp-chaunce ye may them mete.

210 'Whether he be messengere,
    Or a man that myrthës can,
  Of my good he shall haue some,
    Yf he be a porë man.'

211 Forth then stert Lytel Johan,
    Half in tray and tene,
  And gyrde hym with a full good swerde,
    Under a mantel of grene.

212 They went vp to the Sayles,
    These yemen all thre;
  They loked est, they loked west,
    They myght no man se.

213 But as [t]he[y] loked in Bernysdale,
    By the hyë waye,
  Than were they ware of two blacke monkes,
    Eche on a good palferay.

214 Then bespake Lytell Johan,
    To Much he gan say,
  I dare lay my lyfe to wedde,
    That [these] monkes haue brought our pay.

215 'Make glad chere,' sayd Lytell Johan,
    'And frese your bowes of ewe,
    And loke your hertës be seker and sad,
    Your stryngës trusty and trewe.

216 'The monke hath two and fifty [men,]
    And seuen somers full stronge;
    There rydeth no bysshop in this londe
    So ryally, I vnderstond.

217 'Brethern,' sayd Lytell Johan,
    'Here are no more but we thre;
    But we bryngë them to dyner,
    Our mayster dare we not se.

218 'Bende your bowes,' sayd Lytell Johan,
    'Make all yon prese to stonde;
    The formost monke, his lyfe and his deth
    Is closed in my honde.

219 'Abyde, chorle monke,' sayd Lytell Johan,
    'No ferther that thou gone;
    Yf thou doost, by dere worthy God,
    Thy deth is in my honde.

220 'And euyll thryfte on thy hede,' sayd Lytell
    Johan,
    'Ryght vnder thy hattës bonde;
    For thou hast made our mayster wroth,
    He is fastynge so longe.'

221 'Who is your mayster?' sayd the monke;
    Lytell Johan sayd, Robyn Hode;
    'He is a stronge thefe,' sayd the monke,
    'Of hym herd I neuer good.'

222 'Thou lyest,' than sayd Lytell Johan,
    'And that shall rewë the;
    He is a yeman of the forest,
    To dyne he hath bodë the.'

223 Much was redy with a bolte,
    Redly and anone,
    He set the monke to-fore the brest,
    To the grounde that he can gone.

224 Of two and fyfty wyght yonge yemen
    There abode not one,
    Saf a lytell page and a grome,
    To lede the somers with Lytel Johan.

225 They brought the monke to the lodgë-dore,
    Whether he were loth or lefe,

For to speke with Robyn Hode,
    Maugre in theyr tethe.

226 Robyn dyde adowne his hode,
    The monke whan that he se;
    The monke was not so curtëyse,
    His hode then let he be.

227 'He is a chorle, mayster, by dere worthy
    God,'
    Than sayd Lytell Johan:
    'Thereof no force,' sayd Robyn,
    'For curteysy can he none.

228 'How many men,' sayd Robyn,
    'Had this monke, Johan?'
    'Fyfty and two whan that we met,
    But many of them be gone.'

229 'Let blowe a horne,' sayd Robyn,
    'That felaushyp may vs knowe;'
    Seuen score of wyght yemen
    Came pryckynge on a rowe.

230 And eueryche of them a good mantell
    Of scarlet and of raye;
    All they came to good Robyn,
    To wyte what he wolde say.

231 They made the monke to wasshe and wype,
    And syt at his denere,
    Robyn Hode and Lytell Johan
    They serued him both in-fere.

232 'Do gladly, monke,' sayd Robyn.
    'Gramercy, syr,' sayd he.
    'Where is your abbay, whan ye are at home,
    And who is your avowë?'

233 'Saynt Mary abbay,' sayd the monke,
    'Though I be symple here.'
    'In what offyce?' sayd Robyn:
    'Syr, the hyë selerer.'

234 'Ye be the more welcome,' sayd Robyn,
    'So euer mote I the;
    Fyll of the best wyne,' sayd Robyn,
    'This monke shall drynke to me.

235 'But I haue grete meruayle,' sayd Robyn,
    'Of all this longë day;
    I drede Our Lady be wroth with me,
    She sent me not my pay.'

236 'Haue no doute, mayster,' sayd Lytell Johan,
　　'Ye haue no nede, I saye ;
　　This monke it hath brought, I dare well swere,
　　For he is of her abbay.'

237 'And she was a borowe,' sayd Robyn,
　　'Betwene a knyght and me,
　　Of a lytell money that I hym lent,
　　Under the grëne-wode tree.

238 'And yf thou hast that syluer ibrought,
　　I pray the let me se ;
　　And I shall helpë the eftsones,
　　Yf thou haue nede to me.'

239 The monke swore a full grete othe,
　　With a sory chere,
　　'Of the borowehode thou spekest to me,
　　Herde I neuer ere.'

240 'I make myn avowe to God,' sayd Robyn,
　　'Monke, thou art to blame ;
　　For God is holde a ryghtwys man,
　　And so is his dame.

241 'Thou toldest with thyn ownë tonge,
　　Thou may not say nay,
　　How thou arte her seruaunt,
　　And seruest her euery day.

242 'And thou art made her messengere,
　　My money for to pay ;
　　Therfore I cun the morë thanke
　　Thou arte come at thy day.

243 'What is in your cofers ? ' sayd Robyn,
　　'Trewe than tell thou me : '
　　'Syr,' he sayd, 'twenty marke,
　　Al so mote I the.'

244 'Yf there be no more,' sayd Robyn,
　　'I wyll not one peny ;
　　Yf thou hast myster of ony more,
　　Syr, more I shall lende to the.

245 'And yf I fyndë [more,' sayd] Robyn,
　　'I-wys thou shalte it for gone ;
　　For of thy spendynge-syluer, monke,
　　Thereof wyll I ryght none.

246 'Go nowe forthe, Lytell Johan,
　　And the trouth tell thou me ;

　　If there be no more but twenty marke,
　　No peny that I se.'

247 Lytell Johan spred his mantell downe,
　　As he had done before,
　　And he tolde out of the monkës male
　　Eyght [hondred] pounde and more.

248 Lytell Johan let it lye full styll,
　　And went to his mayster in hast ;
　　'Syr,' he sayd, 'the monke is trewe ynowe,
　　Our Lady hath doubled your cast.'

249 'I make myn avowe to God,' sayd Robyn —
　　'Monke, what tolde I the ? —
　　Our Lady is the trewest woman
　　That euer yet founde I me.

250 'By dere worthy God,' sayd Robyn,
　　'To seche all Englond thorowe,
　　Yet founde I neuer to my pay
　　A moche better borowe.

251 'Fyll of the best wyne, and do hym drynke,'
　　sayd Robyn,
　　'And grete well thy lady hende,
　　And yf she haue nede to Robyn Hode,
　　A frende she shall hym fynde.

252 'And yf she nedeth ony more syluer,
　　Come thou agayne to me,
　　And, by this token she hath me sent,
　　She shall haue such thre.'

253 The monke was goynge to London ward,
　　There to holde grete mote,
　　The knyght that rode so hye on hors,
　　To brynge hym vnder fote.

254 'Whether be ye away ? ' sayd Robyn :
　　'Syr, to maners in this londe,
　　Too reken with our reues,
　　That haue done moch wronge.'

255 'Come now forth, Lytell Johan,
　　And harken to my tale ;
　　A better yemen I knowe none,
　　To seke a monkës male.'

256 'How moch is in yonder other corser ? ' sayd
　　Robyn,
　　'The soth must we see : '

'By Our Lady,' than sayd the monke,
  'That were no curteysye,

257 'To bydde a man to dyner,
    And syth hym bete and bynde.'
  'It is our oldë maner,' sayd Robyn,
    'To leue but lytell behynde.'

258 The monke toke the hors with spore,
    No lenger wolde he abyde :
  'Askë to drynkë,' than sayd Robyn,
    'Or that ye forther ryde.'

259 'Nay, for God,' than sayd the monke,
    'Me reweth I cam so nere ;
  For better chepe I myght haue dyned
    In Blythe or in Dankestere.'

260 'Grete well your abbot,' sayd Robyn,
    'And your pryour, I you pray,
  And byd hym send me such a monke
    To dyner euery day.'

261 Now lete we that monke be styll,
    And speke we of that knyght :
  Yet he came to holde his day,
    Whyle that it was lyght.

262 He dyde him streyt to Bernysdale,
    Under the grenë-wode tre,
  And he founde there Robyn Hode,
    And all his mery meynë.

263 The knyght lyght doune of his good palfray ;
    Robyn whan he gan see,
  So curteysly he dyde adoune his hode,
    And set hym on his knee.

264 'God the sauë, Robyn Hode,
    And all this company :'
  'Welcome be thou, gentyll knyght,
    And ryght welcome to me.'

265 Than bespake hym Robyn Hode,
    To that knyght so fre :
  What nedë dryueth the to grenë wode ?
    I praye the, syr knyght, tell me.

266 'And welcome be thou, ge[n]tyll knyght,
    Why hast thou be so longe ?'
  'For the abbot and the hyë iustyce
    Wolde haue had my londe.'

267 'Hast thou thy londe [a]gayne ?' sayd Robyn ;
    'Treuth than tell thou me :'
  'Ye, for God,' sayd the knyght,
    'And that thanke I God and the.

268 'But take not a grefe,' sayd the knyght, 'that
    I haue be so longe ;
  I came by a wrastelynge,
    And there I holpe a porë yeman,
  With wronge was put behynde.'

269 'Nay, for God,' sayd Robyn,
    'Syr knyght, that thanke I the ;
  What man that helpeth a good yeman,
    His frende than wyll I be.'

270 'Haue here foure hondred pounde,' than sayd
    the knyght,
  'The whiche ye lent to me ;
  And here is also twenty marke
    For your curteysy.'

271 'Nay, for God,' than sayd Robyn,
    'Thou broke it well for ay ;
  For Our Lady, by her [hyë] selerer,
    Hath sent to me my pay.

272 'And yf I toke it i-twyse,
    A shame it were to me ;
  But trewely, gentyll knyght,
    Welcom arte thou to me.'

273 Whan Robyn had tolde his tale,
    He leugh and had good chere :
  'By my trouthe,' then sayd the knyght,
    'Your money is redy here.'

274 'Broke it well,' sayd Robyn,
    'Thou gentyll knyght so fre ;
  And welcome be thou, ge[n]tyll knyght,
    Under my trystell-tre.

275 'But what shall these bowës do ?' sayd
    Robyn,
  'And these arowës ifedred fre ?'
  'By God,' than sayd the knyght,
    'A porë present to the.'

276 'Come now forth, Lytell Johan,
    And go to my treasurë,
  And brynge me there foure hondred pounde ;
    The monke ouer-tolde it me.

277 'Haue here foure hondred pounde,
    Thou gentyll knyght and trewe,
    And bye hors and harnes good,
    And gylte thy spores all newe.

278 'And yf thou fayle ony spendynge,
    Com to Robyn Hode,
    And by my trouth thou shalt none fayle,
    The whyles I haue any good.

279 'And broke well thy foure hondred pound,
    Whiche I lent to the,
    And make thy selfe no more so bare,
    By the counsell of me.'

280 Thus than holpe hym good Robyn,
    The knyght all of his care :
    God, that syt in heuen hye,
    Graunte vs well to fare!

THE FYFTH FYTTE.

281 Now hath the knyght his leue i-take,
    And wente hym on his way ;
    Robyn Hode and his mery men
    Dwelled styll full many a day.

282 Lyth and lysten, gentil men,
    And herken what I shall say,
    How the proud[ë] sheryfe of Notyngham
    Dyde crye a full fayre play ;

283 That all the best archers of the north
    Sholde come vpon a day,
    And [he] that shoteth allther best
    The game shall bere a way.

284 He that shoteth allther best,
    Furthest fayre and lowe,
    At a payre of fynly buttes,
    Under the grenë-wode shawe,

285 A ryght good arowe he shall haue,
    The shaft of syluer whyte,
    The hede and the feders of ryche rede golde,
    In Englond is none lyke.

286 This than herde good Robyn,
    Under his trystell-tre :
    'Make you redy, ye wyght yonge men ;
    That shotynge wyll I se.

287 'Buske you, my mery yonge men,
    Ye shall go with me ;
    And I wyll wete the shryuës fayth,
    Trewe and yf he be.'

288 Whan they had theyr bowes i-bent,
    Theyr takles fedred fre,
    Seuen score of wyght yonge men
    Stode by Robyns kne.

289 Whan they cam to Notyngham,
    The buttes were fayre and longe ;
    Many was the bolde archere
    That shoted with bowës stronge.

290 'There shall but syx shote with me ;
    The other shal kepe my he[ue]de,
    And standë with good bowës bent,
    That I be not desceyued.'

291 The fourth outlawe his bowe gan bende,
    And that was Robyn Hode,
    And that behelde the proud[ë] sheryfe,
    All by the but [as] he stode.

292 Thryës Robyn shot about,
    And alway he slist the wand,
    And so dyde good Gylberte
    Wyth the whytë hande.

293 Lytell Johan and good Scatheloke
    Were archers good and fre ;
    Lytell Much and good Reynolde,
    The worste wolde they not be.

294 Whan they had shot aboute,
    These archours fayre and good,
    Euermore was the best,
    For soth, Robyn Hode.

295 Hym was delyuered the good arowe,
    For best worthy was he ;
    He toke the yeft so curteysly,
    To grenë wode wolde he.

296 They cryed out on Robyn Hode,
    And grete hornës gan they blowe :
    'Wo worth the, treason !' sayd Robyn,
    'Full euyl thou art to knowe.

297 'And wo be thou ! thou proudë sheryf,
    Thus gladdynge thy gest ;

Other wyse thou behotë me
    In yonder wylde forest.

298 'But had I the in grenë wode,
    Under my trystell-tre,
    Thou sholdest leue me a better wedde
    Than thy trewe lewtë.'

299 Full many a bowë there was bent,
    And arowës let they glyde;
    Many a kyrtell there was rent,
    And hurt many a syde.

300 The outlawes shot was so stronge
    That no man myght them dryue,
    And the proud[ë] sheryfës men,
    They fled away full blyue.

301 Robyn sawe the busshement to-broke,
    In grenë wode he wolde haue be;
    Many an arowe there was shot
    Amonge that company.

302 Lytell Johan was hurte full sore,
    With an arowe in his kne,
    That he myght neyther go nor ryde;
    It was full grete pytë.

303 'Mayster,' then sayd Lytell Johan,
    'If euer thou loue[d]st me,
    And for that ylkë lordës loue
    That dyed vpon a tre,

304 'And for the medes of my seruyce,
    That I haue serued the,
    Lete neuer the proudë sheryf
    Alyue now fyndë me.

305 'But take out thy brownë swerde,
    And smyte all of my hede,
    And gyue me woundës depe and wyde;
    No lyfe on me be lefte.'

306 'I wolde not that,' sayd Robyn,
    'Johan, that thou were slawe,
    For all the golde in mery Englonde,
    Though it lay now on a rawe.'

307 'God forbede,' sayd Lytell Much,
    'That dyed on a tre,
    That thou sholdest, Lytell Johan,
    Parte our company.'

308 Up he toke hym on his backe,
    And bare hym well a myle;
    Many a tyme he layd hym downe,
    And shot another whyle.

309 Then was there a fayre castell,
    A lytell within the wode;
    Double-dyched it was about,
    And walled, by the rode.

310 And there dwelled that gentyll knyght,
    Syr Rychard at the Lee,
    That Robyn had lent his good,
    Under the grenë-wode tree.

311 In he toke good Robyn,
    And all his company:
    'Welcome be thou, Robyn Hode,
    Welcome arte thou to me;

312 'And moche [I] thanke the of thy confort,
    And of thy curteysye,
    And of thy gretë kyndënesse,
    Under the grenë-wode tre.

313 'I loue no man in all this worlde
    So much as I do the;
    For all the proud[ë] sheryf of Notyngham,
    Ryght here shalt thou be.

314 'Shyt the gates, and drawe the brydge,
a.   And let no man come in,
    And arme you well, and make you redy,
    And to the walles ye wynne.

315 'For one thynge, Robyn, I the behote;
    I swere by Saynt Quyntyne,
    These forty dayes thou wonnest with me,
    To soupe, ete, and dyne.'

316 Bordes were layde, and clothes were spredde,
    Redely and anone;
    Robyn Hode and his mery men
    To metë can they gone.

THE VI. FYTTE.

317 Lythe and lysten, gentylmen,
    And herkyn to your songe;
    Howe the proudë shyref of Notyngham,
    And men of armys stronge,

318 Full fast cam to the hyë shyref,
    The contrë vp to route,
And they besette the knyghtës castell,
    The wallës all aboute.

319 The proudë shyref loude gan crye,
    And sayde, Thou traytour knight,
Thou kepest here the kynges enemys,
    Agaynst the lawe and right.

320 'Syr, I wyll auowe that I haue done,
    The dedys that here be dyght,
Vpon all the landës that I haue,
    As I am a trewë knyght.

321 ' Wende furth, sirs, on your way,
    And do no more to me
Tyll ye wyt oure kyngës wille,
    What he wyll say to the.'

322 The shyref thus had his answere,
    Without any lesynge;
[Fu]rth he yede to London towne,
    All for to tel our kinge.

323 Ther he telde him of that knight,
    And eke of Robyn Hode,
And also of the bolde archars,
    That were soo noble and gode.

324 ' He wyll auowe that he hath done,
    To mayntene the outlawes stronge;
He wyll be lorde, and set you at nought,
    In all the northe londe.'

325 'I wil be at Notyngham,' saide our kynge,
    ' Within this fourteenyght,
And take I wyll Robyn Hode,
    And so I wyll that knight.

326 ' Go nowe home, shyref,' sayde our kynge,
    ' And do as I byd the;
And ordeyn gode archers ynowe,
    Of all the wydë contrë.'

327 The shyref had his leue i-take,
    And went hym on his way,
And Robyn Hode to grenë wode,
    Vpon a certen day.

328 And Lytel John was hole of the arowe
    That shot was in his kne,

And dyd hym streyght to Robyn Hode,
    Vnder the grenë-wode tree.

329 Robyn Hode walked in the forest,
    Vnder the leuys grene;
The proudë shyref of Notyngham
    Thereof he had grete tene.

330 The shyref there fayled of Robyn Hode,
    He myght not haue his pray;
Than he awayted this gentyll knyght,
    Bothe by nyght and day.

331 Euer he wayted the gentyll knyght,
    Syr Richarde at the Lee,
As he went on haukynge by the ryuer-syde,
    And lete [his] haukës flee.

332 Toke he there this gentyll knight,
    With men of armys stronge,
And led hym to Notyngham warde,
    Bounde bothe fote and hande.

333 The sheref sware a full grete othe,
    Bi hym that dyed on rode,
He had leuer than an hundred pound
    That he had Robyn Hode.

334 This harde the knyghtës wyfe,
    A fayr lady and a free;
She set hir on a gode palfrey,
    To grenë wode anone rode she.

335 Whanne she cam in the forest,
    Vnder the grenë-wode tree,
Fonde she there Robyn Hode,
    And al his fayre menë.

336 'God the saüe, godë Robyn,
    And all thy company;
For Our derë Ladyes sake,
    A bonë graunte thou me.

337 ' Late neuer my wedded lorde
    Shamefully slayne be;
He is fast bowne to Notingham warde,
    For the loue of the.'

338 Anone than saide goode Robyn
    To that lady so fre,
What man hath your lorde [i-]take?
    .   .   .   .   .   .

339 . . . . . .
   'For soth as I the say;
   He is nat yet thre mylës
   Passed on his way.'

340 Vp than sterte gode Robyn,
   As man that had ben wode:
   'Buske you, my mery men,
   For hym that dyed on rode.

341 'And he that this sorowe forsaketh,
   By hym that dyed on tre,
   Shall he neuer in grenë wode
   No lenger dwel with me.'

342 Sone there were gode bowës bent,
   Mo than seuen score;
   Hedge ne dyche spared they none
   That was them before.

343 'I make myn auowe to God,' sayde Robyn,
   'The sherif wolde I fayne see;
   And if I may hym take,
   I-quyte shall it be.'

344 And whan they came to Notingham,
   They walked in the strete;
   And with the proudë sherif i-wys
   Sonë can they mete.

345 'Abyde, thou proudë sherif,' he sayde,
   'Abyde, and speke with me;
   Of some tidinges of oure kinge
   I wolde fayne here of the.

346 'This seuen yere, by dere worthy God,
   Ne yede I this fast on fote;
   I make myn auowe to God, thou proudë
     sherif,
   It is nat for thy gode.'

347 Robyn bent a full goode bowe,
   An arrowe he drowe at wyll;
   He hit so the proudë sherife
   Vpon the grounde he lay full still.

348 And or he myght vp aryse,
   On his fete to stonde,
   He smote of the sherifs hede
   With his bright[ë] bronde.

349 'Lye thou there, thou proudë sherife,
   Euyll mote thou cheue!

   There myght no man to the truste
b.   The whyles thou were a lyue.'

350 His men drewe out theyr bryght swerdes,
   That were so sharpe and kene,
   And layde on the sheryues men,
   And dryued them downe bydene.

351 Robyn stert to that knyght,
   And cut a two his bonde,
   And toke hym in his hand a bowe,
   And bad hym by hym stonde.

352 'Leue thy hors the behynde,
   And lerne for to renne;
   Thou shalt with me to grenë wode,
   Through myrë, mosse, and fenne.

353 'Thou shalt with me to grenë wode,
   Without ony leasynge,
   Tyll that I haue gete vs grace
   Of Edwarde, our comly kynge.'

THE VII. FYTTE.

354 The kynge came to Notynghame,
   With knyghtës in grete araye,
   For to take that gentyll knyght
   And Robyn Hode, and yf he may.

355 He asked men of that countrë
   After Robyn Hode,
   And after that gentyll knyght,
   That was so bolde and stout.

356 Whan they had tolde hym the case
   Our kynge vnderstode ther tale,
   And seased in his honde
   The knyghtës londës all.

357 All the passe of Lancasshyre
   He went both ferre and nere,
   Tyll he came to Plomton Parke;
   He faylyd many of his dere.

358 There our kynge was wont to se
   Herdës many one,
   He coud vnneth fynde one dere,
   That bare ony good horne.

359 The kynge was wonder wroth withall,
   And swore by the Trynytë,

'I wolde I had Robyn Hode,
     With eyen I myght hym se.

360 'And he that wolde smyte of the knyghtës
     hede,
     And brynge it to me,
     He shall haue the knyghtës londes,
     Syr Rycharde at the Le.

361 'I gyue it hym with my charter,
     And sele it [with] my honde,
     To haue and holde for euer more,
     In all mery Englonde.'

362 Than bespake a fayre olde knyght,
     That was treue in his fay :
     A, my leegë lorde the kynge,
     One worde I shall you say.

363 There is no man in this countrë
     May haue the knyghtës londes,
     Whyle Robyn Hode may ryde or gone,
     And bere a bowe in his hondes,

364 That he ne shall lese his hede,
     That is the best ball in his hode :
     Giue it no man, my lorde the kynge,
     That ye wyll any good.

365 Half a yere dwelled our comly kynge
     In Notyngham, and well more ;
     Coude he not here of Robyn Hode,
     In what countrë that he were.

366 But alway went good Robyn
     By halke and eke by hyll,
     And alway slewe the kyngës dere,
     And welt them at his wyll.

367 Than bespake a proude fostere,
     That stode by our kyngës kne :
     Yf ye wyll se good Robyn,
     Ye must do after me.

368 Take fyue of the best knyghtës
     That be in your lede,
     And walke downe by yon abbay,
     And gete you monkës wede.

369 And I wyll be your ledës-man,
     And lede you the way,
     And or ye come to Notyngham,
     Myn hede then dare I lay,

370 That ye shall mete with good Robyn,
     On lyue yf that he be ;
     Or ye come to Notyngham,
     With eyen ye shall hym se.

371 Full hast[ë]ly our kynge was dyght,
     So were his knyghtës fyue,
     Euerych of them in monkës wede,
     And hasted them thyder blyve.

372 Our kynge was grete aboue his cole,
     A brode hat on his crowne,
     Ryght as he were abbot-lyke,
     They rode up in-to the towne.

373 Styf botës our kynge had on,
     Forsoth as I you say ;
     He rode syngynge to grenë wode,
     The couent was clothed in graye.

374 His male-hors and his gretë somers
     Folowed our kynge behynde,
     Tyll they came to grenë wode,
     A myle vnder the lynde.

375 There they met with good Robyn,
     Stondynge on the waye,
     And so dyde many a bolde archere,
     For soth as I you say.

376 Robyn toke the kyngës hors,
     Hastëly in that stede,
     And sayd, Syr abbot, by your leue,
     A whyle ye must abyde.

377 'We be yemen of this foreste,
     Vnder the grenë-wode tre ;
     We lyue by our kyngës dere,
     [Other shyft haue not wee.]

378 'And ye haue chyrches and rentës both,
     And gold full grete plentë ;
     Gyue vs some of your spendynge,
     For saynt[ë] charytë.'

379 Than bespake our cumly kynge,
     Anone than sayd he ;
     I brought no more to grenë wode
     But forty pounde with me.

380 I haue layne at Notyngham
     This fourtynyght with our kynge,

And spent I haue full moche good,
　　On many a grete lordynge.

381 And I haue but forty pounde,
　　No more than haue I me;
　　But yf I had an hondred pounde,
　　I wolde vouch it safe on the.

382 Robyn toke the forty pounde,
　　And departed it in two partye;
　　Halfendell he gaue his mery men,
　　And bad them mery to be.

383 Full curteysly Robyn gan say;
　　Syr, haue this for your spendyng;
　　We shall mete another day;
　　'Gramercy,' than sayd our kynge.

384 'But well the greteth Edwarde, our kynge,
　　And sent to the his seale,
　　And byddeth the com to Notyngham,
　　Both to mete and mele.'

385 He toke out the brodë targe,
　　And sone he lete hym se;
　　Robyn coud his courteysy,
　　And set hym on his kne.

386 'I loue no man in all the worlde
　　So well as I do my kynge;
　　Welcome is my lordës seale;
　　And, monke, for thy tydynge,

387 'Syr abbot, for thy tydynges,
　　To day thou shalt dyne with me,
　　For the loue of my kynge,·
　　Under my trystell-tre.'

388 Forth he lad our comly kynge,
　　Full fayre by the honde;
　　Many a dere there was slayne,
　　And full fast dyghtande.

389 Robyn toke a full grete horne,
　　And loude he gan blowe;
　　Seuen score of wyght yonge men
　　Came redy on a rowe.

390 All they kneled on theyr kne,
　　Full fayre before Robyn:
　　The kynge sayd hym selfe vntyll,
　　And swore by Saynt Austyn,

391 'Here is a wonder semely syght;
　　Me thynketh, by Goddës pyne,
　　His men are more at his byddynge
　　Then my men be at myn.'

392 Full hast[ë]ly was theyr dyner idyght,
　　And therto gan they gone;
　　They serued our kynge with al theyr myght,
　　Both Robyn and Lytell Johan.

393 Anone before our kynge was set
　　The fattë venyson,
　　The good whyte brede, the good rede wyne,
　　And therto the fyne ale and browne.

394 'Make good chere,' said Robyn,
　　'Abbot, for charytë;
　　And for this ylkë tydynge,
　　Blyssed mote thou be.

395 'Now shalte thou se what lyfe we lede,
　　Or thou hens wende;
　　Than thou may enfourme our kynge,
　　Whan ye togyder lende.'

396 Up they stertë all in hast,
　　Theyr bowës were smartly bent;
　　Our kynge was neuer so sore agast,
　　He wende to haue be shente.

397 Two yerdës there were vp set,
　　Thereto gan they gange;
　　By fyfty pase, our kynge sayd,
　　The merkës were to longe.

398 On euery syde a rose-garlonde,
　　They shot vnder the lyne:
　　'Who so fayleth of the rose-garlonde,' sayd
　　　　Robyn,
　　'His takyll he shall tyne,

399 'And yelde it to his mayster,
　　Be it neuer so fyne;
　　For no man wyll I spare,
　　So drynke I ale or wyne:

400 'And bere a buffet on his hede,
　　I-wys ryght all bare:'
　　And all that fell in Robyns lote,
　　He smote them wonder sare.

401 Twyse Robyn shot aboute,
　　And euer he cleued the wande,

And so dyde good Gylberte
    With the Whytë Hande.

402 Lytell Johan and good Scathelocke,
    For nothynge wolde they spare ;
When they fayled of the garlonde,
    Robyn smote them full sore.

403 At the last shot that Robyn shot,
    For all his frendës fare,
Yet he fayled of the garlonde
    Thre fyngers and mare.

404 Than bespake good Gylberte,
    And thus he gan say ;
' Mayster,' he sayd, ' your takyll is lost,
    Stande forth and take your pay.'

405 ' If it be so,' sayd Robyn,
    ' That may no better be,
Syr abbot, I delyuer the myn arowe,
    I pray the, syr, serue thou me.'

406 ' It falleth not for myn ordre,' sayd our kynge,
    ' Robyn, by thy leue,
For to smyte no good yeman,
    For doute I sholde hym greue.'

407 ' Smyte on boldely,' sayd Robyn,
    ' I giue the largë leue : '
Anone our kynge, with that worde,
    He folde vp his sleue,

408 And sych a buffet he gaue Robyn,
    To grounde he yede full nere :
' I make myn avowe to God,' sayd Robyn,
    ' Thou arte a stalworthe frere.

409 ' There is pith in thyn arme,' sayd Robyn,
    ' I trowe thou canst well shete : '
Thus our kynge and Robyn Hode
    Togeder gan they mete.

410 Robyn behelde our comly kynge
    Wystly in the face,
So dyde Syr Rycharde at the Le,
    And kneled downe in that place.

411 And so dyde all the wylde outlawes,
    Whan they se them knele :
' My lorde the kynge of Englonde,
    Now I knowe you well.

412 ' Mercy then, Robyn,' sayd our kynge,
    ' Vnder your trystyll-tre,
Of thy goodnesse and thy grace,
    For my men and me ! '

413 ' Yes, for God,' sayd Robyn,
    ' And also God me saue,
I askë mercy, my lorde the kynge,
    And for my men I craue.'

414 ' Yes, for God,' than sayd our kynge,
    ' And therto sent I me,
With that thou leue the grenë wode,
    And all thy company ;

415 ' And come home, syr, to my courte,
    And there dwell with me.'
' I make myn avowe to God,' sayd Robyn,
    ' And ryght so shall it be.

416 ' I wyll come to your courte,
    Your seruyse for to se,
And brynge with me of my men
    Seuen score and thre.

417 ' But me lykë well your seruyse,
    I [wyll] come agayne full soone,
And shote at the donnë dere,
    As I am wonte to done.'

THE VIII. FYTTE.

418 ' Haste thou ony grenë cloth,' sayd our kynge,
    ' That thou wylte sell nowe to me ? '
' Ye, for God,' sayd Robyn,
    ' Thyrty yerdës and thre.'

419 ' Robyn,' sayd our kynge,
    ' Now pray I the,
Sell me some of that cloth,
    To me and my meynë.'

420 ' Yes, for God,' then sayd Robyn,
    ' Or elles I were a fole ;
Another day ye wyll me clothe,
    I trowe, ayenst the Yole.'

421 The kynge kest of his colë then,
    A grene garment he dyde on,
And euery knyght also, i-wys,
    Another had full sone.

422 Whan they were clothed in Lyncolne grene,
    They keste away theyr graye;
'Now we shall to Notyngham,'
    All thus our kynge gan say.

423 They bente theyr bowes, and forth they went,
    Shotynge all in-fere,
Towarde the towne of Notyngham,
    Outlawes as they were.

424 Our kynge and Robyn rode togyder,
    For soth as I you say,
And they shote plucke-buffet,
    As they went by the way.

425 And many a buffet our kynge wan
    Of Robyn Hode that day,
And nothynge spared good Robyn
    Our kynge in his pay.

426 'So God me helpë,' sayd our kynge,
    'Thy game is nought to lere;
I sholde not get a shote of the,
    Though I shote all this yere.'

427 All the people of Notyngham
    They stode and behelde;
They sawe nothynge but mantels of grene
    That couered all the felde.

428 Than euery man to other gan say,
    I drede our kynge be slone;
Comë Robyn Hode to the towne, i-wys
    On lyue he lefte neuer one.'

429 Full hast[ë]ly they began to fle,
    Both yemen and knaues,
And olde wyues that myght euyll goo,
    They hypped on theyr staues.

430 The kynge l[o]ughe full fast,
    And commaunded theym agayne;
When they se our comly kynge,
    I-wys they were full fayne.

431 They ete and dranke, and made them glad,
    And sange with notës hye;
Than bespake our comly kynge
    To Syr Rycharde at the Lee.

432 He gaue hym there his londe agayne,
    A good man he bad hym be;

433 Had Robyn dwelled in the kyngës courte
    But twelue monethes and thre,
That [he had] spent an hondred pounde,
    And all his mennes fe.

434 In euery place where Robyn came
    Euer more he layde downe,
Both for knyghtës and for squyres,
    To gete hym grete renowne.

435 By than the yere was all agone
    He had no man but twayne,
Lytell Johan and good Scathelocke,
    With hym all for to gone.

436 Robyn sawe yonge men shote
    Full fayre vpon a day;
'Alas!' than sayd good Robyn,
    'My welthe is went away.

437 'Somtyme I was an archere good,
    A styffe and eke a stronge;
I was compted the best archere
    That was in mery Englonde.

438 'Alas!' then sayd good Robyn,
    'Alas and well a woo!
Yf I dwele lenger with the kynge,
    Sorowe wyll me sloo.'

439 Forth than went Robyn Hode
    Tyll he came to our kynge:
'My lorde the kynge of Englonde,
    Graunte me myn askynge.

440 'I made a chapell in Bernysdale,
    That semely is to se,
It is of Mary Magdaleyne,
    And thereto wolde I be.

441 'I myght neuer in this seuen nyght
    No tyme to slepe ne wynke,
Nother all these seuen dayes
    Nother ete ne drynke.

442 'Me longeth sore to Bernysdale,
    I may not be therfro;
Barefote and wolwarde I haue hyght
    Thyder for to go.'

443 ' Yf it be so,' than sayd our kynge,
    ' It may no better be,
    Seuen nyght I gyue the leue,
    No lengre, to dwell fro me.'

444 ' Gramercy, lorde,' then sayd Robyn,
    And set hym on his kne ;
    He toke his leuë full courteysly,
    To grenë wode then went he.

445 Whan he came to grenë wode,
    In a mery mornynge,
    There he herde the notës small
    Of byrdës mery syngynge.

446 ' It is ferre gone,' sayd Robyn,
    ' That I was last here ;
    Me lyste a lytell for to shote
    At the donnë dere.'

447 Robyn slewe a full grete harte ;
    His horne than gan he blow,
    That all the outlawes of that forest
    That horne coud they knowe,

448 And gadred them togyder,
    In a lytell throwe.
    Seuen score of wyght yonge men
    Came redy on a rowe,

449 And fayre dyde of theyr hodes,
    And set them on theyr kne :
    ' Welcome,' they sayd, ' our [derë] mayster,
    Under this grenë-wode tre.'

450 Robyn dwelled in grenë wode
    Twenty yere and two ;
    For all drede of Edwarde our kynge,
    Agayne wolde he not goo.

451 Yet he was begyled, i-wys,
    Through a wycked woman,
    The pryoresse of Kyrkësly,
    That nye was of hys kynne :

452 For the loue of a knyght,
    Syr Roger of Donkesly,
    That was her ownë speciall ;
    Full euyll motë they the !

453 They toke togyder theyr counsell
    Robyn Hode for to sle,
    And how they myght best do that dede,
    His banis for to be.

454 Than bespake good Robyn,
    In place where as he stode,
    ' To morow I muste to Kyrke[s]ly,
    Craftely to be leten blode.'

455 Syr Roger of Donkestere,
    By the pryoresse he lay,
    And there they betrayed good Robyn Hode,
    Through theyr falsë playe.

456 Cryst haue mercy on his soule,
    That dyed on the rode !
    For he was a good outlawe,
    And dyde pore men moch god.

---

a. Here begynneth a gest of Robyn Hode.
    1–12. *Printed without division of stanzas or verses.*
    2^{2,3}. *Deficiency supplied from* b.
    4^1. gooe.   4^2. milsers.   4^3. yuch.
    6^4. vnkoutg.   7^1. *lacking in all.*
    8^4. .iij. messis.   9^3. The .iij.   9^4. all ther.
    13^4. tillet.   15^4. mynge.   18^3. vnknuth.
    32^3. ynought.   33^1. felsauntes.   37^1. wened.
    38^3. Late *for* Litell, *which all the others have.*
    39^2. of *for* haue.   39^3. but .xx. : *see* 42^4.
    41^1. nowne.   41^3. .xx. felinges.
    46^2. in strocte.   46^3. And.
    47^3. And.   47^4. haue bene.
    50^{2,3}. *The verses are transposed.*
    50^2. God had.   54^2. Vutyll.   66^3. to may.

68^4. Bo .xxviij.   70^4. To helpe : *cf.* 194^4.
77^3. betes.   78^2. clere.   79^3. .xij.   82^1. ou.
82^3. bernedtale.   83^3. for he.
83^4–118^3. *wanting ; supplied from* b.
119^1. a .M.   120^4. Euen .cccc.   121^2. thon.
123^4. Bi god . . . on tree. *The tops of* d
    and of th, *and a part of* dy, *remain.*
124^1. Sir . . . n of lawe.
124^2. *Only the top of* N *remains.*
124^2–127^3. *wanting, being torn away ; supplied from* b.
128^2. Ha.   130^3. .cccc. li.   131^{1,3}. an .C.
131^3. aros we.   132^1. an ille.
132^3. Worked all.
133^{1,2}. He purneyed hym an. *Only a part of*
    n *in the last word remains.* Well harness.

Only a part of n *and the tops of* ess *re-maining.*

133³–136³. *wanting ; supplied from* b.
138². Bnd. 143¹. louge. 143². doue.
150⁴. tho thy. 160³. Thougt : an C.
160⁴. he be go. 161³. And therfore.
162². gyne. 163². he wol be.
164². *read* hyne ? 165³. anowe.
168⁴. mountnauuce. 175³. wasars.
179². sende the. *Perhaps* sent the, *as in* 384² (b).
180¹. abowe. 181³. v myle.
182². Hnntynge. 183³. Rrynolde.
185³. vij. score. 187¹. shyrel.
199¹. this xij. 201³. thy best. 202³. scade.
206¹. Johū. 206⁴. pray.
208⁴–314¹. *wanting ; supplied from* b.
315³. These xl. : with men. 321³. welle.
330¹. fayles. 331³. ryner. 333³. an C. li.
339³. myeles. 349³. to thy.
From 349⁴ *wanting ; supplied from* b.

b. *Title-page :* Here begynneth a lytell geste of Robyn hode. *At the head of the poem :* Here begynneth a lytell geste of Robyn hode and his meyne, And of the proude Sheryfe of Notyngham.

2⁴. y-founde. 3³. Iohan : *and always.*
4¹. Scathelock. 4³. no. 5¹. be spake hym.
5³. yf ye. 6¹. hym *wanting.* 6². I haue.
6³. that *wanting.* 6⁴. vnketh.
7¹. *wanting.* 7³. knygot or some squyere.
8⁴. Thre. 9². The other.
9³. was of. 9⁴. all other moste.
11³. that *wanting :* gone. 11⁴. that *wanting.*
13¹. than *wanting.* 13⁴. tylleth.
14⁴. wolde. 15⁴. ye *wanting.*
16¹. beholde : Ihoan. 16². shall we.
17¹. Robyn. 17³. Scathelocke.
18³. vnketh. 20. vnto. 20². yemen.
21¹. to *wanting.* 21³. came there.
22¹. then was all his semblaunte.
23¹. hangynge ouer. 23⁴. somers.
24¹. full *wanting.* 24⁴. you. 26¹. is your.
26³. is a. 27². all thre. 28¹. went that.
29¹. vnto. 29². gan hym. 30². thou arte.
30³. abyde. 32². set tyll.
32³. right *wanting.* 33³. neuer so.
35⁴. that *wanting.* 36². whan I haue.
38³. Lytell Iohan : Robyn hode.
39¹. than *wanting.* 39². god haue.
39³, 41³. but .x. s. 40¹. thou haue.
40⁴. len. 41⁴. Not one. 42⁴. halfe a.
43². full lowe. 43³. tydynge. 43⁴. inough.

44⁴. clothynge : thynne. 45¹. one worde.
45³. thou were. 46². in stroke.
46⁴. hast thou. 47¹. of them.
47³. An .C. wynter. 47⁴. haue be.
49¹. within two or thre. 49³. hondreth.
50²˒³. *The verses are transposed.*
50². hath shapen.
51¹. than *wanting.* 53¹. of Lancastshyre.
53⁴. both. · 54¹. beth. 56². What shall.
57⁴. may not. 58³. frendes.
59². knowe me. 60⁴. had *wanting.*
61². Scathelocke and Much also.
62¹. frendes. 62². borowes that wyll.
62⁴. on a. 63¹. waye : than *wanting.*
63³. I wyll. 64³. me *wanting.*
67⁴. loke that it well tolde.
68², 74¹, 77³, 83². Scathelocke.
68⁴. By eyghtene. 69¹. lytell Much.
69². greueth. 70⁴. To helpe. 71². many a.
72². it well mete it be. 73¹. And of.
73². lept ouer. 73³. deuylkyns.
73⁴. for *wanting.* 74³. hym the better.
74⁴. Bygod it cost him. 75¹. than *wanting.*
75². All vnto Robyn. 75³. an hors.
75⁴. al th*i*s. 76⁴. God leue. 78². clere.
80³. Without. 81¹. lene. 82¹. went on.
82². he thought. 83¹. bethought.
87¹. *wanting.* 88³. hondrde.
89². he is ryght. 98¹. *wanting.*
113². gan loke. 118⁴. grete ye.
119². were thou. 121⁴. Rewarde.
123⁴. By god that dyed on a tree.
124¹. Syr abbot, and ye men of lawe.
128². of my. 128³. not be.
130³. got foure hondreth. 131². dyght.
132³. I nocked.
133¹˒². purueyed hym an hondreth men
      Well harneysed in that stede.
135¹. *Qy ?* But at Wentbrydge ther was.
136². bulle I vp pyght. 137². in good fay.
137³. that *wanting.* 138³. frend bestad.
138⁴. I-slayne. 139². where that.
140². hondred : fere *for* free. 145². shote.
146¹. shot. 146². sleste. 146⁴. gan.
147⁴. euer *wanting :* I me. 148⁴. wan.
149¹. sir *wanting :* bore. 150². Wolte.
151³. gete leue. 153². Ge gyue.
155¹. befell. 156³. to *wanting.*
156⁴. me to dyne. 157². so longe to be.
157³. sir *wanting.* 157⁴. gyue thou.
159³. the *wanting.* 160¹. a rap.
160². yede nygh on two. 160³. an .c. wynter.
160⁴. wors he sholde go. 161². went vp.

161³. there : made a.   161⁴. and wyne.

163¹. *second* John *wanting.*

163². whyle he.   164³. an householde to.

165³. to God *wanting.*

165⁴. lyketh : me *wanting.*   166¹. and an.

167¹. ful *wanting.*   168². well *wanting.*

169⁴. I me.   170⁴. I-chaunged.

173⁴. same day.   174³. of full *wanting.*

175³. and spones.   175⁴. they none.

176¹. they toke.   176³. dyde hym.

176⁴. wode tre.   178¹. And also.

179². sende the : *cf.* 384².

181¹. hym there.   181². whyle.

181⁴. at his.   182². hounde.   182³. coud his.

184³. syght.   185¹. I se.   185³. an herde.

186¹. His tynde.   188³. afore.

188⁴. sir *wanting.*   189⁴. now be trayed.

191². well *wanting.*   191³. se his.

192¹. Make good.   192⁴. lyfe is graunted.

193². a gone.   193³. commaunded.

194¹. cote a pye.   194². well fyne.

194³. toke.   195³. They shall lay : sote.

196¹. laye that.   196⁴. sydes do smerte.

199¹. All these.

200¹. Or I here a nother nyght sayd.

200². I praye.   200³. to-morne.

201³. the best.   201⁴. That yet had the.

202³. Thou shalt neuer a wayte me scathe.

203². or by.   204¹. haue : I-swore.

205². that he was gone.   205³. had his.

206⁴. pay.   207⁴. trusty.   208³. Scathelock.

209³. after such.

210³,⁴. Or yf he be a pore man
    Of my good he shall haue some.

214⁴. these *wanting.*

215². frese our : leese your? dress your?

216¹. .lii. : men *wanting.*   218². you *for* yon.

224¹. .lii.   231⁴. serued them.

240³. ryghtwysman.   240⁴. his name.

242¹. art nade.   243⁴. Also.

245¹. more sayd *wanting.*

247⁴. hondred *wanting.*   267¹. gayne.

272¹. I toke it I twyse : *the second I is prob-
    ably a misprint.*

279¹. thy .cccc. li.   280². all of this.

283³. all ther best.   284¹. all theyre best.

292². they slist.   293². acchers.   299¹. beut.

305³. dede, *second* d *inverted.*

314⁴. walle.   315³. These twelue : with me.

316¹. were *wanting.*   316⁴. gan they.

317². vnto.   319³. enemye.

319⁴. Agayne the lawes.   320². dedes thou.

321². doth.   322³. yode.   323¹. tolde.

323⁴. That noble were.

324¹. He wolde : had.   324³. He wolde.

325¹. woll : sayd the.

326¹. nowe *wanting :* thou proud sheryf :
    sayde our kynge *wanting.*

326². the bydde.   329⁴. Therfore.

330¹. fayled.   330⁴. and by.

331¹. a wayted that.   331⁴. let his.

332³. hym home.   332⁴. honde and fote.

333². on a tre.

334¹. harde *wanting :* This the lady, the.

334². and fre.   335¹. to the.   335². tre tre.

336¹. God the good : saue *wanting.*

336³. lady loue.   337¹. Late thou neuer.

337². Shamly I slayne be.

337³. fast I-bounde.   338². lady fre.

338³. I take.   338⁴, 339¹. *wanting.*

339⁴. on your.   340². As a : be.

340³. yonge men.   340⁴. on a.   341². on a.

341³. wode be.   341⁴. Nor.   342¹. i bent.

342³. spare.   343². The knyght.

343⁴. I-quyt than.   344⁴. gan.   346². so fast.

346⁴. At is.   347¹. full *wanting.*

347². at his.   349². thou thryue.

349³. to the.   351². his hoode.

356². vnder-stonde.   363². hane.

368³. walked ; *qy?* walketh : by your.

371⁴. blyth.

377⁴ *repeats verse* 2 : Other shyft haue not
    we, *Copland and Ed. White's copies.*

381⁴. I vouch it halfe on the. **f** *and* **g** : I
    would geue it to thee.

385¹. brode tarpe. *Copland and Ed. White's
    copies :* seale *for* tarpe.

400². A wys.   401⁴. the good whyte.

402⁴. sore.   409². shote.

409⁴. than they met. **f**, they gan : **g**, gan
    they mete.

412¹,². *Copland and Ed. White :* sayd Robyn
    to our king, Vnder this.

417². *Copland and Ed. White :* I wyll come.

421³. had so I wys : so *Copland and Ed.
    White.*

423¹. Theyr bowes bente : *cf.* **f**, **g**.

433². .xii.

433³. he had *in Copland and Ed. White.*

436². ferre : fayre *in* **o**, *Copland and Ed.
    White.*

437³. was commytted. *Copland and Ed.
    White :* was commended for.

440¹. bernysdade.   441³. *Qy?* No tymë slepe.

443¹. he so.   449³. our dere *in* **o**.

454². places.

Explycit. kynge Edwarde and Robyn hode and Lytell Johan Enprented at London in fletestrete at the sygne of the sone By Wynken de Worde.

a bode, a gast, a gone, a nother, a vowe, be fore, be gan, be spake, for gone, i brought, launs gay, out lawes, to gyder, vnder take, *etc., etc., are printed* abode, etc., etc. ; I wys, i-wys ; & and.

It will be understood that not all probable cases of ꝫ have been indicated.

c. 26⁴. myche. 28⁴. ere *for* lere.
29². hym gan, *as in* a. 29⁸. he *wanting*.
30⁸. a byde. 30⁴. oures. 32¹. wesshe.
32². sat tyll. 32⁸. ryght inough, *as in* a.
33⁸. non so lytell, *as in* a. 34². Garmercy.
34⁴. all this. 35⁴. that *wanting, as in* b.
36². it *wanting*. 37². Me thynkc.
38⁸. Lytell Johan, *as in* b.
39¹. then sayd, *as in* a.
39². haue parte of the. 39⁸, 41⁸. .x. s. .
40¹. haue, *as in* b. 40⁴. len, *as in* b.
41⁴. Not one, *as in* b. 42⁴. halfe a.
43². full lowe, *as in* b.
43⁸. tydynge, *as in* b. 44⁸. Myche, thyket.
45¹. one worde, *as in* b. 45⁸. were, *as in* b.
46¹. haste be. 46². stroke.
46⁸. And, *as in* a. 46⁴. hast led, *as in* a.
47¹. nene of tho. 47⁸. An .c. wynter.
47⁴. haue be. 48⁸. that syt.
49¹. this two yere, *as in* a. 49². well knowe.
50²,⁸. *order as in* a, b.
50². hath shapen, *as in* b.
51¹. than *wanting, as in* b. 51². thou lose.
53¹. lancasesshyre. 53⁴. bothe, *as in* a, b.
54¹. bothe, *as in* a.
56². shall fall, *as in* b. 57¹. wher.
57⁴. noo better, *as in* a.
58¹. eyen *has fallen into the next line* (eyen way).
58⁸. frende, *as in* a.
58⁴. I ne haue noo nother. 59¹. the frendes.

d. 280². all of this, *as in* b. 281⁴. full styll.
282². [her] keneth. 283⁸. all thee beste.
284¹. all there beste. 286⁸. ye *wanting*.
287⁴, 288¹,²,⁸. *cut off.* 289¹,². *transposed.*
290⁸. I bent. 291¹. can bende.
291⁴. as he. 292¹. shet. 292². they clyft.
293¹. Scathelocke. 293². good in fere.
295⁴. then wolde. 296². can they.
296⁸. the *wanting*.
297. *cut off, except* ylde forest *in line* 4.
302². on his. 302⁸. go ne. 303². louest.

305¹. all out. 305⁸. woundes depe.
306¹⁻⁸. *cut off.*
306⁴. now *wanting: only the lower part of the words of this line remains.*
307². vpon. 310⁸. Robyn hode lente.
312¹. myche thanket he of the.
312⁸. the grete. 314⁴. walle, *as in* b.
315. *nearly all cut away.* 317². herkeneth to.
319⁸. enmye, *as in* b. 319⁴. lawes, *as in* b.
320². [t]hou here, *as in* b.
323³,⁴, 324¹,². *wanting.*
324¹. He wolde, *as in* b.
326¹. Goo home thou proude sheryf, *as in* b.
326². the bydde, *as in* b.
329⁴. Therfore, *as in* b.
331¹. wayted thys gentyll. 331⁴. his haukes.
332³,⁴, 333¹,². *wanting.*
334². and a, *as in* a. 334⁸. a *wanting*.
336⁸. ladye loue, *as in* b.
337⁸. bounde, *as in* b.
338². so *wanting*. 338⁸. I take.
338⁴, 339¹. *wanting, as in* a, b.
339⁴. *has only* [y]our way. 340². be wode.
340⁸. mery yonge men, *as in* a.
340⁴. on rode, *as in* a.
341². *only* [th]at dyed on *preserved*.
342. *wanting.* 343⁴. then shall, *as in* b.
344⁴. can they, *as in* a.
346². so faste, *as in* b.
346⁴. It is not, *as in* a.
347¹. full godd, *as in* a.
347². at wyll, *as in* a.
349². thryue, *as in* b. 349⁸. to the struste.
350². bothe sharp.

e. 436². Full fayre. 436⁴. is gone.
437⁸. cōmitted. 441². to slepe.
441⁸. Nor of all. 441⁴. Noutter ete nor.
442¹. longeth so sore to be in.
442³,⁴, 443¹,². *wanting.* 446⁴. donde.
447². can he. 447⁸. outlawes in.
449⁸. our dere.

f. *Title :* A mery geste of Robyn Hoode and of hys lyfe, wyth a newe playe for to be played in Maye games, very plesaunte and full of pastyme. *At the head of the poem:* Here begynneth a lyttell geste of Robyn hoode and his mery men, and of the proude Shyryfe of Notyngham.

Insignificant variations of spelling are not noted.

1². freborne. 2⁴. yfounde.
3². lened vpon a. 3⁸. stode *wanting*.
4¹. Scathelocke : *and always.* 4². **mylners.**

4^8. was no. 5^8. if ye. 6^1. hym *wanting*.

6^4. vnketh. 7^1. *wanting*.

7^8. or some squyer. 9^2. The other.

9^8. was of. 9^4. of all other.

11^8. that *wanting* : shall gone.

11^4. that *wanting*. 13^1. than *wanting*.

13^8. husbandeman. 13^4. with the.

14^4. That would. 15^4. ye *wanting*.

16^2. shall we. 16^8. farre.

18^1. Nowe walke ye vp vnto the Sayle.

18^8. vnketh. 18^4. By chaunce some may ye.

19^1. cearle *misprinted for* earle.

19^8. hym then to. 20^1. went anone vnto.

21^1. loked in B.

21^2. deme (*for* derne) strate.

21^8. there *wanting*.

22^1. drousli (droufli ?) than : semblaunt.

23^1. hanged ouer : eyes. 23^4. on sommers.

24^1. full *wanting*. 24^4. are you.

25^8. you *wanting*. 26^1. is your.

26^8. is a. 26^4. haue I harde.

27^1. graunt the : wynde.

27^2. brethren all three. 28^1. went that.

28^8. eyes. 29^1. vnto. 29^2. gan hym.

29^4. downe on. 30^2. thou art.

30^8. you *wanting*. 32^8. right *wanting*.

33^8. fayleth neuer so. 33^4. was spred.

35^4. that *wanting*.

36^1. I thank the, knyght, then said.

36^2. when I haue.

36^8. By god I was neuer so gredy.

37^8. dere *wanting*.

38^8. Lytell John : Robyn hoode.

39^1. than *wanting*. 40^1. thou haue.

40^8. I shall lende. 41^4. Not any penny.

42^4. halfe a. 43^2. full lowe.

43^4. inowe *wanting*. 45^1. me one.

45^8. thou were. 46^1. Or yls els : haste by.

46^2. stroke. 46^4. thou *wanting*.

47^1. of them. $47^8, 49^8, 55^8$, *etc.* hundreth.

48^2. hat be. 49^1. two or three yerers.

49^2. *wanting*. $50^{2,8}$. *transposed*.

50^2. hath shopen. 50^4. god it amende.

51^1. than *wanting*. 51^2. lost thy.

52^8. wenters. 53^1. Lancastshyre.

56^2. What shall. 58^1. eyes. 58^8. frendes.

58^4. ne *wanting*. 59^2. knowe mee.

59^8. Whyles. 59^4. boste that.

60^4. had *wanting* : neuer me.

61^2. Much also. 62^1. frendes.

62^2. borowes : wyll. 62^8. than *wanting*.

62^4. on a. 63^1. than *wanting*.

63^8. I haue. 64^1. made me.

64^8. me *wanting*. 65^8. yf *wanting*.

67^4. it well tolde. 68^4. eyghten score.

69^1. lyttell Much. 69^2. greueth.

70^4. To wrappe. 71^2. muche ryche.

72^2. that well mete it. 73^1. And of.

73^2. lept ouer. 73^8. What the deuils.

73^4. for *wanting*. 74^1. lought.

74^8. hym the better. 74^4. By god it cost.

75^1. than *wanting*. 75^2. All unto R.

75^8. that knight an. 75^4. al this.

76^4. God lende that it. 78^1. shal.

78^2. clene. 78^4. out *wanting*.

79^4. Under the. 81^8. may stande.

82^2. he thought. 83^4. came.

84^1. spake the. 86^8. xij monethes.

87^1. *wanting*. 87^2. his lande and fee.

$87^4, 95^4$. Disherited. 89^2. is his.

89^4. sore. 91^8. came. 92^4. poundes.

93^8. The highe. 94^2. taken.

96^1. not *wanting*. 96^8. teme to.

98^1. *wanting*. 100^8. corese.

101^8. The shal. 102^4. saluted.

103^8. that the. 103^4. me my.

104^2. hath made. 105^4. To desyre you of.

106^4. defend me from. 111^1. then *wanting*.

112^2. Sende. 112^8. a assaye.

113^1. on then gan. 113^2. *wanting*.

115^4. canst not. 118^4. Ye get ye it.

119^2. were thou. 120^8. of *wanting*.

121^8. Haddest thou.

121^4. I would haue rewarded thee.

122^2. royall chere. 122^4. fast gan.

123^4. on a. 124^8. I shall.

128^8. not be. 129^2. is *wanting*.

129^4. came. 130^8. got.

131^2. stringes were well dyght.

132^8. And nocked ye were with.

133^8. sute. 134^8. And rode.

135^1. But *wanting* : by a bridg was.

136^2. vp ypyght. 136^4. burnisshed.

137^2. in good fay. 137^8. that *wanting*.

138^8. fayre and frend. 139^2. where ye he.

140^1. the *wanting*. 140^2. him in fere.

141^1. sholdreth and : come *for* rome.

142^2. laye than. 142^4. And drynke.

143^4. the *wanting*. 145^2. shute.

146^2. alway cleft. 146^4. gan.

147^2. a *wanting*.

147^4. That euer I dyd see. 148^1. me thou.

148^8. thou wast. 148^4. wining.

149^1. sir *wanting*. 150^2. Wylt.

151^8. gete leue. 152^8. gaue to him anone.

153^2. He geue vs. 154^1. me *wanting*.

154⁴. he had yete. 156³. to *wanting*.
156⁴. me meate. 157¹. to long.
157². Fasting so long to. 157³. sir *wanting*.
157⁴. geue thou. 158⁴. had lere.
160¹. rappe. 160². backe yede nygh into.
160³. lyueth an hundreth wynter.
160⁴. worse he should go. 161². went vp.
161³. And there : a *wanting*.
161⁴. of *wanting*. 162³. liue this.
162⁴. shall ye. 163¹. and also dronke.
163². that he. 164². hyne, *perhaps rightly*.
164³. an householde to. 164⁴. For *wanting*.
165³. to God *wanting*.
165⁴. do lyke wel me. 166¹. a hardy.
167¹. ful *wanting*. 167³. for *wanting*.
168². wel *wanting*. 169⁴. I me.
170⁴. Chaunged it should.
173⁴. same day at nyght. 174¹. The hyed.
175¹. the *wanting*. 175³. masers and.
175⁴. they non. 176¹. they toke.
176². and three. 176³. And hyed.
176⁴. wode tree.
177⁴. Welcome thou art to me.
178¹. And so is that good.
178². That thou hast brought wyth the.
179². And he hath send the.
179³. His cope. 180¹. advow.
181¹. there *wanting*. 181⁴. at his.
182³. coulde his. 184¹. haue nowe.
185¹. I se. 185³. of *wanting* : a.
186¹. tyndes be. 187³. Buske the.
188³. afore. 188⁴. sir *wanting*.
189³. worthe the. 189⁴. now betrayed.
191². well *wanting*. 192¹. good chere.
192⁴. lyfe is graunted. 193³. commaunded.
194¹. cote a pye. 194³. toke.
195¹. wight yemen.
195³. shall : in that sorte.
196¹. that proude. 196⁴. sydes do smarte.
197¹. chere *wanting*.
198⁴. dwel longe. 199¹. these.
200¹. Or I here another nyght lye.
201³. the best.
202³. Thou shalt neuer wayte me skathe.
202⁴. nor by. 203². by day. 204¹. swore.
204². he *wanting*. 204⁴. was any man.
205². that he was gone.
206². Hode *wanting*. 206⁴. pay.
209¹. walke *wanting* : into the.
209³. And loke for some straunge.
209⁴. By chaunce you. 210². a *wanting*.
210³·⁴. *as in* b. 211¹. sterte. 211². fraye.
212¹. went than vnto. 213¹. as he.

214². can. 214⁴. these monkes.
215². And bende we.
215³. harte. 216¹. but lii men.
218². Make you yonder preste.
220¹. An euell. 220². vnder the.
221¹. What hyght your.
222². shall sore rewe. 223¹. a bowe.
223². Redy. 223⁴. gan.
224¹. twoo and fifty wyght yemen.
224². abode but. 226². whan he did se.
229¹. an. 231¹. The made.
231⁴. serued them.
234². mote I thryue or the.
236². Ye nede not so to saye.
236³. hath brought it. 237¹. And *wanting*.
238¹. broughte. 238³. the eft agayne.
238⁴. of me. 240³. right wise.
241². mayest. 242¹. made *wanting*.
242³. I do the thanke.
243⁴. So mote I thryue or the.
244². not out one. 244³. hast nede.
244⁴. shall I : to *wanting*.
245¹. fyne more sayd.
245⁴. Thereof I wyll haue.
247¹. John layd. 247³. he *wanting*.
247⁴. hundreth poundes. 248⁴. cost.
249². that tolde. 249³. the trust.
252¹. And she haue nede of ony.
256¹. And what is on the other courser.
256². sothe we must. 256³. than *wanting*.
259⁴. *second* in *wanting*.
263¹. light fro his. 263². can.
263³. Right curteysly. 265¹. good Robin.
266⁴. They would. 267¹. agayne.
267³. than sayd. 267⁴. that *wanting*.
268¹. no grefe : *printed in two lines*.
268³. dyd helpe.
269¹. Now, by my treuthe than sayd.
269². For that, knight, thanke.
270¹. poundes. 270³. there.
270³·⁴. *printed in one line*.
271¹. than *wanting*. 271³. her high.
272¹. And I should take : twyse.
272⁴. thou art. 273¹. And whan.
273². laughed and made.
274⁴. Under this trusty. 275². fethered.
275³. gentyl knyght.
276². My wyll done that it be.
277³. bye the a hors.
277⁴. the *for* thy (*as* me, be *for* my, by).
279². I dyd lende. 280². of all his.
280³. sytteth.
283³. they that shote al of the best.

283^4. The best. 284^1. al of the best.

284^3. of goodly. 285^3. fethers.

286^2. his trusty. $286^3, 288^3$. wyght yemen.

287^1. mery yemen. 287^3. I shall knowe.

288^2. Their arowes fethere free.

289^3. archers. 289^4. shote.

291^1. can. 292^2. he clefte.

292^4. the lylly white. 294^1. Whan that.

294^3. than was. 294^4. good Robin.

295^1. To him. 295^3. gyft full.

295^4. than would. 296^2. gan the.

297^2. Thus chering.

297^3. Another promyse thou made to me.

297^4. Within the wylde.

298^1. And I had y^e in the gr[e]ne forest.

298^2. trusty tree. 298^3. me leue.

300^4. away belyue. 301^4. Amonge the.

302^1. John he was hort. 302^2. in the.

303^2. loues. 304^4. nowe to.

305^2. smite thou of.

305^3. woundes so wyde and longe.

305^4. That I after eate no breade.

306^1. that *wanting*. 306^2. slayne.

306^4. Though I had it all by me.

307^1. forbyd that: Much then.

307^4. Depart. 308^4. another a whyle.

312^1. I do the thankes for thy comfort.

$312^{2,3}$. And for. 313^1. all the. 314^1. Shutte.

314^4. wall. 315^1. the hote.

315^3. Thou shalt these xij dayes abide.

316^2. Redye. 316^4. gan. 317^2. vnto the.

317^3. Howe the proude shirife began.

319^1. can. 319^3. kepest there. 319^4. lawes.

320^4. am true. 321^2. do ye no more vnto.

322^3. he went. 323^4. That noble were and.

324^1. He wolde: had. 324^3. He wold.

325^1. the kynge.

326^1. Go home, thou proude sheryfe.

326^2. the bydde. 329^4. Therfore.

330^1. Ther he. 330^3. that gentyl.

330^4. and by. 331^1. awayted that.

331^4. his hauke. 332^1. *misprinted* To be.

332^3. him home to. 332^4. Ybounde.

333^2. on a tree. 333^4. robin hode had he.

334^1. Then the lady the. 334^2. a *wanting*.

335^1. to the. 335^3. There she found.

336^1. Robyn Hode. 336^3. ladyes loue.

337^1. Let thou. 337^2. to be. 337^3. bound.

338^2. so *wanting*. 338^3. ytake.

338^4. The proude shirife than sayd she.

339. *Only this:* He is not yet passed thre myles, You may them ouertake.

340^2. a man: ben. 340^3. mery yemen.

340^4. on a tree. 341^2. on a tree.

$341^{3,4}$. And by him that al thinges maketh No lenger shall dwell with me.

342^1. ybent. 343^2. The knight would.

343^3. And yf ye he may him take.

343^4. Yquyte than shall he bee.

344^4. gan the. 346^2. so fast. 346^4. That is.

347^1. full *wanting*. 347^2. at his.

349^2. may thou thryue. 349^3. to the.

349^4. thou wast. 351^1. start.

351^2. cut into. 354^4. and *wanting*.

355^1. them *for* men. 356^2. vnderstode.

357^1. the compasse. 357^2. He wend.

358^2. a one. 358^3. fynde any. 359^4. eyes.

360^3. He should. 361^2. it with. 364^3. to no.

366^2. By halte. 366^4. And vsed.

368^2. That we be. 368^4. walked: by your.

369^2. on the. 369^4. I saye. 370^4. eyes.

371^1. hastely. 371^3. They were all in.

371^4. thyther blythe. 375^2. Standinge by.

376^1. toke *wanting*. 376^4. you.

377^4. Other shyft haue not we.

378^2. And good. 380^3. full *wanting*.

381^3. a. 381^4. I would geve it to the.

382^2. And deuyde it than did he.

382^3. Half he gaue to. 384^2. He hath sent.

384^3. to *wanting*. 384^4. and to.

385^1. brode seale. 385^2. lete me.

387^4. trusty tre. 388^1. he had.

388^4. fast was. 389^2. he can it.

389^3. wyght yemen. 389^4. Came runnyng.

391^2. pene. 392^1. hastely: dyght. 392^2. can.

394^4. Blessed may. 395^2. that thou.

395^3. maiest. 395^4. together by lente.

396^4. ben. 397^1. werd. 397^2. can the.

397^3. fifty space. 398^2. The.

$400^{1,2}$. A good buffet on his head bare, For that shalbe his fyne.

400^3. And those: fell to.

401^4. the lilly white hande.

404^2. And than he. 405^4. syr *wanting*.

406^1. the kyng. 407^2. largely. 407^4. folded.

408^1. geue. 408^4. a tall. 409^2. can wel.

409^4. Togeder they gan. 410^1. Stedfastly in.

411^2. they sawe. 411^4. wele.

412^1. than sayd Robin. 412^2. this trusty.

412^4. for me.

413^1. And yet sayd good Robin.

413^2. As good god do me. 413^3. aske the.

413^4. I it. 414^1. than *wanting*.

414^2. Thy peticion I graunt the.

414^3. So y^t thou wylt leue.

415^1. syr *wanting*. 415^2. There to.

417¹. But and I lyke not. 417². I wyll.

417⁴. I was. 418². now sell.

419³. To sel to me. 420¹. for good.

420³. And other. 421¹. his cote.

421³. had so ywys.

421⁴. They clothed them full soone.

422³. shal we. 422⁴. All this our kyng can.

423¹. The bent their bowes. 424². and as.

424³. And all they shot.

425⁴. kyng whan he did paye.

426¹. the kyng. 428¹. to the other can.

429¹. hastely. 430². them to come,

430³. sawe. 431⁴. of the. 432⁶. Robin hode.

433¹. Robin hode : dwelleth.

433³. That he had. 434². lay.

434³. and squyers. 435¹. all gone.

436⁴. wend. 437⁸. commended for.

438². Alas what shall I do. 439⁴. my.

440⁴. And there would I faene be.

441¹. might no time this seuen nightes.

441³. Neyther all this. 441⁴. eate nor.

442³. wolward haue I. 443³. nyghtes.

446³. I haue a lyttell lust. 447². can.

448³. wyght yemen. 448⁴. Came runnyng.

449⁴. Under the. 450¹. dwelleth.

450². yeres. 450³. Than for all.

452². Donkester. 452³. *wanting.*

452⁴. For euyll mot thou the.

Thus endeth the lyfe of Robyn hode.

g. *Title and heading as in* f.

1². free borne. 1⁴. yfound.

2². Whilst : on the. 3². leaned vpon a.

3³. stode *wanting.*

4¹. Scathlock, *and always.* 4². milners.

4³. was no. 5¹. bespake him. 5³. if you.

6¹. hym *wanting* : Robin hood. 6². I haue.

6³. that *wanting.* 6⁴. vnketh. 7¹. *wanting.*

7³. or some squire. 9². The other.

9³. was of. 9⁴. of all other. 10¹. he loued.

11³. what way we : gone. 11⁴. that *wanting.*

13¹. than *wanting.* 13³. you : husbandman.

13⁴. with the. 14¹. you. 14⁴. That would.

15¹. These *wanting.* 15⁴. ye *wanting.*

16¹. be *wanting.* 16². shall we.

17². goe with.

18¹. Now walke ye vp vnto the shore.

18⁴. By chance some may ye meet.

19³. him then. 20¹. went anon vnto.

21¹. looked in. 21². a deme.

21³. came there.

22¹. All drouflye, *perhaps (wrongly)* drouslye :
semblant.

22³. on the. 22⁴. The other.

23¹. ouer his eyes. 23⁴. on summers.

24¹. full *wanting.* 24⁴. you.

25³. you *wanting.* 26¹. is your. 26³. is a.

26⁴. haue I. 27². bretheren all three.

28¹. went that. 28³. eyes. 29¹. vnto the.

29². gan him. 29³. he did. 29⁴. downe on.

30². thou art. 30³. you *wanting.*

32³. right *wanting.* 33³. neuer so.

33⁴. was spread. 35⁴. that *wanting.*

36¹. I thanke thee knight then said.

36². when I haue.

36³. By God I was neuer so greedy.

37¹. ere you. 37². Me thinke is.

37³. dere *wanting.*

38³. Little John : Robin hood.

39¹. than *wanting.* 40¹. thou haue.

40⁴. I shall. 41⁴. Not any peny.

42⁴. halfe a. 43². full lowe.

43⁴. inowe *wanting.* 45¹. one word.

45³. thou wert : a *wanting.* 46¹. hast be.

46². stroke. 46⁴. With whores hast thou.

47¹. of these. 47³. An hundreth winters.

47⁴. haue be. 48¹. of it. 48². disgrast.

49¹. Within 2 or 3 yeares : said he.

49². *wanting.* 49³, 55³, 67³, *etc.* hundreth.

50²,³. *transposed.* 50². hath shapen.

50⁴. God it amend. 51¹. than *wanting.*

51². lost. 52³. winters. 53¹. Lancashire.

54¹. landes be. 56². What shall. 58¹. eyes.

58³. friends. 58⁴. ne *wanting.*

59². a one : knowe me. 59³. Whiles.

60⁴. had *wanting.*

61¹. *misprinted* ruthe they went.

61². Much also. 62¹. friends.

62². borrowes : will. 62³. than *wanting.*

62⁴. on a. 63¹. thy iest : than *wanting.*

63². I will. 63³. will God. 64¹. made me.

64². doth *misprinted for* both.

64³. me *wanting.* 65³. yf *wanting.*

65⁴. faileth. 67⁴. it well tolde.

68³. tolde forth. 68⁴. eighteene score.

69¹. little much. 69². grieued. 69⁴. fallen.

70⁴. To wrap. 71². much rich.

72². that well ymet it. 73¹. And of.

73². leped ouer. 73⁴. for *wanting.*

74¹. full *wanting* : laught.

74³. the better measure. 74⁴. By God it cost.

75¹. than *wanting.* 75². All vnto R.

75³. an. 75⁴. all his good.

76¹. God lend that it be. 78². clene.

78⁴. bring them. 79³. months.

79⁴. Vnder the. 81³. the *wanting.*

82². he thought.
83⁴. came.　84¹. spake the.
85⁸. vpon *wanting*.
86⁸. months : there *wanting*.　87¹. *wanting*.
87². land and fee.　87⁴, 95⁴. Disherited.
88⁸. a.　88⁴. lay it.　89². is his.　89⁴. sore.
90⁴. You doe him.　92⁴. pounds.
93¹. and high.　93². Stert.　93⁸. The high.
94². taken.　95⁸. comes.　96¹. not *wanting*.
96⁸. to them.　98¹. *wanting*.
100⁸. best corse.　100⁴. I *wanting*.
101¹. them to.　101⁸. come there.
102⁴. saluted.　103⁴. me my.
104². hath made.　105⁴. To desire of.
106⁴. defend me against.　109². *wanting*.
110⁸. thy lande.　111¹. then *wanting*.
112². Send.　113¹. on them.　113². *wanting*.
113⁴. Step thee : of the.　116¹. tournaments.
116². farre that.　117². a *wanting*.
117⁸. Or else : safely say.
118⁴. Ye get not my land so.
119¹. thousand pound more.
119². were thou.　121². that *wanting*.
121⁸. Hadst.
121⁴. I would haue rewarded thee.
122². royall cheere.　122⁴. gan.
123². to thee.　123⁴. on a.
124¹. and you.　124². held.
128⁸. had not.　129². is *wanting*.
129⁴. came on the.　130⁸. got.
132⁸. And nocked they were with.
133⁸. suite.　134⁸. And rode.
135¹. As he went vp a bridge was.
136¹⋅². *wanting*.　136⁸. with a.
137². in good.　137⁸. that *wanting*.
138⁸. friend bested.　138⁴. Yslaine.
139². where that.　139⁸. the yeoman.
139⁴. the loue.　140². him in feare.
141¹. all *wanting*.　142¹. markes.
142⁴. And drinke.　143². that the.
143⁴. the *wanting*.　146². alway claue.
146⁴. gan.　147⁴. euer I did see.
148¹. me thou.　148⁸. wast thou.
148⁴. wonning.　149¹. sir *wanting*.
149². al *wanting*.　150². Wilt.
151⁸. ye get leaue.　152⁸. to him anon.
153². He giue vs.　154¹. me *wanting*.
154⁴. he had yet.　155¹. befell.　155⁴. forgot.
156². the *wanting*.　156⁸. to *wanting*.
156⁴. me meat.　157². Fasting so long to.
157⁸. sir *wanting*.　157⁴. giue thou.
158¹. Shalt neither eat nor drinke.
159¹. was vncourteous.　159². on the.

160¹. a rappe.　160². backe yede nigh.
160⁸. liueth : winters.　160⁴. he still shall goe.
161². ope.　161⁸. there : a large.
161⁴. and wine.　162¹. you.
162². you liue this.　162⁴. shall ye.
163¹. eat and also drunke.　163⁸. in the.
164¹. my.　164². hine : *perhaps rightly*.
164⁸. an housholde for.
165¹. to God *wanting*.　165⁴. doe like well.
166¹. and a.　167¹. ful *wanting*.
167². toke *wanting*.　167⁸. for *wanting*.
168². well *wanting*.　169⁴. euer I saw yet.
170⁴. changed it should.　171⁴. we will.
173⁸. ylke day at.　174¹. They hied.
174². they could.　174⁸. full *wanting*.
174⁴. euery one.　175¹. the *wanting*.
175⁸. masers and.　175⁴. they none.
176¹. Also they.　176². and three.
176⁸. And hied them to.　176⁴. wood tree.
177⁸. And thou.
177⁴. Welcome thou art to me.
178¹. And so is that good yeoman.
178². That thou hast brought with.
179². He hath sent thee here.　179⁸. His cup.
180². And by.　181¹. there *wanting*.
181⁸. he ran *wanting*.　181⁴. at his.
182². hound.　182⁸. could his.
183¹. saue thee.　183². you saue.
183⁴. haue you.　184¹. haue now be in the.
185¹. I see.　185⁸. of *wanting*.
186¹. tindes be.　187¹. my.
187⁸. Buske thee.　188². A foote.
188⁸. afore.　188⁴. sir *wanting*.
189⁸. worth thee.　189⁴. nowe *wanting*.
190¹. Litell *wanting*.　191². well *wanting*.
192¹. Make good.　192². of *for* for.
192⁴. life is graunted.　193¹. had all.
193⁸. commanded.　193⁴. hose and shoone.
194¹. coate a pie.　194⁸. tooke.
195¹. wight yeomen.
195⁸. That they shall lie in that sorte.
196¹. lay that.　196⁴. sides doe smart.
197¹. chere *wanting*.　198⁴. dwell long.
199¹. All this.
200¹. Or I heere an other night lie.
200². I pray.　200⁸. my : to morne.
200⁴. *wanting*.　201⁸. the best.
202⁸. Thou shalt : wait : scath.　202⁴. nor by.
203². or else by.　204². home againe to.
204⁸. as *wanting*.　204⁴. was any man.
205². that he was gon.　206². But Robin said.
206⁴. pay.　207⁸. dare sweare.
209¹. walke *wanting* : into the.

209^8. And looke for some strange.
209^4. By chance you. 210^2. a *wanting*.
$210^{3,4}$. *as in* b, *excepting* goods *for* good.
211^2. in a fray. 212^1. went then vnto.
213^1. as they. 213^8. They were ware.
214^4. These monkes. 215^2. And bend we.
215^8. looke our.
216^1. hath but fifty and two man.
216^4. royall. 217^1. Bretheren.
218^2. Make you yonder priest. 220^1. An.
221^1. What hight your. 222^2. sore rue.
223^1. a bowe. 223^2. Ready.
223^4. ground he gan.
224^1. two and fiftie wight yeomen.
224^2. abode but. 225^8. Hode *wanting*.
226^1. downe. 226^2. when he did.
226^4. let it. 229^1. blowe we.
231^4. serued him. 232^8. you.
234^2. So mote I thriue of thee.
236^2. You neede not so to say.
236^8. hath brought it. 237^1. And *wanting*.
238^1. hast the mony brought.
238^8. eft againe. 238^4. need of. 240^1. my.
241^2. not denay. 242^1. made *wanting*.
242^8. I doe thee thanke. 243^2. Truth.
243^4. So mought I thriue and thee.
244^2. not take one. 244^8. hast need of.
244^4. shall I : to *wanting*.
245^1. finde more said. 245^8. spending-money.
245^4. Thereof I will haue.
246^4. penny let me. 247^1. John laid.
247^2. he *wanting*. 247^4. Eight hundreth.
248^8. true now. 248^4. cost.
249^2. Monke that. 251^1. and to.
251^8. need of. 252^1. haue need of any.
256^1. And what is in ye other coffer.
256^2. we must. 256^8. than *wanting*.
258^2. he *wanting*. 259^4. or D.
263^1. light from his. 263^2. can.
263^8. Right *for* So : down.
265^1. bespake good Robin : Hode *wanting*.
266^8. For *wanting*. 266^4. They would.
267^8. then said. 267^4. And that.
268^1. take no griefe. 268^8. did I helpe.
268^4. they put. 269^1. Now by my truth then.
269^2. For that knight thanke.
270^1. than *wanting*.
270^8. there is : also *wanting*.
271^1. then said. 271^8. her hie.
272^1. And I should take it twice.
272^2. for me. 273^1. And when.
273^2. He laughed and made. 274^4. this trusty.
275^1. do he said. 275^2. fethered.

275^8. the gentle.
276^2. My will doone that it be.
276^8. Go and fetch me foure : pounds.
277^8. buye thee. 278^8. shalt not.
278^4. Whilste I. 279^1. well for.
279^2. I did send. 280^2. of all his.
280^8. sitteth. 281^1. take. 281^2. wend.
283^8. And they that shoote all of the best.
283^4. The best. 284^1. all of the best.
284^8. of goodly. 285^1. he should.
285^8. and feathers. 285^4. the like.
286^2. his trusty.
286^8. ye ready you wight yeomen.
287^1. merry yeomen. 287^8. I shall know.
288^2. Their takles.
288^8. of *wanting* : wight yeomen.
289^8. were : archers. 289^4. shot.
291^1. The first. 291^4. the buttes where.
292^2. he claue. 292^4. lilly-white.
293^4. they would. 294^8. then was.
295^1. To him. 295^8. guift full.
295^4. then would. 296^2. A great horn gan he.
297^1. be to thee. 297^2. Thus cheering.
297^8. An other promise thou madest to me.
297^4. Within the greene.
298^1. But and I had thee there againe.
298^2. the trusty. 298^8. giue me.
299^8. was torne. 300^4. away beliue.
301^1. broke. 301^4. the *for* that.
302^1. he was. 302^2. on the knee.
303^2. you loued. 305^2. thou off.
305^8. wounds so wide and long.
305^4. That I after eat no bread.
306^1. that *wanting*. 306^2. wert slaine.
306^4. Though I had it all by me.
307^1. forbid that : Much then.
307^4. Depart.
308^8. he set. 310^2. of the.
311^8. be thou *wanting*.
312^1. I do thee thanke for.
$312^{2,8}$. And for. 313^1. all the.
314^4. the wall. 315^1. thee hite.
315^2. And sweare.
315^8. Thou shalt these twelue daies abide with
me.
316^2. Ready and. 316^4. gan.
317^2. hearken vnto the. 317^8. sheriffe began.
319^8. there : enemies. 319^4. all law.
320^1. what I. 320^4. a *wanting*.
321^2. doe ye. 321^8. you wit your.
322^8. he went. 323^4. noble were and.
324^1. He would : had. 324^8. He would.
325^1. said the. 325^4. will I.

326[1]. Goe home thou proude : sayde our kynge
    wanting.

326[2]. I you bid.   329[4]. Therefore had.

330[1]. there he.   330[3]. that gentle.

331[1]. Euer awaited that.   331[2]. of the.

331[4]. his hauke.

332[1]. To betray this gentle knight.

332[3]. him home.   332[4]. Ybound.

333[2]. on a tree.   333[3]. had rather then a.

333[4]. That Robin hood had hee.

334[1]. Then the lady the.   334[2]. a *wanting.*

335[1]. to the.   335[3]. There found she.

335[4]. merry menye.   336[3]. loue *for* sake.

337[1]. Let thou.   337[3]. bound.

338[2]. so *wanting.*   338[3]. thy lord ytake.

338[4]. The proud sheriffe then said she.

339.   he is not yet passed three miles,
    you may them ouertake :

340.   Vp then start good Robin,
    as a man that had been wake :
    Buske ye, my merry yeomen,
    for him that dyed on a tree.

341[2]. on a tree.

341[3]. And by him that all things maketh.

341[4]. shall dwell.   342[1]. ybent.   342[2]. More.

342[3]. they spared none.   343[2]. The knight.

343[3]. if ye may him ouertake.

343[4]. then shall he.   344[4]. gan.

345[2]. so fast.   345[4]. thy boote.

347[1]. full *wanting.*   347[2]. at his.

349[1]. the *for* thou.   349[2]. may thou.

349[3]. to thee.

350[3]. it on.   350[4]. driue.   351[2]. cut in.

353[2]. leasind.   354[4]. hode if.

355[1]. them *for* men.   356[2]. vnderstood.

356[4]. all the knights land.

357[1]. The compasse of.   357[2]. wend.

358[2]. many a one.   358[3]. finde any.

359[4]. eyes.   360[2]. vnto.   360[3]. He should.

360[4]. of *for* at.   361[2]. it with.   362[3]. O my.

364[2]. his best.   364[3]. to no.   366[2]. halt.

366[3]. he slew.   366[4]. And vsed.

368[2]. now be.   368[3]. by your.

368[4]. a monks.   369[1]. lodesman.

369[2]. on the.   369[4]. come at.

370[4]. eyes.   371[1]. hastily.

371[3]. They were all : monks weeds.

371[4]. thither blithe.   372[4]. to *wanting.*

374[1]. sommer.   374[3]. Vntill.   375[2]. by the.

376[3]. sayd *wanting.*   376[4]. you.

377[4]. Other shift haue not wee.

378[2]. good *for* gold.   380[3]. full *wanting.*

381[1]. I *wanting.*   381[3]. an.

381[4]. I would giue it to thee.

382[2]. And deuided it then did he.

382[3]. Halfe he gaue to.   382[4]. to *wanting.*

383[2]. Syr *wanting.*   384[2]. He hath sent.

385[1]. broad seale.   386[3]. be my.

387[1]. tyding.   387[4]. the trusty.

388[1]. he had.   388[4]. full was fast.

389[2]. gan it.   389[3]. wight yeomen.

389[4]. running *for* redy.   392[1]. hastily : dight.

392[2]. can.   393[4]. the good ale browne.

394[4]. may thou.   395[1]. I *for* we.

395[2]. Or that.   395[3]. maist.   395[4]. be lend.

396[4]. beene.   397[2]. can.

400[1,2]. A good buffet on his head beare for
    this shall be his fine.

400[3]. And those : fell in.   401[2]. claue.

401[4]. lilly white.   403[2]. Fore : freends faire.

403[3]. of *wanting.*   404[2]. then *for* thus.

405[4]. syr *wanting.*   406[1]. said y[e].

406[2]. be *for* by, *as often.*   407[2]. largely.

407[4]. folded.   408[4]. a tall frier.   409[2]. can.

409[4]. gan they meet.   410[2]. Stedfast in.

411[1]. the said !   411[2]. sawe.

412[1]. said Robin to.   412[2]. this trusty.

412[4]. and for mee.

413[1]. And yet said good R.

413[2]. As good God do me.   413[3]. aske thee.

413[4]. I it.   414[1]. than *wanting.*

414[2]. Thy petition I graunt thee.

414[3]. So that thou wilt leaue.

415[1]. syr *wanting.*   415[2]. There to dwell.

417[1]. But and I like not.   417[2]. I will.

417[4]. I was.   418[2]. nowe *wanting.*

419[3]. To sell.   421[1]. his cote.

421[3]. had so ywis.

421[4]. They clothed them full.   422[2]. the gray.

422[3]. Now shall we.   422[4]. All this : can.

423[1]. They bent their.   424[3]. And all they.

425[4]. king when he did pay.   426[1]. said the.

426[4]. I shot.   428[1]. togither can.

428[4]. leaueth not one.   429[1]. hastely.

430[2]. to come againe.   430[3]. saw our.

431[4]. of the.   432[3]. Robin hood.

433[1]. Robin hood dwelled.

433[3]. That he had.   434[3]. and squires.

434[4]. a great.   435[1]. gone.

435[4]. hym *wanting.*   436[2]. faire.

436[4]. wend.   437[3]. was commended for the.

438[2]. Alas what shall I doe.

440[4]. there would I faine be.

441[1]. might no time this : nights.

441[2]. one *for* ne.   441[3]. all this.

441[4]. nor *for* ne.   442[3]. haue I.

443³. nights. 446³. I haue a little lust for.
447². can. 448³. wight yeomen.
448⁴. running *for* redy. 449⁴. Vnder the.
450². yeeres. 450³. Then for dred.
452². Dankastre. 452³. *wanting*.

452⁴. For euill : they thee.
455³. good *wanting*.

Thus endeth the life of Robin hood

118

ROBIN HOOD AND GUY OF GISBORNE

'Guye of Gisborne,' Percy MS., p. 262 ; Hales and Furnivall, II, 227.

FIRST printed in the Reliques of Ancient English Poetry, 1765, I, 74, and, with less deviation from the original, in the fourth edition, 1794, I, 81. Reprinted from the Reliques in Ritson's Robin Hood, 1795, I, 114.

Robin Hood has had a dream that he has been beaten and bound by two yeomen, who have taken away his bow. He vows that he will have vengeance, and sets out in search of them with Little John. Robin and John shoot as they go, till they come to the greenwood and see a yeoman leaning against a tree, clad in a horse-hide, with head, tail, and mane. John proposes to go to the yeoman to ask his intentions. Robin considers this to be forward of John, and speaks so roughly to him that John parts company, and returns to Barnsdale. Things are in a bad way there : the sheriff of Nottingham has attacked Robin's band ; two have been slain ; Scarlett is flying, and the sheriff in pursuit with seven score men. John sends an arrow at the pursuers, which kills one of them ; but his bow breaks, and John is made prisoner and tied to a tree.

Robin learns from the man in horse-hide that he is seeking Robin Hood, but has lost his way. Robin offers to be his guide, and as they go through the wood proposes a shooting-match. Both shoot well, but Robin so much the better that the other breaks out into

expressions of admiration, and asks his name. Tell me thine first, says Robin. "I am Guy of Gisborne ; " "and I Robin Hood, whom thou long hast sought." They fight fiercely for two hours ; Robin stumbles and is hit, but invokes the Virgin's aid, leaps up and kills Guy. He nicks Guy's face so that it cannot be recognized, throws his own green gown over the body, puts on the horse-hide, and blows Guy's horn. The sheriff hears in the sound tidings that Guy has slain Robin, and thinks it is Guy that he sees coming in the horse-hide. The supposed Guy is offered anything that he will ask, but will take no reward but the boon of serving the knave as he has the master. Robin hies to Little John, looses him, and gives him Sir Guy's bow. The sheriff takes to flight, but cannot outrun John's arrow, which cleaves his heart.

The beginning, and perhaps the development, of the story might have been more lucid but for verses lost at the very start. Robin Hood dreams of two yeomen that beat and bind him, and goes to seek them, "in greenwood where they be." Sir Guy being one, the other person pointed at must of course be the sheriff of Nottingham (who seems to be beyond his beat in Yorkshire,* but outlaws can raise no questions of jurisdiction), in league with Sir Guy (a Yorkshireman, who has done

* The sheriff flees from Barnsdale "towards his house in Nottingham," in stanza 57. In fact, though these places are fifty miles apart, this ballad treats them as adjacent. See p. 50 f.

many a curst turn) for the capture or slaying of Robin. The dream simply foreshadows danger from two quarters. But Robin Hood is nowhere informed, as we are, that the sheriff is out against him with seven score men, has attacked his camp, and taken John prisoner. He knows nothing of this so far on as stanza 45³, where, after killing Guy, he says he will go to Barnsdale to see how his men are faring. Why then does he make his arrangements in stanzas 42-45², before he returns to Barnsdale, to pass himself off for Sir Guy? Plainly this device is adopted with the knowledge that John is a prisoner, and as a means of delivering him; which all that follows shows. Our embarrassment is the greater because we cannot point out any place in the story at which the necessary information could have been conveyed; there is no cranny where it could have been thrust in. It will not be enough, therefore, to suppose that verses have dropped out; there must also have been a considerable derangement of the story.

The abrupt transition from the introductory verses, 1, 2¹,², is found in Adam Bell, and the like occurs in other ballads.

A fragment of a dramatic piece founded on the ballad of Guy of Gisborne has been preserved in manuscript of the date of 1475, or earlier.* In this, a knight, not named, engages to take Robin Hood for the sheriff, and is promised gold and fee if he does. The knight accosts Robin, and proposes that they shoot together. They shoot, cast the stone, cast the axle-tree, perhaps wrestle (for the knight has a fall), then fight to the utterance. Robin has the mastery, cuts off the knight's head, and dons his clothes, putting the head into his hood. He hears from a man who comes along that Robin Hood and his men have been taken by the sheriff, and says, Let us go kill the sheriff. Then follows, out of the order of time, as is necessary in so brief a piece, the capture of Friar Tuck and the others by the sheriff. The variations from the Percy MS. story may be arbitrary, or may be those of another version of the ballad. The friar is called Tuck, as in the other play: see Robin Hood and the Potter.

'Syr sheryffë, for thy sakë,
Robyn Hode wull Y takë.'
'I wyll the gyffë golde and fee,
This behestë þou holdë me.'

'Robyn Hode, ffayre and fre,
Vndre this lyndë shotë we.'
'With the shote Y wyll,
Alle thy lustës to full fyll.'

'Have at the prykë!'
'And Y cleuë the stykë.'
'Late vs castë the stone.'
'I grauntë well, be Seynt John.'
'Late vs castë the exaltre.'
'Have a foote be-forë the!
Syr knyght, ye haue a falle.'
'And I the, Robyn, qwytë shall.'
'Owte on the! I blowë myn horne.'
'Hit warë better be vnborne.'
'Lat vs fyght at ottraunce.'
'He that fleth, God gyfe hym myschauncë!

---

* Formerly among Sir John Fenn's papers (for the history of which see Gairdner, Paston Letters, I, vii. ff); now in the possession of Mr William Aldis Wright, of Trinity College, Cambridge. The fragment, Mr Wright informs me, is written on a paper which was evidently the last half-leaf of a folio MS. On the back are various memoranda, and among them this: Itᵐ. Rᵈ of Rechard Wytway, penter [or peuter], for hes hosse rent, in full payment, lx [ix ?] s', the vij day of November, aº Ed. iiijᵗⁱ xv [1475]. The grammatical forms of themselves warrant our putting the composition further back. This interesting relic has already been printed in Notes and Queries, First Series, XII, 321, from a very incorrect copy made by Dr Stukely. It is given here from a transcript made for me by Henry Bradshaw, of honored memory. Mr Wright has compared this with the original, and given me the history of the paper, so far as known.

This paper, as far as we can see, came into Sir John Fenn's hands in company with the Paston Letters. In a letter of the date 1473, Sir John Paston writes: W. Woode, whyche promysed . . . he wold never goo fro me, and ther uppon I have kepyd hym thys iii yer to pleye Seynt Jorge, and Robyn Hod and the Shryff off Nottyngham, and now, when I wolde have good horse, he is gone into Bernysdale, and I without a keeper. Fenn, Original Letters, etc., 1787, II, 134, cited by Ritson; Gairdner, Paston Letters, III, 89. The play cited above might be called one of Robin Hood and the Sheriff of Nottingham, and may possibly have been the very one in which William Wood was used to perform, before he went "into Barnysdale," that is, ran away from service.

Now I hauë the maystry herë,
Off I smytë this sory swyrë.
This knyghtys clothis wolle I werë,
And in my hode his hede woll berë.
Welle mete, felowë myn :
What herst þou of gode Robyn ? '
' Robyn Hode and his menye
With the sheryff takyn be.'
' Sette on footë with gode wyll,
And the sheryffë wull we kyll.'

' Beholde wele Ffrere Tukë,
Howe he dothe his bowë plukë.
Ʒeld yow, syrs, to the sheryff[ë],
Or elles shall your bowës clyffë.'
' Nowe we be bownden alle in samë ;
Frere [T]uke, þis is no gamë.'
' Co[m]e þou forth, þou fals outlawë :
þou shall b[e] hangyde and ydrawë.'
' Now, allas ! what shall we doo !
We [m]ostë to the prysone goo.'
' Opy[n] the yatis faste anon,
An[d] [d]oo theis thevys ynnë gon.' *

Ritson pointed out that Guy of Gisborne is named with " other worthies, it is conjectured of a similar stamp," in a satirical piece of William Dunbar, ' Of Sir Thomas Norray.'

Was never vyld Robeine wnder bewch,
Nor ʒet Roger of Clekkinsklewch,
  So bauld a bairne as he ;
Gy of Gysburne, na Allan Bell,
Nor Simones sonnes of Quhynfell,
  At schot war nevir so slie.†
      Ed. John Small, Part II, p. 193.

Gisburne is in the West Riding of Yorkshire, on the borders of Lancashire, seven miles from Clitheroe.

He that had neither beene a kithe nor kin
  Might haue seene a full fayre sight, 36[1,2],

anticipates Byron : —

By heaven, it is a splendid sight to see,
  For one who hath no friend, no brother, there.
        Childe Harold, I, 40[1,2].

Translated, after Percy's Reliques, by Bodmer, II, 128 ; La Motte Fouqué, in Büsching's Erzählungen, p. 241 ; Doenniges, p. 174 ; Anastasius Grün, p. 103 ; Cesare Cantù, Documenti, etc., p. 799 (the first thirty-seven stanzas).

———◆———

1 WHEN shawes beene sheene, and shradds full
      fayre,
    And leeues both large and longe,
  Itt is merrry, walking in the fayre fforrest,
    To heare the small birds songe.

2 The woodweele sang, and wold not cease,
    Amongst the leaues a lyne :
  And it is by two wight yeomen,
    By deare God, that I meane.

    *   *   *   *   *

3 ' Me thought they did mee beate and binde,
    And tooke my bow mee froe ;
  If I bee Robin a-liue in this lande,
    I 'le be wrocken on both them towe.'

4 ' Sweauens are swift, master,' quoth Iohn,
    ' As the wind that blowes ore a hill ;
  Ffor if itt be neuer soe lowde this night,
    To-morrow it may be still.'

5 ' Buske yee, bowne yee, my merry men all,
    Ffor Iohn shall goe with mee ;
  For I 'le goe seeke yond wight yeomen
    In greenwood where the bee.'

6 Thé cast on their gowne of greene,
    A shooting gone are they,
  Vntill they came to the merry greenwood,
    Where they had gladdest bee ;
  There were the ware of [a] wight yeoman,
    His body leaned to a þree.

* The [d]oo in the last line is not quite certain. I am not sure that the parts are always rightly assigned in the third dialogue.
† Norray should be Nornee, or Norny, the name of a court fool. He is mentioned in James IV's Treasurer's Accounts, 1503-12. See Laing's Dunbar, II, 307 f. Allan Bell being sly at shot, it is probable that Allan is miswritten in the MS. for Adam.

7 A sword and a dagger he wore by his side,
    Had beene many a mans bane,
   And he was cladd in his capull-hyde,
    Topp, and tayle, and mayne.

8 'Stand you still, master,' quoth Litle Iohn,
    'Vnder this trusty tree,
   And I will goe to yond wight yeoman,
    To know his meaning trulye.'

9 'A, Iohn, by me thou setts noe store,
    And that's a ffarley thinge;
   How offt send I my men beffore,
    And tarry my-selfe behinde?

10 'It is noe cunning a knaue to ken,
    And a man but heare him speake;
   And itt were not for bursting of my bowe,
    Iohn, I wold thy head breake.'

11 But often words they breeden bale,
    That parted Robin and Iohn;
   Iohn is gone to Barn[e]sdale,
    The gates he knowes eche one.

12 And when hee came to Barnesdale,
    Great heauinesse there hee hadd;
   He ffound two of his fellowes
    Were slaine both in a slade,

13 And Scarlett a ffoote flyinge was,
    Ouer stockes and stone,
   For the sheriffe with seuen score men
    Fast after him is gone.

14 'Yett one shoote I 'le shoote,' sayes Litle Iohn,
    'With Crist his might and mayne;
   I 'le make yond fellow that flyes soe fast
    To be both glad and ffaine.

15 Iohn bent vp a good veiwe bow,
    And ffetteled him to shoote;
   The bow was made of a tender boughe,
    And fell downe to his foote.

16 'Woe worth thee, wicked wood,' sayd Litle
     Iohn,
    'That ere thou grew on a tree!
   Ffor this day thou art my bale,
    My boote when thou shold bee!'

17 This shoote it was but looselye shott,
    The arrowe flew in vaine,

And it mett one of the sheriffes men;
 Good William a Trent was slaine.

18 It had beene better for William a Trent
    To hange vpon a gallowe
   Then for to lye in the greenwoode,
    There slaine with an arrowe.

19 And it is sayd, when men be mett,
    Six can doe more then three:
   And they haue tane Litle Iohn,
    And bound him ffast to a tree.

20 'Thou shalt be drawen by dale and downe,'
     quoth the sheriffe,
    'And hanged hye on a hill:'
   'But thou may ffayle,' quoth Litle Iohn,
    'If itt be Christs owne will.'

21 Let vs leaue talking of Litle Iohn,
    For hee is bound fast to a tree,
   And talke of Guy and Robin Hood,
    In the green woode where they bee.

22 How these two yeomen together they mett,
    Vnder the leaues of lyne,
   To see what marchandise they made
    Euen at that same time.

23 'Good morrow, good fellow,' quoth Sir Guy;
    'Good morrow, good ffellow,' quoth hee;
   'Methinkes by this bow thou beares in thy
     hand,
    A good archer thou seems to bee.'

24 'I am wilfull of my way,' quoth Sir Guye,
    'And of my morning tyde:'
   'I 'le lead thee through the wood,' quoth Robin,
    'Good ffellow, I 'le be thy guide.'

25 'I seeke an outlaw,' quoth Sir Guye,
    'Men call him Robin Hood;
   I had rather meet with him vpon a day
    Then forty pound of golde.'

26 'If you tow mett, itt wold be seene whether
     were better
    Afore yee did part awaye;
   Let vs some other pastime find,
    Good ffellow, I thee pray.

27 'Let vs some other masteryes make,
    And wee will walke in the woods euen;

Wee may chance mee[t] with Robin Hoode
  Att some vnsett steven.'

28 They cutt them downe the summer shroggs
    Which grew both vnder a bryar,
    And sett them three score rood in twinn,
    To shoote the prickes full neare.

29 'Leade on, good ffellow,' sayd Sir Guye,
    ' Lead on, I doe bidd thee : '
    ' Nay, by my faith,' quoth Robin Hood,
    ' The leader thou shalt bee.'

30 The first good shoot that Robin ledd
    Did not shoote an inch the pricke ffroe ;
    Guy was an archer good enoughe,
    But he cold neere shoote soe.

31 The second shoote Sir Guy shott,
    He shott within the garlande ;
    But Robin Hoode shott it better then hee,
    For he cloue the good pricke-wande.

32 'Gods blessing on thy heart!' sayes Guye,
    ' Goode ffellow, thy shooting is goode ;
    For an thy hart be as good as thy hands,
    Thou were better then Robin Hood.

33 'Tell me thy name, good ffellow,' quoth Guy,
    ' Vnder the leaues of lyne : '
    ' Nay, by my faith,' quoth good Robin,
    ' Till thou haue told me thine.'

34 ' I dwell by dale and downe,' quoth Guye,
    ' And I haue done many a curst turne ;
    And he that calles me by my right name
    Calles me Guye of good Gysborne.'

35 'My dwelling is in the wood,' sayes Robin ;
    ' By thee I set right nought ;
    My name is Robin Hood of Barnesdale,
    A ffellow thou has long sought.'

36 He that had neither beene a kithe nor kin
    Might haue seene a full fayre sight,
    To see how together these yeomen went,
    With blades both browne and bright.

37 To haue seene how these yeomen together
        foug[ht],
    Two howers of a summers day ;
    Itt was neither Guy nor Robin Hood
    That ffettled them to flye away.

38 Robin was reacheles on a roote,
    And stumbled at that tyde,
    And Guy was quicke and nimble with-all,
    And hitt him ore the left side.

39 'Ah, deere Lady!' sayd Robin Hoode,
    ' Thou art both mother and may !
    I thinke it was neuer mans destinye
    To dye before his day.'

40 Robin thought on Our Lady deere,
    And soone leapt vp againe,
    And thus he came with an awkwarde stroke ;
    Good Sir Guy hee has slayne.

41 He tooke Sir Guys head by the hayre,
    And sticked itt on his bowes end :
    ' Thou hast beene traytor all thy liffe,
    Which thing must haue an ende.'

42 Robin pulled forth an Irish kniffe,
    And nicked Sir Guy in the fface,
    That hee was neuer on a woman borne
    Cold tell who Sir Guye was.

43 Saies, Lye there, lye there, good Sir Guye,
    And with me be not wrothe ;
    If thou haue had the worse stroakes at my
        hand,
    Thou shalt haue the better cloathe.

44 Robin did off his gowne of greene,
    Sir Guye hee did it throwe ;
    And hee put on that capull-hyde,
    That cladd him topp to toe.

45 ' The bowe, the arrowes, and litle horne,
    And with me now I 'le beare ;
    Ffor now I will goe to Barn[e]sdale,
    To see how my men doe ffare.'

46 Robin sett Guyes horne to his mouth,
    A lowd blast in it he did blow ;
    That beheard the sheriffe of Nottingham,
    As he leaned vnder a lowe.

47 ' Hearken ! hearken ! ' sayd the sheriffe,
    ' I heard noe tydings but good ;
    For yonder I heare Sir Guyes horne blowe,
    For he hath slaine Robin Hoode.

48 ' For yonder I heare Sir Guyes horne blow,
    Itt blowes soe well in tyde,

For yonder comes *that* wighty yeoman,
　Cladd in his capull-hyde.

49 'Come hither, thou good S*i*r Guy,
　　Aske of mee what thou wilt haue:'
　'I'le none of thy gold,' sayes Robin Hood,
　　'Nor I'le none of itt haue.

50 'But now I haue slaine the m*aster*,' he sayd,
　　'Let me goe strike the knaue;
　This is all the reward I aske,
　　Nor noe other will I haue.'

51 'Thou art a madman,' said the shiriffe,
　　'Thou sholdest haue had a knights ffee;
　Seeing thy asking [hath] beene soe badd,
　　Well granted it shall be.'

52 But Litle Iohn heard his m*aster* speake,
　　Well he knew *that* was his steuen;
　'Now shall I be loset,' q*u*oth Litle Iohn,
　　'With Christs might in heauen.'

53 But Robin hee hyed him towards Litle Iohn,
　　Hee thought hee wold loose him beliue;
　The sheriffe and all his companye
　　Fast after him did driue.

54 'Stand abacke! stand abacke!' sayd Robin;
　　'Why draw you mee soe neere?
　Itt was neu*er* the vse in our countrye
　　One's shrift another shold heere.'

55 But Robin pulled forth an Irysh kniffe,
　　And losed Iohn hand and ffoote,
　And gaue him S*i*r Guyes bow in his hand,
　　And bade it be his boote.

56 But Iohn tooke Guyes bow in his hand —
　　His arrowes were rawstye by the roote —;
　The sherriffe saw Litle Iohn draw a bow
　　And ffettle him to shoote.

57 Towards his house in Nottingam
　　He ffled full fast away,
　And soe did all his companye,
　　Not one behind did stay.

58 But he cold neither soe fast goe,
　　Nor away soe fast runn,
　But Litle Iohn, with an arrow broade,
　　Did cleaue his heart in twinn.

———♦———

1¹. When shales beeene.　1⁴. birds singe.
2¹. woodweete.　2⁸. by 2.　11¹. ball.
12⁸. 2 of.　13⁸. with 7.
15¹. veiwe.　*The word is partly pared away.*
15⁴. footee.　18¹. a w*illia*m.　19². 6 can ... 3.
21⁴. in they green.　22¹. these 2.

23⁴. archer: *an* e *has been added at the end.*
　Furnivall.
25⁴. 40ꭵꭵ.
27⁴. *a stroke before the* v *of steven. Furnivall.*
28⁸. 3 score.　31¹. 2ᵈ.　32⁸. for on.
37². 2 howers.　44¹. did on.　55¹. kniffee.

———

119

ROBIN HOOD AND THE MONK

a. MS. of about 1450: Cambridge University Library, Ff. 5. 48, fol. 128 b.　**b.** One leaf of a MS. of the same age, containing stanzas 69⁸–72, 77²–80² : Bagford Ballads, vol. i, art. 6, British Museum.

———♦———

a is printed from the manuscript in Jamieson's Popular Ballads, II, 54, 1806; Hartshorne's Ancient Metrical Tales, p. 179, 1829; Ritson's Robin Hood, ed. 1832, II, 221, collated by Sir Frederic Madden. Here printed from a fresh transcript, carefully revised by Rev. Professor Skeat.

On a bright Whitsuntide morning, Robin Hood, not having "seen his Savior" for more than a fortnight, resolves to go to mass at Nottingham. Much advises that he take twelve yeomen with him for safety, but Robin will have only Little John. They improve the time, while on their way to church, by shooting for a wager. Robin scornfully offers John three to one; but John nevertheless wins five shillings of his master, at which Robin loses his temper, and strikes John. John will be his man no more, and returns to the wood. Robin, sorry for this consequence of his bad humor, goes on to Nottingham alone. A monk at Saint Mary's church recognizes Robin, and gives information to the sheriff, who comes with a large force to arrest the king's felon. Robin kills or wounds many of the posse, but his sword breaks upon the sheriff's head. In some way which we do not learn, owing to verses lost,[*] Robin's men hear that their master has been taken. They are all out of their wits but Little John. Mild Mary, he tells his comrades, will never forsake one who has been so long devoted to her, and he, with her help, will see to the monk. The next day John and Much waylay the monk, who is carrying letters to the king conveying the tidings of Robin's capture; they kill him, take the letters, and carry them to the king themselves. The king gives them twenty pounds for their news, and makes them yeomen of the crown; he sends his privy seal to the sheriff by John, commanding that Robin Hood shall be brought to him unhurt. The sheriff, upon receiving the seal, makes John good cheer, and goes to bed heavy with wine. John and Much, while the sheriff is sleeping,

make their way to the jail. John rouses the porter, runs him through,[†] and takes his keys, unbinds Robin Hood, and puts a good sword in his hand; they leap from the wall where it is lowest. The sheriff finds the jailer dead in the morning, and searches the town for his captive; but Robin is in merry Sherwood. Farewell now, says John; I have done thee a good turn for an ill. Nay, says Robin, I make thee master of my men and me. So shall it never be, answers John; I care only to be a comrade. The king hears that Robin has escaped, and that the sheriff is afraid to show himself. Little John has beguiled us both, says the king. I made them yeomen of the crown, and gave them pay with my own hand! Little John loves Robin Hood better than he does us. Say no more. John has beguiled us all.

Too much could not be said in praise of this ballad, but nothing need be said. It is very perfection in its kind; and yet we have others equally good, and beyond doubt should have had more, if they had been written down early, as this was, and had not been left to the chances of tradition. Even writing would not have saved all, but writing has saved this (in large part), and in excellent form.

The landscape background of the first two stanzas has been often praised, and its beauty will never pall. It may be called landscape or prelude, for both eyes and ears are addressed, and several others of these woodland ballads have a like symphony or setting: Adam Bell, Robin Hood and the Potter, Guy of Gisborne, even the much later ballad of The Noble Fisherman. It is to be observed that the story of the outlaw Fulk Fitz Warine, which has other traits in common with Robin Hood ballads, begins somewhat after the same fashion.[‡]

---

* The gap at 30[2] occurs between two pages, and is peculiarly regrettable. The former reading of "Robyns men" in 30[1] made matters much worse, since there was no way of accounting for the appearance of his men at this point. We must suppose that some one of Robin's many friends carries the news of his capture to his band, and not simply that; with this there must have come information that their leader was to be held to await knowledge of the king's pleasure, otherwise delay would be dangerous, and summary measures for his deliverance be required.

† The porter or warden, in such cases, may commonly look to have his neck wrung, to be thrown over the wall, into a well, etc.: compare Adam Bell, st. 65; Jock o the Side, sts 13, 14; the Tale of Gamelyn, Skeat, v. 303–05; Fulk Fitz Warine, Wright, pp 44, 82 f; King Horn. ed. Wissmann, vv 1097–99; Romance de don Gaiferos, F. Wolf, Ueber eine Sammlung spanischer Romanzen, p. 76, Wolf y Hofmann, Primavera, II, 148, No 174; etc.

‡ En le temps de Averyl e May, quant les prees e les herbes reverdissent, et chescune chose vivaunte recovre ver-

Robin Hood's devotion to the Virgin, st. 34, is a feature which reappears in Robin Hood and the Potter, Guy of Gisborne, Robin Hood and the Curtal Friar, and above all in The Gest. His profound piety, as evinced in stanzas 6, 7, and again in 8, 9 of The Gest, is commemorated by Bower in a passage in the Scotichronicon, of about the same date as the manuscript of the present ballad (1450), which we have every reason to assume to be derived from a lost ballad.* Robin Hood had mass regularly sung at Barnsdale, nor would he suffer the office to be interrupted for the most pressing occasion. (We know from The Gest, st. 440, that he had a pretty chapel there, dedicated to Mary Magdalen.) One day, while so engaged, he was informed that the sheriff and his men, old foes of his, had tracked him to the very retired part of the forest where the service was going on, and was urged to fly with his best speed. This, for reverence of the sacrament, which he was then most devoutly adoring, he utterly refused to do, and then, while the rest were fearing for their lives, trusting in him whom he worshipped, fell upon his enemies, with a few of his followers who had rallied to him, and easily put them to rout. Enriched with their spoil and ransom, he was led to hold the ministers of the church (but apparently not " bishops and archbishops," Gest, st. 15) and masses in greater veneration than ever, mindful of the common saw, God hears the man who often hears the mass.†

There is a general resemblance between the rescue of Robin Hood in stanzas 61–81 and that of William of Cloudesly in Adam Bell,

56–94, and the precaution suggested by Much in the eighth stanza corresponds to the warning given by Adam in the eighth stanza of the other ballad. There is a verbal agreement in stanzas 71 of the first and 66 of the second.‡ Such agreements or repetitions are numerous in the Robin Hood ballads, and in other traditional ballads, where similar situations occur.

Robin Hood's rescue of Little John, in Guy of Gisborne, after quarrelling with him on a fanciful provocation, is a partial offset for Little John's heart-stirring generosity in this ballad. We have already had several cases of ballads in which the principal actors exchange parts.

That portion of ' Robin Hood's Death ' in which Robin Hood gets angry with Scarlet, and shoots with Little John on his way to be let blood, may have been transferred, at least in part, from Robin Hood and the Monk.

It is hardly worth the while to ask whether the monk in this ballad is the same who is pillaged in The Gest. So rational a suggestion as that more than one monk must have fallen into Robin's hands, in the course of his long and lucrative career, may not be conclusive, but we may rest certain that there were many Robin Hood ballads besides the few old ones which have come down to us; and if so, there would be many variations upon so agreeable a topic as the depleting of overstocked friars.

Translated, after Jamieson, by Grundtvig, Engelske og skotske Folkeviser, p. 148, No 24; by Anastasius Grün, p. 89.

tue, beaute e force, les mountz e les valeys retentissent des douce chauntz des oseylouns, e les cuers de chescune gent, pur la beaute du temps e la sesone, mountent en haut e s'enjolyvent, etc. : Wright, Warton Club, 1855, p. 1; Stevenson, Radulphi de Coggeshall Chronicon Anglicanum, etc., p. 277.

   * Already cited at p. 41. Bower wrote 1441–47, and died 1449 : Skene, Johannis de Fordun Chronica, pp xv, xli.

      † Par cest exemple bien veons
        Que li dous Deux en qui creons
        Ame et chierist et honneure

      Celui qui volentiers demeure
        Pour oïr messe en sainte eglise, etc.

   ' Du chevalier qui ooit la messe, et Notre-Dame estoit pour lui au tournoiement,' Barbazan et Méon, Fabliaux, 1808, I, 86.

   ‡ These resemblances are noted by Fricke, Die Robin Hood Balladen, a dissertation, reprinted in Archiv für das Studium der neueren Sprachen (vol. 69), in which the relations of the ballads in question are discussed with sagacity and vigilance.

1 In somer, when þe shawes be sheyne,
  And leves be large and long,
  Hit is full mery in feyre foreste
    To here þe foulys song :

2 To se þe dere draw to þe dale,
  And leve þe hilles hee,
  And shadow hem in þe levës grene,
    Vnder the grene-wode tre.

3 Hit befel on Whitsontide,
    Erly in a May mornyng,
  The son vp feyre can shyne,
    And the briddis mery can syng.

4 'This is a mery mornyng,' seid Litull
    John,
  'Be hym þat dyed on tre ;
  A more mery man þen I am one
    Lyves not in Cristianté.

5 'Pluk vp þi hert, my dere mayster,'
    Litull John can sey,
  'And thynk hit is a full fayre tyme
    In a mornyng of May.'

6 'Ȝe, on thyng greves me,' seid Robyn,
    'And does my hert mych woo ;
  Þat I may not no solem day
    To mas nor matyns goo.

7 'Hit is a fourtnet and more,' seid he,
    'Syn I my sauyour see ;
  To day wil I to Notyngham,' seid Robyn,
    'With þe myght of mylde Marye.'

8 Than spake Moche, þe mylner sun,
    Euer more wel hym betyde !
  'Take twelue of þi wyght ȝemen,
    Well weppynd, be þi side.
  Such on wolde þi selfe slon,
    Þat twelue dar not abyde.'

9 'Of all my mery men,' seid Robyn,
    'Be my feith I wil non haue,
  But Litull John shall beyre my bow,
    Til þat me list to drawe.'

10 'Þou shall beyre þin own,' seid Litull Jon,
    'Maister, and I wyl beyre myne,
  And we well shete a peny,' seid Litull Jon,
    'Vnder þe grene-wode lyne.'

11 'I wil not shete a peny,' seyd Robyn Hode,
    'In feith, Litull John, with the,
  But euer for on as þou shetis,' seide Robyn,
    'In feith I holde þe thre.'

12 Thus shet þei forth, þese ȝemen too,
    Bothe at buske and brome,
  Til Litull John wan of his maister
    Fiue shillings to hose and shone.

13 A ferly strife fel þem betwene,
    As they went bi the wey ;
  Litull John seid he had won fiue shillings,
    And Robyn Hode seid schortly nay.

14 With þat Robyn Hode lyed Litul Jon,
    And smote hym with his hande ;
  Litul Jon waxed wroth þerwith,
    And pulled out his bright bronde.

15 'Were þou not my maister,' seid Litull John,
    'Þou shuldis by hit ful sore ;
  Get þe a man wher þou w[ilt],
    For þou getis me no more.'

16 Þen Robyn goes to Notyngham,
    Hym selfe mornyng allone,
  And Litull John to mery Scherwode,
    The pathes he knew ilkone.

17 Whan Robyn came to Notyngham,
    Sertenly withouten layn,
  He prayed to God and myld Mary
    To bryng hym out saue agayn.

18 He gos in to Seynt Mary chirch,
    And kneled down before the rode ;
  Alle þat euer were þe church within
    Beheld wel Robyn Hode.

19 Beside hym stod a gret-hedid munke,
    I pray to God woo he be !
  Fful sone he knew gode Robyn,
    As sone as he hym se.

20 Out at þe durre he ran,
    Fful sone and anon ;
  Alle þe ȝatis of Notyngham
    He made to be sparred euerychon.

21 'Rise vp,' he seid, 'þou prowde schereff,
    Buske þe and make þe bowne ;

I haue spyed þe kynggis felon,
   Ffor sothe he is in þis town.

22 'I haue spyed þe false felon,
   As he stondis at his masse;
   Hit is long of þe,' seide þe munke,
   'And euer he fro vs passe.

23 'þis traytur name is Robyn Hode,
   Vnder þe grene-wode lynde;
   He robbyt me onys of a hundred pound,
   Hit shalle neuer out of my mynde.'

24 Vp þen rose þis prowde shereff,
   And radly made hym ȝare;
   Many was þe moder son
   To þe kyrk with hym can fare.

25 In at þe durres þei throly thrast,
   With staves ful gode wone;
   'Alas, alas!' seid Robyn Hode,
   'Now mysse I Litull John.'

26 But Robyn toke out a too-hond sworde,
   þat hangit down be his kne;
   þer as þe schereff and his men stode thyckust,
   Thedurwarde wolde he.

27 Thryes thorowout þem he ran þen,
   For soþe as I yow sey,
   And woundyt mony a moder son,
   And twelue he slew þat day.

28 His sworde vpon þe schireff hed
   Sertanly he brake in too;
   'þe smyth þat þe made,' seid Robyn,
   'I pray to God wyrke hym woo!

29 'Ffor now am I weppynlesse,' seid Robyn,
   'Alasse! agayn my wylle;
   But if I may fle þese traytors fro,
   I wot þei wil me kyll.'

30 Robyn in to the churchë ran,
   Throout hem euerilkon,

     *   *   *   *   *

31 Sum fel in swonyng as þei were dede,
   And lay stil as any stone;
   Non of theym were in her mynde
   But only Litull Jon.

32 'Let be your rule,' seid Litull Jon,
   'Ffor his luf þat dyed on tre,
   Ȝe þat shulde be duȝty men;
   Het is gret shame to se.

33 'Oure maister has bene hard bystode
   And ȝet scapyd away;
   Pluk vp your hertis, and leve þis mone,
   And harkyn what I shal say.

34 'He has seruyd Oure Lady many a day,
   And ȝet wil, securly;
   þerfor I trust in hir specialy
   No wyckud deth shal he dye.

35 'þerfor be glad,' seid Litul John,
   'And let þis mournyng be;
   And I shal be þe munkis gyde,
   With þe myght of mylde Mary.

36 .   .   .   .   .   .
   'We will go but we too;
   And I mete hym,' seid Litul John,

    .   .   .   .   .

37 'Loke þat ȝe kepe wel owre tristil-tre,
   Vnder þe levys smale,
   And spare non of this venyson,
   þat gose in thys vale.'

38 Fforþe þen went these ȝemen too,
   Litul John and Moche on fere,
   And lokid on Moch emys hows,
   þe hye way lay full nere.

39 Litul John stode at a wyndow in þe mornyng,
   And lokid forþ at a stage;
   He was war wher þe munke came ridyng,
   And with hym a litul page.

40 'Be my feith,' seid Litul John to Moch,
   'I can þe tel tithyngus gode;
   I se wher þe munke cumys rydyng,
   I know hym be his wyde hode.'

41 They went in to the way, þese ȝemen boþe,
   As curtes men and hende;
   þei spyrred tithyngus at þe munke,
   As they hade bene his frende.

42 'Ffro whens come ȝe?' seid Litull Jon,
   'Tel vs tithyngus, I yow pray,

Off a false owtlay, [callid Robyn Hode,]
Was takyn ȝisterday.

43 'He robbyt me and my felowes boþe
Of twenti marke in serten;
If þat false owtlay be takyn,
Ffor soþe we wolde be fayn.'

44 'So did he me,' seid þe munke,
'Of a hundred pound and more;
I layde furst hande hym apon,
ȝe may thonke me þerfore.'

45 'I pray God thanke you,' seid Litull John,
'And we wil when we may;
We wil go with you, with your leve,
And bryng yow on your way.

46 'Ffor Robyn Hode hase many a wilde felow,
I tell you in certen;
If þei wist ȝe rode þis way,
In feith ȝe shulde be slayn.'

47 As þei went talking be þe way,
The munke and Litull John,
John toke þe munkis horse be þe hede,
Fful sone and anon.

48 Johne toke þe munkis horse be þe hed,
Ffor soþe as I yow say;
So did Much þe litull page,
Ffor he shulde not scape away.

49 Be þe golett of þe hode
John pulled þe munke down;
John was nothyng of hym agast,
He lete hym falle on his crown.

50 Litull John was so[re] agrevyd,
And drew owt his swerde in hye;
This munke saw he shulde be ded,
Lowd mercy can he crye.

51 'He was my maister,' seid Litull John,
'þat þou hase browȝt in bale;
Shalle þou neuer cum at our kyng,
Ffor to telle hym tale.'

52 John smote of þe munkis hed,
No longer wolde he dwell;
So did Moch þe litull page,
Ffor ferd lest he wolde tell.

53 þer þei beryed hem boþe,
In nouþer mosse nor lyng,
And Litull John and Much infere
Bare þe letturs to oure kyng.

54 .   .   .   .   .   .
He knelid down vpon his kne:
'God ȝow saue, my lege lorde,
Ihesus yow saue and se!

55 'God yow saue, my lege kyng!'
To speke John was full bolde;
He gaf hym þe letturs in his hond,
The kyng did hit vnfold.

56 þe kyng red þe letturs anon,
And seid, So mot I the,
þer was neuer ȝoman in mery Inglond
I longut so sore to se.

57 'Wher is þe munke þat þese shuld haue
brouȝt?'
Oure kyng can say:
'Be my trouth,' seid Litull John,
'He dyed after þe way.'

58 þe kyng gaf Moch and Litul Jon
Twenti pound in sertan,
And made þeim ȝemen of þe crown,
And bade þeim go agayn.

59 He gaf John þe seel in hand,
The sheref for to bere,
To bryng Robyn hym to,
And no man do hym dere.

60 John toke his leve at oure kyng,
þe sothe as I yow say;
þe next way to Notyngham
To take, he ȝede þe way.

61 Whan John came to Notyngham
The ȝatis were sparred ychon;
John callid vp þe porter,
He answerid sone anon.

62 'What is þe cause,' seid Litul Jon,
'þou sparris þe ȝates so fast?'
'Because of Robyn Hode,' seid [þe] porter,
'In depe prison is cast.

63 'John and Moch and Wyll Scathlok,
Ffor sothe as I yow say,

þei slew oure men vpon our wallis,
  And sawten vs euery day.'

64 Litull John spyrred after þe schereff,
  And sone he hym fonde ;
  He oppyned þe kyngus priue seell,
  And gaf hym in his honde.

65 Whan þe scheref saw þe kyngus seell,
  He did of his hode anon :
  ' Wher is þe munke þat bare þe letturs ? '
  He seid to Litull John.

66 ' He is so fayn of hym,' seid Litul John,
  ' Ffor soþe as I yow say,
  He has made hym abot of Westmynster,
  A lorde of þat abbay.'

67 The scheref made John gode chere,
  And gaf hym wyne of the best ;
  At nyȝt þei went to her bedde,
  And euery man to his rest.

68 When þe scheref was on slepe,
  Dronken of wyne and ale,
  Litul John and Moch for soþe
  Toke þe way vnto þe jale.

69 Litul John callid vp þe jayler,
  And bade hym rise anon ;
  He seyd Robyn Hode had brokyn prison,
  And out of hit was gon.

70 The porter rose anon sertan,
  As sone as he herd John calle ;
  Litul John was redy with a swerd,
  And bare hym to þe walle.

71 ' Now wil I be porter,' seid Litul John,
  ' And take þe keyes in honde : '
  He toke þe way to Robyn Hode,
  And sone he hym vnbonde.

72 He gaf hym a gode swerd in his hond,
  His hed [ther]with for to kepe,
  And ther as þe walle was lowyst
  Anon down can þei lepe.

73 Be þat þe cok began to crow,
  The day began to spryng ;
  The scheref fond þe jaylier ded,
  The comyn bell made he ryng.

74 He made a crye thoroout al þe tow[n],
  Wheder he be ȝoman or knave,
  þat cowþe bryng hym Robyn Hode,
  His warison he shuld haue.

75 ' Ffor I dar neuer,' said þe scheref,
  ' Cum before oure kyng ;
  Ffor if I do, I wot serten
  Ffor soþe he wil me heng.'

76 The scheref made to seke Notyngham,
  Bothe be strete and stye,
  And Robyn was in mery Scherwode,
  As liȝt as lef on lynde.

77 Then bespake gode Litull John,
  To Robyn Hode can he say,
  I haue done þe a gode turne for an euyll,
  Quyte þe whan þou may.

78 ' I haue done þe a gode turne,' seid Litull
  John,
  ' Ffor sothe as I yow say ;
  I haue brouȝt þe vnder grene-wode lyne ;
  Ffare wel, and haue gode day.'

79 ' Nay, be my trouth,' seid Robyn Hode,
  ' So shall hit neuer be ;
  I make þe maister,' seid Robyn Hode,
  ' Off alle my men and me.'

80 ' Nay, be my trouth,' seid Litull John,
  ' So shalle hit neuer be ;
  But lat me be a felow,' seid Litull John,
  ' No noder kepe I be.'

81 Thus John gate Robyn Hod out of prison,
  Sertan withoutyn layn ;
  Whan his men saw hym hol and sounde,
  Ffor sothe they were full fayne.

82 They filled in wyne, and made hem glad,
  Vnder þe levys smale,
  And ȝete pastes of venyson,
  þat gode was with ale.

83 Than worde came to oure kyng
  How Robyn Hode was gon,
  And how þe scheref of Notyngham
  Durst neuer loke hym vpon.

84 Then bespake oure cumly kyng,
  In an angur hye :

Litull John hase begyled þe schereff,
In faith so hase he me.

85 Litul John has begyled vs bothe,
And þat full wel I se ;
Or ellis þe schereff of Notyngham
Hye hongut shulde he be.

86 'I made hem ȝemen of þe crowne,
And gaf hem fee with my hond ;
I gaf hem grith,' seid oure kyng,
'Thorowout all mery Inglond.

87 'I gaf theym grith,' þen seid oure kyng ;
'I say, so mot I the,
Ffor sothe soch a ȝeman as he is on
In all Inglond ar not thre.

88 'He is trew to his maister,' seid our kyng ;
'I sey, be swete Seynt John,
He louys better Robyn Hode
Then he dose vs ychon.

89 'Robyn Hode is euer bond to hym,
Bothe in strete and stalle ;
Speke no more of this mater,' seid oure kyng,
'But John has begyled vs alle.'

90 Thus endys the talkyng of the munke
And Robyn Hode i-wysse ;
God, þat is euer a crowned kyng,
Bryng vs all to his blisse !

———————◆———————

a. *A curl over final* n, *as in* Robyn, John, on,
sawten, *etc. ; a crossed* h, *as in* John, mych,
etc. ; crossed ll, *as in* full, litull, well, *etc. ;
a hooked* g, *as in* mornyng, kyng, *etc., have
been treated as not significant. As to*
Robyn, *cf.* 7³, 11¹,³, 13⁴, 14¹, *etc., where
there is simple* n ; *as to* John, 10¹,³, 14³,
31⁴, *etc., where we have* Jon ; *as to* Litull,
14¹,³, 39¹, 68³, 69¹, 70³, 71¹, *where we have*
Litul. *And is printed for* & ; be twene, be
fore, be side, be held, be spake, þer with,
thorow out, with outen, *etc., are joined.*
3¹. tide *no longer legible.*
7¹. seid h . . . , *illegible after* h.
8³,⁶. xij. 10¹. þⁱ nown. 12⁴, 13³. v s'.
14¹. lyed *before* Robyn *struck through.*
23³. of a C li.
27¹. thorow at : *but cf.* 30². 27⁴. xij.
30¹. Robyns men to the churche ran : *Madden.
There are no men with Robin. " This line
is almost illegible. It certainly begins with*
Robyn, *and the second word is not* men.

I read it, Robyn into the churche ran."
Skeat.
30². *A gap here between two pages, and there
are commonly six stanzas to a page. At
least six are required for the capture of
Robin Hood and the conveying of the tid-
ings to his men.*
43². Of xx.
44¹. me me *in my copy, probably by inadver-
tence.*
44². Of a C li.
53¹. hym. 56¹. þᵉ kyng. 58². xx li.
77⁴. b *has* Quit me, *which is perhaps better.*
78². *perhaps* saie ; *nearly illegible.*
90². I wysse.
b. 69³. þe prison. 70⁴. throw to. 71¹. be jayler.
71². toke. 72². hed ther with.
72³. wallis were. 72⁴. down ther they.
77². [t]hen *for* can (?). 77⁴. Quit me.
78². the saye. 78³. þe grene.
79¹,³. Hode *wanting.*

120

ROBIN HOOD'S DEATH

A. 'Robin Hoode his Death,' Percy MS., p. 21; Hales and Furnivall, I, 53.

B. 'Robin Hood's Death and Burial.' **a.** The English Archer, Paisley, John Neilson, 1786 : Bodleian Library, Douce, F. F. 71 (6), p. 81. **b.** The English Archer, York, printed by N. Nickson, in Feasegate, n. d.: Bodleian Library, Douce, F. F. 71 (4), p. 70.

B is given in Ritson's Robin Hood, 1795, II, 183, "from a collation of two different copies" of a York garland, "containing numerous variations, a few of which are retained in the margin."

A. Robin Hood is ailing, and is convinced that the only course for him is to go to Kirklees priory for blooding. Will Scarlet cannot counsel this, unless his master take fifty bowmen with him ; for a yeoman lives there with whom there is sure to be a quarrel. Robin bids Scarlet stay at home, if he is afraid. Scarlet, seeing that his master is wroth, will say no more.* Robin Hood will have no one go with him but Little John, who shall carry his bow. John proposes that they shall shoot for a penny along the way, and Robin assents.

The opening of the ballad resembles that of Robin Hood and the Monk. There Robin's soul is ill at ease, as here his body, and he resolves to go to Nottingham for mass ; Much, the Miller's son, advises a guard of twelve yeomen ; Robin will take none with him except John, to bear his bow ;† and John suggests that they shall shoot for a penny as they go.

A very interesting passage of the story here

followed, of which we can barely guess the contents, owing to nine stanzas having been torn away. Robin Hood and John keep up their shooting all the way, until they come to a black water, crossed by a plank. On the plank an old woman is kneeling, and banning Robin Hood. Robin Hood asks why, but the answer is lost, and it is not probable that we shall ever know : out of her proper malignancy, surely, or because she is a hired witch, for Robin is the friend of lowly folk. But if this old woman is banning, others, no doubt women, are weeping, for somehow they have learned that he is to be let blood that day at the priory, and foresee that ill will come of it. Robin is disturbed by neither banning nor weeping; the prioress is his cousin, and would not harm him for the world. So they shoot on until they come to Kirklees.

Robin makes the prioress a present of twenty pound, with a promise of more when she wants, and she falls to work with her bleeding-irons. The thick blood comes, and then the thin, and Robin knows that there has been treason. John asks, What cheer ? Robin answers, Little good. Nine stanzas are again wanting, and again in a place where we are not helped by the other version. John

---

* "You shall never hear more of me" might mean something stronger, but it is unlikely that Will is so touchy as to throw up fealty for a testy word from a sick man. A stanza or more seems to be lost here. Arthur is equally hasty with Gawain. He makes his vow to be the bane of Cornwall King. It is an unadvised vow, says Gawain.

And then bespake him noble Arthur,
And these were the words said he :

Why, if thou be afraid, Sir Gawaine the gay,
Goe home, and drink wine in thine own country.
I, 285, sts 33–35.

† John is again his sole companion when Robin goes in search of Guy of Gisborne. The yeoman in stanza 3 should be Red Roger; but a suspicion has more than once come over me that the beginning of this ballad has been affected by some version of Guy of Gisborne.

must call from the outside of the building, judging by what follows. An altercation seems to pass between Robin and some one; we should suppose between Robin and Red Roger. Robin slips out of a shot-window, and as he does so is thrust through the side by Red Roger. Robin swoops off Red Roger's head, and leaves him for dogs to eat. Then Red Roger must be below, and John is certainly below. He would have seen to Red Roger had they both been within. But John must be under a window on a different side of the building from that whence Robin issues, for otherwise, again, he would have seen to Red Roger. We are driven to suppose that the words in st. 19 pass between Robin above and Roger below.

Though Robin is near his last breath, he has, he says, life enough to take his housel. He must get it in a very irregular way, but he trusts it will "bestand" him.* John asks his master's leave to set fire to Kirklees, but Robin will not incur God's blame by harming any woman ["widow"] at his latter end. Let John make his grave of gravel and greet, set his sword at his head, his arrows at his feet, and lay his bow by his side.†

B, though found only in late garlands, is in the fine old strain. Robin Hood says to Little John that he can no longer shoot matches, his arrows will not flee; he must go to a cousin to be let blood. He goes, alone, to Kirkley nunnery, and is received with a show of cordiality. His cousin bloods him, locks him up in the room, and lets him bleed all the livelong day, and until the next day at noon. Robin bethinks himself of escaping through a casement, but is not strong enough. He sets his horn to his mouth and blows thrice, but so wearily that Little John, hearing, thinks his master must be nigh to death. John comes to Kirkley, breaks the

locks, and makes his way to Robin's presence. He begs the boon of setting fire to Kirkley, but Robin has never hurt woman in all his life, and will not at his end. He asks for his bow to shoot his last shot, and where the arrow lights there his grave shall be.‡ His grave is to be of gravel and green, long enough and broad enough, a sod under his head, another at his feet, and his bow by his side, that men may say, Here lies bold Robin Hood.

The account of Robin Hood's death which is given in The Gest, agrees as to the main items with what we find in A. The prioress of Kirkesly, his near kinswoman, betrayed him when he went to the nunnery to be let blood, and this she did upon counsel with Sir Roger of Donkester, with whom she was intimate. The Life of Robin Hood in the Sloane MS, which is mostly made up from The Gest, naturally repeats this story.

Grafton, in his Chronicle, 1569, citing "an olde and auncient pamphlet," says: For the sayd Robert Hood, beyng afterwardes troubled with sicknesse, came to a certain nonry in Yorkshire, called Bircklies, where, desiryng to be let blood, he was betrayed and bled to death: edition of 1809, p. 221. So the Harleian MS, No 1233, article 199, of the middle of the seventeenth century, and not worth citing, but cited by Ritson. According to Stanihurst, in Holinshed's Ireland (p. 28 of ed. of 1808), after Robin Hood had been betrayed at a nunnery in Scotland called Bricklies, Little John was fain to flee the realm, and went to Ireland, where he executed an extraordinary shot, by which he thought his safety compromised, and so removed to Scotland, and died there.

Martin Parker's True Tale of Robin Hood, which professes to be collected from chronicles, ascribes Robin Hood's death to a faith-

---

* I can make nothing of "give me mood," in 23¹,². 'Give me God' or 'Give me my God,' seems too bold a suggestion: at any rate I have no example of God used simply for housel.

† A few verses are wanting at the end. The "met-yard" of the last line is one of the last things we should think Robin would care for.

‡ It seemed to me at one time that there was a direction to shoot an arrow to determine the place of a grave also in No 16, **A** 3, I, 185.

Now when that ye hear me gie a loud cry,
Shoot frae thy bow an arrow, and there let me lye.

But upon considering the corresponding passage in 16 **B**, **C**, and in 15 **B**, the idea seems rather to be, that the arrow is to leave the bow at the moment when the soul shoots from the body.

less friar, who pretended "in love to let him blood," when he had a fever, and allowed him to bleed to death. Robin Hood and the Valiant Knight, a late and thoroughly worthless broadside ballad, says simply, He sent for a monk to let him blood, who took his life away.

A Russian popular song has an interesting likeness to the conclusion of Robin Hood's Death. The last survivor of a band of brigands, feeling death to be nigh, exclaims:

Bury me, brothers, between three roads,
The Kief, and the Moscow, and the Murom famed
    in story.
At my feet fasten my horse,
At my head set a life-bestowing cross,
In my right hand place my keen sabre.
Whoever passes by will stop;
Before my life-bestowing cross will he utter a
    prayer,

At the sight of my black steed will he be startled,
At the sight of my keen sword will he be terrified.
'Surely this is a brigand who is buried here,
A son of the brigand, the bold Stenka Razín.'

Sakharof, Skazaniya Russkago Naroda, I, iii, 226.*

Dimos, twenty years a Klepht, tells his comrades to make his tomb wide and high enough for him to fight in it, standing up, and to leave a window, so that the swallows may tell him that spring has come and the nightingales that it is May: Fauriel, I, 56; Zambelios, p. 607, 13; Passow, p. 85. This is a song of the beginning of the present century.

B is translated in Le Magasin Pittoresque, 1838, p. 126 f; by Loève-Veimars, p. 223; by Cantù, Documenti alla Storia Universale, V, III, p. 801; Anastasius Grün, p. 200; Knortz, L. u. R. Alt-Englands, No 20.

A

Percy MS., p. 21; Hales and Furnivall, I, 53.

1 'I WILL neuer eate nor drinke,' Robin Hood
        said,
    'Nor meate will doo me noe good,
    Till I haue beene att merry Churchlees,
        My vaines for to let blood.'

2 'That I reade not,' said Will Scarllett,
    'Master, by the assente of me,
    Without halfe a hundred of your best bowmen
        You take to goe with yee.

3 'For there a good yeoman doth abide
        Will be sure to quarrell with thee,
    And if thou haue need of vs, master,
        In faith we will not flee.'

4 'And thou be feard, thou William Scarlett,
        Att home I read thee bee:'
    'And you be wrothe, my deare master,
        You shall neuer heare more of mee.'

* * * * * *

5 'For there shall noe man with me goe,
        Nor man with mee ryde,
    And Litle Iohn shall be my man,
        And beare my benbow by my side.'

6 'You'st beare your bowe, master, your selfe,
        And shoote for a peny with mee:'
    'To that I doe assent,' Robin Hood sayd,
        'And soe, Iohn, lett it bee.'

7 They two bolde children shotten together,
        All day theire selfe in ranke,
    Vntill they came to blacke water,
        And over it laid a planke.

8 Vpon it there kneeled an old woman,
        Was banning Robin Hoode;
    'Why dost thou bann Robin Hoode?' said
        Robin,

. . . .

* * * * * *

* Ralston, Songs of the Russian People, p. 46, who cites B 17, 18. Mr Ralston observes that most of the so-styled Robber Songs of the Russians are reminiscences of the revolt of the Don Cossacks against Tsar Alexis Mikhailovich.

Stenka Razín, the chief of the insurgents, after setting for several years the forces of the Tsar at defiance, was put to a cruel death in 1672: p. 45, as above.

9 . .   .   .
'To giue to Robin Hoode ;
Wee weepen for his deare body,
That this day must be lett bloode.'

10 'The dame prior is my aunts daughter,
And nie vnto my kinne ;
I know shee wold me noe harme this day,
For all the world to winne.'

11 Forth then shotten these children two,
And they did neuer lin,
Vntill they came to merry Churchlees,
To merry Churchlee[s] *with*-in.

12 And when they came to merry Churchlees,
They knoced vpon a pin ;
Vpp then rose dame prioresse,
And lett good Robin in.

13 Then Robin gaue to dame prioresse
Twenty pound in gold,
And bad her spend while that wold last,
And shee shold haue more when shee wold.

14 And downe then came dame prioresse,
Downe she came in that ilke,
With a p*ai*r off blood-irons in her hands,
Were wrapped all in silke.

15 'Sett a chaffing-dish to the fyer,' s*ai*d dame
prioresse,
'And stripp thou vp thy sleeue :'
I hold him but an vnwise man
That will noe warning leeve.

16 Shee laid the blood-irons to R*obin* Hoods vaine,
Alacke, the more pitye !
And pearct the vaine, and let out the bloode,
That full red was to see.

17 And first it bled, the thicke, thicke bloode,
And afterwards the thinne,
And well then wist good Robin Hoode
Treason there was within.

18 'What cheere my m*aster* ?' said Litle Iohn ;
'In faith, Iohn, litle goode ;'
.   .   .   .
.   .   .   .

*   *   *   *   *   *   *

19 'I haue vpon a gowne of greene,
Is cut short by my knee,
And in my hand a bright browne brand
That will well bite of thee.'

20 But forth then of a shot-windowe
Good R*obin* Hood he could glide ;
Red Roger, with a grounden glaue,
Thrust him through the milke-white side.

21 But R*obin* was light and nimble of foote,
And thought to abate his pride,
Ffor betwixt his head and his shoulders
He made a wound full wide.

22 Says, Ly there, ly there, Red Roger,
The doggs they must thee eate ;
'For I may haue my houzle,' he said,
'For I may both goe and speake.

23 'Now giue me mood,' Robin said to Litle
Iohn,
'Giue me mood w*ith* thy hand ;
I trust to God in heauen soe hye
My houzle will me bestand.'

24 'Now giue me leaue, giue me leaue, m*aster*,'
he said,
'For Christs loue giue leaue to me,
To set a fier within this hall,
And to burne vp all Churchlee.'

25 'That I reade not,' said R*obin* Hoode then,
'Litle Iohn, for it may not be ;
If I shold doe any widow hurt, at my latter
end,
God,' he said, 'wold blame me ;

26 'But take me vpon thy backe, Litle Iohn,
And beare me to yonder streete,
And there make me a full fayre graue,
Of grauell and of greete.

27 'And sett my bright sword at my head,
Mine arrowes at my feete,
And lay my vew-bow by my side,
My met-yard wi .   .   .   .

B

a. The English Archer, Paisley, printed by John Neilson for George Caldwell, Bookseller, near the Cross, 1786, p. 81, No 24. b. The English Archer, York, printed by N. Nickson, in Feasegate, n. d., p. 70.

1 WHEN Robin Hood and Little John
    Down a down a down a down
  Went oer yon bank of broom,
    Said Robin Hood bold to Little John,
  We have shot for many a pound.
    Hey, etc.

2 But I am not able to shoot one shot more,
    My broad arrows will not flee;
  But I have a cousin lives down below,
    Please God, she will bleed me.

3 Now Robin he is to fair Kirkly gone,
    As fast as he can win;
  But before he came there, as we do hear,
    He was taken very ill.

4 And when he came to fair Kirkly-hall,
    He knockd all at the ring,
  But none was so ready as his cousin herself
    For to let bold Robin in.

5 'Will you please to sit down, cousin Robin,'
    she said,
    'And drink some beer with me?'
  'No, I will neither eat nor drink,
    Till I am blooded by thee.'

6 'Well, I have a room, cousin Robin,' she said,
    'Which you did never see,
  And if you please to walk therein,
    You blooded by me shall be.'

7 She took him by the lily-white hand,
    And led him to a private room,
  And there she blooded bold Robin Hood,
    While one drop of blood would run down.

8 She blooded him in a vein of the arm,
    And locked him up in the room;
  Then did he bleed all the live-long day,
    Until the next day at noon.

9 He then bethought him of a casement there,
    Thinking for to get down;
  But was so weak he could not leap,
    He could not get him down.

10 He then bethought him of his bugle-horn,
    Which hung low down to his knee;
  He set his horn unto his mouth,
    And blew out weak blasts three.

11 Then Little John, when hearing him,
    As he sat under a tree,
  'I fear my master is now near dead,
    He blows so wearily.'

12 Then Little John to fair Kirkly is gone,
    As fast as he can dree;
  But when he came to Kirkly-hall,
    He broke locks two or three:

13 Until he came bold Robin to see,
    Then he fell on his knee;
  'A boon, a boon,' cries Little John,
    'Master, I beg of thee.'

14 'What is that boon,' said Robin Hood,
    'Little John, [thou] begs of me?'
  'It is to burn fair Kirkly-hall,
    And all their nunnery.'

15 'Now nay, now nay,' quoth Robin Hood,
    'That boon I'll not grant thee;
  I never hurt woman in all my life,
    Nor men in woman's company.

16 'I never hurt fair maid in all my time,
    Nor at mine end shall it be;
  But give me my bent bow in my hand,
    And a broad arrow I'll let flee;
  And where this arrow is taken up,
    There shall my grave digged be.

17 'Lay me a green sod under my head,
    And another at my feet;
  And lay my bent bow by my side,
    Which was my music sweet;
  And make my grave of gravel and green,
    Which is most right and meet.

18 'Let me have length and breadth enough,
    With a green sod under my head;
  That they may say, when I am dead
    Here lies bold Robin Hood.'

19 These words they readily granted him,
    Which did bold Robin please:
  And there they buried bold Robin Hood,
    Within the fair Kirkleys.

A. 1[8]. church Lees: *cf.* 11[8]. 2[8]. halfe 100[d].
3[1]. there is. 6[2]. nor shoote. 7[1], 11[1]. 2.
8[8], 18[2], 27[4]. *half a page gone.*
12[1]. church lees. 13[2]. 20[ty].
20[1]. shop *for* shot. 20[8]. grounding.
24[4]. church lee.

B. a. Robin Hood's death and burial: shewing
how he was taken ill, and how he went to
his cousin at Kirkly-hall, in Yorkshire, who
let him blood, which was the cause of his
death. Tune of Robin Hood's last fare-
wel, etc.
2[2]. fly. 15[8]. burnt *for* hurt. 19[4]. Kirkly.
The ballad, as Ritson says, "is made to con-
clude with some foolish lines (adopted from
the London copy" of R. H. and the Val-
iant Knight) in order to introduce the
epitaph.

20 Thus he that never feard bow nor spear
     Was murderd by letting blood;
     And so, loving friends, the story it ends
     Of valiant Robin Hood.

21 There's nothing remains but his epitaph now,
     Which, reader, here you have,
     To this very day which read you may,
     As it is upon his grave.
     Hey down a derry derry down

The epitaph, however, does not follow.
b. *Title as in* a, *omitting* in Yorkshire *and* Tune
of, etc. *Printed in stanzas of two long*
lines. The burden is wanting.
1[2]. over. 1[8]. bold *wanting.*
2[2]. broad *wanting:* flee. 3[1]. he *wanting.*
3[2]. coud wen. 4[1]. when that.
4[2]. knocked at. 5[4]. I blood letted be.
6[4]. You blood shall letted be.

7[2]. let him into. 7[4]. Whilst: down *wanting.*
8[1]. in the vein. 8[2]. in a. 8[8]. There.
9[1]. casement door. 9[2]. to be gone.
9[4]. Nor he: him *wanting.*
10[4]. strong blasts. 11[2]. under the.
11[8]. now *wanting.* 12[2]. he could.
13[1]. see *wanting.* 14[1]. quoth *for* said.
14[2]. thou begs. 15. *wanting.* 16[1]. neer.
16[2]. at my. 16[4]. my broad arrows.
17[1,2]. *To go with* 16[3,4].
     With verdant sods most neatly put,
     Sweet as the green wood tree.
19[1]. promisd him. 19[4]. Near to: Kirkleys.
20[1]. that feard neither. 20[8]. it *wanting.*
20[4]. valiant bold. 21[1]. There is.
21[4]. it was upon the.
After 19.
     Kirkleys was beautiful of old,
     Like Winifrid's of Wales,
     By whose fair well strange cures are told
     In legendary tales.
     Upon his grave was laid a stone,
     Declaring that he dy'd,
     And tho so many years ago,
     Time can't his actions hide.

At the end is the epitaph, wanting in a.

Robin Hood's Epitaph, set on his tomb by the
     Prioress of Kirkley Monastry, in Yorkshire.

Robert Earl of Huntington
Lies under this little stone.
No archer was like him so good,
His wildness nam'd him Robin Hood.
Full thirteen years and something more
These no[r]thern parts he vexed sore:
Such out-laws as he and his men
May England never know again.

121

ROBIN HOOD AND THE POTTER

Library of the University of Cambridge, MS. E e. 4. 35, fol. 14 b, of about 1500.

———

PRINTED from the manuscript in Ritson's Robin Hood, 1795, I, 81; here from a transcript of the original, carefully revised by Rev. Professor Skeat.

Robin Hood sees a potter driving over the lea; the potter has been in the habit of passing that way, and never has paid toll. Little John has had a brush with the potter, and offers to lay forty shillings that no man can make him leave a pledge. Robin accepts the wager, stops the potter, and demands a "pledge"; the potter refuses to leave pledge or pay toll, takes a staff from his cart, knocks Robin's buckler out of his hand, and, ere Robin can recover it, fells him with a blow in the neck. Robin owns that he has lost. The potter says it is no courtesy to stop a poor yeoman thus; Robin agrees heartily, and proposes fellowship, also to change clothes with the potter and sell his ware at Nottingham. The potter is willing; John warns his master to beware of the sheriff. Robin takes his stand near the sheriff's gate, and offers his pots so cheap that soon there are but five left; these he sends as a gift to the sheriff's wife, who in return asks him to dinner. While they are at their meal, two of the sheriff's men talk of a shooting-match for forty shillings: this the potter says he will see, and after a good dinner goes with the rest to the butts. All the archers come half a bow's length short of the mark; Robin, at his wish, gets a bow from the sheriff, and his first shot misses the mark by less than a foot, his second cleaves the central pin in three. The sheriff applauds; Robin says there is a bow in his cart which he had of Robin Hood. The sheriff wishes he could see Robin Hood, and the potter offers to gratify this wish on the morrow. They go back to the sheriff's for the night, and early the next day set forth; the sheriff riding, the potter in his cart. When they come to the wood, the potter blows his horn, for so they shall know if Robin be near; the horn brings all Robin's men. The sheriff would now give a hundred pound not to have had his wish; had he known his man at Nottingham, it would have been a thousand year ere the potter had come to the forest. I know that well, says Robin, and therefore shall you leave your horse with us, and your other gear. Were it not for your wife you would not come off so lightly. The sheriff goes home afoot, but with a white palfrey, which Robin presents to his wife. Have you brought Robin home? asks the dame. Devil speed him, answers her spouse, he has taken everything from me; all but this fair palfrey, which he has sent to thee. The merry dame laughs, and swears that the pots have been well paid for. Robin asks the potter how much his pots were worth, gives him ten pounds instead of the two nobles for which they could have been sold, and a welcome to the wood whenever he shall come that way.

The Play of Robin Hood, an imperfect copy of which is printed at the end of Copland's and of White's edition of The Gest, is founded on the ballads of Robin Hood and the Curtal Friar and of Robin Hood and the Potter. The portion which is based on the ballad of Robin and the Potter is given in an appendix.

Robin Hood and the Butcher, No 122, repeats many of the incidents of the present ballad. The sheriff is enticed into the forest (by Little John instead of Robin Hood) in

The Gest, 181 ff. This part of the story, in Robin Hood and the Butcher, is much more like that of The Gest than it is in Robin Hood and the Potter. We shall have only too many variations of the adventure in which Robin Hood unexpectedly meets his match in a hand-to-hand fight, now with a pinder, then with a tanner, tinker, shepherd, beggar, etc. His adversaries, after proving their mettle, are sometimes invited and induced to join his company: not so here. In some broadside ballads of this description, with an extravagance common enough in imitations, Robin Hood is very badly mauled, and made all but contemptible.* In Robin Hood and the Potter, Little John is willing to wager on the result of a trial, from his own experience. Will Scadlock is equally confident in Robin Hood and the Curtal Friar, perhaps for the same reason, although this is not said. In Robin Hood and the Shepherd, Little John takes his turn *after* his master, and so with three of Robin's men in Robin Hood and the Beggar, No 133.

Hereward the Saxon introduces himself into the Norman court as a potter, to obtain information of an attack which William the Conqueror was thought to intend on his stronghold at Ely: De Gestis Herwardi Saxonis, 24, in Michel, Chroniques Anglo-Normandes, II, 69, attributed to the twelfth century. Wallace, in like manner, to scout in the English camp: Blind Harry's poem, ed. Moir, Book Six, v. 435 ff, p. 123 ff. This is also one of the many artifices by which Eustace the Monk deceives his enemy, the Count of Boulogne: Roman d'Eustache le Moine, ed. Michel, p. 39, v. 1071 ff, a poem of the thirteenth century. See, for Hereward and Eustace, T. Wright's Essays on Subjects connected with the Literature, etc., of England in the Middle Ages, II, 108 ff, 135.

Disguise is the wonted and simplest expedient of an outlaw mixing among his foes, "wherein the pregnant enemy does much." Fulk Fitz Warine takes the disguise of an old monk, a merchant, a charcoal-burner; Hereward, that of a potter, a fisherman; Eustace the Monk, of a potter, shepherd, pilgrim, charcoal-burner, woman, leper, carpenter, minstrel, etc.; Wallace, of a potter, pilgrim, woman (twice), etc., in Blind Harry's poem, of a beggar in ballads; Robin Hood, of a potter, butcher, beggar, shepherd, an old woman, a fisherman (?), Guy of Gisborne.

Translated by Anastasius Grün, p. 76.

---

1 In schomer, when the leves spryng,
   The bloschoms on eue*r*y bowe,
So merey doyt the berdys syng
   Yn wodys merey now.

2 Herkens, god yemen,
   Comley, corteys, and god,
On of the best þat yeue*r* bare bowe,
   Hes name was Roben Hode.

3 Roben Hood was the yeman's name,
   That was boyt corteys and ffre;
Ffor the loffe of owre ladey,
   All wemen werschepyd he.

4 Bot as the god yeman stod on a day,
   Among hes mery maney,
He was ware of a prowd potte*r*,
   Cam dryfyng owyr the ley.

5 'Yonder comet a prod potte*r*,' seyde Roben,
   'That long hayt hantyd þi*s* wey;
He was neuer so corteys a man
   On peney of pawage to pay.'

6 'Y met hem bot at Went-breg,' seyde Lytyll John,
   'And therefore yeffeJl mot he the!
Seche thre strokes he me gafe,
   Yet by my seydys cleffe þey.

*The personage may have been varied in the broadside ballads to catch the pence of tanners, tinkers, and the rest; or possibly some member of the respective fraternities might do this for the glory of his craft. A parallel case seems to be afforded by the well-known German ballad, 'Der Zimmergesell und die junge Markgräfin,' which is also sung of a journeyman shoemaker, tailor, locksmith, etc.; as remarked by A. Grün, Robin Hood, Ein Balladenkranz, p. 47 f.

7 'Y ley forty shillings,' seyde Lytyll John,
  'To pay het thes same day,
  Ther ys nat a man among hus all
  A wed schall make hem ley.'

8 'Here ys forty shillings,' seyde Roben,
  'More, and thow dar say,
  þat y schall make þat prowde potter,
  A wed to me schall he ley.'

9 There thes money theẏ leyde,
  They toke het a yeman to kepe;
  Roben beffore the potter he breyde,
  A[nd] bad hem stond stell.

10 Handys apon hes hors he leyde,
  And bad the potter stonde foll stell;
  The potter schorteley to hem seyde,
  Ffelow, what ys they well?

11 'All thes thre yer, and more, potter,' he
    seyde,
  'Thow hast hantyd thes wey,
  Yet were tow neuer so cortys a man
  On peney of pauage to pay.'

12 'What ys they name,' seyde þe potter,
  'Ffor pauage thow aske of me?'
  'Roben Hod ys mey name,
  A wed schall thow leffe me.'

13 'Wed well y non leffe,' seyde þe potter,
  'Nor pavag well y non pay;
  Awey they honde ffro mey hors!
  Y well the tene eyls, be mey ffay.'

14 The potter to hes cart he went,
  He was not to seke;
  A god to-hande staffe þerowt he hent,
  Beffore Roben he leppyd.

15 Roben howt with a swerd bent,
  A bokeler en hes honde;
  The potter to Roben he went,
  And seyde, Ffelow, let mey hors go.

16 Togeder then went thes to yemen,
  Het was a god seyt to se;
  Thereof low Robyn hes men,
  There they stod onder a tre.

17 Leytell John to hes ffelowhe[s] seyde,
  'Yend potter well steffeley stonde:'

The potter, with a acward stroke,
  Smot the bokeler owt of hes honde.

18 A[nd] ar Roben meyt get het agen
  Hes bokeler at hes ffette,
  The potter yn the neke hem toke,
  To the gronde sone he yede.

19 That saw Roben hes men,
  As thay stod onder a bow;
  'Let vs helpe owre master,' seyde Lytell John,
  'Yonder potter,' seyde he, 'els well hem
    slo.'

20 Thes yemen went with a breyde,
  To ther mast[er] they cam.
  Leytell John to hes mast[er] seyde,
  Ho haet the wager won?

21 'Schall y haffe yowre forty shillings,' seyde
    Lytl John,
  'Or ye, master, schall haffe myne?'
  'Yeff they were a hundred,' seyde Roben,
  'Y ffeythe, they ben all theyne.'

22 'Het ys fol leytell cortesey,' seyde þe potter,
  'As y haffe harde weyse men saye,
  Yeffe a pore yeman com drywyng on the wey,
  To let hem of hes gorney.'

23 'Be mey trowet, thow seys soyt,' seyde Roben,
  'Thow seys god yeme[n]rey;
  And thow dreyffe fforthe yeuery day,
  Thow schalt neuer be let ffor me.

24 'Y well prey the, god potter,
  A ffelischepe well thow haffe?
  Geffe me they clothyng, and þow schalt hafe
    myne;
  Y well go to Notynggam.'

25 'Y gra[n]t thereto,' seyde the potter,
  'Thow schalt ffeynde me a ffelow gode;
  Bot thow can sell mey pottys well,
  Com ayen as thow yode.'

26 'Nay, be mey trowt,' seyde Roben,
  'And then y bescro mey hede,
  Yeffe y bryng eny pottys ayen,
  And eney weyffe well hem chepe.'

27 Than spake Leytell John,
  And all hes ffelowhes heynd,

'Master, be well ware of the screffe of Not-
            ynggam,
    Ffor he ys leytell howr ffrende.'

28 'Heyt war howte!' seyde Roben,
    'Ffelowhes, let me a lone;
    Thorow the helpe of Howr Ladey,
    To Notynggam well y gon.'

29 Robyn went to Notynggam,
    Thes pott*ys* ffor to sell;
    The pott*er* abode w*ith* Robens men,
    There he ffered not eylle.

30 Tho Roben droffe on hes wey,
    So merey ower the londe:
    Her es mor*e*, and affter ys to saye,
    The best ys beheynde.

31 When Roben cam to Notynggam,
    The soyt yef y scholde saye,
    He set op hes hors anon,
    And gaffe hem hotys and haye.

32 Yn the medys of the towne,
    There he schowed hes war*e*;
    'Pott*ys*! pott*ys*!' he gan crey foll sone,
    'Haffe hansell ffor the mar*e*!'

33 Ffoll effen agenest the screffeys gate
    Schowed he hes chaffar*e*;
    Weyffes and wedowes abowt hem drow,
    And chepyd ffast of hes war*e*.

34 Yet, 'Pott*ys*, gret chepe!' creyed Robyn,
    'Y loffe yeffell thes to stonde;'
    And all that say hem sell
    Seyde he had be no potter long.

35 The pott*ys* that wer*e* werthe pens ffeyffe,
    He solde tham ffor pens thre;
    Preveley seyde man and weyffe,
    'Ywnder potter schall neu*er* the.'

36 Thos Roben solde ffoll ffast,
    Tell he had pott*ys* bot ffeyffe;
    Op he hem toke of hes car*e*,
    And sende hem to the screffeys weyffe.

37 Thereof sche was ffoll ffayne,
    'Gereamarsey, *ser*,' than seyde sche;

'When ye com to thes contre ayen,
    Y schall bey of the[y] pott*ys*, so mot y the.'

38 'Ye schall haffe of the best,' seyde Roben,
    And swar*e* be the Treneytë;
    Ffoll corteysley [sc]he gan hem call,
    'Com deyne w*ith* the screfe and me.'

39 'God amarsey,' seyde Roben,
    'Yowr*e* bedyng schall be doyn;'
    A mayden yn the pott*ys* gan ber*e*,
    Roben and þe screffe weyffe ffolowed anon.

40 Whan Roben yn to the hall cam,
    The screffë sone he met;
    The pott*er* cowed of corteysey,
    And sone the screffe he gret.

41 'Lo, ser, what thes pott*er* hayt geffe yow and
            me;
    Ffeyffe pottys smalle and gret*e*!'
    'He ys ffoll wellcom,' seyd the screffe;
    'Let os was, and go to mete.'

42 As they sat at her methe,
    W*ith* a nobell cher*e*,
    To of the screffes men gan speke
    Off a gret wager;

43 Off a schotyng, was god and ffeyne,
    Was made the thother daye,
    Off forty shillings, the soyt to saye,
    Who scholde thes wager wen.

44 Styll than sat thes prowde potter,
    Thos than thowt he;
    As y am a trow cerstyn man,
    Thes schotyng well y se.

45 Whan they had ffared of the best,
    W*ith* bred and ale and weyne,
    To the bottys the made them prest,
    W*ith* bowes and boltys ffoll ffeyne.

46 The screffes men schot ffoll ffast,
    As archares þat weren godde;
    There cam non ner ney the marke
    Bey halffe a god archares bowe.

47 Stell then stod the prowde pott*er*,
    Thos than seyde he;
    And y had a bow, be the rode,
    On schot scholde yow se.

48 'Thow schall haffe a bow,' seyde the screffe,
    'The best þat thow well cheys of thre ;
    Thou semyst a stalward and a stronge,
        Asay schall thow be.'

49 The screffe commandyd a yeman þat stod hem
        bey
    Afftyr bowhes to weynde ;
    The best bow þat the yeman browthe
        Roben set on a stryng.

50 'Now schall y wet and thow be god,
    And polle het op to they nere ;'
    'So god me helpe,' seyde the prowde potter,
        'Þys ys bot rygȝt weke gere.'

51 To a quequer Roben went,
    A god bolt owthe he toke ;
    So ney on to the marke he went,
        He ffayled not a fothe.

52 All they schot abowthe agen,
    The screffes men and he ;
    Off the marke he welde not ffayle,
        He cleffed the preke on thre.

53 The screffes men thowt gret schame
    The potter the mastry wan ;
    The screffë lowe and made god game,
        And seyde, Potter, thow art a man.

54 .   .   .   .   .   .
    . . . . . .
    Thow art worthey to bere a bowe
    Yn what plas that þow goe.

55 'Yn mey cart y haffe a bowe,
    Ffor soyt,' he seyde, 'and that a godde ;
    Yn mey cart ys the bow
        That gaffe me Robyn Hode.'

56 'Knowest thow Robyn Hode ?' seyde the
        screffe,
    'Potter, y prey the tell thow me ;'
    'A hundred torne y haffe schot with hem,
        Vnder hes tortyll-tre.'

57 'Y had leuer nar a hundred ponde,' seyde þe
        screffe,
    'And sware be the Trenitë,
    . . . . . .
    þat the ffals outelawe stod be me.'

58 'And ye well do afftyr mey red,' seyde þe
        potter,
    'And boldeley go with me,
    And to morow, or we het bred,
        Roben Hode well we se.'

59 'Y wel queyt the,' kod the screffe,
    'Y swere be God of meythe ;'
    Schetyng thay left, and hom þey went,
        Her soper was reddy deythe.

60 Vpon the morow, when het was day,
    He boskyd hem fforthe to reyde ;
    The potter hes cart fforthe gan ray,
        And wolde not leffe beheynde.

61 He toke leffe of the screffys wyffe,
    And thankyd her of all thyng :
    'Dam, ffor mey loffe and ye well þys were,
        Y geffe yow here a golde ryng.'

62 'Gramarsey,' seyde the weyffe,
    'Ser, god eylde het the ;'
    The screffes hart was neuer so leythe,
        The ffeyre fforeyst to se.

63 And when he cam yn to the fforeyst,
    Yonder the leffes grene,
    Berdys there sange on bowhes prest,
        Het was gret goy to se.

64 'Here het ys merey to be,' seyde Roben,
    'Ffor a man that had hawt to spende ;
    Be mey horne I schall awet
        Yeff Roben Hode be here.'

65 Roben set hes horne to hes mowthe,
    And blow a blast þat was ffoll god ;
    þat herde hes men þat þere stode,
        Ffer downe yn the wodde.

66 'I her mey master blow,' seyde Leytell John,
    . . . . . .
    . . . . . .
    They ran as thay were wode.

67 Whan thay to thar master cam,
    Leytell John wold not spare ;
    'Master, how haffe yow ffare yn Notynggam ?
        How haffe yow solde yowre ware ?'

68 'Ye, be mey trowthe, Leyty[ll] John,
    Loke thow take no care ;

Y haffe browt the screffe of Notynggam,
Ffor all howre chaffare.'

69 'He ys ffoll wellcom,' seyde Lytyll John,
'Thes tydyng ys ffoll godde;
The screffe had leuer nar a hundred ponde
He had [neuer sene Roben Hode.]

70 '[Had I] west þat befforen,
At Notynggam when we were,
Thow scholde not com yn ffeyre fforest
Of all thes thowsande eyre.'

71 'That wot y well,' seyde Roben,
'Y thanke God that ye be here;
Thereffore schall ye leffe yowre hors with hos,
And all yowre hother gere.'

72 'That ffend I Godys fforbod,' kod the screffe,
'So to lese mey godde;

.   .   .   .   .   .

.   .   .   .   .   .

73 'Hether ye cam on hors ffoll hey,
And hom schall ye go on ffote;
And gret well they weyffe at home,
The woman ys ffoll godde.

74 'Y schall her sende a wheyt palffrey,
Het ambellet be mey ffey,

.   .   .   .   .   .

.   .   .   .   .   .

75 'Y schall her sende a wheyt palffrey,
Het hambellet as the weynde;
Nere ffor the loffe of yowre weyffe,
Off more sorow scholde yow seyng.'

76 Thes parted Robyn Hode and the screffe;
To Notynggam he toke the waye;

Hes weyffe ffeyre welcomed hem hom,
And to hem gan sche saye:

77 Seyr, how haffe yow ffared yn grene fforeyst?
Haffe ye browt Roben hom?
'Dam, the deyell spede hem, bothe bodey and
bon;
Y haffe hade a ffoll gret skorne.

78 'Of all the god that y haffe lade to grene wod,
He hayt take het ffro me;
All bot thes ffeyre palffrey,
That he hayt sende to the.'

79 With þat sche toke op a lowde lawhyng,
And swhare be hem þat deyed on tre,
'Now haffe yow payed ffor all þe pottys
That Roben gaffe to me.

80 'Now ye be com hom to Notynggam,
Ye schall haffe god ynowe;'
Now speke we of Roben Hode,
And of the pottyr ondyr the grene bowhe.

81 'Potter, what was they pottys worthe
To Notynggam þat y ledde with me?'
'They wer worthe to nobellys,' seyde he,
'So mot y treyffe or the;
So cowde y [haffe] had ffor tham,
And y had there be.'

82 'Thow schalt hafe ten ponde,' seyde Roben,
'Of money ffeyre and ffre;
And yeuer whan thow comest to grene wod,
Wellcom, potter, to me.'

83 Thes partyd Robyn, the screffe, and the potter,
Ondernethe the grene-wod tre;
God haffe mersey on Roben Hodys solle,
And saffe all god yemanrey!

———

2². cortessey.   3⁴. werschep ye.
4⁴. the lefe.   5¹, 6¹. syde.   6⁸. Seche iij.
6⁴. þey cleffe by my seydys.
7¹, 8¹, 21¹, 43⁸. xl s'.   7⁸. hys all.
7⁴. hem leffe.   11¹. thes iij.   11⁴. I peney.
14². And teke at the beginning of the line
struck through.
16¹. thes ij.   17¹. ffelow he seyde.
17⁸. a caward.   19². onder or ender.
19⁴. hels : sclo.   20¹. went yemen.

20². To thes.   21⁸, 56⁸, 57¹. a c.
25. st. 29 is wrongly put here.
25⁴. yede.   27². ffelow hes.
28. The order of the lines is 3, 2, 1, 4.
30⁸. Heres.   35¹. pens v.
35². pens iij. d.   36². bot v.
37². Gere amarsey seyde sche than, with a
character after sche which is probably an
abbreviation for ser, as in 62².

41[4]. to to. 42[1]. methe. 42[3]. ij of.

43[3]. xl s. 45[3]. the pottys.

45[4]. bolt yt. 48[2]. of iij. 48[3]. senyst.

48[4]. A say.

50[2]. And [thow]? *The* ll *in* polle *is crossed ;*
potte *may have been intended by the writer.*

52[4]. on iij.

54[1,2]. *No blank here, and none at* 57[3], 66[2,3],
72[3,4], 74[3,4].

55[3,4]. Yn mey cart ys the bow þat Robyn
gaffe me.

56[3]. A c. 57[1], 69[3]. a c.

59[2]. & swere : meythey. 59[4]. scoper.

64[3]. he schall. 68[1]. I leyty.

69[4], 70[1]. He had west þat be fforen.

74[1,2]. *Ought perhaps to be dropped. The
writer, having got the second verse wrong,
may have begun the stanza again.*

80[3]. *After this line is repeated,* Ye schall
haffe god ynowhe.

80[4]. bowhes. 81[3]. worthe ij.

81[6]. be there. 82. hafe x li.

Expleycyt Robynhode.

A bowt, a non, be heynde, *etc. are joined.
And* for & throughout. *Some terminal curls
rendered with* e *were, perhaps, mere tricks
of writing ; as marks over final* m, n, *in*
cam, on, yemen, *etc., crossed double* l *in* all,
etc., a curled n *in* Roben, *have been assumed
to be.*

APPENDIX

THE PLAYE OF ROBYN HODE (vv. 121 ff.)

As printed by Copland, at the end of his edition
of the Gest, with a few corrections from White's
edition, 1634 : Ritson's Robin Hood, 1795, II, 199.
I have not thought it necessary to collate Ritson's
reprint with Copland. The collations with White
here are made with the undated copy in the Bod-
leian Library, Z. 3. Art. Seld.

ROBYN HODE

Lysten, to [me], my mery men all,   v. 121
And harke what I shall say ;
Of an adventure I shall you tell,
That befell this other daye.
With a proude potter I met,
And a rose-garlande on his head,
The floures of it shone marvaylous freshe ;
This seven yere and more he hath used this waye,
Yet was he never so curteyse a potter
As one peny passage to paye.   130
Is there any of my mery men all
That dare be so bolde
To make the potter paie passage,
Either silver or golde?

LYTELL JOHN

Not I master, for twenty pound redy tolde,   135
For there is not among us al one
That dare medle with that potter, man for man.
I felt his handes not long agone,
But I had lever have ben here by the;
Therfore I knowe what he is.   140

Mete him when ye wil, or mete him whan ye shal,
He is as propre a man as ever you medle[d] withal.

ROBYN HODE

I will lai with the, Litel John, twenti pound so read,
If I wyth that potter mete,
I wil make him pay passage, maugre his head.   145

LYTTEL JOHN

I consente therto, so eate I bread;
If he pay passage, maugre his head,
Twenti pound shall ye have of me for your mede.

THE POTTERS BOY JACKE

Out alas, that ever I sawe this daye !
For I am clene out of my waye   150
From Notyngham towne ;
If I hye me not the faster,
Or I come there the market wel be done.

ROBYN HODE

Let me se, are the pottes hole and sounde?

JACKE

Yea, meister, but they will not breake the ground. 155

ROBYN HODE

I wil them breke, for the cuckold thi maisters sake ;
And if they will breake the grounde,
Thou shalt have thre pence for a pound.

JACKE

Out alas! what have ye done?
If my maister come, he will breke your crown. 160

THE POTTER

Why, thou horeson, art thou here yet?
Thou shouldest have bene at market.

JACKE

I met with Robin Hode, a good yeman ;
He hath broken my pottes,
And called you kuckolde by your name.   165

THE POTTER

Thou mayst be a gentylman, so God me save,
But thou semest a noughty knave.
Thou callest me cuckolde by my name,
And I swere by God and Saynt John,
Wyfe had I never none :   170
This cannot I denye.
But if thou be a good felowe,
I wil sel mi horse, mi harneis, pottes and paniers to,
Thou shalt have the one halfe, and I will have the other.
If thou be not so content,   175
Thou shalt have stripes, if thou were my brother.

ROBYN HODE

Harke, potter, what I shall say:
This seven yere and more thou hast used this way,
Yet were thou never so curteous to me
As one penny passage to paye.   180

THE POTTER

Why should I pay passage to thee?

ROBYN HODE

For I am Robyn Hode, chiefe gouernoure
Under the grene-woode tree.

THE POTTER

This seven yere have I used this way up and downe,
Yet payed I passage to no man,   185
Nor now I wyl not beginne, to do the worst thou can.

ROBYN HODE

Passage shalt thou pai here under the grene-wode tre,
Or els thou shalt leve a wedde with me.

THE POTTER

If thou be a good felowe, as men do the call,
Laye awaye thy bowe,   190
And take thy sword and buckeler in thy hande,
And se what shall befall.

ROBIN HODE

Lyttle John, where art thou?

LYTTEL [JOHN]

Here, mayster, I make God avowe.
I tolde you, mayster, so God me save,   195
That you shoulde fynde the potter a knave.
Holde your buckeler faste in your hande,
And I wyll styfly by you stande,
Ready for to fyghte ;
Be the knave never so stoute,   200
I shall rappe him on the snoute,
And put hym to flyghte.

The rest is wanting.

---

121. to [me], *wanting in White.*
142. medled, *W.*   153. maryet.
154. the, *C.*; thy, *W.*

186. to do: to *wanting in W.*
188. wedded, *C.*; wed, *W.*
196. your, *C.*; you, *W.*

122

ROBIN HOOD AND THE BUTCHER

A. 'Robin Hood and the Butcher,' Percy MS., p. 7; Hales and Furnivall, I, 19.

B. 'Robin Hood and the Butcher.' **a.** Wood, 401, 19 b.   **b.** Garland of 1663, No 6.   **c.** Garland of 1670, No 5.   **d.** Pepys, II, 102, No 89.

OTHER copies, of the second class, are in the Roxburghe collection, III, 259, and the Douce collection, III, 114. **B a** was printed, with changes, by Ritson, Robin Hood, 1795, II,

23; a copy resembling the Douce by Evans, Old Ballads, 1777, 1784, I, 106.

The story is a variation of Robin Hood and the Potter. According to **A**, the sheriff of Nottingham has resolved to have Robin's head. A butcher is driving through the forest, and his dog flies at Robin, for which Robin kills the dog. The butcher undertakes to let a little of the yeoman's blood for this, and there is a bout between staff and sword, in which we know that the butcher must bear himself well, though just here the first of three considerable gaps occurs. Robin buys the butcher's stock, changes clothes with him, and goes to Nottingham to market his flesh. There he takes up his lodging at the sheriff's, having perhaps conciliated the sheriff's wife with the present of a fine joint. He sells at so low a rate that his stock is all gone before any one else has sold a bit. The butchers ask him to drink, and Robin makes an appointment with them at the sheriff's. A second gap deprives us of the knowledge of what passes here, but we infer that, as in B, Robin is so reckless of his money that the sheriff thinks he can make a good bargain in horned beasts with him. Robin is ready; we see that he has come with a well-formed plan. The next day the sheriff goes to view the livestock, and is taken into the depth of the forest; it turns out that the wild deer are the butcher's

horned beasts. Robin's men come in at the sound of his horn; the sheriff is lightened of all his money, and is told that his head is spared only for his wife's sake. All this the sheriff tells his wife, on his return, and she replies that he has been served rightly for not tarrying at home, as she had begged him to do. The sheriff says he has learned wisdom, and will meddle no more with Robin Hood.

B a omits the brush between Robin and the butcher, mostly wanting, indeed, in A also, but only because of the damage which the manuscript has suffered.

The passage in which the sheriff is inveigled into Robin's haunts has, as already mentioned, close affinity with the Gest, 181 ff.

The first three stanzas of A would not be missed, and apparently belong to some other ballad.*

B a is signed T. R., as is also Robin Hood and the Beggar in two editions, and these we may suppose to be the initials of the person who wrote the story over with middle rhyme in the third line of the stanza, a peculiarity which distinguishes a group of ballads which were sung to the tune of Robin Hood and the Stranger: see Robin Hood and Little John, No 125, and also No 128.

A

Percy MS., p. 7; Hales and Furnivall, I, 19.

1 But Robin he walkes in the g[reene] fforrest,
  As merry as bird on boughe,
But he that feitches good Robins head,
  Hee 'le find him game enoughe.

2 But Robine he walkes in the greene fforrest,
  Vnder his trusty-tree;
Sayes, Hearken, hearken, my merrymen all,
  What tydings is come to me.

3 The sheriffe he hath made a cry,
  Hee 'le have my head i-wis;

But 'ere a tweluemonth come to an end
  I may chance to light on his.

4 Robin he marcht in the greene forrest,
  Vnder the greenwood scray,
And there he was ware of a proud bucher,
  Came driuing flesh by the way.

5 The bucher he had a cut-taild dogg,
  And at Robins face he flew;
But Robin he was a good sword,
  The bucher's dogg he slew.

6 'Why slayes thou my dogg?' sayes the bucher,
  'For he did none ill to thee;

* Fricke, Die Robin-Hood-Balladen, p. 20 f, suggests a ballad of Robin Hood and the Sheriff (How Robin took revenge for the sheriff's setting a price on his head), which may have been blended with another, of the Rescue of a Knight, to form the sixth fit of The Gest; and points to st. 329 of the Gest, 'Robyn Hode walked in the forrest,' etc., as the probable beginning of such a ballad.

By all the *saints* that are in heaven
Thou shalt haue buffetts three.'

7 He tooke his staffe then in his hand,
   And he turnd him round about:
'Thou hast a litle wild blood in thy head,
   Good fellow, thou 'st haue it letten out.'

8 'He that does that deed,' sayes Robin,
   'I 'le count him for a man;
But that while will I draw my sword,
   And fend it if I can.'

9 But Robin he stroke att the bloudy bucher,
   In place were he did stand,

*   *   *   *   *   *   *

10 'I [am] a younge bucher,' sayes Robin,
   'You fine dames am I come amonge;
But euer I beseech you, good Mrs Sheriffe,
   You must see me take noe wronge.'

11 'Thou art verry welcome,' said *Master* Sher-
      riff's wiffe,
   'Thy inne heere up [to] take;
If any good ffellow come in thy companie,
   Hee 'st be welcome for thy sake.'

12 Robin called ffor ale, soe did he for wine,
   And for it he did pay:
'I must to my markett goe,' says Robin,
   'For I hold time itt of the day.'

13 But Robin is to the markett gone,
   Soe quickly and beliue,
He sold more flesh for one peny
   Then othe[r] buchers did for fiue.

14 The drew about the younge bucher,
   Like sheepe into a fold;
Yea neuer a bucher had sold a bitt
   Till Robin he had all sold.

15 When Robin Hood had his markett made,
   His flesh was sold and gone;
Yea he had receiued but a litle mony,
   But thirty pence and one.

16 Seauen buchers, the garded Robin Hood,
   Ffull many time and oft;
Sayes, We must drinke with you, brother
      bucher,
   It 's custome of our crafte.

17 'If that be the custome of *your* crafte,
   As heere you tell to me,
Att four of the clocke in the afternoone
   At the sheriffs hall I wilbe.'

*   *   *   *   *   *   *

18 .   .   .   .
   'If thou doe like it well;
Yea heere is more by three hundred pound
   Then thou hast beasts to sell.'

19 Robyn sayd naught, the more he thought:
   'Mony neere comes out of time;
If once I catch thee in the greene fforest,
   That mony it shall be mine.'

20 But on the next day seuen butchers
   Came to guard the sheriffe that day;
But Robin he was the whigh[t]est man,
   He led them all the way.

21 He led them into the greene fforest,
   Vnder the trusty tree;
Yea, there were harts, and ther were hynds,
   And staggs with heads full high.

22 Yea, there were harts and there were hynds,
   And many a goodly ffawne;
'Now praised be God,' says bold Robin,
   'All these they be my owne.

23 'These are my horned beasts,' says Robin,
   '*Master* Sherriffe, w*hi*ch must make the
      stake;'
'But euer alacke, now,' said the sheriffe,
   '*That* tydings comes to late!'

24 Robin sett a shrill horne to his mouth,
   And a loud blast he did blow,
And then halfe a hundred bold archers
   Came rakeing on a row.

25 But when the came befor bold Robin,
   Even there the stood all bare:
'You are welcome, m*aster*, from Nottingham:
   How haue you sold y*ou*r ware?'

*   *   *   *   *   *   *

26 .   .   .   .
   .   .   .   .
   .   .   .   .
   It proues bold Robin Hood.

27 'Yea, he hath robbed me of all my gold
     And siluer *that* euer I had ;
   But that I had a verry good wife at home,
     I shold haue lost my head.

28 'But I had a verry good wife at home,
     W*h*ich made him gentle cheere,
   And therfor, for my wifes sake,
     I shold haue better favor heere.

29 'But such favor as he shewed me
     I might haue of the devills dam,

That will rob a man of all he hath,
     And send him naked home.'

30 'That is very well done,' then says his wiffe,
     'Itt is well done, I say ;
   You might haue tarryed att Nottingham,
     Soe fayre as I did you pray.'

31 'I haue learned wisdome,' sayes the sherriffe,
     'And, wife, I haue learned of thee ;
   But if Robin walke easte, or he walke west,
     He shall neuer be sought for me.'

B

a. Wood, 401, leaf 19 b.   b. Garland of 1663, No 6.
c. Garland of 1670, No 5.   d. Pepys, II, 102, No 89.

1 COME, all you brave gallants, and listen a while,
     With hey down, down, an a down
   That are in the bowers within ;
   For of Robin Hood, that archer good,
     A song I intend for to sing.

2 Upon a time it chancëd so
     Bold Robin in forrest did spy
   A jolly butcher, with a bonny fine mare,
     With his flesh to the market did hye.

3 'Good morrow, good fellow,' said jolly Robin,
     'What food hast ? tell unto me ;
   And thy trade to me tell, and where thou dost
         dwell,
     For I like well thy company.'

4 The butcher he answered jolly Robin :
     No matter where I dwell ;
   For a butcher I am, and to Notingham
     I am going, my flesh to sell.

5 'What is [the] price of thy flesh ?' said jolly
         Robin,
     'Come, tell it soon unto me ;
   And the price of thy mare, be she never so dear,
     For a butcher fain would I be.'

6 'The price of my flesh,' the butcher repli'd,
     'I soon will tell unto thee ;
   With my bonny mare, and they are not dear,
     Four mark thou must give unto me.'

7 'Four mark I will give thee,' saith jolly Robin,
     'Four mark it shall be thy fee ;
   Thy mony come count, and let me mount,
     For a butcher I fain would be.'

8 Now Robin he is to Notingham gone,
     His butcher's trade for to begin ;
   With good intent, to the sheriff he went,
     And there he took up his inn.

9 When other butchers they opened their meat,
     Bold Robin he then begun ;
   But how for to sell he knew not well,
     For a butcher he was but young.

10 When other butchers no meat could sell,
     Robin got both gold and fee ;
   For he sold more meat for one peny
     Than others could do for three.

11 But when he sold his meat so fast,
     No butcher by him could thrive ;
   For he sold more meat for one peny
     Than others could do for five.

12 Which made the butchers of Notingham
     To study as they did stand,
   Saying, surely he was some prodigal,
     That had sold his father's land.

13 The butchers they stepped to jolly Robin,
     Acquainted with him for to be ;
   'Come, brother,' one said, 'we be all of one
         trade,
     Come, will you go dine with me ?'

14 'Accurst of his heart,' said jolly Robin,
  'That a butcher doth deny;
I will go with you, my brethren true,
  And as fast as I can hie.'

15 But when to the sheriff's house they came,
  To dinner they hied apace,
And Robin he the man must be
  Before them all to say grace.

16 'Pray God bless us all,' said jolly Robin,
  'And our meat within this place;
A cup of sack so good will nourish our blood,
  And so I do end my grace.

17 'Come fill us more wine,' said jolly Robin,
  'Let us merry be while we do stay;
For wine and good cheer, be it never so dear,
  I vow I the reckning will pay.

18 'Come, brother[s], be merry,' said jolly Robin,
  'Let us drink, and never give ore;
For the shot I will pay, ere I go my way,
  If it cost me five pounds and more.'

19 'This is a mad blade,' the butchers then said;
  Saies the sheriff, He is some prodigal,
That some land has sold, for silver and gold,
  And now he doth mean to spend all.

20 'Hast thou any horn-beasts,' the sheriff repli'd,
  'Good fellow, to sell unto me?'
'Yes, that I have, good Master Sheriff,
  I have hundreds two or three.

21 'And a hundred aker of good free land,
  If you please it to see;
And I 'le make you as good assurance of it
  As ever my father made me.'

22 The sheriff he saddled a good palfrey,
  With three hundred pound in gold,
And away he went with bold Robin Hood,
  His horned beasts to behold.

23 Away then the sheriff and Robin did ride,
  To the forrest of merry Sherwood;
Then the sheriff did say, God bless us this day
  From a man they call Robin Hood!

24 But when that a little further they came,
  Bold Robin he chancëd to spy
A hundred head of good red deer,
  Come tripping the sheriff full nigh.

25 'How like you my hornd beasts, good Master Sheriff?
  They be fat and fair for to see;'
'I tell thee, good fellow, I would I were gone,
  For I like not thy company.'

26 Then Robin he set his horn to his mouth,
  And blew but blasts three;
Then quickly anon there came Little John,
  And all his company.

27 'What is your will?' then said Little John,
  'Good master come tell it to me;'
'I have brought hither the sheriff of Noting-ham,
  This day to dine with thee.'

28 'He is welcome to me,' then said Little John,
  'I hope he will honestly pay;
I know he has gold, if it be but well told,
  Will serve us to drink a whole day.'

29 Then Robin took his mantle from his back,
  And laid it upon the ground,
And out of the sheriffe['s] portmantle
  He told three hundred pound.

30 Then Robin he brought him thorow the wood,
  And set him on his dapple gray:
'O have me commended to your wife at home;'
  So Robin went laughing away.

A. 1². bughe.
  1³. d in head has a tag to it: Furnivall.
  6⁴. 3. After 9², 17⁴, 25⁴, half a page gone.
  13⁴. 5. 15⁴. 30ᵇ·ʸ. 17³. 4. 18³. 300ᴵᴵ.
  19³. cacth: in thy. 20¹. 7. 24³. 100ᵈ.
  28³. pro for for.

B. a. Robin Hood and the Butcher. To the Tune of Robin Hood and the Begger.
  At the end, T. R.
  Colophon. London. Printed for F. Grove on Snow Hill. F. Grove printed 1620–55: Chappell.

12⁴. hath sold.

b. Robin Hood and the Butcher; shewing how he robbed the sheriff of Nottingham. To the Tune of Robin Hood and the Begger.

4². I do. 5¹. What is price. 10⁴, 11⁴. Then. 12¹. when *misprinted for* made. 12⁴. had sold. 18¹. brother. 18⁸. go on. 19⁸. hath sold. 21¹. And an. 21⁴. to me. 25¹. Sheriff *wanting*. 27⁴. with me. 29⁸. sheriffs.

c. *Title as in* b.

2, 8, *and after* 8, *burden:* a hey.

5¹. is yᵉ. 10⁴, 11⁴. Then. 12⁴. had sold. 17². do *wanting*. 18¹. brother. 18⁸. go on. 18⁴. costs. 19⁸. hath sold. 21². it please. 21⁸. you *wanting*. 21⁴. did me. 24⁸. red *wanting*. 27². pray tell. 29⁸. sheriffs.

d. Robin Hood and the Butcher. To the Tune of Robin Hood and the Beggar.

Colophon. Printed for I. Clarke, W. Thackeray, and T. Passenger. 1670–86 (?).

Burden. From 2¹ *on*, With a hey (*not* With hey). *Also after the fourth line*, With a hey, &c.

1¹. ye. 1². this bower. 1⁴. for *wanting*. 2². in the. 5¹. What's the. 5⁸. be it. 7⁸. The. 8⁸. a good. 9¹. butchers did open. 10⁴. Then. 12⁴. hath sold. 13⁸. of a. 14². will deny. 15⁸. Robin Hood. 16⁴. do *wanting*. 17². be merry. 18¹. brothers. 18⁴. pound or. 20¹. thou *wanting*: hornd: sheriff then said. 21¹. A hundred acres. 22². And with. 22⁸. And *wanting*. 26². blew out. 27¹. will master said. 27². I pray you come. 27⁸. hither *wanting*. 28¹. then *wanting*. 28⁸. were it but. 29⁴. five *for* three, *wrongly, see* 22². 30¹. he *wanting:* through.

123

ROBIN HOOD AND THE CURTAL FRIAR

A. 'Robine Hood and Ffryer Tucke,' Percy MS., p. 10; Hales and Furnivall, I, 26.

B. 'The Famous Battel between Robin Hood and the Curtal Fryer.' **a.** Garland of 1663, No 11. **b.*** Pepys, I, 78, No 37. **c.** Garland of 1670. **d.** Wood, 401, leaf 15 b. **e.** Pepys, II, 99, No 86. **f.** Douce, II, 184.

B also in the Roxburghe collection, III, 16.

B d was printed in Ritson's Robin Hood, 1795, II, 58, corrected by b and compared with e; and in Evans's Old Ballads, 1777–1784, I, 136, probably from the Aldermary garland.

The opening verses of A are of the same description as those with which Nos 117, 118, 119, and others begin. 1 has been corrupted, and 2 also, one would think, as there is no apparent reason for maids weeping and young men wringing hands in the merry month of May. In the first stanza,

But how many merry monthes be in the yeere?
   There are 13 in May;

The midsummer moone is the merryest of all,
   Next to the merry month of May.

m o n t h in the first and the fourth line might be changed to m o o n, to justify thirteen in the second, and to accord with m o o n in the third. For in May, in the second line, we may read, I say, or many say. The first stanza of No 140, B, runs:

There are twelve months in all the year,
   As I hear many say;
But the merriest month in all the year
   Is the merry month of May.

* b would have taken precedence of a, having been printed earlier (1607–41), but I am at liberty only to collate Pepys copies. The Wood copies of Robin Hood ballads are generally preferable to the Pepys.

Nearly, or quite, one half of A has been torn from the manuscript, but there is no reason to suppose that the story differed much from that of B.

Upon Little John's killing a hart at five hundred foot, Robin Hood exclaims that he would ride a hundred mile to find John's match. Scadlock, with a laugh, says that there is a friar at Fountains Abbey who will beat both John and Robin, or indeed Robin and all his yeomen. Robin Hood takes an oath never to eat or drink till he has seen that friar. (Cf. No 30, I, 275, 279.) Robin goes to Fountains Abbey, and ensconces his men in a fern-brake. He finds the friar walking by the water, well armed, and begs [orders, B] the friar to carry him over.* The friar takes Robin on his back, and says no word till he is over; then draws his sword and bids Robin carry him back, or he shall rue it. Robin takes the friar on his back, and says no word till he is over; then bids the friar carry him over once more. The friar, without a word, takes Robin on his back, and when he comes to the middle of the stream throws him in. When both have swum to the shore, Robin lets an arrow fly, which the friar puts by with his buckler. The friar cares not for his arrows, though Robin shoots till his arrows are all gone. They take to swords, and fight with them for six good hours, when Robin begs the boon of blowing three blasts on his horn. The friar gives him leave to blow his eyes out: fifty bowmen come raking over the lea. The friar in turn asks a boon, to whistle thrice in his fist. Robin cares not how much he whistles: fifty good bandogs come raking in a row. Here there is a divergence. According to A, the friar will match every man with a dog, and himself with Robin. God forbid, says Robin; better be matched with three of the dogs than with thee. Stay thy tikes, and let us be friends. In B, two dogs go at Robin and tear his mantle from his back; all the arrows shot

at them the dogs catch in their mouths. Little John calls to the friar to call off his dogs, and enforces his words by laying half a score of them dead on the plain with his bow. The friar cries, Hold; he will make terms. Robin Hood offers the friar clothes and fee to forsake Fountains Abbey for the green-wood. We must infer, as in the parallel case of the Pinder of Wakefield, that the offer is accepted.† But the Curtal Friar, like the Pinder again, plays no part in Robin Hood story out of his own ballad.

Robin Hood and the Friar, in both versions, is in a genuinely popular strain, and was made to sing, not to print. Verbal agreements show that A and B have an earlier ballad as their common source; but of this, one or the other has retained but little. I cannot think that B 33, 34 are of the original matter. It is a derogation from Robin Hood's prowess that he should have his mantle torn from his back, and we may ask why the dogs do not catch Little John's arrows as well as others.

Fountains Abbey, near Ripon, in the West Riding of Yorkshire, was a Cistercian monastery, dating from the twelfth century. (It is loosely called a nunnery in A 4.) The friar is called "cutted" in A and "curtal" in B, and these words have been held to mean short-frocked, and therefore to make the friar a Franciscan. Staveley, The Romish Horseleech, speaking of the Franciscans, says at p. 214, Experience shews that in some countrys, where friers used to wear short habits, the order was presently contemned and derided, and men called them curtaild friers. Cited by Douce, Illustrations of Shakspere, I, 61. So, according to Douce, we may probably understand the curtal friar to be a curtailed friar, and in like manner of the curtal dogs. "Cutted" in A can signify nothing but short-frocked. In the title of that version, though not in the text, the friar is called Tuck, which means that he is "ytukked hye," like Chau-

---

* "A wet weary man," A 7¹, should probably be "wel weary." Why should R. H. be wet? And if wet, he may as well be a little wetter.

† Like terms are assured the cook by John in the Gest, sts 170, 171, and offered the Tanner by Robin Hood, R. H. and the Tanner, st. 26. Cf. Adam Bell, sts 163–65.

The 'Life' in the Sloane MS., which is put not much before 1600, says: He procurd the Pynner of Wakefeyld to become one of his company, and a freyr called Muchel; though some say he was an other kynd of religious man, for that the order of freyrs was not yet sprung up.

cer's Friar John, but not that he wears a short frock. The friar in the play (see below) has a "long cote," v. 46. But I apprehend that B has the older word in curtal, and that curtal is simply *curtilarius*, and applied to both friar and dogs because they had the care and keeping of the *curtile*, or vegetable garden, of the monastery.*

The title of A in the MS. is Robin Hood and Friar Tuck; from which it follows that the copyist, or some predecessor, considered the stalwart friar of Fountains Abbey to be one with the jocular friar of the May-games and the morris dance. But Friar Tuck, the wanton and the merry, like Maid Marian, owes his association with Robin Hood primarily to these popular sports, and not in the least to popular ballads. In the truly popular ballads Friar Tuck is never heard of, and in only two even of the broadsides, Robin Hood and Queen Katherine and Robin Hood's Golden Prize, is he so much as named; in both no more than named, and in both in conjunction with Maid Marian.

'The Play of Robin Hood,' the first half of which is based on the present ballad, calls the friar Friar Tuck, and represents him accordingly. See the Appendix. He is also called Tuck in the play founded on Guy of Gisborne.

In Munday's Downfall of Robert, Earl of Huntington, Friar Tuck is by implication identified with the friar who fell into the well, Dodsley's Old Plays, ed. Hazlitt, VIII, 185; and Mr Chappell is consequently led to say, at p. 390 of his 'Popular Music,' that the ballad of the Friar in the Well was in all probability a tale of "Robin Hood's fat friar." Cavilling at this phrase of Shakspere's only so far as to observe that the friar of the traditional Robin Hood ballad is as little fat as wanton, I need but say that the truth of the case had been already accurately expressed by Mr Chappell at p. 274 of his invaluable work:

"the story is a very old one, and one of the many against monks and friars in which not only England, but all Europe, delighted."

The boon to blow three blasts on his horn, B 25, is also asked by Robin of the Shepherd, No 134, st. 15. The reply made by the Shepherd, st. 16, is, If thou shouldst blow till to-morrow morn, I scorn one foot to flee. In R. H. Rescuing Three Squires, B 25, when Robin, disguised as a beggar, intimates to the sheriff that he may blow his horn, the answer is nearly the same as here: Blow till both thy eyes fall out. In No 127, st. 34 f, Robin asks a boon of the Tinker, without specifying what the boon is; the Tinker refuses; Robin blows his horn while the Tinker is not looking. In No 135, st. 16 f, Robin asks the three keepers to let him blow one blast on his horn, and they refuse. This boon of [three] blasts on a horn is not an important matter in these Robin Hood ballads, but it may be noticed as a feature of other popular ballads in which an actor is reduced to extremity: as in the Swedish ballad Stolts Signild, Arwidsson, II, 128, No 97, and the corresponding Signild og hendes Broder, Danske Viser, IV, 31, No 170, in both of which the answer to the request is, Blow as much as you will. So in a Russian bylina, when Solomon is to be hanged, he obtains permission three several times to blow his horn, and is told to blow as much as he will, and upon the third blast his army comes to the rescue: Rybnikof, II, No 52, Jagić, in Archiv für slavische Philologie, I, 104 ff; Miss Hapgood's Epic Songs of Russia, p. 287 f; also F. Vogt, Salman und Morolf, p. 104, sts 494 ff.† Three cries take the place of three blasts, upon occasion: as in the case of the unhappy maid in the German forms of No 4, I, 32 ff, where also the maid is sometimes told to cry as much as she wants, and in Gesta Romanorum, Oesterley, cap. 108, p. 440.

B is translated by Anastasius Grün, p. 124.

---

* Curtilarius (Old English curtiler) qui curtile curat aut incolit: Ducange.

† I suppose that it must already have been pointed out that the story of King Ramiro, versified by Southey from the Portuguese, Poetical Works, 1838, VI, 122, is a variety of that of Solomon. There are curious points of resemblance between 'R. H. rescuing Three Squires' and the conclusion of the story of Solomon.

A

Percy MS., p. 10; Hales and Furnivall, I, 26.

1 BUT how many merry monthes be in the
yeere ?
There are thirteen, I say;
The midsummer moone is the merryest of all,
Next to the merry month of May.

2 In May, when mayds beene fast weepand,
Young men their hands done wringe,

*   *   *   *   *   *   *

3 'I 'le . . pe . . . . .
Over may noe man for villanie : '
' I 'le never eate nor drinke,' Robin Hood
sa[id],
'Till I that cutted friar see.'

4 He builded his men in a brake of fearne,
A litle from that nunery ;
Sayes, If you heare my litle horne blow,
Then looke you come to me.

5 When Robin came to Fontaines Abey,
Wheras that fryer lay,
He was ware of the fryer where he stood,
And to him thus can he say.

6 A payre of blacke breeches the yeoman had on,
His coppe all shone of steele,
A fayre sword and a broad buckeler
Beseemed him very weell.

7 'I am a wet weary man,' said Robin Hood,
' Good fellow, as thou may see ;
Wilt beare [me] over this wild water,
Ffor sweete Saint Charity ? '

8 The fryer bethought him of a good deed ;
He had done none of long before ;
He hent up Robin Hood on his backe,
And over he did him beare.

9 But when he came over that wild water,
A longe sword there he drew :
' Beare me backe againe, bold outlawe,
Or of this thou shalt have enoughe.'

10 Then Robin Hood hent the fryar on his back,
And neither sayd good nor ill ;

11 Then Robin Hood wett his fayre greene hoze,
A span aboue his knee ;
S[ay]s, Beare me ore againe, thou cutted
f[ryer]

*   *   *   *   *   *   *

12 .   .   .   .
.   .   .   .   .   .
.   .   .   .   good bowmen
[C]ame raking all on a rowe.

13 ' I beshrew thy head,' said the cutted ffriar,
' Thou thinkes I shall be shente ;
I thought thou had but a man or two,
And thou hast [a] whole conuent.

14 ' I lett thee haue a blast on thy horne,
Now giue me leaue to whistle another ;
I cold not bidd thee noe better play
And thou wert my owne borne brother.'

15 ' Now fute on, fute on, thou cutted fryar,
I pray God thou neere be still ;
It is not the futing in a fryers fist
That can doe me any ill.'

16 The fryar sett his neave to his mouth,
A loud blast he did blow ;
Then halfe a hundred good bandoggs
Came raking all on a rowe.

17 .   .   .   .
.   .   .   .   .   .
' Euery dogg to a man,' said the cutted fryar,
' And I my selfe to Robin Hood.'

18 ' Over God's forbott,' said Robin Hood,
' That euer that soe shold bee ;
I had rather be mached with three of the tikes
Ere I wold be matched on thee.

19 ' But stay thy tikes, thou fryar,' he said,
' And freindshipp I 'le haue with thee ;
But stay thy tikes, 'thou fryar,' he said,
' And saue good yeomanry.'

20 The fryar he sett his neave to his mouth,
A lowd blast he did blow ;

The doggs the coucht downe euery one,
They couched downe on a rowe.

21 'What is thy will, thou yeoman?' he said,
'Haue done and tell it me;'

'If that thou will goe to merry greenwood,

*   *   *   *   *   *   *

B

a. Garland of 1663, No 11.   b. Pepys, I, 78, No 37.
c. Garland of 1670, No 10.   d. Wood, 401, leaf 15 b.
e. Pepys, II, 99, No 86.   f. Douce, II, 184.

1 In summer time, when leaves grow green,
And flowers are fresh and gay,
Robin Hood and his merry men
Were disposed to play.

2 Then some would leap, and some would run,
And some would use artillery:
'Which of you can a good bow draw,
A good archer to be?

3 'Which of you can kill a buck?
Or who can kill a do?
Or who can kill a hart of greece,
Five hundred foot him fro?'

4 Will Scadlock he killd a buck,
And Midge he killd a do,
And Little John killd a hart of greece,
Five hundred foot him fro.

5 'God's blessing on thy heart,' said Robin Hood,
'That hath [shot] such a shot for me;
I would ride my horse an hundred miles,
To finde one could match with thee.'

6 That causd Will Scadlock to laugh,
He laughed full heartily:
'There lives a curtal frier in Fountains Abby
Will beat both him and thee.

7 'That curtal frier in Fountains Abby
Well can a strong bow draw;
He will beat you and your yeomen,
Set them all on a row.'

8 Robin Hood took a solemn oath,
It was by Mary free,
That he would neither eat nor drink
Till the frier he did see.

9 Robin Hood put on his harness good,
And on his head a cap of steel,
Broad sword and buckler by his side,
And they became him weel.

10 He took his bow into his hand,
It was made of a trusty tree,
With a sheaf of arrows at his belt,
To the Fountains Dale went he.

11 And comming unto Fountain[s] Dale,
No further would he ride;
There was he aware of a curtal frier,
Walking by the water-side.

12 The fryer had on a harniss good,
And on his head a cap of steel,
Broad sword and buckler by his side,
And they became him weel.

13 Robin Hood lighted off his horse,
And tied him to a thorn:
'Carry me over the water, thou curtal frier,
Or else thy life's forlorn.'

14 The frier took Robin Hood on his back,
Deep water he did bestride,
And spake neither good word nor bad,
Till he came at the other side.

15 Lightly leapt Robin Hood off the friers back;
The frier said to him again,
Carry me over this water, fine fellow,
Or it shall breed thy pain.

16 Robin Hood took the frier on 's back,
Deep water he did bestride,
And spake neither good word nor bad,
Till he came at the other side.

17 Lightly leapt the fryer off Robin Hoods back;
Robin Hood said to him again,
Carry me over this water, thou curtal frier,
Or it shall breed thy pain.

18 The frier took Robin Hood on 's back again,
  And stept up to the knee;
Till he came at the middle stream,
  Neither good nor bad spake he.

19 And coming to the middle stream,
  There he threw Robin in:
'And chuse thee, chuse thee, fine fellow,
  Whether thou wilt sink or swim.'

20 Robin Hood swam to a bush of broom,
  The frier to a wicker wand;
Bold Robin Hood is gone to shore,
  And took his bow in hand.

21 One of his best arrows under his belt
  To the frier he let flye;
The curtal frier, with his steel buckler,
  He put that arrow by.

22 'Shoot on, shoot on, thou fine fellow,
  Shoot on as thou hast begun;
If thou shoot here a summers day,
  Thy mark I will not shun.'

23 Robin Hood shot passing well,
  Till his arrows all were gone;
They took their swords and steel bucklers,
  And fought with might and maine;

24 From ten oth' clock that day,
  Till four ith' afternoon;
Then Robin Hood came to his knees,
  Of the frier to beg a boon.

25 'A boon, a boon, thou curtal frier,
  I beg it on my knee;
Give me leave to set my horn to my
    mouth,
  And to blow blasts three.'

26 'That will I do,' said the curtal frier,
  'Of thy blasts I have no doubt;
I hope thou 'lt blow so passing well
  Till both thy eyes fall out.'

27 Robin Hood set his horn to his mouth,
  He blew but blasts three;
Half a hundred yeomen, with bows bent,
  Came raking over the lee.

28 'Whose men are these,' said the frier,
  'That come so hastily?'

'These men are mine,' said Robin Hood;
  'Frier, what is that to thee?'

29 'A boon, a boon,' said the curtal frier,
  'The like I gave to thee;
Give me leave to set my fist to my mouth,
  And to whute whutes three.'

30 'That will I do,' said Robin Hood,
  'Or else I were to blame;
Three whutes in a friers fist
  Would make me glad and fain.'

31 The frier he set his fist to his mouth,
  And whuted whutes three;
Half a hundred good ban-dogs
  Came running the frier unto.

32 'Here's for every man of thine a dog,
  And I my self for thee:'
'Nay, by my faith,' quoth Robin Hood,
  'Frier, that may not be.'

33 Two dogs at once to Robin Hood did go,
  The one behind, the other before;
Robin Hoods mantle of Lincoln green
  Off from his back they tore.

34 And whether his men shot east or west,
  Or they shot north or south,
The curtal dogs, so taught they were,
  They kept their arrows in their mouth.

35 'Take up thy dogs,' said Little John,
  'Frier, at my bidding be;'
'Whose man art thou,' said the curtal frier,
  'Comes here to prate with me?'

36 'I am Little John, Robin Hoods man,
  Frier, I will not lie;
If thou take not up thy dogs soon,
  I 'le take up them and thee.'

37 Little John had a bow in his hand,
  He shot with might and main;
Soon half a score of the friers dogs
  Lay dead upon the plain.

38 'Hold thy hand, good fellow,' said the curtal
    frier,
  'Thy master and I will agree;
And we will have new orders taken,
  With all the haste that may be.'

39 'If thou wilt forsake fair Fountains Dale,
   And Fountains Abby free,
Every Sunday throughout the year,
   A noble shall be thy fee.

40 'And every holy day throughout the year,
   Changed shall thy garment be,

If thou wilt go to fair Nottingham,
   And there remain with me.'

41 This curtal frier had kept Fountains Dale
   Seven long years or more;
There was neither knight, lord, nor earl
   Could make him yield before.

———◆———

A. *Half a page is gone after* 2², 11³, 21³.
   1¹. moones? 1². 13 in May.
   1⁴. month *may pass, though* moone *is expected.*
   2¹,². *might perhaps be intelligible with the
      other half of the stanza.*
   10⁴, 20³. They. 11¹. eze.
   13⁴. counent? comment? *F.* 15¹. Now fate.
   16³. 100ᵈ. 17³,⁴. *bis* }
   18¹. Ever. 18³. 3.

B. a. The famous battel between Robin Hood and
   the Curtal Fryer, near Fountain Dale.
   To a new northern tune.
   4¹, 6¹. Sadlock : Scadlock *elsewhere.*
   15¹. stept. *Cf.* 17¹ : leapt *in* b, e.
   19⁴. sing.
   24³. his *wanting, and in all but* b, e.
   24⁴. the *wanting, and in all but* b, e.
   27⁴. ranking : *in* d, e, f, ranging.
   32¹. of thine *wanting : found only in* b.
   34⁴. catcht : kept *in* b, d. 35³. thon.

b. *Title as in* a, *omitting* near Fountain Dale.
   Printed at London for H. Gosson. (1607–41.)
   2⁴. for to. 3⁴, 4⁴, 5³, 27³, 31³. hundreth.
   5³. a *for* an. 5⁴. with *wanting.* 7³. and all.
   7⁴. all a on a. 8¹. Hood he.
   9², 12². And *wanting.* 10⁴. Fountaine.
   11¹. into. 11². he would.
   11³. he was : of the. 12¹. a *wanting.*
   14⁴, 16⁴. th' other. 15¹. leapt *for* stept.
   16¹. on his. 18¹. Hood *wanting.*
   18². in *for* up. 20². wigger. 20⁴. in his.
   22¹. Scot : *a misprint.* 23². gane.
   23⁴. They *for* And. 24¹. of clock of that.
   24². four of th'. 24³. to his. 24⁴. of the.
   25⁴. But to. 26¹. I will. 27⁴. raking.
   28². comes.
   29⁴, 30³, 31². whues, *unobjectionable : in all
      the rest* whutes.
   31¹. he set. 31³. of good band-dogs.
   32¹. man of thine. 32³. said *for* quoth.
   34⁴. kept the. 38⁴. that *wanting.*
   40¹. through the. 41². and more.

c. *Title as in* a, *except* Dales.
   5². hath *wanting.* 6³, 7¹. Fountain.
   8⁴. he the frier did. 15¹. stept. 20¹. swom.
   23¹. shot so. 28³. men *wanting.*
   31³. band-dogs. 34⁴. catcht. 35⁴. to me.
   40². garments.

d. *Title as in* b.
   Printed for F. Coles, T. Vere, W. Gilbertson.
      (1640–80 ?)
   5³. a. 5⁴. with *wanting.* 7⁴. all in.
   11¹. Fountains. 11². farther. 15¹. stept.
   16¹. on his. 20². wigger. 23¹. shot so.
   23⁴. They *for* And. 24³. his *wanting.*
   24⁴. the *wanting.* 27⁴. ranging.
   28³. men *wanting.* 31¹. he *wanting.*
   32¹. of thine *wanting.* 33². and the other.
   34⁴. They kept. 39³. through the.
   40². garments.

e. *Title as in* b.
   Printed for W. Thackeray, J. Millet, and A.
      Milbourn. (1680–97 ?)
   2⁴. for *wanting.* 3⁴, 4⁴. hundreth.
   5². That shot such a shoot. 5³. a *for* an.
   5⁴. with *wanting.* 6³. Fountain.
   7, 8. *wanting.* 10². made *wanting.*
   11¹. Fountain's. 11². farther. 11³. he was.
   12¹. on *wanting.* 15¹. leapt *for* stept.
   15³. thou fine. 16¹. on his. 16³. speak.
   17³. over the. 20². wigger. 20³. to the.
   22². on *wanting.* 23¹. shot so.
   23². were all gane. 23⁴. They *for* And.
   24³. to his. 24⁴. Of the. 26¹. I will.
   27². blew out. 27⁴. ranging.
   31³. bay dogs. 32¹. Here is.
   34³. The cutrtles. 34⁴. caught the.
   38¹. Hold thy hand, hold thy hand, said.
   39¹,², 41¹. Fountain. 40¹. through the.
   40². garments. 41². and *for* or.

f. *Title as in* b.
   London, printed for F. Coles, T. Vere, and
      J. Wright. (1655–80.)
   2². some *wanting.* 5². shot such a shoot.
   5³. a. 5⁴. with *wanting.* 11¹. Fountains.

11². farther. 11⁸. ware. 15¹. step'd.
15⁸. thou fine. 16¹. on his.
20². wigger. 20⁸. to the. 21⁸, 34⁸. curtle.
22². on *wanting*. 23¹. shot so.
23². Till all his arrows were.
23⁴. They *for* And. 24⁸. his *wanting*.
24⁴. the *wanting*. 27⁴. ranging.

28⁸. men *wanting*. 30⁸. fryer.
31¹. he *wanting*. 31⁸. bay-dogs.
32¹. Here is : of thine *wanting*.
33². and the other. 34⁴. caught the.
39², 41¹. Fountain. 39⁸, 40¹. through the.
40². garments. 41². and more.

APPENDIX

THE PLAY OF ROBIN HOOD

(1–110)

a. Ritson's Robin Hood, 1795, II, 192, as printed
   by William Copland, at the end of his edition
   of the Gest.
b. As printed by Edward White, at the end of his
   edition of the Gest: Bodleian Library, Z. 3.
   Art. Seld.

ROBYN HODE

Now stand ye forth, my mery men all,
And harke what I shall say;
Of an adventure I shal you tell,
The which befell this other day.
5 As I went by the hygh way,
With a stout frere I met,
And a quarter-staffe in his hande.
Lyghtely to me he lept,
And styll he bade me stande.
10 There were strypes two or three,
But I cannot tell who had the worse,
But well I wote the horeson lept within me,
And fro me he toke my purse.
Is there any of my mery men all
15 That to that frere wyll go,
And bryng hym to me forth withall,
Whether he wyll or no?

LYTELL JOHN

Yes, mayster, I make God avowe,
To that frere wyll I go,
20 And bring him to you,
Whether he wyl or no.

FRYER TUCKE

Deus hic ! deus hic ! God be here !
Is not this a holy worde for a frere?
God save all this company!
25 But am not I a jolly fryer?
For I can shote both farre and nere,

And handle the sworde and buckler,
And this quarter-staffe also.
If I mete with a gentylman or yeman,
30 I am not afrayde to loke hym upon,
Nor boldly with him to carpe ;
If he speake any wordes to me,
He shall have strypes two or thre,
That shal make his body smarte.
35 But, maisters, to shew you the matter
Wherfore and why I am come hither,
In fayth I wyll not spare.
I am come to seke a good yeman,
In Bernisdale men sai is his habitacion,
40 His name is Robyn Hode.
And if that he be better man than I,
His servaunt wyll I be, and serve him truely;
But if that I be better man than he,
By my truth my knave shall he be,
45 And leade these dogges all three.

ROBYN HODE

Yelde the, fryer, in thy long cote.

FRYER TUCKE

I beshrew thy hart, knave, thou hurtest my throt[e].

ROBYN HODE

I trowe, fryer, thou beginnest to dote ;
Who made the so malapert and so bolde
50 To come into this forest here,
Amonge my falowe dere?

FRYER

Go louse the, ragged knave.
If thou make mani wordes, I will geve the on the
     eare,
Though I be but a poore fryer.
55 To seke Robyn Hode I am com here,
And to him my hart to breke.

ROBYN HODE

Thou lousy frer, what wouldest thou with hym?
He never loved fryer, nor none of freiers kyn.

FRYER

Avaunt, ye ragged knave !
60 Or ye shall have on the skynne.

ROBYN HODE

Of all the men in the morning thou art the worst,
To mete with the I have no lust;
For he that meteth a frere or a fox in the morning,
To spede ill that day he standeth in jeoperdy.
65 Therfore I had lever mete with the devil of hell,
(Fryer, I tell the as I thinke,)
Then mete with a fryer or a fox
In a mornyng, or I drynk.

FRYER

Avaunt, thou ragged knave ! this is but a mock ;
70 If thou make mani words thou shal have a
knock.

ROBYN HODE

Harke, frere, what I say here :
Over this water thou shalt me bere,
The brydge is borne away.

FRYER

To say naye I wyll not;
75 To let the of thine oth it were great pitie and sin ;
But up on a fryers backe, and have even in !

ROBYN HODE

Nay, have over.

FRYER

Now am I, frere, within, and thou, Robin, without,
To lay the here I have no great doubt.
80 Now art thou, Robyn, without, and I, frere, within,
Lye ther, knave ; chose whether thou wilte sinke
or swym.

ROBYN HODE

Why, thou lowsy frere, what hast thou done?

FRYER

Mary, set a knave over the shone.

ROBYN HODE

Therfore thou shalt abye.

FRYER

85 Why, wylt thou fyght a plucke?

ROBYN HODE

And God send me good lucke.

FRYER

Than have a stroke for fryer Tucke.

ROBYN HODE

Holde thy hande, frere, and here me speke.

FRYER

Say on, ragged knave,
90 Me semeth ye begyn to swete.

ROBYN HODE

In this forest I have a hounde,
I wyl not give him for an hundreth pound.
Geve me leve my horne to blowe,
That my hounde may knowe.

FRYER

95 Blowe on, ragged knave, without any doubte,
Untyll bothe thyne eyes starte out.
Here be a sorte of ragged knaves come in,
Clothed all in Kendale grene,
And to the they take their way nowe.

ROBYN HODE

100 Peradventure they do so.

FRYER

I gave the leve to blowe at thy wyll,
Now give me leve to whistell my fyll.

ROBYN HODE

Whystell, frere, evyl mote thou fare !
Untyll bothe thyne eyes stare.

FRYER

105 Now Cut and Bause !
Breng forth the clubbes and staves,
And downe with those ragged knaves !

ROBYN HODE

How sayest thou, frere, wylt thou be my man,
To do me the best servyse thou can?
110 Thou shalt have both golde and fee.

After ten lines of ribaldry, which have no per-
tinency to the traditional Robin Hood and Friar,
the play abruptly passes to the adventure of Robin
Hood and the Potter.

a. *Ritson has been followed, without collation with
Copland.*
35. maister.   64. spede ell.

70. you, you *for* thou, thou.   82. donee.
104. starte.
b. 13. he *wanting.*   15. to the.   23. word of.
31. Not.   35. maister.   41. if he.   43. be a.
59. ye *wanting.*   61. in a.
65. had rather : of hell *wanting.*   70. y^u: y^u shalt.
81. choose either sinke.   97. Here is.
103. might thou.   104. stare.

124

THE JOLLY PINDER OF WAKEFIELD

A. a. Wood, 402, leaf 43. b. Garland of 1663, No 4. B. Percy MS., p. 15; Hales and Furnivall, I, 32.
c. Garland of 1670, No 3. d. Pepys, II, 100, No
87 a. e. Wood, 401, leaf 61 b.

———◆———

PRINTED in Ritson's Robin Hood, 1795, II, 16, from one of Wood's copies, " compared with two other copies in the British Museum, one in black letter:" Evans, Old Ballads, 1777, 1784, I, 99.

There is another copy in the Roxburghe collection, III, 24, and there are two in the Bagford.

'A ballett of Wakefylde and a grene' is entered to Master John Wallye and Mistress Toye, 19 July, 1557–9 July, 1558: Stationers' Registers, Arber, I, 76.

The ballad is one of four, besides the Gest, that were known to the author of the Life of Robin Hood in Sloane MS., 715, which dates from the end of the seventeenth century. It is thoroughly lyrical, and therein " like the old age," and was pretty well sung to pieces before it ever was printed. A snatch of it is sung, as Ritson has observed, in each of the Robin Hood plays, The Downfall of Robert, Earl of Huntington, by Anthony Munday, and The Death of Robert, Earl of Huntington, by A. Munday and Henry Chettle, both printed in 1601.

> At Michaelmas cometh my covenant out,
>   My master gives me my fee;
> Then, Robin, I 'll wear thy Kendall green,
>   And wend to the greenwood with thee.
>
> O there dwelleth a jolly pinder
>   At Wakefield all on a green.*

Silence sings the line 'And Robin Hood, Scarlet, and John,' 3², in the Second Part of

King Henry Fourth, V, 3, and Falstaff addresses Bardolph as Scarlet and John in the first scene of The Merry Wives of Windsor. In Beaumont and Fletcher's Philaster, V, 4, Dyce, I, 295, we have: " Let not . . . your Robinhoods, Scarlets, and Johns tie your affections in darkness to your shops." Scarlet and John, comrades of Robin Hood from the beginning, are prominent in many ballads.

Robin Hood, Scarlet, and John have left the highway and made a path over the corn,† apparently in defiance of the Pinder of Wakefield, who has the fame of being able to exact a penalty of trespassers, whatever their rank. The Pinder bids them turn again; they, being three to one, scorn to comply. The Pinder fights with them till their swords are broken. Robin cries Hold! and asks the Pinder to join his company in the greenwood. This the Pinder is ready to do at Michaelmas, when his engagement to his present master will be terminated. Robin asks for meat and drink, and the Pinder offers him bread, beef, and ale.

The adventure of the ballad is naturally introduced into the play of George a Greene, the Pinner of Wakefield, printed in 1599, reprinted in Dodsley's Old Plays (the third volume of the edition of 1825), and by Dyce among the works of Robert Greene. George a Greene fights with Scarlet, and beats him; then with Much (not John), and beats him; then with Robin Hood. Robin protests he is the stoutest champion that ever he laid hands on, and says:

———

* Dodsley's Old Plays, 4th ed., by W. C. Hazlitt, VIII, 195, 232.

† A very serious offence: see E. Peacock, Hales and Furnivall, Percy Folio Manuscript, I, lxii, note to p. 34.

George, wilt thou forsake Wakefield
  And go with me?
Two liveries will I give thee every year,
  And forty crowns shall be thy fee.

George welcomes Robin to his house, offering him wafer-cakes, beef, mutton, and veal. (Dyce, II, 196 f.)

The scene in the play is found in the prose history of George a Green, London, 1706, of which a copy is known, no doubt substantially the same, of the date 1632. The Pinner here fells 'Slathbatch,' Little John, and the Friar, before his bout with Robin. See Thoms, A Collection of Early Prose Romances, II, 44–47, and the prefaces, p. viii ff, p. xviii f, for more about the popularity of the Pinner's story.

Wakefield is in the West Riding of the county of York.

Richard Brathwayte, in a poetical epistle " to all true-bred northerne sparks of the generous society of the Cottoneers," Strappado for the Divell, 1615 (cited by Ritson, Robin Hood, ed. 1795, I, xxvii–ix), speaks of

The Pindar's valour, and how firme he stood
In th' townes defence gainst th' rebel Robin Hood;
How stoutly he behav'd himselfe, and would,
In spite of Robin, bring his horse to th' fold:

from which we might infer that according to one account the Pinder had impounded Robin's horse. But as Robin Hood, in this passage, is confounded with the rebel Earl of Kendal, or some one of his adherents, it is safe to suppose that Brathwayte has been twice inaccurate.*

The ballad is so imperfect that one might be in doubt whether the Pinder fights with Robin Hood, Scarlet, and John all together or successively. But to suppose the Pinder capable of dealing with all three at once would be monstrous, and we see from the History and from Greene's play that the Pin-

der must take them one after the other, and Robin the last of the three.

There are seven other ballads, besides The Pinder of Wakefield, in which Robin Hood, after trying his strength with a stout fellow, and coming off somewhat or very much the worse, induces his antagonist to enlist in his company. Several of these are very late, and most of them imitations, we may say, of the Pinder, or one of the other. These ballads are: Robin Hood and the Curtal Friar; Robin Hood and Little John; Robin Hood and the Tanner; Robin Hood and the Tinker, 28 ff; Robin Hood Revived; Robin Hood and the Ranger; Robin Hood and the Scotchman. We might add Robin Hood and Maid Marian. The episode of Little John and the Cook, in the Gest, 165–171, is after the same pattern. There is another set in which a contest of a like description does not result in an accession to the outlaw-band. These are Robin Hood and the Potter; Robin Hood and the Butcher; Robin Hood and the Beggar, I; Robin Hood and the Beggar, II (Robin Hood first beaten, then three of his men severely handled); Robin Hood and the Shepherd (Robin Hood overmastered, Little John on the point of being beaten, etc.); The Bold Pedlar and Robin Hood (John outmatched first, then his master); Robin Hood's Delight (combat between Robin Hood, Little John, and Scadlock and three Keepers); Robin Hood and the Pedlars (again three to three).

There are, as might be expected, frequent verbal agreements in these ballads, and many of them are collected by Fricke, Die Robin-Hood-Balladen, pp 91–95.

The fights in these ballads last from an hour, Gest, st. 168, to a long summer's day, in this ballad, st. 6. In Robin Hood and Maid Marian, st. 11, the time is at least an hour, or more; in Robin Hood and the Tanner,

---

* Further on, Brathwayte alludes to a difference between Robin Hood and the Shoemaker of Bradford, which had been treated of by stage-poets. This refers to the fight that Robin Hood and George a Green have with the shoemakers, in chap. xii of the History (Thoms, p. 52 f), which is introduced into Robert Greene's play (Dyce, p. 199 f),

but only George does the fighting there. It is mere carelessness when Munday, 'Downfall,' etc., applies the name of George a Greene to the Shoemaker of Bradford (Hazlitt, as above, p. 151). In the same play and the same scene he makes Scathlock and Scarlet two persons.

st. 20, two hours and more ; in Robin Hood and the Ranger, st. 12, three hours ; in Robin Hood and the Curtal Friar, B 24, and Robin Hood and the Shepherd, st. 11, from ten o'clock till four ; in Robin Hood's Delight, st. 11, from eight o'clock till two, and past.

———✦———

A

a. Wood, 402, leaf 43.   b. Garland of 1663, No 4.
c. Garland of 1670, No 3.   d. Pepys, II, 100, No 87 a.
e. Wood, 401, leaf 61 b.

1 In Wakefield there lives a jolly pinder,
 In Wakefield, all on a green ; (bis)

2 'There is neither knight nor squire,' said the
  pinder,
 ' Nor baron that is so bold, (bis)
Dare make a trespasse to the town of Wake-
 field,
 But his pledge goes to the pinfold.' (bis)

3 All this beheard three witty young men,
 'T was Robin Hood, Scarlet, and John ;
With that they spyed the jolly pinder,
 As he sate under a thorn.

4 'Now turn again, turn again,' said the pinder,
 ' For a wrong way have you gone ;
For you have forsaken the king his highway,
 And made a path over the corn.'

5 'O that were great shame,' said jolly Robin,
 ' We being three, and thou but one : '
The pinder leapt back then thirty good foot,
 'T was thirty good foot and one.

6 He leaned his back fast unto a thorn,
 And his foot unto a stone,
And there he fought a long summer's day,
 A summer's day so long,
Till that their swords, on their broad bucklers,
 Were broken fast unto their hands.

 * * * * * * *

7 'Hold thy hand, hold thy hand,' said Robin
  Hood,
 ' And my merry men euery one ;
For this is one of the best pinders
 That ever I try'd with sword.

8 'And wilt thou forsake thy pinder his craft,
 And live in [the] green wood with me ?
. . . .
. . . .

9 'At Michaelmas next my covnant comes out,
 When every man gathers his fee ;
I 'le take my blew blade all in my hand,
 And plod to the green wood with thee.'

10 'Hast thou either meat or drink,' said Robin
  Hood,
 ' For my merry men and me ?
. . . .
. . . .

11 'I have both bread and beef,' said the pinder,
 ' And good ale of the best ; '
' And that is meat good enough,' said Robin
  Hood,
 ' For such unbidden guest.

12 'O wilt thou forsake the pinder his craft,
 And go to the green wood with me ?
Thou shalt have a livery twice in the year,
 The one green, the other brown [shall be].'

13 'If Michaelmas day were once come and gone
 And my master had paid me my fee,
Then would I set as little by him
 As my master doth set by me.'

———✦———

B

Percy MS., p. 15 ; Hales and Furnivall, I, 32.

 * * * * * * *

1 'But hold y . . hold y . . . ' says Robin,
 ' My merrymen, I bid yee,
For this [is] one of the best pindars
 That euer I saw with mine eye.

2 'But hast thou any meat, thou iolly pindar,
  For my merrymen and me?'

. . . .

. . . .

3 'But I haue bread and cheese,' sayes the
    pindar,
  'And ale all on the best :'
  'That's cheere good enoughe,' said Robin,
  'For any such vnbidden guest.

4 'But wilt be my man?' said good Robin,
  'And come and dwell with me?

And twise in a yeere thy clothing [shall] be
    changed
  If my man thou wilt bee,
The tone shall be of light Lincolne greene,
  The tother of Picklory.'

5 'Att Michallmas comes a well good time,
  When men haue gotten in their ffee ;
I 'le sett as litle by my m*aster*
  As he now setts by me,
I 'le take my benbowe in my hande,
  And come into the grenwoode to thee.'

———•———

A. *The second and fourth lines were repeated in
    singing.*
  a. The Iolly Pinder of Wakefield.
    Printed for F. Coles, T. Vere, and W. G[i]l-
    ber[t]son. (F. Coles, 1646–1674; T. Vere,
    1648–1680; W. Gilbertson, 1640–1663.
    Chappell.)
    1¹. their.
    3¹. witty, *which all have, is a corruption of*
    wight.
    10¹. laid. 13⁴. by my.
  b, c. Robin Hood and the jolly Pinder of Wake-
    field, shewing how he fought with Robin
    Hood, Scarlet, and John a long summer's
    day. To a Northern tune.
  b. 1¹. there dwels. 2⁴. it goes. 4¹. saith.
    5¹. a *for* great: saith. 11². all. 11³. that's.
    12¹. thy *for* the.
  c. 4³. king's high. 6². fast unto.
    6⁴. And a. 6⁵. that *wanting*.
    9¹. covenants. 10¹. thou *wanting*.
  d. The Jolly Pinder of Wakefield with Robin
    Hood, Scarlet, and John.
    Printed by and for Alex. Milbourn, in Green-
    Arbor Court, in the Little Old-Baily. (A.
    Milbourn, 1670–1697. Chappell.)
    3³. espy'd. 3⁴. sat. 4². you have.
    4³. the kings. 5¹. a *for* great.
    6². foot against. 6³. they *for* he.
    6⁶. broke. 8¹. pinders craft.
    8². in the. 13¹. was come.
    13⁴. set *wanting*.
  e. The Jolly Pinder of Wakefield : with Robin
    Hood, Scarlet and John.
    No printer's name.

3³. espyed. 3⁴. sat. 4². you have.
4³. kings. 6¹. foot against. 6⁶. broke.
8¹. pinders craft. 13¹. was come.
13⁴. set *wanting*.

Pepys Penny Merriments Garland : *according
  to Hales and Furnivall.*
6⁴. And a. 6⁵. that *wanting*.
10¹. thou *wanting*. 12¹. thy pinder.

Gutch, Robin Hood, II, 144 f, *says that the
  Roxburghe copy has in* 3¹ *wight yeomen.
  He prints* 7²⁻⁴ :

    And my merry men stand aside ;
    For this is one of the best pinders
    That with sword ever I tryed.

8³,⁴. Thou shalt have a livery twice in the year,
    Th' one greene, tither brown shall be.

These parts of stanzas 7, 8 *he gives as from
  a black-letter copy, which he does not de-
  scribe.*

B. 1¹,² *make half a stanza in the MS., and* 1³,⁴
  are joined with 2¹,². 4⁵,⁶ *and* 5¹,² *make a
  stanza. It is not supposed that* 4 *and* 5
  *were originally stanzas of six lines, but
  rather that, one half of each of two stanzas
  having been forgotten, the other has at-
  tached itself to a complete stanza which
  chanced to have the same rhyme. Stanzas
  of six lines, formed in this way, are com-
  mon in traditional ballads.*
3⁴. guests. 4³. 2ₐ. in.

125

ROBIN HOOD AND LITTLE JOHN

a. A Collection of Old Ballads, 1723, I, 75.   b. Aldermary Garland, by R. Marshall, n. d., No 22.

———

RITSON, Robin Hood, 1795, II, 138 ; Evans, Old Ballads, 1777, 1784, I, 204.   There is a bad copy in a Robin Hood's Garland of 1749. " This ballad," says Ritson, " is named in a schedule of such things under an agreement between W. Thackeray and others in 1689, Col. Pepys, vol. 5." It occurs in a list of ballads printed for and sold by William Thackeray at the Angel in Duck-Lane (see The Ballad Society's reprint of the Roxburghe Ballads, W. Chappell, I, xxiv, from a copy in the Bagford collection), but by some caprice of fortune has not, so far as is known, come down in the broadside form, neither is it found in the older garlands.

Robin Hood and Little John belongs to a set of ballads which have middle rhyme in the third line of the stanza, and are directed to be sung to one and the same tune.   These are: R. H. and the Bishop, R. H. and the Beggar, R. H. and the Tanner, to the tune of R. H. and the Stranger ; R. H. and the Butcher, R. H.'s Chase, Little John and the Four Beggars, to the tune of R. H. and the Beggar ; R. H. and Little John, R. H. and the Ranger, to the tune of Arthur a Bland (that is, R. H. and the Tanner).   There is no ballad with the

title Robin Hood and the Stranger.   Ritson thought it proper to give this title to a ballad which uniformly bears the title of Robin Hood Newly Revived, No 128, because Robin's antagonist is repeatedly called "the stranger" in it.   But Robin's antagonist is equally often called "the stranger" in the present ballad (eleven times in each), and Robin Hood and Little John has the middle rhyme in the third line, which Robin Hood Newly Revived has not (excepting in seven stanzas at the end, which are a portion of a different ballad, Robin Hood and the Scotchman).   Robin Hood and Little John (and Robin Hood Newly Revived as well) would naturally be referred to as Robin Hood and the Stranger, for the same reason that Robin Hood and the Tanner is referred to as Arthur a Bland.   The fact that the middle rhyme in the third line is found in Robin Hood and Little John, but is lacking in Robin Hood Newly Revived, gives a slightly superior probability to the supposition that the former, or rather some older version of it (for the one we have is in a rank seventeenth-century style), had the secondary title of Robin Hood and the Stranger.*

Like Robin Hood's Progress to Nottingham,

* Robin Hood Newly Revived (which, by the way, is in the same bad style as Robin Hood and Little John) is directed to be sung 'to a delightful new Tune.' The tune, as is seen from the burden, was that of Arthur a Bland, etc., called in Robin Hood and the Prince of Aragon (the Second Part of Robin Hood Newly Revived) Robin Hood, or Hey down, down a down. The earliest printed copy of the air is preserved in the ballad-opera of The Jovial Crew, 1731 (Rimbault, in Gutch's Robin Hood, II, 433, Chappell's Popular Music, p. 391), and the song which is there sung to it has middle rhyme in the first line as well as the third, which is the case with no Robin Hood ballad except Robin Hood and the Peddlers.

Robin Hood and Maid Marian, which has the middle

rhyme in the third line, is directed to be sung to Robin Hood Revived. Robin Hood and the Scotchman, as already said, has middle rhyme in the third line ; so have The King's Disguise, etc., R. H. and the Golden Arrow, R. H. and the Valiant Knight ; but the tune assigned to the last is Robin Hood and the Fifteen Foresters, that is, Robin Hood's Progress to Nottingham.

It ought to be added that Robin Hood Newly Revived is found in the Garland of 1663, in company with R. H. and the Bishop, R. H. and the Butcher, etc., and that Robin Hood and Little John is not there ; but I do not consider this circumstance sufficient to offset the probability in favor of the supposition, that by Robin Hood and the Stranger is meant Robin Hood and Little John.

this ballad affects, in the right apocryphal way, to know an adventure of Robin's early life. Though but twenty years old, Robin has a company of threescore and nine bowmen. With all these he shakes hands one morning, and goes through the forest alone, prudently enjoining on the band to come to his help if he should blow his horn. He meets a stranger on a narrow bridge, and neither will give way. Robin threatens the stranger with an arrow, which, as he requires to be reminded, is cowardly enough, seeing that the other man has nothing but a staff. Recalled to ordinary manliness, Robin Hood, laying down his bow, provides himself with an oaken stick, and proposes a battle on the bridge, which he shall be held to win who knocks the other into the water in the end. In the end the stranger tumbles Robin into the brook, and is owned to have won the day. The band are now summoned by the horn, and when they hear what the stranger has done are about to seize and duck him, but are ordered to forbear. Robin Hood proposes to his antagonist that he shall join his men, and John Little, as he declares his name to be, accedes. John Little is seven foot tall.* Will Stutely says his name must be changed, and they rebaptize the "infant" as Little John.

'A pastorall plesant commedie of Robin Hood and Little John, etc.,' is entered to Edward White in the Stationers' Registers, May 14, 1594, and 'Robin Hood and Litle John' to Master Oulton, April 22, 1640. (Arber, II, 649, IV, 507.)

Translated by Anastasius Grün, p. 65.

————◆————

1 WHEN Robin Hood was about twenty years
        old,
    With a hey down down and a down
He happend to meet Little John,
    A jolly brisk blade, right fit for the trade,
    For he was a lusty young man.

2 Tho he was calld Little, his limbs they were
        large,
    And his stature was seven foot high;
Where-ever he came, they quak'd at his name,
    For soon he would make them to fly.

3 How they came acquainted, I'll tell you in
        brief,
    If you will but listen a while;
For this very jest, amongst all the rest,
    I think it may cause you to smile.

4 Bold Robin Hood said to his jolly bowmen,
    Pray tarry you here in this grove;
And see that you all observe well my call,
    While thorough the forest I rove.

5 We have had no sport for these fourteen long
        days,
    Therefore now abroad will I go;

Now should I be beat, and cannot retreat,
    My horn I will presently blow.

6 Then did he shake hands with his merry men all,
    And bid them at present good b'w'ye;
Then, as near a brook his journey he took,
    A stranger he chancd to espy.

7 They happend to meet on a long narrow bridge,
    And neither of them would give way;
Quoth bold Robin Hood, and sturdily stood,
    I'll show you right Nottingham play.

8 With that from his quiver an arrow he drew,
    A broad arrow with a goose-wing:
The stranger reply'd, I'll liquor thy hide,
    If thou offerst to touch the string.

9 Quoth bold Robin Hood, Thou dost prate like
        an ass,
    For were I to bend but my bow,
I could send a dart quite thro thy proud heart,
    Before thou couldst strike me one blow.

10 'Thou talkst like a coward,' the stranger re-
        ply'd;
    'Well armd with a long bow you stand,

---

* Fourteen foot, as proved by his bones, preserved, according to Hector Boece, in the kirk of Pette, in Murrayland.

See Ritson's Robin Hood, 1832, I, cxxxii f; and Gutch, II, 112, note *.

To shoot at my breast, while I, I protest,
  Have nought but a staff in my hand.'

11 'The name of a coward,' quoth Robin, 'I scorn,
    Wherefore my long bow I 'll lay by ;
  And now, for thy sake, a staff will I take,
    The truth of thy manhood to try.'

12 Then Robin Hood stept to a thicket of trees,
    And chose him a staff of ground-oak ;
  Now this being done, away he did run
    To the stranger, and merrily spoke :

13 Lo ! see my staff, it is lusty and tough,
    Now here on the bridge we will play ;
  Whoever falls in, the other shall win
    The battel, and so we 'll away.

14 'With all my whole heart,' the stranger re-
      ply'd ;
    'I scorn in the least to give out ;'
  This said, they fell to 't without more dispute,
    And their staffs they did flourish about.

15 And first Robin he gave the stranger a bang,
    So hard that it made his bones ring :
  The stranger he said, This must be repaid,
    I 'll give you as good as you bring.

16 So long as I 'm able to handle my staff,
    To die in your debt, friend, I scorn :
  Then to it each goes, and followd their blows,
    As if they had been threshing of corn.

17 The stranger gave Robin a crack on the crown,
    Which caused the blood to appear ;
  Then Robin, enrag'd, more fiercely engag'd,
    And followd his blows more severe.

18 So thick and so fast did he lay it on him,
    With a passionate fury and ire,
  At every stroke, he made him to smoke,
    As if he had been all on fire.

19 O then into fury the stranger he grew,
    And gave him a damnable look,
  And with it a blow that laid him full low,
    And tumbld him into the brook.

20 'I prithee, good fellow, O where art thou
      now ?'
    The stranger, in laughter, he cry'd ;

Quoth bold Robin Hood, Good faith, in the
      flood,
    And floating along with the tide.

21 I needs must acknowledge thou art a brave
      soul ;
    With thee I 'll no longer contend ;
  For needs must I say, thou hast got the day,
    Our battel shall be at an end.

22 Then unto the bank he did presently wade,
    And pulld himself out by a thorn ;
  Which done, at the last, he blowd a loud blast
    Straitway on his fine bugle-horn.

23 The eccho of which through the vallies did fly,
    At which his stout bowmen appeard,
  All cloathed in green, most gay to be seen ;
    So up to their master they steerd.

24 'O what 's the matter?' quoth William Stutely ;
    'Good master, you are wet to the skin :'
  'No matter,' quoth he ; 'the lad which you see,
    In fighting, hath tumbld me in.'

25 'He shall not go scot-free,' the others reply'd ;
    So strait they were seizing him there,
  To duck him likewise ; but Robin Hood cries,
    He is a stout fellow, forbear.

26 There 's no one shall wrong thee, friend, be
      not afraid ;
    These bowmen upon me do wait ;
  There 's threescore and nine ; if thou wilt be
      mine,
    Thou shalt have my livery strait.

27 And other accoutrements fit for a man ;
    Speak up, jolly blade, never fear ;
  I 'll teach you also the use of the bow,
    To shoot at the fat fallow-deer.

28 'O here is my hand,' the stranger reply'd,
    'I 'll serve you with all my whole heart ;
  My name is John Little, a man of good mettle ;
    Nere doubt me, for I 'll play my part.'

29 His name shall be alterd,' quoth William
      Stutely,
    'And I will his godfather be ;
  Prepare then a feast, and none of the least,
    For we will be merry,' quoth he.

30 They presently fetchd in a brace of fat does,
       With humming strong liquor likewise ;
   They lovd what was good ; so, in the green-
           wood,
       This pretty sweet babe they baptize.

31 He was, I must tell you, but seven foot high,
       And, may be, an ell in the waste ;
   A pretty sweet lad ; much feasting they had ;
       Bold Robin the christning grac'd.

32 With all his bowmen, which stood in a ring,
       And were of the Notti[n]gham breed ;
   Brave Stutely comes then, with seven yeomen,
       And did in this manner proceed.

33 'This infant was called John Little,' quoth he,
       'Which name shall be changed anon ;
   The words we 'll transpose, so where-ever he
           goes,
       His name shall be calld Little John.'

34 They all with a shout made the elements ring,
       So soon as the office was ore ;
   To feasting they went, with true merriment,
       And tippld strong liquor gillore.

35 Then Robin he took the pretty sweet babe,
       And cloathd him from top to the toe
   In garments of green, most gay to be seen,
       And gave him a curious long bow.

36 'Thou shalt be an archer as well as the best,
       And range in the greenwood with us ;
   Where we 'll not want gold nor silver, be-
           hold,
       While bishops have ought in their purse.

37 'We live here like squires, or lords of renown,
       Without ere a foot of free land ;
   We feast on good cheer, with wine, ale, and
           beer,
       And evry thing at our command.'

38 Then musick and dancing did finish the day ;
       At length, when the sun waxed low,
   Then all the whole train the grove did refrain,
       And unto their caves they did go.

39 And so ever after, as long as he livd,
       Altho he was proper and tall,
   Yet nevertheless, the truth to express,
       Still Little John they did him call.

———◆———

a. *Title.* Robin Hood and Little John. Being
   an account of their first meeting, their fierce
   encounter, and conquest. To which is
   added, their friendly agreement, and how
   he came to be calld Little John.
   To the tune of Arthur a Bland.

b. *Title as in* a.
   2². statue. 3². you would. 3³. among.
   3⁴. it *wanting.* 4³. his *for* my, *wrongly.*
   5¹. for *wanting.* 5³. be *wanting.*
   8⁴. offer. 9². where I do bend.

11². Therefore. 11³. I will.
13¹. it *wanting.* 13². on this.
15¹. And first : he *wanting.* 15². he *for* it.
16¹. a *for* my. 16³. both goes, and follow.
18¹. he did. 19¹. in a fury.
19³. which *for* that. 20¹. O *wanting.*
22³. blew. 23¹. did ring. 23⁴. their matter.
24³. that *for* which. 27¹. fitting also.
30¹. him *for* in. 30⁴. baptiz'd. 31¹. feet.
31³. He was a sweet. 32³. came.
34⁴. liquors. 35². the *wanting.*
39¹. they *for* he. 39². he be.

126

ROBIN HOOD AND THE TANNER

a. Wood, 401, leaf 9 b.

b. Garland of 1663, No 10.

c. Garland of 1670, No 9.

d. Pepys, II, 111, No 98.

PRINTED in Old Ballads, 1723, I, 83.

a was printed by Ritson, Robin Hood, 1795, II, 30. Evans has an indifferent copy, probably edited, in his Old Ballads, 1777, 1784, I, 112.

Arthur a Bland, a Nottingham tanner, goes of a summer's morning into Sherwood forest to see the red deer. Robin Hood pretends to be a keeper and to see cause for staying the Tanner. The Tanner says it will take more than one such to make him stand. They have a two hours' fight with staves, when Robin cries Hold! The Tanner henceforth shall be free of the forest, and if he will come and live there with Robin Hood shall have both gold and fee. Arthur a Bland gives his hand never to part from Robin, and asks for Little John, whom he declares to be his kinsman. Robin Hood blows his horn. Little John comes at the call, and, learning what has been going on, would like to try a bout with the Tanner, but after a little explanation throws himself upon his kinsman's neck. The three take hands for a dance round the oak-tree.

The sturdy Arthur a Bland is well hit off,

and, bating the sixteenth and thirty-fifth stanzas, the ballad has a good popular ring. There is corruption at 8^3, 12^3, and perhaps 13^3.

Little John offers to fight with the Tinker in No 127, and again with the Stranger in No 128, as here with the Tanner, and is forbidden, as here, by his master. In R. H. and the Shepherd, No 135, he undertakes the Shepherd after Robin has owned himself conquered, and the fight is stopped after John has received some sturdy blows. In the Bold Pedlar and Robin Hood, No 132, John begins and Robin follows, and each in turn cries, Pedlar, pray hold your hand. In R. H. and the Potter, No 121, John is ready to bet on the Potter, because he has already had strokes from him which he has reason to remember.

As the Tanner is John's cousin, so, in Robin Hood Revived, No 128, the Stranger turns out to be Robin Hood's nephew, Young Gamwell, thenceforward called Scathlock; and in No 132 the Bold Pedlar proves to be Gamble Gold, Robin's cousin.

Translated by Anastasius Grün, p. 117.

---

1 In Nottingham there lives a jolly tanner,
    With a hey down down a down down
  His name is Arthur a Bland;
  There is nere a squire in Nottinghamshire
  Dare bid bold Arthur stand.

2 With a long pike-staff upon his shoulder,
    So well he can clear his way;

By two and by three he makes them to flee,
  For he hath no list to stay.

3 And as he went forth, in a summer's morning,
    Into the forrest of merry Sherwood,
  To view the red deer, that range here and there,
  There met he with bold Robin Hood.

4 As soon as bold Robin Hood did him espy,
  He thought some sport he would make;
Therefore out of hand he bid him to stand,
  And thus to him he spake:

5 Why, what art thou, thou bold fellow,
  That ranges so boldly here?
In sooth, to be brief, thou lookst like a thief,
  That comes to steal our king's deer.

6 For I am a keeper in this forrest;
  The king puts me in trust
To look to his deer, that range here and
    there,
  Therefore stay thee I must.

7 'If thou beest a keeper in this forrest,
  And hast such a great command,
Yet thou must have more partakers in store,
  Before thou make me to stand.'

8 'Nay, I have no more partakers in store,
  Or any that I do need;
But I have a staff of another oke graff,
  I know it will do the deed.'

9 'For thy sword and thy bow I care not a
    straw,
  Nor all thine arrows to boot;
If I get a knop upon thy bare scop,
  Thou canst as well shite as shoote.'

10 'Speak cleanly, good fellow,' said jolly Robin,
  'And give better terms to me;
Else I'le thee correct for thy neglect,
  And make thee more mannerly.'

11 'Marry gep with a wenion!' quoth Arthur a
    Bland,
  'Art thou such a goodly man?
I care not a fig for thy looking so big;
  Mend thou thyself where thou can.'

12 Then Robin Hood he unbuckled his belt,
  He laid down his bow so long;
He took up a staff of another oke graff,
  That was both stiff and strong.

13 'I'le yield to thy weapon,' said jolly Robin,
  'Since thou wilt not yield to mine;
For I have a staff of another oke graff,
  Not half a foot longer then thine.

14 'But let me measure,' said jolly Robin,
  'Before we begin our fray;
For I'le not have mine to be longer then thine,
  For that will be called foul play.'

15 'I pass not for length,' bold Arthur reply'd,
  'My staff is of oke so free;
Eight foot and a half, it will knock down a
    calf,
  And I hope it will knock down thee.'

16 Then Robin Hood could no longer forbear;
  He gave him such a knock,
Quickly and soon the blood came down,
  Before it was ten a clock.

17 Then Arthur he soon recovered himself,
  And gave him such a knock on the crown,
That on every hair of bold Robin Hoods
    head,
  The blood came trickling down.

18 Then Robin Hood raged like a wild bore,
  As soon as he saw his own blood;
Then Bland was in hast, he laid on so fast,
  As though he had been staking of wood.

19 And about, and about, and about they went,
  Like two wild bores in a chase;
Striving to aim each other to maim,
  Leg, arm, or any other place.

20 And knock for knock they lustily dealt,
  Which held for two hours and more;
That all the wood rang at every bang,
  They ply'd their work so sore.

21 'Hold thy hand, hold thy hand,' said Robin
    Hood,
  'And let our quarrel fall;
For here we may thresh our bones into mesh,
  And get no coyn at all.

22 'And in the forrest of merry Sherwood
    Hereafter thou shalt be free:'
'God-a-mercy for naught, my freedom I bought,
  I may thank my good staff, and not thee.'

23 'What tradesman art thou?' said jolly Robin,
  'Good fellow, I prethee me show:
And also me tell in what place thou dost dwel,
  For both these fain would I know.'

24 'I am a tanner,' bold Arthur reply'd,
   'In Nottingham long have I wrought;
And if thou 'lt come there, I vow and do swear
   I will tan thy hide for naught.'

25 'God a mercy, good fellow,' said jolly Robin,
   'Since thou art so kind to me;
And if thou wilt tan my hide for naught,
   I will do as much for thee.

26 'But if thou 'lt forsake thy tanners trade,
   And live in green wood with me,
My name 's Robin Hood, I swear by the rood
   I will give thee both gold and fee.'

27 'If thou be Robin Hood,' bold Arthur reply'd,
   'As I think well thou art,
Then here 's my hand, my name 's Arthur a
     Bland,
   We two will never depart.

28 'But tell me, O tell me, where is Little John?
   Of him fain would I hear;
For we are alide by the mothers side,
   And he is my kinsman near.'

29 Then Robin Hood blew on the beaugle horn,
   He blew full lowd and shrill,
But quickly anon appeard Little John,
   Come tripping down a green hill.

30 'O what is the matter?' then said Little John,
   'Master, I pray you tell;
Why do you stand with your staff in your hand?
   I fear all is not well.'

31 'O man, I do stand, and he makes me to stand,
   The tanner that stands thee beside;
He is a bonny blade, and master of his trade,
   For soundly he hath tand my hide.'

32 'He is to be commended,' then said Little John,
   'If such a feat he can do;
If he be so stout, we will have a bout,
   And he shall tan my hide too.'

33 'Hold thy hand, hold thy hand,' said Robin
     Hood,
   'For as I do understand,
He 's a yeoman good, and of thine own blood,
   For his name is Arthur a Bland.'

34 Then Little John threw his staff away,
   As far as he could it fling,
And ran out of hand to Arthur a Bland,
   And about his neck did cling.

35 With loving respect, there was no neglect,
   They were neither nice nor coy,
Each other did face, with a lovely grace,
   And both did weep for joy.

36 Then Robin Hood took them both by the hand,
   And danc'd round about the oke tree;
'For three merry men, and three merry men,
   And three merry men we be.

37 'And ever hereafter, as long as I live,
   We three will be all one;
The wood shall ring, and the old wife sing,
   Of Robin Hood, Arthur, and John.'

---

a. Robin Hood and the Tanner, or, Robin Hood met with his match: A merry and pleasant song relating the gallant and fierce combate fought between Arthur Bland, a Tanner of Nottingham, and Robin Hood, the greatest and most noblest archer of England. The ✓ tune is, Robin and the Stranger.
Printed for W. Gilbertson. (1640–63: *Chappell*.)
3². merry Forrest of. 7². hath. 7³. But. 9³. the bare. 11¹. qd. . 13³. straff.
14⁴. *Wanting in my copy, probably by accidental omission: supplied from* b.
17³. That from every side: Old Ballads, 1713, *to restore the middle rhyme.*

21². let your Quiver: *cf.* b, c, d.
21³. thrash: to: *cf.* b. 22⁴. good *wanting.*
26³. the wood: *cf.* d. 35². noice.
36¹. took him by: *cf.* d. 37⁴. Kobin.
b. *Title as in* a. *By the same printer as* a. *Burden sometimes* With hey, etc.
1¹. lives there. 1², 11¹, 27³. Arthur Bland.
3². merry Forrest of. 6². he puts.
7². hath. 7³. Yet. 7⁴. Before that.
8³, 12³, 13³. graft.
9³. thy bare. 11¹. quoth.
13¹. I yield. 13⁴. than. 14³. to *wanting.*
14⁴. For that will be called foul play.
17². He gave. 17³. Hoods *wanting.*
21². let our quarrel. 21³. thresh: into.

22⁴. my good.   23². pray thee.
24³. thou come.   25². kinde and free.
26³. the wood.
28¹. where 's.   29². both *for* full.
30¹. then *wanting.*
33³. thy.   34⁴. he did.   36¹. took him by.
36². round *wanting.*   37¹. so long.

c. *Title as in* a.   *Burden after* 2¹, With
     hey, *etc.*

1², 11¹, 27³. Arthur Bland.
2⁴. not.   3². merry Forrest of.   4³. them to.
7². hath.   7³. Yet you.   7⁴. Before that.
8³, 12³, 13³. graft.
9³. thy bare.   11¹. qd. .
13¹. I yield.   14³. to *wanting.*
14⁴. For that will be called foul play.
16³. blood ran.   17². He gave.
17³. hair on Robins.
17⁴. blood ran.   18⁴. been cleaving wood.
20¹. deal.   20⁴. so fast.
21². let our quarrel.
21³. thresh : into.   22⁴. my good.
24³. thou come.   25². kind and free.
26¹. thou wilt.   26³. the wood.
28³. mother.   29¹. he blew.
29². both *for* full.
29³. and anon.   30³. your *wanting.*
31². me *for* thee.   33¹. Hood *wanting.*
33³. thy blood.   34⁴. he did.   35⁴. they both.
36¹. took him by.   36². round *wanting.*
37¹. And we : so long as we.

d. *Title as in* a, *except :* the greatest archer in.
     London.   Printed for J. Wright, J. Clarke,
     W. Thackeray, and T. Passenger.   (1670–
     1682 ?)   *Burden sometimes,* With hey, *etc.*

1⁴. to stand.   3¹. on a.   3². forrest of merry.
4¹. Robin he did him.   4⁴. he did spake.
5⁴. the kings.
6¹. If thou beest a, *caught from* 7¹.
7². hast.   7³. Then thou.   7⁴. makst.
8². Nor any : do not.   9². thy.
9³. thou get a knock upon thy.
11¹. gip : wernion qd.   11⁴. if thou.
12². And threw it upon the ground.
12³. Says, I have a.
12⁴. That is both strong and sound.
13¹. But let me measure, said.
14³. I 'le have mine no longer.
14⁴. For that will be counted foul play.
16¹. Hood *wanting.*   17¹. he *wanting.*
17³. from every hair of.
18¹. raved *for* raged.   18³. he was.
18⁴. stacking.   19⁴. other *wanting.*
20². for *wanting.*   21². let our quarrel.
21³. thrash our bones to.   22³. I 've.
22⁴. my good.
24³. thou come.   26¹. thou wilt.   26². in the.
26³. name is : rood.   29¹. on his.
29². both *for* full.   29⁴. tripping over the hill.
30². you me.   30³. the staff.   31³. and a.
32³. about.   33³. thy.   35². They was.
37¹. we live.   37². all as (*printed* sa).

127

ROBIN HOOD AND THE TINKER

a. Wood, 401, leaf 17 b.

b. Pepys, II, 107, No 94.

c. Douce, III, 118 b.

IN the Roxburghe collection, III, 22.   Not
in the Garland of 1663 or that of 1670.

a is printed in Ritson's Robin Hood, 1795,
II, 38 ; in Gutch's Robin Hood, II, 264,
" compared with " the Roxburghe copy.   The
ballad was printed by Evans, Old Ballads,
1777, 1784, I, 118.

The fewest words will best befit this con-
temptible imitation of imitations.   Robin Hood
meets a Tinker, and they exchange scurrili-
ties.   The Tinker has a warrant from the
king to arrest Robin, but will not show it when
asked.   Robin Hood suggests that it will be
best to go to Nottingham, and there the two

take one inn and drink together till the Tinker falls asleep; when Robin makes off, and leaves the Tinker to pay the shot. The host informs the Tinker that it was Robin Hood that he was drinking with, and recommends him to seek his man in the parks. The Tinker finds Robin, and they fall to it, crab-tree staff against sword. Robin yields, and begs a boon; the Tinker will grant none. A blast of the horn brings Little John and Scadlock. Little John would fain see whether the Tinker can do for him what he has done for his master, but Robin proclaims a peace, and offers the Tinker terms which induce him to join the outlaws.

It is not necessary to suppose the warrant to arrest Robin a souvenir of 'Guy of Gisborne'; though that noble ballad is in a 17th century MS., it does not appear to have been known to the writers of broadsides.

---

1 In summer time, when leaves grow green,
    Down a down a down
    And birds sing on every tree,
    Hey down a down a down

    Robin Hood went to Nottingham,
    Down a down a down
    As fast as hee could dree.
    Hey down a down a down

2 And as hee came to Nottingham
    A Tinker he did meet,
    And seeing him a lusty blade,
    He did him kindly greet.

3 'Where dost thou live?' quoth Robin Hood,
    'I pray thee now mee tell;
    Sad news I hear there is abroad,
    I fear all is not well.'

4 'What is that news?' the Tinker said;
    'Tell mee without delay;
    I am a tinker by my trade,
    And do live at Banbura.'

5 'As for the news,' quoth Robin Hood,
    'It is but as I hear;
    Two tinkers they were set ith' stocks,
    For drinking ale and bear.'

6 'If that be all,' the Tinker said,
    'As I may say to you,
    Your news it is not worth a fart,
    Since that they all bee true.

7 'For drinking of good ale and bear,
    You wil not lose your part:'
    'No, by my faith,' quoth Robin Hood,
    'I love it with all my heart.

8 'What news abroad?' quoth Robin Hood;
    'Tell mee what thou dost hear;
    Being thou goest from town to town,
    Some news thou need not fear.'

9 'All the news,' the Tinker said,
    'I hear, it is for good;
    It is to seek a bold outlaw,
    Which they call Robin Hood.

10 'I have a warrant from the king,
    To take him where I can;
    If you can tell me where hee is,
    I will make you a man.

11 'The king will give a hundred pound
    That hee could but him see;
    And if wee can but now him get,
    It will serve you and mee.'

12 'Let me see that warrant,' said Robin Hood;
    'I 'le see if it bee right;
    And I will do the best I can
    For to take him this night.'

13 'That will I not,' the Tinker said;
    'None with it I will trust;
    And where hee is if you 'l not tell,
    Take him by force I must.'

14 But Robin Hood perceiving well
    How then the game would go,
    'If you will go to Nottingham,
    Wee shall find him I know.'

15 The Tinker had a crab-tree staff,
    Which was both good and strong;
    Robin hee had a good strong blade,
    So they went both along.

16 And when they came to Nottingham,
   There they both tooke one inn;
And they calld for ale and wine,
   To drink it was no sin.

17 But ale and wine they drank so fast
   That the Tinker hee forgot
What thing he was about to do;
   It fell so to his lot

18 That while the Tinker fell asleep,
   Hee made then haste away,
And left the Tinker in the lurch,
   For the great shot to pay.

19 But when the Tinker wakened,
   And saw that he was gone,
He calld then even for his host,
   And thus hee made his moan.

20 'I had a warrant from the king,
   Which might have done me good,
That is to take a bold outlaw,
   Some call him Robin Hood.

21 'But now my warrant and mony's gone,
   Nothing I have to pay;
And he that promisd to be my friend,
   He is gone and fled away.'

22 'That friend you tell on,' said the host,
   'They call him Robin Hood;
And when that first hee met with you,
   He ment you little good.'

23 'Had I known it had been hee,
   When that I had him here,
Th' one of us should have tri'd our strength
   Which should have paid full dear.

24 'In the mean time I must away;
   No longer here I'le bide;
But I will go and seek him out,
   What ever do me betide.

25 'But one thing I would gladly know,
   What here I have to pay;'
'Ten shillings just,' then said the host;
   'I'le pay without delay.

26 'Or elce take here my working-bag,
   And my good hammer too;

And if that I light but on the knave,
   I will then soon pay you.'

27 'The onely way,' then said the host,
   'And not to stand in fear,
Is to seek him among the parks,
   Killing of the kings deer.'

28 The Tinker hee then went with speed,
   And made then no delay,
Till he had found then Robin Hood,
   That they might have a fray.

29 At last hee spy'd him in a park,
   Hunting then of the deer;
'What knave is that,' quoth Robin Hood,
   'That doth come mee so near?'

30 'No knave, no knave,' the Tinker said,
   'And that you soon shall know;
Whether of us hath done most wrong,
   My crab-tree staff shall show.'

31 Then Robin drew his gallant blade,
   Made then of trusty steel;
But the Tinker laid on him so fast
   That he made Robin reel.

32 Then Robins anger did arise;
   He fought full manfully,
Vntil hee had made the Tinker
   Almost then fit to fly.

33 With that they had a bout again,
   They ply'd their weapons fast;
The Tinker threshed his bones so sore
   He made him yeeld at last.

34 'A boon, a boon,' Robin hee cryes,
   'If thou wilt grant it mee;'
'Before I do it,' the Tinker said,
   'I'le hang thee on this tree.'

35 But the Tinker looking him about,
   Robin his horn did blow;
Then came unto him Little John,
   And William Scadlock too.

36 'What is the matter,' quoth Little John,
   'You sit in th' highway side?'
'Here is a Tinker that stands by,
   That hath paid well my hide.'

37 'That Tinker,' then said Little John,
      'Fain that blade I would see,
   And I would try what I could do,
      If hee 'l do as much for mee.'

38 But Robin hee then wishd them both
      They should the quarrel cease,
   'That henceforth wee may bee as one,
      And ever live in peace.

39 'And for the jovial Tinker's part,
      A hundred pound I 'le give,
   In th' year to maintain him on,
      As long as he doth live.

40 'In manhood hee is a mettle man,
      And a mettle man by trade;
   I never thought that any man
      Should have made me so fraid.

41 'And if hee will bee one of us,
      Wee will take all one fare,
   And whatsoever wee do get,
      He shall have his full share.'

42 So the Tinker was content
      With them to go along,
   And with them a part to take,
      And so I end my song.

———◆———

a. A new song, to drive away cold winter,
   Between Robin Hood and the Jovial Tinker;
      How Robin by a wile
         The Tinker he did cheat,
      But at the length, as you shall hear,
         The Tinker did him beat;
   Whereby the same they then did so agree
   They after livd in love and unity.

To the tune of In Summer Time.
London, Printed for F. Grove, dwelling on
   Snowhill. (1620–55.)
1⁸. Nottingam. 8². here. 10¹. warrand.

b. *Title as in* a: *except that* he *is wanting in
   the fourth line, and* so *in the last line but
   one.*
Printed for I. Clarke, W. Thackeray, and T.
   Passenger. (1670–86?)
3¹. qd. 4⁴. Banburay. 6⁸. it *wanting.*
11¹. king would: an. 14⁸. you would.
16². they took up their.
22¹. speak *for* tell. 24¹. was *for* will.
24⁴. me *wanting.*
25⁸. Ten shillings just I have to pay.
26⁸. if I: on that. 28⁸. then found.
31⁸. Tinker he laid on so fast.
32². right *for* full. 33¹. laid about.
33⁴. That he. 35⁴. Will.
39². pounds: I *for* Ile.

c. Robin Hood and the Jolly Tinker: Shewing
   how they fiercely encountered, and after the
   victorious conquest lovingly agreed. Tune
   of In Summer Time.
London, Printed by J. Hodges, at the Looking
   Glass, on London Bridge. *Not in black
   letter.*
3¹. doth. 4¹. the news. 4⁴. Bullbury.
5⁸. they are. 6⁸. it *wanting.* 8⁴. needs.
11¹. would give an. 11⁴. thee *for* you.
15¹. A crab-tree staff the Tinker had.
16². they took up at their inn.
18². Robin made haste away.
19¹. did awake. 19⁸. even *wanting.*
20⁸. to seek. 21¹. the *for* my.
21⁴. He *wanting.* 22¹. speak *for* tell.
23¹. I but. 23⁸. might *for* strength.
24¹. I will. 24⁴. should betide.
25¹. But *wanting.* 25⁸. just I have to pay.
26¹. bags. 26⁸. that *wanting.* 27⁸. amongst.
29¹. in the. 31². Made of a.
31⁸. he laid: him *wanting.* 32⁸. that he.
32⁴. Then almost. 33¹. they laid about.
33⁸. full *for* so. 33⁴. That he. 34². grant to.
35⁴. also *for* too. 36⁸. There.
37². would I. 37⁸. And would.
38². They would. 39⁸. In a.
40¹. mettle. 40⁴. afraid.

40¹. mettled. 40⁴. afraid. 41¹. with us.

128

ROBIN HOOD NEWLY REVIVED

'Robin Hood Newly Reviv'd.' **a.** Wood, 401, leaf 27 b. **b.** Roxburghe, III, 18, in the Ballad Society's reprint, II, 426. **c.** Garland of 1663, No 3. **d.** Garland of 1670, No 2. **e.** Pepys, II, 101, No 88.

ALSO Douce, III, 120 b, London, by L. How, and Roxburghe, III, 408 : both of these are of the eighteenth century.

a is printed, with not a few changes, in Ritson's Robin Hood, 1795, II, 66. Evans, Old Ballads, 1777, 1784, I, 143, agrees nearly with the Aldermary garland.

Robin Hood, walking the forest, meets a gaily-dressed young fellow, who presently brings down a deer at forty yards with his bow. Robin commends the shot, and offers the youngster a place as one of his yeomen. The offer is rudely received ; each bends his bow at the other. Robin suggests that one of them may be slain, if they shoot : swords and bucklers would be better. Robin strikes the first blow, and is so stoutly answered that he is fain to know who the young man is. His name is Gamwell, and, having killed his father's steward, he has fled to the forest to join his uncle, Robin Hood. The kinsmen embrace, and walk on till they meet Little John. Robin Hood tells John that the stranger has beaten him. Little John would like a bout, to see if the stranger can beat him. This Robin forbids, for this stranger is his own sister's son ; he shall be next in rank to Little John among his yeomen, and be called Scarlet.

The story seems to have been built up on a portion of the ruins, so to speak, of the fine tale of Gamelyn. There the king of the outlaws, sitting at meat with his seven score young men, sees Gamelyn wandering in the wood with Adam, and tells some of his young men to fetch them in. Seven start up to execute the order, and when they come to Gamelyn and his comrade bid the twain hand over their bows and arrows. Gamelyn replies, Not though ye fetch five men, and so be twelve ; but no violence being attempted, the pair go to the king, who asks them what they seek in the woods. Gamelyn answers, No harm ; but to shoot a deer, if we meet one, like hungry men. The king gives them to eat and drink of the best, and, upon learning that the spokesman is Gamelyn, makes him master, under himself, over all the outlaws. Little John having long had the place of first man under Robin, the best that the ballad-maker could do for Gamwell was to make him chief yeoman after John.[*] (The Tale of Gamelyn, ed. Skeat, vv 625–686. The resemblance of the ballad is remarked upon at p. x.)

Ritson gives this ballad the title of Robin Hood and the Stranger, remarking : The title now given to this ballad is that which it seems to have originally borne ; having been foolishly altered to Robin Hood newly Revived. R. H. and the Bishop, R. H. and the Beggar, R. H. and the Tanner, are directed to be sung to the tune of Robin Hood and the Stranger, but no ballad bears such a title in any garland or broadside.[†] The ballad referred to as Robin Hood and the Stranger may possibly have been this, but, for reasons given at

---

[*] The Bold Pedlar and Robin Hood, No 132, is a traditional variation of Robin Hood Revived.

[†] Though Mr W. C. Hazlitt, in his Handbook to the Popular, Poetical, and Dramatic Literature of Great Britain, p. 514, No 25, has : "Robin Hood and the Stranger. In two parts. [Col.] London : printed by and for W. O., and to be

sold at the booksellers. Roxb. and Wood Colls." This colophon belongs only to Robin Hood, Will Scadlock, and Little John, otherwise Robin Hood and the Prince of Aragon, which see. The title Robin Hood and the Stranger is adopted from Ritson.

p. 133, Robin Hood and Little John is, as I think, more likely to be the one meant.

Robin Hood and the Stranger was one name for the most popular of Robin Hood tunes, and this particular tune was sometimes called 'Robin Hood' absolutely (see the note at the end of the next ballad). If the ballad denoted by Robin Hood and the Stranger was also sometimes known as 'Robin Hood' simply, and especially if this ballad was Robin Hood and Little John, an explanation presents itself of the title 'Robin Hood newly Revived.' What is revived is the favorite topic of the process by which Robin Hood enlarged and strengthened his company. The earlier ballad had shown how Little John came to join the band; the second undertakes to tell us how Scarlet was enlisted, the next most important man after John.

The second part, referred to in the last stanza, was separated, Mr Chappell thought, when the present ballad was "newly revived," because the whole was found too long for a penny (one would say that both parts together were "dear enough a leek"), and seven stanzas (incoherent in themselves and not cohering with what lies before us) added to fill up the sheet. These stanzas will be given under No 130, as Robin Hood and the Scotchman; and the "second part," 'R. H. and the Prince of Aragon,' or 'R. H., Will. Scadlock and Little John,' follows immediately.

———◆———

1 COME listen a while, you gentlemen all,
     With a hey down down a down down
   That are in this bower within,
     For a story of gallant bold Robin Hood
   I purpose now to begin.

2 'What time of the day?' quoth Robin Hood
     then;
   Quoth Little John, 'T is in the prime;
   'Why then we will to the green wood gang,
     For we have no vittles to dine.'

3 As Robin Hood walkt the forrest along —
     It was in the mid of the day —
   There was he met of a deft young man
     As ever walkt on the way.

4 His doublet it was of silk, he said,
     His stockings like scarlet shone,
   And he walkt on along the way,
     To Robin Hood then unknown.

5 A herd of deer was in the bend,
     All feeding before his face:
   'Now the best of ye I 'le have to my dinner,
     And that in a little space.'

6 Now the stranger he made no mickle adoe,
     But he bends and a right good bow,
   And the best buck in the herd he slew,
     Forty good yards him full froe.

7 'Well shot, well shot,' quoth Robin Hood then,
     'That shot it was shot in time;
   And if thou wilt accept of the place,
     Thou shalt be a bold yeoman of mine.'

8 'Go play the chiven,' the stranger said,
     'Make haste and quickly go;
   Or with my fist, be sure of this,
     I 'le give thee buffets store.'

9 'Thou hadst not best buffet me,' quoth Robin
     Hood,
   'For though I seem forlorn,
   Yet I can have those that will take my part,
     If I but blow my horn.'

10 'Thou wast not best wind thy horn,' the stran-
     ger said,
   'Beest thou never so much in hast,
   For I can draw out a good broad sword,
     And quickly cut the blast.'

11 Then Robin Hood bent a very good bow,
     To shoot, and that he would fain;
   The stranger he bent a very good bow,
     To shoot at bold Robin again.

12 'O hold thy hand, hold thy hand,' quoth Robin
     Hood,
   'To shoot it would be in vain;
   For if we should shoot the one at the other,
     The one of us may be slain.'

13 'But let's take our swords and our broad
　　bucklers,
　　And gang under yonder tree : '
　'As I hope to be sav'd,' the stranger said,
　　'One foot I will not flee.'

14 Then Robin Hood lent the stranger a blow
　　Most scar'd him out of his wit ;
　'Thou never felt blow,' the stranger he said,
　　'That shall be better quit.'

15 The stranger he drew out a good broad sword,
　　And hit Robin on the crown,
　That from every haire of bold Robins head
　　The blood ran trickling down.

16 'God a mercy, good fellow ! ' quoth Robin
　　Hood then,
　'And for this that thou hast done ;
　Tell me, good fellow, what thou art,
　　Tell me where thou doest woon.'

17 The stranger then answered bold Robin Hood,
　　I 'le tell thee where I did dwell ;
　In Maxfield was I bred and born,
　　My name is Young Gamwell.

18 For killing of my own fathers steward,
　　I am forc'd to this English wood,
　And for to seek an vncle of mine ;
　　Some call him Robin Hood.

19 'But thou art a cousin of Robin Hoods then ?
　　The sooner we should have done : '

'As I hope to be sav'd,' the stranger then said,
　'I am his own sisters son.'

20 But, Lord ! what kissing and courting was there,
　　When these two cousins did greet !
　And they went all that summers day,
　　And Little John did meet.

21 But when they met with Little John,
　　He there unto [him] did say,
　O master, where have you been,
　　You have tarried so long away ?

22 'I met with a stranger,' quoth Robin Hood
　　then,
　'Full sore he hath beaten me : '
　'Then I 'le have a bout with him,' quoth Little
　　John,
　'And try if he can beat me.'

23 'Oh [no], oh no,' quoth Robin Hood then,
　　'Little John, it may [not] be so ;
　For he 's my own dear sisters son,
　　And cousins I have no mo.

24 'But he shall be a bold yeoman of mine,
　　My chief man next to thee ;
　And I Robin Hood, and thou Little John,
　　And Scarlet he shall be :

25 'And wee 'l be three of the bravest outlaws
　　That is in the North Country.'
　If you will have any more of bold Robin Hood,
　　In his second part it will be.

———◆———

a, b, e. Robin Hood newly reviv'd.　To a de-
　lightful new tune.
c, d. Robin Hood newly revived : Or his meeting
　and fighting with his cousin Scarlet.　To a
　delightful new tune.
a. Printed for Richard Burton.　(1641–74.)
　2^1, 7^1, 9^1, 12^1, 16^1, 22^1, 22^3, qd.　6^3. in th.
　11^2. To that shoot and.
　21^2. him *supplied from* c, d.
b. London, Printed for Richard Burton, at the
　Sign of the Horshooe in West Smithfield.
　3^2. midst.　4^1. it *wanting*.　6^4. full *wanting*.
　11^2. To shot and that.　12^4. must be.
　21^2. him *wanting*.　23^1. Oh no.
　23^2. may not.

c. 3^3. ware *for* met.
　7^1, 9^1, 12^1, 16^1, 22^1, 22^3, 23^1, qd.　9^3. can I.
　10^1. blow *for* wind.　11^2. To shoot and that.
　13^3. he said.　16^1, 18^4. bold Robin.
　19^1. art thou.　21^2. unto him.　23^1. Oh no.
　23^2. may not.　25^4. In this.
d. 2^1, 7^1, 9^1, 12^1, 16^1, 22^1, qd.
　3^3. ware *for* met.
　6^4. good *wanting*.　7^2. was in.
　9^2. am *for* seem.　11^1. he bent.
　11^2. To shoot and that.　12^4. must be.
　13^3. he said.　16^2. that *wanting*.
　18^1. own *wanting*.　19^1. art thou.
　21^2. unto him.　23^1. Oh no.　23^2. may not.
　25^3. If thou wilt.　25^4. In this.

e. Printed for J. Clarke, W. Thackeray, and T. Passenger. (1670–82 ?)

1². in *wanting*.

2¹, 7¹, 9¹, 12¹, 16¹, 22¹, 22³. quod.

3². midst. 3³. with *for* of. 4¹. it *wanting*.

6². and *wanting*. 6⁴. full *wanting*.

7³. except. 9³. can *wanting*.

11². To that shot and he.

11³. bent up a noble. 12¹. O *wanting*.

12⁴. must be. 19¹. art thou.

21². him *wanting*. 22¹, 23¹. then *wanting*.

23¹. Oh no. 23². may not.

25³. If you 'l have more. 25⁴. In this.

Followed in all the copies by seven stanzas which belong to a different ballad. See No 130.

129

ROBIN HOOD AND THE PRINCE OF ARAGON

'Robin Hood, Will. Scadlock and Little John.' *

a. Roxburghe, I, 358, in the Ballad Society's reprint, II, 431. b. Pepys, II, 120, No 106.

ALSO Roxburghe, III, 582, without a printer's name.

Ritson, Robin Hood, 1795, II, 71, from a, with changes ; Evans, Old Ballads, 1777, 1784, I, 186.

This is only a pseudo-chivalrous romance, tagged to Robin Hood Newly Revived as a Second Part, with eight introductory stanzas. Both parts are as vapid as possible, and no piquancy is communicated by the matter of the two being as alien as oil and water. The Prince of Aragon, a Turk and an infidel, has beleaguered London, and will have the princess to his spouse, unless three champions can vanquish him and his two giants. Robin Hood, Scadlock, and John undertake the case, and disguise themselves as pilgrims, so as not to be stopped on their way. Robin kills the prince, and John and Scadlock each a giant. The king demands to know who his deliverers are, and Robin Hood avails himself of the opportunity to get the king's pardon for himself and his men. The princess was to be the victor's prize, but cannot marry all three, as might perhaps have been foreseen. She is allowed to pick, and chooses Will Scadlock. The Earl of Maxfield is present, and weeps bitterly at the sight of Scadlock, because, he says, he had a son like Will, of the name of Young Gamwell. Scadlock, whom we know from the First Part to be Gamwell, falls at his father's feet, and the wedding follows.

---

1 Now Robin Hood, Will Scadlock and Little John
    Are walking over the plain,
  With a good fat buck which Will Scadlock
    With his strong bow had slain.

2 'Jog on, jog on,' cries Robin Hood,
    'The day it runs full fast;
  For though my nephew me a breakfast gave,
    I have not yet broke my fast.

3 'Then to yonder lodge let us take our way,
    I think it wondrous good,
  Where my nephew by my bold yeomen
    Shall be welcomd unto the green wood.'

4 With that he took the bugle-horn,
    Full well he could it blow;
  Streight from the woods came marching down
    One hundred tall fellows and mo.

5 'Stand, stand to your arms !' crys Will Scadlock,
    'Lo ! the enemies are within ken :'

* 'Robin Hood and the Prince of Aragon,' in Thackeray's list, Ballad Society, I, xxiv, and in the late Garlands, 1749, etc.

With that Robin Hood he laughd aloud,
  Crys, They are my bold yeomen.

6 Who, when they arriv'd and Robin espy'd,
  Cry'd, Master, what is your will?
  We thought you had in danger been,
  Your horn did sound so shrill.

7 'Now nay, now nay,' quoth Robin Hood,
  'The danger is past and gone;
  I would have you to welcome my nephew
    here,
  That hath paid me two for one.'

8 In feasting and sporting they passed the day,
  Till Phœbus sunk into the deep;
  Then each one to his quarters hy'd,
  His guard there for to keep.

9 Long had they not walked within the green wood,
  But Robin he was espy'd
  Of a beautiful damsel all alone,
  That on a black palfrey did ride.

10 Her riding-suit was of sable hew black,
  Sypress over her face,
  Through which her rose-like cheeks did blush,
  All with a comely grace.

11 'Come, tell me the cause, thou pritty one,'
  Quoth Robin, 'and tell me aright,
  From whence thou comest, and whither · thou
    goest,
  All in this mournful plight?'

12 'From London I came,' the damsel reply'd,
  'From London upon the Thames,
  Which circled is, O grief to tell!
  Besieg'd with forraign arms.

13 'By the proud Prince of Aragon,
  Who swears by his martial hand
  To have the princess for his spouse,
  Or else to waste this land:

14 'Except that champions can be found
  That dare fight three to three,
  Against the prince and giants twain,
  Most horrid for to see:

15 'Whose grisly looks, and eyes like brands,
  Strike terrour where they come,
  With serpents hissing on their helms,
  Instead of feathered plume.

16 'The princess shall be the victors prize,
  The king hath vowd and said,
  And he that shall the conquest win
  Shall have her to his bride.

17 'Now we are four damsels sent abroad,
  To the east, west, north, and south,
  To try whose fortune is so good
  To find these champions forth.

18 'But all in vaine we have sought about;
  Yet none so bold there are
  That dare adventure life and blood,
  To free a lady fair.'

19 'When is the day?' quoth Robin Hood,
  'Tell me this and no more:'
  'On Midsummer next,' the damsel said,
  'Which is June the twenty-four.'

20 With that the teares trickled down her cheeks,
  And silent was her tongue;
  With sighs and sobs she took her leave,
  Away her palfrey sprung.

21 This news struck Robin to the heart,
  He fell down on the grass;
  His actions and his troubled mind
  Shewd he perplexed was.

22 'Where lies your grief?' quoth Will Scadlock,
  'O master, tell to me;
  If the damsels eyes have pierced your heart,
  I'll fetch her back to thee.'

23 'Now nay, now nay,' quoth Robin Hood,
  'She doth not cause my smart;
  But it is the poor distressed princess
  That wounds me to the heart.

24 'I will go fight the giants all
  To set the lady free:'
  'The devil take my soul,' quoth Little John,
  'If I part with thy company.'

25 'Must I stay behind?' quoth Will Scadlock;
  'No, no, that must not be;
  I'le make the third man in the fight,
  So we shall be three to three.'

26 These words cheerd Robin at the heart,
  Joy shone within his face;
  Within his arms he huggd them both,
  And kindly did imbrace.

27 Quoth he, We'll put on mothly gray,
  With long staves in our hands,
  A scrip and bottle by our sides,
  As come from the Holy Land.

28 So may we pass along the high-way;
  None will ask from whence we came,
  But take us pilgrims for to be,
  Or else some holy men.

29 Now they are on their journey gone,
   As fast as they may speed,
Yet for all haste, ere they arriv'd,
   The princess forth was led :

30 To be deliverd to the prince,
   Who in the list did stand,
Prepar'd to fight, or else receive
   His lady by the hand.

31 With that he walkt about the lists,
   With giants by his side :
' Bring forth,' said he, ' your champions,
   Or bring me forth my bride.

32 ' This is the four and twentieth day,
   The day prefixt upon ;
Bring forth my bride, or London burns,
   I swear by Acaron.'

33 Then cries the king, and queen likewise,
   Both weeping as they speak,
Lo ! we have brought our daughter dear,
   Whom we are forcd to forsake.

34 With that stept out bold Robin Hood,
   Crys, My liege, it must not be so ;
Such beauty as the fair princess
   Is not for a tyrants mow.

35 The prince he then began to storm ;
   Crys, Fool, fanatick, baboon !
How dares thou stop my valours prize?
   I 'll kill thee with a frown.

36 ' Thou tyrant Turk, thou infidel,'
   Thus Robin began to reply,
' Thy frowns I scorn ; lo ! here 's my gage,
   And thus I thee defie.

37 ' And for these two Goliahs there,
   That stand on either side,
Here are two little Davids by,
   That soon can tame their pride.'

38 Then did the king for armour send,
   For lances, swords, and shields :
And thus all three in armour bright
   Came marching to the field.

39 The trumpets began to sound a charge,
   Each singled out his man ;
Their arms in pieces soon were hewd,
   Blood sprang from every vain.

40 The prince he reacht Robin a blow —
   He struck with might and main —
Which forcd him to reel about the field,
   As though he had been slain.

41 ' God-a-mercy,' quoth Robin, ' for that blow !
   The quarrel shall soon be try'd ;
This stroke shall shew a full divorce
   Betwixt thee and thy bride.'

42 So from his shoulders he 's cut his head,
   Which on the ground did fall,
And grumbling sore at Robin Hood,
   To be so dealt withal.

43 The giants then began to rage,
   To see their prince lie dead :
' Thou 's be the next,' quoth Little John,
   ' Unless thou well guard thy head.'

44 With that his faulchion he whirld about —
   It was both keen and sharp —
He clove the giant to the belt,
   And cut in twain his heart.

45 Will Scadlock well had playd his part,
   The giant he had brought to his knee;
Quoth he, The devil cannot break his fast,
   Unless he have you all three.

46 So with his faulchion he run him through,
   A deep and gashly wound ;
Who damd and foamd, cursd and blasphemd,
   And then fell to the ground.

47 Now all the lists with cheers were filld,
   The skies they did resound,
Which brought the princess to herself,
   Who was faln in a swound.

48 The king and queen and princess fair
   Came walking to the place,
And gave the champions many thanks,
   And did them further grace.

49 ' Tell me,' quoth the king, ' whence you are,
   That thus disguised came,
Whose valour speaks that noble blood
   Doth run through every vain.'

50 ' A boon, a boon,' quoth Robin Hood,
   ' On my knees I beg and crave : '
' By my crown,' quoth the king, ' I grant;
   Ask what, and thou shalt have.'

51 ' Then pardon I beg for my merry men,
   Which are within the green wood,
For Little John, and Will Scadlock,
   And for me, bold Robin Hood.'

52 ' Art thou Robin Hood ? ' then quoth the king ;
   ' For the valour you have shewn,
Your pardons I doe freely grant,
   And welcome every one.

53 'The princess I promised the victors prize ;
   She cannot have you all three : '
'She shall chuse,' quoth Robin ; saith Little John,
   Then little share falls to me.

54 Then did the princess view all three,
   With a comely lovely grace,
Who took Will Scadlock by the hand,
   Quoth, Here I make my choice.

55 With that a noble lord stept forth,
   Of Maxfield earl was he,
Who lookt Will Scadlock in the face,
   Then wept most bitterly.

56 Quoth he, I had a son like thee,
   Whom I lovd wondrous well;
But he is gone, or rather dead ;
   His name is Young Gamwell.

57 Then did Will Scadlock fall on his knees,
   Cries, Father ! father ! here,
Here kneels your son, your Young Gamwell
   You said you lovd so dear.

58 But, lord ! what imbracing and kissing was there,
   When all these friends were met !
They are gone to the wedding, and so to bedding,
   And so I bid you good night.

a. Robin Hood, Will. Scadlock, and Little John, or, A narrative of their victory obtained against the Prince of Aragon and the two Giants : and how Will. Scadlock married the Princess.
Tune of Robin Hood, or, Hey down, down a down. London, Printed by and for W. O[nley], and are to be sold by the booksellers. (1650–1702.)
1¹. Will., *and always, except* 55⁸. 27¹. moth-ly. 32². perfixt. 47¹. sheers.

b. A new ballad of Robin Hood, *etc.*, *as in* a. To the tune of, *etc.* London : Printed for A. M[ilbourne], W. O[nley], and T. Thackeray in Duck Lane. (1670–89 ?)
1⁸. William. 7⁸. I should. 7⁴. has. 10². Cypress. 11⁸. whether. 13⁸. to his. 27¹. mothly. 32¹. twenty day. 32². prefixt. 32⁸. or *wanting*. 37¹. those. 38¹. the king did. 40⁸. him rell. 42⁸. grumbled. 46⁸. ramb'd *for* dam'd. 47¹. with sheets. 56⁴. it is. 58⁸. and so the bedding.

130

ROBIN HOOD AND THE SCOTCHMAN

A. a. Wood, 401, leaf 27 b.   **b.** Roxburghe, III, 18, in the Ballad Society's reprint, II, 426.   **c.** Garland of 1663, No 3.   **d.** Garland of 1670, No 2.   **e.** Pepys, II, 101, No 88.

B. Gutch's Robin Hood, II, 392, from an Irish garland, printed at Monaghan, 1796.

A is simply the conclusion given to Robin Hood Newly Revived in the broadsides, and has neither connection with that ballad nor coherence in itself, being on the face of it the beginning and the end of an independent ballad, with the break after the third stanza. 3 may possibly refer to the Scots giving up Charles I to the parliamentary commissioners, in 1647. In B, four stanzas appear to have been added to the first three of A in order to make out a story, — the too familiar one of Robin being beaten in a fight with a fellow whom he chances to meet, and consequently enlisting the man as a recruit.

A

a. Wood, 401, leaf 27 b. b. Roxburghe, III, 18, in the Ballad Society's reprint, II, 426. c. Garland of 1663, No 3. d. Garland of 1670, No 2. e. Pepys, II, 101, No 88.

1 THEN bold Robin Hood to the north he would
     go,
  With a hey down down a down down
With valour and mickle might,
  With sword by his side, which oft had been
     tri'd,
  To fight and recover his right.

2 The first that he met was a bony bold Scot,
    His servant he said he would be ;
  'No,' quoth Robin Hood, 'it cannot be good,
  For thou wilt prove false unto me.

3 'Thou hast not bin true to sire nor cuz : '
    'Nay, marry,' the Scot he said,
  'As true as your heart, I 'le never part,
    Gude master, be not afraid.'

*   *   *   *   *   *   *

4 Then Robin Hood turnd his face to the east ;
    'Fight on my merry men stout,
  Our cause is good,' quoth brave Robin Hood,
    'And we shall not be beaten out.'

5 The battel grows hot on every side,
    The Scotchman made great moan ;
  Quoth Jockey, Gude faith, they fight on each
     side ;
    Would I were with my wife Ione !

6 The enemy compast brave Robin about,
    'T is long ere the battel ends ;
  Ther 's neither will yeeld nor give up the field,
    For both are supplied with friends.

*   *   *   *   *   *   *

7 This song it was made in Robin Hoods dayes ;
    Let 's pray unto Iove above
  To give us true peace, that mischief may cease,
    And war may give place unto love.

B

Gutch's Robin Hood, II, 392, from an Irish garland, printed at Monaghan, 1796.

1 Now bold Robin Hood to the north would go,
    With valour and mickle might,
  With sword by his side, which oft had been
     try'd,
    To fight and recover his right.

2 The first that he met was a jolly stout Scot,
    His servant he said he would be ;
  'No,' quoth Robin Hood, 'it cannot be good,
  For thou wilt prove false unto me.

3 'Thou hast not been true to sire or cuz ; '
    'Nay, marry,' the Scot he said,
  'As true as your heart, I never will part ;
    Good master, be not afraid.'

4 'But eer I employ you,' said bold Robin Hood,
    'With you I must have a bout ; '
  The Scotchman reply'd, Let the battle be try'd,
    For I know I will beat you out.

5 Thus saying, the contest did quickly begin,
    Which lasted two hours and more ;
  The blows Sawney gave bold Robin so brave
    The battle soon made him give oer.

6 'Have mercy, thou Scotchman,' bold Robin
     Hood cry'd,
    'Full dearly this boon have I bought ;
  We will both agree, and my man you shall be,
    For a stouter I never have fought.'

7 Then Sawny consented with Robin to go,
    To be of his bowmen so gay ;
  Thus ended the fight, and with mickle delight
    To Sherwood they hasted away.

A. *For the printer, etc.,* see No 128, Robin Hood
     newly Revived.
a. 1³. trid. 1⁴. rigth. 4³, 5³. qd.
b. 1³. tri'd. 3¹. or *for* nor. 4³. case.

c. 4³, 5³. qd.
d. 4³. case.
e. 2¹. met with was a bold. 2³. qd.
     4³. case : quod.

131

ROBIN HOOD AND THE RANGER

'Robin Hood and the Ranger.' a. Robin Hood's Garland, London, C. Dicey, in Bow Church-Yard, n. d., but before 1741, p. 78. b. R. H.'s Garland, London, W. & C. Dicey, n. d. c. R. H.'s Garland, London, L. How, in Peticoat Lane, n. d. d. The English Archer, etc., York, N. Nickson, in Feasegate, n. d. e. The English Archer, etc., Paisley, John Neilson, 1786. f. R. H.'s Garland, York, T. Wilson & R. Spence, n. d. (All in the Bodleian Library.)

In Ritson's Robin Hood, 1795, II, 133, from a York edition of Robin Hood's Garland. Evans, Old Ballads, 1777, 1784, I, 200, apparently from an Aldermary garland.

Mr Halliwell, in Notices of Fugitive Tracts, etc., Percy Society, vol. xxix. p. 19, refers to an edition of Robin Hood's Garland printed for James Hodges, at the Looking-glass, London-bridge, n. d., as containing "the earliest copy yet known" of Robin Hood and the Ranger, but does not indicate how the alleged fact was ascertained. Inside of the cover of a is written, William Stukely, 1741. b appears in advertisements as early as 1753.

Robin Hood, while about to kill deer, is forbidden by a forester, and claiming the forest as his own, the cause has to be tried with weapons. They break their swords on one another, and take to quarter-staves. Robin Hood is so sorely cudgelled that he gives up the fight, declaring that he has never met with so good a man. He summons his yeomen with his horn; the forester is induced to join them.

---

1 When Phœbus had melted the sickles of ice,
  With a hey down, &c.
 And likewise the mountains of snow,
 Bold Robin Hood he would ramble to see,
  To frolick abroad with his bow.

2 He left all his merry men waiting behind,
  Whilst through the green vallies he passd;
 There did he behold a forester bold,
  Who cry'd out, Friend, whither so fast?

3 'I'm going,' quoth Robin, 'to kill a fat buck,
  For me and my merry men all;
 Besides, eer I go, I'll have a fat doe,
  Or else it shall cost me a fall.'

4 'You'd best have a care,' said the forester then,
  'For these are his majesty's deer;
 Before you shall shoot, the thing I'll dispute,
  For I am head-forester here.'

5 'These thirteen long summers,' quoth Robin,
  'I'm sure,
 My arrows I here have let fly,
 Where freely I range; methinks it is strange,
  You should have more power than I.

6 'This forest,' quoth Robin, 'I think is my own,
  And so are the nimble deer too;
 Therefore I declare, and solemnly swear,
  I wont be affronted by you.'

7 The forester he had a long quarter-staff,
  Likewise a broad sword by his side;
 Without more ado, he presently drew,
  Declaring the truth should be try'd.

8 Bold Robin Hood had a sword of the best,
  Thus, eer he would take any wrong,
 His courage was flush, he'd venture a brush,
  And thus they fell to it ding dong.

9 The very first blow that the forester gave,
   He made his broad weapon cry twang;
   'T was over the head, he fell down for dead,
   O that was a damnable bang!

10 But Robin he soon did recover himself,
   And bravely fell to it again;
   The very next stroke their weapons were
   broke,
   Yet never a man there was slain.

11 At quarter-staff then they resolved to play,
   Because they would have t'other bout;
   And brave Robin Hood right valiantly stood,
   Unwilling he was to give out.

12 Bold Robin he gave him very hard blows,
   The other returnd them as fast;
   At every stroke their jackets did smoke,
   Three hours the combat did last.

13 At length in a rage the bold forester grew,
   And cudgeld bold Robin so sore
   That he could not stand, so shaking his hand,
   He said, Let us freely give oer.

14 Thou art a brave fellow, I needs must con-
   fess
   I never knew any so good;
   Thou 'rt fitting to be a yeoman for me,
   And range in the merry green wood.

15 I 'll give thee this ring as a token of love,
   For bravely thou 'st acted thy part;
   That man that can fight, in him I delight,
   And love him with all my whole heart.

16 Then Robin Hood setting his horn to his
   mouth,
   A blast he merrily blows;

His yeomen did hear, and strait did appear,
   A hundred, with trusty long bows.

17 Now Little John came at the head of them all,
   Cloathd in a rich mantle of green;
   And likewise the rest were gloriously drest,
   A delicate sight to be seen.

18 'Lo, these are my yeomen,' said Robin Hood,
   'And thou shalt be one of the train;
   A mantle and bow, a quiver also,
   I give them whom I entertain.'

19 The forester willingly enterd the list,
   They were such a beautiful sight;
   Then with a long bow they shot a fat doe,
   And made a rich supper that night.

20 What singing and dancing was in the green
   wood,
   For joy of another new mate!
   With mirth and delight they spent the long
   night,
   And liv'd at a plentiful rate.

21 The forester neer was so merry before
   As then he was with these brave souls,
   Who never would fail, in wine, beer or ale,
   To take off their cherishing bowls.

22 Then Robin Hood gave him a mantle of green,
   Broad arrows, and a curious long bow;
   This done, the next day, so gallant and gay,
   He marched them all on a row.

23 Quoth he, My brave yeomen, be true to your
   trust,
   And then we may range the woods wide:
   They all did declare, and solemnly swear,
   They 'd conquer, or die by his side.

---

a. Robin Hood and the Ranger, or True Friend-
   ship after a fierce Fight. Tune of Arthur
   a Bland.
   2⁴. whether. 8³. he 'll. 12¹. a very hard blow.
b. 2⁴. whither. 6². are all. 11². the other.
   12¹. very hard blows. 14². any one.
   15². thou hast. 18². And wanting.
   23⁴. They would.
c. Burden: With a hey down down down and a
   down.

2⁴. whither. 5³. methink'. 6². deers.
8³. he 'd. 10¹. soon recoverd.
10². to wanting. 10³. they broke.
12¹. very hard blows. 12⁴. this combat.
13⁴. He cry'd. 14⁴. And live. 16². blast then.
19². a wanting. 21². with the.
d. Tune of, etc. wanting. Burden wanting.
   1¹. the circles. 1³. he wanting: ramble away.
   2⁴. whither. 5². arrows here I 've. 5⁴. then I.
   6². so is. 7¹. he wanting. 8¹. he had.

8³. he 'd.   9¹. that *wanting*.   9³. his head.
10¹. soon recoverd.   10³. they broke.
12¹. he *wanting* : many hard blows.
13⁴. He cry'd.
16¹. Then *wanting* : Hood set his bugle horn.
16². blast then.   16³. and soon.   16⁴. An.
17³. rest was.   18¹. said bold.   18⁴. I 'll.
20³. the whole.   21². with the.   21³. beer and.
21⁴. take of the.   22². a *wanting*.
23⁴. They would.

e. *Burden :* With a hey down down derry down:
   or Hey down derry derry down.
1¹. circle.   1³. he *wanting* : ramble away.
2³. he did.   2⁴. whither.
3¹. quoth Robin *wanting*.   3³. ere.
5². here *wanting*.   6². so is.   7¹. he *wanting*.
8². neer.   8³. he 'd.   8⁴. thus *wanting*.

9³. his head.   10¹. soon recovered.
10³. they broke.   11¹. then *wanting*.
12¹. many hard blows.   13⁴. He cry'd.
15⁴. whole *wanting*.   16¹. set his brave.
16². blast then.   16³. and soon.   16⁴. An.
18¹. said bold.   18³. and a bow.   18⁴. I 'll.
20¹. were in.   20³. the whole.   21². with the.
22². a *wanting*.

f. 1¹. ickles of ice.   1³. would frolicksome be.
1⁴. And ramble about with his bow.
2⁴. whither.   8¹. Hood *wanting*.   8³. he 'd.
10¹. recovered.   10³. they broke.
10⁴. Yet neither of them were slain.
11². the other.   12¹. very hard blows.
12⁴. this combat.   13⁴. He cry'd.
14¹. And live.   18¹. said bold.   19⁴. a good.
21². As when.   21³. beer and.

132

THE BOLD PEDLAR AND ROBIN HOOD

J. H. Dixon, Ancient Poems, Ballads, and Songs of the Peasantry of England, p. 71, Percy Society, vol. xvii, 1846.

"An aged female in Bermondsey, Surrey, from whose oral recitation the editor took down the present version, informed him, that she had often heard her grandmother sing it, and that it was never in print; but he has of late met with several common stall copies."

Robin Hood and Little John fall in with a pedlar. Little John asks what goods he carries, and says he will have half his pack. The pedlar says he shall have the whole if he can make him give a perch of ground. They fight, and John cries Hold.   Robin Hood undertakes the pedlar, and in turn cries Hold.

Robin asks the pedlar's name.   He will not give it till they have told theirs, and when they have so done says it still lies with him to tell or not.   However, he is Gamble Gold, forced to flee his country for killing a man. If you are Gamble Gold, says Robin, you are my own cousin.   They go to a tavern and dine and drink.

Stanzas 11, 12, 15 recall Robin Hood's Delight, No 136, 19, 20, 24 ; 13, 14 Robin Hood Revived, No 128, 17, 18.   As remarked under No 128, this is a traditional variation of Robin Hood Revived.

1 There chanced to be a pedlar bold,
    A pedlar bold he chanced to be ;
  He rolled his pack all on his back,
    And he came tripping oer the lee.
        Down a down a down a down,
        Down a down a down

2 By chance he met two troublesome blades,
    Two troublesome blades they chanced to be;
  The one of them was bold Robin Hood,
    And the other was Little John so free.

3 'O pedlar, pedlar, what is in thy pack?
    Come speedilie and tell to me:'
  'I've several suits of the gay green silks,
    And silken bow-strings two or three.'

4 'If you have several suits of the gay green
    silk,
    And silken bow-strings two or three,
  Then it's by my body,' cries Little John,
    'One half your pack shall belong to me.'

5 'O nay, o nay,' says the pedlar bold,
    'O nay, o nay, that never can be;
  For there's never a man from fair Nottingham
    Can take one half my pack from me.'

6 Then the pedlar he pulled off his pack,
    And put it a little below his knee,
  Saying, If you do move me one perch from
    this,
    My pack and all shall gang with thee.

7 Then Little John he drew his sword,
    The pedlar by his pack did stand;
  They fought until they both did sweat,
    Till he cried, Pedlar, pray hold your hand!

8 Then Robin Hood he was standing by,
    And he did laugh most heartilie;
  Saying, I could find a man, of a smaller scale,
    Could thrash the pedlar and also thee.

9 'Go you try, master,' says Little John,
    'Go you try, master, most speedilie,

Or by my body,' says Little John,
    'I am sure this night you will not know me.'

10 Then Robin Hood he drew his sword,
    And the pedlar by his pack did stand;
  They fought till the blood in streams did flow,
    Till he cried, Pedlar, pray hold your hand!

11 Pedlar, pedlar, what is thy name?
    Come speedilie and tell to me:
  'My name! my name I neer will tell,
    Till both your names you have told to me.'

12 'The one of us is bold Robin Hood,
    And the other Little John so free:'
  'Now,' says the pedlar, 'it lays to my good will,
    Whether my name I chuse to tell to thee.

13 'I am Gamble Gold of the gay green woods,
    And travelled far beyond the sea;
  For killing a man in my father's land
    From my country I was forced to flee.'

14 'If you are Gamble Gold of the gay green
    woods,
    And travelled far beyond the sea,
  You are my mother's own sister's son;
    What nearer cousins then can we be?'

15 They sheathed their swords with friendly
    words,
    So merrilie they did agree;
  They went to a tavern, and there they dined,
    And bottles cracked most merrilie.

——◆——

3¹, 5¹, 5². Oh.

———

133

ROBIN HOOD AND THE BEGGAR, I

a. Wood, 401, leaf 23 b.   **c.** Garland of 1670, No 7.

b. Garland of 1663, No 8.   **d.** Pepys, II, 116, No 100.

——◆——

a is printed, with changes, by Ritson, Robin
Hood, 1795, II, 122. Evans, Old Ballads, 1777, 1784, I, 180, agrees with the Aldermary
garland.

There is a copy in the Roxburghe Collection, III, 20.

Robin Hood, riding towards Nottingham, comes upon a beggar, who asks charity. Robin says he has no money, but must have a bout with him. The beggar with his staff gives three blows for every stroke of Robin's with his sword. Robin cries truce, and at the suggestion, we might almost say upon the requisition, of the beggar, exchanges his horse and finery for the beggar's bags and rags. Thus equipped, he proceeds to Nottingham, and has the adventure with the sheriff and three yeomen which is the subject of No 140.

The copy in the Wood and in the Roxburghe collections is signed T. R., like Robin Hood and the Butcher, B, and, like the latter ballad, this is a *rifacimento*, with middle rhyme in the third line. It is perhaps made up from two distinct stories; the Second Part, beginning at stanza 20, from Robin Hood rescuing Three Squires, and what precedes from a ballad resembling Robin Hood and the Beggar, II.

But no seventeenth-century version of Robin Hood and the Beggar, II, is known, and it is more likely that we owe the fight between Robin Hood and the Beggar to the folly and bad taste of T. R. Robin has no sort of provocation to fight with the beggar, and no motive for changing clothes, the proposition actually coming from the beggar, st. 15, and it is an accident that his disguise proves useful (cf. Guy of Gisborne). The beggar should have reported that three men were to be hanged, but instead of this is forced into a fight, in order that one more ignominious defeat may be scored against Robin.

The verses,

$9^{3,4}$, I am an outlaw, as many do know,
My name it is Robin Hood,

occur also in Robin Hood and the Bishop, No 143, $6^{3,4}$. 'And this mantle of mine I'le to thee resign,' 16^3, looks very like a reminiscence of Robin Hood and the Bishop, 10^3, 'Thy spindle and twine unto me resign.' *

---

1 COME light and listen, you gentlemen all,
    Hey down, down, and a down
  That mirth do love for to hear,
  And a story true I'le tell unto you,
    If that you will but draw near.

2 In elder times, when merriment was,
    And archery was holden good,
  There was an outlaw, as many did know,
    Which men called Robin Hood.

3 Vpon a time it chanced so
    Bold Robin was merry disposed,
  His time to spend he did intend,
    Either with friends or foes.

4 Then he got vp on a gallant brave steed,
    The which was worth angels ten ;
  With a mantle of green, most brave to be seen,
    He left all his merry men.

5 And riding towards fair Nottingham,
    Some pastime for to spy,
  There was he aware of a jolly beggar
    As ere he beheld with his eye.

6 An old patcht coat the beggar had on,
    Which he daily did vse for to wear ;
  And many a bag about him did wag,
    Which made Robin Hood to him repair.

7 'God speed, God speed,' said Robin Hood,
    'What countryman? tell to me :'
  'I am Yorkeshire, sir ; but, ere you go far,
    Some charity give vnto me.'

8 'Why, what wouldst thou have?' said Robin
      Hood,
    'I pray thee tell vnto me :'
  'No lands nor livings,' the beggar he said,
    'But a penny for charitie.'

9 'I have no money,' said Robin Hood then,
    'But, a ranger within the wood,
  I am an outlaw, as many do know,
    My name it is Robin Hood.

10 'But yet I must tell thee, bonny beggar,
    That a bout with [thee] I must try ;

---

* Remarked by Fricke, p. 88 f.

Thy coat of gray, lay down I say,
   And my mantle of green shall lye by.'

11 'Content, content,' the beggar he cry'd,
   'Thy part it will be the worse;
For I hope this bout to give thee the rout,
   And then have at thy purse.'

12 The beggar he had a mickle long staffe,
   And Robin had a nut-brown sword;
So the beggar drew nigh, and at Robin let fly,
   But gave him never a word.

13 'Fight on, fight on,' said Robin Hood then,
   'This game well pleaseth me;'
For every blow that Robin did give,
   The beggar gave buffets three.

14 And fighting there full hard and sore,
   Not far from Nottingham town,
They never fled, till from Robin['s] head
   The blood came trickling down.

15 'O hold thy hand,' said Robin Hood then,
   'And thou and I will agree;'
'If that be true,' the beggar he said,
   'Thy mantle come give vnto me.'

16 'Nay a change, a change,' cri'd Robin Hood;
   'Thy bags and coat give me,
And this mantle of mine I 'le to thee resign,
   My horse and my braverie.'

17 When Robin Hood had got the beggars clothes,
   He looked round about;
'Methinks,' said he, 'I seem to be
   A beggar brave and stout.

18 'For now I have a bag for my bread,
   So have I another for corn;
I have one for salt, and another for malt,
   And one for my little horn.

19 'And now I will a begging goe,
   Some charitie for to find:'
And if any more of Robin you 'l know,
   In this second part it 's behind.

20 Now Robin he is to Nottingham bound,
   With his bags hanging down to his knee,
His staff, and his coat, scarce worth a groat,
   Yet merrilie passed he.

21 As Robin he passed the streets along,
   He heard a pittifull cry;
Three brethren deer, as he did hear,
   Condemned were to dye.

22 Then Robin he highed to the sheriffs [house],
   Some reliefe for to seek;
He skipt, and leapt, and capored full high,
   As he went along the street.

23 But when to the sheriffs doore he came,
   There a gentleman fine and brave,
'Thou beggar,' said he, 'come tell vnto me
   What is it that thou wouldest have?'

24 'No meat, nor drink,' said Robin Hood then,
   'That I come here to crave;
But to beg the lives of yeomen three,
   And that I fain would have.'

25 'That cannot be, thou bold beggar,
   Their fact it is so cleer;
I tell to thee, hangd they must be,
   For stealing of our kings deer.'

26 But when to the gallows they did come,
   There was many a weeping eye:
'O hold your peace,' said Robin then,
   'For certainly they shall not dye.'

27 Then Robin he set his horn to his mouth,
   And he blew but blastes three,
Till a hundred bold archers brave
   Came kneeling down to his knee.

28 'What is your will, master?' they said,
   'We are here at your command:'
'Shoot east, shoot west,' said Robin Hood then,
   'And look that you spare no man.'

29 Then they shot east, and they shot west;
   Their arrows were so keen
The sheriffe he, and his companie,
   No longer must be seen.

30 Then he stept to these brethren three,
   And away he had them tane;
But the sheriff was crost, and many a man lost,
   That dead lay on the plain.

31 And away they went into the merry green wood,
   And sung with a merry glee,
And Robin took these brethren good
   To be of his yeomandrie.

a. Robin Hood and the Beggar : Shewing how Robin Hood and the Beggar fought, and how he changed clothes with the Beggar, and how he went a begging to Nottingham, and how he saved three brethren from being hangd for stealing of deer.   To the tune of Robin Hood and the Stranger.   *Signed* T. R.

London, Printed for Francis Grove, on Snow-hill. (1620–55.)

Burden : an a.

1^1. light *in all : a corruption of* lyth.

2^2. archrey. 3^4. friend or foe : *cf.* b, c.

4^2. angell. 6^1. had one. 10^1. tell the.

12^1. saffe. 21^3. brethred. 27^4. dow.

31^4. yeomandriee.

b, c. *Title as in* a.   *Not signed.   Burden sometimes,* With hey, *etc.,* or, With a hey, *etc. ; once, in* c, Hey derry derry down.

b. 3^4. friends or foes. 4^2. angels.

7^1. Hood then. 7^2. unto. 8^3. he *wanting.*

9^3. doth know. 10^2. with thee. 10^4. lay.

16^1. said *for* cri'd. 20^1. he *wanting.*

21^4. was for to. 22^1. sheriffs house.

27^2. he *wanting.* 30^2. them had.

c. 3^4. friends or foes. 4^2. angels.

7^1. Hood then. 7^2. unto. 8^3. living.

10^2. with thee. 19^4. known *for* behind.

21^4. for to. 22^1. sheriffs house.

25^3. they hanged. 27^2. he *wanting.*

30^2. them had.

d. *Title as in* a : *except* of the king's deer.   *Not signed.*

Printed for I. Clarke, W. Thackeray, and T. Passinger. (1670–86.)

Burden : With a hey down down and a down.

3^2. merrily. 3^4. friend or foe. 4^2. angels.

5^1. brave *for* fair. 7^1. Hood then.

7^2. unto. 10^2. with thee. 11^1. he said.

12^1. muckle. 12^4. But he. 13^3. Robin gave.

14^3. Robin Hood's head. 15^3. If it.

17^1. Hood *wanting.* 17^3. Methink.

18^3. for mault : for salt.

19^4. In the.   house *wanting, as in* a.

22^3. and he leapt. 23^4. is 't : would'st.

25^4. of the. 26^3. O *wanting :* Robin Hood.

27^4. down on their. 28^2. here *wanting.*

29^1. east then. 30^2. has. 30^3. many men.

31^1. And *wanting.*

31^3. Then Robin Hood.

134

ROBIN HOOD AND THE BEGGAR, II

a. ' The History of Robin Hood and the Beggar,' Aberdeen, Printed by and for A. Keith : Bodleian Library, Douce, HH 88, pasted between pp 68, 69 of Robin Hood's Garland, London, C. Dicey. A. Keith of Aberdeen printed from 1810 to 1835.

b. ' A pretty dialogue betwixt Robin Hood and a Beggar,' Newcastle, in Ritson's Robin Hood, 1795, I, 97.

a is printed by Gutch, Robin Hood, II, 230, with deviations. Of b Ritson says : The corruptions of the press being equally numerous and minute, some of the most trifling have been corrected without notice. Despite the corruptions, b is, in some readings, preferable to a. Motherwell, Minstrelsy, p. xliii, says that pretty early stall copies were printed both at Aberdeen and Glasgow.

Robin Hood attempts to stop a beggar, from whom he thinks he may get some money. The beggar gives no heed to his summons, but hies on. Robin, getting a surly answer upon a second essay, says that if there be but a farthing he will have it, orders the beggar to loose the strings of his pocks, and threatens him with an arrow. The beggar defies him, and upon Robin's drawing his bow, reaches him such a stroke with a staff that bow and arrow are broken to bits.

Robin takes to his sword; the beggar lights on his hand with his staff and disables him completely, then follows in with lusty blows, till Robin falls in a swoon. The beggar moves on with entire unconcern. Three of Robin's men come by and revive him with water. Their master tells them of his disgrace; he had never been in so hard a place in forty year. He bids them bring the beggar back or slay him. Two of the three will be enough for that, they say, and one shall stay with him. Two set forth, accordingly, with a caution to be wary, take a short cut, which brings them out ahead of the beggar, and leap on him from a hiding, one gripping his staff and the other putting a dagger to his breast. The beggar sues for his life in vain; they will bind him and will take him back to their master, to be slain or hanged. He offers them a hundred pound and more for his liberty. They decide together to take the money, and say nothing about it, simply reporting that they have killed the old carl. The beggar spreads his cloak on the ground and many a pock on it; then, standing between them and the wind, takes a great bag of meal from his neck and flings the meal into their eyes. Having thus blinded them, he seizes his staff, which they had stuck in the ground, and gives each of them a dozen. The young men take to their heels, the beggar calling after them to stop for their pay. Robin, after a jest at the meal on their cloaths, makes them tell how they have fared. We are shamed forever, he cries; but smiles to see that they have had their taste of the beggar's tree.

This tale is rightly called by Ritson a North Country composition of some antiquity, "perhaps Scottish." Fragments of Robin Hood ballads, Motherwell informs us, were traditionally extant in his day which had not (and have not) found their way into printed collections, and we know from very early testimony that such ballads were current in Scotland. This is by far the best of the Robin Hood ballads of the secondary, so to speak cyclic, period. It has plenty of homely humor, but the heroic sentiment is gone. It does not belong to the iron, the cast-iron, age of Robin Hood's Birth, Breeding, etc.; but neither does it belong to the golden age of Robin Hood and the Monk, or the Gest. It would be no gain to have Thersites drubbing Odysseus. Robin finds his match, for the nonce, in the Potter, but he does not for that depute two of his men to be the death of the Potter. It never occurred to Little John and Much to get a hundred pound from a beggar, kill him, and pocket the money.

A story resembling that of the second part of this ballad occurs, as Ritson has observed, in Le moyen de parvenir, "1739, I, 304;" II, 94, London, 1786; p. 171, Paris, 1841. A friar encounters two footpads, who offer to relieve him of the burden of his frock. He asks them to let him take it off peaceably, puts his staff under his foot, takes off the frock and throws it before them. While one of the pair stoops to get it, the friar picks up the staff and hits the knave a blow which sends him headlong; the other runs off.

Translated by Anastasius Grün, p. 180.

———◆———

1 LYTH and listen, gentlemen,
   That's come of high born blood;
   I'll tell you of a brave booting
   That befel Robin Hood.

2 Robin Hood upon a day,
   He went forth him alone,
   And as he came from Barnesdale
   Into a fair evening,

3 He met a beggar on the way,
   That sturdily could gang;
   He had a pike-staff in his hand,
   That was baith stark and strang.

4 A clouted cloak about him was,
   That held him from the cold;
   The thinnest bit of it, I guess,
   Was more than twenty fold.

5 His meal-pock hang about his neck,
    Into a leathern fang,
Well fastened with a broad buckle,
    That was both stark and strang.

6 He had three hats upon his head,
    Together sticked fast;
He cared neither for wind nor weet,
    In lands wherever he past.

7 Good Robin coost him in his way,
    To see what he might be;
If any beggar had money,
    He thought some part had he.

8 'Tarry, tarry,' good Robin says,
    'Tarry, and speak with me;'
He heard him as he heard [him] not,
    And fast his way can hie.

9 'It be's not so,' says good Robin,
    'Nay, thou must tarry still;'
'By my troth,' says the bold beggar,
    'Of that I have no will.

10 'It is far to my lodging-house,
    And it is growing late;
If they have supt ere I come in,
    I will look wondrous blate.'

11 'Now, by my troth,' says good Robin,
    'I see well by thy fare,
If thou chear well to thy supper,
    Of mine thou takes no care;

12 'Who wants my dinner all the day,
    And wots not where to lie,
And should I to the tavern go,
    I want money to buy.

13 'Sir, thou must lend me some money,
    Till we two meet again:'
The beggar answerd cankerdly,
    I have no money to lend.

14 Thou art as young a man as I,
    And seems to be as sweer;
If thou fast till thou get from me,
    Thou shalt eat none this year.

15 'Now, by my troth,' says good Robin,
    'Since we are sembled so,

If thou have but a small farthing,
    I'll have it ere thou go.

16 'Therefore, lay down thy clouted cloak,
    And do no longer stand,
And loose the strings of all thy pocks;
    I'll ripe them with my hand.

17 'And now to thee I make a vow,
    If thou make any din,
I shall see if a broad arrow
    Can pierce a beggar's skin.'

18 The beggar smil'd, and answer made:
    Far better let me be;
Think not that I will be afraid
    For thy nip crooked tree.

19 Or that I fear thee any whit
    For thy curn nips of sticks;
I know no use for them so meet
    As to be pudding-pricks.

20 Here I defy thee to do me ill,
    For all thy boistrous fare;
Thou's get nothing from me but ill,
    Would thou seek it evermair.

21 Good Robin bent his noble bow —
    He was an angry man —
And in it set a broad arrow;
    Yet er 't was drawn a span,

22 The beggar, with his noble tree,
    Reacht him so round a rout
That his bow and his broad arrow
    In flinders flew about.

23 Good Robin bound him to his brand,
    But that provd likewise vain;
The beggar lighted on his hand
    With his pike-staff again.

24 I wot he might not draw a sword
    For forty days and more;
Good Robin could not speak a word,
    His heart was never so sore.

25 He could not fight, he could not flee,
    He wist not what to do;
The beggar, with his noble tree,
    Laid lusty flaps him to.

26 He paid good Robin back and side,
   And beft him up and down,
   And with his pike-staff still on laid
   Till he fell in a swoon.

27 'Fy! stand up, man,' the beggar said,
   ' 'T is shame to go to rest;
   Stay still till thou get thy mony [told],
   I think it were the best.

28 'And syne go to the tavern-house,
   And buy both wine and ale;
   Hereat thy friends will crack full crouse,
   Thou has been at a dale.'

29 Good Robin answerd never a word,
   But lay still as a stane;
   His cheeks were white as any clay,
   And closed were his eyne.

30 The beggar thought him dead but fail,
   And boldly bownd away;
   I would you had been at the dale,
   And gotten part of the play.

31 Now three of Robin's men, by chance,
   Came walking on the way,
   And found their master in a trance,
   On ground where he did lie.

32 Up have they taken good Robin,
   Making a piteous bier,
   Yet saw they no man there at whom
   They might the matter spear.

33 They looked him all round about,
   But wounds on him saw none,
   Yet at his mouth came bocking out
   The blood of a good vein.

34 Cold water they have taken syne,
   And cast into his face;
   Then he began to lift his eyne,
   And spake within short space.

35 'Tell us, dear master,' says his men,
   'How with you stands the case?'
   Good Robin sighd ere he began
   To tell of his disgrace.

36 'I have been watchman in this wood
   Near hand this forty year,
   Yet I was never so hard bestead
   As you have found me here.

37 'A beggar with a clouted cloak,
   In whom I feard no ill,
   Hath with a pike-staff clawd my back;
   I fear 't shall never be well.

38 'See, where he goes out oer yon hill,
   With hat upon his head;
   If ever you lovd your master well,
   Go now revenge this deed.

39 'And bring him back again to me,
   If it lie in your might,
   That I may see, before I die,
   Him punisht in my sight.

40 'And if you may not bring him back,
   Let him not go loose on;
   For to us all it were great shame
   If he escapt again.'

41 'One of us shall with you remain,
   Because you 're ill at ease;
   The other two shall bring him back,
   To use him as you please.'

42 'Now, by my troth,' says good Robin,
   'I trow there 's enough said;
   If he get scouth to weild his tree,
   I fear you 'll both be paid.'

43 'Be ye not feard, our good master,
   That we two can be dung
   With any blutter base beggar,
   That hath nought but a rung.

44 'His staff shall stand him in no stead;
   That you shall shortly see;
   But back again he shall be led,
   And fast bound shall he be,
   To see if you will have him slain,
   Or hanged on a tree.'

45 'But cast you slily in his way,
   Before he be aware,
   And on his pike-staff first lay hands;
   You 'll speed the better far.'

46 Now leave we Robin with his man,
      Again to play the child,
   And learn himself to stand and gang
      By haulds, for all his eild.

47 Now pass we to the bold beggar,
      That raked oer the hill,
   Who never mended his pace no more
      Nor he had done no ill.

48 The young men knew the country well,
      So soon where he would be,
   And they have taken another way,
      Was nearer by miles three.

49 They rudely ran with all their might,
      Spar'd neither dub nor mire,
   They stirred neither at laigh nor hight,
      No travel made them tire,

50 Till they before the beggar wan,
      And coost them in his way;
   A little wood lay in a glen,
      And there they both did stay.

51 They stood up closely by a tree,
      In ilk side of the gate,
   Until the beggar came them to,
      That thought not of such fate.

52 And as he was betwixt them past,
      They leapt upon him baith;
   The one his pike-staff gripped fast,
      They feared for its scaith.

53 The other he held in his sight
      A drawn dirk to his breast,
   And said, False carl, quit thy staff,
      Or I shall be thy priest.

54 His pike-staff they have taken him frae,
      And stuck it in the green;
   He was full leath to let [it] gae,
      If better might have been.

55 The beggar was the feardest man
      Of one that ever might be;
   To win away no way he can,
      Nor help him with his tree.

56 He wist not wherefore he was tane,
      Nor how many was there;

He thought his life-days had been gone,
      And grew into despair.

57 'Grant me my life,' the beggar said,
      'For him that died on tree,
   And take away that ugly knife,
      Or then for fear I 'll die.

58 'I grievd you never in all my life,
      By late nor yet by ayre;
   Ye have great sin, if ye should slay
      A silly poor beggar.'

59 'Thou lies, false lown,' they said again,
      'By all that may be sworn;
   Thou hast near slain the gentlest man
      That ever yet was born.

60 'And back again thou shalt be led,
      And fast bound shalt thou be,
   To see if he will have thee slain,
      Or hanged on a tree.'

61 The beggar then thought all was wrong;
      They were set for his wrack;
   He saw nothing appearing then
      But ill upon worse back.

62 Were he out of their hands, he thought,
      And had again his tree,
   He should not be had back for nought,
      With such as he did see.

63 Then he bethought him on a wile,
      If it could take effect,
   How he the young men might beguile,
      And give them a begeck.

64 Thus for to do them shame or ill
      His beastly breast was bent;
   He found the wind grew something shril,
      To further his intent.

65 He said, Brave gentlemen, be good,
      And let the poor man be;
   When ye have taken a beggar's blood,
      It helps you not a flee.

66 It was but in my own defence,
      If he hath gotten skaith;
   But I will make a recompence,
      Much better for you baith.

67 If ye will set me safe and free,
    And do me no danger,
  An hundred pounds I will you give,
    And much more good silver,

68 That I have gathered these many years,
    Under this clouted cloak,
  And hid up wonder privately,
    In bottom of my pock.

69 The young men to a council yeed,
    And let the beggar gae ;
  They wist how well he had no speed
    From them to run away.

70 They thought they would the money take,
    Come after what so may,
  And then they would not bring him back,
    But in that part him slay.

71 By that good Robin would not know
    That they had gotten coin ;
  It would content him for to show
    That there they had him slain.

72 They said, False carl, soon have done
    And tell forth that money ;
  For the ill turn thou hast done
    'T is but a simple fee.

73 And yet we will not have thee back,
    Come after what so may,
  If thou will do that which thou spake,
    And make us present pay.

74 O then he loosd his clouted cloak,
    And spread it on the ground,
  And thereon laid he many a pock,
    Betwixt them and the wind.

75 He took a great bag from his hase ;
    It was near full of meal ;
  Two pecks in it at least there was,
    And more, I wot full well.

76 Upon his cloak he laid it down,
    The mouth he opend wide,
  To turn the same he made him bown,
    The young men ready spy'd.

77 In every hand he took a nook
    Of that great leathern meal,

And with a fling the meal he shook
    Into their faces hail.

78 Wherewith he blinded them so close
    A stime they could not see ;
  And then in heart he did rejoice,
    And clapt his lusty tree.

79 He thought, if he had done them wrong
    In mealing of their cloaths,
  For to strike off the meal again
    With his pike-staff he goes.

80 Or any one of them could red their eyne,
    Or yet a glimmering could see,
  Ilk ane of them a dozen had,
    Well laid on with the tree.

81 The young men were right swift of foot,
    And boldly ran away ;
  The beggar could them no more hit,
    For all the haste he may.

82 'What ails this haste ?' the beggar said,
    'May ye not tarry still,
  Until your money be receivd ?
    I 'll pay you with good will.

83 'The shaking of my pocks, I fear,
    Hath blown into your eyne ;
  But I have a good pike-staff here
    Will ripe them out full clean.'

84 The young men answerd neer a word,
    They were dumb as a stane ;
  In the thick wood the beggar fled,
    Eer they riped their eyne.

85 And syne the night became so late,
    To seek him was but vain :
  But judge ye, if they looked blate
    When they came home again.

86 Good Robin speard how they had sped ;
    They answerd him, Full ill ;
  'That cannot be,' good Robin says ;
    'Ye have been at the mill.

87 'The mill it is a meatrif place,
    They may lick what they please ;
  Most like ye have been at that art,
    Who would look to your cloaths.'

88 They hangd their heads, and droped down,
   A word they could not speak:
Robin said, Because I fell a-swoon,
   I think you'll do the like.

89 Tell on the matter, less and more,
   And tell me what and how
Ye have done with the bold beggar
   I sent you for right now.

90 And then they told him to an end,
   As I have said before,
How that the beggar did them blind,
   What misters process more.

91 And how he lin'd their shoulders broad
   With his great trenchen tree,
And how in the thick wood he fled,
   Eer they a stime could see.

92 And how they scarcely could win home,
   Their bones were beft so sore:
Good Robin cry'd, Fy! out, for shame!
   We're sham'd for evermore.

93 Altho good Robin would full fain
   Of his wrong revenged be,
He smil'd to see his merry young men
   Had gotten a taste of the tree.

———◆———

a. The History of Robin Hood and the Beggar:
in two Parts. Part I: Shewing how Robin
Hood, in attempting to rob a Beggar near
Barnesdale, was shamefully defeated, and
left for dead, till taken up by three of his
men. Part II: How the beggar blinded
two of his men with a bag of meal, who
were sent to kill him or bring him back.
Title prefixed to the ballad: Robin Hood and
the Beggar.
In stanzas of two long lines. After 30: The
Second Part.
22³. arrows. 30¹. but sail: *that is,* but fail.
38³. you *for* your.
41². ill a case: *which perhaps should be re-
tained.*
46¹. and *for* with. 46⁴. the eild.
48³. a another.
51⁴. fate: b, late, *that is,* let. 53³. quite.
65⁴. fly: b, flee. 77³. sling: *that is,* fling.
79³. strick. 89². where and.
b. *In stanzas of two long lines.*
*Some of these readings may be Ritson's cor-
rections.*
1². That be. 2⁴. a *wanting.*
3². Who *for* That. 4². frae the. 5². whang.
5³. to a. 7¹. cast. 8³. heard him not.
8⁴. on his. 9¹. 'Tis be. 9³. said.
11³. shares well. 11⁴. dost not care.
12¹. all this. 12³. would I. 13¹. you must.
13². two *wanting.* 14¹. art a.
15². asembled. 15³. has. 16¹. Come lay.
17³. if *wanting.* 20⁴. Wouldst: it *wanting.*
21⁴. Lo eer. 22³. arrow. 24²,⁴. mair, sair.
25³. flaps. 26². baift.

26³. laid on loud *for* still on laid.
27¹. Fy *wanting.* 27³. still till: money told.
28⁴. hast been at the. 29³. pale *for* white.
30¹. but fail. 30². his way. 30³. ye.
31². by the. 31⁴. where that he lay.
33². wound. 34¹. gotten *for* taken.
34². unto. 34³. to hitch his ear. 34⁴. speak.
35¹. said. 36². this twenty. 36⁴. ye.
37². Of whom. 37³. with his. 37⁴. 't will.
38¹. out *wanting.* 38³. eer ye.
40⁴. escape. 41². ill at ease. 42³. And he.
43¹. ye, good *wanting.* 43⁴. has. 44⁵. ye.
45³. hands lay. 45⁴. Ye. 46¹. with his.
46⁴. his eild. 47³. no *wanting.*
47⁴. Then he. 48¹,². *wanting.*
49¹. They stoutly.
49³. They started at neither how nor height.
50². cast them. 51². In each.
51³. them nigh. 51⁴. thought of no such late.
54³. let it. 54⁴. An better might it been.
55². any *for* one. 56¹. Nor wist he.
56⁴. He *for* And. 57². on the.
57³. And hold. 57⁴. Or else.
58². Neither by late or air.
58³. You have great sin if you would.
59². For all. 59⁴. Of one that eer.
60¹. shall. 62³. led back.
63³. he might the young men.
63⁴. gave them a begack.
64¹. for *wanting:* for ill.
64³. blew *for* grew. 65². a poor. 65⁴. flee.
66². has. 66⁴. Is better. 67¹. fair and.
67². no more dear. 67⁴. odd *for* good.
68¹. this. 69¹. to the. 69³. full well.
70³. And yet: not take. 70⁴. that place.

71⁸. for *wanting*. 72². forth thy.
72⁸. turn that. 72⁴. It's : plee *for* fee.
74⁸. lay he. 75¹. half, *that is*, half.
76¹. this cloak : set it. 76⁸. bound.
77². bag *for* meal. 77⁸. fling.
77⁴. face all hail. 79². cloath.
79⁸. strike. 80¹. Eer any of.
80². Or a glimmering might. 80⁴. with his.
81². boldly bound. 82¹. What's all this.

82². May not thou. 83⁴. Can ripe.
85². in vain. 87¹. meat rife part.
87⁸. at the. 87⁴. at your.
88¹. they drooped. 88⁸. a sound. 88⁴. ye.
89¹. less or. 89². what and.
90¹. And when. 90⁴. presses *for* process.
91¹,². *wanting*. 91⁸. woods.
92². were baste. 93². his wrath.

135

ROBIN HOOD AND THE SHEPHERD

a. Garland of 1663, No 13.

b. Garland of 1670, No 12.

c. Wood, 401, leaf 13 b.

d. Pepys, II, 115, No 102.

ROXBURGHE, II, 392, III, 284 ; Douce, III, 115 b, by L. How, of the eighteenth century. A manuscript copy in the British Museum, Add. 15072, fol. 59, is a, with omission of 12²–15⁴, and a few errors of carelessness.

Printed in Ritson's Robin Hood from c and one of the Roxburghe broadsides. Evans, Old Ballads, 1777, 1784, I, 136, seems to have followed the Aldermary garland, with slight deviation.

Robin Hood, walking in the forest, finds a shepherd lying on the ground, and bids him rise and show what he has in his bottle and bag. The shepherd tells him that he shall not see a drop of his bottle until his valor has been tried. Robin stakes twenty pound on the issue of a fight, and the shepherd his bag and bottle. They fight from ten to four, hook against sword. Robin Hood falls to the ground, and the shepherd calls on him to own himself beaten. Robin demands the boon of three blasts on his horn. These bring Little John, who undertakes the shepherd, and is so roughly handled that Robin is fain to yield his wager, to which Little John heartily agrees.

It is but the natural course of exaggeration that the shepherd, having beaten Robin Hood, should beat Little John. This is descending low enough, but we do not see the bottom of this kind of balladry here.

In King Alfred and the Shepherd, Old Ballads, 1723, I, 43, stanzas 6–17, the king plays Robin's part, fighting four hours with the Shepherd and then craving a truce. Further on Alfred blows his horn. There are also verbal agreements.

---

1 ALL gentlemen and yeomen good,
    Down a down a down a down
  I wish you to draw near ;
For a story of gallant brave Robin Hood
    Vnto you I wil declare.
    Down, etc.

2 As Robin Hood walkt the forrest along,
    Some pastime for to spie,
  There was he aware of a jolly shepherd,
    That on the ground did lie.

3 'Arise, arise,' cryed jolly Robin,
  'And now come let me see
What is in thy bag and bottle, I say;
  Come tell it unto me.'

4 'What's that to thee, thou proud fellow?
  Tell me as I do stand
What thou hast to do with my bag and bottle?
  Let me see thy command.'

5 'My sword, which hangeth by my side,
  Is my command I know;
Come, and let me taste of thy bottle,
  Or it may breed thee wo.'

6 'Tut, the devil a drop, thou proud fellow,
  Of my bottle thou shalt see,
Untill thy valour here be tried,
  Whether thou wilt fight or flee.'

7 'What shall we fight for?' cries bold Robin
  Hood;
  'Come tell it soon to me;
Here is twenty pounds in good red gold;
  Win it, and take it thee.'

8 The Shepherd stood all in a maze,
  And knew not what to say:
'I have no money, thou proud fellow,
  But bag and bottle I'le lay.'

9 'I am content, thou shepherd-swain,
  Fling them down on the ground;
But it will breed thee mickle pain,
  To win my twenty pound.'

10 'Come draw thy sword, thou proud fellow,
  Thou stands too long to prate;
This hook of mine shall let thee know
  A coward I do hate.'

11 So they fell to it, full hardy and sore;
  It was on a summers day;
From ten till four in the afternoon
  The Shepherd held him play.

12 Robins buckler proved his chief defence,
  And saved him many a bang,
For every blow the Shepherd gave
  Made Robins sword cry twang.

13 Many a sturdy blow the Shepherd gave,
  And that bold Robin found,

Till the blood ran trickling from his head;
  Then he fell to the ground.

14 'Arise, arise, thou proud fellow,
  And thou shalt have fair play,
If thou wilt yield, before thou go,
  That I have won the day.'

15 'A boon, a boon,' cried bold Robin;
  'If that a man thou be,
Then let me take my beaugle-horn,
  And blow but blasts three.'

16 'To blow three times three,' the Shepherd said,
  'I will not thee deny;
For if thou shouldst blow till to-morrow morn,
  I scorn one foot to fly.'

17 Then Robin set his horn to his mouth,
  And he blew with mickle main,
Until he espied Little John
  Come tripping over the plain.

18 'O who is yonder, thou proud fellow,
  That comes down yonder hill?'
'Yonder is Little John, bold Robin Hoods
  man,
Shall fight with thee thy fill.'

19 'What is the matter?' saies Little John,
  'Master, come tell to me:'
'My case is great,' saies Robin Hood,
  'For the Shepherd hath conquered me.'

20 'I am glad of that,' cries Little John,
  'Shepherd, turn thou to me;
For a bout with thee I mean to have,
  Either come fight or flee.'

21 'With all my heart, thou proud fellow,
  For it never shall be said
That a shepherds hook of thy sturdy look
  Will one jot be dismaid.'

22 So they fell to it, full hardy and sore,
  Striving for victory;
'I will know,' saies John, 'ere we give ore,
  Whether thou wilt fight or flye.'

23 The Shepherd gave John a sturdy blow,
  With his hook under the chin;
'Beshrew thy heart,' said Little John,
  'Thou basely dost begin.'

24 'Nay, that's nothing,' said the Shepherd;
   'Either yield to me the day,
Or I will bang thee back and sides,
   Before thou goest thy way.

25 'What? dost thou think, thou proud fellow,
   That thou canst conquer me?
Nay, thou shalt know, before thou go,
   I 'le fight before I 'le flee.'

26 With that to thrash Little John like mad
   The Shepherd he begun;

'Hold, hold,' cryed bold Robin Hood,
   'And I 'le yield the wager won.'

27 'With all my heart,' said Little John,
   'To that I will agree;
For he is the flower of shepherd-swains,
   The like I never did see.'

28 Thus have you heard of Robin Hood,
   Also of Little John,
How a shepherd-swain did conquer them;
   The like did never none.

———◆———

a, b. Robin Hood and the Shepard: Shewing how
   Robin Hood, Little John and the Shep-
   heard fought a sore combate.
   Tune is, Robin Hood and Queen Katherine.
a. *Burden: a third* a down *is not printed after
   the first line, but is after the last.*
   4³. hast thou. 5⁴. thy wo. 7². Gome.
   20⁴. Eihter. 26². Sheherd.
b. *Burden:* Down a down a down a down.
   After 9¹, 21⁴, With a, &c.
   1³. bold *for* brave. 4³. thou hast.
   5³. tast. 5⁴. thee *for* thy.
   7¹. bold *wanting.* 7³. pound. 10². standst.
   12¹. chiefest. 13³. tickling.
   16¹. Then said the Shepherd to bold Robin.
   16². *wanting.* 17¹. Robin he.
   18³. Little *wanting.* 19³. is very bad, cries.
   26¹. Again the Shepherd laid on him.
   26⁴. And *wanting:* I will. 27⁴. I did never.
   28⁴. was never known.
c. Robin Hood and the Shepheard: Shewing how
   Robin Hood, Little John and the Shep-
   heard fought a sore combat.

   The Shepherd fought for twenty pound,
      And Robin for bottle and bag,
   But the Shepheard stout gave them the rout
      So sore they could not wag.

   The tune is Robin and Queen Katherine.

London, Printed for John Andrews, at the
   White Lion, in Pie-Corner. (1660.)
Burden: Down a down a down a down.
1³. bold *for* brave. 4³. thou hast.
5⁴. my wo. 8¹. amaze. 11³. four till ten.
12¹. chiefest. 13⁴. And then. 16¹. *wanting.*
19³. cries *for* saies. 19⁴. hath beaten.
22³. ile know saith. 22⁴. flee. 25¹. doest.
26¹. *wanting.* 26². began.
26⁴. And *wanting:* I will. 27³. Shepheards.
27⁴. I did never.
d. *Title as in* a, b.
Printed for William Thackeray, at the Angel
   in Duck Lane. (1689.)
Burden: Down a down down.
1³. bold *for* brave. 2³. he was.
4³. hast thou, *as in* a. 5¹. that *for* which.
5⁴. thy woe, *as in* a. 6¹. Tut *wanting.*
7¹. bold *wanting.* 7³. pound. 10². standest.
11¹. hard. 12¹. chiefest. 15³. beagle.
16¹. Then said the Shepherd to bold Robin.
16². To that will I agree. 16⁴. flee.
17¹. he set. 17². with might and main.
18³. Little *wanting.* 19³. bad cries.
21². shall never. 21³. at thy. 22⁴. flee.
24³. thy *for* thee.
26¹. Again the Shepherd laid on him.
26². began. 26³. Hood *wanting.*
26⁴. And *wanting:* I will. 27⁴. I did never.
28⁴. The like was never known.

136

ROBIN HOOD'S DELIGHT

(ROBIN HOOD, JOHN, SCARLOCK AND THREE KEEPERS)

a. Wood, 401, leaf 41 b.

c. Garland of 1670, No 16.

b. Garland of 1663, No 17.

d. Pepys, II, 112, No 99.

———◆———

RITSON, Robin Hood, 1795, II, 116, from a, with changes. Evans, Old Ballads, 1777, 1784, I, 176.

Robin Hood, Scarlock, and John, walking in Sherwood, are charged to stand by three of King Henry's keepers. There is a fight from eight till two o'clock, in which the outlaws are at some disadvantage. Robin asks that he may blow his horn, then he will fight again. The keepers refuse; he must fall on or yield. Robin owns them to be stout fellows; he will not fight it out there with swords, but at Nottingham with sack. They go to Nottingham accordingly, and drink themselves good friends.

The Bold Pedlar and Robin Hood, No 132, a late traditional copy, shows traces of st. 20 of this ballad in st. 12, where the Pedlar says it lies with him whether he will tell his name, and again at the end, where Robin Hood, John, and the Pedlar drink friendship at the tavern. Robin Hood's antagonists are again foresters and keepers in the Progress to Nottingham, and in Robin Hood and the Ranger. There are numerous verbal agreements between Robin Hood's Delight and Robin Hood and the Shepherd.

Translated by Loève-Veimars, p. 199.

———◆———

1 THERE is some will talk of lords and knights,
      Doun a doun a doun a doun
   And some of yeoman good,
   But I will tell you of Will Scarlock,
      Little John and Robin Hood.
         Doun a doun a doun a doun

2 They were outlaws, as 't is well known,
      And men of a noble blood;
   And a many a time was their valour shown
      In the forrest of merry Sheerwood.

3 Vpon a time it chanced so,
      As Robin Hood would have it be,
   They all three would a walking go,
      Some pastime for to see.

4 And as they walked the forest along,
      Upon a midsummer day,
   There was they aware of three keepers,
      Clade all in green aray.

5 With brave long faucheons by their sides,
      And forest-bills in hand,
   They calld aloud to those bold outlaws,
      And charged them to stand.

6 'Why, who are you,' cry'd bold Robin,
      'That speaks so boldly here?'
   'We three belong to King Henry,
      And are keepers of his deer.'

7 'The devil thou art!' sayes Robin Hood,
      'I am sure that it is not so;

We be the keepers of this forest,
And that you soon shall know.

8 'Come, your coats of green lay on the ground,
And so will we all three,
And take your swords and bucklers round,
And try the victory.'

9 'We be content,' the keepers said,
'We be three, and you no less;
Then why should we be of you afraid,
And we never did transgress?'

10 'Why, if you be three keepers in this forest,
Then we be three rangers good,
And we will make you to know, before you do
go,
You meet with bold Robin Hood.'

11 'We be content, thou bold outlaw,
Our valour here to try,
And we will make you know, before we do go,
We will fight before we will fly.'

12 'Then, come draw your swords, you bold out-
laws,
And no longer stand to prate,
But let us try it out with blows,
For cowards we do hate.

13 'Here is one of us for Will Scarlock,
And another for Little John,
And I my self for Robin Hood,
Because he is stout and strong.'

14 So they fell to it full hard and sore;
It was on a midsummers day;
From eight a clock till two and past,
They all shewed gallant play.

15 There Robin, and Will, and Little John,
They fought most manfully,
Till all their winde was spent and gone,
Then Robin aloud did cry:

16 'O hold, O hold,' cries bold Robin,
'I see you be stout men;
Let me blow one blast on my bugle-horn,
Then I 'le fight with you again.'

17 'That bargain 's to make, bold Robin Hood,
Therefore we it deny;
Though a blast upon thy bugle-horn
Cannot make us fight nor fly.

18 'Therefore fall on, or else be gone,
And yield to us the day:
It shall never be said that we were afraid
Of thee, nor thy yeomen gay.'

19 'If that be so,' cries bold Robin,
'Let me but know your names,
And in the forest of merry Sheerwood
I shall extol your fames.'

20 'And with our names,' one of them said,
'What hast thou here to do?
Except that you will fight it out,
Our names thou shalt not know.'

21 'We will fight no more,' sayes bold Robin,
'You be men of valour stout;
Come and go with me to Nottingham,
And there we will fight it out.

22 'With a but of sack we will bang it out,
To see who wins the day;
And for the cost, make you no doubt
I have gold and money to pay

23 'And ever after, so long as we live,
We all will brethren be;
For I love those men with heart and hand
That will fight, and never flee.'

24 So away they went to Nottingham,
With sack to make amends;
For three dayes space they wine did chase,
And drank themselves good friends.

———◆———

a. Robin Hood's Delight, or, A merry combat
fought between Robin Hood, Little John
and Will Scarelock and three stout Keepers
in Sheerwood Forrest.

Robin was valiant and stout, so was Scarelock
and John, in the field,
But these keepers stout did give them the rout,
and made them all for to yield;

But after the battel ended was, bold Robin did make them amends,
For claret and sack they did not lack, so drank themselves good friends.

To the tune of Robin Hood and Quene Katherine, or, Robin Hood and the Shepheard.
London, Printed for John Andrews, at the White Lion, near Pye Corner. (1660.)

b, c. *Title the same, without the verses :* Scarlet *for* Scarelock.
1². b, yeomen. 1⁸, 13¹. Scarlet.
2¹. it is. 2⁸. And many.
4⁸. was he : c, forresters *for* keepers.
5¹. side. 5². c, forrests bils.
5⁸. c, bold *wanting.*
7¹. b, bold Robin, Hood *wanting :* c, said Robin Hood.
7². b, it *wanting :* c, that *wanting.*

10⁴. met. 11⁸. do *wanting.* 11⁴, b. wee 'l.
16¹. c. thy hand cryes. 17¹. is.
19⁸. c. in that. 19⁴. b. I will.
20⁸. thou wilt. 23¹. hereafter.

d. *Title as in* b, c, *except :* fought against.
Printed for William Thackeray, at the Angel in Duck Lane. (1689.)
1¹. There 's. 1². yeomen. 1⁸, 13¹. Scarlet.
2⁸. And many. 4⁸. forresters *for* keepers.
5⁸. bold *wanting.* 6². speak. 7¹. said.
7². that *wanting.* 7⁸. the *wanting :* in *for* of.
8¹. Come *wanting.* 9². you *wanting.*
9⁸. we of you be. 10¹. the *for* three.
10⁸. we 'l : to *wanting.*
11⁸. *first* we, do *wanting.* 14¹. hardy.
15⁸. spend. 16⁸. with my beagle. 17¹. is.
17⁸. Thy blast : beagle.
18⁸. never shall : we are. 20⁸. thou wilt.
23¹. hereafter. 23⁸. these.

137

ROBIN HOOD AND THE PEDLARS

' Robinhood and the Peddlers,' the fourth ballad in a MS. formerly in the possession of J. Payne Collier, now in the British Museum ; previously printed in Gutch's Robin Hood, II, 351.

THE manuscript in which this ballad occurs contains a variety of matters, and, as the best authority * has declared, may in part have been written as early as 1650, but all the ballads are in a nineteenth-century hand, and some of them are maintained to be forgeries. I see no sufficient reason for regarding this particular piece as spurious, and therefore, though I should be glad to be rid of it, accept it for the present as perhaps a copy of a broadside, or a copy of a copy.

The story resembles that of Robin Hood's Delight, pedlars taking the place of keepers; but Robin is reduced to an ignominy paralleled only in the second ballad of Robin Hood and the Beggar. Robin Hood, accompanied by Scarlet and John, bids three pedlars stand. They pay no heed, and he sends an arrow through the pack of one of them. Hereupon they throw down their packs and wait for their assailants to come up. Robin's bow is broken by a blow from a staff of one of the pedlars. Robin calls a truce until he and his men can get staves. There is then an equal fight, the end of which is that Robin Hood is knocked senseless and left in a swoon, tended by Scarlet and John. But before the pedlars set forward, Kit o Thirske, the best man of the three, and the one who has fought with Robin, administers a balsam to his fallen foe,

* Mr E. Maunde Thompson, Keeper of the Manuscripts in the British Museum, in an obliging letter to Harvard College Library, and in The Academy, 1885, March 7, p. 170. No 8 C of this collection is in this manuscript.

which he says will heal his hurts, but which operates unpleasantly.

Thirsk is about twenty miles from York, in the North Riding.

1 WILL you heare a tale of Robin Hood,
  Will Scarlett, and Little John ?
  Now listen awhile, it will make you smile,
  As before it hath many done.

2 They were archers three, of hie degree,
  As good as ever drewe bowe;
  Their arrowes were long and their armes were strong,
  As most had cause to knowe.

3 But one sommers day, as they toke their way
  Through the forrest of greene Sherwood,
  To kill the kings deare, you shall presently heare
  What befell these archers good.

4 They were ware on the roade of three peddlers with loade,
  Ffor each had his packe,
  Ffull of all wares for countrie faires,
  Trusst up upon his backe.

5 A good oke staffe, a yard and a halfe,
  Each one had in his hande ;
  And they were all bound to Nottingham towne,
  As you shall understand.

6 'Yonder I see bolde peddlers three,'
  Said Robin to Scarlett and John ;
  'We 'le search their packes upon their backes
  Before that they be gone.

7 'Holla, good fellowes !' quod Robin Hood,
  'Whither is it ye doe goe ?
  Now stay and rest, for that is the best,
  'T is well ye should doe soe.'

8 'Noe rest we neede, on our roade we speede,
  Till to Nottingham we get : '
  'Thou tellst a lewde lye,' said Robin, ' for I
  Can see that ye swinke and swet.'

9 The peddlers three crosst over the lee,
  They did not list to fight :
  'I charge you tarrie,' quod Robin, 'for marry,
  This is my owne land by right.

10 'This is my mannor and this is my parke,
  I would have ye for to knowe ;
  Ye are bolde outlawes, I see by cause
  Ye are so prest to goe.'

11 The peddlers three turned round to see
  Who it might be they herd ;
  Then agen went on as they list to be gone,
  And never answered word.

12 Then toke Robin Hood an arrow so good,
  Which he did never lacke,
  And drew his bowe, and the swift arrowe
  Went through the last peddlers packe.

13 Ffor him it was well on the packe it fell,
  Or his life had found an ende ;
  And it pierst the skin of his backe within,
  Though the packe did stand his frend.

14 Then downe they flung their packes eche one,
  And stayde till Robin came :
  Quod Robin, I saide ye had better stayde ;
  Good sooth, ye were to blame.

15 'And who art thou ? by S. Crispin, I vowe
  I 'le quickly cracke thy head ! '
  Cried Robin, Come on, all three, or one ;
  It is not so soone done as said.

16 My name, by the roode, is Robin Hood,
  And this is Scarlett and John ;
  It is three to three, ye may plainelie see,
  Soe now, brave fellowes, laye on.

17 The first peddlars blowe brake Robins bowe
  That he had in his hand ;
  And Scarlett and John, they eche had one
  That they unneath could stand.

18 'Now holde your handes,' cride Robin Hood,
  'Ffor ye have got oken staves ;
  But tarie till wee can get but three,
  And a fig for all your braves.'

19 Of the peddlers the first, his name Kit o
    Thirske,
  Said, We are all content;
  Soe eche tooke a stake for his weapon, to
    make
    The peddlers to repent.

20 Soe to it they fell, and their blowes did ring
    well
  Uppon the others backes;
  And gave the peddlers cause to wish
    They had not cast their packes.

21 Yet the peddlers three of their blowes were so
    free
  That Robin began for to rue;
  And Scarlett and John had such loade laide on
    It made the sunne looke blue.

22 At last Kits oke caught Robin a stroke
  That made his head to sound;
  He staggerd, and reelde, till he fell on the
    fielde,
  And the trees with him went round.

23 'Now holde your handes,' cride Little John,
  And soe said Scarlett eke;
  'Our maister is slaine, I tell you plaine,
  He never more will speake.'

24 'Now, heaven forefend he come to that ende,'
  Said Kit, 'I love him well;

But lett him learne to be wise in turne,
  And not with pore peddlers mell.

25 'In my packe, God wot, I a balsame have got
  That soone his hurts will heale;'
  And into Robin Hoods gaping mouth
  He presentlie powrde some deale.

26 'Now fare ye well, tis best not to tell
  How ye three peddlers met;
  Or if ye doe, prithee tell alsoe
  How they made ye swinke and swett.'

27 Poore Robin in sound they left on the ground,
  And hied them to Nottingham,
  While Scarlett and John Robin tended on,
  Till at length his senses came.

28 Noe soone[r], in haste, did Robin Hood taste
  The balsame he had tane,
  Than he gan to spewe, and up he threwe
  The balsame all againe.

29 And Scarlett and John, who were looking on
  Their maister as he did lie,
  Had their faces besmeard, both eies and beard,
  Therewith most piteously.

30 Thus ended that fray; soe beware alwaye
  How ye doe challenge foes;
  Looke well aboute they are not to stoute,
  Or you may have worst of the blowes.

138

ROBIN HOOD AND ALLEN A DALE

a. 'Robin Hood and Allin of Dale,' Douce, II, leaf 185.   c. 'Robin Hood and Allen a Dale,' Douce, III, 119 b.

b. 'Robin Hood and Allin of Dale,' Pepys, II, 110, No 97.

PRINTED in A Collection of Old Ballads, 1723, II, 44, and Evans's Old Ballads, 1777, 1784, I, 126, after a copy very near to c. In Ritson's Robin Hood, 1795, II, 46, probably after Roxburghe II, 394. Not included in the garlands of 1663, 1670; in a garland of 1749, the Aldermary garland, R. Marshall, and the Lichfield, M. Morgan, both not dated, No 8; in the York garland, 1811, No 9. In the Kinloch MSS, V, 183, there is a copy, derived from the broadside, but Scotticised, and improved in the process.

A young man, Allen a Dale, whom Robin Hood has seen passing, one day singing and the next morning sighing, is stopped by Little John and the Miller's Son, and brought before their master, who asks him if he has any money. He has five shillings and a ring, and was to have been married the day before, but his bride has been given to an old knight. Robin asks what he will give to get his true-love. All that he can give is his faithful service. Robin goes to the church and declares the match not fit: the bride shall choose for herself. He blows his horn, and four-and-twenty of his men appear, the foremost of whom is Allen a Dale. Robin tells Allen that he shall be married on the spot. The bishop says no; there must be three askings. Robin puts the bishop's coat on Little John, and Little John asks seven times. Robin gives Allen the maid, and bids the man take her away that dare.

The ballad, it will be observed, is first found in broadside copies of the latter half of the seventeenth century. The story is told of Scarlock in the life of Robin Hood in Sloane MS, 715, 7, fol. 157, of the end of the sixteenth century; Thoms, Early Prose Romances, II, p. 39.

" Scarlock he induced [to become one of his company] upon this occacion. One day meting him as he walked solitary and lyke to a man forlorne, because a mayd to whom he was affyanced was taken from [him] by the violence of her frends, and given to another, that was auld and welthy; whereupon Robin, understandyng when the maryage-day should be, came to the church as a beggar, and having his company not far of, which came in so sone as they hard the sound of his horne, he ' took ' the bryde perforce from him that was in hand to have maryed her, and caused the preist to wed her and Scarlocke togeyther."

Translated by Anastasius Grün, p. 146.

---

1 COME listen to me, you gallants so free,
    All you that loves mirth for to hear,
  And I will you tell of a bold outlaw,
    That lived in Nottinghamshire. (*bis.*)

2 As Robin Hood in the forrest stood,
    All under the green-wood tree,
  There was he ware of a brave young man,
    As fine as fine might be.

3 The youngster was clothed in scarlet red,
    In scarlet fine and gay,
  And he did frisk it over the plain,
    And chanted a roundelay.

4 As Robin Hood next morning stood,
    Amongst the leaves so gay,
  There did he espy the same young man
    Come drooping along the way.

5 The scarlet he wore the day before,
    It was clean cast away;
  And every step he fetcht a sigh,
    ' Alack and a well a day ! '

6 Then stepped forth brave Little John,
    And Nick the millers son,
  Which made the young man bend his bow,
    When as he see them come.

7 ' Stand off, stand off,' the young man said,
    ' What is your will with me ? '
  ' You must come before our master straight,
    Vnder yon green-wood tree.'

8 And when he came bold Robin before,
    Robin askt him courteously,
  O hast thou any money to spare
    For my merry men and me ?

9 'I have no money,' the young man said,
    ' But five shillings and a ring ;
  And that I have kept this seven long years,
    To have it at my wedding.

10 ' Yesterday I should have married a maid,
    But she is now from me tane,
  And chosen to be an old knights delight,
    Whereby my poor heart is slain.'

11 'What is thy name?' then said Robin Hood,
  'Come tell me, without any fail:'
  'By the faith of my body,' then said the young
      man,
  'My name it is Allin a Dale.'

12 'What wilt thou give me,' said Robin Hood,
  'In ready gold or fee,
  To help thee to thy true-love again,
  And deliver her unto thee?'

13 'I have no money,' then quoth the young man,
  'No ready gold nor fee,
  But I will swear upon a book
  Thy true servant for to be.'

14 'How many miles is it to thy true-love?
  Come tell me without any guile:'
  'By the faith of my body,' then said the young
      man,
  'It is but five little mile.'

15 Then Robin he hasted over the plain,
  He did neither stint nor lin,
  Vntil he came unto the church
  Where Allin should keep his wedding.

16 'What dost thou do here?' the bishop he said,
  'I prethee now tell to me:'
  'I am a bold harper,' quoth Robin Hood,
  'And the best in the north countrey.'

17 'O welcome, O welcome,' the bishop he said,
  'That musick best pleaseth me;'
  'You shall have no musick,' quoth Robin Hood,
  'Till the bride and the bridegroom I see.'

18 With that came in a wealthy knight,
  Which was both grave and old,
  And after him a finikin lass,
  Did shine like glistering gold.

19 'This is no fit match,' quoth bold Robin Hood,
  'That you do seem to make here;

For since we are come unto the church,
  The bride she shall chuse her own dear.'

20 Then Robin Hood put his horn to his mouth,
  And blew blasts two or three;
  When four and twenty bowmen bold
  Came leaping over the lee.

21 And when they came into the church-yard,
  Marching all on a row,
  The first man was Allin a Dale,
  To give bold Robin his bow.

22 'This is thy true-love,' Robin he said,
  'Young Allin, as I hear say;
  And you shall be married at this same time,
  Before we depart away.'

23 'That shall not be,' the bishop he said,
  'For thy word shall not stand;
  They shall be three times askt in the church,
  As the law is of our land.'

24 Robin Hood pulld off the bishops coat,
  And put it upon Little John;
  'By the faith of my body,' then Robin said,
  'This cloath doth make thee a man.'

25 When Little John went into the quire,
  The people began for to laugh;
  He askt them seven times in the church,
  Least three times should not be enough.

26 'Who gives me this maid,' then said Little
      John;
  Quoth Robin, That do I,
  And he that doth take her from Allin a Dale
  Full dearly he shall her buy.

27 And thus having ended this merry wedding,
  The bride lookt as fresh as a queen,
  And so they returnd to the merry green wood,
  Amongst the leaves so green.

---

a. Robin Hood and Allin of Dale: Or, a pleasant
relation how a young gentleman being in love
with a young damsel, which was taken from
him to be an old knight's bride, and how
Robin Hood, pittying the young mans case,
took her from the old knight, when they

were going to be marryed, and restored her
to her own true love again.

Bold Robin Hood he did the young man right,
And took the damsel from the doteing knight.

To a pleasant northern tune, or, Robin Hood in the green wood stood.

With allowance. Printed for F. Cole, T. Vere, J. Wright and J. Clarke. (Coles, Vere and Wright, 1655–80, J. Clarke, 1650–82: *Chappell*.)

11⁴. Alllin. 18¹. wealhty. 22³. marrid.

b. *Title, etc., as in* a.

With allowance. Printed for Alex. Milbourn, in Green-Arbor-Court, in the Little-Old-Baily. (Alexander Milbourne 1670–97: *Chappell*.)

1³. tell you. 2³. he was aware. 10². she was from me tane. 16¹. dost thou here. 16². unto. 18⁴. like the. 19¹. not a fit: qd. 25². for *wanting*. 26¹. then *wanting*. 26³. And *wanting*. 27¹. having ende of. 27². lookt like a.

c. Robin Hood and Allen a Dale: Or, the man-

ner of Robin Hood's rescuing a young lady from an old knight to whom she was going to be married, and restoring her to Allen a Dale, her former love.

To the tune of Robin Hood in the green wood. *No printer.* Sold in Bow-Church-Yard, London.

1³. tell you. 2³. aware. 4³. spy. 5². quite *for* clean. 6². Midge *for* Nick. 9³. these seven. 10². she was from me taen. 11². any *wanting*. 13⁴. for *wanting*. 16¹. do *wanting*: then *for* he. 16². unto me. 17¹. then *for* he. 18⁴. Who shone like the glittering. 19¹. not a fit. 19⁴. she *wanting*. 22³. at the. 24³. Robin he. 24⁴. This coat. 25¹. to *for* into. 25². for *wanting*. 26¹. me *wanting*: maid, says. 27². bride she lookd like a.

139

ROBIN HOOD'S PROGRESS TO NOTTINGHAM

a. Wood, 402, leaf 14 b. b. Wood, 401, leaf 37 b. c. Garland of 1663, No 2. d. Garland of 1670, No 1.
e. Pepys, II, 104, No 92.

THIS piece occurs also in the Roxburghe Ballads, III, 270, 845, the Douce, III, 120, was among Heber's ballads (a copy by W. Onley), and is probably in all collections of broadsides.

a or b was printed by Ritson, Robin Hood, 1795, II, 12. A copy in Evans's Old Ballads, 1777, 1784, I, 96, is later, and very like Douce, III, 120.

When Robin Hood is but fifteen years of age, he falls in with fifteen foresters who are drinking together at Nottingham. They hear with scorn that he intends to take part in a shooting-match. He wagers with them that he will kill a hart at a hundred rod, and does this. They refuse to pay, and bid him begone if he would save his sides from a basting. Robin kills them all with his bow; people

come out from Nottingham to take him, but get very much hurt. Robin goes to the green wood; the townsmen bury the foresters.

This is evidently a comparatively late ballad, but has not come down to us in its oldest form. The story is told to the following effect in the life of Robin Hood in Sloane MS. 715, 7, fol. 157, written, as it seems, says Ritson, towards the end of the sixteenth century. Robin Hood, going into a forest with a bow of extraordinary strength, fell in with some rangers, or woodmen, who gibed at him for pretending to use a bow such as no man could shoot with. Robin said that he had two better, and that the one he had with him was only a "birding-bow"; nevertheless he would lay his head against a certain sum of money that he would kill a deer with it at a great distance. When the chance offered, one of the rangers sought to disconcert him by reminding him that he would lose his head if he missed his mark. Robin won the wager, and gave every man his money back except the one who had tried to fluster him. A quarrel followed, which ended with Robin's killing them all, and consequently betaking himself to life in the woods. Thoms, Early Prose Romances, II, Robin Hood, 37 ff.

Douce notes in his copy of Ritson's Robin Hood (Bodleian Library) the second stanza of this ballad as it is cited in the Duke of Newcastle's play, 'The Varietie':

When Robin came to Nottingham,
    His dinner all for to dine,
There met him fifteen jolly foresters,
    Were drinking ale and wine.
                        Gutch's Robin Hood, II, 123.

Translated by A. Grün, p. 61 ; Doenniges, p. 170.

———•———

1 ROBIN HOOD hee was and a tall young man,
        Derry derry down
    And fifteen winters old,
And Robin Hood he was a proper young man,
        Of courage stout and bold.
            Hey down derry derry down

2 Robin Hood he would and to fair Nottingham,
        With the general for to dine ;
    There was he ware of fifteen forresters,
        And a drinking bear, ale, and wine.

3 'What news ? What news ?' said bold Robin Hood ;
    'What news, fain wouldest thou know ?
Our king hath provided a shooting-match : '
    'And I 'm ready with my bow.'

4 'We hold it in scorn,' then said the forresters,
    'That ever a boy so young
Should bear a bow before our king,
    That 's not able to draw one string.'

5 'I 'le hold you twenty marks,' said bold Robin Hood,
    'By the leave of Our Lady,
That I 'le hit a mark a hundred rod,
    And I 'le cause a hart to dye.'

6 'We 'l hold you twenty mark,' then said the forresters,
    'By the leave of Our Lady,
Thou hitst not the marke a hundred rod,
    Nor causest a hart to dye.'

7 Robin Hood he bent up a noble bow,
    And a broad arrow he let flye,
He hit the mark a hundred rod,
    And he caused a hart to dy.

8 Some said hee brake ribs one or two,
    And some said hee brake three ;
The arrow within the hart would not abide,
    But it glanced in two or three.

9 The hart did skip, and the hart did leap,
    And the hart lay on the ground ;
'The wager is mine,' said bold Robin Hood,
    'If 't were for a thousand pound.'

10 'The wager 's none of thine,' then said the forresters,
    'Although thou beest in haste ;
Take up thy bow, and get thee hence,
    Lest wee thy sides do baste.'

11 Robin Hood hee took up his noble bow,
    And his broad arrows all amain,
And Robin Hood he laught, and begun to smile,
    As hee went over the plain.

12 Then Robin Hood hee bent his noble bow,
    And his broad arrows he let flye,
Till fourteen of these fifteen forresters
    Vpon the ground did lye.

13 He that did this quarrel first begin
    Went tripping over the plain ;
But Robin Hood he bent his noble bow,
    And hee fetcht him back again.

14 'You said I was no archer,' said Robin Hood,
    'But say so now again ; '
With that he sent another arrow
    That split his head in twain.

15 'You have found mee an archer,' saith Robin Hood,
    'Which will make your wives for to wring,

And wish that you had never spoke the word,
  That I could not draw one string.'

16 The people that lived in fair Nottingham
      Came runing out amain,
    Supposing to have taken bold Robin Hood,
      With the forresters that were slain.

17 Some lost legs, and some lost arms,
      And some did lose their blood,

But Robin Hood hee took up his noble bow,
  And is gone to the merry green wood.

18 They carryed these forresters into fair Not-
      tingham,
      As many there did know;
    They digd them graves in their church-yard,
      And they buried them all a row.

---

a, b. Robin Hoods Progresse to Nottingham,

  Where hee met with fifteen forresters, all on a
    row,
  And hee desired of them some news for to
    know,
  But with crosse graind words they did him
    thwart,
  For which at last hee made them smart.

  To the tune of Bold Robin Hood.
a. London, Printed for Fran. Grove. And en-
    tred according to order. (1620–55 : *Chap-
    pell.*)
b. London, Printed for F. Coles, T. Vere, and
    J. Wright. (1655–80 : *Chappell.*)
    3. *Commonly punctuated as if spoken entirely
    by Robin. There would certainly be an
    antecedent probability against three speeches
    in one stanza, in an older ballad.*
c, d. Robin Hoods Progress to Notingham, where

he slew fifteen Forresters. To the tune of
Bold Robin Hood.
c. 6^3. an. 7^3. a mark. 15^3. spake.
d. 7^3. an hundred. 11^3. began. 12^3. of the.
14^2. say you so.
14^3. he another arrnw let fly. 18^1. to fair.
e. *Title as in* **a, b,** *above, with these variations
in the verse :*
2, news to.   3, And with.   4, them for to.
Printed for J. Clarke, W. Thackeray, and T.
  Passenger. (1670–82 ?)
1^1. and *wanting*. 2^1. would unto.
2^3. aware. 4^1. scorn said bold R. Hood.
5^3. the mark an. 5^4, 7^4. one hart.
6^1. marks. 6^3. That thou : an. 7^3. an.
8^2. some say. 8^3. in *for* within.
11^2. all *wanting*. 11^3. began.
14^4. Which split. 15^1. said.
15^2. for *wanting*. 15^3. wish you ne'r had.
17^3. R. Hood he bent. 18^3. yards.
18^4. all on a row.

140

ROBIN HOOD RESCUING THREE SQUIRES

A. Percy MS., p. 5 ; Hales and Furnivall, I, 13 ;
Jamieson's Popular Ballads, II, 49.

B. a. 'Robin Hood rescuing the Widow's Three Sons
from the Sheriff, when going to be executed,' The
English Archer, York, N. Nickson, n. d. **b.** The
English Archer, Paisley, John Neilson, 1786. **c.**
Adventures of . . . Robin Hood, Falkirk, T. John-
ston, 1808. All in the Bodleian Library, Douce,
F.F. 71.

C. 'Robin Hood rescuing the Three Squires from Not-
tingham Gallows.' **a.** Robin Hood's Garland, Lon-
don, Printed by W. & C. Dicey, n. d. **b.** R. H.'s
Garland, London, L. How, in Peticoat Lane, n. d.
c. R. H.'s Garland, York, T. Wilson and R. Spence,
n. d. **d.** R. H.'s Garland, Preston, W. Sergent,
n. d. **e.** R. H.'s Garland, London, J. Marshall &
Co., n. d. **f.** R. H.'s Garland, Wolverhampton, J.
Smart, n. d. a–d, Douce, FF. 71, **f,** Douce, Add.
262, Bodleian Library.

B is given by Ritson, Robin Hood, 1795, II, 151, "from the York edition of Robin Hood's garland;" C, the same, II, 216, from an Aldermary Churchyard garland, and by Evans, Old Ballads, 1777, 1784, I, 215.

B. Robin Hood, while on his way to Nottingham, meets an old woman who is weeping for three squires condemned to die that day, not for recognized crimes, but for killing the king's deer. These seem to be his own men: st. 6. Pursuing his way, he meets an old "palmer," really a beggar, who confirms the bad news. He changes clothes with the palmer (who at first thinks the proposal a mock), and at Nottingham comes upon the sheriff, and asks what he will give an old fellow to be his hangman. The sheriff offers suits and pence; Robin says, hangmen be cursed, he will never take to that business. He has a horn in his pocket which would blow the sheriff little good; the sheriff bids him blow his fill. The first blast brings a hundred and fifty of Robin's men; the second brings three score more. They free their own men and hang the sheriff.

In C the three squires are expressly said to be the woman's sons; * for the palmer we have a beggar; Robin asks it as a boon that he may be hangman, and will have nothing for his service but three blasts on his horn, 'that their souls to heaven may flee.' The horn brings a hundred and ten men, and the sheriff surrenders the three squires.

In the fragment A, Robin changes clothes with an old man, who appears by stanza 11 to be a beggar. His men are with him meanwhile, and he orders them to conceal themselves in a wood until they hear his horn. A blast brings three hundred of them; Robin casts off his beggar's gear and stands in his red velvet doublet; † his men bend their bows and beset the gallows. The sheriff throws up his hands and begs for terms; Robin demands the three squires. The sheriff objects, for they are the king's felons; Robin will

have them, or the sheriff shall be the first man to flower the tree.

'Robin Hood and the Beggar,' No 133, from stanza 16, is another version of this ballad. Robin changes clothes with a beggar, after a hard fight in which he has had the worse, goes to Nottingham, and hears that three brothers are condemned to die. He hies to the sheriff to plead for them; a gentleman at the door tells him they must be hanged for deer-stealing clearly proved. At the gallows Robin blows his horn; a hundred archers present themselves, and ask his will. He commands them to shoot east and west and spare no man. The sheriff and his men, all that are not laid low, fly, and the three brothers, who have already shown their quality, are added to Robin's company.

A Scottish version of B, derived from the English, is given in an appendix. It occurs in Kinloch MSS, V, 288, and may be as old as the York garland used by Ritson, or older.

Ritson was informed by his friend Edward Williams, the Welsh bard, that C and its tune were well known in South Wales by the name of Marchog Glas, or Green Knight. As to the tune, says Dr Rimbault, it is not to be found in the collections of Welsh airs, nor was *his* friend John Parry, then representing the Welsh bards, able to give any account of it. Nothing further is said by Rimbault, either way, of the ballad.

B 6, in which Robin reminds the old woman that she had once given him to sup and dine, implicitly as a reason for his exerting himself in behalf of the three squires (who, according to the title of the ballad, but not the text, are her three sons), looks like a reminiscence of st. 9 of R. H. and the Bishop, No 143, where an old woman shows her gratitude to Robin Hood for having given her shoes and hose, and may not originally have belonged here.‡

B 1, A $9^{1,2}$, $11^{3,4}$, B 25, $28^{1,2}$ are almost repetitions of Robin Hood and the Curtal Friar, A 1, A $4^{3,4}$, $12^{3,4}$, B 26, $28^{1,2}$.‡

* A verse in the passage from Drayton's Polyolbion, Song xxvi, cited by Ritson, I, viii of Robin Hood, 1795, may refer to this version of the ballad: "The widow in distress he graciously relievd."

† In st. 2 Robin is in his proper Lincoln green. He wears

scarlet red again in No. 141, st. 6 and in No 145, st. 18, his men being in green.

‡ Fricke has observed this, pp 59, 69, and at p. 58 the resemblance to Wallace.

The rescue in the ballad is introduced into Anthony Munday's play of The Downfall of Robert Earl of Huntington, Act II, Scene 2. Scarlet and Scathlock, sons of Widow Scarlet, are to be hanged. Friar Tuck attends them as confessor. Robin Hood, disguised as an old man, pretends that they have killed his son, and asks the sheriff that they may be delivered to him for revenge. The sheriff allows them to be unbound. Robin, for a feigned reason, blows his horn; Little John and Much come in and begin a fight; Friar Tuck, pretending to help the sheriff, knocks down his men; the sheriff and his men run away. (Dodsley's Old Plays, ed. Hazlitt, VIII, 134–41.)

Ritson, Robin Hood, 1832, II, 155, suggests that the circumstance of Robin's changing clothes with the palmer may possibly be taken from " the noble history of Ponthus of Galyce," printed by Wynkyn de Worde, 1511, and cites this passage, which resembles the narrative in **B** 8, 10, 11 : " And as he [Ponthus] rode, he met with a poore palmer, beggynge his brede, the whiche had his gowne all to-clouted and an olde pylled hatte : so he alyght, and sayd to the palmer, frende, we shall make a chaunge of all our garmentes,

for ye shall have my gowne and I shall have yours and your hatte. A, syr, sayd the palmer, ye bourde you with me. In good fayth, sayd Ponthus, I do not ; so he dyspoyled hym and cladde hym with all his rayment, and he put vpon hym the poore mannes gowne, his gyrdell, his hosyn, his shone, his hatte and his bourden."

This noble history is taken from one in French which is merely the romance of Horn turned into prose, and it is also possible that the passage in the English ballad may be derived from some version of Hind Horn: see No 17.

Wallace changes clothes with a beggar in ' Gude Wallace,' No 157, **F, G**, where there is a general likeness to this ballad of Robin Hood. It may be noted that Wulric the Heron, one of the comrades of Hereward, rescues four brothers who were about to be hanged, killing some of their common enemies: Michel, Chroniques Anglo-Normandes, II, 51.

B is translated by Anastasius Grün, p. 135, Doenniges, p. 135, Knortz L. u. R. Altenglands, No 19; combined with **C**, by Talvj, Charakteristik, p. 489.

———✦———

* * * * * * *

1 ' .   .   .   .
   In faith thou shal[t] haue mine,
And twenty pound in thy purse,
   To spend att ale and wine.'

2 ' Though your clothes are of light Lincolne
     green,
   And mine gray russett and torne,
Yet it doth not you beseeme
   To doe an old man scorne.'

3 ' I scorne thee not, old man,' says Robin,
   ' By the faith of my body ;
Doe of thy clothes, thou shalt haue mine,
   For it may noe better bee.'

4 But Robin did on this old mans hose,
   The were torne in the wrist ;

' When I looke on my leggs,' said Robin,
   ' Then for to laugh I list.'

5 But Robin did on the old mans shooes,
   And the were cliitt full cleane ;
' Now, by my faith,' sayes Little Iohn,
   ' These are good for thornës keene.'

6 But Robin did on the old mans cloake,
   And it was torne in the necke ;
' Now, by my faith,' said William Scarlett,
   ' Heere shold be set a specke.'

7 But Robin did on this old mans hood,
   Itt gogled on his crowne ;
' When I come into Nottingham,' said Robin,
   ' My hood it will lightly downe.

8 ' But yonder is an outwood,' said Robin,
   ' An outwood all and a shade,

And thither I reede you, my merrymen all,
  The ready way to take.

9 'And when you heare my litle horne blow,
  Come raking all on a rowte

.   .   .   .

   .   .   .   .

*   *   *   *   *   *   *

10 But Robin he lope, and Robin he threw,
  He lope over stocke and stone;
  But those that saw Robin Hood run
  Said he was a liuer old man.

11 [Then Robin set his] horne to his mowth,
  A loud blast cold h[e] blow;
  Ffull three hundred bold yeomen
  Came rakinge all on a row.

12 But Robin cast downe his baggs of bread,
  Soe did he his staffe with a face,
  And in a doublet of red veluett
  This yeoman stood in his place.

13 'But bend your bowes, and stroke your strings,
  Set the gallow-tree aboute,

And Christs cursse on his heart,' said Robin,
  'That spares the sheriffe and the sergiant!'

14 When the sheriffe see gentle Robin wold
    shoote,
  He held vp both his hands;
  Sayes, Aske, good Robin, and thou shalt haue,
  Whether it be house or land.

15 'I will neither haue house nor land,' said
    Robin,
  'Nor gold, nor none of thy ffee,
  But I will haue those three squires
  To the greene fforest with me.

16 'Now marry, Gods forbott,' said the sheriffe,
  'That euer *that* shold bee;
  For why, they be the kings ffelons,
  They are all condemned to dye.'

17 'But grant me my askinge,' said Robin,
  'Or by the faith of my body
  Thou shalt be the first man
  Shall flower this gallow-tree.'

18 'But I wi[ll haue t]hose three squires

.   .   .   .

B

a. The English Archer, Robin Hood's Garland, York,
N. Nickson, n. d., p. 65. b. The English Archer, etc., Pais-
ley, John Neilson, 1786. c. Adventures of Robin Hood,
Falkirk, T. Johnston, 1808.

1 THERE are twelve months in all the year,
  As I hear many men say,
  But the merriest month in all the year
  Is the merry month of May.

2 Now Robin Hood is to Nottingham gone,
  With a link a down and a day,
  And there he met a silly old woman,
  Was weeping on the way.

3 'What news? what news, thou silly old woman?
  What news hast thou for me?'
  Said she, There's three squires in Nottingham
    town
  To-day is condemned to die.

4 'O have they parishes burnt?' he said,
  'Or have they ministers slain?

Or have they robbed any virgin,
  Or with other men's wives have lain?'

5 'They have no parishes burnt, good sir,
  Nor yet have ministers slain,
  Nor have they robbed any virgin,
  Nor with other men's wives have lain.'

6 'O what have they done?' said bold Robin
    Hood,
  'I pray thee tell to me:'
  'It's for slaying of the king's fallow deer,
  Bearing their long bows with thee.'

7 'Dost thou not mind, old woman,' he said,
  'Since thou made me sup and dine?
  By the truth of my body,' quoth bold Robin
    Hood,
  'You could not tell it in better time.'

8 Now Robin Hood is to Nottingham gone,
  With a link a down and a day,
  And there he met with a silly old palmer,
  Was walking along the highway.

9 'What news? what news, thou silly old man?
    What news, I do thee pray?'
Said he, Three squires in Nottingham town
    Are condemnd to die this day.

10 'Come change thy apparel with me, old man,
    Come change thy apparel for mine;
Here is forty shillings in good silver,
    Go drink it in beer or wine.'

11 'O thine apparel is good,' he said,
    'And mine is ragged and torn;
Whereever you go, wherever you ride,
    Laugh neer an old man to scorn.'

12 'Come change thy apparel with me, old churl,
    Come change thy apparel with mine;
Here are twenty pieces of good broad gold,
    Go feast thy brethren with wine.'

13 Then he put on the old man's hat,
    It stood full high on the crown:
'The first bold bargain that I come at,
    It shall make thee come down.'

14 Then he put on the old man's cloak,
    Was patchd black, blew, and red;
He thought no shame all the day long
    To wear the bags of bread.

15 Then he put on the old man's breeks,
    Was patchd from ballup to side;
'By the truth of my body,' bold Robin can say,
    'This man lovd little pride.'

16 Then he put on the old man's hose,
    Were patchd from knee to wrist;
'By the truth of my body,' said bold Robin
    Hood,
    'I'd laugh if I had any list.'

17 Then he put on the old man's shoes,
    Were patchd both beneath and aboon;
Then Robin Hood swore a solemn oath,
    It's good habit that makes a man.

18 Now Robin Hood is to Nottingham gone,
    With a link a down and a down,
And there he met with the proud sheriff,
    Was walking along the town.

19 'O save, O save, O sheriff,' he said,
    'O save, and you may see!

And what will you give to a silly old man
    To-day will your hangman be?'

20 'Some suits, some suits,' the sheriff he said,
    'Some suits I'll give to thee;
Some suits, some suits, and pence thirteen
    To-day's a hangman's fee.'

21 Then Robin he turns him round about,
    And jumps from stock to stone;
'By the truth of my body,' the sheriff he
    said,
    'That's well jumpt, thou nimble old man.'

22 'I was neer a hangman in all my life,
    Nor yet intends to trade;
But curst be he,' said bold Robin,
    'That first a hangman was made.

23 'I've a bag for meal, and a bag for malt,
    And a bag for barley and corn;
A bag for bread, and a bag for beef,
    And a bag for my little small horn.

24 'I have a horn in my pocket,
    I got it from Robin Hood,
And still when I set it to my mouth,
    For thee it blows little good.'

25 'O wind thy horn, thou proud fellow,
    Of thee I have no doubt;
I wish that thou give such a blast
    Till both thy eyes fall out.'

26 The first loud blast that he did blow,
    He blew both loud and shrill;
A hundred and fifty of Robin Hood's men
    Came riding over the hill.

27 The next loud blast that he did give,
    He blew both loud and amain,
And quickly sixty of Robin Hood's men
    Came shining over the plain.

28 'O who are yon,' the sheriff he said,
    'Come tripping over the lee?'
'The 're my attendants,' brave Robin did say,
    'They'll pay a visit to thee.'

29 They took the gallows from the slack,
    They set it in the glen,
They hangd the proud sheriff on that,
    Releasd their own three men.

C

Robin Hood's Garland. **a.** London, printed by W. & C. Dicey, in St. Mary Aldermary Church Yard, Bow Lane, Cheapside, and sold at the Warehouse at Northampton, n. d. : p. 74, No 24. **b.** London, printed by L. How, in Peticoat Lane, n. d. : p. 23. **c.** York, T. Wilson and R. Spence, n. d. : p. 27. **d.** Preston, W. Sergent, n. d. : p. 62. **e.** London, printed and sold by J. Marshall & Co., Aldermary Church Yard, Bow Lane, n. d. : No 24. **f.** Wolverhampton, printed and sold by J. Smart, n. d.

1 Bold Robin Hood ranging the forest all round,
    The forest all round ranged he ;
  O there did he meet with a gay lady,
    She came weeping along the highway.

2 'Why weep you, why weep you?' bold Robin
    he said,
  'What, weep you for gold or fee?
  Or do you weep for your maidenhead,
    That is taken from your body?'

3 'I weep not for gold,' the lady replyed,
    'Neither do I weep for fee ;
  Nor do I weep for my maidenhead,
    That is taken from my body.'

4 'What weep you for then?' said jolly Robin,
    'I prithee come tell unto me ;'
  'Oh! I do weep for my three sons,
    For they are all condemned to die.'

5 'What church have they robbed?' said jolly
    Robin,
  'Or parish-priest have they slain?
  What maids have they forced against their
    will ?
  Or with other men's wives have lain?'

6 'No church have they robbd,' this lady replied,
    'Nor parish-priest have they slain ;
  No maids have they forc'd against their will,
    Nor with other men's wives have lain.'

7 'What have they done then?' said jolly Robin,
    'Come tell me most speedily :'
  'Oh! it is for killing the king's fallow deer,
    And they are all condemned to die.'

8 'Get you home, get you home,' said jolly
    Robin,
  'Get you home most speedily,
  And I will unto fair Nottingham go,
    For the sake of the squires all three.'

9 Then bold Robin Hood for Nottingham goes,
    For Nottingham town goes he,
  O there did he meet with a poor beggar-man,
    He came creeping along the highway.

10 'What news, what news, thou old beggar-man?
    What news, come tell unto me :'
  'O there is weeping and wailing in fair Not-
    tingham,
  For the death of the squires all three.'

11 This beggar-man had a coat on his back,
    'T was neither green, yellow, nor red ;
  Bold Robin Hood thought 't was no disgrace
    To be in a beggar-man's stead.

12 'Come, pull off thy coat, you old beggar-man,
    And you shall put on mine ;
  And forty good shillings I 'll give thee to boot,
    Besides brandy, good beer, ale and wine.'

13 Bold Robin Hood then unto Nottingham came,
    Unto Nottingham town came he ;
  O there did he meet with great master sheriff,
    And likewise the squires all three.

14 'One boon, one boon,' says jolly Robin,
    'One boon I beg on my knee ;
  That, as for the deaths of these three squires,
    Their hangman I may be.'

15 'Soon granted, soon granted,' says great mas-
    ter sheriff,
  'Soon granted unto thee ;
  And you shall have all their gay cloathing,
    Aye, and all their white money.'

16 'O I will have none of their gay cloathing,
    Nor none of their white money,
  But I 'll have three blasts on my bugle-horn,
    That their souls to heaven may flee.'

17 Then Robin Hood mounted the gallows so high,
    Where he blew loud and shrill,
  Till an hundred and ten of Robin Hood's
    men
  They came marching all down the green hill.

18 'Whose men are they all these?' says great
    master sheriff,
  'Whose men are they? tell unto me :'
  'O they are mine, but none of thine,
    And they 're come for the squires all three.'

19 'O take them, O take them,' says great master
  sheriff,
  'O take them along with thee;

For there's never a man in all Nottingham
Can do the like of thee.'

———————

A. 1³. 20¹.
  5². *Only one of the* i's *is dotted in* cliit: *Fur-*
  nivall.
  6⁸. said wᵐ. 9². *half a page wanting.*
  10 *follows* 12. 11³. 300ᵈ.
  15³, 18¹. 3. 17². or be me.
  18¹. *half a page wanting.*
B. a. 3⁸. Knews. 4¹, 6¹, 11¹, 19¹,², 25¹, 28¹. Oh.
  8². and a down a.
  12¹. chur. 15¹. Teen. 16². Where.
  17⁴. Itts. 24⁴. For me. 28¹. are you.
  b. Robin Hood rescu'd the Widow's three Sons
  from the Sheriff when going to be hanged.
  c. How Robin Hood rescued, etc., . . . to be
  hanged.
  b, c. 2¹. Hood *wanting*. 2². a down down.
  2⁸. met with. 2⁴. along the highway.
  3². to me. 3⁴. To-day are.
  5². Nor have they.
  6⁸. 'T is for. 7⁸. quoth *wanting*.
  8¹. Robin he is. 8². a down down and a day.
  8⁸. old *wanting*. 9¹. silly palmer.
  10². with *for* for. 10⁸. of *for* in.
  10⁴. beer and good wine.
  12¹. churl. 14⁸. not *for* no.
  14⁴. the poor bags. 15¹. Then.
  15². Were *for* Was. 15⁸. did say.
  16², 17². Were *wanting*. 17². both *wanting*.
  17⁴. 'T is. 18¹. Robin is unto.
  18². a down down and a day.
  18⁴. the highway. 19². you may you [may
  you ?].
  19⁴. That to-day. 20⁴. day is.
  21². stone to stone. 22¹. never: in *wanting*.
  23². And *wanting*. 24¹. a small horn now in.
  24². it *wanting*. 24⁴. For thee. 25⁴. fly out.
  26⁸. An: Robin's men. 27⁸. Robin's men.
  28¹. are you. 28². Comes. 28⁸. bold Robin.
  29⁴. And released.
  b. 18⁸. with *wanting*. 20². unto thee.
  20⁸. pence fourteen.
  c. 6². unto me. 7². mad'st. 15¹. poor *for* old.
  20¹. suits and pence fourteen. 20²,³. *wanting*.
  21¹. turnd. 21². jumpd. 22². the trade.
  24⁸. I put. 25⁸. gave. 29². let *for* set.

C. a. *The Garland is not earlier, and probably not*
  much later, than 1753, "The Arguments . . .
  in the . . . affair of Eliz. Canning . . . robbed
  . . . in* Janʸ, 1753," *occurring in advertise-*
  ments printed therewith.
  16¹. of ther.
  b. 5⁴. have they. 6⁴. have they. 11⁴. in the.
  12⁴. beside. 16⁸. buglee. 17². blew both.
  18⁸. are all. 19⁴. That can.
  c. 1¹. ranged. 3¹. this lady. 4⁴. all *wanting*.
  5⁴. have they. 6⁸. they have. 6⁴. have they.
  7⁸. it's all. 7⁴. they're. 8⁸. will then to.
  9¹. bold *wanting*: to *for* for. 11². It was.
  11². or red. 11⁸. it was. 11⁴. in the.
  12¹. thou old. 12⁸. give you. 13¹. then to.
  13⁸. And there. 13⁴. Aye and.
  14². upon my. 14⁸. the three.
  15¹. great *wanting*.
  15². Soon grant it I will unto thee.
  15⁴. Aye *wanting*. 16¹. I'll. 16⁸. of my.
  17². blew both. 17⁴. They *wanting*.
  18⁸. are all. 19⁴. That can.
  d. 1⁸. he did. 3². I *wanting*. 6². No.
  7². Come tell unto me speedily. 8⁸. will for.
  10⁸. there's: fair *wanting*. 11⁴. in the.
  12¹. thou old. 12². thou shalt.
  15¹. great *wanting*. 17¹. When.
  17⁸. Hood's *wanting*.
  17⁴. They *wanting*: all *wanting*.
  18¹. all *wanting*: great *wanting*.
  18⁴. And are. 19⁸. in fair.
  e. 5⁴. have they. 6⁴. have they.
  10⁸. there's: fair *wanting*. 11⁴. in the.
  12¹. thou old. 12². thou shalt. 14⁸. death.
  15¹. great *wanting*. 17¹. When.
  17⁴. They wanting: all *wanting*.
  18¹. are they: great *wanting*. 18². come tell.
  18⁴. And are. 19⁸. in fair.
  f. 5⁴. have they. 6⁴. have they. 7⁴. they're.
  10⁸. there's: fair *wanting*. 11⁴. in the.
  12¹. thou old. 12². thou shalt. 14⁸. death.
  15¹. great *wanting*. 17¹. When.
  17⁴. They *wanting*: all *wanting*.
  18¹. are they: great *wanting*. 18². come tell.
  18⁴. And are come. 19⁸. in fair.

APPENDIX

ROBIN HOOD AND THE SHERIFF

Kinloch MSS, V, 288, in Kinloch's handwriting.

1 ROBIN HOOD 's to Nottinghame gane,
    Wi a linkie down and a day,
  And there he met wi an auld woman,
    Coming weeping alang the highway.

2 ' Weep ye for any of my gold, auld woman?
    Or weep ye for my fee?
  Or weep ye for any warld's gear
    This day I can grant to thee? '

3 ' I weep not for your gold, kind sir,
    I weep not for your fee;
  But I weep for my three braw sons,
    This day condemned to die.'

4 ' O have they parishes burned? ' he said,
    ' Or have they ministers slain?
  Or have they forced maidens against their will?
    Or wi other men's wives hae they lain? '

5 ' They have not parishes burned, kind sir,
    They have not ministers slain ;
  They neer forced a maid against her will,
    Nor wi no man's wife hae they lain.'

6 ' O what hae they done then? ' quo Robin Hood,
    ' I pray thee tell unto me : '
  ' O they killed the king's fallow deer,
    And this day are condemned to die.'

7 ' O have you mind, old mother,' he said,
    ' Since you made my merry men to dine?
  And for to repay it back unto thee
    Is come in a very good time.'

8 Sae Robin Hood 's to Nottinghame gane,
    With a linkie down and a day,
  And there he met an old beggar man,
    Coming creeping along the high way.

9 ' What news, what news, old father? ' he said,
    ' What news hast thou for me? '
  ' There 's three merry men,' quo the poor auld man,
    ' This day condemned to die.'

10 ' Will you change your apparel wi me, old father?
    Will you change your apparel for mine?
  And twenty broad shillings I 'll gie ye to the boot,
    To drink gude beer or wine.'

11 ' Thine is of the scarlet fine,
    And mine is baith ragged and torn;
  Sae never let a young supple youth
    Laugh a gude auld man to scorn.'

12 ' Change your apparel wi me, old churl,
    And quickly change it for mine,
  And thirty broad shillings I 'll gie to the boot,
    To drink gude beer or wine.'

13 When Robin put on the auld man's hat,
    It was weary high in the crown ;
  ' By the hand of my body,' quo Robin Hood,
    ' I am lang whan I loot down.'

14 Whan Robin put on the auld man's cloak,
    There was mony a pock therein;
  A pock for meal, and a pock for maut,
    And a pock for groats and corn,
  And a little wee pockie that hung by his side
    That he put in his bugle-horn.

15 Sae Robin Hood 's [to] Nottinghame gane,
    Wi a linkie down and a day,
  And there he met wi the high sheriff,
    Coming riding alang the high way.

16 ' O save you, O save you, high sheriff,' he
      said,
    ' And weel saved mote you be !
  And what will you gie to the silly auld man
    Your hangman for to be? '

17 ' Thirteen pence,' the sheriff replied,
    ' That is the hangman's fee,
  But an the claiths of the three young men
    This day condemned to die.'

18 ' I never hanged a man in a' my life,
    And intend not to begin ;
  But ever I hang a man in my life,
    High sheriff, thou 's be the ane.

19 ' But I have a horn in my pocket,
    I gat it frae Robin Hood,
  And gif I tak out my little horn,
    For thee it will no blaw gude.'

20 ' Blaw, blaw, bauld beggar,' he said,
    ' Blaw, and fear nae doubt ;
  I wish you may gie sic a blast
    Till your eyne loup out.'

21 Then Robin he gave a skip,
    And he skipped frae a stick till a stane;
  ' By the hand of my body,' quo the high sheriff,
    ' You are a supple auld man.'

22 Then Robin set his horn to his mouth,
   And he blew baith loud and shrill,
   Till sixty-four of bold Robin's men
   Cam marching down the green hill.

23 'What men are these,' quo the high sheriff,
   'That comes sae merrily?'
   'They are my men,' quo Robin Hood,
   'And they 'll pay a visit to thee.'

24 They tack the gallows out of the glen,
   And they set it in a slap ;
   They hanged the sheriff upon it,
   And his best men at his back.

25 They took the gallows out o the slap,
   And they set [it] back in the glen,
   And they hanged the sheriff upon it,
   Let the three young men gae hame.

141

ROBIN HOOD RESCUING WILL STUTLY

a. Wood, 401, leaf 35 b.

b. Garland of 1663, No 7.

c. Garland of 1670, No 6.

d. Pepys, II, 106, No 93.

THIS ballad probably occurs in all the larger collections of broadsides. It was given in Old Ballads, 1723, I, 90. a is printed by Ritson, Robin Hood, 1795, II, 102. Evans, Old Ballads, 1777, 1784, I, 164, follows an Aldermary copy.

Robin Hood learns that Will Stutly has been captured and is to be hanged the next day. Robin and his men go to the rescue, and ask information of a palmer who is standing under the wall of the castle in which Stutly is confined; the palmer confirms the news. Stutly is brought out by the sheriff, of whom he asks to have a sword and die in fight, not on the tree. This refused, he asks only to have his hands loosed. The sheriff again refuses; he shall die on the gallows. Little John comes out from behind a bush, cuts Stutly's bonds, and gives him a sword twitched by John from one of the sheriff's men. An arrow shot by Robin Hood puts the sheriff to flight, and his men follow. Stutly rejoices that he may go back to the woods.

This is a ballad made for print, with little of the traditional in the matter and nothing in the style. It may be considered as an imitation of The Rescue of the Three Squires, whence the ambush in st. 9 and the palmer 'fair' in 10.

---

1 WHEN Robin Hood in the green-wood livd,
      Derry derry down
   Vnder the green-wood.tree,
   Tidings there came to him with speed,
   Tidings for certainty,
      Hey down derry derry down

2 That Will Stutly surprized was,
      And eke in prison lay ;
   Three varlets that the sheriff had hired
   Did likely him betray.

3 I, and to-morrow hanged must be,
      To-morrow as soon as it is day ;
   But before they could this victory get,
   Two of them did Stutly slay.

4 When Robin Hood he heard this news,
      Lord ! he was grieved sore,
   I, and unto his merry men [said],
   Who altogether swore,

5 That Will Stutly should rescued be,
   And be brought safe again;
Or else should many a gallant wight
   For his sake there be slain.

6 He cloathed himself in scarlet then,
   His men were all in green;
A finer show, throughout the world,
   In no place could be seen.

7 Good lord! it was a gallant sight
   To see them all on a row;
With every man a good broad sword,
   And eke a good yew bow.

8 Forth of the green wood are they gone,
   Yea, all couragiously,
Resolving to bring Stutly home,
   Or every man to die.

9 And when they came the castle neer
   Whereas Will Stutly lay,
'I hold it good,' saith Robin Hood,
   'Wee here in ambush stay,

10 'And send one forth some news to hear,
   To yonder palmer fair,
That stands under the castle-wall;
   Some news he may declare.'

11 With that steps forth a brave young man,
   Which was of courage bold;
Thus hee did say to the old man:
   I pray thee, palmer old,

12 Tell me, if that thou rightly ken,
   When must Will Stutly die,
Who is one of bold Robins men,
   And here doth prisoner lie?

13 'Alack, alass,' the palmer said,
   'And for ever wo is me!
Will Stutly hanged must be this day,
   On yonder gallows-tree.

14 'O had his noble master known,
   Hee would some succour send;
A few of his bold yeomandree
   Full soon would fetch him hence.'

15 'I, that is true,' the young man said;
   'I, that is true,' said hee;

'Or, if they were neer to this place,
   They soon would set him free.

16 'But fare thou well, thou good old man,
   Farewell, and thanks to thee;
If Stutly hanged be this day,
   Revengd his death will be.'

17 He was no sooner from the palmer gone,
   But the gates was opened wide,
And out of the castle Will Stutly came,
   Guarded on every side.

18 When hee was forth from the castle come,
   And saw no help was nigh,
Thus he did say unto the sheriff,
   Thus he said gallantly:

19 Now seeing that I needs must die,
   Grant me one boon, says he;
For my noble master nere had man
   That yet was hangd on the tree.

20 Give me a sword all in my hand,
   And let mee be unbound,
And with thee and thy men I 'le fight,
   Vntill I lie dead on the ground.

21 But his desire he would not grant,
   His wishes were in vain;
For the sheriff had sworn he hanged should be,
   And not by the sword be slain.

22 'Do but unbind my hands,' he saies,
   'I will no weapons crave,
And if I hanged be this day,
   Damnation let me have.'

23 'O no, O no,' the sheriff he said,
   'Thou shalt on the gallows die,
I, and so shall thy master too,
   If ever in me it lie.'

24 'O dastard coward!' Stutly cries,
   'Thou faint-heart pesant slave!
If ever my master do thee meet,
   Thou shalt thy paiment have.

25 'My noble master thee doth scorn,
   And all thy cowardly crew;
Such silly imps unable are
   Bold Robin to subdue.'

26 But when he was to the gallows come,
  And ready to bid adiew,
  Out of a bush leaps Little John,
  And steps Will Stutly to.

27 'I pray thee, Will, before thou die,
  Of thy dear friends take leave ;
  I needs must borrow him a while,
  How say you, master sheriff ? '

28 'Now, as I live,' the sheriff he said,
  ' That varlet will I know ;
  Some sturdy rebell is that same,
  Therefore let him not go.'

29 With that Little John so hastily
  Away cut Stutly's bands,
  And from one of the sheriff his men,
  A sword twicht from his hands.

30 'Here, Will, here, take thou this same,
  Thou canst it better sway ;
  And here defend thy self a while,
  For aid will come straight way.'

31 And there they turnd them back to back,
  In the middle of them that day,
  Till Robin Hood approached neer,
  With many an archer gay.

32 With that an arrow by them flew,
  I wist from Robin Hood ;

' Make haste, make haste,' the sheriff he said,
  ' Make haste, for it is good.'

33 The sheriff is gone ; his doughty men
  Thought it no boot to stay,
  But, as their master had them taught,
  They run full fast away.

34 'O stay, O stay,' Will Stutly said,
  ' Take leave ere you depart ;
  You nere will catch bold Robin Hood
  Vnless you dare him meet.'

35 'O ill betide you,' quoth Robin Hood,
  ' That you so soon are gone ;
  My sword may in the scabbord rest,
  For here our work is done.'

36 'I little thought when I came here,
  When I came to this place,
  For to have met with Little John,
  Or seen my masters face.'

37 Thus Stutly was at liberty set,
  And safe brought from his foe ;
  'O thanks, O thanks to my master,
  Since here it was not so.'

38 'And once again, my fellows,
  We shall in the green woods meet,
  Where we will make our bow-strings twang,
  Musick for us most sweet.'

---

a. Robin Hood his rescuing Will Stutly from the
  sheriff and his men, who had taken him
  prisoner, and was going to hang him.
  To the tune of Robin Hood and Queen Kathe-
  rine.
  London, Printed for F. Grove, on Snow-hill.
  Entred according to order. (1620–55 :
  Chappell.)
  25¹. thou dost. 26⁴. too. 29². Stutli's.
  33¹. doubtless.
b. *Title as in* a, *except* rescuing of : were going.
  4³. said *wanting*. 6³. in all the.
  11¹. steps out. 13¹. Alas, alas.
  13⁴. yonders gallow. 14². would soon.
  16⁴. shall be. 19⁴. the *wanting*.
  25¹. thou dost. 26⁴. too.
  28¹. he *wanting*. 33¹. doubtless.
c. *Title as in* a, *except* were going.
  1⁴. Tiding for certainly. 3⁴. stay.

4³. men said. 13¹. Alass, alass.
17². was *wanting*. 24². hearted.
25¹. thee dost. 26⁴. too. 29². Stutli's.
33¹. doubtless. 36². came hereto.
d. *Title as in* a.
Printed for J. Clarke, W. Thackeray, and T.
  Passenger. (1670–86 ?)
  1¹. livd *wanting*. 3². as 'tis.
  4³. and to : men said. 5². brought back.
  8¹. they are. 9³. said. 13¹. Alas, alas.
  13³. to day. 14³. yeomanry.
  17². gates were. 19²₁ said.
  19⁴. the *wanting*. 21¹. But this.
  21³. swore. 24². hearted. 25¹. thee doth.
  26¹. gone *for* come. 28¹. he *wanting*.
  29¹. And Little. 29³. sheriffs.
  33¹. doubtless. 35¹. said *for* quoth.
  36². came here.

142

LITTLE JOHN A BEGGING

A. Percy MS., p. 20; Hales and Furnivall, I, 47.

B. 'Little John and the Four Beggers.' **a.** Wood,

401, leaf 33 b. **b.** Garland of **1663**, No 16.
c. Garland of 1670, No 15. **d.** Pepys, II, 119,
No 105.

B is also in the Roxburghe collection, III, 10.

B **a** is printed in Ritson's Robin Hood, 1795, II, 128. Evans, Old Ballads, 1777, 1784, I, 196 follows the Aldermary garland.

A. Little John, meaning to go a begging, induces an old mendicant to change clothes with him and to give him some hints how to conduct himself. Thus prepared he attempts to attach himself to three palmers, who, however, do not covet his company. One of the palmers gives John a whack on the head. We may conjecture, from the course of the story in B, that John serves them all accordingly, and takes from them so much money that, if he had kept on in this way, he might, as he says, have bought churches.

The beginning of **A** is very like that of Robin Hood rescuing Three Squires, **A**; but the disguise is for a different object. We are reminded again of Hind Horn, and particularly of versions C, G, **H**, in which the beggar, after change of clothes, is asked for instructions.

B. John is deputed by Robin to go a begging, and asks to be provided with staff, coat, and bags. He joins four sham beggars, one of whom takes him a knock on the crown. John makes the dumb to speak and the halt to run, and bangs them against the wall, then gets from one's cloak three hundred pound, and from another's bag three hundred and three, which he thinks is doing well enough to warrant his return to Sherwood.

B is translated by Anastasius Grün, p. 155.

A

Percy MS., p. 20; Hales and Furnivall, I, 47.

*   *   *   *   *   *   *

1 .   .   .   .

    .   .   .   .

    .   .   .   beggar,' he sayes,
  'With none such fellows as thee.'

2 'I am not in iest,' said Litle Iohn,
    'I sweare all by the roode;
  Change with mee,' said Litle Iohn,
    ' And I will giue thee some boote.'

3 But he has gotten on this old mans gowne,
    It reacht not to his wrist;
  ' Christ's curse on 's hart,' said Litle Iohn,
    ' That thinkes my gowne amisse.'

4 But he has gotten on this old mans shoes,
    Are clouted nine fold about;
  ' Beshrew his hart,' says Litle Iohn,
    ' That bryer or thorne does doubt.

5 'Wilt teach me some phrase of thy begging?'
    says Iohn;
    ' I pray thee, tell it mee,
  How I may be as beggar-like
    As any in my companie.'

6 ' Thou must goe two foote on a staffe,
    The third vpon a tree;
  Full loud that thou must cry and fare,
    When nothing ayleth thee.'

7 But Iohn he walket the hills soe high,
    Soe did [he] the hills soe browne;

The ready way that he cold take
  Was towards Nottingham towne.

8 But as he was on the hills soe high,
  He mett with palmers three ;
  Sayes, God you saue, my brethren all,
  Now God you saue and see !

9 This seuen yeere I haue you sought ;
  Before I cold neuer you see !
  Said they, Wee had leuer such a cankred carle
  Were neuer in our companie.

10 But one of them tooke Litle Iohn on his head,
  The blood ran over his eye ;
  Little Iohn turned him twise about
  . . . .

  * * * * * * *

11 'If I . . . . . .
  As I haue beene but one day,
  I shold haue purcchased three of the best
    churches
  That stands by any highway.'

B

a. Wood, 401, leaf 33 b. b. Garland of 1663, No 16.
c. Garland of 1670, No 15. d. Pepys, II, 119, No 105.

1 ALL you that delight to spend some time
    With a hey down down a down down
  A merry song for to sing,
  Vnto me draw neer, and you shall hear
  How Little John went a begging.

2 As Robin Hood walked the forrest along,
  And all his yeomandree,
  Sayes Robin, Some of you must a begging go,
  And, Little John, it must be thee.

3 Sayes John, If I must a begging go,
  I will have a palmers weed,
  With a staff and a coat, and bags of all sort,
  The better then I shall speed.

4 Come, give me now a bag for my bread,
  And another for my cheese,
  And one for a peny, when as I get any,
  That nothing I may leese.

5 Now Little John he is a begging gone,
  Seeking for some relief ;
  But of all the beggers he met on the way,
  Little John he was the chief.

6 But as he was walking himself alone,
  Four beggers he chanced to spy,
  Some deaf, and some blind, and some came
    behind ;
  Says John, Here 's brave company !

7 'Good-morrow,' said John, 'my brethren dear,
  Good fortune I had you to see ;
  Which way do you go ? pray let me know,
  For I want some company.

8 'O what is here to do ? ' then said Little John,
  ' Why rings all these bells ? ' said he ;
  'What dog is a hanging ? come, let us be
    ganging,
  That we the truth may see.'

9 'Here is no dog a hanging,' then one of them
    said,
  'Good fellow, we tell unto thee ;
  But here is one dead wil give us cheese and
    bred,
  And it may be one single peny.'

10 'We have brethren in London,' another he said,
  'So have we in Coventry,
  In Barwick and Dover, and all the world over,
  But nere a crookt carril like thee.

11 'Therefore stand thee back, thou crooked carel,
  And take that knock on the crown ;'
  'Nay,' said Little John, 'I 'le not yet be gone,
  For a bout will I have with you round.

12 'Now have at you all,' then said Little John,
  'If you be so full of your blows ;
  Fight on, all four, and nere give ore,
  Whether you be friends or foes.'

13 John nipped the dumb, and made him to rore,
  And the blind that could not see,
  And he that a cripple had been seven years,
  He made him run faster then he.

14 And flinging them all against the wall,
  With many a sturdie bang,

It made John sing, to hear the gold ring,
    Which against the walls cryed twang.

15 Then he got out of the beggers cloak
    Three hundred pound in gold ;
    ' Good fortune had I,' then said Little John,
    'Such a good sight to behold.'

16 But what found he in a beggers bag,
    But three hundred pound and three ?
    ' If I drink water while this doth last,
    Then an ill death may I dye !

17 ' And my begging-trade I will now give ore,
    My fortune hath bin so good ;
    Therefore I 'le not stay, but I will away
    To the forrest of merry Sherwood.'

18 And when to the forrest of Sherwood he came,
    He quickly there did see
    His master good, bold Robin Hood,
    And all his company.

19 ' What news ? What news ? ' then said Robin Hood,
    ' Come, Little John, tell unto me ;
    How hast thou sped with thy beggers trade ?
    For that I fain would see.'

20 ' No news but good,' then said Little John,
    ' With begging ful wel I have sped ;
    Six hundred and three I have here for thee,
    In silver and gold so red.'

21 Then Robin took Little John by the hand,
    And danced about the oak-tree :
    ' If we drink water while this doth last,
    Then an il death may we die ! '

22 So to conclude my merry new song,
    All you that delight it to sing,
    'T is of Robin Hood, that archer good,
    And how Little John went a begging.

———◆———

A. *Half a page wanting at the beginning, and after* 10⁸. 3². his crest.
4². 9. 6¹. 2. 6². 3ᵈ. 8², 11⁸. 3. 9¹. 7.
9⁸. had neuer. 10². him 2⁸ᵢ.

B. a. Little John and the Four Beggers: A new merry song of Robin Hood and Little John, shewing how Little John went a begging, and how he fought with Four Beggers, and what a prize he got of the Four Beggers.
The tune is, Robin Hood and the Begger.
Printed for William Gilber[t]son. (1640–63.)
13⁴. them *for* him. 14⁴. Whih again.
22⁴. beggiug.

b. *Title as in* a.
11². on thy. 11⁴. I will. 12⁸. never.
13⁴. made him. 14⁴. again.
20⁸. Three hundred.

c. *Title as in* a, *except :* from these four Beg-
gers. To the tune of Robin Hood and the Begger.
Burden : last down *wanting.*
8⁸. a *wanting :* let 's. 9². I *for* we.
10¹. he *wanting.* 12⁸. never.
13⁴. made him : than. 14⁴. against.
19⁴. I fain would fain. 20¹. then *wanting.*
20⁸. Three hundred. 22². it *wanting.*

d. *Title as in* a, *except :* Or, a new. To the tune of Robin Hood, &c.
Printed for J. Wright, J. Clarke, W. Thackeray, and T. Passenger. (1670–86 ?)
1². for *wanting.* 3⁸. sorts. 3⁴. then shall I.
4⁸. as *wanting.* 5¹·⁴. he *wanting.*
7¹. my children. 10². in the Country.
13⁴. made run then. 14⁴. against.
16¹. in the. 17². it hath. 18¹. But when.
19⁸. with the. 22². And you.

143

ROBIN HOOD AND THE BISHOP

'Robin Hood and the Bishop.' a. Wood, 401, leaf 11 b.
b. Garland of 1663, No 5.
c. Garland of 1670, No 4.
d. Pepys, II, 109, No 96.
e. Roxburghe, I, 362, in the Ballad Societys reprint, II, 448.

ALSO Pepys, II, 122, No 107, by Alexander Milbourne (1670–97) : Old Ballads, 1723, II, 39.

a is printed in Ritson's Robin Hood, 1795, II, 19. Evans, Old Ballads, 1777, 1784, I, 102, apparently follows the Aldermary Churchyard garland.

Robin Hood, while ranging the forest, sees a bishop and all his men coming, and, knowing that if he is taken no mercy will be given him, asks the help of an old woman, to whom he makes himself known. The old woman has had a kindness from him, and wishes to return it. She consents to exchange her gray coat and spindle for his green mantle and arrows, and Robin makes for his band in this disguise. The bishop carries off the old woman on a horse, making no doubt that he has Robin in custody, but, as he proceeds through the wood, sees a hundred bowmen, and asks his prisoner what this may be. I think it be Robin Hood, says the supposed outlaw. "And who are you?" "Why, I am an old woman." The bishop turns about, but Robin stays him, ties him to a tree, takes

five hundred pound from his portmantle, and then is willing he should go. But Little John will not let him off till he has sung a mass ; after which the bishop is mounted on his dapple-gray, with his face to the tail, and told to pray for Robin Hood.

This ballad and the following are variations upon the theme of Robin Hood and the Monk, in the Gest. The disguise as a woman occurs in other outlaw stories; as in Eustace the Monk, Michel, p. 43. Also in Blind Harry's Wallace, ed. Moir, Book I, 239, and Book IV, 764, pp 9, 72 : in the first case Wallace has a rock and sits spinning. See also the ballad of Gude Wallace, further on.

We hear again of the forced mass, st. 23, in Robin Hood and Queen Katherine, A 31, B 40; and of money borrowed against the bishop's will, in A 32 of the same. It is the Bishop of Hereford who suffers : see the ballad which follows.

Translated by Doenniges, p. 203 ; Anastasius Grün, p. 113.

1 COME, gentlemen all, and listen a while,
    Hey down down an a down
    And a story I 'le to you unfold ;
    I 'le tell you how Robin Hood served the Bishop,
    When he robbed him of his gold.

2 As it fell out on a sun-shining day,
    When Phebus was in his prime,
    Then Robin Hood, that archer good,
    In mirth would spend some time.

3 And as he walkd the forrest along,
    Some pastime for to spy,
    There was he aware of a proud bishop,
    And all his company.

4 'O what shall I do ?' said Robin Hood then,
    ' If the Bishop he doth take me,
    No mercy he 'l show unto me, I know,
    But hanged I shall be.'

5 Then Robin was stout, and turnd him about,
    And a little house there he did spy;
And to an old wife, for to save his life,
    He loud began for to cry.

6 'Why, who art thou?' said the old woman,
    'Come tell it to me for good:'
'I am an out-law, as many do know,
    My name it is Robin Hood.

7 'And yonder's the Bishop and all his men,
    And if that I taken be,
Then day and night he'l work me spight,
    And hanged I shall be.'

8 'If thou be Robin Hood,' said the old wife,
    'As thou dost seem to be,
I 'le for thee provide, and thee I will hide
    From the Bishop and his company.

9 'For I well remember, one Saturday night
    Thou bought me both shoos and hose;
Therefore I 'le provide thy person to hide,
    And keep thee from thy foes.'

10 'Then give me soon thy coat of gray,
    And take thou my mantle of green;
Thy spindle and twine unto me resign,
    And take thou my arrows so keen.'

11 And when that Robin Hood was so araid,
    He went straight to his company;
With his spindle and twine, he oft lookt be-
        hind
    For the Bishop and his company.

12 'O who is yonder,' quoth Little John,
    'That now comes over the lee?
An arrow I will at her let flie,
    So like an old witch looks she.'

13 'O hold thy hand, hold thy hand,' said Robin
        then,
    'And shoot not thy arrows so keen;
I am Robin Hood, thy master good,
    And quickly it shall be seen.'

14 The Bishop he came to the old womans house,
    And he called with furious mood,
'Come let me soon see, and bring unto me,
    That traitor Robin Hood.'

15 The old woman he set on a milk-white steed,
    Himselfe on a dapple-gray,
And for joy he had got Robin Hood,
    He went laughing all the way.

16 But as they were riding the forrest along,
    The Bishop he chanc'd for to see
A hundred brave bow-men bold
    Stand under the green-wood tree.

17 'O who is yonder,' the Bishop then said,
    'That's ranging within yonder wood?'
'Marry,' says the old woman, 'I think it to be
    A man calld Robin Hood.'

18 'Why, who art thou,' the Bishop he said,
    'Which I have here with me?'
'Why, I am an old woman, thou cuckoldly
        bishop;
    Lift up my leg and see.'

19 'Then woe is me,' the Bishop he said,
    'That ever I saw this day!'
He turnd him about, but Robin so stout
    Calld him, and bid him stay.

20 Then Robin took hold of the Bishops horse,
    And ty'd him fast to a tree;
Then Little John smil'd his master upon,
    For joy of that company.

21 Robin Hood took his mantle from 's back,
    And spread it upon the ground,
And out of the Bishops portmantle he
    Soon told five hundred pound.

22 'So now let him go,' said Robin Hood;
    Said Little John, That may not be;
For I vow and protest he shall sing us a
        mass
    Before that he goe from me.

23 Then Robin Hood took the Bishop by the hand,
    And bound him fast to a tree,
And made him sing a mass, God wot,
    To him and his yeomandree.

24 And then they brought him through the wood,
    And set him on his dapple-gray,
And gave the tail within his hand,
    And bade him for Robin Hood pray.

a. Robin Hood and the Bishop : Shewing how
   Robin Hood went to an old womans house
   and changed cloaths with her, to scape
   from the Bishop ; and how he robbed the
   Bishop of all his gold, and made him sing
   a mass. To the tune of Robin Hood and
   the Stranger.
   London, Printed for F. Grove on Snow-Hill.
   (1620–55.)
   Burden : sometimes With a hey, *etc.* ; With
   hey, *etc.*
   2². her *for* his : *cf.* b, c.
   8². doth : *cf.* b, c, d, e. 9¹. on *for* one : *cf.* e.
   16². chance.
b. *Title as in* a. *Burden : with the same varia-
   tions as in* a.
   2². in his. 5⁴. for *wanting*. 8¹. then said.
   8². dost. 9¹. on. 14³. soon *wanting.*
   16². chanc'd. 17¹. then *wanting.*
   17². yonders. 18³. cuckoldy. 19¹. to me.
   19³. Robin Hood.
c. *Title as in* a. *Burden : always* With a hey,
   etc.
   2². in his. 4⁴. *wanting.* 5³,⁴. for *wanting.*
   8². dost. 9¹. on. 16¹. long. 16². chanced.
   17¹. he said. 18³. cuckoldy. 19¹. to me.
   19³. Robin Hood. 24⁴. bid.
d. *Title as in* a, except, escape : robbed him :
   sing mass.
   Burden : With a hey down down and a down.

2¹. of a. 2². in her.
2³. That *for* Then. 4⁴. shall I.
5⁴. for *wanting.* 7³. my *for* me.
8¹. old woman. 8². dost.
9¹. well *wanting :* on.
11¹. that *wanting :* thus *for* so.
13¹. Robin Hood. 16². chanc'd.
18³. am a woman : cuckoldy.
19³. Robin Hood. 20⁴. of his.
22¹. So *wanting.* 23¹. by'th.
24¹. And when.
e. *Title as in* a, *except,* escape : robbed him : sing
   mass.
   London, Printed by and for W. O[nley], *etc.*
   (1650–1702.)
   Burden : With a hey down down an a down.
   1². to you I 'll. 1³. to you. 2¹. of a.
   2². in her. 2³. Bold Robin Hood.
   3³. he *wanting.*(?) 4¹. saith. 4⁴. shall I.
   5². did he. 5³. for *wanting.*
   5⁴. aloud began to. 7³. my *for* me.
   7⁴. shall I. 8¹. then said the old woman.
   8². dost. 9¹. well *wanting :* one.
   9². brought. 10². the *for* my.
   11¹. thus *for* so. 11³. and *wanting.*
   12³. at her I will. 13¹. saith.
   16². chanc'd. 17⁴. A *wanting.*
   18³. am a woman. 19³. Robin Hood.
   19⁴. to him. 20⁴. of this. 22¹. So *wanting.*
   23¹. by th'.

144

ROBIN HOOD AND THE BISHOP OF HEREFORD

A. a. Robin Hood's Garland, London, J. Marshall &
Co., Aldermary Churchyard, No 23. b. 'Robin
Hood and the Bishop of Hereford,' Douce Ballads,
III, 123 b, London, C. Sheppard, 1791. c. Chap-
pell's Popular Music of the Olden Time, p. 395, from

a broadside printed for Daniel Wright, next the
Sun Tavern in Holborn. d. Robin Hood's Garland,
1749, No 23.

B. E. Cochrane's Song-Book, p. 149, No 113.

A a in Ritson's Robin Hood, 1795, II, 146,
"compared with the York copy," that is,
with two or three slight changes: Evans, Old
Ballads, 1777, 1784, I, 211. B, the Scottish
copy, is very likely only an imperfect remem-
brance of a broadside, but the date of the

MS., though this is perhaps not determinable,
has been put as early as 1730.
   Robin Hood, expecting the Bishop of Here-
ford to pass near Barnsdale, has a deer killed
for his dinner. He dresses himself and six
of his men in shepherd's attire, and when the

Bishop approaches they make an ado to attract his attention. The Bishop interrogates them. Robin owns that they mean to make merry with the king's venison. The Bishop will show them no mercy; they must go before the king with him. Robin summons his band with his horn and it is the Bishop's turn to cry mercy. Robin will not let him off, but takes him to Barnsdale, and makes him great cheer. The Bishop foresees that there will be a heavy reckoning. Little John searches the Bishop's portmanteau, and takes out three hundred pound; enough, he says, to make him in charity with the churchman. They make the Bishop dance in his boots, A, or sing a mass, B, and he is glad to get off so lightly.

The Bishop of Hereford appears in the next ballad, Robin Hood and Queen Katherine. He there tells us that Robin had made him sing a mass out of hours, and had borrowed money of him against his will.

The conclusion of this ballad is to the same effect as that of the preceding, and was probably suggested by the Gest. No copy has been found, in print or writing, earlier than the last century; a fact of no special importance. Whenever written, if written it was, it is far superior to most of the seventeenth century broadsides. Mr Chappell speaks of it as being now (thirty years ago) the most popular of the Robin Hood set.

Translated by Talvj, Charakteristik, p. 493; Anastasius Grün, p. 151; Loève-Veimars, p. 204.

A

a. Robin Hood's Garland, Aldermary Churchyard, No 23. b. Douce Ballads, III, 123 b, 1791. c. Chappell's Popular Music of the Olden Time, p. 395, from a broadside printed for Daniel Wright. d. Robin Hood's Garland, without place, 1749, No 23, p. 98.

1 SOME they will talk of bold Robin Hood,
  And some of barons bold,
  But I'll tell you how he servd the Bishop of Hereford,
  When he robbd him of his gold.

2 As it befel in merry Barnsdale,
  And under the green-wood tree,
  The Bishop of Hereford was to come by,
  With all his company.

3 'Come, kill a venson,' said bold Robin Hood,
  'Come, kill me a good fat deer;
  The Bishop of Hereford is to dine with me to-day,
  And he shall pay well for his cheer.

4 'We'll kill a fat venson,' said bold Robin Hood,
  'And dress it by the highway-side;
  And we will watch the Bishop narrowly,
  Lest some other way he should ride.'

5 Robin Hood dressd himself in shepherd's attire,
  With six of his men also;
  And, when the Bishop of Hereford came by,
  They about the fire did go.

6 'O what is the matter?' then said the Bishop,
  'Or for whom do you make this a-do?
  Or why do you kill the king's venson,
  When your company is so few?'

7 'We are shepherds,' said bold Robin Hood,
  'And we keep sheep all the year,
  And we are disposed to be merry this day,
  And to kill of the king's fat deer.'

8 'You are brave fellows!' said the Bishop,
  'And the king of your doings shall know;
  Therefore make haste and come along with me,
  For before the king you shall go.'

9 'O pardon, O pardon,' said bold Robin Hood,
  'O pardon, I thee pray!
  For it becomes not your lordship's coat
  To take so many lives away.'

10 'No pardon, no pardon,' says the Bishop,
  'No pardon I thee owe;
  Therefore make haste, and come along with me,
  For before the king you shall go.'

11 Then Robin set his back against a tree,
  And his foot against a thorn,
And from underneath his shepherd's coat
  He pulld out a bugle-horn.

12 He put the little end to his mouth,
  And a loud blast did he blow,
Till threescore and ten of bold Robin's men
  Came running all on a row ;

13 All making obeysance to bold Robin Hood ;
  'T was a comely sight for to see :
' What is the matter, master,' said Little John,
  ' That you blow so hastily ? '

14 ' O here is the Bishop of Hereford,
  And no pardon we shall have : '
' Cut off his head, master,' said Little John,
  ' And throw him into his grave.'

15 ' O pardon, O pardon,' said the Bishop,
  ' O pardon, I thee pray !
For if I had known it had been you,
  I 'd have gone some other way.'

16 ' No pardon, no pardon,' said Robin Hood,
  ' No pardon I thee owe ;
Therefore make haste and come along with me,
  For to merry Barnsdale you shall go.'

17 Then Robin he took the Bishop by the hand,
  And led him to merry Barnsdale ;
He made him to stay and sup with him that
  night,
  And to drink wine, beer, and ale.

18 ' Call in the reckoning,' said the Bishop,
  ' For methinks it grows wondrous high : '
' Lend me your purse, Bishop,' said Little
  John,
  ' And I 'll tell you bye and bye.'

19 Then Little John took the bishop's cloak,
  And spread it upon the ground,
And out of the bishop's portmantua
  He told three hundred pound.

20 ' Here 's money enough, master,' said Little
  John,
  ' And a comely sight 't is to see ;
It makes me in charity with the Bishop,
  Tho he heartily loveth not me.'

21 Robin Hood took the Bishop by the hand,
  And he caused the music to play,
And he made the Bishop to dance in his boots,
  And glad he could so get away.

B

E. Cochrane's Song-Book, p. 149, No 113.

1 SOME talk of lords, and some talk of lairds,
  And some talk of barrons bold,
But I 'll tell you a story of bold Robin Hood,
  How he robbed the Bishop of his gold.

2 ' Cause kill us a venison,' says Robin Hood,
  ' And we 'll dress it by the high-way side,
And we will watch narrowly for the Bishop,
  Lest some other way he do ride.'

3 ' Now who is this,' sayes the Bishop,
  ' That makes so boldly here
To kill the king's poor small venison,
  And so few of his company here ? '

4 ' We are shepherds,' says Robin Hood,
  ' And do keep sheep all the year ;

And we thought it fit to be merry on a day,
  And kill one of the king's fallow deer.'

5 ' Thou art a bold fellow,' the Bishop replyes,
  ' And your boldness you do show ;
Make hast, make hast, and go along with me,
  For the king of your doings shall know.'

6 He leand his back unto a brae,
  His foot against a thorn,
And out from beneath his long shepherds coat
  He pulled a blowing-horn.

7 He put his horn in to his mouth,
  And a snell blast he did blow,
Till four and twenty of bold Robins men
  Came riding up all in a row.

8 ' Come, give us a reckoning,' says the Bishop,
  ' For I think you drink wondrous large : '

'Come, give me your purse,' said bold Robin
   Hood,
  'And I will pay all your charge.'

9 He pulled off his long shepherds coat,
   And he spread it on the ground,
   And out of the Bishops long trunk-hose,
   He pulled a hundred pound.

10 'O master,' quoth Litle John,
   'It's a very bony sight for to see;
   It makes me to favour the Bishop,
   Tho in heart he loves not me.'

11 'Come, sing us a mass,' sayes bold Robin Hood,
   'Come, sing us a mass all anon;
   Come, sing us a mass,' sayes bold Robin Hood,
   'Take a kick in the a—se, and be gone.'

A. a. The Bishop of Hereford's Entertainment by
Robin Hood and Little John, &c., in merry
Barnsdale.
  8⁴. Forr. 18⁸. master *for* Bishop: *cf.* b.
b. London, Published April 7th, 1791, by C.
Sheppard, No 19, Lambert Hill, Doctors
Commons.
  3⁸. 's to. 7⁴. to taste. 10¹. said. 11⁴. out his.
12². he did. 12⁸. Robin Hood's.
13². for *wanting.* 13⁸. What's.
14². Says no. 17¹. he *wanting.*
17⁸. him stay and dine with him that day.
18². For I think. 18⁸. bishop *for* master.
20⁸. me have charity for.
21⁸. And *wanting:* the old.
c. *Title as in* **a.**
  1¹. O some: of brave. 1⁸. ye.
1⁴. And robbd. 2¹. All under. 3¹. kill me.
3⁸. 's to. 10¹. said. 16¹. said bold.
18¹. in a. 18⁸. purse, master. 21⁸. the old.
d. *Title as in* **a**: &c *wanting.*

1¹. they *wanting.* 1⁸. of Hereford *wanting.*
1⁴. his *wanting.* 3¹. Hood *wanting.*
3⁸. to-day *wanting.* 3⁴. well *wanting.*
4¹. kill the vension. 5¹. Hood he.
5². And six: men likewise.
5⁴. Then *for* They. 6¹. then *wanting.*
6⁸. of the. 6⁴. And your: so small.
7¹. Hood *wanting.* 9¹. bold *wanting.*
10¹. said. 10⁴. you must. 11⁴. out his fine.
12². he did. 12⁴. marching down in a.
13⁸. master *wanting.* 14⁴. into the.
15⁴. I would: gone another.
16¹. bold Robin: Hood *wanting.*
17¹. he *wanting.* 17². And he.
17⁸. to *wanting.* 18¹. in a.
18². Methinks it runs. 18⁸. master *wanting.*
19⁸. portmantle. 19⁴. He took.
20¹. master *wanting.*
20². And it is: 't is *wanting.*
21¹. Robin he took. 21². he *wanting.*
21⁸. And *wanting.* 21⁴. so *wanting.*

145

ROBIN HOOD AND QUEEN KATHERINE

A. 'Robin Hoode and Quene Kath[erine],' Percy MS.,
p. 15; Hales and Furnivall, I, 37.

B. 'Renowned Robin Hood,' etc. **a.** Wood, 502, leaf
10. **b.** Roxburghe, I, 356, in the Ballad Society's
reprint, II, 419. **c.** Garland of 1663, No 9. **d.** Gar-
land of 1670, No 8. **e.** Wood, 401, leaf 31 b.
f. Pepys, II, 103, No 90.

C. 'Robin Hood, Scarlet and John,' etc., Garland of
1663, No 1.

A COPY in Roxburghe, III, 450, printed by
L. How, in Petticoat Lane, is of the eigh-
teenth century. In Ritson's Robin Hood,
1795, II, 82, "from an old black-letter copy

in a private collection, compared with another in that of Anthony a Wood." In Evans's Old Ballads, 1777, 1784, I, 149, from an Aldermary garland.

Robin Hood has made Queen Katherine his friend by presenting her with a sum of gold which he had taken from the king's harbingers. The king has offered a heavy wager that his archers cannot be excelled, and the queen may have her choice of all other bowmen in England. Availing herself of these terms, the queen summons Robin Hood and his men, who are to come to London on St George's day, under changed names. She hopes to have Robin relieved of his outlawry. The king's archers lead off, and make three. The ladies think the queen has no chance. She asks Sir Richard Lee, known to us already from the Gest, to be on her side. Sir Richard Lee, we are told, is sprung from Gawain's blood (A, Gower's, Gowrie's in other texts), and naturally would deny nothing to a lady. The Bishop of Hereford declines to be of the queen's party, but stakes a large sum on the king's men. The queen's archers shoot, and the game stands three and three; the queen bids the king beware. The third three shall pay for all, says the king. It is now time for the outlaws to do their best. Loxly, as Robin Hood is called, leads off. The particulars of the outlaws' exploits are wanting in A.

In B, C, Robin's feat is obscurely described. Clifton, who represents Scarlet (for in B, C, contrary to older tradition, Scarlet seems to be put before John), cleaves the willow wand, and Midge (Mutch), the Miller's Son, who, according to A 10, is John, is but little behind him.* The queen, to assure the safety of her men, begs the boon that the king will not be angry with any of her party, and the king replies, Welcome, friend or foe.

After this there is no occasion for concealment. The Bishop of Hereford, learning who Loxly is, says that Robin is only too old an acquaintance; Robin had once made him say a mass at two in the afternoon, and borrowed money of him which had never been repaid. Robin offers to pay him for the mass by giving half of the gold back. Small thanks, says the bishop, for paying me with my own money. King Henry, quite outstripping even the easiness of Edward in the Gest, says he loves Robin never the worse, and invites him to leave his outlaws and come live at the court, a proposal which is peremptorily rejected. This is a very pleasant ballad, with all the exaggeration, and it is much to be regretted that one half of A is lost.

C is a piece of regular hack-work, and could not maintain itself in competition with B, upon which, perhaps, it was formed. It will be observed that Sir Richard Lee is changed into Sir Robert Lee in C, and that the thirty-fourth stanza represents the king as subsequently making Robin Hood Earl of Huntington.

The adventure of the Bishop of Hereford with Robin Hood is the subject of a separate ballad, now found only in a late form: see No 144.

Loxly, the name given to Robin in the present ballad, is, according to the Life in the Sloane MS., a town in Yorkshire, " or after others in Nottinghamshire," where Robin was born. The ballad of Robin Hood's Birth, Breeding, etc., following the same tradition, or invention, says " Locksly town in Nottinghamshire." It appears from Spencer Hall's Forester's Offering, London, 1841, that there is a Loxley Chase near Sheffield, in Yorkshire, and a Loxley River too: Gutch, I, 75.

Finsbury field was long a noted place for the practice of archery. In the year 1498, says Stow, all the gardens which had continued time out of mind without Moorgate, to wit, about and beyond the lordship of Fensbury, were destroyed. And of them was made a

---

* Even the author of A seems not to be aware that Much, the Miller's Son, is the standing name of one of Robin Hood's men, and therefore would not answer for a disguise. In B, C, nothing is expressly said about the change of names, and in fact this arrangement seems not to be understood, since in B 21¹ Clifton is spoken of as one Clifton. Comparing B 33, 34, 37, we see that Clifton should be Little John, but Midge, the Miller's Son, himself, not Scathlock, still less John.

plain field for archers to shoot in. Survey of
London, 1598, p. 351, cited, with other things
pertinent, by Ritson, Robin Hood, 1795, II,
86 f.

R. H. and the Shepherd, R. H. rescuing
Will Stutly, and R. H.'s Delight, are directed
to be sung to the tune of R. H. and Queen
Katherine, B, and may therefore be inferred
to be of later date. R. H.'s Progress to
Nottingham is to be sung to "Bold Robin
Hood," and as this conjunction of words oc-
curs several times in R. H. and Queen Kath-
erine, and the burden and its disposition, in
the Progress to Nottingham, are the same as
in R. H. and Queen Katherine, "Bold Robin
Hood" may indicate this present ballad. R.
H. and Queen Katherine, C, is directed to be
sung to the tune of The Pinder of Wakefield.

R. H.'s Chase is a sequel to R. H. and
Queen Katherine.

Translated by Anastasius Grün, p. 172.

A

Percy MS., p. 15 ; Hales and Furnivall, I, 37.

1 Now list you, lithe you, gentlemen,
    A while for a litle space,
And I shall tell you how Queene Katterine
    Gott Robin Hood his grace.

2 Gold taken from the kings harbengers
    Seldome times hath beene seene,

.   .   .   .

.   .   .   .

*   *   *   *   *   *   *

3 .   .   .   .
    'Queene Katherine, I say to thee ; '
'That 's a princly wager,' quoth Queene Kath-
    erine,
    ' Betweene your grace and me.

4 'Where must I haue mine archers?' says
    Queene Katherine ;
    ' You haue the flower of archery : '
'Now take your choice, dame,' he sayes,
    'Thorow out all England free.

5 ' Yea from North Wales to Westchester,
    And also to Couentry ;
And when you haue chosen the best you can,
    The wager must goe with mee.'

6 'If that prooue,' says Queene Katherine,
    'Soone that wilbe tride and knowne ;
Many a man counts of another mans pursse,
    And after looseth his owne.'

7 The queene is to her palace gone,
    To her page thus shee can say :
Come hither to me, Dicke Patrinton,
    Trusty and trew this day.

8 Thou must bring me the names of my archers
    all,
    All strangers must they bee,
Yea from North Wales to West Chester,
    And alsoe to Couentrie.

9 Commend me to Robin Hood, says Queene
    Katherine,
    And alsoe to Litle John,
And specially to Will Scarlett,
    Ffryar Tucke and Maid Marryan.

10 Robin Hood we must call Loxly,
    And Little John the Millers sonne ;
Thus wee then must change their names,
    They must be strangers euery one.

11 Commend mee to Robin Hood, sayes Queene
    Katherine,
    And marke, page, what I say ;
In London they must be with me
    [Vpon St Georges day.]

*   *   *   *   *   *   *

12 .   .   .   .
    'These words hath sent by me ;
Att London you must be with her
    Vpon St Georg[e]s day.

13 'Vpon St Georg[e]s day att noone
    Att London needs must you bee ;

Shee wold not misse your companie
For all the gold in Cristinty.

14 'Shee hath tane a shooting for your sake,
   The greatest in Christentie,
   And her part you must needs take
   Against her prince, Henery.

15 'Shee sends you heere her gay gold ring
   A trew token for to bee;
   And, as you are [a] banisht man,
   Shee trusts to sett you free.'

16 'And I loose that wager,' says bold Robin
   Hoode,
   'I 'le bring mony to pay for me;
   And wether that I win or loose,
   On my queenes part I will be.'

17 In sommer time when leaues grow greene,
   And flowers are fresh and gay,
   Then Robin Hood he deckt his men
   Eche one in braue array.

18 He deckt his men in Lincolne greene,
   Himselfe in scarlett red;
   Fayre of theire brest then was it seene
   When his siluer armes were spread.

19 With hattis white and fethers blacke,
   And bowes and arrowes keene,
   And thus he ietted towards louly London,
   To present Queene Katherine.

20 But when they cam to louly London,
   They kneeled vpon their knee;
   Sayes, God you saue, Queene Katherine,
   And all your dignitie!

   *   *   *   *   *   *   *

21 . . . . of my guard,'
   Thus can King Henry say,
   'And those that wilbe of Queene Katerines
   side,
   They are welcome to me this day.'

22 'Then come hither to me, Sir Richard Lee,
   Thou art a knight full good;
   Well it is knowen ffrom thy pedygree
   Thou came from Gawiins blood.

23 'Come hither, Bishopp of Hereford,' quoth
   Queene Katherine —
   A good preacher I watt was hee —
   'And stand thou heere vpon a odd side,
   On my side for to bee.'

24 'I like not that,' sayes the bishopp then,
   'By faikine of my body,
   For if I might haue my owne will,
   On the kings I wold bee.'

25 'What will thou be[t] against vs,' says Loxly
   then,
   'And stake it on the ground?'
   'That will I doe, fine fellow,' he says,
   'And it drawes to fiue hundreth pound.'

26 'There is a bett,' says Loxly then;
   'Wee 'le stake it merrily;'
   But Loxly knew full well in his mind
   And whose that gold shold bee.

27 Then the queenes archers they shot about
   Till it was three and three;
   Then the lady 's gaue a merry shout,
   Sayes, Woodcocke, beware thine eye!

28 'Well, gam and gam,' then quoth our king,
   'The third three payes for all;'
   Then Robine rounded with our queene,
   Says, The kings part shall be small.

29 Loxly puld forth a broad arrowe,
   He shott it vnder hand,
   .   .   .   .   . s vnto   .   .
   .   .   .   .

   *   *   *   *   *   *   *

30 .   .   .   .   .   .
   'For once he vndidd mee;
   If I had thought it had beene bold Robin
   Hoode,
   I wold not haue betted one peny.

31 'Is this Robin Hood?' says the bishopp againe;
   'Once I knew him to soone;
   He made me say a masse against my will,
   Att two a clocke in the afternoone.

32 'He bound me fast vnto a tree,
   Soe did he my merry men;

He borrowed ten pound against my will,
   But he neuer paid me againe.'

33 'What and if I did?' says bold Ro*bin* Hood,
   'Of that masse I was full faine;
In recompence, befor king and queene
   Take halfe of thy gold againe.'

34 'I thanke thee for nothing,' says the bishopp,
   'Thy large gift to well is knowne,
That will borrow a mans mony against his will,
   And pay him againe *with* his owne.'

35 'What if he did soe?' says King Henery,
   'For that I loue him neuer the worsse;
Take vp thy gold againe, bold Robin Hood,
   And put [it] in thy pursse.

36 'If thou woldest leaue thy bold **outlawes**,
   And come and dwell *with* me,
Then I wold say thou art welcome, bold Ro*bin*
   Hood,
   The flower of archery.'

37 'I will not leaue my bold outlawes
   For all the gold in Christentie;
In merry Sherwood I 'le take my end,
   Vnder my trusty tree.

38 'And gett *your* shooters, my leeig[e], where
   you will,
   For in faith you shall haue none of me;
And when Queene Katherine puts up her
   f[inger]
   Att her Graces com*m*andement I 'le bee.'

*   *   *   *   *   *   *   *

B

a. Wood, 402, leaf 10.   b. Roxburghe, I, 356, in the Ballad Society's reprint, II, 419.   c. Garland of 1663, No 9. d. Garland of 1670, No 8.   e. Wood, 401, leaf 31 b.   f. Pepys, II, 103, No 90.

1 GOLD tane from the kings harbengers,
   Down a down a down
As seldome hath been seen,
   Down a down a down
And carried by bold Robin Hood
   For a present to the queen.
   Down a down a down

2 'If that I live a year to an end,'
   Thus gan Queen Katherin say,
'Bold Robin Hood, I will be thy friend,
   And all thy yeomen gay.'

3 The queen is to her chamber gone,
   As fast as she can wen;
She cals unto her her lovely page,
   His name was Richard Patringten.

4 'Come hither to mee, thou lovely page,
   Come thou hither to mee;
For thou must post to Notingham,
   As fast as thou canst dree.

5 'And as thou goest to Notingham,
   Search all those English wood;

Enquire of one good yeoman or another
   That can tell thee of Robin Hood.'

6 Sometimes he went, sometimes hee ran,
   As fast as he could win;
And when hee came to Notingham,
   There he took up his inne.

7 And when he came to Notingham,
   And had took up his inne,
He calls for a pottle of Renish wine,
   And drank a health to his queen.

8 There sat a yeoman by his side;
   'Tell mee, sweet page,' said hee,
'What is thy business or the cause,
   So far in the North Country?'

9 'This is my business and the cause,
   Sir, I 'le tell it you for good,
To inquire of one good yeoman or another
   To tell mee of Robin Hood.'

10 'I 'le get my horse betime in the morn,
   By it be break of day,
And I will shew thee bold Robin Hood,
   And all his yeomen gay.'

11 When that he came at Robin Hoods place,
   Hee fell down on his knee:

'Queen Katherine she doth greet you well,
    She greets you well by mee.

12 'She bids you post to fair London court,
        Not fearing any thing;
    For there shall be a little sport,
        And she hath sent you her ring.'

13 Robin took his mantle from his back —
        It was of the Lincoln green —
    And sent it by this lovely page,
        For a present unto the queen.

14 In summer time, when leaves grow green,
        It is a seemly sight to see
    How Robin Hood himself had drest,
        And all his yeomandry.

15 He cloathed his men in Lincoln green,
        And himself in scarlet red,
    Black hats, white feathers, all alike;
        Now bold Robin Hood is rid.

16 And when he came at Londons court,
        Hee fell downe on his knee:
    'Thou art welcome, Locksly,' said the queen,
        'And all thy good yeomendree.'

17 The king is into Finsbury field,
        Marching in battel ray,
    And after follows bold Robin Hood,
        And all his yeomen gay.

18 'Come hither, Tepus,' said the king,
        'Bow-bearer after mee,
    Come measure mee out with this line
        How long our mark shall be.'

19 'What is the wager?' said the queen,
        'That must I now know here:'
    'Three hundred tun of Renish wine,
        Three hundred tun of beer.

20 'Three hundred of the fattest harts
        That run on Dallom lee;
    That's a princely wager,' said the king,
        'That needs must I tell thee.'

21 With that bespake one Clifton then,
        Full quickly and full soon;
    'Measure no mark for us, most soveraign leige,
        Wee 'l shoot at sun and moon.'

22 'Ful fifteen score your mark shall be,
        Ful fifteen score shall stand;'
    'I 'le lay my bow,' said Clifton then,
        'I 'le cleave the willow wand.'

23 With that the kings archers led about,
        While it was three and none;
    With that the ladies began to shout,
        Madam, your game is gone!

24 'A boon, a boon,' Queen Katherine cries,
        'I crave on my bare knee;
    Is there any knight of your privy counsel
        Of Queen Katherines part will be?

25 'Come hither to mee, Sir Richard Lee,
        Thou art a knight full good;
    For I do know by thy pedigree
        Thou springst from Goweres blood.

26 'Come hither to me, thou Bishop of Hereford-
            shire' —
        For a noble priest was he —
    'By my silver miter,' said the bishop then,
        'I 'le not bet one peny.

27 'The king hath archers of his own,
        Full ready and full light,
    And these be strangers every one,
        No man knows what they height.'

28 'What wilt thou bet,' said Robin Hood,
        'Thou seest our game the worse?'
    'By my silver miter,' said the bishop then,
        'All the mony within my purse.'

29 'What is in thy purse?' said Robin Hood,
        'Throw it down on the ground;'
    'Fifteen score nobles,' said the bishop then,
        'It's neer an hundred pound.'

30 Robin Hood took his bagge from his side,
        And threw it down on the green;
    William Scadlocke went smiling away,
        'I know who this mony must win.'

31 With that the queens archers led about,
        While it was three and three;
    With that the ladies gave a shout,
        'Woodcock, beware thyn ee!'

32 'It is three and three, now,' said the king,
        'The next three pays for all;'

Robin Hood went and whispered to the queen,
  'The kings part shall be but small.'

33 Robin Hood he led about,
    He shot it under hand,
    And Clifton, with a bearing arrow,
    He clave the willow wand.

34 And little Midge, the Miller's son,
    Hee shot not much the worse;
    He shot within a finger of the prick;
    'Now, bishop, beware thy purse!'

35 'A boon, a boon,' Queen Katherine cries,
    'I crave on my bare knee, —
    That you will angry be with none
    That is of my party.'

36 'They shall have forty days to come,
    And forty days to go,
    And three times forty to sport and play;
    Then welcome friend or fo.'

37 'Then thou art welcome, Robin Hood,' said
      the queen,
    'And so is Little John,

So is Midge, the Miller's son;
  Thrice welcome every one.'

38 'Is this Robin Hood?' the king now said;
    'For it was told to mee
    That he was slain in the pallace-gate,
    So far in the North Country.'

39 'Is this Robin Hood,' said the bishop then,
    'As I see well to be?
    Had I knowne that had been that bold outlaw,
    I would not have bet one peny.

40 'Hee took me late one Saturday at night,
    And bound mee fast to a tree,
    And made mee sing a mass, God wot,
    To him and his yeomendree.'

41 'What and if I did?' says Robin Hood,
    'Of that mass I was full fain;
    For recompense to thee,' he says,
    'Here 's half thy gold again.'

42 'Now nay, now nay,' saies Little John,
    'Master, that shall not be;
    We must give gifts to the kings officers;
    That gold will serve thee and mee.'

———————

C

The Garland of 1663, No 1.

1 STOUT Robin Hood, a most lusty out-law,
    As ever yet lived in this land,
    As ever yet lived in this land.
    His equal I 'm sure you never yet saw,
    So valiant was he of his hand,
    So valiant was he of his hand.

2 No archers could ever compare with these
      three,
    Although from us they are gone;
    The like was never, nor never will be,
    To Robin Hood, Scarlet and John.

3 Many stout robberies by these men were done,
    Within this our kingdom so wide;
    Vpon the highway much treasure they have
      won,
    No one that his purse ere deny'd.

4 Great store of money they from the kings men
    Couragiously did take away;
    Vnto fair Queen Katherine they gave it again,
    Who to them these words did say.

5 If that I live but another fair year,
    Kind Robin Hood, said the fair queen,
    The love for this courtesie that I thee bear,
    Assure thy self it shall be seen.

6 Brave Robin Hood courteously thanked her
      Grace,
    And so took his leave of the queen;
    He with his bold archers then hied him apace,
    In summer time, to the woods green.

7 'Now wend we together, my merry men all,
    To the green wood to take up our stand:'
    These archers were ready at Robin Hoods call,
    With their bent bows all in their hand.

8 'Come, merrily let us now valiantly go
   With speed unto the green wood,
And there let us kill a stout buck or a do,
   For our master, Robin Hood.'

9 At London must now be a game of shooting,
   Where archers should try their best skill;
It was so commanded by their gracious king;
   The queen then thought to have her will.

10 Her little foot-page she sent with all speed,
   To find out stout Robin Hood,
Who in the North bravely did live, as we read,
   With his bow-men in the green wood.

11 When as this young page unto the North came,
   He staid under a hill at his inn;
Within the fair town of sweet Nottingham,
   He there to enquire did begin.

12 The page then having enquired aright
   The way unto Robin Hoods place,
As soon as the page had obtained of him sight,
   He told him strange news from her Grace.

13 'Her Majestie praies you to haste to the court,'
   And therewithall shewd him her ring;
We must not delay his swift haste to this sport,
   Which then was proclaimd by the king.

14 Then Robin Hood hies him with all speed he
     may,
   With his fair men attired in green,
And towards fair London he then takes his
     way;
   His safety lay all on the queen.

15 Now Robin Hood welcome was then to the
     court,
   Queen Katharine so did allow;
Now listen, my friends, and my song shal re-
     port
   How the queen performed her vow.

16 The king then went marching in state with his
     peers
   To Finsbury field most gay,
Where Robin Hood follows him, void of all
     fears,
   With his lusty brave shooters that day.

17 The king did command that the way should be
   Straight mete with a line that was good;

The answer was made to him presently,
   By lusty bold Robin Hood.

18 'Let there be no mark measured,' then said he
     soon;
   'I,' so said Scarlet and John,
'For we will shoot to the sun or the moon;
   We scorn to be outreacht with none.'

19 'What shall the wager be?' then said the
     queen,
   'Pray tell me before you begin:'
'Three hundred tuns of good wine shall be
     seen,
   And as much of strong bear for to win.

20 'Three hundred of lusty fat bucks, sweet, beside,
   Shall now be our royal lay:'
Quoth Robin Hood, What ere does betide,
   I 'le bear this brave purchase away.

21 'Full fifteenscore,' saith the king, 'it shall be;'
   Then straight did the bow-men begin,
And Robin Hoods side gave them leave cer-
     tainly
   A while some credit to win.

22 The royal queen Katharine aloud cried she,
   Is here no lord, nor yet knight,
That will take my part in this bold enmity?
   Sir Robert Lee, pray do me right.

23 Then to the bold Bishop of Herefordshire
   Most mildly spoke our good queen;
But he straight refused to lay any more,
   Such ods on their parties were seen.

24 'What wilt thou bet, seeing our game is the
     worse?'
   Unto him then said Robin Hood:
'Why then,' quoth the bishop, 'all that's in
     my purse;'
   Quoth Scarlet, That bargain is good.

25 'A hundred good pounds there is in the same,'
   The bishop unto him did say;
Then said Robin Hood, Now here 's for the
     game,
   And to bear this your money away.

26 Then did the kings archer his arrows com-
     mand
   Most bravely and with great might,

But brave jolly Robin shot under his hand,
  And then did hit the mark right.

27 And Clifton he then, with his arrow so good,
  The willow-wood cleaved in two;
The Miller's young son came not short, by the
    rood,
  His skill he most bravely did show.

28 Thus Robin Hood and his crew won the rich
    prize,
  From all archers that there could be;
Then loudly unto the king Queen Katherine
    cries,
  Forgive all my company!

29 The king then did say, that for forty daies,
  Free leave then to come or go,
For any man there, though he got the praise,
  'Be he friend,' quoth he, 'or be he foe.'

30 Then quoth the queen, Welcome thou art,
    Robin Hood,
  And welcome, brave bow-men all three;
Then straight quoth the king, I did hear, by
    the rood,
  That slain he was in the countrey.

31 'Is this Robin Hood?' the bishop did say,
  'Is this Robin Hood certainly?
He made me to say him mass last Saturday,
  To him and his bold yeomendry.'

32 'Well,' quoth Robin Hood, 'in requital thereof,
  Half thy gold I give unto thee;'
'Nay, nay,' then said Little John in a scoff,
  ''T will serue us ith' North Countrey.'

33 Then Robin Hood pardon had straight of the
    king,
  And so had they every one;
The fame of these days most loudly does ring,
  Of Robin Hood, Scarlet and John.

34 Great honours to Robin Hood after were done,
  As stories for certain do say;
The king made him Earl of fair Huntington,
  Whose fame will never decay.

35 Thus have you heard the fame of these men,
  Good archers they were every one;
We never shal see the like shooters again
  As Robin Hood, Scarlet and John.

A. *After* 2², 11³, 20⁴, 29³, 38⁴, *half a page is gone.*
  2¹. *Perhaps* harvengers. 5². cauentry.
  9³. *Perhaps* William. *After* 16: The 2d part.
  18². hinselfe. 25⁴. 500ᵗʰ. 27², 28². 3.
  31⁴. 2. 32³. 10ˡⁱ.
B. Renowned Robin Hood: or, his famous arch-
  ery truly related; with the worthy exploits
  hee acted before Queen Katherine, hee be-
  ing an outlaw-man; and how shee for the
  same obtained of the king his own and his
  fellows pardon. To a new tune.
a. London, Printed for F. Grove, on Snow-hill.
  Entred according to order. (1620–55.)
  16⁴. yeomen three: *so* b–e, *but* yeomendree,
    the reading of f, *must be right, since the*
    whole band is present, and only two yeomen
    besides Robin are distinguished.
  23², 31². While, *if preserved, must be taken*
    in the sense of till, *which occurs in* f, 23²,
    as in A, 27².
  31¹. the kings: *so all.* A, 27 *has* queenes,
    rightly.

  31⁴. thy knee: *so all except* b, *which has* thy
    nee.
  35². crave that on.
  39⁴. have *wanting: cf.* A 30, c, f.
  40⁴. yeomen three: *so all. See* 16⁴.
b. Printed at London for Francis Grove.
  2². can. 3. unto her lovely. 3⁴. Parringten.
  4⁴. can. 6³, 7¹. came at. 8¹. sate. 8⁴. in this.
  10². Be it the. 11¹. Hood. 13³. sent that.
  14². It's. 21³. markes. 23¹. archer.
  25⁴. sprungst. 31¹. the kings. 31⁴. thy nee.
  33³. baring. 33⁴. clove. 35¹. cryed.
  35². crave that on. 38¹. now said the king.
  38². so told. 38³. in Pallace gates.
  39⁴. not bet. 40⁴. yeomen three.
  41¹. an if. 41². full *wanting.*
c. 3³. unto her lovelie. 5³, 9³. or other.
  8¹. sate. 9¹. is the. 10⁴. yeoman.
  16⁴. yeomen three. 17¹. gone *for* field.
  20⁴. must I needs. 23³. shoot.
  24⁴. On *for* Of. 25⁴. sprangst from Gowries.
  30³. Sadlock. 30⁴. whose this money must be.

31^1. the kings. 31^4. thy knee.
32^3. to *wanting*. 35^2. crave that on.
39^4. have bet. 40^1. on *for* one.
40^4. yeomen three.
d. 3^3. unto her lovely. 3^4. Patrington.
13^4. to *for* unto. 14^4. his *wanting*.
16^4. yeomen three. 24^4. On *for* Of.
25^4. sprangst. 31^1. the kings.
31^4. thy knee. 35^2. crave that on.
36^4. welcome every one. 39^1. quoth *for* said.
39^4. not bet. 40^1. on *for* one.
40^4. yeomen three.
e. London, Printed for F. Coles, T. Vere & J.
   Wright. (1655–80.)
3^4. Patrington. 7^3. calld. 8^1. sate.
8^3. thy cause. 10^1. betimes.
16^4. good *wanting* : yeomen three.
17^2. gallant ray. 19^2. needs *for* now.
20^2. runs. 22^3. quoth *for* said.
31^1. the kings. 31^3. shoot. 31^4. thy knee.
35^2. that *wanting*. 38^3. the *wanting*.
39^3. I thought it had. 39^4. not bet.
40^4. yeomen three. 42^2. may not.
f. *In the title :* being an outlaw man (hee *want-ing*) : how he *for* how shee.
   Printed for J. W[right], J. C[larke], W.
   T[hackeray], and T. Passenger. (1670–86 ?)
3^3. unto her lovely. 3^4. Parington.

4^1. Come thou : my *for* thou. 4^3. now *for* post.
5^2. woods. 6^2. wen. 7^3. bottle. 7^4. drinks.
8^1. sate. 8^3. or thy. 10^1. betimes.
11^1. to *for* at. 13^2. the *wanting*.
13^4. to *for* unto. 14^2. It was.
16^4. thy yeomandree. 17^1. is gone to.
17^2. array. 18^4. must be. 20^4. to the.
23^1. lead. 23^2. Till it. 24^2. crave it.
24^3. ever a *for* any. 24^4. side *for* part.
25^4. sprangest. 28^3. then said the bishop.
29^1. in it said. 30^3. Will. 31^1. the kings.
31^4. thy knee. 32^4. part *wanting*.
35^2. crave it. 35^3. would *for* will.
36^4. welcome every one. 37^3. And so.
38^1. said now. 39^1. quoth *for* said.
39^3. it had. 39^4. not a bet.
40^1. on Saturday night. 40^4. yeomen three.
41^1. then says. 42^2. may not.
C. Robin Hood, Scarlet and John : Wherein you
   may see how Robin Hood, having lived an
   out-law many years, the Queen sent for him,
   and shooting a match before the King and
   Queen at London, and winning the rich
   prize, the Queen gained his pardon, and he
   was afterwards Earl of Huntington.
   To the tune of The Pinder of Wakefield.
   20^3. what or. 26^1. archers. 27^3. yonng.
   28^3. Katheline. $30^{1,3}$. qd.

146

ROBIN HOOD'S CHASE

a. Garland of 1663, No 15.

b. Garland of 1670, No 14.

c. Wood, 401, leaf 29 b.

d. Pepys, II, 104, No 91.

ROXBURGHE, III, 14, 418 ; Douce, III, 121 b, London, by L. How, an eighteenth-century copy. c is signed T. R., and has no printer's name.

Reprinted in Ritson's Robin Hood, 1795, II, 92, from c. Evans, Old Ballads, 1777, 1784, I, 156, agrees nearly with the Aldermary garland.

Robin Hood's Chase is a sequel to Robin Hood and Queen Katherine, and begins with a summary of that ballad. King Henry, who has been gracious, and over-gracious, to the outlaw, has a revulsion of feeling after Robin has left his presence, and sets out in pursuit of him. When the king reaches Nottingham, Robin leaves Sherwood for Yorkshire, whence he speeds successively to Newcastle, Berwick, Carlisle, Lancaster, Chester, the king always following him close. At Chester the happy idea occurs to him of going back to London, as if to inquire whether he were wanted. Queen Katherine informs Robin that the king has gone to Sherwood to seek him, and Robin says he will return to the forest immediately to learn the king's will. King Henry, coming home weary and vexed, is told by his queen that Robin has been there to seek him. A cunning knave, quoth the king. The queen intercedes for Robin.

This is a well-conceived ballad, and only needs to be older.

Translated by A. Grün, p. 169, with omission of stanzas 1–7, 24.

---

1 COME you gallants all, to you I do call,
  With a hey down down a down down
That now is within this place,
For a song I will sing of Henry the king,
How he did Robin Hood chase.

2 Queen Katherine she a match then did make,
  As plainly doth appear,
For three hundred tun of good red wine,
And three hundred tun of beer.

3 But yet her archers she had to seek,
  With their bows and arrows so good ;
But her mind it was bent, with a good intent,
To send for bold Robin Hood.

4 But when bold Robin Hood he came there,
  Queen Katherine she did say,
Thou art welcome, Locksley, said the queen,
And all thy yeomen gay.

5 For a match at shooting I have made,
  And thou my part must be :
'If I miss the mark, be it light or dark,
Then hanged I will be.'

6 But when the game came to be playd,
  Bold Robin he then drew nigh ;
With his mantle of green, most brave to be
  seen,
He let his arrows fly.

7 And when the game it ended was,
  Bold Robin wan it with a grace,
But after, the king was angry with him,
And vowed he would him chase.

8 What though his pardon granted was
  While he with them did stay,
But yet the king was vexed at him
When as he was gone his way.

9 Soon after the king from the court did hie,
  In a furious angry mood,
And often enquire, both far and near,
  After bold Robin Hood.

10 But when the king to Nottingham came,
  Bold Robin was then in the wood ;
'O come now,' said he, 'and let me see
  Who can find me bold Robin Hood.'

11 But when that Robin Hood he did hear
  The king had him in chase,
Then said Little John, T is time to be gone,
  And go to some other place.

12 Then away they went from merry Sherwood,
  And into Yorkshire he did hie,
And the king did follow, with a hoop and a
  hallow,
But could not come him nigh.

13 Yet jolly Robin he passed along,
  He [went] straight to Newcastle town,
And there stayed he hours two or three,
  And then he for Berwick was gone.

14 When the king he did see how Robin did
  flee,
He was vexed wondrous sore ;
With a hoop and a hallow he vowed to follow,
  And take him, or never give ore.

15 'Come now, let's away,' then cries Little John,
  'Let any man follow that dare ;
To Carlile wee'l hie with our company,
  And so then to Lancaster.'

16 From Lancaster then to Chester they went,
  And so did king Henery ;
But Robin away, for he durst not stay,
  For fear of some treachery.

17 Saies Robin, Come, let us to London go,
   To see our noble queens face ;
   It may be she wants our company,
   Which makes the king so us chase.

18 When Robin he came Queen Katherine before,
   He fell upon his knee :
   'If it please your Grace, I am come to this
   place,
   To speak with king Henery.'

19 Queen Katherine she answered bold Robin
   again,
   The king is gone to merry Sherwood ;
   And when he went he to me did say
   He would go seek Robin Hood.

20 'Then fare you well, my gracious queen,
   For to Sherwood I will hie apace ;
   For fain would I see what he would with me,
   If I could but meet with his Grace.'

21 But when King Henery he came home,
   Full weary, and vexed in mind,
   When he did hear Robin had been there,
   He blamed Dame Fortune unkind.

22 'You are welcome home,' Queen Katherine
   cried,
   'Henry, my soveraign liege ;
   Bold Robin Hood, that archer good,
   Your person hath been to seek.'

23 But when King Henry he did hear
   That Robin had been there him to seek,
   This answer he gave, He 's a cunning knave,
   For I have sought him this whole three
   weeks.

24 'A boon ! a boon !' Queen Katherine cried,
   'I beg it here on your Grace,
   To pardon his life, and seek no more strife : '
   And so endeth Robin Hoods chase.

———◆———

a, b, c. Robin Hood's Chase : or, A merry progress between Robin Hood and King Henry, shewing how Robin Hood led the King his chase from London to London, and when he had taken his leave of the Queen he returned to merry Sherwood.
To the tune of Robin Hood and the Begger.
a. *Burden : variously printed* With a hey, etc., With hey, etc.; *twice* Down a down a down.
5²,³. Robin *between the lines, to show that what follows is his speech. So* b, c. *In* d Robin *stands at the head of the third line.*
21³. But when : *so* b, c. 23⁴, 3 weeks.
b. *Burden :* With hey, etc., *or,* With a hey, etc.
2¹. she then a match.
3¹. she had her archers. 6¹. game it.
7². a *wanting.* 10². then *wanting.*
11¹. that bold. 13². went *wanting.*
14⁴. and *for* or. 15¹. cry'd.
16². good King Henry. 18⁴. Henry.
21³. But when. 23². there *wanting.*
23⁴. 3 weeks. 24². here on my knee.
c. *Signed* T. R. *No printer.*
Burden : With hey down down an a down.

2⁴. hundred *wanting.* 3³. it *wanting.*
5¹. of *for* at. 6¹. it came. 8³. after *for* yet.
10². then *wanting.* 13². went *wanting.*
16², 18⁴, 21¹. Henry. 16³. to stay.
18². fell low. 18⁴. For to. 21³. But when.
22². leech. 23⁴. 3 weeks.
d. *Title as in* a, b, c, *except :* The tune is.
Printed for William Thackeray at the Angel in Duck-Lane. (1689.)
Burden : With hey down down a down.
2¹. then a match did.
3¹. yet she had her archers. 5¹. of *for* at.
5². on my. 5⁴. will I. 6². he *wanting.*
7². a *wanting.* 8⁴. had *for* was.
10². O bold : then *wanting.*
10³. Come said he. 11¹. that bold Robin he.
13². And went strait. 13³. he stayed.
13⁴, 14¹. he *wanting.* 14⁴. gave.
15¹. than said Little. 16², 18⁴, 21¹. Henry.
17¹. for London. 18². fell low.
18⁴. For to. 19³. he *wanting.*
19⁴. go to. 20³. what he 'd have.
21³. And that he. 22¹. You 're.
23². there *wanting.* 23³. He is a.
23⁴. 3 week. 24². of your.

147

ROBIN HOOD'S GOLDEN PRIZE

a. Wood, 401, leaf 39 b.

b. Garland of 1663, No 14.

c. Garland of 1670, No 13.

d. Pepys, II, 114, No 101.

———+———

ALSO Roxburghe, III, 12, 486; Old Ballads, 1723, II, 121; Douce, III, 121, London, by L. How, of the last century.

Ritson's Robin Hood, 1795, II, 97, from a, with changes. Evans, Old Ballads, 1777, 1784, I, 160, agrees nearly with the Aldermary garland.

Entered, says Ritson, in the Stationers' book, by Francis Grove, 2d June, 1656.* Being directed to be sung to the tune " R. H. was a tall young man," that is, R. H.'s Progress to Nottingham, this ballad is the later of the two.

Robin Hood, disguised as a friar, asks charity of two priests. They pretend to have been robbed, and not to have a penny. Robin pulls them from their horses, saying, Since you have no money, we will pray for some, and keeps them at their prayers for an hour. Now, he says, we will see what heaven has sent us; but the monks can find nothing in their pockets. We must search one another, Robin says, and beginning the operation finds five hundred pounds on the monks. Of this he gives fifty pounds to each of the priests to pay for their prayers, keeping the remainder. The priests would now move on, but Robin

requires three oaths of them, of truth, chastity and charity, before he lets them go.

The kernel of the story is an old tale which we find represented in Pauli's Schimpf und Ernst, 1533, Österley, p. 397, Anhang, No 14, 'Wie drey lantzknecht vmb ein zerung batten.' Three soldiers, out of service, meet the cellarer of a rich Benedictine cloister, who has a bag hanging at his saddle-bow, with four hundred ducats in it. They ask for some money, for God's sake and good fellowship's. The cellarer answers that he has no money: there is nothing but letters in his bag. Then, since we all four are without money, they say, we will kneel down and pray for some. After a brief orison, the three jump up, search the bag, and find four hundred ducats. The cellarer offers them a handsome douceur, and says he had the money in the bag before; but to this they will give no credence. They give the monk his share of one hundred, and thank God devoutly for his grace. Retold by Waldis, with a supplement, Esopus, IV, 21, ed. Kurz, II, 64; and by others, see Oesterley's notes, p. 552, Kurz's, p. 156.

a seems to be signed L. P., and these would most naturally be the initials of the versifier.

* Also says Ritson, Robin Hood, II, 97, by Francis Coule, 13th June, 1631; but the ballad there entered is The Noble Fisherman.

Translated by Doenniges, p. 198, by Anastasius Grün, p. 131.

1 I HAVE heard talk of bold Robin Hood,
    Derry derry down
And of brave Little John,
Of Fryer Tuck, and Will Scarlet,
    Loxley, and Maid Marion.
      Hey down derry derry down

2 But such a tale as this before
    I think there was never none ;
For Robin Hood disguised himself,
    And to the wood is gone.

3 Like to a fryer, bold Robin Hood
    Was accoutered in his array ;
With hood, gown, beads and crucifix,
    He past upon the way.

4 He had not gone [past] miles two or three,
    But it was his chance to spy
Two lusty priests, clad all in black,
    Come riding gallantly.

5 ' Benedicete,' then said Robin Hood,
    ' Some pitty on me take ;
Cross you my hand with a silver groat,
    For Our dear Ladies sake.

6 ' For I have been wandring all this day,
    And nothing could I get ;
Not so much as one poor cup of drink,
    Nor bit of bread to eat.'

7 ' Now, by my holydame,' the priests repli'd,
    ' We never a peny have ;
For we this morning have been robd,
    And could no mony save.'

8 ' I am much afraid,' said bold Robin Hood,
    ' That you both do tell a lye ;
And now before that you go hence,
    I am resolvd to try.'

9 When as the priests heard him say so,
    Then they rode away amain ;
But Robin Hood betook him to his heels,
    And soon overtook them again.

10 Then Robin Hood laid hold of them both,
    And pulld them down from their horse :
' O spare us, fryer ! ' the priests cry'd out,
    ' On us have some remorse ! '

11 ' You said you had no mony,' quoth he,
    ' Wherefore, without delay,
We three will fall down on our knees,
    And for mony we will pray.'

12 The priests they could not him gainsay,
    But down they kneeled with speed ;
' Send us, O send us,' then quoth they,
    ' Some mony to serve our need.'

13 The priests did pray with mournful chear,
    Sometimes their hands did wring,
Sometimes they wept and cried aloud,
    Whilst Robin did merrily sing.

14 When they had been praying an hours space,
    The priests did still lament ;
Then quoth bold Robin, Now let 's see
    What mony heaven hath us sent.

15 We will be sharers now all alike
    Of the mony that we have ;
And there is never a one of us
    That his fellows shall deceive.

16 The priests their hands in their pockets put,
    But mony would find none :
' We 'l search our selves,' said Robin Hood,
    ' Each other, one by one.'

17 Then Robin Hood took pains to search them both,
    And he found good store of gold ;
Five hundred peeces presently
    Vpon the grass was told.

18 ' Here is a brave show,' said Robin Hood,
    ' Such store of gold to see,
And you shall each one have a part,
    Cause you prayed so heartily.'

19 He gave them fifty pound a-peece,
    And the rest for himself did keep ;
The priests durst not speak one word,
    But they sighed wondrous deep.

20 With that the priests rose up from their knees,
    Thinking to have parted so ;
' Nay, stay,' said Robin Hood, ' one thing more
    I have to say ere you go.

21 'You shall be sworn,' said bold Robin Hood,
    'Vpon this holy grass,
That you will never tell lies again,
    Which way soever you pass.

22 'The second oath that you here must take,
    All the days of your lives
You never shall tempt maids to sin,
    Nor lye with other mens wives.

23 'The last oath you shall take, it is this,
    Be charitable to the poor;
Say you have met with a holy fryer,
    And I desire no more.'

24 He set them upon their horses again,
    And away then they did ride;
And hee returnd to the merry green-wood,
    With great joy, mirth and pride.

a. Robin Hoods Golden Prize.

He met two priests upon the way,
And forced them with him to pray.
For gold they prayed, and gold they had,
Enough to make bold Robin glad.
His share came to four hundred pound,
That then was told upon the ground;
Now mark, and you shall hear the jest;
You never heard the like exprest.

Tune is, Robin Hood was a tall young man.
London, Printed for F. Grove on Snow-hill.
    Entred according to order. Finis, L. P.
    F. Grove's *date, according to Mr Chappell,*
    is 1620–55. *Ritson says that the ballad*
    was entered in the Stationers' book by
    Francis Grove, 2d June, 1656.

b. Robin Hoods Golden Prize: Shewing how he
    robbed two priests of five hundred pound.
    The tune is, Robin Hood was a tall young
    man.
    4^1. gone past. 6^1. all the.
    7^1. holy dame: priest. 9^2. Then *wanting*.

10^1. hold on. 13^1. with a. 15^4. fellow.
17^4. he *for* was. 18^4. For praying so.
19^1. pounds. 19^3. not to. 23^1. it *wanting*.

c. *Title the same: except,* Tune is.
    2^4. he is. 4^1. gone past. 7^1. holy dame.
    9^2. Then *wanting*. 10^1. holt of. 13^1. with a.
    15^1. now *wanting*. 15^4. fellow.
    17^1. pain: both *wanting*. 18^3. each one shall.
    19^1. pounds. 24^1. upon *wanting*.

d. *Title as in* c. Printed for William Thackeray
    at the Angel in Duck-lane. (1689.)
    1^1. bold *wanting*. 2^2. think was never known.
    4^1. gone past. 7^1. holy dame.
    8^3. before you do go. 9^1. so say.
    10^1. hold on. 11^1. you'd: quoth Robin Hood.
    12^2. kneel. 13^1. with a. 14^3. let us.
    15^1. now *wanting*. 15^2. the *wanting*.
    15^4. fellow. 16^2. could.
    17^1. pain: both *wanting*. 17^4. he *for* was.
    18^3. each one shall. 19^1. pounds.
    19^2. doth *for* did. 20^1. up *wanting*.
    22^3. unto sin. 23^3. with *wanting*.
    24^1. on *for* upon.

148

THE NOBLE FISHERMAN, OR, ROBIN HOOD'S PREFER–MENT

a. Wood, 402, p. 18. **b.** Wood, 401, leaf 25 b. **c.** Garland of 1663, No 12. **d.** Garland of 1670, No 11. **e.** Rawlinson, 566. **f.** Pepys, II, 108, No 95. **g.** Pepys, II, 123, No 108.

ALSO Roxburghe, II, 370, III, 524; The Noble Fisherman's Garland, 1686; Bagford, 643. m. 10, 22.

'The Noble Ffisherman, or, Robin Hoods great Prize' is receipted for to Francis Coules in the Stationers' Registers, June 13, 1631: Arber, IV, 254.

Ritson, Robin Hood, II, 110, 1795, "from three old black-letter copies, one in the collection of Anthony a Wood, another in the British Museum, and the third in a private collection." Evans, Old Ballads, 1777, 1784, I, 171, from an Aldermary garland.

Robin Hood is here made to try his fortunes on the sea, like Eustace the Monk and Wallace. He goes to Scarborough and gives himself out as a fisherman, and is engaged as such by a widow with whom he lodges, who is the owner of a ship. Out of his wantonness, rather than his ignorance, we must suppose, Simon, as he calls himself, when others cast baited hooks into the water, casts in bare lines; for which he is laughed to scorn. A French cruiser bears down on the fishermen, and the master gives up all for lost. Simon asks for his bow; not a Frenchman will he spare. The master, not strangely, takes such talk for brag. Simon requests to be tied to a mast, 'that at his mark he may stand fair,' and to have his bow in his hand, when never a Frenchman will he spare. He shoots one of the enemy through the heart, and then asks to be loosed and to have his bow in his hand, when, again, never a Frenchman will he spare. The Englishmen board, and find a booty of twelve thousand pound. Simon announces that he shall give half the ship to the dame who employed him, and the other half to his comrades. The master objects; Simon has won the vessel with his own hand (a point which might have been made more distinctly to appear in the narrative), and he shall have her. But the outlaw afloat has still his munificent old ways; so it shall be as to the ship, and the twelve thousand pound shall build an asylum 'for the opprest'! All this may strike us as infantile, but the ballad was evidently in great favor two hundred years ago.

Translated (not entirely) by A. Grün, p. 295.

---

1 IN summer time, when leaves grow green,
   When they doe grow both green and long,
 Of a bould outlaw, calld Robin Hood,
   It is of him I sing this song.

2 When the lilly leafe and the elephant
   Doth bud and spring with a merry good
     cheere,

This outlaw was weary of the wood-side,
   And chasing of the fallow deere.

3 'The fishermen brave more mony have
   Then any merchant, two or three;
 Therefore I will to Scarborough goe,
   That I a fisherman brave may be.'

4 This outlaw calld his merry men all,
　　As they sate under the green-wood tree :
' If any of you have gold to spend,
　　I pray you heartily spend it with me.

5 ' Now,' quoth Robin, ' I 'le to Scarborough goe,
　　It seemes to be a very faire day ; '
Who tooke up his inne at a widdow-womans
　　　house,
Hard by upon the water gray.

6 Who asked of him, Where wert thou borne ?
　　Or tell to me, where dost thou fare ?
' I am a poore fisherman,' saith he then,
　　' This day intrapped all in care.'

7 ' What is thy name, thou fine fellow ?
　　I pray thee heartily tell to me ; '
' In mine own country where I was borne,
　　Men called me Simon over the Lee.'

8 ' Simon, Simon,' said the good wife,
　　' I wish thou maist well brook thy name ; '
The outlaw was ware of her courtesie,
　　And rejoycd he had got such a dame.

9 ' Simon, wilt thou be my man ?
　　And good round wages I 'le give thee ;
I have as good a ship of mine owne
　　As any sayle upon the sea.

10 ' Anchors and planks thou shalt want none,
　　Masts and ropes that are so long ; '
' And if that you thus furnish me,'
　　Said Simon, ' nothing shall goe wrong.'

11 They pluckt up anchor, and away did sayle,
　　More of a day then two or three ;
When others cast in their baited hooks,
　　The bare lines into the sea cast he.

12 ' It will be long,' said the master then,
　　' Ere this great lubber do thrive on the sea ;
I 'le assure you he shall have no part of our fish,
　　For in truth he is of no part worthy.'

13 ' O woe is me,' said Simon then,
　　' This day that ever I came here !
I wish I were in Plomton Parke,
　　In chasing of the fallow deere.

14 ' For every clowne laughs me to scorne,
　　And they by me set nought at all ;

If I had them in Plomton Park,
　　I would set as little by them all.'

15 They pluckt up anchor, and away did sayle,
　　More of a day then two or three ;
But Simon spied a ship of warre,
　　That sayld towards them most valourously.

16 ' O woe is me,' said the master then,
　　' This day that ever I was borne !
For all our fish we have got to-day
　　Is every bit lost and forlorne.

17 ' For your French robbers on the sea,
　　They will not spare of us one man,
But carry us to the coast of France,
　　And ligge us in the prison strong.'

18 But Simon said, Doe not feare them,
　　Neither, master, take you no care ;
Give me my bent bow in my hand,
　　And never a Frenchman will I spare.

19 ' Hold thy peace, thou long lubber,
　　For thou art nought but braggs and boast ;
If I should cast the over-board,
　　There were nothing but a lubber lost.'

20 Simon grew angry at these words,
　　And so angry then was he
That he tooke his bent bow in his hand,
　　And to the ship-hatch goe doth he.

21 ' Master, tye me to the mast,' saith he,
　　' That at my mark I may stand fair,
And give me my bended bow in my hand,
　　And never a Frenchman will I spare.'

22 He drew his arrow to the very head,
　　And drew it with all might and maine,
And straightway, in the twinkling of an eye,
　　Doth the Frenchmans heart the arow gain.

23 The Frenchman fell downe on the ship-hatch,
　　And under the hatches down below ;
Another Frenchman that him espy'd
　　The dead corps into the sea doth throw.

24 ' O master, loose me from the mast,' he said,
　　' And for them all take you no care,
And give me my bent bow in my hand,
　　And never a Frenchman will I spare.'

25 Then streight [they] did board the French-
     mans ship,
   They lying all dead in their sight;
   They found within the ship of warre
     Twelve thousand pound of money bright.

26 'The one halfe of the ship,' said Simon then,
     'I 'le give to my dame and children small;
   The other halfe of the ship I 'le bestow
     On you that are my fellowes all.'

27 But now bespake the master then,
     For so, Simon, it shall not be;
   For you have won her with your own hand,
     And the owner of it you shall bee.

28 'It shall be so, as I have said;
     And, with this gold, for the opprest
   An habitation I will build,
     Where they shall live in peace and rest.'

---

a. The Noble Fisher-man, or, Robin Hoods Pre-
ferment: shewing how he won a great prize
on the sea, and how he gave the one halfe
to his dame and the other to the building of
almes-houses.
The tune is, In summer time.
London, Printed for F. Coles, in the Old
Baily. (1631?)
3¹. fisher-man, *which perhaps should stand.*
5¹. with *for* quoth. 20⁴. hatchs. 21². fare.
22⁴. Frenchman. 23¹. fell owne. 25². lyin.
28². for thee.

b. *Title as in* a, *except:* won a prize, gave one
half.
Printed for F. Coles, T. Vere, and W. Gilbert-
son. (1648–63?)
2¹. Clephant. 2². good *wanting.*
3¹. fisherman. 3³. will I. 5¹. with *for* quoth.
12⁴. of *wanting.* 14². set nothing.
16³. fish that we have got: to-day *wanting.*
17¹. For yon. 19⁴. There 's but a simple.
20⁴. ship-hatch. 21¹. mast he said. 21². fare.
21³. bent. 22⁴. Frenchmans. 23¹. downe.
25¹. streight they boarded the French ship.
25². lying. 25⁴. in mony.
26³. of my ship I 'le give. 26⁴. To you.
27³. hands. 27⁴. must be. 28². for thee.

c, d. *Title as in* a, *except:* won a prize, gave one.
The tune is, Summer time.
2². good *wanting.* 3¹. fisher men.
3². Than. 5¹. Now quoth. 6². c, thou dost.
6³. said. 6⁴. d, cares. 7⁴. call. 9⁴. sails.
11². d, than. 12³. you *wanting.*
12⁴. of *wanting.* 14². set nothing.
15². than. 15⁴. most *wanting.*
16³. fish that we have got: to-day *wanting.*
17¹. yon: robber. 18². you any.
19⁴. There 's but a simple. 20⁴. shiphatch.
21¹. mast he said. 21². fair. 21³. bent.
21⁴. d, a *wanting.* 22⁴. Frenchmans.
23¹. down. 24¹. c, mast side.

25¹. they boarded the French ship. 25². lying.
25⁴. in *for* of. 26³. of my ship I 'le give.
26⁴. To you. 27¹. c, But *wanting.*
27³. hands. 27⁴. you must: d, of you it.
28². for the.

e. *Title as in* b. *Variations found also in* b
are not given.
Printed for F. Coles, T. Vere, J. Wright, and
J. Clarke. (1650–80?)
5¹. Now quoth. 5⁴. waters. 6¹. of *wanting.*
9⁴. sails. 15³. espy'd. 17⁴. And lay.
18². any *for* no. 23³. that him did espy.

f. *Title as in* b.
Printed for Alex. Milbourn, Will. Ownley,
Tho. Thackeray at the Angel in Duck-lane.
(*Date indeterminable: after* 1670.)
1². doe *wanting.* 1⁴. my song.
2². good *wanting.* 3¹. fishermen.
3². merchants. 3⁴. fisherman might be.
4³. If you have any.
5¹. Now quoth Robin Hood. 5⁴. waters.
6¹. of *wanting.* 6³. said. 7². tell it.
7⁴. call. 9². I will. 9³. of my. 9⁴. sails.
10¹. shalt not want. 10³. that *wanting.*
12³. you *wanting.* 12⁴. of *wanting.*
14². set nothing. 15³. espyed.
15⁴. most *wanting.*
16³. fish that we have got. 17¹. robber.
17⁴. And lay. 18². you any.
19⁴. There 's but a simple lubber lost.
20⁴. And in. 21¹. saith he *wanting.*
21². fair. 21³. bent. 22⁴. Frenchmans.
23¹. ship-catch: *so* g. 23². there below.
25¹. Then they boarded the French: *so* g.
25⁴. in *for* of. 26³. other part: I 'le give.
26⁴. To you. 27³. hands.
27⁴. owner thereof you must. 28². for the.

g. *Title as in* b.
Printed for I. Wright, I. Clarke, W. Thack-
eray, and T. Passinger. (1670–86?)
Agrees generally with f. 17¹. For yon.

149

ROBIN HOOD'S BIRTH, BREEDING, VALOR AND MARRIAGE

a. Roxburghe, I, 360, in The Ballad Society's reprint, II, 440.   **b.** Pepys, II, 116, No 103.   **c.** Pepys, II, 118, No 104.

PRINTED in Dryden's Miscellany, VI, 346, ed. 1716; A Collection of Old Ballads, 1723, I, 64; Ritson's Robin Hood, 1795, II, 1 (a); Evans, Old Ballads, 1777, 1784, I, 86.

The jocular author of this ballad, who would certainly have been diverted by any one's supposing him to write under the restraints of tradition, brings Adam Bell, Clim, and Cloudesly into company with Robin Hood's father. So again the silly Second Part of Adam Bell in one of the copies, that of 1616. Robin Hood's father's bow, st. 3, carried two north-country miles and an inch. The son, then, was only half his father, though, in Ritson's words, " Robin Hood and Little John have frequently shot an arrow a measured mile."

Robin Hood's mother was niece to Guy of Warwick, and sister to Gamwel of Gamwel Hall. In Robin Hood newly Revived, Young Gamwel is Robin Hood's sister's son. According to this ballad, Robin Hood goes with his mother to keep Christmas with old Gamwell, his uncle, whose seat is forty miles from Locksly town. Little John is a member of the household, a fine lad at gambols and juggling, and twenty such tricks. Robin Hood, however, puts Little John down in this way, and everybody else. His uncle is so much pleased that he tells Robin he shall be his heir, and no more go home. Robin asks the boon that Little John may be his page. All the while, for how long we know not, Robin Hood has had his band of yeomen in Sherwood. Thither he goes (the time is not specified, but birds are singing in st. 50), and while he is collecting his men, Clorinda, queen of the shepherds and archeress, passes, and arrests his at-

tention. The favorable impression which she makes at first sight is confirmed by her presently shooting a deer through side and side. Robin takes her to his bower for a refection, which is served by four-and-twenty yeomen. She inquires his name; he gives it, and asks her to be his bride. After a blush and a pause, Clorinda says, With all my heart, and it is no wonder that Robin proposes to send for a priest immediately. Clorinda is, however, engaged to go to Titbury feast, whither she invites Robin to keep her company. On the way he has an affray with eight yeomen, who bid him hand over the buck which Clorinda had killed, and which he is somehow taking along with him. With Little John's help, five of the eight are killed; the rest are spared. A bull-baiting is going on at Titbury, which one wonders that a person of Clorinda's imputed " wisdom and modesty" should care for; but somehow Clorinda throws off her dignity in the 45th stanza. After dinner the parson is sent for, the marriage ceremony is performed, and Robin and Clorinda return to Sherwood.

The author of this ballad ("the most beautiful and one of the oldest extant" of the series, says the editor of the collection of 1723) knew nothing of the Earl of Huntington and Matilda Fitzwater, but represents Robin Hood as the son of a forester. In everything except keeping Robin a yeoman, he writes " as the world were now but to begin, antiquity forgot, custom not known;" but poets in his day, to quote the critic of 1723, " were looked upon like other Englishmen, born to live and write with freedom."

Concerning the bull-running at Tutbury,

or Stutesbury, Staffordshire (a hideously bru-
tal custom, of long standing), a compendium of
antiquarian information is given by Gutch, II,

118. Arthur a Bradley, a rollicking ballad of
a Merry Wedding, mentioned in stanza 46, is
printed by Ritson, Robin Hood, 1795, II, 210.

---

1 KIND gentlemen, will you be patient awhile?
   Ay, and then you shall hear anon
A very good ballad of bold Robin Hood,
   And of his man, brave Little John.

2 In Locksly town, in Nottinghamshire,
   In merry sweet Locksly town,
There bold Robin Hood he was born and was
      bred,
   Bold Robin of famous renown.

3 The father of Robin a forrester was,
   And he shot in a lusty long bow,
Two north country miles and an inch at a shot,
   As the Pinder of Wakefield does know.

4 For he brought Adam Bell, and Clim of the Clugh,
   And William a Clowdesle
To shoot with our forrester for forty mark,
   And the forrester beat them all three.

5 His mother was neece to the Coventry knight,
   Which Warwickshire men call Sir Guy ;
For he slew the blue bore that hangs up at the
      gate,
   Or mine host of The Bull tells a lye.

6 Her brother was Gamwel, of Great Gamwel Hall,
   And a noble house-keeper was he,
Ay, as ever broke bread in sweet Nottinghamshire,
   And a squire of famous degree.

7 The mother of Robin said to her husband,
   My honey, my love, and my dear,
Let Robin and I ride this morning to Gamwel,
   To taste of my brothers good cheer.

8 And he said, I grant thee thy boon, gentle Joan,
   Take one of my horses, I pray ;
The sun is a rising, and therefore make haste,
   For to-morrow is Christmas-day.

9 Then Robin Hoods fathers grey gelding was
      brought,
   And sadled and bridled was he ;
God wot, a blew bonnet, his new suit of cloaths,
   And a cloak that did reach to his knee.

10 She got on her holiday kirtle and gown,
   They were of a light Lincoln green ;
The cloath was homespun, but for colour and make
   It might a beseemed our queen.

11 And then Robin got on his basket-hilt sword,
   And his dagger on his tother side,
And said, My dear mother, let 's haste to be gone,
   We have forty long miles to ride.

12 When Robin had mounted his gelding so grey,
   His father, without any trouble,
Set her up behind him, and bad her not fear,
   For his gelding had oft carried double.

13 And when she was settled, they rode to their
      neighbours,
   And drank and shook hands with them all ;
And then Robin gallopt, and never gave ore,
   Till they lighted at Gamwel Hall.

14 And now you may think the right worshipful squire
   Was joyful his sister to see ;
For he kist her and kist her, and swore a great oath,
   Thou art welcome, kind sister, to me.

15 To-morrow, when mass had been said in the chap-
      pel,
   Six tables were coverd in the hall,
And in comes the squire, and makes a short speech,
   It was, Neighbours, you 're welcome all.

16 But not a man here shall taste my March beer,
   Till a Christmas carrol he sing :
Then all clapt their hands, and they shouted and
      sung,
   Till the hall and the parlour did ring.

17 Now mustard and braun, roast beef and plumb pies,
   Were set upon every table :
And noble George Gamwel said, Eat and be merry,
   And drink too, as long as you 're able.

18 When dinner was ended, his chaplain said grace,
   And, ' Be merry, my friends,' said the squire ;
' It rains, and it blows, but call for more ale,
   And lay some more wood on the fire.

19 ' And now call ye Little John hither to me,
   For Little John is a fine lad'
At gambols and juggling, and twenty such tricks
   As shall make you merry and glad.'

20 When Little John came, to gambols they went,
   Both gentleman, yeoman and clown ;
And what do you think? Why, as true as I live,
   Bold Robin Hood put them all down.

21 And now you may think the right worshipful
     squire
     Was joyful this sight for to see ;
     For he said, Cousin Robin, thou 'st go no more
     home,
     But tarry and dwell here with me.

22 Thou shalt have my land when I dye, and till
     then
     Thou shalt be the staff of my age ;
     ' Then grant me my boon, dear uncle,' said Robin,
     ' That Little John may be my page.'

23 And he said, Kind cousin, I grant thee thy boon;
     With all my heart, so let it be;
     ' Then come hither, Little John,' said Robin Hood,
     ' Come hither, my page, unto me.

24 ' Go fetch me my bow, my longest long bow,
     And broad arrows, one, two, or three ;
     For when it is fair weather we 'll into Sherwood,
     Some merry pastime to see.'

25 When Robin Hood came into merry Sherwood,
     He winded his bugle so clear,
     And twice five and twenty good yeomen and bold
     Before Robin Hood did appear.

26 ' Where are your companions all ? ' said Robin
     Hood,
     ' For still I want forty and three ; '
     Then said a bold yeoman, Lo, yonder they stand,
     All under a green-wood tree.

27 As that word was spoke, Clorinda came by ;
     The queen of the shepherds was she ;
     And her gown was of velvet as green as the grass,
     And her buskin did reach to her knee.

28 Her gait it was graceful, her body was straight,
     And her countenance free from pride ;
     A bow in her hand, and quiver and arrows
     Hung dangling by her sweet side.

29 Her eye-brows were black, ay, and so was her
     hair,
     And her skin was as smooth as glass;
     Her visage spoke wisdom, and modesty too;
     Sets with Robin Hood such a lass !

30 Said Robin Hood, Lady fair, whither away?
     O whither, fair lady, away?
     And she made him answer, To kill a fat buck;
     For to-morrow is Titbury day.

31 Said Robin Hood, Lady fair, wander with me
     A little to yonder green bower ;
     There sit down to rest you, and you shall be sure
     Of a brace or a lease in an hour.

32 And as we were going towards the green bower,
     Two hundred good bucks we espy'd ;
     She chose out the fattest that was in the herd,
     And she shot him through side and side.

33 ' By the faith of my body,' said bold Robin Hood,
     ' I never saw woman like thee ;
     And comst thou from east, ay, or comst thou from
     west,
     Thou needst not beg venison of me.

34 ' However, along to my bower you shall go,
     And taste of a forresters meat : '
     And when we come thither, we found as good
     cheer
     As any man needs for to eat.

35 For there was hot venison, and warden pies cold,
     Cream clouted, with honey-combs plenty ;
     And the sarvitors they were, beside Little John,
     Good yeomen at least four and twenty.

36 Clorinda said, Tell me your name, gentle sir ;
     And he said, 'T is bold Robin Hood :
     Squire Gamwel 's my uncle, but all my delight
     Is to dwell in the merry Sherwood.

37 For 't is a fine life, and 't is void of all strife.
     ' So 't is, sir,' Clorinda reply'd ;
     ' But oh,' said bold Robin, ' how sweet would
     it be,
     If Clorinda would be my bride ! '

38 She blusht at the motion ; yet, after a pause
     Said, Yes, sir, and with all my heart ;
     ' Then let 's send for a priest,' said Robin Hood,
     ' And be married before we do part.'

39 But she said, It may not be so, gentle sir,
     For I must be at Titbury feast;
     And if Robin Hood will go thither with me,
     I 'll make him the most welcome guest.

40 Said Robin Hood, Reach me that buck, Little
     John,
     For I 'll go along with my dear ;
     Go bid my yeomen kill six brace of bucks,
     And meet me to-morrow just here.

41 Before we had ridden five Staffordshire miles,
     Eight yeomen, that were too bold,
     Bid Robin Hood stand, and deliver his buck ;
     A truer tale never was told.

42 ' I will not, faith ! ' said bold Robin : ' come, John,
     Stand to me, and we 'll beat em all : '
     Then both drew their swords, an so cut em and
     slasht em
     That five of them did fall.

43 The three that remain calld to Robin for quarter,
  And pitiful John beggd their lives;
When John's boon was granted, he gave them good
    counsel,
  And so sent them home to their wives.

44 This battle was fought near to Titbury town,
  When the bagpipes bated the bull;
I am king of the fidlers, and sware 't is a truth,
  And I call him that doubts it a gull.

45 For I saw them fighting, and fidld the while,
  And Clorinda sung, Hey derry down!
The bumpkins are beaten, put up thy sword, Bob,
  And now let 's dance into the town.

46 Before we came to it, we heard a strange shouting,
  And all that were in it lookd madly;
For some were a bull-back, some dancing a morris,
  And some singing Arthur-a-Bradly.

47 And there we see Thomas, our justices clerk,
  And Mary, to whom he was kind;
For Tom rode before her, and calld Mary, Madam,
  And kist her full sweetly behind.

48 And so may your worships. But we went to din-
    ner,
  With Thomas and Mary and Nan;
They all drank a health to Clorinda, and told her
  Bold Robin Hood was a fine man.

49 When dinner was ended, Sir Roger, the parson
  Of Dubbridge, was sent for in haste;

He brought his mass-book, and he bade them take
    hands,
  And he joynd them in marriage full fast.

50 And then, as bold Robin Hood and his sweet bride
  Went hand in hand to the green bower,
The birds sung with pleasure in merry Sherwood,
  And 't was a most joyful hour.

51 And when Robin came in thé sight of the bower,
  ' Where are my yeomen? ' said he;
And Little John answered, Lo, yonder they stand,
  All under the green-wood tree.

52 Then a garland they brought her, by two and by
    two,
  And plac'd them upon the bride's head;
The music struck up, and we all fell to dance,
  Till the bride and the groom were a-bed.

53 And what they did there must be counsel to me,
  Because they lay long the next day,
And I had haste home, but I got a good piece
  Of the bride-cake, and so came away.

54 Now out, alas! I had forgotten to tell ye
  That marryd they were with a ring;
And, so will Nan Knight, or be buried a maiden,
  And now let us pray for the king:

55 That he may get children, and they may get more,
  To govern and do us some good;
And then I 'll make ballads in Robin Hood's bower,
  And sing em in merry Sherwood.

———◆———

a. A new ballad of bold Robin Hood, shewing his
    Birth, Breeding, Valour and Marriage, at Tit-
    bury Bull-running: calculated for the meridian
    of Staffordshire, but may serve for Derbyshire
    or Kent.
  London, Printed by and for W. O[nley], and are
    to be sold by the booksellers. (1650–1702.)
  15¹. Morrow. 16². be sung.
  17¹. mustards, braun : *cf.* b.
  20². gentlemen, yeomen : *cf.* b. 30². Oh.
  38⁴. be merry : *cf.* b. 40³. Go *wanting* : *cf.* b.
  43⁸. good *wanting* : *cf.* b. 52¹. the brought.
  52². them at the bride's bed : *cf.* b.
b. A proper new ballad of bold Robin Hood, shewing
    his Birth, his Breeding, his Valour, *etc.*, *as above.*
  To a pleasant new northern tune.
  Printed for I. Wright, I. Clarke, W. Thackeray,
    and T. Passenger. (1670–86?)
  1², 6³, 29¹, 33³. I *for* Ay.
  2¹. And, *by mistake, for* In : in merry Nottingham-
    shire.
  3⁸. shoot. 4⁴. beat um. 5³. at that.

9⁸. Got on his. 13¹. And *wanting.* 13². drunk.
13⁴. at greát. 15¹. To-morrow. 15². ith hall.
15⁴. y're. 16². be sung. 17¹. mustard and braun.
17⁴. y' are. 18¹. this *for* his. 19⁴. you both.
20². gentleman, yeoman. 21⁴. here *wanting.*
24¹. Go and fetch my bow. 24². and *for* or.
24⁸. 'tis. 26⁴. the *for* a. 27⁴. buskins.
28⁸. quiver of. 30². O. 30⁸. him an.
30⁴. Tilbery. 34⁸. came. 38⁸. let us.
38⁴. be married. 40⁸. Go bid.
41². Six *for* Eight : too too. 42². beat um.
42⁸. slasht um. 42⁴. of the six.
43⁸. good counsel. 45⁸. Rob. 46¹. came in we.
51¹. in sight. 51⁴. a *for* the.
52¹. they. 52². upon the bride's head.
55⁴. sing um.
c. Printed by and for Alex. Milbourn, at the Station-
    ers-Arms, in Green-Arbor-Court, in the Little-
    Old-Baily. (1670–97.) *Compared only here and*
    there.
  9¹. God wot his. 30⁴. Tilbury.
  41². Eight : too too. 42⁴. of the eight. 45⁸. Bob.

150

ROBIN HOOD AND MAID MARIAN

Wood, 401, leaf 21 b.

RITSON, Robin Hood, 1795, II, 157, from Wood's copy. In none of the garlands.

The Earl of Huntington, *alias* Robin Hood, is forced by fortune's spite to part from his love Marian, and take to the green wood. Marian dresses herself "like a page," and, armed with bow, sword, and buckler, goes in quest of Robin. Both being disguised, neither recognizes the other until they have had an hour at swords, when Robin Hood, who has lost some blood, calls to his antagonist to give over and join his band. Marian knows his voice, and discovers herself. A banquet follows, and Marian remains in the wood.

Though Maid Marian and Robin Hood had perhaps been paired in popular sports, no one thought of putting more of her than her name into a ballad, until one S. S. (so the broadside is signed) composed this foolish ditty. The bare name of Maid Marian occurs in No 145 A, 9[4] and in No 147, 1[4].

Even in Barclay's fourth eclogue, written not long after 1500, where, according to Ritson,[*] the earliest notice of Maid Marian occurs, and where, he says, "she is evidently connected with Robin Hood," the two are really kept distinct; for the lusty Codrus in that eclogue wishes to hear "some mery fit of Maide Marion, *or els* of Robin Hood."

In Munday's play of The Downfall of Robert Earl of Huntington, Matilda, otherwise Marian, daughter to Lord Lacy, accompanies Earl Robert to Sherwood, upon his being outlawed for debt the very day of their troth-plight. There she lives a spotless maiden, awaiting the time when the outlawry shall be repealed and Robin may legally take her to wife. Neither the author of the play nor that of the ballad was, so far as is known, repeating any popular tradition.

The ordinary partner of Maid Marian is Friar Tuck, not Robin Hood. There is no ground for supposing that there ever were songs or tales about the Maid and Friar, notwithstanding what is cursorily said by one of the characters in Peele's Edward I:

> Why so, I see, my mates, of old
> All were not lies that *beldames told*
> Of Robin Hood and Little John,
> Friar Tuck and Maid Marian.
>   ed. Dyce, I, 133.

Translated by Anastasius Grün, p. 72, Loève-Veimars, p. 208.

---

1 A BONNY fine maid of a noble degree,
    With a hey down down a down down
    Maid Marian calld by name,
Did live in the North, of excellent worth,
    For she was a gallant dame.

2 For favour and face, and beauty most rare,
    Queen Hellen shee did excell ;
For Marian then was praisd of all men
    That did in the country dwell.

3 'T was neither Rosamond nor Jane Shore,
    Whose beauty was clear and bright,

That could surpass this country lass,
    Beloved of lord and knight.

4 The Earl of Huntington, nobly born,
    That came of noble blood,
To Marian went, with a good intent,
    By the name of Robin Hood.

5 With kisses sweet their red lips meet,
    For shee and the earl did agree ;
In every place, they kindly imbrace,
    With love and sweet unity.

---

* Robin Hood, ed. 1832, p. xxxvi, note, p. lxxxvii.

6 But fortune bearing these lovers a spight,
   That soon they were forced to part,
To the merry green wood then went Robin Hood,
   With a sad and sorrowfull heart.

7 And Marian, poor soul, was troubled in mind,
   For the absence of her friend ;
With finger in eye, shee often did cry,
   And his person did much comend.

8 Perplexed and vexed, and troubled in mind,
   Shee drest her self like a page,
And ranged the wood to find Robin Hood,
   The bravest of men in that age.

9 With quiver and bow, sword, buckler, and all,
   Thus armed was Marian most bold,
Still wandering about to find Robin out,
   Whose person was better then gold.

10 But Robin Hood, hee himself had disguisd,
   And Marian was strangly attir'd,
That they provd foes, and so fell to blowes,
   Whose vallour bold Robin admir'd.

11 They drew out their swords, and to cutting they
      went,
   At least an hour or more,
That the blood ran apace from bold Robins face,
   And Marian was wounded sore.

12 'O hold thy hand, hold thy hand,' said Robin
      Hood,
   ' And thou shalt be one of my string,
To range in the wood with bold Robin Hood,
   To hear the sweet nightingall sing.'

13 When Marian did hear the voice of her love,
   Her self shee did quickly discover,
And with kisses sweet she did him greet,
   Like to a most loyall lover.

14 When bold Robin Hood his Marian did see,
   Good lord, what clipping was there !

With kind imbraces, and jobbing of faces,
   Providing of gallant cheer.

15 For Little John took his bow in his hand,
   And wandring in the wood,
To kill the deer, and make good chear,
   For Marian and Robin Hood.

16 A stately banquet the[y] had full soon,
   All in a shaded bower,
Where venison sweet they had to eat,
   And were merry that present hour.

17 Great flaggons of wine were set on the board,
   And merrily they drunk round
Their boules of sack, to strengthen the back,
   Whilst their knees did touch the ground.

18 First Robin Hood began a health
   To Marian his onely dear,
And his yeomen all, both comly and tall,
   Did quickly bring up the rear.

19 For in a brave veine they tost off the[ir] bouls,
   Whilst thus they did remain,
And every cup, as they drunk up,
   They filled with speed again.

20 At last they ended their merryment,
   And went to walk in the wood,
Where Little John and Maid Marian
   Attended on bold Robin Hood.

21 In sollid content together they livd,
   With all their yeomen gay;
They livd by their hands, without any lands,
   And so they did many a day.

22 But now to conclude, an end I will make
   In time, as I think it good,
For the people that dwell in the North can tell
   Of Marian and bold Robin Hood.

———◆———

A Famous Battle between Robin Hood and Maid
   Marian, declaring their Love, Life, and Liberty.
   Tune, Robin Hood Reviv'd.
No printer : black-letter. S. S. at the end.
11¹. out rheir. 19¹. vente. 21³. there : wirhout.

A MS. copy in Percy's papers has in 16¹ *he had,
and in* 19¹, *in a brave venie they tost off their
bowles. It is barely possible that* venie, *which
Ritson prints, may be right.*

151

THE KING'S DISGUISE, AND FRIENDSHIP WITH ROBIN HOOD

a. Robin Hood's Garland, London, W. & C. Dicey, in St Mary Aldermary Church Yard, Bow Lane, Cheapside, n. d. (but not older than 1753), p. 76, No 25. **b.** Robin Hood's Garland, London, Printed by L. How, in Peticoat Lane, n. d. **c.** 'The King's Disguise and True Friendship with Robin Hood,' London, Printed by L. How, in Petticoat Lane, Douce Ballads, III, 113 b (not black letter). **d.** Robin Hood's Garland, London, R. Marshall, in Aldermary Church-Yard, Bow-Lane, n. d., p. 80, No 25.

Ritson, Robin Hood, 1795, II, 162, "from the common collection of Aldermary Church Yard;" Evans, Old Ballads, 1777, 1784, I, 218; Gutch, Robin Hood, II, 281, Ritson's copy "compared with one in the York edition."

The ballad is not found in a garland of 1749; but this garland has only twenty-four pieces.

The story, as far as st. 38, is a loose paraphrase, with omissions, of the seventh and eighth fits of the Gest, and seems, like the two which here follow it, " to have been written by some miserable retainer to the press, merely to eke out the book; being, in fact, a most contemptible performance: " Ritson.

12[1] may have been borrowed from Martin Parker's True Tale, No 154, 15[1]. By the clergyman who was first Robin Hood's bane, 29[1], is meant the prior of York, who in Munday's play, The Downfall of Robert Earl of Huntington, procures his outlawry. The forcing of the sheriff to give the king a supper may be the beggarly author's own invention. The last two lines are intended to serve as a link with Robin Hood and the Valiant Knight, which, however, does not immediately succeed in the garlands, Robin Hood and the Golden Arrow being interposed.

Translated by Doenniges, p. 185; A. Grün, p. 159; Loève-Veimars, p. 212.

---

1 King Richard hearing of the pranks
  Of Robin Hood and his men,
He much admir'd, and more desir'd,
  To see both him and them.

2 Then with a dozen of his lords
  To Nottingham he rode;
When he came there, he made good cheer,
  And took up his abode.

3 He having staid there some time,
  But had no hopes to speed,
He and his lords, with [free] accord,
  All put on monk's weeds.

4 From Fountain-abby they did ride,
  Down to Barnsdale;

Where Robin Hood prepar'd stood
  All company to assail.

5 The king was higher then the rest,
  And Robin thought he had
An abbot been whom he did spleen;
  To rob him he was glad.

6 He took the king's horse by the head,
  'Abbot,' says he, 'abide;
I am bound to rue such knaves as you,
  That live in pomp and pride.'

7 'But we are messengers from the king,'
  The king himself did say;
'Near to this place his royal Grace
  To speak with thee does stay.'

8 'God save the king,' said Robin Hood,
   'And all that wish him well ;
He that does deny his sovereignty,
   I wish he was in hell.'

9 'O thyself thou curses,' says the king,
   'For thou a traitor art : '
'Nay, but that you are his messenger,
   I swear you lie in heart.

10 'For I never yet hurt any man
   That honest is and true ;
But those that give their minds to live
   Upon other men's due.

11 'I never hurt the husbandman,
   That use to till the ground ;
Nor spill their blood that range the wood
   To follow hawk or hound.

12 'My chiefest spite to clergy is,
   Who in these days bear a great sway ;
With fryars and monks, with their fine sprunks,
   I make my chiefest prey.

13 'But I am very glad,' says Robin Hood,
   'That I have met you here ;
Come, before we end, you shall, my friend,
   Taste of our green-wood cheer.'

14 The king did then marvel much,
   And so did all his men ;
They thought with fear, what kind of cheer
   Robin would provide for them.

15 Robin took the king's horse by the head,
   And led him to the tent ;
'Thou would not be so usd,' quoth he,
   'But that my king thee sent.

16 'Nay, more than that,' said Robin Hood,
   'For good king Richard's sake,
If you had as much gold as ever I told,
   I would not one penny take.'

17 Then Robin set his horn to his mouth,
   And a loud blast he did blow,
Till a hundred and ten of Robin Hood's men
   Came marching all of a row.

18 And when they came bold Robin before,
   Each man did bend his knee ;
'O,' thought the king, ''t is a gallant thing,
   And a seemly sight to see.'

19 Within himself the king did say,
   These men of Robin Hood's
More humble be than mine to me ;
   So the court may learn of the woods.

20 So then they all to dinner went,
   Upon a carpet green ;
Black, yellow, red, finely minglëd,
   Most curious to be seen.

21 Venison and fowls were plenty there,
   With fish out of the river :
King Richard swore, on sea or shore,
   He neer was feasted better.

22 Then Robin takes a can of ale :
   'Come, let us now begin ;
Come, every man shall have his can ;
   Here 's a health unto the king.'

23 The king himself drank to the king,
   So round about it went ;
Two barrels of ale, both stout and stale,
   To pledge that health were spent.

24 And after that, a bowl of wine
   In his hand took Robin Hood ;
'Until I die, I 'll drink wine,' said he,
   'While I live in the green-wood.

25 'Bend all your bows,' said Robin Hood,
   'And with the grey goose wing
Such sport now shew as you would do
   In the presence of the king.'

26 They shewd such brave archery,
   By cleaving sticks and wands,
That the king did say, Such men as they
   Live not in many lands.

27 'Well, Robin Hood,' then says the king,
   'If I could thy pardon get,
To serve the king in every thing
   Wouldst thou thy mind firm set ? '

28 'Yes, with all my heart,' bold Robin said,
   So they flung off their hoods ;
To serve the king in every thing,
   They swore they would spend their bloods.

29 'For a clergyman was first my bane,
   Which makes me hate them all ;
But if you 'll be so kind to me,
   Love them again I shall.'

30 The king no longer could forbear,
   For he was movd with ruth ;
['Robin,' said he, 'I now 'tell thee
   The very naked truth.]

31 'I am the king, thy sovereign king,
   That appears before you all ; '
When Robin see that it was he,
   Strait then he down did fall.

32 'Stand up again,' then said the king,
  'I 'll thee thy pardon give ;
Stand up, my friend ; who can contend,
  When I give leave to live?'

33 So they are all gone to Nottingham,
  All shouting as they came ;
But when the people them did see,
  They thought the king was slain,

34 And for that cause the outlaws were come,
  To rule all as they list ;
And for to shun, which way to run
  The people did not wist.

35 The plowman left the plow in the fields,
  The smith ran from his shop ;
Old folks also, that scarce could go,
  Over their sticks did hop.

36 The king soon let them understand
  He had been in the green wood,
And from that day, for evermore,
  He 'd forgiven Robin Hood.

37 When the people they did hear,
  And the truth was known,
They all did sing, ' God save the king !
  Hang care, the town 's our own ! '

38 'What 's that Robin Hood ?' then said the sheriff ;
  ' That varlet I do hate ;

  Both me and mine he causd to dine,
  And servd us all with one plate.'

39 ' Ho, ho,' said Robin, ' I know what you mean ;
  Come, take your gold again ;
Be friends with me, and I with thee,
  And so with every man.

40 ' Now, master sheriff, you are paid,
  And since you are beginner,
As well as you give me my due ;
  For you neer paid for that dinner.

41 ' But if that it should please the king
  So much your house to grace
To sup with you, for to speak true,
  [I] know you neer was base.'

42 The sheriff could not [that] gain say,
  For a trick was put upon him ;
A supper was drest, the king was guest,
  But he thought 't would have undone him.

43 They are all gone to London court,
  Robin Hood, with all his train ;
He once was there a noble peer,
  And now he 's there again.

44 Many such pranks brave Robin playd
  While he lived in the green wood :
Now, my friends, attend, and hear an end
  Of honest Robin Hood.

The King's Disguise, and Friendship with Robin
  Hood.
To a Northern Tune.
a. 9¹. thyself, thyself. 9³. yon. 28⁴. spent.
29¹. ban. 30². with truth.
30³,⁴. *Supplied from R. H.'s Garland, York, Thomas*
  Wilson & Son, 1811.
b, c. 3⁸. with free. 6¹. c, livd. 9¹. O thyself thou.
13¹. said. 14⁸. that kind. 18¹. bold *wanting.*
21¹. was. 23⁴. was. 26⁴. c, Lived.
27². I [s]hould. 27⁴. would. 28². they *wanting.*
28⁴. they 'd. 29¹. ban. 30². with truth.
30³,⁴. *wanting.* 33¹. c, they 're. 34¹. was.

35¹. his plow : field. 36⁴. b, Ha'd : c, Had.
37². And that. 38⁴. b, with plate : c, in plate.
40². are the. 41¹. c, it *wanting.*
41⁴. b, I *wanting* : c, I know. 42¹. that gain say.
42⁴. it would undone. 43¹. They 're.
d. 3⁸. with one. 5⁸. he had seen. 6⁴. lives.
9¹. Thyself thou cursest said. 10⁸. who give.
14¹. king he then did. 16¹. quoth *for* said.
21⁴. never. 22⁸. And every. 23⁴. was spent.
28⁴. blood. 29¹. bane. 30². with truth.
30³,⁴. *wanting.* 31⁸. saw *for* see. 36¹. did let.
37¹. Then. 41⁴. I *wanting.* 42¹. that *wanting.*
42⁴. a guest.

152

ROBIN HOOD AND THE GOLDEN ARROW

a. Robin Hood's Garland, London, W. and C. Dicey, St Mary Aldermary Church-yard, Bow-Lane, n. d., p. 80, No 26. b. Robin Hood's Garland, London, R. Marshall, in Aldermary Church-yard, Bow-Lane, n. d., p. 84, No 26. c. Robin Hood's Garland, Preston, Printed and sold by W. Sergent, n. d.

———•———

EVANS, Old Ballads, 1777, 1784, I, 226, and Ritson, Robin Hood, 1795, II, 171, from an Aldermary garland. Gutch, II, 289, from Ritson, "compared with the York edition."

The ballad is not found in a garland of 1749.

The first twenty-three stanzas are based upon The Gest, sts 282–95. The remainder is mostly taken up with John's astute device for sending information to the sheriff. The two concluding lines are for connection with R.

H. and the Valiant Knight, which follows in some garlands, as here.

According to Martin Parker's True Tale, Robin Hood shot a letter addressed to the king into Nottingham, on an arrow-head, offering to submit upon terms: sts 78–81. Two cases of a message shot on an arrow are cited by Rochholz, Tell u. Gessler in Sage u. Geschichte, p. 28 and note.

Translated by A. Grün, p. 140.

———•———

1 WHEN as the sheriff of Nottingham
  Was come, with mickle grief,
  He talkd no good of Robin Hood,
  That strong and sturdy thief.
      Fal lal dal de

2 So unto London-road he past,
  His losses to unfold
  To King Richard, who did regard
  The tale that he had told.

3 'Why,' quoth the king, 'what shall I do?
  Art thou not sheriff for me?
  The law is in force, go take thy course
  Of them that injure thee.

4 'Go get thee gone, and by thyself
  Devise some tricking game
  For to enthral yon rebels all ;
  Go take thy course with them.'

5 So away the sheriff he returnd,
  And by the way he thought
  Of the words of the king, and how the thing
  To pass might well be brought.

6 For within his mind he imagined
  That when such matches were,
  Those outlaws stout, without [all] doubt,
  Would be the bowmen there.

7 So an arrow with a golden head
  And shaft of silver white,
  Who won the day should bear away
  For his own proper right.

8 Tidings came to brave Robin Hood,
  Under the green-wood tree :
  'Come prepare you then, my merry men,
  We 'll go yon sport to see.'

9 With that stept forth a brave young man,
  David of Doncaster :
  'Master,' said he, ' be ruld by me,
  From the green-wood we 'll not stir.

10 'To tell the truth, I 'm well informed
   Yon match is a wile ;
   The sheriff, I wiss, devises this
   Us archers to beguile.'

11 ' O thou smells of a coward,' said Robin Hood,
    ' Thy words does not please me ;
    Come on 't what will, I 'll try my skill
    At yon brave archery.'

12 O then bespoke brave Little John :
    Come, let us thither gang ;
    Come listen to me, how it shall be
    That we need not be kend.

13 Our mantles, all of Lincoln green,
    Behind us we will leave ;
    We 'll dress us all so several
    They shall not us perceive.

14 One shall wear white, another red,
    One yellow, another blue ;
    Thus in disguise, to the exercise
    We 'll gang, whateer ensue.

15 Forth from the green-wood they are gone,
    With hearts all firm and stout,
    Resolving [then] with the sheriff's men
    To have a hearty bout.

16 So themselves they mixed with the rest,
    To prevent all suspicion ;
    For if they should together hold
    They thought [it] no discretion.

17 So the sheriff looking round about,
    Amongst eight hundred men,
    But could not see the sight that he
    Had long expected then.

18 Some said, If Robin Hood was here,
    And all his men to boot,
    Sure none of them could pass these men,
    So bravely they do shoot.

19 ' Ay,' quoth the sheriff, and scratchd his head,
    ' I thought he would have been here ;
    I thought he would, but, tho he 's bold,
    He durst not now appear.'

20 O that word grieved Robin Hood to the heart ;
    He vexëd in his blood ;
    Eer long, thought he, thou shalt well see
    That here was Robin Hood.

21 Some cried, Blue jacket! another cried, Brown !
    And the third cried, Brave Yellow!
    But the fourth man said, Yon man in red
    In this place has no fellow.

22 For that was Robin Hood himself,
    For he was cloathd in red ;

At every shot the prize he got,
    For he was both sure and dead.

23 So the arrow with the golden head
    And shaft of silver white
    Brave Robin Hood won, and bore with him
    For his own proper right.

24 These outlaws there, that very day,
    To shun all kind of doubt,
    By three or four, no less no more,
    As they went in came out.

25 Until they all assembled were
    Under the green-wood shade,
    Where they report, in pleasant sport,
    What brave pastime they made.

26 Says Robin Hood, All my care is,
    How that yon sheriff may
    Know certainly that it was I
    That bore his arrow away.

27 Says Little John, My counsel good
    Did take effect before,
    So therefore now, if you 'll allow,
    I will advise once more.

28 ' Speak on, speak on,' said Robin Hood,
    ' Thy wit 's both quick and sound ;
    [I know no man amongst us can
    For wit like thee be found.']

29 ' This I advise,' said Little John ;
    ' That a letter shall be pend,
    And when it is done, to Nottingham
    You to the sheriff shall send.'

30 ' That is well advised,' said Robin Hood,
    ' But how must it be sent ? '
    ' Pugh! when you please, it 's done with ease,
    Master, be you content.

31 ' I 'll stick it on my arrow's head,
    And shoot it into the town ;
    The mark shall show where it must go,
    When ever it lights down.'

32 The project it was full performd ;
    The sheriff that letter had ;
    Which when he read, he scratchd his head,
    And rav'd like one that 's mad.

33 So we 'll leave him chafing in his grease,
    Which will do him no good ;
    Now, my friends, attend, and hear the end
    Of honest Robin Hood.

a. 12². hither. 25⁸. relate *for* report. 28³·⁴. *supplied from R. H.'s Garland, York, Thomas Wilson & Son*, 1811.

b, c. 3⁸. to take. 6⁸. without all. 10¹. the *wanting*. 10². it is. 11¹·• O *wanting*. 11². do not. 12². thither. 14⁸. in the.

15⁸. then *wanting*. 16⁴. thought it. 17⁴. suspected. 19⁸. **c**, but *wanting*. 21². a third. 22¹. **c**, bold Robin. 24². kinds. 24⁸. nor more. 25⁸. relate. 28³·⁴. *wanting*. 31⁸. must show. 32¹. well *for* full. 33¹. in the.

153

ROBIN HOOD AND THE VALIANT KNIGHT

a. Robin Hood's Garland, London, C. Dicey, Bow Church Yard, n. d., but before 1741, p. 88, Bodleian Library, Douce H H, 88. **b.** Robin Hood's Garland, 1749, without place or printer, p. 101, No 24.

c. Robin Hood's Garland, London, R. Marshall, in Aldermary Church-Yard, Bow-Lane, n. d., p. 87, No 27.

EVANS, Old Ballads, 1777, 1784, I, 232, from an Aldermary garland; Ritson, Robin Hood, 1795, II, 178, from an Aldermary garland, corrected by a York copy.

Written, perhaps, because it was thought that authority should in the end be vindicated against outlaws, which may explain why this piece surpasses in platitude everything that goes before.

Translated by Loève-Veimars, p. 219.

1 WHEN Robin Hood, and his merry men all,
    Derry, etc.
  Had reigned many years,
  The king was then told they had been too bold
  To his bishops and noble peers.
    Hey, etc.

2 Therefore they called a council of state,
  To know what was best to be done
  For to quell their pride, or else, they reply'd,
  The land would be over-run.

3 Having consulted a whole summers day,
  At length it was agreed
  That one should be sent to try the event,
  And fetch him away with speed.

4 Therefore a trusty and worthy knight
  The king was pleasd to call,
  Sir William by name; when to him he came,
  He told him his pleasure all.

5 'Go you from hence to bold Robin Hood,
  And bid him, without more a-do,
  Surrender himself, or else the proud elf
  Shall suffer with all his crew.

6 'Take here a hundred bowmen brave,
  All chosen men of might,
  Of excellent art for to take thy part,
  In glittering armour bright.'

7 Then said the knight, My sovereign liege,
  By me they shall be led;
  I'll venture my blood against bold Robin Hood,
  And bring him alive or dead.

8 One hundred men were chosen straight,
  As proper as eer men saw;
  On Midsummer-day they marched away,
  To conquer that brave outlaw.

9 With long yew bows and shining spears,
  They marchd in mickle pride,
  And never delayd, or halted, or stayd,
  Till they came to the greenwood-side.

10 Said he to his archers, Tarry here;
  Your bows make ready all,
  That, if need should be, you may follow me;
  And see you observe my call.

11 ' I 'll go in person first,' he cry'd,
    ' With the letters of my good king,
Both signd and seald, and if he will yield,
    We need not draw one string.'

12 He wanderd about till at length he came
    To the tent of Robin Hood ;
The letter he shews ; bold Robin arose,
    And there on his guard he stood.

13 ' They 'd have me surrender,' quoth bold Robin
       Hood,
    ' And lie at their mercy then ;
But tell them from me, that never shall be,
    While I have full seven-score men.'

14 Sir William the knight, both hardy and bold,
    Did offer to seize him there,
Which William Locksly by fortune did see,
    And bid him that trick forbear.

15 Then Robin Hood set his horn to his mouth,
    And blew a blast or twain,
And so did the knight, at which there in sight
    The archers came all amain.

16 Sir William with care he drew up his men,
    And plac'd them in battle array ;
Bold Robin, we find, he was not behind ;
    Now this was a bloody fray.

17 The archers on both sides bent their bows,
    And the clouds of arrows flew ;
The very first flight, that honoured knight
    Did there bid the world adieu.

18 Yet nevertheless their fight did last
    From morning till almost noon ;
Both parties were stout, and loath to give out ;
    This was on the last [day] of June.

19 At length they went off ; one part they went
    To London with right good will ;
And Robin Hood he to the green-wood tree,
    And there he was taken ill.

20 He sent for a monk, who let him blood,
    And took his life away ;
Now this being done, his archers they run,
    It was not a time to stay.

21 Some got on board and crossd the seas,
    To Flanders, France, and Spain,
And others to Rome, for fear of their doom,
    But soon returnd again.

22 Thus he that never feard bow nor spear
    Was murderd by letting of blood ;
And so, loving friends, the story doth end
    Of valiant bold Robin Hood.

23 There 's nothing remains but his epitaph now,
    Which, reader, here you have ;
To this very day, and read it you may,
    As it was upon his grave.

Robin Hood's Epitaph,
Set on his tomb
By the Prioress of Birkslay Monastery, in
Yorkshire.

Robin, Earl of Huntington,
Lies under this little stone.
No archer was like him so good ;
His wildness nam'd him Robin Hood.
Full thirteen years, and something more,
These northern parts he vexed sore.
Such outlaws as he and his men
May England never know again !

———◆———

Robin Hood and the Valiant Knight; together
    with an account of his Death and Burial, &c.
    Tune of Robin Hood and the Fifteen Foresters.
a. *Inside the cover is written, William Stukely*, 1741.
    18⁴. day *found in* b.
b. *A carelessly printed book, with only twenty-four*
    ballads. It belonged to Bishop Percy. Burden
    omitted.
    1¹. When bold Robin and.   1³. had been told he.
    1⁴. With his.   2¹. the best.   2⁴. will be.
    3. *wanting.*   6¹. Take an.   6³. art to.
    7³. again Robin.   12¹. till at last.   12². of bold.
    13¹. would have : bold, Hood, *wanting.*
    13³. that it.   13⁴. Whilst.   15¹. Robin he set.

17⁴. there *wanting.*   18¹. the fight.   18⁴. last day.
19². For London.   19³. he *wanting.*   20¹. to let.
20². done away they ran.   21. *wanting.*
22¹. that neither.   24³. it *wanting.*   24⁴. it were.
The epitaph is not given.
c. *Burden :* Derry down down : Hey down derry
    derry down.
    1³. that they had been bold.   2². best *wanting.*
    5¹. Go you.   6¹. an.   7³. bold *wanting.*
    10⁴. see that.   11³. Well signd.
    14⁴. bid them : to forbear.   18⁴. day *wanting.*
    19¹. party.   19². For London.   20¹. to let.
    20². Who took.   20⁴. a *wanting.*   21¹. Some went.
    23³. and *wanting.*

154

A TRUE TALE OF ROBIN HOOD

MARTIN PARKER'S True Tale of Robin Hood was entered to Francis Grove the 29th of February, 1632: Stationers' Registers, Arber, IV, 273. A copy in the British Museum (press-mark C. 39. a. 52), which is here reprinted, is assumed by Mr W. C. Hazlitt, Handbook, p. 439, and Mr George Bullen, Brit. Mus. Catalogue, to be of this first edition. The title of this copy is: A True Tale of Robbin [Hood], or, A briefe touch of the life and death o[f that] Renowned Outlaw, Robert Earle of Huntin[gton] vulgarly called Robbin Hood, who lived and died in [A. D.] 1198, being the 9. yeare of the reigne of King Ric[hard] the first, commonly called Richard Cuer de Lyon. Carefully collected out of the truest Writers of our English C[hroni]cles. And published for the satisfaction of those who desire to s[ee] Truth purged from falsehood. By Martin Parker. Printed at London for T. Cotes, and are to be sold by F. Grove dwellin[g] upon Snow-hill, neare the Saracen[s head].*

Martin Parker professes in st. 117 to follow chronicles, not "fained tales." Perhaps he regards broadside-ballads with historical names in them as chronicles: at any rate, though he reports some things which are found in Grafton, and in Major as cited by Grafton, much the larger part of his True Tale is now to be found only in ballads. When he does not agree with ballads which have come down to us, he may have used earlier copies, or he may have invented. The story of the abbot in 23–26 is at least from the same source as Robin Hood and the Bishop; the plundering of King Richard's receivers in 33 is evidently the same event as that referred to in the first stanza of Robin Hood and Queen Katherine; Robin Hood is said to have built eight almshouses in 71, and one in the last stanza of The Noble Fisherman. The Gest could hardly have been unknown to Parker. Stanzas 3–9, concerning Robin's rank, prodigality, and outlawry, may have been based upon Munday's play; but nothing is said of Maid Marian. 44–50 and 56–65 may report the substance of some lost broadside.

Perhaps Parker calls his compilation a *True* Tale because a tale of Robin Hood was a proverb for an incredible story: "Tales of Robin Hood are good for fools."

---

1 BOTH gentlemen, or yeomen bould,
  Or whatsoever you are,
To have a stately story tould,
  Attention now prepare.

2 It is a tale of Robin Hood,
  Which I to you will tell,

Which being rightly understood,
  I know will please you well.

3 This Robbin, so much talked on,
  Was once a man of fame,
Instiled Earle of Huntington,
  Lord Robert Hood by name.

---

* The mutilated parts are supplied, to a slight extent, from a copy in the Bodleian Library (L. 78. Art., 5th tract), which happens to be injured on the right side of the title-page in nearly the same places as the Museum copy, and also has the lower portion cut off, to the loss of the printer's name; the rest from an edition printed for J. Clark, W. Thackeray, and T. Passinger, 1686. Mr J. P. Collier possessed a copy with the same imprint as that of the Museum, which he lent Gutch, and which Gutch says he used for his text. If Gutch followed the Collier copy, then that was not identical with the Museum copy. Ritson reprinted the text of 1686.

4 In courtship and magnificence,
   His carriage won him prayse,
And greater favour with his prince
   Than any in his dayes.

5 In bounteous liberality
   He too much did excell,
And loved men of quality
   More than exceeding well.

6 His great revennues all he sould
   For wine and costly cheere;
He kept three hundred bowmen bold,
   He shooting lovd so deare.

7 No archer living in his time
   With him might well compare ;
He practisd all his youthfull prime
   That exercise most rare.

8 At last, by his profuse expence,
   He had consumd his wealth,
And being outlawed by his prince,
   In woods he livd by stealth.

9 The abbot of *Saint* Maries rich,
   To whom he mony ought,
His hatred to this earle was such
   That he his downefall wrought.

10 So being outlawed, as 't is told,
   He with a crew went forth
Of lusty cutters, stout and bold,
   And robbed in the North.

11 Among the rest, one Little John,
   A yeoman bold and free,
Who could, if it stood him upon,
   With ease encounter three.

12 One hundred men in all he got,
   With whom, the story sayes,
Three hundred common men durst not
   Hold combate any wayes.

13 They Yorkshire woods frequented much,
   And Lancashire also,
Wherein their practises were such
   That they wrought mickle woe.

14 None rich durst travell to and fro,
   Though nere so strongly armd,
But by these theeves, so strong in show,
   They still were robd and harmd.

15 His chiefest spight to the clergie was,
   That lived in monstrous pride ;
No one of them he would let passe
   Along the high-way side,

16 But first they must to dinner goe,
   And afterwards to shrift :
Full many a one he served so,
   Thus while he livd by theft.

17 No monkes nor fryers he would let goe,
   Without paying their fees :
If they thought much to be usd so,
   Their stones he made them leese.

18 For such as they the country filld
   With bastards in those dayes ;
Which to prevent, these sparkes did geld
   All that came by their wayes.

19 But Robbin Hood so gentle was,
   And bore so brave a minde,
If any in distresse did passe,
   To them he was so kinde

20 That he would give and lend to them,
   To helpe them at their neede :
This made all poore men pray for him,
   And wish he well might speede.

21 The widdow and the fatherlesse
   He would send meanes unto,
And those whom famine did oppresse
   Found him a friendly foe.

22 Nor would he doe a woman wrong,
   But see her safe conveid ;
He would protect with power strong
   All those who crav'd his ayde.

23 The abbot of Saint Maries then,
   Who him undid before,
Was riding with two hundred men,
   And gold and silver store.

24 But Robbin Hood upon him set
   With his couragious sparkes,
And all the coyne perforce did get,
   Which was twelve thousand markes.

25 He bound the abbot to a tree,
   And would not let him passe
Before that to his men and he
   His lordship had sayd masse.

26 Which being done, upon his horse
   He set him fast astride,
And with his face towards his ar—
   He forced him to ride.

27 His men were faine to be his guide,
   For he rode backward home ;
The abbot, being thus villifide,
   Did sorely chafe and fume.

28 Thus Robbin Hood did vindicate
    His former wrongs receivd ;
 For 't was this covetous prelate
    That him of land bereavd.

29 The abbot he rode to the king
    With all the haste he could,
 And to his Grace he every thing
    Exactly did unfold.

30 And sayd if that no course were tane,
    By force or stratagem,
 To take this rebell and his traine,
    No man should passe for them.

31 The king protested by and by
    Unto the abbot then
 That Robbin Hood with speed should dye,
    With all his merry men.

32 But ere the king did any send,
    He did another feate,
 Which did his Grace much more offend ;
    The fact indeed was great.

33 For in a short time after that,
    The kings receivers went
 Towards London with the coyne they got,
    For 's Highnesse northerne rent.

34 Bold Robbin Hood and Little John,
    With the rest of their traine,
 Not dreading law, set them upon,
    And did their gold obtaine.

35 The king much moved at the same,
    And the abbots talke also,
 In this his anger did proclaime,
    And sent word to and fro,

36 That whosoere, alive or dead,
    Could bring him Robbin Hood,
 Should have one thousand markes, well payd
    In gold and silver good.

37 This promise of the king did make
    Full many yeomen bold
 Attempt stout Robbin Hood to take,
    With all the force they could.

38 But still when any came to him,
    Within the gay greene wood,
 He entertainement gave to them,
    With venison fat and good.

39 And shewd to them such martiall sport,
    With his long bow and arrow,
 That they of him did give report,
    How that it was great sorow,

40 That such a worthy man as he
    Should thus be put to shift,
 Being late a lord of high degree,
    Of living quite bereft.

41 The king, to take him, more and more
    Sent men of mickle might,
 But he and his still beate them sore,
    And conquered them in fight.

42 Or else, with love and courtesie,
    To him he won their hearts :
 Thus still he lived by robbery,
    Throughout the northerne parts.

43 And all the country stood in dread
    Of Robbin Hood and 's men ;
 For stouter lads nere livd by bread,
    In those dayes nor since then.

44 The abbot which before I nam'd
    Sought all the meanes he could
 To have by force this rebell tane,
    And his adherents bold.

45 Therefore he armd five hundred men,
    With furniture compleate,
 But the outlawes slew halfe of them,
    And made the rest retreate.

46 The long bow and the arrow keene
    They were so usd unto
 That still they kept the forest greene,
    In spight o th' proudest foe.

47 Twelve of the abbots men he tooke,
    Who came him to have tane,
 When all the rest the field forsooke ;
    These he did entertaine

48 With banquetting and merriment,
    And, having usd them well,
 He to their lord them safely sent,
    And willd them him to tell

49 That if he would be pleasd at last
    To beg of our good king
 That he might pardon what was past,
    And him to favour bring,

50 He would surrender backe agen
    The money which before
 Was taken by him and his men,
    From him and many more.

51 Poore men might safely passe by him,
    And some that way would chuse,
 For well they knew that to helpe them
    He evermore did use.

52 But where he knew a miser rich,
　　That did the poore oppresse,
　To feele his coyne his hand did itch ;
　　Hee 'de have it, more or lesse.

53 And sometimes, when the high-way fayld,
　　Then he his courage rouses ;
　He and his men have oft assayld
　　Such rich men in their houses.

54 So that, through dread of Robbin then
　　And his adventurous crew,
　The mizers kept great store of men,
　　Which else maintaynd but few.

55 King Richard, of that name the first,
　　Sirnamed Cuer de Lyon,
　Went to defeate the Pagans curst,
　　Who kept the coasts of Syon.

56 The Bishop of Ely, chancelor,
　　Was left as vice-roy here,
　Who like a potent emperor
　　Did proudly domminere.

57 Our chronicles of him report
　　That commonly he rode
　With a thousand horse from court to court,
　　Where he would make abode.

58 He, riding downe towards the north,
　　With his aforesayd traine,
　Robbin and his did issue forth,
　　Them all to entertaine.

59 And, with the gallant gray-goose wing,
　　They shewed to them such play,
　That made their horses kicke and fling,
　　And downe their riders lay.

60 Full glad and faine the bishop was,
　　For all his thousand men,
　To seeke what meanes he could to passe
　　From out of Robbins ken.

61 Two hundred of his men were kil'd,
　　And fourescore horses good ;
　Thirty, who did as captives yeeld,
　　Were carryed to the greene wood.

62 Which afterwards were ransomed,
　　For twenty markes a man ;
　The rest set spurres to horse, and fled
　　To th' town of Warrington.

63 The bishop, sore enraged then,
　　Did, in King Richards name,
　Muster a power of northerne men,
　　These outlawes bold to tame.

64 But Robbin, with his courtesie,
　　So wonne the meaner sort,
　That they were loath on him to try
　　What rigor did import.

65 So that bold Robbin and his traine
　　Did live unhurt of them,
　Vntill King Richard came againe
　　From faire Jerusalem.

66 And then the talke of Robbin Hood
　　His royall eares did fill ;
　His Grace admir'd that ith' greene wood
　　He thus continued still.

67 So that the country farre and neare
　　Did give him great applause ;
　For none of them neede stand in feare,
　　But such as broke the lawes.

68 He wished well unto the king,
　　And prayed still for his health,
　And never practised any thing
　　Against the common wealth.

69 Onely, because he was undone
　　By th' crewell clergie then,
　All meanes that he could thinke upon
　　To vexe such kinde of men

70 He enterprized, with hatefull spleene ;
　　In which he was to blame,
　For fault of some, to wreeke his teene
　　On all that by him came.

71 With wealth which he by robbery got
　　Eight almes-houses he built,
　Thinking thereby to purge the blot
　　Of blood which he had spilt.

72 Such was their blinde devotion then,
　　Depending on their workes ;
　Which, if 't were true, we Christian men
　　Inferiour were to Turkes.

73 But, to speake true of Robbin Hood,
　　And wrong him not a iot,
　He never would shed any mans blood
　　That him invaded not.

74 Nor would he iniure husbandmen,
　　That toyld at cart and plough ;
　For well he knew, were 't not for them,
　　To live no man knew how.

75 The king in person, with some lords,
　　To Notingham did ride,
　To try what strength and skill affords
　　To crush these outlawes pride.

76 And, as he once before had done,
 He did againe proclaime,
 That whosoere would take upon
 To bring to Notingham,

77 Or any place within the land,
 Rebellious Robbin Hood,
 Should be preferd in place to stand
 With those of noble blood.

78 When Robbin Hood heard of the same,
 Within a little space,
 Into the towne of Notingham
 A letter to his Grace

79 He shot upon an arrow-head,
 One evening cunningly ;
 Which was brought to the king, and read
 Before his Maiestie.

80 The tennour of this letter was
 That Robbin would submit,
 And be true leigeman to his Grace,
 In any thing that 's fit,

81 So that his Highnesse would forgive
 Him and his merry men all ;
 If not, he must i th' greene wood live,
 And take what chance did fall.

82 The king would faine have pardoned him,
 But that some lords did say,
 This president will much condemne
 Your Grace another day.

83 While that the king and lords did stay
 Debating on this thing,
 Some of these outlawes fled away
 Unto the Scottish king.

84 For they supposd, if he were tane,
 Or to the king did yeeld,
 By th' commons all the rest on 's traine
 Full quickely would be quelld.

85 Of more than full a hundred men
 But forty tarryed still,
 Who were resolvd to sticke to him,
 Let fortune worke her will.

86 If none had fled, all for his sake
 Had got their pardon free ;
 The king to favour meant to take
 His merry men and he.

87 But ere the pardon to him came,
 This famous archer dy'd :
 His death, and manner of the same,
 I 'le presently describe.

88 For, being vext to thinke upon
 His followers revolt,
 In melancholly passion
 He did recount their fault.

89 ' Perfideous traytors ! ' sayd he then,
 ' In all your dangers past
 Have I you guarded as my men
 To leave me thus at last ? '

90 This sad perplexity did cause
 A fever, as some say,
 Which him unto confusion drawes,
 Though by a stranger way.

91 This deadly danger to prevent,
 He hide him with all speede
 Vnto a nunnery, with intent
 For his healths sake to bleede.

92 A faithlesse fryer did pretend
 In love to let him blood ;
 But he by falshood wrought the end
 Of famous Robbin Hood.

93 The fryer, as some say, did this
 To vindicate the wrong
 Which to the clergie he and his
 Had done by power strong.

94 Thus dyed he by trechery,
 That could not dye by force ;
 Had he livd longer, certainely,
 King Richard, in remorse,

95 Had unto favour him receavd ;
 He brave men elevated ;
 'T is pitty he was of life bereavd
 By one which he so hated.

96 A treacherous leech this fryer was,
 To let him bleed to death ;
 And Robbin was, me thinkes, an asse,
 To trust him with his breath.

97 His corpes the priores of the place,
 The next day that he dy'd,
 Caused to be buried, in mean case,
 Close by the high-way side.

98 And over him she caused a stone
 To be fixed on the ground ;
 An epitaph was set thereon,
 Wherein his name was found.

99 The date o th' yeare, and day also,
 Shee made to be set there,
 That all who by the way did goe
 Might see it plaine appeare

100 That such a man as Robbin Hood
    Was buried in that place ;
  And how he lived in the greene wood,
    And robd there for a space.

101 It seemes that though the clergie he
    Had put to mickle woe,
  He should not quite forgotten be,
    Although he was their foe.

102 This woman, though she did him hate,
    Yet loved his memory ;
  And thought it wondrous pitty that
    His fame should with him dye.

103 This epitaph, as records tell,
    Within this hundred yeares
  By many was discerned well,
    But time all things outweares.

104 His followers, when he was dead,
    Were some received to grace ;
  The rest to forraigne countries fled,
    And left their native place.

105 Although his funerall was but meane,
    This woman had in minde
  Least his fame should be buried cleane
    From those that came behind.

106 For certainely, before nor since,
    No man ere understood,
  Vnder the reigne of any prince,
    Of one like Robbin Hood.

107 Full thirteene yeares, and something more,
    These outlawes lived thus,
  Feared of the rich, loved of the poore,
    A thing most marvelous.

108 A thing impossible to us
    This story seemes to be ;
  None dares be now so venturous ;
    But times are chang'd, we see.

109 We that live in these latter dayes
    Of civill government,
  If neede be, have a hundred wayes
    Such outlawes to prevent.

110 In those dayes men more barbarous were,
    And lived lesse in awe ;

Now, God be thanked ! people feare
    More to offend the law.

111 No roaring guns were then in use,
    They dreampt of no such thing ;
  Our English men in fight did chuse
    The gallant gray-goose wing.

112 In which activity these men,
    Through practise, were so good,
  That in those dayes non equald them,
    Specially Robbin Hood.

113 So that, it seemes, keeping in caves,
    In woods and forrests thicke,
  Thei 'd beate a multitude with staves,
    Their arrowes did so pricke.

114 And none durst neare unto them come,
    Unlesse in courtesie ;
  All such he bravely would send home,
    With mirth and iollity.

115 Which courtesie won him such love,
    As I before have told ;
  'T was the cheefe cause that he did prove
    More prosperous than he could.

116 Let us be thankefull for these times
    Of plenty, truth and peace,
  And leave our great and horrid crimes,
    Least they cause this to cease.

117 I know there 's many fained tales
    Of Robbin Hood and 's crew ;
  But chronicles, which seldome fayles,
    Reports this to be true.

118 Let none then thinke this a lye,
    For, if 't were put to th' worst,
  They may the truth of all discry
    I th' raigne of Richard the first.

119 If any reader please to try,
    As I direction show,
  The truth of this brave history,
    Hee 'l finde it true I know.

120 And I shall thinke my labour well
    Bestowed, to purpose good,
  When 't shall be sayd that I did tell
    True tales of Robbin Hood.

At the end of the Tale:

The Epitaph which the Prioresse of the Monastery of Kirkes Lay in Yorke-shire set over Robbin Hood, which, as is before mentioned, was to bee reade within these hundreth yeares, though in old broken English, much to the same sence and meaning.

Decembris quarto die, 1198: anno regni Richardii Primi 9.

Robert Earle of Huntington
Lies under this little stone.
No archer was like him so good :
His wildnesse named him Robbin Hood.
Full thirteene yeares, and something more,
These northerne parts he vexed sore.

Such out-lawes as he and his men
May England never know agen.

Some other superstitious words were in it, which I thought fit to leave out.*

Bodl. L. 78. 2^2. That *for* which. 20^4. wisht.
59^8. kicke *for* kickle. 70^2. In *for* For.
94^2. Who *for* That.
108^1. impossible *for* unpossible. 116^8. our *for* out.

* "Now, under this precise gentleman's favor, one would be glad to know what these same superstitious words were; there not being anything of the kind in Dr Gale's copy, which seems to be the original, and which is shorter by two lines than the above.   Thirteen should be thirty."   Ritson, Robin Hood, ed. 1832, II, 127 f.   For the epitaph and the gravestone, see the same volume, pp. liv–lvii.

155

SIR HUGH, OR, THE JEW'S DAUGHTER

A. 'Hugh of Lincoln,' Jamieson's Popular Ballads, I, 151.

B. 'The Jew's Daughter,' Percy's Reliques, 1765, I, 32.

C. 'The Jewis Daughter,' Bishop Percy's Papers.

D. 'Sir Hugh,' Herd's MSS, I, 213; stanzas 7–10, II, 219.   Herd's Scottish Songs, 1776, I, 96.

E. 'Sir Hugh, or, The Jew's Daughter,' Motherwell's Minstrelsy, p. 51.

F. A. Hume, Sir Hugh of Lincoln, p. 35.

G. From the recitation of an American lady.

H. 'The Jew's Daughter,' from the recitation of an American lady.

I. Sir Egerton Brydges, Restituta, I, 381.

J. 'Sir Hugh.'   **a.** Notes and Queries, First Series, XII, 496.   **b.** The same, VIII, 614.

K. Notes and Queries, First Series, IX, 320 ; Salopian

Shreds and Patches, in Miss C. S. Burne's Shropshire Folk-Lore, p. 539.

L. a. Communicated by the Rev. E. Venables.   **b.** A Walk through Lincoln Cathedral, by the same, p. 41.

M. F. H. Groome, In Gipsy Tents, Edinburgh, 1880, p. 145.

N. 'Little Harry Hughes and the Duke's Daughter,' Newell, Games and Songs of American Children, p. 75.

O. G. A. Sala, Illustrated London News, LXXXI, 415, October 21, 1882, and Living London, 1883, p. 465.

P. Halliwell, Ballads and Poems respecting Hugh of Lincoln, p. 37, Popular Rhymes and Nursery Tales, p. 192 : two stanzas.

Q. 'The Jew's Daughter,' Motherwell's Note-Book, p. 54 : two stanzas.

R. 'Sir Hew, or, The Jew's Daughter,' Motherwell's Minstrelsy, Appendix, p. xvii, VII : one stanza.

THE copy in Pinkerton's Tragic Ballads, 1781, p. 50, is made up of eight stanzas of D and six of B, slightly retouched by the editor; that in Gilchrist's collection, 1815, I, 210, is eight stanzas of D and nine of A; that in Stenhouse's edition of Johnson's Museum, IV, 500, "communicated by an intelligent antiquarian correspondent," is compounded from A, B, D, E and Pinkerton, with a little chaff of its own; that printed by W. C. Atkinson, of Brigg, Lincolnshire, in the London Athenæum, 1867, p. 96, is Pinkerton's, with two trifling changes. Allen, History of the County of Lincoln, 1834, p. 171 (repeating Wilde, Lincoln Cathedral, 1819, p. 27, as appears from Notes and Queries, 4th Series, II, 60), says that a complete manuscript of the ballad was once in the library of the cathedral, and cites the first stanza, which differs from Pinkerton's only in having " Mary Lincoln " for " merry Lincoln."

The several versions agree in the outline of the story, and in many of the details. According to A, boys who are playing football are joined by Sir Hugh, who kicks the ball through the Jew's window. Sir Hugh sees the Jew's daughter looking out of the window, and asks her to throw down the ball. She tells him to come and get it; this he is afraid to do, for fear she may do to him " as she did to his father." The Jew's daughter entices him in with an apple, leads him through nine dark doors, lays him on a table, and sticks him like a swine; then rolls him in a cake of lead, and throws him into a draw-well fifty fathoms deep, Our Lady's draw-well. The boy not returning at eve, his mother sets forth to seek him; goes to the Jew's castle, the Jew's garden, and to the draw-well, entreating in each case Sir Hugh to speak. He answers from the well, bidding his mother go make his winding-sheet, and he will meet her at the back of merry Lincoln the next morning. His mother makes his winding-sheet, and the dead corpse meets her at the back of merry Lincoln: all the bells of Lincoln are rung without men's hands, and all the books of Lincoln are read without man's tongue.

The boy's name is Sir Hugh in A-F, etc.;

in K the name is corrupted to Saluter, and in the singular and interesting copy obtained in New York, N, to Harry Hughes, the Jew's Daughter in this becoming the Duke's Daughter. The place is Merry Lincoln in A, D, L (Lincoln, J; Lincolnshire, Q); corrupted in B, C, to Mirryland town,* in E to Maitland town; changed to Merry Scotland, I, J, O, which is corrupted to Merrycock land, K; in G, H, old Scotland, fair Scotland. The ball is tossed [patted] into the Jew's garden, G, H, I, L, M, O, P, where the Jews are sitting a-row, I, O. The boy will not come in without his play-feres, B, C, D, F, G, I, J, K; if he should go in, his mother would cause his heart's blood to fall, etc., G, I, K.† The boy is rolled in a cake [case] of lead, A-E (L, b?); in a quire of tin, N. The draw-well is Our Lady's only in A (L, b?); it is the Jew's in C, D; it is a [the] deep draw-well, simply, in B, E, F, G; a little draw-well, N, a well, O; fifty fathoms deep, A-F, N; G, eighteen fathoms, O, five and fifty feet. In G, the Jew's daughter lays the Bible at the boy's head, and the Prayer-Book at his feet (how came these in the Jew's house?) before she sticks him; in I, K, the Bible and Testament after; in I, the Catechism in his heart's blood. In H, the boy, at the moment of his death, asks that the Bible may be put at his head, and the Testament at his feet, and in M, wants " a seven-foot Bible " at his head and feet. In E, F, the boy makes this request from the draw-well ("and pen and ink at every side," E), and in N with the variation that his Bible is to be put at his head, his " busker " at his feet, and his Prayer-Book at his right side. In O there is a jumble:

' Oh lay a Bible at my head,
　　And a Prayer-Book at my feet,
　In the well that they did throw me in,' etc.

* Percy : " As for Mirryland Town, it is probably a corruption of Milan (called by the Dutch Meylandt) town ; the Pa is evidently the river Po, although the Adige, not the Po, runs through Milan." B¹ is unintelligible. Do the lads run down the Pa ?

† In J, 4, he will be beaten for losing his ball. In the Irish F, 8, the mother takes a little rod in her hand, meaning to bate him for staying so long: cf. J 10, N 4, 12, and the last verse of T. Hood's ' Lost Heir.'

The boy asks his mother to go and make ready his winding-sheet in A, B, C, E, F; and appoints to meet her at the back of the town, A, B, E; at the birks of Mirryland town, C.

The fine trait of the ringing of the bells without men's hands, and the reading of the books without man's tongue, occurs only in A. When Florence of Rome approached a church, " the bellys range thorow Godys grace, withowtyn helpe of hande:" Le Bone Florence of Rome, Ritson, Met. Rom., III, 80, v. 1894 f. Bells which ring without men's hands are very common in popular tradition. See Jamieson's Popular Ballads, I, 140 ; Wunderhorn, II, 272, ed. 1808; Luzel, C. P. de la Basse-Bretagne, I, 446 f., 496 f., II, 44 f., 66 f., 308 f., 542 f.; Maurer, Isländische Volkssagen, p. 215; Weckenstedt, Wendische Sagen, p. 379, No 5; Temme, Volkssagen der Altmark, p. 29, No 31; Münsterische Geschichten, u. s. w., p. 186; Bartsch, Sagen aus Meklenburg, I, 390, No 539; Mone's Anzeiger, VIII, 303 f., No 41 and note, and VII, 32; Birlinger, Aus Schwaben, Neue Sammlung, I, 72; Birlinger u. Buck, I, 144, No 223, 145, No 225, a, b, c; Schöppner, Sagenbuch der bayerischen Lande, I, 294, No 301, etc.*

The story of Hugh of Lincoln is told in the Annals of Waverley, under the year 1255, by a contemporary writer, to this effect.† A boy in Lincoln, named Hugh, was crucified by the Jews in contempt of Christ, with various preliminary tortures. To conceal the act from Christians, the body, when taken from the cross, was thrown into a running stream; but the water would not endure the wrong done its maker, and immediately ejected it upon dry land. The body was then buried in the earth, but was found above ground the next day. The guilty parties were now very much frightened and quite at their wit's end; as a last resort they threw the corpse into a drinking-well. Thereupon the whole place was filled with so brilliant a light and so sweet an odor that it was clear to everybody that there must be something holy and prodigious in the well. The body was seen floating on the water, and, upon its being drawn up, the hands and feet were found to be pierced, the head had, as it were, a crown of bloody points, and there were various other wounds: from all which it was plain that this was the work of the abominable Jews. A blind woman, touching the bier on which the blessed martyr's corpse was carrying to the church, received her sight, and many other miracles followed. Eighteen Jews, convicted of the crime, and confessing it with their own mouth, were hanged.

Matthew Paris, also writing contemporaneously, supplies additional circumstances, one of which, the mother's finding of the child, is prominent in the ballad.‡ The Jews of Lincoln stole the boy Hugh, who was some eight years old, near Peter and Paul's day, June 29, and fed him properly for ten days, while they were sending to all parts of England to convoke their co-believers to a crucifixion of him in contempt of Jesus. When they were assembled, one of the Lincoln Jews was appointed judge, a Pilate, as it were, and the boy was sentenced to various torments; he was scourged till the blood ran, crowned with thorns, spit upon, pricked with knives, made to drink gall, mocked and scoffed at, hailed as false prophet; finally he was crucified, and a lance thrust into his heart. He was then taken down and disembowelled; for what reason is not known, but, as it was said, for magical purposes. The mother (whose name, not given by this chronicler, is known to have been Beatrice) made diligent search for her lost child for several days, and was told by her neighbors that they had seen the boy playing with Jewish children, and going into

* Dem Volke war die Glocke nicht herzlos ; sie war ihm eine beseelte Persönlichkeit, und stand als solche mit dem Menschen in lebendigem Verkehr. . . . Die Glocken . . . scheinen auch von höheren Mächten berührt zu werden; sie sprechen wie Gottesstimmen, ertönen oft von selbst, als Mahnung von oben, als Botschaft vom Tode bedeutender Personen, als Wahrzeichen der Unschuld eines Angeklagten, zur Bewährung der Heiligkeit eines von Gott erwählten Rüstzeugs. Uhland, Schriften zur Geschichte der Dichtung u. Sage, VIII, 588 f.

† Annales Monastici, ed. Luard, II, 346 ff. "From 1219 to 1266 the MS. was written contemporaneously with the events described, from year to year:" p. xxxvi.

‡ Chronica Majora, ed. Luard, V, 516–19. Matthew Paris died in 1259.

a Jew's house. This house the mother entered, and saw the boy's body, which had been thrown into a well. The town officers were sent for, and drew up the corpse. The mother's shrieks drew a great concourse to the place, among whom was Sir John of Lexington, a long-headed and scholarly man (a priest of the cathedral), who declared that he had heard of the Jews doing such things before. Laying hands on the Jew into whose house the boy had been known to go, John of Lexington told him that all the gold in England would not buy him off; nevertheless, life and limb should be safe if he would tell everything. The Jew, Copin by name, encouraged and urged by Sir John, made a full confession: all that the Christians had said was true; the Jews crucified a boy every year, if they could get hold of one, and had crucified this Hugh; they had wished to bury the body, after they had come to the conclusion that an innocent's bowels were of no use for divination, but the earth would not hold it; so they had thrown it into a well, but with no better success, for the mother had found it, and reported the fact to the officers. The canons of Lincoln Cathedral begged the child's body, and buried it in their church with the honors due to so precious a martyr. The king, who had been absent in the North, being made acquainted with these circumstances, blamed Sir John for the promise which he had so improperly made the wretch Copin. But Copin was still in custody, and, seeing he had no chance for life, he volunteered to complete his testimony! almost all the Jews in England had been accessory to the child's death, and almost every city of England where Jews lived had sent delegates to the ceremony of his immolation, as to a Paschal sacrifice. Copin was then tied to a horse, and dragged to the gallows, and ninety-one other Jews carried to London and imprisoned. The inquisition made by the king's justices showed that the crime had been virtually the common act of the Jews of England, and the mother's appeal to the king, which was pressed unremittingly, had such effect that on St Clement's day eighteen of the richer and more considerable Jews

of Lincoln were hanged on gallows specially constructed for the purpose, more than sixty being reserved for a like sentence in the tower of London.*

The Annals of Burton give a long report of this case, which is perhaps contemporary, though the MS. is mostly of the next century. On the last day of July, at a time when all the principal Jews of England were collected at Lincoln, Hugh, a school-boy (*scholaris*) of nine, the only son of a poor woman, was kidnapped towards sunset, while playing with his comrades, by Jopin, a Jew of that place. He was concealed in Jopin's house six and twenty days, getting so little to eat and drink that he had hardly the strength to speak. Then, at a council of all the Jews, resident and other, it was determined that he should be put to death. They stripped him, flogged him, spat in his face, cut off the cartilage of the nose and the upper lip, and broke the main upper teeth; then crucified him. The boy, fortified by divine grace, maintained himself with cheerfulness, and uttered neither complaint nor groan. They ran sharp points into him from the sole of his foot to the crown of his head, till the body was covered with the blood from these wounds, then pierced his side with a lance, and he gave up the ghost. The boy not coming home as usual, his mother made search for him. As he was not found, the information given by his playmates as to when and where they had last seen him roused a strong suspicion among the Christians that he had been carried off and killed by the Jews; all the more because there were so many of them present in the town at that time, and from all parts of the kingdom, though the Jews pretended that the occasion for this unusual congregation was a grand wedding. The truth becoming every day clearer, the mother set off for Scotland, where the king then chanced to be, and laid the complaint at his feet. The Jews, meanwhile, knowing that the business would be

---

* Seventy-one were thus reserved, but escaped, by the use of money or by the intercession of the Franciscans, or both. See the same volume, p. 546; but also the account which follows, from the Annals of Burton.

looked into, were in great consternation; they took away the body in the night, and threw it into a well. In the well it was found in the course of an inquisition ordered by the king, and, when it was drawn out, a woman, blind for fifteen years, who had been very fond of the boy, laid her hand on the body in faith, exclaiming, Alas, sweet little Hugh, that it so happened! and then rubbed her eyes with the moisture of the body, and at once recovered her sight. The miracle drew crowds of people to the spot, and every sick or infirm person that could get near the body went home well and happy: hearing whereof, the dean and canons of the cathedral went out in procession to the body of the holy martyr, and carried it to the minster with all possible ceremony, where they buried it very honorably (disregarding the passionate protests of a brother canon, of the parish to which the boy belonged, who would fain have retained so precious, and also valuable, an object within his own bounds). The king stopped at Lincoln, on his way down from Scotland, looked into the matter, found the charges against the Jews to be substantiated, and ordered an arrest of the whole pack. They shut themselves up in their houses, but their houses were stormed. In the course of the examination which followed, John of Lessington promised Jopin, the head of the Jews, and their priest (who was believed to be at the bottom of the whole transaction), that he would do all he could to save his life, if Jopin would give up the facts. Jopin, delighted at this assurance, and expecting to be able to save the other Jews by the use of money, confessed everything. But considering what a disgrace it would be to the king's majesty if the deviser and perpetrator of such a felony escaped scot-free, Jopin was, by sentence of court, tied to the tail of a horse, dragged a long way through the streets, over sticks and stones, and hanged. Such other Jews as had been taken into custody were sent to London, and a good many more, who were implicated but had escaped, were arrested in the provinces. Eighteen suffered the same fate as Jopin. The Dominicans

exerted themselves to save the lives of the others, — bribed so to do, as some thought; but they lost favor by it, and their efforts availed nothing. It was ordered by the government that all the Jews in the land who had consented to the murder, and especially those who had been present, namely, seventy-one who were in prison in London, should die the death of Jopin. But Richard of Cornwall, the king's brother, to whom the king had pledged all the Jews in England as security for a loan, stimulated also by a huge bribe, withstood this violation of vested rights, and further execution was stayed.*

An Anglo-French ballad of ninety-two stanzas, which also appears to be contemporary with the event, agrees in many particulars with the account given in the Annals of Burton, adding several which are found in none of the foregoing narratives.† Hugh of Lincoln was kidnapped one evening towards the beginning of August, by Peitevin, the Jew.‡ His mother at once missed him, and searched for him, crying, I have lost my child! till curfew. She slept little and prayed much, and immediately after her prayer the suspicion arose in her mind that her child had been abducted by the Jews. So, with the break of day, the woman went weeping

* Annales de Burton, in Annales Monastici, Luard, I, 340–48. Hugh of Lincoln is commemorated in the Acta Sanctorum, July (27), VI, 494.

† Michel, Hugues de Lincoln, etc., from a MS. in the "Bibliothèque royale, No 7268, 3. 3. A. Colb. 3745, fol. 135, 1°, col. 1." Reprinted by Halliwell, Ballads and Poems respecting Hugh of Lincoln, p. 1, and from Halliwell by Hume, Sir Hugh of Lincoln, etc., p. 43 ff. In stanzas 13, 75, there is an invocation in behalf of King Henry (Qui Deu gard et tenge sa vie!), which implies that he is living. The ballad shows an acquaintance with the localities.

‡ "A la gule de aust." The day, according to the Annals of Burton, was the vigil of St Peter ad vincula. We find in Henschel's Ducange, "ad festum S. Petri, in gula Augusti," and "le jour de feste S. Pere, en goule Aoust." Strictly taken, goule should be the first day, Lammas. Peitevin was actually resident in Lincoln at the time. "He was called Peitevin the Great, to distinguish him from another person who bore the appellation of Peitevin the Little. The Royal Commission issued in 1256 directs an inquisition to be taken of the names of all those who belonged to the school of Peytevin Magnus, who had fled on account of his implication in the crucifixion of a Christian boy." London Athenæum, 1849, p. 1270 f.

through the Jewry, calling at the Jews' doors, Where is my child? Impelled by the suspicion which, as it pleased God, she had of the Jews, she kept on till she came to the court. When she came before King Henry (whom God preserve!), she fell at his feet and begged his grace: "Sire, my son was carried off by the Lincoln Jews one evening; see to it, for charity!" The king swore by God's pity, If it be so as thou hast told, the Jews shall die; if thou hast lied on the Jews, by St Edward, doubt not thou shalt have the same judgment. Soon after the child was carried off, the Jews of Lincoln made a great gathering of all the richest of their sect in England. The child was brought before them, tied with a cord, by the Jew Jopin. They stripped him, as erst they did Jesus. Then said Jopin, thinking he spoke to much profit, The child must be sold for thirty pence, as Jesus was. Agim, the Jew, answered, Give me the child for thirty pence; but I wish that he should be sentenced to death, since I have bought him. The Jews said, Let Agim have him, but let him be put to death forthwith: worse than this, they all cried with one voice, Let him be put on the cross! The child was unbound and hanged on the cross, vilely, as Jesus was. His arms were stretched to the cross, and his feet and hands pierced with sharp nails, and he was crucified alive. Agim took his knife and pierced the innocent's side, and split his heart in two. As the ghost left the body, the child called to his mother, Pray Jesus Christ for me! The Jews buried the body, so that no one might know of their privity, but some of them, passing the place the next morning, found it lying above ground. When they heard of this marvel, they determined in council that the corpse should be thrown into a jakes; but the morning after it was again above ground. While they were in agonies of terror, one of their number came and told them that a woman, who had been his nurse, had agreed for money to take the body out of the city; but he recommended that all the wounds should first be filled with boiling wax. The body was taken off by this nurse and thrown into a well behind the castle.* A woman coming for water the next day discovered it lying on the ground, so filthy that she scarce durst touch it. This woman bethought herself of the child which had been stolen. She went back to Lincoln, and gave information to Hugh's stepfather, who found her tale probable by reason of the suspicion which he already had of the Jews. The woman went through the city proclaiming that she had found the child, and everybody flocked to the well. The coroners were sent for, and came with good will to make their inspection. The body was taken back to Lincoln. A woman came up, who had long before lost her sight, and calling out, Alas, pretty Hugh, why are you lying here! applied her hands to the corpse and then to her eyes, and regained her sight. All who were present were witnesses of the miracle, and gave thanks to God. A converted † Jew presented himself, and suggested that if they wished to know how the child came by its death they should wash the body in warm water; and this being done, the examination which he made enabled him to show that this treason had been done by the Jews, for the very wounds of Jesus were found upon the child. They of the cathedral, hearing of the miracle, came out and carried the body to the church, and buried it among other saints with great joy: mult ben firent, cum m' est avis. Soon after, the mother arrived from the court, very unhappy because she had not been able to find her child. The Lincoln Jews were apprehended and thrown into prison; they said, We have been betrayed by Falsim. The next day King Henry came to Lincoln, and ordered the Jews before him for an inquest. A wise man who was there took it upon him to say that the Jew who would tell the truth to the king should fare the better for it. Jopin, in whose house the treason had been done, told the whole story as already related. King Henry, when all had been told, cried, Right ill did he that

---

* The site of the Jewry was on the hill and about the castle : London Athenæum, 1849, p. 1271.

† These renegades play a like part in many similar cases.

killed him! The justices * went to council, and condemned Jopin to death : his body was to be drawn through the city " de chivals forts et ben ferré[s] " till life was extinct, and then to be hanged. And this was done. I know well where, says the singer : by Canewic, on the high hill.† Of the other Jews it is only said that they had much shame.

The English ballads, the oldest of which were recovered about the middle of the last century, must, in the course of five hundred years of tradition, have departed considerably from the early form ; in all of them the boy comes to his death for breaking a Jew's window, and at the hands of the Jew's daughter. The occurrence of Our Lady's draw-well, in A, is due to a mixing, to this extent, of the story of Hugh with that of the young devotee of the Virgin who is celebrated in Chaucer's Prioresses Tale. In Chaucer's legend, which somewhat strangely removes the scene to a city in Asia, a little " clergeon " (cf. the scholaris of the Annals of Burton) excites, not very unnaturally, the wrath of the Jews by singing the hymn " Alma redemptoris mater " twice a day, as he passes, schoolward and homeward, through the Jewry. For this they cut his throat and throw him into a privy. The Virgin comes to him, and bids him sing the anthem still, till a grain which she lays upon his tongue shall be removed. The mother, in the course of her search for her boy, goes to the pit, under divine direction, and hears him singing.

Another version of this legend occurs in a collection of the Miracles of Our Lady in the Vernon MS., c. 1375, leaf cxxiii, back ; printed by Dr. Horstmann in Herrig's Archiv, 1876, LVI, 224, and again in the Chaucer Society's Originals and Analogues, p. 281. The boy, in this, contributes to the support of his family by singing and begging in the streets of Paris. His song is again Alma redemptoris mater, and he sings it one Saturday as he goes through the Jewry. He is

killed, disposed of, and discovered as in Chaucer's tale, and the bishop, who " was come to see that wonder," finds in the child's throat a lily, inscribed all over with Alma redemptoris mater, which being taken out the song ceases. But when the child's body is carried to the minster, and a requiem mass is begun, the corpse rises up, and sings Salve, sancta parens.

Another variety of the legend is furnished by the Spanish Franciscan Espina, Fortalicium Fidei, 1459, in the edition of Lyons, 1500, fol. ccviii, reprinted by the Chaucer Society, Originals and Analogues, p. 108.‡ The boy is here called Alfonsus of Lincoln. The Jews, having got him into their possession, deliberate what shall be done to him, and decide that the tongue with which he had sung Alma redemptoris shall be torn out, likewise the heart in which he had meditated the song, and the body be thrown into a jakes. The Virgin comes to him, and puts a precious stone in his mouth, to supply the place of his tongue, and the boy at once begins to sing the anthem, and keeps on incessantly for four days ; at the end of which time the discovery is made by the mother, as before. The body is taken to the cathedral, where the bishop delivers a sermon, concluding with an injunction upon all present to pour out their supplications to heaven that this mystery may be cleared up. The boy rises to his feet, takes the jewel from his mouth, explains everything that has passed, hands the jewel to the bishop, to be preserved with other reliques, and expires.

A miracle versified from an earlier source by Gautier de Coincy, some thirty or forty years before the affair of Hugh of Lincoln, is obviously of the same ultimate origin as the Prioresses Tale. A poor woman in England had an only son with a beautiful voice, who did a good deal for the support of his mother by his singing. The Virgin took a particular interest in this clerçoncel, among whose songs was Gaude Maria, which he used to give in a style that moved many to tears. One day, when he was playing in the streets

* Les Jus, 82[1] ; but this is impossible, and we have li justis in 91[1].

† " Canwick is pleasantly situated on a bold eminence, about a mile northward of Lincoln." Allen, History of the County of Lincoln, I, 208.

‡ I do not find this story in the Basel edition of c. 1475.

with his comrades, they came to the Jews' street, where some entertainment was going on which had collected a great many people, who recognized the boy, and asked him to give them a song about Our Lady. He sang with his usual pathos and applause. Jews were listening with the rest, and one of them was so exasperated by a passage in the hymn that he would have knocked the singer on the head then and there, had he dared. When the crowd was dispersed, this Jew enticed the child into his house by flattery and promises, struck him dead with an axe, and buried him. His mother went in search of him, and learned the second day that the boy had been singing in the Jewry the day before, and it was intimated that the Jews might have laid hands on him and killed him. The woman gave the Virgin to understand that if she lost her child she should never more have confidence in her power; nevertheless, more than twenty days passed before any light was thrown on his disappearance. At the end of that time, being one day in the Jews' street, and her wild exclamations having collected a couple of thousand people, she gave vent to her conviction that the Jews had killed her son. Then the Virgin made the child, dead and buried as he was, sing out Gaude Maria in a loud and clear voice. An assault was made on the Jews and the Jews' houses, including that of the murderer; and here, after much searching, guided by the singing, they found the boy buried under the door, perfectly well, and his face as red as a fresh cherry. The boy related how he had been decoyed into the house and struck with an axe; the Virgin had come to him in what seemed a sleep, and told him that he was remiss in not singing her response as he had been wont, upon which he began to sing. Bells were rung, the Virgin was glorified, some Jews were converted, the rest massacred. (G. de Coincy, ed. Poquet, col. 557 ff; Chaucer Society, Originals and Analogues, p. 253 ff.) The same miracle, with considerable variations, occurs in Mariu Saga, ed. Unger, p. 203, No 62, ' Af klerk ok gyðingum ; ' also in Collin de Plancy, Légendes des Saintes

Images, p. 218, ' L'Enfant de Chœur de Notre-Dame du Puy,' under the date 1325.

Murders like that of Hugh of Lincoln have been imputed to the Jews for at least seven hundred and fifty years,* and the charge, which there is reason to suppose may still from time to time be renewed, has brought upon the accused every calamity that the hand of man can inflict, pillage, confiscation, banishment, torture, and death, and this in huge proportions. The process of these murders has often been described as a parody of the crucifixion of Jesus. The motive most commonly alleged, in addition to the expression of contempt for Christianity, has been the obtaining of blood for use in the Paschal rites, — a most unhappily devised slander, in stark contradiction with Jewish precept and practice. That no Christian child was ever killed by a Jew, that there never even was so much truth as that (setting aside the object) in a single case of these particular criminations, is what no Christian or Jew would undertake to assert; but of these charges in the mass it may safely be said, as it has been said, that they are as credible as the miracles which, in a great number of cases, are asserted to have been worked by the reliques of the young saints, and as well substantiated as the absurd sacrilege of stabbing, baking, or boiling the Host,† or the enormity of poisoning springs, with which the Jews have equally been taxed.‡ And these pretended child-mur-

---

* A case cited by Eisenmenger, Entdecktes Judenthum, 2ʳ Theil, p. 220, from Socrates, Ecclesiastical History, l. vii, 16, differs from later ones by being a simple extravagance of drunkenness. Some Jews in Syria, " A. D. 419," who were making merry after their fashion, and indulging in a good deal of tomfoolery, began, as they felt the influence of wine, to jeer at Christ and Christians; from which they proceeded to the seizing of a Christian boy and tying him to a cross. At first they were contented to make game of him, but, growing crazy with drink, they fell to beating him, and even beat him to death; for which they were properly punished.

† See the ballads ' Vom Judenmord zu Deggendorf,' 1337, ' Von den Juden zu Passau,' 1478, in Liliencron, I, 45, No 12, II, 142, No 153.

‡ Nothing could be more just than these words of Percy: " If we consider, on the one hand, the ignorance and superstition of the times when such stories took their rise, the virulent prejudices of the monks who record them, and the eagerness with which they would be catched up by the bar-

ders, with their horrible consequences, are only a part of a persecution which, with all moderation, may be rubricated as the most disgraceful chapter in the history of the human race.*

Cases in England, besides that of Hugh of Lincoln, are William of Norwich, 1137, the Saxon Chronicle, Earle, p. 263, Acta Sanctorum, March (25), III, 588; a boy at Gloucester, 1160, Brompton, in Twysden, col. 1050, Knyghton, col. 2394; Robert of St Edmondsbury, 1181, Gervasius Dorobornensis, Twysden, col. 1458; a boy at Norwich, stolen, circumcised, and kept for crucifixion, 1235, Matthew Paris, Chronica Majora, Luard, III, 305 (see also III, 543, 1239, IV, 30, 1240); a boy at London, 1244, Matthew Paris, IV, 377 (doubtful, but solemnly buried in St. Paul's); a boy at Northampton, 1279, crucified, but not quite killed, the continuator of Florence of Worcester, Thorpe, II, 222.

It would be tedious and useless to attempt to make a collection of the great number of similar instances which have been mentioned by chroniclers and ecclesiastical writers; enough come readily to hand without much research.

A boy was crucified and thrown into the Loire by the Jews of Blois in 1171: Sigiberti Gemblacensis Chronica, auctarium Roberti de Monte, in Pertz, Mon. Germ. Hist. Script., VI, 520, Grätz, Geschichte der Juden, VI, 217-19. Philip Augustus had heard in his early years from playmates that the Jews sacrificed a Christian annually (and, according to some, partook of his heart), and this is represented as having been his reason for expelling the Jews from France. Richard of Pontoise was one of these victims, in 1179: Rigordus,

barous populace as a pretence for plunder; on the other hand, the great danger incurred by the perpetrators, and the inadequate motives they could have to excite them to a crime of so much horror, we may reasonably conclude the whole charge to be groundless and malicious." Reliques, 1795, I, 32.

* Read the indictment against Christians filed by Zunz, Die synagogale Poesie des Mittelalters, pp 19–58, covering the time from the eleventh century to the middle of the sixteenth. It is regrettable that Zunz has not generally cited his authorities. See also Stobbe, Die Juden in Deutschland, p. 183 ff., and notes, p. 280 ff., where the authorities are given.

Gesta Philippi Augusti, p. 14 f., § 6, and Guillelmus Armoricus, p. 179, § 17, in the edition of 1882; Acta Sanctorum, March (25), III, 591. France had such a martyr as late as 1670: see the case of Raphaël Lévy in Eisenmenger, Entdecktes Judenthum, 2ʳ Theil, 224; Drumont, La France Juive, II, 402–09.

Alfonso the Wise has recorded in the Siete Partidas, 1255, that he had heard that the Jews were wont to crucify on Good Friday children that they had stolen (or waxen images, when children were not to be had), Partida VII, Tit. XXIV, Ley iiª, III, 670, ed. 1807, and this was one of the most effective grounds offered in justification of the expulsion of the Jews under Ferdinand and Isabella: Amador de los Rios, Historia de los Judíos de España, I, 483 f. San Dominguito de Val, a choir-boy of seven, Chaucer's clergeon over again, was said to have been stolen and crucified at Saragossa in 1250: Basnage, Histoire des Juifs, 1726, vol. ix, 2d part, pp. 484–86; Acta SS., Aug. (31), VI, 777. Several children were crucified at Valladolid in 1452, and like outrages occurred near Zamora in 1454, and at Sepulveda in 1468: Grätz, VIII, 238. Juan Passamonte, "el niño de Guardia," was kidnapped in 1489, and crucified in 1490: Llorente (Pellier), Histoire de l'Inquisition, ed. 1818, I, 258 f.

Switzerland affords several stories of the sort: a boy at Frisingen in 1287, Ulrich, Sammlung jüdischer Geschichten, p. 149; Rudolf of Bern, 1288 or 1294, Ulrich, pp. 143–49, Acta Sanctorum, April (17), II, 504, Stobbe, Die Juden in Deutschland, p. 283; a boy at Zürich, 1349, another at Diessenhofen, 1401, Ulrich, pp. 82, 248 f.

Examples are particularly numerous in Germany. 1181, Vienna, Zunz, p. 25; 1198, Nuremberg, Stobbe, p. 281'; about 1200, Erfurt, Zunz, p. 26; 1220, St Henry, Weissenburg, Acta SS., April, II, 505 (but 1260, Schœpflin, Alsatia Illustrata, II, 394 f.); 1235–6, Fulda, Grätz, Geschichte der Juden, VII, 109, 460; 1261, Magdeburg, Stobbe, p. 282; 1283, Mayence, Grätz, VII, 199; 1285, Munich, Grätz, VII, 200, Aretin, Geschichte der Juden in Baiern, p. 18; 1286, Oberwesel, near Bacharach, Werner (boy or man), Grätz, VII, 201, 479, Stobbe, p. 282, Acta Sanctorum, April (19), II, 697; 1292, Colmar, Stobbe, p. 283; 1293, Krems, *ib.*; 1302, Remken, *ib.*; 1303, Conrad, at Weissensee, *ib.*; 1345, Henry, at Munich, Acta SS., May (27), VI, 657; 1422, Augsburg, or 1429, Ravensburg, Ulrich, p. 88 ff; 1454, Breslau, Grätz, VIII, 205; 1462, Andrew, in Tyrol, Acta SS., July (12), III, 462; 1474 and 1476, Ratisbon, Zeitschrift für die historische Theologie (Train, Geschichte der Juden in Regensburg), 1837, Heft 3, p. 98 ff., 104 ff., and (Saalschütz), 1841, Heft 4, p. 140 ff., Grätz, VIII, 279 ff.; 1475, Simon of Trent, Muratori, Rer. Ital. Script., XX, 945–49 (Annals of Placentia), Liliencron, Historische V. l. der Deutschen, II, 13, No 128, Grätz, VIII, 269 ff., Acta SS., March (24), III, 494, La Civiltà Cattolica, 1881 and 1882;* a little before 1478, Baden, Train, as above, p. 117; 1540, Zappenfeld, near Neuburg (nothing "proved"), Aretin, p. 44 f.; 1562, Andrew, Tyrol, Acta SS., July (12), III, 462, with a picture,† p. 464; 1650, Caden (and others in Styria, Carinthia, and Carniola), Eisenmenger, Entdecktes Judenthum, 1711, 2ʳ Theil, p. 223; near Sigeberg, in the diocese of Cologne, Joanettus, Acta SS., March, III, 502, with no year.

Italy appears to be somewhat behind the rest of Europe. The Fortalicium Fidei re-

* In vol. viii, pp 225, 344, 476, 598, 730, vol. ix, 107, 219, 353, 472, 605, the confessions of the defendants are given from the original minutes of the trial; and it fully appears from these confessions that blood is requisite for a proper performance of the Paschal ceremonies, and also that the blood must be got from a boy, and from a boy while he is undergoing torment. Only it is to be remembered that the inducements to these confessions were the same as those which led the Jews of Passau to acknowledge that blood exuded from the Host when it was stabbed, and that when two bits of the wafer were thrown into an oven two doves flew out: Train, as above, p. 116, note 57.

† For other pictures of these martyrdoms, see the Nuremberg Chronicle, 1493, fol. ccliiii, v°, for Simon of Trent; Lacroix, Mœurs, Usages, etc., 1875, p. 473, for Richard of Pontoise, p. 475, for Simon, repeated from the N. Chron.; that of Munich, 1285, and the children of Ratisbon, reproduced in Cosmos, March 30, 1885 (according to Drumont, II, 418, note). See also Michel, Hugues de Lincoln, p. 54, note 41.

ports a case at Pavia some time before 1456, and another at Savona of about 1452: Basel ed. (c. 1475), fol. 116 f. 1480, Venice, Beato Sebastiano da Porto Buffolè del Bergamasco, Civiltà Cattolica, X, 737. Israel, one of the culprits of Trent, revealed his knowledge of similar transactions at Padova, Mestre, Serravalle and Bormio, in the course of his own life, besides several in Germany: Civ. Catt., X, 737.

Further, 1305, Prague, Eisenmenger, p. 221; 1407, Cracow, "Dlugosz, Hist. Polonicæ, l. x, p. 187;" 1494, Tyrnau, Ungerische Chronica, 1581, p. 375; 1505, Budweis, Stobbe, p. 292; 1509, Bösing, Hungary, Eisenmenger, p. 222; 1569, Constantinople, Fickler, Theologia Juridica, 1575, p. 505 (cited by Michel); 1598, Albertus, in Polonia, Acta SS., April (circa 20), II, 835.

Train, as above, p. 98, note, adds, with authorities, Pforzheim, Ueberlingen, Swäbisch-Hall, Friuli, Halle, Eichstädt, Berlin. See also Acta SS., April, III, 838 (De pluribus innocentibus per Judæos excruciatis), March, III, 589, and April, II, 505; and Drumont, La France Juive, II, 392 f.

The charge against the Jews of murdering children for their blood is by no means as yet a thing of the past. The accusation has been not infrequently made in Russia during the present century. Although the entertaining of such an inculpation was forbidden by an imperial ukase in 1817, a criminal process on this ground, involving forty-three persons, was instituted in 1823, and was brought to a close only in 1835, when the defendants were acquitted on account of the entire failure of proof: Stobbe, p. 186. The murder of a child of six in Neuhoven, in the district of Düsseldorf, in 1834, occasioned the demolition of two Jewish houses and a synagogue: Illgen, in Zeitschrift für die historische Theologie, 1837, Heft 3, 40, note. In February, 1840, a Greek boy of ten disappeared in Rhodes. The Jews were believed to have killed him for his blood. Torture was freely used to extort confessions. The case was removed to Constantinople, and in July, upon the report of the supreme court, the Divan pronounced the innocence of the defendants: Illgen, Z. f. d. Hist. Theol., 1841, Heft 4, p. 172, note, Hume, Sir Hugh of Lincoln, p. 30.[*] In 1881, the Jews were in suspicion on account of a boy at Alexandria, and of a girl at Calarasi, Wallachia: Civiltà Cattolica, VIII, 225, 737. The Moniteur de Rome, June 15, 1883, affords several more of these too familiar tales. A Greek child was stolen at Smyrna, a few years before the date last mentioned, towards the time of the Passover, and its body found four days after, punctured with pins in a thousand places. The mother, like Beatrice in 1255, denounced the Jews as the culprits; the Christian population rose in a mass, rushed to the Jews' quarter, and massacred more than six hundred. An affair of the same nature took place at Balata, the Ghetto of Constantinople, in 1842, of which the consequences to the Jews are not mentioned; and again at Galata, "where the Jews escaped by bribing the Turkish police to suppress testimony" (Drumont, II, 412). A young girl disappeared at Tisza-Eszlár, in Hungary, in April, 1882, and the Jews were suspected of having made away with her. The preliminary judicial inquiry was marked by the intimidation and torture of several persons examined for evidence. Fifteen who were held for trial were absolutely acquitted in August, 1883, after more than a year of imprisonment. The shops of Jews in Budapest were plundered by Christians disappointed in the verdict! (Der Blut-Prozess von Tisza-Eszlár,.New York, 1883.)

B is translated by Herder, I, 120; by Bodmer, I, 59; in Seckendorf's Musenalmanach für das Jahr 1808, p. 5; by Doering, p. 163; by Von Marées, p. 48. Allingham's ballad by Knortz, Lieder u. Romanzen Alt-Englands, p. 118.

———

A

Jamieson's Popular Ballads, I, 151, as taken down by the editor from Mrs Brown's recitation.

1   FOUR and twenty bonny boys
      Were playing at the ba,
   And by it came him sweet Sir Hugh,
      And he playd oer them a'.

2   He kickd the ba with his right foot,
      And catchd it wi his knee,
   And throuch-and-thro the Jew's window
      He gard the bonny ba flee.

3   He's doen him to the Jew's castell,
      And walkd it round about;
   And there he saw the Jew's daughter,
      At the window looking out.

4   'Throw down the ba, ye Jew's daughter,
      Throw down the ba to me!'

'Never a bit,' says the Jew's daughter,
   'Till up to me come ye.'

5   'How will I come up? How can I come up?
      How can I come to thee?
   For as ye did to my auld father,
      The same ye 'll do to me.'

6   She 's gane till her father's garden,
      And pu'd an apple red and green;
   'T was a' to wyle him sweet Sir Hugh,
      And to entice him in.

7   She 's led him in through ae dark door,
      And sae has she thro nine;
   She 's laid him on a dressing-table,
      And stickit him like a swine.

8   And first came out the thick, thick blood,
      And syne came out the thin,
   And syne came out the bonny heart's blood;
      There was nae mair within.

[*] The extraordinary occurrence in Damascus in the same year, 1840, which excited the indignation, sympathy, and active interposition of nearly all the civilized world, requires but the briefest allusion. A capuchin friar was in this instance the victim immolated, and for blood to mix with the Paschal bread. The most frightful torture was used, under the direction of the Turkish pacha, assisted by the French consul, under which three unhappy men succumbed. See Illgen's detailed account of this persecution in the periodical and article above cited, pp. 153 ff. Drumont is of the same mind as he would have been four or five hundred years ago: "les faits étaient prouvés, démontrés, indiscutables" (La France Juive, II, 411).

9　She's rowd him in a cake o lead,
　　Bade him lie still and sleep;
　She's thrown him in Our Lady's draw-well,
　　Was fifty fathom deep.

10　When bells were rung, and mass was sung,
　　And a' the bairns came hame,
　When every lady gat hame her son,
　　The Lady Maisry gat nane.

11　She's taen her mantle her about,
　　Her coffer by the hand,
　And she's gane out to seek her son,
　　And wanderd oer the land.

12　She's doen her to the Jew's castell,
　　Where a' were fast asleep:
　'Gin ye be there, my sweet Sir Hugh,
　　I pray you to me speak.'

13　She's doen her to the Jew's garden,
　　Thought he had been gathering fruit:

'Gin ye be there, my sweet Sir Hugh,
　　I pray you to me speak.'

14　She neard Our Lady's deep draw-well,
　　Was fifty fathom deep:
　'Whareer ye be, my sweet Sir Hugh,
　　I pray you to me speak.'

15　'Gae hame, gae hame, my mither dear,
　　Prepare my winding sheet,
　And at the back o merry Lincoln
　　The morn I will you meet.'

16　Now Lady Maisry is gane hame,
　　Made him a winding sheet,
　And at the back o merry Lincoln
　　The dead corpse did her meet.

17　And a' the bells o merry Lincoln
　　Without men's hands were rung,
　And a' the books o merry Lincoln
　　Were read without man's tongue,
　And neer was such a burial
　　Sin Adam's days begun.

B

Percy's Reliques, I, 32, 1765; from a manuscript copy sent from Scotland.

1　THE rain rins doun through Mirry-land toune,
　　Sae dois it doune the Pa;
　Sae dois the lads of Mirry-land toune,
　　Whan they play at the ba.

2　Than out and cam the Jewis dochter,
　　Said, Will ye cum in and dine?
　'I winnae cum in, I cannae cum in,
　　Without my play-feres nine.'

3　Scho powd an apple reid and white,
　　To intice the yong thing in:
　Scho powd an apple white and reid,
　　And that the sweit bairne did win.

4　And scho has taine out a little pen-knife,
　　And low down by her gair;
　Scho has twin'd the yong thing and his life,
　　A word he nevir spak mair.

5　And out and cam the thick, thick bluid,
　　And out and cam the thin,

And out and cam the bonny herts bluid;
　　Thair was nae life left in.

6　Scho laid him on a dressing-borde,
　　And drest him like a swine,
　And laughing said, Gae nou and pley
　　With your sweit play-feres nine.

7　Scho rowd him in a cake of lead,
　　Bade him lie stil and sleip;
　Scho cast him in a deip draw-well,
　　Was fifty fadom deip.

8　Whan bells wer rung, and mass was sung,
　　And every lady went hame,
　Than ilka lady had her yong sonne,
　　Bot Lady Helen had nane.

9　Scho rowd hir mantil hir about,
　　And sair, sair gan she weip,
　And she ran into the Jewis castel,
　　Whan they wer all asleip.

10　'My bonny Sir Hew, my pretty Sir Hew,
　　I pray thee to me speik:'
　'O lady, rinn to the deip draw-well,
　　Gin ye your sonne wad seik.'

11 Lady Helen ran to the deip draw-well,
   And knelt upon her kne :
   'My bonny Sir Hew, an ye be here,
   I pray thee speik to me.'

12 'The lead is wondrous heavy, mither,
   The well is wondrous deip ;

C

Percy papers; communicated to Percy by Paton, in 1768
or 69, and derived from a friend of Paton's.

1 FOUR and twenty bonny boys
   War playing at the ba ;
   Then up and started sweet Sir Hew,
   The flower amang them a'.

2 He hit the ba a kick wi 's fit,
   And kept it wi his knee,
   That up into the Jew's window
   He gart the bonny ba flee.

3 ' Cast doun the ba to me, fair maid,
   Cast doun the ba to me ; '
   ' O neer a bit o the ba ye get
   Till ye cum up to me.

4 'Cum up, sweet Hew, cum up, dear Hew,
   Cum up and get the ba ; '
   ' I canna cum, I darna cum,
   Without my play-feres twa.'

5 'Cum up, sweet Hew, cum up, dear Hew,
   Cum up and play wi me ; '
   ' I canna cum, I darna cum,
   Without my play-feres three.'

6 She's gane into the Jew's garden,
   Where the grass grew lang and green ;
   She powd an apple red and white,
   To wyle the young thing in.

7 She wyl'd him into ae chamber,
   She wyl'd him into twa,
   She wyl'd him to her ain chamber,
   The fairest o them a'.

8 She laid him on a dressing-board,
   Where she did sometimes dine ;
   She put a penknife in his heart,
   And dressed him like a swine.

A keen pen-knife sticks in my hert,
   A word I dounae speik.

13 ' Gae hame, gae hame, my mither deir,
   Fetch me my windling sheet,
   And at the back o Mirry-land toun,
   It 's thair we twa sall meet.'

9 Then out and cam the thick, thick blude,
   Then out and cam the thin ;
   Then out and cam the bonny heart's blude,
   Where a' the life lay in.

10 She rowd him in a cake of lead,
   Bad him lie still and sleep ;
   She cast him in the Jew's draw-well,
   Was fifty fadom deep.

11 She's tane her mantle about her head,
   Her pike-staff in her hand,
   And prayed Heaven to be her guide
   Unto some uncouth land.

12 His mither she cam to the Jew's castle,
   And there ran thryse about :
   ' O sweet Sir Hew, gif ye be here,
   I pray ye to me speak.'

13 She cam into the Jew's garden,
   And there ran thryse about :
   ' O sweet Sir Hew, gif ye be here,
   I pray ye to me speak.'

14 She cam unto the Jew's draw-well,
   And there ran thryse about :
   ' O sweet Sir Hew, gif ye be here,
   I pray ye to me speak.'

15 ' How can I speak, how dare I speak,
   How can I speak to thee ?
   The Jew's penknife sticks in my heart,
   I canna speak to thee.

16 ' Gang hame, gang hame, O mither dear,
   And shape my winding sheet,
   And at the birks of Mirryland town
   There you and I shall meet.'

17 Whan bells war rung, and mass was sung,
   And a' men bound for bed,
   Every mither had her son,
   But sweet Sir Hew was dead.

D

Herd's MS., I, 213 ; stanzas 7-10, II, 219.

1 A' THE boys of merry Linkim
   War playing at the ba,
An up it stands him sweet Sir Hugh,
   The flower amang them a'.

2 He keppit the ba than wi his foot,
   And catchd it wi his knee,
And even in at the Jew's window
   He gart the bonny ba flee.

3 'Cast out the ba to me, fair maid,
   Cast out the ba to me ! '
'Ah never a bit of it,' she says,
   'Till ye come up to me.

4 'Come up, sweet Hugh, come up, dear Hugh,
   Come up and get the ba' ! '
'I winna come up, I mayna come [up],
   Without my bonny boys a'.'

5 'Come up, sweet Hugh, come up, dear Hugh,
   Come up and speak to me ! '

'I mayna come up, I winna come up,
   Without my bonny boys three.'

6 She 's taen her to the Jew's garden,
   Where the grass grew lang and green,
She 's pu'd an apple reid and white,
   To wyle the bonny boy in.

7 She 's wyl'd him in thro ae chamber,
   She 's wyl'd him in thro twa,
She 's wyl'd him till her ain chamber,
   The flower out owr them a'.

8 She 's laid him on a dressin-board,
   Whare she did often dine ;
She stack a penknife to his heart,
   And dressd him like a swine.

9 She rowd him in a cake of lead,
   Bade him lie still and sleep ;
She threw him i the Jew's draw-well,
   'T was fifty fathom deep.

10 Whan bells was rung, and mass was sung,
   An a' man bound to bed,
Every lady got hame her son,
   But sweet Sir Hugh was dead.

E

Motherwell's Minstrelsy, p. 51, as taken down from the recitation of a lady.

1 YESTERDAY was brave Hallowday,
   And, above all days of the year,
The schoolboys all got leave to play,
   And little Sir Hugh was there.

2 He kicked the ball with his foot,
   And kepped it with his knee,
And even in at the Jew's window
   He gart the bonnie ba flee.

3 Out then came the Jew's daughter :
   'Will ye come in and dine ? '
'I winna come in, and I canna come in,
   Till I get that ball of mine.

4 'Throw down that ball to me, maiden,
   Throw down the ball to me ! '
'I winna throw down your ball, Sir Hugh,
   Till ye come up to me.'

5 She pu'd the apple frae the tree,
   It was baith red and green ;
She gave it unto little Sir Hugh,
   With that his heart did win.

6 She wiled him into ae chamber,
   She wiled him into twa,
She wiled him into the third chamber,
   And that was warst o't a'.

7 She took out a little penknife,
   Hung low down by her spare,
She twined this young thing o his life,
   And a word he neer spak mair.

8 And first came out the thick, thick blood,
   And syne came out the thin,
And syne came out the bonnie heart's blood,
   There was nae mair within.

9 She laid him on a dressing-table,
   She dressd him like a swine ;
Says, Lie ye there, my bonnie Sir Hugh,
   Wi yere apples red and green !

10 She put him in a case of lead,
    Says, Lie ye there and sleep!
  She threw him into the deep draw-well,
    Was fifty fathom deep.

11 A schoolboy walking in the garden
    Did grievously hear him moan;
  He ran away to the deep draw-well,
    And fell down on his knee.

12 Says, Bonnie Sir Hugh, and pretty Sir
    Hugh,
  I pray you speak to me!
  If you speak to any body in this world,
    I pray you speak to me.

13 When bells were rung, and mass was sung,
    And every body went hame,
  Then every lady had her son,
    But Lady Helen had nane.

14 She rolled her mantle her about,
    And sore, sore did she weep;
  She ran away to the Jew's castle,
    When all were fast asleep.

15 She cries, Bonnie Sir Hugh, O pretty Sir
    Hugh,
  I pray you speak to me!
  If you speak to any body in this world,
    I pray you speak to me.

16 'Lady Helen, if ye want your son,
    I'll tell ye where to seek;

    Lady Helen, if ye want your son,
      He's in the well sae deep.'

17 She ran away to the deep draw-well,
    And she fell down on her knee.
  Saying, Bonnie Sir Hugh, O pretty Sir Hugh,
    I pray ye speak to me!
  If ye speak to any body in the world,
    I pray ye speak to me.

18 'Oh the lead it is wondrous heavy, mother,
    The well it is wondrous deep;
  The little penknife sticks in my throat,
    And I downa to ye speak.

19 'But lift me out o this deep draw-well,
    And bury me in yon churchyard;

.   .   .   .
    .   .   .   .   .

20 'Put a Bible at my head,' he says,
    'And a Testament at my feet,
  And pen and ink at every side,
    And I'll lie still and sleep.

21 'And go to the back of Maitland town,
    Bring me my winding sheet;
  For it's at the back of Maitland town
    That you and I shall meet.'

22 O the broom, the bonny, bonny broom,
    The broom that makes full sore,
  A woman's mercy is very little,
    But a man's mercy is more.

F

Hume's Sir Hugh of Lincoln, p. 35, obtained from recitation in Ireland.

1 'T was on a summer's morning
    Some scholars were playing at ball,
  When out came the Jew's daughter
    And leand her back against the wall.

2 She said unto the fairest boy,
    Come here to me, Sir Hugh;
  'No! I will not,' said he,
    'Without my playfellows too.'

3 She took an apple out of her pocket,
    And trundled it along the plain,

    And who was readiest to lift it
    Was little Sir Hugh again.

4 She took him by the milk-white han,
    An led him through many a hall,
  Until they came to one stone chamber,
    Where no man might hear his call.

5 She set him in a goolden chair,
    And jaggd him with a pin,
  And called for a goolden cup
    To houl his heart's blood in.

6 She tuk him by the yellow hair,
    An also by the feet,
  An she threw him in the deep draw-well;
    It was fifty fadom deep.

7 Day bein over, the night came on,
    And the scholars all went home;
  Then every mother had her son,
    But little Sir Hugh's had none.

8 She put her mantle about her head,
    Tuk a little rod in her han,
  An she says, Sir Hugh, if I fin you here,
    I will bate you for stayin so long.

9 First she went to the Jew's door,
    But they were fast asleep;
  An then she went to the deep draw-well,
    That was fifty fadom deep.

10 She says, Sir Hugh, if you be here,
    As I suppose you be,
  If ever the dead or quick arose,
    Arise and spake to me.

11 'Yes, mother dear, I am here,
    I know I have staid very long;
  But a little penknife was stuck in my heart,
    Till the stream ran down full strong.

12 'And mother dear, when you go home,
    Tell my playfellows all
  That I lost my life by leaving them,
    When playing that game of ball.

13 'And ere another day is gone,
    My winding-sheet prepare,
  And bury me in the green churchyard,
    Where the flowers are bloomin fair.

14 'Lay my Bible at my head,
    My Testament at my feet;
  The earth and worms shall be my bed,
    Till Christ and I shall meet.'

G

a. Written down by Mrs Dulany, January 14, 1885, from the recitation of her mother, Mrs Nourse, aged above ninety, as learned when a child, in Philadelphia. b. From the same source, furnished several years earlier by Miss Perine, of Baltimore.

1 IT rains, it rains in old Scotland,
    And down the rain does fa,
  And all the boys in our town
    Are out a playing at ba.

2 'You toss your balls too high, my boys,
    You toss your balls too low;
  You 'll toss them into the Jew's garden,
    Wherein you darst not go.'

3 Then out came one of the Jew's daughters,
    All dressed in red and green:
  'Come in, come in, my pretty little boy,
    And get your ball again.'

4 'I winna come in, and I canna come in,
    Without my playmates all,
  And without the will of my mother dear,
    Which would cause my heart's blood to fall.'

5 She shewed him an apple as green as grass,
    She shewed him a gay gold ring,
  She shewed him a cherry as red as blood,
    Which enticed the little boy in.

6 She took him by the lily-white hand,
    And led him into the hall,
  And laid him on a dresser-board,
    And that was the worst of all.

7 She laid the Bible at his head,
    The Prayer-Book at his feet,
  And with a penknife small
    She stuck him like a sheep.

8 Six pretty maids took him by the head,
    And six took him by the feet,
  And threw him into a deep draw-well,
    That was eighteen fathoms deep.

*   *   *   *   *   *   *

9 'The lead is wondrous heavy, mother,
    The well is wondrous deep,
  A keen pen-knife sticks in my heart,
    And nae word more can I speak.'

H

Communicated by Miss Perine, of Baltimore, Maryland, as sung by her mother about 1825.

1 IT rains, it rains in fair Scotland,
  It rains both great and small

. . . .

. . . .

2 He tossed the ball so high, so low,
  He tossed the ball so low,
  He tossed it over the Jew's garden-wall,
  Where no one dared to go.

3 Out came one of the Jew's daughters,
  All dressed in apple-green;
  Said she, My dear little boy, come in,
  And pick up your ball again.

4 'I dare not come, I will not come,
  I dare not come at all;
  For if I should, I know you would
  Cause my blood to fall.'

5 She took him by the lily-white hand,
  And led him thro the kitchen;
  And there he saw his own dear maid
  A roasting of a chicken.

6 She put him in a little chair,
  And pinned him with a pin,
  And then she called for a wash-basin,
  To spill his life blood in.

7 'O put the Bible at my head,
  And the Testament at my feet,
  And when my mother calls for me,
  You may tell her I'm gone to sleep.'

I

Sir E. Brydges, Restituta, I, 381, "obtained some years since" (1814) from the recitation of an aged lady.

1 IT rains, it rains in merry Scotland,
  It rains both great and small,
  And all the children in merry Scotland
  Are playing at the ball.

2 They toss the ball so high, so high,
  They toss the ball so low,
  They toss the ball in the Jew's garden,
  Where the Jews are sitting a row.

3 Then up came one of the Jew's daughters,
  Cloathed all in green:

'Come hither, come hither, my pretty Sir Hugh,
  And fetch thy ball again.'

4 'I durst not come, I durst not go,
  Without my play-fellowes all;
  For if my mother should chance to know,
  She'd cause my blood to fall.'

*   *   *   *   *   *   *

5 She laid him upon the dresser-board,
  And stuck him like a sheep;
  She laid the Bible at his head,
  The Testament at his feet,
  The Catechise-Book in his own heart's blood,
  With a penknife stuck so deep.

*   *   *   *   *   *   *

J

a. Notes and Queries, First Series, XII, 496, B. H. C., from the manuscript of an old lacemaker in Northamptonshire. b. N. and Q., First Series, VIII, 614, B. H. C., from memory, stanzas 1–6.

1 IT rains, it rains in merry Scotland,
  Both little, great and small,
  And all the schoolfellows in merry Scotland
  Must needs go play at ball.

2 They tossd the ball so high, so high,
  With that it came down so low;
  They tossd it over the old Jew's gates,
  And broke the old Jew's window.

3 The old Jew's daughter she came out,
  Was clothed all in green:
  'Come hither, come hither, you young Sir Hugh,
  And fetch your ball again.'

4 'I dare not come, nor I will not come,
   Without my schoolfellows come all ;
For I shall be beaten when I go home
   For losing of my ball.'

5 She 'ticed him with an apple so red,
   And likewise with a fig ;
She threw him over the dresser-board,
   And sticked him like a pig.

6 The first came out the thickest of blood,
   The second came out so thin,
The third came out the child's heart-blood,
   Where all his life lay in.

7 'O spare my life ! O spare my life !
   O spare my life ! ' said he ;
'If ever I live to be a young man,
   I 'll do as good chare for thee.'

8 'I 'll do as good chare for thy true love
   As ever I did for the king ;
I will scour a basin as bright as silver
   To let your heart-blood run in.'

9 When eleven o'clock was past and gone,
   And all the school-fellows came home,
Every mother had her own child
   But young Sir Hugh's mother had none.

10 She went up Lincoln and down Lincoln,
   And all about Lincoln street,
With her small wand in her right hand,
   Thinking of her child to meet.

11 She went till she came to the old Jew's gate,
   She knocked with the ring ;
Who should be so ready as the old Jew herself
   To rise and let her in !

12 'What news, fair maid ? what news, fair maid ?
   What news have you brought to me ?
.   .   .   .
   .   .   .   .

13 'Have you seen any of my child today,
   Or any of the rest of my kin ? '
'No, I 've seen none of your child today,
   Nor none of the rest of your kin.'

K

Notes and Queries, First Series, IX, 320 ; taken down by
S. P. Q. from the recitation of a nurse-maid in Shropshire
about 1810. Salopian Shreds and Patches, July 21, 1875,
in Miss Burne's Shropshire Folk-Lore, p. 539.

1 It hails, it rains, in Merry-Cock land,
   It hails, it rains, both great and small,
And all the little children in Merry-Cock land
   They have need to play at ball.

2 They tossd the ball so high,
   They tossd the ball so low,
mongst all the Jews' cattle,
   And amongst the Jews below.

3 Out came one of the Jew's daughters,
   Dressed all in green :
'Come, my sweet Saluter,
   And fetch the ball again.'

4 'I durst not come, I must not come,
   Unless all my little playfellows come along ;
For if my mother sees me at the gate,
   She 'll cause my blood to fall.

5 'She showd me an apple as green as grass,
   She showd me a gay gold ring ;
She showd me a cherry as red as blood,
   And so she entic'd me in.

6 'She took me in the parlor,
   She took me in the kitchen,
And there I saw my own dear nurse,
   A picking of a chicken.

7 'She laid me down to sleep,
   With a Bible at my head and a Testament
      at my feet ;
And if my playfellows come to quere for me,
   Tell them I am asleep.'

L

a. Communicated in a letter from the Rev. E. Venables, Precentor of Lincoln, as sung to him by a nurse-maid nearly sixty years ago, January 24, 1885. A Buckinghamshire version. b. A Walk through Lincoln Minster, by the Rev. E. Venables, p. 41, 1884.

1 It rains, it hails in merry Lincoln,
  It rains both great and small,
  And all the boys and girls today
  Do play at pat the ball.

2 They patted the ball so high, so high,
  They patted the ball so low,
  They patted it into the Jew's garden,
  Where all the Jews do go.

3 Then out it spake the Jew's daughter,
  As she leant over the wall ;
  'Come hither, come hither, my pretty play-
  fellow,
  And I'll give you your ball.'

4 She tempted him [in] with apple so red,
  But that wouldnt tempt him in ;
  She tempted him in with sugar so sweet,
  And so she got him in.

5 Then she put forth her lilly-white hand,
  And led him through the hall :
  'This way, this way, my pretty play-fellow,
  And you shall have your ball.'

6 She led him on through one chamber,
  And so she did through nine,
  Until she came to her own chamber,
  Where she was wont to dine,
  And she laid him on a dressing-board,
  And sticket him like a swine.

7 Then out it came the thick, thick blood,
  And out it came the thin,
  And out it came the bonnie heart's blood,
  There was no more within.

M

F. H. Groome, In Gipsy Tents, 1880, p. 145 : "first heard at Shepherd's Bush, in 1872, from little Amy North."

1 Down in merry, merry Scotland
  It rained both hard and small ;
  Two little boys went out one day,
  All for to play with a ball.

2 They tossed it up so very, very high,
  They tossed it down so low ;
  They tossed it into the Jew's garden,
  Where the flowers all do blow.

3 Out came one of the Jew's daughters,
  Dressëd in green all :

'If you come here, my fair pretty lad,
  You shall have your ball.'

4 She showed him an apple as green as grass ;
  The next thing was a fig ;
  The next thing a cherry as red as blood,
  And that would 'tice him in.

5 She set him on a golden chair,
  And gave him sugar sweet ;
  Laid him on some golden chest of drawers,
  Stabbed him like a sheep.

6 'Seven foot Bible
  At my head and my feet ;
  If my mother pass by me,
  Pray tell her I'm asleep.'

N

Newell's Games and Songs of American Children, p. 75, as sung by a little girl in New York : derived, through her mother, from a grandmother born in Ireland.

1 It was on a May, on a midsummer's day,
  When it rained, it did rain small ;
  And little Harry Hughes and his playfellows
  all
  Went out to play the ball.

2 He knocked it up, and he knocked it down,
  He knocked it oer and oer ;
  The very first kick little Harry gave the ball,
  He broke the duke's windows all.

3 She came down, the youngest duke's daughter,
  She was dressed in green :
  'Come back, come back, my pretty little boy,
  And play the ball again.'

4 'I wont come back, and I daren't come back,
  Without my playfellows all ;
  And if my mother she should come in,
  She 'd make it the bloody ball.'

5 She took an apple out of her pocket,
  And rolled it along the plain ;
  Little Harry Hughes picked up the apple,
  And sorely rued the day.

6 She takes him by the lily-white hand,
  And leads him from hall to hall,
  Until she came to a little dark room,
  That no one could hear him call.

7 She sat herself on a golden chair,
  Him on another close by,
  And there's where she pulled out her little
      penknife,
  That was both sharp and fine.

8 Little Harry Hughes had to pray for his soul,
  For his days were at an end ;
  She stuck her penknife in little Harry's heart,
  And first the blood came very thick, and
      then came very thin.

9 She rolled him in a quire of tin,
  That was in so many a fold ;
  She rolled him from that to a little draw-well,
  That was fifty fathoms deep.

10 'Lie there, lie there, little Harry,' she cried,
   'And God forbid you to swim,

If you be a disgrace to me,
  Or to any of my friends.'

11 The day passed by, and the night came on,
   And every scholar was home,
   And every mother had her own child,
   But poor Harry's mother had none.

12 She walked up and down the street,
   With a little sally rod in her hand,
   And God directed her to the little draw-well,
   That was fifty fathoms deep.

13 'If you be there, little Harry,' she said,
   'And God forbid you to be,
   Speak one word to your own dear mother,
   That is looking all over for thee.'

14 'This I am, dear mother,' he cried,
   'And lying in great pain,
   With a little penknife lying close to my heart,
   And the duke's daughter she has me slain.

15 'Give my blessing to my schoolfellows all,
   And tell them to be at the church,
   And make my grave both large and deep,
   And my coffin of hazel and green birch.

16 'Put my Bible at my head,
   My busker (?) at my feet,
   My little prayer-book at my right side,
   And sound will be my sleep.'

O

G. A. Sala, Illustrated London News, October 21, 1882,
LXXXI, 415, repeated in Living London, 1883, p. 465 :
heard from a nurse in childhood.

1 IT rains, it rains, in merry Scotland,
  It rains both great and small,
  And all the children in merry Scotland
  Must needs play at ball.

2 They toss the ball so high,
  And they toss the ball so low ;
  They toss it into the Jew's garden,
  Where the Jews sate all of a row.

3 .   .   .   .
  A-dressèd all in green :
  'Come in, come in, my pretty lad,
  And you shall have your ball again.'

4 'They set me in a chair of state,
  And gave me sugar sweet ;
  They laid me on a dresser-board,
  And stuck me like a sheep.

5 'Oh lay a Bible at my head,
  And a Prayer-Book at my feet !
  In the well that they did throw me in,
  Full five-and-fifty feet deep.'

P

Halliwell, Ballads and Poems respecting Hugh of Lincoln, p. 37, Halliwell's Popular Rhymes and Nursery Tales, p. 192, ed. 1849: communicated by Miss Agnes Strickland, from oral tradition at Godalming, Surrey.

1 HE tossed the ball so high, so high,
  He tossed the ball so low,

He tossed the ball in the Jew's garden,
  And the Jews were all below.

2 Oh then out came the Jew's daughter,
  She was dressed all in green :
'Come hither, come hither, my sweet pretty
    fellow,
  And fetch your ball again.'

Q

Motherwell's Note-Book, p. 54, as sung by Widow Michael, an old woman in Barhead.

1 A' the bairns o Lincolnshire
  Were learning at the school,

And every Saturday at een
  They learnt their lessons weel.

2 The Jew's dochter sat in her bower-door,
  Sewing at her seam ;
She spied a' the bonnie bairns,
  As they cam out and hame.

R

Motherwell's Minstrelsy, Appendix, p. xvii, VII.

IT was in the middle o the midsimmer tyme,
  When the scule weans playd at the ba, ba,

Out and cam the Jew's tochter,
  And on little Sir Hew did ca, ca,
  And on little Sir Hew did ca.

B. *Initial* quh *is changed to* wh : z, *for* ʒ, *to* y.
C. " ' The Jew's Daughter,' which you say was transmitted to Mr Dodsley by a friend of yours, never reached me, and Mr Dodsley says he knows nothing of it. I wish you would prevail on your friend to try to recollect or recover it, and send me another copy by you." *Percy to Paton, Jan.* 12, 1769. *The copy in the Percy papers is in Paton's hand.*
  1^4. *First written :* The fairest o them a'.
  7^4. *First written :* The flower amang them a'.
D. 10^4. bells were, *in the second copy.*
E. 9^2. a swan.
F. *Hume says, p.* 5, *that he first heard the ballad in early boyhood ;* "it was afterwards readily identified with Sir Hugh of Lincoln, though the rustic minstrel from whom I received it made no allusion to locality." *One cannot tell whether this copy is the ballad heard in early boyhood.*
  14^1. " *This and the next verse are transposed.*" *Hume.*

G. a. 2^4. darest.
  b. 1^2. doth fall. 1^3. When all.
    1^4. Were out a playing ball.
    2^1. We toss the balls so.
    2^2. We toss the balls so. 2^3. We 've tossed it.
    2^4. Where no one dares to.
    3^1. out and came the Jew's daughter.
    3^3. Said, Come.
    4^1. will not come in, I cannot.
    4^2. playfellows. 4^3. Nor *for* And.
    4^4. Which will. *After* 4 :

     I must not come, I dare not come,
      I cannot come at all,
     For if my mother should call for me,
      I cannot hear her call.

    5^4. To entice this.
    After 5 (*compare Miss Perine's own version,* H 6) :

     She put him in a little chair,
     She pinned him with a pin,

And then she called for a wash-basin,
    To spill his heart's blood in.

6^3. dressing. 7^2. And the.   8 *comes before* 6.
8^3. they threw : deep dark well.
8^4. Was fifty fathoms.   9 *wanting.*
J. a. 6^4. Whereer.
  b. 1^2. It rains both great.
    2^2. And yet it. 3^3. thou young.
    4^1. I dare not come, I dare not come.
    4^2. Unless my.
    4^3. And I shall be flogged when I get.
    5^3. She laid him on the.
    6^1. The thickest of blood did first come out.
    6^3. The third that came was his dear heart's
      blood.
    6^4. Where all his.   7–13 *wanting.*
K. *There are slight changes in the second copy.*
    4^2. all *wanting.* $5^{1,3}$. *The first as wanting.*
L. a. " After nearly sixty years my memory is not
    altogether trustworthy, and I am not alto-
    gether sure how far I have mixed up my
    childish recollections with later forms of the
    ballad which I have read."
    The singer tagged on to this fragment version
    c *of* The Maid *freed from the* Gallows,
    given at II, 352.
  b. 1^3. For all. 3^1. it *wanting.* 4^1. him in.
    4^4. And wiled the young thing in.
    5. *wanting.* 6^1. him in through one dark door.

6^2. she has. $6^{3,4}$ *wanting.*
6^5. She 's laid him.   *After* 7 :

She 's rolled him in a cake of lead,
    Bade him lie still and sleep,
And thrown him in St Mary's well,
    'T was fifty fathoms deep.

When bells were rung, and mass was sung,
    And all the boys came home,
Then every mother had her own son,
    But Lady Maisy had none.

N. " The writer was not a little surprised to hear
    from a group of colored children, in the
    streets of New York city (though in a more
    incoherent form), the following ballad. He
    traced the song to a little girl living in one
    of the cabins near Central Park, from whom
    he obtained this version. . . . The mother of
    the family had herself been born in New
    York, of Irish parentage, but had learned
    from her own mother, and handed down to
    her children, such legends of the past as the
    ballad we cite." *Communicated to me by*
    Mr. Newell some considerable time before
    publication.

O. 3. " One of the Jew's daughters, ' a-dressed all
    in green,' issues from the garden and says,
    Come in, etc."

THE

ENGLISH AND SCOTTISH

POPULAR BALLADS

EDITED BY

FRANCIS JAMES CHILD

PART VI

156

QUEEN ELEANOR'S CONFESSION

A. a. 'Queen Eleanor's Confession,' a broadside, London, Printed for C. Bates, at the Sun and Bible in Gilt-spur-street, near Pye-corner, Bagford Ballads, II, No 26, British Museum (1685 ?). b. Another broadside, Printed for C. Bates in Pye-corner, Bagford Ballads, I, No 33 (1685 ?). c. Another copy, Printed for C. Bates, in Pye-corner, reprinted in Utterson's Little Book of Ballads, p. 22. d. A Collection of Old Ballads, 1723, I, 18.

B. Skene MS., p. 39.

C. 'Queen Eleanor's Confession,' Buchan's Gleanings, p. 77.

D. 'The Queen of England,' Aytoun, Ballads of Scotland, 1859, I, 196.

E. 'Queen Eleanor's Confession,' Kinloch's Ancient Scottish Ballads, p. 247.

F. 'Earl Marshall,' Motherwell's Minstrelsy, p. 1.

GIVEN in Percy's Reliques, 1765, II, 145, "from an old printed copy," with some changes by the editor, of which the more important are in stanzas 2–4. F, "recovered from recitation" by Motherwell, repeats Percy's changes in 2, 3, 10⁴, and there is reason to question whether this and the other recited versions are anything more than traditional variations of printed copies. The ballad seems first to have got into print in the latter part of the seventeenth century, but was no doubt circulating orally some time before that, for it is in the truly popular tone. The fact that *two* friars hear the confession would militate against a much earlier date. In E there might appear to be some consciousness of this irregularity; for the Queen sends for a single friar, and the King says he will be "a prelate old" and sit in a dark corner; but none the less does the King take an active part in the shrift.*

There is a Newcastle copy, "Printed and sold by Robert Marchbank, in the Customhouse-Entry," among the Douce ballads in the Bodleian Library, 3, fol. 80, and in the Roxburghe collection, British Museum, III, 634. This is dated in the Museum catalogue 1720?

Eleanor of Aquitaine was married to Henry II of England in 1152, a few weeks after her divorce from Louis VII of France, she being then about thirty and Henry nineteen years of age. "It is needless to observe," says Percy, "that the following ballad is altogether fabulous; whatever gallantries Eleanor encouraged in the time of her first husband, none are imputed to her in that of her second."

In Peele's play of Edward I, 1593, the story of this ballad is transferred from Henry II and Eleanor of Aquitaine to Edward Longshanks and that model of women and wives, Eleanor of Castile, together with other slanders which might less ridiculously have been invented of Henry II's Eleanor.† Edward's brother Edmund plays the part of the Earl Marshall. The Queen dies; the King bewails his loss in terms of imbecile affection, and orders crosses to be reared at all the stages of the funeral convoy. Peele's Works, ed. Dyce, I, 184 ff.

There are several sets of tales in which a

---

* The threat implied in E 3⁴ has no motive; and the phrase "haly spark" in 5⁴ is an unadvised anticipation.

† Found also in the ballad, A Warning-Piece to England against Pride and Wickedness: Being the Fall of Queen Eleanor, Wife to Edward the First, King of England, who, for her Pride, by God's Judgments, sunk into the Ground at Charing-Cross and rose at Queen-Hithe. A Collection of Old Ballads, I, 97.

husband takes a shrift-father's place and hears his wife's confession. 1. A fabliau "Du chevalier qui fist sa fame confesse," Barbazan et Méon, III, 229 ; Montaiglon, Recueil Général, I, 178, No 16 ; Legrand, Fabliaux, etc., 1829, IV, 132, with circumstances added by Legrand. 2. Les Cent Nouvelles Nouvelles, 1432, No 78 ; Scala Celi, 1480, fol. 49 ;* Mensa Philosophica, cited by Manni, Istoria del Decamerone, p. 476 ; Doni, Novelle, Lucca, 1852, Nov. xiii ; Malespini, Ducento Novelle, No 92, Venice, 1609, I, 248 ; Kirchhof, Wendunmuth, No 245, Oesterley, II, 535 ; La Fontaine, " Le Mari Confesseur," Contes, I, No 4. 3. Boccaccio, VII, 5.

In 1, 2, the husband discovers himself after the confession ; in 3 he is recognized by the wife before she begins her shrift, which she frames to suit her purposes. In all these, the wife, on being reproached with the infidelity which she had revealed, tells the husband that she knew all the while that he was the confessor, and gives an ingenious turn to her

apparently compromising disclosures which satisfies him of her innocence. All these tales have the cynical Oriental character, and, to a healthy taste, are far surpassed by the innocuous humor of the English ballad.

Oesterley, in his notes to Kirchhof, V, 103, cites a number of German story-books in which the tale may, in some form, be found ; also Hans Sachs, 4, 3, 7b.† In Bandello, Parte Prima, No 9, a husband, not disguising himself, prevails upon a priest to let him overhear his wife's confession, and afterwards kills her.

Svend Grundtvig informed me that he had six copies of an evidently recent (and very bad) translation of Percy's ballad, taken down from recitation in different parts of Denmark. In one of these Queen Eleanor is exchanged for a Queen of Norway. Percy's ballad is also translated by Bodmer, II, 40 ; Ursinus, p. 59 ; Talvj, Charakteristik, p. 513 ; Döring, p. 373 ; Knortz, L. u. R. Alt-Englands, No 51.

A

a. A broadside, London, Printed for C. Bates, at the Sun & Bible in Gilt-spur-street, near Pye-corner, Bagford Ballads, II, No 26, 1685 ? b. A broadside, Printed for C. Bates, in Pye-corner, Bagford Ballads, I, No 33, 1685 ? c. Another copy of b, reprinted in Utterson's Little Book of Ballads, p. 22. d. A Collection of Old Ballads, 1723, I, 18.

1 QUEEN ELENOR was a sick woman,
    And afraid that she should dye ;
Then she sent for two fryars of France,
    For to speak with them speedily.

2 The King calld down his nobles all,
    By one, by two, and by three,
And sent away for Earl Martial,
    For to speak with him speedily.

3 When that he came before the King,
    He fell on his bended knee ;

'A boon, a boon ! our gracious king,
    That you sent so hastily.'

4 'I'll pawn my living and my lands,
    My septer and my crown,
That whatever Queen Elenor says,
    I will not write it down.

5 'Do you put on one fryar's coat,
    And I'll put on another,
And we will to Queen Elenor go,
    One fryar like another.'

6 Thus both attired then they go ;
    When they came to Whitehall,
The bells they did ring, and the quiristers sing,
    And the torches did light them all.

7 When that they came before the Queen,
    They fell on their bended knee :

---

* There attributed to Jacques de Vitry, but not found in his Exempla. Professor Crane informs me that, though the Scala Celi cites Jacques de Vitry sixty-two times, only fourteen of such *exempla* occur among J. de V.'s.

† The story does not occur in Doni's Marmi, iii, 27, as has been said. What is there found is somewhat after the fashion of ' The Baffled Knight,' No 112.

'A boon, a boon! our gracious queen,
   That you sent so hastily.'

8 'Are you two fryars of France?' she said,
   'Which I suppose you be;
But if you are two English fryars,
   Then hanged shall you be.'

9 'We are two fryars of France,' they said,
   'As you suppose we be ;
We have not been at any mass
   Since we came from the sea.'

10 'The first vile thing that ere I did
   I will to you unfold ;
Earl Martial had my maidenhead,
   Underneath this cloath of gold.'

11 'That is a vile sin,' then said the king,
   'God may forgive it thee ! '
'Amen ! Amen ! ' quoth Earl Martial,
   With a heavy heart then spoke he.

12 'The next vile thing that ere I did
   To you I 'll not deny ;
I made a box of poyson strong,
   To poyson King Henry.'

13 'That is a vile sin,' then said the King,
   'God may forgive it thee ! '
'Amen ! Amen ! ' quoth Earl Martial,
   'And I wish it so may be.'

14 'The next vile thing that ere I did
   To you I will discover ;

I poysoned Fair Rosamond,
   All in fair Woodstock bower.'

15 'That is a vile sin,' then said the King,
   'God may forgive it thee ! '
'Amen ! Amen ! ' quoth Earl Martial,
   'And I wish it so may be.'

16 'Do you see yonders little boy,
   A tossing of that ball?
That is Earl Martial['s] eldest son,
   And I love him the best of all.

17 'Do you see yonders little boy,
   A catching of the ball?
That is King Henry's son,' she said,
   'And I love him the worst of all.

18 'His head is like unto a bull,
   His nose is like a boar ; '
'No matter for that,' King Henry said,
   'I love him the better therefore.'

19 The King pulld of his fryar's coat,
   And appeard all in red ;
She shriekd and she cry'd, she wrong her
   hands,
And said she was betrayd.

20 The King lookd over his left shoulder,
   And a grim look looked he,
And said, Earl Martial, but for my oath,
   Then hanged shouldst thou be.

B

Skene MS., p. 39.

1 OUR queen 's sick, an very sick,
   She 's sick an like to die ;
She has sent for the friars of France,
   To speak wi her speedilie.

2 'I 'll put on a friar's robe,
   An ye 'll put on anither,
An we 'll go to Madam the Queen,
   Like friars bath thegither.'

3 'God forbid,' said Earl Marishall,
   'That ever the like shud be,

That I beguile Madam the Queen!
   I wad be hangit hie.'

4 The King pat on a friar's robe,
   Earl Marishall on anither ;
They 're on to the Queen,
   Like friars baith thegither.

5 'Gin ye be the friars of France,
   As I trust well ye be —
But an ye be ony ither men,
   Ye sall be hangit hie.'

6 The King he turnd him roun,
   An by his troth sware he,

We hae na sung messe
  Sin we came frae the sea.

7 'The first sin ever I did,
  An a very great sin 't was tee,
I gae my maidenhead to Earl Marishall,
  Under the greenwood tree.'

8 'That was a sin, an a very great sin,
  But pardond it may be;'
'Wi mendiment,' said Earl Marshall,
  But a heavy heart had he.

9 'The next sin ever I did,
  An a very great sin 't was tee,
I poisened Lady Rosamond,
  An the King's darling was she.'

10 'That was a sin, an a very great sin,
  But pardond it may be;'
'Wi mendiment,' said King Henry,
  But a heavy heart had he.

11 'The next sin ever I did,
  An a very great sin 't was tee,
I keepit poison in my bosom seven years,
  To poison him King Henrie.'

12 'That was a sin, an a very great sin,
  But pardond it may be;'
'Wi mendiment,' said King Henry,
  But a heavy heart had he.

13 'O see na ye yon bonny boys,
  As they play at the ba?
An see na ye Lord Marishal's son?
  I lee him best of a'.

14 'But see na ye King Henry's son?
  He's headit like a bull, and backit like a boar,
  I like him warst awa:'
'And by my sooth,' says him King Henry,
  'I like him best o the twa.'

15 The King he turned him roun,
  Pat on the coat o goud,
  .   .   .   .   .   .
The Queen turnd the King to behold.

16 .   .   .   .
  .   .   .   .   .   .
'Gin I hadna sworn by the crown and sceptre
    roun,
Earl Marishal sud been gart die.'

C

Buchan's Gleanings, p. 77.

1 THE Queen's faen sick, and very, very sick,
  Sick, and going to die,
And she's sent for twa friars of France,
  To speak with her speedilie.

2 The King he said to the Earl Marischal,
  To the Earl Marischal said he,
The Queen she wants twa friars frae France,
  To speak with her presentlie.

3 Will ye put on a friar's coat,
  And I'll put on another,
And we'll go in before the Queen,
  Like friars both together.

4 'But O forbid,' said the Earl Marischal,
  'That I this deed should dee!
For if I beguile Eleanor our queen,
  She will gar hang me hie.'

5 The King he turned him round about,
  An angry man was he;
He's sworn by his sceptre and his sword
  Earl Marischal should not die.

6 The King has put on a friar's coat,
  Earl Marischal on another,
And they went in before the Queen,
  Like friars both together.

7 'O, if ye be twa friars of France,
  Ye're dearly welcome to me;
But if ye be twa London friars,
  I will gar hang you hie.'

8 'Twa friars of France, twa friars of France,
  Twa friars of France are we,
And we vow we never spoke to a man
  Till we spake to Your Majesty.'

9 'The first great sin that eer I did,
  And I'll tell you it presentlie,

Earl Marischal got my maidenhead,
  When coming oer the sea.'

10 'That was a sin, and a very great sin,
  But pardoned it may be;'
'All that with amendment,' said Earl Mari-
  schal,
But a quacking heart had he.

11 'The next great sin that eer I did,
  I'll tell you it presentlie;
I carried a box seven years in my breast,
  To poison King Henrie.'

12 'O that was a sin, and a very great sin,
  But pardoned it may be;'
'All that with amendment,' said Earl Mari-
  schal,
But a quacking heart had he.

13 'The next great sin that eer I did,
  I'll tell you it presentlie;
I poisoned the Lady Rosamond,
  And a very good woman was she.

14 'See ye not yon twa bonny boys,
  As they play at the ba?
The eldest of them is Marischal's son,
  And I love him best of a';
The youngest of them is Henrie's son,
  And I love him none at a'

15 'For he is headed like a bull, a bull,
  He is backed like a boar;'
'Then by my sooth,' King Henrie said,
  'I love him the better therefor.'

16 The King has cast off his friar's coat,
  Put on a coat of gold;
The Queen she's turned her face about,
  She could not's face behold.

17 The King then said to Earl Marischal,
  To the Earl Marischal said he,
Were it not for my sceptre and sword,
  Earl Marischall, ye should die.

———

D

Aytoun's Ballads of Scotland, 2d edition, I, 196, from the recitation of a lady residing in Kirkcaldy; learned of her mother.

1 THE queen of England she has fallen sick,
  Sore sick, and like to die;
And she has sent for twa French priests,
  To bear her companie.

2 The King he has got word o this,
  And an angry man was he;
And he is on to the Earl-a-Marshall,
  As fast as he can gae.

3 'Now you'll put on a priest's robe,
  And I'll put on anither,
And we will on unto the Queen,
  Like twa French priests thegither.'

4 'No indeed!' said the Earl-a-Marshall,
  'That winna I do for thee,
Except ye swear by your sceptre and crown
  Ye'll do me nae injurie.'

5 The King has sworn by his sceptre and crown
  He'll do him nae injurie,
And they are on unto the Queen,
  As fast as they can gae.

6 'O, if that ye be twa French priests,
  Ye're welcome unto me;
But if ye be twa Scottish lords,
  High hanged ye shall be.

7 'The first sin that I did sin,
  And that to you I'll tell,
I sleeped wi the Earl-a-Marshall,
  Beneath a silken bell.

8 'And wasna that a sin, and a very great sin?
  And I pray ye pardon me;'
'Amen, and amen!' said the Earl-a-Marshall,
  And a wearied man was he.

9 'The neist sin that I did sin,
  And that to you I'll tell,
I keeped the poison seven years in my bosom,
  To poison the King himsel.

10 'And wasna that a sin, and a very great sin?
　　And I pray ye pardon me ; '
　'Amen, and amen ! ' said the Earl-a-Marshall,
　　And a wearied man was he.

11 'O see ye there my seven sons,
　　A' playing at the ba ?
　There 's but ane o them the King's himsel,
　　And I like him warst of a'.

12 'He's high-backed, and low-breasted,
　　And he is bald withal ; '
　' And by my deed,' and says the King,
　　' I like him best mysel !

13 'O wae betide ye, Earl-a-Marshall,
　　And an ill death may ye die !
　For if I hadna sworn by my sceptre and crown,
　　High hanged ye should be.'

E

Kinloch's Ancient Scottish Ballads, p. 247.

1 THE Queen fell sick, and very, very sick,
　　She was sick, and like to dee,
　And she sent for a friar oure frae France,
　　Her confessour to be.

2 King Henry, when he heard o that,
　　An angry man was he,
　And he sent to the Earl Marshall,
　　Attendance for to gie.

3 'The Queen is sick,' King Henry cried,
　　'And wants to be beshriven ;
　She has sent for a friar oure frae France ;
　　By the rude, he were better in heaven !

4 'But tak you now a friar's guise,
　　The voice and gesture feign,
　And when she has the pardon crav'd,
　　Respond to her, Amen !

5 'And I will be a prelate old,
　　And sit in a corner dark,
　To hear the adventures of my spouse,
　　My spouse, and her haly spark.'

6 'My liege, my liege, how can I betray
　　My mistress and my queen ?
　O swear by the rude that no damage
　　From this shall be gotten or gien ! '

7 'I swear by the rude,' quoth King Henry,
　　'No damage shall be gotten or gien ;
　Come, let us spare no cure nor care
　　For the conscience o the Queen.'

*　　*　　*　　*　　*

8 'O fathers, O fathers, I 'm very, very sick,
　　I 'm sick, and like to dee ;
　Some ghostly comfort to my poor soul
　　O tell if ye can gie ! '

9 'Confess, confess,' Earl Marshall cried,
　　' And you shall pardoned be ; '
　'Confess, confess,' the King replied,
　　' And we shall comfort gie.'

10 'Oh, how shall I tell the sorry, sorry tale !
　　How can the tale be told !
　I playd the harlot wi the Earl Marshall,
　　Beneath yon cloth of gold.

11 'Oh, wasna that a sin, and a very great sin ?
　　But I hope it will pardoned be ; '
　'Amen ! Amen ! ' quoth the Earl Marshall,
　　And a very feart heart had he.

12 'O down i the forest, in a bower,
　　Beyond yon dark oak-tree,
　I drew a penknife frae my pocket
　　To kill King Henerie.

13 'Oh, wasna that a sin, and a very great sin ?
　　But I hope it will pardoned be ; '
　'Amen ! Amen ! ' quoth the Earl Marshall,
　　And a very feart heart had he.

14 'O do you see yon pretty little boy,
　　That 's playing at the ba ?
　He is the Earl Marshall's only son,
　　And I loved him best of a'.

15 'Oh, wasna that a sin, and a very great sin ?
　　But I hope it will pardoned be ; '
　'Amen ! Amen ! ' quoth the Earl Marshall,
　　And a very feart heart had he.

16 'And do you see yon pretty little girl,
    That's a' beclad in green?
  She's a friar's daughter, oure in France,
    And I hoped to see her a queen.

17 'Oh, wasna that a sin, and a very great sin?
    But I hope it will pardoned be;'
  'Amen! Amen!' quoth the Earl Marshall,
    And a feart heart still had he.

18 'O do you see yon other little boy,
    That's playing at the ba?

He is King Henry's only son,
    And I like him warst of a'.

19 'He's headed like a buck,' she said,
    'And backed like a bear;'
  'Amen!' quoth the King, in the King's ain
    voice,
  'He shall be my only heir.'

20 The King lookd over his left shoulder,
    An angry man was he:
  'An it werna for the oath I sware,
    Earl Marshall, thou shouldst dee.'

———◆———

F

Motherwell's Minstrelsy, p. 1; from recitation.

1 QUEENE ELEANOR was a sick woman,
    And sick just like to die,
  And she has sent for two fryars of France,
    To come to her speedilie.
  And she has sent, etc.

2 The King called downe his nobles all,
    By one, by two, by three:
  'Earl Marshall, I'll go shrive the Queene,
    And thou shalt wend with mee.'

3 'A boone, a boone!' quoth Earl Marshall,
    And fell on his bended knee,
  'That whatsoever the Queene may say,
    No harm thereof may bee.'

4 'O you'll put on a gray-friar's gowne,
    And I'll put on another,
  And we will away to fair London town,
    Like friars both together.'

5 'O no, O no, my liege, my king,
    Such things can never bee;
  For if the Queene hears word of this,
    Hanged she'll cause me to bee.'

6 'I swear by the sun, I swear by the moon,
    And by the stars so hie,
  And by my sceptre and my crowne,
    The Earl Marshall shall not die.'

7 The King's put on a gray-friar's gowne,
    The Earl Marshall's put on another,

And they are away to fair London towne,
    Like fryars both together.

8 When that they came to fair London towne,
    And came into Whitehall,
  The bells did ring, and the quiristers sing,
    And the torches did light them all.

9 And when they came before the Queene,
    They kneeled down on their knee:
  'What matter, what matter, our gracious
    queene,
  You've sent so speedilie?'

10 'O, if you are two fryars of France,
    It's you that I wished to see;
  But if you are two English lords,
    You shall hang on the gallowes-tree.'

11 'O we are not two English lords,
    But two fryars of France we bee,
  And we sang the Song of Solomon,
    As we came over the sea.'

12 'Oh, the first vile sin I did commit
    Tell it I will to thee;
  I fell in love with the Earl Marshall,
    As he brought me over the sea.'

13 'Oh, that was a great sin,' quoth the King,
    'But pardond it must bee;'
  'Amen! Amen!' said the Earl Marshall,
    With a heavie heart spake hee.

14 'Oh, the next sin that I did commit
    I will to you unfolde;

Earl Marshall had my virgin dower,
 Beneath this cloth of golde.'

15 'Oh, that was a vile sin,' said the King,
 'May God forgive it thee!'
'Amen! Amen!' groaned the Earl Marshall,
 And a very frightened man was hee.

16 'Oh, the next sin that I did commit
 Tell it I will to thee;
I poisoned a lady of noble blood,
 For the sake of King Henrie.'

17 'Oh, that was a great sin,' said the King,
 'But pardoned it shall bee;'
'Amen! Amen!' said the Earl Marshall,
 And still a frightened man was he.

18 'Oh, the next sin that ever I did
 Tell it I will to thee;
I have kept strong poison this seven long years,
 To poison King Henrie.'

19 'Oh, that was a great sin,' said the King,
 'But pardoned it must bee;'
'Amen! Amen!' said the Earl Marshall,
 And still a frightened man was hee.

20 'O don't you see two little boys,
 Playing at the football?
O yonder is the Earl Marshall's son,
 And I like him best of all.

21 'O don't you see yon other little boy,
 Playing at the football?
O that one is King Henrie's son,
 And I like him worst of all.

22 'His head is like a black bull's head,
 His feet are like a bear;'
'What matter! what matter!' cried the King,
 'He's my son, and my only heir.'

23 The King plucked off his fryar's gowne,
 And stood in his scarlet so red;
The Queen she turned herself in bed,
 And cryed that she was betrayde.

24 The King lookt oer his left shoulder,
 And a grim look looked he;
'Earl Marshall,' he said, 'but for my oath,
 Thou hadst swung on the gallowes-tree.'

––––––––

A. a. Queen Eleanor's Confession: Shewing how King Henry, with the Earl Martial, in Fryars Habits, came to her, instead of two Fryars from France, which she sent for. To a pleasant New Tune. *Both* a *and* b *are dated in the Museum Catalogue* 1670? "C. Bates, at Sun & Bible, near St. Sepulchre's Church, in Pye Corner, 1685." *Chappell.*
10¹. thta ere. 14². disdover. 17¹. younders.
b. *Title the same, except* came to see her.
16³. Martial's. 17¹. see then yonders.
20¹. his let.
c. *Title as in* a. 4³. whatsoever. 8⁴. you shall.
16². catching of the. 16³. Marshal's.
17¹. see then yonders.

d. Queen Eleanor's Confession to the Two supposed Fryars of France.
1⁴. To speak with her. 2². and *wanting*.
2⁴. For *wanting*.
4¹. I'll pawn my lands the King then cry'd.
4³. whatsoere. 5¹. on a.
5⁴. Like fryar and his brother.
6³. they *wanting*. 7⁴. you. 8². As I.
10⁴. Beneath this. 11¹, 13¹, 15¹. That's.
11⁴. then *wanting*.
16². of the. 16³. Marshal's.
16⁴, 17⁴. And *wanting*. 18³. Henry cry'd.
19³. shriekd, she cry'd, and wrung.
20⁴. Or hanged.
E. 14⁴. loved; love *in Kinloch's annotated copy.*
F. 10¹, 11¹, 20¹,³, 21¹,³. Oh.

157

GUDE WALLACE

A. 'On an honourable Achievement of Sir William Wallace, near Falkirk,' a chap-book of Four New Songs and a Prophecy, 1745? Johnson's Museum, ed. 1853, D. Laing's additions, IV, 458 *; Maidment's Scotish Ballads and Songs, 1859, p. 83.

B. 'Sir William Wallace,' communicated to Percy by Robert Lambe, of Norham, probably in 1768.

C. 'Gude Wallace,' Johnson's Museum, p. 498, No 484, communicated by Robert Burns.

D. 'Gude Wallace,' communicated to Robert Chambers by Elliot Anderson, 1827.

E. 'Willie Wallace,' communicated to James Telfer by A. Fisher.

F. 'Willie Wallace,' Buchan's Gleanings, p. 114.

G. 'Sir William Wallace,' Alexander Laing's Thistle of Scotland, p. 100; Motherwell's MS., p. 487.

H. 'Wallace and his Leman,' Buchan's Ballads of the North of Scotland, II, 226.

———◆———

C is reprinted by Finlay, I, 103. It is made the basis of a long ballad by Jamieson, II, 166, and serves as a thread for Cunningham's 'Gude Wallace,' Scottish Songs, I, 262.* F is repeated by Motherwell, Minstrelsy, p. 364, and by Aytoun, I, 54. A copy in the Laing MSS, University of Edinburgh, Div. II, 358, is C.

Blind Harry's Wallace (of about 1460, earlier than 1488) is clearly the source of this ballad. A-F are derived from vv 1080–1119 of the Fifth Book. Here Wallace, on his way to a hostelry with a comrade, met a woman, who counselled them to pass by, if Scots, for southrons were there, drinking and talking of Wallace; twenty are there, making great din, but no man of fence. "Wallace went in and bad Benedicite." The captain said, Thou art a Scot, the devil thy nation quell. Wallace drew, and ran the captain through; "fifteen he straik and fifteen has he slayn;" his comrade killed the other five.

The story of A-E is sufficiently represented by that of **A**. Wallace comes upon a woman washing, and asks her for tidings. There are fifteen Englishmen at the hostelry seeking Wallace. Had he money he would go thither. She tells him out twenty shillings (for which he takes off *both* hat and hood, and thanks her reverently). He bows himself over a staff and enters the hostelry, saying, Good ben be here (in C, he bad Benedicite, in the words of Blind Harry). The captain asks the crooked carl where he was born, and the carl answers that he is a Scot. The captain offers the carl twenty shillings for a sight of Wallace. The carl wants no better bode, or offer.† He strikes the captain such a blow over the jaws that he will never eat more, and sticks the rest. Then he bids the goodwife get him food, for he has eaten nothing for two days. Ere the meal is ready, fifteen other Englishmen light at the door. These he soon disposes of, sticking five, trampling five in the gutter, and hanging five in the wood.

F makes Wallace change clothes with a

---

* Cunningham, in his loose way, talks of several fragments which he had endeavored to combine, but can spare room for only one couplet:

    Though lame of a leg and blind of an ee,
    You're as like William Wallace as ever I did see.

But this is the William of 'The Knight and the Shepherd's Daughter,' No 110.

† **A** 15, **B** 12, **D** 12, are somewhat corrupted. In **F** 14 Wallace says he never *had* a better bode. In **E** 10 Wallace's reply is, Pay down, for if your answer be not good you shall have the downfall of Robin Hood; and in **G** 30, Tell down, and ye shall see William Wallace with the downcome of Robin Hood; that is, I suppose, you shall be knocked down as if by Robin Hood.

beggar, and ask charity at the inn.   He kills
his thirty men between eight and four, and
then returning to the North-Inch (a common
lying along the Tay, near Perth) finds the
maid who was washing her lilie hands in st. 3
still "washing tenderlie." He pulls out twenty
of the fifty pounds which he got from the
captain, and hands them over to the maid for
the good luck of her half-crown.

G has the change of clothes with the beg-
gar, found in F, and prefixes to the story of
the other versions another adventure of Wal-
lace, taken from the Fourth Book of Blind
Harry, vv 704–87.   Wallace's enemies have
seen him leaving his mistress's house.   They
seize her, threaten to burn her unless she
'tells,' and promise to marry her to a knight
if she will help to bring the rebel down.
Wallace returns, and she seeks to detain
him, but he says he must go back to his
men.   Hereupon she falls to weeping, and
ends with confessing her treason.   He asks
her if she repents ; she says that to mend
the miss she would burn on a hill, and is for-
given.   Wallace puts on her gown and curches,
hiding his sword under his weed, tells the
armed men who are watching for him that
Wallace is locked in, and makes good speed
out of the gate.   Two men follow him, for
he seems to be a stalwart quean ; Wallace
turns on them and kills them.   This is Blind

Harry's story, and it will be observed to be
followed closely in the ballad, with the addi-
tion of a pitcher in each hand to complete
the female disguise, and two more southrons
to follow and be killed.   The first half of
this version is plainly a late piece of work,
very possibly of this century, much later than
the other, which itself need not be very old.
But the portions of Blind Harry's poem out
of which these ballads were made were per-
haps themselves composed from older ballads,
and the restitution of the lyrical form may
have given us something not altogether un-
like what was sung in the fifteenth, or even
the fourteenth, century.   The fragment H is,
as far as it goes, a repetition of G.

Bower (1444–49) says that after the battle
of Roslyn, 1298, Wallace took ship and went
to France, distinguishing himself by his valor
against pirates on the sea and against the
English on the continent, as ballads both in
France and Scotland testify.*   A fragment
of a ballad relating to Wallace is preserved
in Constable's MS. Cantus: Leyden's Com-
playnt of Scotland, p. 226.

> Wallace parted his men in three
> And sundrie gaits are gone.

C is translated by Arndt, Blütenlese, p.
198 ; F by Knortz, Schottische Balladen, p.
69, No 22.

A

A chap-book of Four New Songs and a Prophecy, 1745 ?
The Scots Musical Museum, 1853, D. Laing's additions, IV,
458 * ; Maidment, Scotish Ballads and Songs, 1859, p. 83.

1 'HAD we a king,' said Wallace then,
   'That our kind Scots might live by their
     own !
  But betwixt me and the English blood
  I think there is an ill seed sown.'

2 Wallace him over a river lap,
   He lookd low down to a linn ;

He was war of a gay lady
   Was even at the well washing.

3 'Well mot ye fare, fair madam,' he said,
   ' And ay well mot ye fare and see !
  Have ye any tidings me to tell,
   I pray you 'll show them unto me.'

4 'I have no tidings you to tell,
   Nor yet no tidings you to ken ;
  But into that hostler's house
   There 's fifteen of your Englishmen.'

* Post enim conflictum de Roslyn, Wallace, ascensa navi,
Franciam petit, ubi quanta probitate refulsit, tam super
mare a piratis quam in Francia ab Anglis perpessus est dis-
crimina, et viriliter se habuit, nonnulla carmina, tam in ipsa
Francia quam Scotia, attestantur. Scotichronicon, Goodall,
II, 176, note.

5 'And they are seeking Wallace there,
    For they 've ordained him to be slain : '
 'O God forbid ! ' said Wallace then,
    ' For he 's oer good a kind Scotsman.

6 ' But had I money me upon,
    And evn this day, as I have none,
 Then would I to that hostler's house,
    And evn as fast as I could gang.'

7 She put her hand in her pocket,
    She told him twenty shillings oer her knee ;
 Then he took off both hat and hood,
    And thankd the lady most reverently.

8 ' If eer I come this way again,
    Well paid [your] money it shall be ; '
 Then he took off both hat and hood,
    And he thankd the lady most reverently.

9 He leand him twofold oer a staff,
    So did he threefold oer a tree,
 And he 's away to the hostler's house,
    Even as fast as he might dree.

10 When he came to the hostler's house,
    He said, Good-ben be here ! quoth he :
 An English captain, being deep load,
    He asked him right cankerdly,

11 Where was you born, thou crooked carle,
    And in what place, and what country ?
 ' T is I was born in fair Scotland,
    A crooked carle although I be.'

12 The English captain swore by th' rood,
    ' We are Scotsmen as well as thee,
 And we are seeking Wallace ; then
    To have him merry we should be.'

13 ' The man,' said Wallace, ' ye 're looking for,
    I seed him within these days three ;

And he has slain an English captain,
    And ay the fearder the rest may be.'

14 ' I 'd give twenty shillings,' said the captain,
    ' To such a crooked carle as thee,
 If you would take me to the place
    Where that I might proud Wallace see.'

15 ' Hold out your hand,' said Wallace then,
    ' And show your money and be free,
 For tho you 'd bid an hundred pound,
    I never bade a better bode ' [, said he].

16 He struck the captain oer the chafts,
    Till that he never chewed more ;
 He stickd the rest about the board,
    And left them all a sprawling there.

17 ' Rise up, goodwife,' said Wallace then,
    ' And give me something for to eat ;
 For it 's near two days to an end
    Since I tasted one bit of meat.'

18 His board was scarce well covered,
    Nor yet his dine well scantly dight,
 Till fifteen other Englishmen
    Down all about the door did light.

19 ' Come out, come out,' said they, ' Wallace ! '
        then,
    ' For the day is come that ye must die ; '
 And they thought so little of his might,
    But ay the fearder they might be.

20 The wife ran but, the gudeman ran ben,
    It put them all into a fever ;
 Then five he sticked where they stood,
    And five he trampled in the gutter.

21 And five he chased to yon green wood,
    He hanged them all out-oer a grain ;
 And gainst the morn at twelve o'clock,
    He dined with his kind Scottish men.

B

Communicated to Percy by R. Lambe, of Norham, apparently in 1768.

1 ' I WISH we had a king,' says Wallace,
    ' That Scotland might not want a head ;

In England and in Scotland baith,
    I 'm sure that some have sowed ill seed.'

2 Wallace he oer the water did luke,
    And he luked law down by a glen,

And he was aware of a gay lady,
  As she was at the well washing.

3 'Weel may ye save, fair lady !' he says,
  'Far better may ye save and see !
If ye have ony tidings to tell,
  I pray cum tell them a' to me.'

4 'I have no tidings you to tell,
  And as few tidings do I ken ;
But up and to yon ostler-house
  Are just gane fifteen gentlemen.

5 'They now are seeking Gude Wallace,
  And ay they're damning him to hang ;'
'Oh God forbid,' says Wallace then,
  'I'm sure he is a true Scotsman.

6 'Had I but ae penny in my pocket,
  Or in my company ae baubee,
I woud up to yon ostler-house,
  A' these big gentlemen to see.'

7 She pat her hand into her pocket,
  She powd out twenty shillings and three :
'If eer I live to come this way,
  Weel payed shall your money be.'

8 He leaned him twafold oer a staff,
  Sae did he twafold oer a tree,
And he's gane up to the ostler-house,
  A' these fine gentlemen to see.

9 When he cam up among them a',
  He bad his benison be there ;
The captain, being weel buke-learnd,
  Did answer him in domineer.

10 'Where was ye born, ye eruked carl,
  Or in what town, or what countree ?'
'O I was born in fair Scotland,
  A cruked carl although I be.'

11 The captain sware by the root of his sword,
  Saying, I'm a Scotsman as weel as thee ;
Here's twenty shillings of English money
  To such a cruked carl as thee,
If thou 'll tell me of that Wallace ;
  He's ay the creature I want to see.

12 'O hawd your hand,' says Wallace then,
  'I'm feard your money be not gude ;
If 't were as muckle and ten times mair,
  It shoud not bide anither bode.'

13 He's taen the captain alang the chaps,
  A wat he never chawed mair ;
The rest he sticked about the table,
  And left them a' a sprawling there.

14 'Gude wife,' he said, 'for my benison,
  Get up and get my dinner dight ;
For it is twa days till an end
  Syne I did taste ane bit of meat.'

15 Dinner was not weel made ready,
  Nor yet upon the table set,
When fifteen other Englishmen
  Alighted all about the yate.

16 'Come out, come out now, Wallace,' they say,
  'For this is the day ye are to dee ;
Ye trust sae mickle in God's might,
  And ay the less we do fear thee.'

17 The gude wife ran but, the gude man ran ben,
  They pat the house all in a swither ;
Five sune he sticked where he stude,
  And five he smitherd in a gutter.

18 Five he chac'd to the gude green-wood,
  And hanged them a' out-oer a pin ;
And at the morn at eight o'clock
  He din'd with his men at Lough-mabin.

———◆———

C

Johnson's Museum, p. 498, No 484, communicated by Robert Burns.

1 'O FOR my ain king,' quo Gude Wallace,
  'The rightfu king of fair Scotland !
Between me and my soverign blude
  I think I see some ill seed sawn.'

2 Wallace out over yon river he lap,
  And he has lighted low down on yon plain,
And he was aware of a gay ladie,
  As she was at the well washing.

3 'What tydins, what tydins, fair lady ?' he says,
  'What tydins hast thou to tell unto me ?

What tydins, what tydins, fair lady?' he says,
'What tydins hae ye in the south countrie?'

4 'Low down in yon wee ostler-house
There is fyfteen Englishmen,
And they are seekin for Gude Wallace,
It's him to take and him to hang.'

5 'There's nocht in my purse,' quo Gude Wallace,
'There's nocht, not even a bare pennie;
But I will down to yon wee ostler-house,
Thir fyfteen Englishmen to see.'

6 And when he cam to yon wee ostler-house
He bad bendicite be there;
. . . .
. . . .

7 'Where was ye born, auld crookit carl?
Where was ye born, in what countrie?'
'I am a true Scot born and bred,
And an auld crookit carl just sic as ye see.'

8 'I wad gie fifteen shillings to onie crookit carl,
To onie crookit carl just sic as ye,
If ye will get me Gude Wallace;
For he is the man I wad very fain see.'

9 He hit the proud captain alang the chafft-blade,
That never a bit o meal he ate mair;

And he sticket the rest at the table where they sat,
And he left them a' lyin sprawlin there.

10 'Get up, get up, gudewife,' he says,
'And get to me some dinner in haste;
For it will soon be three lang days
Sin I a bit o meat did taste.'

11 The dinner was na weel readie,
Nor was it on the table set,
Till other fifteen Englishmen
Were a' lighted about the yett.

12 'Come out, come out now, Gude Wallace!
This is the day that thou maun die:'
'I lippen nae sae little to God,' he says,
'Altho I be but ill wordie.'

13 The gudewife had an auld gudeman;
By Gude Wallace he stiffly stood;
Till ten o the fyfteen Englishmen
Before the door lay in their blude.

14 The other five to the greenwood ran,
And he hangd these five upon a grain,
And on the morn, wi his merry men a',
He sat at dine in Lochmaben town.

D

Communicated to Robert Chambers by Elliot Anderson, Galashiels, 21 April, 1827, in a letter preserved among Kinloch's papers. Copied, with changes, in Kinloch MSS, I, 177. Furnished me by Mr. Macmath.

1 'I WISH we had our king,' quo Gude Wallace,
'An ilka true Scotsman had his nawn;
For between us an the southron louns
I doubt some ill seed has been sawn.'

2 Wallace he owre the water gaed,
An looked low down by a glen,
An there he saw a pretty, pretty maid,
As she was at the well washin.

3 'O weel may ye wash, my bonny, bonny maid!
An weel may ye saep, an me to see!

If ye have ony tidins to tell,
I pray you tell them unto me.'

4 'I have no tidins for to tell,
Nor ony uncos do I ken;
But up into yon little alehouse
An there sits fyfteen Englishmen.'

5 'An ay they are speakin o Gude Wallace,
An ay they are doomin him to hang:'
'O forbid!' quo Gude Wallace,
'He's owre truehearted a Scotsman.

6 'Had I but a penny in my pouch,
As I have not a single bawbee,
I would up into yon little alehouse,
An ay thae southron blades to see.'

7 She 's put her hand into her pouch,
    An counted him out pennies three ;
'If ever I live to come back this way,
    Weel paid the money it shall be.'

8 He 's taen a staff into his hand,
    An leand himsel outowre a tree,
An he 's awa to yon little alehouse,
    An ay the southron louns to see.

9 When he gaed in to that little alehouse,
    He bad his bennison be there ;
The captain answered him [in] wrath,
    He answerd him with domineer.

10 'O whare was ye born, ye crooked auld carle?
    An how may this your dwellin be ? '
'O I was born in fair Scotland,
    A crooked carle altho I be.'

11 'O I would een gie twenty shillins
    To ony sic crooked carle as thee
That wad find me out Gude Wallace ;
    For ay that traitor I lang to see.'

12 'Haud out your hand,' quo Gude Wallace,
    'I doubt your money be not gude ;

If ye 'll gie ither twenty shillins,
    It neer shall bide ye anither bode.'

13 He 's taen the captain outowre the jaws,
    Anither word spak he neer mair ;
An five he sticket whare they sat,
    The rest lay scramblin here an there.

14 'Get up, get up, gudewife,' he says,
    'An get some meat ready for me,
For I hae fasted this three lang days ;
    A wat right hungry I may be.'

15 The meat it wasna weel made ready,
    Nor as weel on the table set,
Till there cam fyfteen Englishmen
    An lighted a' about the yett.

16 The gudewife ran but, the gudeman ran ben ;
    It put them a' in sic a stoure
That five he sticket whare they sat,
    An five lay sprawlin at the door.

17 An five are to the greenwood gane,
    An he 's hangd them a' outowre a tree,
An before the mornin twal o clock
    He dined wi his men at Loch Marie.

E

Communicated to James Telfer by A. Fisher, as written
down from the mouth of a serving-man, who had learned it
in the neighborhood of Lochmaben. Mr Robert White's
papers.

1 WILLIE WALLACE the water lap,
    And lighted low down in a glen ;
There he came to a woman washing,
    And she had washers nine or ten.

2 'O weel may ye wash !' said Willie Wallace,
    'O weel may ye wash !' said fair Willie,
'And gin ye have any tidings to tell,
    I pray ye tell them unto me.'

3 'I have nae tidings for to tell,
    And as few will I let ye ken ;
But down into yon hosteler-ha
    Lies fifteen English gentlemen.'

4 'O had I ae penny in my pocket,
    Or had I yet ane bare bawbee,

I would go to yon hosteler-ha,
    All for these Englishmen to see.

5 'O wil ye len me ane pennie,
    Or will ye len me a bare bawbee,
I would go to yon hosteler-ha,
    All for these Englishmen to see.'

6 She 's put her hand into her pocket,
    And she 's gaen him out guineas three,
And he 's away to yon ostler-ha,
    All for these Englishmen to see.

7 Before he came to the hosteler-ha,
    He linkit his armour oer a tree ;
These Englishmen, being weel book-learned,
    They said to him, Great Dominie !

8 Where was ye born, ye crookit carle ?
    Where was ye born, or in what countrie ?
'In merry Scotland I was born,
    A crookit carle altho I be.'

9 'Here's fifteen shillings,' one of them said,
  'Here's other fifteen I'll gie to thee,
If you will tell me where the traitor Willie
    Wallace is,
  Or where away thou thinks he'll be.'

10 'Pay down, pay down your money,' he said,
  'Pay down, pay down richt speedilie,
For if your answer be not good,
  You shall have the downfall of Robin Hood,'
    [said he].

11 He struck the captain on the jaw,
  He swore that he would chow nae mair
    cheese ;
He's killed all the rest with his good broad-
    sword,
  And left them wallowing on their knees.

12 'Go cover the table,' said Willie Wallace,
  'Go cover the table, get me some meat,

For it is three days and rather mair
  Since I did either drink or eat.'

13 They had not the table weel covered,
  Nor yet the candle weel gaen licht,
Till fifteen other Englishmen
  They a' down at the door did light.

14 'Come out, come out, Willie Wallace,' they
    said.
  'Come out, come out, and do not flee,
For we have sworn by our good broadswords
  That this is the nicht that you sall dee.'

15 He's killed five with his good broadsword,
  He's drowned other five in the raging sea,
And he's taen other five to the merry green-
    wood,
  And hanged them oer the highest tree.

————◆————

F

Buchan's Gleanings, p. 114 ; from a gypsy tinker, p. 199.

1 WALLACE in the high highlans,
  Neither meat nor drink got he ;
Said, Fa me life, or fa me death,
  Now to some town I maun be.

2 He's put on his short claiding,
  And on his short claiding put he ;
Says, Fa me life, or fa me death,
  Now to Perth-town I maun be.

3 He steped oer the river Tay,
  I wat he steped on dry land ;
He was aware of a well-fared maid,
  Was washing there her lilie hands.

4 'What news, what news, ye well-fared maid ?
  What news hae ye this day to me ? '
'No news, no news, ye gentle knight,
  No news hae I this day to thee,
But fifteen lords in the hostage-house
  Waiting Wallace for to see.'

5 'If I had but in my pocket
  The worth of one single pennie,
I would go to the hostage-house,
  And there the gentlemen to see.'

6 She put her hand in her pocket,
  And she has pulld out half-a-crown ;
Says, Take ye that, ye belted knight,
  'T will pay your way till ye come down.

7 As he went from the well-fared maid,
  A beggar bold I wat met he,
Was coverd wi a clouted cloak,
  And in his hand a trusty tree.

8 'What news, what news, ye silly auld man ?
  What news hae ye this day to gie ? '
'No news, no news, ye belted knight,
  No news hae I this day to thee,
But fifteen lords in the hostage-house
  Waiting Wallace for to see.'

9 'Ye'll lend me your clouted cloak,
  That covers you frae head to shie,
And I'll go to the hostage-house,
  Asking there for some supplie.'

10 Now he's gone to the West-muir wood,
  And there he's pulld a trusty tree ;
And then he's on to the hostage gone,
  Asking there for charitie.

11 Down the stair the captain comes,
  ·Aye the poor man for to see :

'If ye be a captain as good as ye look,
  Ye 'll give a poor man some supplie ;
If ye be a captain as good as ye look,
  A guinea this day ye 'll gie to me.'

12 'Where were ye born, ye crooked carle ?
    Where were ye born, in what countrie ? '
  'In fair Scotland I was born,
    Crooked carle that I be.'

13 'I would give you fifty pounds,
    Of gold and white monie,
  I would give you fifty pounds,
    If the traitor Wallace ye 'd let me see.'

14 'Tell down your money,' said Willie Wallace,
    'Tell down your money, if it be good ;
  I 'm sure I have it in my power,
    And never had a better bode.

15 'Tell down your money,' said Willie Wallace,
    'And let me see if it be fine ;
  I 'm sure I have it in my power
    To bring the traitor Wallace in.'

16 The money was told on the table,
    Silver bright of pounds fiftie ;
  'Now here I stand,' said Willie Wallace,
    'And what hae ye to say to me ? '

17 He slew the captain where he stood,
    The rest they did quack an roar ;

He slew the rest around the room,
  And askd if there were any more.

18 'Come, cover the table,' said Willie Wallace,
    'Come, cover the table now, make haste ;
  For it will soon be three lang days
    Sin I a bit o meat did taste.'

19 The table was not well covered,
    Nor yet was he set down to dine,
  Till fifteen more of the English lords
    Surrounded the house where he was in.

20 The guidwife she ran but the floor,
    And aye the guidman he ran ben ;
  From eight o clock till four at noon
    He has killd full thirty men.

21 He put the house in sick a swither
    That five o them he sticket dead,
  Five o them he drownd in the river,
    And five hung in the West-muir wood.

22 Now he is on to the North-Inch gone,
    Where the maid was washing tenderlie ;
  'Now by my sooth,' said Willie Wallace,
    'It 's been a sair day's wark to me.'

23 He 's put his hand in his pocket,
    And he has pulld out twenty pounds ;
  Says, Take ye that, ye weel-fared maid,
    For the gude luck of your half-crown.

———◆———

G

The Thistle of Scotland, Alexander Laing, p. 100, from the repetition of an old gentlewoman in Aberdeenshire. Also Motherwell's MS., p. 487, communicated by Peter Buchan of Peterhead, "who had it from an old woman in that neighborhood."

1 Woud ye hear of William Wallace,
    An sek him as he goes,
  Into the lan of Lanark,
    Amang his mortel faes ?

2 There was fyften English sogers
    Unto his ladie cam,
  Said, Gie us William Wallace,
    That we may have him slain.

3 Woud ye gie William Wallace,
    That we may have him slain,

And ye 's be wedded to a lord,
  The best in Christendeem.

4 'This verra nicht at seven,
    Brave Wallace will come in,
  And he 'll come to my chamber-door,
    Without or dread or din.'

5 The fyften English sogers
    Around the house did wait,
  And four brave southron foragers
    Stood hie upon the gait.

6 That verra nicht at seven
    Brave Wallace he came in,
  And he came to his ladie's bouir,
    Withouten dread or din.

7 When she beheld him Wallace,
   She star'd him in the face;
'Ohon, alas!' said that ladie,
   'This is a woful case.

8 'For I this nicht have sold you,
   This nicht you must be taen,
And I 'm to be wedded to a lord,
   The best in Christendeem.'

9 'Do you repent,' said Wallace,
   'The ill you 've dane to me?'
'Ay, that I do,' said that ladie,
   'And will do till I die.

10 'Ay, that I do,' said that ladie,
   'And will do ever still,
And for the ill I 've dane to you,
   Let me burn upon a hill.'

11 'Now God forfend,' says brave Wallace,
   'I shoud be so unkind;
Whatever I am to Scotland's faes,
   I 'm aye a woman's friend.

12 'Will ye gie me your gown, your gown,
   Your gown but and your kirtle,
Your petticoat of bonny brown,
   And belt about my middle?

13 'I 'll take a pitcher in ilka hand,
   And do me to the well;
They 'll think I 'm one of your maidens,
   Or think it is yoursell.'

14 She has gien him her gown, her gown,
   Her petticoat and kirtle,
Her broadest belt, wi silver clasp,
   To bind about his middle.

15 He 's taen a pitcher in ilka hand,
   And dane him to the well;
They thought him one of her maidens,
   They kend it was nae hersell.

16 Said one of the southron foragers,
   See ye yon lusty dame?
I woud nae gie muckle to thee, neebor,
   To bring her back agen.

17 Then all the southrons followd him,
   And sure they were but four;

But he has drawn his trusty brand,
   And slew them pair by pair.

18 He threw the pitchers frae his hands,
   And to the hills fled he,
Until he cam to a fair may,
   Was washin on yon lea.

19 'What news, what news, ye weel-far'd may?
   What news hae ye to gie?'
'Ill news, ill news,' the fair may said,
   'Ill news I hae to thee.

20 'There is fyften English sogers
   Into that thatched inn,
Seeking Sir William Wallace;
   I fear that he is slain.'

21 'Have ye any money in your pocket?
   Pray lend it unto me,
And when I come this way again,
   Repaid ye weel shall be.'

22 She['s] put her hand in her pocket,
   And taen out shillings three;
He turnd him right and round about,
   And thankd the weel-far'd may.

23 He had not gone a long rig length,
   A rig length and a span,
Until he met a bold beggar,
   As sturdy as coud gang.

24 'What news, what news, ye bold beggar?
   What news hae ye to gie?'
'O heavy news,' the beggar said,
   'I hae to tell to thee.

25 'There is fyften English sogers,
   I heard them in yon inn,
Vowing to kill him Wallace;
   I fear the chief is slain.'

26 'Will ye change apparell wi me, auld man?
   Change your apparell for mine?
And when I come this way again,
   Ye 'll be my ain poor man.'

27 When he got on the beggar's coat,
   The pike-staff in his hand,
He 's dane him down to yon tavern,
   Where they were drinking wine.

28 'What news, what news, ye staff-beggar?
    What news hae ye to gie?'
  'I hae nae news, I heard nae news,
    As few I 'll hae frae thee.'

29 'I think your coat is ragged, auld man;
    But woud you wages win,
  And tell where William Wallace is,
    We 'll lay gold in your hand.'

30 'Tell down, tell down your good red gold,
    Upon the table-head,
  And ye sall William Wallace see,
    Wi the down-come of Robin Hood.'

31 They had nae tauld the money down,
    And laid it on his knee,
  When candles, lamps, and candlesticks,
    He on the floor gard flee.

32 And he has drawn his trusty brand,
    And slew them one by one,
  Then sat down at the table-head,
    And called for some wine.

33 The goodwife she ran but, ran but,
    The goodman he ran ben,
  The verra bairns about the fire
    Were a' like to gang brain.

34 'Now if there be a Scotsman here,
    He 'll come and drink wi me;
  But if there be an English loun,
    It is his time to flee.'

35 The goodman was an Englishman,
    And to the hills he ran;
  The goodwife was a Scots woman,
    And she came to his hand.

H

Buchan's Ballads of the North of Scotland, II, 226.

1 WALLACE wight, upon a night,
    Came riding oer the linn,
  And he is to his leman's bower,
    And tirld at the pin.

2 'O sleep ye, wake ye, lady?' he said,
    'Ye 'll rise, lat me come in.'
  'O wha 's this at my bower-door,
    That knocks, and knows my name?'
  'My name is William Wallace,
    Ye may my errand ken.'

3 'The truth to you I will rehearse,
    The secret I 'll unfold;
  Into your enmies' hands this night
    I fairly hae you sold.'

4 'If that be true ye tell to me,
    Do ye repent it sair?'
  'O that I do,' she said, 'dear Wallace,
    And will do evermair!

5 'The English did surround my house,
    And forced me theretill;
  But for your sake, my dear Wallace,
    I coud burn on a hill.'

6 Then he gae her a loving kiss,
    The tear droppd frae his ee;
  Says, Fare ye well for evermair,
    Your face nae mair I 'll see.

7 She dressd him in her ain claithing,
    And frae her house he came;
  Which made the Englishmen admire,
    To see this stalwart dame.

8 He is to Saint Johnston gane,
    And there he playd him well;
  For there he saw a well-far'd may,
    Was washing at a well.

9 'What news, what news, ye well-far'd may?
    What news hae ye to me?
  What news, what news, ye well-far'd may,
    All from your north countrie?'

10 'See ye not yon tavern-house,
    That stands on yonder plain?
  This very day have landet in it
    Full fifteen Englishmen;

11 'In search of Wallace, our dear champion,
    Ordaining that he shoud dee.'
  'Then on my troth,' said Wallace wight,
    'These Englishmen I 'se see.'

A. 2³. was not war. F 3 *has* wasna aware.
B, C, *have the obviously right reading.*
5¹. Wallace then. *Maidment,* there.
5⁴. *Maidment,* ouer good.
10¹. *Maidment,* When come.
10². quoth he be here.
12⁴. *Maidment,* should we.

B. 8². oer a stree. Stree *is glossed by Lambe as
stick, but this is impossible: the* s *was in-
duced by the* s *in* staff *above.*
10⁸, 12¹. Oh.
11¹. root of his sword *simply from ignorance
of the meaning of the* rood, *by which the
captain swears in* A 12; *rood of his sword
is hardly to be thought of.*
12². A word *for* A wat. *See* D 14⁴.
16³,⁴. *Corrupted: the words should be Wal-
lace's. Cf.* C 12.

C. 9². meal: *perhaps* meat.
D. 1². *Var. (or gloss),* his ain.
2¹. went *changed to* gaed (*for rhyme?*).
9⁴. *Var.* with angry jeer.
E. 2³. gin he. *A. Fisher says that lines are
wanting, and has supplied two after* 7²
(*making a stanza of* 7³,⁴, 8¹,², *and leaving*
8³,⁴ *as a half stanza) and two after* 10²
(*leaving* 10³,⁴ *as the second half of another
stanza). The arrangement here adopted is
in conformity with that of the other copies.*
F. 3³. wasna. 22¹. Insch.
G. *Buchan's variations.* 2³. And *for* Said.
3⁴. Christendeen.
9², 10⁸, 15², 27⁸. done. 10⁴. on a.
12¹. me *wanting.*
20². I heard them in yon inn. 21¹. you.
32². ane by ane.

158

HUGH SPENCER'S FEATS IN FRANCE

A. 'Hugh Spencer,' Percy MS., p. 281; Hales and
Furnivall, II, 290.

B. 'Hugh Spencer,' Percy Papers, communicated by
the Duchess Dowager of Portland.

C. Dr Joseph Robertson's Journal of Excursions, No 4.

THE king of England, A, B, sends Hugh
Spencer as ambassador to France, to know
whether there is to be peace or war between
the two lands. Spencer takes with him a
hundred men-at-arms, A; twenty ships, B.
The French king, Charles, A 30, declares for
war, A, C; says that the last time peace was
broken it was not along of him, B. The queen,
Maude, B 9, is indignant that the king should
parley with traitors, A, with English shep-
herds, B. She proposes to Spencer a joust
with one of her knights. The Englishman
has no jousting-horse. Three horses are
brought out for him, all of which he rejects,
A, B; in C, two. In A he calls for his old
hack which he had brought over sea; in B, C,
he accepts a fourth [third], a fiery-eyed black.

Spencer breaks his spear, a French shaft, upon
his antagonist; three spears [two] are tied to-
gether to make something strong enough for
him to wield. He unhorses the Frenchman,
then rides through the French camp and kills
some thirteen or fourteen score of King
Charles's men, A. The king says he will
have his head, A, with some provocation cer-
tainly; the queen says as much in B, though
Spencer has only killed her champion in fair
fight. Spencer has but four true brethren
left, A 33; we are not told what had become
of the rest of his hundred. With these, or, in
B, with two, he makes a stand against the
royal guard, and kills scores of them. The
French king begs him to hold his hand, A 34,
B 35. There shall never be war with England

while peace may be kept, A; he shall take back with him all the ships he brought, B.*

Hugh is naturally turned into a Scotsman in the Scottish version, C. The shepherd's son that he is matched with, 7, 15, is explained by traditional comment to be the queen's cousin.

These feats of Hugh Spencer do not outstrip those of the Breton knight Les Aubrays, when dealing with the French, Luzel, I, 286–305, II, 564–581; nor is his *fanfaronnerie* much beyond that of Harry Fifth. The Breton knight was explicitly helped by St Anne, but then Spencer and Harry have God and St George to borrow.

Liebrecht well remarks, Göttinger Gelehrte Anzeigen, 1868, p. 1900, that Spencer's rejecting the three French horses and preferring his old hack is a characteristically traditional trait, and like what we read of Walter of Aquitania in the continuation of his story in the chronicle of the cloister of Novalesa. After Walter, in his old age, had entered this monastery, he was deputed to obtain redress for a serious depredation on the property of the brethren. Asking the people of the cloister whether they have a horse serviceable for fight in case of necessity, he is told that there are good strong cart-horses at his disposal. He has these brought out, mounts one and another, and condemns all. He then inquires whether the old steed which he had brought with him is still alive. It is, but very old, and only used to carry corn to the mill. " Let me see him," says Walter, and, mounting, cries, " Oh, this horse has not forgotten what I taught him in my younger days." Grimm u. Schmeller, Lateinische Gedichte des X. u. XI. Jahrhunderts, p. 109. See ' Tom Potts,' II, 441.†

Of the many Hugh Spensers if we select the younger of the favorites of Edward II, his exploits, had they any foundation in reality, would necessarily fall between 1322, when Charles IV came to the French throne, and 1326, when the Spensers, father and son, ended their career. The French king says in B 8 that Spenser had sunk his ships and slain his men. Hugh Spenser the younger (both, according to Knyghton, col. 2539, but the father was a very old man) was engaged in piracy in 1321. The quarrel between Edward II and Charles IV, touching the English possessions in France, was temporarily arranged in 1325, but not through the mediation of the younger Spenser, who never was sent on an embassy to France. Another Sir Hugh Spenser was a commander in the Earl of Arundel's fleet in the operations against the French in Charles VI's time, 1387, and was taken prisoner in consequence of his ship grounding: Knyghton, col. 2693; Nicolas, History of the Royal Navy, II, 322f. No one of the three queens of Charles IV bore the name of Maude, which is assigned to the French queen in B, neither did the queen of Charles VI.

A

Percy MS., p. 281 ; Hales and Furnivall, II, 290.

1   THE court is kept att leeue London,
     And euermore shall be itt ;
     The King sent for a bold embassador,
     And Sir Hugh Spencer that he hight.

2   'Come hither, Spencer,' saith our kinge,
     ' And come thou hither vnto mee ;
     I must make thee an embassadour
     Betweene the king of Ffrance and mee.

3   'Thou must comend me to the king of Ffrance,
     And tell him thus and now ffrom mee,

---

* " Thou hadst twenty ships hither, thou'st have twenty away," B 37. It would be more in the ballad-way were the second twenty doubled.

† In the London Athenæum, about twenty-five years ago, there was (I think) a story of an Englishman in Russia resembling Hugh Spencer's. I have wrongly noted the number as 1871, and have not recovered the story after much rummaging. This ballad is not very unlike Russian *bylinas*.

I wold know whether there shold be peace in
   his land,
   Or open warr kept still must bee.

4 'Thou 'st haue thy shipp at thy comande,
   Thou 'st neither want for gold nor ffee ;
   Thou 'st haue a hundred armed men,
   All att thy bidding ffor to bee.'

5 The wind itt serued, and they sayled,
   And towards Ffrance thus they be gone ;
   The wind did bring them safe to shore,
   And safelye landed euerye one.

6 The Ffrenchmen lay on the castle-wall,
   The English souldiers to behold :
   ' You are welcome, traitors, out of England ;
   The heads of you are bought and sold.'

7 With that spake proud Spencer :
   My leege, soe itt may not bee ;
   I am sent an embassador
   Ffrom our English king to yee.

8 The king of England greetes you well,
   And hath sent this word by mee ;
   He wold know whether there shold be peace in
   your land,
   Or open warres kept still must bee.

9 ' Comend me to the English kinge,
   And tell this now ffrom mee ;
   There shall neuer peace be kept in my land
   While open warres kept there may bee.'

10 With that came downe the queene of Ffrance,
   And an angry woman then was shee ;
   Saies, Itt had beene as ffitt now for a king
   To be in his chamber with his ladye,
   Then to be pleading with traitors out of Eng-
   land,
   Kneeling low vppon their knee.

11 But then bespake him proud Spencer,
   For noe man else durst speake but hee :
   You haue not wiped your mouth, madam,
   Since I heard you tell a lye. '

12 ' O hold thy tounge, Spencer ! ' shee said,
   ' I doe not come to plead with thee ;
   Darest thou ryde a course of warr
   With a knight that I shall put to thee ? '

13 ' But euer alacke ! ' then Spencer sayd,
   ' I thinke I haue deserued Gods cursse ;
   Ffor I haue not any armour heere,
   Nor yett I haue noe iusting-horsse.'

14 ' Thy shankes,' quoth shee, ' beneath the knee
   Are verry small aboue the shinne
   Ffor to doe any such honourablle deeds
   As the Englishmen say thou has done.

15 ' Thy shankes beene small aboue thy shoone,
   And soe the beene aboue thy knee ;
   Thou art to slender euery way
   Any good iuster ffor to bee.'

16 ' But euer alacke,' said Spencer then,
   ' For one steed of the English countrye ! '
   With that bespake and one Ffrench knight,
   This day thou 'st haue the choyce of three.

17 The first steed he ffeiched out,
   I-wis he was milke-white ;
   The ffirst ffoot Spencer in stirropp sett,
   His backe did from his belly tyte.

18 The second steed that he ffeitcht out,
   I-wis that hee was verry browne ;
   The second ffoot Spencer in stirropp settt,
   That horsse and man and all ffell downe.

19 The third steed that hee ffeitched out,
   I-wis that he was verry blacke ;
   The third ffoote Spencer into the stirropp
   sett,
   He leaped on to the geldings backe.

20 ' But euer alacke,' said Spencer then,
   ' For one good steed of the English coun-
   trye !
   Goe ffeitch me hither my old hacneye,
   That I brought with me hither beyond the
   sea.'

21 But when his hackney there was brought,
   Spencer a merry man there was hee ;
   Saies, With the grace of God and St George of
   England,
   The ffeild this day shall goe with mee.

22 ' I haue not fforgotten,' Spencer sayd,
   ' Since there was ffeild foughten att Wal-
   singam,

When the horsse did heare the trumpetts
    sound,
  He did beare ore both horsse and man.'

23 The day was sett, and togetther they mett,
    With great mirth and melodye,
  With minstrells playing, and trumpetts sound-
    inge,
  With drumes striking loud and hye.

24 The ffirst race that Spencer run,
    I-wis hee run itt wonderous sore;
  He [hitt] the knight vpon his brest,
    But his speare itt burst, and wold touch noe
    more.

25 'But euer alacke,' said Spencer then,
    'For one staffe of the English countrye!
  Without you 'le bind me three together,'
    Quoth hee, 'they 'le be to weake ffor mee.'

26 With that bespake him the Ffrench knight,
    Sayes, Bind him together the whole thirtye,
  For I haue more strenght in my to hands
    Then is in all Spencers bodye.

27 'But proue att parting,' Spencer sayes,
    'Ffrench knight, here I tell itt thee;
  For I will lay thee five to four
    The bigger man I proue to bee.'

28 But the day was sett, and together they mett,
    With great mirth and melodye,
  With minstrells playing, and trumpetts sound-
    inge,
  With drummes strikeing loud and hye.

29 The second race that Spencer run,
    I-wis hee ridd itt in much pride,

And he hitt the knight vpon the brest,
    And draue him ore his horsse beside.

30 But he run thorrow the Ffrench campe;
    Such a race was neuer run beffore;
  He killed of King Charles his men
    Att hand of thirteen or fourteen score.

31 But he came backe againe to the K[ing],
    And kneeled him downe vpon his knee;
  Saies, A knight I haue slaine, and a steed I
    haue woone,
  The best that is in this countrye.

32 'But nay, by my faith,' then said the King,
    'Spencer, soe itt shall not bee;
  I 'le haue that traitors head of thine,
    To enter plea att my iollye.'

33 But Spencer looket him once about,
    He had true bretheren left but four;
  He killed ther of the Kings gard
    About twelve or thirteen score.

34 'But hold thy hands,' the King doth say,
    'Spencer, now I doe pray thee;
  And I will goe into litle England,
    Vnto that cruell kinge with thee.'

35 'Nay, by my ffaith,' Spencer sayd,
    'My leege, for soe itt shall not bee;
  For an you sett ffoot on English ground,
    You shall be hanged vpon a tree.'

36 'Why then, comend [me] to that Englishe
    kinge,
  And tell him thus now ffrom mee,
    That there shall neuer be open warres kept in
    my land
  Whilest peace kept that there may bee.'

———◆———

B

Percy Papers: communicated by the Duchess Dowager of
Portland.

1 OUR king lay at Westminster,
    as oft times he had done,
  And he sent for Hugh Spencer,
    to come to him anon.

2 Then in came Hugh Spencer,
    low kneeling on his knee:
  'What 's the matter, my liege,
    you sent so speedily for me?'

3 'Why you must go ambassadour
    to France now, to see
  Whether peace shall be taken,
    aye, or open wars must be.'

4 ' Who shall go with me ? '
   says Hugh Spencer, he :
' That shall Hugh Willoughby
   and John of Atherly.'
' O then,' says Hugh Spencer,
   ' we 'll be a merry company.'

5 When they came before the French king,
   they kneeled low on the knee :
' O rise up, and stand up,
   whose men soer you be.'

6 The first that made answer
   was Hugh Spencer, he :
' We are English ambassad*ou*rs,
   come hither to see
Whether peace shall be taken,
   aye, or open wars must be.'

7 Then spoke the French king,
   and he spoke courteously :
The last time peace was broken,
   it was neer along of me.

8 For you sunk my ships, slew my men,
   and thus did ye ;
And the last time peace was broken,
   it was neer along of me.

9 Then in came Queen Maude,
   and full as ill was she :
' A chamber of presence
   is better for thee,
Then amongst English shepherds,
   low bending on the knee.'

10 The first that made answer
   was Hugh Spencer, he :
' We are no English shepherds,
   Queen Maude, I tell thee,
But we 're knights, and knights fellows,
   the worst man in our company.'

11 O then spoke Queen Maude,
   and full as ill was she :
Thou shouldst be Hugh Spencer,
   thou talkst so boldly.

12 And if thou beest Hugh Spencer,
   as well thou seemst to be,
I 've oft heard of thy justling,
   and some of it would fain see.

13 I have a steed in my stable
   that thou canst not ride ;
I have a spear in my keeping
   that thou canst not guide ;
And I have a knight in my realm
   that thou darest not abide.

14 Then Spencer askd Willoughby
   and John of Atherly
Whether he should take this justling in
   hand,
   aye, or let it be.

15 O then spoke Hugh Willoughby
   and John of Atherly :
If you won't take it [in] hand,
   why turn it unto we.

16 ' It shall neer be said in England,'
   says Hugh Spencer, he,
' That I refused a good justling
   and turned it to ye.

17 ' Alas,' says Hugh Spencer,
   ' full sore may I moan,
I have nought here but an ambler,
   my good steed 's at home.'

18 Then spoke a French knight,
   and he spoke courteously :
I have thirty steeds in my stables,
   the best of them take to thee.

19 ' Gramercy,' says Spencer,
   ' aye, and gramercy ;
If eer thou comest to England,
   well rewarded shalt thou be.'

20 The first steed they brought him,
   he was a milk-white :
' Take that away,' says Spencer,
   ' for I do not him like.'

21 The next steed they brought him,
   he was a good dun :
' Take that away,' says Spencer,
   ' for he 's not for my turn.'

22 The next steed they brought him,
   he was a dapple-grey :
' Take that away,' says Spencer,
   ' for he is not used to the way.'

23 The next steed they brought him,
　　he was a coal-black;
His eyes burnt in his head,
　　as if fire were in flax;
' Come saddle me that horse,' says Spencer,
　　' for I 'll have none but that.'

24 When that horse was saddled,
　　and Spencer got on,
With his spear at his foot,
　　O he was portly man!

25 ' Now I am on that steede-back
　　that I could not ride,
That spear in my keeping
　　that I could not guide,
Come shew me that French knight
　　that I dare not abide.'

26 ' It is a sign by thy sharp shin,
　　ay, and thy cropped knee,
That you are no fit match
　　to justle with me :'
' Why it makes no matter,' says Spencer,
　　' you hear no brags of me.'

27 The first time they rode together,
　　now Sir Hugh and he,
He turnd him in his saddle
　　like an apple on a tree.

28 The next time they rode together,
　　now Sir Hugh and he,
He lit upon his breast-plate,
　　and he broke his spear in three.

29 ' A spear now,' says Spencer,
　　' a spear now get me :'
' Thou shalt have one,' says Willoughby,
　　' if in France one there be.'

30 ' O tye two together,
　　and the stronger they 'l be,
For the French is the better,
　　and the better shall be :'

' Why it makes no matter,' says Spencer,
　　' you hear no brags of me.'

31 The next time they rode together,
　　now Sir Hugh and he,
He threw him fifteen foot from his saddle,
　　and he broke his back in three :
' Now I have slain thy justler,
　　Queen Maude, I tell thee.'

32 O then spoke Queen Maude,
　　and full as ill was she :
If thou 'st slain my justler,
　　by the Kings laws thou 'st dye.

33 ' It shall neer be said in England,'
　　says Hugh Spencer, he ;
' It shall neer be said in England,'
　　says Hugh Willoughby ;

34 ' It shall neer be said in England,'
　　says John of Atherly,
' That a queen of another nation
　　eer had her will of we.'

35 They laid their heads together,
　　and their backs to the wall ;
There were four score of the Queen's guards,
　　and they slew them all.

36 Then spoke the French king,
　　and he spoke courteously :
O hold thy hand, Spencer,
　　I dearly pray thee.

37 Thou art sharp as thy spear,
　　and as fierce as thy steed,
And the stour of thy lilly-white hand
　　makes my heart bleed.

38 Thou hadst twenty ships hither,
　　thou 'st have twenty away ;
Then hold thy hand, Spencer,
　　I dearly thee pray.

C

Dr Joseph Robertson's Journal of Excursions, No 4 ; taken down from a man in the parish of Leochel, Aberdeenshire, 12 February, 1829.

1 It fell about the Martinmas time
  The wind blew loud and cauld,
And all the knichts of fair Scotland
  They drew them to sum hald.

2 Unless it was him young Sir Hugh,
  And he beet to sail the sea,
Wi a letter between twa kings, to see an they
  wald lat down the wars,
And live and lat them be.

3 On Friday shipped he, and lang
  Ere Wodensday at noon
In fair France landed he,

. . . . . .

4 He fell down before the King,
  On his bare knees :
' Gude mak ye safe and soun ; '
  ' Fat news o your contrie ? ' he says.

5 ' The news o our countrie,' he says,
  ' Is but news brought over the sea,
To see an ye 'll lat down the wars,
  And live and lat them be.'

6 ' Deed no,' he says ;
  ' I 'm but an auld man indeed,
But I 'll no lat down the wars,
  And live and lat them be.'

7 It 's out it spak the Queen hersel: I have a
    shepherd's sin
  Would fight an hour wi you ;
' And by my seeth,' says young Sir Hugh,
  ' That sight fain would I see.'

8 The firsten steed that he drew out,
  He was the penny-gray ;
He wad hae ridden oer meel or mor
  A leve-lang summer's day.

9 O girths they brak, and great horse lap,
  But still sat he on he :
' A girth, a girth,' says young Sir Hugh,
  ' A girth for charity ! '
' O every girth that you shall have,
  Its gude lord shall hae three.'

10 The nexten steed that he drew out,
  He was the penny-brown ;
He wad hae ridden oer meel or mor
  As ever the dew drap down.

11 O bridles brak, and great horse lap,
  But still sat he on he :
' A bridle, a bridle,' says young Sir Hugh,
  ' A bridle for charitie ! '
' O every bridle that you shall have,
  And its gude lord shall have three.'

12 The nexten steed that he drew out
  He was the raven-black ;
His een was glancin in his head
  Like wild-fire in a slack ;
' Get here a boy,' says young Sir Hugh,
  ' Cast on the saddle on that.'

13 O brands there brak, and great horse lap,
  But still sat he on he :
' A brand, a brand,' says young Sir Hugh,
  ' A brand for charitie ! '
' O every brand that you sall have,
  And its gude lord sall have three.'

14 He gave him a dep unto the heart,
  And over the steed fell he :
' I rather had gane you money,' she says,
  ' And free lands too,
That ye had foughten an hour wi him,
  And than had latten him be.'

15 ' If ye hae ony mair shepherd's sins,' he says,
  ' Or cooks i your kitchie,
Or ony mair dogs to fell,
  Ye 'll bring them here to me ;
And gin they be a true-hearted Scotsman,
  They 'll no be scorned by thee.'

———◆———

A. 4^3. 100. $5^{1,3}$. They.
  6^1. walls ? *There is a tag at the end of this word in the MS. Furnivall.*

16^4. of 3. 17^4. *MS.,* tylpe, *with the* l *crossed at top. Furnivall.*
$18^{1,3}$. 2^d. 18^2. *I should read* berry-browne *were it not for* verry blacke *in* 19^2.

19^{1,3}.   3^d.   25^3. 3.
26^2. 30^{tye}.   27^3. 5 to 4.   29^1.   2^d.
30^4. 13 or 14.
32^4. *No emendation of this unintelligible line occurs to me.*
33^2. 4.   33^3. therof.
33^4. 2 or 3 : *cf.* 30^4, *and observe the metre.*

35^3. for on : seitt *or* settt.
And *for* & *always.*

C. 14^4. too : *pronounced* tee.
15. The shepherd's son was the Queen's own son : *comment of the reciter. I do not understand the last two lines; indeed they are obviously corrupt.*

159

DURHAM FIELD

'Durham ffeilde,' Percy MS., p. 245 ; Hales and Furnivall, II, 190.

WHILE Edward Third was absent in France, and for the time engaged with the siege of Calais, David Bruce, the young king of Scotland, at the instance of Philip of Valois, but also because he "yearned to see fighting," invaded England with a large army. Having taken by storm the Border castle of Liddel, he was advised by William of Douglas to turn back, which, it was represented by Douglas, he could do with credit after this success. Other lords said that Douglas had filled his bags, but theirs were toom, and that the way lay open to London, for there were no men left in England but souters, skinners, and traders.* The Scots moved on to Durham, and encamped in a park not far from the town, in a bad position. In the mean while a powerful force had been collected by the northern nobility and the English churchmen, without the knowledge of the Scots. William of Douglas, going out to forage, rode straight to the ground where his foes lay, and in the attempt to retreat lost five hundred of his men. King David drew up his army in three divisions : one under his own command, another under the Earl of Murray and William Douglas, the third under the Steward of Scotland and the Earl of March. The operations of the Scots were impeded by the ditches and fences that traversed the ground on which they stood, and their situation made them an almost helpless mark for the ten thousand archers of the English army. Murray's men were completely routed by a charge of cavalry, and their leader killed. The English then fell upon the King's division, which, after a desperate fight, was "vanquished utterly." David, who had received two wounds from arrows, was taken prisoner by John Copland, "by force, not yolden," after knocking out two of the Englishman's teeth with a knife. Wyntoun's Chronykil, ed. Laing, II, 470 ff ; Scotichronicon, ed. Goodall, II, 339 ff. The battle was fought on the 17th of October, 1346.

According to the English chronicle of Lanercost, John of Douglas, 'germanus domini Willelmi,' fought with the Earl of Murray in the first Scottish division, and the Earl of Buchan was associated with King David in the command of the second. The English were also in three bodies. The leaders of the first were the Earl of Angus, 'inter omnes Angliæ nobilis persona,' Henry Percy, Ralph

---

* Presbyteri, fratres et clerici, sutores et mechanici, Bower ; agricolœ ac pastores, et capellani imbecilles et decrepiti, Knyghton ; miseri monachi, improbi presbyteri, porcorum pastores, sutores et pelliparii, Chronicon de Lanercost ; clericos et pastores, Walsingham, Hist. Angl.

Neville, and Henry Scrope; the Archbishop of York led the second; Mowbray, Rokeby, and John of Copland were in the third. Ed. Stevenson, pp. 349–51.

David, in the ballad, proposes to himself nothing less than the conquest of England and the distribution of the territory among his chief men. He is not a youth of twenty-two; William Douglas has served him four and thirty years. Still he will brook no advice, and kills his own squire for warning him of the danger of his enterprise. The Earl of Angus is to lead the van; but Angus, as we have seen, was engaged on the other side. The title of Angus might have deceived the minstrel, but it was hardly to be expected that Neville should be turned into a Scot as he is in st. 17. Angus, and also 'Vaughan,' that is Baughan, or Buchan,* are to be in the king's coat-armor, sts 11, 13, imitating Blunt and the rest at Shrewsbury, and the five false Richmonds at Bosworth. James† Douglas offers to lead the van, 14; so does William Douglas in 21. An Englishman who does not know a Neville would surely not be very precise about a Douglas, and it must be conceded that the Douglases have not always been kept perfectly distinct by historians. James Douglas, whoever he may be supposed to be, "went before;" that is, he plays the part which belongs historically to the Knight of Liddesdale, loses all his men, and returns, with an arrow in his thigh, to report that one Englishman is worth five Scots: 26–33.‡ But the Scots, even at that rate, have the advantage, for a herald, sent out to reconnoitre, tells their king that they are ten to one.

The commanders on the English side are the Bishop of Durham, Earl Percy, the Archbishop of York, the Bishop of Carlisle, and "Lord Fluwilliams." § The Bishop of Durham orders that no man shall fight before he has 'served his God,' and five hundred priests say mass in the field who afterwards take part in the fray. (The monks of Durham, Knyghton tells us, had made terms with the Scots, and were to pay a thousand pounds for ransom-money the next day; and so, when they saw the Scots yielding, they raised their voices in a Te Deum, which sounded to the clouds and quickened the courage of the English.) The king of Scots is wounded by an arrow through his nose, and, stepping aside to bleed, is taken prisoner by John of Copland, whom he first smites angrily. Copland sets the king on a palfrey and leads him to London. King Edward, newly arrived from France, asks him how he likes the shepherds, millers, and priests. There's not a yeoman in England, says David, but he is worth a Scottish knight. Aye, says King Edward, laughing, that is because you were fighting against the right. Shortly after this the Black Prince brings the king of France captive from the field of Poitiers. Says David to John, Welcome, brother, but I would I had gone to Rome! And I, would I had gone to Jerusalem! replies John. Thus ends the battle of Durham, fought, says the minstrel, on a morning of May, sts 27, 64, and within the same month as the battles of Crécy and Poitiers.|| Though Poitiers was fought ten years after Durham, the king of Scots and the king of France no doubt met in London, for John was taken thither in April,

---

* It is very doubtful whether there was an Earl of Buchan in 1346. Henry de Beaumont, according to the peerages, died in 1341. He was an Englishman, had fought against the Scots at Duplin, 1332, and was after that in the service of Edward III.

† 'Famous,' the MS. reading in 14¹, may probably be an error for James, which occurs so often in 28–33. William Douglas, the Knight of Liddesdale, had a brother James, but this James had been killed in 1335. He had also a brother John, Scotichronicon and Chronicon de Lanercoste, and the latter, as has been mentioned, puts John in Murray's division. Knyghton, col. 2590, gives as among the prisoners dominus Willielmus Duglas et frater ejusdem Willielmi.

‡ When William Douglas, in the Chronicle of Lanercost, tells the king that the English are at hand, and David replies, there is nothing in England but monks, priests, swineherds, etc., Douglas says, 'aliter invenietis; sunt varii validi viri.'

§ Froissart says that the English force was in four battalions: the first commanded by the Bishop of Durham and Lord Percy; the second by the Archbishop of York and Lord Neville; the third by the Bishop of Lincoln and Lord Mowbray; the fourth by Edward Balliol and the Archbishop of Canterbury.

|| Crécy, 26 August, 1346; Durham, 17 October, 1346; Poitiers, 19 September, 1356.

1357, and David was not released from his captivity until the following November.

Stanza 18 affords us an upper limit for a date. Lord Hambleton is said to be of the king's kin full nigh. James Hamilton, the first lord, married the princess Mary, sister of James III, in 1474, and his descendants were the next heirs to the throne after the Stewarts, whose line was for a time but barely kept up.

———◆———

1 LORDINGES, listen, and hold you still;
    Hearken to me a litle;
I shall you tell of the fairest battell
    That eu*er* in England beffell.

2 For as it befell in Edward the Thirds dayes,
    In England, where he ware the crowne,
Then all the cheefe chiualry of England
    They busked and made them bowne.

3 They chosen all the best archers
    *Tha*t in England might be found,
And all was to fight w*i*th the k*ing* of Ffrance,
    W*i*thin a litle stounde.

4 And when our k*ing* was ou*er* the water,
    And on the salt sea gone,
Then tydings into Scotland came
    *Tha*t all England was gone.

5 Bowes and arrowes they were all forth,
    At home was not left a man
But shepards and millers both,
    And preists w*i*th shauen crownes.

6 Then the k*ing* of Scotts in a study stood,
    As he was a man of great might;
He sware he wold hold his parlam*ent* in leeue London,
    If he cold ryde there right.

7 Then bespake a sq*uier*, of Scottland borne,
    And sayd, My leege, apace,
Before you come to leeue London,
    Full sore you 'le rue *that* race.

8 Ther beene bold yeomen in merry England,
    Husbandmen stiffe and strong;
Sharpe swords they done weare,
    Bearen bowes and arrowes longe.

9 The K*ing* was angrye at that word;
    A long sword out hee drew,

And there befor his royall companye
    His owne squier hee slew.

10 Hard hansell had the Scottes *tha*t day,
    *Tha*t wrought them woe enoughe,
For then durst not a Scott speake a word
    Ffor hanging att a boughe.

11 'The Earle of Anguish, where art thou?
    In my coate-armor thou shalt bee,
And thou shalt lead the forward
    Thorrow the English countrye.

12 'Take thee Yorke,' then sayd the K*ing*,
    'In stead wheras it doth stand;
I 'le make thy eldest sonne after thee
    Heyre of all Northumberland.

13 'The Earle of Vaughan, where be yee?
    In my coate-armor thou shalt bee;
The high Peak and Darbyshire
    I giue it thee to thy fee.'

14 Then came in famous Douglas,
    Saies, What shall my meede bee?
And I 'le lead the vawward, lord,
    Thorow the English countrye.

15 'Take thee Worster,' sayd the K*ing*,
    'Tuxburye, Killingworth, Burton vpon Trent;
Doe thou not say another day
    But I haue giuen thee lands and rent.

16 'Sir Rich*ard* of Edenborrow, where are yee?
    A wise man in this warr!
I 'le giue thee Bristow and the shire
    The time *that* wee come there.

17 'My lo*rd* Nevill, where beene yee?
    You must in this warres bee;
I 'le giue thee Shrewsburye,' saies the K*ing*,
    'And Couentrye faire and free.

18 'My lord of Hambleton, where art thou?
　　Thou art of my kin full nye;
　　I 'le giue thee Lincolne and Lincolneshire,
　　And *that*'s enouge for thee.'

19 By then came in W*illia*m Douglas,
　　As breeme as any bore;
　　He kneeled him downe vpon his knees,
　　In his hart he sighed sore.

20 Saies, I haue serued you, my louelye leege,
　　This thirty winters and four,
　　And in the Marches betweene England and
　　　　Scottland
　　I haue beene wounded and beaten sore.

21 For all the good service *that* I haue done,
　　What shall my meed bee?
　　And I will lead the vanward
　　Thorrow the English countrye.

22 'Aske on, Douglas,' said the king,
　　'And granted it shall bee:'
　　'Why then, I aske litle London,' saies W*illia*m
　　　　Douglas,
　　'Gotten giff *that* it bee.'

23 The King was wrath, and rose away,
　　Saies, Nay, *that* cannot bee!
　　For *that* I will keepe for my cheefe chamber,
　　Gotten if it bee.

24 But take thee North Wales and Weschaster,
　　The cuntrye all round about,
　　And rewarded thou shalt bee,
　　Of *that* take thou noe doubt.

25 Fiue score k*nigh*ts he made on a day,
　　And dubbd them w*i*th his hands;
　　Rewarded them right worthilye
　　With the townes in merry England.

26 And when the fresh k*nigh*ts they were made,
　　To battell the buske them bowne;
　　Iames Douglas went before,
　　And he thought to haue wonnen him shoone.

27 But the were mett in a morning of May
　　With the com*m*inaltye of litle England;
　　But there scaped neu*er* a man away,
　　Through the might of Chrisẗes hand.

28 But all onely Iames Douglas;
　　In Durham in the ffeild

An arrow stroke him in the thye;
　　Fast flinge[s he] towards the K*ing*.

29 The K*ing* looked toward litle Durham,
　　Saies, All things is not well!
　　For Iames Dowglas beares an arrow in his
　　　　thye,
　　The head of it is of steele.

30 'How now Iames?' then said the K*ing*,
　　'How now, how may this bee?
　　And where beene all thy merrymen
　　That thou tooke hence w*i*th thee?'

31 'But cease, my k*in*g,' saies Iames Douglas,
　　'Aliue is not left a man!'
　　'Now by my faith,' saies the k*in*g of Scottes,
　　'*Tha*t gate was euill gone.

32 'But I 'le reuenge thy quarrell well,
　　And of *tha*t thou may be faine;
　　For one Scott will beate fiue Englishmen,
　　If the meeten them on the plaine.'

33 'Now hold y*ou*r tounge,' saiés Iames Douglas,
　　'For in faith *tha*t is not soe;
　　For one English man is worth fiue Scotts,
　　When they meeten together thoe.

34 'For they are as egar men to fight
　　As a faulcon vpon a pray;
　　Alas! if eu*er* the winne the vanward,
　　There scapes noe man away.'

35 'O peace thy talking,' said the K*ing*,
　　'They bee but English knaues,
　　But shepards and millers both,
　　And preists w*i*th their staues.'

36 The K*ing* sent forth one of his heralds of
　　　　armes
　　To vew the Englishmen:
　　'Be of good cheere,' the herald said,
　　'For against one wee bee ten.'

37 'Who leades those ladds?' said the k*in*g of
　　　　Scottes,
　　'Thou herald, tell thou mee:'
　　The herald said, The Bishopp of Durham
　　Is captaine of *tha*t companye.

38 'For the Bishopp hath spred the K*ing*'s banner,
　　And to battell he buskes him bowne:'

'I sweare by St. Andrewes bones,' saies the
 King,
'I 'le rapp *that* preist on the crowne.'

39 The King looked towards litle Durham,
 And *that* hee well beheld,
That the Earle Percy was well armed,
 With his battell-axe entred the feild.

40 The King looket againe towards litle Durham,
 Four ancyents there see hee;
There were to standards, six in a valley,
 He cold not see them with his eye.

41 My Lord of Yorke was one of them,
 My Lord of Carlile was the other,
And my Lord Ffluwilliams,
 The one came with the other.

42 The Bishopp of Durham commanded his men,
 And shortlye he them bade,
That neuer a man shold goe to the feild to fight
 Till he had serued his God.

43 Fiue hundred preists said masse *that* day
 In Durham in the feild,
And afterwards, as I hard say,
 They bare both speare and sheeld.

44 The Bishopp of Durham orders himselfe to
 fight,
 With his battell-axe in his hand;
He said, This day now I will fight
 As long as I can stand!

45 'And soe will I,' sayd my Lord of Carlile,
 'In this faire morning gay;'
'And soe will I,' said my Lord Ffluwilliams,
 'For Mary, *that* myld may.'

46 Our English archers bent their bowes.
 Shortlye and anon;
They shott ouer the Scottish oast
 And scantlye toucht a man.

47 'Hold downe your hands,' sayd the Bishopp
 of Durham,
 'My archers good and true:'
The second shoote *that* the shott,
 Full sore the Scottes itt rue.

48 The Bishopp of Durham spoke on hye,
 That both partyes might heare:

'Be of good cheere, my merrymen all,
 The Scotts flyen, and changen there cheere.'

49 But as the saidden, soe the didden,
 They fell on heapes hye;
Our Englishmen laid on with their bowes,
 As fast as they might dree.

50 The king of Scotts in a studye stood
 Amongst his companye;
An arrow stoke him thorrow the nose,
 And thorrow his armorye.

51 The King went to a marsh-side
 And light beside his steede;
He leaned him downe on his sword-hilts,
 To let his nose bleede.

52 There followed him a yeaman of merry Eng-
 land,
 His name was Iohn of Coplande:
'Yeeld thee, traytor!' saies Coplande then,
 'Thy liffe lyes in my hand.'

53 'How shold I yeeld me,' says the King,
 'And thou art noe gentleman?'
'Noe, by my troth,' sayes Copland there,
 'I am but a poore yeaman.

54 'What art thou better then I, Sir King?
 Tell me if that thou can!
What art thou better then I, Sir King,
 Now we be but man to man?'

55 The King smote angerly at Copland then,
 Angerly in that stonde;
And then Copland was a bold yeaman,
 And bore the King to the ground.

56 He sett the King upon a palfrey,
 Himselfe upon a steede;
He tooke him by the bridle-rayne,
 Towards London he can him lead.

57 And when to London *that* he came,
 The King from Ffrance was new come
 home,
And there unto the king of Scottes
 He sayd these words anon.

58 'How like you my shepards and my millers?
 My priests with shaven crownes?'

'By my fayth, they are the sorest fighting
men
That ever I mett on the ground.

59 'There was never a yeaman in merry England
But he was worth a Scottish knight : '
'I, by my troth,' said King Edward, and
laughe,
'For you fought all against the right.'

60 But now the prince of merry England,
Worthilye under his sheelde,
Hath taken the king of Ffrance,
At Poytiers in the ffeelde.

61 The prince did present his father with that
food,
The louely king off Ffrance,
And fforward of his iourney he is gone :
God send us all good chance !

62 'You are welcome, brother ! ' sayd the king of
Scotts, to the king of Ffrance,
'For I am come hither to soone ;

Christ leeve that I had taken my way
Unto the court of Roome ! '

63 'And soe wold I,' said the king of Ffrance,
'When I came over the streame,
That I had taken my iourney
Unto Ierusalem ! '

64 Thus ends the battell of ffaire Durham,
In one morning of May,
The battell of Cressey, and the battle of
Potyers,
All within one monthës day.

65 Then was welthe and welfare in mery Eng-
land,
Solaces, game, and glee,
And every man loved other well,
And the King loved good yeomanrye.

66 But God that made the grasse to growe,
And leaves on greenwoode tree,
Now save and keepe our noble king,
And maintaine good yeomanry !

———◆———

And for & throughout.
1¹. Perhaps lesten : yo. 1². a litle spell ?
2¹. 3ᵈˢ. 8³. sharpes.
11³. forward has a tag to the d. Furnivall.
12¹. thy for thee.
13¹. in Earle the l is made over an e. Furnivall.
15². Tuxburye doubtful in the MS.
20². 30 : 4. 25. 5 score. 31¹. Janes.
32³, 33³. 5. After 39. 2d part. 40². 4.

40³. 6. 43¹. 500. 44¹. Durhan. 47³. 2d.
62¹. brothers.
66. Pencil note in Percy's late hand.
This and 2 following leaves being unfortunately
torn out, in sending the subsequent piece
[' King Estmere '] to the press, the conclusion
of the preceding ballad has been carefully tran-
scribed ; and indeed the fragments of the other
leaves ought to have been so.

160

THE KNIGHT OF LIDDESDALE

Hume of Godscroft, History of the Houses of Douglas and Angus, 1644, p. 77.

WILLIAM DOUGLAS, the Knight of Liddesdale, who figures in the foregoing ballad, was assassinated in 1353, while hunting in Ettrick forest, by his kinsman and godson, Lord William Douglas.

According to the Scotichronicon, the motive was said to be revenge for Alexander Ramsay, one of the first men among the Scots, whom Liddesdale had assaulted while he was holding a court, wounded, carried off, and suffered to die by starving; and for Sir David Berkeley, whom Liddesdale was charged with procuring to be murdered in 1350, in return for the death of his brother, Sir John Douglas, brought to pass by Berkeley. (Scotichronicon, ed. Goodall, II, 348, 335, XIV, 8, XIII, 50, XIV, 7.)

Hume of Godscroft considers the motive assigned to be quite unnatural, and at best a pretence. A ballad known to him gave a different account. "The Lord of Liddesdale, being at his pastime, hunting in Attrick forest, is beset by William Earle of Douglas, and such as hee had ordained for that purpose, and there assailed, wounded, and slain, beside Galsewood, in the yeare 1353; upon a jealousie that the Earle had conceived of him with his lady, as the report goeth, for so sayes the old song." After citing the stanza which follows, Hume goes on to say: "The song also declareth how shee did write her love-letters to Liddisdale, to disswade him from that hunting. It tells likewise the manner of the taking of his men, and his owne killing at Galsewood, and how hee was carried the first night to Lindin Kirk, a mile from Selkirk, and was buried within the Abbacie of Melrosse."

"The sole basis for this statement of Hume's," says Sir William Fraser, The Douglas Book, I, 223 f, 1885, "seems to be the anonymous Border ballad, part of which he quotes, to which he adds the tradition that the lady wrote to her lover to dissuade him from that hunting. Apart from the fact that this tradition is opposed to contemporary history, which states that Sir William was wholly unsuspicious of danger, the story told by Godscroft is otherwise erroneous. He assumes that Douglas was made earl in 1346, and that he was married to a daughter of the Earl of March, neither of which assumptions is true. Douglas was not created earl until 26th January, 1357–8, and there was therefore no 'Countess of Douglas' to wait for the Knight of Liddesdale. Douglas's only wife was Lady Margaret of Mar, who survived him. The exact date of their marriage has not been ascertained, but it is certain that Douglas had no countess of the family of March in 1353, while it is doubtful if at that date he was married at all. Popular tradition is therefore at fault in assigning matrimonial jealousy as a motive for killing the Knight of Liddesdale."

"Some fragments of this ballad are still current, and will be found in the ensuing work," says Scott, Minstrelsy, I, 221, note, ed. 1833. It may be that Sir Walter became convinced that these fragments were not genuine; at any rate, they do not appear in his collection.

> The Countesse of Douglas out of her boure
>   she came,
>   And loudly there that she did call :
> 'It is for the Lord of Liddesdale
>   That I let all these teares downe fall.'

161

THE BATTLE OF OTTERBURN

A. a. Cotton MS. Cleopatra, C. iv, leaf 24, of about 1550. b. Harleian MS. 293, leaf 52. Both in the British Museum.

B. a. Herd's MSS, I, 149, II, 30 ; Herd's Scottish Songs, 1776, I, 153. b. Minstrelsy of the Scottish Border, 1802, I, 31.

C. Minstrelsy of the Scottish Border, 1833, I, 354.

D. Finlay's Scottish Ballads, I, xviii f., two stanzas.

E. Motherwell's Minstrelsy, p. lxxi, note 30, one stanza.

A a was first printed in the fourth edition of Percy's Reliques, 1794, I, 18, and **A** b in the first edition, 1765, I, 18.

By far the most circumstantial account of the battle of Otterburn is given by Froissart (Chroniques, Buchon, XI, 362 ff, chap. 115 ff), and his highly felicitous narrative may be briefly summarized as follows.

The quarrels of Richard II with his uncles and a consequent feud between the great northern families of Neville and Percy furnished the Scots an inviting opportunity for an invasion of England on a large scale. Under the pretext of a festive meeting, a preliminary conference of barons and knights was held at Aberdeen, and it was there agreed that they should muster, the middle of August, 1388, at a place on the border near Jedburgh, with such forces as they could command. In all this they took no counsel with the king, who was then past seventy, and was regarded as of no account for their purposes. The result was a larger gathering than had been seen for sixty years, quite twelve hundred lances and forty thousand ordinary fighting-men.

The Earl of Northumberland and his sons, the Seneschal of York, and the Captain of Berwick had heard of the intended meeting at Aberdeen, and had sent heralds and minstrels thither, to get further information.

These agents reported that all Scotland was astir, and that there was to be another parley in the forest of Jedburgh. The barons and knights of Northumberland made due preparations, and, the better to keep these secret, remained quiet in their houses, ready to sally as soon as they learned that the Scots were in motion. Feeling themselves incapable of coping with so large a body as had been collected, they decided upon a simultaneous counter-raid, and that from the east or from the west, according as the enemy should take the road from the west or the east. Of this plan of the English the Scots obtained knowledge from a spy whom they had captured, and to foil it they divided their army, directing the main body towards Carlisle, under command of Archibald Douglas, of the Earl of Fife, son of the king, and many other nobles, while a detachment of three or four hundred picked men-at-arms, supported by two thousand stout fellows, partly archers, all well mounted,* and commanded by James, Earl of Douglas, the Earl of March and Dunbar, and the Earl of Murray, were to strike for Newcastle, cross the river, and burn and ravage the bishopric of Durham.

The eastern division (with which alone we are concerned) carried out their program to the letter. They advanced at speed, stopping for nothing, and meeting with no resistance,

---

* " Froissart describes a Scottish host of the same period as consisting of '.iiii. M. of armes, knightis and squiers, mounted on good horses, and other .x. M. men of warre, armed after their gyse, right hardy and firse, mounted on lytle hackeneys, the whiche were never tyed nor kept at hard meate, but lette go to pasture in the feldis and busshes.' " Happily cited by Scott, in illustration of **C** 16 : Lord Berners' translation, cap. xvii, Pynson, 1523, fol. viii.

and the burning and pillaging had begun in Durham before the Earl of Northumberland knew of their arrival. Fire and smoke soon showed what was going on. The earl dispatched his sons Henry and Ralph Percy to Newcastle, where the whole country rallied, gentle and simple; he himself remaining at Alnwick, in the hope of being able to enclose the Scots, when they should take the way north, between two bodies of English. The Scots attained to the very gates of Durham; then, having burned every unfortified town between there and Newcastle, they turned northward, with a large booty, repassed the Tyne, and halted at Newcastle. There was skirmishing for two days before the city, and in the course of a long combat between Douglas and Henry Percy the Scot got possession of the Englishman's pennon. This he told Percy he would raise on the highest point of his castle at Dalkeith; Percy answered that he should never accomplish that vaunt, nor should he carry the pennon out of Northumberland. 'Come then to-night and win it back,' said Douglas; 'I will plant it before my tent.' It was then late, and the fighting ceased; but the Scots kept good guard, looking for Percy to come that very night for his pennon. Percy, however, was constrained to let that night pass.

The Scots broke up their camp early the next morning and withdrew homewards. Taking and burning the tower and town of Ponteland on their way, they moved on to Otterburn, thirty miles northwest from Newcastle, where there was a strong castle or tower, in marshy ground, which they assailed for a day without success. At the end of the day they held a council, and the greater part were in favor of making for Carlisle in the morning, to rejoin their countrymen. But the Earl of Douglas would not hear of this; Henry Percy had said that he would challenge his pennon; they would stay two or three days more and assault the castle, and see if Percy would be as good as his word. So the Scots encamped at their ease, making themselves huts of trees, and availing themselves of the marshes to fortify their position. At the entrance of the

marshes, which was on the Newcastle road, they put their servants and foragers, and they drove their cattle into the bogs.

Henry Percy was greatly vexed and mortified at the loss of his pennon, and in the evening he represented to the knights and squires of Northumberland how much it concerned his honor to make good what he had said to Douglas, that the pennon should never be carried out of England. But these gentlemen were all convinced that Douglas was backed by the whole power of Scotland, of which they had seen only the van, by forty thousand men who could handle them at their will; at any rate, it was better to lose a pennon than two or three hundred knights and squires, and expose the country to risk. As for the loss of the pennon, it was one of the chances of arms; Douglas had won it handsomely; another time Percy would get as much from him, or more.* To this the Percys were fain to yield. Later there came scouts with information that Douglas was encamped at Otterburn, that the main army was not acting in conjunction with him, and that his forces, all told, did not exceed three thousand. Henry Percy was overjoyed at the news, and cried, To horse! by the faith I owe to God and my father, I will go seek my pennon, and the Scots shall be ousted before this night is over. The evening of that same day the Bishop of Durham was expected to arrive with a great many men, but Henry Percy would not wait. Six hundred lances and eight thousand foot were enough, he said, to serve the Scots, who had but three hundred lances and two thousand other folk. The English set forth as soon as they could get together, by the road which the Scots had taken, but were not able to move very fast by reason of their infantry.

Some of the Scots knights were supping, and more were asleep (for they had had hard work at the assault on the tower, and were meaning to be up betimes to renew the attack), when the English were upon the camp, crying, Percy! Percy! There was naturally

* A consolation as old as wise. So Paris, for himself: νίκη δ' ἐπαμείβεται ἄνδρας, Iliad, vi, 339.

great alarm. The English made their attack at that part of the camp where, as before said, the servants and foragers were lodged. This was, however, strong, and the knights sent some of their men to hold it while they themselves were arming. Then the Scots formed, each under his own earl and captain. It was night, but the weather was fair and the moon shining. The Scots did not go straight for the English, but took their way along by the marshes and by a hill, according to a plan which they had previously arranged against the case that their camp should be attacked. The English made short work with the underlings, but, as they advanced, always found fresh people to keep up a skirmish. And now the Scots, having executed a flank movement, fell upon their assailants in a mass, from a quarter where nothing was looked for, shouting their battle-cries with one voice. The English were astounded, but closed up, and gave them Percy! for Douglas! Then began a fell battle. The English, being in excess and eager to win, beat back the Scots, who were at the point of being worsted. James Douglas, who was young, strong, and keen for glory, sent his banner to the front, with the cry, Douglas! Douglas! Henry and Ralph Percy, indignant against the earl for the loss of the pennon, turned in the direction of the cry, responding, Percy! Knights and squires had no thought but to fight as long as spears and axes would hold out. It was a hand-to-hand fight; the parties were so close together that the archers of neither could operate; neither side budged, but both stood firm. The Scots showed extraordinary valor, for the English were three to one; but be this said without disparagement of the English, who have always done their duty.

As has been said, the English were so strong that they were forcing their foes back, and this James Douglas saw. To regain the ground, he took a two-handed axe, plunged into the thickest, and opened a path before him; for there was none so well armed in helmet or plate as not to fear his strokes. So he made his way till he was hit by three spears, all at once, one in the shoulder, an-

other in the chest, another in the thigh, and borne to the ground. The English did not know that it was Earl Douglas that had fallen; they would have been so much elated that the day would have been theirs. Neither did the Scots; if they had, they would have given up in despair. Douglas could not raise himself from the ground, for he was wounded to the death. The crush about him was great, but his people had kept as close to him as they could. His cousin, Sir James Lindsay, reached the spot where he was lying, and with Lindsay Sir John and Sir Walter Sinclair, and other knights and squires. Near him, and severely wounded, they found his chaplain, William of North Berwick, who had kept up with his master the whole night, axe in hand; also Sir Robert Hart, with five wounds from lances and other weapons. Sir John Sinclair asked the earl, Cousin, how fares it with you? 'Indifferently,' said the earl; 'praised be God, few of my ancestors have died in their beds. Avenge me, for I count myself dead. Walter and John Sinclair, up with my banner, and cry, Douglas! and let neither friend nor foe know of my state.' The two Sinclairs and Sir John Lindsay did as they were bidden, raised the banner, and shouted, Douglas! They were far to the front, but others, who were behind, hearing the shout loudly repeated, charged the English with such valor as to drive them beyond the place where Douglas now lay dead, and came up with the banner which Sir John Lindsay was bearing, begirt and supported by good Scots knights and squires. The Earl of Murray came up too, and the Earl of March and Dunbar as well, and they all, as it were, took new life when they saw that they were together and that the English were giving ground. Once more was the combat renewed. The English had the disadvantage of the fatigue of a rapid march from Newcastle, by reason whereof their will was better than their wind, whereas the Scots were fresh; and the effects appeared in this last charge, in which the Scots drove the English so far back that they could not recover their lost ground. Sir Ralph Percy had already been taken prisoner. Like Douglas, he had advanced so far as to be surrounded, and being so badly wounded that his hose and boots were full of blood, he surrendered to Sir John Maxwell. Henry Percy, after a valorous fight with the Lord Montgomery, became prisoner to the Scottish knight.

It was a hard battle and well fought, but such are the turns of fortune that, although the English were the greater number, and all bold men and practised in arms, and although they attacked the enemy valiantly, and at first drove them back a good distance, the Scots in the end won the day. The losses of the English were put by their antagonists at 1040 prisoners, 1860 killed in the fight and the pursuit, and more than 1000 wounded; those of the Scots were about 100 killed and 200 captured.* The Scots retired without molestation, taking the way to Melrose Abbey, where they caused the Earl of Douglas to be interred, and his obsequies to be reverently performed. Over his body a tomb of stone was built, and above this was raised the earl's banner.

Such is the story of the battle of Otterburn, fought on Wednesday, the 19th day of August,† in the year of grace 1388, as related by Froissart (with animated tributes to the hardihood and generosity of both parties) upon the authority of knights and squires

actually present, both English and Scots, and also French.

Wyntoun, ix, 840–54, 900f (Laing, III, 36f) says that the alarm was given the Scots by a young man that came right fast riding (cf. A 20, 21, B 4, C 17), and that many of the Scots were able to arm but imperfectly; among these Earl James, who was occupied with getting his men into order and was "reckless of his arming," and the Earl of Murray, who forgot his basnet (cf. C 20). Earl James was slain no man knew in what way. Bower, Scotichronicon, II, 405, agrees with Wyntoun. English chroniclers, Knyghton, col. 2728, Walsingham (Riley, II, 176 ‡), Malverne, the continuator of Higden (Polychronicon, Lumby, IX, 185), assert that Percy killed Douglas with his own hand, Knyghton adding that Percy also wounded the Earl of Murray to the point of death.

That a Scots ballad of Otterburn was popular in the sixteenth century appears from The Complaynte of Scotlande, 1549, where a line is cited, The Perssee and the Mongumrye met, p. 65, ed. Murray: cf. B 9^1, C 30^1.§ In the following century Hume of Godscroft writes: ‖ The Scots song made of Otterburn telleth the time, about Lammasse, and the occasion, to take preyes out of England; also the dividing of the armies betwixt the Earles of Fife and Douglas, and their severall journeys,

---

* Buchanan has these numbers, with the exception of 1840, for 1860, killed: ed. 1582, fol. 101. " That there was a memorable slaughter in this affair, a slaughter far beyond the usual proportion to the numbers engaged, cannot be doubted; nor was there ever bloodshed more useless for the practical ends of war. It all came of the capture of the Percy's pennon. The Scots might have got clear off with all their booty; the English forgot all the precautions of war when they made a midnight rush on a fortified camp without knowledge of the ground or the arrangements of their enemy. It was for these specialties that Froissart admired it so. He saw in it a fight for fighting's sake, a great passage at arms in which no bow was drawn, but each man fought hand to hand; in fact, about the greatest and bloodiest tournament he had to record. Hence his narrative is ever interrupted with bursts of admiration as his fancy contemplates the delightful scene raised before it." Burton, History of Scotland, II, 364, ed. 1873 (who, perhaps by an error of the press, makes the losses of the English in killed eight hundred and forty, in place of Buchanan's eighteen hundred and forty).

† Bower and Barry say St Oswald's day, Wednesday, the 5th, Scotichronicon, II, 405, 407; Knyghton also; the con-

tinuator of Higden's Polychronicon, August 12, Wednesday. The ballad; A 18⁴, gives the day as Wednesday. There was a full moon August 20, which makes the 19th of itself far more probable, and Froissart says the moon was shining. See White, Battle of Otterburn, p. 133.

‡ Walsingham writes in the vein of Froissart: " Erat ibidem cernere pulchrum spectaculum, duos tam præclaros juvenes manus conserere et pro gloria decertare." Walsingham says that the English were few. Malverne puts the Scots at 30,000, and here, as in the ballad A 35, the cronykle does not layne (indeed, the ballad is all but accurate), if the main body of the Scots be included, which was at first supposed to be supporting Douglas.

§ ' The perssee and the mongumrye met, that day, that day, that gentil day,' which I suppose to be either a different reading from any that has come down, or a blending of a line from Otterburn with one from The Hunting of the Cheviot, A 24¹; indicating in either case the present ballad only, for The Hunttis of Cheuet had been cited before. Furnivall holds that the second line means another ballad: Captain Cox, p. clix.

‖ The History of the Houses of Douglas and Angus, 1644, p. 104.

almost as in the authentick history. It beginneth thus:

It fell about the Lammas tide,
When yeomen wonne their hay,
The doughtie Douglas gan to ride,
In England to take a prey.

Motherwell maintains that the ballad which passes as English is the Scots song altered to please the other party. His argument, however, is far from conclusive. "That The Battle of Otterbourne was thus dealt with by an English transcriber appears obvious, for it studiously omits dilating on Percy's capture, while it accurately details his combat with Douglas;" that is to say, the ballad as we have it is just what a real English ballad would have been, both as to what it enlarges on and what it slights. "Whereas it would appear that in the genuine Scottish version the capture of Percy formed a prominent incident, seeing it is the one by which the author of The Complaynt refers to the ballad [The Perssee and the Mongumrye met]:" from which Motherwell was at liberty to deduce that B and C represent the genuine Scottish version, several stanzas being given to the capture of Percy in these; but this he would not care to do, on account of the great inferiority of these forms. A Scotsman could alter an English ballad "to suit political feeling and flatter national vanity," as Motherwell says the Scots *did* with Chevy Chace. (See further on, p. 303.) There is no reason to doubt that a Scots ballad of Otterburn once existed, much better than the two inferior, and partly suspicious, things which were printed by Herd and Scott, and none to doubt that an English minstrel would deal freely with any Scots ballad which he could turn to his purpose; but then there is no evidence, positive or probable, that this particular ballad was "adapted" from the Scots song made of Otterburn; rather are we to infer that the few verses of B and C which repeat or resemble the text of A were borrowed from A, and, as likely as not, Hume's first stanza too.*

A, in the shape in which it has come down to us, must have a date long subsequent to the battle, as the grammatical forms show; still, what interested the borderers a hundred years or more after the event must have interested people of the time still more, and it would be against the nature of things that there should not have been a ballad as early as 1400. The ballad we have is likely to have been modernized from such a predecessor, but I am not aware that there is anything in the text to confirm such a supposition, unless one be pleased to make much of the Wednesday of the eighteenth stanza. The concluding stanza implies that Percy is dead, and he was killed at Shrewsbury, in 1403.

A. 3. Hoppertope hyll, says Percy, is a corruption for Ottercap Hill (now Ottercaps Hill) in the parish of Kirk Whelpington, Tynedale Ward, Northumberland. Rodclyffe Cragge (now Rothley Crags) is a cliff near Rodeley, a small village in the parish of Hartburn, in Morpeth Ward, south-east of Ottercap; and Green Leyton, corruptly Green Lynton, is another small village, south-east of Rodeley, in the same parish. Reliques, 1794, I, 22.

8. Henry Percy seems to have been in his twenty-third year. As for his having been a march-man "all his days," he is said to have begun fighting ten years before, in 1378, and to have been appointed Governor of Berwick and Warden of the Marches in 1385: White, History of the Battle of Otterburn, p. 67 f. Walsingham calls both Percy and Douglas young men, and Froissart speaks at least twice of Douglas as young. Fraser, The Douglas Book, 1885, I, 292, says that Douglas was probably born in 1358. White, as above, p. 91, would make him somewhat older.

17. The chivalrous trait in this stanza, and that in the characteristic passage 36–44, are peculiar to this transcendently heroic ballad.

26, 27. The earldom of Menteith at the time of this battle, says Percy, following Douglas's Peerage, was possessed by Robert

* For Motherwell's views, see his Minstrelsy, li, lii, and lxxi, note 30.

Stewart, Earl of Fife, third son of King Robert II; but the Earl of Fife was in command of the main body and not present. (As Douglas married a daughter of King Robert II, the Earl of Fife was not his uncle, but his brother-in-law.) The mention of Huntley, says Percy, shows that the ballad was not composed before 1449; for in that year Alexander, Lord of Gordon and Huntley, was created Earl of Huntley by King James II. The Earl of Buchan at that time was Alexander Stewart, fourth son of the king. Reliques, 1794, I, 36.

35². 'The cronykle will not layne.' So in 'The Rose of England,' No 166, st. 22⁴, 'The cronickles of this will not lye,' and also 17²; and in 'Flodden Field,' appendix, p. 360, st. 121⁴.

43, 49. It will be remembered that the archers had no part in this fight.

45, 46. "The ancient arms of Douglas are pretty accurately emblazoned in the former stanza, and if the readings were, The crowned harte, and, Above stode starres thre, it would be minutely exact at this day. As for the Percy family, one of their ancient badges or cognizances was a white lyon statant, and the silver crescent continues to be used by them to this day. They also give three luces argent for one of their quarters." Percy, as above, p. 30.

48. So far as I know, St George does not appear as Our Lady's knight in any legendary, though he is so denominated or described elsewhere in popular tradition. So in the spell for night-mare, which would naturally be of considerable antiquity,

S. George, S. George, Our Ladies knight,
He walkt by day, so did he by night, etc.:

Reginald Scot, The Discoverie of Witchcraft, 1584, as reprinted by Nicholson, p. 68, ed. 1665, p. 48; and Fletcher's Monsieur Thomas, iv. 6, Dyce, VII, 388. In Nicholas Udall's

'Roister Doister,' known to be as old as 1551, Matthew Merrygreek exclaims, "What then? sainct George to borow, Our Ladie's knight!" Ed. W. D. Cooper, p. 77, Shakespeare Society, 1847. The Danish ballad of St George, 'St Jørgen og Dragen,' Grundtvig, No 103, II, 559 ff, the oldest version of which is from a 16th century MS., begins, "Knight St George, thou art my man" (svend); and in the second version, George, declining the princess whom he has rescued, says he has vowed to Mary to be her servant.* In the corresponding Swedish ballad, of the same age as the Danish, George is called Mary's knight (Maria honom riddare gjorde, st. 2): Geijer and Afzelius, ed. Bergström, II, 402. This is also his relation in German ballads: Meinert, p. 254; Ditfurth, I, 55, No 68.†

B. 1, 9, 14 nearly resemble A 1, 50, 68, and must have the same origin. In B 9 Douglas is changed to Montgomery; in 14 Douglas is wrongly said to have been buried on the field, instead of at Melrose Abbey, where his tomb is still to be seen.

7 is founded upon a tradition reported by Hume of Godscroft: "There are that say that he was not slain by the enemy, but by one of his owne men, a groome of his chamber, whom he had struck the day before with a truncheon in the ordering of the battell, because hee saw him make somewhat slowly to; and they name this man John Bickerton of Luffenesse, who left a part of his armour behinde unfastned, and when hee was in the greatest conflict, this servant of his came behinde his back and slew him thereat." Ed. 1644, p. 105.

11. The summons to surrender to a braken-bush is not in the style of fighting-men or fighting-days, and would justify Hotspur's contempt of metre-ballad-mongers.

12, 13. B agrees with Froissart in making a Montgomery to be the captor of Henry Percy, whereas A represents that Montgom-

---

* B 20.   Ingen iomfru maa ieg loffue,
           huerchen lønlig eller aaben-bahre;
           det haffuer ieg iomfru Maria loffuet
           hindis tienere skall ieg verre.

† The burden is 'O kiennicheinn Maria' in the first, 'Hiif Maria' in the second; in both George declines the king's

daughter, and orders a church to be built 'mit Mariabeild,' or to himself and Mary. This, and perhaps the hint for St George's addiction to Mary altogether, is from the Golden Legend, where the king "in honorem beatæ Mariæ et beati Georgii ecclesiam miræ magnitudinis construxit": Grässe, p. 261.

ery was taken prisoner and exchanged for Percy. In The Hunting of the Cheviot Sir Hugh Montgomery kills Percy, and in return is shot by a Northumberland archer.

C. Scott does not give a distinct account of this version. He says that he had obtained two copies, since the publication of the earlier edition, "from the recitation of old persons residing at the head of Ettrick Forest, by which the story is brought out and completed in a manner much more correspondent to the true history." C is, in fact, a combination of four copies; the two from Ettrick Forest, B a, and the MS. copy used in B b to "correct" Herd.

8, it scarcely requires to be said, is spurious, modern in diction and in conception.

19. Perhaps derived from Hume of Godscroft rather than from tradition. When Douglas was dying, according to this historian,* he made these last requests of certain of his kinsmen: "First, that yee keep my death close both from our owne folke and from the enemy; then, that ye suffer not my standard to be lost or cast downe; and last, that ye avenge my death, and bury me at Melrosse

with my father. If I could hope for these things," he added, "I should die with the greater contentment; for long since I heard a prophesie that a dead man should winne a field, and I hope in God it shall be I." Ed. 1644, p. 100.

22 must be derived from the English version. As the excellent editor of The Ballad Minstrelsy of Scotland, Glasgow, 1871, remarks, "no Scottish minstrel would ever have dreamt of inventing such a termination to the combat between these two redoubted heroes . . . as much at variance with history as it is repulsive to national feeling:" p. 431.

Genealogical matters, in this and the following ballad, are treated, not always to complete satisfaction, in Bishop Percy's notes, Reliques, 1794, I, 34 ff; Scott's Minstrelsy, 1833, I, 351, 363 ff: White's History of the Battle of Otterburn, p. 67 ff; The Ballads and Songs of Ayrshire, I, 66 f.

A is translated by Doenniges, p. 87; C by Grundtvig, Engelske og skotske Folkeviser, No 12, p. 74, and by Talvj, Charakteristik, p. 537.

A

a. Cotton MS. Cleopatra, C. iv, leaf 64, of about 1550.
b. Harleian MS. 293, leaf 52.

1 YT fell abowght the Lamasse tyde,
  Whan husbondes wynnes ther haye,
  The dowghtye Dowglasse bowynd hym to ryde,
  In Ynglond to take a praye.

2 The yerlle of Fyffe, wythowghten stryffe,
  He bowynd hym over Sulway;
  The grete wolde ever to-gether ryde;
  That raysse they may rewe for aye.

3 Over Hoppertope hyll they cam in,
  And so down by Rodclyffe crage:
  Vpon Grene Lynton they lyghted dowyn,
  Styrande many a stage.

4 And boldely brente Northomberlond,
  And haryed many a towyn;
  They dyd owr Ynglyssh men grete wrange,
  To batell that were not bowyn.

5 Than spake a berne vpon the bent,
  Of comforte that was not colde,
  And sayd, We haue brente Northomberlond,
  We haue all welth in holde.

6 Now we haue haryed all Bamborowe schyre,
  All the welth in the worlde haue wee,
  I rede we ryde to Newe Castell,
  So styll and stalworthlye.

7 Vpon the morowe, when it was day,
  The standers schone full bryght;

* Following in part Buchanan, who, however, says nothing of Melrose, or of the prophecy, which is the point here. Illa vero a vobis postrema peto: primum, vt mortem meam et nostros et hostes cœletis; deinde, ne vexillum meum de-jectum sinatis; demum, vt meam cædem vlciscamini. Hæc si sperem ita fore, cætera æquo animo feram. Fol. 101, ed. 1582.

To the Newe Castell the toke the waye,
    And thether they cam full ryght.

8 S*yr* Henry Perssy laye at the New Castell,
    I tell yow w*ythow*tten drede ;
    He had byn a march-man all hys dayes,
    And kepte Barwyke vpon Twede.

9 To the Newe Castell when they cam,
    The Skottes they cryde on hyght,
'Syr Hary Perssy, and thou byste w*ith*in,
    Com to the fylde, and fyght.

10 'For we haue brente Northomberlonde,
    Thy erytage good and ryght,
    And syne my logeyng I haue take
    W*yth* my brande dubbyd many a knyght.'

11 S*yr* Harry Perssy cam to the wall*es*,
    The Skottyssch oste for to se,
    And sayd, And thou hast brente Northomber-
        lond,
    Full sore it rewyth me.

12 Yf thou hast haryed all Bamborowe schyre,
    Thow hast done me grete envye ;
    For the trespasse thow hast me done,
    The tone of vs schall dye.

13 'Where schall I byde the ? ' sayd the Dowglas,
    'Or where wylte thow com to me ? '
'At Otterborne, in the hygh way,
    [T]her mast thow well logeed be.

14 '[T]he roo full rekeles ther sche rinnes,
    [T]o make the game a[nd] glee ;
[T]he fawken and the fesaunt both,
    Among the holtes on hye.

15 'Ther mast thow haue thy welth at wyll,
    Well looged ther mast be ;
Yt schall not be long or I com the tyll,'
    Sayd Syr Harry Perssye.

16 'Ther schall I byde the,' sayd the Dowglas,
    'By the fayth of my bodye : '
'Thether schall I com,' sayd S*yr* Harry Perssy,
    'My trowth I plyght to the.'

17 A pype of wyne he gaue them over the walles,
    For soth as I yow saye ;
Ther he mayd the Dowglasse drynke,
    And all hys ost that daye.

18 The Dowglas turnyd hym homewarde agayne,
    For soth w*ith*owghten naye ;
He toke hys logeyng at Oterborne,
    Vpon a Wedynsday.

19 And ther he pyght hys standerd dowyn,
    Hys gettyng more and lesse,
And syne he warned hys men to goo
    To chose ther geldyng*es* gresse.

20 A Skottysshe knyght hoved vpon the bent,
    A wache I dare well saye ;
So was he ware on the noble Perssy,
    In the dawnyng of the daye.

21 He prycked to hys pavyleon-dore,
    As faste as he myght ronne ;
'Awaken, Dowglas,' cryed the knyght,
    ' For hys love that syttes in trone.

22 ' Awaken, Dowglas,' cryed the knyght,
    ' For thow maste waken wyth wynne ;
Yender haue I spyed the prowde Perssye,
    And seven stondardes wyth hym.'

23 'Nay by my trowth,' the Dowglas sayed,
    ' It ys but a fayned taylle ;
He durst not loke on my brede banner
    For all Ynglonde so haylle.

24 ' Was I not yesterdaye at the Newe Castell,
    That stond*es* so fayre on Tyne ?
For all the men the Perssy had,
    He coude not garre me ones to dyne.'

25 He stepped owt at his pavelyon-dore,
    To loke and it were lesse :
' Araye yow, lordyng*es*, one and all,
    For here bygynnes no peysse.

26 ' The yerle of Mentaye, thow arte my eme,
    The fowarde I gyve to the :
The yerlle of Huntlay, cawte and kene,
    He schall be w*yth* the.

27 ' The lorde of Bowghan, in armure bryght,
    On the other hand he schall be ;
Lord Jhonsto*u*ne and Lorde Maxwell,
    They to schall be w*yth* me.

28 'Swynton, fayre fylde vpon y*our* pryde !
    To batell make yow bowen

Syr Davy Skotte, Syr Water Stewarde,
  Syr Jhon of Agurstone ! '

29 The Perssy cam byfore hys oste,
    Wych was ever a gentyll knyght;
  Vpon the Dowglas lowde can he crye,
    ' I wyll holde that I haue hyght.

30 ' For thou haste brente Northomberlonde,
    And done me grete envye ;
  For thys trespasse thou hast me done,
    The tone of vs schall dye.'

31 The Dowglas answerde hym agayne,
    Wyth grett wurdes vpon hye,
  And sayd, I haue twenty agaynst thy one,
    Byholde, and thou maste see.

32 Wyth that the Perssy was grevyd sore,
    For soth as I yow saye ;
  He lyghted dowyn vpon his foote,
    And schoote hys horsse clene awaye.

33 Euery man sawe that he dyd soo,
    That ryall was euer in rowght;
  Euery man schoote hys horsse hym froo,
    And lyght hym rowynde abowght.

34 Thus Syr Hary Perssye toke the fylde,
    For soth as I yow saye ;
  Jhesu Cryste in hevyn on hyght
    Dyd helpe hym well that daye.

35 But nyne thowzand, ther was no moo,
    The cronykle wyll not layne ;
  Forty thowsande of Skottes and fowre
    That day fowght them agayne.

36 But when the batell byganne to ioyne,
    In hast ther cam a knyght;
  The letters fayre furth hath he tayne,
    And thus he sayd full ryght:

37 ' My lorde your father he gretes yow well,
    Wyth many a noble knyght;
  He desyres yow to byde
    That he may see thys fyght.

38 ' The Baron of Grastoke ys com out of the
      west,
    Wyth hym a noble companye ;
  All they loge at your fathers thys nyght,
    And the batell fayne wolde they see.'

39 ' For Jhesus love,' sayd Syr Harye Perssy,
    ' That dyed for yow and me,
  Wende to my lorde my father agayne,
    And saye thow sawe me not wyth yee.

40 ' My trowth ys plyght to yonne Skottysh
      knyght,
    It nedes me not to layne,
  That I schulde byde hym vpon thys bent,
    And I haue hys trowth agayne.

41 ' And if that I w[e]ynde of thys growende,
    For soth, onfowghten awaye,
  He wolde me call but a kowarde knyght
    In hys londe another daye.

42 ' Yet had I lever to be rynde and rente,
    By Mary, that mykkel maye,
  Then ever my manhood schulde be reprovyd
    Wyth a Skotte another day.

43 ' Wherfore schote, archars, for my sake,
    And let scharpe arowes flee ;
  Mynstrells, playe vp for your waryson,
    And well quyt it schall bee.

44 ' Euery man thynke on hys trewe-love,
    And marke hym to the Trenite ;
  For to God I make myne avowe
    Thys day wyll I not flee.'

45 The blodye harte in the Dowglas armes,
    Hys standerde stode on hye,
  That euery man myght full well knowe ;
    By syde stode starrës thre.

46 The whyte lyon on the Ynglyssh perte,
    For soth as I yow sayne,
  The lucettes and the cressawntes both ;
    The Skottes favght them agayne.

47 Vpon Sent Androwe lowde can they crye,
    And thrysse they schowte on hyght,
  And syne merked them one owr Ynglysshe men,
    As I haue tolde yow ryght.

48 Sent George the bryght, owr ladyes knyght,
    To name they were full fayne ;
  Owr Ynglyssh men they cryde on hyght,
    And thrysse the schowtte agayne.

49 Wyth that scharpe arowes bygan to flee,
    I tell yow in sertayne ;

Men of armes byganne to joyne,
  Many a dowghty man was ther slayne.

50 The Perssy and the Dowglas mette,
    That ether of other was fayne ;
  They swapped together whyll that the swette,
    Wyth swordes of fyne collayne :

51 Tyll the bloode from ther bassonnettes ranne,
    As the roke doth in the rayne ;
  'Yelde the to me,' sayd the Dowglas,
    ' Or elles thow schalt be slayne.

52 'For I see by thy bryght bassonet,
    Thow arte sum man of myght ;
  And so I do by thy burnysshed brande ;
    Thow arte an yerle, or elles a knyght.'

53 ' By my good faythe,' sayd the noble Perssye,
    ' Now haste thow rede full ryght ;
  Yet wyll I never yelde me to the,
    Whyll I may stonde and fyght.'

54 They swapped together whyll that they swette,
    Wyth swordës scharpe and long ;
  Ych on other so faste thee beette,
    Tyll ther helmes cam in peyses dowyn.

55 The Perssy was a man of strenghth,
    I tell yow in thys stounde ;
  He smote the Dowglas at the swordës length
    That he felle to the growynde.

56 The sworde was scharpe, and sore can byte,
    I tell yow in sertayne ;
  To the harte he cowde hym smyte,
    Thus was the Dowglas slayne.

57 The stonderdes stode styll on eke a syde,
    Wyth many a grevous grone ;
  Ther the fowght the day, and all the nyght,
    And many a dowghty man was slayne.

58 Ther was no freke that ther wolde flye,
    But styffely in stowre can stond,
  Ychone hewyng on other whyll they myght
      drye,
    Wyth many a bayllefull bronde.

59 Ther was slayne vpon the Skottës syde,
    For soth and sertenly,
  Syr James a Dowglas ther was slayne,
    That day that he cowde dye.

60 The yerlle of Mentaye he was slayne,
    Grysely groned vpon the growynd ;
  Syr Davy Skotte, Syr Water Stewarde,
    Syr Jhon of Agurstoune.

61 Syr Charllës Morrey in that place,
    That never a fote wold flee ;
  Syr Hewe Maxwell, a lorde he was,
    Wyth the Dowglas dyd he dye.

62 Ther was slayne vpon the Skottës syde,
    For soth as I yow saye,
  Of fowre and forty thowsande Scottes
    Went but eyghtene awaye.

63 Ther was slayne vpon the Ynglysshe syde,
    For soth and sertenlye,
  A gentell knyght, Syr Jhon Fechewe,
    Yt was the more pety.

64 Syr James Hardbotell ther was slayne,
    For hym ther hartes were sore ;
  The gentyll Lovell ther was slayne,
    That the Perssys standerd bore.

65 Ther was slayne vpon the Ynglyssh perte,
    For soth as I yow saye,
  Of nyne thowsand Ynglyssh men
    Fyve hondert cam awaye.

66 The other were slayne in the fylde ;
    Cryste kepe ther sowlles from wo !
  Seyng ther was so fewe fryndes
    Agaynst so many a foo.

67 Then on the morne they mayde them beerys
    Of byrch and haysell graye ;
  Many a wydowe, wyth wepyng teyres,
    Ther makes they fette awaye.

68 Thys fraye bygan at Otterborne,
    Bytwene the nyght and the day ;
  Ther the Dowglas lost hys lyffe,
    And the Perssy was lede awaye.

69 Then was ther a Scottysh prisoner tayne,
    Syr Hewe Mongomery was hys name ;
  For soth as I yow saye,
    He borowed the Perssy home agayne.

70 Now let vs all for the Perssy praye
    To Jhesu most of myght,
  To bryng hys sowlle to the blysse of heven,
    For he was a gentyll knyght.

B

a. Herd's MS., I, 149, II, 30 ; Herd's Scottish Songs, 1776, I, 153. b. Scott's Minstrelsy, I, 31, 1802, "corrected" from Herd, 1776, "by a MS. copy."

1 IT fell and about the Lammas time,
　　When husbandmen do win their hay,
　　Earl Douglass is to the English woods,
　　And a' with him to fetch a prey.

2 He has chosen the Lindsays light,
　　With them the gallant Gordons gay,
　　And the Earl of Fyfe, withouten strife,
　　And Sir Hugh Montgomery upon a grey.

3 They have taken Northumberland,
　　And sae hae they the north shire,
　　And the Otter Dale, they hae burnt it hale,
　　And set it a' into fire.

4 Out then spake a bonny boy,
　　That servd ane o Earl Douglass kin ;
　　Methinks I see an English host,
　　A-coming branken us upon.

5 ' If this be true, my little boy,
　　And it be troth that thou tells me,
　　The brawest bower in Otterburn
　　This day shall be thy morning-fee.

6 ' But if it be fase, my little boy,
　　But and a lie that thou tells me,
　　On the highest tree that 's in Otterburn
　　With my ain hands I 'll hing thee high.'

7 The boy 's taen out his little penknife,
　　That hanget low down by his gare,

And he gaed Earl Douglass a deadly wound,
　　Alack ! a deep wound and a sare.

8 Earl Douglas said to Sir Hugh Montgomery,
　　Take thou the vanguard o the three,
　　And bury me at yon braken-bush,
　　That stands upon yon lilly lee.

9 Then Percy and Montgomery met,
　　And weel a wot they warna fain ;
　　They swaped swords, and they twa swat,
　　And ay the blood ran down between.

10 ' O yield thee, yield thee, Percy,' he said,
　　' Or else I vow I 'll lay thee low ; '
　　' Whom to shall I yield,' said Earl Percy,
　　' Now that I see it maun be so ? '

11 ' O yield thee to yon braken-bush,
　　That grows upon yon lilly lee ;
· · · · · · ·
· · · · · · ·

12 ' I winna yield to a braken-bush,
　　Nor yet will I unto a brier ;
　　But I would yield to Earl Douglass,
　　Or Sir Hugh Montgomery, if he was here.'

13 As soon as he knew it was Montgomery,
　　He stuck his sword's point in the ground,
　　And Sir Hugh Montgomery was a courteous knight,
　　And he quickly broght him by the hand.

14 This deed was done at Otterburn,
　　About the breaking of the day ;
　　Earl Douglass was buried at the braken-bush,
　　And Percy led captive away.

C

Minstrelsy of the Scottish Border, 1833, I, 345. B completed by two copies "obtained from the recitation of old persons residing at the head of Ettrick Forest."

1 IT fell about the Lammas tide,
　　When the muir-men win their hay,
　　The doughty Douglas bound him to ride
　　Into England, to drive a prey.

2 He chose the Gordons and the Græmes,
　　With them the Lindsays, light and gay ;

But the Jardines wald not with him ride,
　　And they rue it to this day.

3 And he has burnd the dales of Tyne,
　　And part of Bambrough shire,
　　And three good towers on Reidswire fells,
　　He left them all on fire.

4 And he marchd up to Newcastle,
　　And rode it round about :
　　' O wha 's the lord of this castle?
　　Or wha 's the lady o 't ? '

5 But up spake proud Lord Percy then,
    And O but he spake hie!
  I am the lord of this castle,
    My wife's the lady gay.

6 'If thou 'rt the lord of this castle,
    Sae weel it pleases me,
  For, ere I cross the Border fells,
    The tane of us shall die.'

7 He took a lang spear in his hand,
    Shod with the metal free,
  And for to meet the Douglas there
    He rode right furiouslie.

8 But O how pale his lady lookd,
    Frae aff the castle-wa,
  When down before the Scottish spear
    She saw proud Percy fa.

9 'Had we twa been upon the green,
    And never an eye to see,
  I wad hae had you, flesh and fell;
    But your sword sall gae wi me.'

10 'But gae ye up to Otterbourne,
    And, wait there dayis three,
  And, if I come not ere three dayis end,
    A fause knight ca ye me.'

11 'The Otterbourne 's a bonnie burn;
    'T is pleasant there to be;
  But there is nought at Otterbourne
    To feed my men and me.

12 'The deer rins wild on hill and dale,
    The birds fly wild from tree to tree;
  But there is neither bread nor kale
    To fend my men and me.

13 'Yet I will stay at Otterbourne,
    Where you shall welcome be;
  And, if ye come not at three dayis end,
    A fause lord I 'll ca thee.'

14 'Thither will I come,' proud Percy said,
    'By the might of Our Ladye;'
  'There will I bide thee,' said the Douglas,
    'My troth I plight to thee.'

15 They lighted high on Otterbourne,
    Upon the bent sae brown;
  They lighted high on Otterbourne,
    And threw their pallions down.

16 And he that had a bonnie boy,
    Sent out his horse to grass;
  And he that had not a bonnie boy,
    His ain servant he was.

17 But up then spake a little page,
    Before the peep of dawn:
  'O waken ye, waken ye, my good lord,
    For Percy 's hard at hand.'

18 'Ye lie, ye lie, ye liar loud!
    Sae loud I hear ye lie:
  For Percy had not men yestreen
    To dight my men and me.

19 'But I have dreamd a dreary dream,
    Beyond the Isle of Sky;
  I saw a dead man win a fight,
    And I think that man was I.'

20 He belted on his guid braid sword,
    And to the field he ran,
  But he forgot the helmet good,
    That should have kept his brain.

21 When Percy wi the Douglas met,
    I wat he was fu fain;
  They swakked their swords, till sair they swat,
    And the blood ran down like rain.

22 But Percy with his good broad sword,
    That could so sharply wound,
  Has wounded Douglas on the brow,
    Till he fell to the ground.

23 Then he calld on his little foot-page,
    And said, Run speedilie,
  And fetch my ain dear sister's son,
    Sir Hugh Montgomery.

24 'My nephew good,' the Douglas said,
    'What recks the death of ane!
  Last night I dreamd a dreary dream,
    And I ken the day 's thy ain.

25 'My wound is deep; I fain would sleep;
    Take thou the vanguard of the three,
  And hide me by the braken-bush,
    That grows on yonder lilye lee.

26 'O bury me by the braken-bush,
    Beneath the blooming brier;
  Let never living mortal ken
    That ere a kindly Scot lies here.'

27 He lifted up that noble lord,
     Wi the saut tear in his ee ;
   He hid him in the braken-bush,
     That his merrie men might not see.

28 The moon was clear, the day drew near,
     The spears in flinders flew,
   But mony a gallant Englishman
     Ere day the Scotsmen slew.

29 The Gordons good, in English blood
     They steepd their hose and shoon ;
   The Lindsays flew like fire about,
     Till all the fray was done.

30 The Percy and Montgomery met,
     That either of other were fain ;
   They swapped swords, and they twa swat,
     And aye the blood ran down between.

31 'Now yield thee, yield thee, Percy,' he said,
     'Or else I vow I 'll lay thee low ! '

'To whom must I yield,' quoth Earl Percy,
  'Now that I see it must be so ? '

32 'Thou shalt not yield to lord nor loun,
     Nor yet shalt thou yield to me ;
   But yield thee to the braken-bush,
     That grows upon yon lilye lee.'

33 'I will not yield to a braken-bush,
     Nor yet will I yield to a brier ;
   But I would yield to Earl Douglas,
     Or Sir Hugh the Montgomery, if he were
       here.'

34 As soon as he knew it was Montgomery,
     He struck his sword's point in the gronde ;
   The Montgomery was a courteous knight,
     And quickly took him by the honde.

35 This deed was done at the Otterbourne,
     About the breaking of the day ;
   Earl Douglas was buried at the braken-bush,
     And the Percy led captive away.

— ⬩ —

D

Finlay's Scottish Ballads, I, xviii f ; from recitation.

1 THEN out an spak a little wee boy,
     And he was near o Percy's kin :
   Methinks I see the English host
     A coming branking us upon.

2 Wi nine waggons scaling wide,
     And seven banners bearing high ;
   It wad do any living gude
     To see their bonny colours fly.

— ⬩ —

E

Motherwell's Minstrelsy, p. lxxi, note 30 ; from a recited copy.

'O YIELD thee to yon braken-bush,
   That grows upon yon lilly lie ;

For there lies aneth yon braken-bush
  What aft has conquerd mae than thee.'

— ⬩ —

A. a. 3⁴. many a styrande.
    "The reading of the MS. is, I suspect,
    right ; for stage, or staig, in Scotland
    means a young horse unshorn of its mas-
    culine attributes, and the obvious inten-
    tion of the poet is merely to describe that
    the Scottish alighted from many a pranc-
    ing steed, in order to prepare for action."
    Motherwell, Minstrelsy, p. lxxi, note 30,

who would read accordingly, [Off] many
a styrande stage. *The fourth line, as
amended by Motherwell, would be a
superfluity, whereas Percy's reading,
here adopted, adds a pleasing incident,
the rousing of the deer as the troopers
passed their haunts.*
20¹. beste, *corrected to* bent.
22¹. *repeated at the top of fol.* 65 *back.*

31⁸. the one; b, thy one.   34². soth soth.
41¹. b, weynde.   46⁸. cressaw*tte*s.
50⁸. schapped : *cf.* 54¹.
60⁴. S*yr* James : *cf.* 28⁴.   64⁸. Covell.
Crossed final ll, *in* all, styll, Castell, schall,
   well, *etc., has not been rendered* lle.
b. A Songe made in R. 2. his tyme of the Bat-
   telle at Otterburne betweene the Lord Henry
   Percye, Earle of Northomberland, and the
   Earle Douglas of Scotland, An⁰ 1388.
Either b *is a transcript of* a, *or both are
from the same source.*
   3². Redclyffe.   3⁴. Many a stirande.
   4⁴. bound.   7⁴. they ranne.
   11¹. Sr Henry came.   13². wille.
   14². game and.   15⁸. maiste thou.
   15⁴. Henrye.
   20¹. houered vppon the beste bent.
   24⁴. gare me oute to.   28⁴. Aguiston.
   31⁸. thy one.   35¹. no more.   35². cronicles.
   37⁸. abyde.   39⁴. wth thie eye.
   40¹. yonde Skot*es*.   41¹. Ffor yf I weynde.
   44⁸. my avowe.   46². I *wanting*.
   49¹. arrowes gan vpe to.
   50⁸. schapped : swatte.   51¹. from the.
   54¹. swotte.   57¹. stonderes ; elke syde.
   59⁸. a *wanting*.   60⁴. Sr James.
   63⁸. Ffitzhughe.   64¹. Harbotle.
   64⁸. Covelle.   66⁴. a *wanting*.
   67¹. the morowe.   70¹. Percyes.
A pencil note on the first leaf of b *(signed
   F. M., Sir F. Madden) states that it is in
   Ralph Starkey's hand.*
B. a. 2⁸. Fuife *in my transcript of* Herd, I ; Fyfe
   in II.

3⁸. hae *is omitted in* II *and the printed copy.*
3⁴. *printed* into a fire.
5⁸. bravest *in my transcript of* Herd, I ;
   brawest, II ; *printed* brawest.
7⁸. *The second MS. has* gae ; *printed* gae.
8⁸. bring me *in my transcript of* Herd, I ;
   bury *in the second MS., and so printed.*
12². II, into.
b. 1¹. and *wanting*.   2⁴. Hugh the.
   3¹. have harried.   3². they Bambroshire.
   3⁸. And *wanting*.   3⁴. a' in a blaze o fire.
   5¹. true, thou little foot-page.
   5². If this be true thou tells to me.
   5⁴. This day *wanting ;* morning's.
   6¹. thou little.   6². lie thou tells to.
   6⁸. that's *wanting*.   6⁴. hang.   7¹. boy has.
   7². hung right low.   7⁸. gave Lord.
   7⁴. I wot a.
   8¹. Douglas to the Montgomery said.
   8⁸. me by the.   8⁴. that grows.
   9¹. The Percy.
   9². That either of other were fain.
   10¹. Yield thee, O yield.   10⁴. it must.

11 Thou shalt not yield to lord nor loun,
      Nor yet shalt thou yield to me ;
   But yield thee to the braken-bush,
      That grows upon yon lilye lee.

12¹. I will not.   12². I to.
12⁴. Hugh the : he were.
13^{1,8}. And the Montgomery.
13⁴. And quickly took him.   14⁴. the Percy.
C. 34¹. *In one copy :* As soon as he knew it was
   Sir Hugh.

162

THE HUNTING OF THE CHEVIOT

A. MS. Ashmole, 48, 1550 or later, Bodleian Library, in Skeat's Specimens of English Literature, etc., third edition, 1880, p. 67.*

B. a. 'Chevy Chase,' Percy MS., p. 188, Hales and Furnivall, II, 7. b. Pepys Ballads, I, 92, No 45, Magdalene College, Cambridge, broadside, London, printed for M. G. c. Douce Ballads, fol. 27ᵇ, Bod-

leian Library, and Roxburghe Ballads, III, 66, British Museum, broadside, printed for F. Coles, T. Vere, and J. Wright. d. Wood Ballads, 401, 48, Bodleian Library, broadside, printed for F. Coles, T. Vere, and W. Gilbertson. e. Bagford Ballads, I, No 32, British Museum, broadside, printed by and for W. Onley. f. A Scottish copy, without printer, Harvard College Library.

A was first printed by Hearne in Guilielmi Neubrigensis Historia, I, lxxxii ff, 1719; then by Percy, Reliques, I, 1, 1765, with a judicious preface. The whole manuscript, in which this piece is No 8, was edited by Thomas Wright for the Roxburghe Club in 1860: Songs and Ballads, with other short Poems, chiefly of the Reign of Philip and Mary.

B may probably be found in any of the larger sets of broadsides. It is included in such collections as Dryden's Miscellanies, II, 238, 1702; Pills to purge Melancholy, IV, 289, 1719; Old Ballads, I, 111, 1723; Percy's Reliques, I, 235, 1765. b has many readings of a, the copy in the Percy MS. There is a second Bagford copy, II, No 37, printed like e, for W. Onley. f, the Scottish copy, is probably of a date near 1700. Like the edition printed at Glasgow, 1747, it is, in the language of Percy, "remarkable for the wilful corruptions made in all the passages which concern the two nations": Folio Manuscript, Hales and Furnivall, II, 1, note, and Reliques, 1765, I, 234. The Scots are made fifteen hundred, the English twenty, in 6, 13, 53, 54; the speeches of King James and King Henry are interchanged in 58, 60; 62, 63, are dropped.

The 'Hunttis of Chevet' is among the "sangis of natural music of the antiquite" mentioned as sung by the "shepherds" in The Complaynt of Scotland, a book assigned to 1549. It was an old and a popular song at the middle of the sixteenth century. The copy in the Ashmolean manuscript is subscribed Expliceth, quod Rychard Sheale, upon which ground Sheale has been held to be the author,† and not, as Percy and Ritson assumed, simply the transcriber, of the ballad. Sheale describes himself as a minstrel living at Tamworth, whose business was to sing and talk, or to chant ballads and tell stories. He was the author of four pieces of verse in the same manuscript, one of which is of the date 1559 (No 56). This and another piece (No 46), in which he tells how he was robbed of above three score pound, give a sufficient idea of his dialect and style and a measure of his ability. This ballad was of course part of his stock as minstrel; the supposition that he was the author is preposterous in the extreme.

The song "which is commonly sung of the Hunting of Chiviot," says Hume of Godscroft, "seemeth indeed poeticall and a meer fiction, perhaps to stirre up vertue; yet a fiction whereof there is no mention, neither in the Scottish nor English chronicle": p. 104. To

---

* I have not resorted to the MS. in this case, for the reason that I could not expect to get a transcript which would merit the confidence which must attach to one made by the hand of Professor Skeat.

† British Bibliographer, IV, 99 f; Wright, Songs and Ballads, p. viii; etc.

this the general replication may be made that the ballad can scarcely be a deliberate fiction. The singer is not a critical historian, but he supposes himself to be dealing with facts; he may be partial to his countrymen, but he has no doubt that he is treating of a real event; and the singer in this particular case thought he was describing the battle of Otterburn, the Hunting of the Cheviot being indifferently so called: st. 65. The agreement to meet, in A, st. 9, corresponds with the plight in Otterburn, st. 16; 17[4] corresponds to Otterburn 12[4], 30[4]; 47, 56, 57, are the same as Otterburn 58, 61, 67; 31, 32, 66, are variants of Otterburn 51, 52, 68; Douglas's summons to Percy to yield, Percy's refusal, and Douglas's death, 33[1], 35–37[2], may be a variation of Otterburn, 51[3], 55–56; Sir John of Agarstone is slain with Percy in 52, and with Douglas in Otterburn 60; Sir Hugh Montgomery appears in both.

The differences in the story of the two ballads, though not trivial, are still not so material as to forbid us to hold that both may be founded upon the same occurrence, the Hunting of the Cheviot being of course the later version,* and following in part its own tradition, though repeating some portions of the older ballad. According to this older ballad, Douglas invades Northumberland in an act of public war; according to the later, Percy takes the initiative, by hunting in the Scottish hills without the leave and in open defiance of Douglas, lieutenant of the Marches. Such trespasses,† whether by the English or the Scots, were not less common, we may believe, than hostile incursions, and the one would as naturally as the other account for a bloody collision between the rival families of Percy and Douglas, to those who consulted "old men" instead of histories: cf. stanza 67. The older and the later ballad concur (and herein are in harmony with some chroniclers,

though not with the best) as to Percy's slaying Douglas. In the older ballad Percy is taken prisoner, an incident which history must record, but which is somewhat insipid, for which reason we might expect tradition to improve the tale by assigning a like fate to both of the heroic antagonists.

The singer all but startles us with his historical lore when he informs us in 63 that King Harry the Fourth "did the battle of Hombylldown" to requite the death of Percy; for though the occasion of Homildon was really another incursion on the part of the Scots, and the same Percy was in command of the English who in the ballad meets his death at Otterburn, nevertheless the battle of Homildon was actually done fourteen years subsequent to that of Otterburn and falls in the reign of Henry Fourth. The free play of fancy in assigning the cause of Homildon must be allowed to offset the servility to an accurate chronology; and such an extenuation is required only in this instance.‡ Not only is the fourth Harry on the throne of England at the epoch of Otterburn, but Jamy is the Scottish king, although King James I was not crowned until 1424, the second year of Henry VI.

But here we may remember what is well said by Bishop Percy: "A succession of two or three Jameses, and the long detention of one of them in England, would render the name familiar to the English, and dispose a poet in those rude times to give it to any Scottish king he happened to mention." The only important inference from the mention of a King James is that the minstrel's date is not earlier than 1424.

The first, second, and fourth James were contemporary with a Henry during the whole of their reign, and the third during a part of his; with the others we need not concern ourselves. It has given satisfaction to some

---

* The grammatical forms of the Hunting of the Cheviot are, however, older than those of the particular copy of Otterburn which has been preserved. The plural of the noun is very often in -ës or -ys, as lordës, 23[1]; longës, 37[1]; handdës, 60[1]; sydis, 8[2]; bowys, 13[2], 25[1], 29[1], etc., at least sixteen cases. We find, also, sydë at 6[2], and possibly should read faÿllë at 9[3]. The plural in -ës is rare in The Battle of

Otterburn: starrës, 45[4]; swordës, 54[2]; Skottës, 59[1], 62[1]. Probably we are to read swordës length in 55[3].

† See the passage in the Memoirs of Carey, Earl of Monmouth, referred to in Percy's Reliques, 1765, I, 235, and given at length in Hales and Furnivall, II; 3 f.

‡ The minstrel was not too nice as to topography either: Otterburn is not in Cheviot.

who wish to reconcile the data of the ballad with history to find in a Scottish historiographer a record of a fight between a Percy and a Douglas in 1435 or 1436, at the very end of the reign of James I. Henry Percy of Northumberland, says Hector Boece, made a raid into Scotland with four thousand men (it is not known whether of his own motion or by royal authority), and was encountered by nearly an equal force under William Douglas, Earl of Angus, and others, at Piperden, the victory falling to the Scots, with about the same slaughter on both sides: Scotorum Historia, 1526, fol. ccclxvi, back. This affair is mentioned by Bower, Scotichronicon, 1759, II, 500 f, but the leader of the English is not named,* wherefore we may doubt whether it was a Percy. Very differently from Otterburn, this battle made but a slight impression on the chroniclers.

Sidney's words, though perhaps a hundred times requoted since they were cited by Addison, cannot be omitted here: " Certainly I must confesse my own barbarousnes. I never heard the olde song of Percy and Duglas that I found not my heart mooved more then with a trumpet; and yet is it sung but by some blinde crouder, with no rougher voyce then rude stile : which, being so evill apparrelled in the dust and cobwebbes of that uncivill age, what would it worke trymmed in the gorgeous eloquence of Pindar ! "† Sidney's

commendation is fully justified by the quality of The Battle of Otterburn, but is merited in even a higher degree by The Hunting of the Cheviot, and for that reason (I know of no other) The Hunting of the Cheviot may be supposed to be the ballad he had in mind. The song of Percy and Douglas, then, was sung about the country by blind fiddlers about 1580 in a rude and ancient form, much older than the one that has come down to us; for that, if heard by Sidney, could not have seemed to him a song of an uncivil age, meaning the age of Percy and Douglas, two hundred years before his day. It would give no such impression even now, if chanted to an audience three hundred years later than Sidney.‡

B is a striking but by no means a solitary example of the impairment which an old ballad would suffer when written over for the broadside press. This very seriously enfeebled edition was in circulation throughout the seventeenth century, and much sung (says Chappell) despite its length. § It is declared by Addison, in his appreciative and tasteful critique, Spectator, Nos 70, 74, 1711, to be the favorite ballad of the common people of England.‖ Addison, who knew no other version, informs us that Ben Jonson used to say that he had rather have been the author of Chevy Chase than of all his works. The broadside copy may possibly have been the only one

* Tytler, History of Scotland, III, 293, though citing only the Scotichronicon, says Sir Robert Ogle, and also Scott, I, 270; for reasons which do not appear.

† An Apologie for Poetrie, p. 46 of Arber's reprint of the first edition, 1595. For the date of the writing, 1581–85, see Arber, p. 7 f.

‡ The courtly poet deserves much of ballad-lovers for avowing his barbarousness (one doubts whether he seriously believed that the gorgeous Pindar could have improved upon the ballad), but what would he not have deserved if he had written the blind crowder's song down !

§ Popular Music, I, 198. Chevy Chase is entered in the Stationers' Registers, among a large parcel of ballads, in 1624, and clearly was no novelty : Arber, IV, 131. " Had it been printed even so early as Queen Elizabeth's reign," says Percy, " I think I should have met with some copy wherein the first line would have been, God prosper long our noble queen." " That it could not be much later than that time appears from the phrase *doleful dumps*, which in that age carried no ill sound with it, but to the next generation became ridiculous. We have seen it pass uncensured in a sonnet that was at that time in request, and where it could

not fail to have been taken notice of had it been in the least exceptionable; see above, Book ii, song v, ver. 2 [by Richard Edwards, 1596 ?]. Yet, in about half a century after, it was become burlesque. Vide Hudibras, Pt. I, c. 3, v. 95." Reliques, 1794, I, 268, note, 269.

The copy in the Percy MS., B a, though carelessly made, retains, where the broadsides do not, two of the readings of A : bade on the bent, 28^2; to the hard head haled he, 45^4.

‖ Addison was not behind any of us in his regard for traditional songs and tales. No 70 begins : " When I travelled, I took a particular delight in hearing the songs and fables that are come from father to son and are most in vogue among the common people of the countries through which I passed ; for it is impossible that anything should be universally tasted and approved by a multitude, tho they are only the rabble of a nation, which hath not in it some peculiar aptness to please and gratify the mind of man. Human nature is the same in all reasonable creatures, and whatever falls in with it will meet with admirers amongst readers of all qualities and conditions."

known to Jonson also, but in all probability the traditional ballad was still sung in the streets in Jonson's youth, if not later.

A 3. By these "shyars thre" is probably meant three districts in Northumberland which still go by the name of *shires* and are all in the neighborhood of Cheviot. These are Islandshire, being the district so named from Holy Island; Norehamshire, so called from the town and castle of Noreham or Norham; and Bamboroughshire, the ward or hundred belonging to Bamborough castle and town. Percy's Reliques, 1794, I, 5, note.

15. Chyviat Chays, well remarks Mr Wheatley in his edition of the Reliques, I, 22, becomes Chevy Chace by the same process as that by which Teviotdale becomes Tividale, and there is no sufficient occasion for the suggestion that Chevy Chase is a corruption of chevauchée, raid, made by Dr. E. B. Nicholson, Notes and Queries, Third Series, XII, 124, and adopted by Burton, History of Scotland, II, 366.

38 f. "That beautiful line *taking the dead man by the hand* will put the reader in mind of Æneas's behavior towards Lausus, whom he himself had slain as he came to the rescue of his aged father" (Ingemuit miserans graviter, dextramque tetendit, etc., Æn. X, 823, etc.): Addison, in Spectator, No 70.

54³,⁴, and B 50³,⁴. Witherington's prowess was not without precedent, and, better still, was emulated in later days. Witness the battle of Ancrum Muir, 1545, or "Lilliard's Edge," as it is commonly called, from a woman that fought with great bravery there, to whose memory there was a monument erected on the field of battle with this inscription, as the traditional report goes:

"Fair maiden Lilliard lies under this stane;
Little was her stature, but great her fame;
On the English lads she laid many thumps,
And when her legs were off, she fought upon her stumps." *

The giant Burlong also fought wonderfully on his stumps after Sir Triamour had smitten his legs off by the knee: Utterson's Popular Poetry, I, 67, 1492–94, cited by Motherwell; Percy MS., Hales and Furnivall, II, 131. Sir Graysteel fights on one leg: Eger and Grine, Percy MS., I, 386 f, 1032, 1049. Nygosar, in Kyng Alisaunder, after both his armes have been cut off, bears two knights from their steeds "with his heved and with his cors": 2291–2312, Weber, I, 98 f. Still better, King Starkaðr, in the older Edda, fights after his head is off: Helgakviða Hundingsbana, ii, 27, Bugge, p. 196.†

"Sed, etiam si ceciderit, de genu pugnat," Seneca, De Providentia 2, 4 (cited in The Gentleman's Magazine, 1794, I, 306), is explained by Seneca himself, Epis. lxvi, 47: "qui, succisis poplitibus, in genua se excepit nec arma dimisit." "In certaminibus gladiatorum hoc sæpe accidisse et statuæ existentes docent, imprimis gladiator Borghesinus." Senecæ Op. Phil., Bouillet, II, 12.

61¹. "Lovely London," as Maginn remarks, Blackwood's Magazine, VII, 327, is like the Homeric Αὐγειὰς ἐρατεινάς, Ἀρήνην ἐρατεινήν, Il., ii, 532, 591, etc. Leeve, or lovely, London, is of frequent occurrence: see No 158, 1¹, No 168, appendix, 7⁵, No 174, 35¹, etc. So "men of pleasant Tivydale," B 14¹, wrongly in B a, f, "pleasant men of Tiuydale."

64³. Glendale is one of the six wards of Northumberland, and Homildon is in this ward, a mile northwest of Wooler.

---

* A Description of the Parish of Melrose [by the Revd. Adam Milne], Edinburgh, 1743, p. 21. Scott cites the epitaph, with some slight variations (as "English louns"), Appendix to The Eve of St. John, Minstrelsy, IV, 199, ed. 1833. The monument was "all broken in pieces" in Milne's time; seems to have been renewed and again broken up (The Scotsman, November 12, 1873); but, judging from Murray's Handbook of Scotland, has again been restored.

Squire Meldrum's valor was inferior to nobody's, but as his fortune was happier than Witherington's and Lilliard's, a note may suffice for him. "Quhen his schankis wer schorne in sunder, vpon his knees he wrocht greit wounder:" Lindsay, ed. 1594, Cv. recto, v. 30 f, Hall, p. 358, v.

1349 f. But really he was only "hackit on his hochis and theis," or as Pittscottie says, Dalyell, p. 306, "his hochis war cutted and the knoppis of his elbowis war strikin aff," and by and by he is "haill and sound" again, according to the poet, and according to the chronicler he "leived fyftie yeires thairefter."

† As stanch as some of these was a Highlander at the battle of Gasklune, 1392, who, though nailed to the ground by a horseman's spear, held fast to his sword, writhed himself up, and with a last stroke cut his foeman above the foot to the bone, "through sterap-lethire and the bute, thre ply or foure": Wyntoun's Chronicle, B. ix, ch. 14, Laing, III, 59.

65². That tear begane this spurn "is said to be a proverb, meaning that tear, or pull, brought about this kick": Skeat. Such a proverb is unlikely and should be vouched. There may be corruption, and perhaps we should read, as a lamentation, That ear (ever) begane this spurn! Or possibly, That tear is for That there, meaning simply there.

For genealogical illustrations may be consulted, with caution, Percy's Reliques, 1794, I, 34 ff, 282 ff. With respect to 53¹, Professor Skeat notes: "Loumle, Lumley; always hitherto printed louele (and explained Lovel), though the MS. cannot be so read, the word being written loūle. 'My Lord Lumley' is mentioned in the ballad of Scotish Feilde,

Percy Fol. MS., I, 226, l. 270; and again in the ballad of Bosworth Feilde, id., III, 245, l. 250."

A is translated by Herder, II, 213; by R. v. Bismarck, Deutsches Museum, 1858, I, 897; by Von Marées, p. 63; by Grundtvig, Engelske og skotske Folkeviser, p. 84, No 13. Into Latin by Dr. William Maginn, in Blackwood's Magazine, 1819–20, VI, 199, VII, 323.

B is translated by Bothe, p. 6; by Knortz, L. u. R. Alt-Englands, p. 24, No 7; by Loève-Veimars, p. 55; (in part) by Cantù, p. 802. Into Latin by Henry Bold, Dryden's Miscellanies, ed. 1702, II, 239; by Rev. John Anketell, Poems, etc., Dublin, 1793, p. 264.

A

MS. Ashmole, 48, Bodleian Library, in Skeat's Specimens of English Literature, 1394–1579, ed. 1880, p. 67.

1 THE Persë owt off Northombarlonde,
    and avowe to God mayd he
That he wold hunte in the mowntayns
    off Chyviat within days thre,
In the magger of doughtë Dogles,
    and all that euer with him be.

2 The fattiste hartes in all Cheviat
    he sayd he wold kyll, and cary them away:
'Be my feth,' sayd the dougheti Doglas agayn,
    'I wyll let that hontyng yf that I may.'

3 The[n] the Persë owt off Banborowe cam,
    with him a myghtee meany,
With fifteen hondrith archares bold off blood
    and bone;
the wear chosen owt of shyars thre.

4 This begane on a Monday at morn,
    in Cheviat the hillys so he;
The chylde may rue that ys vn-born,
    it wos the mor pittë.

5 The dryvars thorowe the woodës went,
    for to reas the dear;
Bomen byckarte vppone the bent
    with ther browd aros cleare.

6 Then the wyld thorowe the woodës went,
    on euery sydë shear;
Greahondes thorowe the grevis glent,
    for to kyll thear dear.

7 This begane in Chyviat the hyls abone,
    yerly on a Monnyn-day;
Be that it drewe to the oware off none,
    a hondrith fat hartës ded ther lay.

8 The blewe a mort vppone the bent,
    the semblyde on sydis shear;
To the quyrry then the Persë went,
    to se the bryttlynge off the deare.

9 He sayd, It was the Duglas promys
    this day to met me hear;
But I wyste he wolde faylle, verament;
    a great oth the Persë swear.

10 At the laste a squyar off Northomberlonde
    lokyde at his hand full ny;
He was war a the doughetie Doglas commynge,
    with him a myghttë meany.

11 Both with spear, bylle, and brande,
    yt was a myghtti sight to se;
Hardyar men, both off hart nor hande,
    wear not in Cristiantë.

12 The wear twenti hondrith spear-men good,
    withoute any feale ;
  The wear borne along be the watter a Twyde,
    yth bowndẻs of Tividale.

13 ' Leave of the brytlyng of the dear,' he sayd,
  ' and to your boÿs lock ye tayk good hede ;
  For neuer sithe ye wear on your mothars borne
    had ye neuer so mickle nede.'

14 The dougheti Dogglas on a stede,
    he rode alle his men beforne ;
  His armor glytteryde as dyd a glede ;
    a boldar barne was never born.

15 ' Tell me whos men ye ar,' he says,
  ' or whos men that ye be :
  Who gave youe leave to hunte in this Chyviat
    chays,
    in the spyt of myn and of me.'

16 The first mane that ever him an answear mayd,
    yt was the good lord Persë :
  ' We wyll not tell the whoys men we ar,' he
    says,
  ' nor whos men that we be ;
  But we wyll hounte hear in this chays,
    in the spyt of thyne and of the.

17 ' The fattiste hartẻs in all Chyviat
    we haue kyld, and cast to carry them away : '
  ' Be my troth,' sayd the doughetë Dogglas
    agay[n],
  ' therfor the ton of vs shall de this day.'

18 Then sayd the doughtë Doglas
    unto the lord Persë :
  ' To kyll alle thes giltles men,
    alas, it wear great pittë !

19 ' But, Persë, thowe art a lord of lande,
    I am a yerle callyd within my contrë ;
  Let all our men vppone a parti stande,
    and do the battell off the and of me.'

20 ' Nowe Cristes cors on his crowne,' sayd the
    lorde Persë,
  ' who-so-euer ther-to says nay !
  Be my troth, doughttë Doglas,' he says,
  ' thow shalt neuer se that day.

21 ' Nethar in Ynglonde, Skottlonde, nar France,
    nor for no man of a woman born,

But, and fortune be my chance,
    I dar met him, on man for on.'

22 Then bespayke a squyar off Northombarlonde,
    Richard Wytharyngton was him nam ;
  ' It shall neuer be told in Sothe-Ynglonde,' he
    says,
  ' to Kyng Herry the Fourth for sham.

23 ' I wat youe byn great lordẻs twaw,
    I am a poor squyar of lande ;
  I wylle neuer se my captayne fyght on a fylde,
    and stande my selffe and loocke on,
  But whylle I may my weppone welde,
    I wylle not [fayle] both hart and hande.'

24 That day, that day, that dredfull day !
    the first fit here I fynde ;
  And youe wyll here any mor a the hountynge
    a the Chyviat,
    yet ys ther mor behynde.

25 The Yngglyshe men hade ther bowys yebent,
    ther hartes wer good yenoughe ;
  The first off arros that the shote off,
    seven skore spear-men the sloughe.

26 Yet byddys the yerle Doglas vppon the bent,
    a captayne good yenoughe,
  And that was sene verament,
    for he wrought hom both woo and wouche.

27 The Dogglas partyd his ost in thre,
    lyk a cheffe cheften off pryde ;
  With suar spears off myghttë tre,
    the cum in on euery syde ;

28 Thrughe our Yngglyshe archery
    gave many a wounde fulle wyde ;
  Many a doughetë the garde to dy,
    which ganyde them no pryde.

29 The Ynglyshe men let ther boÿs be,
    and pulde owt brandes that wer brighte ;
  It was a hevy syght to se
    bryght swordes on basnites lyght.

30 Thorowe ryche male and myneyeple,
    many sterne the strocke done streght ;
  Many a freyke that was fulle fre,
    ther vndar foot dyd lyght.

31 At last the Duglas and the Persë met,
   lyk to captayns of myght and of mayne;
The swapte togethar tylle the both swat,
   with swordes that wear of fyn myllan.

32 Thes worthë freckys for to fyght,
   ther-to the wear fulle fayne,
Tylle the bloode owte off thear basnetes sprente,
   as euer dyd heal or ra[y]n.

33 'Yelde the, Persë,' sayde the Doglas,
   'and i feth I shalle the brynge
Wher thowe shalte haue a yerls wagis
   of Jamy our Skottish kynge.

34 'Thoue shalte haue thy ransom fre,
   I hight the hear this thinge;
For the manfullyste man yet art thowe
   that euer I conqueryd in filde fighttynge.'

35 'Nay,' sayd the lord Persë,
   'I tolde it the beforne,
That I wolde neuer yeldyde be
   to no man of a woman born.'

36 With that ther cam an arrowe hastely,
   forthe off a myghttë wane;
Hit hathe strekene the yerle Duglas
   in at the brest-bane.

37 Thorowe lyvar and longës bathe
   the sharpe arrowe ys gane,
That neuer after in all his lyffe-days
   he spayke mo wordës but ane:
That was, Fyghte ye, my myrry men, whyllys
   ye may,
   for my lyff-days ben gan.

38 The Persë leanyde on his brande,
   and sawe the Duglas de;
He tooke the dede mane by the hande,
   and sayd, Wo ys me for the!

39 'To haue savyde thy lyffe, I wolde haue par-
   tyde with
my landes for years thre,
For a better man, of hart nare of hande,
   was nat in all the north contrë.'

40 Off all that se a Skottishe knyght,
   was callyd Ser Hewe the Monggombyrry;
He sawe the Duglas to the deth was dyght,
   he spendyd a spear, a trusti tre.

41 He rod vppone a corsiare
   throughe a hondrith archery:
He neuer stynttyde, nar neuer blane,
   tylle he cam to the good lord Persë.

42 He set vppone the lorde Persë
   a dynte that was full soare;
With a suar spear of a myghttë tre
   clean thorow the body he the Persë ber,

43 A the tothar syde that a man myght se
   a large cloth-yard and mare:
Towe bettar captayns wear nat in Cristiantë
   then that day slan wear ther.

44 An archar off Northomberlonde
   say slean was the lord Persë;
He bar a bende bowe in his hand,
   was made off trusti tre.

45 An arow that a cloth-yarde was lang
   to the harde stele halyde he;
A dynt that was both sad and soar
   he sat on Ser Hewe the Monggombyrry.

46 The dynt yt was both sad and sar
   that he of Monggomberry sete;
The swane-fethars that his arrowe bar
   with his hart-blood the wear wete.

47 Ther was neuer a freake wone foot wolde fle,
   but still in stour dyd stand,
Heawyng on yche othar, whylle the myghte
   dre,
   with many a balfull brande.

48 This battell begane in Chyviat
   an owar befor the none,
And when even-songe bell was rang,
   the battell was nat half done.

49 The tocke .. on ethar hande
   be the lyght off the mone;
Many hade no strenght for to stande,
   in Chyviat the hillys abon.

50 Of fifteen hondrith archars of Ynglonde
   went away but seuenti and thre;
Of twenti hondrith spear-men of Skotlonde,
   but even five and fifti.

51 But all wear slayne Cheviat within;
   the hade no streng[th]e to stand on hy;

The chylde may rue that ys unborne,
   it was *th*e mor pittë.

52 Thear was slayne, withe the lord Persë,
   S*er* Johan of Ager*st*one,
   S*er* Rogar, the hinde Hartly,
   S*er* Wyllyam, the bolde Hearone.

53 Ser Jorg, the worthë Lou*m*le,
   a knyghte of great renowen,
   Ser Raff, the ryche Rugbe,
   with dynt*es* wear beaten dowene.

54 For Wetharryngton my harte was wo,
   *tha*t eu*er* he slayne shulde be ;
   For when both his leggis wear hewyne in to,
   yet he knyled and fought on hys kny.

55 Ther was slayne, w*ith th*e dougheti Duglas,
   S*er* Hewe the Monggo*m*byrry,
   S*er* Dauy Lwdale, *that* worthë was,
   his sistars sou was he.

56 S*er* Charls a Murrë in that place,
   *tha*t neu*er* a foot wolde fle ;
   S*er* Hewe Maxwell*e*, a lorde he was,
   w*ith th*e Doglas dyd he dey.

57 So on the morrowe the mayde them byears
   off birch and hasell so g[r]ay ;
   Many wedous, w*ith* wepyng tears,
   cam to fache *the*r makys away.

58 Tivydale may carpe off care,
   Northo*m*barlond may mayk great mon,
   For towe such captayns as slayne wear thear
   on the March-p*ar*ti shall neu*er* be non.

59 Word ys co*m*men to Eddenburrowe,
   to Jamy *th*e Skottishe kynge,
   That dougheti Duglas, lyff-tenant of the
     Ma*r*ches,
   he lay slean Chyviot w*ith*in.

60 His handdës dyd he weal and wryng,
   he sayd, Alas, and woe ys me !
   Such an othar captayn Skotland w*ith*in,
   he sayd, ye-feth shuld neu*er* be.

61 Worde ys co*m*myn to lovly Londone,
   till the fourth Harry our kynge,
   That lord Persë, leyff-tenante of the Ma*r*chis,
   he lay slayne Chyviat w*ith*in.

62 'God haue me*r*ci on his soll*e*,' sayde Kyng
     Harry,
   'good lord, yf thy will it be !
   I haue a hondrith captayns in Ynglonde,' he
     sayd,
   'as good as eu*er* was he :
   But, Persë, and I brook my lyffe,
   thy deth well quyte shall be.'

63 As our noble kynge mayd his avowe,
   lyke a noble prince of renowen,
   For the deth of the lord Persë
   he dyde the battell of Ho*m*byll-down ;

64 Wher syx and thrittë Skottishe knygh*tes*
   on a day wear beaten down ;
   Glendale glytteryde on ther armor bryght,
   ov*er* castille, towar, and town.

65 This was the hontynge off the Cheviat,
   that tear begane this spurn ;
   Old men that knowen the grownde well
     yenoughe
   call it *th*e battell of Otterburn.

66 At Otterburn begane this spurne,
   vppone a Monnynday ;
   Ther was the doughtë Doglas slean,
   *th*e Persë neu*er* went away.

67 Ther was neu*er* a tym on the Marche-p*ar*tës
   sen *th*e Doglas and *th*e Persë met,
   But yt ys me*r*vele and the rede blude ro*n*ne
     not,
   as the reane doys in *th*e stret.

68 Ihesue Crist our balys bete,
   and to the blys vs brynge !
   Thus was the hountynge of the Chivyat :
   God send vs all*e* good endyng !

B

a. Percy MS., p. 188, Hales and Furnivall, II, 7. b. Pepys Ballads, I, 92, No 45, broadside printed for M. G. c. Douce Ballads, fol. 27ᵇ, and Roxburghe Ballads, III, 66, broadside printed for F. Coles, T. Vere, and J. Wright. d. Wood's Ballads, 401, 48, broadside printed for F. Coles, T. Vere, and W. Gilbertson. e. Bagford Ballads, I, No 32, broadside printed by and for W. Onley. f. A Scottish copy, without printer.

1 GOD prosper long our noble k*ing*,
    our liffes and saftyes all!
  A woefull hunting once there did
    in Cheuy Chase befall.

2 To dr*i*ue the deere w*i*th hound and horne
    Erle Pearcy took the way:
  The child may rue *that* is vnborne
    the hunting of *that* day!

3 The stout Erle of Northumberland
    a vow to God did make
  His pleasure in the Scottish woods
    three som*m*ers days to take,

4 The cheefest harts in Cheuy C[h]ase
    to kill and beare away:
  These tydings to Erle Douglas came
    in Scottland, where he lay.

5 Who sent Erle Pearcy p*r*esent word
    he wold p*r*event his sport;
  The English erle, not fearing that,
    did to the woods resort,

6 W*i*th fifteen hundred bowmen bold,
    all chosen men of might,
  Who knew ffull well in time of neede
    to ayme their shafts arright.

7 The gallant greyhound[s] swiftly ran
    to chase the fallow deere;
  On Munday they began to hunt,
    ere daylight did appeare.

8 And long before high noone the had
    a hundred fat buckes slaine;
  Then hauing dined, the drouyers went
    to rouze the deare againe.

9 The bowmen mustered on the hills,
    well able to endure;
  Theire backsides all w*i*th speciall care
    that day were guarded sure.

10 The hounds ran swiftly through the woods
    the nimble deere to take,
  That with their cryes the hills and dales
    an eccho shrill did make.

11 Lord Pearcy to the querry went
    to veiw the tender deere;
  Q*uo*th he, Erle Douglas p*r*omised once
    this day to meete me heere;

12 But if I thought he wold not come,
    noe longer wold I stay.
  W*i*th *that* a braue younge gentlman
    thus to the erle did say:

13 'Loe, yonder doth Erle Douglas come,
    hys men in armour bright;
  Full twenty hundred Scottish speres
    all marching in our sight.

14 'All men of pleasant Tiuydale,
    fast by the riuer Tweede:'
  'O ceaze y*ou*r sportts!' Erle Pearcy said,
    'and take y*ou*r bowes w*i*th speede.

15 'And now w*i*th me, my countrymen,
    y*ou*r courage forth advance!
  For there was neuer champion yett,
    in Scottland nor in Ffrance,

16 '*That* euer did on horsbacke come,
    [but], and if my hap it were,
  I durst encounter man for man,
    w*i*th him to breake a spere.'

17 Erle Douglas on his milke-white steede,
    most like a baron bold,
  Rode formost of his company,
    whose armor shone like gold.

18 'Shew me,' sayd hee, 'whose men you bee
    that hunt soe boldly heere,
  That w*i*thout my consent doe chase
    and kill my fallow deere.'

19 The first man *that* did answer make
    was noble Pearcy hee,
  Who sayd, Wee list not to declare
    nor shew whose men wee bee;

20 'Yett wee will spend our deerest blood
    thy cheefest harts to slay.'

Then Douglas swore a solempne oathe,
  and thus in rage did say :

21 ' Ere thus I will outbraued bee,
  one of vs tow shall dye ;
I know thee well, an erle thou art ;
  Lord Pearcy, soe am I.

22 ' But trust me, Pearcye, pittye it were,
  and great offence, to kill
Then any of these our guiltlesse men,
  for they haue done none ill.

23 ' Let thou and I the battell trye,
  and set our men aside :'
' Accurst bee [he !] ' Erle Pearcye sayd,
  ' by whome it is denyed.'

24 Then stept a gallant squire forth —
  Witherington was his name —
Who said, ' I wold not haue it told
  to Henery our k*ing*, for shame,

25 ' *That* ere my captaine fought on foote,
  and I stand looking on.
You bee two Erles,' q*uot*h Witheringhton,
  and I a squier alone ;

26 ' I 'le doe the best *that* doe I may,
  while I haue power to stand ;
While I haue power to weeld my sword,
  I 'le fight w*i*th hart and hand.'

27 Our English archers bent their bowes ;
  their harts were good and trew ;
Att the first flight of arrowes sent,
  full foure score Scotts the slew.

28 To driue the deere w*i*th hound and horne,
  Dauglas bade on the bent ;
Two captaines moued w*i*th mickle might,
  their speres to shiuers went.

29 They closed full fast on eu*er*ye side,
  noe slacknes there was found,
But many a gallant gentleman
  lay gasping on the ground.

30 O Christ ! it was great greeue to see
  how eche man chose his spere,
And how the blood out of their brests
  did gush like water cleare.

31 At last these two stout erles did meet,
  like captaines of great might ;
Like lyons woode they layd on lode ;
  the made a cruell fight.

32 The fought vntill they both did sweat,
  with swords of tempered steele,
Till blood downe their cheekes like raine
  the trickling downe did feele.

33 ' O yeeld thee, Pearcye ! ' Douglas sayd,
  ' and in faith I will thee bringe
Where thou shall high advanced bee
  by Iames our Scottish k*ing*.

34 ' Thy ransome I will freely giue,
  and this report of thee,
Thou art the most couragious k*night*
  [that ever I did see.] '

35 ' Noe, Douglas ! ' q*uot*h Erle Percy then,
  ' thy pr*o*fer I doe scorne ;
I will not yeelde to any Scott
  *tha*t eu*er* yett was borne ! '

36 W*i*th *that* there came an arrow keene,
  out of an English bow,
Which stroke Erle Douglas on the brest
  a deepe and deadlye blow.

37 Who neu*er* sayd more words then these :
  Fight on, my merry men all !
For why, my life is att [an] end,
  lo*rd* Pearcy sees my fall.

38 Then leauing liffe, Erle Pearcy tooke
  the dead man by the hand ;
Who said, ' Erle Dowglas, for thy life,
  wold I had lost my land !

39 ' O Christ ! my verry hart doth bleed
  for sorrow for thy sake,
For sure, a more redoubted k*night*
  mischance cold neu*er* take.'

40 A k*night* amongst the Scotts there was
  w*h*ich saw Erle Douglas dye,
Who streight in hart did vow revenge
  vpon the Lord Pearcye.

41 S*i*r Hugh Mountgomerye was he called,
  who, w*i*th a spere full bright,

Well mounted on a gallant steed,
  ran feircly through the fight,

42 And past the English archers all,
  without all dread or feare,
And through Erle Percyes body then
  he thrust his hatfull spere.

43 With such a vehement force and might
  his body he did gore,
The staff ran through the other side
  a large cloth-yard and more.

44 Thus did both those nobles dye,
  whose courage none cold staine;
An English archer then perceiued
  the noble erle was slaine.

45 He had [a] good bow in his hand,
  made of a trusty tree;
An arrow of a cloth-yard long
  to the hard head haled hee.

46 Against Sir Hugh Mountgomerye
  his shaft full right he sett;
The grey-goose-winge *that* was there-on
  in his harts bloode was wett.

47 This fight from breake of day did last
  till setting of the sun,
For when the rung the euening-bell
  the battele scarse was done.

48 With stout Erle Percy there was slaine
  Sir Iohn of Egerton,
Sir Robert Harcliffe and Sir William,
  Sir Iames, that bold barron.

49 And with Sir George and Sir Iames,
  both knights of good account,
Good Sir Raphe Rebbye there was slaine,
  whose prowesse did surmount.

50 For Witherington needs must I wayle
  as one in dolefull dumpes,
For when his leggs were smitten of,
  he fought vpon his stumpes.

51 And with Erle Dowglas there was slaine
  Sir Hugh Mountgomerye,
And Sir Charles Morrell, *that* from feelde
  one foote wold neuer flee;

52 Sir Roger Heuer of Harcliffe tow,
  his sisters sonne was hee;
Sir David Lambwell, well esteemed,
  but saved he cold not bee.

53 And the Lord Maxwell, in like case,
  with Douglas he did dye;
Of twenty hundred Scottish speeres,
  scarce fifty-fiue did flye.

54 Of fifteen hundred Englishmen
  went home but fifty-three;
The rest in Cheuy Chase were slaine,
  vnder the greenwoode tree.

55 Next day did many widdowes come
  their husbands to bewayle;
They washt their wounds in brinish teares,
  but all wold not prevayle.

56 Theyr bodyes, bathed in purple blood,
  the bore with them away;
They kist them dead a thousand times
  ere the were cladd in clay.

57 The newes was brought to Eddenborrow,
  where Scottlands king did rayne,
That braue Erle Douglas soddainlye
  was with an arrow slaine.

58 'O heauy newes!' King Iames can say;
  'Scottland may wittenesse bee
I haue not any captaine more
  of such account as hee.'

59 Like tydings to King Henery came,
  within as short a space,
That Pearcy of Northumberland
  was slaine in Cheuy Chase.

60 'Now God be with him!' said our king,
  'sith it will noe better bee;
I trust I haue within my realme
  fiue hundred as good as hee.

61 'Yett shall not Scotts nor Scottland say
  but I will vengeance take,
And be revenged on them all
  for braue Erle Percyes sake.'

62 This vow the king did well performe
  after on Humble-downe;

In one day fifty k*nigh*ts were slayne,
with lords of great renowne.

63 And of the rest, of small account,
did many hundreds dye:
Thus endeth the hunting in Cheuy Chase,
made by the Erle Pearcye.

64 God saue our k*ing*, and blesse this land
with plentye, ioy, and peace,
And grant hencforth *that* foule debate
twixt noble men may ceaze !

———◆———

A. *Without division of stanzas, and in long lines,*
in the MS., and so printed by Hearne,
Wright, and Skeat.
" The MS. is a mere scribble, and the spelling
very unsatisfactory : " Skeat.
1^2. and A vowe : *for* avowe, *see* 63^1.
1^4. days iij. 3^2. xv. C archarde*s*. 3^4. iij.
$5^1, 30^1, 37^1$. throrowe. 7^1. *The*r : *cf.* 4^1.
8^1. mot. 10^3. war ath the. 11^1. brylly and.
12^1. xx. C. 22^4. Herry *the* iiij. .
24^3. mor athe : athe chyviat.
27^1. in iii. . 36^1. A narrowe. 39^2. years iij. .
43^1. athe. 44^1. A narchar. 45^2. haylde.
48^2. A nowar. 50^1. xvC. 50^2. vij^x.
50^3. xxC. 60^3. A-nothar. 61^2. the iiij. .
61^3. cheyff tenante. 62^3. a C. . 68^1. ballys.
And *for* & *always.*
Expliceth quoth Rychard Sheale.
B. **a.** 1^3. there was. 3^4. 3. 6^1. 1500.
8^1. a 100. 9^4. *that* they. 13^3. 20.
14^1. pleasant men of. 25^3. 2.
27^1. bend. $28^3, 31^1$. 2. 31^3. Lyons moods.
36^3. who scorke Erle.
38^3. thy sake ; *but compare* A 41^1. b, c, *have*
life ; sake *was caught from* 39^2.
41. 2^d parte. 43^2. *that* his body.
48^1. slaine. *There is a dot for the* i, *but*
nothing more in the MS.: Furnivall.
49^3. & good.
50^2. in too full ; *perhaps* wofull. 53^3. 20.
53^4. 55. 54^1. 1500. 54^2. 53.
55^3. They washt they. 56^3. a 1000.
59^1. in Cheuy chase was slaine. 60^4. 500.
62^3. 50. And *always for* &.
b, c, d, e. b, c, d (*and I suppose* e), *in stanzas*
of eight lines.
b. A memorable song vpon the vnhappy hunt-
ing in Cheuy Chase betweene the Earle
Pearcy of England and Earle Dowglas of
Scotland. To the tune of Flying Fame.
London, Printed for M. G. *Error for* H. G.?
Henry Gosson (1607–41).

c. A Memorable song on the unhappy Hunting
in Chevy-Chase between Earl Piercy of Eng-
land and Earl Dowglas of Scotland. Tune
of Flying Fame.
Printed for F. Coles, T. Vere and J. Wright.
(1655–80 ?)
d. Title as in c. To the tune, etc.
Printed for F. Coles, T. Vere and W. Gilbert-
son. (1648–61 ?)
e. An Unhappy Memorable Song of the Hunting ;
the rest as in d.
Licensd and Enterd according to Order.
London, Priented by and for W. Onley, and
are to be sold by C. Bates, at the Sun and
Bible in Pye-corner, (1650–1702?)
1^3. d. The woful. 1^4. there did.
2^2. his way. 4^3. e. The tidings.
5^3. fearing this. 7^1. gray-hounds.
7^4. when day light. 8^2. b, c, d. an.
8^4. c, d, e. rouze them up. 9^3. d. The.
9^4. that day. 10^3. c, d, e. And with.
11^3. c, d, e. once *wanting.*
12^1. e. If that I.
14^1. b. pleasant men of. c, d, e. men of
pleasant.
14^3. Then cease your sport.
15^3. c, d, e. For never was their (there).
15^4. or in. 16^2. b, c. but if. d. but since.
16^3. d. I *wanting.* 17^1. c, d, e. on a.
17^3. c, d, e. of the. 18^1. c, d, e. he said.
19^1. The man that first. 19^4. c, d. now shew.
20^1. b, c, d. Yet will we.
22^3. b, c, d. Then *wanting.* e. And *for* any.
c, e. harmless.
22^4. c, d, e. no ill.
23^3. be he. c, d, e. Lord P.
23^4. c, d, e. this is. 24^3. c, d. said he would.
25^1. d. ever. 25^2. c, d, e. I stood.
25^3. d. two be. b. quod W. c, d, e. said W.
27^1. bent. 27^4. c, e. threescore.
28^2. c, d, e. Earl D. c. had the bent. d.
bad the bent.

28³. A captain : mickle pride.

28⁴. The spears. e. sent *for* went.

29³. And many. 30¹. b. a *for* great.

30². b. each one chose. c, d, e. and likewise for to hear.

30³,⁴. c, d, e. The cries of men lying in their gore, and scattered here and there.

31³. lions mov'd. 31⁴. and made.

32³. Vntill the blood like drops of raine.

33¹. Yeeld thee Lord Piercy.

33². and *wanting.* 33³. shalt.

33⁴. b. with Iames. d. the *for* our.

34¹. c, d. will I. 34². and thus.

34⁴. that ever I did see. 35¹. e. To *for* Noe.

36³. b. And stroke E. D. to the heart. c, d, e. Which struck E. D. to the heart.

36⁴. e. and a.

37¹. c, d, e. never spake (spoke).

37³. at an end.

38³. c, d, e. And said. b, c, d, e. thy life.

39². with sorrow.

39³. c, d, e. more renowned.

39⁴. c, d. did. e. did ever. 40¹. b. among.

40³. in wrath. 40⁴. the Earl.

41². c, e. most bright.

43². b. his body he did. c, d, e. he did his body.

43³. c, d, e. The spear went.

44¹. c, d, e. So thus. b. both these two. c, e. these.

45¹. b. a good bow in. c, d, e. a bow bent in.

45⁴. c, d, e. unto the head drew he.

46¹. d. Montgomery then.

46². so right his shaft. 46⁴. heart.

47¹. fight did last from break of day.

48¹. c, d, e. With the Earl. 48². Ogerton.

48³. c, d, e. Ratcliff and Sir Iohn.

49¹. and good. 49³. And (*of* a) *wanting.*

50². b. wofull. c, d, e. doleful.

50⁴. b. still vpon.

51³. And *wanting :* the field. c, e. Charles Currel. 51⁴. flye.

52¹. b. Sir Robert. c, d, e. Sir Charles Murrel of Ratcliff too. 52². d. sisters sisters.

52³. c, d, e. Lamb so well.

52⁴. yet saved could.

53¹. Markwell : c, d, e. in likewise.

53². did with E. Dowglas dye.

53³. b, d. peers *for* speeres.

54³. c, d, e. rest were slain in C. C.

56⁴. c, d, e. when *for* ere.

57¹. c, d, e. This news. 58¹. did say.

58². can *for* may.

59⁴. was slain in Chevy Chase.

60². twill. 61¹. c, e. Scot.

61⁴. e. Lord *for* Erle.

62¹. c, d, e. vow full well the king performd.

62⁴. b. of high.

63³. ended. d. of *for* in.

63⁴. b. Lord *for* Erle.

64¹. c, d, e. the king : the land.

64². c, d, e. in plenty.

f. *The copy reprinted by Maidment, Scotish Ballads and Songs Historical and Traditionary,* 1868, *I,* 80. *This copy was given Maidment by Mr Gibb,* " for many years one of the sub-librarians in the library of the Faculty of Advocates. It had belonged to his grandmother, and was probably printed in Edinburgh about the beginning of the last or end of the preceding century."

5³. fearing him. 6¹. twenty hundred.

13³. fifteen hundred.

14¹. All pleasant men, *as in* a, b.

27¹. Our Scotish archers bent.

27⁴. they four score English slew.

28². Douglas bade on the bent.

30¹. O but it was a grief to see ; *and again,* 39¹, O but *for* O Christ.

46³. wings that were. 46⁴. were.

50⁴. fought still on the stumps.

53³. Of fifteen hundred.

53⁴. went hame but fifty three.

54¹. twenty hundred.

54². scarce fifty five did flee.

55⁴. could. 56⁴. when they were cold as clay.

58¹. 60 *is substituted here.*

60. 58 *is substituted, with change of* James *to* Henry, *and, in the next line, of* Scotland *to* England.

61, 62 are omitted. 63¹. Now of.

64³. debates.

163

THE BATTLE OF HARLAW

A. a. Communicated by Charles Elphinstone Dalrymple, Esq., of Kinaldie, Aberdeenshire. **b.** Notes and Queries, Third Series, VII, 393, communicated by A. Ferguson.

B. The Thistle of Scotland, 1823, p. 92.

⎯⎯⎯⎯◆⎯⎯⎯⎯

THE copy of this ballad which was printed by Aytoun, 1858, I, 75, was derived by Lady John Scott from a friend of Mr Dalrymple's, and when it left Mr Dalrymple's hands was in the precise form of **A a.** Some changes were made in the text published by Aytoun, and four stanzas, 14–16, 18, were dropped, the first three to the advantage of the ballad, and quite in accordance with the editor's plan. Mr Dalrymple informs me that in his younger days he had essayed to improve the last two lines of stanza 7 by the change,

> We 'd best cry in our merry men
> And turn our horses' head,

and had rearranged stanzas 18, 19, " which were absolutely chaotic," adhering, however, closely to the sense. **A b,** given in Notes and Queries, from a manuscript, as " the original version of this ballad," exhibits the changes made by Mr Dalrymple, and was therefore, one would suppose, founded upon his copy. Half a century ago the ballad was familiar to the people, and the variations of **b,** which are not few, may be traditional, and not arbitrary; for this reason it has been thought best not to pass them over. The Great North of Scotland Railway, A Guide, by W. Ferguson, Edinburgh, 1881, contains, p. 8 f, a copy which is evidently compounded from **A b** and Aytoun. It adds this variation of the last stanza:

> Gin ony body spier at ye
> For the men ye took awa,
> They 're sleepin soun and in their sheen
> I the howe aneath Harlaw.

The editor of The Thistle of Scotland treats the ballad as a burlesque, and "not worth the attention of the public," on which ground he refrains from printing more than three stanzas, one of these being 15; and certainly both this and that which follows it have a dash of the unheroic and even of the absurd. Possibly there were others in the same strain in the version known to Laing, but all such may fairly be regarded as wanton depravations, of a sort which other and highly esteemed ballads have not escaped.

The battle of Harlaw was fought on the 24th July, 1411. Donald of the Isles, to maintain his claim to the Earldom of Ross,* invaded the country south of the mountains with ten thousand islanders and men of Ross (ravaging everywhere as he advanced) in the hope of sacking Aberdeen, and reducing to his power the country as far as the Tay. There was universal alarm in those parts. He was met at Harlaw, eighteen miles northwest of Aberdeen, by Alexander Stewart, Earl of Mar, and Alexander Ogilby, sheriff of Angus, with the forces of Mar, Garioch, Angus, and The Mearns, and his further progress was stayed. The Celts lost more than nine hundred, the Lowlanders five hundred, including nearly all the gentry of Buchan. (Scotichronicon, II, 444 f.) This defeat was in the interest of civilization against savagery, and was felt, says Burton, " as a more memorable deliverance even than that of Bannockburn." (History of Scotland, 1883, II, 394.)

---

* Legally just: Maidment, Scotish Ballads and Songs, Historical and Traditionary, I, 349 ff.

As might be expected, the Lowlanders made a ballad about this hard fight. 'The battel of the Hayrlau' is noted among other popular songs, in immediate connection with 'The Hunttis of Chevet,' by the author of The Complaint of Scotland, 1549 (Murray's edition, p. 65), but most unfortunately this ancient song, unlike Chevy Chase, has been lost. There is a well-known poem upon the battle, in thirty-one eight-line stanzas, printed by Ramsay, in his Ever Green, 1724, I, 78.* David Laing believed that it had been printed long before. "An edition," he says, "printed in the year 1668, was in the curious library of old Robert Myln" (Early Metrical Tales, p. xlv.) In the catalogue of Myln's books there is entered, apparently as one of a bundle of pamphlets, "Harlaw, The Battle yrof, An. 1411 .... 1668," † and the entry may reasonably be taken to refer to the poem printed by Ramsay. This piece is not in the least of a popular character. It has the same artificial rhyme as The Raid of the Reid Swyre and The Battle of Balrinnes, but in every other respect is prose. Mr Norval Clyne, Ballads from Scottish History, p. 244 ff, has satisfactorily shown that the author used Boece's History, and even, in a way, translated some of Boece's phrases.

The story of the traditional ballad is, at the start, put into the mouth of a Highlander, who meets Sir James the Rose and Sir John the Gryme, and is asked for information about Macdonell; but after stanza 8, these gentlemen having gone to the field, the narrator describes what he saw as he went on and further on. It is somewhat surprising

that John Highlandman should be strolling about in this idle way when he should have been with Macdonell. The narrator ‡ in the Ever Green poem reports at second hand: as he is walking, he meets a man who, upon request, tells him the beginning and the end. § Both pieces have nearly the same first line. The borrowing was more probably on the part of the ballad, for a popular ballad would be likely to tell its tale without preliminaries.

A ballad taken down some four hundred years after the event will be apt to retain very little of sober history. It is almost a matter of course that Macdonell should fall, though in fact he was not even routed, but only forced to retire. It was vulgarly said in Major's time that the Highlanders were beaten: they turned and ran awa, says the ballad. Donaldum non fugarunt, says Major, and even the ballad, inconsistently, 'Ye'd scarce known who had won.' We are not disconcerted at the Highland force being quintupled, or the battle's lasting from Monday morning till Saturday gloaming: diuturna erat pugna, says Major. But the ignoring of so marked a personage as Mar, and of other men of high local distinction that fell in the battle, ‖ in favor of the Forbeses, who, though already of consequence in Aberdeenshire, are not recorded to have taken any part in the fight, is perhaps more than might have been looked for, and must dispose us to believe that this particular ballad had its rise in comparatively recent times.

Dunidier is a conspicuous hill on the old road to Aberdeen, and Netherha is within

* And afterwards, 1748, by Robert Foulis, Glasgow: "Two old Historical Scots Poems, giving an account of the Battles of Harlaw and the Reid-Squair."

† Ane Catalogue of the Books, Manuscripts and Pamphlets Belonging to Robert Mylne, Wryter in Edr, 1709: Advocates Library. Mr Macmath, who has come to my aid here, writes: "So far as I can make out, this catalogue contains no MSS. It is in two divisions: 1st, Printed Books; 2d, Pamphlets. The following is in the second division, and I understand the reference to be, year of publication, volume, or bundle of pamphlets, number of piece in bundle or volume:
"Harlaw The Battle yrof An: 1411 .... 1668, 79, 5."
Mylne died in 1747, at the age, it is said, of 103 or 105: [Maidment], A Book of Scotish Pasquils, p. 423.

‡ He talks like a canny packman:

> I wist nocht quha was fae or freind;
> Yet quietly I did me carrie,
>
> . . . . . .
>
> And thair I had nae tyme to tairie,
> For bissiness in Aberdene.

§ So with The Battle of Balrinnes and The Haughs of Cromdale. The first line of The Battle of Balrinnes is, 'Betuixt Dunother and Aberdein.'

‖ Not only were these long and affectionately remembered, but their heirs were exempted from certain feudal taxes, because the defeat of the Celts was regarded as a national deliverance: Burton's History, II, 394.

two miles of it. (Overha and Netherha are only a mile apart, and the one reading is as good as the other.) Harlaw is a mile north from Balquhain (pronounced Bawhyne), and precisely at a right angle to John Highlandman's route from the West. Drumminor (to which Brave Forbes sends for his mail-coat in stanza 15) was above twenty miles away, and the messenger would have to pass right through the Highland army. The fact that Drumminor ceased to be the head-castle of that powerful name in the middle of the last century tells in some degree in favor of the age of the ballad. (Notes of Mr Dalrymple.)

" The tune to which the ballad is sung, a particularly wild and simple one, I venture to believe," says Mr Dalrymple, " is of the highest antiquity." A tune of The Battle of Har-law, as Motherwell pointed out, Minstrelsy lxii, is referred to in Polemo Middiana; * and a " march, or rather pibroch," held to be this same air, is given in the Lute Book of Sir William Mure of Rowallan, p. 30, and is reproduced in Dauney's Ancient Scotish Melodies, p. 349 (see the same work, p. 138 f, note b.) Sir William Mure is said to have died in 1657. The Ever Green Harlaw is adapted to an air in Johnson's Museum, No 512, and " The Battle of Hardlaw, a pibroch," is given in Stenhouse's Illustrations, IV, 447, 1853, " from a folio MS. of Scots tunes, of considerable antiquity." This last air occurs, says Maidment, in the rare Collection of Ancient Scots Music (c. 1776) by Daniel Dow, " The Battle of Hara Law," p. 28 : Scotish Ballads, etc., I, 200.

A

a. Communicated by Charles Elphinstone Dalrymple, Esq., of Kinaldie, Aberdeenshire, in 1888, as obtained from the country people by himself and his brother fifty years before. b. Notes and Queries, Third Series, VII, 393, communicated by A. Ferguson.

1 As I cam in by Dunidier,
    An doun by Netherha,
  There was fifty thousand Hielanmen
    A-marching to Harlaw.
  Wi a dree dree dradie drumtie dree.

2 As I cam on, an farther on,
    An doun an by Balquhain,
  Oh there I met Sir James the Rose,
    Wi him Sir John the Gryme.

3 ' O cam ye frae the Hielans, man ?
    An cam ye a' the wey ?
  Saw ye Macdonell an his men,
    As they cam frae the Skee ? '

4 ' Yes, me cam frae ta Hielans, man,
    An me cam a' ta wey,
  An she saw Macdonell an his men,
    As they cam frae ta Skee.'

5 ' Oh was ye near Macdonell's men ?
    Did ye their numbers see ?
  Come, tell to me, John Hielanman,
    What micht their numbers be ? '

6 ' Yes, me was near, an near eneuch,
    An me their numbers saw ;
  There was fifty thousan Hielanmen
    A-marchin to Harlaw.'

7 ' Gin that be true,' says James the Rose,
    ' We 'll no come meikle speed ;
  We 'll cry upo our merry men,
    And lichtly mount our steed.'

8 ' Oh no, oh no,' says John the Gryme,
    ' That thing maun never be ;
  The gallant Grymes were never bate,
    We 'll try phat we can dee.'

9 As I cam on, an farther on,
    An doun an by Harlaw,

* A macaronic ascribed to Drummond of Hawthornden.
    Interea ante alios dux piperlarius heros
    Præcedens, magnamque gestans cum burdine pipam,
    Incipit Harlai cunctis sonare Batellum.
        (Poems, Maitland Club, p. 413, after the first
            dated edition of 1684.)

They fell fu close on ilka side;
  Sic fun ye never saw.

10 They fell fu close on ilka side,
    Sic fun ye never saw;
  For Hielan swords gied clash for clash,
    At the battle o Harlaw.

11 The Hielanmen, wi their lang swords,
    They laid on us fu sair,
  An they drave back our merry men
    Three acres breadth an mair.

12 Brave Forbës to his brither did say,
    Noo brither, dinna ye see?
  They beat us back on ilka side,
    An we 'se be forced to flee.

13 'Oh no, oh no, my brither dear,
    That thing maun never be;
  Tak ye your good sword in your hand,
    An come your wa's wi me.'

14 'Oh no, oh no, my brither dear,
    The clans they are ower strang,
  An they drive back our merry men,
    Wi swords baith sharp an lang.'

15 Brave Forbës drew his men aside,
    Said, Tak your rest a while,
  Until I to Drumminnor send,
    To fess my coat o mail.

16 The servan he did ride,
    An his horse it did na fail,
  For in twa hours an a quarter
    He brocht the coat o mail.

17 Then back to back the brithers twa
    Gaed in amo the thrang,
  An they hewed doun the Hielanmen,
    Wi swords baith sharp an lang.

18 Macdonell, he was young an stout,
    Had on his coat o mail,
  An he has gane oot throw them a',
    To try his han himsell.

19 The first ae straik that Forbës strack,
    He garrt Macdonell reel,
  An the neist ae straik that Forbës strack,
    The great Macdonell fell.

20 An siccan a lierachie
    I 'm sure ye never saw
  As wis amo the Hielanmen,
    When they saw Macdonell fa.

21 An whan they saw that he was deid,
    They turnd an ran awa,
  An they buried him in Leggett's Den,
    A large mile frae Harlaw.

22 They rade, they ran, an some did gang,
    They were o sma record;
  But Forbës an his merry men,
    They slew them a' the road.

23 On Monanday, at mornin,
    The battle it began,
  On Saturday, at gloamin,
    Ye 'd scarce kent wha had wan.

24 An sic a weary buryin
    I 'm sure ye never saw
  As wis the Sunday after that,
    On the muirs aneath Harlaw.

25 Gin ony body speer at you
    For them ye took awa,
  Ye may tell their wives and bairnies
    They 're sleepin at Harlaw.

————•————

B

The Thistle of Scotland, 1823, p. 92.

1 As I cam thro the Garrioch land,
    And in by Over Ha,
  There was sixty thousan Highland men
    Marching to Harlaw.

11 The Highland men, with their broad sword,
    Pushd on wi might and power,
  Till they bore back the red-coat lads
    Three furlongs long, and more.

15 Lord Forbës calld his men aside,
    Says, Take your breath awhile,
  Until I send my servant now
    To bring my coat o mail.

A. a. 1¹. *Var.* Garioch land.

    4⁸. she : *so delivered, notwithstanding the inconsistency with* me *in lines* 1, 2.

    11⁸. *Var.* back the red-coats.

    20¹. *Sometimes* pitleurachie.

    25. "*There are different versions of this stanza :*" C. E. D.

A. b. *Printed in two long lines.*

    Burden : In a dree, etc.

    1². Wetherha. 1⁴. a' marchin.

    3⁴, 4⁴. Come marchin frae. 4¹,². she cam.

    5¹. Oh were ye near an near eneuch.

    6¹. she was. 6². An she.

    6⁴. a' marchin for Harlaw. 7¹. quo James.

    7³,⁴. So we 'd best cry in our merry men,
    And turn our horses' heeds.

    8¹. quo John. 10⁸. gaed *for* gied.

    11⁴. or mair. 12¹. did to his brither say.

    12⁴. And we 'll be.

    15¹. Forbes to his men did say.

    15². Noo, tak.

    16¹. Brave Forbes' hinchman, *var.* servant, then did.

    19². Made the great M'Donell.

    19⁸. The second stroke that.

    20¹. a 'pilleurichie.' 20². The like ye.

    20⁸. As there was amang.

    21⁸. in 'Leggatt's lan :' "*the manuscript is indistinct, and it would read equally well,* Leggalt's lan."

    21⁴. Some twa three miles awa.

    22². But they were. 22⁸. For Forbes.

    22⁴. Slew maist a' by the.

    23⁴. Ye 'd scarce tell wha.

    24². The like ye never. 24⁸. As there was.

    24⁴. muirs down by.

    25¹. An gin Hielan lasses speer.

    25². them that gaed awa.

    25⁸. tell them plain an plain eneuch.

B. 15¹. man.

164

KING HENRY FIFTH'S CONQUEST OF FRANCE

a–d, broadsides. a. Among Percy's papers. b. Roxburghe Ballads, III, 358. c. Jewitt's Ballads and Songs of Derbyshire, p. 1. d. Chetham's Library, Manchester, in Hales and Furnivall, Percy's Folio MS., II, 597. e. Percy papers, "taken down from memory." f. Nicolas, History of the Battle of Agincourt, 1832, Appendix, p. 78, from the recitation of a very aged person. g. The same, p. 80, source not mentioned. h. Tyler, Henry of Monmouth, II, 197, apparently from memory. i. Percy Society, XVII, Dixon, Ancient Poems, etc., p. 52, from singing. j. Skene MS., p. 42. k. Macmath MS., p. 27, from tradition. l, m. Buchan's MSS, I, 176, II, 124, probably broadside or stall copies.

ALL the known copies of this ballad are recent. It is not in Thackeray's list of broadsides, which dates perhaps as late as 1689 (Chappell, The Roxburghe Ballads, I, xxiv–xxvii) ; and it is not included in the collection of 1723–25, which showed particular favor to historical pieces. In a manuscript index of first lines to a large collection of songs and ballads " formed in 1748," I find, " As our king lay on his bed," and the ballad may probably have first been published in the second quarter of the last century. In a woodcut below the title of a, b, there are two soldiers with G R on the flap of the coat and G on the cap (no doubt in c as well) ; the date of these broadsides cannot therefore be earlier than the accession of George I, 1714. The broadside is in a popular manner, but has no mark of antiquity. It may, however, represent an older ballad, disfigured by some purveyor for the Aldermary press.

It is probable that the recited versions had their ultimate source in print, and that printed copies were in circulation which, besides the usual slight variations,* contained two more stanzas, one after 2 and another after 8, such as are found in h and elsewhere; which stanzas are likely to have formed part of the original matter.

After 2, h (see also g, i, j):

> Tell him to send me my tribute home,
> Ten ton of gold that is due to me;
> Unless he send me my tribute home,
> Soon in French land I will him see.

After 8, h (see also g, i, k, m):

> O then bespoke our noble king,
> A solemn vow then vowed he:
> I 'll promise him such English balls †
> As in French lands he neer did see!

g has several stanzas which are due to the hand of some improver.

Another, and much more circumstantial, ballad on Agincourt, written from the chronicles, was current in the seventeenth century. It begins, 'A councell braue [grave] our king did hold,' and may be seen in the Percy Manuscript, p. 241, Hales and Furnivall, II, 166, in The Crown Garland of Golden Roses (with seven stanzas fewer), ed. 1659, p. 65 of the reprint by the Percy Society, vol. xv; Pepys' Ballads, I, 90, No 44; Old Ballads, II, 79; Pills to purge Melancholy, V, 49; etc.

The story of the Tennis-Balls is not mentioned by the French historians, by Walsingham, Titus Livius, or the anonymous biographer of Henry in Cotton MS., Julius E. iv.‡ It occurs, however, in several contemporary writings, as in Elmham's Liber Metricus de Henrico Quinto, cap. xii (Quod filius regis Francorum, in derisum, misit domino regi pilas, quibus valeret cum pueris ludere potius quam pugnare, etc.), Cole, Memorials of Henry the Fifth, 1858, p. 101; but not in Elmham's prose history. So in Capgrave, De illustribus Henricis, with a *fertur*, ed. Hingeston, 1858, p. 114; but not in Capgrave's chronicle. We might infer, in these two cases, that the tale was thought good enough for verses and good enough for eulogies, though not good enough for history.

Again, in verses of Harleian MS. 565, "in a hand of the fifteenth century," the Dolphin says to the English ambassadors:

> Me thinke youre kyng he is nought [so] old
> No werrys for to maynteyn.
> Grete well youre kyng, he seyde, so yonge,
> That is both gentill and small;
> A tonne of tenys-ballys I shall hym sende,
> For hym to pleye with all.

Henry sends back this message:

> Oure Cherlys of Fraunce gret well or ye wende,
> The Dolfyn prowed withinne his wall;
> Swyche tenys-ballys I schal hym sende
> As schall tere the roof all of his [h]all. §

But there is a chronicler who has the tale still. Otterbourne writes: Eodem anno [1414], in quadragesima, rege existente apud Kenilworth, Karolus, regis Francorum filius, Delphinus vocatus, misit pilas Parisianas ad ludendum cum pueris. Cui rex Anglorum rescripsit, dicens se in brevi pilas missurum Londoniarum, quibus terreret et confunderet sua tecta.

And once more, the author of an inedited "Chronicle of King Henry the Fifth that was Kyng Henries son," Cotton MS., Claudius A. viii, of the middle of the fifteenth century, fol. 1, back: ||

And than the Dolphine of Fraunce aunswered to our embassatours, and said in this maner, 'that the kyng was ouer yong and to tender of age to make any warre ayens hym, and was not lyke yet to be noo good werrioure to doo and to make suche a conquest there vpon hym. And somwhat in scorne

---

* 3². Away and away and away, e, f, i, k. 12¹. The first that fired it was the French, f, g, h. 12⁴. were forced to flee, f, i, m (first to flee, e). 14³. in all French land, e, f, g, (in our) h, m. Etc.

† English balls again in m, tennis-balls in i, k.

‡ Whose work was printed in 1850, ed. Benjamin Williams. I am for the most part using Sir Harris Nicolas's excellent History of the Battle of Agincourt, 2d ed., 1832, here; see pp. 8–13, 301 f.

§ Nicolas, p. 302 f, slightly corrected; much the same in another copy of the poem, *ib.*, Appendix, p. 69 f. The jest in Henry's reply is carried out in detail when he comes to Harfleur, *ib.*, pp. 308–310.

|| Nicolas, p. 10, as corrected by Hales and Furnivall, II, 161, and in one word emended by me. By several of the above writers the Dauphin Louis is called Charles, through confusion with his father or his younger brother.

and dispite he sente to hym a tonne fulle of tenys-
ballis, be-cause he wolde haue some-what for to
play with*alle* for hym and for his lordis, and that
be-came hym better than to mayntayn any werre.
And than anone oure lordes that was embassatours
token hir leue and comen in to England ayenne,
and tolde the kyng and his counceill*e* of the vn-
goo*d*ly aunswer that they had of the Dolphy*n*, and
of the present the which*e* he had sent vnto the
kyng. And whan the kyng had hard her wordis,
and the answere of the Dolp[h]ynne, he was
wondre sore agreued, and right*e* euell*e* apayd to-
warde the Frensshemen, and toward the kyng, and
the Dolphynne, and thought*e* to auenge hym vpon
hem as sone as God wold send hym grace and
myght*e*; and anon lette make tenys-ballis for the
Dolp[h]ynne in all the hast that the myght*e* be
made, and they were grete gonne-stones for the
Dolp[h]ynne to play wyth*e-alle*.'

The Dolphin, whom two of these writers
make talk of Henry as if he were a boy, was
himself in his nineteenth year, and the Eng-
lish king more than eight years his senior.
" Hume has justly observed," says Sir Harris
Nicolas, " that the great offers made by the
French monarch, however inferior to Henry's
demands, prove that it was his wish rather to
appease than exasperate him ; and it is almost
incredible that, whilst the advisers of Charles
evinced so much forbearance, his son should
have offered Henry a personal insult. . . .
It should be observed, as additional grounds
for doubting that the message or gift was sent
by the Dauphin, that such an act must have
convinced both parties of the hopelessness of
a pacific arrangement afterwards, and would,
it may be imagined, have equally prevented
the French court and Henry from seeking
any other means of ending the dispute than
by the sword. This, however, was not the
case ; for even supposing that the offensive

communication was made on the occasion of
the last, instead . . . . of that of the first em-
bassy, it is certain that overtures were again
sent to Henry whilst he was on his journey
to the place of embarkation, and that even
when there, he wrote to the French monarch
with the object of adjusting his claims with-
out a recourse to arms : " pp. 9, 12 f.

History repeats itself. Darius writes to
Alexander as if he were a boy, and sends
him, with other things, a ball to play with ;
and Alexander, in his reply to Darius, turns
the tables upon the Persian king by his in-
terpretation of the insolent gifts : Pseudo-
Callisthenes, I, 36, ed. Müller, p. 40 f.* The
parallel is close. It is not inconceivable that
the English story is borrowed, but I am not
prepared to maintain this.

It does not appear from any testimony ex-
ternal to the ballad that married men or
widows' sons had the benefit of an exemption
in the levy for France, or that Cheshire,
Lancashire, and Derby † were particularly
called upon to furnish men : st. 9. The Rev.
J. Endell Tyler believes the ballad to be
unquestionably of ancient origin, "probably
written and sung within a very few years of
the expedition," " before Henry's death, and
just after his marriage ; " which granted, this
stanza would have a certain interest. But,
says Mr Tyler, " whether there is any founda-
tion at all in fact for the tradition of Henry's
resolution to take with him no married man
or widow's son, the tradition itself bears such
strong testimony to the general estimate of
Henry's character for bravery at once and
kindness of heart that it would be unpardon-
able to omit every reference to it," and he has
both printed the ballad in the body of his
work and placed " that golden stanza " on his
title-page. ‡ The question of Henry's kind-

---

* The gifts are a whip (σκῦτος), a ball, and a casket of
gold. In Julius Valerius's version, Müller, as above,
σκῦτος is rendered habena, whip or reins ; in Leo's Historia
de Preliis, ed. Landgraf, p. 54, we have virga for habena ;
in Lamprecht's Alexander, Weismann, I, 74, 1296–1301,
the habena is a pair of shoe-strings. The French romance,
Michelant, p. 52, 25 ff, to make sure, gives us both rod
(verge) and reins ; the English Alexander, Weber, I, 75,
1726–28, has a top, a scourge, and a small purse of gold.
Weber has noticed the similarity of the stories, Romances,

III, 299, and he remarks that in ' The Famous Victories of
Henry Fifth ' a carpet is sent with the tun of tennis-balls,
to intimate that the prince is fitter for carpet than camp.

† Cheshire, Lancashire, and *the Earl of* Derby are made
to carry off the honors in ballad-histories of Bosworth and
Flodden : see the appendix to No 168. Perhaps the hand of
some minstrel of the same clan as the author or authors of
those eulogies may be seen in this passage.

‡ Henry of Monmouth, or Memoirs of the Life and Char-
acter of Henry the Fifth, II, 121, 197. Jewitt, Derbyshire

ness of heart does not require to be discussed here, but it may be said in passing that there is not quite enough in this ballad to remove the impression which is ordinarily made by his conduct of the siege of Rouen.

The Battle of Agincourt was fought Oc-tober 25, 1415. It is hardly necessary to say, with reference to the marching to Paris gates, that Henry had the wisdom to evacuate French ground as soon after the battle as convoy to England could be procured.

———◆———

1 As our king lay musing on his bed,
　　He bethought himself upon a time
Of a tribute that was due from France,
　　Had not been paid for so long a time.
　　　Fal, lal, etc.

2 He called for his lovely page,
　　His lovely page then called he,
Saying, You must go to the king of France,
　　To the king of France, sir, ride speedily.

3 O then went away this lovely page,
　　This lovely page then away went he;
And when he came to the king of France,
　　Low he fell down on his bended knee.

4 'My master greets you, worthy sir;
　　Ten ton of gold that is due to he,
That you will send him his tribute home,
　　Or in French land you soon will him see.'

5 'Your master's young and of tender years,
　　Not fit to come into my degree,
And I will send him three tennis-balls,
　　That with them he may learn to play.'

6 O then returned this lovely page,
　　This lovely page then returned he,
And when he came to our gracious king,
　　Low he fell down on his bended knee.

7 'What news, what news, my trusty page?
　　What is the news you have brought to me?'
　　'I have brought such news from the king of France
　　That you and he will never agree.

8 'He says you 're young and of tender years,
　　Not fit to come into his degree,
And he will send you three tennis-balls,
　　That with them you may learn to play.'

9 'Recruit me Cheshire and Lancashire,
　　And Derby Hills that are so free;
No marryd man nor no widow's son;
　　For no widow's curse shall go with me.'

10 They recruited Cheshire and Lancashire,
　　And Derby Hills that are so free;
No marryd man, nor no widow's son;
　　Yet there was a jovial bold company.

11 O then we marchd into the French land,
　　With drums and trumpets so merrily;
And then bespoke the king of France,
　　'Lo, yonder comes proud King Henry.'

12 The first shot that the Frenchmen gave,
　　They killd our Englishmen so free;
We killd ten thousand of the French,
　　And the rest of them they ran away.

13 And then we marched to Paris gates,
　　With drums and trumpets so merrily:
O then bespoke the king of France,
　　'The Lord have mercy on my men and me!

14 'O I will send him his tribute home,
　　Ten ton of gold that is due to he,
And the finest flower that is in all France
　　To the Rose of England I will give free.'

Ballads, p. 2, says that there is a tradition in the Peak of Derby that Henry V would take no married man or widow's son, when recruiting for Agincourt; but he goes on to say that the ballad is not unfrequently sung by the hardy sons of the Peak, which adequately accounts for the tradition.

a. King Henry V. his Conquest of France, in revenge for the affront offered him by the French king in sending him, instead of the Tribute due, a Ton of Tennis-Balls.

Printed and sold at the Printing Office in Bow Church-Yard, London.

1[8]. due to.

b. *Title the same, with omission of the first* him *and* due.

Printed and sold in Aldermary Church Yard, Bow Lane, London. st.

1[8]. due from.　3[8]. Low he came.

3[4]. And when fell.　7[1] *wanting.*

7[4]. he and you will ne'er.

10[8]. man or widow's.　12[4]. run.

c. *Title as in* b.　*Printed as in* b.

1[8]. due from.　3[1]. away went.　3[8]. Lo he.

3[4]. And then he.　7[4]. he and you will ne'er.

9[8]. man or widow's.　12[4]. run.

d. *Title as in* b.　*Imprint not given.*

1[8]. due from.　3[8]. Low he came.

3[4]. And when fell.　7[4]. he and you will ne'er.

9[8]. man or.　12[4]. run.

e. 2[1]. Then he called on.

2[4]. With a message from King Henry.

3[1]. Away then went.

3[2]. Away and away and away.

3[4]. He fell low down.　4[2]. of gold *wanting.*

4[8]. And you must send him this.

4[4]. you 'll soon.　5[1], 8[1]. tender age.

5[2], 8[2]. not meet to come in.

5[8]. So I 'll send him home some.

6[1,2,4] *as in* 3[1,2,4].　7[1]. my lovely.

7[2]. what news bring you to me?

7[4]. That I 'm sure with him you 'll neer **agree.**

8[8]. So he 's sent you here some.

9[2]. that be.　9[8], 10[8]. man nor widow's.

9[4]. For *wanting.*

10[1,2]. Then they recruited Lankashire, Cheshire and Derby Hills so free.

10[4]. brave *for* bold.　11[2], 13[2]. so *wanting.*

11[8], 13[1]. O then.　12[8]. But we.

12[4]. them were forsd to free.

13[4]. Lord have mercy on [my] men and me.

14[1]. send this.

14[8]. fairest flower in all French land.

14[4]. make free.

f. "Communicated by Bertram Mitford, of Mitford Castle, in Northumberland, who wrote it from the dictation of a very aged relative."

1[1]. As a.

1[8]. Those tributes due from the French king.

2[4]. Those tributes that are due to me.

3[1,2], 6[1,2]. Away, away went this lovely page, Away and away and away went he, *nearly as in* e.

4[1,2]. My master he does greet you well, He doth greet you most heartily.

4[8]. If you don't.　5[2], 8[2]. come within.

5[4]. And in French land he ne'er dare me see.

7[1]. my lovely, *as in* e.

7[8]. from the French king.

7[4]. That with him I 'm sure you can ne'er agree.

8[4]. And in French land you ne'er dare him see.

9[1]. Go, 'cruit me.　10[4]. jovial brave, *as in* e.

12[1]. The first that fired it was the French.

12[4]. them were forced to flee.

13[8]. The first that spoke was the French king.

13[4]. Lord a mercy on my poor men and me.

14[1,2]. O go and take your tributes home, Five tons of gold I will give thee.

14[4]. in all French land, *as in* e.

f *was clearly derived from the same source as* e.

g. *The fourth line repeated as burden.*

2. O then calld he his lovely page,
　His lovely page then called he,
Who, when he came before the king,
　Lo, he fell down on his bended knee.

'Welcome, welcome, thou lovely page,
　Welcome, welcome art thou here;
Go sped thee now to the king of France,
　And greet us well to him so dear.

'And when thou comst to the king of
　France,
　And hast greeted us to him so dear,
Thou then shall ask for the tribute due,
　That has not been paid for many a year.'

3[1,2]. Away then went this lovely page, Away, away, O then went he.

3[4]. Lo, he.　*Between 3 and 4:*

'What news, what news, thou royal page?
　What news, what news dost thou bring
　to me?'
'I bring such news from our good king
　That him and you may long agree.

4. 'My master then does greet you well,
    Does greet you well and happy here,
And asks from you the tribute due,
    That has not been paid this many a year.'

$6^{1,2}$. Away, away went this lovely page,
    Away, away, then away went he.*

7^4. That he and you can ne'er agree.
After 8 :

O then in wroth rose our noble king,
    In anger great then up rose he :
' I 'll send such balls to the king in France
    As Frenchmen ne'er before did see.'

9^1. Go 'cruit me.
$10^{3,4}$. Tho no married man, nor no widow's son,
    They recruited three thousand men and
    three.

Between 10 *and* 11 :

And when the king he did them see,
    He greeted them most heartily :
' Welcome, welcome, thou trusty band,
    For thou art a jolly brave company.

' Go now make ready our royal fleet,
    Make ready soon, and get to sea ;
I then will shew the king of France
    When on French ground he does me see.'

And when our king to Southampton came,
    There the ships for him did wait a while ;
Sure such a sight was ne'er seen before,
    By any one in this our isle.

Their course they then made strait for
    France,
    With streamers gay and sails well filld ;
But the grandest ship of all that went
    Was that in which our good king saild.

$11^{3,4}$. The Frenchmen they were so dismayd,
    Such a sight they ne'er did wish to see.
12^1. The first that fired it was the French, *as
in* f.
13^3. The first that spoke was the French king,
    as in f.
13^4. Lo yonder comes proud King Henry.

   * *Cf.* g 6 and ' Lord Bateman,' 14, II, 508.

After 13 :

' Our loving cousin, we greet you well,
    From us thou now hast naught to fear ;
We seek from you our tribute due,
    That has not been paid for this many a
    year.'

$14^{1,2}$. ' O go and take your tributes home,
    Five tons of gold I will give to thee,'
as in f.

14^3. And the fairest flower in all French land,
    as in e, f.
h. " The author, to whom the following Song of
    Agincourt has been familiar from his child-
    hood, cannot refrain from inserting it here."
1^1. musing *wanting*.
1^2. All musing at the hour of prime : " con-
    jectural."
1^3. He bethought him of the king of France.
1^4. And tribute due for so long a time.
$2^{3,4}$, 3^3. king in.
After 2 :

Tell him to send me my tribute home,
    Ten ton of gold that is due to me ;
Unless he send me my tribute home,
    Soon in French land I will him see.

$3^{1,2}$, $6^{1,2}$. Away then goes this lovely page,
    As fast, as fast as he could hie.

4^2. gold is due to me.
5^3. send him home some.
7^4. That you and he can. 8^2. come up to.
8^3. He has sent you home some. *After* 8 :

Oh ! then bespoke our noble king,
    A solemn vow then vowed he :
I 'll promise him such English balls
    As in French lands he ne'er did see.
Cf. g.

9^1. Go ! call up. 9^3, 10^3. But neither . . . nor.
9^4. For *wanting*. 10^1. They called up.
After 10 :

He called unto him his merry men all,
    And numbered them by three and three,
Until their number it did amount
    To thirty thousand stout men and three.
Cf. g $10^{3,4}$.

11¹. Away then marched they.

11², 13². and fifes.

12¹. The first that fired it was the French, *as in* f, g.

13¹. Then marched they on to.

14². due from me. 14³. the very best flower.

i. *From the singing of a Yorkshire minstrel, with "*one or two verbal corrections*" from a modern broadside.*

2¹,², 3¹, 6¹. trusty *for* lovely. *After* 2 :

> And tell him of my tribute due,
>   Ten ton of gold that's due to me ;
> That he must send me my tribute home,
>   Or in French land he soon will me see.

3², 6². Away and away and away, *as in* e, f.

After 8: Oh! then, etc., *as in* h, *but* tennis-balls *in line three.*

9¹. Go call up, *as in* h.

10¹. They called up, *as in* h.

12⁴. And the rest of them they were forced to flee, *nearly as in* f.

13⁴. Lord have mercy on my poor men and me, *as in* f.

14³. And the fairest flower that is in our French land : *cf.* e, f, g.

14⁴. shall go free, *as in* g.

j. *A Scottish version of the broadside from recitation of the beginning of this century : of slight value.*

1². On his bed lay musing he : *for the* ee *rhyme.*

After 2 (*cf.* g, h, i) :

> Ye gae on to the king of France,
>   Ye greet him well and speedily,
> And ye bid him send the tributes due,
>   Or in French lands he'll soon see me.

5³, 8³. some tennis.

5⁴. may play him merrilie.

6¹. Away, away went. 7⁴. him an you.

8⁴. may play fu merrilie.

9¹, 10¹. Chester and Lincolnshire.

11². wi drum an pipe. 12 *wanting.*

13². wi pipe an drum.

13⁴. God hae mercie on my poor men and me : *cf.* f, i.

14 *wanting.*

k. Received, 1886, from Mr Alexander Kirk, Inspector of Poor, Dalry, Kirkcudbrightshire, who learned it many years ago from David Rae, Barlay, Balmaclellan.

3¹,², 6¹,². Away, away . . . Away, away, and away : *cf.* e, f, g, i.

7³,⁴. No news, no news, . . . But just what my two eyes did see : *cf.* No 114, A 11, E 10, F 10.

After 8 (*cf.* g, h, i) :

> Go call to me my merry men all,
>   All by thirties and by three,
> And I will send him such tennis-balls
>   As on French ground he did never see.

12 *wanting.*

13¹. But when they came to the palace-gates.

l. 'Henry V and King of France.'

2³,⁴, 3³. king in. 5². come unto.

7⁴. him and you. 8². come to.

11¹. Then they. 13⁴. Have mercy, Lord.

m. 'The Two Kings.'

> 3, 4. When he came to the king of France,
>   He fell down on his bended knee :
> 'My master greets you, noble sir,
>   For a tribute that is due to he.'

5², 8². come to. 5³. send him home ten.

> 6, 7. When he came to our noble king,
>   He fell low on his bended knee :
> 'What news, what news, my lovely page ?
>   What news have ye brought unto me ?'

8³. He's sent you hame ten.

After 8 :

> Out then spake our noble king,
>   A solemn vow then vowed he :
> 'I shall prepare such English balls
>   That in French land he ne'er did see.'

9¹. You do recruit. 10¹. They did recruit.

11 *wanting.*

12⁴. The rest of them were forced to flee.

13¹. As we came in at the palace-gates.

13⁴. Have mercy on my men and me.

14³. The fairest flower in a' French land.

165

SIR JOHN BUTLER

'Sir Iohn Butler,' Percy MS., p. 427 ; Hales and Furnivall, III, 205.

———◆———

THE subject of this ballad is the murder of a Sir John Butler at Bewsey Hall, near Warrington, Lancashire.

The story, which may be imperfect at the beginning, is that a party of men cross the moat in a leathern boat, and among them William Savage is one of the first. Sir John Butler's daughter Ellen wakens her father and tells him that his uncle Stanley is within his hall. If that be true, says Sir John, a hundred pound will not save me. Ellen goes down into the hall, and is asked where her father is ; she avers that he is ridden to London, but the men know better, and search for him. Little Holcroft loses his head in trying to keep the door of the room where Sir John is ; they enter, and call on him to yield. He will yield to his uncle Stanley, but never to false Peter Legh. Ellen Butler calls for a priest ; William Savage says, He shall have no priest but my sword and me. Lady Butler was at this time in London ; had she been at home she might have begged her husband's life of her good brother John. She dreams that her lord is swimming in blood, and long before day sets out for Bewsey Hall. On her way she learns that her husband is slain, and the news impels her to go back to London, where she begs of the king the death of false Peter Legh, her brother Stanley, William Savage, and all. Would ye have three men to die for one ? says the king ; if thou wilt come to London, thou shalt go home Lady Gray.

The papers of Roger Dodsworth,* the antiquarian († 16 . .), give the following account of the transaction, according to the tradition of his time. " Sir John Boteler, Knight, was slaine in his bed by the Lord Standley's procurement, Sir Piers Leigh and Mister William Savage joininge with him in that action, currupting his servants, his porter settinge a light in a windowe to give knowledge upon the water that was about his house at Bewsaye, when the watch that watched about his howse at Bewsaye, where your way to . . . [i. e. Bold] comes, were gone awaye to their owne homes ; and then they came over the moate in lether boates, and soe to his chambre, where one of his servants, called Hontrost [Holcroft], was slaine, being his chamberlaine ; the other brother betrayed his master. They promised him a great reward, and he going with them a way, they hanged him at a tree in Bewsaye Park. After this Sir John Boteler's lady pursued those that slewe her husband, and indyted xx. men for that ' saute,' but being marryed to Lorde Gray, he made her suites voyd, for which cause she parted from her husband, the Lorde Graye, and came into Lancastershyre, and sayd, If my lord wyll not helpe me that I may have my wyll of mine enemies, yet my bodye shall be berryed by him ; and she caused a tombe of alabaster to be made, where she lyeth upon the right hand of her husband, Sir John Butler." †

Another paper in the same collection as-

* Vol. cxiii, fol. 14, Bodleian Library : cited (p. 303 f.) in Beamont's Annals of the Lords of Warrington, Chetham Society, 1872, where may be found the fullest investigation yet attempted of this obscure matter. I have freely and

thankfully used chapters 17–19 of that highly interesting work.

† For Lord Grey's making the suit void, and his lady's resolution to be buried near Sir John, see Beamont, p. 319 f, pp. 297–99.

sumes to give the cause of the murder. " The occasion of the murther was this. The king being to come to Lathom, the Erle of Derby, his brother-in-law, sent unto hym [Sir John Butler] a messenger to desire him to wear his cloath [appear as his retainer] at that tyme; but in his absence his lady said she scorned that her husband should wayte on her brother, being as well able to entertayne the kynge as he was; which answer the erle tooke in great disdayne, and persecuted the said Sir John Butler with all the mallice that cowd be." After mutual ill-services, they took arms one against the other, Sir Piers Legh and William Savage siding with the earl, and in the end these three corrupted Sir John Butler's servants and murdered him in his bed. " Hys lady, at that instant being in London, did dreame the same night that he was slayne, that Bewsaye Hall did swym with blood; whereupon she presently came homewards, and heard by the way the report of his death." *

Sir John Boteler, son of Sir John, born in 1429, married for his third wife Margaret Stanley, widow of Sir Thomas Troutbeck, daughter of Thomas first Lord Stanley, and sister of Thomas the second lord, whom Dodsworth calls by anticipation Earl of Derby, which he was not until 1485. Sir John Boteler had by his first wife four daughters, but no Ellen; by Margaret Stanley he had a son Thomas, born in 1461. He died in 1463, and his wife afterwards married for her third husband Henry Lord Grey of Codnor.

According to st. 23 of the ballad, Dame Margaret's brother Stanley, that is Lord Thomas, is directly concerned in the murder which in the Dodsworth story he is said only to have procured. But an uncle Stanley appears to be a prominent member of the hostile party in sts 5, 12; how, we cannot explain. A 'good' brother John is mentioned in st. 15, of whom Lady Butler might have begged her husband's

life, and who must, therefore, have been present. Lady Butler had a brother John. But the alleged participation of Sir Peter Legh and William Savage in this murder, perpetrated in 1463, is an impossibility. Sir Peter Legh was born in 1455, and was only eight years old at that time, and William Savage, nephew of Lord Thomas Stanley, was also a mere child. As to the part ascribed to Lord Thomas Stanley, Sir Thomas Butler, the son of Sir John, is said to have lived on the most friendly terms with him in after days, and to have limited " an estate in remainder, after the limitation to himself and his heirs, to the Earl of Derby in fee," which we can hardly suppose he would have done if the earl had been his father's murderer.

The occasion of the murder is represented in the tradition reported by Dodsworth to have been Sir John Butler's refusal (through his wife) to wear the Earl of Derby's livery at the time of the king's coming to Lathom. The king (Henry VII) did indeed come to Lathom, but not until the year 1495, thirty-two years after Sir John's death, and three years after that of his wife. It is true that other accounts make Sir Thomas, the son of Sir John, to have been the victim of the murder; but Sir Thomas died in 1522, and the Earl of Derby in 1504.† There is not, as Dr. Robson says, a tittle of evidence to show that there was any murder at all, whether of Sir John or any other of the Butler family. But it was an unquiet time, and the conjecture has been offered " that, being a consistent Lancastrian," Sir John " may have incurred some Yorkist resentments, and have been sacrificed by a confederacy of some of those who, though his private friends, were his political enemies." ‡

Sir John Butler, son of Sir John, is of course the only person that the ballad and the parallel tradition can intend, for Margaret Stanley was the only Stanley that ever mar-

---

* Beamont, p. 304.

† Pennant, in the second half of the last century, heard that both Sir Thomas and his lady were murdered in his house by assassins, who, in the night, crossed the moat in leathern boats. Again, Sir Peter Legh, simply, was said to

have slain Sir Thomas Butler. Sir Thomas died quietly in his bed, and Sir Peter, who had turned priest, administered ghostly consolations to him not long before his decease.

† See Beamont, p. 308; and also p. 296 for another hypothesis.

ried a Butler, and Margaret Stanley's third husband was Lord Grey of Codnor. But Sir John the elder, who died in 1430, had a daughter Ellen, " old enough to raise an alarm when her father was attacked, while he was actually nephew by marriage to the second Sir John Stanley of Lathom, who survived him." (If we might proceed according to established mythological rules, and transfer to the son what is told of the father, we might account for the " uncle Stanley " and the Ellen of the ballad.) Sir John the senior's widow, Lady Isabella, was in 1437 violently carried off and forced into marriage by one William Poole, and her petition to Parliament for redress calls this Poole an outlaw " for felony for man's death by him murdered and slain." It has been thought a not overstrained presumption that this language may refer to the death of Lady Isabella's husband, the earlier Sir John, though it would be strange, if such were the reference, that no name should be given.*

The Bewsey murder has been narrated, with the variations of later tradition, by John Fitchett in ' Bewsey, a Poem,' Warrington, 1796 ; in a ballad by John Roby, Traditions of Lancashire, 1879, II, 72 ; and in another ballad in Ballads and Songs of Lancashire, Harland and Wilkinson, 1882, p. 13 (at p. 15 Fitchett's verses are cited). See also Dr Robson, in the preface to the Percy ballad, p. 208, and Beamont, Annals of the Lords of Warrington, p. 318.

————•————

1 BUT word is come to Warrington,
    And Busye Hall is laid about ;
    Sir Iohn Butler and his merry men
    Stand in ffull great doubt.

2 When they came to Busye Hall
    Itt was the merke midnight,
    And all the bridges were vp drawen,
    And neuer a candle-light.

3 There they made them one good boate,
    All of one good bull skinn ;
    William Sauage was one of the ffirst
    That euer came itt within.

4 Hee sayled ore his merrymen,
    By two and two together,
    And said itt was as good a bote
    As ere was made of lether.

5 ' Waken you, waken you, deare ffather !
    God waken you within !
    For heere is your vnckle Standlye
    Come your hall within.'

6 ' If that be true, Ellen Butler,
    These tydings you tell mee,
    A hundred pound in good redd gold
    This night will not borrow mee.'

7 Then came downe Ellen Butler
    And into her ffathers hall,
    And then came downe Ellen Butler,
    And shee was laced in pall.

8 ' Where is thy ffather, Ellen Butler ?
    Haue done, and tell itt mee : '
    ' My ffather is now to London ridden,
    As Christ shall haue part of mee.'

9 ' Now nay, now nay, Ellen Butler,
    Ffor soe itt must not bee ;
    Ffor ere I goe fforth of this hall,
    Your ffather I must see.'

10 The sought that hall then vp and downe
    Theras Iohn Butler lay ;
    The sought that hall then vp and downe
    Theras Iohn Butler lay.

11 Ffaire him ffall, litle Holcrofft !
    Soe merrilye he kept the dore,
    Till that his head ffrom his shoulders
    Came tumbling downe the ffloore.

12 ' Yeeld thee, yeelde thee, Iohn Butler !
    Yeelde thee now to mee ! '
    ' I will yeelde me to my vnckle Stanlye,
    And neere to ffalse Peeter Lee.'

* Beamont, pp. 259, 321.

13 'A preist, a preist,' saies Ellen Butler,
　　'To housle and to shriue !
　A preist, a preist,' sais Ellen Butler,
　　'While *that* my father is a man aliue ! '

14 Then bespake him Will*iam* Sauage,
　　A shames death may hee dye !
　Sayes, He shall haue no other preist
　　But my bright sword and mee.

15 The Ladye Butler is to London rydden,
　　Shee had better haue beene att home ;
　Shee might haue beggd her owne marryed l*ord*
　　Att her good brother Iohn.

16 And as shee lay in leeue London,
　　And as shee lay in her bedd,
　Shee dreamed her owne marryed l*ord*
　　Was swiminnge in blood soe red.

17 Shee called vp her merry men all,
　　Long ere itt was day ;
　Saies, Wee must ryde to Busye Hall,
　　With all speed *that* wee may.

18 Shee mett w*i*th three Kendall men,
　　Were ryding by the way :
　'Tydings, tydings, Kendall men,
　　I pray you tell itt mee ! '

19 'Heauy tydings, deare madam ;
　　Ffrom you wee will not leane ;

The worthyest k*nigh*t in merry England,
　　Iohn Butler, Lord ! hee is slaine ! '

20 'Ffarewell, ffarwell, Iohn Butler !
　　Ffor thee I must neuer see :
　Ffarewell, ffarwell, Busiye Hall !
　　For thee I will neu*er* come nye.'

21 Now Ladye Butler is to London againe,
　　In all the speed might bee,
　And when shee came before her prince,
　　Shee kneeled low downe on her knee.

22 'A boone, a boone, my leege ! ' shee sayes,
　　'Ffor Gods loue grant itt mee ! '
　'What is thy boone, Lady Butler ?
　　Or what wold thou haue of mee ?

23 'What is thy boone, Lady Butler ?
　　Or what wold thou haue of mee ? '
　' *Tha*t ffalse Peeres of Lee, and my brother
　　　Stanley,
　　And Will*iam* Sauage, and all, may dye.'

24 'Come you hither, Lady Butler,
　　Come you ower this stone ;
　Wold you haue three men ffor to dye,
　　All ffor the losse off one ?

25 'Come you hither, Lady Butler,
　　With all the speed you may ;
　If thou wilt come to London, L*ady* Butler,
　　Thou shalt goe home Lady Gray.'

———◆———

2². merke *may be* merle *in the MS.: Furni-*
　vall.
4². 2 and 2.　6⁸. a 100ʰ.
7¹. them *for* Then.
10¹,². *These two lines only are in the MS.,*

but they are marked with a bracket and
bis : Furnivall.
18¹, 24⁸. 3.
22⁸,⁴. *These two lines are bracketed, and*
marked bis in the MS. : Furnivall.

166

THE ROSE OF ENGLAND

'The Rose of Englande,' Percy MS., p. 423; Hales and Furnivall, III, 187.

———•———

THE title of this ballad, as Percy notes in his manuscript, is quoted in Fletcher's Monsieur Thomas (printed in 1639), act third, scene third, Dyce, VII, 364. The subject is the winning of the crown of England from Richard III by Henry VII, and the parties on both sides, though some of them are sometimes called by their proper names, are mostly indicated by their badges or cognizances,* which were perfectly familiar, so that though there is a "perpetual allegory," it is not a "dark conceit."

The red rose of Lancaster was rooted up by a boar, Richard, who was generally believed to have murdered Henry VI and his son Edward, the Prince of Wales; but the seed of the rose, the Earl of Richmond, afterwards wore the crown. The sixth stanza gives us to understand that the young Earl of Richmond was under the protection of Lord Stanley at Lathom before his uncle, the Earl of Pembroke, fled with him to Brittany, in 1471; but this does not appear in the histories. The Earl of Richmond came back to claim his right (in 1485), and brought with him the blue boar, the Earl of Oxford, to encounter, with Richard, the white boar. Richmond sends a messenger to the old eagle, Lord Stanley, his stepfather, to announce his arrival; Stanley thanks God, and hopes that the rose shall flourish again. The Welshmen rise in a mass under Rice ap Thomas and shog on to Shrewsbury. Master Mitton, bailiff of Shrewsbury, refuses at first to let Richmond enter, but, upon receiving letters from Sir William Stanley of Holt Castle, opens the

gates. The Earl of Oxford is about to smite off the bailiff's head; Richmond interferes, and asks Mitton why he was kept out. The bailiff knows no king but him that wears the crown; if Richmond shall put down Richard, he will, when sworn, be as true to Richmond as to Richard now. Richmond recognizes this as genuine loyalty, and will not have the bailiff harmed. The earl moves on to Newport, and then has a private meeting at Atherstone with Lord Stanley, who makes great moan because the young eagle, Lord Strange, his eldest son, is a hostage in the hands of the white boar. At the battle Oxford has the van; Lord Stanley follows 'fast'! The Talbot-dog (Sir Gilbert Talbot) bites sore; the unicorn (Sir John Savage) quits himself well; then comes in the hart's head (Sir William Stanley), the field is fought, the white boar slain, and the young eagle saved as by fire.†

How the Earl of Richmond compassed the crown of England is told at more length in two histories in the ballad-stanza, 'Bosworth Field' and 'Lady Bessy.' The first of these (656 verses) occurs only in the Percy MS., Hales and Furnivall, III, 235. It is on the whole a tame performance. Richmond is kept quite subordinate to the Stanleys, kneeling to Sir William, v. 371, and "desiring" the van of Lord Stanley, who grants his request, 449–51. The second exists in two versions: (1) Harleian MS. 367, printed by Mr Halliwell-Phillipps, Percy Society, vol. xx, 1847, p. 43, and Palatine Anthology, 1850, p. 60; Percy MS., Hales and Furnivall, III, 321 (each of about 1100 verses); (2) Percy Society and

* These are duly interpreted in Hales and Furnivall.
† Lord Strange's hair-breadth escape is, however, perhaps

apocryphal: see Croston, County Families of Lancashire and Cheshire, 1887, p. 25 f.

Palatine Anthology again, p. 1, p. 6, and previously by Thomas Heywood, 1829 (about 1250 vv). In this second poem the love, ambition, and energy of Elizabeth of York sets all the instruments at work, and the Stanleys are not so extravagantly prominent. It is a remarkably lively narrative, with many curious details, and in its original form (which we cannot suppose we have) must have been nearly contemporary. 'Bosworth Field' borrows some verses from it.

17^2, 22^4. This affirmation of the trustworthiness of the chronicle occurs in 'The Battle of Otterburn,' No 161, 35^2, and again in 'Flodden Field,' No 178, appendix, 121^4.

1 THROUGHOUT a garden greene and gay,
  A seemlye sight itt was to see
How fflowers did flourish fresh and gay,
  And birds doe sing melodiouslye.

2 In the midst of a garden there sprange a tree,
  Which tree was of a mickle price,
And there vppon sprang the rose soe redd,
  The goodlyest that euer sprange on rise.

3 This rose was ffaire, ffresh to behold,
  Springing with many a royall lance;
A crowned king, with a crowne of gold,
  Ouer England, Ireland, and of Ffrance.

4 Then came in a beast men call a bore,
  And he rooted this garden vpp and downe;
By the seede of the rose he sett noe store,
  But afterwards itt wore the crowne.

5 Hee tooke the branches of this rose away,
  And all in sunder did them teare,
And he buryed them vnder a clodd of clay,
  Swore they shold neuer bloome nor beare.

6 Then came in an egle gleaming gay,
  Of all ffaire birds well worth the best;
He took the branche of the rose away,
  And bore itt to Latham to his nest.

7 But now is this rose out of England exiled,
  This certaine truth I will not laine;
But if itt please you to sitt a while,
  I 'le tell you how the rose came in againe.

8 Att Milford Hauen he entered in;
  To claime his right, was his delight;
He brought the blew bore in with him,
  To encounter with the bore soe white.

9 The[n] a messenger the rose did send
  To the egles nest, and bidd him hye:

'To my ffather, the old egle, I doe [me] comend,
  His aide and helpe I craue speedylye.'

10 Saies, I desire my father att my cominge
  Of men and mony att my need,
And alsoe my mother of her deer blessing;
  The better then I hope to speede.

11 And when the messenger came before thold egle,
  He kneeled him downe vpon his knee;
Saith, Well greeteth you my lord the rose,
  He hath sent you greetings here by me.

12 Safe ffrom the seas Christ hath him sent,
  Now he is entered England within:
'Let vs thanke God,' the old egle did say,
  'He shall be the fflower of all his kine.

13 'Wend away, messenger, with might and maine;
  Itt 's hard to know who a man may trust;
I hope the rose shall fflourish againe,
  And haue all things att his owne lust.'

14 Then Sir Rice ap Thomas drawes Wales with him;
  A worthy sight itt was to see,
How the Welchmen rose wholy with him,
  And shogged them to Shrewsburye.

15 Att that time was baylye in Shrewsburye
  One Master Mitton, in the towne;
The gates were strong, and he mad them ffast,
  And the portcullis he lett downe.

16 And throug a garrett of the walls,
  Ouer Severne these words said hee;
'Att these gates no man enter shall;'
  But he kept him out a night and a day.

17 These words Mitton did Erle Richmond tell
   (I am sure the chronicles of this will not lye);
   But when *lett*res came from *Sir Willia*m Stan-
      ley of the Holt castle,
   Then the gates were opened p*r*esentlye.

18 Then entred this towne the noble lord,
   The Erle Richmond, the rose soe redd ;
   The Erle of Oxford, w*i*th a sword,
      Wold haue smitt of the bailiffes head.

19 'But hold y*ou*r hand,' saies Erle Richmond,
   'Ffor his loue *that* dyed vpon a tree !
   Ffor if wee begin to head so soone,
      In England wee shall beare no degree.'

20 'What offence haue I made thee,' sayd Erle
      Richmonde,
   ' *Tha*t thou kept me out of my towne ? '
   'I know no king,' sayd Mitton then,
   ' But Richa*rd* now, *that* weares the crowne.'

21 'Why, what wilt tho*u* say,' said Erle Rich-
      monde,
   'When I haue put K*ing* Richard downe ? '
   'Why, then Ile be as true to you, my lo*r*d,
      After the time *that* I am sworne.'

22 'Were itt not great pitty,' sayd Erle Rich-
      mond,
   ' *Tha*t such a man as this shold dye,
   Such loyall service by him done ?
      (The cronickles of this will not lye.)

23 'Thou shalt not be harmed in any case ; '
   He p*ar*done[d] him p*r*esentlye ;
   They stayd not past a night and a day,
      But towards Newp*or*t did they hye.

24 But [at] Attherston these lords did meete ;
   A worthy sight itt was to see,
   How Erle Richmond tooke his hatt in his hand,
   And said, Cheshire and Lancashire, welcome
      to me !

25 But now is a bird of the egle taken ;
   Ffrom the white bore he cannot fflee ;
   Therfore the old egle makes great moane,
      And prayes to God most certainly.

26 ' O stedfast God, verament,' he did say,
   ' Thre p*er*sons in one god in Trinytye,
   Saue my sonne, the young egle, this day
      Ffrom all ffalse craft and trecherye ! '

27 Then the blew bore the vanward had ;
   He was both warry and wise of witt ;
   The right hand of them he tooke,
      The sunn and wind of them to gett.

28 Then the egle ffollowed fast vpon his pray,
   W*i*th sore dints he did them smyte ;
   The talbott he bitt wonderous sore,
      Soe well the vnicorne did him quite.

29 And then came in the harts head ;
   A worthy sight itt was to see,
   The iacketts *that* were of white and redd,
      How they laid about them lustilye.

30 But now is the ffeirce ffeeld foughten and
      ended,
   And the white bore there lyeth slaine,
   And the young egle is p*r*eserued,
      And come to his nest againe.

31 But now this garden fflourishes ffreshly and
      gay,
   W*i*th ffragrant fflowers comely of hew,
   And gardners itt doth maintaine ;
      I hope they will proue iust and true.

32 Our k*ing*, he is the rose soe redd,
   *Tha*t now does fflourish ffresh and gay :
   Confound his ffoes, Lo*rd*, wee beseeche,
      And loue His Grace both night and day !

10⁴. Then better.
12¹. him *is apparently altered from* mim *in
   the MS.: Furnivall.*

14⁴. shogged him. 17³. cane *for* came.
26². 3. 29³. They.

167

SIR ANDREW BARTON

A. 'Sir Andrew Bartton,' Percy MS. p. 490; Hales and Furnivall, III, 399.

B. 'The Life and Death of Sir Andrew Barton,' etc. **a.** Douce Ballads, I, 18 b. **b.** Pepys Ballads, I, 484, No 249. **c.** Wood Ballads, 401, 55. **d.** Rox-burghe Ballads, I, 2 ; reprinted by the Ballad Society, I, 10. **e.** Bagford Ballads, 643, m. 9. (61). **f.** Bagford Ballads, 643, m. 10 (77). **g.** Wood Ballads, 402, 37. **h.** 'Sir Andrew Barton,' Glenriddell MSS, XI, 20.

GIVEN in Old Ballads, 1723, I, 159; in Percy's Reliques, 1765, II, 177, a copy made up from the Folio MS. and **B b**, with editorial emendations ; Ritson's Select Collection of English Songs, 1783, I, 313. **B f** is reprinted by Halliwell, Early Naval Ballads, Percy Society, vol. ii, p. 4, 1841 ; by Moore, Pictorial Book of Ancient Ballad Poetry, p. 256, 1853. There is a Bow - Churchyard copy, of no value, in the Roxburghe collection, III, 726, 727, dated in the Museum catalogue 1710.

A collation of **A** and **B** will show how ballads were retrenched and marred in the process of preparing them for the vulgar press.[*] **B a–g** clearly lack two stanzas after 11 (12, 13, of **A**). This omission is perhaps to be attributed to careless printing rather than to reckless cutting down, for the stanzas wanted are found in **h**. **h** is a transcript, apparently from recitation or dictation, of a Scottish broadside. It has but fifty-six stanzas, against the sixty-four of **B a** and the

eighty-two of **A**, and is extremely corrupted. Besides the two stanzas not found in the English broadside, it has one more, after 50, which is perhaps borrowed from ' Adam Bell ' :

> ' Foul fa the hands,' says Horsley then,
> ' This day that did that coat put on ;
> For had it been as thin as mine,
>   Thy last days had been at an end.' [†]

A has a regrettable gap after 35, and is corrupted at 29² [‡], 47².

In the year 1476 a Portuguese squadron seized a richly loaded ship commanded by John Barton, in consequence of which letters of reprisal were granted to Andrew, Robert, and John Barton, sons of John, and these letters were renewed in 1506,[§] " as no opportunity had occurred of effectuating a retaliation ; " that is to say, as the Scots, up to the later date, had not been supplied with the proper vessels. The king of Portugal remonstrated against reprisals for so old an offence, but he had put himself in the wrong four

---

[*] **B** begins vilely, but does not go on so ill. The forty merchants coming 'with fifty sail' to King Henry on a mountain top, 3¹,², requires to be taken indulgently.

[†]   'God's curse on his hartt,' saide William,
>   'Thys day thy cote dyd on ;
>   If it had ben no better then myne,
>   It had gone nere thy bone.'
>   (Vol. iii, 23, st. 27.)

[‡] An approach to sense may be had by reading ' either in hach-bord or in hull,' that is, by striking with his beam either the side or the body of the vessel ; but I do not think so well of this change as to venture it.

[§] The letters granted to the Bartons authorized them to seize all Portuguese ships till repaid 12,000 ducats of Portugal. Pinkerton, whose excellent account, everywhere justified by documents, I have been indebted to above, remarks : " The justice of letters of reprisal after an interval of thirty years may be much doubted. At any rate, one prize was sufficient for the injury, and the continuance of their captures, and the repeated demands of our kings, even as late as 1540, cannot be vindicated. Nay, these reprisals on Portugal were found so lucrative that, in 1543, Arran, the regent, gave similar letters to John Barton, grandson of the first John. In 1563 Mary formally revoked the letters of marque to the Bartons, because they had been abused into piracy." Pinkerton's History of Scotland, II, 60 f, 70.

years before by refusing to deal with a herald sent by the Scottish king for the arrangement of the matter in dispute. It is probable that there was justice on the Scottish side, "yet there is some reason to believe that the Bartons abused the royal favor, and the distance and impunity of the sea, to convert this retaliation into a kind of piracy against the Portuguese trade, at that time, by the discoveries and acquisitions in India, rendered the richest in the world." All three of the brothers were men of note in the naval history of Scotland. Andrew is called Sir Andrew, perhaps, in imitation of Sir Andrew Wood; but his brother attained to be called Sir Robert.*

We may now hear what the writers who are nearest to the time have to say of the subject-matter of our ballad.

Hall's Chronicle, 1548. In June [1511], the king being at Leicester, tidings were brought to him that Andrew Barton, a Scottish man and a pirate of the sea, saying that the king of Scots had war with the Portingales, did rob every nation, and so stopped the king's streams that no merchants almost could pass, and when he took the Englishmen's goods, he said they were Portingales' goods, and thus he haunted and robbed at every haven's mouth. The king, moved greatly with this crafty pirate, sent Sir Edmund Howard, Lord Admiral of England,† and Lord Thomas Howard, son and heir to the Earl of Surrey, in all the haste to the sea, which hastily made ready two ships, and without any more abode took the sea, and by chance of weather were severed. The Lord Howard, lying in the Downs, perceived where Andrew was making toward Scotland, and so fast the said lord chased him that he overtook him, and there was a sore battle. The Englishmen were fierce, and the Scots defended them manfully, and ever Andrew blew his whistle to encourage his men, yet for all

that, the Lord Howard and his men, by clean strength, entered the main deck; then the Englishmen entered on all sides, and the Scots fought sore on the hatches, but in conclusion Andrew was taken, which was so sore wounded that he died there; then all the remnant of the Scots were taken, with their ship, called The Lion. All this while was the Lord Admiral in chase of the bark of Scotland called Jenny Pirwyn, which was wont to sail with The Lion in company, and so much did he with other that he laid him on board and fiercely assailed him, and the Scots, as hardy and well stomached men, them defended; but the Lord Admiral so encouraged his men that they entered the bark and slew many, and took all the other. Then were these two ships taken, and brought to Blackwall the second day of August, and all the Scots were sent to the Bishop's place of York, and there remained, at the king's charge, till other direction was taken for them. [They were released upon their owning that they deserved death for piracy, and appealing to the king's mercy, says Hall.] The king of Scots, hearing of the death of Andrew of Barton and taking of his two ships, was wonderful wroth, and sent letters to the king requiring restitution according to the league and amity. The king wrote with brotherly salutations to the king of Scots of the robberies and evil doings of Andrew Barton, and that it became not one prince to lay a breach of a league to another prince in doing justice upon a pirate or thief, and that all the other Scots that were taken had deserved to die by justice if he had not extended his mercy. (Ed. of 1809, p. 525.)

Buchanan, about twenty years later, writes to this effect. Andrew Breton ‡ was a Scots trader whose father had been cruelly put to death by the Portuguese, after they had plundered his ship. This outrage was committed within the dominion of Flanders, and the

---

* Robert was skipper of the Great Michael, a ship two hundred and forty feet long, with sides ten feet thick, and said to be larger and stronger than any vessel in the navy of England or of France.

† A mistake of Edmund for Edward and an anticipation. Sir Edward Howard was not made admiral till the next

year. Edmund was his younger brother. Lesley has Edmund again; Stowe has Edward.

‡ Britanus. "Breton, whom our chroniclers call Barton," says Lord Herbert of Cherbury, Life of Henry VIII, 1649, p. 15.

Flemish admiralty, upon suit of the son, gave judgment against the Portuguese; but the offending parties would not pay the indemnity, nor would their king compel them, though the king of Scots sent a herald to make the demand. The Scot procured from his master a letter of marque, to warrant him against charges of piracy and freebooting while prosecuting open war against the Portuguese for their violation of the law of nations, and in the course of a few months inflicted great loss on them. Portuguese envoys went to the English king and told him that this Andrew was a man of such courage and enterprise as would make him a dangerous enemy in the war then impending with the French, and that he could now be conveniently cut off, under cover of piracy, to the advantage of English subjects and the gratification of a friendly sovereign. Henry was easily persuaded, and dispatched his admiral, Thomas Howard,* with two of the strongest ships of the royal navy, to lie in wait at the Downs for Andrew, then on his way home from Flanders. They soon had sight of the Scot, in a small vessel, with a still smaller in company. Howard attacked Andrew's ship, but, though the superior in all respects, was barely able to take it after the master and most of his men had been killed. The Scots captain, though several times wounded and with one leg broken by a cannon-ball, seized a drum and beat a charge to inspirit his men to fight until breath and life failed. The smaller ship was surrendered with less resistance, and the survivors of both vessels, by begging their lives of the king (as they were instructed to do by the English), obtained a discharge without punishment. The Scottish king made formal complaint of this breach of peace, but the answer was ready: the killing of pirates broke no leagues and furnished no decent

ground for war. (Rer. Scot. Historia, 1582, fol. 149 b, 150.)

Bishop Lesley, writing at about the same time as Buchanan, openly accuses the English of fraud. "In the month of June," he says, "Andrew Barton, being on the sea in warfare contrar the Portingals, against whom he had a letter of mark, Sir Edmund Howard, Lord Admiral of England, and Lord Thomas Howard, son and heir to the Earl of Surrey, past forth at the king of England's command, with certain of his best ships; and the said Andrew, being in his voyage sailing toward Scotland, having only but one ship and a bark, they set upon at the Downs, and at the first entry did make sign unto them that there was friendship standing betwix the two realms, and therefore thought them to be friends; wherewith they, nothing moved, did cruelly invade, and he manfully and courageously defended, where there was many slain, and Andrew himself sore wounded, that he died shortly; and his ship, called The Lion, and the bark, called Jenny Pirrvyne, which, with the Scots men that was living, were had to London, and kept there as prisoners in the Bishop of Yorks house, and after was sent home in Scotland. When that the knowledge hereof came to the king, he sent incontinent a herald to the king of England, with letters requiring dress for the slaughter of Andrew Barton, with the ships to be rendered again; otherwise it might be an occasion to break the league and peace contracted between them. To the which it was answered by the king of England that the slaughter being a pirate, as he alleged, should be no break to the peace; yet not the less he should cause commissioners meet upon the borders, where they should treat upon that and all other enormities betwix the two realms." † (History of Scotland, Edinburgh, 1830, p. 82 f.)

---

* Another anticipation. Sir Thomas Howard became admiral only after his brother Edward's death, in 1513. The expedition of the Howards against Barton appears to have been a private one, though with the consent of the king.

† The commissioners met, and "the wrongs done unto Scotland many ways, specially of the slaughter of Andrew Barton and taking of his ships, were conferred," but the

commissioners of England would not consent to make any redress or restitution till after a certain date when they expected to know the issue of their king's invasion of France. Hereupon a herald was sent to King Henry in France, with a letter from King James, rehearsing the great wrongs and unkindnesses done to himself and his lieges, and among these the slaughter of Andrew Barton by Henry's own command, though he had done no offence to him or his lieges;

The ballad displaces Sir Thomas and Sir Edward Howard, and puts in their place Lord Charles Howard, who was not born till twenty-five years after the fight. Lord Charles Howard, son of William, a younger half-brother of Thomas and Edward, was, in his time, like them, Lord High Admiral, and had the honor of commanding the fleet which served against the Armada. He was created Earl of Nottingham in 1596, and this circumstance, adopted into A 78,* puts this excellent ballad later than one would have said, unless, as is quite possible, the name of the English commander has been changed. There is but one ship in the ballad, as there is but a single captain, but Henry Hunt makes up for the other when we come to the engagement. The dates are much deranged in A. The merchants make their complaint at midsummer, the summer solstice (in May, B 1), and here there is agreement with Hall and Lesley. The English ship sails the day before midsummer-even, A 17; the fight occurs not more than four days after (A 18, 33, 34; B 16, 31); four days is a large allowance for returning, but the ship sails into Thames mouth on the day before New Year's even, A 71, 72, 74.† In B the English do not sail till winter, and although the interval from May is long for fitting out a ship, inconsistency is avoided. According to Hall, the English ships brought in their prizes August 2d.

A. King Henry Eighth, having been informed by eighty London merchants that navigation is stopped by a Scot who would rob them were they twenty ships to his one,

asks if there is never a lord who will fetch him that traitor, and Lord Charles Howard volunteers for the service, he to be the only man. The king offers him six hundred fighting men, his choice of all the realm. Howard engages two noble marksmen, Peter Simon to be the head of a hundred gunners, and William Horsley to be the head of a hundred bowmen, and sails, resolved to bring in Sir Andrew and his ship, or never again come near his prince. On the third day he falls in with a fine ship commanded by Henry Hunt, and asks whether they have heard of Barton. Henry Hunt had been Barton's prisoner the day before, and can give the best intelligence and advice. Barton is a terrible fellow; his ship is brass within and steel without; and although there is a deficiency at A 36, there is enough to show that it was not less magnificent than strong, 36^2, 75^2. He has a pinnace of thirty guns, and the voluble and not too coherent Hunt makes it a main point to sink this pinnace first. But above all, Barton carries beams in his topcastle, and with these, if he can drop them, his own ship is a match for twenty; ‡ therefore, let no man go to his topcastle. Hunt borrows some guns from Lord Howard, trusting to be forgiven for breaking the oath upon which he had been released by his captor the day before, and sets a 'glass' (lantern?) to guide Howard's ship to Barton's, which they see the next day. Barton is lying at anchor, 45^3, 46^1; the English ship, feigning to be a merchantman, passes him without striking topsails or topmast, 'stirring neither top nor

and no satisfaction being obtained, the herald, according to his instructions, "denounced war to the king of England," August, 1513. (Lesley, pp. 87–91.)

* B 63^3, "Lord Howard shall Earl Bury hight." Admiral Thomas Howard, for his good service at Flodden and elsewhere, was created Earl of Surrey in 1514. Bury is, one would suppose, a corruption of Surrey, and if so, Surrey may have been the reading of earlier copies, and perhaps Thomas again, instead of Charles.

† By reading midwinter in A 17^3 this difficulty would be removed.

‡ These beams, Henry Hunt intimates in 32, would be dangerous to boarders, which is conceivable should they chance to hit the right heads; but they are evidently meant to be dropped on the adversary's vessel, and this by a process which is not distinctly described, and was, I fear, not

perfectly grasped by the minstrel. The veriest landsman must think that a magazine of heavy timbers stowed in either castle (there is an upper and a lower in the pictures of Henry VII's Great Harry and of Henry VIII's Grace de Dieu, and the lower is well up the mast) would not be favorable to sailing; but this is a minor difficulty. Stones and fire-balls were sometimes thrown from the topcastle, which, properly, should be a stage at the very tip of the mast, as we find it in old prints: see Nicolas's History of the Royal Navy, II, 170. Stones and iron bars thrown from the high decks of Spanish ships did much harm to the English in a fight in 1372: Froissart, Buchon, V, 276. An intelligible way of operating the ancient "dolphins," heavy masses of metal dropped from the end of a yard, is suggested in Graser, De veterum re navali, 1864, p. 82 f.

mast.' Sir Andrew has been admiral on the
sea for more than three years, and no Eng-
lishman or Portingal passes without his leave :
he orders his pinnace to bring the pedlars
back ; they shall hang at his main-mast tree.
The pinnace fires on Lord Howard and brings
down his foremast and fifteen of his men,
but Simon sinks the pinnace with one dis-
charge, which, to be sure, includes nine yards
of chain besides other great shot, less and
more. Sir Andrew cuts his ropes to go for
the pedlar himself. Lord Howard throws off
disguise, sounds drums and trumpets, and
spreads his ensign. Simon's son shoots and
kills sixty ; the perjured Henry Hunt comes
in on the other side, brings down the fore-
mast, and kills eighty. One wonders that
Barton's guns do not reply ; in fact he never
fires a shot ; but then he has that wonder-
ful apparatus of the beams, which, whether
mechanically perfect or not, is worked well
by the poet, for not many better passages are
met with in ballad poetry than that which
tells of the three gallant attempts on the
main-mast tree, 52–66. Sir Andrew had not
taken the English archery into his reckoning.
Gordon, the first man to mount, is struck
through the brain ; so is James Hamilton,
Barton's sister's son. Sir Andrew dons his
armor of proof and goes up himself. Hors-
ley hits him under his arm ; Barton will not
loose his hold, but a second mortal wound
forces him to come down. He calls on his
men to fight on ; he will lie and bleed awhile,
and then rise and fight again ; " fight on for
Scotland and St Andrew, while you hear my
whistle blow ! " Soon the whistle is mute,
and they know that Barton is dead ; the Eng-
lish board ; Howard strikes off Sir Andrew's
head, while the Scots stand by weeping, and

throws the body over the side, with three
hundred crowns about the middle to secure it
a burial. So Jon Rimaardssøn binds three
bags about his body when he jumps into the
sea, saying, He shall not die poor that will
bury my body : Danske Viser, II, 225, st. 30.
Lord Howard sails back to England, and is
royally welcomed. England before had but
one ship of war, and Sir Andrew's made the
second, says the ballad, but therein seems to
be less than historically accurate : see South-
ey's Lives of the British Admirals, 1833, II,
171, note. Hunt, Horsley, and Simon are
generously rewarded, and Howard is made
Earl of Nottingham. When King Henry
sees Barton's ghastly head, he exclaims that
he would give a hundred pounds if the man
were alive as he is dead : ambiguous words,
which one would prefer not to interpret by
the later version of the ballad, in which
Henry is eager himself to give the doom, B
58 ; nor need we, for in the concluding stanza
the king, in recognition of the manful part
that he hath played, both here and beyond the
sea, says that each of Barton's men shall have
half a crown a day to take them home.

The variations of B, as to the story, are of
slight importance. There is no pinnace in
B. Horsley's shots are somewhat better ar-
ranged : Gordon is shot under the collar-bone,
the nephew through the heart ; the first ar-
row rebounds from Barton's armor, the second
smites him to the heart. ' Until you hear
my whistle blow,' in 53^4, is a misconception,
coming from not understanding that till (as
in A 66^4) may mean while.

The copy in Percy's Reliques is translated
by Von Marées, p. 88.

A

Percy MS., p. 490 ; Hales and Furnivall, III, 399.

1 As itt beffell in m[i]dsumer-time,
　　When burds singe sweetlye on euery tree,
　　Our noble king, King Henery the Eighth,
　　Ouer the riuer of Thames past hee.

2 Hee was no sooner ouer the riuer,
　　Downe in a fforrest to take the ayre,
　　But eighty merchants of London cittye
　　Came kneeling before King Henery there.

3 ' O yee are welcome, rich merchants,
　　[Good saylers, welcome unto me ! ']

They swore by the rood the were saylers good,
 But rich merchants they cold not bee.

4 'To Ffrance nor Fflanders dare we nott passe,
 Nor Burdeaux voyage wee dare not ffare,
And all ffor a ffalse robber *that* lyes on the
  seas,
 And robb[s] vs of our merchants-ware.'

5 K*ing* Henery was stout, and he turned him
  about,
 And swore by the Lord *that* was mickle of
  might,
'I thought he had not beene in the world
  throughout
That durst haue wrought England such vn-
  right.'

6 But euer they sighed, and said, alas!
 Vnto K*ing* Harry this answere againe:
'He is a proud Scott *that* will robb vs all
 If wee were twenty shipps and hee but
  one.'

7 The k*ing* looket ouer his left shoulder,
 Amongst his lords and barrons soe ffree:
'Haue I neuer lo*rd* in all my realme
 Will ffeitch yond traitor vnto mee?'

8 'Yes, *that* dare I!' sayes my lo*rd* Chareles
  Howard,
 Neere to the k*ing* wheras hee did stand;
'If *that* Yo*ur* Grace will giue me leaue,
 My selfe wilbe the only man.'

9 'Thou shalt haue six hundred men,' saith our
  k*ing*,
 'And chuse them out of my realme soe ffree;
Besids marriners and boyes,
 To guide the great shipp on the sea.'

10 'I'le goe speake w*ith* Si*r* Andrew,' sais Ch*arles*,
  my lo*rd* Haward;
 'Vpon the sea, if hee be there;
I will bring him and his shipp to shore,
 Or before my prince I will neu*er* come
  neere.'

11 The ffirst of all my lo*rd* did call,
 A noble gunner hee was one;
This man was three score yeeres and ten,
 And Peeter Simon was his name.

12 'Peeter,' sais hee, 'I must sayle to the sea,
 To seeke out an enemye; God be my speed!'
Before all others I haue chosen thee;
 Of a hundred guners thoust be my head.'

13 'My lo*rd*,' sais hee, 'if you haue chosen mee
 Of a hundred gunners to be the head,
Hange me att yo*ur* maine-mast tree
 If I misse my marke past three pence bread.'

14 The next of all my lo*rd* he did call,
 A noble bowman hee was one;
In Yorekeshire was this gentleman borne,
 And William Horsley was his name.

15 'Horsley,' sayes hee, 'I must sayle to the
  sea,
 To seeke out an enemye; God be my speede!
Before all others I haue chosen thee;
 Of a hundred bowemen thoust be my head.'

16 'My lo*rd*,' sais hee, 'if you haue chosen mee
 Of a hundred bowemen to be the head,
Hang me att yo*ur* mainemast-tree
 If I misse my marke past twelue pence
  bread.'

17 W*ith* pikes, and gunnes, and bowemen bold,
 This noble Howard is gone to the sea
On the day before midsummer-euen,
 And out att Thames mouth sayled they.

18 They had not sayled dayes three
 Vpon their iourney they tooke in hand,
But there they mett w*ith* a noble shipp,
 And stoutely made itt both stay and stand.

19 'Thou must tell me thy name,' sais Ch*arles*,
  my lo*rd* Haward,
 'Or who thou art, or ffrom whence thou
  came,
Yea, and where thy dwelling is,
 To whom and where thy shipp does belong.'

20 'My name,' sayes hee, 'is Henery Hunt,
 With a pure hart and a penitent mind;
I and my shipp they doe belong
 Vnto the New-castle *that* stands vpon Tine.'

21 'Now thou must tell me, Harry Hunt,
 As thou hast sayled by day and by night,
Hast thou not heard of a stout robber?
 Men calls him Si*r* Andrew Bartton, k*night*.'

22 But euer he sighed, and sayd, Alas!
    Ffull well, my lord, I know *that* wight;
    He robd me of my merchants ware,
    And I was his prisoner but yesternight.

23 As I was sayling vppon the sea,
    And [a] Burdeaux voyage as I did ffare,
    He clasped me to his archborde,
    And robd me of all my merchants-ware.

24 And I am a man both poore and bare,
    And euery man will haue his owne of me,
    And I am bound towards London to ffare,
    To complaine to my prince Henerye.

25 ' *That* shall not need,' sais my lord Haward;
    ' If thou canst lett me this robber see,
    Ffor euery peny he hath taken thee ffroe,
    Thou shalt be rewarded a shilling,' q*uo*th
    hee.

26 ' Now God fforefend,' saies Henery Hunt,
    ' My lord, you shold worke soe ffarr amisse!
    God keepe you out of *that* traitors hands!
    For you wott ffull litle what a man hee is.

27 ' Hee is brasse *wi*thin, and steele *wi*thout,
    And beames hee beares in his topcastle
    stronge;
    His shipp hath ordinance cleane round about;
    Besids, my lord, hee is verry well mand.

28 ' He hath a pinnace, is deerlye dight,
    *Sai*nt Andrews crosse, *that* is his guide;
    His pinnace beares nine score men and more,
    Besids fifteen cannons on euery side.

29 ' If you were twenty shippes, and he but one,
    Either in archbord or in hall,
    He wold ouercome you euerye one,
    And if his beames they doe downe ffall.'

30 ' This is cold comfort,' sais my Lord Haward,
    ' To wellcome a stranger thus to the sea;
    I 'le bring him and his shipp to shore,
    Or else into Scottland hee shall carrye mee.'

31 ' Then you must gett a noble gunner, my lord,
    That can sett well *wi*th his eye,
    And sinke his pinnace into the sea,
    And soone then ou*er*come will hee bee.

32 ' And when *that* you haue done this,
    If you chance *Si*r Andrew for to bord,

Lett no man to his topcastle goe;
    And I will giue you a glasse, my lord,

33 ' And then you need to ffeare no Scott,
    Whether you sayle by day or by night;
    And to-morrow, by seuen of the clocke,
    You shall meete wi*th* *Si*r Andrew Bartton,
    k*night*.

34 ' I was his prisoner but yester night,
    And he hath taken mee sworne,' qu*o*th
    hee;
    ' I trust my L[ord] God will me fforgiue
    And if *that* oath then broken bee.

35 ' You must lend me sixe peeces, my lord,'
    qu*o*th hee,
    ' Into my shipp, to sayle the sea,
    And to-morrow, by nine of the clocke,
    Yo*ur* Hono*ur* againe then will I see.'

*   *   *   *   *   *   *

36 And the hache-bord where *Si*r Andrew lay
    Is hached *wi*th gold deerlye dight:
    ' Now by my ffaith,' sais C*harl*es, my lord
    Haward,
    ' Then yonder Scott is a worthye wight!

37 ' Take in yo*ur* ancyents and yo*ur* standards,
    Yea *that* no man shall them see,
    And put me fforth a white willow wand,
    As merchants vse to sayle the sea.'

38 But they stirred neither top nor mast,
    But *Si*r Andrew they passed by:
    ' Whatt English are yonder,' said *Si*r Andrew,
    ' *That* can so litle curtesye?

39 ' I haue beene admirall ou*er* the sea
    More then these yeeres three;
    There is neu*er* an English dog, nor Portingall,
    Can passe this way *wi*thout leaue of mee.

40 ' But now yonder pedlers, they are past,
    *Whi*ch is no litle greffe to me:
    Ffeich them backe,' sayes *Si*r Andrew Bartton,
    ' They shall all hang att my maine-mast tree.'

41 With *tha*t the pinnace itt shott of,
    That my Lord Haward might itt well ken;
    Itt stroke downe my lords fforemast,
    And killed fourteen of my lo*r*d his men.

42 'Come hither, Simon!' sayes my lord Haward,
   'Looke *that* thy words be true thou sayd;
  I 'le hang thee att my maine-mast tree
    If thou misse thy marke past twelue pence
     bread.'

43 Simon was old, but his hart itt was bold;
   Hee tooke downe a peece, and layd itt ffull
    lowe;
  He put in chaine yeards nine,
    Besids other great shott lesse and more.

44 With *that* hee lett his gun-shott goe;
   Soe well hee settled itt with his eye,
  The ffirst sight *that* Sir Andrew sawe,
   Hee see his pinnace sunke in the sea.

45 When hee saw his pinace sunke,
   Lord! in his hart hee was not well:
  'Cutt my ropes! itt is time to be gon!
  I 'le goe ffeitch yond pedlers backe my selfe!'

46 When my lord Haward saw Sir Andrew loose,
   Lord! in his hart *that* hee was ffaine:
  'Strike on your drummes! spread out your
    ancyents!
    Sound out your trumpetts! sound out
     amaine!'

47 'Ffight on, my men!' sais Sir Andrew Bartton;
   'Weate, howsoeuer this geere will sway,
  Itt is my lord Adm[i]rall of England
   Is come to seeke mee on the sea.'

48 Simon had a sonne; with shott of a gunn —
   Well Sir Andrew might itt ken —
  He shott itt in att a priuye place,
   And killed sixty more of Sir Andrews men.

49 Harry Hunt came in att the other syde,
   And att Sir Andrew hee shott then;
  He droue downe his fformast-tree,
   And killed eighty more of Sir Andriwes
    men.

50 'I haue done a good turne,' says Harry Hunt;
   'Sir Andrew is not our kings ffreind;
  He hoped to haue vndone me yesternight,
   But I hope I haue quitt him well in the end.'

51 'Euer alas!' sayd Sir Andrew Barton,
   'What shold a man either thinke or say?
  Yonder ffalse theeffe is my strongest enemye,
   Who was my prisoner but yesterday.

52 'Come hither to me, thou Gourden good,
   And be thou readye att my call,
  And I will giue thee three hundred pound
   If thou wilt lett my beames downe ffall.'

53 With *that* hee swarued the maine-mast tree,
   Soe did he itt with might and maine;
  Horseley, with a bearing arrow,
   Stroke the Gourden through the braine.

54 And he ffell into the haches againe,
   And sore of this wound *that* he did bleed;
  Then word went throug Sir Andrews men,
   That the Gourden hee was dead.

55 'Come hither to me, Iames Hambliton,
   Thou art my sisters sonne, I haue no more;
  I will giue [thee] six hundred pound
   If thou will lett my beames downe ffall.'

56 With *that* hee swarued the maine-mast tree,
   Soe did hee itt with might and maine:
  Horseley, with another broad arrow,
   Strake the yeaman through the braine.

57 *That* hee ffell downe to the haches againe;
   Sore of his wound *that* hee did bleed;
  Couetousness getts no gaine,
   Itt is verry true, as the Welchman sayd.

58 But when hee saw his sisters sonne slaine,
   Lord! in his heart hee was not well:
  'Goe ffeitch me downe my armour of proue,
   Ffor I will to the topcastle my-selfe.

59 'Goe ffeitch me downe my armour of prooffe,
   For itt is guilded with gold soe cleere;
  God be with my brother, Iohn of Bartton!
   Amongst the Portingalls hee did itt weare.'

60 But when hee had his armour of prooffe,
   And on his body hee had itt on,
  Euery man *that* looked att him
   Sayd, Gunn nor arrow hee neede feare none.

61 'Come hither, Horsley!' sayes my lord Ha-
   ward,
   'And looke your shaft *that* itt goe right;
  Shoot a good shoote in the time of need,
   And ffor thy shooting thoust be made a
    knight.'

62 'I 'le doe my best,' sayes Horslay then,
   'Your Honor shall see beffore I goe;

If I shold be hanged att yo*u*r mainemast,
 I haue in my shipp but arrowes tow.'

63 But att S*i*r Andrew hee shott then ;
 Hee made sure to hitt his marke ;
 Vnder the spole of his right arme
 Hee smote S*i*r Andrew quite throw the hart.

64 Yett ffrom the tree hee wold not start,
 But hee clinged to itt w*i*th might and maine ;
 Vnder the coller then of his iacke,
 He stroke S*i*r Andrew thorrow the braine.

65 ' Ffight on my men,' sayes Sir Andrew Bartton,
 ' I am hurt, but I am not slaine ;
 I 'le lay mee downe and bleed a-while,
 And then I 'le rise and ffight againe.

66 ' Ffight on my men,' sayes S*i*r Andrew Bartton,
 ' These English doggs they bite soe lowe ;
 Ffight on ffor Scottland and S*ain*t Andrew
 Till you heare my whistle blowe ! '

67 But when the cold not heare his whistle blow,
 Sayes Harry Hunt, I 'le lay my head
 You may bord yonder noble shipp, my lo*r*d,
 For I know S*i*r Andrew hee is dead.

68 W*i*th *tha*t they borded this noble shipp,
 Soe did they itt w*i*th might and maine ;
 The ffound eighteen score Scotts aliue,
 Besids the rest were maimed and slaine.

69 My lo*r*d Haward tooke a sword in his hand,
 And smote of S*i*r Andrews head ;
 The Scotts stood by did weepe and mourne,
 But neu*er* a word durst speake or say.

70 He caused his body to be taken downe,
 And ou*er* the hatch-bord cast into the sea,
 And about his middle three hundred crownes :
 ' Whersoeuer thou lands, itt will bury thee.'

71 W*i*th his head they sayled into England againe,
 W*i*th right good will, and fforce and main,
 And the day beffore Newyeeres euen
 Into Thames mouth they came againe.

72 My lo*r*d Haward wrote to K*ing* Heneryes
 grace,
 W*i*th all the newes hee cold him bring :
 ' Such a Newyeeres gifft I haue brought to
 yo*u*r Gr[ace]
 As neu*er* did subiect to any king.

73 ' Ffor merchandyes and manhood,
 The like is nott to be ffound ;
 The sight of these wold doe you good,
 Ffor you haue not the like in yo*u*r English
 ground.'

74 But when hee heard tell *tha*t they were come,
 Full royally hee welcomed them home ;
 Sir Andrews shipp was the k*ing*s Newyeeres
 guifft ;
 A brauer shipp you neu*er* saw none.

75 Now hath our k*ing* Sir Andrews shipp,
 Besett w*i*th pearles and pr*e*cyous stones ;
 Now hath England two shipps of warr,
 Two shipps of warr, before but one.

76 ' Who holpe to this ? ' sayes K*ing* Henerye,
 ' *Tha*t I may reward him ffor his paine : '
 ' Harry Hunt, and Peeter Simon,
 William Horseleay, and I the same.'

77 ' Harry Hunt shall haue his whistle and chaine,
 And all his iewells, whatsoeuer they bee,
 And other rich giffts *tha*t I will not name,
 For his good service he hath done mee.'

78 ' Horslay, right thoust be a k*night*,
 Lands and liuings thou shalt haue store ;
 Howard shalbe erle of Nottingham,
 And soe was neuer Haward before.

79 ' Now, Peeter Simon, thou art old ;
 I will maintaine thee and thy sonne ;
 Thou shalt haue fiue hundred pound all in gold
 Ffor the good service *tha*t thou hast done.'

80 Then K*ing* Henerye shiffted his roome ;
 In came the Queene and ladyes bright ;
 Other arrands they had none
 But to see S*i*r Andrew Bartton, k*night*.

81 But when they see his deadly fface,
 His eyes were hollow in his head ;
 ' I wold giue a hundred pound,' sais K*ing*
 Henerye,
 ' The man were aliue as hee is dead !

82 ' Yett ffor the manfull p*ar*t *tha*t hee hath
 playd,
 Both heere and beyond the sea,
 His men shall haue halfe a crowne a day
 To bring them to my brother, K*ing* Iamye.'

B

a. Douce Ballads, I, 18 b. **b.** Pepys Ballads, I, 484, No 249. **c.** Wood Ballads, 401, 55. **d.** Roxburghe Ballads, I, 2. **e.** Bagford Ballads, 643, m. 9 (61). **f.** Bagford Ballads, 643, m. 10 (77). **g.** Wood Ballads, 402, 37. **h.** Glenriddell MSS, XI, 20.

1 WHEN Flora, with her fragrant flowers,
  Bedeckt the earth so trim and gay,
  And Neptune, with his dainty showers,
  Came to present the month of May,

2 King Henry would a progress ride;
  Over the river of Thames past he,
  Unto a mountain-top also
  Did walk, some pleasure for to see.

3 Where forty merchants he espy'd,
  With fifty sail, come towards him,
  Who then no sooner were arriv'd,
  But on their knees did thus complain.

4 'An't please Your Grace, we cannot sail
  To France no voyage, to be sure,
  But Sir Andrew Barton makes us quail,
  And robs us of our merchant-ware.'

5 Vext was the king, and turned him,
  Said to the lords of high degree,
  Have I ner a lord within my realm
  Dare fetch that traytor unto me?

6 To him repli'd Lord Charles Howard:
  I will, my liege, with heart and hand;
  If it please you grant me leave, he said,
  I will perform what you command.

7 To him then spake King Henry:
  I fear, my lord, you are too young.
  'No whit at all, my liege,' quoth he;
  'I hope to prove in valour strong.

8 'The Scottish knight I vow to seek,
  In what place soever he be,
  And bring a shore, with all his might,
  Or into Scotland he shall carry me.'

9 'A hundred men,' the king then said,
  'Out of my realm shall chosen be,
  Besides saylors and ship-boys
  To guide a great ship on the sea.

10 'Bow-men and gunners of good skill
  Shall for this service chosen be,

And they at thy command and will
  In all affairs shall wait on thee.'

11 Lord Howard calld a gunner then
  Who was the best in all the realm;
  His age was threescore years and ten,
  And Peter Simon was his name.

12 My lord calld then a bow-man rare,
  Whose active hands had gained fame,
  A gentleman born in Yorkshire,
  And William Horsly was his name.

13 'Horsly,' quoth he, 'I must to sea,
  To seek a traytor, with great speed;
  Of a hundred bow-men brave,' quoth he,
  'I have chosen thee to be the head.'

14 'If you, my lord, have chosen me
  Of a hundred men to be the head,
  Upon the main-mast I 'le hanged be,
  If twelve-score I miss one shillings breadth.'

15 Lord Howard then, of courage bold,
  Went to the sea with pleasant chear,
  Not curbd with winters piercing cold,
  Though it was the stormy time of the year.

16 Not long he had been on the sea,
  No more in days then number three,
  Till one Henry Hunt he there espied,
  A merchant of Newcastle was he.

17 To him Lord Howard cald out amain,
  And strictly charged him to stand;
  Demanding then from whence he came,
  Or where he did intend to land.

18 The merchant then made him answer soon,
  With heavy heart and careful mind,
  'My lord, my ship it doth belong
  Unto Newcastle upon Tine.'

19 'Canst thou shew me,' the lord did say,
  'As thou didst sail by day and night,
  A Scottish rover on the sea,
  His name is Andrew Barton, knight?'

20 Then to him the merchant sighd and said,
  With grieved mind and well a way,
  'But over well I know that wight,
  I was his prisoner but yesterday.

21 'As I, my lord, did pass from France,
    A Burdeaux voyage to take so far,
  I met with Sir Andrew Barton thence,
    Who robd me of my merchant-ware.

22 'And mickle debts, God knows, I owe,
    And every man did crave his own;
  And I am bound to London now,
    Of our gracious king to beg a boon.'

23 'Shew me him,' said [Lord] Howard then,
    'Let me but once the villain see,
  And one penny he hath from the tane,
    I 'le double the same with shillings three.'

24 'Now, God forbid,' the merchant said;
    'I fear your aim that you will miss;
  God bless you from his tyranny,
    For little you know what man he is.

25 'He is brass within and steel without,
    His ship most huge and mighty strong,
  With eighteen pieces strong and stout,
    He carrieth on each side along.

26 'With beams for his top-castle,
    As also being huge and high,
  That neither English nor Portugal
    Can pass Sir Andrew Barton by.'

27 'Hard news thou shewst,' then said the lord,
    'To welcome strangers to the sea;
  But, as I said, I 'le bring him aboard,
    Or into Scotland he shall carry me.'

28 The merchant said, If you will do so,
    Take counsel, then, I pray withal:
  Let no man to his top-castle go,
    Nor strive to let his beam[s] down fall.

29 'Lend me seven pieces of ordnance then,
    Of each side of my ship,' quoth he,
  'And to-morrow, my lord, twixt six and seven,
    Again I will Your Honour see.

30 'A glass I 'le set that may be seen
    Whether you sail by day or night;
  And to-morrow, be sure, before seven,
    You shall see Sir Andrew Barton, knight.'

31 The merchant set my lord a glass,
    So well apparent in his sight
  That on the morrow, as his promise was,
    He saw Sir Andrew Barton, knight.

32 The lord then swore a mighty oath,
    'Now by the heavens that be of might,
  By faith, believe me, and by troth,
    I think he is a worthy knight.

33 'Fetch me my lyon out of hand,'
    Saith the lord, 'with rose and streamer high;
  Set up withal a willow-wand,
    That merchant-like I [may] pass by.'

34 Thus bravely did Lord Howard pass,
    And did on anchor rise so high;
  No top-sail at all he cast,
    But as his foe he did him defie.

35 Sir Andrew Barton seeing him
    Thus scornfully to pass by,
  As though he cared not a pin
    For him and all his company,

36 Then called he his men amain,
    'Fetch back yon pedler now,' quoth he,
  'And against this way he comes again
    I 'le teach him well his courtesie.'

37 A piece of ordnance soon was shot
    By this proud pirate fiercely then
  Into Lord Howards middle deck,
    Which cruel shot killd fourteen men.

38 He calld then Peter Simon, he:
    'Look now thy word do stand in stead,
  For thou shalt be hanged on main-mast
    If thou miss twelve score one penny breadth.'

39 Then Peter Simon gave a shot
    Which did Sir Andrew mickle scare,
  In at his deck it came so hot,
    Killd fifteen of his men of war.

40 'Alas!' then said the pyrate stout,
    'I am in danger now, I see;
  This is some lord, I greatly doubt,
    That is set on to conquer me.'

41 Then Henry Hunt, with rigor hot,
    Came bravely on the other side,
  Who likewise shot in at his deck,
    And kild fifty of his men beside.

42 Then 'Out, alas!' Sir Andrew cri'd,
    'What may a man now think or say!
  Yon merchant thief that pierceth me,
    He was my prisoner yesterday.'

43 Then did he on Gordion call,
  Unto top-castle for to go,
  And bid his beams he should let fall,
  'For I greatly fear an overthrow.'

44 The lord cald Horsly now in hast :
  'Look that thy word stand now in stead,
  For thou shalt be hanged on main-mast
  If thou miss twelve score one shillings
    breadth.'

45 Then up [the] mast-tree swarved he,
  This stout and mighty Gordion ;
  But Horsly, he most happily
  Shot him under the collar-bone.

46 Then calld he on his nephew then,
  Said, Sisters sons I have no mo ;
  Three hundred pound I will give thee,
  If thou wilt to top-castle go.

47 Then stoutly he began to climb,
  From off the mast scornd to depart ;
  But Horsly soon prevented him,
  And deadly piercd him to the heart.

48 His men being slain, then up amain
  Did this proud pyrate climb with speed,
  For armour of proof he had put on,
  And did not dint of arrow dread.

49 'Come hither, Horsly,' said the lord,
  'See thine arrow aim aright ;
  Great means to thee I will afford,
  And if you speed, I 'le make you a knight.'

50 Sir Andrew did climb up the tree,
  With right good will and all his main ;
  Then upon the breast hit Horsly he,
  Till the arrow did return again.

51 Then Horsly spied a private place,
  With a perfect eye, in a secret part ;
  His arrow swiftly flew apace,
  And smote Sir Andrew to the heart.

52 'Fight on, fight on, my merry men all,
  A little I am hurt, yet not slain ;
  I 'le but lie down and bleed a while,
  And come and fight with you again.

53 'And do not,' he said, 'fear English rogues,
  And of your foes stand not in awe,

But stand fast by St Andrews cross,
  Until you hear my whistle blow.'

54 They never heard his whistle blow,
  Which made them [all] sore afraid :
  Then Horsly said, My lord, aboard,
  For now Sir Andrew Barton 's dead.

55 Thus boarded they this gallant ship,
  With right good will and all their main,
  Eighteen score Scots alive in it,
  Besides as many more were slain.

56 The lord went where Sir Andrew lay,
  And quickly thence cut off his head :
  'I should forsake England many a day,
  If thou wert alive as thou art dead.'

57 Thus from the wars Lord Howard came,
  With mickle joy and triumphing ;
  The pyrates head he brought along
  For to present unto our king :

58 Who briefly then to him did say,
  Before he knew well what was done,
  'Where is the knight and pyrate gay ?
  That I my self may give the doom.'

59 'You may thank God,' then said the lord,
  'And four men in the ship,' quoth he,
  'That we are safely come ashore,
  Sith you had never such an enemy :

60 'That is Henry Hunt, and Peter Simon,
  William Horsly, and Peters son ;
  Therefore reward them for their pains,
  For they did service at their turn.'

61 To the merchant then the king did say,
  'In lue of what he hath from the tane,
  I give to the a noble a day,
  Sir Andrews whistle and his chain :

62 'To Peter Simon a crown a day,
  And half-a-crown a day to Peters son,
  And that was for a shot so gay,
  Which bravely brought Sir Andrew down.

63 'Horsly, I will make thee a knight,
  And in Yorkshire thou shalt dwell :
  Lord Howard shall Earl Bury hight,
  For this title he deserveth well.

64 'Seven shillings to our English men,　　　And twelve pence a-day to the Scots, till they
　　Who in this fight did stoutly stand,　　　　　Come to my brother kings high land.'

All the copies in stanzas of eight lines.

A. 1³. 8ᵗʰ. 2³. 80.

3². *MS. pared away. From the Reliques.
Percy's marginal reading is* For sailors
good are welcome to me. *The tops of letters
left do not suit either of Percy's lines, says
Furnivall.*

3³. swore : *MS. pared away. Percy's read-
ing.*

6⁴. 20. 9¹. 600. 11³. 60 : **B,** three score.

12⁴, 13², 15⁴, 16². 100ᵈ, 100. 13⁴, 18¹. 3.

16². they *for* the. 16⁴, 42⁴. 12ᵈ̣.

15¹. sayes, *a letter blotted out before* a : *Fur-
nivall.*

20². poor *would read better than* pure (*cf.* B,
18², heavy heart), *but is not satisfactory.*

23³. archborde *for* hachborde ? : *cf.* 36¹, 70².

27², 29⁴, 52⁴, 55⁴. beanes, *or* beaues. 28³. 9.

28⁴. 15. 29¹. 20.

29². charke-bord : *should perhaps be* hach-
bord.

33¹. fferae. 33³. 7. 35³, 43³. 9.

36 *is perhaps out of place.* 36¹. lies *for* lay ?

37. Part II. 41¹. they *for* the.

41³. strokes. 44⁴. sumke.

47². Weate *I cannot emend.* 48⁴. 60.

49³. fformost. 49⁴. 80 : Andirwes. 52³. 300ˡⁱ.

53¹, 56¹. *perhaps* swarned : *Furnivall.*

55³. 600ˡⁱ.

57³,⁴. *three follows four : transposed for
rhyme.*

64⁴. they *for* the.

65⁴. *Only half the* n *of* againe *in the MS. :
Furnivall.*

68³. 18. 70³. 300. 71². meanye *for* main.

71⁴. againe they came. 75³,⁴. 2.

76². paime. 79³. 500ˡⁱ. 81³. 100ˡⁱ.

B. a. The Relation of the life and death of Sir
Andrew Barton, a Pyrate and Rover on the
Seas.

The tune is, Come follow my love.

Printed for F. Coles, T. Vere, and J. Wright
[1655–80].

13¹. ly *in* Horsly *is worn or torn away, and
so is* to *in the next line.*

20³. But ever.

24¹. the Lord he : c, g, my Lord he : *the
others,* the merchant.

26⁴. Can S. A. B. pass by. *So all but* h.

28⁴. beam. 33, 34 *follow* 36.

38². to *for* do. 45². Thus.

47³. *Cut off : supplied from* b, c.

53³. Sir Andrews, *and so* b, c, d.

54². all *supplied from* c.

63³. bright *for* hight.

64³. ey *of* they *cut off, and* land *in the follow-
ing line.*

b. A True Relation, *etc.* Tune is, *etc.*

Printed for J. Wright, J. Clarke, W. Thack-
eray, and T. Passinger [1670–82 ?].

*From a transcript made for Bishop Percy,
who has in a few places made corrections
which are not always easily distinguished
from those of the copyist.*

5². to his. 10¹. great *changed to* good.

13². To seek : good speed.

14⁴. Of : I *wanting.* 15⁴. was stormy.

16³. But one : there he 'spy'd.

17⁴. did *inserted by Percy, but perhaps in the
text.*

18¹. him *wanting.* 20³. over well.

20⁴. but *wanting.* 21¹. did sail.

22¹. deps. 23¹. [Lord] *wanting.*

24¹. the merchant. 25³. pieces of ordnance.

28⁴. beams. 29³. twix. 33, 34 *follow* 36.

33⁴. [may] *wanting.* 36¹. is men.

36³. And again. 38². to *for* do.

38⁴, 44⁴. breath. 44⁴. a shilling.

47³. But Horsly soon prevented him.

49⁴. if thou. 53¹. said he.

53³. Sir : *corrected by Percy to* St. 54¹. hear.

54². [all] *wanting.* 57⁴. unto the.

59⁴. never *wanting.* 61². lieu. 63². shall.

63³. hight. 64³. they. 64⁴. land.

c. A true Relation, *etc.* The tune is, *etc.*

Printed for F. Coles, T. Vere, and W. Gil-
bertson. [1648–80. Coles, Vere, Wright,
and Gilbertson *are found together as early
as* 1655.]

4¹. An 't like. 5³. lord in all.

8². In place wheresoever. 8³. on shore.

11³. year. 13². To see. 14³. the *wanting.*

18¹. him *wanting.* 20³. ever : knew.

21³. with *wanting.* 21⁴. wares.

23². that villain. 24¹. my Lord he.

24⁴. you little know. 26¹. for her.

31^2. to his. 33, 34 *follow* 36.
33^2. streamers. 34^2. ride *for* rise.
35^3. Although. 36^1. he on. 36^3. come.
38^2. do stand. 39^2. care *for* scare.
39^4. fifty. 41^3. shot it. 41^4. five *for* fifty.
42^4. but yesterday. 44^4. shilling bred.
45^1. then swarded he. 46^2. son: no more.
47^3. *As in* b. 49^2. that thine.
49^4. a *wanting.* 53^3. Sir Andrews.
54^2. them all sore. 57^3. he *wanting.*
59^3. are come safely to the shore.
62^2. half crown. 63^2. there shalt thou.
63^3. hight. 63^4. he hath deserved.
64^2. to this.

d, e, f. *Title as in* b. Tune, Come follow my love, etc.

d. Printed by and for W. O[nley], and sold by the Booksellers of Pye-corner and London-Bridge. [1650–1702.]

e. Printed by and for W. O., and sold by C. Bates at the Sun and Bible in Pye-corner.

f. Printed by and for W. O., and sold by the booksellers.

d *and* e *are dated in the Museum Catalogue* 1670; f. 1672.

2^1. a hunting. 5^1. turning. 5^2. d, e. to his.
6^1. Charles Lord Howard.
7^1. d, e. speak. f. spoke. 8^1. Scotch.
13^2. with good. 15^4. the *wanting.*
16^1. f. the *wanting.* 16^2. f. no *wanting.*
16^3. But one: there he. 18^1. him *wanting.*
20^1. to him *wanting.* 20^3. over well.
20^4. but *wanting.* 21^1. did sail.
22^2. doth: *but* And *means* if.
23^1. Lord Howard. 23^2. but *wanting.*
23^3. And e'ry. 24^1. the merchant.
24^4. you think. 25^3. pieces of ordnance.
27^2. stranger. 28^4. beams.
29^3. twixt six and seven *wanting.*
30^1. d, e. set as. f. I set as.
33, 34 *follow* 36. 33^4. I may.
34^2. did *wanting.* 34^3. at last.
34^4. as a foe did. 36^3. And ere. 37^2. e. By his.
38^2. how thy word do. 38^3. shall.
38^4. f. breath. 40^3. greatly fear.
43^2. Unto the. 43^4. For he: feard.
44^2. d, e. now stand. f. now *wanting.*
44^4. d, e. a shilling. f. shilling's breath.
45^1. swerved. 45^4. f. under his.
47^3. *As in* b, c. 48^4. arrows.
49^2. See thou thy arrows.
49^4. if thou speedst: make the[e] knight.
52^4. f. with *wanting.* 53^1. he said.

53^2. e. inwe. 53^3. Sir Andrews.
54^2. all full sore. 56^4. were.
58^1. unto *for* then to. 59^4. never had.
61^1. f. merchant therefore the king he said.
63^3. hight. 63^4. e. this girle. f. this act.
64^1. f. Ninety pound.

g. A true Relation, etc. To the tune of Come follow me, love.

London, Printed for E. W.

This copy has been considerably corrected, and only a part of the variations is given.

2^2. of *wanting.* 2^3. mountaines.
3^2. with swiftest. 4^1. An't like. 5^2. to his.
5^3. in all my. 11^4. One *for* And.
14^4. shilling.
16^2. No more then dayes in number three.
18^1. him *wanting.* 20^1. said and sighd.
20^2. a g. m. and a w. 20^3. over.
20^4. For I. 21^3. with *wanting.*
23^1. Lord Howard. 23^2. that *for* the.
23^3. for one. 24^1. my Lord, quoth he.
26^1. beams from her. 28^4. beames.
32^4. weight (*that is,* wight) *for* knight.
33^2. streamers. 33^4. I may. 34^2. ride.
34^4. he *wanting.* 35, 36 *wanting.*
38^2. do stand. 38^4. bred. 39^4. fifty.
41^4. five. 42^4. but yesterday.
43^1. on one Gordion. 45^1. then swarmed.
48^2. this stout. 49^2. See that thy arrow.
49^4. if thou: thee knight.
53^2. stand in no awe. 53^3. S. Andrew's.
54^2. them all full sore. 55^4. moe.
56^3. I would forsweare. 57^4. the king.
59^2. in this ship with me. 59^3. to shore.
59^4. never had. 60^3. paine.
63^2. there shalt thou.
63^4. his title he hath deserved. 64^2. to this.
64^4. king his land.

Old Ballads, 1723, *and* Roxburghe, III, 726, *have Iris for the* Neptune *of B, in* 1^3; *Charles Lord Howard in* 6^1; *Ninety pounds in* 64^1.

h. *This being a Scottish copy, and the variations also numerous, it seems advisable to give the whole text rather than only the divergent readings. The transcript may be inferred, from passages phonetically misrendered, to have been made from recitation or reading, more probably from recitation, since many of the differences from the printed copies are of the sort which are made by reciters; that is, immaterial expressions are imperfectly remembered; and again*, 16² *is adopted from popular ballad phraseology, and, as already observed, the stanza following 50 is borrowed from* 'Adam Bell.' *Cases of writing sound for sense are* 4³, makes us squails *for* makes us quail; 7³, I quitted all *for* No whit at all; 48², The spirit *for* This pīrate; 61³, A nobler day *for* A noble a day. *Verses of* 25, 26 *have been interchanged.* 8, 9³,⁴, 10¹,², 21, 28, 29, 30, 32, 36, 44, 49, 52²,³,⁴, 53¹ *are wanting.* 33, 34 *are in the right order. It is a little surprising that a Scottish copy should have* Sir Andrew Cross *for* St Andrew's cross, 53³. a–d *have* Sir Andrews Cross.

1 WHEN Febus, with her fragrant flours,
    bedect the earth so trim and gay,
And Neptan, with his denty shours,
    came to present the month o May,

2 King Hendry would a hunting ride,
    and over the river Thames past he,
Unto a mountain-top also
    he walkd, some pleasures to espy.

3 There fortie merchants he espy'd,
    with fiftie sail, come towards him;
No sooner there they were arrived
    but on their knees they did complain.

4 'My lodge,' said they, 'we cannot sail
    to France nor Spain, for to be sure;
Sir Andrew Barton makes us squails,
    and berubs (?) us of our merchant-wair.'

5 The king was grievd and turnd him,
    said to his lords of high degree,
Is there not a lord in my realm
    can fetch yon traitor unto me?

6 Then out bespoke Lord Charles Howard,
    and says, My ludge, with heart and hand,
If that you 'l give me leave, said he,
    I will perform what you command.

7 But out bespoke King Hendrie:
    'I fear, my lord, you are too young;'
'I quitted all, my lodge,' said he,
    'for I think to prove one valient strong.'

9¹,² 'A hundred men out of my realm
    shall for this service chosen be,

10³,⁴ And they, at thy command and will,
    in all affairs, shall wait on thee.'

11 The king calld on a gunner then,
    whose age was 'bove three score and ten;
He was the best in that realm,
    and Petter Simon height his name.

[A 12] 'Now Peter,' said he, 'wee'r bound to sea,
    to fetch a traitor with good speed,
And over a hundred gunners good
    I 've chosen thee to be the head.'

[A 13] 'My lodge,' says he, 'if he have chosen me
    oer a hundred men to be the head,
Upon mine mast I hangd shall be,
    if I mess twelve score on a shilling breadth.'

12 My lord calld on a bow-man then,
    whose hands and acts had gained fame;
He was the best in that realm,
    and William Horsley height his name.

13 'Now Horsley,' says he, 'wee'r bound to sea,
    to fetch a traitor wi good speed,
And over a hundred archers good
    I 've chosen thee to be the head.'

14 'My lord,' sais he, 'if ye hae chosen me
    oer a hundred men to be the head,
Upon my mast I hangd shall be,
    if I mess twelve score a shilling breadth.'

15 Lord Howard he 's gone to the wars,
    wi muckle mirth and merrie cheer;
He was not curbd with winters cold,
    tho it was the stormy time a year.

16 He had not been upon the seas,
    no not a day but only three,
Till he espy'd Sir Hendry Hunt,
    a merchant of Newcastle he.

17 A peice of ordinance was shot,
    which straitly charged him to stand;
Demanding of him from whence he came,
    and where he was intend to land.

18 The merchant he made answer then,
    with a heavy heart and carefull mind,

'If it please Your Grace, my ship belongs
    unto Newcastle upon Tine.'

19 'Canst thou but show me,' said the lord,
    ' as those did sail by day or night,
  A Scotish rubber on the seas,
      whose name's Sir Andrew Burton,
      knight?'

20 The merchant sighd, and said, Alas !
    full over well I do him know ;
  Good keep you frae his tiranie !
    for I was his prisoner yesterday.

22 And muckle debt, God knows, I owe,
    if every man would crave his oun ;
  But I am bound for London nou,
    of our gracious king to beg a bon.

23 'Wilt you go with me,' said the lord,
    ' and once that villain let me see,
  For every pennie he's from thee taen
    I double the same wi shillings three.'

24 But the merchant sighd, and said, Alas !
    I fear, my lord, your aims you miss ;
  Good keep you frae his tiranie !
    for little you ken what a man he is.

25[1] For he's brass within and steel without,
26[2]   and his great ship's mighty hugie high,
  So that neither English nor Portugees
    can pass Sir Andrew Burton by.

26[1] And he has beams for his top-castle
25[2]   which is both mighty huge and strong ;
  He has eighteen peice of ordinance
    he carries on each side along.

27 'Bad news thou tells,' then said the lord,
    ' to welcome strangers to the sea ;
  But as I have said, I'll bring him abord,
    or into Scotland he's carry me.'

31 So the merchant set my lord a glass,
    that well appeared in his eye,
  And the morning, as his promise was,
    he did Sir Andrew Burton see.

33 'Fetch me my lyon out of hand,
    set up our rose on streamers high ;
  Set up likewise a willie wand,
    that merchant like we may pass by.'

34 Thus bravely did Lord Howard pass,
    upon an anchor rose so high ;
  No topsail at last he did upcast,
    but like a foe did him defie.

35 Sir Andrew Barton, seeing him
    thus scornfull-like for to pass by,
  As tho he cared not a pin
    for him and all his company,

37 Sir Andrew Barton gave a shott
    which did Lord Howard muckle dear ;
  For it came so hotly in at his deck
    killd fifteen of his men a ware.

38 My lord calld on o' Petter Seymore,
    says, See thy words does stand in steed ;
  For upon main-mast thou hangd shall be,
    if thou miss twelve score a shilling
    breed.

39 Then Petter Symore gave a shot
    which did Sir Andrew muckle scarr ;
  It came so hotly in his deck
    killd fifty of his men a ware.

40 Then 'Out, alas !' Sir Andrew cryes,
    ' and aye alas, and woe's me !
  This is some lord, I greatly fear,
    that is set out to conquer me.'

41 Then Hendry Hunt, with rigor hot,
    came bravely on the other side ;
  He shot so hotly in at his deck
    killd fiftie of his men beside.

42 Then 'Out, alas !' Sir Andrew cryes,
    ' what can a man now do or say ?
  This merchant thief it percies me,
    he was my prisoner yesterday.'

43 Sir Andrew calld on Gordon then,
    and bad him to top-castle go
  And strive to let his beems doun fall,
    for he greatly feard an overthrow.

45 Then up mass'-tree then climed he,
    that stout and mighty Gordon ;
  But Horsley soon prevented him,
    and shot him in at collar-bone.

46 Sir Andrew calld his nephew then ;
    says, Sisters son I hi nè mae ;

A hundred pounds I 'll to thee give
  if thou 'l up to top-castle gae.

47 Then up mast-tree then climed he,
  from of the deck for to depart;
But Horsley soon prevented him,
  and deadly peirced him to the heart.

48 His men being slain, then up amain
  the spirit proud did climb wi speed;
Armour of proof he did put on,
  and of arrows dint he had nè dread.

50 Then up mast-tree then climbed he,
  the spirit proud did climb amain;
But Horsley hat him upon the breast,
  till his arrow did return again.

  ' Foul fà the hands,' says Horsley then,
  ' this day that did that coat put on!
For had it been as thin as mine,
  thy last days had been at an end.'

51 But Horsley spy'd a private part,
  with a canie hand and secret art,
And his arrows swiftly flew amain,
  and pierced Sir Andrew to the heart.

52¹ ' Fight on, fight on, my mirrie men all,
53²   and of English rogues stand ye nè aw;
But stand fast by Sir Andrew cross
  till that ye hear my whistle blà.'

54 But they never heard his whistle blà,
  which made them mightyly to dread;
Say Horsley, My lord, we 'll go abord,
  for now I know Sir Andrew 's dead.

55 Then boarded they this great ship then,
  with muckle might and a' their main,
And in her was eighteen score o Scots
  alive,
besides there mony maē were slain.

56 My lord went where Sir Andrew lay,
  and hastely cut of his head:
' I 'd forsake England this mony a day,
  if thou were alive as thou art dead.'

57 So Lord Howard he 's come from the wars,
  with muckle mirth and triumphing,
And the pirot's head he brought along,
  for to present unto their king.

58 But out bespoke King Hendry,
  before he knew well what was done:
' Bring here to me that villain strong,
  that I mysell may give the doom.'

59 ' Ye may be thankfà,' said the lord,
  ' at what is done, my ludge,' said he,
' That we 'r returned alive again;
  for ye 'd never such an enemy.

60 ' There 's Hendry Hunt, and Petter Sy-
    more,
  and William Horsley, and Petter's son;
Therefore reward them for their pain,
  for they did service at their turn.'

61 The king he said to Hendry Hunt,
  ' For every pennie he 's from the tane,
A nobler day I 'l to thee give,
  and Sir Andrew's whistle and his chain.

62 ' A croun a day to Petter Symore,
  and half a croun to Petter's son;
And that was for the shots they gave,
  which bravely brought Sir Andrew
    doun.

63 ' Horsley, I 'l make of thee a knight,
  and in Yorkshire thou shall dwell;
Lord Howard shall Earl Bewry height,
  for the tittle he deserves full well.

64 ' Seven rosenobles to our English men,
  which in the feight did stoutly stand,
And twelve pence a day unto the Scots,
  till they come to my brother king's
    land.'

———◆———

38¹. on O'.   o' *may mean* old.
62 *follows* 63.

168

FLODDEN FIELD

From Deloney's Pleasant History of John Winchcomb, in his younger yeares called Jacke of Newberie, etc., London, 1633; reprinted by J. O. Halliwell, London, 1859, p. 48.

PRINTED in Ritson's Ancient Songs, 1790, p. 115; Evans's Old Ballads, 1810, III, 55.

A booke called Jack of Newbery was entered to Thomas Millington, March 7, 1597: Arber, Stationers' Registers, III, 81. The edition of 1633, the earliest which Mr Halliwell-Phillipps had met with, was the ninth, published by Cuthbert Wright. The author has introduced several pieces of verse into his tale, two of them popular ballads, 'The Fair Flower of Northumberland' and this of Flodden, of which Deloney says, "in disgrace of the Scots, and in remembrance of the famous atchieved historie, the commons of England made this song, which to this day is not forgotten of many:" p. 47.

King James has made a vow to be in London on St James's day. Queen Margaret begs him to keep faith with her brother Henry, and reminds him that England is hard to win; for which James says she shall die. Lord Thomas Howard, the queen's chamberlain, comes to the defence of his mistress, but the king in his rage declares that he shall be hanged and she burned as soon as he comes back. But James never came back; he was slain at Bramstone Green with twelve thousand of his men.

1, 2. St James's day is selected, as being the king's. King James's letter to King Henry is dated the 26th of July, the day following St James's day, and the Scottish herald delivered it in France, and announced war to the king of England, in consequence of the unsatisfactory answer, on the 12th of August, or shortly before.

3-5. Queen Margaret's remonstrance is historical. James, says Lindsay, would "give

no credence to no counsel, sign nor token that made against his purpose, but refused all godly counsel which was for the weal of his crown and country; neither would he use any counsel of his wise and prudent wife, Margaret, queen of Scotland, for no prayer nor supplication that she could make him. . . . She assured him, if he past in England at that time, that he would get battle. Yet this wise and loving counsel could not be taken in good part by him, because she was the king of England's sister." Cronicles, 1814, p. 267 f.

6. The Earl of Surrey, uncle by marriage to Margaret Tudor, had the charge of escorting her to Scotland in 1503, and this is ground enough for the ballad's making him her chamberlain ten years later.

8. "This battle was called the Field of Flodden by the Scotsmen and Brankston [Bramstone] by the Englishmen, because it was stricken on the hills of Flodden beside a town called Brankston; and was stricken the ninth day of September, 1513." Lesley, History, 1830, p. 96.

10. Hall says that the English slew "twelve thousand, at the least, of the best gentlemen and flower of Scotland." The gazette of the battle (Pinkerton's History, II, 457), Polydore Vergil, and modern Scottish historians, say ten thousand. Among these were twelve earls, thirteen lords, and many other persons of high rank.

12. 'Iack with a feather' is said in contempt of the Scottish king's levity or foolhardiness. "Then was the body bowelled, embawmed and cered:" Hall, p. 564, ed. 1809. "His body was bowelled, rebowelled, and enclosed in lead," "lapped in lead:" Stowe,

Chronicle, p. 494 b, ed. 1631; Survey, Book III, p. 81 a, ed. 1710. Fair Rosamond's bones, when they were exhumed at Godstow, says Leland, were closed in lead and within that closed in leather: Dugdale's Monasticon, ed. 1823, IV, 365, No VIII.

In the letter sent to Henry VIII in France James included the slaughter of Andrew Barton among the unredressed grievances of which he had to complain. A few days before the battle of Flodden, Lord Thomas Howard, then admiral, used the occasion of his father's dispatching a herald to the King of Scots to say that "inasmuch as the said king had divers and many times caused the said lord to be called at days of true to make redress for Andrew Barton, a pirate of the sea long before that vanquished by the same Lord Admiral, he was now come, in his own proper person, to be in the vanguard of the field, to justify the death of the said Andrew against him and all his people, and would see what could be laid to his charge the said day:" Hall's Chronicle, ed. 1809, p. 558.

There is a slight resemblance in one or two particulars, such as might be expected from similarity of circumstances, between this ballad and 'Durham Field.' In the latter the King of Scots swears that he will hold his parliament in leeve London, st. 6. A squire warns him that there are bold yeomen in England; the king is angry, draws his sword, and kills the squire, 7-9. In 'Scotish Ffeilde,' Percy Folio, Hales and Furnivall, I, 217,* the French king says there is nothing left in England save millers and mass-priests, v. 109; and in the poem on Flodden, reprinted by Weber, and recently by Federer,† Lord Home makes this same assertion, Weber, p. 10, 187-92; Federer, p. 8, sts 46, 47. Cf. 'Durham Field,' p. 282.

The forged manuscript formerly in the possession of J. Payne Collier, containing thirty ballads alleged to be of the early part of the seventeenth century, has for the second piece in the volume a transcript of this ballad, with variations.

The battle of Flodden called out a great deal of verse. The most notable pieces are two already referred to, and a third which will be given here in an appendix; the less important will be found in Weber's volume.

———◆———

1   KING JAMIE hath made a vow,
     Keepe it well if he may!
   That he will be at lovely London
     Upon Saint James his day.

2   'Upon Saint James his day at noone,
     At faire London will I be,
   And all the lords in merrie Scotland,
     They shall dine there with me.'

3   Then bespake good Queene Margaret,
     The teares fell from her eye:
   'Leave off these warres, most noble king,
     Keepe your fidelitie.

4   'The water runnes swift and wondrous deepe,
     From bottome unto the brimme;
   My brother Henry hath men good enough;
     England is hard to winne.'

5   'Away,' quoth he, 'with this silly foole!
     In prison fast let her lie:
   For she is come of the English bloud,
     And for these words she shall dye.'

6   With that bespake Lord Thomas Howard,
     The queenes chamberlaine that day:
   'If that you put Queene Margaret to death,
     Scotland shall rue it alway.'

7   Then in a rage King Jamie did say,
     'Away with this foolish mome!
   He shall be hanged, and the other be burned,
     So soone as I come home.'

8   At Flodden Field the Scots came in,
     Which made our English men faine;
   At Bramstone Greene this battaile was seene,
     There was King Jamie slaine.

* A better, but defective, copy is in the second volume of Chetham Miscellanies, edited by Dr J. Robson, 1855.

† Harleian MS. No 3526, date of about 1636; a printed copy of 1664, from which the poem was edited by Weber, Edinburgh, 1808; a printed copy of 1755-62, from a different source, excellently edited by Charles A. Federer, Manchester, 1884. See further this last, pp. 134-37.

9 Then presently the Scots did flie,
  Their cannons they left behind ;
  Their ensignes gay were won all away,
  Our souldiers did beate them blinde.

10 To tell you plaine, twelve thousand were slaine
   That to the fight did stand,
   And many prisoners tooke that day,
   The best in all Scotland.

11 That day made many [a] fatherlesse child,
   And many a widow poore,
   And many a Scottish gay lady
   Sate weeping in her bower.

12 Jack with a feather was lapt all in leather,
   His boastings were all in vaine ;
   He had such a chance, with a new morrice-
     dance,
   He never went home againe.

3¹. he spake.
The copy followed by Ritson puts st. 11 *after*
5. *The principal variations of the Collier
copy may be given, though they are without
authority or merit.*

After 2 :
  March out, march out, my merry men,
  Of hie or low degree;
  I 'le weare the crowne in London towne,
  And that you soone shall see.

4⁴. To venture life and limme.

  Then doe not goe from faire Scotland,
  But stay thy realm within ;
  Your power, I weene, is all to weake,
  And England hard to winne.

5¹. this sillie mome.
7². this other mome.

After 8 :
  His bodie never could be found,
  When he was over throwne,
  And he that wore faire Scotlands crowne
  That day could not be knowne.

For 12, *to adapt the piece to the seventeenth
century :*

  Now heaven we laude that never more
  Such tiding shall come to hand ;
  Our king, by othe, is king of both
  England and faire Scotland.

APPENDIX

FLODDEN FIELD

a. 'Flodden Ffeilde,' Percy MS., p. 117; Hales and Furni-
vall, I, 313. b. Harleian MS. 293, fol. 55. c. Harleian
MS. 367, fol. 120.

A TEXT made from b and c is printed by Weber,
Flodden Field, p. 366, and by R. H. Evans, Old
Ballads, 1810, III, 58. b, c lack all that follows
102 except 103, with which all three copies alike
end. This stanza makes a natural conclusion to
the vindication of Lancashire, Cheshire and the
Earl of Derby, and what intervenes in a, after 102,
seems to be an interpolation. Nevertheless I have
preferred to give the Percy text (though the others
are not inferior to it, and possess the unity which
has to be brought about in this case by transferring
the last stanza), on account of the pleasing story
How Rowland Egerton came to the lordship of
Ridley, 107–119, which would make no bad ballad
by itself.

At the battle of Flodden, the right wing of the
van, commanded by Sir Edmund Howard, the third
son of the Earl of Surrey, was routed by the Scots
under Lord Home, Chamberlain of Scotland, and
the Earl of Huntly. "Edmund Howard had with
him a thousand Cheshire men, and five hundred
Lancashire men, and many gentlemen of Yorkshire,
on the right wing of the lord Howard ; and the
Lord Chamberlain of Scotland, with many lords,
did set on him, and the Cheshire and Lancashire
men never abode stroke, and few of the gentlemen
of Yorkshire abode, but fled. . . . And the said
Edmund Howard was thrice felled, and to his relief

the lord Dacre came, with fifteen hundred men." *
On the other hand, the Cheshire and Lancashire
men of the extreme left, under command of Sir
Edward Stanley, discomfited the Scottish division
of Lennox and Argyle. King Henry received the
news of the victory while he was lying before Tour-
nay, "and highly praised the Earl, and the Lord
Admiral and his son, and all the gentlemen and
commons that were at that valiant enterprise; how-
beit, the king had a secret letter that the Cheshire
men fled from Sir Edmund Howard, which letter
caused great heart-burning and many words; but
the king thankfully accepted all thing, and would
no man to be dispraised." †

This poem, a history in the ballad style, was com-
posed to vindicate the behavior of Lancashire and
Cheshire at Flodden, and to glorify the Stanleys; ‡
in the accomplishment of which objects it becomes
incumbent upon the minstrel to expose the malice of
the Earl of Surrey, to whom he imputes the "wrong
writing" which caused such heart-burning.

The Earl of Surrey sends a letter by a herald to
King Henry, then at Tournay. The king asks the
news before he breaks the seal, and who fought and
who fled. The herald answers that King James is
slain, and that Lancashire and Cheshire fled; no
man of the Earl of Derby's durst face the foe.
The king opens the letter, which confirms the her-
ald's report, and calls for the Earl of Derby. Sir
Ralph Egerton suggests that if Lancashire and Che-
shire fled, it must have been because they had a
Howard, and not a Stanley, for their captain. The
Earl of Derby comes before the king, and says the
same; let him have Lancashire and Cheshire, and
he will burn up all Scotland and conquer to Paris
gate. The king says cowards will fight to retrieve
what they have lost. We were never cowards, re-
joins Derby; who brought in your father at Mil-
ford Haven? (It was not precisely the Stanleys.)
The king turns away; the Duke of Buckingham is
ready to lay his life that all this comes from a false
writing of the Earl of Surrey.§ Derby is not to be
comforted, and breaks out in farewells to all his
kith and kin, Edward Stanley, John Stanley, and
many more; they must be slain, for they never
would flee. The Earl of Shrewsbury bids him
take heart; Derby goes on with farewells to Lan-

caster, Latham, and all familiar places. In the
midst of his exclamations, James Garsed, "Long
Jamie," a yeoman of the guard, comes flying to the
Earl of Derby for protection: he had killed two
men, and wounded three. Derby's intercession can
do only harm now, but he will ask friends to speak
for Jamie. A messenger arrives from the king
ordering Long Jamie to be delivered up; he is to
be hanged. Buckingham takes Jamie by one arm
and Shrewsbury takes him by the other, and with
Derby in front and many gentlemen following, they
go to the king. Welcome, dukes and earls, says
the king, but most welcome of all our traitor, Long
Jamie! Jamie, how durst thou show thyself in our
presence after slaying thy brethren? Jamie explains
that his fellows had called him coward, and bidden
him flee to that coward the Earl of Derby. The
Earl of Derby had befriended him when he was little
and maintained him till he was able to shoot. Then
one day a Scottish minstrel brought King Henry a
bow which none of his guard could bend. Jamie
shot seven times with it, and the eighth time broke
it; then told the Scot to pick up the pieces and
take them to his king; upon which Henry had
made him yeoman of the guard, thanks to His
Grace and to the Earl of Derby who had brought
him up. And now, to have the earl taunted, to be
false to the man who had been true to him — he
had rather die. Stand up, Jamie, says the King;
have here my charter; but let there be no more
fighting while you are in France. Then you must
grant me one thing, says Jamie — that he that
abuses Lancashire or Cheshire shall die; and the
king commands proclamation to be made that any
man abusing Lancashire or Cheshire shall have his
judgment on the next tree. The next morning
comes a messenger from the queen wishing the
king joy, for his brother-in-law, King Jamie, is slain.
Henry asks again, Who fought and who fled?
"Lancashire and Cheshire have done the deed," is
the reply; "had not the Earl of Derby been true
to thee, England had been in great hazard." The
king on the moment promotes Edward and John
Stanley and 'Rowland' Egerton, who had fought
with Edward. Buckingham runs for Derby, and
the king welcomes the earl, and returns to him
all that he had taken from him. But one thing

---

* Articles of the bataill betwix the Kinge of Scottes and
the Erle of Surrey in Brankstone Feld, the 9 day of Sep-
tember: State Papers, vol. iv, King Henry the Eighth,
Part iv, p. 2, 1836.

† Hall's Chronicle, p. 564.

‡ Who are celebrated also in three other pieces, 'Scottish

Field,' 'Bosworth Field,' and 'Lady Bessie:' Percy MS.,
Hales and Furnivall, I, 212, III, 235, 321.

§ "He never loved thee, for thy uncle [that is, Sir Wil-
liam Stanley] slew his father" [the Duke of Norfolk];
which, however, is not true.

grieveth me still, says Derby — to have been called coward yesterday. "It was a wrong writing that came from the Earl of Surrey," says the king, "but I shall teach him to know his prince." Derby asks no more than to be judge over Surrey, and the king makes him so; as he says, so it shall be. "Then his life is saved," says the earl; "if my uncle slew his father" (but, as before said, there was no occasion for uneasiness on that score), "he would have taken vengeance on me." And so the glory is all shifted to Derby, and nothing remains for Surrey.

The minstrel goes on to speak of the surrender of Tournay, and then of an essay of the king's to reward an Egerton for good service done.* Egerton would be glad to have his reward in Cheshire. The king has nothing there to give but five mills at Chester; Egerton does not wish to be called a miller. The king offers the forest of Snowdon; Egerton, always kneeling on his knee, does not wish to be called a ranger. Nothing will please thee, Egerton, says the king; but Egerton asks for Ridley in Cheshire, and gets it.

The last twelve verses profess to enumerate Henry Eighth's victories in France: 'Hans and Gynye' (neither of which I recognize, unless Gynye stands for Guinegatte, the Battle of the Spurs), Tournay and Thérouanne, these in the campaign of 1513, and Boulogne and Montreuil † during the invasion of 1544.

1 Now let vss talke of [the] Mount of Flodden,
  Fforsooth such is our chance,
And let vs tell what tydings the Ear[l]e of Surrey
  Sent to our king into France.

2 The earle he hath a writting made,
  And sealed it with his owne hand;
From the Newcastle vpon Tine
  The herald passed from the land.

3 And after to Callice hee arriued,
  Like a noble leed of high degree,
And then to Turwin soone he hyed,
  There he thought to haue found King Henery.

4 But there the walls were beaten downe,
  And our English soldiers therin laine;
Sith to Turnay the way hee nume,
  Wheras lay the emperour of Almaine,

* Sir Ralph Egerton is made marshal in st. 91; but this Rowland is really Ralph over again. Ralph was knighted at Tournay, and was granted the manor of Ridley in February of the next year.

And there he found the king of England,
  Blessed Iesus, preserve that name !

5 When the herald came before our king,
  Lowlye he fell downe on his knee,
And said, Christ, christen king, that on the crosse dyed,
  Noble King Henery, this day thy speed may bee !

6 The first word that the prince did minge,
  Said, Welcome, herald, out of England, to me !
How fares my leeds ? how fares my lords?
  My knights, my esquiers, in their degree ?

7 'Heere greeteth you well your owne leaetenant,
  The Honorable Erle of Surrey;
He bidds you in Ffrance to venter your chance,
  For slaine is your brother, King Iamye,
And att louelie London you shall him finde,
  My comelye prince, in the presence of thee.'

8 Then bespake our comlye king,
  Said, Who did fight and who did flee ?
And who bore him best of the Mount of Fflodden?
  And who was false, and who was true to me ?

9 'Lancashire and Cheshire,' sayd the messenger,
  'Cleane they be fled and gone ;
There was nere a man that longd to the Erle of Darby
  That durst looke his enemyes vpon.'

10 S[t]ill in a study stood our noble king,
  And tooke the writting in his hand ;
Shortlye the seale he did vnclose,
  And readilye he read as he found.

11 Then bespake our comlye king,
  And called vpon his chiualree,
And said, Who will feitch me the King of Man,
  The Honnorable Thomas Erle of Darbye ?

12 He may take Lancashire and Cheshire,
  That he hath called the cheefe of chiualree;
Now falsely are they fled and gone,
  Neuer a one of them is true to mee !

13 Then bespake Sir Raphe Egerton, the knight,
  And lowlye kneeled vpon his knee,
And said, My soueraigne lord, King Henery,
  If it like your Grace to pardon mee,

14 If Lancashire and Cheshire be fled and gone,
  Of those tydings wee may be vnfaine ;

† "Where they lay a long time, and left the town as they found it:" Hall, p. 861.

But I dare lay my life and lande
 It was for want of their cap*taine*.

15 For if the Erle of Derby our cap*taine* had beene,
 And vs to lead in our arraye,
Then noe Lancashire man nor Cheshire
 That euer wold haue fled awaye.

16 ' Soe it prooued well,' said our noble k*ing*,
 ' By him *that* deerlye dyed vpon a tree !
Now when wee had the most neede,
 Falslye they serued then to mee.'

17 Then spake W*illia*m Brewerton, k*night*,
 And lowlye kneeled his prince before,
And sayd, My soueraigne k*ing*, Henery the Eighth,
 If *your* Grace sett by vs soe little store,

18 Wheresoeuer you come in any feild to fight,
 Set the Earle of Darby and vs before ;
Then shall you see wether wee fight or flee,
 Trew or false whether we be borne.

19 Compton rowned w*ith* our k*ing*,
 And said, Goe wee and leaue the cowards right;
' Heere is my gloue to thee,' q*u*oth Egerton,
 ' Compton, if thou be a k*night*.

20 ' Take my gloue, and w*ith* me fight,
 Man to man, if thou wilt turne againe ;
For if our prince were not *p*resent right,
 The one of vs two shold be slaine,

21 ' And neu*er* foote beside the ground gone
 Vntill the one dead shold bee.'
Our prince was moued theratt anon,
 And returned him right teenouslye.

22 And to him came on the other hand
 The Honno*ra*ble Erle of Darbye ;
And when he before our prince came,
 He lowlye kneeled vpon his knee,

23 And said, Iesu Christ, *that* on the crosse dyed,
 This day, noble Henery, thy speed may bee !
The first word *that* the k*ing* did speake,
 Sayd, Welcome, K*ing* of Man and Erle of
  Darbye !

24 How likest thou Cheshire and Lancashire both,
 W*h*ich were counted cheefe of chiualree?
Falslye are they fled and gone,
 And neu*er* a one is trew to mee.

25 ' If *that* be soe,' said the erle free,
 ' My leege, therof I am not faine;
My comlye prince, rebuke not mee,
 I was not there to be there cap*taine*.

26 ' If I had beene their cap*taine*,' the erle said then,
 ' I durst haue layd both liffe and land
He neu*er* came out of Lancashire nor Cheshire
 That wold haue fledd beside the ground.

27 ' But if it like y*our* noble Grace
 A litle boone to grant itt mee,
Lett me haue Lancashire and Cheshire both,
 I desire noe more helpe trulye ;

28 ' If ffayle to burne vp all Scottland,
 Take me and hang me vpon a tree!
I, I shall conquer to Paris gate,
 Both comlye castles and towers hye.

29 ' Wheras the walls beene soe stronge,
 Lancashire and Cheshire shall beate them
  downe.'
' By my fathers soule,' sayd our k*ing*,
 ' And by him *that* dyed on the roode,

30 ' Thou shalt neu*er* haue Lancashire nor Cheshire
  right
 Att thy owne obedyence for to bee!
Cowards in a feild felly will fight
 Againe to win the victorye.'

31 ' Wee were neu*er* cowards,' said the erle,
 ' By him *that* deerlye dyed on tree !
Who brought in y*our* father att Milford Hauen?
 K*ing* Henery the Seuenth forsooth was hee.

32 ' Thorow the towne of Fortune wee did him
  bring,
 And soe convayd him to Shrewsburye,
And soe crowned him a noble k*ing*;
 And Rich*ar*d *that* day wee deemed to dye.'

33 Our prince was greatlye moued at *that* worde,
 And returned him hastilye againe;
To comfort the erle came on the other hande
 The doughtye Edward, Duk of Buckingam.

34 ' Plucke vp thy hart, brother Stanlye,
 And lett nothing greeiue thee!
For I dare lay my liffe to wedd
 It is a false writing of the Erle of Surrey.

35 ' Sith K*ing* Rich*ar*d felle, he neu*er* loued thee,
 For thy vnckle slue his father deere,
And deerlye deemed him to dye ;
 S*ir* Chr*isto*pher Savage his standard away did
  beare.'

36 ' Alas, brother,' sayd the Erle of Darbye,
 ' Woe be the time *that* I was made k*night*,
Or were ruler of any lande,
 Or euer had manhood in feild to fight !

37 ' Soe bold men in battle as were they,
    Forsooth had neither lord nor swaine;
Ffarwell my vnckle, Sir Edward Stanley!
    For well I wott that thou art slaine.

38 ' Surelye whiles thy liffe wold last
    Thou woldest neuer shrinke beside the plaine;
Nor Iohn Stanley, that child soe younge;
    Well I wott that thou art slaine.

39 ' Ffarwell Kighlye ! coward was thou neuer ;
    Old Sir Henery, the good knight,
I left the[e] ruler of Latham,
    To be [my] deputye both day and night.

40 ' Ffarwell Townlye, that was soe true !
    And that noble Ashton of Middelton !
And the sad Southwarke, that euer was sure!
    For well I wott that thou art gone.

41 ' Farwell Ashton vnde[r] Line !
    And manlye Mullenax ! for thou art slaine ;
For doubtlesse while your liues wold last
    You wold never shun beside the plaine.

42 ' Ffarwell Adderton with the leaden mall !
    Well I know thow art deemed to dye ;
I may take my leaue att you all ;
    The flower of manhoode is gone from mee.

43 ' Ffarwell Sir Iohn Booth of Barton, knight !
    Well I know that thou art slaine;
While thy liffe wold last to fight,
    Thou wold neuer be-sids the plaine.

44 ' Ffarwell Butler, and Sir Bode !
    Sure you haue beene euer to mee ;
And soe I know that [still] you wold,
    If that vnslaine you bee.

45 ' Ffarwell Christopher Savage, the wighte !
    Well I know that thou art slaine ;
For whiles thy life wold last to fight,
    Thou wold neuer besids the plaine.

46 ' Ffarwell Dutton, and Sir Dane !
    You haue beene euer trew to mee;
Ffarwell the Baron of Kinderton !
    Beside the feild thou wold not flee.

47 ' Ffarwell Ffitton of Gawsworth !
    Either thou art taken or slaine;
Doubtelesse while thy life wold last,
    Thou wold neuer beside the plaine.'

48 As they stood talkinge together there,
    The duke and the erle trulye,
Came ffor to comfort him th[e] trew Talbott,
    And the noble Erle of Shrewsburye.

49 ' Plucke vp thy hart, sonne Thomas, and be merry,
    And let noe tydings greeve thee !
Am not I godfather to our king ?
    My owne god-sonne forsooth is hee.'

50 He tooke the Duke of Buckingam by the arme,
    And the Erle of Sh[r]ewsburye by the other :
' To part with you it is my harme ;
    Farwell, my father and my brother !

51 ' Farwell Lancaster, that litle towne !
    Farwell now for euer and aye !
Many pore men may pray for my soule
    When they lye weeping in the lane.

52 ' Ffarwell Latham, that bright bower !
    Nine towers thou beares on hye,
And other nine thou beares on the outer walls ;
    Within thee may be lodged kings three.

53 ' Ffarwell Knowsley, that litle tower
    Vnderneth the holtes soe hore !
Euer when I thinke on that bright bower,
    Wite me not though my hart be sore.

54 ' Ffarwell Tocstaffe, that trustye parke,
    And the fayre riuer that runes there beside,
There I was wont to chase the hinde and hart!
    Now therin will I neuer abide.

55 ' Ffarwell bold Birkhead ! there was I boorne,
    Within the abbey and that monesterye;
The sweet covent for mee may mourne;
    I gaue to you the tythe of Beeston, trulye.

56 ' Ffarwell Westchester for euermore !
    And the Watter Gate ! it is my owne;
I gaue a mace for the serieant to weare,
    To waite on the maior, as it is knowne.

57 ' Will I neuer come that citye within ;
    But, sonne Edward, thou may clayme it of
      right:
Ffarwell Westhardin! I may thee [call] myn,
    Knight and lord I was of great might.

58 ' Sweete sonne Edward, white bookes thou make,
    And euer haue pittye on the pore cominaltye!
Ffarwell Hope and Hopedale !
    Mould and Moulesdale, God be with thee !
I may take leaue with a sorry cheere,
    For within thee will I neuer bee.'

59 As they stoode talking together there,
    The duke and the lords trulye,
Came Iamie Garsed, a yeman of the guard,
    That had beene brought vp with the Erle of
      Derbye ;
Like the devill with his fellowes he had fared,
    He s[t]icked two, and wounded three.

60 After, with his sword drawen in his hand,
  He fled to the noble Earle of Derbye :
' Stand vp, Iamye ! ' the erle said,
  ' These tydings nothing liketh mee.

61 ' I haue seene the day I cold haue saued thee,
  Such thirty men if thou hads slaine,
And now if I shold speake for thee,
  Sure thow weret to be slaine.

62 ' I will once desire my bretheren eche one
  That they will speake for thee.'
He prayd the Duke of Buckingam,
  And alsoe the Erle of Shrewsburye,

63 Alsoe my lord Fitzwater soe wise,
  And the good Lord Willowbye,
Sir Rice Ap Thomas, a knight of price ;
  They all spoke for Long Iamye.

64 They had not stayd but a litle while there,
  The duke and the erles in their talkinge,
But straight to the erle came a messenger,
  That came latelye from the king,

65 And bad *that* Long Iamie shold be sent ;
  There shold neither be grith nor grace,
But on a boughe he shold be hanged,
  In middest the feild, before the erles face.

66 ' If *that* be soe,' said the Erle of Derbye,
  ' I trust our prince will better bee ;
Such tydings maketh my hart full heavye
  Afore his Grace when *that* wee bee.'

67 The Duke of Buckingam tooke Iamie by the one
    arme,
  And the Erle of Shrewsburye by the other ;
Afore them they put the King of Man,
  It was the Erle of Darbye and noe other.

68 The lord Fitzwater followed fast,
  And soe did the lord Willowbyghe ;
The comfortable Cobham mad great hast ;
  All went with the noble Erle of Derbye.

69 The hind Hassall hoved on fast,
  With the lusty Lealand trulye ;
Soe did Sir Alexander Osbaston,
  Came in with the Erle of Derbye.

70 The royall Ratcliffe, *that* rude was neuer,
  And the trustye Trafford, keene to trye,
And wight Warburton, out of Cheshire,
  All came with the Erle of Darbye.

71 Sir Rice ap Thomas, a knight of Wales,
  Came with a feirce menye ;
He bent his bowes on the bent to abyde,
  And cleane vnsett the gallow-tree.

72 When they came afore our king,
  Lowlye they kneeled vpon their knees ;
The first word *that* our prince did myn,
  ' Welcome, dukes and erles, to mee !

73 ' The most welcome hither of all
  Is our owne traitor, Long Iamie :
Iamie, how durst thou be soe bold
  As in our presence for to bee ?

74 ' To slay thy bretheren within their hold !
  Thou was sworne to them, and they to thee.'
Then began Long Iamie to speake bold :
  ' My leege, if it please your Grace to pardon mee,

75 ' When I was to my supper sett,
  They called me coward to my face,
And of their talking they wold not lett,
  And thus with them I vpbrayded was.

76 ' The bade me flee from them apace
  To *that* coward the Erle of Derbye !
When I was litle, and had small grace,
  He was my helpe and succour trulye.

77 ' He tooke [me] from my father deere,
  And keeped me within his woone
Till I was able of my selfe
  Both to shoote and picke the stone.

78 ' Then after, vnder Grenwich, vpon a day
  A Scottish minstrell came to thee,
And brought a bow of yew to drawe,
  And all the guard might not stirr *that* tree.

79 ' Then the bow was giuen to the Erle of Derbye,
  And the erle deliuered it to mee ;
Seven shoots before your face I shott,
  And att the eighth in sunder it did flee.

80 ' Then I bad the Scott bow downe his face,
  And gather vp the bow, and bring it to his
    king ;
Then it liked your noble Grace
  Into your guard for me to bring.

81 ' Sithen I haue liued a merry liffe,
  I thanke your Grace and the Erle of Darbye ;
But to haue the erle rebuked thus,
  That my bringer-vp forsooth was hee,

82 ' I had rather suffer death,' he said,
  ' Then be false to the erle *that* was true to me.'
' Stand vp Iamie ! ' said our king,
  ' Haue heere my charter, I giue it thee.

83 ' Let me haue noe more fighting of thee
  Whilest thou art within Ffrance lande.'
' Then one thing you must grant,' said Iamie,
  ' *That* your word theron may stand :

84 'Whosoe rebuketh Lancashire or Chesshire
  Shortlye shall be deemed to dye.'
  Our king comanded a cry i-wis
  To be proclaimed hastilye.

85 'If the dukes and erles kneele on their knees,
  Itt getteth on sturr the comonaltye ;
  If wee be vpbrayded thus,
  Manye a man is like to dye.'
  The king said, He that rebuket Lancashire or
      Cheshire
  Shall haue his iudgment on the next tree.

86 Then soe they were in rest
  For the space of a night, as I weene,
  And on the other day, without leasinge,
  There came a messenger from the queene.

87 And when he came before our king,
  Lowlye he kneeled vpon his knee,
  And said, Chr[i]st thee saue, our noble king,
  And thy speed this day may bee !
  Heere greeteth thee well thy loue and liking,
  And our honorable queene and ladye,

88 And biddeth you in Ffrance to be glad,
  For slaine is your brother-in-law King Iamie,
  And att louelye London he shalbe found,
  My comlye prince, in the presence of thee.

89 Then bespake our comlye prince,
  Saiinge, Who did fight and who did flee ?
  And who bare them best of the Mount of Fflod-
      den ?
  And who is false, and who is true to mee?

90 'Lancashire and Cheshire,' said the messenger,
  ' They haue done the deed with their hand ;
  Had not the Erle of Derbye beene to thee true,
  In great aduenture had beene all England.'

91 Then bespake our prince on hye,
  ' Sir Raphe Egertton, my marshall I make thee ;
  Sir Edward Stanley, thou shalt be a lord,
  Lord Mounteagle thou shalt bee.

92 ' Yonge Iohn Stanley shalbe a knight,
  And he is well worthy for to bee.'
  The Duke of Buckingham the tydings hard,
  And shortlye ran to the Erle of Darbye :

93 ' Brother, plucke vp thy hart and be merrye,
  And let noe tydings greeve thee !
  Yesterday, thy men called cowerds were,
  And this day they haue woone the victorye.'

94 The duke tooke the erle by the arme,
  And thus they ledden to the prince [trulye].

Seven roods of ground the king he came,
  And sayd, ' Welcome, King of Man and Erle of
      Derbye !
  The thing that I haue taken from thee,
  I geeve it to thee againe whollye.

95 'The manrydden of Lancashire and Cheshire
      both,
  Att thy bidding euer to bee ;
  Ffor those men beene true, Thomas, indeed ;
  They beene trew both to thee and mee.'

96 ' Yett one thing greeveth me,' said the erle,
  ' And in my hart maketh me heavye,
  This day to heare the wan the feild,
  And yesterday cowards to bee.'

97 ' It was a wronge wryting,' sayd our king,
  ' That came ffrom the Erle of Surrey ;
  But I shall him teach his prince to know,
  If euer wee come in our countrye.'

98 ' I aske noe more,' sayd the noble erle,
  ' Ffor all that my men haue done trulye,
  But that I may be iudge my selfe
  Of that noble Erle of Surreye.'

99 ' Stand vp, Thomas !' sayd our prince,
  ' Lord Marshall I make thee,
  And thou shalt be iudge thy selfe,
  And as thou saiest, soe shall it bee.'

100 ' Then is his liffe saued,' sayd the erle,
  ' I thanke Iesu and your Grace trulye ;
  If my vnckle slew his father deere,
  He wold haue venged him on mee.'

101 ' Thou art verry patient,' sayd our king ;
  ' The Holy Ghost remaines, I thinke, in thee ;
  On the south side of Turnay thou shalt stande,
  With my godfather the Erle of Shrewsburye.'

102 And soe to that seege forth the went,
  The noble Shrewsburye and the Erle of Derbye,
  And the laid seege vnto the walls,
  And wan the towne in dayes three.

103 Thus was Lancashire and Cheshire rebuked
  Thorow the pollicye of the Erle of Surrey.
  Now God, that was in Bethlem borne,
  And for vs dyed vpon a tree,
  Saue our noble prince that wereth the crowne,
  And haue mercy on the Erles soule of Derbye !

_____

104 And then bespake our noble king,
  These were the words said hee ;
  Sayes, Come, Alexander Ratcliffe, knight,
  Come hither now vnto mee,

Ffor thou shalt goe on the south side of Tournay,
   And with thee thou shalt haue thousands three.

105 Then forth is gone Alexander Ratcliffe, knight;
   With him he leads men thousand three;
   But or ere three dayes were come to an end,
   The Ffrenchmen away did flee.

106 Then King Henery planted three hundred English-
   men
   That in the citye shold abyde and bee :
   Alexander Ratcliffe, he wold haue mad him gouer-
   nour there,
   But he forsooke it certainelye,
   And made great intreatye to our king
   That he might come into England in his com-
   pa[n]ye.

---

107 And then bespake noble King Henery,
   And these were the words said hee :
   Sayes, Come hither, Rowland Egerton, knight,
   And come thou hither vnto mee ;

108 For the good service that thou hast done,
   Well rewarded shalt thou bee.
   Then forth came Rowland Egerton,
   And kneeled downe vpon his knee.

109 Saies, If it like your Grace, my gracious king,
   The reward that you will bestow on mee,
   I wold verry gladlye haue it in Cheshire,
   Ffor that's att home in my owne country.

110 And then bespake him noble King Henery,
   And these were the words said hee;
   'I haue nothing, Egerton, in all Cheshire
   That wilbe any pleasure for thee
   But fiue mills stands att Chester townes end ;
   The gone all ouer the water of Dee.'

111 Still kneeled Rowland Egerton,
   And did not rise beside his knee ;
   Sayes, If it like your Highnesse, my gracious king,
   A milner called I wold neuer bee.

112 And then bespake him noble King Harrye,
   These were the words said hee;
   Saith, I'le make mine avow to God,
   And alsoe to the Trinitye,
   There shall neuer be king of England
   But the shalbe miller of the mills of Dee !

113 I haue noe other thing, Egerton,
   That wilbe for thy delight;
   I will giue thee the forrest of Snoden in Wales,
   Wherby thou may giue the horne and lease ;

In siluer it wilbe verry white,
   And meethinkes shold thee well please.

114 .   .   .   .
   Still kneeled Rowland Egerton on his knee ;
   He sayes, If itt like your Highnes, my gracious
   king,
   A ranger called wold I neuer bee.

115 Then our king was wrathe, and rose away,
   Sayes, I thinke, Egerton, nothing will please
   thee.
   And then bespake him, Rowland Egerton,
   Kneeling yet still on his knee :

116 Sayes, If itt like your Highnesse, my gracious
   king,
   That your Highnes pleasure will now heer
   mee,
   In Cheshire there lyes a litle grange-house,
   In the lordsh[i]ppe of Rydeley it doth lyee.

117 A tanner there in it did dwell;
   My leege, it is but a cote with one eye,
   And if your Grace wold bestow this on mee,
   Ffull well it wold pleasure me.

118 Then bespake our noble King Harrye,
   And these were the words saith hee ;
   Saies, Take thee that grange-house, Egerton,
   And the lordshippe of Rydley, faire and free.

119 For the good service thou hast to me done,
   I will giue it vnto thy heyres and thee :
   And thus came Row[land] Egertton
   To the lordshippe of Rydley, faire and free.

---

120 This noble King Harry wan great victoryes in
   France,
   Thorrow the might that Christ Jesus did him
   send.

   First our king wan Hans and Gynye,
   And [two] walled townes, the truth to say;
   And afterwards wan other two townes,
   The names of them were called Turwin and
   Turnay.

121 High Bullen and Base Bullen he wan alsoe,
   And other village-townes many a one,
   And Muttrell he wan alsoe —
   The cronicles of this will not lye —
   And kept to Calleis, plainsht with Englishmen,
   Vnto the death that he did dye.

a. 4². soliders. 16⁴. them. 17⁸. 8ᵗʰ. 20⁸. wright. 20⁴. vs 2. 31⁴. 7ᵗʰ. 35¹. feele.

35⁴. xopher Savage, *and again* 45¹: always *for* away.

41¹. vndeline. 45¹. K*night for* wighte. 52²˒³. 9. 52⁴. 3. 53². whore. 53⁴. white. 56⁸. giue : pro *for* for. 57². wright. 58¹. Lookes *for* bookes. 2d Parte *at* 59⁸. 59⁶. 2 : 3. 61². 30. 65¹. Ianie. 79⁸. 7. 79⁴. 8ᵗʰ: breake *for* flee, *cf.* **b, c.** 83⁴. ward : *cf.* **b.** 84⁸. I cry *for* a cry: a *in* **b, c.** 89⁴. who his *for the first* who is. 94⁸. 7. 95¹. Maurydden. 102⁴, 104⁴. 3. 103. 121 *in the MS.* 104⁶. 1000⁸˒ 3. 105². 1000ᵈ 3. 106¹. 300ᵈ. 110⁵. 5. 112⁶. he *for* the ? 117⁴. me pleasure. 120⁵. 2. And *for* & *always.*

b, c. *In stanzas of eight lines.* **b.** A ballate of the Battalle of Ffloden Ffeeld betweene the Earle of Surrey and the King of Scots. **c.** Flowden Feilde.

Trivial variations of spelling are not regarded.

1¹. of the. 1². our fortune and chaunce. 1⁸. tell of. **b.** tythandes. **c.** tythance. 2². surly *after* And : his *wanting.* 3¹. at *for* to. 3². **b.** lorde *for* leed. **b, c.** great *for* high. 3⁴. **b.** found Henry our kynge. 4⁵⁻⁷⁶. *Two stanzas, the first ending at* 6². 4⁵. the prince. 4⁶. **c.** Iesu. 5². he kneeled vppon. 5⁴. King *wanting.* 6⁴. and *for the second* my. 7⁸. biddethe. 7⁵. ye. 8². *Prefix* And. 8⁸. bare : uppon, upon, *for* of. **b.** them *for* him. 9². they bene both. 9⁸. non *for* nere. **b.** belonged. 10¹. **b.** a stand. 10². And he. 10⁴. *First* he *wanting.* **b.** tould (*corrected from* coulde ?) *for* found. 11¹. **b.** noble *for* comlye. 11². And he. 12¹. **b.** C. and L. **b, c** *add* bothe. 12². the *wanting.* 12⁴. Not a. 13⁸. King *wanting.* 13⁴. **b,** And it, **c,** Yf it, like you my souereigne lord. 14¹. **c.** bene. 14². **c.** tythandes. 15⁸. **b.** L. nor C. mene. 15⁴. **b.** wold euer. 16². on *for* vpon a. 16⁸. For now : greatest *for* most. 16⁴. then served they *for* they serued then. 17⁴. And *for* If. 18¹. ye : any *wanting.* 18⁸. **c.** ye. 18⁴. **b.** whether (*altered from* wher) that wee are. 19¹. **b.** rounded. **b, c.** anon *added to* king. 19². And *wanting.* **b.** Sayenge. 19⁸. to thee *wanting.* 21¹. **b.** neuer a : besydes. 21⁴. **b.** right angerly. 22¹. other syde. 22⁴. lowly he. 23⁸. **b.** our king sayde. **c.** speake. 23⁴. **b.** Was *for* Sayd. 24¹. **c.** L. and C. 24². was *for* were. 24⁸. nowe *inserted before* are. 24⁴. **b.** Neuer a one of them. **c.** Neuer one of them ys (*but are, in a later hand*).

25¹. **c.** then *for* free. 26⁴. **b.** fled a foote. 27². **b.** to *for* itt. 28¹. to brene, bren. 28². *First* me *wanting.* 28⁸. *First* I *wanting* : all to. **b.** gates. 28⁴. **b.** Bothe the. 29¹. walles they. 29⁸. then sayd. 30¹. and *for* nor. 30². **c.** thyne. 30⁸. **b.** freely *for* felly. 31². for me *for* on tree. 32². **b.** To the towne of. 32⁸. we *after* soe. 33². **b.** vppon the same *for* againe. **c.** in same, *but* on the *for* in, *in a later hand.* 33⁸. side, syde, *for* hande. 34⁴. **b.** duke *for* erle. 35¹. Synce : feelde, feylde. 35². **c.** thyne : theare, there *for* deere. 35⁴. awaye *for* always. 36⁸. **c.** therby *added by a later hand.* 37⁸. **c.** myne. 37⁴. **c.** art *altered to* weart. 38¹. whileste that, whiles that. 38². schunte besides. 38⁴. nowe *before* that. 39¹. **b.** for *before* coward. **b, c.** none *for* neuer. 39⁴. be my. 40². the *for* that. 40⁸. **b.** Sotheworthe. **c.** Sothewarke *altered to* Sotheworthe. 41⁸. **c.** whilest. 41⁴. schunte. 42¹. **b.** Anderton. 42⁸. leaue nowe. **b.** at *altered to* of. 43⁸. For whileste, For whiles. 43⁴. wouldeste (**c** woulde) neuer beside the playne. 44¹. **b.** Bolde. 44². ye. 44⁸. stylle, still. 44⁴. Vnslayne nowe yf, (**b**) that you bee, (**c**) you had bee. 45¹. weighte, wighte. 45⁸. **b.** whileste. 45⁴. woldeste, wouldest : beside. 46¹. Done, Downe. 46². Ye. 46⁴. **b.** woldeste. 47¹. **b.** Seton *altered to* Fitton. 47². Other. 47⁸. *Prefix* For : whiles. 47⁴. woldeste, wouldest. 48⁸. ffor *wanting.* 49². **c.** tythands. 49⁴. myne. 51⁴. **c.** lawne. 52². beareste, bearest. 52⁸. in the vtter. 53². whore. 53⁴. Wyte. 54². ronnethe, renneth. **b.** besydes. 54⁸. **b.** was I. 54⁴. **b.** I will. 55¹. Berkenhede, Byrkhead *altered to* Byrkenhead. 55⁴. **c.** the *wanting.* 56². myn, myne. 56⁸. gaue : pro (*or* for) *wanting.* 57². mayeste, maiest. **c.** yt clayme. 57⁸. **c.** call *after* may, *in a later hand.* 58¹. bookes, bokes. 58². comentye, comyntie. 58⁸. Hopesdalle. 58⁴. Mouldesdalle, Mouldesdale. 58⁵. take my : hevie, heavie, *for* sorry. 59⁸. Iames : Garsye, Garsyde. 59⁶. stycked, sticked. 60¹. **b.** And after. 60⁸. **b.** Iames. 60⁴, 66⁸. **c.** tythandes. 61². hadeste, had. 61⁴. wearte for, were for. 62². will nowe. 63¹. **b.** Fitzwaters. **c.** Feighwater *altered to* Fitzwater. 63⁸, 71¹. **c.** vp *for* ap. 63⁴. And all they spake. 64¹. standen. 64⁸. But *wanting.* 65¹, 73⁸, 74⁸, 82⁸. **b.** Iames. 65¹. **c.** send. 65⁴. Amydeste. 66¹. **c.** soe *wanting.*

66³. **b.** makes. 67⁴. non.

68¹. **c.** Feighwater. **b.** he followed.

69¹. **b.** hied *for* hoved. 69³. **b.** Osboldstone.

69⁴. **b.** come. 70³. **b.** wighty.

71². came forthe even with. 71³. **c.** bend.

71⁴. gallowes. 72¹. When as. **b.** the king.

72³. **b.** minge. 72⁴. *Prefix* Said : vnto.

73¹. *Prefix* But.

73². **c.** our owne *altered to* yondere.

74². **c.** waste. 74⁴. lyke, like, *for* please.

75⁴. vpbrayded that I *for* I vpbrayded.

77¹. tooke me. 77². **b.** kepte. 78³. of vewe.

79⁴. **b.** did flee. **c.** be *altered to* flie.

80ᴸ·². **b.** Then I layd the bowe one his face, and bade him gather vpe the bowe, *etc.* **c.** geder.

80⁴. for *wanting.* 82¹. had lyuer, leaver.

83². **c.** whiles. **b.** Frenche. 83³. ye.

83⁴. **b.** word. 84³. Our prince : a cry.

85². **b.** settethe one and. 85³. Yf that.

85⁵. rebuketh. **b.** and *for* or. 86¹. stylle at rest.

86². **b.** as *wanting.* 87¹. **b.** prince *for* king.

87². **b.** kneene, *rhyming with* 86²·⁴.

87³. prince *for* king.

87⁴. This owere (**c** our) noble kynge this (**c** thy) speede may be.

87⁵. greetes (**c** gretteth) yow well your lyffe and spouse (**c** liking).

87⁶. Your honorable : fair ladye. 88¹. for to.

88². **b.** in-law *wanting.* 89². And sayd.

89³. vppon, vpon, the *for* of the.

89⁴. And who weare, were, *bis.*

91¹. **b.** on highe, *originally; altered in the same hand to* with ane highe word.

91⁴. Ye, yea, *prefixed :* shalt thou.

92². As *for* And.

92³. **b.** thes *for* the. **c.** tythands. **b.** *adds* righte *at the end.*

93¹. Brother *after* hart. 93². **c.** tythandes.

93³. **b.** this (*written upon* thy) men cowards were they. **c.** cowardes called *for* called cowerds.

93⁴. they *wanting.* 94¹. **b.** him *for* the erle.

94² *adds* trulye *at the end.* **b.** and lede him *for* thus they ledden.

94⁵. haue from the taken. 94⁶. agayne to thee.

95¹. **b.** marshallynge. **c.** manratten. **b.** men *for* both.

95². for to. **b** *omits* euer. 95³. these. **b.** be.

95⁴. **b.** be. 96¹. **b.** the earle saide. 96⁴. for to.

97¹. **b.** our kinge sayd.

97⁴. And *for* If.

98¹. **b.** the earle nowe.

98³. **b.** That I my selfe his iudgmente maye pronounce. **c.** But that I gyve iudgment my selfe.

99². **b.** will I. **c.** that I shall.

99³. shalt geue (gyue) the iudgment.

100¹. **b.** Then sayd the earle, saved is his lyfe.

100³. If *wanting.* 101¹. **b.** our kyng sware.

101². remayneth : I thinke *wanting.*

101⁴. **c.** the *wanting.* 102¹. **b.** they ganged.

102³. **b** *adds* batled *at the end.*

102⁴. **b.** toweres. **c.** townes. **b, c.** within.

103⁵. **b.** weres.

103⁶. **b.** And shewe thie mersye one the Earle of Derby.

104–121 *wanting.*

169

JOHNIE ARMSTRONG

A. a. 'A Northern Ballet,' Wit Restord in severall Select Poems not formerly publisht, London, 1658, p. 30, in Facetiæ, London, 1817, I, 132. **b.** 'A Northern Ballad,' Wit and Drollery, London, 1682, p. 57.

B. a. 'John Arm-strongs last Good - Night,' etc., Wood, 401, fol. 93 b, Bodleian Library. **b.** Pepys Ballads, II, 133, No 117. **c.** 'Johnny Armstrongs last Good-Night,' Old Ballads, 1723, I, 170.

C. 'Johnie Armstrang,' The Ever Green, 1724, II, 190.

A b is not found in Wit and Drollery, 1661; it is literally repeated in Dryden's Miscellanies, 1716, III, 307. B is in the Roxburghe collection, III, 513, the Bagford, I, 64, II, 94, and no doubt in others. It was printed by Evans, 1777, II, 64, and by Rit-son, English Songs, 1783, II, 322. C was printed by Herd, 1769, p. 260, 1776 (with spelling changed), I, 13; by Ritson, Scotish Songs, 1794, II, 7; by Scott, 1802, I, 49, 1833, I, 407 (with a slight change or two).

'Ihonne Ermistrangis dance' is mentioned

in The Complaynt of Scotland, 1549, ed. Murray, p. 66. The tune of C is No 356 of Johnson's Museum; see further Stenhouse, in the edition of 1853, IV, 335 f.

Of his copy C, Ramsay says: "This is the true old ballad, never printed before. . . . This I copied from a gentleman's mouth of the name of Armstrang, who is the sixth generation from this John. He tells me this was ever esteemd the genuine ballad, the common one false." Motherwell remarks, Minstrelsy, p. lxii, note 3: "The common ballad alluded to by Ramsay [A, B] is the one, however, which is in the mouths of the people. His set I never heard sung or recited; but the other frequently." A manuscript copy of B, entitled Gillnokie, communicated to Percy by G. Paton, Edinburgh, December 4, 1778, which has some of the peculiar readings of B a, introduces the 27th stanza of C * in place of 12, and has 'Away, away, thou traitor strong' for 12^1. A copy in Buchan's MSS, I, 61, 'The Death of John Armstrong,' has the first half of C 18 and also of C 19 (with very slight variations). Another Scottish copy, which was evidently taken from recitation, introduces C 23 after 14.†

Both forms of the ballad had been too long printed to allow validity to any known recited copy. Besides the three already mentioned, there is one in Kinloch's MSS, V, 263, which intermixes two stanzas from Johnie Scot. The Scottish copies naturally do not allow 'Scot' to stand in 17^3. Paton's substitutes 'chiell'; the others 'man,' and so a broadside reprinted by Maidment, Scotish Ballads and Songs, Historical and Traditionary, I, 130.

The Armstrongs were people of consideration in Liddesdale from the end, or perhaps from the middle, of the fourteenth century, and by the sixteenth had become the most important sept, as to numbers, in that region, not only extending themselves over a large part of the Debateable Land,‡ but spreading also into Eskdale, Ewesdale, Wauchopedale, and Annandale. The Earl of Northumberland, in 1528, puts the power of the Armstrongs, with their adherents, above three thousand horsemen. Mangerton, in Liddesdale, on the east bank of the Liddel, a little north of its junction with the Kersope, was the seat of the chief. John Armstrong, known later as Gilnockie, a brother of Thomas, laird of Mangerton, is first heard of in 1525. Removing from Liddesdale early in the century, as it is thought, he settled on the church lands of Canonby, and at a place called The Hollows, on the west side of the Esk, built a tower, which still remains.§

---

* 'Where got thou these targits, Jony,
   That hings so low down by thy knee ?'
 'I got them, cukel king, in the field,
   Where thow and thy men durst not come see.'

† This copy I have in MS. and have not noted, neither can I remember, how I came by it, but it is probably a transcript from recent print. It diverges from the ordinary text more than any that I have seen. After 17 comes this stanza (cf. 'Robin Hood rescuing Three Squires,' No 140, B 29):

   They took the gallows frae the slack,
     An there they set it on a plain,
   An there they hanged Johnnie Armstrong,
     Wi fifty of his warlike men.

18–20, 23 are wanting. A "pretty little boy," in what corresponds to 21, 22, says, 'Johnnie Armstrong you'll never see,' and the lady ends the ballad with:

   If that be true, my pretty little boy,
     Aye the news you tell to me,
   You'll be the heir to a' my lands,
     You an your young son after thee.

‡ A tract on the extreme western border, beginning between the mouths of the Sark and Esk and stretching north and east eight miles, with a greatest breadth of four miles. The particulars of the boundaries are given from an old roll in Nicolson and Burn's Westmorland and Cumberland, I, xvi, and as follows by Mr T. J. Carlyle, The Debateable Land, Dumfries, 1868, p. 1 : "bounded on the west by the Sark and Pingleburn, on the north by the Irvine burn, Tarras, and Reygill, on the east by the Mereburn, Liddal, and Esk, and on the south by the Solway Frith." The land was parted between England and Scotland in 1552, with no great gain to good order for the half century succeeding.

§ It has been maintained that there was a Gilnockie tower on the eastern side of the Esk, a very little lower than the Hollows tower. "We can also inform our readers that Giltknock Hall was situate on a small rocky island on the river Esk below the Langholm, the remains of which are to be seen:" Crito in the Edinburgh Evening Courant, March 8, 1773. "Many vestiges of strongholds can be traced within the parish, although there is only one, near the new bridge already described, that makes an appearance at this point, its walls being yet entire:" Statistical Account of Canoby, Sinclair, XIV, 420.

Sir John Sinclair, 1795, says, in a note to this last pas-

Others of the Armstrongs erected strong houses in the neighborhood. Lord Dacre, the English warden of the West Marches, essayed to surprise these strengths in the early part of 1528, but was foiled by John and Sym Armstrong, though he had a force of two thousand men. The Armstrongs, if nominally Scots, were so far from being " in due obeysaunce " that, at a conference of commissioners of both realms in November of the year last named, the representatives of the Scottish king could not undertake to oblige them to make redress for injuries done the English, though a peace depended upon this condition. Perhaps the English border suffered more than the Scottish from their forays (and the English border, we are informed, was not nearly so strong as the Scottish, neither in " capetayns nor the commynnaltie "), but how little Scotland was spared appears from what Sym Armstrong, the laird of Whitlaugh, in the same year again, told the Earl of Northumberland: that himself and his adherents had laid waste in the said realm sixty miles, and laid down thirty parish churches, and that there was not one in the realm of Scotland dare remedy the same. Indeed, our John, Thomas of Mangerton, Sym of Whitlaugh, and the rest, seem to be fairly enough described in an English indictment as " enemies of the king of England, and traitors, fugitives, and felons of the king of Scots." *

Other measures having failed, King James the Fifth, in the summer of 1530, took the pacifying of his borders into his own hand, and for this purpose levied an army of from eight to twelve thousand men. The particulars of this noted expedition are thus given by Lindsay of Pitscottie.†

" The king . . . made a convention at Edinburgh with all the lords and barons, to consult how he might best stanch theiff and river within his realm, and to cause the commons to live in peace and rest, which long time had been perturbed before. To this effect he gave charge to all earls, lords, barons, freeholders and gentlemen, to compeir at Edinburgh with a month's victual, to pass with the king to daunton the thieves of Teviotdale and Annandale, with all other parts of the realm; also the king desired all gentlemen that had dogs that were good to bring them with them to hunt in the said bounds, which the most part of the noblemen of the Highlands did, such as the earls of Huntly, Argyle, and Athol, who brought their deer-hounds with them and hunted with his majesty. These lords, with many other lords and gentlemen, to the number of twelve thousand men, assembled at Edinburgh, and therefrom went with the king's grace to Meggat-land, in the which bounds were slain at that time eighteen score of deer. After this hunting the king hanged John Armstrong, laird of Kilnokie; which many a Scotsman heavily lamented, for he was a doubtit man, and as good a chieftain as ever was upon the borders, either of Scotland or of England. And albeit he was a loose-living man, and sustained the number of twenty-four well-horsed able gentlemen with him, yet he never molested no Scotsman.‡ But it is said, from the Scots border to Newcastle of England, there was not one, of whatsoever estate, but paid to this John Armstrong a tribute, to be free of his cumber, he was so doubtit in England. So when he entered in before the king, he came very reverently, with his foresaid number very richly appareled, trusting that in respect he had come to the king's grace willingly and voluntarily, not being taken nor apprehended by the king, he should obtain the more favor. But when the king saw him and his men so gorgeous

---

sage, that the spot of ground at the east end of " the new bridge " is, "indeed, called to this day, Gill-knocky, but it does not exhibit the smallest vestige of mason-work." Mr. T. J. Carlyle, The Debateable Land, p. 17, gives us to understand that the foundations of the tower were excavated and removed when the bridge was built; but this does not appear to be convincingly made out.

* The History of Liddesdale, Eskdale, Ewesdale, Wau-

chopedale, and The Debateable Land, by Robert Bruce Armstrong, 1883, pp 177 f, 227 f, 245, 259 f; Appendix, pp. xxvi, xxxi.

† The Cronicles of Scotland, etc., edited by J. G. Dalyell, 1814, II, 341 ff. (partially modernized, for more comfortable reading).

‡ Wherein, if this be true, John differed much from Sym.

in their apparel, and so many braw men under a tyrant's commandment, throwardlie he turned about his face, and bade take that tyrant out of his sight, saying, What wants yon knave that a king should have? But when John Armstrong perceived that the king kindled in a fury against him, and had no hope of his life, notwithstanding of many great and fair offers which he offered to the king — that is, that he should sustain himself, with forty gentlemen, ever ready to await upon his majesty's service, and never to take a penny of Scotland nor Scotsmen; secondly, that there was not a subject in England, duke, earl, lord, or baron, but within a certain day he should bring any of them to his majesty, quick or dead — he, seeing no hope of the king's favor towards him, said very proudly, I am but a fool to seek grace at a graceless face. But had I known, sir, that ye would have taken my life this day, I should have lived upon the borders in despite of King Harry and you both; for I know King Harry would down weigh my best horse with gold to know that I were condemned to die this day. So he was led to the scaffold, and he and all his men hanged."

Buchanan's account is, that the king undertook an expedition for the suppressing of freebooters in July, 1530, with an army of about eight thousand men, and encamped at Ewes water, near which was the hold of John Armstrong, a chief of a band of thieves, who had struck such terror into the parts adjacent that even the English for many miles about paid him tribute. Under enticement of the king's officers, John set out to pay a visit to the king with about fifty horsemen, both unarmed and without a safe-conduct, and on his way fell in with a body of scouts, who took him to their master as a pretended prisoner, and he and most of his men were hanged. The authors of his death averred that Armstrong had promised the English to put the neighboring Scots territory under their sway,

if they would make it for his interest; whereas the English were extremely pleased at his death, because they were rid of a redoubtable enemy.*

Bishop Lesley says simply that in the month of June (apparently 1529) the king passed to the borders with a great army, where he caused forty-eight of the most noble thieves, with John Armstrong, their captain, to be taken, who being convict of theft, reiff, slaughter, and treason, were all hanged upon growing trees.†

Another account gives us positively and definitely to understand that the Armstrongs were not secured without artifice. " On the eighth of June the principals of all the surnames of the clans on the borders came to the king, upon hope of a proclamation proclaimed in the king's name that they should all get their lives if they would come in and submit themselves in the king's will. And so, upon this hope, John Armstrong, who kept the castle of Langholm (a brother of the laird of Mangerton's, a great thief and oppressor, and one that kept still with him four and twenty well-horsed men), came in to the king; and another called Ill Will Armstrong, another stark thief, with sundry of the Scotts and Elliotts, came all forward to the camp where the king was, in hope to get their pardons. But no sooner did the king perceive them, and that they were come afar off, when direction was given presently to enclose them round about; the which was done, accordingly, and were all apprehended, to the number of thirty-five persons, and at a place called Carlaverock Chapel were all committed to the gallows. . . . The English people was exceeding glad when they understood that John Armstrong was executed, for he did great robberies and stealing in England, maintaining twenty-four men in household every day upon reiff and oppression." ‡

The place of execution is mentioned by no other historian than Anderson, just quoted,

* Rerum Scoticarum Historia, 1582, fol. 163 b, 164.
† History of Scotland, Bannatyne Club, 1830, p. 143.
‡ Anderson's History, MS., Advocates Library, I, fol. 153 f. Anderson flourished about 1618–35. He gives the

year both as 1527 and 1528. Cited by Armstrong, History of Liddesdale, etc., p. 274 f. For what immediately follows, Armstrong, pp. 273, 279.

and he gives it as Carlaverock Chapel. But this must be a mistake for Carlenrig Chapel, Carlaverock not being in the line of the king's progress. James is known to have been at Carlenrig * on the 5th of July, and Johnie Armstrong not to have been alive on the eighth. It has been popularly believed that Johnie and his band were buried in Carlenrig churchyard (where the graves used to be shown), and their execution made so deep an impression on the people † that it is not unplausible that the fact should be remembered, and that the ballad C, in saying that John was murdered at Carlenrig, has followed tradition rather than given rise to it.

It appears from Lindsay's narrative that Johnie Armstrong came to the king voluntarily, and that he was not "taken or apprehended." Buchanan says that he was enticed by the king's officers, and Anderson that the heads of the border-clans were induced to come in by a proclamation that their lives should be safe. It is but too likely, therefore, that the capture was not effected by honorable means, and this is the representation of the ballads. There is no record of a trial,‡ and the execution was probably as summary as the arrest was perfidious.

The ballads treat facts with the customary freedom and improve upon them greatly. In A, B, English ballads, Johnie is oddly enough a Westmorland man,§ though in B 11 he admits himself to be a subject of the Scots king. The king writes John a long letter promising to do him no wrong, A 4; a loving letter, to come and speak with him speedily, B 4, C 2. Johnie goes to Edinburgh with the eight-score men that he keeps in his hall, all in a splendid uniform, asks grace, and is told that he and his eight-score shall be hanged the next morning. They are not unarmed, and resolve to fight it out rather than be hanged. They kill all the king's guard but three, B

16, but all Edinburgh rises; four-score and ten of Johnie's men lie gasping on the ground, A 14. A cowardly Scot comes behind Johnie and runs him through; like Sir Andrew Barton, he bids his men fight on; he will bleed awhile, then rise and fight again. Most of his company are killed, but his foot-page escapes and carries the bad news to Giltnock Hall. His little son, by or on the nurse's knee, vows to revenge his father's death.

C differs extensively from A, B, indeed resembles or repeats the English ballad only in a few places: C 2 = A 4, B 4; C 6 = B 10; C 7 = A g, B 11; C 22³,⁴ = A 11³,⁴, B 13³,⁴. The Eliots go with the Armstrongs according to C 3, and it is the intention to bring the king to dine at Gilnockie. In C 9-17 Johnie offers twenty-four steeds, four of them laden with as much gold as they can carry, twenty-four mills, and as much wheat as their hoppers can hold, twenty-four sisters-sons, who will fight to the utterance, tribute from all the land between 'here' and Newcastle, — all this for his life. The king replies to each successive offer that he never has granted a traitor's life, and will not begin with him. Johnie gives the king the lie as to his being a traitor; he could make England find him in meal and malt for a hundred years, and no Scot's wife could say that he had ever hurt her the value of a fly. Had he known how the king would treat him, he would have kept the border in spite of all his army. England's king would be a blithe man to hear of his capture. At this point the king is attracted by Johnie's splendid girdle and hat, and exclaims, What wants that knave that a king should have! Johnie bids farewell to his brother, Laird of Mangerton (Thomas, here called Kirsty), and to his son Kirsty, and to Gilnock-Hall, and is murdered at Carlenrig with all his band.

It will be observed that the substance, or

---

* A place two miles north of Mosspaul, on the road from Langholm to Hawick.

† Scott remarks that the "common people of the high parts of Teviotdale, Liddesdale, and the country adjacent, hold the memory of Johnie Armstrong in very high respect." "They affirm, also," he adds, "that one of his at-

tendants broke through the king's guard, and carried to Gilnockie Tower the news of the bloody catastrophe:" but that is in the English ballad, B 20.

‡ Dr Hill Burton has made a slight slip here, III, 146, ed. 1863; compare Pitcairn's Criminal Trials, I, 154.

§ He lived in the West March, if that helps to an explanation.

at least the hint, of C 21[3,4], 17[3,4], 26, 15, 22[3,4], 23, 24[1,2], is to be found in Lindsay's narrative.

In the last stanza of A and of B, Johnie Armstrong's son (afterwards known as Johnie's Christy) sitting on his nurse's knee, B (cf. C 30), or standing by his nurse's knee, A, vows, if he lives to be a man, to have revenge for his father's death.* Not infrequently, in popular ballads, a very young (even unborn) child speaks, by miracle, to save a life, vindicate innocence, or for some other kindly occasion;† sometimes again to threaten revenge, as here. So a child in the cradle in 'Frændehævn,' Grundtvig, I, 28, No 4, B 34 (= C 63), and in 'Hævnersværdet,' I, 351, No 25, sts 29, 30; and Kullervo in his third month, Kalevala, Rune 31, Schiefner, p. 194, vv. 109–112.‡

Johnie's plain speech to the king in C 19, 'Ye lied, ye lied, now, king!' is such as we have often heard before in these ballads: see I, 427, No 47, A 14; I, 446, No 50, A 8, 9; I, 452 f, No 52, C 10, D 7; II, 25 f, No 58, G 7, H 10; II, 269 ff, No 83, D 13, E 16, F 22; II, 282, No 86, A 6; III, 62, 67, No 117, sts 114, 222. It is not unexampled elsewhere. So Sthenelus to Agamemnon, Il. iv, 204; Ἀτρείδη, μὴ ψεύδε', ἐπιστάμενος σάφα εἰπεῖν; and Bernardo del Carpio, on much the same occasion as here,

> Mentides, buen rey, mentides,
> que no decides verdad,
> que nunca yo fuí traidor,

Wolf & Hofmann, Primavera, I, 38 and 41; see also I, 186, II, 100, 376.

This ballad was an early favorite of Goldsmith's: "The music of the finest singer is dissonance to what I felt when our old dairymaid sung me into tears with Johnny Armstrong's Last Good Night, or the Cruelty of Barbara Allen." Essays, 1765, p. 14.

C is translated by Talvi, Versuch, u. s. w., p. 543; by Schubart, p. 179; by Loève-Veimars, p. 270.

A

a. Wit Restord in severall Select Poems not formerly publisht, London, 1658, p. 30, in Facetiæ, London, 1871, I, 132.
b. Wit and Drollery, London, 1682, p. 57.

1 THERE dwelt a man in faire Westmerland,
  Ionnë Armestrong men did him call,
He had nither lands nor rents coming in,
  Yet he kept eight score men in his hall.

2 He had horse and harness for them all,
  Goodly steeds were all milke-white;
O the golden bands an about their necks,
  And their weapons, they were all alike.

3 Newes then was brought unto the king
  That there was sicke a won as hee,
That livëd lyke a bold out-law,
  And robbëd all the north country.

4 The king he writt an a letter then,
  A letter which was large and long;
He signëd it with his owne hand,
  And he promised to doe him no wrong.

---

* Found also in one copy of Hugh the Græme, Buchan's MSS, I, 63, st. 15. Borrowed by Sir Walter Scott in The Lay of the Last Minstrel, Canto I, ix.

† See many cases in Liebrecht, Zur Volkskunde, p. 210 f, to which may be added: Milà, Romancerillo, No 243, pp. 219–21; Briz, II, 222; Amador de los Rios, Historia de la Lit. Esp., VII, 449; El Folk-Lore Andaluz, 1882, pp. 41, 77; Almeida- Garrett, II, 56, note; Nigra, C. P. del Piemonte, No 1, E–I, N, O; 'Le serpent vert,' Poésies p. de la France, MS., III, fol. 126, 508, now printed by Rolland, III, 10; Kolberg, Pieśni ludu polskiego, No 18, p. 208; Luzel,

I, 81, II, 357, 515; Brewer, Dictionary of Miracles, pp. 205, 355 f.; Gaidoz, and others, Mélusine, IV, 228 ff., 272 ff., 298, 323 f., 405.

‡ Grundtvig, No 84, 'Hustru og Mands Moder,' is not so good a case, though a boy just born announces that he will revenge his mother, because the boy is born nine years old; II, 412, D 30, E 18. This again in Kristensen, I, 202 f, No 74, B 12, C 11, and II, 113 ff, No 35, A 18, B 14, C 11. The stanza cited by Dr Prior, I, 37, from 'Hammen von Reystett,' Wunderhorn, 1808, II, 179, is hardly to the purpose.

5 When this letter came Ionnë untill,
   His heart it was as blythe as birds on the
      tree :
  'Never was I sent for before any king,
   My father, my grandfather, nor none but
      mee.

6 'And if wee goe the king before,
   I would we went most orderly ;
  Every man of you shall have his scarlet cloak,
   Laced with silver laces three.

7 'Every won of you shall have his velvett
      coat,
   Laced with sillver lace so white ;
  O the golden bands an about your necks,
   Black hatts, white feathers, all alyke.'

8 By the morrow morninge at ten of the clock,
   Towards Edenburough gon was hee,
  And with him all his eight score men ;
   Good lord, it was a goodly sight for to
      see !

9 When Ionnë came befower the king,
   He fell downe on his knee ;
  'O pardon, my soveraine leige,' he said,
   'O pardon my eight score men and mee ! '

10 'Thou shalt have no pardon, thou traytor
      strong,
    For thy eight score men nor thee ;
   For to-morrow morning by ten of the clock,
    Both thou and them shall hang on the gal-
      low-tree.'

11 But Ionnë looke'd over his left shoulder,
    Good Lord, what a grevious look looked hee !
   Saying, Asking grace of a graceles face —
    Why there is none for you nor me.

12 But Ionnë had a bright sword by his side,
    And it was made of the mettle so free,
   That had not the king stept his foot aside,
    He had smitten his head from his faire boddë.

13 Saying, Fight on, my merry men all,
    And see that none of you be taine ;
   For rather then men shall say we were hange'd,
    Let them report how we were slaine.

14 Then, God wott, faire Eddenburrough rose,
    And so besett poore Ionnë rounde,
   That fowerscore and tenn of Ionnës best men
    Lay gasping all upon the ground.

15 Then like a mad man Ionnë laide about,
    And like a mad man then fought hee,
   Untill a falce Scot came Ionnë behinde,
    And runn him through the faire boddee.

16 Saying, Fight on, my merry men all,
    And see that none of you be taine ;
   For I will stand by and bleed but awhile,
    And then will I come and fight againe.

17 Newes then was brought to young Ionnë Arme-
      strong,
    As he stood by his nurses knee,
   Who vowed if ere he live'd for to be a man,
    O the treacherous Scots revengd hee'd be.

B

a. Wood, 401, fol. 93 b, London, printed for Francis
Grove (1620–55 ?).
b. Pepys, II, 133, No 117, London, printed for W. Thack-
eray and T. Passenger (1660–82 ?).
c. A Collection of Old Ballads, 1723, I, 170.

1 Is there never a man in all Scotland,
   From the highest state to the lowest degree,
  That can shew himself now before the king ?
   Scotland is so full of their traitery.

2 Yes, there is a man in Westmerland,
   And John Armstrong some do him call ;
  He has no lands nor rents coming in,
   Yet he keeps eightscore men within his hall.

3 He has horse and harness for them all,
   And goodly steeds that be milk-white,
  With their goodly belts about their necks,
   With hats and feathers all alike.

4 The king he writ a lovely letter,
   With his own hand so tenderly,
  And has sent it unto John Armstrong,
   To come and speak with him speedily.

5 When John he looked the letter upon,
   Then, Lord ! he was as blithe as a bird in
      a tree :
  'I was never before no king in my life,
   My father, my grandfather, nor none of us
      three.

6 'But seeing we must [go] before the king,
   Lord! we will go most valiantly;
You shall every one have a velvet coat,
   Laid down with golden laces three.

7 'And you shall every one have a scarlet cloak,
   Laid down with silver laces five,
With your golden belts about your necks,
   With hats [and] brave feathers all alike.'

8 But when John he went from Guiltknock Hall!
   The wind it blew hard, and full sore it did
    rain:
'Now fare you well, brave Guiltknock Hall!
   I fear I shall never see thee again.'

9 Now John he is to Edenborough gone,
   And his eightscore men so gallantly,
And every one of them on a milk-white steed,
   With their bucklers and swords hanging
    down to the knee.

10 But when John he came the king before,
   With his eightscore men so gallant to see,
The king he moved his bonnet to him;
   He thought he had been a king as well as
    he.

11 'O pardon, pardon, my soveraign leige,
   Pardon for my eightscore men and me!
For my name it is John Armstrong,
   And a subject of yours, my leige,' said he.

12 'Away with thee, thou false traitor!
   No pardon I will grant to thee,
But, to-morrow before eight of the clock,
   I will hang thy eightscore men and thee.'

13 O how John looked over his left shoulder!
   And to his merry men thus said he:
I have asked grace of a graceless face,
   No pardon here is for you nor me.

14 Then John pulld out a nut-brown sword,
   And it was made of mettle so free;
Had not the king moved his foot as he did,
   John had taken his head from his body.

15 'Come, follow me, my merry men all,
   We will scorn one foot away to fly;

It never shall be said we were hung like doggs;
   No, wee 'l fight it out most manfully.'

16 Then they fought on like champions bold —
   For their hearts was sturdy, stout, and free —
Till they had killed all the kings good guard;
   There was none left alive but onely three.

17 But then rise up all Edenborough,
   They rise up by thousands three;
Then a cowardly Scot came John behind,
   And run him thorow the fair body.

18 Said John, Fight on, my merry men all,
   I am a little hurt, but I am not slain;
I will lay me down for to bleed a while,
   Then I 'le rise and fight with you again.

19 Then they fought on like mad men all,
   Till many a man lay dead on the plain;
For they were resolved, before they would
    yield,
That every man would there be slain.

20 So there they fought couragiously,
   'Till most of them lay dead there and slain,
But little Musgrave, that was his foot-page,
   With his bonny grissell got away untain.

21 But when he came up to Guiltknock Hall,
   The lady spyed him presently:
'What news, what news, thou little foot-page?
   What news from thy master and his com-
    pany?'

22 'My news is bad, lady,' he said,
   'Which I do bring, as you may see;
My master, John Armstrong, he is slain,
   And all his gallant company.

23 'Yet thou are welcome home, my bonny grisel!
   Full oft thou hast fed at the corn and hay,
But now thou shalt be fed with bread and wine,
   And thy sides shall be spurred no more, I
    say.'

24 O then bespoke his little son,
   As he was set on his nurses knee:
'If ever I live for to be a man,
   My fathers blood revenged shall be.'

C

Allan Ramsay, The Ever Green, II, 190, "copied from a gentleman's mouth of the name of Armstrang, who is the 6th generation from this John."

1 Sum speiks of lords, sum speiks of lairds,
   And siclyke men of hie degrie;
Of a gentleman I sing a sang,
   Sumtyme calld Laird of Gilnockie.

2 The king he wrytes a luving letter,
   With his ain hand sae tenderly:
And he hath sent it to Johny Armstrang,
   To cum and speik with him speidily.

3 The Eliots and Armstrangs did convene,
   They were a gallant company:
'We 'ill ryde and meit our lawful king,
   And bring him safe to Gilnockie.

4 'Make kinnen and capon ready, then,
   And venison in great plenty;
We 'ill welcome hame our royal king;
   I hope he 'ill dyne at Gilnockie!'

5 They ran their horse on the Langum howm,
   And brake their speirs with mekle main;
The ladys lukit frae their loft-windows,
   'God bring our men weil back again!'

6 When Johny came before the king,
   With all his men sae brave to see,
The king he movit his bonnet to him;
   He weind he was a king as well as he.

7 'May I find grace, my sovereign liege,
   Grace for my loyal men and me?
For my name it is Johny Armstrang,
   And subject of yours, my liege,' said he.

8 'Away, away, thou traytor, strang!
   Out of my sicht thou mayst sune be!
I grantit nevir a traytors lyfe,
   And now I 'll not begin with thee.'

9 'Grant me my lyfe, my liege, my king,
   And a bony gift I will give to thee;
Full four-and-twenty milk-whyt steids,
   Were a' foald in a yeir to me.

10 'I 'll gie thee all these milk-whyt steids,
   That prance and nicher at a speir,

With as mekle gude Inglis gilt
   As four of their braid backs dow beir.'

11 'Away, away, thou traytor strang!
   Out o' my sicht thou mayst sune be!
I grantit nevir a traytors lyfe,
   And now I 'll not begin with thee.'

12 'Grant me my lyfe, my liege, my king,
   And a bony gift I 'll gie to thee;
Gude four-and-twenty ganging mills,
   That gang throw a' the yeir to me.

13 'These four-and-twenty mills complete
   Sall gang for thee throw all the yeir,
And as mekle of gude reid wheit
   As all their happers dow to bear.'

14 'Away, away, thou traytor, strang!
   Out of my sicht thou mayst sune be!
I grantit nevir a traytors lyfe,
   And now I 'll not begin with thee.'

15 'Grant me my lyfe, my liege, my king,
   And a great gift I 'll gie to thee;
Bauld four-and-twenty sisters sons,
   Sall for the fecht, tho all sould flee.'

16 'Away, away, thou traytor, strang!
   Out of my sicht thou mayst sune be!
I grantit nevir a traytors lyfe,
   And now I 'll not begin with thee.'

17 'Grant me my lyfe, my liege, my king,
   And a brave gift I 'll gie to thee;
All betwene heir and Newcastle town
   Sall pay thair yeirly rent to thee.'

18 'Away, away, thou traytor, strang!
   Out of my sicht thou mayst sune be!
I grantit nevir a traytors lyfe,
   And now I 'll not begin with thee.'

19 'Ye lied, ye lied, now, king,' he says,
   'Althocht a king and prince ye be,
For I luid naithing in all my lyfe,
   I dare well say it, but honesty;

20 'But a fat horse, and a fair woman,
   Twa bony dogs to kill a deir:
But Ingland suld haif found me meil and malt,
   Gif I had livd this hundred yeir!

21 'Scho suld haif found me meil and malt,
    And beif and mutton in all plentie;
But neir a Scots wyfe could haif said
    That eir I skaithd her a pure flie.

22 'To seik het water beneth cauld yce,
    Surely it is a great folie;
I haif asked grace at a graceless face,
    But there is nane for my men and me.

23 'But had I kend, or I came frae hame,
    How thou unkynd wadst bene to me,
I wad haif kept the border-syde,
    In spyte of all thy force and thee.

24 'Wist Englands king that I was tane,
    O gin a blyth man wald he be!
For anes I slew his sisters son,
    And on his breist-bane brak a tree.'

25 John wore a girdle about his midle,
    Imbroiderd owre with burning gold,
Bespangled with the same mettle,
    Maist beautifull was to behold.

26 Ther hang nine targats at Johnys hat,
    And ilk an worth three hundred pound:
'What wants that knave that a king suld haif,
    But the sword of honour and the crown!

27 'O whair gat thou these targats, Johnie,
    That blink sae brawly abune thy brie?'

'I gat them in the field fechting,
    Wher, cruel king, thou durst not be.

28 'Had I my horse, and my harness gude,
    And ryding as I wont to be,
It sould haif bene tald this hundred yeir
    The meiting of my king and me.

29 'God be withee, Kirsty, my brither,
    Lang live thou Laird of Mangertoun!
Lang mayst thou live on the border-syde
    Or thou se thy brither ryde up and doun.

30 'And God be withee, Kirsty, my son,
    Whair thou sits on thy nurses knee!
But and thou live this hundred yeir,
    Thy fathers better thoult never be.

31 'Farweil, my bonny Gilnock-Hall,
    Whair on Esk-syde thou standest stout!
Gif I had lived but seven yeirs mair,
    I wald haif gilt thee round about.'

32 John murdred was at Carlinrigg,
    And all his galant companie:
But Scotlands heart was never sae wae,
    To see sae mony brave men die.

33 Because they savd their country deir
    Frae Englishmen; nane were sae bauld,
Whyle Johnie livd on the border-syde,
    Nane of them durst cum neir his hald.

A. a. 3^3. syke a. 17^4. O th' the.
  b. 3^2. sick a man. 5^2. it *wanting*.
    6^1. And therefore if. 7^4. and white.
    8^4. an it: for *wanting*. 9^1. Johnnee.
    10^2. Ne for. 11. There Johnne.
    11^3. Said he. 11^4. yee. 12^2. the *wanting*.
    13^4. that we. 14^3. Johnnee's.
    15^4. thorough.
B. a. Iohn Arm-strongs last good night. Declaring How John Arm-strong and his eightscore men fought a bloody bout with a Scottish king at Edenborough. To a pretty northern tune called, Fare you well, guilt Knock-hall.
    6^1. we must before; *perhaps rightly*.
    $8^{1,3}$, 21^1. guilt Knock-hall.
    Signed T. R.

London, Printed for Francis Grove on S[n]ow-hill.
Entered according to order.
b. *Title*: with the Scottish. To a pretty new northern tune: called, &c., *omitted*.
    1^2. estate. 1^4. of treachery.
    2^2. Jonny: they do. 4^1. writes a loving.
    4^2. And with. 4^3. hath. 5^1. this letter.
    5^1. Good Lord. 5^2. he lookt. 5^3. a king.
    6^1. must go.
    6^2. most gallantly. 7^1. And ye.
    7^4. hats and. $8^{1,3}$, 21^1. guilt Knock-hall.
    8^2. full fast. 8^3. fare thee well thou guilt.
    9^1. Johnny. 9^4. to their. 10^1. he *wanting*.
    12^3. to morrow morning by eight.
    12^4. hang up. 13^1. Johnny. 14^1. out his.
    15^2. It shall ne'r. 15^4. We will.

16². were. 16⁴. but two or. 17¹,². rose.

17³. Then *wanting*.

18². little wounded but am. 19². up on.

20⁸. Musgrove. 21¹. up *wanting*.

22³. Johnny Armstrong is.

23². been fed with. 24¹. bespake.

24³. for *wanting*. 24⁴. father's death.

Signed T. R.

London, Printed for W. Thackeray and T. Passenger.

c. Johnny Armstrongs, last Good-night, shewing how John Armstrong, with his Eightscore Men, fought a bloody Battle with the Scotch King at Edenborough. To a Northern Tune.

1¹. ever. 1². estate. 1³. our king.

1⁴. full of treachery. 2². Johnny : they do.

3¹. horses. 4¹. writes a loving.

4². And with. 4³. hath : letter.

5¹. this letter. 5². He lokd as blith.

5³. a king. 6¹. must go. 6². most gallantly.

6³. Ye. 7¹. And every one shall.

6⁴. hats and feathers.

8¹. Johnny went : Giltnock. 8². full fast.

8³. fare thee well thou Giltnock.

9¹. Johnny. 9². With his.

9⁴. hanging to their.

10¹. he *wanting*. 11³. Johnny.

11⁴. a *wanting*. 12². will I.

12³. to-morrow morning by eight.

12⁴. hang up. 13¹. Then Johnny.

13⁴. there is : you and.

14¹. his good broad sword.

14². That was made of the. 14⁴. his fair.

15². foot for to. 15³. shall never be : hangd.

15⁴. We will. 16². were.

16⁴. were : but one, two or three.

17¹,². rose. 17³. Then *wanting*.

17⁴. through. 18². little wounded but am.

18³. for *wanting*. 21¹. up *wanting*.

21¹. Giltnock. 22³. Iohnny Armstrong is.

23². hast been fed with corn. 24¹. bespake.

24². he sat on. 24³. for *wanting*.

24⁴. fathers death.

C. *Printed in stanzas of eight lines.*

Zours, zeir, *etc.*, *are here printed* yours, yeir, etc.; quhair, quheit, *here*, whair, wheit.

5¹. hown.

11, 14, 16, 18, *only* Away, away thou traytor, etc., *is printed*.

19⁴. sayit.

170

THE DEATH OF QUEEN JANE

A. Percy papers, 1776. **B.** 'Queen Jeanie,' Kinloch's Ancient Scottish Ballads, p. 116. **C. a.** Jamieson's Popular Ballads, I, 182.* **b.** Herd's MSS, I, 103. **D.** 'The Death of Queen Jane,' Bell's Ancient Poems, Ballads and Songs of the Peasantry of England, p. 113. **E.** 'Queen Jeanie,' Macmath MS., p. 68. **F.** Notes and Queries, Second Series, XI, 131. **G.** A fragment from William Motherwell's papers.

THIS threnody is said to have been current throughout Scotland. There is another, not in the popular style, in the Crowne Garland of Golden Roses, 1612, Percy Society, vol. vi, p. 29 : The Wofull Death of Queene Jane, wife to King Henry the Eight, and how King Edward was cut out of his mother's belly. This is reprinted in Old Ballads, 1723, II, 115, and Evans's Collection, 1777, 1784, II, 54, and is among Pepys's Penny Merriments, vol. iii. 'A ballett called The Lady Jane' and another piece entitled The Lamentation of Quene Jane were licensed in 1560; Stationers' Registers, Arber, I, 151 f.

Jane Seymour gave birth to Prince Edward October 12, 1537, and by a natural process, but, in consequence of imprudent management, died twelve days after. There was a

---

* Jamieson cites the first two verses in The Scots Magazine, October, 1803, and says : Of this affecting composition I have two copies, both imperfect, but they will make a pretty good and consistent whole between them.

belief that severe surgery had been required, under which the queen sank. The editor of Old Ballads, II, 116 f, cites Sir John Hayward as saying: "All reports do constantly run that he [Prince Edward] was not by natural passage delivered into the world, but that his mother's belly was opened for his birth, and that she died of the incision the fourth day following." And Du Chesne: " Quand ce vint au terme de l'accouchement, elle eut tant de tourment et de peine qu'il lui fallut fendre le costé, par lequel on tira son fruit, le douzième jour d'Octobre. Elle mourut douze jours après." But Echard again: " Contrary to the opinion of many writers," the queen "died twelve days after the birth of this prince, having been well delivered, and without any incision, as others have maliciously reported."

————◆————

A

Communicated to Percy by the Dean of Derry, as written from memory by his mother, Mrs. Bernard, February, 1776.

1 QUEEN JANE was in labour full six weeks and more,
    And the women were weary, and fain would give oer:
  'O women, O women, as women ye be,
    Rip open my two sides, and save my baby!'

2 'O royal Queen Jane, that thing may not be;
    We'll send for King Henry to come unto thee.'
  King Henry came to her, and sate on her bed:
    'What ails my dear lady, her eyes look so red?'

3 'O royal King Henry, do one thing for me:
    Rip open my two sides, and save my baby!'
  'O royal Queen Jane, that thing will not do;
    If I lose your fair body, I'll lose your baby too.'

4 She wept and she waild, and she wrung her hands sore;
    O the flour of England must flurish no more!
  She wept and she waild till she fell in a swoond,
    They opend her two sides, and the baby was found.

5 The baby was christened with joy and much mirth,
    Whilst poor Queen Jane's body lay cold under earth:
  There was ringing and singing and mourning all day,
    The princess Eliz[abeth] went weeping away.

6 The trumpets in mourning so sadly did sound,
    And the pikes and the muskets did trail on the ground.

. . . .
. . . .

————◆————

B

Kinloch's Ancient Scottish Ballads, p. 116.

1 QUEEN JEANIE, Queen Jeanie, traveld six weeks and more,
    Till women and midwives had quite gien her oer:
  'O if ye were women as women should be,
    Ye would send for a doctor, a doctor to me.'

2 The doctor was called for and set by her bedside:
    'What aileth thee, my ladie, thine eyes seem so red?'

'O doctor, O doctor, will ye do this for me,
    To rip up my two sides, and save my babie?'

3 'Queen Jeanie, Queen Jeanie, that's the thing I'll neer do,
    To rip up your two sides to save your babie:'
  Queen Jeanie, Queen Jeanie, traveld six weeks and more,
    Till midwives and doctors had quite gien her oer.

4 'O if ye were doctors as doctors should be,
    Ye would send for King Henry, King Henry to me:'

King Henry was called for, and sat by her bedside,
'What aileth thee, Jeanie? what aileth my bride?'

5 'King Henry, King Henry, will ye do this for me,
To rip up my two sides, and save my babie?'
'Queen Jeanie, Queen Jeanie, that's what I'll never do,
To rip up your two sides to save your babie.'

6 But with sighing and sobbing she's fallen in a swoon,
Her side it was ript up, and her babie was found;
At this bonie babie's christning there was meikle joy and mirth,
But bonnie Queen Jeanie lies cold in the earth.

7 Six and six coaches, and six and six more,
And royal King Henry went mourning before;
O two and two gentlemen carried her away,
But royal King Henry went weeping away.

8 O black were their stockings, and black were their bands,
And black were the weapons they held in their hands;
O black were their mufflers, and black were their shoes,
And black were the cheverons they drew on their luves.

9 They mourned in the kitchen, and they mournd in the ha,
But royal King Henry mournd langest of a':
Farewell to fair England, farewell for evermore!
For the fair flower of England will never shine more.

———•———

C

a. Jamieson's Popular Ballads, I, 182; "from two fragments, one transmitted from Arbroath and another from Edinburgh." b. Herd's MSS, I, 103.

1 QUEEN JEANY has traveld for three days and more,
Till the ladies were weary, and quite gave her oer:
'O ladies, O ladies, do this thing for me,
To send for King Henry, to come and see me.'

2 King Henry was sent for, and sat by her bedside:
'Why weep you, Queen Jeany? your eyes are so red.'
'O Henry, O Henry, do this one thing for me,
Let my side straight be opend, and save my babie!'

3 'O Jeany, O Jeany, this never will do,
It will leese thy sweet life, and thy young babie too.'
She wept and she wailed, till she fell in a swoon:
Her side it was opened, the babie was found.

4 Prince Edward was christened with joy and with mirth,
But the flower of fair England lies cold in the earth.
O black was King Henry, and black were his men,
And black was the steed that King Henry rode on.

5 And black were the ladies, and black were their fans,
And black were the gloves that they wore on their hands,
And black were the ribbands they wore on their heads,
And black were the pages, and black were the maids.

* * * * * * *

6 The trumpets they sounded, the cannons did roar,
But the flower of fair England shall flourish no more.

. . . .
. . . .

D

Robert Bell's Ancient Poems, Ballads, and Songs of the Peasantry of England, p. 113; "taken down from the singing of a young gipsy girl, to whom it had descended orally through two generations."

1 QUEEN JANE was in travail for six weeks or
  more,
    Till the women grew tired and fain would
      give oer:
  'O women, O women, good wives if ye be,
    Go send for King Henrie, and bring him to
      me!'

2 King Henrie was sent for, he came with all
  speed,
    In a gownd of green velvet from heel to the
      head:
  'King Henrie, King Henrie, if kind Henrie
    you be,
    Send for a surgeon, and bring him to me!'

3 The surgeon was sent for, he came with all
  speed,
    In a gownd of black velvet from heel to the
      head;
  He gave her rich caudle, but the death-sleep
    slept she,

Then her right side was opened, and the
  babe was set free.

4 The babe it was christened, and put out and
  nursed,
    While the royal Queen Jane she lay cold in
      the dust.

5 So black was the mourning, and white were
    the wands,
    Yellow, yellow the torches they bore in their
      hands;
    The bells they were muffled, and mournful did
      play,
    While the royal Queen Jane she lay cold in
      the clay.

6 Six knights and six lords bore her corpse
    through the grounds,
    Six dukes followed after, in black mourning
      gownds;
    The flower of Old England was laid in cold
      clay,
    Whilst the royal King Henrie came weeping
      away.

E

Macmath MS., p. 68. "From my aunt, Miss Jane Webster, 1886–1887. She learned it at Airds of Kells, Kirkcudbrightshire, over fifty years ago, from the singing of James Smith."

1 'YE midwives and women-kind, do one thing
    for me;
  Send for my mother, to come and see me.'

2 Her mother was sent for, who came speedilie:
  'O Jeanie, Queen Jeanie, are ye gaun to dee?'

3 'O mother, dear mother, do one thing for me;
  O send for King Henry, to come and see me.'

4 King Henry was sent for, who came speedilie:
  'O Jeanie, Queen Jeanie, are ye gaun to dee?'

5 'King Henry, King Henry, do one thing for
    me;
  O send for a doctor, to come and see me.'

6 The doctor was sent for, who came speedilie:
  'O Jeanie, Queen Jeanie, are ye gaun to dee?'

7 'O doctor, oh doctor, do one thing for me;
  Open my left side, and let my babe free.'

8 He opened her left side, and then all was oer,
  And the best flower in England will flourish
    no more.

F

Notes and Queries, Second Series, XI, 131 ; sung by an illiterate nursemaid " some forty years since " (1861).

1 QUEEN JANE lies in labour six weeks or
    more,
    Till the women were tired, go see her no
      more :
  ' Oh women, oh women, if women you be,
    You 'll send for King Henry, to come and
      see me.

G

In pencil, in Motherwell's handwriting, inside of the cover of what appears to be a sketch of his Introduction to his Minstrelsy ; communicated by Mr Macmath.

1 QUEEN JEANIE was in labour full three days
    and more,
    Till a' the good women was forced to gie
      her oer :
  ' O guide women, gude women, gude women,'
    quo she,
    ' Will ye send for King Henry, to come and
      see me ? '

B. 3¹, 5⁸. do *is to be pronounced* dee.
C. b. *Only six lines :* 2³,⁴, 4¹,², 5¹,²
    2³. This thing.
    2⁴. Straight open my two sides : save your.
    4¹. The babie was.
    4². But royal Queen Jeany lay low.
    5¹. Then black were their mournings.
E. *The first seven stanzas taken down October*
    15, 1886, and the last sent on February 3,
    1887.

2 ' Oh King Henry, King Henry, if King Henry
    you be,
    You 'll send for the doctor, to come and see
      me :
  Oh doctor, oh doctor, if a doctor you be,
    You 'll open my right side, and save my
      baby.'

3 They churchd her, they chimed her, they dug
    her her grave,
    They buried her body, and christend her
      babe.

Wi weeping and wailing, lamenting full sore,
    That the flower of all Eng*land* should flourish
    no more.

2 K*ing* He*nry* was sent for, wh*o* came in *great*
    speed,
    Stand*ing* weep*ing* and wail*ing* at *Queen*
    Jeanie's bedside ;
    Stand*ing* weep*ing* and wail*ing*, etc.

3 ' O King He*nry*, Ki*ng* He*nry*, K*ing* He*nry*,'
    quo she,
    ' Will ye send for my mothe*r* . . . .

24th March, 1887. " I can never remember
them, sitting thinking about them. Yester-
day I was humming away, not knowing
what I was singing, until I sung this :

8 He opened her left side, Queen Jeanie's life 's
    oer,
    And the last rose of England will flourish no
    more."

171

THOMAS CROMWELL

Percy MS., p. 55; Hales and Furnivall, I, 129.

JUNE 10, 1540, Thomas Lord Cromwell, "when he least expected it," was arrested at the council-table by the Duke of Norfolk for high-treason, and on the 28th of July following he was executed. Cromwell, says Lord Herbert of Cherbury, judged "his perdition more certain that the duke was uncle to the Lady Katherine Howard, whom the king began now to affect." Later writers * have asserted that Katherine Howard exerted herself to procure Cromwell's death, and we can understand nobody else but her to be doing this in the third stanza of this fragment; nevertheless there is no authority for such a representation. The king had no personal interview with the minister whom he so suddenly struck down, but he did send the Duke of Norfolk and two others to visit Cromwell in prison, for the purpose of extracting confessions pertaining to Anne of Cleves. Cromwell wrote a letter to the king, imploring the mercy which, as well as confession, he refuses in stanza five.

Percy inserted in the Reliques, 1765, II, 58, a song against Cromwell, printed in 1540, and apparently before his death, and he observes, 1767, II, 86, that there was a succession of seven or eight more, for and against, which were then preserved, and of course are still existing, in the archives of the Antiquarian Society.

---

* * * * * * *

1 . . . .
  . . . .
  'Ffor if your boone be askeable,
    Soone granted it shalbe:

2 'If it be not touching my crowne,' he said,
    'Nor hurting poore comminaltye.'
  'Nay, it is not touching your crowne,' shee sayes,
    'Nor hurting poore cominaltye,

3 'But I begg the death of Thomas Cromwell,
    For a false traitor to you is hee.'
  'Then feitch me hither the Earle of Darby
    And the Earle of Shrewsbury,

4 'And bidde them bring Thomas Cromawell;
    Let 's see what he can say to mee;'
  For Thomas had woont to haue carryed his head vp,
    But now he hanges it vppon his knee.

5 'How now? How now?' the king did say,
    'Thomas, how is it with thee?'
  'Hanging and drawing, O king!' he saide;
    'You shall neuer gett more from mee.'

Half of the page is gone before the beginning.
2⁸. it it is.

* Burnet; Rapin-Thoyras, 1724, V, 401.

172

MUSSELBURGH FIELD

'Musleboorrowe ffeild,' Percy MS., p. 54; Hales and Furnivall, I, 123.

———+———

THE Protector Somerset, to overcome or to punish the opposition of the Scots to the marriage of Mary Stuart with Edward VI, invaded Scotland at the end of the summer of 1547 with eighteen thousand men, supported by a fleet. The Scots mustered at Musselburgh, a town on the water five or six miles east of Edinburgh, under the Earls of Arran, Angus, and Huntly, each of whom, according to Buchanan, had ten thousand men, and there the issue was tried on the 10th of September. The northern army abandoned an impregnable position, and their superior, but illmanaged, and partly ill-composed, force, after successfully resisting a cavalry charge, was put to flight by the English, who had an advantage in cannon and cavalry as well as generalship. A hideous slaughter followed; Leslie admits that, in the chase and battle, there were slain above ten thousand of his countrymen. Patten, a Londoner who saw and described the fight, says that the one anxiety of the Scots was lest the English should get away, and that they were so sure of victory that, the night before the battle, they fell "to playing at dice for certain of our noblemen and captains of fame" (cf. stanza 3), as the French diced for prisoners on the eve of Agincourt. The dates are wrong in $1^{1,2}$, 5^1;

Huntly is rightly said to have been made prisoner, 7^1.

6, 8. When the Scots were once turned, says Patten, "it was a wonder to see how soon and in how sundry sorts they were scattered; the place they stood on like a wood of staves, strewed on the ground as rushes in a chamber, unpassable, they lay so thick, for either horse or man." Some made their course along the sands by the Frith, towards Leith; some straight toward Edinburgh; "and the residue, and (as we noted then) the most, of them toward Dalkeith, which way, by means of the marsh, our horsemen were worst able to follow." *

The battle is known also by the name of Pinkie or Pinkie Cleuch, appellations of an estate, a burn and a hill ("a hill called Pinkincleuche," Leslie), near or within the field of operations.

Percy remarks upon 3^3: "It should seem from hence that there was somewhat of a uniform among our soldiers even then." There are jackets white and red in No 166, 29^3. Sir William Stanley has ten thousand red coats at his order in 'Lady Bessy,' vv 593, 809–11, 937 f, Percy MS., III, 344, 352, 358; Sir John Savage has fifteen hundred white hoods in the same piece, v. 815.

———+———

1 ON the tenth day of December,
    And the fourth yeere of King Edwards
        raigne,
  Att Musleboorrowe, as I remember,
    Two goodly hosts there mett on a plaine.

2 All that night they camped there,
    Soe did the Scotts, both stout and stubborne;

* W. Patten, The Expedicion into Scotlande, etc., reprinted in Dalyell's Fragments of Scottish History, pp. 51, 66.

But "wellaway," it was their song,
  For wee haue taken them in their owne
    turne.

3 Over night they carded for our English mens
      coates;
  They fished before their netts were spunn;
  A white for sixpence, a red for two groates;
  Now wisdome wold haue stayed till they had
    been woone.

4 Wee feared not but that they wold fight,
  Yett itt was turned vnto their owne paine;
  Thoe against one of vs that they were eight,
  Yett with their owne weapons wee did them
    beat.

5 On the twelfth day in the morne
  The made a face as the wold fight,

But many a proud Scott there was downe
    borne,
  And many a ranke coward was put to flight.

6 But when they heard our great gunnes cracke,
  Then was their harts turned into their hose;
  They cast down their weapons, and turned
    their backes,
  They ran soe fast that the fell on their nose.

7 The Lord Huntley, wee had him there;
  With him hee brought ten thousand men,
  Yett, God bee thanked, wee made them such a
    banquett
  That none of them returned againe.

8 Wee chased them to D[alkeith]

*   *   *   *   *   *   *

1¹. 10th. 1². 4th. 1⁴. 2. 2¹. all night that.
2⁴. horne *may be the reading, instead of* turne.

3³. 6^{d}: *pro* 2. 4³. 8^{t}. 5¹. 12th.
7². 10000. 8¹. *Half a page gone.*

173

MARY HAMILTON

A. a. 'Marie Hamilton,' Sharp's Ballad Book, 1824, p. 18. b. Communicated by the late John Francis Campbell. c. Aungervyle Society's publications, No V, p. 18.

B. 'Mary Hamilton,' Motherwell's MS., p. 337; printed in part in Motherwell's Minstrelsy, p. 313 ff.

C. 'Mary Myles,' Motherwell's MS., p. 265.

D. 'Mary Hamilton,' Motherwell's MS., p. 267; Motherwell's Minstrelsy, p. 316.

E. 'Lady Maisry,' Buchan's MSS, II, 186; Buchan's Ballads of the North of Scotland, II, 190.

F. Skene MS., p. 61.

G. 'Mary Hamilton,' MS. of Scottish Songs and Ballads copied by a granddaughter of Lord Woodhouselee, p. 51.

H. 'Mary Hamilton,' Kinloch's Ancient Scottish Ballads, p. 252.

I. a. 'The Queen's Marie,' Scott's Minstrelsy, 1833, III, 294. b. Scott's Minstrelsy, 1802, II, 154, three stanzas.

J. 'Marie Hamilton,' Harris MS., fol. 10 b.

K. 'The Queen's Mary,' Motherwell's MS., p. 96.

L. 'Mary Hamilton,' Motherwell's MS., p. 280.

M. 'Mary Hamilton,' Maidment's North Countrie Garland, p. 19. Repeated in Buchan's Gleanings, p. 164.

N. 'The Queen's Maries,' Murison MS., p. 33.

O. 'The Queen's Marie,' Finlay's Scottish Ballads, I, xix.

P. Kinloch MSS, VII, 95, 97; Kinloch's Ancient Scottish Ballads, p. 252.

Q. 'Queen's Marie,' Letters from and to Charles

Kirkpatrick Sharpe, ed. Allardyce, II, 272, two stanzas.

R. Burns, Letter to Mrs Dunlop, 25 January, 1790, Currie, II, 290, 1800, one stanza.

THE scene is at the court of Mary Stuart, A–N, Q. The unhappy heroine is one of the queen's Four Maries, A a 18, b 14, c 1, 18, 23, B 19, D 21, F 3, 12, G 16, H 18, I 19, J 8, 10, K 8, M 7, N 1; Mary Hamilton, A a 1, b 2, c 2, B 3, D 8, G 1, H 4, I 1, J 6; Lady Mary, F 5, 6; Mary Mild, Myle, C 5, M 1, N 1, also A c 6, Moil, O, but Lady Maisry, E 6. She gangs wi bairn; it is to the highest Stewart of a', A a 1, A c 2, B 3, C 5; cf. D 3, G 1–3, I 1–6, L 9, P 1. She goes to the garden to pull the leaf off the tree, in a vain hope to be free of the babe, C 3; it is the savin-tree, D 4, the deceivin-tree, N 3, the Abbey-tree (and pulled by the king), I 6.* She rolls the bairn in her apron, handkerchief, and throws it in the sea, A a 3, A b 3, A c 4, C 4, D 5, 9, I 7, K 2, 4, L 5 (inconsistently), O 3; cf. B 7. The queen asks where the babe is that she has heard greet, A a 4, b 4, c 6, B 4, 6, C 6, D 6, 8, E 6, 7, F 6, G 5, H 5, I 9, J 3, L 1, M 1; there is no babe, it was a stitch in the side, colic, A a 5, b 5, c 7, B 5, C 7, D 7, E 8, F 7, G 6, H 6, I 10, J 4, L 2, M 2; search is made and the child found in the bed, dead, E 9, F 9, H 7, J 5, L 4, M 4 (and A c 8 inconsistently). The queen bids Mary make ready to go to Edinburgh (i. e., from Holyrood), A a 6, A b 6, A c 10, C 8, D 11, E 10, F 12, H 8, I 11. The purpose is concealed in A, a, b, c, and for the best effect should be concealed, or at least simulated, as in B, D, G, I, where a wedding is the pretence, Mary Hamilton's own wedding in D. The queen directs Mary to put on black or brown, A a 6, A b 6, A c 10; she will not put on black or brown, but white, gold, red, to shine through Edinburgh town, A a 7, A b 7, A c 11, B 9, C 9, D 13, E 11, H 10, K 6, N 5,

O 5. When she went up the Canongate, A a 8, b 8, c 13, L 6, up the Parliament stair, A a 9, b 9, c 14, D 16, up the Tolbooth stair, C 12, E 14, H 15, I 17, came to the Netherbow Port, G 10, I 18, M 6, she laughed loudly or lightly, A a 8, b 8, c 13, D 16, E 14, G 10, H 15, I 18, L 6, M 6; the heel, lap, came off her shoe, A a 9, b 9, c 14, C 12, the corks from her heels did flee, I 17; but ere she came down again she was condemned to die, A a 9, b 9, c 14, C 12, D 16, E 14, H 15, I 17; but when she reached the gallows-foot, G 10, I 18, M 6, ere she came to the Cowgate Head, L 6, when she came down the Canongate, A a 8, b 8, c 13, the tears blinded her eyes. She calls for a bottle of wine, that she may drink to her well-wishers and they may drink to her, A a 12, b 10, c 17, B 14; cf. D 19, 20, G 13. She adjures sailors, travellers, not to let her father and mother get wit what death she is to die, A a 14, b 12, c 19, B 15, C 13, D 20, F 15, G 13, H 21, I 23, L 7, M 8, or know but that she is coming home, A a 13, b 11, B 16, C 14, D 19, E 15, F 16, G 14, H 20, I 22, L 8. Little did her mother think when she cradled her (brought her from home, F 18) what lands she would travel and what end she would come to, A a 15, c 21, B 17, 18, C 15, D 17, G 15, I 25, J 9, N 9, R; as little her father, when he held her up, A a 16, c 22, C 16, brought her over the sea, F 17. Yestreen the queen had four Maries, to-night she'll have but three (see above); yestreen she washed Queen Mary's feet, etc., and the gallows is her reward to-day, A a 17, b 13, B 20, C 17, G 11, 12, H 19, I 20, 21, N 8.

It is impossible to weave all the versions into an intelligible and harmonious story. In E 10, F 12, H 8 the intention to bring Mary to trial is avowed, and in A c 9, B 8[5,6]. F 10, K 5, M 5 she is threatened with death. In

* Deceivin, Abbey, are of course savin misunderstood. One of the reciters of D (4²) gave 'saving.'

D 12, H 9, J 7, N 4, the queen is made to favor, and not inhibit, gay colors. Mary may laugh when she goes up the Parliament stair, but not when she goes up the Tolbooth stair. She goes up the Canongate to the Parliament House to be tried, but she would not go down the Canongate again, the Tolbooth being in the High Street, an extension of the Canongate, and the Parliament House in the rear. The tears and alaces and ohones as Mary goes by, A a 10, c 15, B 10, C 10, D 14, E 12, F 13, H 11, I 16, are a sufficiently effective incident as long as Mary is represented to be unsuspicious of her doom, as she is in D 15, G 9, I 15, 16 ; but in A a 11, c 16, B 11, C 11, H 12, 22, she forbids condolement, because she deserves to die for killing her babe, which reduces this passage to commonplace. Much better, if properly introduced, would be the desperate ejaculation, Seek never grace at a graceless face ! which we find in E 13, F 14, H 13, N 7.

At the end of B the king tells Mary Hamilton to come down from the scaffold, but she scorns life after having been put to public shame. So in D, with queen for king.

In A a 4, b 4, 13, G 5 the queen is " the auld queen," and yet Mary Stuart.

E, from 16, F, from 19, are borrowed from No 95, ' The Maid freed from the Gallows : ' see II, 346. G 8 (and I 13, taken from G) is derived from ' Lord Thomas and Fair Annet,' D a 11, e 10, g 11 : see II, 187, 196, 197. The rejection of black and brown, A 7, C 9, D 13, etc., or of green, K 6, is found in the same ballad, C 10, E 16, F 12, 15, etc., B 20. B 21 is perhaps from ' The Laird of Waristoun : ' see further on, A 9, B 10, C 4. I 12, 14 look like a souvenir of ' Fair Janet,' No 64.

There are not a few spurious passages. Among these are the extravagance of the queen's bursting in the door, F 8 ; the platitude, of menial stamp, that the child, if saved, might have been an honor to the mother, D 10, L 3, O 4 ; the sentimentality of H 3, 16.

Allan Cunningham has put the essential incidents of the story into a rational order,

that of A, for example, with less than usual of his glistering and saccharine phraseology : Songs of Scotland, I, 348. Aytoun's language is not quite definite with regard to the copy which he gives at II, 45, ed. 1859 : it is, however, made up from versions previously printed.

When Mary Stuart was sent to France in 1548, she being then between five and six, she had for companions " sundry gentlewomen and noblemen's sons and daughters, almost of her own age, of the which there were four in special of whom every one of them bore the same name of Mary, being of four sundry honorable houses, to wit, Fleming, Livingston, Seton, and Beaton of Creich ; who remained all four with the queen in France during her residence there, and returned again in Scotland with her Majesty in the year of our Lord 1561 : " Lesley, History of Scotland, 1830, p. 209. We still hear of the Four Maries in 1564, Calendar of State Papers (Foreign), VII, 213, 230 ; cited by Burton, IV, 107. The ballad substitutes Mary Hamilton and Mary Carmichael for Mary Livingston and Mary Fleming ; but F 3, 12 has Livingston. N, of late recitation, has Heaton for Seton and Michel for Carmichael.

D 4, etc. In ' Tam Lin,' No 39, Janet pulls the rose to kill or scathe away her babe ; A 19, 20, F 8, I 24, 25 (probably repeated from A). In G 18, 19, the herb of 15 and the rose of 17 becomes the pile of the gravil green, or of the gravil gray ; in H 5, 6 Janet pulls an unspecified flower or herb (I, 341 ff).

We have had in ' The Twa Brothers,' No 49, a passage like that in which Mary begs sailors and travellers not to let her parents know that she is not coming home ; and other ballads, Norse, Breton, Romaic, and Slavic, which present a similar trait, are noted at I, 436 f, II, 14. To these may be added Passow, p. 400, No 523 ; Jeannaraki, p. 116, No 118 ; Sakellarios, p. 98, No 31 ; Puymaigre, 1865, p. 62, Bujeaud, II, 210 (Liebrecht) ; also Guillon, p. 107, Nigra, No 27, A, B, pp. 164, 166, and many copies of ' Le Déserteur,' and some of ' Le Plongeur,' ' La ronde du Battoir.'

Scott thought that the ballad took its rise

from an incident related by Knox as occurring in "the beginning of the regiment of Mary, Queen of Scots." " In the very time of the General Assembly," says Knox, "there comes to public knowledge a heinous murder committed in the court, yea, not far from the queen's own lap; for a French woman that served in the queen's chamber had played the whore with the queen's own apothecary. The woman conceived and bare a child, whom, with common consent, the father and the mother murdered. Yet were the cries of a new-born bairn heard; search was made, the child and mother was both deprehended, and so were both the man and the woman damned to be hanged upon the public street of Edinburgh." *
"It will readily strike the reader," says Scott, " that the tale has suffered great alterations, as handed down by tradition; the French waiting - woman being changed into Mary Hamilton, and the queen's apothecary † into Henry Darnley. Yet this is less surprising when we recollect that one of the heaviest of the queen's complaints against her ill-fated husband was his infidelity, and that even with her personal attendants." This General Assembly, however, met December 25, 1563, and since Darnley did not come to Scotland until 1565, a tale of 1563, or of 1563–4, leaves him unscathed.

Charles Kirkpatrick Sharpe, in his preface to A, Ballad Book, 1824, p. 18, observes: "It is singular that during the reign of the Czar Peter, one of his empress's attendants, a Miss Hamilton, was executed for the murder of a natural child. . . . I cannot help thinking that the two stories have been confused in the ballad, for if Marie Hamilton was exe-

cuted in Scotland, it is not likely that her relations resided beyond seas; and we have no proof that Hamilton was really the name of the woman who made a slip with the queen's apothecary." Sharpe afterwards communicated details of the story ‡ to Scott, who found in them " a very odd coincidence in name, crime and catastrophe; " Minstrelsy, 1833, III, 296, note. But Sharpe became convinced " that the Russian tragedy must be the original " (note in Laing's edition of the Ballad Book, 1880, p. 129); and this opinion is the only tenable one, however surprising it may be or seem that, as late as the eighteenth century, the popular genius, helped by nothing but a name, should have been able so to fashion and color an episode in the history of a distant country as to make it fit very plausibly into the times of Mary Stuart.

The published accounts of the affair of the Russian Mary Hamilton differ to much the same degree as some versions of the Scottish ballad. The subject has fortunately been reviewed in a recent article founded on original and authentic documents. §
When the Hamiltons first came to Russia does not appear. Artemon Sergheievitch Matveief, a distinguished personage, minister and friend of the father of Peter the Great, married a Hamilton, of a Scottish family settled at Moscow, after which the Hamilton family ranked with the aristocracy. The name of Mary's father, whether William or Daniel, is uncertain, but it is considered safe to say that she was niece to Andrei Artemonovitch Matveief, son of the Tsar Alexei's friend. Mary Hamilton was cre-

* History of the Reformation, Knox's Works, ed. Laing, II, 415 f. Knox continues: "But yet was not the court purged of whores and whoredom, which was the fountain of such enormities; for it was well known that shame hasted marriage betwix John Semple, called the Dancer, and Mary Livingston, surnamed the Lusty. What bruit the Maries and the rest of the dancers of the court had, the ballads of that age did witness, which we for modesty's sake omit." This Mary Livingston is one of the Four Marys, but, as already said, is mentioned in version F only of our ballad.
† "In this set of the ballad" [D], says Motherwell, " from its direct allusion to the use of the savin tree, a clue is perhaps afforded for tracing how the poor mediciner mentioned by Knox should be implicated in the crime of Mary

Hamilton." Maidment goes further: " The reference to the use of the savin tree in Motherwell induces a strong suspicion that the lover was a mediciner." Maidment should have remembered that there is a popular pharmacopœia quite independent of the professional. No apothecary prescribes in ' Tam Lin.'
‡ In an extract from Gordon's History of Peter the Great, Aberdeen, 1755, II, 308 f.
§ 'Maid - of - Honor Hamilton,' by M. I. Semefsky, in Slovo i Dyelo (Word and Deed), 1885, St Petersburg, 3d edition, p. 187. I am indebted to Professor Vinogradof, of the University of Moscow, for pointing out this paper, and to Miss Isabel Florence Hapgood for a summary of its contents.

ated maid-of-honor to the Empress Catharine chiefly on account of her beauty. Many of Catharine's attendants were foreigners; not all were of conspicuous families, but Peter required that they should all be remarkably handsome. Mary had enjoyed the special favor of the Tsar, but incurred his anger by setting afloat a report that Catharine had a habit of eating wax, which produced pimples on her face. The empress spoke to her about this slander; Mary denied that she was the author of it; Catharine boxed her ears, and she acknowledged the offence. Mary Hamilton had been having an amour with Ivan Orlof, a handsome aide-de-camp of Tsar Peter, and while she was under the displeasure of her master and mistress, the body of a child was found in a well, wrapped in a court-napkin. Orlof, being sent for by Peter on account of a missing paper, thought that his connection with Mary had been discovered, and in his confusion let words escape him which Peter put to use in tracing the origin of the child. The guilt was laid at Mary's door; she at first denied the accusation, but afterwards made a confession, exonerating Orlof, however, from all participation in the death of the babe; and indeed it was proved that he had not even known of its birth till the information came to him in the way of court-gossip. Both were sent to the Petropaulovsk fortress, Orlof on April 4, Mary on April 10, 1718. Orlof was afterwards discharged without punishment. Mary, after being twice subjected to torture, under which she confessed to having previously destroyed two children,* was condemned to death November 27, 1718, and executed on March 14, 1719, the Tsar attending. She had attired herself in white silk, with black ribbons, hoping thereby to touch Peter's heart. She fell on her knees and implored a pardon. But a law against the murder of illegitimate children had recently been promulgated afresh

and in terms of extreme severity. Peter turned aside and whispered something to the executioner; those present thought he meant to show grace, but it was an order to the headsman to do his office. The Tsar picked up Mary's head and kissed it, made a little discourse on the anatomy of it to the spectators, kissed it again, and threw it down. That beautiful head is said to have been kept in spirits for some sixty years at the Academy of Sciences in St Petersburg.

It will be observed that this adventure at the Russian court presents every material feature in the Scottish ballad, and even some subordinate ones which may or may not have been derived from report, may or may not have been the fancy-work of singers or reciters. We have the very name, Mary Hamilton; she is a maid-of-honor; she has, as some versions run, an intrigue with the king, and has a child, which she destroys; she rolls the child in a napkin and throws it into a well (rolls the child in her handkerchief, apron, and throws it in the sea); she is charged with the fact and denies; according to some versions, search is made and overwhelming proof discovered;† she is tried and condemned to die; she finds no grace. The appeal to sailors and travellers in the ballad shows that Mary Hamilton dies in a foreign land — not that of her ancestors. The king's coming by in **B** 22 (cf. **D** 22, 23) may possibly be a reminiscence of the Tsar's presence at the execution, and Mary's dressing herself in white, etc., to shine through Edinburgh town a transformation of Mary's dressing herself in white to move the Tsar's pity at the last moment; but neither of these points need be insisted on.

There is no trace of an admixture of the Russian story with that of the French woman and the queen's apothecary, and no ballad about the French woman is known to have existed.

---

* The parentage of these was not ascertained. Some accounts make Mary Hamilton to have been Peter's mistress: for example [J. B. Schérer's], Anecdotes intéressantes et secrètes de la cour de Russie, London, 1792, II, 272 ff. See also Mélanges de Littérature, etc., par François-Louis,

comte d'Escherny, Paris, 1811, I, 7 f. (The white gown with black ribbons is here.)

† "Hamilton, imperturbable, niait. Menzikoff engagea l'empereur à faire une perquisition dans les coffres d'Hamilton, ou l'on trouva le corps du délit, l'arrière-faix et du linge ensanglanté." Schérer, Anecdotes, p. 274.

We first hear of the Scottish ballad in 1790, when a stanza is quoted in a letter of Robert Burns (see R). So far as I know, but one date can be deduced from the subject-matter of the ballad; the Netherbow Port is standing in G, I, M, and this gate was demolished in 1764. The ballad must therefore have arisen between 1719 and 1764. It is remark-able that one of the very latest of the Scottish popular ballads should be one of the very best.

I a is translated by Gerhard, p. 149; Aytoun's ballad by Knortz, Schottische Balladen, p. 76, No 24.

———•———

A

a. Sharpe's Ballad Book, 1824, p. 18. **b.** Communicated by the late John Francis Campbell, as learned from his father about 1840. **c.** Aungervyle Society's publications, No V, p. 5 (First Series, p. 85); "taken down early in the present century from the lips of an old lady in Annandale."

1 WORD's gane to the kitchen,
    And word's gane to the ha,
That Marie Hamilton gangs wi bairn
    To the hichest Stewart of a'.

2 He's courted her in the kitchen,
    He's courted her in the ha,
He's courted her in the laigh cellar,
    And that was warst of a'.

3 She's tyed it in her apron
    And she's thrown it in the sea;
Says, Sink ye, swim ye, bonny wee babe!
    You'l neer get mair o me.

4 Down then cam the auld queen,
    Goud tassels tying her hair:
'O Marie, where's the bonny wee babe
    That I heard greet sae sair?'

5 'There never was a babe intill my room,
    As little designs to be;
It was but a touch o my sair side,
    Come oer my fair bodie.'

6 'O Marie, put on your robes o black,
    Or else your robes o brown,
For ye maun gang wi me the night,
    To see fair Edinbro town.'

7 'I winna put on my robes o black,
    Nor yet my robes o brown;
But I'll put on my robes o white,
    To shine through Edinbro town.'

8 When she gaed up the Cannogate,
    She laughd loud laughters three;
But whan she cam down the Cannogate
    The tear blinded her ee.

9 When she gaed up the Parliament stair,
    The heel cam aff her shee;
And lang or she cam down again
    She was condemnd to dee.

10 When she cam down the Cannogate,
    The Cannogate sae free,
Many a ladie lookd oer her window,
    Weeping for this ladie.

11 'Ye need nae weep for me,' she says,
    'Ye need nae weep for me;
For had I not slain mine own sweet babe,
    This death I wadna dee.

12 'Bring me a bottle of wine,' she says,
    'The best that eer ye hae,
That I may drink to my weil-wishers,
    And they may drink to me.

13 'Here's a health to the jolly sailors,
    That sail upon the main;
Let them never let on to my father and mother
    But what I'm coming hame.

14 'Here's a health to the jolly sailors,
    That sail upon the sea;
Let them never let on to my father and mother
    That I cam here to dee.

15 'Oh little did my mother think,
    The day she cradled me,
What lands I was to travel through,
    What death I was to dee.

16 'Oh little did my father think,
    The day he held up me,
    What lands I was to travel through,
    What death I was to dee.

17 'Last night I washd the queen's feet,
    And gently laid her down;

    And a' the thanks I've gotten the nicht
    To be hangd in Edinbro town!

18 'Last nicht there was four Maries,
    The nicht there 'l be but three;
    There was Marie Seton, and Marie Beton,
    And Marie Carmichael, and me.'

B

Motherwell's MS., p. 337.

1 THERE were ladies, they lived in a bower,
    And oh but they were fair!
    The youngest o them is to the king's court,
    To learn some unco lair.

2 She hadna been in the king's court
    A twelve month and a day,
    Till of her they could get na wark,
    For wantonness and play.

3 Word is to the kitchen gane,
    And word is to the ha,
    And word is up to Madame the Queen,
    And that is warst of a',
    That Mary Hamilton has born a bairn,
    To the hichest Stewart of a'.

4 'O rise, O rise, Mary Hamilton,
    O rise, and tell to me
    What thou did with thy sweet babe
    We sair heard weep by thee.'

5 'Hold your tongue, madame,' she said,
    'And let your folly be;
    It was a shouir o sad sickness
    Made me weep sae bitterlie.'

6 'O rise, O rise, Mary Hamilton,
    O rise, and tell to me
    What thou did with thy sweet babe
    We sair heard weep by thee.'

7 'I put it in a piner-pig,
    And set it on the sea;
    I bade it sink, or it might swim,
    It should neer come hame to me.'

8 'O rise, O rise, Mary Hamilton,
    Arise, and go with me;

    There is a wedding in Glasgow town
    This day we'll go and see.'

9 She put not on her black clothing,
    She put not on her brown,
    But she put on the glistering gold,
    To shine thro Edinburgh town.

10 As they came into Edinburgh town,
    The city for to see,
    The bailie's wife and the provost's wife
    Said, Och an alace for thee!

11 'Gie never alace for me,' she said,
    'Gie never alace for me;
    It's all for the sake of my poor babe,
    This death that I maun die.'

12 As they gaed up the Tolbuith stair,
    The stair it was sae hie,
    The bailie's son and the provost's son
    Said, Och an alace for thee!

13 'Gie never alace for me,' she said,
    'Gie never alace for me!
    It's all for the sake of my puir babe,
    This death that I maun die.

14 'But bring to me a cup,' she says,
    'A cup bot and a can,
    And I will drink to all my friends,
    And they ll drink to me again.

15 'Here's to you all, travellers,
    Who travels by land or sea;
    Let na wit to my father nor mother
    The death that I must die.

16 'Here's to you all, travellers,
    That travels on dry land;
    Let na wit to my father nor mother
    But I am coming hame.

17 'Little did my mother think,
    First time she cradled me,
What land I was to travel on,
    Or what death I would die.

18 'Little did my mother think,
    First time she tied my head,
What land I was to tread upon,
    Or whare I would win my bread.

19 'Yestreen Queen Mary had four Maries,
    This night she 'll hae but three;
She had Mary Seaton, and Mary Beaton,
    And Mary Carmichael, and me.

20 'Yestreen I wush Queen Mary's feet,
    And bore her till her bed;

This day she 's given me my reward,
    This gallows-tree to tread.

21 'Cast off, cast off my goun,' she said,
    ' But let my petticoat be,
And tye a napkin on my face,
    For that gallows I downa see.'

22 By and cum the king himsell,
    Lookd up with a pitiful ee:
' Come down, come down, Mary Hamilton,
    This day thou wilt dine with me.'

23 ' Hold your tongue, my sovereign leige,
    And let your folly be;
An ye had a mind to save my life,
    Ye should na shamed me here.'

C

Motherwell's MS. p. 265; from Mrs Crum, Dumbarton,
7 April, 1825.

1 THERE lived a lord into the west,
    And he had dochters three,
And the youngest o them is to the king's court,
    To learn some courtesie.

2 She was not in the king's court
    A twelvemonth and a day,
Till she was neither able to sit nor gang,
    Wi the gaining o some play.

3 She went to the garden,
    To pull the leaf aff the tree,
To tak this bonnie babe frae her breast,
    But alas it would na do!

4 She rowed it in her handkerchief,
    And threw it in the sea:
' O sink ye, swim ye, wee wee babe!
    Ye 'll get nae mair o me.'

5 Word is to the kitchen gane,
    And word is to the ha,
That Mary Myle she goes wi child
    To the highest Steward of a'.

6 Down and came the queen hersell,
    The queen hersell so free:

' O Mary Myle, whare is the child
    That I heard weep for thee?'

7 ' O hold your tongue now, Queen,' she says,
    ' O hold your tongue so free!
For it was but a shower o the sharp sickness,
    I was almost like to die.'

8 ' O busk ye, busk ye, Mary Myle,
    O busk, and go wi me;
O busk ye, busk ye, Mary Mile,
    It 's Edinburgh town to see.'

9 ' I 'll no put on my robes o black,
    No nor yet my robes [o] brown;
But I 'll put on my golden weed,
    To shine thro Edinburgh town.'

10 When she went up the Cannongate-side,
    The Cannongate-side so free,
Oh there she spied some ministers' lads,
    Crying Och and alace for me!

11 ' Dinna cry och and alace for me!
    Dinna cry o[c]h and alace for me!
For it 's all for the sake of my innocent babe
    That I come here to die.'

12 When she went up the Tolbooth-stair,
    The lap cam aff her shoe;
Before that she came down again,
    She was condemned to die.

13 'O all you gallant sailors,
    That sail upon the sea,
Let neither my father nor mother know
    The death I am to die!

14 'O all you gallant sailors,
    That sail upon the faem,
Let neither my father nor mother know
    But I am coming hame!

15 'Little did my mother know,
    The hour that she bore me,

What lands I was to travel in,
    What death I was to die.

16 'Little did my father know,
    When he held up my head,
What lands I was to travel in,
    What was to be my deid.

17 'Yestreen I made Queen Mary's bed,
    Kembed doun her yellow hair;
Is this the reward I am to get,
    To tread this gallows-stair!'

D

Motherwell's MS., p. 267; from the recitation of Miss Nancy Hamilton and Mrs Gentles, January, 1825.

1 THERE lives a knight into the north,
    And he had daughters three;
The ane of them was a barber's wife,
    The other a gay ladie.

2 And the youngest of them is to Scotland gane,
    The queen's Mary to be,
And a' that they could say or do,
    Forbidden she woudna be.

3 The prince's bed it was sae saft,
    The spices they were sae fine,
That out of it she couldna lye
    While she was scarce fifteen.

4 She's gane to the garden gay
    To pu of the savin tree;
But for a' that she could say or do,
    The babie it would not die.

5 She's rowed it in her handkerchief,
    She threw it in the sea;
Says, Sink ye, swim ye, my bonnie babe!
    For ye'll get nae mair of me.

6 Queen Mary came tripping down the stair,
    Wi the gold strings in her hair:
'O whare's the little babie,' she says,
    'That I heard greet sae sair?'

7 'O hold your tongue, Queen Mary, my dame,
    Let all those words go free!

It was mysell wi a fit o the sair colic,
    I was sick just like to die.'

8 'O hold your tongue, Mary Hamilton,
    Let all those words go free!
O where is the little babie
    That I heard weep by thee?'

9 'I rowed it in my handkerchief,
    And threw it in the sea;
I bade it sink, I bade it swim,
    It would get nae mair o me.'

10 'O wae be to thee, Marie Hamilton,
    And an ill deid may you die!
For if ye had saved the babie's life
    It might hae been an honour to thee.

11 'Busk ye, busk ye, Marie Hamilton,
    O busk ye to be a bride!
For I am going to Edinburgh toun,
    Your gay wedding to bide.

12 'You must not put on your robes of black,
    Nor yet your robes of brown;
But you must put on your yellow gold stuffs,
    To shine thro Edinburgh town.'

13 'I will not put on my robes of black,
    Nor yet my robes of brown;
But I will put on my yellow gold stuffs,
    To shine thro Edinburgh town.'

14 As she went up the Parliament Close,
    A riding on her horse,
There she saw many a cobler's lady,
    Sat greeting at the cross.

15 'O what means a' this greeting?
    I'm sure its nae for me;
For I'm come this day to Edinburgh town
    Weel wedded for to be.'

16 When she gade up the Parliament stair,
    She gied loud lauchters three;
But ere that she came down again,
    She was condemned to die.

17 'O little did my mother think,
    The day that she prinned my gown,
That I was to come sae far frae hame
    To be hangid in Edinburgh town.

18 'O what'll my poor father think,
    As he comes thro the town,
To see the face of his Molly fair
    Hanging on the gallows-pin!

19 'Here's a health to the marineres,
    That plough the raging main!
Let neither my mother nor father know
    But I'm coming hame again!

20 'Here's a health to the sailors,
    That sail upon the sea!
Let neither my mother nor father ken
    That I came here to die!

21 'Yestreen the queen had four Maries,
    This night she'll hae but three;
There was Mary Beaton, and Mary Seaton,
    And Mary Carmichael, and me.'

22 'O hald your tongue, Mary Hamilton,
    Let all those words go free!
This night eer ye be hanged
    Ye shall gang hame wi me.'

23 'O hald your tongue, Queen Mary, my dame,
    Let all those words go free!
For since I have come to Edinburgh toun,
    It's hanged I shall be,
And it shall neer be said that in your court
    I was condemned to die.'

E

Buchan's MSS, II, 186.

1 'My father was the Duke of York,
    My mother a lady free,
Mysell a dainty damsell,
    Queen Mary sent for me.

2 'Yestreen I washd Queen Mary's feet,
    Kam'd down her yellow hair,
And lay a' night in the young man's bed,
    And I'll rue t for evermair.

3 'The queen's kale was aye sae het,
    Her spice was aye sae fell,
Till they gart me gang to the young man's bed,
    And I'd a' the wyte mysell.

4 'I was not in the queen's service
    A twelvemonth but barely ane,
Ere I grew as big wi bairn
    As ae woman could gang.

5 'But it fell ance upon a day,
    Was aye to be it lane,

I did take strong travilling
    As ever yet was seen.'

6 Ben it came the queen hersell,
    Was a' gowd to the hair;
'O where's the bairn, Lady Maisry,
    That I heard greeting sair?'

7 Ben it came the queen hersell,
    Was a' gowd to the chin:
'O where's the bairn, Lady Maisry,
    That I heard late yestreen.'

8 'There is no bairn here,' she says,
    'Nor never thinks to be;
'T was but a stoun o sair sickness
    That ye heard seizing me.'

9 They sought it out, they sought it in,
    They sought it but and ben,
But between the bolster and the bed
    They got the baby slain.

10 'Come busk ye, busk ye, Lady Maisdry,
    Come busk, an go with me;

For I will on to Edinburgh,
And try the verity.'

11 She woud not put on the black, the black,
Nor yet wad she the brown,
But the white silk and the red scarlet,
That shin'd frae town to town.

12 As she gaed down thro Edinburgh town
The burghers' wives made meen,
That sic a dainty damsel
Sud ever hae died for sin.

13 'Make never meen for me,' she says,
'Make never meen for me;
Seek never grace frae a graceless face,
For that ye 'll never see.'

14 As she gaed up the Tolbooth stair,
A light laugh she did gie;
But lang ere she came down again
She was condemned to die.

15 'A' you that are in merchants-ships,
And cross the roaring faem,
Hae nae word to my father and mother,
But that I 'm coming hame.

16 'Hold your hands, ye justice o peace,
Hold them a little while!
For yonder comes my father and mother,
That 's travelld mony a mile.

17 'Gie me some o your gowd, parents,
Some o your white monie,
To save me frae the head o yon hill,
Yon greenwood gallows-tree.'

18 'Ye 'll get nane o our gowd, daughter,
Nor nane o our white monie;
For we hae travelld mony a mile,
This day to see you die.'

19 'Hold your hands, ye justice o peace,
Hold them a little while!
For yonder comes him Warenston,
The father of my chile.

20 'Give me some o your gowd, Warenston,
Some o your white monie,
To save me frae the head o yon hill,
Yon greenwood gallows-tree.'

21 'I bade you nurse my bairn well,
And nurse it carefullie,
And gowd shoud been your hire, Maisry,
And my body your fee.'

22 He 's taen out a purse o gowd,
Another o white monie,
And he 's tauld down ten thousand crowns,
Says, True love, gang wi me.

———◆———

F

Skene MS., p. 61.

1 My father was the Duke of York,
My mother a lady free,
Mysel a dainty demosell,
Queen Mary sent for me.

2 The queen's meat, it was sae sweet,
Her clothing was sae rare,
It made me lang for Sweet Willie's bed,
An I 'll rue it ever maer.

3 Mary Beaton, and Mary Seaton,
And Lady Livinston, three,
We 'll never meet in Queen Mary's bower,
Now Maries tho ye be.

4 Queen Mary sat in her bower,
Sewing her silver seam;
She thought she heard a baby greet,
But an a lady meen.

5 She threw her needle frae her,
Her seam out of her hand,
An she is on to Lady Mary's bower,
As fast as she could gang.

6 'Open yer door, Lady Mary,' she says,
'And lat me come in;
For I hear a baby greet,
But an a lady meen.'

7 'There is na bab in my bower, madam,
Nor never thinks to be,

But the strong pains of gravel
　　This night has seized me.'

8 She pat her fit to the door,
　　But an her knee,
Baith of brass and iron bands
　　In flinders she gard flee.

9 She pat a hand to her bed-head,
　　An ither to her bed-feet,
An bonny was the bab
　　Was blabbering in its bleed.

10 'Wae worth ye, Lady Mary,
　　An ill dead sall ye die !
For an ye widna kept the bonny bab,
　　Ye might ha sen 't to me.'

11 'Lay na the wate on me, madam,
　　Lay na the wate on me !
For my fas love bare the brand at his side
　　That gared my barrine die.'

12 'Get up, Lady Beaton, get up, Lady Seton,
　　And Lady Livinstone three,
An we will on to Edinburgh,
　　An try this gay lady.'

13 As she came to the Cannongate,
　　The burgers' wives they cryed
Hon ohon, ochree !　.　.　.

　.　　.　　.　　.　　.

14 'O had you still, ye burgers' wives,
　　An make na meen for me ;
Seek never grace of a graceless face,
　　For they hae nane to gie.

15 'Ye merchants and ye mariners,
　　That trade upon the sea,
O dinna tell in my country
　　The dead I 'm gaen to die !

16 'Ye merchants and ye mariners,
　　That sail upo the faeme,
O dinna tell in my country
　　But that I 'm comin hame !

17 'Little did my father think,
　　Whan he brought me our the sea,
That he wad see me yellow locks
　　Hang on a gallow's tree.

18 'Little did my mither think
　　Whan she brought me fra hame,
That she maught see my yellow loks
　　Han[g] on a gallow-pin.

19 'O had your hand a while !

　.　　.　　.　　.　　.

For yonder comes my father,
　　I 'm sure he 'l borrow me.

20 'O some of your goud, father,
　　An of your well won fee,
To save me [frae the high hill]
　　[And] frae the gallow-tree ! '

21 'Ye 's get nane of my goud,
　　Nor of my well won fee,
For I would gie five hundred pown
　　To see ye hangit hie.'

22 'O had yer hand a while !

　.　　.　　.　　.　　.

Yonder is my love Willie,
　　Sure he will borrow me.

23 'O some o your goud, my love Willie,
　　An some o yer well won fee,
To save me frae the high hill,
　　And fra the gallow-tree ! '

24 'Ye 's get a' my goud,
　　And a' my well won fee,
To save ye fra the headin-hill,
　　And frae the gallow-tree.'

————◆————

G

Manuscript of Scottish Songs and Ballads, copied by a granddaughter of Lord Woodhouselee, 1840–50, p. 51.

1 O MARY HAMILTON to the kirk is gane,
　　Wi ribbons in her hair ;

An the king thoct mair o Marie
　　Then onie that were there.

2 Mary Hamilton 's to the preaching gane,
　　Wi ribbons on her breast ;
An the king thocht mair o Marie
　　Than he thocht o the priest.

3 Syne word is thro the palace gane,
   I heard it tauld yestreen,
The king loes Mary Hamilton
   Mair than he loes his queen.

4 A sad tale thro the town is gaen,
   A sad tale on the morrow ;
Oh Mary Hamilton has born a babe,
   An slain it in her sorrow !

5 And down then cam the auld queen,
   Goud tassels tied her hair :
' What did ye wi the wee wee bairn
   That I heard greet sae sair ? '

6 ' There neer was a bairn into my room,
   An as little designs to be ;
'T was but a stitch o my sair side,
   Cam owre my fair bodie.'

7 ' Rise up now, Marie,' quo the queen,
   ' Rise up, an come wi me,
For we maun ride to Holyrood,
   A gay wedding to see.'

8 The queen was drest in scarlet fine,
   Her maidens all in green ;
An every town that they cam thro
   Took Marie for the queen.

9 But little wist Marie Hamilton,
   As she rode oure the lea,
That she was gaun to Edinbro town
   Her doom to hear and dree.

10 When she cam to the Netherbow Port,
   She laughed loud laughters three ;
But when she reached the gallows-tree,
   The tears blinded her ee.

11 ' Oh aften have I dressed my queen,
   An put gowd in her hair ;
The gallows-tree is my reward,
   An shame maun be my share !

12 ' Oh aften hae I dressed my queen,
   An saft saft made her bed ;
An now I 've got for my reward
   The gallows-tree to tread !

13 ' There 's a health to all gallant sailors,
   That sail upon the sea !
Oh never let on to my father and mither
   The death that I maun dee !

14 ' An I charge ye, all ye mariners,
   When ye sail owre the main,
Let neither my father nor mither know
   But that I 'm comin hame.

15 ' Oh little did my mither ken,
   That day she cradled me,
What lands I was to tread in,
   Or what death I should dee.

16 ' Yestreen the queen had four Maries,
   The nicht she 'll hae but three ;
There 's Marie Seaton, an Marie Beaton,
   An Marie Carmichael, an me.'

H

Kinloch's Ancient Scottish Ballads, p. 252 ; a North Country version.

1 ' WHAN I was a babe, and a very little babe,
   And stood at my mither's knee,
Nae witch nor warlock did unfauld
   The death I was to dree.

2 ' But my mither was a proud woman,
   A proud woman and a bauld ;
And she hired me to Queen Mary's bouer,
   When scarce eleven years auld.

3 ' O happy, happy is the maid,
   That 's born of beauty free !

It was my dimpling rosy cheeks
   That 's been the dule o me ;
And wae be to that weirdless wicht,
   And a' his witcherie ! '

4 Word 's gane up and word 's gane doun,
   An word 's gane to the ha,
That Mary Hamilton was wi bairn,
   An na body kend to wha.

5 But in and cam the queen hersel,
   Wi gowd plait on her hair :
Says, Mary Hamilton, whare is the babe
   That I heard greet sae sair ?

6 'There is na babe within my bouer,
　　And I hope there neer will be ;
　But it 's me wi a sair and sick colic,
　　And I 'm just like to dee.'

7 But they looked up, they looked down,
　　Atween the bowsters and the wa,
　It 's there they got a bonnie lad-bairn,
　　But its life it was awa.

8 'Rise up, rise up, Mary Hamilton,
　　Rise up, and dress ye fine,
　For you maun gang to Edinbruch,
　　And stand afore the nine.

9 'Ye 'll no put on the dowie black,
　　Nor yet the dowie brown ;
　But ye 'll put on the robes o red,
　　To sheen thro Edinbruch town.'

10 'I 'll no put on the dowie black,
　　Nor yet the dowie brown ;
　But I 'll put on the robes o red,
　　To sheen thro Edinbruch town.'

11 As they gaed thro Edinbruch town,
　　And down by the Nether-bow,
　There war monie a lady fair
　　Siching and crying, Och how !

12 'O weep na mair for me, ladies,
　　Weep na mair for me !
　Yestreen I killed my ain bairn,
　　The day I deserve to dee.

13 'What need ye hech and how, ladies ?
　　What need ye how for me ?
　Ye never saw grace at a graceless face,
　　Queen Mary has nane to gie.'

14 'Gae forward, gae forward,' the queen she said,
　　'Gae forward, that ye may see ;

For the very same words that ye hae said
　Sall hang ye on the gallows-tree.'

15 As she gaed up the Tolbooth stairs,
　　She gied loud lauchters three ;
　But or ever she cam down again,
　　She was condemnd to dee.

16 'O tak example frae me, Maries,
　　O tak example frae me,
　Nor gie your luve to courtly lords,
　　Nor heed their witchin' ee.

17 'But wae be to the Queen hersel,
　　She micht hae pardond me ;
　But sair she 's striven for me to hang
　　Upon the gallows-tree.

18 'Yestreen the Queen had four Maries,
　　The nicht she 'll hae but three ;
　There was Mary Beatoun, Mary Seaton,
　　And Mary Carmichael, and me.

19 'Aft hae I set pearls in her hair,
　　Aft hae I lac'd her gown,
　And this is the reward I now get,
　　To be hangd in Edinbruch town !

20 'O a' ye mariners, far and near,
　　That sail ayont the faem,
　O dinna let my father and mither ken
　　But what I am coming hame !

21 'O a' ye mariners, far and near,
　　That sail ayont the sea,
　Let na my father and mither ken
　　The death I am to dee !

22 'Sae, weep na mair for me, ladies,
　　Weep na mair for me ;
　The mither that kills her ain bairn
　　Deserves weel for to dee.'

———◆———

I

a. Scott's Minstrelsy, 1833, III, 294, made up from various copies. b. Three stanzas (23, 18, 19) in the first edition of the Minstrelsy, 1802, II, 154, from recitation.

1 MARIE HAMILTON 's to the kirk gane,
　　Wi ribbons in her hair ;

The king thought mair o Marie Hamilton
　Than ony that were there.

2 Marie Hamilton 's to the kirk gane,
　　Wi ribbons on her breast ;
　The king thought mair o Marie Hamilton
　　Then he listend to the priest.

3 Marie Hamilton 's to the kirk gane,
    Wi gloves upon her hands ;
  The king thought mair o Marie Hamilton,
    Than the queen and a' her lands.

4 She hadna been about the king's court
    A month, but barely one,
  Till she was beloved by a' the king's court,
    And the king the only man.

5 She hadna been about the king's court
    A month, but barely three,
  Till frae the king's court Marie Hamilton,
    Marie Hamilton durstna be.

6 The king is to the Abbey gane,
    To pu the Abbey-tree,
  To scale the babe frae Marie's heart,
    But the thing it wadna be.

7 O she has rowd it in her apron,
    And set it on the sea :
  'Gae sink ye, or swim ye, bonny babe !
    Ye 's get nae mair o me.'

8 Word is to the kitchen gane,
    And word is to the ha,
  And word is to the noble room,
    Amang the ladyes a',
  That Marie Hamilton 's brought to bed,
    And the bonny babe 's mist and awa.

9 Scarcely had she lain down again,
    And scarcely fa'en asleep,
  When up then started our gude queen,
    Just at her bed-feet,
  Saying, Marie Hamilton, where 's your babe ?
    For I am sure I heard it greet.

10 'O no, O no, my noble queen,
    Think no such thing to be !
  'T was but a stitch into my side,
    And sair it troubles me.'

11 'Get up, get up, Marie Hamilton,
    Get up and follow me ;
  For I am going to Edinburgh town,
    A rich wedding for to see.'

12 O slowly, slowly raise she up,
    And slowly put she on,
  And slowly rode she out the way,
    Wi mony a weary groan.

13 The queen was clad in scarlet,
    Her merry maids all in green,
  And every town that they cam to,
    They took Marie for the queen.

14 'Ride hooly, hooly, gentlemen,
    Ride hooly now wi me !
  For never, I am sure, a wearier burd
    Rade in your cumpanie.'

15 But little wist Marie Hamilton,
    When she rade on the brown,
  That she was gaen to Edinburgh town,
    And a' to be put down.

16 'Why weep ye so, ye burgess-wives,
    Why look ye so on me ?
  O I am going to Edinburgh town
    A rich wedding for to see !'

17 When she gaed up the Tolbooth stairs,
    The corks frae her heels did flee ;
  And lang or eer she cam down again
    She was condemnd to die.

18 When she cam to the Netherbow Port,
    She laughed loud laughters three ;
  But when she cam to the gallows-foot,
    The tears blinded her ee.

19 'Yestreen the queen had four Maries,
    The night she 'll hae but three ;
  There was Marie Seaton, and Marie Beaton,
    And Marie Carmichael, and me.

20 'O often have I dressd my queen,
    And put gold upon her hair ;
  But now I 've gotten for my reward
    The gallows to be my share.

21 'Often have I dressd my queen,
    And often made her bed ;
  But now I 've gotten for my reward
    The gallows-tree to tread.

22 'I charge ye all, ye mariners,
    When ye sail ower the faem,
  Let neither my father nor mother get wit
    But that I 'm coming hame !

23 'I charge ye all, ye mariners,
    That sail upon the sea,
  Let neither my father nor mother get wit
    This dog's death I 'm to die !

24 'For if my father and mother got wit,
    And my bold brethren three,
    O mickle wad be the gude red blude
    This day wad be spilt for me !

25 'O little did my mother ken,
    That day she cradled me,
    The lands I was to travel in,
    Or the death I was to die ! '

J

Harris MS., fol. 10 b ; " Mrs Harris and others."

1 My mother was a proud, proud woman,
    A proud, proud woman and a bold ;
    She sent me to Queen Marie's bour,
    When scarcely eleven years old.

2 Queen Marie's bread it was sae sweet,
    An her wine it was sae fine,
    That I hae lien in a young man's arms,
    An I rued it aye synsyne.

3 Queen Marie she cam doon the stair,
    Wi the goud kamis in her hair :
    'Oh whare, oh whare is the wee wee babe
    I heard greetin sae sair ? '

4 'It's no a babe, a babie fair,
    Nor ever intends to be ;
    But I mysel, wi a sair colic,
    Was seek an like to dee.'

5 They socht the bed baith up an doon,
    Frae the pillow to the straw,
    An there they got the wee wee babe,
    But its life was far awa.

6 'Come doon, come doon, Marie Hamilton,
    Come doon an speak to me ;

  .   .   .   .   .   .
    .   .   .   .   .   .

7 'You 'll no put on your dowie black,
    Nor yet your dowie broun ;
    But you 'll put on your ried, ried silk,
    To shine through Edinborough toun.'

*   *   *   *   *   *   *

8 'Yestreen the queen had four Maries,
    The nicht she 'll hae but three ;
    There was Marie Bethune, an Marie Seaton,
    An Marie Carmichael, an me.

9 'Ah, little did my mother ken,
    The day she cradled me,
    The lands that I sud travel in,
    An the death that I suld dee.'

10 Yestreen the queen had four Maries,
    The nicht she has but three ;
    For the bonniest Marie amang them a'
    Was hanged upon a tree.

K

Motherwell's MS., p. 96 ; from Jean Macqueen, Largs.

1 Queen Mary had four serving-maids,
    As braw as braw could be,
    But ane o them has fa'n wi bairn,
    And for it she maun die.

2 But whan the babie it was born,
    A troubled woman was she ;
    She rowed it up in a handkerchief,
    And flang it in the sea.

3 Out then spoke a bonnie wee burd,
    And it spak sharp and keen :
    'O what did ye do wi your wee babie,
    Ye had in your arms yestreen ? '

4 'O I tyed it up in a napkin,
    And flang it in the sea ;
    I bade it sink, I bade it soom,
    'T wad get nae mair o me.'

5 Out and spak King Henrie,
    And an angry man was he :
    'A' for the drowning o that wee babe
    High hanged ye shall be.'

*   *   *   *   *   *

6 'I 'll no put on a goun o black,
    Nor yet a goun o green,
    But I 'll put on a goun o gowd,
    To glance in young men's een.

7 'O gin ye meet my father or mother,
　　Ye may tell them frae me,
　'T was for the sake o a wee wee bairn
　　That I came here to die.

8 'Yestreen four Maries made Queen Mary's
　　　bed,
　　This nicht there 'll be but three,

　　　A Mary Beaton, a Mary Seaton,
　　　　A Mary Carmichael, and me.

9 'O what will my three brithers say,
　　When they come hame frae see,
　When they see three locks o my yellow hair
　　Hinging under a gallows-tree !'

L

Motherwell's MS., p. 280; from the recitation of Mrs
Trail of Paisley.

1 Doun and cam the queen hersell,
　　Wi the goud links in her hair :
　'O what did you do wi the braw lad bairn
　　That I heard greet sae sair ?'

2 'There was never a babe into my room,
　　Nor ever intends to be ;
　It was but a fit o the sair colic,
　　That was like to gar me die.'

3 Doun and cam the king himsell,
　　And an angry man was he :
　'If ye had saved that braw child's life,
　　It might hae been an honour to thee.'

4 They socht the chamer up and doun,
　　And in below the bed,
　And there they fand a braw lad-bairn
　　Lying lapperin in his blood.

5 She rowed it up in her apron green,
　　And threw it in the sea :

'Een sink or swim, you braw lad bairn !
　Ye 'll neer get mair o me.'

* 　 * 　 * 　 * 　 * 　 * 　 *

6 When she gaed up the Cannogate,
　　She gied loud lauchters three ;
　But or she cam to the Cowgate Head
　　The tears did blind her ee.

7 'Come a' ye jovial sailors,
　　That sail upon the sea,
　Tell neither my father nor mother
　　The death that I 'm to die !

8 'Come a' ye jovial sailors,
　　That sail upon the main,
　See that ye tell baith my father and mother
　　That I 'm coming sailing hame !

9 'My father he 's the Duke of York,
　　And my mother 's a gay ladie,
　And I mysell a pretty fair lady,
　　And the king fell in love with me.'

M

Maidment's North Countrie Garland, p. 19.

1 Then down cam Queen Marie,
　　Wi gold links in her hair,
　Saying, Marie Mild, where is the child,
　　That I heard greet sae sair ?

2 'There was nae child wi me, madam,
　　There was nae child wi me ;
　It was but me in a sair cholic,
　　When I was like to die.'

3 'I 'm not deceived,' Queen Marie said,
　　' No, no, indeed not I !
　So Marie Mild, where is the child ?
　　For sure I heard it cry.'

4 She turned down the blankets fine,
　　Likewise the Holland sheet,
　And underneath, there strangled lay
　　A lovely baby sweet.

5 'O cruel mother,' said the queen,
　　' Some fiend possessed thee ;

But I will hang thee for this deed,
　My Marie tho thou be!'

*　　*　　*　　*　　*　　*　　*

6 When she cam to the Netherbow Port
　She laught loud laughters three;
　But when she cam to the gallows-foot,
　The saut tear blinded her ee.

7 'Yestreen the Queen had four Maries,
　The night she'll hae but three;

There was Marie Seton, and Marie Beaton,
　And Marie Carmichael, and me.

8 'Ye mariners, ye mariners,
　That sail upon the sea,
　Let not my father or mother wit
　The death that I maun die!

9 'I was my parents' only hope,
　They neer had ane but me;
　They little thought when I left hame,
　They should nae mair me see!'

N

Murison MS., p. 33; from recitation at Old Deer, 1876.

1 THE streen the queen had four Maries,
　This nicht she'll hae but three;
　There's Mary Heaton, an Mary Beaton,
　An Mary Michel, an me,
　An I mysel was Mary Mild,
　An flower oer a' the three.

2 Mary's middle was aye sae neat,
　An her clothing aye sae fine,
　It caused her lie in a young man's airms,
　An she's ruet it aye sin syne.

3 She done her doon yon garden green,
　To pull the deceivin tree,
　For to keep back that young man's bairn,
　But forward it would be.

4 'Ye winna put on the dowie black,
　Nor yet will ye the broon,
　But ye'll put on the robes o red,
　To shine through Edinburgh toon.'

5 She hasna pitten on the dowie black,
　Nor yet has she the broon,
　But she's pitten on the robes o red,
　To shine thro Edinburgh toon.

6 When she came to the mariners' toon,
　The mariners they were playin,

· 　· 　· 　· 　· 　·
　· 　· 　· 　· 　·

7 'Ye needna play for me, mariners,
　Ye needna play for me;
　Ye never saw grace in a graceless face,
　For there's nane therein to be.

8 'Seven years an I made Queen Mary's bed,
　Seven years an I combed her hair,
　An a hansome reward noo she's gien to me,
　Gien me the gallows-tows to wear!

9 'Oh little did my mither think,
　The day she cradled me,
　What road I'd hae to travel in,
　Or what death I'd hae to dee!'

O

Finlay's Scottish Ballads, I, xix, from recitation.

1 THERE lived a lord into the south,
　And he had dochters three,
　And the youngest o them went to the king's
　　court,
　To learn some courtesie.

2 She rowd it in a wee wee clout
　· 　· 　· 　· 　· 　·

· 　· 　· 　· 　· 　·
　· 　· 　· 　· 　·

3 She rowd it in a wee wee clout
　And flang't into the faem,
　Saying, Sink ye soon, my bonny babe!
　I'll go a maiden hame.

4 'O woe be to you, ye ill woman,
　An ill death may ye die!
　Gin ye had spared the sweet baby's life,
　It might hae been an honour to thee.'

5 She wadna put on her gowns o black,
  Nor yet wad she o brown,
But she wad put on her gowns o gowd,
  To glance through Embro town.

———◆———

P

Kinloch's MSS, VII, 95, 97.

MY father's the Duke of Argyll,
  My mither's a lady gay,
And I mysel am a dainty dame,
  And the king desired me.

———◆———

Q

Letters from and to Charles Kirkpatrick Sharpe, ed.
Allardyce, 1888, II, 272, in a letter from Sharpe to W.
Scott [1823].

1 THE Duke of York was my father,
  My mother a lady free,

———◆———

R

Burns, in a letter to Mrs Dunlop, January 25, 1790;
Currie, II, 290, 1800.

LITTLE did my mother think,
  That day she cradled me,

———◆———

6 'Come saddle not to me the black,' she says,
  'Nor yet to me the brown,
But come saddle to me the milk-white steed,
  That I may ride in renown.'

He schawd [me] up, he shawed me doun,
  He schawd me to the ha;
He schawd me to the low cellars,
  And that was waurst of a'.

Myself a dainty damosell,
  Queen Marie sent for me.

2 The queen's meat it was sae sweet,
  Her cleiding was sae rare,
It gart me grien for sweet Willie,
  And I'll rue it evermair.

What land I was to travel in,
  Or what death I should die!

———◆———

A. b. 1. There's news is gaen in the kitchen,
    There's news is gaen in the ha,
    There's news is gaen in the laigh cellar,
    And that was warst of a'.

  2. There's news is gaen in the kitchen,
    There's news is gaen in the ha',
    That Mary Hamilton's gotten a wean,
    And that was warst of a'.

3^1. She's rowed. 3^2. She's cuist it.
3^3. My bonnie bairn ga sink or swim.
3^4. Ye's no hear mair. 4^1. Then doon.
4^2. Wi tasslets.
4^3. Cri'n, M. H., whaur's the bairn.
4^4. That *wanting*.
5^1. There's no a bairn in a' the toon.
5^2. Nor yet. 5^3. 'T was but a steek in.
6^1. And ye maun.

6^4. And ye maun awa wi me the morn.
7^1. I'se no. 7^4. To see fair. 8^1. And when.
8^3. And when. 8^4. tear stood in.
9^1. And when. 9^2. heel slipped off.
9^3. And when she cam doon the Parliament
  stair.
10, 11 *wanting*. 12^1. But bring: she cried.
$13^1, 14^1$. And here's to the jolly sailor lad.
$13^2, 14^2$. sails: faem.
13^3. And let not my father nor mother get wit.
13^4. that I shall come again.
14^3. But let, *as in* 13^3.
14^4. O the death that I maun dee.
15, 16 *wanting*. 17^1. auld queen's.
17^2. And I laid her gently.
17^3. I hae gotten the day. 17^4. Is to.
18^1. night the queen had.
18^2. This night she'll hae.
18^4. M. Beton and M. Seton.

c. *Begins:* This nicht the queen has four Maries,
          Each fair as she can be ;
        There's Marie Seton, etc.

3¹. The bairn's tyed.   3². And thrown intill.
4³. O sink.

After 3 :
     Oh I have born this bonnie wee babe
        Wi mickle toil and pain ;
     Gae hame, gae hame, you bonnie wee babe !
        For nurse I dare be nane.

4¹. Then down cam Queen Marie.
4³. Saying, Marie mild, where is the babe.
5¹. There was nae babe.
5². There was na babe wi me.
5³. o a sair cholic.

After 5 (*mostly spurious*) :
     The queen turned down the blankets fine,
        Likewise the snae-white sheet,
     And what she saw caused her many a tear,
        And made her sair to greet.

     O cruel mither, said the queen,
        A fiend possessed thee :
     But I will hang thee for this deed,
        My Marie though thou be.

After 7 :
     And some they mounted the black steed,
        And some mounted the brown,
     But Marie mounted her milk-white steed,
        And rode foremost thro the town.

8³. But when.   *After* 12 :

     Yestreen the queen had four Maries,
        The nicht she 'll hae but three ;
     There was M. S., and M. B.
        And M. C., and me.

13 *wanting.* 14¹. Ye mariners, ye mariners.
14³. L[et] not my father and mother wit.
14⁴. The death that I maun dee.

After 14 :
     I was my parents' only hope,
        They neer had ane but me ;
     They little thought, when I left hame,
        They should nae mair me see.

17 *wanting.* 18¹. there were.
Largely taken from a, 1, 2, 6–12, 15, 16 *being
     literally repeated.*

B. 3³. us up.   8⁵,⁶. *wrongly :*
     And we 'll ride into Edinburgh town,
        High hanged thou shalt be.

C. 9². *Altered from* I 'll put on my brown.
     Var. between 9² *and* 9³ :
        Nor I 'll no put on my suddling silks,
           That I wear up and down.
     up and down *altered from* ilka day.

10¹. went *altered from* gaed.
13¹, 14¹. Oh.

D. *From two reciters, which accounts for the
     alterations and insertions.*
     1¹. *Altered from* There was a lord lived in
        the north.
     2¹. *Altered from* And the third.
     2³. *Altered from* that he.
     4¹. gay *added later.*
     4². *Altered from* And pued the saving tree.
     4³. for *inserted later.* 4⁴. it *inserted later.*
     7³. a fit o *inserted later.*
     7⁴. *Altered from* I am just.
     9. *After* 9, *Motherwell wrote* A stanza want-
        ing, *and subsequently added* 10, 11.
     12³. *Originally,* gold stars.
     13. *Originally,*
        She did not put on her robes of black,
           Nor yet her robes of brown,
        But she put on her yellow gold stars (stays?).

     14. *Originally,*
        And when she came into Edinborugh, (bad
           reading)
        And standing at the cross,
        There she saw all the coblers' wifes,
           Sat greeting at the cross.

     15³,⁴. *Originally,* For I am come to, etc.,
        Weeded for to be.
     *A marginal note by Motherwell, opposite the
        last line, but erased, has* A rich wedding to
        sie.
     16¹. stair *altered from* close.
     19, 20. *Written in the margin, after those
        which follow.*
     23³,⁴ *and* And, 23⁵, *are of later insertion.*

E. *For the seven stanzas after* 15, *see No* 95, II,
     346.

F. 3. Mary Beaton & Mary Seaton & Lady Livin-
       ston
       Three we 'll [*or* will] never meet
       In queen Mary's bower
       Now Maries tho ye be.

    13². then cryed. 14¹. had your. 18⁴. pine.
    For the six stanzas after 18, *see No* 95, II,
    346.
G. 1¹. Oh.
H. 3, 16, 17, 22 *are put into smaller type as
    being evidently spurious.*
I. a. 24 *is certainly spurious, and reduces the
    pathos exceedingly.*
   b. 18⁴. tear.

    23. O ye mariners, mariners, mariners,
        That sail upon the sea,
        Let not my father nor mother to wit
        The death that I maun die!

K. From Jean Macqueen, Largo, *in the MS.*

    " More likely to be Largs, which is on the
    Clyde, than Largo, on the east coast " : *note
    of Mr J. B. Murdoch.*
    4¹. Oh.
    6 *is the last stanza but one in the MS.*
L. 9 *might better be* 1.
N. *Variations.*

    1³⁻⁶. There 's Mary Beaton, an Mary Seaton,
          An Mary Carmichael, an me;
          An I mysel, Queen Mary's maid,
          Was flower oer a' the three.

    2¹. sae jimp.   2³. She loved to lie.
    3². the savin tree.

    3³,⁴. But the little wee babe came to her back,
          An forward it would be.

    8 *is* 4 *in the MS.*
O. " The unfortunate heroine's name is Mary
    Moil " : Finlay, p. xix.

174

EARL BOTHWELL

'Earle Bodwell,' Percy MS., p. 272; Hales and Furnivall, II, 260.

———

PRINTED in Percy's Reliques, with changes,
1765, II, 197, ' The Murder of the King of
Scots ; ' with some restorations of the original
readings, 1794, II, 200.

This ballad represents, 8, 13, that the
murder of Darnley was done in revenge for
his complicity in the murder of Riccio ; in
which there may be as much truth as this,
that the queen's resentment of Darnley's par-
ticipation in that horrible transaction may
have been operative in inducing her assent —
such assent as she gave — to the conspiracy
against the life of her husband.

2. Darnley came to Scotland in February,
1565 (being then but just turned of nine-
teen), not sent for, but very possibly with
some hope of pleasing his cousin, ' the queen
[dowager] of France,' to whom he was mar-
ried in the following July. His inglorious
career was closed in February, 1567.

5. On the fatal evening of the ninth of
March, 1566, Riccio was sitting in the queen's
cabinet with his cap on ; " and this sight was
perhaps the more offensive that a few Scots-
men of good rank seem to have been in at-
tendance as domestics." *

6. The ballad should not be greatly in
excess as to the number of the daggers, since
Riccio had fifty-six [fifty-two] wounds.

* Bedford and Randolph to the Council, Wright's Queen
Elizabeth, etc., p. 227; Burton, History of Scotland, IV,
145.

7. After Riccio had been dragged out of the queen's cabinet, Darnley fell to charging the queen with change in her ways with him since "yon fellow Davie fell in credit and familiarity" with her. In answer to his reproaches and interpellations her Majesty said to him that he was to blame for all the shame that was done to her; "for the which I shall never be your wife nor lie with you, nor shall never like well till I gar you have as sore a heart as I have presently." *

9–14. A large quantity of powder was fired in the room below that in which "the worthy king" slept, but the body of Darnley and that of his servant were found lying at a considerable distance from the house, without any marks of having been subject to the explosion. One theory of the circumstances was that the two had been strangled in their beds, and removed before the train was lighted; another account is that Darnley, who would naturally hear some stir in the house, made his escape with his page, but "was intercepted and strangled after a desperate resistance, his cries for mercy being heard by some women in the nearest house." † Bothwell, though the author of all these proceedings and personally superintending the execution of them, did not openly appear.

It will be observed that King James says that his father [MS. mother] was hanged on a tree, in 'King James and Brown,' No 180, 8².

Bothwell and Huntly, who by virtue of their offices had apartments in the palace, not being in sympathy with the conspirators, are said in the Diurnal of Occurrents, p. 90, to have broken through a window, in fear of their lives, and to have let themselves down by a cord. Bothwell, as the champion of the queen against the confederate lords, might naturally be supposed by the minstrel to take a personal interest in revenging Riccio.

15, 16. The Regent Murray is here described as 'bitterly banishing' Mary, wherefore she durst not remain in Scotland, but fled to England. The queen escaped from Lochleven Castle on the second of May, 1568, and took refuge in England on the sixteenth. We must suppose the ballad to have been made not long after.

Translated by Bodmer, II, 51, from Percy's Reliques.

————◆————

1 WOE worth thee, woe worth thee, false Scottlande !
    Ffor thou hast euer wrought by a sleight;
    For the worthyest prince *that* euer was borne,
    You hanged vnder a cloud by night.

2 The Queene of France a letter wrote,
    And sealed itt w*i*th hart and ringe,
    And bade him come Scottland w*i*thin,
    And shee wold marry him and crowne him ki*ng*.

3 To be a ki*ng*, itt is a pleasant thing,
    To bee a prince vnto a peere ;
    But you haue heard, and so haue I too,
    A man may well by gold to deere.

4 There was an Italyan in that place,
    Was as wel beloued as euer was **hee** ;
    Lo*rd* David was his name,
    Chamberlaine vnto the queene was hee.

5 Ffor if the king had risen forth of his place,
    He wold haue sitt him downe in the cheare,
    And tho itt beseemed him not soe well,
    Altho the king had beene p*r*esent there.

6 Some lords in Scottland waxed wonderous wroth,
    And quarrelld w*i*th him for the nonce ;
    I shall you tell how itt beffell ,
    Twelue daggers were in him all att once.

* Ruthven's Relation, p. 30 f, London, 1699.

† The Historie of King James the Sext, p. 6 ; Diurnal of Occurrents, p. 105 f ; Tytler's History, VII, 83.

7 When this queene see the chamberlaine was
    slaine,
  For him her cheeks shee did weete,
  And made a vow for a twelue month and a
    day
  The k*ing* and shee wold not come in one
    sheete.

8 Then some of the lo*rd*s of Scottland waxed
    wrothe,
  And made their vow vehementlye,
  'For death of the queenes chamberlaine
  The k*ing* himselfe he shall dye.'

9 They strowed his chamber ou*er* w*ith* gunpow-
    der,
  And layd greene rushes in his way;
  Ffor the traitors thought *that* night
  The worthy king for to betray.

10 To bedd the worthy k*ing* made him bowne,
   To take his rest, *that* was his desire;
  He was noe sooner cast on sleepe,
  But his chamber was on a blasing fyer.

11 V*p* he lope, and a glasse window broke,
   He had thirty foote for to ffall;
  Lo*rd* Bodwell kept a priuy wach
  Vnderneath his castle-wall:

'Who haue wee heere?' sayd Lo*rd* Bodwell;
  'Answer me, now I doe call.'

12 'K*ing* Henery the Eighth my vnckle was;
   Some pitty show for his sweet sake!
  Ah, Lo*rd* Bodwell, I know thee well;
  Some pitty on me I pray thee take!'

13 'I 'le pitty thee as much,' he sayd,
   'And as much favor I 'le show to thee
  As thou had on the queene's chamberlaine
  That day thou deemedst him to dye.'

14 Through halls and towers this k*ing* they ledd,
   Through castles and towers *that* were hye,
  Through an arbor into an orchard,
  And there hanged him in a peare tree.

15 When the gou*er*nor of Scotland he heard tell
   That the worthye king he was slaine,
  He hath banished the queene soe bitterlye
  That in Scottland shee dare not remaine.

16 But shee is ffled into merry England,
   And Scottland to a side hath laine,
  And through the Queene of Englands good
    grace
  Now in England shee doth remaine.

———◆———

6². noncett, *with* tt *blotted out.* (?) *Furnivall.*
6⁴, 7³. 12. 10³. sleepee. 11². 30.

12¹. 8ᵗʰ. 13¹. *Partly pared away. Furnivall.*
16². to aside.

———◆———

175

THE RISING IN THE NORTH

'Risinge in the Northe,' Percy MS., p. 256; Hales and Furnivall, II, 210.

———◆———

PRINTED in Percy's Reliques, 1765, I, 250,
"from two MS. copies, one of them in the edi-
tor's folio collection. They contained con-
siderable variations, out of which such read-
ings were chosen as seemed most poetical and
consonant to history." Bearing in mind Per-
cy's express avowal that he "must plead
guilty to the charge of concealing his own
share in amendments under some such gen-
eral title as a modern copy, or the like," one

would conclude without hesitation that there was but a single authentic text in this case, as in others. Percy notes on the margin of his manuscript: " N. B. To correct this by my other copy, which seems more modern. The other copy in many parts preferable to this." But this note would seem to be a private memorandum. Or are we to suppose that Percy might employ, from habit perhaps, the same formula, not to say artifice, with himself as with the public? In notes in the Folio to ' Northumberland betrayed by Douglas ' (No 176), Percy speaks of a second copy of that ballad also as being in his possession, and describes it as containing much which is omitted in the other, and as beginning like ' The Earl of Westmoreland,' (No 177). Of the beginning of this last he says, in a note in the Folio, " these lines are given in one of my *old* copies to Lord Northumberland." " Old copies " is staggering; for any one who examines the variations of the texts in the Reliques from the texts in the Folio will find them of the same character and style as Percy's acknowledged improvements of other ballads, and will be compelled to impute them to the editor or his double.*

The earls of Northumberland and Westmoreland, having for a time succeeded, by exuberant professions, in allaying very sufficiently grounded suspicions of their loyal dealing, at last, upon receiving the Queen's summons to London, found compliance unsafe, and went into rebellion. They took this step with but half a heart and against their judgment, overcome by the clamor and urgency of a portion of their fellow-conspirators. The intent of the insurgents was, in Northumberland's own words, " the reformation of religion, and the preservation of the Queen of Scots, whom they accounted by God's law and man's law to be right heir, if want

should be of issue of the Queen's Majesty's body." These two causes, they were confident, were favored by the larger number of noblemen within the realm.† Protestantism had no hold in the north, and the Queen's officers in those parts were, for the moment, not strong enough to make opposition. With leaders of energy and military skill, and a good chest to draw upon,‡ the rising would have been highly dangerous. As things were, it collapsed in five weeks without the shedding of a drop of blood; but hundreds of simple people were subsequently hanged.

The earls, with others, among whom Richard Norton, then sheriff of York, was the most conspicuous, entered Durham in arms on Sunday, the fourteenth of November (1569). They went to the minster, overthrew the communion-table, tore the Bible and service-books, replaced the old altar (which had been thrown into a rubbish-heap), and had mass said. The next day they turned southwards, with nobody to molest or stop them in their rear or in front. The Earl of Sussex was collecting a force at York, but it came in slowly, and it could not be trusted. " To get the more credit among the favorers of the old Romish religion, they had a cross, with a banner of the five wounds, borne after them, sometime by old Norton, sometime by others " (Holinshed). They proceeded to Ripon, Wetherby, and Clifford Moor (Bramham Moor) near Tadcaster. " Their main body was at Wetherby and Tadcaster, their advanced horse were far down across the Ouse." Their numbers, according to Holinshed, never exceeded about two thousand horse and five thousand foot. Tutbury, where Mary Stuart was confined, was but a little more than fifty miles from their advance; they proposed to release the Queen of Scots, and then to move on London, or wait for a rising in the south.

---

* To save appearances, we may understand "old copies" to mean copies restored or brought nearer to what is imagined to have been the original form. The variations will be given in notes as *pièces justificatives*.

† Sir Cuthbert Sharp, Memorials of the Rebellion of 1569, p. 202; a collection of many original papers pertaining to this rising, with much subsidiary information. But the story should be read in the eighteenth chapter of Mr

Froude's Reign of Elizabeth. Both works have been used here *passim*; Froude in the edition of New York, 1870.

‡ Northumberland, on being asked how much money he spent in the quarrel, says, "about one hundred and twenty pound." The Queen's proclamation, Nov. 24, declares that the earls were two persons as ill chosen for the reformation of any great matters as any could be in the realm, for they were both in poverty, etc. Sharp, pp. 208, 66; also 290.

Mary Stuart, at the nick of time, was removed to Coventry. On the twenty-fourth we hear that the rebels were drawn back to Knaresborough and Boroughbridge; on the thirtieth, that they are returned into the Bishopric. There they laid siege to Barnard Castle, which Sir George Bowes was obliged to surrender on December twelfth; on the fifteenth the earls were still at Durham. On the thirteenth the earls of Warwick and Clinton, commanders of the Army of the South, met at Wetherby with a combined force of eleven thousand foot and above twelve hundred horse, "eager to encounter the rebels, if they would abide." But on the sixteenth the "lords rebels" warned their footmen to shift for themselves, and fled with such horse as they had left into Northumberland. The twenty-second of December, the Earl of Sussex, qui cunctando restituit rem, Lord Hunsdon, who had been joined with him in command, and Sir Ralph Sadler, who had been deputed to watch him, write to the Queen: "The earls rebels, with their principal confederates and the Countess of Northumberland, did the twentieth of this present in the night, flee into Liddesdale with about a hundred horse; and there remain under the conduction of Black Ormiston, one of the murtherers of the Lord Darnley, and John of the Side and the Lord's Jock, two notable thieves of Liddesdale, and the rest of the rebels be utterly scaled." *

The ballad, which is the work of a loyal but not unsympathetic minstrel, gives but a cursory and imperfect account of "this geere." Earl Percy has come to the conclusion that he must fight or flee; his lady urges him thrice over to go to the court, and right himself, but he tells her that his treason is known well enough; if he follows her advice she will never see him again. He sends a letter to Master Norton, urging that gentleman to ride with him. Norton asks counsel of his son Christopher, who advises him not to go back from the word he has spoken, and much

pleases his father thereby. He asks his nine sons how many of them will take part with him. All but the eldest at once answer that they will stand by him till death: Francis Norton, the eldest, will not advise acting against the crown. Coward Francis, thou never tookest that of me! says the father. Francis will go with his father, but unarmed, and he wishes an ill death to them that strike the first stroke against the crown. There is a muster at Wetherby, and Westmoreland and Northumberland are there with their proper banners,† and with another setting forth the Lord on the cross. Sir George Bowes "rising to make a spoil," they besiege him in a castle to which he retires, easily win the outer walls, but cannot win the inner. Word comes to the Queen of the rebels in the north; she sends thirty thousand men against them, under the "false" Earl of Warwick, and they never stop till they reach York. (A gap occurs here, which need not be a large one, considering the leaps taken already.) Northumberland is gone, Westmoreland vanished, and Norton and his eight sons fled.

5–10. The Countess of Northumberland would have been the last person to give such advice as is attributed to her. "His wife, being the stouter of the two, doth encourage him to persevere, and rideth up and down with the army, so as the grey mare is the better horse." Hunsdon to Cecil, November twenty-sixth, MS. cited by Froude.

11–27. Richard Norton, miscalled Francis in 40, was a man of seventy-one when he engaged in the rising, and the father of eleven sons and eight daughters. Seven of the sons were involved in the rebellion. Francis, the eldest son, so far from standing out, took a prominent part with his father. But what is said of Francis is true of William, the fourth son. Sir George Bowes says of him: "I neither heard or could perceive William Norton to deal with any office or charge amongst the rebels, but, as I have heard

* Sharp, p. 113.
† The dun-bull of the Nevilles is given in Sharp, p. 87, and one greyhound's head, with what may pass for a golden

collar, at p. 316; the three dogs are not warranted. Percy's half-moon is improperly mixed up with the banner of the five wounds in 31.

it affirmed, he both refused the taking charge of horsemen when it was offered unto him, and also *would wear no armor*. Farther, upon my departure from the castle [Barnard Castle], he came to me, and in the way as he rode with me, he entered to declare that he greatly misliked of all their doings and practices, saying that he was there amongst them for his father's sake, and to accompany him, and otherways he never had been with them," etc. MS. cited by Sharp, p. 284.

Christopher Norton deserves the distinction accorded him in the ballad. "Christopher had been among the first to enroll himself a knight of Mary Stuart. His religion had taught him to combine subtlety with courage, and through carelessness or treachery, or his own address, he had been admitted into Lord Scrope's guard at Bolton Castle. There he was allowed to assist his lady's escape, should escape prove possible; there he was able to receive messages and carry them; there, to throw the castellan off his guard, he pretended to flirt with her attendants, and twice at least, by his own confession, closely as the prisoner was watched, he contrived to hold private communications with her." (Froude, Reign of Elizabeth, III, 505, where follow lively particulars of these two encounters.) Christopher was the only one of the Nortons who is known to have suffered the death-pen-

alty of treason; it was "after he had beheld the death of his uncle, as well his quartering as otherwise, knowing and being well assured that he himself must follow the same way." (Sharp, p. 286.) Richard Norton, the father, fled to Flanders with his sons Francis and Sampson, and all three seem to have died there.

33 f. Sussex to Cecil: Dec. 6. "The rebels have shot three days together at the wall of the outer ward, but they have done no hurt." Dec. 8. "The rebels have won the first ward." Sir George Bowes' men leaped the walls, one day some eighty at a time, and the next day seven or eight score of the best disposed, who had been appointed to guard the gates, suddenly set them open, and went to the rebels; whereupon Sir George was driven to composition, and there was no need to take the inner walls.*

A considerable number of "balletts" were called forth by the northern rebellion, and a few of these have been preserved. See Arber, Stationers' Registers, I, 404–6, 407–9, 413–15; A Collection of Seventy-Nine Blackletter Ballads, etc., 1870, pp. xxv, 1, 56, 231, 239.

The copy in the Reliques is translated by Seckendorf, Musenalmanach, 1807, p. 103; by Doenniges, p. 102.

---

1 LISTEN, liuely lordings all,
  And all *that* beene this place within:
If you 'le giue eare vnto my songe,
  I will tell you how this geere did begin.

2 It was the good Erle of Westmorlande,
  A noble erle was callëd hee,
And he wrought treason against the crowne;
  Alas, itt was the more pittye!

3 And soe itt was the Erle of Northumberland,
  Another good noble erle was hee;
They tooken both vpon one p*a*rt,
  Against the crowne they wolden bee.

4 Earle Pearcy is into his garden gone,
  And after walkes his awne ladye:
' I heare a bird sing in my eare
  That I must either flight or fflee.'

5 ' God fforbidd,' shee sayd, ' good my lord,
  That euer soe *that* it shalbee !
But goe to London to the court,
  And faire ffall truth and honestye ! '

6 ' But nay, now nay, my ladye gay,
  That eu*er* it shold soe bee ;
My treason is knowen well enoughe ;
  Att the court I must not bee.'

* Sharp, pp. 92, 95, 97 f.

7 'But goe to the court yet, good my lord,
　　Take men enowe with thee ;
　If any man will doe you wronge,
　　Your warrant they may bee.'

8 'But nay, now nay, my lady gay,
　　For soe itt must not bee;
　If I goe to the court, ladye,
　　Death will strike me, and I must dye.'

9 'But goe to the court yett, [good] my lord,
　　I my-selfe will ryde with thee ;
　If any man will doe you wronge,
　　Your borrow I shalbee.'

10 'But nay, now nay, my lady gay,
　　For soe it must not bee ;
　For if I goe to the court, ladye,
　　Thou must me neuer see.

11 'But come hither, thou litle foot-page,
　　Come thou hither vnto mee,
　For thou shalt goe a message to Master Norton,
　　In all the hast that euer may bee.

12 'Comend me to that gentleman ;
　　Bring him here this letter from mee,
　And say, I pray him earnestlye
　　That hee will ryde in my companye.'

13 But one while the foote-page went,
　　Another while he rann ;
　Vntill he came to Master Norton,
　　The ffoot-page neuer blanne.

14 And when he came to Master Nortton,
　　He kneeled on his knee,
　And tooke the letter betwixt his hands,
　　And lett the gentleman it see.

15 And when the letter itt was reade,
　　Affore all his companye,
　I-wis, if you wold know the truth,
　　There was many a weeping eye.

16 He said, Come hither, Kester Nortton,
　　A ffine ffellow thou seemes to bee ;
　Some good councell, Kester Nortton,
　　This day doe thou giue to mee.

17 'Marry, I 'le giue you councell, ffather,
　　If you 'le take councell att me,

That if you haue spoken the word, father,
　　That backe againe you doe not flee.'

18 'God a mercy ! Christopher Nortton,
　　I say, God a mercye !
　If I doe liue and scape with liffe,
　　Well advanced shalt thou bee.

19 'But come you hither, my nine good sonnes,
　　In mens estate I thinke you bee ;
　How many of you, my children deare,
　　On my part that wilbe ? '

20 But eight of them did answer soone,
　　And spake ffull hastilye ;
　Sayes, We wilbe on your part, ffather,
　　Till the day that we doe dye.

21 'But God a mercy ! my children deare,
　　And euer I say God a mercy !
　And yett my blessing you shall haue,
　　Whether-soeuer I liue or dye.

22 'But what sayst thou, thou Ffrancis Nortton,
　　Mine eldest sonne and mine heyre trulye ?
　Some good councell, Ffrancis Nortton,
　　This day thou giue to me.'

23 'But I will giue you councell, ffather,
　　If you will take councell att mee ;
　For if you wold take my councell, father,
　　Against the crowne you shold not bee.'

24 'But ffye vpon thee, Ffrancis Nortton !
　　I say ffye vpon thee !
　When thou was younge and tender of age
　　I made ffull much of thee.'

25 'But your head is white, ffather,' he sayes,
　　'And your beard is wonderous gray ;
　Itt were shame ffor your countrye
　　If you shold rise and fflee away.'

26 'But ffye vpon thee, thou coward Ffrancis !
　　Thou neuer tookest that of mee !
　When thou was younge and tender of age
　　I made too much of thee.'

27 'But I will goe with you, father,' quoth hee ;
　　'Like a naked man will I bee ;
　He that strikes the first stroake against the
　　crowne,
　　An ill death may hee dye ! '

28 But then rose vpp M*aster* Nortton, *that*
  esq*uier*,
   W*i*th him a ffull great companye ;
   And then the erles they comen downe
     To ryde in his companye.

29 Att Whethersbye the mustered their men,
   Vpon a ffull fayre day ;
   Thirteen thousand there were seene
     To stand in battel ray.

30 The Erle of Westmoreland, he had in his
   ancyent
   The dunn bull in sight most hye,
   And three doggs w*i*th golden collers
     Were sett out royallye.

31 The Erle of Northumberland, he had in his
   ancyent
   The halfe moone in sight soe hye,
   As the L*ord* was crucifyed on the crosse,
     And set forthe pleasantlye.

32 And after them did rise good S*i*r George
   Bowes,
   After them a spoyle to make ;
   The erles returned backe againe,
     Thought eu*er that* k*night* to take.

33 This barron did take a castle then,
   Was made of lime and stone ;
   The vttermost walls were ese to be woon ;
     The erles haue woon them anon.

34 But tho they woone the vttermost walls,
   Quickly and anon,
   The innermust walles the cold not winn ;
     The were made of a rocke of stone.

35 But newes itt came to leeue London,
   In all the speede *that* eu*er* might bee ;
   And word it came to our royall queene
     Of all the rebells in the north countrye.

36 Shee turned her grace then once about,
   And like a royall queene shee sware ;
   Sayes, I will ordaine them such a breake-fast
     As was not in the north this thousand yeere !

37 Shee caused thirty thousand men to be made,
   W*i*th horsse and harneis all quicklye ;
   And shee caused thirty thousand men to be
     made,
   To take the rebells in the north countrye.

38 They tooke w*i*th them the false Erle of War-
   wicke,
   Soe did they many another man ;
   Vntill they came to Yorke castle,
     I-wis they neu*er* stinted nor blan.

*   *   *   *   *   *   *

39 . . . .
   . . . .
   'Spread thy ancyent, Erle of Westmoreland !
     The halfe-moone ffaine wold wee see ! '

40 But the halfe-moone is fled and gone,
   And the dun bull vanished awaye ;
   And Ffrancis Nortton and his eight sonnes
     Are ffled away most cowardlye.

41 Ladds w*i*th mony are counted men,
   Men w*i*thout mony are counted none ;
   But hold yo*ur* tounge ! why say you soe ?
     Men wilbe men when mony is gone.

———◆———

3⁴. their *for* the.
7⁴. they *altered in MS. from* them.
18¹. amercy : *and afterwards.* 19¹. 9.
20¹. 8ᵗʰ. 21². godamercy. 29³. 13000.
30². Dum̄ : m *for* nn. *Furnivall.*
30³. 3.
34³. imermust. 35². all they. 36⁴. 1000.
37¹,³. 30000.
38². *Only half the* n *in* many. *Furnivall.*
And *for* & *throughout.*

Variations of the copy in Percy's Reliques,
  1765, I, 250.

1²⁻⁴. Lithe and listen unto mee,
   And I will sing of a noble earle,
     The noblest earle in the north countrie.

2, 3 *wanting.*
4². after him walkes his faire.
4³. mine.

5[1,2]. Now heaven forefend, my dearest lord,
    That eer such harm should hap to
      thee.

6[1], 8[1], 10[1], 24[1]. Now *for* But.
6[2,3]. Alas thy counsell suits not mee ;
    Mine enemies prevail so fast.

6[4]. That at : I may. 7[1]. O goe.
7[2]. And take thy gallant men.
7[3]. any dare to doe.
7[4]. Then your warrant.
8[1]. thou lady faire.
8[2]. The court is full of subtiltie. 8[3]. And if.
8[4]. Never more I may thee see.
9[1]. Yet goe to the court, my lord, she sayes.
9[2]. And I : will goe wi. ryde *in ed.* 1794.
9[3]. At court then for my dearest lord.
9[4]. His faithfull borrowe I will.
10[1]. lady deare.

10[2,4]. Far lever had I lose my life,
    Than leave among my cruell foes
      My love in jeopardy and strife.

11[1]. come thou : my little.
11[3]. To maister Norton thou must goe.
12[2]. And beare this letter here fro mee.
12[3]. And say that earnestly I praye.
12[4]. That *wanting.*
13[1]. But *wanting :* little footpage.
13[2]. And another.
13[3]. to his journeys end.
13[4]. little footpage.
14[1]. When to that gentleman he came.
14[2]. Down he knelt upon.

14[3,4]. Quoth he, My lord commendeth him,
    And sends this letter unto thee.
The reading of the Folio is restored in ed.
1794.
15[2]. Affore that goodlye.
15[3]. you the truthe wold know.
16[1]. thither, Christopher.
16[2]. A gallant youth thou seemst.

16[3,4]. What doest thou counsell me, my sonne,
    Now that good earle 's in jeopardy.

17. Father, my counselle 's fair and free ;
    That earle he is a noble lord,
    And whatsoever to him you hight,
      I wold not have you breake your word.

18[1-3]. Gramercy, Christopher, my sonne,
    Thy counsell well it liketh mee,
    And if we speed, and

18[4]. thou shalt. 19[1]. But *wanting.*
19[2]. Gallant men I trowe.
19[4]. Will stand by that good earle and mee.
20[1]. But *wanting :* answer make.
20[2]. Eight of them spake hastilie.

20[3,4]. O father, till the daye we dye,
    We 'll stand by that good earle and
      thee.

21[1]. Gramercy now, my children deare,
    You showe yourselves right bold and
      brave ;
    And whethersoeer I live or dye,
      A fathers blessing you shal have.

22[1]. O Francis.

22[2-4]. Thou art mine eldest sonn and heire ;
    Somewhat lyes brooding in thy breast,
    Whatever it bee, to mee declare.

23 *wanting, and instead, this stanza, like* 25 :
    Father, you are an aged man,
      Your head is white, your bearde is gray ;
    It were a shame, at these your yeares,
      For you to ryse in such a fray.

24, 26. *For these :*
    Now fye upon thee, coward Francis,
      Thou never learnedst this of mee ;
    When thou wert yong and tender of age,
      Why did I make soe much of thee ?

27[1,2]. But, father, I will wend with you,
    Unarmd and naked will I bee.

27[3]. And he : the first stroake *wanting.*
27[4]. Ever an.

28. Then rose that reverend gentleman,
    And with him came a goodlye band,
    To join with the brave Earl Percy,
    And all the flower o Northumberland.

29. With them the noble Nevill came,
    The earle of Westmorland was hee ;
    At Wetherbye they mustred their host,
    Thirteen thousand faire to see.

30[1,2]. Lord Westmorland his ancyent raisde,
 The dun bull he raysd on hye.

30[3]. And *wanting :* collars brave.
30[4]. Were there sett out most.

31. Earl Percy there his ancyent spred,
 The half moone shining all soe faire ;
The Nortons ancyent had the crosse,
 And the five wounds our Lord did
  beare.

32[1]. Then Sir George Bowes he straitwaye
rose.
32[2]. some spoyle.
32[3]. Those noble earles turnd.
32[4]. And aye they vowed that.

33. That baron he to his castle fled,
 To Barnard castle then fled hee ;
The uttermost walles were eathe to win,
 The earles have wonne them presentlie.

34. The uttermost walles were lime and bricke ;
 But thoughe they won them soon anone,
Long eer they wan the innermost walles,
 For they were cut in rocke of stone.

35[1]. Then newes unto leeve London came.
35[2]. ever may. 35[3]. word is brought.
35[4]. Of the rysing in.
36[1]. Her grace she turned her round about.

36[2]. swore. 36[3]. Sayes *wanting.*
36[4]. As never was in the North before.
37[1]. be raysd. 37[2]. harneis faire to see.
37[3]. And *wanting :* be raised.
37[4]. the earles i th'.

38[1,2]. Wi them the false Earle Warwick went,
 Th' earle Sussex and the lord Hunsdèn.

38[3]. to Yorke castle came. 38[4]. stint ne.

39. Now spread thy ancyent, Westmorland,
 Thy dun bull faine would we spye ;
And thou, the Earl o Northumberland,
 Now rayse thy half moone up on hye.

40[1]. the dun bulle is.
40[2]. the half moone vanished.
40[3,4]. The Earles, though they were brave and
 bold,
 Against soe many could not stay.

41. Thee, Norton, wi thine eight good sonnes,
 They doomd to dye, alas ! for ruth !
Thy reverend lockes thee could not save,
 Nor them their faire and blooming
  youthe.

Wi them full many a gallant wight
 They cruellye bereavd of life,
And many a childe made fatherlesse,
 And widowed many a tender wife.

176

NORTHUMBERLAND BETRAYED BY DOUGLAS

'Northumberland betrayd by Dowglas,' Percy MS., p. 259 ; Hales and Furnivall, II, 217.

PRINTED in Percy's Reliques, 1765, I, 257, "from two copies [which contained great variations, 1794, I, 297], one of them in the Editor's folio MS." In this manuscript Percy makes these notes. " N. B. My other copy is more correct than this, and contains much which is omitted here. N. B. The other copy begins with lines the same as that in page 112 [that is, the 'Earl of Westmoreland']. The minstrels often made such changes."

See the preface to the foregoing ballad as to the probable character of the copy, which " contains much that is omitted here."

The Earl of Sussex writes on December 22d that, the next morning after Northumberland and Westmorland took refuge in Liddesdale, Martin Eliot and others of the principal men of the dale raised a force against the earls, Black Ormiston, and the rest of their company, and offered fight; but in the end, Eliot, wishing to avoid a feud, said to Ormiston that " he would charge him and the rest before the Regent for keeping of the rebels of England, if he did not put them out of the country, and that if they [the earls] were in the country after the next day, he would do his worst against them and all that maintained them." Whereupon the earls were driven to quit Liddesdale and to fly to one of the Armstrongs in the Debateable Land, leaving the Countess of Northumberland "at John of the Sydes house, a cottage not to be compared to any dog-kennel in England." Three days later Sussex and Sadler write that " the Earl of Northumberland was yesterday [the 24th], at one in the afternoon, delivered by one Hector, of Harlaw wood, of the surname of the Armstrongs, to Alexander Hume, to be carried to the Regent." * The Regent took Northumberland to Edinburgh, and on the second of January, 1570, committed him to the castle of Lochleven, attended by two servants.†

The sentiment of Scotsmen, and especially of borderers, was outraged by this proceeding: " for generally, all sorts, both men and women, cry out for the liberty of their country; which is, to succor banisht men, as themselves have been received in England not long

since, and is the freedom of all countries, as they allege." ‡

Northumberland remained in confinement at Lochleven until June, 1572. Meanwhile the Countess of Northumberland, who had escaped to Flanders, had been begging money to buy her husband of the Scots, and had been negotiating with Douglas of Lochleven to that effect. She was ready to give the sum demanded, which seems to have been two thousand pounds, as soon as sufficient assurance could be had that her husband would be liberated upon payment of the money. Lord Hunsdon discussed the surrender of Northumberland with the Earl of Morton and the Commendator of Dunfermling, on the occasion of their coming to Berwick to treat about the pacification of the troubles in Scotland. " They made recital of the charges that the lord of Lochleven hath been at with the said earl, and how the earl hath offered the lord of Lochleven four thousand marks sterling, to be paid presently to him in hand, to let him go. Notwithstanding, both he and the rest shall be delivered to her Majesty upon reasonable consideration of their charges." (November 22, 1571.) Political considerations turned the scale, and on the seventh of June Lord Hunsdon paid the two thousand pounds which the countess had offered, and Northumberland was put into his hands. Hunsdon had the earl in custody at Berwick until the following August. He was then made over to Sir John Forster, Warden of the Middle Marches, taken to York and there beheaded (August 27th, 1572).§

---

* Sharp, pp. 114 f, 118. "My lord Regent convened with Martin Eliot that he should betray Thomas, Earl of Northumberland, who was fled in Liddesdale out of England for refuge, in this manner: that is to say, the said Martin caused Heckie Armstrong desire my lord of Northumberland to come and speak with him under trust, and caused the said earl believe that, after speaking, if my lord Regent would pursue him, that he and his friends should take plain part with the Earl of Northumberland. And when the said earl came with the same Heckie Armstrong to speak the said Martin, he caused certain light-horsemen of my lord Regent's, with others his friends, to lie at await, and when they should see the said earl and the said Martin speaking together, that they should come and take the said earl; and so as was devised, so came to pass." Diurnal of Occurrents, p. 154.

† From a letter of January 6, we learn that the Earl of Northumberland was then in Edinburgh, attended by James Swyno, William Burton, and others. James Swyno is apparently the chamberlain of the ballad. Sharp, p. 139.

‡ Lord Hunsdon, Sharp, p. 125.

§ Sharp, pp. 324–29. To whom the money went, if to anybody besides William Douglas, we are not distinctly told. Tytler intimates that Morton had a share: " this base and avaricious man sold his unhappy prisoner to Elizabeth," VII, 395. There was baseness enough without the addition of avarice: "The Earl of Northumberland was rendered to the Queen of England, forth of the castle of Lochleven, by a certain condition made betwix her and the Earl of Morton for gold. . . . And indeed this was unthankfully remembered, for when Morton was banisht from Scotland he found no such kind man to him in England as this earl

The ballad - minstrel acquaints us with circumstances concerning the surrender of Northumberland which are not known to any of the historians. One night, when many gentlemen are supping at Lochleven Castle, William Douglas, the laird of the castle, rallies the earl on account of his sadness; there is to be a shooting in the north of Scotland the next day, and to this Douglas has engaged his word that Percy shall go. Percy is ready to ride to the world's end in Douglas's company. Mary Douglas, William's sister, interposes: her brother is a traitor, and has taken money from the Earl [Morton?] to deliver Percy to England. Northumberland will not believe this; the surrender of a banisht man would break friendship forever between England and Scotland. Mary Douglas persists; he had best let her brother ride his own way, and he can tell the English lords that he cannot be of the party because he is in an isle of the sea (an obstacle which must appear to us not greater for one than for the other); and while her brother is away she will carry Percy to Edinburgh Castle, and deliver him to Lord Hume, who has already suffered loss in his behalf. But if he will not give credence to her, let him come on her right hand, and she will shew him something. Percy never loved witchcraft, but permits his chamberlain to go with the lady. Mary Douglas's mother was a witch-woman, and had taught her daughter something of her art. She shows the chamberlain through the belly of a ring many Englishmen who are on the await for his master, among them Lord Hunsdon, Sir William Drury, and Sir John Forster, though at that moment they are thrice fifty mile distant. The chamberlain goes back to his lord weeping, but the relation of what he has seen produces no effect. Percy says he has been in Lochleven almost three years and has never had an 'outrake' (outing); he will not hear a word to hinder him from going to the shooting. He twists

from his finger a gold ring — left him when he was in Harlaw wood — and gives it to Mary Douglas, with an assurance that, though he may drink, he will never eat, till he is in Lochleven again. Mary faints when she sees him in the boat, and Percy once and again proposes to go back to see how she fares; but William Douglas treats the fainting very lightly; his sister is crafty enough to beguile thousands like them. When they have sailed the first fifty mile (it will be borne in mind that the Douglas castle is described as being on an isle of the sea), James Swynard, the chamberlain,* asks how far it is to the shooting, and gets an alarming answer: fair words make fools fain; whenever they come to the shooting, they will think they have come soon enough! Jamie carries this answer to his master, who finds nothing discouraging in it; it was meant only to try his mettle. But after sailing fifty miles more, Percy himself calls to Douglas and asks what his purpose is. "Look that your bridle be strong and your spurs be sharp," says Douglas (but 49[1] is probably corrupted). "This is mere flouting," replies Percy; "one Armstrong has my horse, another my spurs and all my gear." Fifty miles more of the sea, and they land Lord Percy at Berwick, a deported, "extradited" man!

14. The Countess of Northumberland was sheltered for some time at Hume Castle (Sir C. Sharp's Memorials, pp. 143, 146, 150, 344, ff). The castle was invested, and by direction of Lord Hume, then absent in Edinburgh, was surrendered without resistance, in the course of Sussex's destructive raid in April, 1570. Cabala, ed. 1663, p. 175. See also Diurnal of Occurrents, p. 170.

19. Witchcraft was rife at the epoch of this ballad, nor was the imputation of it confined to hags of humble life. The Lady Buccleuch, the Countess of Athole, and the Lady Foullis were all accused of practising the black art. Nothing in that way was charged upon Lady

---

was." Historie of King James the Sext, p. 106 f. Sir Richard Maitland, who spares Morton and Lochleven no epithets in his spirited invective against those who delivered the Earl of Northumberland, says that they "of his bluide

resavit the pygrall pryce," but does not charge Morton with an act of ingratitude.

* Stanza 43 is corrupted.

Douglas of Lochleven, the mother of William Douglas and of the Regent Murray; but Lady Janet Douglas, sister of the Earl of Angus, had been burnt in 1537 for meditating the death of James V by poison or witchcraft, and it is possible, as Percy has suggested, that this occurrence may have led to the attribution of sorcery to Lady Douglas of Lochleven.*

Mary Douglas shows Northumberland's chamberlain, through the hollow of her ring, the English lords who are waiting for his master "thrice fifty mile" distant, at Berwick. In a Swiss popular song the infidelity of a lover is revealed by a look through a finger-ring. People on the Odenberg hear a drum-beat, but see nothing. A wizard makes one after another look through a ring made by bowing the arm against the side; they see armed men going into and coming out of the hill. So Biarco is enabled to see Odin on his white horse by looking through Ruta's bent arm.†

32, 33. The day after Northumberland was put into his hands, Hunsdon writes to Burghley: "For the earl, I have had no great talk with him; but truly he seems to follow his old humours, readier to talk of hawks and hounds than anything else." (Sharp, p. 330.)

51. It was their old manner, as Robin Hood says, to leave but little behind; but what is recorded is that, when "the earls were driven to leave Liddesdale and to fly to one of the Armstrongs upon the Bateable, ... the Liddesdale men stole my lady of Northumberland's horse, and her two women's horses, and ten other horses." Sussex to Cecil, Sharp, p. 114 f.

52. Percy "left Lochleven with joy, under the assurance that he should be conveyed in a Scottish vessel to Antwerp. To his surprise and dismay he found himself, after a short voyage, at Coldingham." Lingard's History, VI, 137, London, 1854.

The copy in the Reliques is translated by Doenniges, p. 111.

---

1 Now list and lithe, you gentlemen,
　　And I 'st tell you the veretye,
How they haue dealt with a banished man,
　　Driuen out of his countrye.

2 When as hee came on Scottish ground,
　　As woe and wonder be them amonge!
Ffull much was there traitorye
　　The wrought the Erle of Northumberland.

3 When they were att the supper sett,
　　Beffore many goodly gentlemen,
The ffell a fflouting and mocking both,
　　And said to the Erle of Northumberland:

4 'What makes you be soe sad, my lord,
　　And in your mind soe sorrowffullye?
In the north of Scotland to-morrow there 's a
　　shooting,
　　And thither thou 'st goe, my Lord Percye.

5 'The buttes are sett, and the shooting is
　　made,
　　And there is like to be great royaltye,
And I am sworne into my bill
　　Thither to bring my Lord Pearcy.'

6 'I 'le giue thee my hand, Douglas,' he sayes,
　　'And be the faith in my bodye,
If that thou wilt ryde to the worlds end,
　　I 'le ryde in thy companye.'

7 And then bespake the good ladye,
　　Marry a Douglas was her name:
'You shall byde here, good English lord;
　　My brother is a traiterous man.

8 'He is a traitor stout and stronge,
　　As I 'st tell you the veretye;
For he hath tane liuerance of the Erle,
　　And into England he will liuor thee.'

---

* Kirkpatrick Sharpe's Historical Account of Witchcraft in Scotland, pp. 38–54, ed. 1884.

† Rochholz, Schweizersagen aus dem Aargau, II, 162; Grimm, Deutsche Mythologie, p. 783 f, ed. 1876, and Saxo Grammaticus (p. 34, ed. 1576, Holder, p. 66), quoted by Grimm. These citations are furnished by Liebrecht, Göttingen Gelehrte Anzeigen, 1868, p. 1899, who finds hydromancy in st. 26, where, however, all that seems to be meant is that the mother would let her daughter see *from* Lochleven what was doing in London. Of dactyliomancy proper there is something in Delrio, IV, ii, 6, **4, 5,** p. 547, ed. 1624.

9 'Now hold thy tounge, thou goodlye ladye,
   And let all this talking bee;
  Ffor all the gold that's in Loug Leuen,
   William wold not liuor mee.

10 'It wold breake truce betweene England and
   Scottland,
   And freinds againe they wold neuer bee,
  If he shold liuor a bani[s]ht erle,
   · Was driuen out of his owne countrye.'

11 'Hold your tounge, my lord,' shee sayes,
   'There is much ffalsehood them amonge;
  When you are dead, then they are done,
   Soone they will part them freinds againe.

12 'If you will giue me any trust, my lord,
   I'le tell you how you best may bee;
  You'st lett my brother ryde his wayes,
   And tell those English lords, trulye,

13 'How that you cannot with them ryde,
   Because you are in an ile of the sea;
  Then, ere my brother come againe,
   To Edenborrow castle I'le carry thee.

14 'I'le liuor you vnto the Lord Hume,
   And you know a trew Scothe lord is hee,
  For he hath lost both land and goods
   In ayding of your good bodye.'

15 'Marry, I am woe, woman,' he sayes,
   'That any freind fares worse for mee;
  For where one saith it is a true tale,
   Then two will say it is a lye.

16 'When I was att home in my [realme],
   Amonge my tennants all trulye,
  In my time of losse, wherin my need stoode,
   They came to ayd me honestlye.

17 'Therfore I left a many a child ffatherlese,
   And many a widdow to looke wanne;
  And therfore blame nothing, ladye,
   But the woeffull warres which I began.'

18 'If you will giue me noe trust, my lord,
   Nor noe credence you will give mee,
  And you'le come hither to my right hand,
   Indeed, my lorid, I'le lett you see.'

19 Saies, I neuer loued noe witchcraft,
   Nor neuer dealt with treacherye,

But euermore held the hye way;
   Alas, that may be seene by mee!

20 'If you will not come your selfe, my lord,
   You'le lett your chamberlaine goe with mee,
  Three words that I may to him speake,
   And soone he shall come againe to thee.'

21 When Iames Swynard came that lady before,
   Shee let him see thorrow the weme of her
   ring
  How many there was of English lords
   To wayte there for his master and him.

22 'But who beene yonder, my good ladye,
   That walkes soe royallye on yonder greene?'
  'Yonder is Lord Hunsden, Iamye,' she
   saye[d],
   'Alas, hee'le doe you both tree and teene!'

23 'And who beene yonder, thou gay ladye,
   That walkes soe royallye him beside?'
  'Yond is Sir William Drurye, Iamy,' shee
   sayd,
   'And a keene captain hee is, and tryde.'

24 'How many miles is itt, thou good ladye,
   Betwixt yond English lord and mee?'
  'Marry, thrise fifty mile, Iamy,' shee sayd,
   'And euen to seale and by the sea.

25 'I neuer was on English ground,
   Nor neuer see itt with mine eye,
  But as my witt and wisedome serues,
   And as [the] booke it telleth mee.

26 'My mother, shee was a witch woman,
   And part of itt shee learned mee;
  Shee wold let me see out of Lough Leuen
   What they dyd in London cytye.'

27 'But who is yonde, thou good laydye,
   That comes yonder with an osterne fface?'
  'Yond's Sir Iohn Forster, Iamye,' shee sayd;
   'Methinkes thou sholdest better know him
   then I.'
  'Euen soe I doe, my goodlye ladye,
   And euer alas, soe woe am I!'

28 He pulled his hatt ouer his eyes,
   And, Lord, he wept soe tenderlye!
  He is gone to his master againe,
   And euen to tell him the veretye.

29 'Now hast thou beene with Marry, Iamy,' he
    sayd,
  'Euen as thy tounge will tell to mee;
But if thou trust in any womans words,
  Thou must refraine good companye.'

30 'It is noe words, my lord,' he sayes;
  'Yonder the men shee letts me see,
How many English lords there is
  Is wayting there for you and mee.

31 'Yonder I see the Lord Hunsden,
  And hee and you is of the third degree;
A greater enemye, indeed, my Lord,
  In England none haue yee.'

32 'And I haue beene in Lough Leven
  The most part of these yeeres three:
Yett had I neuer noe out-rake,
  Nor good games that I cold see.

33 'And I am thus bidden to yonder shooting
  By William Douglas all trulye;
Therfore speake neuer a word out of thy
  mouth
  That thou thinkes will hinder mee.'

34 Then he writhe the gold ring of his ffingar
  And gaue itt to that ladye gay;
Sayes, That was a legacye left vnto mee
  In Harley woods where I cold bee.

35 'Then ffarewell hart, and farewell hand,
  And ffarwell all good companye!
That woman shall neuer beare a sonne
  Shall know soe much of your priuitye.'

36 'Now hold thy tounge, ladye,' hee sayde,
  'And make not all this dole for mee,
For I may well drinke, but I'st neuer eate,
  Till againe in Lough Leuen I bee.'

37 He tooke his boate att the Lough Leuen,
  For to sayle now ouer the sea,
And he hath cast vpp a siluer wand,
  Saies, Fare thou well, my good ladye!
The ladye looked ouer her left sholder;
  In a dead swoone there fell shee.

38 'Goe backe againe, Douglas!' he sayd,
  'And I will goe in thy companye,
For sudden sicknesse yonder lady has tane,
  And euer, alas, shee will but dye!

39 'If ought come to yonder ladye but good,
  Then blamed sore that I shall bee,
Because a banished man I am,
  And driuen out of my owne countrye.'

40 'Come on, come on, my lord,' he sayes,
  'And lett all such talking bee;
There's ladyes enow in Lough Leuen
  And for to cheere yonder gay ladye.'

41 'And you will not goe your selfe, my lord,
  You will lett my chamberlaine go with
  mee;
Wee shall now take our boate againe,
  And soone wee shall ouertake thee.'

42 'Come on, come on, my lord,' he sayes,
  'And lett now all this talking bee;
Ffor my sister is craftye enoughe
  For to beguile thousands such as you and
  mee.'

43 When they had sayled fifty myle,
  Now fifty mile vpon the sea,
Hee had fforgotten a message that hee
  Shold doe in Lough Leuen trulye:
Hee asked, how ffarr it was to that shooting
  That William Douglas promised mee.

44 'Now faire words makes fooles faine,
  And that may be seene by thy master and
  thee;
Ffor you may happen think itt soone enoughe
  When-euer you that shooting see.'

45 Iamye pulled his hatt now ouer his browe,
  I wott the teares fell in his eye;
And he is to his master againe,
  And ffor to tell him the veretye.

46 'He sayes fayre words makes fooles faine,
  And that may be seene by you and mee,
Ffor wee may happen thinke itt soone enoughe
  When-euer wee that shooting see.

47 'Hold vpp thy head, Iamye,' the erle sayd,
  'And neuer lett thy hart fayle thee;
He did itt but to proue thee with,
  And see how thow wold take with death
  trulye.'

48 When they had sayled other fifty mile,
  Other fifty mile vpon the sea,

Lord Peercy called to him, himselfe,
  And sayd, Douglas, what wilt thou doe with
    mee?

49 'Looke *that* your brydle be wight, my lord,
    That you may goe as a shipp att sea;
  Looke *that* your spurres be bright and sharpe,
    That you may pricke her while shee 'le
    awaye.'

50 'What needeth this, Douglas,' he sayth,
    ' *That* thou needest to ffloute mee?

For I was counted a horsseman good
  Before *that* euer I mett with thee.

51 'A ffalse Hector hath my horsse,
    And euer an euill death may hee dye!
  And Willye Armestronge hath my spurres
    And all the geere belongs to mee.'

52 When the had sayled other fifty mile,
    Other fifty mile vpon the sea,
  The landed low by Barwicke-side;
    A deputed lord landed Lord Percye.

———◆———

6¹. my Land. 15⁴. 2.
16¹. *This line is partly pared away.   Fur-*
  nivall.
18⁴. Lorid, *or* Louerd; *or* Lord, *with one*
  stroke too many.   Furnivall.
20³. 3. 22¹. ny *for* my. 24³. 3ˢᵉ 50.
31². 3ᵈ. 32². 3.
33⁴. *Partly cut away by the binder.   Furni-*
  vall.
43¹,². 48¹,². 52¹,². 50.
52⁴. land *for* lord.   And *for* & *throughout.*

Variations of Percy's Reliques, 1765, I, 258.
1–3. *Cf. the next ballad,* 1–3.
  How long shall fortune faile me nowe,
    And harrowe me with fear and dread?
  How long shall I in bale abide,
    In misery my life to lead?

  To fall from my bliss, alas the while!
    It was my sore and heavye lott;
  And I must leave my native land,
    And I must live a man forgot.

  One gentle Armstrong I doe ken,
    A Scot he is much bound to mee;
  He dwelleth on the border-side,
    To him I 'll goe right privilie.

  Thus did the noble Percy 'plaine,
    With a heavy heart and wel-away,
  When he with all his gallant men
    On Bramham moor had lost the day.

  But when he to the Armstrongs came,
    They dealt with him all treacherouslye;
  For they did strip that noble earle,
    And ever an ill death may they dye!

  False Hector to Earl Murray sent,
    To shew him where his guest did hide,
  Who sent him to the Lough-levèn,
    With William Douglas to abide.

  And when he to the Douglas came,
    He halched him right courteouslie;
  Sayd, Welcome, welcome, noble earle,
    Here thou shalt safelye bide with mee.

  When he had in Lough-leven been
    Many a month and many a day,
  To the regent the lord-warden sent,
    That bannisht earle for to betray.

  He offered him great store of gold,
    And wrote a letter fair to see,
  Saying, Good my lord, grant me my boon,
    And yield that banisht man to mee.

  Earle Percy at the supper sate,
    With many a goodly gentleman;
  The wylie Douglas then bespake,
    And thus to flyte with him began.

4³ ⁴. To-morrow a shootinge will bee held
    Among the lords of the North countrye.

5¹. sett, the shooting's.
5². there will be.
6¹. hand, thou gentle Douglas : he sayes *want-*
  ing.
6². And here by my true faith, quoth hee.
6³. If thou: worldes.   6⁴. I will.
7¹. bespake a lady faire.
8². As I tell you in privitie.
8³. he has.   hath, 1794.
8⁴. Into England nowe to 'liver.

9. Now nay, now nay, thou goodly lady,
   The regent is a noble lord ;
Ne for the gold in all Englànd
   The Douglas wold not break his word.

When the regent was a banisht man,
   With me he did faire welcome find ;
And whether weal or woe betide,
   I still shall find him true and kind.

10¹. Tween England and Scotland 't wold break
    truce. Betweene : it, 1794.
10³. If they.

11, 12. Alas ! alas ! my lord, she sayes,
   Nowe mickle is their traitorìe ;
Then let my brother ride his ways,
   And tell those English lords from thee.

13¹. with him.

14–17. ' To the Lord Hume I will thee bring ;
   He is well knowne a true Scots lord,
And he will lose both land and life
   Ere he with thee will break his word.'

' Much is my woe,' Lord Percy sayd,
   ' When I thinke on my own countrìe ;
When I thinke on the heavye happe
   My friends have suffered there for mee.

' Much is my woe,' Lord Percy sayd,
   ' And sore those wars my minde distresse ;
Where many a widow lost her mate,
   And many a child was fatherlesse.

' And now that I, a banisht man,
   Shold bring such evil happe with mee,
To cause my faire and noble friends
   To be suspect of treacherie,

' This rives my heart with double woe ;
   And lever had I dye this day
Then thinke a Douglas can be false,
   Or ever will his guest betray.'   he will,
    1794.

18. ' If you 'll give me no trust, my lord,
   Nor unto mee no credence yield,
Yet step one moment here aside,
   Ile showe you all your foes in field.'

19¹,². Lady, I never loved witchcraft,
   Never dealt in privy wyle.

19⁴. Of truth and honoure, free from guile.
20¹. If you 'll.
20². Yet send your chamberlaine with.
20³. Let me but speak three words with him.
20⁴. And he.
21¹. James Swynard with that lady went.
21³. She showed him through.
21³. many English lords there were.
21⁴. Waiting for.
22¹. And who walkes yonder.
22². That walkes *wanting*.
22³. O yonder is the lord Hunsdèn.
22⁴. you drie and teene. 23¹. who beth.
23². so proudly.
23³. That is : Iamy *wanting*.
23⁴. And *wanting*. 24¹. itt, madàme.
24². lords.
24³,⁴. Marry, it is thrice fifty miles,
    To sayl to them upon the sea.
25². Ne never sawe.
25³,⁴. But as my book it sheweth mee,
    And through my ring I may descrye.
26¹. witch ladye. 26². And of her skille she.
27¹. thou lady faire.
27². That looketh with sic an.
27³,⁴. Yonder is Sir John Foster, quoth shee,
    Alas ! he 'll do ye sore disgrace.
27⁵,⁶ *wanting*.
28¹. downe over his browe.
28². And in his heart he was full woe. He
    wept ; his heart he was full of woe, 1794.

28³,⁴. And he is gone to his noble lord,
    Those sorrowfull tidings him to show.

29. Now nay, now nay, good James Swynàrd,
   I may not believe that witch ladìe ;
The Douglasses were ever true,
   And they can neer prove false to mee.

30, 31 *wanting*.
32¹. I have now in Lough-leven been.
32³. And I have never had. Yett have I never
    had, 1794.
32⁴. Ne no good.

33. Therefore I 'll to yond shooting wend,
   As to the Douglas I have hight ;
Betide me weale, betide me woe,
   He neer shall find my promise light.

34¹. He writhe a gold ring from.
34². that faire ladìe. that gay ladìe, 1794.
34³. Sayes, It was all that I cold save.

35. And wilt thou goe, thou noble lord?
    Then farewell truth and honestie!
    And farewell heart, and farewell hand!
    For never more I shall thee see.

36 *wanting.*

37^{1,2}. The wind was faire, the boatmen calld,
    And all the saylors were on borde;
    Then William Douglas took to his boat,
    And with him went that noble lord.

37^{3,4}. Then he cast up a silver wand,
    Says, Gentle lady, fare thee well!
    The lady fett a sigh soe deepe,
    And in a dead swoone down shee fell.

38, 39. Now let us goe back, Douglas, he sayd,
    A sickness hath taken yond faire ladìe;
    If ought befall yond lady but good,
    Then blamed for ever I shall bee.

40^2. Come on, come on, and let her bee.
40^4. For to: that gay.

41. 'If you 'll not turne yourself, my lord,
    Let me goe with my chamberlaine;
    We will but comfort that faire lady,
    And wee will return to you againe.

42$^{2-4}$. 'Come on, come on, and let her bee;
    My sister is crafty, and wold beguile
    A thousand such as you and mee.

43^2. Now *wanting: restored*, 1794.
43^{3,4} *wanting.*

43$^{5-6}$. Hee sent his man to ask the Douglas
    When they shold that shooting see.
44^1. Faire words, quoth he, they make.
44^2. And that by thee and thy lord is seen.
44^3. You may hap to.
44^4. Ere you that shooting reach, I ween.
45^1. his hatt pulled over.
45$^{2-4}$. He thought his lord then was betrayd;
    And he is to Earle Percy againe,
    To tell him what the Douglas sayd.

46 *wanting.*
47^1. head, man, quoth his lord,
47$^{2-4}$. Nor therfore let thy courage fail;
    He did it but to prove thy heart,
    To see if he cold make it quail.

48^1. had other fifty sayld.
48^3. calld to the Douglas himselfe. to D., 1794.
48^4. Sayd, What wilt thou nowe doe.
49^2. And your horse goe swift as ship.
50^1. sayd. sayth, 1794.
50^2. What needest thou to flyte with mee.
51^1. he hath. hath, 1794.
51^2. Who dealt with mee so treacherouslìe.
51^3. A false Armstrong he hath. hath, 1794.
51^4. geere that. geere, 1794.
52^3. landed him at Berwick towne. *MS. reading restored*, 1794.
52^4. The Douglas landed Lord Percie.
    MS. reading restored with ' laird ' *for* land.

Then he at Yorke was doomde to dye,
    It was, alas! a sorrowful sight;
Thus they betrayed that noble earle,
    Who ever was a gallant wight.

177

THE EARL OF WESTMORELAND

' Earle of Westmorlande,' Percy MS., p. 112; Hales and Furnivall, I, 292.

—◆—

" THESE lines," says Percy in a note in his MS. to 1^1, " are given in one of my old copies to Lord Northumberland; they seem here corrupted."   The first three stanzas, with extensive variations, begin ' Northumberland betrayed by Douglas,' as printed in the Reliques,

I, 258, 1765. It will be remarked that Percy does not allege that he has an old copy of this ballad, though he implies he has one of the other, 'Northumberland betrayed by Douglas.'

The earls of Westmoreland and Northumberland, as has been seen, upon being forced to leave Liddesdale, took refuge for a short time with one of the Armstrongs, John of the Side (cf. st. 3). They parted company, and Westmoreland, Lady Northumberland, Francis Norton, and others, were received by Sir Thomas Ker at Fernihurst, near Jedburgh; Old Norton, Markenfield, and others, by Buccleuch at Branxholm. Lady Northumberland shortly after removed to Hume Castle. The Regent Murray sent a secret messenger to persuade Fernihurst and Buccleuch to render into his hands the "Earl of Westmoreland and the other her Majesty's principal rebels being in their bounds," Jan. 14, 1570 (cf. st. 9). Westmoreland escaped to Flanders in the autumn of 1570, "with very slight means." He was very desirous to make his peace with Elizabeth, but the efforts he made were unsuccessful, and he wore out thirty-one years in the Low Countries, a pensioner of Spain, dying at Newport in November, 1601. The countess, his wife, daughter of the poet Surrey, a highly educated and in every way admirable woman, was treated by Elizabeth as innocent of treason (she was a zealous Protestant), and was granted a decent annuity for the support of herself and her three daughters. The Countess of Northumberland fled to Flanders in 1570, and lived on the King of Spain's bounty, separated from her children, and with no consolation but such as she derived from her intense religious and theological convictions, until 1596.*

The ballad-story is that after the flight (as it is described) from Bramham ('Bramaball') Moor, Westmoreland sought refuge with Jock Armstrong on the west border, who also "took"† or sheltered Old Norton and other of the rebels. Neville does not think the Debateable Land safe, and goes to Scotland, to Hume Castle, where all the banished men find welcome. The Regent is minded to write to Lord Hume to see whether he can be brought to surrender the fugitives, but on second thoughts, being at deadly feud with Hume, he concludes that writing will serve no purpose. (10⁴ is not very intelligible.) He will rather send for troops from Berwick, and take the men by force. Lord Hume gets knowledge of the Regent's intention, and removes his guests to the castle of 'Camelye.' But still Neville sees that there is no biding even in Scotland, and he and his comrades take a noble ship, to be mariners on the sea.

So far the ballad, it will be perceived, has an historical substratum, though details are incorrect; what follows is pure fancy work, or rather an imitation of stale old romance.

After cruising three months, a large ship is sighted. Neville calls Markenfield to council. The latter, who knows every banner that is borne, knows whether any man that he has once laid eyes on is friend or foe, knows every language that is spoken, and who has besides (st. 39) a gift of prophecy. By the serpent and the serpent's head and the mole in the midst, Markenfield is able to say that the ship is Don John of Austria's, and he advises flight. This counsel (which would have lost Neville much glory and a hundred pounds a day) does not please the earl; he orders his own standard of the Dun Bull to be displayed. Don John sends a pinnace, with a herald, to fetch the name of the master of the ship he has met. Neville refuses to give up his name until he knows the master of the other vessel; the herald informs him that it is Duke John of Austria, who lives in Seville; then says the Briton, Charles Neville is my name, and in England I was Earl of Westmoreland. The herald makes his report, and is sent back to invite the nobleman to Don John's ship; for Don John had read in the 'Book of Mable' that a Briton, Charles Neville, 'with a child's voice,' should come over

---

* Sharp's Memorials, pp. 138, 142, 298 ff, 346 ff.

† The most favorable interpretation has been given to 'Now hath Armstrong taken. The meaning is rather, perhaps, that Armstrong has detained Neville and his followers.

the sea. Neville is courteously received; Don John desires to see his men; it is but a small company, says the earl, and calls in Markenfield the prophet, Dacres, Master Norton and four sons, and John of Carnabye. These are all my company, says Neville; when we were in England, our prince and we could not agree. The duke says Norton and his sons shall go to France, and also Dacres, who shall be a captain; Neville and Markenfield shall go to Seville, and the two others (there is but one other, John of Carnabye) are to go with Dacres. Neville will not part with men who have known him in weal and woe, and the duke says that, seeing he has so much manhood, he shall part with none of them. Both ships land at Seville, where the duke recommends Neville to the queen as one who wished to serve her as captain. The queen, first acquainting herself with his name, makes Neville captain over forty thousand men, to keep watch and ward in Seville, and to war against the heathen soldan. The soldan, learning in Barbary that a venturesome man is in Seville, sends him, through the queen, a challenge to single combat, both lands to be joined in one according to the issue of the fight. The queen declines this particular challenge, but promises the soldan a fight every day for three weeks, if he wishes it. Neville overhears all this and offers the queen to fight the soldan; she thinks it great pity that Neville should die, though he is a banished man. Don John informs the queen that he has read in the Book of Mable that a Briton was to come over the sea, Charles Neville by name, with a child's voice, and that this man there present hath heart and hand. (62 is corrupted.) The queen's council put their heads together, and it is determined that Neville shall fight with the soldan. The battle is to come off at the Headless Cross. Neville wishes to see the queen's ensign. In the ensign is a broken sword, with bloody hands and a headless cross. The all-knowing Markenfield pronounces that these are a token that the prince has suffered a sore overthrow. Neville orders his Dun Bull to be set up and trumpets to blow, makes

Markenfield captain over his host during his absence, and rides to the headless cross, where he finds the soldan, a foul man to see. The soldan cries out, Is it some kitchen-boy that comes to fight with me? Neville replies with a commonplace: thou makest* so little of God's might, the less I care for thee. After a fierce but indecisive fight of an hour, the soldan, with a glance at his antagonist, says, No man shall overcome me except it be Charles Neville. Neville, without avowing his name, waxes bold, and presently strikes off the soldan's head. The queen comes out of the city with a procession, takes the crown from her head, and wishes to make him king on the spot, but Neville informs her that he has a wife in England. So the queen calls for a penman and writes Neville down for a hundred pound a day, for which he returns thanks, and proffers his services as champion if ever her Grace shall stand in need.

4. Martinfield is Thomas Markenfield of York, one of the most active promoters of the rising. He had been long a voluntary exile on account of religion, but returned to England the year before the rebellion. He fled to the continent with Westmoreland and the Nortons, and had a pension of thirty-six florins a month from Spain.

By Lord Dakers should be meant Edward, son of William, Lord Dacre, for he is in the list of fugitive rebels demanded of the Regent Murray by Lord Sussex. He fled to Flanders. But Leonard Dacre may be intended, who, though he did not take part with the earls, engaged in a rebellion of his own in February, 1570, fought and lost a battle, and like the rest fled to Flanders.

5. Only two of Richard Norton's sons went to the Low Countries with their father, Francis and Sampson. John Carnaby of Langley is in a list of persons indicted for rebellion. (Sharp, p. 230.) No reason appears why he should be distinguished.

11. Captain Reed, one of the captains of Berwick, was suspected of having to do with the rebels, and on one occasion was observed

---

* 71³. 'spekest soe litle.'

to be in company with some of the Nortons, in arms. He was committed to ward, but Lord Hunsdon stood his friend and brought him through safely. Sharp, p. 15 f.

21 ff. Don John's sole connection with the rebels seems to have been the paying of their pensions for the short time during which he was governor of the Netherlands, 1576–78. Westmoreland's pension was two hundred florins a month. (Sharp, p. 223, note.)

——◆——

1 'How long shall fortune faile me now,
    And keepe me heare in deadlye dreade?
  How long shall I in bale abide,
    In misery my life to leade?

2 'To ffall from my rose, it was my chance;
    Such was the Queene of England free;
  I tooke a lake, and turned my backe,
    On Bramaball More shee caused me flye.

3 'One gentle Armstrong *that* I doe ken,
    Alas, with thee I dare not mocke!
  Thou dwellest soe far on the west border,
    Thy name is called the Lord Iocke.'

4 Now hath Armstrong taken noble Nevill,
    And as one Martinfield did profecye;
  He hath taken the Lord Dakers,
    A lords sonne of great degree.

5 He hath taken old *Master* Nortton,
    And sonnes four in his companye;
  Hee hath taken another gentleman,
    Called Iohn of Carnabie.

6 Then bespake him Charles Nevill;
    To all his men, I wott, sayd hee,
  Sayes, I must into Scottland fare;
    Soe nie the borders is noe biding for me.

7 When he came to Humes Castle,
    And all his noble companye;
  The Lord Hume halched them right soone,
    Saying, Banished men, welcome to mee!

8 They had not beene in Humes Castle
    Not a month and dayes three,
  But the regent of Scottland and he got witt
    That banished men there shold be.

9 'I 'le write a letter,' sayd the regent then,
    'And send to Humes Castle hastilye,
  To see whether Lord Hume wilbe soe good
    To bring the banished men vnto mee.

10 '*That* lord and I haue beene att deadlye fuyde,
    And hee and I cold neuer agree;
   Writting a letter, *that* will not serue;
     The banished men must not speake with me.

11 'But I will send for the garrison of Barwicke,
    That they will come all with speede,
   And with them will come a noble captaine,
     Which is called Captain Reade.'

12 Then the Lord Hume he got witt
    They wold seeke vnto Nevill, where he did lye;
   He tooke them out of the castle of Hume,
     And brought them into the castle of Camelye.

13 Then bespake him Charles Nevill,
    To all his men, I wott, spoke hee,
   Sayes, I must goe take a noble shippe,
     And wee 'le be marriners vpon the sea.

14 I 'le seeke out fortune where it doth lye;
    In Scottland there is noe byding for mee;
   Then the tooke leaue with fayre Scottland,
     For they are sealing vpon the sea.

15 They had not sayled vpon the sea
    Not one day and monthes three,
   But they were ware of a Noble shippe,
     That fiue topps bare all soe hye.

16 Then Nevill called to Martinfeeld,
    Sayd, Martinffeeld, come hither to mee;
   Some good councell, Martinfeeld,
     I pray thee giue it vnto mee.

17 Thou told me when I was in England fayre,
    Before *that* I did take the sea,
   Thou neuer sawst noe banner borne
     But thou wold ken it with thine eye.

18 Thou neuer saw noe man in the face,
    Iff thou had seene before with thine eye,
    [But] thou coldest haue kend thy freind by
      thy foe,
    And then haue told it vnto mee.

19 Thou neuer heard noe speeche spoken,
    Neither in Greeke nor Hebrewe,
    [But] thou coldest haue answered them in any
      language,
    And then haue told it vnto mee.

20 'Master, master, see you yonder faire an-
      cyent?
    Yonder is the serpent and the serpents head,
    The mould-warpe in the middest of itt,
    And itt all shines with gold soe redde.

21 'Yonder is Duke Iohn of Austria,
    A noble warryour on the sea,
    Whose dwelling is in Ciuill land,
    And many men, God wot, hath hee.'

22 Then bespake him Martinfeelde,
    To all his fellowes, I wot, said hee,
    Turne our noble shipp about,
    And that's a token that wee will flee.

23 'Thy councell is not good, Martinfeeld;
    Itt falleth not out fitting for mee;
    I rue the last time I turnd my backe;
    I did displease my prince and the countrye.'

24 Then bespake him noble Nevill,
    To all his men, I wott, sayd hee,
    Sett me vp my faire Dun Bull,
    With gilden hornes hee beares all soe hye.

25 And I will passe yonder noble Duke,
    By the leaue of mild Marye;
    For yonder is the Duke of Austria,
    That trauells now vpon the sea.

26 And then bespake this noble Duke,
    Vnto his men then sayd hee,
    Yonder is sure some nobleman,
    Or else some youth that will not flee.

27 I will put out a pinace fayre,
    A harold of armes vpon the sea,
    And goe thy way to yonder noble shippe,
    And bring the masters name to mee.

28 When the herald of armes came before noble
      Nevill,
    He fell downe low vpon his knee:
    'You must tell me true what is your name,
    And in what countrye your dwelling may
      bee.'

29 'That will I not doe,' sayd noble Nevill,
    'By Mary mild, that mayden ffree,
    Except I first know thy masters name,
    And in what country his dwelling may bee.'

30 Then bespake the herald of armes,
    O that he spoke soe curteouslye!
    Duke Iohn of Austria is my masters name,
    He will neuer lene it vpon the sea.

31 He hath beene in the citye of Rome,
    His dwelling is in Ciuillee:
    'Then wee are poore Brittons,' the Nevill can
      say,
    'Where wee trauell vpon the sea.

32 'And Charles Nevill itt is my name,
    I will neuer lene it vpon the sea;
    When I was att home in England faire,
    I was the Erle of Westmoreland,' sayd hee.

33 Then backe is gone this herald of armes
    Whereas this noble duke did lye;
    'Loe, yonder are poore Brittons,' can he say,
    'Where the trauell vpon the sea.

34 'And Charles Nevill is their masters name,
    He will neuer lene it vpon the sea;
    When he was at home in England fayre,
    He was the Erle of Westmoreland, said hee.'

35 Then bespake this noble duke,
    And euer he spake soe hastilye,
    And said, Goe backe to yonder noble-man,
    And bid him come and speake with me.

36 For I haue read in the Booke of Mable,
    There shold a Brittaine come ouer the sea,
    Charles Nevill with a childs voice:
    I pray God that it may be hee.

37 When these two nobles they didden meete,
    They halched eche other right curteouslye;
    Yett Nevill halched Iohn the sooner
    Because a banished man, alas! was hee.

38 'Call in your men,' sayd this noble duke,
   'Faine your men *that* I wold see;'
'Euer alas!' said noble Nevill,
   'They are but a litle small companye.'

39 First he called in Martinfield,
   That Martinffeeld *that* cold prophecye;
He call[ed] in then Lord Dakers,
   A lords sonne of high degree.

40 Then called he in old *Master* Nortton,
   And sonnes four in his companye;
He called in one other gentleman,
   Called Iohn of Carnabye.

41 'Loe! these be all my men,' said noble Nevill,
   'And all *that*'s in my companye;
When we were att home in England fayre,
   Our prince and wee cold not agree.'

42 Then bespake this noble duke:
   To try your manhood on the sea,
Old *Master* Nortton shall goe ou*er* into France,
   And his sonnes four in his companye.

43 And my lord Dakers shall goe over into
   Ffrance,
There a captaine ffor to bee;
And those two other gentlemen wold goe with
   him,
And for to fare in his companye.

44 And you your-selfe shall goe into Ciuill land,
   And Marttinffeild *that* can prophecye;
'*That* will I not doe,' sayd noble Nevill,
   'By Mary mild, *that* mayden free.

45 'For the haue knowen me in wele and woe,
   In neede, scar[s]nesse and pouertye;
Before I'le p*ar*t with the worst of them,
   I'le rather p*ar*t with my liffe,' sayd hee.

46 And then bespake this noble duke,
   And euer he spake soe curteouslye;
Sayes, You shall p*ar*t with none of them,
   There is soe much manhood in your bodye.

47 Then these two noblemen labored together,
   Pleasantlye vpon the sea;
Their landing was in Ciuill land,
   In Ciuilee that ffaire citye.

48 Three nights att this dukes Nevill did lye,
   And serued like a nobleman was hee;

Then the duke made a supplication,
   And sent it to the queene of Ciuilee.

49 Saying, Such a man is your citye within,
   I mett him pleasantlye vpon the sea;
He seemes to be a noble man,
   And captaine to your Grace he faine wold
   bee.

50 Then the queene sent for [these] noble men
   For to come into her companye;
When Nevill came before the queene,
   Hee kneeled downe vpon his knee.

51 Shee tooke him vp by the lilly-white hand,
   Said, Welcome, my lord, hither to me;
You must first tell me your name,
   And in what countrye thy dwelling may bee.

52 He said, Charles Nevill is my name;
   I will neu*er* lene it in noe countrye;
When I was att home in England fayre,
   I was the Erle of Westmorland trulye.

53 The queene made him captaine ou*er* forty
   thousand,
Watch and ward within Ciuill land to keepe,
   And for to warr against the heathen soldan,
   And for to helpe her in her neede.

54 When the heathen soldan he gott witt,
   In Barbarye where he did lye,
Sainge, Such a man is in yonder citye within,
   And a bold venturer by sea is hee,

55 Then the heathen soldan made a letter,
   And sent it to the queene instantlye,
And all that heard this letter reade
   Where it was rehersed in Ciuillee.

56 Saying, Haue you any man your land within
   Man to man dare fight with mee?
And both our lands shalbe ioyned in one,
   And cristened lands they both shalbe.

57 Shee said, I haue noe man my land within
   Man to man dare fight with thee;
But euery day thou shalt haue a battell,
   If it be for these weekes three.

58 All beheard him Charles Nevill,
   In his bedd where he did lye,
And when he came the queene before,
   He fell downe low vpon his knee.

59 'Grant me a boone, my noble dame,
　　For Chrissts loue *that* dyed on tree;
　Ffor I will goe fight *with* yond heathen soldan,
　　If you will bestowe the manhood on mee.'

60 Then bespake this curteous queene,
　　And eu*er* shee spoke soe curteouslye :
　Though you be a banished man out of *your*
　　realme,
　　It is great pitye *that* thou shold dye.

61 Then bespake this noble duke,
　　As hee stood hard by the queenes knee :
　As I haue read in the Booke of Mable,
　　There shall a Brittone come ou*er* the sea,

62 And Charles Nevill shold be his name;
　　But a childs voyce, I wott, hath hee,
　And if he be in Christendome;
　　For hart and hand this man hath hee.

63 Then the queenes councell cast their heads to
　　gether,
　.　.　.　.　.　.　.
　That Nevill shold fight *with* the heathen sol-
　　dan
　That dwelt in the citye of Barbarye.

64 The battell and place appointed was
　　In a fayre greene, hard by the sea,
　And they shood meete att the Headless Crosse,
　　And there to fight right manfullye.

65 Then Nevill cald for the queenes ancient,
　　And faine *that* ancient he wold see;
　The brought him forth the broken sword,
　　With bloodye hands therein trulye.

66 The brought him forth the headless crosse,
　　In *that* ancyent it was seene;
　' O this is a token,' sayd Martinfeeld,
　　' *That* sore ouerthrowen this prince hath
　　beene.

67 ' O sett me vp my fayre Dun Bull,
　　And trumpetts blow me farr and nee,
　Vntill I come *with*in a mile of the Headlesse
　　Crosse,
　　That the Headlesse Crosse I may see.'

68 Then lighted downe noble Nevill,
　　And sayd, Marttinffeeld, come hither to me;
　Heere I make thee choice cap*tain* over my host
　　Vntill againe I may thee see.

69 Then Nevill rode to the Headless Crosse,
　　W*hi*ch stands soe fayre vpon the sea;
　There was he ware of the heathen soldan,
　　Both fowle and vglye for to see.

70 Then the soldan began for to call;
　　Twise he called lowd and hye,
　And sayd, What is this?　Some kitchin boy
　　That comes hither to fight *with* mee?

71 Then bespake him Charles Nevill,
　　But a childs voice, I wott, had hee :
　' Thou spekest soe litle of Gods might,
　　Much more lesse I doe care for thee.'

72 Att the first meeting *that* these two mett,
　　The heathen soldan and the christen man,
　The broke their speares quite in sunder,
　　And after *that* on foote did stand.

73 The next meeting *that* these two mett,
　　The swapt together *with* swords soe fine;
　The fought together till they both swett,
　　Of blowes *that* were both derf and dire.

74 They fought an houre in battell strong;
　　The soldan marke[d] Nevill *with* his eye;
　' There shall neuer man me ouercome
　　Except it be Charles Nevill,' sayd hee.

75 Then Nevill he waxed bold,
　　And cunning in fight, I wott, was hee;
　Euen att the gorgett of the soldans iacke
　　He stroke his head of p*re*sentlye.

76 Then kneeled downe noble Nevill,
　　And thanked God for his great grace,
　That he shold come soe farr into a strang[e]
　　land,
　　To ouercome the soldan in place.

77 Hee tooke the head vpon his sword-poynt,
　　And carryed it amongst his host soe fayre;
　When the saw the soldans head,
　　They thanked God on their knees there.

78 Seuen miles from the citye the queene him
　　mett,
　　With p*ro*cession *that* was soe fayre;
　Shee tooke the crowne beside her heade,
　　And wold haue crowned him k*ing* there.

79 ' Now nay!　Now nay! my noble dame,
　　For soe, I wott, itt cannott bee;

I haue a ladye in England fayre,
And wedded againe I wold not bee.'

80 The queene shee called for her penman,
I wot shee called him lowd and hye,
Saying, Write him downe a hundred pound a
day,
To keepe his men more merrylye.

81 'I thanke your Grace,' sayd noble Nevill,
'For this worthy gift you haue giuen to me;
If euer your Grace doe stand in neede,
Champion to your Highnesse again I 'le
bee.'

1¹. feare *for* dreade. 2². fayre *for* free.
2⁴. my *for* me. 5², 40², 42⁴. 4.
5⁴. Carnakie : *cf.* 40⁴. 8², 15², 48¹, 57⁴. 3.
8³. he & god. 14¹. fortume. 15⁴. 5.
20³. middest ffitt. 35. The Second Part.
37¹, 43³, 47¹, 72¹, 73¹. 2. 48⁴. Ciuilee. *In
this and the like names following, the* u

*has only one stroke in the MS., as often
happens. The letter is not meant for* c,
*clearly, as it has not the accent or beak of
a* c. *Furnivall.*
53¹. 40000. 55³. all they ? all these ?
62³. ben. 70². 2ˢᵉ. 78¹. 7. 80². 100ᴸᴵ.
And *for* & *always.*

178

CAPTAIN CAR, OR, EDOM O GORDON

A. Cotton MS. Vespasian, A. xxv, No 67, fol. 187, of
the last quarter of the 16th century,* British Museum;
Ritson's Ancient Songs, 1790, p. 137 ; Böddeker, in
Jahrbuch für romanische und englische Sprache und
Literatur, XV, 126, 1876 (very incorrectly) ; Trans-
actions of the New Shakspere Society, 1880–86, Ap-
pendix, p. 52 †, edited by F. J. Furnivall.

B. Percy MS., p. 34 ; Hales and Furnivall, I, 79.

C. Percy Papers, from a servant of Rev. Robert
Lambe's, 1766.

D. 'Edom of Gordon,' an ancient Scottish Poem. Never

before printed. Glasgow, printed and sold by
Robert and Andrew Foulis, 1755, small 4⁰, 12 pages.
Ritson, Scotish Songs, II, 17.

E. ' Edom o Gordon,' Kinloch MSS, V, 384.

F. The New Statistical Account of Scotland, V, 846,
1845 ; 'Loudoun Castle,' The Ballads and Songs of
Ayrshire, J. Paterson and C. Gray, 1st Series, p. 74,
Ayr, 1846.

G. ' The Burning o Loudon Castle,' Motherwell's MS.,
p. 543.

FIRST printed by the Foulises, Glasgow,
1755, after a copy furnished by Sir David
Dalrymple, " who gave it as it was preserved
in the memory of a lady." This information
we derive from Percy, who inserted the Dal-
rymple ballad in his Reliques, 1765, I, 99,

* This is the date given me. It is very near to that of
the event.

" improved, and enlarged with several fine
stanzas recovered from a fragment . . . in the
Editor's folio MS." Seven stanzas of the en-
larged copy were adopted from this MS., with
changes ; 16²·⁴, 30, 35, 36, are Percy's own ;
the last three of the Glasgow edition are
dropped. Herd's copy, The Ancient and
Modern Scots Songs, 1769, p. 234, is from

Percy's Reliques; so is Pinkerton's, Scottish Tragic Ballads, 1781, p. 43, with the omission of the seventh stanza and many alterations. Ritson, Scotish Songs, 1794, II, 17, repeats the Glasgow copy; so the Campbell MSS, I, 155, and Finlay, I, 85. The copy in Buchan's Gleanings, p. 180, is Percy's, with one stanza from Ritson. Of twelve stanzas given in Burton's History of Scotland, V, 70 f., 3–6 are from Percy's Reliques (modified by E, a fragment obtained by Burton), the rest from D.

During the three wretched and bloody years which followed the assassination of the regent Murray, the Catholic Earl of Huntly, George Gordon, was one of the most eminent and active of the partisans of the queen. Mary created him her lieutenant-governor, and his brother, Adam Gordon, a remarkably gallant and able soldier, whether so created or not, is sometimes called the queen's deputy-lieutenant in the north. Our ballad is concerned with a minor incident of the hostilities in Aberdeenshire between the Gordons and the Forbeses, a rival but much less powerful clan, who supported the Reformed faith and the regency or king's party.*

"The queen's lieutenant - deputy in the north, called Sir Adam Gordon of Auchindown, knight, was very vigilant in his function; for suppressing of whom the Master of Forbes was directed, with the regent's commission. But the first encounter, which was upon the ninth day of October [1571], Auchindown obtained such victory that he slew of the Forbeses a hundred and twenty persons, and lost very few of his own." This was the battle of Tulliangus, on the northern slope of the hills of Coreen, some thirty miles northwest of Aberdeen. Both parties having been reinforced, an issue was tried again on the twentieth of November at Crabstane, in the vicinity of Aberdeen, where Adam Gordon inflicted a severe defeat on the Forbeses.†

" But what glory and renown," says the contemporary History of King James the Sixth, " he [Gordon] obtained of these two victories was all cast down by the infamy of his next attempt; for immediately after this last conflict he directed his soldiers to the castle of Towie, desiring the house to be rendered to him in the queen's name; which was obstinately refused by the lady, and she burst forth with certain injurious words. And the soldiers being impatient, by command of their leader, Captain Ker, fire was put to the house, wherein she and the number of twenty-seven persons were cruelly burnt to the death."

Another account, reported by a contemporary who lived in Edinburgh, is that " Adam Gordon sent Captain Ker to the place of Toway, requiring the lady thereof to render the place of Carrigill to him in the queen's name, which she would noways do; whereof the said Adam having knowledge, moved in ire towards her, caused raise fire thereintill, wherein she, her daughters, and other persons were destroyed, to the number of twenty-seven or thereby." ‡ This was in November, 1571.

We have a third report of this outrage from Richard Bannatyne, also a contemporary, a man, it may be observed, bitterly hostile to the queen's party. " Adam of Gordon . . . went to the house of Towie, which he burnt and twenty four persons in the same, never one escaping but one woman that came through the corns and hather which was cast to the house-sides, whereby they were smothered. This was done under assurance; for the laird of Towie's wife, being sister to the lady Crawfurd (and also died within the house), sent a boy to the laird in time of the truce (which was for the space of twelve hours) to see on what conditions they should render the house. In the mean time, Adam Gordon's men laid the corns and timbers and hather about the house, and set all on fire." *

Buchanan puts the incident which mainly concerns us between the fights of Tulliangus and Crabstone; so does Archbishop Spottiswood. "Not long after" the former, says the archbishop, who was a child of six when the affair occurred, Adam Gordon " sent to summon the house of Tavoy, pertaining to Alexander Forbes. The lady refusing to yield without direction from her husband, he put fire unto it and burnt her therein with children and servants, being twenty-seven persons in all. This inhuman and barbarous cruelty made his name odious, and stained all his former doings; otherwise he was held both active and fortunate in his enterprises." †

Buchanan dispatches the burning of the house in a line: Domus Alexandri Forbosii, cum uxore pregnante, liberis et ministris, cremata. Ed. 1582, fol. 248 b.

Towie was a place of no particular importance; judging both by the square keep that remains, which is described as insignificant, and by the number of people that the house contained, it must have been a small place. It is therefore more probable that Captain Ker burnt Towie while executing a general commission to harry the Forbeses than that this house should have been made a special object. But whether this were so or not, it is evident from the terms in which the transaction is spoken of by contemporaries, who were familiarized to a ferocious kind of warfare,‡ that there must have been something quite beyond the common in Captain Ker's proceedings on this occasion, for they are denounced even in those days as infamous, inhuman, and barbarously cruel, and the name of Adam Gordon is said to have been made odious by them.

It is not to be disguised that the language employed by Spottiswood might be so interpreted as to signify that Ker did not act in this dreadful business entirely upon his own responsibility; and the second of the four writers who speak circumstantially of the affair even intimates that Ker applied to his superior for instructions. On the other hand, the author of the History of James the Sixth says distinctly that the house was fired by the command of Ker, whose soldiers were rendered impatient by an obstinate refusal to surrender, accompanied with opprobrious words. The oldest of the ballads, also, which is nearly coeval with the occurrence, speaks only of Captain Car, knows nothing of Adam Gordon. On the other hand, Bannatyne knows nothing, or chooses to say nothing, of Captain Car: Adam Gordon burns the house, and even does this during a truce. It may be said that, even if the act were done without the orders or knowledge of Adam Gordon, he deserves all the ill fame which has fallen to him, for not punishing, or at least discharging, the perpetrator of such an outrage. But this would be applying the standards of the nineteenth century (and its very best standards) to the conduct of the sixteenth. It may be doubted whether there was at that time a man in Scotland, nay, even a man in Europe, who would have turned away a valuable servant because he had cruelly exceeded his instructions.§

A favorable construction, where the direct evidence is conflicting, is due to Adam Gordon because of his behavior on two other occasions, one immediately preceding, and the other soon following, the burning of the house of Towie. We are told that he used his victory at Crabstone "very moderately, and suffered no man to be killed after the fury of the fight was past. Alexander Forbes of Strath-gar-neck, author of all these troubles

* Journal of the Transactions in Scotland during the contest between the adherents of Queen Mary and those of her son, 1570, 1571, 1572, 1573, p. 302 f., Edinburgh, 1806.

† History of the Church of Scotland, ed. 1666, p. 259.

‡ "For many miserable months Scotland presented a sight which might have drawn pity from the hardest heart: her sons engaged in a furious and constant butchery of each other; . . . nothing seen but villages in flames, towns be-

leagured by armed men, women and children flying from the cottages where their fathers or husbands had been massacred; . . . prisoners tortured, or massacred in cold blood, or hung by forties and fifties at a time." Tytler, VII, 370.

§ These are nearly the words of Lieut.-Col. Lumsden, upon whom I am very glad to lean. That Ker was a valuable officer is well known.

betwixt these two families, was taken at this battle, and as they were going to behead him Auchindown caused stay his execution. He entertained the Master of Forbes and the rest of the prisoners with great kindness and courtesy, he carried the Master of Forbes along with him to Strathbogie, and in end gave him and all the rest leave to depart." * And again, after another success in a fight called The Bourd of Brechin, in the ensuing July, he caused all the prisoners to be brought before him, they expecting nothing but death, and said to them: " My friends and brethren, have in remembrance how God has granted to me victory and the upper hand of you, granting me the same vantage [' vand and sching'] to punish you wherewith my late father and brother were punished at the Bank of Fair; and since, of the great slaughter made on the Queen's Grace's true subjects, and most filthily of the hanging of my soldiers here by the Earl of Lennox; and since, by the hanging of ten men in Leith, with other unlawful acts done contrary to the laws of arms; and I doubt not, if I were under their dominion, as you are under mine, that I should die the death most cruelly. Yet notwithstanding, my good brethren and countrymen, be not afraid nor fear not, for at this present ye shall incur no danger of your bodies, but shall be treated as brethren, and I shall do to you after the commandment of God, in doing good for evil, forgetting the cruelty done to the queen and her faithful subjects, and receiving you as her faithful subjects in time coming. Who promised to do the same, and for assurance hereof each found surety. After which the Regent past hastily out of Sterling to Dundee, charging all manner of man to follow him, with twenty days victuals, against the

said Adam Gordon. But there would never a man in those parts obey the charge, by reason of the bond made before and of the great gentleness of the said Adam." †

After the Pacification of February, 1573, Adam Gordon obtained license to go to France and other parts beyond sea, for certain years, on condition of doing or procuring nothing to the hurt of the realm of Scotland; but for private practices of his, contrary to his promise, in conjunction with Captain Ker and others, he was ordered to return home, 12th May, 1574. His brother, the Earl of Huntly, upon information of these unlawful practices in France, was committed to ward, and when released from ward had to give security to the amount of £20,000. Adam Gordon returned in July, 1575, " at the command of the regent," with twenty gentlemen who had gone to France with him, and was in ward in 1576. He died at St. Johnston in October, 1580, " of a bleeding." As he was of tender age in 1562, he must still have been a young man.‡

Thomas Ker was a captain " of men of war "; that is, a professional soldier. As such he is mentioned in one of the articles of the Pacification, where it is declared that Captain Thomas Ker, Captain James Bruce, and Captain Gilbert Wauchop, with their respective lieutenants and ensigns, and two other persons, " shall be comprehended in this present pacification, as also all the soldiers who served under their charges, for deeds of hostility and crimes committed during the present troubles." He was accused of being engaged in practices against the regency, as we have already seen, in 1574. He was released from ward upon caution in February, 1575. 1578, 26th July, he was summoned to appear be-

---

* The History of the Feuds and Conflicts among the Clans, p. 54 f.

† Diurnal of Occurrents, p. 304 f. Also The Historie of King James the Sext, p. 111.

As to the ' Bank of Fair,' otherwise called Corrichie, the Earl of Huntly and two of his sons, John and Adam, were made prisoners at the battle there in 1562. The father, a corpulent man, " by reason of the throng that pressed him, expired in the hands of his takers." John was executed, but Adam was spared because of his tender age. (Spottiswood, p. 187.)

Tytler observes of Adam Gordon: " In his character we find a singular mixture of knightly chivalry with the ferocity of the highland freebooter. . . . Such a combination as that exhibited by Gordon was no infrequent production in these dark and sanguinary times." VII, 367. But it would have been a good thing to cite other instances.

‡ Register of the Privy Council of Scotland, II, 355 f., 420, 480, 720. Diurnal of Occurrents, p. 350. Chronicle of Aberdeen, in The Miscellany of the Spalding Club, II, 53.

fore the king and council to answer to such things as should be inquired of him. He is mentioned as a burgher of Aberdeen 1588, 1591. 1593, 3d March, he is required to give caution to the amount of 1000 merks that he will not assist the earls of Huntly and Errol. His "counsail and convoy was chiefly usit" in an important matter at Balrinnes in 1594, at which battle he "behavit himself so valiantly" that he was knighted on the field. November 4, 1594, Captain Thomas Ker and James Ker, his brother, are ordered to be denounced as rebels, having failed to appear to answer touching their treasonable assistance to George, sometime Earl of Huntly; and this seems to be the latest notice of him that has been recovered.*

In the Genealogy of the family of Forbes drawn up by Matthew Lumsden in 1580, and continued to 1667 by William Forbes, p. 43 f., ed. 1819, we read: "John Forbes of Towie married —— Grant, daughter to John Grant of Bandallach, who did bear to him a son who was unmercifullie murdered in the castle of Corgaffe; and after the decease of Bandallach's daughter, the said John Forbes married Margaret Campbell, daughter to Sir John Campbell of Calder, knight, who did bear him three sons, Alex. Forbes of Towie, John Forbes, thereafter of Towie, and William

Forbes. . . . The said John Forbes of Towie, after the murder of Margaret Campbell, married — Forbes, a daughter to the Reires," by whom he had a son, who, as also a son of his own, died in Germany. Alexander and William, sons of Margaret Campbell, died without succession, and by the death of an only son of John, junior, the house of Towie became extinct. "The rest of the said Margaret Campbell's bairns, with herself, were unmercifullie murdered in the castle of Corgaffe." †

According to the Lumsden genealogy, then, Margaret Campbell, with her younger children, and also a son of her husband, John Forbes of Towie, by a former marriage, were murdered at the castle of Corgaffe. Corgarf is a place "exigui nominis," some fifteen miles west of Towie, and, so far as is known, there is nothing to connect this place with the Forbes family. ‡ Three sixteenth-century accounts, and a fourth by an historian who was born before the event, make Towie to be the scene of the "murder," and Towie we know to have been in the possession of a member of the house of Forbes for several generations. Since Lumsden wrote only nine years after the event, and was more particularly concerned with the Forbes family than any of the other writers referred to, his statement cannot be peremptorily set aside. But we

---

* Register of the Privy Council, II, 199, 725; III, 10; V, 46, 187. Register of the Great Seal, No 1554, vol. V. Miscellany of the Spalding Club, III, 163. Historie of King James the Sext, pp 339 f., 342. The so-called ballad in Dalzell's Scotish Poems of the Sixteenth Century, II, 347, which was in circulation as a broadside.

† That a Margaret Campbell was the wife of John Forbes of Towie in 1556–63 appears from the Register of the Great Seal of Scotland, Nos 1124, 1404, 1469. But Lieut.-Col. Lumsden remarks that Sir John Campbell of Calder had no daughter of the name of Margaret, and that there is no record of such a marriage in the Cawdor papers. It may be observed in passing that Buchanan's and Spottiswood's error (as it seems to be) of substituting Alexander Forbes for John might easily arise, since, according to the Genealogy, John's father, one of his brothers, a son, and a grandson, all bore the name Alexander.

‡ "After making considerable researches upon the subject, I am come to the conclusion that it was Towie House that was burnt. Cargarf never was in possession of a Forbes." (Joseph Robertson, Kinloch MSS, VI, 28.) What is said of Corgarf in the View of the Diocese of Aberdeen, 1732, Robertson, Collections for a History of the Shires of Aberdeen and Banff, pp. 611, 616, is derived from Lumsden.

Robert Gordon, writing about 1654, says, "Non procul a fontibus [Donæ] jacet Corgarf, exigui nominis." A description of the parish of Strathdon, written about 1725, in Macfarlane's Geographical Collections, MS., says of Curgarf, "This is an old castle belonging to the earls of Mar, but nothing remarkable about it:" pp. 26, 616, of the work last cited. The Statistical Accounts of Scotland give no light; the older tells the story of Corgarf, the later of both Corgarf and Towie, and the one is as uncritical as the other.

John Forbes of Towie (Tolleis) is one of a long list of that name in an order of the Lords of Council concerning an action of the Forbes clan against the Earl of Huntly in 1573; and in another paper, dated July, 1578, which has reference to the same action, the Forbeses complain that "sum of thair housiss, wyiffis and bairnis being thairin, were all uterlie wraikit and brount." (Robertson, Illustrations, etc., IV, 762, 765.) Bearing in mind the latitude of phraseology customary in indictments, we are perhaps under no necessity of thinking that the atrocity of Towie was but one of several instances of houses burnt, wives (women) and bairns being therein. There may be those who will think it plausible that "Carrigill" in the Diurnal of Occurrents should be Corgarf, and that both were burnt.

may owe Corgarf to the reviser of 1667, although he professes not to have altered the substance of his predecessor's work.

Reverting now to the ballad, we observe that none of the seven versions, of which one is put towards the end of the sixteenth century, one is of the seventeenth century, two are of the eighteenth, and the remainder from tradition of the present century, lay the scene at Towie. E, which is of this century, has Cargarf. A, B, the oldest copies (both English), give no name to the castle. Crecrynbroghe in A, Bittonsborrow in B, are not the name of the castle that is burned, but of a castle suggested for a winter retirement by one of Car's men, and rejected by the captain. The fragment C (English again) also names no place. D transfers the scene from the north to the house of Rodes, near Dunse, in Berwickshire, and F, G to Loudoun castle in Ayrshire; the name of Gordon probably helping to the localizing of the ballad in the former case, and that of Campbell, possibly, in the other.

Captain Car is the leader of the bloody band in A, B; he is lord of Eastertown A 6, 13, of Westertown B 5, 9; but 'Adam' is said to fire the house in B 14. Adam Gordon is the captain in C–G. The sufferers are in A Hamiltons,* in F, G, Campbells. The name Forbes is not preserved in any version.

A, B. Martinmas weather forces Captain Car to look for a hold. Crecrynbroghe, A, Bittonsborrow, B, is proposed, but he knows of a castle where there is a fair lady whose lord is away, and makes for that. The lady sees from the wall a host of men riding towards the castle, and thinks her lord is coming home, but it was the traitor Captain Car. By supper-time he and his men have lighted about the place. Car calls to the lady to give up the house; she shall lie in his arms that night, and the morrow heir his land. She will not give up the house, but fires on

Car and his men. [Orders are given to burn the house.] The lady entreats Car to save her eldest son. Lap him in a sheet and let him down, says Car; and when this is done, cuts out tongue and heart, ties them in a handkerchief, and throws them over the wall. The youngest son begs his mother to surrender, for the smoke is smothering him. She would give all her gold and fee for a wind to blow the smoke away; but the fire falls about her head, and she and her children are burned to death. Captain Car rides away, A. The lord of the castle dreams, learns by a letter, at London, that his house has been fired, and hurries home. He finds the hall still burning, and breaks out into expressions of grief, A. In B, half of which has been torn from the manuscript, after reading the letter he says he will find Car wherever Car may be, and, long ere day, comes to Dractonsborrow, where the miscreant is. If nine or ten stanzas were not lost at this point, we should no doubt learn of the revenge that was taken.

In the short fragment C, upon surrender being demanded, reply is made by a shot which kills seven of the beleaguerers. An only daughter, smothered by the reek, asks her mother to give up the house. Rather would I see you burnt to ashes, says the mother. The boy on the nurse's knee makes the same appeal; her mother would sooner see him burnt than give up her house to be Adam of Gordon's whore.

D makes the lady try fair speeches with Gordon, and the lady does not reply with firearms to the proposal that she shall lie by his side. Nevertheless she has spirit enough to say, when her youngest son beseeches her to give up the house, Come weal, come woe, you must take share with me. The daughter, and not the eldest son, is wrapped in sheets and let down the wall; she gets a fall on the

---

* The making Gordon burn a house of the Hamiltons, who were of the queen's party, is a heedless perversion of history such as is to be found only in 'historical' ballads. The castle of Hamilton had been burnt in 1570, " and the toun and palice of Hamiltoun thairwith," more than a year before the burning of Towie, but by Lennox and his English allies. (Diurnal of Occurrents, p. 177.)

"The old castle of Loudoun," says the Rev. Norman Macleod, " was destroyed by fire about 350 years ago [that is, about 1500]. The current tradition regarding the burning of the old castle ascribes that event to the clan Kennedy at the period above mentioned, and the remains of an old tower at Achruglen, on the Galston side of the valley, is still pointed out as having been their residence."

point of Gordon's spear. Then follow deplorable interpolations, beginning with st. 19. Edom o Gordon, having turned the girl over with his spear, and wished her alive, turns her owr and owr again! He orders his men to busk and away, for he cannot look on the bonnie face. One of his men hopes he will not be daunted with a dame, and certainly three successive utterances in the way of sentiment show that the captain needs a little toning up. At this point the lord of the castle is coming over the lea, and sees that his castle is in flames. He and his men put on at their best rate; lady and babes are dead ere the foremost arrives; they go at the Gordons, and but five of fifty of these get away.

> And *round and round* the wae's he went,
>   *Their ashes for to view:*
> *At last* into the flames he flew,
>   And bad the world adieu.

This is superior to turning her owr and owr again, and indeed, in its way, not to be improved.

Nothing need be said of the fragment **E** further than that the last stanza is modern.

F is purely traditional, and has one fine stanza not found in any of the foregoing:

> Out then spake the lady Margaret,
>   As she stood on the stair;
> The fire was at her goud garters,
>   The lowe was at her hair.

There is no firing at the assailants (though the lady wishes that her only son could charge a gun). Lady Margaret, with the flame in her hair, would give the black and the brown for a drink of the stream that she sees below. Anne asks to be rowed in a pair of sheets and let down the wall; her mother says that she must stay and die with her. Lord Thomas, on the nurse's knee, says, Give up, or the reek will choke me. The mother would rather be burned to small ashes than give up the castle, her lord away. And burnt she is with her children nine.

* **F.** 1, 2, 3, 4, 5, 6, 7, 8, 9, 10, 11, 12, 13, 14, 15, 16, 17, 18.
  G. 1, 2, 3, 4, 13, 14, 5, 6, 30, 20, 15, 16, 22, 24, 25, 26, 34, 35.

G has the eighteen stanzas of **F**,* neglecting slight variations, and twenty more (among them the bad **D** 21), nearly all superfluous, and one very disagreeable. Lady Campbell, having refused to "come down" and be "kept" (caught) on a feather-bed, 5, 6, is ironically asked by Gordon to come down and be kept on the point of his sword, 7. Since you will not come down, says Gordon, fire your death shall be. The lady had liefer be burnt to small ashes than give up the castle while her lord is from home, 10. Fire is set. The oldest daughter asks to be rolled in a pair of sheets and flung over the wall. She gets a deadly fall on the point of Gordon's sword, and is turned over and over again, 18, over and over again, 19. Lady Margaret cries that the fire is at her garters and the flame in her hair. Lady Ann, from childbed where she lies, asks her mother to give up the castle, and is told that she must stay and dree her death with the rest. The youngest son asks his mother to go down, and has the answer that was given Gordon in 10. The waiting-maid begs to have a baby of hers saved; her lady's long hair is burnt to her brow, and how can she take it? So the babe is rolled in a feather-bed and flung over the wall, and gets a deadly fall on the point of Gordon's ever-ready sword. Several ill-connected stanzas succeed, three of which are clearly recent, and then pity for Lady Ann Campbell, who was burnt with her nine bairns. Lord Loudon comes home a "sorry" man, but comforts himself with tearing Gordon with wild horses.

A slight episode has been passed over. It is a former servant of the family that breaks through the house-wall and kindles the fire, **A** 21, **D** 12-14, **F** 5, 6, **G** 13, 14. In all but **A** he makes the excuse that he is now Gordon's man, and must do or die.

There is a Danish ballad of about 1600 (communicated to me by Svend Grundtvig, and, I think, not yet printed) in which Karl grevens søn, an unsuccessful suitor of Lady Linild, burns Lady Linild in her bower, and taking refuge in Maribo church, is there burned himself by Karl kejserens søn, Lady

Linild's preferred lover. See also 'Liden En-gel,' under 'Fause Foodrage,' No 89, II, 298.

The copy in Percy's Reliques is translated by Bodmer, I, 126, and by Doenninges, p. 69 ;

Pinkerton's copy by Grundtvig, No 9, and by Loève-Veimars, p. 307 ; Knortz, Schottische Balladen, No 13, apparently translates Alling-ham's.

A

Cotton MS. Vespasian, A. xxv, No 67, fol. 187 ; Furni-vall, in Transactions of the New Shakspere Society, 1880–86, Appendix, p. 52†.

1 It befell at Martynmas,
　　When wether waxed colde,
Captaine Care said to his men,
　　We must go take a holde.

　　　　Syck, sike, and to-towe sike,
　　　　　And sike and like to die ;
　　　　The sikest nighte that euer I abode,
　　　　　God lord haue mercy on me !

2 'Haille, master, and wether you will,
　　And wether ye like it best ; '
'To the castle of Crecrynbroghe,
　　And there we will take our reste.'

3 'I knowe wher is a gay castle,
　　Is builded of lyme and stone ;
Within their is a gay ladie,
　　Her lord is riden and gone.'

4 The ladie she lend on her castle-walle,
　　She loked vpp and downe ;
There was she ware of an host of men,
　　Come riding to the towne.

5 'Se yow, my meri men all,
　　And se yow what I see ?
Yonder I see an host of men,
　　I muse who they bee.'

6 She thought he had ben her wed lord,
　　As he comd riding home ;
Then was it traitur Captaine Care
　　The lord of Ester-towne.

7 They wer no soner at supper sett,
　　Then after said the grace,
Or Captaine Care and all his men
　　Wer lighte aboute the place.

8 'Gyue ouer thi howsse, thou lady gay,
　　And I will make the a bande ;
To-nighte thou shall ly within my armes,
　　To-morrowe thou shall ere my lande.'

9 Then bespacke the eldest sonne,
　　That was both whitt and redde :
O mother dere, geue ouer your howsse,
　　Or elles we shalbe deade.

10 'I will not geue ouer my hous,' she saithe,
　　'Not for feare of my lyffe ;
It shalbe talked throughout the land,
　　The slaughter of a wyffe.

11 'Fetch me my pestilett,
　　And charge me my gonne,
That I may shott at yonder bloddy butcher,
　　The lord of Easter-towne.'

12 Styfly vpon her wall she stode,
　　And lett the pellettes flee ;
But then she myst the blody bucher,
　　And she slew other three.

13 '[I will] not geue ouer my hous,' she saithe,
　　'Netheir for lord nor lowne ;
Nor yet for traitour Captaine Care,
　　The lord of Easter-towne.

14 'I desire of Captine Care,
　　And all his bloddye band,
That he would saue my eldest sonne,
　　The eare of all my lande.'

15 'Lap him in a shete,' he sayth,
　　'And let him downe to me,
And I shall take him in my armes,
　　His waran shall I be.'

16 The captayne sayd unto him selfe :
　　Wyth sped, before the rest,
He cut his tonge out of his head,
　　His hart out of his brest.

17 He lapt them in a handkerchef,
And knet it of knotes three,
And cast them ouer the castell-wall,
At that gay ladye.

18 'Fye vpon the, Captayne Care,
And all thy bloddy band !
For thou hast slayne my eldest sonne,
The ayre of all my land.'

19 Then bespake the yongest sonne,
That sat on the nurses knee,
Sayth, Mother gay, geue ouer your house ;
It smoldereth me.

20 'I wold geue my gold,' she saith,
'And so I wolde my ffee,
For a blaste of the westryn wind,
To dryue the smoke from thee.

21 'Fy vpon the, John Hamleton,
That euer I paid the hyre !
For thou hast broken my castle-wall,
And kyndled in the ffyre.'

22 The lady gate to her close parler,
The fire fell aboute her head ;
She toke vp her children thre,
Seth, Babes, we are all dead.

23 Then bespake the hye steward,
That is of hye degree ;
Saith, Ladie gay, you are in close,
Wether ye fighte or flee.

24 Lord Hamleton dremd in his dream,
In Caruall where he laye,
His halle were all of fyre,
His ladie slayne or daye.

25 'Busk and bowne, my mery men all,
Even and go ye with me ;
For I dremd that my haal was on fyre,
My lady slayne or day.'

26 He buskt him and bownd hym,
And like a worthi knighte ;
And when he saw his hall burning,
His harte was no dele lighte.

27 He sett a trumpett till his mouth,
He blew as it plesd his grace ;
Twenty score of Hamlentons
Was light aboute the place.

28 'Had I knowne as much yesternighte
As I do to-daye,
Captaine Care and all his men
Should not haue gone so quite.

29 'Fye vpon the, Captaine Care,
And all thy blody bande !
Thou haste slayne my lady gay,
More wurth then all thy lande.

30 'If thou had ought eny ill will,' he saith,
'Thou shoulde haue taken my lyffe,
And haue saved my children thre,
All and my louesome wyffe.'

B

Percy MS., p. 34 ; Hales and Furnivall, I, 79.

1 'Ffaith, master, whither you will,
Whereas you like the best ;
Vnto the castle of Bittons-borrow,
And there to take your rest.'

2 'But yonder stands a castle faire,
Is made of lyme and stone ;
Yonder is in it a fayre lady,
Her lord is ridden and gone.'

3 The lady stood on her castle-wall,
She looked vpp and downe ;
She was ware of an hoast of men,
Came rydinge towards the towne.

4 'See you not, my merry men all,
And see you not what I doe see ?
Methinks I see a hoast of men ;
I muse who they shold be.'

5 She thought it had beene her louly lord,
He had come ryding home ;
It was the traitor, Captaine Carre,
The lord of Westerton-towne.

6 They had noe sooner super sett,
And after said the grace,
But the traitor, Captaine Carre,
Was light about the place.

7 'Giue over thy house, thou lady gay,
I will make thee a band ;

All night with-in mine armes thou 'st lye,
  To-morrow be the heyre of my land.'

8 'I 'le not giue over my house,' shee said,
  'Neither for ladds nor man,
Nor yet for traitor Captaine Carre,
  Vntill my lord come home.

9 'But reach me my pistoll pe[c]e,
  And charge you well my gunne;
I 'le shoote at the bloody bucher,
  The lord of Westerton.'

10 She stood vppon her castle-wall
  And let the bulletts flee,
And where shee mist   .   .
  .   .   .   .   .   .

11 But then bespake the litle child,
  That sate on the nurses knee;
Saies, Mother deere, giue ore this house,
  For the smoake it smoothers me.

12 'I wold giue all my gold, my childe,
  Soe wold I doe all my fee,
For one blast of the westerne wind
  To blow the smoke from thee.'

13 But when shee saw the fier
  Came flaming ore her head,
Shee tooke then vpp her children two,
  Sayes, Babes, we all beene dead!

14 But Adam then he fired the house,
  A sorrowfull sight to see;
Now hath he burned this lady faire
  And eke her children three.

15 Then Captaine Carre he rode away,
  He staid noe longer at that tide;
He thought that place it was to warme
  Soe neere for to abide.

16 He calld vnto his merry men all,
  Bidd them make hast away;
'For we haue slaine his children three,
  All and his lady gay.'

17 Worde came to louly London,
  To London wheras her lord lay,
His castle and his hall was burned,
  All and his lady gay.

18 Soe hath he done his children three,
  More dearer vnto him
Then either the siluer or the gold,
  That men soe faine wold win.

19 But when he looket this writing on,
  Lord, in is hart he was woe!
Saies, I will find thee, Captaine Carre,
  Wether thou ryde or goe!

20 Buske yee, bowne yee, my merrymen all,
  With tempered swords of steele,
For till I haue found out Captaine Carre,
  My hart it is nothing weele.

21 But when he came to Dractons-borrow,
  Soe long ere it was day,
And ther he found him Captaine Carre;
  That night he ment to stay.

*   *   *   *   *   *   *

C

Communicated to Percy by Robert Lambe, Norham, October 4, 1766, being all that a servant of Lambe's could remember.

*   *   *   *   *   *   *

1 'Luk ye to yon hie castel,
  Yon hie castel we see;
A woman's wit's sun oercum,
  She 'll gie up her house to me.'

2 She ca'd to her merry men a',
  'Bring me my five pistols and my lang gun;'
The first shot the fair lady shot,
  She shot seven of Gordon's men.

3 He turned round about his back,
  And sware he woud ha his desire,
And if that castel was built of gowd,
  It should gang a' to fire.

4 Up then spak her doughter deere,
  She had nae mair than she:

'Gie up your house, now, mither deere,
  The reek it skomfishes me.'

5 'I d rather see you birnt,' said she,
  'And doun to ashes fa,
  Ere I gie up my house to Adam of Gordon,
  And to his merry men a'.

6 'I 've four and twenty kye
  Gaing upo the muir;
  I 'd gie em for a blast of wind,
  The reek it blaws sae sour.'

7 Up then spak her little young son,
  Sits on the nourrice knee:

'Gie up your house, now, mither deere,
  The reek it skomfishes me.'

8 'I 've twenty four ships
  A sailing on the sea;
  I 'll gie em for a blast of southern wind,
  To blaw the reek frae thee.

9 'I 'd rather see you birnt,' said she,
  'And grund as sma as flour,
  Eer I gie up my noble house,
  To be Adam of Gordon's hure.'

*   *   *   *   *   *   *

D

Robert and Andrew Foulis, Glasgow, 1755; "as preserved in the memory of a lady."

1 It fell about the Martinmas,
  When the wind blew schrile and cauld,
  Said Edom o Gordon to his men,
  We maun draw to a hald.

2 'And what an a hald sall we draw to,
  My merry men and me?
  We will gae to the house of the Rhodes,
  To see that fair lady.'

3 She had nae sooner busket her sell,
  Nor putten on her gown,
  Till Edom o Gordon and his men
  Were round about the town.

4 They had nae sooner sitten down,
  Nor sooner said the grace,
  Till Edom o Gordon and his men
  Were closed about the place.

5 The lady ran up to her tower-head,
  As fast as she could drie,
  To see if by her fair speeches
  She could with him agree.

6 As soon he saw the lady fair,
  And hir yates all locked fast,
  He fell into a rage of wrath,
  And his heart was aghast.

7 'Cum down to me, ye lady fair,
  Cum down to me; let 's see;

This night ye 's ly by my ain side,
  The morn my bride sall be.'

8 'I winnae cum down, ye fals Gordon,
  I winnae cum down to thee;
  I winnae forsake my ane dear lord,
  That is sae far frae me.'

9 'Gi up your house, ye fair lady,
  Gi up your house to me,
  Or I will burn yoursel therein,
  Bot and your babies three.'

10 'I winnae gie up, you fals Gordon,
  To nae sik traitor as thee,
  Tho you should burn mysel therein,
  Bot and my babies three.'

11 'Set fire to the house,' quoth fals Gordon,
  'Sin better may nae bee;
  And I will burn hersel therein,
  Bot and her babies three.'

12 'And ein wae worth ye, Jock my man!
  I paid ye weil your fee;
  Why pow ye out my ground-wa-stane,
  Lets in the reek to me?

13 'And ein wae worth ye, Jock my man!
  For I paid you weil your hire;
  Why pow ye out my ground-wa-stane,
  To me lets in the fire?'

14 'Ye paid me weil my hire, lady,
  Ye paid me weil my fee,

But now I 'm Edom of Gordon's man,
  Maun either do or die.'

15 O then bespake her youngest son,
  Sat on the nurses knee,
'Dear mother, gie owre your house,' he says,
  'For the reek it worries me.'

16 'I winnae gie up my house, my dear,
  To nae sik traitor as he;
Cum weil, cum wae, my jewels fair,
  Ye maun tak share wi me.'

17 O then bespake her dochter dear,
  She was baith jimp and sma;
'O row me in a pair o shiets,
  And tow me owre the wa.'

18 They rowd her in a pair of shiets,
  And towd her owre the wa,
But on the point of Edom's speir
  She gat a deadly fa.

19 O bonny, bonny was hir mouth,
  And chirry were her cheiks,
And clear, clear was hir yellow hair,
  Whereon the reid bluid dreips!

20 Then wi his speir he turnd hir owr;
  O gin hir face was wan!
He said, You are the first that eer
  I wist alive again.

21 He turned hir owr and owr again;
  O gin hir skin was whyte!
He said, I might ha spard thy life
  To been some mans delyte.

22 'Busk and boon, my merry men all,
  For ill dooms I do guess;

I cannae luik in that bonny face,
  As it lyes on the grass.'

23 'Them luiks to freits, my master deir,
  Then freits will follow them;
Let it neir be said brave Edom o Gordon
  Was daunted with a dame.'

24 O then he spied hir ain deir lord,
  As he came owr the lee;
He saw his castle in a fire,
  As far as he could see.

25 'Put on, put on, my mighty men,
  As fast as ye can drie!
For he that 's hindmost of my men
  Sall neir get guid o me.'

26 And some they raid, and some they ran,
  Fu fast out-owr the plain,
But lang, lang eer he coud get up
  They were a' deid and slain.

27 But mony were the mudie men
  Lay gasping on the grien;
For o fifty men that Edom brought out
  There were but five ged heme.

28 And mony were the mudie men
  Lay gasping on the grien,
And mony were the fair ladys
  Lay lemanless at heme.

29 And round and round the waes he went,
  Their ashes for to view;
At last into the flames he flew,
  And bad the world adieu.

E

Kinloch MSS, V, 384, in the handwriting of John Hill Burton.

1 IT fell about the Martinmas time,
  When the wind blew shrill and cauld,
Said Captain Gordon to his men,
  We 'll a' draw to som hauld.

2 'And whatena hauld shall we draw to,
  To be the nearest hame?'

'We will draw to the ha o bonny Cargarff;
  The laird is na at hame.'

3 The lady sat on her castle-wa,
  Beheld both dale and down;
And she beheld the fause Gordon
  Come halycon to the town.

4 'Now, Lady Cargarff, gie ower yer house,
  Gie ower yer house to me;

Now, Lady Cargarff, gie ower yer house,
    Or in it you shall die.'

5 'I 'll no gie ower my bonny house,
    To lord nor yet to loun;
I 'll no gie ower my bonny house
    To the traitors of Auchindown.'

*   *   *   *   *   *   *

6 Then up and spak her youngest son,
    Sat at the nourice's knee:

'O mother dear, gie ower yer house,
    For the reek o 't smothers me.'

7 'I would gie a' my goud, my child,
    Sae would I a' my fee,
For ae blast o the westlan win,
    To blaw the reek frae thee.'

8 Then up and spak her eldest heir,
    He spak wi muckle pride:
'Now mother dear, keep weel yer house,
    And I 'll fight by yer side.'

—◆—

F

The New Statistical Account of Scotland, V, 846, Parish of Loudoun, by Rev. Norman Macleod: "known among the peasantry from time immemorial."

1 It fell about the Martinmas time,
    When the wind blew snell and cauld,
That Adam o Gordon said to his men,
    Where will we get a hold?

2 See [ye] not where yonder fair castle
    Stands on yon lily lee?
The laird and I hae a deadly feud,
    The lady fain would I see.

3 As she was up on the househead,
    Behold, on looking down,
She saw Adam o Gordon and his men,
    Coming riding to the town.

4 The dinner was not well set down,
    Nor the grace was scarcely said,
Till Adam o Gordon and his men
    About the walls were laid.

5 'It 's fause now fa thee, Jock my man!
    Thou might a let me be;
Yon man has lifted the pavement-stone,
    An let in the low unto me.'

6 'Seven years I served thee, fair ladie,
    You gave me meat and fee;
But now I am Adam o Gordon's man,
    An maun either do it or die.'

7 'Come down, come down, my lady Loudoun,
    Come down thou unto me!

I 'll wrap thee on a feather-bed,
    Thy warrand I shall be.'

8 'I 'll no come down, I 'll no come down,
    For neither laird no[r] loun;
Nor yet for any bloody butcher
    That lives in Altringham town.

9 'I would give the black,' she says,
    'And so would I the brown,
If that Thomas, my only son,
    Could charge to me a gun.'

10 Out then spake the lady Margaret,
    As she stood on the stair;
The fire was at her goud garters,
    The lowe was at her hair.

11 'I would give the black,' she says,
    'And so would I the brown,
For a drink of yon water,
    That runs by Galston Town.'

12 Out then spake fair Annie,
    She was baith jimp and sma
'O row me in a pair o sheets,
    And tow me down the wa!'

13 'O hold thy tongue, thou fair Annie,
    And let thy talkin be;
For thou must stay in this fair castle,
    And bear thy death with me.'

14 'O mother,' spoke the lord Thomas,
    As he sat on the nurse's knee,
'O mother, give up this fair castle,
    Or the reek will worrie me.'

15 'I would rather be burnt to ashes sma,
    And be cast on yon sea-foam,
    Before I'd give up this fair castle,
    And my lord so far from home.

16 'My good lord has an army strong,
    He's now gone oer the sea;
    He bad me keep this gay castle,
    As long as it would keep me.

17 'I've four-and-twenty brave milk kye,
    Gangs on yon lily· lee;
    I'd give them a' for a blast of wind,
    To blaw the reek from me.'

18 O pittie on yon fair castle,
    That's built with stone and lime!
    But far mair pittie on Lady Loudoun,
    And all her children nine!

—◆—

G

Motherwell's MS., p. 543, from the recitation of May Richmond, at the Old Kirk of Loudon.

1 IT was in and about the Martinmas time,
    When the wind blew schill and cauld,
    That Adam o Gordon said to his men,
    Whare will we get a hauld?

2 'Do ye not see yon bonnie castell,
    That stands on Loudon lee?
    The lord and I hae a deadlie feed,
    And his lady fain wuld I see.'

3 Lady Campbell was standing in the close,
    A preenin o her goun,
    Whan Adam o Gordon and his men
    Cam riding thro Galston toun.

4 The dinner was na weel set doun,
    Nor yet the grace weel said,
    Till Adam o Gordon and a' his men
    Around the wa's war laid.

5 'Come doun, come down, Ladie Campbell,' he said,
    'Come doun and speak to me;
    I'll kep thee in a feather bed,
    And thy warraner I will be.'

6 'I winna come doun and speak to thee,
    Nor to ony lord nor loun;
    Nor yet to thee, thou bloody butcher,
    The laird o Auchruglen toun.'

7 'Come doun, come doun, Ladye Campbell,' he said,
    'Cum doun and speak to me;
    I'll kep thee on the point o my sword,
    And thy warraner I will be.'

8 'I winna come doun and speak to thee,
    Nor to ony lord or loun,
    Nor yet to thee, thou bludie butcher,
    The laird o Auchruglen toun.'

9 'Syne gin ye winna come doun,' he said,
    'A' for to speak to me,
    I'll tye the bands around my waist,
    And fire thy death sall be.'

10 'I'd leifer be burnt in ashes sma,
    And cuist in yon sea-faem,
    Or I'd gie up this bonnie castell,
    And my gude lord frae hame.

11 'For my gude lord's in the army strong,
    He's new gane ower the sea;
    He bade me keep this bonnie castell,
    As lang's it wuld keep me.'

12 'Set fire to the house,' said bauld Gordon,
    'Set fire to the house, my men;
    We'll gar Lady Campbell come for to rew
    As she burns in the flame.'

13 'O wae be to thee, Carmichael,' she said,
    'And an ill death may ye die!
    For ye hae lifted the pavement-stane,
    And loot up the lowe to me.

14 'Seven years ye war about my house,
    And received both meat and fee:'
    'And now I'm Adam o Gordon's man,
    I maun either do or dee.'

15 'Oh I wad gie the black,' she said,
    'And I wuld gie the brown,
    All for ae cup o the cauld water
    That rins to Galstoun toun.'

16 Syne out and spak the auld dochter,
    She was baith jimp and sma:
  'O row me in a pair o sheets,
    And fling me ower the wa!'

17 They row't her in a pair o sheets,
    And flang her ower the wa,
  And on the point o Gordon's sword
    She gat a deadlie fa.

18 He turned her ower, and ower again,
    And oh but she looked wan!
  'I think I've killed as bonnie a face
    As ere the sun shined on.'

19 He turned her ower, and ower again,
    And oh but she lookt white!
  'I micht hae spared this bonnie face,
    To hae been some man's delight!'

20 Syne out and spak Lady Margaret,
    As she stood on the stair:
  'The fire is at my gowd garters,
    And the lowe is at my hair.'

21 Syne out and spak fair Ladie Ann,
    Frae childbed whare she lay:
  'Gie up this bonnie castell, mother,
    And let us win away.'

22 'Lye still, lye still, my fair Annie,
    And let your talking be;
  For ye maun stay in this bonnie castell
    And dree your death wi me.'

23 'Whatever death I am to dree,
    I winna die my lane:
  I'll tak a bairn in ilka arm
    And the third is in my wame.'

24 Syne out and spak her youngest son,
    A bonnie wee boy was he:
  'Gae doun, gae doun, mother,' he said,
    'Or the lowe will worry me.'

25 'I'd leifer be brent in ashes sma
    And cuist in yon sea-faem,
  Or I'd gie up this bonnie castell,
    And my guid lord frae hame.

26 'For my gude lord 's in the army strong,
    He 's new gane ower the sea;

But gin he eer returns again,
    Revenged my death sall be.'

27 Syne out and spak her waitin-maid:
    Receive this babe frae me,
  And save the saikless babie's life,
    And I 'll neer seek mair fee.

28 'How can I tak the bairn?' she said,
    'How can I tak 't?' said she,
  'For my hair was ance five quarters lang,
    And 't is now brent to my bree.'

29 She rowit it in a feather-bed,
    And flang it ower the wa,
  But on the point o Gordon's sword
    It gat a deidlie fa.

30 'I wuld gie Loudon's bonnie castell,
    And Loudon's bonnie lee,
  All gin my youngest son Johnnie
    Could charge a gun to me.

31 'Oh, I wuld gie the black,' she said,
    'And sae wuld I the bay,
  Gin young Sir George could take a steed
    And quickly ride away.'

32 Syne out and spak her auldest son,
    As he was gaun to die:
  'Send doun your chamber-maid, mother,
    She gaes wi bairn to me.'

33 'Gin ye were not my eldest son,
    And heir o a' my land,
  I 'd tye a sheet around thy neck,
    And hang thee with my hand.

34 'I would gie my twenty gude milk-kye,
    That feed on Shallow lee,
  A' for ae blast o the norland wind,
    To blaw the lowe frae me.'

35 Oh was na it a pitie o yon bonnie castell,
    That was biggit wi stane and lime!
  But far mair pity o Lady Ann Campbell,
    That was brunt wi her bairns nine.

36 Three o them war married wives,
    And three o them were bairns,
  And three o them were leal maidens,
    That neer lay in men's arms.

37 And now Lord Loudon he 's come hame,
　　And a sorry man was he:
' He micht hae spared my lady's life,
　　And wreakit himsell on me!

38 ' But sin we 've got thee, bauld Gordon,
　　Wild horses shall thee tear,
For murdering o my ladie bricht,
　　Besides my children dear.'

———•———

A.　*Stanzas 1–15 have been revised, or altered,
　　in another hand.*
　2¹. master *in my copy:* mary, Furnivall.
　3¹. wher is *is inserted.*
　3². ed *in* builded *has been run through with
　　a line.*
　3⁴. riden & gone *struck out, and* ryd from
　　hom *written over.*
　4¹. she *struck out.*
　5¹. Se yow *changed to* Com yow hether:
　　merimen *in MS.*
　5². *Changed to* And look what I do see.
　　And (&), *both in the original text and in
　　the revised, is rendered* O *in my copy.*
　5³. *Changed to* Yonder is ther.
　5⁴. musen, *as a correction: Furnivall.*
　6¹. own wed, *as a correction: Furnivall.*
　6². yᵗ had *for* As he.
　8³. thou shall ly in *altered to* thoust ly
　　wᵗin.
　10². Not *is a correction: Furnivall.　My
　　copy has* no.
　11³. this *substituted for* yonder.
　12¹. *Changed to* She styfly stod on her castle
　　wall.
　12³. but then *struck out.*
　12⁴. she *struck out.*
　13¹. I will: *MS. torn.*
　15³. arme, *Furnivall: my copy,* armes.
　15⁴. wyll *substituted for* shall.

　19⁴. *Editors supply* The smoke *at the begin-
　　ning of the line.*
　20³. westeyn: *Furnivall.*　21⁴. *MS. has* thee.
　23³. Saith: no close, *Furnivall.　South:* in
　　close, *my copy.　to* chose, *Böddeker.*
　24². *Perhaps* carnall: *Furnivall.*
　25¹. Bush *in my copy:* merymen *in MS.*
　25³. dreme, hall *in my copy: Furnivall as
　　printed.*
　26¹. busht *in my copy:* buskt, *Furnivall.*
　26²,³. *My copy renders* And (&) O: *Furni-
　　vall as printed.*
　28⁴. *Editors supply* awaye *at the end of the
　　line.　Böddeker reads* so gai.
　29². bande *looks like* baides, *one stroke of
　　the* n *wanting.*
　30¹. *Should we not read* me *for* eny? she *for*
　　he *in my copy:* he, *Furnivall.*
　And *for* & *throughout.*
　Finis per me Will*elmu*m Asheton, clericum.
　*By my copy is meant a collation made for me
　　by Miss Lucy Toulmin Smith.*

B.　13³. 2.　14⁴, 16³, 18¹. 3.
　10³, 21⁴. *Half a page gone.*
　And *for* &.

D.　27¹, 28¹. Mudiemen, Mudie men.
　Quhen, ze, zour, *etc., are here spelled* when,
　　ye, your, *etc.*

F.　5⁴. the loun to: *cf.* G 13⁴.

G.　6⁴. *Another recitation gave* Auchindown.

179

ROOKHOPE RYDE

The Bishopric Garland, or Durham Minstrel [edited by Joseph Ritson], 2d ed., Newcastle, 1792 ; here, from the reprint by Joseph Haslewood, 1809, p. 54, in Northern Garlands, London, 1810. " Taken down from the chanting of George Collingood the elder, late of Boltsburn, in the neighborhood of Ryhope," who died in 1785.

PRINTED in Bell's Rhymes of Northern Bards, 1812, p. 276 ; Minstrelsy of the Scottish Border, 1833, II, 101 ; [Sir Cuthbert Sharp's] Bishoprick Garland, 1834, p. 14.

The date of this ryde, or raid, may be precisely ascertained from the ballad itself; it is shown by 13⁴, 11 to be December 6, 1569.

The thieves of Thirlwall (Northumberland) and Williehaver, or Willeva (Cumberland), avail themselves of the confusion incident to the Rising in the North and of the absence of a part of the fencible men (some of whom were with the earls, others with Bowes in Barnard castle) to make a foray into Rookhope, in Weardale, Durham. In four hours they get together six hundred sheep. But the alarm is given by a man whose horses they have taken ; the cry spreads through the dale ; word comes to the bailiff, who instantly arms, and is joined by his neighbors to the number of forty or fifty. The thieves are a hundred, the stoutest men and best in gear.

When the Weardale men come up with them, the marauders get fighting enough. The fray lasts an hour ; four of the robbers are killed, a handsome number wounded, and eleven taken prisoners, with the loss of only one of those who fought for the right.

Rookhope is the name of a valley, about five miles in length, at the termination of which Rookhope burn empties itself into the river Wear. Rookhope-head is the top of the vale. (Ritson.)

The Weardale man who was killed was Rowland Emerson, perhaps a kinsman of the bailiff. The family of Emerson of Eastgate, says Surtees, long exercised the offices of bailiff of Wolsingham (the chief town and borough of Weardale) and of forester, etc., etc., under successive prelates. (Surtees to Scott, Memoir by Taylor and Raine, p. 33.)

34. The thieves bare 'three banners' against the Weardale men. They choose three captains in 9.

---

1 ROOKHOPE stands in a pleasant place,
 If the false thieves wad let it be ;
But away they steal our goods apace,
 And ever an ill death may they die !

2 And so is the men of Thirlwa 'nd Williehaver,
 And all their companies thereabout,
That is minded to do mischief,
 And at their stealing stands not out.

3 But yet we will not slander them all,
 For there is of them good enough ;

It is a sore consumed tree
 That on it bears not one fresh bough.

4 Lord God ! is not this a pitiful case,
 That men dare not drive their goods to t' fell,
But limmer thieves drives them away,
 That fears neither heaven nor hell ?

5 Lord, send us peace into the realm,
 That every man may live on his own !
I trust to God, if it be his will,
 That Weardale men may never be overthrown.

6 For great troubles they 've had in hand,
   With borderers pricking hither and thither,
But the greatest fray that eer they had
   Was with the 'men' of Thirlwa 'nd Willie-
      haver.

7 They gatherd together so royally,
   The stoutest men and the best in gear,
And he that rade not on a horse,
   I wat he rade on a weil-fed mear.

8 So in the morning, before they came out,
   So well, I wot, they broke their fast;
In the [forenoon they came] unto a bye fell,
   Where some of them did eat their last.

9 When they had eaten aye and done,
   They sayd some captains here needs must
      be :
Then they choosed forth Harry Corbyl,
   And 'Symon Fell,' and Martin Ridley.

10 Then oer the moss, where as they came,
   With many a brank and whew,
One of them could to another say,
   'I think this day we are men enew.

11 'For Weardale men is a journey taen ;
   They are so far out-oer yon fell
That some of them 's with the two earls,
   And others fast in Barnard castell.

12 'There we shal get gear enough,
   For there is nane but women at hame ;
The sorrowful fend that they can make
   Is loudly cries as they were slain.'

13 Then in at Rookhope-head they came,
   And there they thought tul a had their
      prey,
But they were spy'd coming over the Dry Rig,
   Soon upon Saint Nicholas' day.

14 Then in at Rookhope-head they came,
   They ran the forest but a mile ;
They gatherd together in four hours
   Six hundred sheep within a while.

15 And horses I trow they gat
   But either ane or twa,
And they gat them all but ane
   That belanged to great Rowley.

16 That Rowley was the first man that did them
      spy ;
   With that he raised a mighty cry ;
The cry it came down Rookhope burn,
   And spread through Weardale hasteyly.

17 Then word came to the bailif's house,
   At the East Gate, where he did dwell ;
He was walkd out to the Smale Burns,
   Which stands above the Hanging Well.

18 His wife was wae when she heard tell,
   So well she wist her husband wanted
      gear ;
She gard saddle him his horse in haste,
   And neither forgqt sword, jack, nor spear.

19 The bailif got wit before his gear came
   That such news was in the land ;
He was sore troubled in his heart,
   That on no earth that he could stand.

20 His brother was hurt three days before,
   With limmer thieves that did him prick ;
Nineteen bloody wounds lay him upon ;
   What ferly was 't that he lay sick ?

21 But yet the bailif shrinked nought,
   But fast after them he did hye,
And so did all his neighbours near,
   That went to bear him company.

22 But when the bailiff was gathered,
   And all his company,
They were numberd to never a man
   But forty [or] under fifty.

23 The thieves was numberd a hundred men,
   I wat they were not of the worst
That could be choosed out of Thirlwa 'nd
      Williehaver,
   .   .   .   .

24 But all that was in Rookhope-head,
   And all that was i Nuketon Cleugh,
Where Weardale men oertook the thieves,
   And there they gave them fighting eneugh.

25 So sore they made them fain to flee,
   As many was 'a'' out of hand,
And, for tul have been at home again,
   They would have been in iron bands ;

26 And for the space of long seven years,
    As sore they mighten a had their lives;
But there was never one of them
    That ever thought to have seen their 'wives.'

27 About the time the fray began,
    I trow it lasted but an hour,
Till many a man lay weaponless,
    And was sore wounded in that stour.

28 Also before that hour was done,
    Four of the thieves were slain,
Besides all those that wounded were,
    And eleven prisoners there was taen.

29 George Carrick and his brother Edie,
    Them two, I wot, they were both slain;
Harry Corbyl and Lennie Carrick
    Bore them company in their pain.

30 One of our Weardale men was slain,
    Rowland Emerson his name hight;
I trust to God his soul is well,
    Because he 'fought' unto the right.

31 But thus they sayd : 'We 'll not depart
    While we have one; speed back again!'
And when they came amongst the dead men,
    There they found George Carrick slain.

32 And when they found George Carrick slain,
    I wot it went well near their 'heart;'
Lord, let them never make a better end
    That comes to play them sicken a 'part!'

33 I trust to God, no more they shal,
    Except it be one for a great chance;
For God wil punish all those
    With a great heavy pestilence.

34 Thir limmer thieves, they have good hearts,
    They nevir think to be oerthrown;
Three banners against Weardale men they bare,
    As if the world had been all their own.

35 Thir Weardale men, they have good hearts,
    They are as stif as any tree;
For, if they 'd every one been slain,
    Never a foot back man would flee.

36 And such a storm amongst them fell
    As I think you never heard the like,
For he that bears his head so high,
    He oft-times falls into the dyke.

37 And now I do entreat you all,
    As many as are present here,
To pray for [the] singer of this song,
    For he sings to make blithe your cheer.

———•———

2⁸. mischief hither *in Bell, who, however, prints from Ritson.*
2⁴. as : at *in Scott, who had his copy, as printed in* 1792, *from Ritson's nephew.* at *also in Bell.*
9⁸, 29⁸. Corbyl, *it is thought, should be Corbyt, which is a northern name. Both Corbyl and* Carrick *were new to Surtees.*
10⁸. *Bell reads* would, *not understanding that* could *means* did.

11¹. *Scott, wrongly,* have *for* is : *Bell, who aims at grammar,* are.
17⁸. He had, *Bell, for improvement again.*
23⁴. *The reciter, from his advanced age, could not recollect this line : Ritson.*
25². *Bell,* land *for* hand.
30⁸. *Bell,* in *for* to.
Ritson's emendations, indicated by ' ', have necessarily been allowed to stand.

180

KING JAMES AND BROWN

'Kinge James and Browne,' Percy MS., p. 58; Hales and Furnivall, I, 135.

———

As the minstrel is walking by himself, he hears a young prince lamenting. The prince says to him, Yonder comes a Scot who will do me wrong. Douglas comes with armed men, who beset the king with swords and spears. Are you lords of Scotland, come for council, asks the king, or are you traitors, come for my blood? They say that they are traitors, come for his blood. Fie on you, false Scots! exclaims the king; you have slain my grandfather, caused my mother to flee, and hanged my father. [About nine stanzas are lost here.] Douglas offers Brown his daughter in marriage to betray the king; Brown will never be a traitor. Douglas is making off fast, but Brown takes him prisoner and conducts him to the king. Douglas prays for pardon. The king replies that Douglas has sought to kill him ever since he was born. Douglas swears to be a true subject if pardoned. The king pardons him freely, and all traitors in Scotland, great and small. Douglas mutters to himself (we may suppose), If I live a twelvemonth you shall die, and I will burn Edinburgh to-morrow. This irredeemable traitor hies to Edinburgh with his men, but the people shut the gates against him. Brown is always where he is wanted, and takes Douglas prisoner again; the report that Douglas is secured goes to the king, who demands his taker to be brought into his presence, and promises him a thousand pound a year. So they call Brown; we may imagine that the distance is no greater than Holyrood. How often hast thou fought for me, Brown? asks James. Brown's first service was in Edinburgh; had he not stood stoutly there, James had never been king.

The second was his killing the sheriff of Carlisle's son, who was on the point of slaying his Grace. The third was when he killed the Bishop of St Andrews, who had undertaken to poison the king. James had already made the faithful Englishman (for such he is) knight; now he makes him an earl, with professions of fidelity to the English queen.

This third service of Brown is the subject of a poem by William Elderton, here given in an appendix. The bishop is about to give the king (then a child) a poisoned posset. The lady nurse calls for aid. Brown, an Englishman, hears, goes to help, meets the bishop hurrying off with the posset in his hand, and forces him to drink it, though the bishop makes him handsome offers not to interfere. The venom works swiftly, the bishop's belly bursts. The king knights Brown, and gives him lands and livings.

John Hamilton, Archbishop of St Andrews, must be the person whom Brown slays in the ballad for an attempt to poison the young king. He was, however, hanged by his political enemies, April 7, 1571. This prelate was credited with being an accomplice to the murder of Darnley and to that of the Regent Murray. His elder brother was heir to the throne after the progeny of Mary Stuart, and both of these persons were more or less in the way. Mary Stuart's son was a step on which the Hamiltons must "fall down or else oerleap," and the archbishop is said to have sneered at the Duke of Chatelherault for letting an infant live between him and the throne. A report that the archbishop had undertaken to poison this infant would readily be believed. Sir William

Drury thought it worth his while to write to Cecil that Queen Mary had done the same before her son was a year old.*

Of Browne's two previous performances, his standing stoutly for the king at Edinburgh, st. 26, and his killing the son of the sheriff of Carlisle, st. 27, we are permitted to know only that, since these preceded the killing of the bishop, they occurred at some time before James was five years old. The epoch of the adventure with Douglas, which is the principal subject of the ballad, could be determined beyond question if we could ascertain when Brown was made an earl. It falls after the murder of the Regent Lennox, 8¹, that is, later than September, 1571, and the king is old enough to know something of the unhappy occurrences in his family, to forget and forgive, and to make knights and earls. There are correspondences between the ballad and the proceedings by which the Earl of Morton, after his resignation of the regency, obtained possession of the young king's person and virtually reëstablished himself in his former power. This was in April, 1578, when James was not quite twelve years old. Morton was living at Lochleven "for policie, devysing the situation of a fayre gardene with allayis, to remove all suspicion of his consavit treason." James was in the keeping of Alexander Erskine, his guardian, at Stirling Castle, of which Erskine was governor; and the young Earl of Mar, nephew of the governor, was residing there. This young man became persuaded, perhaps through Morton's representations, that he himself was entitled to the custody of the castle, and incidentally of the king. Early in the morning of the 26th of April, before the garrison were astir, Mar (who was risen under pretence of a hunting-party), supported by two Abbot Erskines, his uncles, and a retinue of his own, demanded the castle-keys of the governor. An affray followed, in which a son of Alexander Erskine lost his life. The young king, wakened by the noise, rushed in terror from his chamber, tearing his hair. Mar overpowered resistance and seized the keys. Shortly after this, he and his uncle the governor came to terms at the instance of the king, Mar retaining Stirling Castle and the wardenship of the king, and the uncle being made keeper of the castle of Edinburgh. Morton was received into Stirling Castle, and resumed his sway. All this did not pass without opposition. The citizens of Edinburgh rose in arms against Morton (cf. sts 21, 22), and large forces collected from other parts of the country for the liberation of the king. A civil war was imminent, and was avoided, it would seem, chiefly through the influence of the English minister, Bowes, who offered himself as peacemaker, in the name of his queen (cf. sts 31, 32).†

The Douglas of this ballad is clearly William Douglas of Lochleven, who joined Mar at Stirling as Morton's intermediary. He was afterwards engaged in the Raid of Ruthven.

It may be added that Robert Brown, a servant of the king's, played a very humble part, for the defence of his master, in the Gowrie Conspiracy, but that was nearly twenty years after Andrew Brown was celebrated by Elderton, and when James was no young prince, but in his thirty-fifth year.

---

1   As I did walke my selfe alone,
    And by one garden greene,
  I heard a yonge prince make great moane,
    Which did turne my hart to teene.

2   'O Lord!' he then said vntou me,
    ' Why haue I liued soe long?
  For yonder comes a cruell Scott,'
    Quoth hee, ' that will doe me some ronge.'

---

* "At the queen last being at Stirling, the prince being brought unto her, she offered to kiss him, but he would not, but put her away, and did to his strength scratch her. She offered him an apple, but it would not be received of him, and to a greyhound bitch having whelps was thrown, who eat it, and she and her whelps died presently. A sugar-loaf also for the prince was brought at the same time; it is judged to be very ill compounded." Calendar of State Papers, Foreign, May 20, 1567, p. 235 : cited by Burton. Considering that the prince had only just passed his eleventh month, it would seem that the apple or the sugar-loaf might have served without any compounding.

† Historie of King James the Sext, p. 165 ff; Tytler's History, VIII, 35 ff; Burton, V, 163 ff.

3 And then came traitor Douglas there,
    He came for to betray his king ;
Some they brought bills, and some they brought
        bowes,
    And some the brought other things.

4 The king was aboue in a gallery,
    With a heauy heart ;
Vnto his body was sett about
    With swords and speares soe sharpe.

5 ' Be you the lordes of Scotland,' he said,
    ' That hither for councell seeke to me ?
Or bee yoe traitors to my crowne,
    My blood that you wold see ? '

6 ' Wee are the lords of Scottland,' they said,
    ' Nothing we come to craue of thee ;
But wee be traitors to thy crowne,
    Thy blood that wee will see.'

7 ' O fye vpon you, you false Scotts !
    For you neuer all trew wilbe ;
My grandfather you haue slaine,
    And caused my mother to flee.

8 ' My grandfather you haue slaine,
    And my owne father you hanged on a tree ;
And now,' quoth he, ' the like treason
    You haue now wrought for me.

9 ' Ffarwell hart, and farwell hand !
    Farwell all pleasures alsoe !
Farwell th   .   .   .   my head
    .   .   .   .   .   .

10 .   .   .   .   .   .
    .   .   .   .   .   .
' If thou wilt   .   .   .   .
    And soe goe away with mee.'

11 ' Goe marry thy daughter to whome thou wilt,'
    Quoth Browne ; ' thou marrys none to me ;
For I 'le not be a traitor,' quoth Browne,
    ' For all the gold that euer I see.'

12 This Douglas, hearing Browne soe say,
    Began to flee away full fast ;
' But tarry a while,' saies lusty Browne,
    ' I 'le make you to pay before you passe.'

13 He hath taken the Douglas prisoner,
    And hath brought him before the king ;

He kneeled low vpon his knee,
    For pardon there prainge.

14 ' How shold I pardon thee,' saith the king,
    ' And thou 'le remaine a traitor still ?
For euer since that I was borne,'
    Quoth he, ' thou hast sought my blood to
        spill.'

15 ' For if you will grant me my pardon,' he said,
    ' Out of this place soe free,
I wilbe sworne before your Grace
    A trew subiect to bee.'

16 ' God for-gaue his death,' said the king,
    ' When he was nayled vpon a tree ;
And as free as euer God forgaue his death,
    Douglas,' quoth he, ' I 'le forgiue thee.

17 ' And all the traitors in Scottland,'
    Quoth he, ' both great and small ;
As free as euer God forgaue his death,
    Soe free I will forgiue them all.'

18 ' I thanke you for your pardon, king,
    That you haue granted forth soe plaine ;
If I liue a twelue month to an end,
    You shall not aliue remaine.

19 ' Tomorrow yet, or ere I dine,
    I meane to doo thee one good turne ;
For Edenborrow, that is thine owne,'
    Quoth he, ' I will both h[arry] and [burne].'

20 Thus Douglas hied towards Edenborrow,
    And many of his men were gone beffore;
And after him on euery side,
    With him there went some twenty score.

21 But when that they did see him come,
    They cryed lowd with voices, saying,
' Yonder comes a false traitor,
    That wold haue slaine our king.'

22 They chaynd vp the gates of Edenborrow,
    And there the made them wonderous fast,
And there Browne sett on Douglas againe,
    And quicklye did him ouer cast.

23 But worde came backe againe to the king,
    With all the speed that euer might bee,
That traitor Douglas there was taken,
    And his body was there to see.

24 'Bring me his taker,' quoth the king,
　'Come, quickly bring him vnto me!
　I 'le giue a thousand pound a yeere,
　What man soeuer he bee.'

25 But then they called lusty Browne;
　Sayes, 'Browne, come thou hither to mee.
　How oft hast thou foughten for my sake,
　And alwayes woone the victory?'

26 'The first time that I fought for you,
　It was in Edenborrow, king;
　If there I had not stoutly stood,
　My leege, you neuer had beene king.

27 'The second time I fought for you,
　Here I will tell you in this place;
　I killd the sheriffs sonne of Carlile,'
　Quoth he, 'that wold haue slaine your
　　Grace.

28 'The third time that I fought for you,
　Here for to let you vnderstand,

I slew the Bishopp of St Andrew[s],'
　Quoth he, 'with a possat in [his hand].'

29 .   .   .   .   .   quoth hee,
　'That euer my manhood I did trye;
　I 'le make a vow for Englands sake
　That I will neuer battell flee.'

30 'God amercy, Browne,' then said the king,
　'And God amercy heartilye!
　Before I made thee but a knight,
　But now an earle I will make thee.

31 'God saue the queene of England,' he said,
　'For her blood is verry neshe;
　As neere vnto her I am
　As a colloppe shorne from the fleshe.

32 'If I be false to England,' he said,
　'Either in earnest or in iest,
　I might be likened to a bird,'
　Quoth he, 'that did defile it nest.'

5³. yoe bee. 5⁴. by my: cf. 6⁴. 6¹. are they.
8². mother for father.
9⁴. Half a page torn away.

18³. a 12. 20⁴. 20 score. 24⁸. a 1000.
28¹. the 3ᵈ.
28⁴. possat? MS. rubbed: Hales.

APPENDIX

THE KING OF SCOTS AND ANDREW BROWNE

A new Ballad, declaring the great treason conspired against the young King of Scots, and how one Andrew Browne, an Englishman, which was the king's chamberlaine, preuented the same. To the tune of Milfield, or els to Greenesleeues.

This piece, which is contained in a collection of ballads and proclamations in the library of the Society of Antiquaries, London, is signed W. Elderton, and was "imprinted at London for Yarathe Iames, dvvelling in Nevvgate Market, ouer against Christes Church." It was licensed to James, May 30, 1581: Arber II, 393. Reprinted by Percy, Reliques, 1765, II, 204; here from the original. There is an imperfect and incorrect copy in the Percy MS., p. 273; Hales and Furnivall, II, 265.

Morton was beheaded only three days after these verses were licensed, and had been in durance for several months before at the castle of Edinburgh. Elderton cannot be supposed to have the last news from Scotland, and he was not a man to keep his compositions by him nine years. The exhortation of Morton to his confederate, Douglas, in the last stanza but one is divertingly misplaced. The fictions of the privie banket and the selling of the king beyond seas are of the same mint as those in the ballad.

JESUS, God! what a griefe is this,
　That princes subiects cannot be true,
But still the deuill hath some of his
　Will play their parts, whatsoeuer ensue;
Forgetting what a greeuous thing
It is to offend the annointed kinge.

Alas for woe ! why should it be so ?
This makes a sorowfull heigh ho.

In Scotland is a bonie kinge,
    As proper a youthe as neede to be,
Well giuen to euery happy thing
    That can be in a kinge to see;
Yet that vnluckie countrie still
Hath people giuen to craftie will.
        Alas for woe ! etc.

On Whitson eue it so befell
    A posset was made to give the kinge,
Whereof his ladie-nurse hard tell,
    And that it was a poysoned thing.
She cryed, and called piteouslie,
'Now helpe, or els the king shall die ! '
        Alas for woe ! etc.

One Browne, that was an English man,
    And hard the ladies piteous crye,
Out with his sword, and besturd him than
    Out of the doores in haste to flie ;
But all the doores were made so fast,
Out of a window he got at last.
        Alas for woe ! etc.

He met the bishop comming fast,
    Hauing the posset in his hande ;
The sight of Browne made him agast,
    Who bad him stoutly staie and stand.
With him were two that ranne away,
For feare that Browne would make a fray.
        Alas for woe ! etc.

' Bishop,' quoth Browne, ' what hast thou there? '
    ' Nothing at all, my freend,' sayde he,
' But a posset to make the king good cheere.'
    ' Is it so? ' sayd Browne, ' that will I see.
First I will haue thy selfe begin,
Before thou goe any further in ;
        Be it weale or woe, it shall be so.'
        This makes a sorowfull heigh ho.

The bishop saide, Browne, I doo know
    Thou art a young man poore and bare ;
Liuings on thee I will bestowe ;
    Let me go on, take thee no care.
' No, no,' quoth Browne, ' I will not be
A traitour for all Christiantie.
        Happe weal or woe, it shall be so :
        Drinke now, with a sorowfull heigh ho.'

The bishop dranke, and by and by
    His belly burst and he fell downe :
A iust reward for his traytery.
    ' This was a posset in deede! ' quoth Browne.
He serched the bishop, and found the keyes
To come to the kinge when he did please.
        Alas for woe! etc.

As soone as the king gat word of this,
    He humbly fell vppon his knee,
And praysed God that he did misse
    To tast of that extremity :
For that he did perceaue and know
His clergie would betray him so.
        Alas for woe! etc.

' Alas,' he said, ' vnhappy realme !
    My father and godfather slaine,
My mother banished, O extreame
    Vnhappy fate, and bitter bayne !
And now like treason wrought for me.
What more vnhappy realme can be ! '
        Alas for woe ! etc.

The king did call his nurse to his grace,
    And gave her twentie pound a yeere ;
And trustie Browne to, in like case,
    He knighted him, with gallant geere,
And gaue him . . . liuings great,
For dooing such a manly feat
        As he did sho[w]e, to the bishops woe,
        Which made, etc.

When all this treason don and past
    Tooke not effect of traytery,
Another treason at the last
    They sought against his Maiestie ;
How they might make their kinge away
By a priuie banket on a daye.
        Alas for woe ! etc.

Wherat they ment to sell the king
    Beyonde the seas, it was decreede:
Three noble earles heard of this thing,
    And did preuent the same with speede.
For a letter came, with such a charme,
That they should doo they[r] king no harme,
        For further woe, if they did so;
        Which made a sorowfull heigh ho.

The Earle Mourton told the Douglas then,
    ' Take heede you doo not offend the kinge;
But shew your selues like honest men,
    Obediently in euery thing ;
For his godmother will not see
Her noble childe misvsde to be
        With any woe ; for if it be so,
        She will make a sorowfull heigh ho '

God graunt all subiects may be true,
    In England, Scotland, and euerie where,
That no such daunger may ensue,
    To put the prince or state in feare;
That God, the highest king, may see
Obedience as it ought to be.
        In wealth or woe, God graunt it be so!
        To auoide the sorowfull heigh ho.

181

THE BONNY EARL OF MURRAY

A. 'The Bonny Earl of Murray,' Ramsay's Tea-Table Miscellany, 11th ed., London, 1750, p. 356 (vol. iv).

B. 'The Bonnie Earl o Murray,' Finlay's Scottish Ballads, II, 11.

A is not in the ninth edition of the Tea-Table Miscellany, 1733, but may be in the tenth (1736 ? 1740 ?), which I have not seen. It is printed in Percy's Reliques, 1765, II, 210, and in many subsequent collections : Herd's Scots Songs, 1769, p. 32; Ritson's Scottish Songs, 1794, II, 29; Johnson's Museum, No 177; etc.

James Stewart, son of Sir James Stewart of Doune, became Earl of Murray in consequence of his marriage with the oldest daughter and heiress of the Regent Murray. "He was a comely personage, of a great stature, and strong of body like a kemp." * There was a violent hostility between Murray and the Earl of Huntly. The occurrence which is the subject of the ballad may be narrated in the least space by citing the account given by Spottiswood. After his assault on Holyrood House in December (or September), 1591, "Bothwell went into the north, looking to be supplied by the Earl of Murray, his cousin-german; which the king suspecting, Andrew Lord Ochiltrie was sent to bring Murray unto the south, of purpose to work a reconcilement betwixt him and Huntly. But a rumor being raised in the mean while that the Earl of Murray was seen in the palace with Bothwell on the night of the enterprise, the same was entertained by Huntly (who waited then at court) to make him suspected of the king, and prevailed so far as he did purchase a commission to apprehend and bring Murray to his trial. The nobleman, not fearing that any such course should be used, was come to Donibristle, a house situated on the north side of Forth, and belonging to his

mother the lady Doune. Huntly, being advertised of his coming, and how he lay there secure, accompanied only with the Sheriff of Murray and a few of his own retinue, went thither and beset the house, requiring him to render. The Earl of Murray refusing to put himself in the hands of his enemy, after some defence made, wherein the sheriff was killed, fire was set to the house, and they within forced by the violence of the smoke and flame to come forth. The earl staid a great space after the rest, and, the night falling down, ventured among his enemies, and, breaking through the midst of them, did so far outrun them all as they supposed he was escaped; yet searching him among the rocks, he was discovered by the tip of his head-piece, which had taken fire before he left the house, and unmercifully slain. The report went that Huntly's friends, fearing he should disclaim the fact (for he desired rather to have taken him alive), made him light from his horse and give some strokes to the dead corpse. . . . The death of the nobleman was universally lamented, and the clamors of the people so great . . . that the king, not esteeming it safe to abide at Edinburgh, removed with the council to Glasgow, where he remained until Huntly did enter himself in ward in Blackness, as he was charged. But he staid not there many days, being dimitted, upon caution, to answer before the justice whensoever he should be called. The corpses of the Earl and Sheriff of Murray were brought to the church of Leith in two coffins, and there lay divers months unburied, their friends refusing to commit their bodies to the earth till the slaughter was punished. Nor did any

* Historie of King James the Sext, p. 246.

man think himself so much interested in that fact as the Lord Ochiltrie, who had persuaded the Earl of Murray to come south; whereupon he fell afterwards away to Bothwell, and joined with him for revenge of the murder."

This outrage was done in the month of February, 1592. Huntly sheltered himself under the king's commission, and was not punished. He was no doubt a dangerous man to discipline, but the king, perhaps because he believed Murray to be an abettor of Bothwell, showed no disposition that way.

According to Sir James Balfour, "the queen, more rashly than wisely, some few days before had commended" Murray, "in the king's hearing, with too many epithets of a proper and gallant man." Balfour may have had gossip, or he may have had a ballad, for his authority (see **A** 5); the suggestion deserves no attention.*

In **B** the Countess of Murray is treated as the sister of Huntly.

A is translated by Grundtvig, Engelske og skotske Folkeviser, No 8, p. 52; by Herder, II, 71. **B** by Arndt, Blütenlese, p. 196.

———✦———

A

Ramsay's Tea-Table Miscellany, 1763, p. 356.

1 YE Highlands, and ye Lawlands,
    Oh where have you been?
  They have slain the Earl of Murray,
    And they layd him on the green.

2 'Now wae be to thee, Huntly!
    And wherefore did you sae?
  I bade you bring him wi you,
    But forbade you him to slay.'

3 He was a braw gallant,
    And he rid at the ring;
  And the bonny Earl of Murray,
    Oh he might have been a king!

4 He was a braw gallant,
    And he playd at the ba;
  And the bonny Earl of Murray
    Was the flower amang them a'.

5 He was a braw gallant,
    And he playd at the glove;
  And the bonny Earl of Murray,
    Oh he was the Queen's love!

6 Oh lang will his lady
    Look oer the castle Down,
  Eer she see the Earl of Murray
    Come sounding thro the town!
  Eer she, etc.

———✦———

B

Finlay's Scottish Ballads, II, 11; from recitation.

1 'OPEN the gates,
    and let him come in;
  He is my brother Huntly,
    he 'll do him nae harm.'

2 The gates they were opent,
    they let him come in,
  But fause traitor Huntly,
    he did him great harm.

3 He 's ben and ben,
    and ben to his bed,

And with a sharp rapier
  he stabbed him dead.

4 The lady came down the stair,
    wringing her hands:
  'He has slain the Earl o Murray,
    the flower o Scotland.'

5 But Huntly lap on his horse,
    rade to the king:
  'Ye 're welcome hame, Huntly,
    and whare hae ye been?

* Spottiswood's History, ed. 1666, p. 387. See also The Historie of King James the Sext, p. 246 ff.; Moysie's Memoirs, p. 88 ff.; Birrel's Diary, p. 26 f.

6 'Whare hae ye been?
   and how hae ye sped?'
'I've killed the Earl o Murray,
   dead in his bed.'

7 'Foul fa you, Huntly!
   and why did ye so?
You might have taen the Earl o Murray,
   and saved his life too.'

8 'Her bread it's to bake,
   her yill is to brew;
My sister's a widow,
   and sair do I rue.

9 'Her corn grows ripe,
   her meadows grow green,
But in bonny Dinnibristle
   I darena be seen.'

182

THE LAIRD O LOGIE

A. 'The Laird o Logie,' Scott's Minstrelsy, 1833, III, 128. The same, with the insertion of one stanza from recitation, Motherwell's Minstrelsy, p. 56.

B. 'The young Laird of Ochiltrie,' Herd, The Ancient and Modern Scots Songs, 1769, p. 240; ed. 1776, I, 21. Repeated in Campbell MSS, I, 142.

C. 'The Laird of Logie,' a stall-copy printed by M.

Randall, Stirling. The same in Motherwell's MS., p. 504, and in Maidment's Scotish Ballads and Songs, p. 8, 'The young Laird of Logie.'

D. 'Young Logie,' Harris MS., fol. 16.

E. 'The Laird o Logie, or, May Margaret,' Motherwell's Minstrelsy, p. 56, one stanza.

FRANCIS STEWART, Earl of Bothwell, a madcap cousin of the king, had been guilty of a violent assault upon Holyrood House in December (or September), 1591, and in June, 1592, had "conspired the apprehension of the king's person" while James was residing at Falkland. In August following he attempted to force himself into the king's presence to "make his reconciliation."

"The lairds of Burlie and Logie, delated to [have] had intelligence with the Earl Bothwell, were taken and apprehended by the Duke of Lennox the ninth day of August, 1592, and committed to ward within Dalkeith; where being examined they both confessed the same. Burley gat his life for telling the truth, but Logie, being a great courtier with the king, and dealer with the Earl Bothwell in Bothwell's enterprise which should [have] been done at Dalkeith, to wit, that they should come in at the back gate through the yard and [have] gotten the king in their

hands, the said laird of Logie was ordained to be tried by an assize and executed to the death. But the same night that he was examined, he escaped out by the means of a gentlewoman whom he loved, a Dane, who conveyed him out of his keepers' hands, through the queen's chamber, where his Majesty and the queen were lying in their beds, to a window in the backside of the place, where he went down upon a tow [rope], and shot three pistols in token of his onlouping [mounting his horse] where some of his servants, with the laird of Niddry, were awaiting him." (Moysie's Memoirs, p. 95.)

Another account may be added, from The Historie of King James the Sext (p. 253 f.):

"It fortuned that a gentleman called Wemyss of Logie, being also in credence at court, was delated as a trafficker with Francis Earl Bothwell; and he, being examined before king and council, confessed his accusation to be of verity; that sundry times he had spoken with him, expressly against the king's inhibition proclaimed in the contrary ; which confession he subscribed with his hand. . . .

"Queen Anne, our noble princess, was served with divers gentlewomen of her own country, and namely with one called Mistress Margaret Twynstoun, to whom this gentleman, Wemyss of Logie, bore great honest affection, tending to the godly band of marriage ; the which was honestly requited by the said gentlewoman, yea, even in his greatest mister (need). For how soon she understood the said gentleman to be in distress, and apparently by his confession, to be punisht to the death, and she having privilege to lie in the queen's chamber that same very night of his accusation, where the king was also reposing that same night, she came forth of the door privily, both the princes being then at quiet rest, and past to the chamber where the said gentleman was put in custody to certain of the guard, and commanded them that immediately he should be brought to the king and queen ; whereunto they giving sure credence obeyed. But how soon she was come back to the chamberdoor, she desired the watches to stay till he should come forth again ; and so she closed the door and conveyed the gentleman to a window, where she ministered a long cord unto him to convey himself down upon, and so, by her good charitable help, he happily escaped, by the subtlety of love."

Calderwood gives the following account : "Upon Monday the seventh of August, the king being in Dalkeith, the young laird of Logie and Burlie promised to Bothwell to bring him in before the king to seek his pardon. The king was forewarned, and Bothwell, howbeit brought in quietly within the castle, was conveyed out again. Burlie was accused and confessed ; Logie denied, and therefore would have suffered trial. The night before, one of the queen's dames, Mistress Margaret, a Dutchwoman, came to the guard and desired that he might be suffered to

come to the queen, who had something to inquire of him. Two of the guard brought him to the king's chamber-door, and staid upon his coming forth, but she conveyed him in the mean time out at a window in a pair of sheets. . . . Logie married the gentlewoman after, when he was received into the king's favor again." * Logie, according to Calderwood, was " a varlet of the king's chamber."

Spottiswood says : John Weymis younger of Logie, gentleman of his Majesty's chamber, and in great favor both with the king and queen, was discovered to have the like dealing with Bothwell, and, being committed to the keeping of the guard, escaped by the policy of one of the Dutch maids, with whom he entertained a secret love. The gentlewoman, named Mistress Margaret Twinslace, coming one night, whilst the king and queen were in bed, to his keepers, shewed that the king called for the prisoner, to ask of him some question. The keepers, suspecting nothing, for they knew her to be the principal maid in the chamber, conveyed him to the door of the bed-chamber, and making a stay without, as they were commanded, the gentlewoman did let him down at a window, by a cord that she had prepared. The keepers, waiting upon his return, staid there till the morning, and then found themselves deceived. This, with the manner of the escape, ministered great occasion of laughter ; and not many days after, the king being pacified by the queen's means, he was pardoned, and took to wife the gentlewoman who had in this sort hazarded her credit for his safety.†

The lady, called by Calderwood and Spottiswood a Dutchwoman, but rightly by Moysie a Dane, was one of a train of her countrywomen who attended Queen Anne when she came to Scotland in May, 1590. She is called Mistress Margaret Vinstar in a letter of Robert Bowes to Lord Burghley of August 12, 1592 ; ‡ Margaret Weiksterne in a charter dated 25th December, 1594.§

---

* History of the Church of Scotland, published by the Wodrow Society, Edinburgh, 1844, V, 173 ; in Maidment's Scotish Ballads and Songs, 1859, p. 8.
† History of the Church of Scotland, ed. 1666, p. 389.

‡ Calendar of the State Papers relating to Scotland, Thorpe, II, 611.
§ Carta Ioanni, filio natu maximo et heredi Andreæ Weymis de Myrecarny, et Margarete Weiksterne, sue

Young Logie cannot have received a complete pardon within a few days of his escape. At a council meeting, September 14, 1592, it is ordered that Wemyss of Logie the younger, having failed to appear this day to answer touching the 'intercommuning and having intelligence with Francis, sometime Earl Bothwell,' be denounced rebel.*

A. Young Logie is a prisoner, in Carmichael's † keeping, and May Margaret, who is enamored of him, is weeping for his expected death. The queen can do nothing, and tells her that she must go to the king himself to beg the life of her lover. She goes, accordingly, but gets an ill answer: all the gold in Scotland shall not save Young Logie. In this strait she steals the king's comb and the queen's knife, and sends them to Carmichael as tokens that Logie is to be discharged. She provides the young man with money, and gives him a pair of pistols, which he is to fire in sign that he is at liberty. The king hears the 'volley' from his bed, and by his peculiar sagacity recognizes the shot of Young Logie. He sends for Carmichael, and learning that the prisoner was set free in virtue of a royal token, says, You will make his place good tomorrow. Carmichael hurries to Margaret, and wants a word with Logie. Margaret, with a laugh, tells him that the bird is flown. The young pair severally take ship and are married.

In B, the queen, instead of referring Margaret to the king as the only resource, herself undertakes to save the young man's life. She asks it of her consort as her first boon; the king makes her the same answer which he gives Margaret in A, All the gold in Scotland will not buy mercy. Margaret, in desperation, wishes to kill herself, but the queen will put her in a better way to save her lover. The queen steals the prison-keys, and the story proceeds as before. The king threatens to hang all his gaolers, to the number of thirty and three. The gaolers plead that they received the keys (which are also thirty and three) with a strict command to enlarge the prisoner. The queen says that, if the gaolers are to hang, a beginning must be made with her.

B substitutes Ochiltrie for Logie. Andrew Stewart, Lord of Ochiltrie, was an active partisan of Bothwell (see the preceding ballad), and at a council-meeting on May 2, 1594 (the same meeting at which a caution of three hundred merks was required for Young Logie), was ordered to be denounced rebel for not appearing to answer touching his " tressounable attemptattis " ; that is, for having been Bothwell's main helper in the Raid of Leith, April 3 preceding.‡ So far his case resembles Young Logie's, and it may be that the two became confounded in tradition earlier than the middle of the eighteenth century, about which time B was taken down. But an interchange of names is of the commonest occurrence in traditional ballads, and perhaps Ochiltrie's appearance here no more requires to be accounted for than his figuring, as he does, in one of the versions of ' The Broom of Cowdenknows.'

Although the queen had no hand in the freeing of Young Logie, and is not known even to have winked at it, she stood by Mistress Margaret, and refused to give her up when requested.§

sponse, Terrarum de Myrecarny, etc. Fife, 25 Dec[rs], 1594. Weymis de Myrecarny and Wemys de Logy are one, as appears by a charter of July 25, 1564. Register of the Great Seal of Scotland, Index, in the Signet Library, noted for me by Mr Macmath.

* Register of the Privy Council of Scotland, V, 11. And again : 1594, April 13. Caution in £2000 by —— Wemys, apparent of that Ilk, for Johnne Wemyss, apparent of Logy, that he shall remain in ward with David Wemys of that Ilk till relieved.

May 2. Caution in 300 merks by Johnne Wemys, younger of that Ilk, for Johnne Wemys of Logy, that he shall answer before the Privy Council at Edinburgh upon 22d instant "to sic thingis as salbe inquirit of him."

September 27. Sir Johnne Wemys of Tullibrck, Michaell Balfour of Monquhaine, and Andro Wemyss of Myrecairny, for Johnne Wemyss, son and apparent heir of Andro, £20,000, to go abroad by the 15th October next and not return without licence. Deleted by warrant subscribed by the king and treasurer–depute at Haliruidhous 20th February, 1594. *Ib.*, pp 141 f., 144, 638. The entries in 1594 may have reference to later offences.

† Sir John Carmichael was appointed captain of the king's guard in 1588, and usually had the keeping of state criminals of rank. Scott.

‡ The Historie of King James the Sext, p. 303 f. ; Register of the Privy Council of Scotland, V, 144.

§ Calendar of State Papers relating to Scotland, Thorpe, II, 611, No 6.

C agrees with B as to the part taken by the queen in the rescue. There are but three keepers, and presumably but three keys to steal from under the king's head, and the queen sends her wedding-ring with the keys, as a warrant to the keepers. In 5, Anne is queen of England as well as queen of Scotland; but we cannot expect that a stall-ballad of this century should be nice about a matter of eleven years.

The offence for which Young Logie is to die in D is the stealing of a kiss "from the queen's marie," which shows a high appreciation of the discipline at James's court.

The queen counterfeits the king's hand and steals his right glove, and sends the forged paper and the glove to " Pitcairn's walls " as authority for the liberation of the prisoner. The king, looking over his castle-wall, sees Young Logie approaching, and his exclamation at the sight brings the queen to an instantaneous confession of what she has done. The king very good-naturedly overlooks the offence and absolves the lover for whom it was committed.

Translated from Motherwell by Wolff, Halle der Völker, I, 73.

———•———

A

Scott's Minstrelsy, 1833, III, 128, "as recited by a gentleman residing near Biggar."

1 I WILL sing, if ye will hearken,
    If ye will hearken unto me;
    The king has taen a poor prisoner,
    The wanton laird o Young Logie.

2 Young Logie's laid in Edinburgh chapel,
    Carmichael's the keeper o the key;
    And May Margaret's lamenting sair,
    A' for the love of Young Logie.

3 'Lament, lament na, May Margaret,
    And of your weeping let me be;
    For ye maun to the king himsell,
    To seek the life of Young Logie.'

4 May Margaret has kilted her green cleiding,
    And she has curld back her yellow hair:
    'If I canna get Young Logie's life,
    Farewell to Scotland for evermair!'

5 When she came before the king,
    She knelit lowly on her knee:
    'O what's the matter, May Margaret?
    And what needs a' this courtesie?'

6 'A boon, a boon, my noble liege,
    A boon, a boon, I beg o thee,
    And the first boon that I come to crave
    Is to grant me the life of Young Logie.'

7 'O na, O na, May Margaret,
    Forsooth, and so it mauna be;
    For a' the gowd o fair Scotland
    Shall not save the life of Young Logie.'

8 But she has stown the king's redding-kaim,
    Likewise the queen her wedding knife,
    And sent the tokens to Carmichael,
    To cause Young Logie get his life.

9 She sent him a purse o the red gowd,
    Another o the white monie;
    She sent him a pistol for each hand,
    And bade him shoot when he gat free.

10 When he came to the Tolbooth stair,
    There he let his volley flee;
    It made the king in his chamber start,
    Een in the bed where he might be.

11 'Gae out, gae out, my merrymen a',
    And bid Carmichael come speak to me;
    For I'll lay my life the pledge o that
    That yon's the shot o Young Logie.'

12 When Carmichael came before the king,
    He fell low down upon his knee;
    The very first word that the king spake
    Was, Where's the laird of Young Logie?

13 Carmichael turnd him round about,
    I wot the tear blinded his ee:
    'There came a token frae your Grace
    Has taen away the laird frae me.'

14 'Hast thou playd me that, Carmichael?
    And hast thou playd me that?' quoth he;
  'The morn the Justice Court's to stand,
    And Logie's place ye maun supplie.'

15 Carmichael's awa to Margaret's bower,
    Even as fast as he may dree:
  'O if Young Logie be within,
    Tell him to come and speak with me.'

16 May Margaret turnd her round about,
    I wot a loud laugh laughed she:
  'The egg is chippd, the bird is flown,
    Ye'll see nae mair of Young Logie.'

17 The tane is shipped at the pier of Leith,
    The tother at the Queen's Ferrie,
  And she's gotten a father to her bairn,
    The wanton laird of Young Logie.

———◆———

B

Herd, The Ancient and Modern Scots Songs, 1769, p. 240.

1 O LISTEN, gude peopell, to my tale,
    Listen to what I tel to thee;
  The king has taiken a poor prisoner,
    The wanton laird of Ochiltrie.

2 When news came to our guidly queen,
    Sche sicht, and said right mournfullie,
  'O what will cum of Lady Margret!
    Wha beirs sick luve to Ochiltrie.'

3 Lady Margret tore hir yellow hair
    When as the queen tald hir the saim:
  'I wis that I had neir bin born,
    Nor neir had knawn Ochiltrie's naim!'

4 'Fie, na!' quoth the queen, 'that maunna be;
    Fie, na! that maunna be;
  I'll fynd ye out a better way
    To saif the lyfe of Ochiltrie.'

5 The queen sche trippit up the stair,
    And lowlie knielt upon hir knie:
  'The first boon which I cum to craive
    Is the life of gentel Ochiltrie.'

6 'O iff you had askd me castels or towirs,
    I wad hae gin thaim, twa or thrie;
  Bot a' the monie in fair Scotland
    Winna buy the lyfe of Ochiltrie.'

7 The queen sche trippit down the stair,
    And down she gade richt mournfullie:
  'It's a' the monie in fair Scotland
    Winna buy the lyfe of Ochiltrie!'

8 Lady Margaret tore her yellow hair
    When as the queen tald hir the saim:

  'I'll tak a knife and end my lyfe,
    And be in the grave as soon as him!'

9 'Ah, na! Fie, na!' quoth the queen,
    'Fie, na! Fie, na! this maunna be;
  I'll set ye on a better way
    To loose and set Ochiltrie frie.'

10 The queen sche slippit up the stair,
    And sche gaid up richt privatlie,
  And sche has stoun the prison-keys,
    And gane and set Ochiltrie frie.

11 And sche's gien him a purse of gowd,
    And another of whyt monie;
  Sche's gien him twa pistoles by's syde,
    Saying to him, Shute, when ye win
      frie.

12 And when he cam to the queen's window,
    Whaten a joyfou shute gae he!
  'Peace be to our royal queen,
    And peace be in hir companie!'

13 'O whaten a voyce is that?' quoth the
      king,
  'Whaten a voyce is that?' quoth he;
  'Whaten a voyce is that?' quoth the
      king;
  'I think it's the voyce of Ochiltrie.

14 'Call to me a' my gaolours,
    Call thaim by thirtie and by thrie;
  Whairfoir the morn, at twelve a clock,
    It's hangit schall they ilk ane be.'

15 'O didna ye send your keyis to us?
    Ye sent thaim be thirtie and be thrie,
  And wi thaim sent a strait command
    To set at lairge young Ochiltrie.'

16 'Ah, na! Fie, na!' quoth the queen,
   'Fie, my dear luve, this maunna be!
   And iff ye 're gawn to hang thaim a',
   Indeed ye maun begin wi me.'

17 The tane was schippit at the pier of Leith,
   The ither at the Queen's Ferrie,
   And now the lady has gotten hir luve,
   The winsom laird of Ochiltrie.

—•—

C

A stall-copy, printed by M. Randall, Stirling.

1 THE young laird of Logie is to prison cast;
   Carmichael 's the keeper of the key;
   Lady Margaret, the queen's cousin, is very
       sick,
   And it 's all for love of Young Logie.

2 She 's into the queen's chamber gone,
   She has kneeld low down on her knee;
   Says she, You must go to the king yourself;
   It 's all for a pardon to Young Logie.

3 The queen is unto the king's chamber gone,
   She has kneeld low down on her knee:
   'O what is the matter, my gracious queen?
   And what means all this courtesie?

4 'Have I not made thee queen of fair Scot-
       land?
   The queen of England I trow thou be;
   Have not I made thee my wedded wife?
   Then what needs all this courtesie?'

5 'You have made me queen of [fair] Scotland,
   The queen of England I surely be;
   Since you have made me your wedded wife,
   Will you grant a pardon for Young Logie?'

6 The king he turned him right round about,
   I think an angry man was he:
   'The morrow, before it is twelve o'clock,
   O hangd shall the laird of Logie be.'

7 The queen she 's into her chamber gone,
   Amongst her maries, so frank and free;
   'You may weep, you may weep, Margaret,'
       she says,
   'For hanged must the laird of Logie be.'

8 She has torn her silken scarf and hood,
   And so has she her yellow hair:
   'Now fare you well, both king and queen,
   And adieu to Scotland for ever mair!'

9 She has put off her goun of silk,
   And so has she her gay clothing:
   'Go fetch me a knife, and I 'll kill myself,
   Since the laird of Logie is not mine.'

10 Then out bespoke our gracious queen,
   And she spoke words most tenderlie;
   'Now hold your hand, Lady Margaret,' she said,
   'And I 'll try to set Young Logie free.'

11 She 's up into the king's chamber gone,
   And among his nobles so free;
   'Hold away, hold away!' says our gracious
       king,
   'No more of your pardons for Young Logie.

12 'Had you but askd me for houses and land,
   I would have given you castles three;
   Or anything else shall be at your command,
   But only a pardon for Young Logie.'

13 'Hold your hand now, my sovereign liege,
   And of your anger let it be;
   For the innocent blood of Lady Margret
   It will rest on the head of thee and me.'

14 The king and queen are gone to their bed,
   But as he was sleeping so quietly,
   She has stole the keys from below his head,
   And has sent to set Young Logie free.

15 Young Logie he 's on horseback got,
   Of chains and fetters he 's got free;
   As he passd by the king's window,
   There he has fired vollies three.

16 The king he awakend out of his sleep,
   Out of his bed came hastilie;
   Says, I 'll lay all my lands and rents
   That yonder 's the laird of Logie free.'

17 The king has sent to the prison strong,
   He has calld for his keepers three;
   Says, How does all your prisoners?
   And how does the young laird of Logie?

18 'Your Majesty sent me your wedding-ring,
       With your high command to set him free;'
   'Then tomorrow, before that I eat or drink,
       I surely will hang you keepers three.'

19 Then out bespoke our gracious queen,
       And she spoke words most tenderlie;

   'If ever you begin to hang a man for this,
       Your Majesty must begin with me.'

20 The one took shipping at [the pier of] Leith,
       The other at the Queen's Ferrie;
   Lady Margaret has gotten the man she loves,
       I mean the young laird of Logie.

D

Harris MS., fol. 16; from Mrs Harris's recitation.

1 PRETTY is the story I hae to tell,
       Pretty is the praisin o itsel,
   An pretty is the prisner oor king's tane,
       The rantin young laird o Logie.

2 Has he brunt? or has he slain?
       Or has he done any injurie?
   Oh no, no, he's done nothing at all,
       But stown a kiss frae the queen's marie.

3 Ladie Margaret cam doon the stair,
       Wringin her hands an tearin her hair;
   Cryin, Oh, that ever I to Scotland cam,
       Aye to see Young Logie dee!

4 'Had your tongue noo, Lady Margaret,
       An a' your weepin lat a bee!
   For I'll gae to the king my sell,
       An plead for life to Young Logie.'

5 'First whan I to Scotland cam,
       You promised to gie me askens three;
   The first then o these askens is
       Life for the young laird o Logie.'

6 'If you had asked house or lands,
       They suld hae been at your command;
   But the morn, ere I taste meat or drink,
       High hanged sall Young Logie be.'

7 Lady Margaret cam doon the stair,
       Wringin her hands an tearin her hair;

Cryin, Oh, that ever I to Scotland cam,
       A' to see Young Logie dee!

8 'Haud your tongue noo, Lady Margaret,
       An a' your weepin lat a bee!
   For I'll counterfiet the king's hand-write,
       An steal frae him his richt hand gloe,
   An send them to Pitcairn's wa's,
       A' to lat Young Logie free.'

9 She counterfieted the king's hand-write,
       An stole frae him his richt hand gloe,
   An sent them to Pitcairn's wa's,
       A' to let Young Logie free.

10 The king luikit owre his castle-wa,
       Was luikin to see what he cald see:
   'My life to wad an my land to pawn,
       Yonder comes the young laird o Logie!'

11 'Pardon, oh pardon! my lord the king,
       Aye I pray you pardon me;
   For I counterfieted your hand-write,
       An stole frae you your richt hand gloe,
   An sent them to Pitcairn's wa's,
       A' to set Young Logie free.'

12 'If this had been done by laird or lord,
       Or by baron of high degree,
   I'se mak it sure, upon my word,
       His life suld hae gane for Young Logie.

13 'But since it is my gracious queen,
       A hearty pardon we will gie,
   An for her sake we'll free the loon,
       The rantin young laird o Logie.'

E

Motherwell's Minstrelsy, p. 56, the third stanza; from recitation.

MAY MARGARET sits in the queen's bouir,
   Knicking her fingers ane be ane,
Cursing the day that she ere was born,
   Or that she ere heard o Logie's name.

B. 6¹. and towirs *in ed.* 1776.
Qu *in* what, etc., *is rendered by* w, *and* z *in* ze, *etc., by* y.

C. *Maidment's copy has some slight variations, such as often occur in different issues of stall-prints.*
1⁸. very very. 1⁴. the love. 3¹. into.

4². you be. 6⁴. It's hanged. 7¹. her own.
7². and so free. 7³. Lady Margret. 8¹. tore.
8², 9². she has. 8³. ye. 11¹. up to.
14². beds. 18². commands.
19⁸. you do hang. 20¹. at the pier of.

D. 2¹. *Perhaps* brent. 6¹. *Perhaps* houses.
10². *Perhaps* culd.

183

WILLIE MACINTOSH

A. 'Burning of Auchindown.' **a.** The Thistle of Scotland, p. 106. **b.** Whitelaw, The Book of Scottish Ballads, p. 248.

B. 'Willie Mackintosh,' Finlay's Scottish Ballads, II, 89.

THE murder of the "Bonny Earl of Murray" was the occasion of serious commotions in the North Highlands. Towards the end of the year 1592, the Macintoshes of the Clan Chattan, who of all the faction of Murray "most eagerly endeavored to revenge his death," invaded the estates of the Earl of Huntly, and killed four gentlemen of the surname of Gordon. Huntly retaliated, "and rade into Pettie (which was then in the possession of the Clan Chattan), where he wasted and spoiled all the Clan Chattan's lands, and killed divers of them. But as the Earl of Huntly had returned home from Pettie, he was advertised that William Macintosh with eight hundred of Clan Chattan were spoiling his lands of Cabrach: whereupon Huntly and his uncle Sir Patrick Gordon of Auchindown, with some few horsemen, made speed towards the enemy, desiring the rest of his company to follow him with all possible diligence, knowing that if once he were within sight of them they would desist from spoiling the country.

Huntly overtook the Clan Chattan before they left the bounds of Cabrach, upon the head of a hill called Stapliegate, where, without staying for the rest of his men, he invaded them with these few he then had. After a sharp conflict he overthrew them, chased them, killed sixty of their ablest men, and hurt William Macintosh with divers others of his company." [*]

Two William Macintoshes are confounded in the ballad. The burning of Auchindown is attributed, rightly or wrongly, to an earlier William, captain of the clan, who, in August, 1550, was formally convicted of conspiracy against the life of the Earl of Huntly, then lieutenant in the north, sentenced to lose his life and lands, and, despite a pledge to the contrary, executed shortly after by the Countess of Huntly. [†]

Auchindown castle is on the banks of the Fiddich, **B** 1. By Cairn Croom, **A** 4, is meant, I suppose, the noted Cairngorm mountain, at the southern extremity of Banffshire.

---

[*] The History of the Feuds and Conflicts among the Clans, etc., p. 41 f, in Miscellanea Scotica. Spottiswood, ed. 1666, p. 390.

[†] Lesley, History of Scotland, p. 235; Gregory, History of the Western Highlands, ed. 1881, p. 184; Browne, History of the Highlands, IV, 476. For the traditional story, Finlay, II, 95, note; Laing's Thistle of Scotland, p. 107 f.; Whitelaw, p. 248.

A

a. The Thistle of Scotland, p. 106, 1823. b. Whitelaw, The Book of Scottish Ballads, p. 248; from an Aberdeen newspaper of about 1815.

1 'TURN, Willie Macintosh,
    Turn, I bid you;
    Gin ye burn Auchindown,
    Huntly will head you.'

2 'Head me or hang me,
    That canna fley me;
    I'll burn Auchendown
    Ere the life lea me.'

3 Coming down Deeside,
    In a clear morning,

Auchindown was in flame,
    Ere the cock-crawing.

4 But coming oer Cairn Croom,
    And looking down, man,
    I saw Willie Macintosh
    Burn Auchindown, man.

5 'Bonny Willie Macintosh,
    Whare left ye your men?'
    'I left them in the Stapler,
    But they'll never come hame.'

6 'Bonny Willie Macintosh,
    Whare now is your men?'
    'I left them in the Stapler,
    Sleeping in their sheen.'

B

Finlay's Scottish Ballads, II, 89, 1808, as recollected by a lady and communicated by Walter Scott.

1 As I came in by Fiddich-side,
    In a May morning,
    I met Willie Mackintosh,
    An hour before the dawning.

2 'Turn again, turn again,
    Turn again, I bid ye;
    If ye burn Auchindown,
    Huntly he will head ye.'

3 'Head me, hang me,
    That sall never fear me;

I'll burn Auchindown
    Before the life leaves me.'

4 As I came in by Auchindown,
    In a May morning,
    Auchindown was in a bleeze,
    An hour before the dawning.

*   *   *   *   *   *

5 Crawing, crawing,
    For my crowse crawing,
    I lost the best feather i my wing
    For my crowse crawing.

A. b. 1². Turn, turn. 1³. If you.
    2². That winna. 3 *wanting*.
    4¹. But *wanting*.
    After 4:

Light was the mirk hour
    At the day-dawing,
    For Auchindoun was in flames
    Ere the cock-crawing.

5, 6 *wanting*.

184

THE LADS OF WAMPHRAY

Glenriddell MSS, XI, 34, 1791.

———•———

'LADS of Wamphray, ane old ballad, sometimes called The Galiard,' is the superscription in the manuscript. Printed in Scott's Minstrelsy, I, 208, 1802, II, 148, 1833; with the omission of 4 and 36, the insertion of four verses after 8, two transpositions, and some changes of language.

"The following song celebrates the skirmish, in 1593, betwixt the Johnstones and Crichtons, which led to the revival of the ancient quarrel betwixt Johnstone and Maxwell, and finally to the battle of Dryffe Sands, in which the latter lost his life. Wamphray is the name of a parish in Annandale. Lethenhall was the abode of Johnstone of Wamphray, and continued to be so till of late years. William Johnstone of Wamphray, called the Galliard, was a noted freebooter. A place near the head of Teviotdale retains the name of the Galliard's Faulds (folds), being a valley, where he used to secrete and divide his spoil with his Liddesdale and Eskdale associates. His *nom de guerre* seems to have been derived from the dance called the galliard. The word is still used in Scotland to express an active, gay, dissipated character. Willie of the Kirkhill, nephew to the Galliard, and his avenger, was also a noted Border robber."

" Leverhay, Stefenbiggen, Girth-head, etc., are all situated in the parish of Wamphray. The Biddes-burn, where the skirmish took place betwixt the Johnstones and their pursuers, is a rivulet which takes its course among the mountains on the confines of Nithesdale and Annandale. The Wellpath is a pass by which the Johnstones were re-

treating to their fastnesses in Annandale. Ricklaw-holm is a place upon the Evan water, which falls into the Annan below Moffat. Wamphray-gate was in these days an alehouse." Scott's Minstrelsy, I, 208 ff., ed. 1802.

This affair is briefly noticed in the Historie of King James the Sext in the following terms: "Sum unbrydlit men of Johnstons . . . hapnit to ryd a steiling in the moneth of Julij this present yeir of God 1593, in the lands and territoreis pertening to the Lord Sanquhar and the knyghtis of Drumlanryg, Lag and Closburne, upon the watter of Nyth; whare, attoure the great reaf and spulye that thay tuik away with violent hand, thay slew and mutilat a great nomber of men wha stude for defence of thair awin geir and to reskew the same from the hands of sik vicious revers." * P. 297.

It is hard to determine whether the first eight stanzas of the ballad are anything more than a prelude, and whether 5, 7 note the customary practice of the Lads of Wamphray, or anticipate, as is done in 3, certain points in the story which follows. The gap after 8 is filled by Scott with verses which describe the Galliard as incapable of keeping his hands from another man's horse, and as having gone to Nithsdale to steal Sim Crichton's dun. The Galliard makes an unlucky selection from the Crichton stable, and takes a blind horse instead of the coveted dun. Under the impression that he has the right beast, he calls out to Sim to come out and see a Johnstone ride. The Crichtons mount for pursuit; the Gal-

* "In the end of this year [1593] there fell out great troubles in the west marches. Some of the surname of Johnston having in the July preceding made a great depre-
dation upon the lands of Sanwhare and Drumlanrig, and killed eighteen persons that followed for rescue of their goods," etc. Spottiswood, p. 400, ed. 1666.

liard sees that they will be up with him, and tries to hide behind a willow-bush. Resistance is vain, for there is no other man by but Will of Kirkhill; entreaties and promises are bootless; the Crichtons hang the Galliard high. Will of Kirkhill vows to avenge his uncle's death, and to this end goes back to Wamphray and raises a large band of riders, who proceed to Nithsdale and drive off the Crichtons' cattle. On the return the Johnstones are followed or intercepted by the Crichtons; a fight ensues, and the Crichtons

suffer severely. Will of Kirkhill boasts that he has killed a man for every finger of the Galliard. The Johnstones drive the Crichtons' nout to Wamphray.*

There is a story, not sufficiently authenticated, that Lord Maxwell, while engaged in single combat with Johnstone, at the battle of Dryfesands, "was slain behind his back by the cowardly hands of Will of Kirkhill." The New Statistical Account of Scotland, IV, 148, note *.

---

1 TWIXT the Girthhead and Langwood-end
Livd the Galiard and Galiard's men.

2 It is the lads of Lethenha,
The greatest rogues among them a'.

3 It is the lads of Leverhay,
That drove the Crichtons' gier away.

4 It is the lads o the Kirkhill,
The gay Galiard and Will o Kirkhill,

5 But and the lads o Stefenbiggin,
They broke the house in at the riggin.

6 The lads o Fingland and Hellbackhill,
They were neer for good, but aye for ill.

7 Twixt the Staywood Bass and Langside Hill,
They stelld the broked cow and branded bull.

8 It is the lads o the Girthhead,
The diel's in them for pride and greed.

9 .   .   .   .
  .   .   .   .

10 The Galiard is to the stable gane;
Instead of the Dun, the Blind he's taen.

11 'Come out now, Simmy o the Side,
Come out and see a Johnston ride!

12 'Here's the boniest horse in a' Nithside,
And a gentle Johnston aboon his hide.'

13 Simmy Crichton's mounted then,
And Crichtons has raised mony a ane.

14 The Galiard thought his horse had been fleet,
But they did outstrip him quite out o sight.

15 As soon as the Galiard the Crichton he saw,
Beyond the saugh-bush he did draw.

16 The Crichtons there the Galiard hae taen,
And nane wi him but Willy alane.

17 'O Simmy, Simmy, now let me gang,
And I vow I'll neer do a Crichton wrang!

18 'O Simmy, Simmy, now let me be,
And a peck o goud I'll gie to thee!

19 'O Simmy, Simmy, let me gang,
And my wife shall heap it wi her hand!'

20 But the Crichtons wadna let Willy bee,
But they hanged him high upon a tree.

21 O think then Will he was right wae,
When he saw his uncle guided sae.

22 'But if ever I live Wamphray to see,
My uncle's death revenged shall be!'

* 37 does not come in happily. Scott put this stanza after 29, omitting 'Sin'; but there is no rational sense gained, unless the Johnstones are supposed to deny the cattle-lifting. Admitting a bold anacoluthon in the first verse (a mixture of since — so and neither — nor), 37 might stand as and where it is. The Johnstones have done no wanton injury; they have only revenged in a proper way the death of the Galliard. But even then the Johnstones would be made to blink the Galliard's horse-stealing.

23 Back to Wamphray Willy's gane,
   And riders has raised mony a ane.

24 Saying, My lads, if ye'll be true,
   Ye's a' be clad in the noble blue.

25 Back to Nidsdale they are gane,
   And away the Crichtons' nout they hae taen.

26 As they came out at the Wallpath-head,
   The Crichtons bad them light and lead.

27 And when they came to the Biddess-burn,
   The Crichtons bad them stand and turn.

28 And when they came to the Biddess-strand,
   The Crichtons they were hard at hand.

29 But when they cam to the Biddess-law,
   The Johnstons bad them stand and draw.

30 Out then spake then Willy Kirkhill:
   'Of fighting, lads, ye's hae your fill.'

31 Then off his horse Willy he lap,
   And a burnishd brand in his hand he took.

32 And through the Crichtons Willy he ran,
   And dang them down both horse and man.

33 O but these lads were wondrous rude,
   When the Biddess-burn ran three days blood!

34 'I think, my lads, we've done a noble deed;
   We have revengd the Galiard's blood.

35 'For every finger o the Galiard's hand,
   I vow this day I've killed a man.'

36 And hame for Wamphray they are gane,
   And away the Crichtons' nout they've taen.

37 'Sin we've done na hurt, nor we'll
          take na wrang,
   But back to Wamphray we will gang.'

38 As they came in at Evanhead,
   At Reaklaw-holm they spred abroad.

39 'Drive on, my lads, it will be late;
   We'll have a pint at Wamphray Gate.

40 'For where eer I gang, or eer I ride,
   The lads o Wamphr[a]y's on my side.

41 'For of a' the lads that I do ken,
   The lads o Wamphr[a]y's king o men.'

---

*Not divided into stanzas in the MS. Scott
  makes stanzas of four lines.*
3¹. Leuerhay.
After 8 Scott inserts:

For the Galliard, and the gay Galliard's men,
They neer saw a horse but they made it their ain.

The Galliard to Nithside is gane,
To steal Sim Crichton's winsome dun.

20¹. let Willy bee, *in the text:* or the Galiard,
   in the margin.
21¹. *In the margin:* Will of Kirkhill.
38². Breaklaw: *changed in the MS. to* Reak-
   law.

185

DICK O THE COW

a. ' An excelent old song cald Dick of the Cow.' Percy Papers, 1775.   b. Caw's Poetical Museum, p. 22, 1784.
c. Campbell, Albyn's Anthology, II, 31, 1818.

———◆———

a seems to have been communicated to Percy by Roger Halt in 1775. b was contributed to Caw's Museum by John Elliot of Reidheugh, a gentleman, says Scott, well skilled in the antiquities of the western border. c was taken down "from the singing and recitation of a Liddesdale-man, namely, Robert Shortreed, sheriff-substitute of Roxburghshire, in the autumn of 1816;" but it differs from b in no important respect except the omission of thirteen stanzas, 17, 18, 24, 32, 35–38, 51, 52, 56–58.

Scott's copy, I, 137, 1802, II, 63, 1833, is c with the deficient stanzas supplied from b. A copy in the Campbell MSS, I, 204, is b.

Ritson pointed out to Scott a passage in Nashe's Have with you to Saffren Walden which shows that this ballad was popular before the end of the sixteenth century: "Dick of the Cow, that mad demi-lance northren borderer, who plaied his prizes with the lord Jockey so bravely," 1596, in Grosart's Nashe, III, 6.

An allusion to it likewise occurs in Parrot's Laquei Ridiculosi, or Springes for Woodcocks, London, 1613, Epigr. 76.

Owenus wondreth, since he came to Wales,
What the description of this isle should be,
That nere had seen but mountains, hills, and dales;
Yet would he boast, and stand on pedigree
From Rice ap Richard, sprung from Dick a Cow;
Be cod, was right gud gentleman, look ye now!
Scott's Minstrelsy, II, 62, 1833.

In a list of books printed for and sold by P. Brooksby, 1688, occurs Dick-a-the-Cow, containing north-country songs: Ritson, in Scott's Minstrelsy, I, 223, 1833.

Two stanzas are cited in Pennant's Tour in Scotland and Voyage to the Hebrides in 1772, Part II, p. 276, ed. 1776.

Then Johnie Armstrong to Willie gan say,
' Billie, a riding then will we;
England and us have been long at feud;
Perhaps we may hit on some bootie.'

Then they 're come on to Hutton-Ha;
They rade that proper place about;
But the laird he was the wiser man,
For he had left na geir without.

Fair Johnie Armstrong * and Willie his brother, having lain long in, ride out on the chance of some booty. They come to Hutton Hall, but find no gear left without by the experienced laird, except six sheep, which they scorn to take. Johnie asks Willie who the man was that they last met, and learning that it was Dick o the Cow, a fool whom he knows to have three as good kine as are in Cumberland, says, These kine shall go with me to Liddesdale. They carry off Dick's three kine, and also three coverlets from his wife's bed. When daylight reveals the theft, Dick's wife raises a wail; he bids her be still, he will bring her three cows for one. Dick goes to his master and makes his loss known, and asks

———

* As there was no great "routh" of Christian names among the clansmen of the borders, to-names became necessary for the distinction of the numerous Jocks, Christies, Watties and Archies. The name of parent, or of parent and grandparent, was sometimes prefixed, as John's Christie, Agnes' Christie, Peggie's Wattie, Gibb's Jack's Johnie, Pat-

tie's Geordie's Johnie; sometimes the place of abode was added, as Jock o the Side; sometimes there was distinction by personal peculiarities, dress, or arms, as Fair Johnie, Red Cloak, John with the Jack, etc., etc. See lists of all varieties in Mr R. B. Armstrong's History of Liddesdale, etc., p. 78 f.

leave to go to Liddesdale to steal; his troth is required that he will steal from none but those who have stolen from him. Dickie goes on to Puddingburn, where there are three and thirty Armstrongs, and complains to the Laird's Jock of the wrong which Fair Johnie Armstrong and Willie have done him. Fair Johnie is for hanging Dick, Willie for slaying him, and another young man for tossing him in a sheet, beating him, and letting him go. The Laird's Jock, who is a better fellow than the rest, tells Dick that if he will sit down he shall have a bit of his own cow. Dick observes that a key has been flung over the doorhead by lads who have come in late. With this key he opens the stable where are the Armstrongs' three and thirty horses. He ties all but three with a triple knot,* leaps on one, takes another in his hand, and makes off. Fair Johnie discovers in the morning that his own horse and Willie's have been stolen, borrows the Laird's-Jock's, which Dick (for improvement of the story) happens not to have tied, arms himself, and sets out in pursuit. Overtaking Dick on Canoby lee, Johnie sends a spear at him, which only pierces the innocent's jerkin. Dick turns on Johnie, and has the good fortune to fell him with the pommel of his sword. He strips Johnie of armor and sword, takes the third horse, and goes home to his master, who threatens to hang him for his thieving. The fool plants himself upon the terms his master had made with him: he had stolen from none but those that had stolen from him. His having the Laird Jock's horse requires explanation; but Dick is able to give such satisfaction on that point that his master offers twenty pound and one of his best milk-kye for the horse. Dick exacts and gets thirty, and

makes the same bargain with his master's brother for Fair Johnie Armstrong's horse. So he goes back to his wife, and gives her three-score pound for her three coverlets, two kye as good as her three, and has the third horse over and above. But Dick sees that he cannot safely remain on the border after this reprisal upon the Armstrongs, and removes to Burgh (Brough) under Stainmoor, in the extreme south of Cumberland.†

Henry Lord Scroop of Bolton was warden of the West Marches for thirty years from 1563, and his son Thomas for the next ten years, down to the union of the crowns. Which of the two is intended in this ballad might be settled beyond question by identifying my lord's brother, Ralph Scroop, Bailif Glazenberrie, or Glozenburrie, st. 54 f.; but the former is altogether more probable.

The Laird's Jock, in the opinion of Mr R. B. Armstrong, was a son of Thomas of Mangerton, the elder brother of Gilnockie. There are notices of him from 1569 to 1599. In 1569 Archibald Armstrong of Mangerton declined to be pledge for John Armstrong, called the Lardis Jok, Reg. P. Council; in 1599 he and other principal Armstrongs executed a bond,‡ and he is mentioned (in what fashion will presently appear) at various intermediate dates.

Jock, the Laird's son, an Armstrong of Liddesdale, had a brother called John,§ MS. General Register House, 1569. (He is not called Fair John in any document besides the ballad.) In a later MS. there is an entry of the marriage of John Armstrong, called the Lord's John. John Armstrong, son to the laird of Mangerton, is witness to two bonds in which John of the Syde is a party, in 1562, 1563: R. B. Armstrong, History of Liddes-

---

* Ties them with St Mary's knot: hamstrings them, says Caw, and say others after him. A St John's knot is double, a St Mary's triple. Observe that in 31 it is simply said that there is only one horse loose in the stable.

† "The Armstrongs at length got Dick o the Cow in their clutches, and, out of revenge, they tore his flesh from his bones with red-hot pincers:" note in Caw's Museum, p. 35. "At the conclusion of the ballad, the singer used invariably to add that Dickie's removal to Burgh under Stainmuir did not save him from the clutches of the Armstrongs. Having fallen into their power, several years after this exploit, he

was plunged into a large boiling pot, and so put to death. The scene of this cruel transaction is pointed out somewhere in Cumberland." Chambers, Scottish Ballads, p. 55, note. No well-wisher of Dick has the least occasion to be troubled by these puerile supplements of the singers.

‡ I am indebted to Mr R. B. Armstrong for all information not hitherto published.

§ "It was not unusual to call two sons by a favorite name, and the brother of Gilnockie would have probably called his sons by that name:" R. B. A.

dale, etc., Appendix, pp. ciii, civ. In a London MS. the Lord's John is said to have been executed.

The Laird's Jock, his father the laird of Mangerton, Sim's Thom, and their accomplices, are complained of in November, 1582, by Sir Simon Musgrave for burning of his barns, wheat, etc., worth £1,000 sterling: Nicolson and Burn, History of Westmoreland and Cumberland, I, xxxi. The commendation of the Laird's Jock's honesty in st. 47, as Scott says, seems but indifferently founded; "for in July, 1586, a bill was fouled against him, Dick of Dryup, and others, by the deputy of Bewcastle, at a warden-meeting, for four hundred head of cattle taken in open foray from the Drysike in Bewcastle; and in September, 1587, another complaint appears, at the instance of one Andrew Rutledge of the Nook, against the Laird's Jock and his accomplices, for fifty kine and oxen, besides furniture to the amount of one hundred merks sterling:" Nicolson and Burn, as above. To be sure, we find the laird of Mangerton, on the next page, making complaints of the same kind against various persons, but it is to be feared that the Laird's Jock, at least, did not keep to the innocent's golden rule, 'to steal frae nane but them that sta from thee.' Sir Richard Maitland gives him his character:

> Thay spuilye puire men of thair pakis,
> Thay leife tham nocht on bed nor bakis;
> Baith henne and cok,
> With reill and rok,
> The Lairdis Jok all with him takis. (MS.)

Hutton Hall, 3, being more than twenty miles from the border, seems remote for the Armstrongs' first *reconnaissance*, and it is no wonder that Fair Johnie stickled at driving six sheep to such a distance. We might ask how Dick, who evidently lives near Carlisle (for, besides other reasons, he is intimately acquainted with the Armstrongs), should have been met so far from home.

Harribie, 14, mentioned also in 'Kinmont Willie,' was the place of execution at Carlisle.

Puddingburn House, 16, according to Chambers, Scottish Ballads, p. 48, was a strong place on the side of the Tinnis Hill, about three miles westward from the Syde (and therefore a very little further from the house of Mangerton), of which the ruins now serve for a sheepfold. A MS. cited by Mr R. B. Armstrong says: "Joke Armestronge, called the Lord's Joke, dwelleth under Denys Hill besides Kyrsoppe in Tenisborne;" and in another MS. the Lord Jock of Tennesborne is stated to have lived a mile west from Kersopp-foote. The name Puddingburn has not been found on any map.*

Cannobei, 34, is on the east of the Esk, just above its juncture with the Liddel. Mattan, 52, 58 (Morton in b), is perhaps the small town a few miles east of Whitehaven. There were cattle-fairs at Arlochden, which is very nigh, in the early part of this century: Lysons, Cumberland, p. 10.

The Cow in Dick's name can have no reference to his cattle, for then his style would have been Dick o the Kye. Cow may possibly denote the hut in which he lived; or bush, or broom.

Translated by Knortz, Schottische Balladen, No 15, p. 42.

---

* "The place which is alluded to by Scott was pointed out to me about thirty years since. There then were the remains of a tower which stood on a small plateau where the Dow Sike and the Blaik Grain join the Stanygillburn, a tributary of the Tinnisburn. Some remains of the building may still be traced at the northern angle of the sheepfold of which it forms part. The walls that remain are 4 feet 3 inches thick, and measured on the inside about 6 feet high. They extend about 18 feet 6 inches in one direction and 14 feet in another, forming portions of two sides with the angle of the tower. . . . There must have been a considerable building of a rude kind. . . . This place, as the crow flies, is quite two miles and a quarter from Kershope-foot, and by the burn two miles and a half. . . . The Laird's Jock's residence is marked on a sketch map of Liddesdale by Lord Burleigh, drawn when Simon was laird of Mangerton. (Simon, son of Thomas, was laird in 1578-9.) It is also marked at the mouth of the Tinnisburn on a 'platt' of the country, of 1590." R. B. A.

1 Now Liddisdale has lain long in,
    Fa la
  There is no rideing there a ta;
    Fa la
  Their horse is growing so lidder and fatt
    That are lazie in the sta.
    Fa la la didle

2 Then Johnë Armstrang to Willie can say,
    Billie, a rideing then will we;
  England and us has been long at a feed;
    Perhaps we may hitt of some bootie.

3 Then they 'r comd on to Hutton Hall,
    They rade that proper place about;
  But the laird he was the wiser man,
    For he had left nae gear without.

4 Then he had left nae gear to steal,
    Except six sheep upon a lee;
  Says Johnie, I 'de rather in England die
    Before their six sheep good to Liddisdale
    with me.

5 'But how cald they the man we last with mett,
    Billie, as we came over the know?'
  'That same he is an innocent fool,
    And some men calls him Dick o the Cow.'

6 'That fool has three as good kyne of his own
    As is in a' Cumberland, billie,' quoth he:
  'Betide my life, betide my death,
    These three kyne shal go to Liddisdaile with
    me.'

7 Then they 're comd on to the poor fool's house,
    And they have broken his wals so wide;
  They have loosd out Dick o the Cow's kyne
    three,
    And tane three coerlets off his wife's bed.

8 Then on the morn, when the day grew light,
    The shouts and crys rose loud and high:
  'Hold thy tongue, my wife,' he says,
    'And of thy crying let me bee.

9 'Hald thy tongue, my wife,' he says,
    ' And of thy crying let me bee,
  And ay that where thou wants a kow,
    Good sooth that I shal bring the three.'

10 Then Dick 's comd on to lord and master,
    And I wate a drerie fool [was] he:

'Hald thy tongue, my fool,' he says,
    'For I may not stand to jest with thee.'

11 'Shame speed a your jesting, my lord,' quo
    Dickie,
  'For nae such jesting grees with me;
  Liddesdaile has been in my house this last
    night,
    And they have tane my three kyne from me.

12 'But I may nae langer in Cumberland dwel,
    To be your poor fool and your leel,
  Unless ye give me leave, my lord,
    To go to Liddisdale and steal.'

13 'To give thee leave, my fool,' he says,
    ' Thou speaks against mine honour and me;
  Unless thou give me thy trouth and thy right
    hand
    Thou 'l steal frae nane but them that sta
    from thee.'

14 'There is my trouth and my right hand;
    My head shal hing on Hairibie,
  I 'le never crose Carlele sands again,
    If I steal frae a man but them that sta frae
    me.'

15 Dickie has tane leave at lord and master,
    And I wate a merrie fool was he;
  He has bought a bridle and a pair of new spurs,
    And has packed them up in his breek-thigh.

16 Then Dickie 's come on for Puddinburn,
    Even as fast as he may drie;
  Dickie 's come on for Puddinburn,
    Where there was thirty Armstrongs and
    three.

17 'What 's this comd on me!' quo Dickë,
    'What meakle wae 's this happend on me,'
    quo he,
  'Where here is but ae innocent fool,
    And there is thirty Armstrongs and three!'

18 Yet he 's comd up to the hall among them all;
    So wel he became his courtisie:
  'Well may ye be, my good Laird's Jock!
    But the deil bless all your companie.

19 'I 'm come to plain of your man Fair Johnie
    Armstrong,
    And syne his billie Willie,' quo he;

'How they have been in my house th*is* last
     night,
   And they have tane my three ky frae me.'

20 Quo Johnie Armstrong, We 'll him hang;
     'Nay,' thain quo Willie, ' we 'll him slae ;'
   But up bespake another young man, We 'le
       nit him in a four-nooked sheet,
     Give him his burden of batts, and lett him
       gae.

21 Then up bespake the good Laird's Jock,
     The best falla in the companie :
   Fitt thy way down a little while, Dickë,
     And a peice of thine own cow's hough I 'l
       give to thee.

22 But Dicki's heart it grew so great
     That never a bitt of it he dought to eat ;
   But Dickie was warr of ane auld peat-house,
     Where there al the night he thought for to
       sleep.

23 Then Dickie was warr of that auld peat-house,
     Where there al the night he thought for to
       ly ;
   And a' the prayers the poor fool prayd was,
     'I wish I had a mense for my own three
       kye ! '

24 Then it was the use of Puddinburn,
     And the house of Mangertoun, all haile !
   These that came not at the first call
     They gott no more meat till the next meall.

25 The lads, that hungry and aevery was,
     Above the door-head they flang the key ;
   Dickie took good notice to that ;
     Says, There 's a bootie younder for me.

26 Then Dickie 's gane into the stable,
     Where there stood thirty horse and three ;
   He has ty'd them a' with St Mary knot,
     All these horse but barely three.

27 He has ty'd them a' with St Mary knott,
     All these horse but barely three ;
   He has loupen on one, taken another in his
       hand,
     And out at the door and gane is Dickie.

28 Then on the morn, when the day grew light,
     The shouts and cryes rose loud and high ;

'What 's that theife ? ' quo the good Laird's
     Jock ;
   'Tel me the truth and the verity.

29 'What 's that theife ? ' quo the good Laird's
     Jock ;
   'See unto me ye do not lie : '
   'Dick o the Cow has been in the stable this
       last night,
     And has my brother's horse and mine frae
       me.'

30 'Ye wad never be teld it,' quo the Laird's
     Jock ;
   'Have ye not found my tales fu leel ?
   Ye wade never out of England bide,
     Till crooked and blind and a' wad steal.'

31 'But will thou lend me thy bay ? ' Fair Johnë
     Armstrong can say,
   'There 's nae mae horse loose in the stable
       but he ;
   And I 'le either bring ye Dick o the Kow again,
     Or the day is come that he must die.'

32 'To lend thee my bay,' the Laird's Jock can
     say,
   'He 's both worth gold and good monie ;
   Dick o the Kow has away twa horse,
     I wish no thou should no make him three.'

33 He has tane the Laird's jack on his back,
     The twa-handed sword *that* hang lieugh by
       his thigh ;
   He has tane the steel cap on his head,
     And on is he to follow Dickie.

34 Then Dickie was not a mile off the town,
     I wate a mile but barely three,
   Till John Armstrang has oertane Dick o the
       Kow,
     Hand for hand on Cannobei lee.

35 'Abide th[e], bide now, Dickie than,
     The day is come that thow must die ; '
   Dickie looked oer his left shoulder ;
     'Johnie, has thow any mo in thy company ?

36 'There is a preacher in owr chapell,
     And a' the lee-lang day teaches he ;
   When day is gane, and night is come,
     There 's never a word I mark but three.

37 'The first and second's Faith and Conscience;
     The third is, Johnie, Take head of thee;
   But what faith and conscience had thow, trai-
       tor,
     When thou took my three kye frae me?

38 'And when thou had tane my three kye,
     Thou thought in thy heart thou was no wel
       sped;
   But thou sent thi billie Willie oer the know,
     And he took three coerlets of my wife's bed.'

39 Then Johne lett a spear fa leaugh by his thigh,
     Thought well to run the innocent through;
   But the powers above was more than his,
     He ran but the poor fool's jerkin through.

40 Together they ran or ever they blan —
     This was Dickie, the fool, and hee —
   Dickie could net win to him with the blade of
       the sword,
     But he feld [him] with the plummet under
       the eye.

41 Now Dickie has [feld] Fair Johnë Armstrong,
     The prettiest man in the south countrey;
   'Gramercie,' then can Dickie say,
     'I had twa horse, thou has made me three.'

42 He has tane the laird's jack off his back,
     The twa-handed sword that hang leiugh by
       his thigh;
   He has tane the steel cape off his head:
     'Johnie, I 'le tel my master I met with thee.'

43 When Johnë wakend out of his dream,
     I wate a dreiry man was he:
   'Is thou gane now, Dickie, than?
     The shame gae in thy company!

44 'Is thou gane now, Dickie, than?
     The shame go in thy companie!
   For if I should live this hundred year,
     I shal never fight with a fool after thee.'

45 Then Dickie comed home to lord and master,
     Even as fast as he may driee:
   'Now Dickie, I shal neither eat meat nor drink
     Till high hanged that thou shall be!'

46 'The shame speed the liars, my lord!' quo
       Dickie,
     'That was no the promise ye made to me;

For I 'd never gane to Liddesdale to steal
     Till that I sought my leave at thee.'

47 'But what gart thow steal the Laird's-Jock's
       horse?
     And, limmer, what gart thou steal him?'
       quo he;
   'For lang might thow in Cumberland dwelt
     Or the Laird's Jock had stoln ought frae
       thee.'

48 'Indeed I wate ye leed, my lord,
     And even so loud as I hear ye lie;
   I wan him frae his man, Fair Johnë Arm-
       strong,
     Hand for hand on Cannobie lee.

49 'There 's the jack was on his back,
     The twa-handed sword that hung lewgh by
       his thigh;
   There 's the steel cap was on his head;
     I have a' these takens to lett you see.'

50 'If that be true thou to me tels—
     I trow thou dare not tel a lie —
   I 'le give thee twenty pound for the good horse,
     Wel teld in thy cloke-lap shall be.

51 'And I 'le give thee one of my best milk-
       kye,
     To maintain thy wife and children three;
   [And that may be as good, I think,
     As ony twa o thine might be.']

52 'The shame speed the liars, my lord!' quo
       Dicke,
     'Trow ye ay to make a fool of me?
   I 'le either have thirty pound for the good
       horse,
     Or els he 's gae to Mattan fair wi me:'

53 Then he has given him thirty pound for the
       good horse,
     All in gold and good monie;
   He has given him one of his best milk-kye,
     To maintain his wife and children three.

54 Then Dickie 's come down through Carlile
       town,
     Even as fast as he may drie:
   The first of men that he with mett
     Was my lord's brother, Bailife Glazenberrie.

55 'Well may ye be, my good Ralph Scrupe!'
  'Welcome, my brother's fool!' quo he;
  'Where did thou gett Fair Johnie Armstrong's
    horse?'
  'Where did I get him but steall him,' quo he.

56 'But will thou sell me Fair Johnie Arm-
    strong['s] horse?
  And, billie, will thou sel him to me?' quo he:
  'Ay, and tel me the monie on my cloke-lap,
    For there's not one fathing I'le trust thee.'

57 'I'le give thee fifteen pound for the good horse,
  Wel teld on thy cloke-lap shal be;
  And I'le give [thee] one of my best milk-kye,
    To maintain thy wife and thy children three.'

58 'The shame speed the liars, my lord!' quo
    Dickë,
  'Trow ye ay to make a fool of me?' quo he:
  'I'le either have thirty pound for the good
    horse,
    Or else he's to Mattan Fair with me.'

59 He has given him thirty pound for the good
    horse,
  All in gold and good monie;

He has given him one of his best milk-kye,
  To maintain his wife and children three.

60 Then Dickie lap a loup on high,
  And I wate a loud laughter leugh he:
  'I wish the neck of the third horse were
    browken,
    For I have a better of my own, and onie
    better can be.'

61 Then Dickie comd hame to his wife again;
  Judge ye how the poor fool he sped;
  He has given her three score of English pounds
    For the three auld coerlets was tane of her
    bed.

62 'Hae, take thee there twa as good kye,
  I trow, as al thy three might be;
  And yet here is a white-footed naigg;
    I think he'le carry booth thee and me.

63 'But I may no langer in Cumberland dwell;
  The Armstrongs the'le hang me high:'
  But Dickie has tane leave at lord and master,
    And Burgh under Stanemuir there dwels
    Dickie.

---

a. 4^4. *Over* good *is written* went.
  10^2. I wats: *cf.* 15^2, 34^2, 43^2.
  21^3. Fitt: *Caw*, Sit. *I take* fitt *in the sense
    of* fettle.
  23^4. a mense. 38^3. Sent y^e.
  47^2. steal the Laird Jock horse *erroneously
    repeated from the line above: corrected
    from Caw.*
  $51^{3,4}$ *wanting: supplied from* b.
  55^1. Srcupe.
  62^2. *for* thy, thyee, *corrected from* three.
b. *Burden, after the first and fourth line,* Fala,
  fala, fala, faliddle.
  1^3. horses are grown sae lidder fat.
  1^4. They downa stur out o the sta.
  2^2. then we'll gae. 2^4. Ablins we'll hit on.
  3^2. rade the. 4^3. Quo J. 4^4. Ere thir: gae.
  5^1. with *wanting*. 5^4. men ca.
  $6^{1,4}$, 11^4, 19^4. ky. 6^2. As there's.
  6^3. me *for* my, *twice*. 7^3. three ky.
  8^1. day was. 8^3, 9^1. O had.
  9^4. In good sooth I'll. 10^1. on for's.

10^2. was he. 10^3. Now had.
11^3. this *wanting*. 13^1. I gi.
13^2. speakest: my. 13^3. right *wanting*.
13^4. but wha sta frae. 14^2. hang.
14^4. but wha sta. 16^2. might.
16^3. Now Dickie's. 16^4. were.
17^1. O what's this comd o me now.
18^2. Sae weil's. 19^2. o his. 19^3. the last.
20^3, 21^1. up and.
20^3. We'll nit him in a four-nooked sheet
  wanting.
20^4. We'll gie im his batts. 21^2. in a' the.
21^3. Sit thy ways: Dickie. 21^4. thy: gi thee.
22^3. Then Dickie. 22^4, 23^2. there *wanting*.
23^1. o an auld. 23^3. was *wanting*.
23^4. a mense. 24^3. came na. 24^4. t' the.
25^1. weary *for* aevery: were.
25^2. Aboon: hang *for* flang. 25^3. Dickie he.
26^1. Then D. into the stable is gane.
26^2, 27^2. horses. 26^3, 27^1. Mary's.
27^3. tane: his *wanting*. 28^3, 29^1. O where's.
29^2. dinna. 29^3. Dickie's been: this *wanting*.

30[1]. it *wanting.*
31[1]. But lend me thy bay, Johnie.
31[2]. mae *wanting.* 31[3]. ye *wanting.*
31[4]. he shall. 32[2]. worth baith.
32[4]. na thou may make. 33[2]. lieugh *wanting.*
33[4]. he gane. 34[1]. was na.
34[3]. Till he's oertane by Johnie A.
35[1]. Abide, abide. 35[2]. maun die.
35[3]. Then *wanting.* 35[4]. thy *wanting.*
36[4]. neer ae.
37[2]. third, neer let a traitor free.
37[3]. But Johnie: hadst: traitor *wanting.*
38[1]. tane away. 38[3]. But sent thy.
39[2]. to hae slain the innocent, I trow.
39[3]. were mair than he. 39[4]. For he.
40[4]. But feld 'im. 41[1]. has feld.
42[2]. leiugh *wanting.* 43[1]. Johnie.
43[3], 44[1]. And is. 44[3]. years.
44[4]. I neer shall. 45[1]. come.
45[3]. I'll neither eat nor.
45[4]. hanged thou shalt.
46[4]. Till I had got my.
47[2]. gard thou steal him, quo he.
47[4]. Ere: stawn frae. 48[3]. Johnie.
49[3]. And there's. 49[4]. let thee. 50[2]. dare na.
50[3], 52[3], 53[1], 57[1], 58[3], 59[1]. punds.
51[3,4]. And that may be as good, I think, As
ony twa o thine might be.
52[4]. els *wanting*: Mortan. 53[1]. He's gien.
54[1]. Dickie came. 54[2]. he might.
54[3]. met with. 54[4]. Glozenburrie. 56[1,2]. wilt.
56[4]. no ae fardin. 57[3]. gi thee.
57[4]. thy *wanting.* 58[4]. Or he's gae: Mortan.
60[1]. fu hie. 60[2]. laugh laughed.
60[4]. if better can be. 61[1]. Dickie's.
61[2]. fool sped. 62[1]. these *for* there.
62[3]. a *accidentally wanting*: nagie.
63[1]. bide *for* dwell. 63[4]. dwells he.
*Simple Scotticisms and ordinary contractions
have generally not been noted.*

c. *Reading of* b *are not repeated.*
Burden: after the first and the second verse,
Lal de ral, *thrice,* la lal de ; *at the end of
the stanza:*
Lal lal de ridle la di, fal lal de ridle la di,
Fal lal di lal la, fal lal di ridle la.

2[1]. Fair Johnie. 2[2]. riding we will.
2[3]. have been: at feid. 2[4]. we'll light.
3[1]. they are come. 3[2]. that proper, *as* a.
4[1]. For he. 5[1]. ca. 5[4]. And men they call.
6[2]. there are. 7[1]. they have come.
7[4]. frae his. 8[2]. rase.
9[2]. ay where thou hast lost ae.

9[4]. suith I shall.
10[1]. Now Dickie's gane to the gude Lord
Scroop.
11[1]. Shame fa your. 11[4]. hae awa.
12[3]. you. 13[4]. Thou'lt. 15[1]. leave o.
15[2]. And *wanting.*
16[1]. on to Pudding-burn house.
16[3]. Then: on to. 17, 18 *wanting.*
19[3]. house last. 20[1]. Ha quo fair.
20[2]. then *wanting.*
20[3]. Then up and spak: young Armstrang.
21[1]. But up and spak. 21[3]. down thy ways.
21[4]. gie ye. 22[2]. the neer.
22[3]. Then was he aware.
23[4]. Were I: amends: my gude.
24 *wanting.* 25[2]. they threw. 25[3]. o that.
25[4]. There will be a bootie for.
26[1]. has into the stable gane.
27[4]. And away as fast as he can hie.
28[1]. But. 28[2]. raise.
28[3]. Ah, whae has done this.
29[1]. Whae has done this deed.
29[2]. See that to me. 29[4]. has taen.
31[1]. But lend me thy bay, Fair Johnie can say.
31[2]. save he. 31[3]. either fetch. 32 *wanting.*
33[2]. A: to hang by. 33[3]. a *for* the.
33[4]. And galloped on to.
34[1]. Then *wanting*: frae aff.
34[3]. When he was: Fair J. A.
35–38 *wanting.* 39[1]. fu *for* fa : *misprint?*
40[3]. at him. 41[1]. Thus. 41[4]. hast.
42[1]. the steil-jack aff Johnie's back.
42[2]. hang low.
43[4]. The shame and dule is left wi me.
44[2]. The deil. 44[3]. these h. years.
45[1]. hame to the good Lord Scroop.
45[2]. he might hie.
46[4]. Had I not got my leave frae.
47[1]. garrd thee. 47[2]. garrd ye.
47[3]. thou mightst.
48[3]. wan the horse frae Fair.
48[4]. Hand to. 49[2]. This: sword hang.
49[4]. brought a'. 50[2]. And I think thou dares.
50[3]. fifteen pounds for the horse. 50[4]. on thy.
51, 52 *wanting.* 53[1]. twenty pounds.
54[2]. could drie. 55[1]. Well be ye met.
55[3]. didst. 56, 57, 58 *wanting.*
59[1]. twenty punds. 59[2]. Baith in.
60[4]. If ony of the twa were better than he.
61[1]. Dickie's come. 61[2]. had sped.
61[3]. twa score. 61[4]. was *wanting.*
62[1]. And tak. 63[2]. they would. 63[3]. So D.
63[4]. And at.

186

KINMONT WILLIE

Minstrelsy of the Scottish Border, I, 111, 1802; II, 32, 1833.

———•———

THIS ballad celebrates a bold and masterly exploit of Sir Walter Scott of Branxholm, laird of Buccleuch, which is narrated as follows by a contemporary, Archbishop Spotiswood: *

"The Lord Scroop being then Warden of the West-Marches of England, and the Laird of Bacleugh having the charge of Lidisdale, they sent their deputies to keep a day of truce for redress of some ordinary matters. The place of meeting was at the Dayholme of Kershop, where a small brook divideth England from Scotland, and Lidisdale from Bawcastle. There met, as deputy for the Laird of Bacleugh, Robert Scott of Hayninge, and for the Lord Scroop, a gentleman within the West-Wardenry called Mr Salkeld. These two, after truce taken and proclaimed, as the custom was, by sound of trumpet, met friendly, and, upon mutual redress of such wrongs as were then complained of, parted in good terms, each of them taking his way homewards. Meanwhile it happened one William Armstrong, commonly called Will of Kinmouth, to be in company with the Scottish deputy; against whom the English had a quarrel for many wrongs he had committed, as he was indeed a notorious thief. This man having taken his leave of the Scots deputy, and riding down the river of Liddell on the Scottish side, towards his own house, was pursued by the English that espied him from the other side of the river, and after a chase of three or four miles taken prisoner, and brought back to the English deputy, who carried him away to the castle of Carlile.

"The Laird of Bacleugh complaining of the breach of truce (which was always taken from the time of meeting unto the next day at sun-rising) wrote to Mr Salkeld and craved redress. He excused himself by the absence of the Lord Scroop. Whereupon Bacleugh sent to the Lord Scroop, and desired the prisoner might be set at liberty, without any bond or condition, seeing he was unlawfully taken. Scroop answered that he could do nothing in the matter, it having so happened, without a direction from the queen and council of England, considering the man was such a malefactor. Bacleugh, loath to inform the king of what was done, lest it might have bred some misliking betwixt the princes, dealt with Mr Bowes, the resident ambassador of England, for the prisoner's liberty: who wrote very seriously to the Lord Scroop in that business, advising him to set the man free, and not to bring the matter to a farther hearing. But no answer was returned; the matter thereupon was imparted to the king, and the queen of England solicited by letters to give direction for his liberty; yet nothing was obtained. Which Bacleugh perceiving, and apprehending both the king, and himself as the king's officer, to be touched in honor, he resolved to work the prisoner's relief by the best means he could.

"And upon intelligence that the castle of Carlile, wherein the prisoner was kept, was surprisable, he employed some trusty persons to take a view of the postern-gate, and measure the height of the wall, which he meant to scale by ladders; and if those failed, to

* The Archbishop's account is apparently based upon a more minute "relation of the maner of surprizeing of the Castell of Cairlell by the lord of Buccleugh," given, from a manuscript of the period, in the later edition of the Minstrelsy, II, 32. There is another account of the rescue in The Historie of King James the Sext, p. 366 ff.

break through the wall with some iron instruments, and force the gates. This done so closely as he could, he drew together some two hundred horse, assigning the place of meeting at the tower of Morton,* some ten miles from Carlile, an hour before sun-set. With this company passing the water of Esk about the falling, two hours before day he crossed Eden beneath Carlile bridge (the water through the rain that had fallen being thick), and came to the Sacery [Sacray], a plain under the castle. There making a little halt at the side of a small bourn which they call Cadage [Caday, Caldew], he caused eighty of the company to light from their horses, and take the ladders and other instruments which he had prepared with them. He himself, accompanying them to the foot of the wall, caused the ladders to be set to it; which proving too short, he gave order to use the other instruments for opening the wall, nigh the postern, and finding the business like to succeed, retired to the rest whom he had left on horseback, for assuring those that entered upon the castle against any eruption from the town. With some little labor a breach was made for single men to enter, and they who first went in brake open the postern for the rest. The watchmen and some few the noise awaked made a little restraint, but they were quickly repressed and taken captive. After which they passed to the chamber wherein the prisoner was kept, and having brought him forth, sounded a trumpet, which was a signal to them without that the enterprise was performed. My Lord Scroop and Mr Salkeld were both within the house, and to them the prisoner cried a good-night. The captives taken in the first encounter were brought to Bacleugh, who presently returned them to their master, and would not suffer any spoil, or booty, as they term it, to be carried away. He had straightly forbidden to break open any door but that where the prisoner was kept, though he might have made prey of all the goods within the castle and taken the warden himself captive; for he would

have it seen that he did intend nothing but the reparation of his Majesty's honor. By this time the prisoner was brought forth, the town had taken the alarm, the drums were beating, the bells ringing, and a beacon put on the top of the castle to give warning to the country. Whereupon Bacleugh commanded those that entered the castle, and the prisoner, to horse, and marching again by the Sacery, made to the river at the Stony bank, on the other side whereof certain were assembled to stop his passage; but he, causing sound the trumpet, took the river, day being then broken; and they choosing to give him way, he retired in order through the Grahams of Esk (men at that time of great power and his unfriends) and came back into Scottish ground two hours after sun-rising, and so homewards. This fell out the thirteenth of April, 1596." (History of the Church of Scotland, 1639, in the second edition, 1666, p. 413 ff.)

Lord Scroope, on the morning after, wrote thus to the Privy Council of England:

"Yesternight, in the dead time thereof, Walter Scott of Hardinge and Walter Scott of Goldylands, the chief men about Buclughe, accompanied with five hundred horsemen of Buclughe and Kinmont's friends, did come, armed and appointed with gavlocks and crows of iron, hand-picks, axes, and scaling-ladders, unto an outward corner of the base-court of this castle, and to the postern-door of the same, which they undermined speedily and quickly, and made themselves possessors of the base-court, brake into the chamber where Will of Kinmont was, carried him away, and, in their discovery by the watch, left for dead two of the watchmen, hurt a servant of mine, one of Kinmont's keepers, and were issued again out of the postern before they were descried by the watch of the inner ward, and ere resistance could be made. The watch, as it should seem, by reason of the stormy night, were either on sleep or gotten under some covert to defend themselves from the violence of the weather, by means whereof

---

* Near the water of Sark, in the Debateable Land, and belonging to Kinmont Willie: "William Armstrong, in

Morton Tower, called Will of Kinmouth, 1569." Register of the Privy Council of Scotland, II, 44.

the Scots achieved their enterprise with less difficulty. . . . If Buclughe himself have been thereat in person, the captain of this proud attempt, as some of my servants tell me they heard his name called upon (the truth whereof I shall shortly advertise) then I humbly beseech that her Majesty may be pleased to send unto the king to call for and effectually to press his delivery, that he may receive punishment as her Majesty shall find that the quality of his offence shall demerit." * MS. of the State Paper Office, in Tytler's History, IX, 436.

Kinmont's rapacity made his very name proverbial. "Mas James Melvine, in urging reasons against subscribing the act of supremacy, in 1584, asks ironically, Who shall take order with vice and wickedness? The court and bishops? As well as Martine Elliot and Will of Kinmont with stealing upon the borders!" Scott, Minstrelsy, 1833, II, 46.

Accordingly, when James was taking measures for bringing the refractory ministers and citizens of Edinburgh into some proper subjection, at the end of the year 1596, a report that Kinmont Willie was to be let loose upon the city caused a lively consternation; "but too well grounded," says Scott, "considering what had happened in Stirling ten years before, when the Earl of Angus, attended by Home, Buccleuch, and other border chief-

tains, marched thither to remove the Earl of Arran from the king's councils: the town was miserably pillaged by the borderers, particularly by a party of Armstrongs, under this very Kinmont Willie, who not only made prey of horses and cattle, but even of the very iron grating of the windows." Minstrelsy, II, 45.

The ballad gives Buccleuch only forty men, and they are all of the name of Scott except Sir Gilbert Elliot of Stobs: st. 16. A partial list of the men who forced the castle was obtained by Lord Scroope. It includes, as might be expected, not a few Armstrongs, and among them the laird of Mangerton, Christy of Barngleish (son of Gilnockie), and four sons of Kinmont Willie (he had at least seven); two Elliots, but not Sir Gilbert; four Bells.† Scott of Satchells, in his History of the Name of Scott, 1688, makes Sir Gilbert Elliot one of the party, but may have taken this name from the ballad. (Scott's Minstrelsy, 1833, II, 43.) Dick of Dryhope, 24, 25, was an Armstrong.‡ The ballad, again, after cutting down Buccleuch's men to thirty (st. 33) or forty (18, 19), assigns the very liberal garrison of a thousand to the castle, 33; the ladders are long enough, Buccleuch mounts the first,§ the castle is won, and Kinmont Willie, in his irons, is borne down the ladder on Red Rowan's ‖ shoulders: all of

* "The queen of England, having notice sent her of what was done, stormed not a little," and her ambassador was instructed to say that peace could not continue between the two realms unless Buccleuch were delivered to England, to be punished at the queen's pleasure. Buccleuch professed himself willing to be tried, according to ancient treaties, by commissioners of the respective kingdoms, and the Scots made the proposal, but Elizabeth did not immediately consent to this arrangement. At last, to satisfy the queen, Buccleuch was put in ward at the castle of St Andrews. Spotiswood adds that he was "afterwards entered in England, where he remained not long" (and Tytler to the same effect, IX, 226). According to one of the MSS of The Historie of King James the Sext, the king, to please and pleasure her Majesty, entered Buccleuch in ward at Berwick with all expedition possible, and the queen, of her courtesy, released him back in due and sufficient time: p. 421. But Buccleuch seems to have been entered in England only once, and that in 1597, and not for the assault on Carlisle castle, or for a raid which he made in the next year, but because he did not deliver up his pledges, as he was under obligation to do according to a treaty made by a joint commission in 1597. See Ridpath's Border History, 1848, pp. 473, 477.

† Tytler's History, IX, 437. "The greatest nomber whareof war ordinar nycht-walkers" (H. of K. J. the Sext, p. 369).

‡ "Dike Armestronge of Dryup dwelleth neare High Morgarton" (Mangerton). Dike Armestronge of Dryup appears in a list of the principal men in Liddesdale, drawn up when Simon Armstrong was laird of Mangerton, among Simon's uncles or uncles' sons. Dick of Dryup is complained of, with others, for reif and burning, in 1583, 1586, 1587, 1603, and his name is among the outlaws proclaimed at Carlisle July 23, 1603. (Notes of Mr R. B. Armstrong.)

§ "The informer saith that Buclughe was the fifth man which entered the castle:" Lord Scroop's letter, Tytler, IX, 437. But the MS. used by Scott, Spotiswood's account (founded chiefly or altogether upon that MS.), and The Historie of King James the Sext agree in saying that Buccleuch remained outside, "to assure the retreat of his awin from the castell againe."

‖ "Red Rowy Forster" is one of the list complained of to the Bishop of Carlisle, about 1550 (see 'Hughie Grame'), and he is in company with Jock of Kinmont, one of Will's four sons, Archie of Gingles, Jock of Gingles, and George of the Gingles, who may represent "The Chingles" in the informer's list already cited. Nicolson and Burn, I, lxxxii.

which is as it should be in a ballad. And so with the death of the fause Sakelde, though not a life seems to have been lost in the whole course of the affair.

"This ballad," says Scott, "is preserved by tradition in the West Borders, but much mangled by reciters, so that some conjectural emendations have been absolutely necessary to render it intelligible. In particular, the Eden has been substituted for the Esk [in 26²], the latter name being inconsistent with geography." It is to be suspected that a great deal more emendation was done than the mangling of reciters rendered absolutely necessary. One would like, for example, to see stanzas 10–12 and 31 in their mangled condition.*

1. William Armstrong, called Will of Kinmonth, lived in Morton Tower, a little above the Marchdike-foot. He appears, says Mr R. B. Armstrong, to have been a son of Sandy, *alias* Ill Will's Sandy. Haribee is the place of execution outside of Carlisle. 3. The Liddel-rack is a ford in that river, which, for a few miles before it empties into the Esk, is the boundary of England and Scotland. 8. Branxholm, or Branksome, is three miles southwest, and Stobs, 16, some four miles southeast, of Hawick. 19. Woodhouselee was a house on the Scottish border, a little west of the junction of the Esk and Liddel, "belonging to Buccleuch," says Scott.

---

1 O HAVE ye na heard o the fause Sakelde?
   O have ye na heard o the keen Lord
     Scroop?
  How they hae taen bauld Kinmont Willie,
   On Hairibee to hang him up?

2 Had Willie had but twenty men,
   But twenty men as stout as he,
  Fause Sakelde had never the Kinmont taen,
   Wi eight score in his companie.

3 They band his legs beneath the steed,
   They tied his hands behind his back;
  They guarded him, fivesome on each side,
   And they brought him ower the Liddel-
     rack.

4 They led him thro the Liddel-rack,
   And also thro the Carlisle sands;
  They brought him to Carlisle castell,
   To be at my Lord Scroope's commands.

5 'My hands are tied, but my tongue is free,
   And whae will dare this deed avow?
  Or answer by the border law?
   Or answer to the bauld Buccleuch?'

6 'Now haud thy tongue, thou rank reiver!
   There 's never a Scot shall set ye free;
  Before ye cross my castle-yate,
   I trow ye shall take farewell o me.'

7 'Fear na ye that, my lord,' quo Willie;
   'By the faith o my bodie, Lord Scroop,'
    he said,
  'I never yet lodged in a hostelrie
   But I paid my lawing before I gaed.'

8 Now word is gane to the bauld Keeper,
   In Branksome Ha where that he lay,
  That Lord Scroope has taen the Kinmont
    Willie,
  Between the hours of night and day.

9 He has taen the table wi his hand,
   He garrd the red wine spring on hie;
  'Now Christ's curse on my head,' he said,
   'But avenged of Lord Scroop I 'll be!

10 'O is my basnet a widow's curch?
   Or my lance a wand of the willow-tree?
  Or my arm a ladye's lilye hand?
   That an English lord should lightly me.

* This is also to be observed: "There are in this collection no fewer than three poems on the rescue of prisoners, the incidents in which nearly resemble each other, though the poetical description is so different that the editor did not think himself at liberty to reject any one of them, as borrowed from the others. As, however, there are several verses which, in recitation, are common to all these three songs, the editor, to prevent unnecessary and disagreeable repetition, has used the freedom of appropriating them to that in which they seem to have the best poetic effect." 'Jock o the Side,' Minstrelsy, II, 76, ed. 1833.

11 'And have they taen him Kinmont Willie,
    Against the truce of Border tide,
    And forgotten that the bauld Bacleuch
    Is keeper here on the Scottish side?

12 'And have they een taen him Kinmont Willie,
    Withouten either dread or fear,
    And forgotten that the bauld Bacleuch
    Can back a steed, or shake a spear?

13 'O were there war between the lands,
    As well I wot that there is none,
    I would slight Carlisle castell high,
    Tho it were builded of marble-stone.

14 'I would set that castell in a low,
    And sloken it with English blood;
    There's nevir a man in Cumberland
    Should ken where Carlisle castell stood.

15 'But since nae war's between the lands,
    And there is peace, and peace should be,
    I'll neither harm English lad or lass,
    And yet the Kinmont freed shall be!'

16 He has calld him forty marchmen bauld,
    I trow they were of his ain name,
    Except Sir Gilbert Elliot, calld
    The Laird of Stobs, I mean the same.

17 He has calld him forty marchmen bauld,
    Were kinsmen to the bauld Buccleuch,
    With spur on heel, and splent on spauld,
    And gleuves of green, and feathers blue.

18 There were five and five before them a',
    Wi hunting-horns and bugles bright;
    And five and five came wi Buccleuch,
    Like Warden's men, arrayed for fight.

19 And five and five like a mason-gang,
    That carried the ladders lang and hie;
    And five and five like broken men;
    And so they reached the Woodhouselee.

20 And as we crossd the Bateable Land,
    When to the English side we held,
    The first o men that we met wi,
    Whae sould it be but fause Sakelde!

21 'Where be ye gaun, ye hunters keen?'
    Quo fause Sakelde; 'come tell to me!'

'We go to hunt an English stag,
    Has trespassd on the Scots countrie.'

22 'Where be ye gaun, ye marshal-men?'
    Quo fause Sakelde; 'come tell me true!'
'We go to catch a rank reiver,
    Has broken faith wi the bauld Buccleuch.'

23 'Where are ye gaun, ye mason-lads,
    Wi a' your ladders lang and hie?'
'We gang to herry a corbie's nest,
    That wons not far frae Woodhouselee.'

24 'Where be ye gaun, ye broken men?'
    Quo fause Sakelde; 'come tell to me!'
Now Dickie of Dryhope led that band,
    And the nevir a word o lear had he.

25 'Why trespass ye on the English side?
    Row-footed outlaws, stand!' quo he;
The neer a word had Dickie to say,
    Sae he thrust the lance thro his fause bodie.

26 Then on we held for Carlisle toun,
    And at Staneshaw-bank the Eden we crossd;
    The water was great, and meikle of spait,
    But the nevir a horse nor man we lost.

27 And when we reachd the Staneshaw-bank,
    The wind was rising loud and hie;
    And there the laird garrd leave our steeds,
    For fear that they should stamp and nie.

28 And when we left the Staneshaw-bank,
    The wind began full loud to blaw;
    But 't was wind and weet, and fire and sleet,
    When we came beneath the castel-wa.

29 We crept on knees, and held our breath,
    Till we placed the ladders against the wa;
    And sae ready was Buccleuch himsell
    To mount the first before us a'.

30 He has taen the watchman by the throat,
    He flung him down upon the lead:
'Had there not been peace between our lands,
    Upon the other side thou hadst gaed.

31 'Now sound out, trumpets!' quo Buccleuch;
    'Let's waken Lord Scroope right merrilie!'
Then loud the Warden's trumpets blew
    'O whae dare meddle wi me?'

32 Then speedilie to wark we gaed,
    And raised the slogan ane and a',
And cut a hole thro a sheet of lead,
    And so we wan to the castel-ha.

33 They thought King James and a' his men
    Had won the house wi bow and speir ;
It was but twenty Scots and ten
    That put a thousand in sic a stear !

34 Wi coulters and wi forehammers,
    We garrd the bars bang merrilie,
Untill we came to the inner prison,
    Where Willie o Kinmont he did lie.

35 And when we cam to the lower prison,
    Where Willie o Kinmont he did lie,
' O sleep ye, wake ye, Kinmont Willie,
    Upon the morn that thou 's to die ? '

36 ' O I sleep saft, and I wake aft,
    It 's lang since sleeping was fleyd frae me ;
Gie my service back to my wyfe and bairns,
    And a' gude fellows that speer for me.'

37 Then Red Rowan has hente him up,
    The starkest men in Teviotdale :
' Abide, abide now, Red Rowan,
    Till of my Lord Scroope I take farewell.

38 ' Farewell, farewell, my gude Lord Scroope !
    My gude Lord Scroope, farewell ! ' he cried ;
' I 'll pay you for my lodging-maill
    When first we meet on the border-side.'

39 Then shoulder high, with shout and cry,
    We bore him down the ladder lang ;

At every stride Red Rowan made,
    I wot the Kinmont's airns playd clang.

40 ' O mony a time,' quo Kinmont Willie,
    ' I have ridden horse baith wild and wood ;
But a rougher beast than Red Rowan
    I ween my legs have neer bestrode.

41 ' And mony a time,' quo Kinmont Willie,
    ' I 've pricked a horse out oure the furs ;
But since the day I backed a steed
    I nevir wore sic cumbrous spurs.'

42 We scarce had won the Staneshaw-bank,
    When a' the Carlisle bells were rung,
And a thousand men, in horse and foot,
    Cam wi the keen Lord Scroope along.

43 Buccleuch has turned to Eden Water,
    Even where it flowd frae bank to brim,
And he has plunged in wi a' his band,
    And safely swam them thro the stream.

44 He turned him on the other side,
    And at Lord Scroope his glove flung he :
' If ye like na my visit in merry England,
    In fair Scotland come visit me ! '

45 All sore astonished stood Lord Scroope,
    He stood as still as rock of stane ;
He scarcely dared to trew his eyes
    When thro the water they had gane.

46 ' He is either himsell a devil frae hell,
    Or else his mother a witch maun be ;
I wad na have ridden that wan water
    For a' the gowd in Christentie.'

187

JOCK O THE SIDE

A. 'John a Side,' Percy MS., p. 254; Hales and Furnivall, II, 203.

B. 'Jock o the Side.' **a.** Caw's Poetical Museum, 1784, p. 145. **b.** Campbell, Albyn's Anthology, II, 28, 1818.

C. 'John o the Side,' Percy Papers, as collected from the memory of an old person in 1775.

D. Percy Papers, fragment from recitation, 1774.

THE copy in Scott's Minstrelsy, 1802, I, 154, 1833, II, 76, is B b, with the insertion of three stanzas (6, 7, 23) from B a. Neither Campbell nor Scott has the last stanza of B a. Campbell says, in a note to his copy: The melody and particularly the words of this Liddesdale song were taken down by the editor from the singing and recitation of Mr Thomas Shortreed, who learnt it from his father. As to the words (except in the omission of four stanzas), b does not differ significantly from a, and it may, with little hesitation, be said to have been derived from a. Campbell seems to have given this copy to Scott, who published it sixteen years before it appeared in the Anthology, with the addition already mentioned.* The copy in the Campbell MSS, I, 220, is B a.

The earliest appearance of John o the Side is, perhaps, in the list of the marauders against whom complaint was made to the Bishop of Carlisle "presently after" Queen Mary Stuart's departure for France; not far, therefore, from 1550: "John of the Side (Gleed John)."

Mr R. B. Armstrong has printed two bonds in which John Armstrong of the Syde is a party, with others, of the date 1562 and 1563. History of Liddesdale, etc., Appendix, pp ciii, civ, Nos LXV, LXVI.

The earls of Northumberland and Westmoreland, after the failure of the Rising in the North, fled first to Liddesdale, and thence " to one of the Armstrongs," in the Debateable Land. The Liddesdale men stole the Countess of Northumberland's horses, and the earls, continuing their flight, left her " on foot, at John of the Syde's house, a cottage not to be compared to any dog-kennel in England." At his departing, " my lord of Westmoreland changed his coat of plate and sword with John of the Syde, to be the more unknown:" Sussex to Cecil, December 22, 1569, printed in Sharp's Memorials of the Rebellion, p. 114 f.

John is nephew to the laird of Mangerton in B 1, 3, 4, C 1, 3, and therefore cousin to the Laird's Jock and the Laird's Wat: † but this does not appear in A.

Sir Richard Maitland commemorates both John of the Syde and the Laird's Jock in his verses on the thieves of Liddesdale :

> He is weill kend, Johne of Syde,
> A greater theife did never ryd :
> > He never tyres
> > For to brek byres,
> Our muire and myres our guid ane gyde.
> (MS., fol. 4, back, line 13.)

An Archie Armstrang in Syde is complained of, with others, in 1596, for burning eleven houses (Register of the Privy Council of Scotland, V, 294), and Christie of the Syde

---

* Campbell " projected " his work as early as 1790, and he intimates in his preface, p. viii (if I have rightly understood him), that he gave help to Scott.

† For the Laird's Jock, see 'Dick o the Cow,' No 185.

" I do not say there never was a Laird's Wat, but I do not recollect having met with an Armstrong called Walter during the sixteenth century : " Mr R. B. Armstrong.

is "mentioned in the list of border clans, 1597" (Scott).

In Blaeu's map of Liddesdale, "Syid" is on the right bank of the Liddel, nearly opposite Mangerton, but a little higher up the stream.

A. John a Side has been taken in a raid[*] and carried prisoner to Newcastle. Sybill o the Side (his mother, 20) runs by the water with the news to Mangerton, where lords and ladies are ready to sell all their cattle and sheep for John's ransom. But Hobby Noble says that with five men he would fetch John back. The laird offers five thousand, but Hobby will take only five. They will not go like men of war, but like poor corn-dealers, and their steeds must be barefoot. When they come to Chollerton, on the Tyne, the water is up. Hobby asks an old man the way over the ford. The old man in three-score years and three has never seen horse go over except a horse of tree; meaning, we may suppose, a foot-bridge. In spite of the old man they find a way where they can cross in pairs. In Howbram wood they cut a tree of three-and-thirty foot, and with help of this, or without it, they climb to the top of the castle, where John is making his farewells to his mother, the lord of Mangerton, Much the Miller's son, and "Lord Clough." Hobby Noble calls to John to say that he has come to loose him; [†] John fears that it will not be done. Two men keep the horses, and four break the outer door (John himself breaking five doors within) and come to the iron door. The bell strikes twelve. Much the Miller fears they will be taken, and even John despairs of success. Hobby is not daunted; he files down the iron door and takes John out. John in his bolts can neither sit nor stride; Hobby ties the chains to John's feet, and says John rides like a bride. As they go through Howbram town John's horse stumbles, and

Much is again in a panic, which seems to show that John's commendation of him in 22 applies rather to his capacity as a thief than to his mettle. In Howbram wood they file off John's bolts at the feet. Now, says Hobby, leap over a horse! and John leaps over five. They have no difficulty in fording the Tyne on their return, and bring John home to Mangerton without further trouble.

It is Hobby Noble, then, that looses John in A, as he is said to have done in his own ballad, st. 27; but in B, C the Laird's Jock takes the lead, and Hobie plays a subordinate part. The Laird's Wat replaces the faint-hearted Much (who, however, is again found in the fragment D); Sybil of the Side becomes Downie (in D Dinah); the liberating party is but three instead of six.

The laird in B orders the horses to be shod the wrong way,[‡] whereas in A the shoes were taken off; and the party must not seem to be gentlemen, Heaven save the mark! but look like corn-cadgers, as in A. At Cholerford they cut a tree with fifteen nags, B 11, C with fifty nags, on each side, D twenty snags, and three long ones on the top; but when they come to Newcastle it proves to be too short, as the ladders are in the historical account of the release of Kinmont Willie. The Laird's Jock says they must force the gate. A proud porter withstands them; they wring his neck, and take his keys, B 13, 14, C 10 (cf. No 116, st. 65, No 119, 70, 71, and III, 95 note †). When they come to the jail, they let Jock know that they mean to free him; he is hopeless; the day is come he is to die; fifteen stone of iron (fifty, C) is laid on him. Work thou within and we without, says the Laird's Jock. One door they open and one they break. The Laird's Jock gets John o the Side on his back and takes him down the stair, declining help from Hobie. They put the prisoner on a horse, with the

---

[*] If the text is right, John (or was it Hobbie Noble?) had killed Peeter a Whifeild. See 'Hobbie Noble,' 9[4].

[†] "I am a bastard brother of thine," says Hobby in 26[3]; cf. 28[2]. But in B 7 and 'Hobie Noble,' 3, he is an Englishman, born in Bewcastle, and banished to Liddesdale.

[‡] This device, whether of great practical use or not, has much authority to favor it: Hereward, De Gestis Herwardi,

Michel, Chroniques A. Normandes, p. 81; Fulk Fitz-Warin, Wright, p. 92; Eustache le Moine, Michel, p. 55, vv. 1505 ff. (see Michel's note, p. 104 f.); Robert Bruce, Scotichronicon, Goodall, II, 226; other cases in Miss Burne's Shropshire Folk-Lore, pp. 16, 20, 93 note. It is repeated in 'Archie o Cawfield.'

same jest as before; the night is wet, as it was when Kinmont Willie was loosed, but they hie on merrily. They had no trouble in crossing the Tyne when they were coming, but now it is running like a sea. The old man had never seen it so big; the Laird Wat says they are all dead men. Set the prisoner on behind me, cries the gallant Laird's Jock, and they all swim through. Hardly have they won the other side when twenty Englishmen who are pursuing them reach the river. The land-sergeant says that the water will not ride, and calls to them to throw him the irons; they may have the rogue. The Laird's Jock answers that he will keep the irons to shoe his grey mare.* They bring John to Liddesdale, and there they free him of his irons, **B**. Now, John, they say, 'the day was come thou wast to die;' but thou 'rt as well at thy own fireside.

In **D** 5 they cut their mares' tails before starting, and never stop running till they come to Hathery Haugh. Tyne is running like a sea when they come to Chollerton, on their way to the rescue, as in **A**. They cut their tree in Swinburn wood. When they are to re-cross the river, Much says his mare is young and will not swim; the Laird's Jock (?) says, Take thou mine, and I 'll take thine.

The ballad is one of the best in the world, and enough to make a horse-trooper of any young borderer, had he lacked the impulse. In deference to history, it is put after Kinmont Willie, for it may be a free version of his story.

———◆———

A

Percy MS., p. 254; Hales and Furnivall, II, 203.

*   *   *   *   *   *   *

1   PEETER a Whifeild he hath slaine,
    And Iohn a Side, he is tane,
    And Iohn is bound both hand and foote,
    And to the New-castle he is gone.

2   But tydinges came to the Sybill o the Side,
    By the water-side as shee rann;
    Shee tooke her kirtle by the hem,
    And fast shee runn to Mangerton.

3 .   .   .   .
    The lord was sett downe at his meate;
    When these tydings shee did him tell,
    Neuer a morsell might he eate.

4   But lords, the wrunge their fingars white,
    Ladyes did pull themselues by the haire,
    Crying, Alas and weladay!
    For Iohn o the Side wee shall neuer see
      more.

5   ' But wee 'le goe sell our droues of kine,
    And after them our oxen sell,
    And after them our troopes of sheepe,
    But wee will loose him out of the New Cas-
      tell.'

6   But then bespake him Hobby Noble,
    And spoke these words wonderous hye;
    Sayes, Giue me fiue men to my selfe,
    And I 'le feitch Iohn o the Side to thee.

7   ' Yea, thou 'st haue fiue, Hobby Noble,
    Of the best *that* are in this countrye;
    I 'le giue thee fiue thousand, Hobby Noble,
    That walke in Tyuidale trulye.'

8   ' Nay, I 'le haue but fiue,' saies Hobby Noble,
    ' *That* shall walke away with mee;
    Wee will ryde like noe men of warr;
    But like poore badgers wee wilbe.'

9   They stuffet vp all their baggs with straw,
    And their steeds barefoot must bee;
    ' Come on, my bretheren,' sayes Hobby Noble,
    ' Come on your wayes, and goe with mee.'

10   And when they came to Culerton ford,
    The water was vp, they cold it not goe;
    And then they were ware of a good old man,
    How his boy and hee were at the plowe.

11   ' But stand you still,' says Hobby Noble,
    ' Stand you still heere at this shore,
    And I will ryde to yonder old man,
    And see w[h]ere the gate it lyes ore.

* Bay and grey should be exchanged in **B** 10, **C** 7.

12 'But Christ you saue, father!' quoth hee,
   'Crist both you saue and see!
Where is the way ouer this fford?
   For Christ's sake tell itt mee!'

13 'But I haue dwelled heere three score yeere,
   Soe haue I done three score and three;
I neuer sawe man nor horsse goe ore,
   Except itt were a horse of tree.'

14 'But fare thou well, thou good old man!
   The devill in hell I leave with thee,
Noe better comfort heere this night
   Thow giues my bretheren heere and me.'

15 But when he came to his brether againe,
   And told this tydings full of woe,
And then they found a well good gate
   They might ryde ore by two and two.

16 And when they were come ouer the fforde,
   All safe gotten att the last,
'Thankes be to God!' sayes Hobby Nobble,
   'The worst of our perill is past.'

17 And then they came into Howbrame wood,
   And there then they found a tree,
And cutt itt downe then by the roote;
   The lenght was thirty ffoote and three.

18 And four of them did take the planke,
   As light as it had beene a fflee,
And carryed itt to the New Castle,
   Where as Iohn a Side did lye.

19 And some did climbe vp by the walls,
   And some did climbe vp by the tree,
Vntill they came vpp to the top of the castle,
   Where Iohn made his moane trulye.

20 He sayd, God be with thee, Sybill o the Side!
   My owne mother thou art, quoth hee;
If thou knew this night I were here,
   A woe woman then woldest thou bee.

21 And fare you well, Lord Mangerton!
   And euer I say God be with thee!
For if you knew this night I were heere,
   You wold sell your land for to loose mee.

22 And fare thou well, Much, Millers sonne!
   Much, Millars sonne, I say;

Thou has beene better att merke midnight
   Then euer thou was att noone o the day.

23 And fare thou well, my good Lord Clough!
   Thou art thy ffathers sonne and heire;
Thou neuer saw him in all thy liffe
   But with him durst thou breake a speare.

24 'Wee are brothers childer nine or ten,
   And sisters children ten or eleven.
We neuer came to the feild to fight,
   But the worst of us was counted a man.'

25 But then bespake him Hoby Noble,
   And spake these words vnto him;
Saies, Sleepest thou, wakest thou, Iohn o the Side,
   Or art thou this castle within?

26 'But who is there,' quoth Iohn oth Side,
   '*That* knowes my name soe right and free?'
'I am a bastard-brother of thine;
   This night I am comen for to loose thee.'

27 'Now nay, now nay,' quoth Iohn o the Side;
   'Itt ffeares me sore *that* will not bee;
Ffor a pecke of gold and silver,' Iohn sayd,
   'In faith this night will not loose mee.'

28 But then bespake him Hobby Noble,
   And till his brother thus sayd hee;
Sayes, Four shall take this matter in hand,
   And two shall tent our geldings ffree.

29 Four did breake one dore without,
   Then Iohn brake fiue himsell;
But when they came to the iron dore,
   It smote twelue vpon the bell.

30 'Itt ffeares me sore,' sayd Much, the Miller,
   '*That* heere taken wee all shalbee;'
'But goe away, bretheren,' sayd Iohn a Side,
   'For euer alas! this will not bee.'

31 'But ffye vpon thee!' sayd Hobby Noble;
   'Much, the Miller, fye vpon thee!
'It sore feares me,' said Hobby Noble,
   'Man *that* thou wilt neuer bee.'

32 But then he had Fflanders files two or three,
   And hee fyled downe *that* iron dore,

And tooke Iohn out of the New Castle,
    And sayd, Looke thou neu*er* come heere
        more !

33 When he had him fforth of the New Castle,
    ' Away *with* me, Iohn, thou shalt ryde : '
    But eu*er* alas ! itt cold not bee ;
    For Iohn cold neither sitt nor stryde.

34 But then he had sheets two or three,
    And bound Iohns boults fast to his ffeete,
    And sett him on a well good steede,
    Himselfe on another by him seete.

35 Then Hobby Noble smiled and loug[h]e,
    And spoke these worde in mickle pryde :
    Thou sitts soe finely on thy geldinge
    That, Iohn, thou rydes like a bryde.

36 And when they came thorrow Howbra*i*ne
      towne,
    Iohns horsse there stumbled at a stone ;
    ' Out and alas ! ' cryed Much, the Miller,
    ' Iohn, thou 'le make vs all be tane.'

37 ' But fye vpon thee ! ' saies Hobby Noble,
    ' Much, the Millar, fye on thee !
    I know full well,' sayes Hobby Noble,
    ' Man *that* thou wilt neu*er* bee.'

38 And when the came into Howbrame wood,
    He had Fflanders files two or three
    To file Iohns bolts beside his ffeete,
    That hee might ryde more easilye.

39 Sayes, ' Iohn, now leape ou*er* a steede ! '
    And Iohn then hee lope ou*er* fiue :
    ' I know well,' sayes Hobby Noble,
    ' Iohn, thy ffellow is not aliue.'

40 Then he brought him home to Mangerton ;
    The lo*rd* then he was att his meate ;
    But when Iohn o the Side he there did see,
    For faine hee cold noe more eate.

41 He sayes, Blest be thou, Hobby Noble,
    That euer thou wast man borne !
    Thou hast feitched vs home good Iohn oth
      Side,
    That was now cleane ffrom vs gone.

———◆———

B

a. Caw's Poetical Museum, 1784, p. 145 ; "from an old
manuscript copy." b. Campbell's Albyn's Anthology, II,
28 ; "taken down from the recitation of Mr Thomas Short-
reed," of Jedburgh, "who learnt it from his father."

1 ' Now Liddisdale has ridden a raid,
    But I wat they had better staid at hame ;
    For Mitchel o Winfield he is dead,
    And my son Johnie is prisner tane.'
      With my fa ding diddle, la la dow diddle.

2 For Mangerton House auld Downie is gane ;
    Her coats she has kilted up to her knee,
    And down the water wi speed she rins,
    While tears in spaits fa fast frae her eie.

3 Then up and bespake the lord Mangerton :
    ' What news, what news, sister Downie, to
      me ? '
    ' Bad news, bad news, my lord Mangerton ;
    Mitchel is killd, and tane they hae my son
      Johnie.'

4 ' Neer fear, sister Downie,' quo Mangerton ;
    ' I hae yokes of oxen four and twentie,

My barns, my byres, and my faulds, a' weel
      filld,
    And I 'll part wi them a' ere Johnie shall
      die.

5 ' Three men I 'll take to set him free,
    Weel harnessd a' wi best o steel ;
    The English rogues may hear, and drie
    The weight o their braid swords to feel.

6 ' The Laird's Jock ane, the Laird's Wat twa,
    Oh, Hobie Noble, thou ane maun be ;
    Thy coat is blue, thou has been true,
    Since England banishd thee, to me.'

7 Now Hobie was an English man,
    In Bewcastle-dale was bred and born ;
    But his misdeeds they were sae great,
    They banishd him neer to return.

8 Lord Mangerton them orders gave,
    ' Your horses the wrang way maun a' be
      shod ;
    Like gentlemen ye must not seem,
    But look like corn-caugers gawn ae road.

9 'Your armour gude ye maunna shaw,
    Nor ance appear like men o weir;
As country lads be all arrayd,
    Wi branks and brecham on ilk mare.'

10 Sae now a' their horses are shod the wrang
        way,
    And Hobie has mounted his grey sae fine,
Jock his lively bay, Wat's on his white horse
        behind,
    And on they rode for the water o Tyne.

11 At the Choler-ford they a' light down,
    And there, wi the help o the light o the
        moon,
A tree they cut, wi fifteen naggs upo ilk side,
    To climb up the wa o Newcastle town.

12 But when they cam to Newcastle town,
    And were alighted at the wa,
They fand their tree three ells oer laigh,
    They fand their stick baith short and sma.

13 Then up and spake the Laird's ain Jock,
    'There's naething for't, the gates we maun
        force;'
But when they cam the gates unto,
    A proud porter withstood baith men and
        horse.

14 His neck in twa I wat they hae wrung,
    Wi hand or foot he neer playd paw;
His life and his keys at anes they hae tane,
    And cast his body ahind the wa.

15 Now soon they reach Newcastle jail,
    And to the prisner thus they call:
'Sleips thou, wakes thou, Jock o the Side?
    Or is thou wearied o thy thrall?'

16 Jock answers thus, wi dolefu tone:
    Aft, aft I wake, I seldom sleip;
But wha's this kens my name sae weel,
    And thus to hear my waes do[es] seik?

17 Then up and spake the good Laird's Jock,
    'Neer fear ye now, my billie,' quo he;
'For here's the Laird's Jock, the Laird's Wat,
    And Hobie Noble, come to set thee free.'

18 'Oh, had thy tongue, and speak nae mair,
    And o thy tawk now let me be!

For if a' Liddisdale were here the night,
    The morn's the day that I maun die.

19 'Full fifteen stane o Spanish iron
    They hae laid a' right sair on me;
Wi locks and keys I am fast bound
    Into this dungeon mirk and drearie.'

20 'Fear ye no that,' quo the Laird's Jock;
    'A faint heart neer wan a fair ladie;
Work thou within, we'll work without,
    And I'll be bound we set thee free.'

21 The first strong dore that they came at,
    They loosed it without a key;
The next chaind dore that they cam at,
    They gard it a' in flinders flee.

22 The prisner now, upo his back,
    The Laird's Jock's gotten up fu hie;
And down the stair him, irons and a',
    Wi nae sma speed and joy brings he.

23 'Now, Jock, I wat,' quo Hobie Noble,
    'Part o the weight ye may lay on me;'
'I wat weel no,' quo the Laird's Jock,
    'I count him lighter than a flee.'

24 Sae out at the gates they a' are gane,
    The prisner's set on horseback hie;
And now wi speed they've tane the gate,
    While ilk ane jokes fu wantonlie.

25 'O Jock, sae winsomely's ye ride,
    Wi baith your feet upo ae side!
Sae weel's ye're harnessd, and sae trig!
    In troth ye sit like ony bride.'

26 The night, tho wat, they didna mind,
    But hied them on fu mirrilie,
Until they cam to Cholerford brae,
    Where the water ran like mountains hie.

27 But when they came to Cholerford,
    There they met with an auld man;
Says, Honest man, will the water ride?
    Tell us in haste, if that ye can.

28 'I wat weel no,' quo the good auld man;
    'Here I hae livd this thretyyeirs and three,
And I neer yet saw the Tyne sae big,
    Nor rinning ance sae like a sea.'

29 Then up and spake the Laird's saft Wat,
   The greatest coward in the company;
'Now halt, now halt, we needna try 't;
   The day is comd we a' maun die!'

30 'Poor faint-hearted thief!' quo the Laird's
   Jock,
'There 'll nae man die but he that's fie;
I 'll lead ye a' right safely through;
   Lift ye the prisner on ahint me.'

31 Sae now the water they a' hae tane,
   By anes and twas they a' swam through;
'Here are we a' safe,' says the Laird's Jock,
   'And, poor faint Wat, what think ye now?'

32 They scarce the ither side had won,
   When twenty men they saw pursue;
Frae Newcastle town they had been sent,
   A' English lads, right good and true.

33 But when the land-sergeant the water saw,
   'It winna ride, my lads,' quo he;

Then out he cries, Ye the prisner may take,
   But leave the irons, I pray, to me.

34 'I wat weel no,' cryd the Laird's Jock,
   'I 'll keep them a', shoon to my mare they 'll
   be;
My good grey mare, for I am sure,
   She 's bought them a' fu dear frae thee.'

35 Sae now they 're away for Liddisdale,
   Een as fast as they coud them hie;
The prisner 's brought to his ain fire-side,
   And there o 's airns they make him free.

36 'Now, Jock, my billie,' quo a' the three,
   'The day was comd thou was to die;
But thou 's as weel at thy ain fire-side,
   Now sitting, I think, tween thee and me.'

37 They hae gard fill up ae punch-bowl,
   And after it they maun hae anither,
And thus the night they a' hae spent,
   Just as they had been brither and brither.

C

Percy Papers. " The imperfect copy sent me from Keel-
der, as collected from the memory of an old person by Mr
William Hadley, in 1775."

1 'Now Liddisdale has ridden a rade,
   But I wat they had a better staid at home;
For Michel of Windfield he is slain,
   And my son Jonny, they have him tane.'
      With my fa dow diddle, lal la dow didle

2 Now Downy 's down the water gone,
   With all her cots unto her arms,
And she gave never over swift running
   Untill she came to Mengertown.

3 Up spack Lord Mengertown and says,
   What news, what news now, sister Downy?
   what news hast thou to me?
'Bad news, bad news, Lord Mengertown,
   For Michal of Windfield he is slain, and my
   son Jonny they have him tain.'

4 Up speaks Lord Mengertown and says, I have
      four and twenty yoke of oxen,
   And four and twenty good milk-ky,

And three times as mony sheep,
   And I 'll gie them a' before my son Jonny die.

5 I will tak three men unto myself;
   The Laird's Jack he shall be ane,
The Laird's Wat another,
   For, Hobbie Noble, thow must be ane.

6 . . . .
      . .   thy cot is of the blue;
   For ever since thou cam to Liddisdale
   To Mengertown thou hast been true.

7 Now Hobbie hath mounted his frienged gray,
   And the Laird's Jack his lively bey,
And Watt with the ald horse behind,
   And they are away as fast as they can ride.

8 Till they are come to the Cholar foord,
   And there they lighted down;
And there they cut a tree with fifty nags upo
   each side,
   For to clim Newcastle wall.

9 And when they came there . . .
   It wad not reach by ellish three;

'There 's nothing for 't,' says the Laird's Jack,
'But forceing o New Castle gate.'

10 And when they came there,
There was a proud porter standing,
And I wat they were obliged to wring his
neck in twa.

11 Now they are come to New Castle gile:
Says they, Sleep thou, wakes thou, John o the
Side?

12 Says he, Whiles I wake, but seldom sleep;
Who is there that knows my name so well?

13 Up speaks the Laird's Jack and says,
. . . .
Here is Jack and Watt and Hobby Noble,
Come this night to set thee free.

14 Up speaks John of the Side and says,
O hold thy tongue now, billy, and of thy talk
now let me be;
For if a' Liddisdale were here this night,
The morn is the day that I must die.

15 For their is fifty stone of Spanish iron
Laid on me fast wee lock and key,
. . . .

. . . .

16 Then up speaks the Laird's Jack and says,
A faint heart neer wan a fair lady;
Work thou within and we without,
And this night we'el set the free.

17 The first door that they came at
They lowsed without either lock or key,
. . . .
And the next they brock in flinders three.

18 Till now Jack has got the prisner on his
back,
And down the tolbooth stair came he;
. . . .

. . . .

19 Up spack Hobby Noble and says,
O man, I think thou may lay some weight o
the prisner upo me;
'I wat weel no,' says the Laird's Jack,
'For I do not count him as havy as ane
poor flee.'

20 So now they have set him upo horse back,
And says, O now so winsomly as thou dost
ride,
Just like a bride, wee beth thy feet
Unto a side.

21 Now they are away wee him as fast as they
can heye,
Till they are come to the Cholar foord brae
head;
And they met an ald man,
And says, Will the water ride?

22 'I wat well no,' says the ald man,
'For I have lived here this thirty years and
three,
. . . .
And I think I never saw Tyne running so
like a sea.'

23 Up speaks the Laird's Watt and says —
The greatest coward of the companie —
. . . .
'Now, dear billies, the day is come that we
must a' die.'

24 Up speaks the Laird's Jack and says, Poor
cowardly thief,
They will never one die but him that 's fee;
. . . .
Set the prisner on behind me.

25 So they have tain the water by ane and two,
Till they have got safe swumd through.

26 Be they wan safe a' through,
There were twenty men pursueing them from
New Castle town.

27 Up speaks the land-sergant and says,
If you be gone with the rog, cast me my irons.

28 'I wat weel no,' says the Laird's Jack,
'For I will keep them to shew my good
grey mere;
. . . .
For I am sure she has bought them dear.'

29 'Good sooth,' says the Laird's Jack,
'The worst perel is now past.'

30 So now they have set him upo hoseback,
And away as fast as they could hye,

Till they brought him into Liddisdale,
And now they have set him down at his own
  fireside.

31 And says, now John,
The day was come that thou was to die,
But thou is full as weel sitting at thy own fire-
  side.

*   *   *   *   *   *   *   *   *

———◆———

D

Percy Papers. "These are scraps of the old song re-
peated to me by Mr Leadbeater, from the neighborhood of
Hexham, 1774."

1 LIDDISDAILL has ridden a raid,
  But they had better ha staid at hame;
For Michael a Wingfield he is slain,
  And Jock o the Side they hae taen.

2 Dinah 's down the water gane,
  Wi a' her coats untill her knes,

*   *   *   *   *   *   *   *
  To Mangerton came she.

3 .   *   *   *   *   *   *   *   *
  How now? how now? What 's your will
    wi me?

*   *   *   *   *   *   *   *
  *   *   *   *   *   *   *   *

4 To the New Castle h[e] is gane.

5 They have cuttin their yad's tailes,
  They 've cut them a little abune the hough,

And they nevir gave oer s . . . . d running
  Till they came to Hathery Haugh.

6 And when they came to Chollerton ford
  Tyne was mair running like a sea.
*   *   *   *   *   *   *   *
  *   *   *   *   *   *   *   *

7 And when they came to Swinburne wood,
  Quickly they ha fellen a tree;
Twenty snags on either side,
  And on the top it had lang three.

8 'My mare is young, she wul na swim,'
*   *   *   *   *   *   *   *
  *   *   *   *   *   *   *   *

9 .   *   *   *   *   *   *   *
  'Now Mudge the Miller, fie on thee!
Tak thou mine, and I 'll tak thine,
  And the deel hang down thy yad and
    thee.'

32 And now they are falln to drink,
  And they drank a whole week one day after
    another,
  And if they be not given over,
  They are all drinking on yet.

———◆———

A. 1¹. whifeild: *the first* i *may be* t: *Furnivall.*
6³, 7¹, 8¹. 5. 7³. 5000. 13¹, 13². 3.
13⁴. 3: *Percy queries,* tree? 15⁴. 2 and 2.
17⁴. 30: 3. 18¹. 4.
19². by. *MS. eaten through by ink: Furni-*
  vall.
20³. knight *for* night. 24¹. 9: or: 10:.
24². 10: or: 11:. *The first and the second*
  line might be transposed to the advantage
  of the rhyme.
25¹. hobynoble. 27⁴. infaith. 28³. 4.
28⁴. 2. 29¹. for 4. 29². 5. 29⁴. 12.
32¹, 34¹, 38². 2 or 3. 39². 5.

B. a. 13². wi' maun. 16⁴. do seik (= dos seik).
  34³. grey mare, *but* bay *in* 10³. b *has* bay *in*
    both.
b. *Burden after the first and the fourth line:*
  Wi my fa ding diddle, lal low dow diddle.
  1². hae staid. 1³, 3⁴. Michael.
  1⁴. And Jock o the Side. 2¹. Lady Downie has. 2⁴. the *wanting.*
  3¹. and spoke our gude auld lord.
  3⁴. and they hae taen.
  4². ousen eighty and three. 5¹. I 'll send.
  5². A' harneist wi the.
  5³. louns *for* rogues. 6, 7 *wanting.*

8¹. then *for* them.   8². maun be.

8³. ye mauna.   8⁴. the road.   9¹. you.

9². yet *for* ance.   9⁴. on each.

10¹. a' *wanting :* the wrang way shod.

10³. Jock 's on his.   11³. nogs on each.

13³. the gate untill.

14¹. twa the Armstrangs wrang.

14². Wi fute or hand.   14⁴. cast the.

15⁴. Art thou weary.

16⁴. to mese my waes does.   17¹. out and.

17². Now fear ye na.   17³. here are.

18¹. Now haud thy tongue, my gude Laird's Jock.

18². For ever alas this canna be.   18³. was.

19⁴. dark and.   20⁴. be sworn we 'll.

21⁴. a' to.   22². Jock has.   23 *wanting*.

28². I hae lived here threty.   29¹. out and.

29⁴. come.   30¹. cried the Laird's ane Jock.

30². but him.   30³. I 'll guide thee.

31¹. Wi that: they hae.   31³. quo the.

32¹. the other brae.   32⁴. lads baith stout.

33². says he.

33³. Then cried aloud, The prisoner take.

33⁴. the fetters.   34¹. quo the.

34³. bay mare.   34⁴. She has : right dear.

35¹. are onto.   36². is comd.   36³. ingle side.

36⁴. twixt thee.   37 *wanting*.

Scott changes Campbell's readings for Caw's now and then, and Caw's for his own.

C.   *Written continuously after the first stanza, and mostly without punctuation.   The end of a stanza is indicated after 3 by the insertion of the burden.   Some one, probably Percy, has attempted to show the proper separation by marks between the lines.   B has been taken as a guide for the divisions here adopted.*

9¹. And when they came there *ends* 8⁴ *in the MS.*

11². Jn° *for* John.

14². And of thy talk, etc., *is a line by itself in the MS.*

16³. And me.   19². *Two lines in the MS.*

20². *Perhaps* dos'.   20³. Unto *&.*

21²,³, 24, 28. The lines are run together.

31. And says now John the day *continues* 30⁴ *in the MS.*

D.   5³. s . . . . d, *illegible.*

7¹. *Perhaps* Swinburin.

9³. gang *has been changed to* hang, *or* hang *to* gang : *neither is quite intelligible.*

1, 2, 3 *are in the MS.* 2, 3, 1.

188

ARCHIE O CAWFIELD

A. 'Archie of the Cawfield,' communicated to Percy by Miss Fisher of Carlisle, 1780.

B. a. 'Archie of Cafield,'* Glenriddell MSS, XI, 14, 1791; Scott's Minstrelsy, 1802, I, 177. b. 'Archie of Ca'field,' Scott's Minstrelsy, 1833, II, 116.

C. 'The Three Brothers,' Buchan's Ballads of the North of Scotland, I, 111.

D. 'Billie Archie,' Motherwell's MS., p. 467, communicated by Buchan, and by him derived from James Nicol of Strichen; Motherwell's Minstrelsy, p. 335.

E. Macmath MS., p. 76, fragments.

F. Communicated by Mr J. M. Watson, of Clark's Island, Plymouth Harbor, Massachusetts.

B a was printed by Scott in the first edition of his Minstrelsy, with the omission of stanzas 11, 13, 15³⁻⁶ (15³,⁴, 16¹,², of the MS.), 17³,⁴ (18¹,² of the MS.), 27, 28, and with many editorial improvements, besides Scotticising

* Miswritten Capeld; again in 12⁴.

of the spelling.   Of B b, the form in which the ballad appears in the later edition of the Minstrelsy, the editor says that he has been enabled to add several stanzas obtained from recitation, of which he remarks that, "as they contrast the brutal indifference of the elder brother with the zeal and spirit of his associates, they add considerably to the dramatic effect of the whole." The new stanzas are ten, and partly displace some of a. None of the omitted stanzas are restored, and the other changes previously made are retained, except of course where new stanzas have been introduced.

This ballad is in all the salient features a repetition of 'Jock o the Side,' Halls playing the parts of Armstrongs. The Halls are several times complained of for reif and away-taking of ky, oxen, etc., in 1579. There is a Jok Hall of the Sykis, Jok Hall, called Paitti's Jok, a Jokie Hall in the Clintis, and the name Archie Hall occurs, which is, to be sure, a matter of very slight consequence. See the Register of the Privy Council of Scotland, III, 236 f., 354 f. Cafield is about a mile west of Langholm, in Wauchopedale. The Armstrongs had spread into Wauchopedale in the sixteenth century, and Jock Armstrong of the Caffeild appears in the Registers of the Privy Council, III, 43, 85, 133, 535. I have not found Halls of Caffeild, and hope not to do them injustice by holding that some friend or member of that sept has substituted their name, for the glory of the family.*

From a passage in A History of Dumfries, by William Bennet, in The Dumfries Monthly Magazine, III, 9 f., July, 1826 (kindly brought to my attention by Mr Macmath), there appears to have been a version of this ballad in which the Johnstones played the part of the Halls, or Armstrongs; but against their enemies the Maxwells, not against the public authority. A gentleman of Dumfries informed Bennet that he had "often, in early life, listened to an interesting ballad, sung by an old female chronicle of the town, which was founded upon the following circumstance. In some fray between the Maxwells and Johnstones, the former had taken the chief of the latter prisoner, and shut him up in the jail of Dumfries, in Lochmaben gate; for in Dumfries they possessed almost the same power as in the Stewartry of Annandale, Crichton of

* "Tradition says that his [Archie's] name was Archibald Armstrong." (Note at the end of the MS.)

Sanquhar, who was then hereditary sheriff of Nithsdale, being their retainer. In a dark night shortly afterwards, a trusty band of the Johnstones marched secretly into Dumfries, and, surprising the jail-keepers, bore off their chief, manacled as he then was, and, placing him behind one of their troopers, galloped off towards the head of Locher, there to regain the Tinwald side and strike into the mountains of Moffat before their enemies should have leisure to start in pursuit. A band of the Maxwells, happening to be in town, and instantly receiving the alarm, started in pursuit of the fugitives, and overtook them about the dawn of morning, just as they had suddenly halted upon the banks of the Locher, and seemed to hesitate about risking its passage; for the stream was much swollen by a heavy rain which had lately fallen, and seemed to threaten destruction to any who should dare to enter it. On seeing the Maxwells, however, and reflecting upon the comparative smallness of their own party, they plunged in, and, by dextrous management, reached in safety the opposite bank at the moment their pursuers drew up on the brink of that which they had left. The Johnstones had now the decided advantage, for, had their enemies ventured to cross, they could, while struggling against the current, have been easily destroyed. The bloodthirsty warriors raged and shook their weapons at each other across the stream; but the flood rolled on as if in mockery of their threatenings, and the one party at length galloped off in triumph, while the other was compelled to return in disgrace."

There are three Halls in A, B, C, brothers, of whom Archie is a prisoner, condemned to die. The actors in D are not said to be brothers or Halls; the prisoner is Archie, as before. In A, Jock the laird and Dickie effect the rescue, assisted by Jocky Ha, a cousin. Dick is the leader, Jocky Ha subordinate, and Jock the laird is the despondent and repining personage, corresponding to Much in Jock o the Side, A, D, and to the Laird's Wat, B, C. In B, Dick is the only brother named; he and Jokie Hall from Teviotdale effect the rescue; Jokie Hall is prominent, and Dickie has the second place; Archie the prisoner is faint-hearted, but, properly speaking, that part is omitted. Jokie Hall represents Hobie Noble, who is the leader in A of the other ballad, as Jokie is here in B, and also C; whereas Dick is the leader in A, D of the ballad before us, and represents the Laird's Jock, who is principal in B, C of the other. In B, C, only two are concerned in breaking the jail. In C, Dick loses heart, or has the place of Much; in D, Caff o Lin.

In A 38, Jock the laird says his colt will drown him if he attempts to cross the river; so Dick in B 23 (for it can be no other, though Dick is not named) and in C 24, and Caff o Lin in D 14. They have not two attacks of panic, as Much has in 'Jock o the Side,' A, with such excellent effect in bringing out Hobie Noble's steadiness. To make up for this, however, the laird has an unheroic qualm after all is well over, in A 44: the dearsome night has cost him Cawfield! It is a fine-spirited answer that Dick makes: 'Light o thy lands! we should not have been three brothers.' In one of the stanzas which Scott added in B b, "coarse Ca'field," that is, the laird again, is addressed (inconsecutively, as the verses stand) with the like reproach: 'Wad ye even your lands to your born billy!'

Archie is prisoner at Dumfries in A, B, at Annan in C; in D no place is mentioned. The route followed in A is Barnglish,* only two or three miles westward, where the horse-shoes are turned, 8; Bonshaw wood, where they take counsel, 10; over the Annan at Hoddam, 12, to Dumfries, 13; back by Bonshaw Shield, where they again take counsel, 29; over the Annan at Annan Holm (Annan Bank?), opposite Wamphray (where the Johnstones would be friendly), 31, to Cafield. Bonshaw Shield would have to be somewhere

between Dumfries and Annan Water; it seems to be an erroneous repetition of the Bonshaw on the left of the Annan.

The route in B is The Murraywhat, where shoes are turned, 6; Dumfries, 8; back by Lochmaben, 17; The Murraywhat, where they file off the shackles, 18; to and across the Annan. Here we may ask why the shoes are not changed earlier; for The Murraywhat is on the west side of the Annan. The route in C is not described; there is no reason, if they start from Cafield (see 23), why they should cross the Annan, the town being on the eastern side. All difficulties are escaped in D by giving no names.

The New England copy, F, naturally enough, names no places. There are three brothers, as in A, B, C, and Dickie is the leader. The prisoner, here called Archer, gives up hope when he comes to the river; his horse is lame and cannot swim; but horses are shifted, and he gets over. His spirits are again dashed when he sees the sheriff in pursuit.

A, 6², 14², 16⁴, 'for leugh o Liddesdale cracked he,' is explained by B a, 10², 'fra the laigh of Tiviotdale was he;' he bragged for lower Liddesdale, was from lower Liddesdale; it seems to be a sort of $εὔχετο εἶναι$. B b reads (that is, Scott corrects), 'The luve of Teviotdale was he.' B a, 16⁴, 'And her girth was the gold-twist to be,' is unintelligible to me, and appears to be corrupt. b reads, And that was her gold-twist to be, an emendation of Scott's, gold-twist meaning "the small gilded chains drawn across the chest of a war-horse." The three stanzas introduced in B b after 7 (the colloquy with the smith) are indifferent modern stuff. This and something worse are C 14, where Johnny Ha takes the prisoner on his back and *leads* the mare, the refreshments in 16, 17, and the sheriff in 19–21, 28, 29.

---

* Belonging to John's Christie, son of Johnie Armstrong. Christie of Barnglish was in Kinmont Willie's rescue. R.

B. Armstrong, Appendix, p. cii, No LXIV; T. J. Carlyle, The Debateable Land, p. 22. Tytler, IX, 437.

A

Communicated to Percy by Miss Fisher of Carlisle, 1780.

1 LATE in an evening forth as I went,
   'T was on the dawning of the day;
I heard two brothers make their moan,
   I listend well what they did say.

2 .   .   .   .   .   .
   .   .   .   .   .
We were three born brethren,
   There[s] one of us condemnd to die.

3 Then up bespake Jock the laird:
   ' If I had but a hundre men,
A hundred o th best i Christenty,
   I wad go on to fair Dumfries, I wad loose
      my brother and set him free.'

4 So up bespak then Dicky Ha,
   He was the wisest o the three:
' A hundre men we 'll never get,
   Neither for gold nor fee,
But some of them will us betray;
   They 'l neither fight for gold nor fee.

5 ' Had I but ten well-wight men,
   Ten o the best i Christenty,
I wad gae on to fair Dumfries,
   I wad loose my brother and set him free.

6 ' Jocky Ha, our cousin, 's be the first man '
   (For leugh o Liddesdale cracked he);
' An ever we come till a pinch,
   He 'll be as good as ony three.'

7 They mounted ten well-wight men,
   Ten o the best i Christenty;
   .   .   .   .   .   .
    .   .   .   .   .   .

8 There was horsing and horsing of haste,
   And cracking o whips out oer the lee,
Till they came to fair Barngliss,
   And they ca'd the smith right quietly.

9 He has shod them a' their horse,
   He 's shod them siccer and honestly,
And he as turnd the cawkers backwards oer,
   Where foremost they were wont to be.

10 And there was horsing, horsing of haste,
   And cracking of whips out oer the lee,

Until they came to the Bonshaw wood,
   Where they held their council privately.

11 Some says, We 'll gang the Annan road,
   It is the better road, said they;
Up bespak then Dicky Ha,
   The wisest of that company.

12 ' Annan road 's a publick road,
   It 's no the road that makes for me;
But we will through at Hoddam ford,
   It is the better road,' said he.

13 And there was horsing, horsing o haste,
   And cracking of whips out oer the lea,
Until they came to fair Dumfries,
   And it was newly strucken three.

14 Up bespake then Jocky Ha,
   For leugh o Liddesdale cracked he:
' I have a mare, they ca her Meg,
   She is the best i Christenty;
An ever we come till a pinch,
   She 'll bring awa both thee and me.'

15 ' But five we 'll leave to had our horse,
   And five will watch, guard for to be;
Who is the man,' said Dicky then,
   ' To the prison-door will go with me?'

16 Up bespak then Jocky Ha,
   For leugh o Liddesdale cracked he:
' I am the man,' said Jocky than,
   ' To the prison-door I 'll go with thee.'

17 They are up the jail-stair,
   They stepped it right soberly,
Until they came to the jail-door;
   They ca'd the prisoner quietly.

18 ' O sleeps thou, wakest thou, Archie, my
      billy?
   O sleeps thou, wakes thou, dear billy?'
' Sometimes I sleep, sometimes I wake;
   But who 's that knows my name so well?'
      [said he.]
' I am thy brother Dicky,' he says;
   ' This night I'm come to borrow thee.'

19 But up bespake the prisoner then,
   And O but he spake woefully!
' Today has been a justice-court,
   .   .   .   .   .

And a' Liddesdale were here the night,
  The morn 's the day at I 'se to die.'

20 'What is thy crime, Archie, my billy?
  What is the crime they lay to thee?'
'I brake a spear i the warden's breast,
  For saving my master's land,' said he.

21 'If that be a' the crime they lay to thee, Ar-
  chie, my billy,
  If that be the crime they lay to thee,
  Work thou within, and me without,
  And thro good strength I 'll borrow thee.'

22 'I cannot work, billy,' he says,
  'I cannot work, billy, with thee,
  For fifteen stone of Spanish iron
  Lyes fast to me with lock and key.'

23 When Dicky he heard that,
  'Away, thou crabby chiel!' cried he;
  He 's taen the door aye with his foot,
  And fast he followd it with his knee.
  Till a' the bolts the door hung on,
  O th' prison-floor he made them flee.

24 'Thou 's welcome, welcome, Archy, my billy,
  Thou 's aye right dear welcome to me;
  There shall be straiks this day,' he said,
  'This day or thou be taen from me.'

25 He 's got the prisoner on o his back,
  He 's gotten him irons and aw,
  .   .   .   .   .   .
    .   .   .   .   .   .

26 Up bespake then Jocky Ha,
  'Let some o th' prisoner lean on me;'
  'The diel o there,' quo Dicky than,
  'He 's no the wightdom of a flea.'

27 They are on o that gray mare,
  And they are on o her aw three,
  And they linked the irons about her neck,
  And galloped the street right wantonly.

28 'To horse, to horse,' then, 'all,' he says,
  'Horse ye with all the might ye may,
  For the jailor he will waken next;
  And the prisoners had a' wan away.'

29 There was horsing, horsing of haste,
  And cracking o whips out oer the lea,

Until they came to the Bonshaw Shield;
  There they held their council privately.

30 Some says, 'We 'll gang the Annan road;
  It is the better road,' said they;
  But up bespak than Dicky Ha,
  The wisest of that company:

31 'Annan road 's a publick road,
  It 's not the road that makes for me;
  But we will through at Annan Holme,
  It is the better road,' said he;
  'An we were in at Wamfrey Gate,
  The Johnstones they will a' help me.'

32 But Dicky lookd oer his left shoulder,
  I wait a wiley look gave he;
  He spied the leiutenant coming,
  And a hundre men of his company.

33 'So horse ye, horse ye, lads!' he said,
  'O horse ye, sure and siccerly!
  For yonder is the lieutenant,
  With a hundred men of his company.'

34 There was horsing, horsing of haste,
  And cracking o whips out oer the lea,
  Until they came to Annan Holme,
  And it was running like a sea.

35 But up bespake the lieutenant,
  Until a bonny lad said he,
  'Who is the man,' said the leiutenant,
  'Rides foremost of yon company?'

36 Then up bespake the bonny lad,
  Until the lieutenant said he,
  'Some men do ca him Dicky Ha,
  Rides foremost of yon company.'

37 'O haste ye, haste ye!' said the leiutenant,
  'Pursue with a' the might ye may!
  For the man had needs to be well saint
  That comes thro the hands o Dicky Ha.'

38 But up bespak Jock the laird,
  'This has been a dearsome night to me;
  I 've a colt of four years old,
  I wait he wannelld like the wind;
  If ever he come to the deep,
  He will plump down, leave me behind.'

39 'Wae light o thee and thy horse baith, Jock,
    And even so thy horse and thee!
Take thou mine, and I 'll take thine,
    Foul fa the warst horse i th' company!
I 'll cast the prisoner me behind;
    There 'll no man die but him that 's fee.'

40 There they 've a' taen the flood,
    And they have taen it hastily;
Dicky was the hindmost took the flood,
    And foremost on the land stood he.

41 Dicky 's turnd his horse about,
    And he has turnd it hastilly:
'Come through, come thro, my lieutenant,
Come thro this day, and drink wi me,
And thy dinner 's be dressd in Annan Holme,
    It sall not cost thee one penny.'

42 'I think some witch has bore the, Dicky,
    Or some devil in hell been thy daddy;

I woud not swum that wan water double-
    horsed,
    For a' the gold in Christenty.

43 'But throw me thro my irons, Dicky,
    I wait they cost me full dear;'
'O devil be there,' quo Jocky Hall,
    'They 'l be good shoon to my gray mare.'

44 O up bespoke then Jock the laird,
    'This has been a dearsome night to me;
For yesternight the Cawfield was my ain,
    Landsman again I neer sall be.'

45 'Now wae light o thee and thy lands baith,
    Jock,
    And even so baith the land and thee!
For gear will come and gear will gang,
    But three brothers again we never were to
    be.'

B

a. Glenriddell MSS, XI, 14, 1791, " an old West Border ballad." **b.** Scott's Minstrelsy, 1833, II, 116.

1 As I was walking mine alane,
    It was by the dawning o the day,
I heard twa brothers make their maine,
    And I listned well what they did say.

2 The eldest to the youngest said,
    'O dear brother, how can this be!
There was three brethren of us born,
    And one of us is condemnd to die.'

3 'O chuse ye out a hundred men,
    A hundred men in Christ[e]ndie,
And we 'll away to Dumfries town,
    And set our billie Archie free.'

4 'A hundred men you cannot get,
    Nor yet sixteen in Christendie;
For some of them will us betray,
    And other some will work for fee.

5 'But chuse ye out eleven men,
    And we ourselves thirteen will be,
And we 'ill away to Dumfries town,
    And borrow bory billie Archie.'

6 There was horsing, horsing in haste,
    And there was marching upon the lee,
Untill they came to the Murraywhat,
    And they lighted a' right speedylie.

7 'A smith, a smith!' Dickie he crys,
    'A smith, a smith, right speedily,
To turn back the cakers of our horses feet!
    For it is forward we woud be.'

8 There was a horsing, horsing in haste,
    There was marching on the lee,
Untill they came to Dumfries port,
    And there they lighted right manfulie.

9 'There['s] six of us will hold the horse,
    And other five watchmen will be;
But who is the man among you a'
    Will go to the Tolbooth door wi me?'

10 O up then spake Jokie Hall
    (Fra the laigh of Tiviotdale was he),
'If it should cost my life this very night,
    I 'll ga to the Tollbooth door wi thee.'

11 'O sleepst thou, wakest thow, Archie laddie?
    O sleepst thou, wakest thow, dear billie?'
'I sleep but saft, I waken oft,
    For the morn 's the day that I man die.'

12 'Be o good cheer now, Archie lad,
   Be o good cheer now, dear billie;
Work thow within and I without,
   And the morn thou 's dine at Cafield wi me.'

13 'O work, O work, Archie?' he cries,
   'O work, O work? ther 's na working for
      me;
For ther 's fifteen stane o Spanish iron,
   And it lys fow sair on my body.'

14 O Jokie Hall stept to the door,
   And he bended it back upon his knee,
And he made the bolts that the door hang on
   Jump to the wa right wantonlie.

15 He took the prisoner on his back,
   And down the Tollbooth stairs came he;
Out then spak Dickie and said,
   Let some o the weight fa on me;
'O shame a ma!' co Jokie Ha,
   'For he 's no the weight of a poor flee.'

16 The gray mare stands at the door,
   And I wat neer a foot stirt she,
Till they laid the links out oer her neck,
   And her girth was the gold-twist to be.

17 And they came down thro Dumfries town,
   And O but they came bonily!
Untill they came to Lochmaben port,
   And they leugh a' the night manfulie.

18 There was horsing, horsing in haste,
   And there was marching on the lee,
Untill they came to the Murraywhat,
   And they lighted a' right speedilie.

19 'A smith, a smith!' Dickie he cries,
   'A smith, a smith, right speedilie,
To file off the shakles fra my dear brother!
   For it is forward we wad be.'

20 They had not filtt a shakle of iron,
   A shakle of iron but barely three,
Till out then spake young Simon brave,
   'Ye do na see what I do see.

21 'Lo yonder comes Liewtenant Gordon,
   And a hundred men in his company:'

'O wo is me!' then Archie cries,
   'For I 'm the prisoner, and I must die.'

22 O there was horsing, horsing in haste,
   And there was marching upon the lee,
Untill they came to Annan side,
   And it was flowing like the sea.

23 'I have a colt, and he 's four years old,
   And he can amble like the wind,
But when he comes to the belly deep,
   He lays himself down on the ground.'

24 'But I have a mare, and they call her Meg,
   And she 's the best in Christendie;
Set ye the prisoner me behind;
   Ther 'll na man die but he that 's fae!'

25 Now they did swim that wan water,
   And O but they swam bonilie!
Untill they came to the other side,
   And they wrang their cloathes right drunk-
      [i]lie.

26 'Come through, come through, Lieutenant
      Gordon!
   Come through, and drink some wine wi me!
For ther 's a ale-house neer hard by,
   And it shall not cost thee one penny.'

27 'Throw me my irons, Dickie!' he cries,
   'For I wat they cost me right dear;'
'O shame a ma!' cries Jokie Ha,
   'For they 'll be good shoon to my gray mare.'

28 'Surely thy minnie has been some witch,
   Or thy dad some warlock has been;
Else thow had never attempted such,
   Or to the bottom thow had gone.

29 'Throw me my irons, Dickie!' he cries,
   'For I wot they cost me dear enough;'
'O shame a ma!' cries Jokie Ha,
   'They 'll be good shakles to my plough.'

30 'Come through, come through, Liewtenant
      Gordon!
   Come throw, and drink some wine wi me!
For yesterday I was your prisoner,
   But now the night I am set free.'

C

Buchan's Ballads of the North of Scotland, I, 111.

1 As I walked on a pleasant green —
    'T was on the first morning of May —
    I heard twa brothers make their moan,
    And hearkend well what they did say.

2 The first he gave a grievous sigh,
    And said, Alas, and wae is me!
    We hae a brother condemned to death,
    And the very morn must hanged be.

3 Then out it speaks him Little Dick,
    I wat a gude fellow was he:
    'Had I three men unto mysell,
    Well borrowed shoud Bell Archie be.'

4 Out it speaks him Johnny Ha,
    A better fellow by far was he:
    'Ye shall hae six men and yoursell,
    And me to bear you companie.

5 'Twa for keepers o the guard,
    See that to keep it sickerlie,
    And twa to come, and twa to gang,
    And twa to speak wi Bell Archie.

6 'But we winna gang like men o weir,
    Nor yet will we like cavalliers;
    But we will gang like corn-buyers,
    And we 'll put brechens on our mares.'

7 Then they are to the jail-house doors,
    And they hae tirled at the pin:
    'Ye sleep ye, wake ye, Bell Archie?
    Quickly rise, lat us come in.'

8 'I sleep not aft, I lie not saft;
    Wha 's there that knocks and kens my
        name?'
    'It is your brothers Dick and John;
    Ye 'll open the door, lat us come in.'

9 'Awa, awa, my brethren dear,
    And ye 'll had far awa frae me;
    If ye be found at jail-house door,
    I fear like dogs they 'll gar ye die.'

10 'Ohon, alas! my brother dear,
    Is this the hearkning ye gie to me?

If ye 'll work therein as we thereout,
    Well borrowd shoud your body be.'

11 'How can I work therein, therein,
    Or yet how can I work thereout,
    When fifty tons o Spanish iron
    Are my fair body round about?'

12 He put his fingers to the lock,
    I wat he handled them sickerlie,
    And doors of deal, and bands of steel,
    He gart them all in flinders flee.

13 He 's taen the prisoner in his arms,
    And he has kissd him cheek and chin:
    'Now since we 've met, my brother dear,
    There shall be dunts ere we twa twine.'

14 He 's taen the prisoner on his back,
    And a' his heavy irons tee,
    But and his marie in his hand,
    And straight to Annan gate went he.

15 But when they came to Annan water,
    It was roaring like the sea:
    'O stay a little, Johnny Ha,
    Here we can neither fecht nor flee.

16 'O a refreshment we maun hae,
    We are baith dry and hungry tee;
    We 'll gang to Robert's at the mill,
    It stands upon yon lily lee.'

17 Up in the morning the jailor raise,
    As soon 's 't was light that he coud see;
    Wi a pint o wine and a mess sae fine,
    Into the prison-house went he.

18 When he came to the prison-door,
    A dreary sight he had to see;
    The locks were shot, the doors were broke,
    And a' the prisoners won free.

19 'Ye 'll gae and waken Annan town,
    Raise up five hundred men and three;
    And if these rascals may be found,
    I vow like dogs I 'll gar them die.

20 'O dinna ye hear proud Annan roar,
    Mair loud than ever roard the sea?
    We 'll get the rascals on this side,
    Sure they can neither fecht nor flee.

21 'Some gar ride, and some gar rin,
      Wi a' the haste that ye can make;
  We 'll get them in some tavern-house,
      For Annan water they winna take.'

22 As Little Dick was looking round,
      All for to see what he could see,
  Saw the proud sheriff trip the plain,
      Five hundred men his companie.

23 'O fare ye well, my bonny wife,
      Likewise farewell, my children three!
  Fare ye well, ye lands o Cafield!
      For you again I neer will see.

24 'For well I kent, ere I came here,
      That Annan water woud ruin me;
  My horse is young, he 'll nae lat ride,
      And in this water I maun die.'

25 Out it speaks him Johnny Ha,
      I wat a gude fellow was he:
  'O plague upo your cowardly face!
      The bluntest man I eer did see.

26 'Gie me your horse, take ye my mare,
      The devil drown my mare and thee!

Gie me the prisoner on behind,
      And nane will die but he that 's fay.'

27 He quickly lap upo the horse,
      And strait the stirrups siccarlie,
  And jumpd upo the other side,
      Wi the prisoner and his irons tee.

28 The sheriff then came to the bank,
      And heard its roaring like the sea;
  Says, How these men they hae got ower,
      It is a marvel unto me.

29 'I wadna venture after them,
      For a' the criminals that I see;
  Nevertheless now, Johnny Ha,
      Throw ower the fetters unto me.'

30 'Deil part you and the fetters,' he said,
      'As lang as my mare needs a shee;
  If she gang barefoot ere they be done,
      I wish an ill death mat ye die.'

31 'Awa, awa, now Johnny Ha,
      Your talk to me seems very snell;
  Your mither 's been some wild rank witch,
      And you yoursell an imp o hell.'

———•———

D

Motherwell's MS., p. 467, "received in MS. by Buchan
from Mr Nicol, of Strichen, who wrote as he had learned
early in life from old people:" Motherwell's Minstrelsy,
p. 335.

1 'SEVEN years have I loved my love,
      And seven years my love 's loved me,
  But now to-morrow is the day
      That billy Archie, my love, must die.'

2 O then out spoke him Little Dickie,
      And still the best fellow was he:
  'Had I but five men and my self,
      Then we would borrow billy Archie.'

3 Out it spoke him Caff o Lin,
      And still the worst fellow was he:
  'You shall have five men and yourself,
      And I will bear you companye.'

4 'We will not go like to dragoons,
      Nor yet will we like grenadiers,

But we will go like corn-dealers,
      And lay our brechams on our meares.

5 'And twa of us will watch the road,
      And other twa will go between,
  And I will go to jail-house door,
      And hold the prisoner unthought lang.'

6 'Who is this at jail-house door,
      So well as they do know the gin?'
  'It 's I myself,' [said] him Little Dickie,
      'And oh sae fain 's I would be in!'

7 'Away, away, now, Little Dickie!
      Away, let all your folly be!
  If the Lord Lieutenant come on you,
      Like unto dogs he 'll cause you die.'

8 'Hold you, hold you, billy Archie,
      And now let all your folly be!
  Tho I die without, you 'll not die within,
      For borrowed shall your body be.'

9 'Away, away, now, Little Dickie!
　　Away, let all this folly be!
　An hundred pounds of Spanish irons
　　Is all bound on my fair bodie.'

10 Wi plough-culters and gavellocks
　　They made the jail-house door to flee;
　'And in God's name,' said Little Dickie,
　　'Cast you the prisoner behind me!'

11 They had not rode a great way off,
　　With all the haste that ever could be,
　Till they espied the Lord Lieutenant,
　　With a hundred men in 's companie.

12 But when they came to wan water,
　　It now was rumbling like the sea;
　Then were they got into a strait,
　　As great a strait as well could be.

13 Then out did speak him Caff o Lin,
　　And aye the warst fellow was he:
　'Now God be with my wife and bairns!
　　For fatherless my babes will be.

14 'My horse is young, he cannot swim;
　　The water 's deep, and will not wade;
　My children must be fatherless,
　　My wife a widow, whateer betide.'

15 O then cried out him Little Dickie,
　　And still the best fellow was he:
　'Take you my mare, I 'll take your horse,
　　And Devil drown my mare and thee!'

16 Now they have taken the wan water,
　　Tho it was roaring like the sea,
　And whan they got to the other side,
　　I wot they bragged right crouselie.

17 'Come thro, come thro now, Lord Lieutenant!
　　O do come thro, I pray of thee!
　There is an alehouse not far off,
　　We 'll dine you and your companye.'

18 'Away, away, now, Little Dickie!
　　O now let all your taunting be!
　There 's not a man in the king's army
　　That would have tried what 's done by thee.

19 'Cast back, cast back my fetters again!
　　Cast back my fetters! I say to thee;
　And get you gane the way you came,
　　I wish no prisoners like to thee.'

20 'I have a mare, she 's called Meg,
　　The best in all our low countrie;
　If she gang barefoot till they are done,
　　An ill death may your lordship die!'

———·———

E

Macmath MS, p. 76. "Taken down by me, September, 1886, from my aunt, Miss Jane Webster: heard by her in her youth, at Airds."

1 .　.　.　.　.　.　.
　.　.　.　.　.　.　.
　'We 'll awa to bonnie Dundee,
　　And set our brither Archie free.'

*　*　*　*　*　*　*

2 They broke through locks, and they broke
　　through bars,
　And they broke through everything that
　　cam in their way,

Until they cam to a big iron gate,
　And that 's where brother Archie lay.

[Little John says]

3 .　.　.　.　.　.　.
　'O brither Archie speak to me,
　.　.　.　.　.　.　.
　For we are come to set ye free.'

4 .　.　.　.　.　.　.
　'Such a thing it canna be,
　For there 's fifty pund o gude Spanish airn
　Atween my neckbane and my knee.'

F

Communicated by Mr J. M. Watson, of Clark's Island, Plymouth Harbor, Massachusetts, April 10, 1889, as remembered by him from the singing of his father.

1 As I walked out one morning in May,
　　Just before the break of day,
　I heard two brothers a making their moan,
　　And I listened a while to what they did say.
　　　I heard, etc.

2 'We have a brother in prison,' said they,
　　'Oh in prison lieth he !
　If we had but ten men just like ourselves,
　　The prisoner we would soon set free.'

3 'Oh no, no, no!' Bold Dickie said he,
　　'Oh no, no, no, that never can be !
　For forty men is full little enough
　　And I for to ride in their companie.

4 'Ten to hold the horses in,
　　Ten to guard the city about,
　Ten for to stand at the prison-door,
　　And ten to fetch poor Archer out.'

5 They mounted their horses, and so rode they,
　　Who but they so merrilie !
　They rode till they came to a broad river's side,
　　And there they alighted so manfullie.

6 They mounted their horses, and so swam they,
　　Who but they so merrilie !
　They swam till they came to the other side,
　　And there they alighted so manfullie.

7 They mounted their horses, and so rode they,
　　Who but they so merrilie !
　They rode till they came to that prison-door,
　　And then they alighted so manfullie.

8 .　.　.　.　.　.
　　.　.　.　.　.　.
　'For I have forty men in my companie,
　　And I have come to set you free.'

9 'Oh no, no, no!' poor Archer says he,
　· 'Oh no, no, no, that never can be !
　For I have forty pounds of good Spanish iron
　　Betwixt my ankle and my knee.'

10 Bold Dickie broke lock, Bold Dickie broke key,
　　Bold Dickie broke everything that he could see ;
　He took poor Archer under one arm,
　　And carried him out so manfullie.

11 They mounted their horses, and so rode they,
　　Who but they so merrilie !
　They rode till they came to that broad river's side,
　　And there they alighted so manfullie.

12 'Bold Dickie, Bold Dickie,' poor Archer says he,
　　'Take my love home to my wife and children three ;
　For my horse grows lame, he cannot swim,
　　And here I see that I must die.'

13 They shifted their horses, and so swam they,
　　Who but they so merrilie !
　They swam till they came to the other side,
　　And there they alighted so manfullie.

14 'Bold Dickie, Bold Dickie,' poor Archer says he,
　　'Look you yonder there and see ;
　For the high-sheriff he is a coming,
　　With an hundred men in his companie.'

15 'Bold Dickie, Bold Dickie,' High-sheriff said he,
　　'You're the damndest rascal that ever I see !
　Go bring me back the iron you've stole,
　　And I will set the prisoner free.'

16 'Oh no, no, no!' Bold Dickie said he,
　　'Oh no, no, no, that never can be !
　For the iron 't will do to shoe the horses,
　　The blacksmith rides in our companie.'

17 'Bold Dickie, Bold Dickie,' High-sheriff says he,
　　'You're the damndest rascal that ever I see !'
　'I thank ye for nothing,' Bold Dickie says he,
　　'And you're a damned fool for following me.'

A. *Written in long lines, without division into stanzas, excepting a few instances.*

1^1. folk I saw went. 13^2. And cracking, etc. 13^4. 3. 29^2. o whips, etc. 42^3. one water. 42^4. Xtenty.

43^1. *Perhaps we should read,* But throw me, throw me.

B. a. 12^4. Capeld. $15^{5,6}$ *are* $16^{1,2}$: $16^{1,2}$ *are* $16^{3,4}$: $16^{3,4}$, $17^{1,2}$: $17^{1,2}$, $17^{3,4}$: $17^{3,4}$, $18^{1,2}$: 18^{1-4}, 18^{3-6}.

b. 1^1. a-walking. 1^4. weel to what.

$2^{1,2}$. The youngest to the eldest said, Blythe and merrie how can we be.

2^3. were.

3–5.

'An ye wad be merrie, an ye wad be sad,
    What the better wad billy Archie be?
Unless I had thirty men to mysell,
    And a' to ride in my cumpanie.

'Ten to hald the horses' heads,
    And other ten the watch to be,
And ten to break up the strong prison
    Where billy Archie he does lie.'

Then up and spak him mettled John Hall
    (The luve of Teviotdale aye was he) ;
'An I had eleven men to mysell,
    It 's aye the twalt man I wad be.'

Then up bespak him coarse Ca'field
    (I wot and little gude worth was he) ;
'Thirty men is few anew,
    And a' to ride in our companie.'

6^2. on the. 6^3. the *wanting.*
6^4, 18^4. there *for* a'. 7^3. shoon *for* feet.
7^4. it 's unkensome.

After 7 :

'There lives a smith on the water-side
    Will shoe my little black mare for me,
And I 've a crown in my pocket,
    And every groat of it I wad gie.'

'The night is mirk, and it 's very mirk,
    And by candle-light I canna weel see ;
The night is mirk, and it 's very pit mirk,
    And there will never a nail ca right for me.'

'Shame fa you and your trade baith !
    Canna beet a good fellow by your mystery ;
But leeze me on thee, my little black mare !
    Thou 's worth thy weight in gold to me.'

8^1. a *wanting.* 8^2. And there : upon.
8^4. And they lighted there right speedilie.
9^1. There 's five. 9^2. will watchmen be.
9^3. ye a'. 10^1. spak him mettled John Hall.
10^2. of *wanting.* 11 *wanting.* 12^3. and we.
12^4. Ca'field. 13 *wanting.*
14^2. bended low back his knee.
14^3. that *wanting.* 14^4. Loup frae the.
15^2. stair. 15^{3-6} *wanting.*
16^1. The black mare stood ready at.
16^2. And *wanting :* I wot a foot neer stirred she.
16^3. Till *wanting.* 16^4. And that was her gold.
17^2. And wow : speedilie. $17^{3,4}$ *wanting.*
$18^{1,2}$. The live-lang night these twelve men rade, And aye till they were right wearie.
18^4. lighted there right.
19^1. then Dickie. 19^3. file the irons frae.
19^4. For forward, forward. 20^1. hadna filed.
20^3. When out and spak.
20^4. O dinna you see. 21^2. Wi a.
$21^{3,4}$. This night will be our lyke-wake night, The morn the day we a' maun die.
22^1. was mounting, mounting.
22^3. Annan water.

23, 24.

'My mare is young and very skeigh,
    And in o the weil she will drown me ; '
'But ye 'll take mine, and I 'll take thine,
    And sune through the water we sall be.'

Then up and spak him coarse Ca'field
    (I wot and little gude worth was he) :
'We had better lose ane than lose a' the lave ;
    We 'll lose the prisoner, we 'll gae free.'

'Shame fa you and your lands baith !
    Wad ye een your lands to your born billy ?
But hey ! bear up, my bonnie black mare,
    And yet thro the water we sall be.'

25^2. And wow. 25^4. drunkily.
26^3. there is an ale-house here.
26^4. thee ae. 27, 28 *wanting.*
29^1. irons, quo Lieutenant Gordon.
29^2. For *wanting.*
29^3. The shame a ma, quo mettled John Ha.
30^3. Yestreen I was.
30^4. now this morning am I free.

C. 5^2. Sae that ?

D. *Slightly changed by Motherwell in printing.* 2^1, 15^1, 18^2. Oh.

E. The ancient and veritable ballad of 'Bold Dickie,' as sung by A. M. Watson, and remembered and rendered by his son, J. M. Watson.

ADDITIONS AND CORRECTIONS

VOL. I.

1. Riddles Wisely Expounded.

P. 1 a. Guess or die. A grim kemp, an unco knicht, asks nine riddles of a young man ; all are guessed ; wherefore the kemp says it shall go well with him. Kristensen, Skattegraveren, II, 97 ff., 154 f., Nos 457, 458, 724; V, 49, No 454.

2. The Elfin Knight.

P. 6. Nigra, No 118, p. 483, ' Che mestiere è il vostro? ' A sempstress to make a shirt without stitch or seam; a mason to make a room without bricks and mortar.

7 b, second paragraph. Add: ' Store Fordringer,' Kristensen's Skattegraveren, II, 8, No 6.

3. The Fause Knight upon the Road.

P. 20. ' Kall og svein ungi,' Hammershaimb, Færøsk Anthologi, p. 283, No 36 (three versions), is another piece of this kind. The boat is in all the copies, Scottish, Swedish, and Färöe.

M. Gaidoz, Mélusine, IV, 207, cites a passage from Plutarch's life of Numa, c. 15, which is curiously like this ballad. The question being what is the proper expiatory sacrifice when divine displeasure has been indicated by thunderbolts, Zeus instructs Numa that it must be made with heads. Onions'? interposes Numa. With m e n 's — says Zeus. Hairs? suggests Numa. With LIVE — says Zeus. Sardines? puts in Numa.

4. Lady Isabel and the Elf-Knight.

P. 22. E is given from singing and recitation in Shropshire Folk-Lore, edited by Charlotte Sophia Burne, 1883–86, p. 548.

Mr W. H. Babcock has recently printed the following version, as sung in a Virginian family from "the corner between the Potomac and the Blue Ridge:" The Folk-Lore Journal, VII, 28.

WILSON.

1 Wilson, sitting in his room one day,
   With his true-love on his knee,
  Just as happy as happy could be, be, be,
  Just as happy as happy could be,

2 ' Do you want for fee? ' said she,
   ' Or do you want for gold?
  Or do you want a handsome ladye,
   More handsomer than me? '

3 ' I do want for fee,' said he,
   ' And I do want for gold;
  But I don't want a handsomer ladye,
   More handsomer than thee.

4 ' Go get some of your father's fee,
   And some of your father's gold,
  And two of the finest horses he has,
   And married we will be, be, be,
   And married we will be.'

5 She mounted on the milk-white steed,
   And he the iron-grey,
  And when they got to the broad waterside
   It was six hours and a half till day.

6 ' Get down, get down! my pretty fair maid,
   Get down, get down!' said he;
  ' For it's nine of the king's daughters I 've drowned here,
   And the tenth one you shall be.

7 ' Take off, take off that costly silk,
   For it is a costly thing ;
  It cost your father too much bright gold
   To drown your fair body in.

8 ' In stooping down to cut the cords round,
   Sing, Turn your back on me;'
  And with all the strength this lady had,
   She pushed him right into the sea.

9 ' Help me out! my pretty fair miss,
   O help me out!' said he,
  ' And we 'll go down to the Catholic church,
   And married we will be.'

10 ' Lie there, lie there! you false-hearted man,
   Lie there, lie there!' said she,
  ' For it 's nine of the king's daughters you 've drowned here,
   But the tenth one 's drowned thee.'

11 She mounted on the milk-white steed,
   And led the iron-grey,
  And when she got to her own father's house
   It was three hours and a half till day.

12 While she was walking in the room,
  Which caused the parrot to wake,
  Said he, What 's the matter, my pretty fair miss,
    That you 're up so long before day?

13 'Hush up, hush up! my pretty little parrot,
  Don't tell no tales on me;
  Your cage shall be lined with sweet may gold,
    And the doors of ivorie.'

14 While they were talking all of this,
  Which caused the old man to wake,
  Said, What 's the matter, my pretty little parrot,
    That you chatter so long before day?

15 'The cat she sprung against my cage,
  And surely frightened me,
  And I called for the pretty fair miss
    To drive the cat away.'

(1 lacks the third verse; in $2^{1.2}$, $3^{1.2}$, $4^{1.2}$, *fee* and *gold* should be exchanged; in 12^2, 14^2, *wake* should perhaps be *say*.)

26 b. Add these Danish copies: Kristensen, Skatte-graveren, I, 210 ff., Nos 1198, 1199. (Some stanzas of 'Kvindemorderen' are inserted in No 932, III, 177.)

29, 34 f. **O, P.** **O** is repeated in Lütolf, Sagen, Bräuche u. Legenden, u. s. w., p. 71, No 29, 'Schön Anneli;' **P** in Kurz, Aeltere Dichter, u. s. w., der Schweizer, I, 117. ' Schön Anneli,' Töbler, Schweizer-ische Volkslieder, II, 170, No 6, is an edited copy, mainly **O**, with use of **P**.

42. A variety of **A** in Revue des Traditions popu-laires, II, 293, communicated by A. Gittée, Chanson wallonne, de Bliquy, environs d'Ath.

42 f. A robber has his hand cut off by a girl. Later he marries her. The day after the marriage they go on horseback to see his relations. On coming to a wood he says, Do you remember the night when you cut off my hand? It is now my turn. He orders her to strip, threatening her with his dagger. When she is in her shift, she begs him to turn away his eyes, seizes the dagger, and cuts his throat. 'Le Voleur des Crêpes,' Sébillot, Contes pop. de la Haute-Bretagne, I, 341, No 62. (G. L. K.)

43 b. 'La Fille de Saint-Martin,' etc. Add: Rol-land, II, 171, obtained by Nérée Quépat.

44 a. Nigra, Canti popolari del Piemonte, 1888, p. 90 ff., No 13, 'Un' Eroina,' gives five unpublished ver-sions (**B–F**), 'La Monferrina,' **D**, being **A** of this large and beautiful collection.

Add also: Giannini, Canti p. della Montagna Luc-chese, 1889, p. 143, 'La Liberatrice;' Finamore, Storie p. abruzzesi, in Archivio, I, 207, 'Lu Pringepe de Meláne.'

44 b. 'Il Corsaro,' in Nigra's collection, No 14, p. 106 ff., with the addition of another version. For 'La

Monferrina incontaminata,' see Nigra again, 'La Fuga,' No 15, pp. 111 ff.; Finamore, in Archivio, I, 87, 'La Fandell' e lu Cavaljiere' (mixed).

Spanish, Nos 38–41, 'Venganza de Honor,' No 42, 'La Hija de la Viudina,' Pidal, Asturian Romances, have the incident of the girl's killing with his own sword or dagger a caballero who offers her violence. The weapon is dropped in the course of a struggle in all but No 40; in this the damsel says, Give me your sword, and see how I would wear it.

It is a commonplace for a pair on horseback to go a long way without speaking. So Pidal, pp. 114, 115, 130, 133, 135, 159:

Siete leguas anduvieron
  sin hablar una palabra.

60 a. **A.** Burden. The song in the Tea-Table Mis-cellany and the music are found in John Squair's MS., fol. 22, Laing collection, library of the Univer-sity of Edinburgh, handwriting about 1700. (W. Mac-math.

5. Gil Brenton.

P. 65 b. A ballad from Normandy, published by Le-grand, Romania, X, 367, III, which I am surprised to find that I have not mentioned, is a very interesting variety of 'Gil Brenton,' more particularly of the Da-nish 'Peder og Malfred.' It has the attempt at substi-tution (a sister); the wife acknowledges that she had been forced (par ses laquais les bras il me bandit); the husband reveals, and proves, that he was the ravisher. The beginning of the Norman ballad, which is lost, would probably have had the feature of the informa-tion given the husband by the shepherdess. Another French ballad, corrupted (environs de Redon, Ille-et-Vilaine), has this and the attempt to pass off the sister; the husband kills his wife. Music is ordered in the last stanza. Rolland, IV, 70. An Italian and a Breton ballad which begin like the Danish, but proceed differ-ently, are spoken of under 'Fair Janet,' No 64, II, 102 f.. See now Nigra's 'Fidanzata infedele' in his collection, No 34, p. 197.

6. Willie's Lady.

P. 82. 'Hustru og mands moder,' Kristensen, Skatte-graveren, I, 73, No 436, VII, 97, No 651; 'Barsel-kvinden,' the same, II, 10, No 7. (The tale, p. 83 b, is reprinted by inadvertence, I, 73, No 234.)

7. Earl Brand.

P. 88 a. **B.** "The copy principally used in this edi-tion of the ballad was supplied by Mr Sharpe." Scott. "The Douglas Tragedy was taught me by a nursery-maid, and was so great a favorite that I committed it to paper as soon as I was able to write." Sharpe's

Letters, ed. Allardyce, I, 135, August 5, 1802. Sharpe was born in 1781.

88 b. 'Hr. Ribolt,' Kristensen, Skattegraveren, VI, 17, No 257, is a good copy of ' Ribold og Guldborg.' It has the testaments at the end, like several others (see I, 144 b).

89–91 a. 'Stolt Hedelil,' Kristensen, Skattegraveren, I, 68, No 231, is another version of 'Hildebrand og Hilde,' closely resembling **G**. So is ' Den mislykkede flugt,' the same, VIII, 17, No 24, with the proper tragic conclusion. Both are inferior copies.

92 a and 489 b. Add: **K**, 'Kung Vallemo ock liten Kerstin,' Bergström ock Nordlander, Nyare Bidrag, o. s. v., p. 101.

95 b, 96, 489. I have omitted to mention the effect of *naming* on ' Clootie' in No 1, **C** 19, I, 5:

> As sune as she the fiend did name,
> He flew awa in a blazing flame.

The Alpthier loses its power to harm and appears in its proper shape, as this or that person, if called by name: Wuttke, Der deutsche Volksaberglaube der Gegenwart, 2d ed., p. 257. Were-wolves appear in their proper human shape on being addressed by their name: Wilhelm Hertz, Der Werwolf, pp. 61, 84, Ulrich Jahn, Volkssagen aus Pommern u. Rügen, pp. 386–7. An enchanted prince is freed when his name is pronounced: Meier, No 53, p. 188 and n., p. 311. "There was in the engagement a man [on the side of Hades] who could not be vanquished unless his name could be discovered:" Myvyrian Archaiology of Wales, I, 167, as quoted by Rhys, Celtic Mythology, Hibbert Lectures, p. 244. (G. L. K.)

96 ff., 489, II, 498. Plants from lovers' graves.

Add : **Portuguese**, Roméro, II, 157, two pines.

Italian, Nigra, No 18, ' Le due Tombe,' p. 125 ff..

A. The lovers are buried apart, one in the church, one outside, a pomegranate springs from the man's grave, an almond-tree from the maid's; they grow large enough to shade three cities ! **B**. A pomegranate is planted on the man's grave, a hazel on the maid's; they shade the city, and interlock. **C**. An almond-tree is planted on the maid's grave, and is cut down. **D**. The lovers are buried as in **A** (and **C**), an almond-tree grows from the grave of the man, a jessamine from the maid's. See also No 19, ' Fior di Tomba,' where, however, there is but one grave, which is to contain the maid's parents as well as her lover. The same phenomenon in the fragments **E**, **F**. ' Il Castello d'Oviglio,' Ferraro, Canti p. monferrini, No 45, p. 64, is another version of this ballad. A pomegranate springs up at the maid's feet, and shades three cities. Cf. ' La Mort des deux Amants,' Rolland, I, 247, No 125.

Roumanian. ' Ring and Handkerchief' also in Marienescu, Balade, p. 50 : cited in Mélusine, IV. 142.

97 b and 489 f., II, 498 a. **Bulgarian**, Miladinof, Bùlgarski narodni pěsni, p. 455, No 497, translated by Krauss, Sagen u. Märchen der Südslaven, II, 427; the youth as rose-tree, the maid as grape-vine. Cited by G. Meyer in Mélusine, IV, 87. **Little-Russian**, plane-trees of the two sexes ; cited by J. Karlowicz, *ib.*, 87 f. Ruthenian (mother attempting to poison her son's wife poisons both wife and son), Herrmann, Ethnologische Mittheilungen, 205 f. ; buried on different sides of the church, plants meet over the roof of the church, the mother tries to cut them down, and while so engaged is turned into a pillar.

Servian. Vuk, I, No 342, II, No 30; youth, pine, maid, grape-vine. Krasić, p. 105, No 21, p. 114, No 26; vine and pine, vine twines round pine. **Bulgarian**, Miladinof, p. 375, No 288, rose and vine. **Magyar-Croat**, Kurelac, p. 147, No 444, grape-vine and rose; No 445, youth behind the church, maid before, grape-vine and rose ; p. 154, No 454, rosemary and a white flower (aleluja?). (W. W.)

Breton. Mélusine, III, 453 f. A tree springs from over the young man's heart (but this is an insertion, and not quite beyond suspicion), a rose from the maid's. There is another version of the ballad at p. 182 f., in which une fleur dorée grows over the man's grave, nothing being said of his mistress's grave, or even of her death.

Italo-Albanian. Also in Vigo, Canti p. siciliani, 1857, p. 345, V, and the edition of 1870–74, p. 698 : cited in Mélusine, IV, 87.

Gaelic. Of Naisi (Naois) and Deirdre. King Conor caused them to be buried far apart, but for some days the graves would be found open in the morning and the lovers found together. The king ordered stakes of yew to be driven through the bodies, so that they might be kept asunder. Yew trees grew from the stakes, and so high as to embrace each other over the cathedral of Armagh. Transactions of the Gaelic Society of Dublin, I, 133, 1808.

In a Scotch-Gaelic version recently obtained, after Naois is put into his grave, Deirdre jumps in, lies down by his side and dies. The bad king orders her body to be taken out and buried on the other side of a loch. Firs shoot out of the two graves and unite over the loch. The king has the trees cut down twice, but the third time his wife makes him desist from his vengeance on the dead. The original in Transactions of the Gaelic Society of Inverness, XIII, 257 ; a translation in The Celtic Magazine, XIII, 138. (All of these cited by Gaidoz, Mélusine, IV, 12, and 62, note.)

8. Erlinton.

107 b, and also No 53, ' Young Beichan,' I, 463 b. For the Magyar ballads of Szilágyi and Hagymási, see Herrmann, Ethnologische Mittheilungen, cols 65–66; also col. 215. (A Transylvanian-Saxon ballad, a Roumanian tale, and a Transylvanian-Gipsy ballad, which follow, are of more or less questionable authenticity : Herrmann, col. 216.)

109. **C**, as well as 'Robin Hood and the Pedlars,' III, 170, are found in a manuscript pretended to be of about 1650, but are written in a forged hand of this century. I do not feel certain that the ballads themselves, bad as they are, are forgeries, and accordingly give the variations of Gutch's Robin Hood from the manuscript, not regarding spelling.

3^2. hold good. 3^4. thou will. 7^1. thus he. 10^1. Thorough : I run. 11^1. [kine ?] 16^2. while. 19^1. Ile. 21^2. he lent. 24^3. be not. 25^2. eldest. 28^1. leant. 29^2. wield. No "Finis" at the end.

9. The Fair Flower of Northumberland.

P. 113. The Servian hero Marko Kraljević is guilty of the same ingratitude. The daughter of the Moorish king releases him from a long captivity and makes him rich gifts. He promises to marry her and they go off together. During a halt the princess embraces him, and he finds her black face and white teeth so repulsive that he strikes off her head. He seeks to atone for his sin by pious foundations. Servian, Vuk, II, No 44 [Bowring, p. 86]; Croat, Bogišić, p. 16; Bulgarian, Miladinof, No 54, Kačanofskij, No 132. (W. W.)

10. The Twa Sisters.

P. 119. A Danish fragment of nine stanzas in Kristensen's Skattegraveren, IV, 161, No 509.

119 b. Three copies of the Swedish ballad are printed by Wahlfisk, Bidrag till Södermanlands äldere Kulturhistoria, No VI, p. 33 f..

124 b, 493 b, II, 498 b.

Rudchenko, South Russian Popular Tales, I, No 55: murder of brother revealed by a flute made from a reed that grows from his grave (No 56, flute from a willow). II, No 14, murder of a boy killed and eaten by his parents revealed by a bird that rises from his bones. (W. W.)

In a Flemish tale reported in the Revue des Traditions populaires, II, 125, Janneken is killed by Milken for the sake of a golden basket. The murder is disclosed by a singing rose. In 'Les Roseaux qui chantent' a sister kills her brother in a dispute over a bush covered with *pain-prunelle*. Roses grow from his grave. A shepherd, hearing them sing, cuts a stem of the rose-bush and whistles in it. The usual words follow. Revue des Traditions populaires, II, 365 ff. ; cf. Sébillot's long note, p. 366 ff.. Das Flötenrohr (two prose versions), U. Jahn, Volkssagen aus Pommern und Rügen, No 510, pp. 399–401. (G. L. K.

11. The Cruel Brother.

Pp. 142 b, 496 a. 'Rizzardo bello,' **E**, 'Ruggiero,' in Mazzatinti, Canti p. umbri, p. 286, Bologna, 1883.

143 b. 'Hr. Adelbrant og jomfru Lindelil,' with a

testament, again in Skattegraveren, I, 5, No I, and V, 17, No 12.

144 a, 496 b. Testaments. A wife who has been gone from home in pursuit of her pleasure is so beaten by her husband on her return that she dies. She leaves valuable legacies to her children and a rope to him. Nigra, No 25, 'Testamento della Moglie,' p. 159.

144 b. 'Ravens Arvegods,' Kristensen, Skattegraveren, II, 192 ff, Nos 774–78, and VIII, 209, No 810.

12. Lord Randal.

Pp. 152, 498. **Italian.** Add **G, H, I**, Nigra, No 26, **A, B, C**, 'Testamento dell' Avvelenato.' **J.** 'L'Amante avvelenato,' Giannini, No 27, p. 199. **K.** 'Mamma e Figghiolo,' Nerucci, in Archivio, II, 526.

154 b, 498 b. 'A megetétt János' in Arany and Gyulai, III, 7, Kriza.

156 a. 'Donna Lombarda' is now No 1 of Nigra's collection, where it is given in sixteen versions.

156 b, 499 a, II, 499 a. Slavic ballads of the sister that poisons her brother, etc. Add : Servian, Rajkowić, No 251. Compare, Bulgarian, Miladinof, No 262; Croat, Mažuranić, p. 152, Sammlung der Zeitschrift 'Naša Sloga,' II, No 158 ; Slovenian, Koritko, IV, No 47. — In Golovatsky, II, 584, a mother asks her son whether he supped with the widow. He supped with her, the witch. What did she cook for him ? A small fish. Where did she catch it, dress it ? Did she eat any of it? No, her head ached. Did the children ? No, they went to bed. — In Verković, No 317, p. 350, the fair Stana is poisoned by her husband's parents with a snake given as a fish. (W. W.)

A Ruthenian ballad of a mother attempting to poison her son's wife, and poisoning the pair, Herrmann, in Ethnologische Mittheilungen, col. 205 f.

A Slovak ballad of this sort in Kollár, Narodnie Zpiewanky, II, 32, translated by Herrmann, 91 f., No 3 ; and another version of the same col. 204 f., No 7. Roumanian versions, cols 206, 207 f., 209 f., Nos 9, 10, 12, the last with another story prefixed. See also Herrmann, col. 90, No 1, 92 f., Nos 4, 5, 208 f., No 11, for poisoning-ballads, and his references at the top of col. 211

13. Edward.

Pp. 167 b, 501 b. Another copy of 'Sven i Rosengård,' **F**, is printed by Aminson in Bidrag till Södermanlands äldere Kulturhistoria, No V, p. 12, eleven stanzas. The swain has killed his sister.

168 b. **Danish.** Four concluding stanzas (When ?) in Kristensen's Skattegraveren, II, 100, No 459.

14. Babylon, or, The Bonnie Banks o Fordie.

P. 170. Add :

F

"In Gipsy Tents," by Francis Hindes Groome, p. 143.

1 There were three sisters going from home,
    All in a lea and alony, oh
  They met a man, and he made them stand,
    Down by the bonny banks of Airdrie, oh.

2 He took the first one by the hand,
  He turned her round, and he made her stand.

3 Saying, Will you be a robber's wife?
  Or will you die by my penknife?

4 'Oh, I wont be a robber's wife,
  But I will die by your penknife.'

5 Then he took the second by her hand,
  He turned her round, and he made her stand.

6 Saying, Will you be a robber's wife?
  Or will you die by my penknife?

7 'Oh, I wont be a robber's wife,
  But I will die by your penknife.'

8 He took the third one by the hand,
  He turned her round, and he made her stand.

9 Saying, Will you be a robber's wife?
  Or will you die by my penknife?

10 'Oh, I wont be a robber's wife,
  And I wont die by your penknife.

11 'If my two brothers had been here,
  You would not have killed my sisters two.'

12 'What was your two brothers' names?'
  'One was John, and the other was James.'

13 'Oh, what did your two brothers do?'
  'One was a minister, the other such as you.'

14 'Oh, what is this that I have done?
  I have killed my sisters, all but one.

15 'And now I 'll take out my penknife,
  And here I 'll end my own sweet life.'

P. 173, II, 499. Add to the French ballad: 'Le Passage du Bois,' V. Smith, Chants p. du Velay et du Forez, Romania, X, 205; 'La Doulento,' Arbaud, I,

120; Poésies p. de la France, MS., IV, fol. 442, printed in Rolland, III, 55. With these belong 'La Ragazza assassinata,' Nigra, No 12, three versions, p. 85 ff. ; 'La Vergine uccisa,' Ferraro, Canti p. monferrini, p. 17.

15. Leesome Brand.

P. 179 a. **Danish**, II. 'Rosenelle og hr. Agervold,' Kristensen, Skattegraveren, I, 65, No 230, is an important variety of Redselille og Medelvold. Another version, III, 82, No 260, 'Rosenelle og hr. Medervold.' In both of these the knight is the lady's brother.

Swedish, II. A copy of 'Lilla Lisa och Herr Nedervall' is printed by Aminson, Bidrag, o. s. v., No 5, p. 17.

16. Sheath and Knife.

P. 185. Mr Macmath has found the following ballad in Motherwell's handwriting, on a half-sheet of paper. It is not completely intelligible (why should Lady Ann be left in the death-throe, to bury herself?), but undoubtedly belongs here. The first stanza agrees with **D**.

E

1 One king's daughter said to anither,
    Brume blumes bonnie and grows sae fair
  'We 'll gae ride like sister and brither.'
    And we 'll neer gae down to the brume nae mair

2 'We 'll ride doun into yonder valley,
  Whare the greene green trees are budding sae gaily.

3 'Wi hawke and hounde we will hunt sae rarely,
  And we 'll come back in the morning early.'

4 They rade on like sister and brither,
  And they hunted and hawket in the valley thegether.

5 'Now, lady, hauld my horse and my hawk,
  For I maun na ride, and I downa walk.

6 'But set me doun be the rute o this tree,
  For there hae I dreamt that my bed sall be.'

7 The ae king's dochter did lift doun the ither,
  And she was licht in her armis like ony fether.

8 Bonnie Lady Ann sat doun be the tree,
  And a wide grave was houkit whare nane suld be.

9 The hawk had nae lure, and the horse had nae
    master,
  And the faithless hounds thro the woods ran
    faster.

10 The one king's dochter has ridden awa,
  But bonnie Lady Ann lay in the deed-thraw.

Some words are difficult to read.
2. sae *wanting in burden* 1.
3¹. hunt? growis fair *in burden* 1.
5¹. *Originally* Oh hauld my bridle and stirrup.
    Ann, *or come, is written over* Oh.
9². faithless?

The lost knife here in **A** 8–10, **B** 5, and in ' Lee-
some Brand,' No 15, 36–41, appears in ' The
Squire of Low Degree,' Percy Folio, III, 267, vv.
117–126 (not in the version printed by Ritson and
by Hazlitt).

' Daughter,' he sais, ' ffor whose sake
  Is *that* sorrow *that* still thou makes ? '
' Ffather,' shee sais, ' as I doe see,
  Itt is ffor no man in Christentye ;
Ffather,' shee sayes, ' as I doe thriue,
  Itt is ffor noe man this day aliue.
Ffor yesterday I lost my kniffe ;
  Much rather had I haue lost my liffe ! '
' My daughter,' he sayes, ' if itt be but a blade,
  I can gett another as good made.'
' Ffather,' shee sais, ' there is neuer a smith but one
  That [can] smith you such a one.'

(G. L. K.)

17. Hind Horn.

P. 193 (2). ' Hr. Lovmand' in Kristensen's Skatte-
graveren, VIII, 49, No 115.

194 ff., 502 f., II, 499 b.

According to a Devonshire tradition given by Mrs
Bray, Traditions of Devonshire, II, 172 (II, 32, of the
new ed. of 1879, which has a fresh title, The Borders
of the Tamar and the Tavy), Sir Francis Drake, hav-
ing been abroad seven years, was apprised by one of
his devils that his wife was about to marry again.
He immediately discharged one of his great guns up
through the earth. The cannon-ball " fell with a loud
explosion between the lady and her intended bride-
groom," who were before the altar. In another ver-
sion, known to Southey and communicated by him to
Mrs Bray (as above, II, 174; new ed., II, 33, 34), the
marriage is broken off by a large stone (no doubt a gun-
stone) which falls on the lady's train as she is on her
way to church. Drake, in this version, returns in dis-
guise, but is recognized by his smile. See for various
stories of the same kind, ' Iouenn Kerménou,' Luzel,
Contes pop. de Basse-Bretagne, I, 416; ' Der todte

Schuldner,' Zingerle, Zeitschrift für deutsche Mytho-
logie, II, 367 ; ' De witte Swâne,' Woeste, the same,
III, 46, translated from the Markish dialect by Sim-
rock, ' Der gute Gerhard,' u. s. w., p. 75; Vernaleken,
Mythen u. Bräuche des Volkes in Oesterreich, p. 372;
Vernaleken, Kinder- u. Hausmärchen, No 54, p. 315 f.;
J. H. Knowles, Folk-Tales of Kashmir, p. 184 f.; Prym
u. Socin, Syrische Sagen u. Märchen, No 20, II, 72.
(G. L. K.)

Pp. 198 b, 502 b, II, 499 b. An Italian form of ' Le
Retour du Mari ' is ' Il Ritorno del Soldato,' Nigra, No
28b, p. 174.

Another Italian ballad has some of the points in the
story of Horn. A man goes off for seven years im-
mediately after marriage ; the woman looking out to-
wards the sea perceives a pilgrim approaching ; he asks
for charity, and makes what seems an impudent sugges-
tion, for which she threatens him with punishment. But
how if I were your husband ? Then you would give me
some token. He pulls out his wedding-ring from under
his cloak. ' Il finto [falso] Pellegrino,' Bernoni, ix, no
7, Ferraro, C. p. monferrini, p. 33, Giannini, p. 151
(nearly the same in Archivio, VI, 361); ' La Moglie
fedele,' Wolf, p. 59, No 81, Ive, p. 334; ' Bennardo,'
Nerucci, in Archivio, III, 44.

To the Portuguese ballads, I, 502 b, add ' A bella In-
fanta,' Bellermann, p. 100.

Add to the Polish ballads, p. 502 b : Roger, p. 13,
Nos 25, 26.

With the Slavic ballads belong : Servian, Vuk, III,
No 25; Bulgarian, Miladinof, Nos 65, 66, 111, 573, Ka-
čanovskiy, Nos 68–73, 112. (W. W.)

202 a. The three singing laverocks in **B** 3, **F** 4, (cf.
A 3,) are to be taken as curiosities of art. Artificial
singing-birds are often mentioned in the earlier times,
(by Sir John Mandeville for instance) : see Liebrecht,
Volkskunde, p. 89 f., No 5. Such birds, and artificially
hissing snakes, occur in the Great-Russian bylina of
Djuk Stepanović; cf. Wollner, Untersuchungen ü. d.
grossr. Volksepik, p. 134 f. (W. W.)

205. **G** would have been printed as it stands in
Kinloch MSS VII, 117, had the volume been in my
possession. The copy principally used in Kinloch's
Ancient Scottish Ballads, p. 138, was derived from the
editor's niece, M. Kinnear. Readings of another copy
are written in pencil over the transcript of the first in
places, and as the name " Christy Smith " is also writ-
ten at the beginning in pencil, it may be supposed that
these readings were furnished by this Christy Smith.
Kinloch adopted some of these readings into the copy
which appears in his book, and he introduced others
which seem to be his own. The readings of the Kin-
near copy not retained by Kinloch will now be given
under **a**, and those supplied (as may be supposed) by
Christy Smith under **b**.

a. 1². Whare was ye born ? or frae what cuntrie ?
  3¹. a gay gowd wand. 4¹. a silver ring.
  5¹. Whan that ring. 6¹. Whan that ring.

7². Till he cam. 8¹. Whan he lookit to.
8². Says, I wish. 9². Until he cam till.
10¹. met with. 10². It was with.
11¹. my puir auld man. 13¹. to me.
13². I'll lend you.
15¹. He has changed wi the puir auld.
16¹. What is the way that ye use. 16². words that.
18¹, 22¹. to yon town end.
19². your Hynde (your *struck out*).
23². his Hynde (his *struck out*).
24¹. he took na frae ane.
27¹. But he drank his glass. 27². Into it he dropt.
30². to your. 34². him evermair.
36¹. The red : oure them aw.
b. 1². in what. 2¹. greenwud's. 2². have left.
3¹. a silver wand.
4¹. And my love gave me a gay gowd ring.
5¹. As lang as that ring. 7². Till that he cam.
9². Until that. 10². a jolly beggar man.
15¹. *struck out in pencil.*
18¹. And whan : yonder down.
20². Unless it be frae. 22¹. yonder down.
24¹. But he wad tak frae nane. 34². for evermair.

19. King Orfeo.

P. 217. The first half of the Norse burden is more likely to have been, originally, what would correspond to the Danish Skoven [er] herlig grön, or, Skoven herlig grönnes. In the other half, grün forbids us to look for hjort in giorten, where we are rather to see Danish urt (English wort), Icelandic jurt: so that this would be, in Danish, Hvor urten hun grönnes herlig. (Note of Mr. Axel Olrik.)

20. The Cruel Mother.

P. 218 b. **Danish.** 'I dølgsmål,' Kristensen, Skattegraveren, V, 98, No 644 ; corrupted.

(**N, O** should be **O, P**, II, 500: see I, 504.)

Q

'The Cruel Mother,' Shropshire Folk-Lore, edited by Charlotte Sophia Burne, 1883–86, p. 540; "sung by Eliza Wharton and brothers, children of gipsies, habitually travelling in North Shropshire and Staffordshire, 13th July, 1885."

1 There was a lady, a lady of York,
  Ri fol i diddle i gee wo
  She fell a-courting in her own father's park.
  Down by the greenwood side, O

2 She leaned her back against the stile,
  There she had two pretty babes born.

3 And she had nothing to lap 'em in,
  But she had a penknife sharp and keen.

4 . . . .
  There she stabbed them right through the heart.

5 She wiped the penknife in the sludge ;
  The more she wiped it, the more the blood showed.

6 As she was walking in her own father's park,
  She saw two pretty babes playing with a ball.

7 'Pretty babes, pretty babes, if you were mine,
  I'd dress you up in silks so fine.'

8 'Dear mother, dear mother, [when we were thine,]
  You dressed us not in silks so fine.

9 'Here we go to the heavens so high,
  You'll go to bad when you do die.'

219 b, 504 a, II, 500 a. (**M** at this last place should be **O**.) Add : **P**, 'Die Schäferstochter,' as sung in the neighborhood of Köslin, Ulrich Jahn, Volkssagen aus Pommern u. Rügen, No 393, p. 310 f. (G. L. K.)

A Magyar-Croat ballad of the same tenor as the German, Kurelac, p. 150, No 451. (W. W.)

21. The Maid and the Palmer.

P. 228 a. **Danish.** Another copy of 'Synderinden' in Kristensen's Skattegraveren, VII, 81, No 505.

230 b. **Slavic.** Sušil, No 3, p. 2, closely resembles Moravian **A**; the woman is turned to stone. In a variant, p. 3, she has had fifty paramours, and again in a Little-Russian ballad, Golovatsky, I, 235, No 68, seventy. In this last, after shrift, the sinner is dissipated in dust. (W. W.)

231. **French.** Add: Victor Smith, Chants du Velay et du Forez, Romania IV, 439 (the conversion, p. 438); Chabaneau, Revue des Langues Romanes, XXIX, 265, 267, 268.

Catalan. 'Santa Magdalena,' conversion and penance, Miscelánea Folk-Lórica, 1887, p. 119, No 8. The Samaritan Woman, simply, p. 118, No 7.

22. St Stephen and Herod.

P. 234 a. 'Rudisar vísa' is now No 11 of Hammershaimb's Færøsk Anthologi, p. 39. There are two other copies.

237. 'Skuin over de groenelands heide,' Dykstra en van der Meulen, p. 121, resembles the Breton stories, but lacks the miracle of the capon.

239. Miracle of the roasted cock. Jesus visits a Jew on Easter Sunday and reproaches him with not believing in the resurrection. The Jew replies that Jesus

having been put to death it was as impossible for him to come to life again as it would be for a roast chicken which lies before them. Faith can do anything, says Jesus. The fowl comes to life and lays eggs; the Jew has himself baptized. Kostomarof, Monuments of the older Russian Literature, I, 217. In a note, a Red-Russian ballad is mentioned which seems to be identical with Golovatsky, II, 6, No 8. A young Jewess, who was carrying water, was the first to see Jesus after his resurrection. She tells her father, as he sits at meat, that the God of the Russians is risen from the dead. "If you were not my daughter, I would have you drowned," says the father. "The God of the Russians will not rise again till that capon flies up and crows." The capon does both; the Jew is turned to stone. (W. W.)

25. Willie's Lyke-Wake.

Pp. 247–49 a. **Danish.** Add : 'Vågestuen,' in Kristensen's Skattegraveren, II, 17, No 17; IV, 17, 115, Nos 26, 285.

249 b and 506 a. **Swedish.** Bröms Gyllenmärs' visbok has been printed in Nyare Bidrag, o. s. v., 1887, and the ballad of Herr Carl is No 77, p. 252. There is an imperfect copy in Bergström ock Nordlander, Nyare Bidrag, p. 102, No 9.

250. 'Il Genovese' is given in eight versions, one a fragment, by Nigra, No 41, p. 257.

250, 506 a, II, 502 a. **Bulgarian.** Stojan, who wants to carry off Bojana, does, at his mother's advice, everything to bring her within his reach. He builds a church, digs a well, plants a garden. All the maids come but her. He then feigns death ; she comes with flowers and mourns over him; he seizes her; the priest blesses their union. Miladinof, p. 294, No 185. An old woman, in a like case, advises a young man to feign death, and brings Bojana to see the body. "Why," asks Bojana, "do his eyes look as if they had sight, his arms as if they would lay hold of me, his feet as if ready to jump up?" "That is because he died so suddenly," says the beldam. The youth springs up and embraces Bojana. Verković, p. 334, No 304. A Magyar-Croat version begins like this last, but has suffered corruption : Kurelac, p. 148, No. 447. (W. W.)

28. Burd Ellen and Young Tamlane.

P. 256. The first paragraph was occasioned by a misprint in Motherwell (corrected at p. cv of his Introduction), and may be dropped. In Pitcairn's MS. it is noted that this fragment was obtained from Mrs Gamnell.

29. The Boy and the Mantle.

Pp. 268 ff., 507, II, 502.
On going to war a king gives each of his two daugh-

ters a rose. "Si vous tombez en faute, quoi que ce soit," says he, "vos roses flétriront." Both princesses yield to the solicitations of their lovers, so that the king, on returning, finds both roses withered, and is grieved thereat. Vinson, Folk-Lore du Pays Basque, p. 102.

Wer ein ausgelöschtes Licht wieder anblasen kann ist noch Jungfrau oder Junggeselle. Wer ein ganz volles Glas zum Munde führen kann, ohne einen Tropfen su verschütten, ist Junggeselle. Zingerle, Sitten der Tiroler, p. 35.

There is a shield in Perceval le Gallois which no knight can wear with safety in a tournament if he is not all that a knight should be, and if he has not, also, "bele amie qui soit loiaus sans trecerie." Several of Arthur's knights try the shield with disastrous results ; Perceval is more fortunate. (See 31805–31, 31865, 32023–48, 32410 ff., Potvin, IV, 45 ff..)

"Vpon the various earth's embrodered gowne
There is a weed vpon whose head growes downe;
Sow-thistle 'tis ycleepd; whose downy wreath
If any one can blow off at a breath,
We deeme her for a maid."

(William Browne, Britannia's Pastorals, Book I,
Song 4, Works, ed. Hazlitt, p. 103.)

Eodem auxilii genere, Tucciae virginis Vestalis, incesti criminis reae, castitas infamiae nube obscurata emersit. Quae conscientia certae sinceritatis suae spem salutis ancipiti argumento ausa petere est. Arrepto enim cribro, 'Vesta,' inquit, 'si sacris tuis castas semper admovi manus, effice ut hoc hauriam e Tiberi aquam et in aedem tuam perferam.' Audaciter et temere iactis votis sacerdotis rerum ipsa natura cessit. Valerius Maximus, viii, 1, 5. Cf. also Pliny, Hist. Nat., xxviii, 2 (3), and the commentators.

There was a (qualified) test of priestesses of Ge at Ægæ by drinking bull's blood, according to Pausanias, VIII, xxv, 8 ; cited by H. C. Lea, Superstition and Force, 3d ed., 1878, p. 236 f. (All the above by G. L. K.)

A spring in Apollonius Heinrichs von Neustadt blackens the hand of the more serious offender, but in a milder case only the ring-finger, "der die geringste Befleckung nicht erträgt." W. Grimm's Kleinere Schriften, III, 446. (C. R. Lanman.)

30. King Arthur and King Cornwall.

P. 274. That this ballad is a traditional variation of Charlemagne's Journey to Jerusalem and Constantinople, was, as I am convinced, too hastily said. See M. Gaston Paris's remarks at p. 110 f. of his paper, Les romans en vers du cycle de la Table Ronde (Extrait du tome xxx de l'Histoire Littéraire de la France). The king who thinks himself the best king in the world, etc., occurs (it is Arthur) also in the romance of Rigomer: the same, p. 92.

34. Kemp Owyne.

P. 307 b. Add 'Linden,' Kristensen's Skattegraveren, V, 50, No 455.

A princess in the form of a toad is kissed three times and so disenchanted : Revue des Traditions populaires, III, 475–6. A princess in the form of a black wolf must be kissed thrice to be disenchanted: Vernaleken, Alpensagen, p. 123. A princess persuades a man to attempt her release from enchantment. Three successive kisses are necessary. On the first occasion she appears as a serpent ; he can kiss her but once. The second attempt is also unsuccessful ; she appears as a salamander and is kissed twice. The third time she takes the form of a toad, and the three kisses are happily given. Luzel, in the Annuaire de la Soc. des Traditions populaires, II, 53. (G. L. K.)

35. Allison Gross.

P. 314 a. Hill-maid's promises. Add : 'Bjærgjomfruens frieri,' Kristensen's Skattegraveren, II, 100, No 460.

37. Thomas Rymer.

P. 319 b, last paragraph. In a Breton story, 'La Fleur du Rocher,' Sébillot, Contes pop. de la Haute-Bretagne, II, 31, Jean Cate addresses the fairy, when he first sees her, as the Virgin Mary. (G. L. K.)

39. Tam Lin.

P. 335. Mr Macmath has found an earlier transcript of B in Glenriddel's MSS, VIII, 106, 1789. The variations (except those of spelling, which are numerous) are as follows :

1². that wears. 1³. go. 3³. has snoded.
3⁵. is gaen. 5¹. had not. 6³. comes. 7². give.
8²⁴, 16²⁴, 35²⁴. above.
11¹. Out then: gray-head.
11³. And ever alas, fair Janet, he says.
13³. fair Janet. 13⁴, thow gaes. 14¹. If I.
14³. Ther'e not. 14⁴, 34⁴. bairns.
15⁴. ye nae, *wrongly*. 16⁵. she is on.
19². groves green. 20¹. Thomas. 20². for his.
20³. Whether ever. 22³. from the.
22⁴. Then from. 23³. The Queen o Fairies has.
23⁴. do dwell. 23⁶. Fiend, *wrongly*.
24¹. is a Hallow-een. 24³. And them.
25³. Amongst. 27¹. ride on. 27⁶. gave.
30⁴. wardly. 31³. Hald me. 34². then in.
37⁴. And there. 38³. Them that hes. 38⁴. Has.
40³·⁴. eyes. 41¹. I kend. 41³. I'd.

J.

'The Queen of the Fairies,' Macmath MS., p. 57.
"Taken down by me 14th October, 1886, from the reci-

tation of Mr Alexander Kirk, Inspector of Poor, Dalry, in the Stewartry of Kirkcudbright, who learned it about fifty years ago from the singing of David Ray, Barlay, Balmaclellan."

This copy has been considerably made over, and was very likely learned from print. The cane in the maid's hand, already sufficiently occupied, either with the Bible or with holy water, is an imbecility such as only the "makers" of latter days are capable of. (There is a cane in another ballad which I cannot at this moment recall.)

1 The maid that sits in Katherine's Hall,
    Clad in her robes so black,
  She has to yon garden gone,
    For flowers to flower her hat.

2 She had not pulled the red, red rose,
    A double rose but three,
  When up there starts a gentleman,
    Just at this lady's knee.

3 Says, Who's this pulls the red, red rose ?
    Breaks branches off the tree ?
  Or who's this treads my garden-grass,
    Without the leave of me ?

4 'Yes, I will pull the red, red rose,
    Break branches off the tree,
  This garden in Moorcartney wood,
    Without the leave o thee.'

5 He took her by the milk-white hand
    And gently laid her down,
  Just in below some shady trees
    Where the green leaves hung down.

6 'Come tell to me, kind sir,' she said,
    'What before you never told ;
  Are you an earthly man ? ' said she,
    'A knight or a baron bold?'

7 'I'll tell to you, fair lady,' he said,
    'What before I neer did tell ;
  I'm Earl Douglas's second son,
    With the queen of the fairies I dwell.

8 'When riding through yon forest-wood,
    And by yon grass-green well,
  A sudden sleep me overtook,
    And off my steed I fell.

9 'The queen of the fairies, being there,
    Made me with her to dwell,
  And still once in the seven years
    We pay a teind to hell.

10 'And because I am an earthly man,
    Myself doth greatly fear,

For the cleverest man in all our train
To Pluto must go this year.

11 'This night is Halloween, lady,
And the fairies they will ride ;
The maid that will her true-love win
At Miles Cross she may bide.'

12 'But how shall I thee ken, though, sir?
Or how shall I thee know,
Amang a pack o hellish wraiths,
Before I never saw?'

13 'Some rides upon a black horse, lady,
And some upon a brown,
But I myself on a milk-white steed,
And I aye nearest the toun.

14 'My right hand shall be covered, lady,
My left hand shall be bare,
And that's a token good enough
That you will find me there.

15 'Take the Bible in your right hand,
With God for to be your guide,
Take holy water in thy left hand,
And throw it on every side.'

16 She's taen her mantle her about,
A cane into her hand,
And she has unto Miles Cross gone,
As hard as she can gang.

17 First she has letten the black pass by,
And then she has letten the brown,
But she's taen a fast hold o the milk-white steed,
And she's pulled Earl Thomas doun.

18 The queen of the fairies being there,
Sae loud she's letten a cry,
'The maid that sits in Katherine's Hall
This night has gotten her prey.

19 'But hadst thou waited, fair lady,
Till about this time the morn,
He would hae been as far from thee or me
As the wind that blew when he was born.'

20 They turned him in this lady's arms
Like the adder and the snake ;
She held him fast; why should she not?
Though her poor heart was like to break.

21 They turned him in this lady's arms
Like two red gads of airn ;
She held him fast; why should she not?
She knew they could do her no harm.

22 They turned him in this lady's arms
Like to all things that was vile ;

She held him fast; why should she not?
The father of her child.

23 They turned him in this lady's arms
Like to a naked knight ;
She's taen him hame to her ain bower,
And clothed him in armour bright.

338 a, 507, II, 505 b.
A king transformed into a nightingale being plunged three times into water resumes his shape : Vernaleken, K.- u. H. Märchen, No 15, p. 79. In Guillaume de Palerne, ed. Michelant, v. 7770 ff., pp. 225, 226, the queen who changes the werewolf back into a man takes care that he shall have a warm bath as soon as the transformation is over ; but this may be merely the bath preliminary to his being dubbed knight (as in Li Chevaliers as Deus Espees, ed. Förster, vv. 1547–49, p. 50, and L'Ordene de Chevalerie, vv. 111–124, Barbazan-Méon, I, 63, 64). A fairy maiden is turned into a wooden statue. This is burned and the ashes thrown into a pond, whence she immediately emerges in her proper shape. She is next doomed to take the form of a snake. Her lover, acting under advice, cuts up a good part of the snake into little bits, and throws these into a pond. She emerges again. J. H. Knowles, Folk-Tales of Kashmir, p. 468 ff.. (G. L. K.)

339 b, II, 505 b.
Fairy salve and indiscreet users of it. See also Sébillot, Contes pop. de la Haute-Bretagne, II, 41, 42, cf. I, 122–3 ; the same, Traditions et Superstitions de la Haute-Bretagne, I, 89, 109 ; the same, Litt. orale de la Haute-B., pp. 19–23, 24–27, and note ; Mrs Bray, Traditions of Devonshire, 1838, I, 184–188, I, 175 ff. of the new ed. called The Borders of the Tamar and the Tavy ; "Lageniensis" [J. O'Hanlon], Irish Folk-Lore, Glasgow, n. d., pp. 48–49. In a Breton story a fairy gives a one-eyed woman an eye of crystal, warning her not to speak of what she may see with it. Disregarding this injunction, the woman is deprived of the gift. Sébillot, Contes pop. de la Haute-Bretagne, II, 24–25. (G. L. K.)

340. The danger of lying under trees at noon. "Is not this connected with the belief in a δαιμόνιον μεσημβρινόν (LXX, Psalm xci, 6)? as to which see Rochholz, Deutscher Unsterblichkeitsglaube, pp. 62 ff., 67 ff., and cf. Lobeck, Aglaophamus, pp. 1092–3." Kittredge, Sir Orfeo, in the American Journal of Philology, VII, 190, where also there is something about the dangerous character of orchards. Of processions of fairy knights, see p. 189 of the same.

Tam o Lin. Add : Tom a Lin, Robert Mylne's MS. Collection of Scots Poems, Part I, 8, 1707. (W. Macmath.)

40. The Queen of Elfan's Nourice.

P. 358 f., II, 505 b.
Mortal women as midwives to fairies, elves, water-

sprites, etc. Further examples are : Sébillot, Littérature orale de la Haute-Bretagne, pp. 19–23 ; the same, Traditions et Superstitions de la Haute-Bretagne, I, 89, 109 ; Vinson, Folk-Lore du Pays Basque, pp. 40, 41 ; Meier, Deutsche Sagen, u. s. w., aus Schwaben, pp. 16–18, 59, 62 ; Mrs Bray, Traditions of Devonshire, 1838, I, 184–188 (in the new ed., which is called The Borders of the Tamar and the Tavy, I, 174 ff.) ; " Lageniensis " [J. O'Hanlon], Irish Folk Lore, Glasgow, n. d., pp. 48, 49 ; U. Jahn, Volkssagen aus Pommern und Rügen, pp. 50, 72 ; Vonbun, Die Sagen Vorarlbergs, p. 16, cf. p. 6 ; Vernaleken, Alpensagen, p. 183. — Mortal woman as nurse for fairy child. Sébillot, Contes populaires de la Haute - Bretagne, I, 121. (G. L. K.)

41. Hind Etin.

P. 361 f. **Danish.** Add : 'Jomfruen og dværgen,' Kristensen, Skattegraveren, III, 98, No 393. A fragment of four stanzas, IV, 193, No 570.

364. **Danish.** Add : ' Angenede og havmanden,' Kristensen, Skattegraveren, III, 17, No 34.

42. Clerk Colvill.

P. 379 a, II, 506. Breton **F** is now printed entire (twenty-one stanzas instead of eleven) by Gaidoz, in Mélusine, IV, 301 ff. (The language appears to be Cornish.)

380, II, 506. **A** is printed by Rolland, III, 39 ; **P, Q**, *ib.*, p. 41, p. 37 ; **T**, *ib.*, p. 32, and in Revue des Traditions pop., I, 33 ; **X**, by Rolland, III, 45 ; **GG**, in Revue des T. p., III, 195. The five stanzas in Poés. pop. de la F., MS., VI, 491 **(MM)**, by Rolland, III, 36.

Add : **NN**, 38 verses, without indication of place, by C. de Sivry in Rev. des T. p., II, 24 ; **OO**, ' Le roi Léouis,' Haute-Bretagne, 60 verses, P. Sébillot, in the same, III, 196.

A Basque version, with a translation, in Rev. des Trad. pop., III, 198.

382 a. **Italian. C–F, H–K** now in Nigra's collection, ' Morte Occulta,' **A–G**, No 21, p. 142, in a different order. **C, D, E, F, H, I, K** are in Nigra now **A, C, D, E, G, F, B**. The fragment spoken of p. 383 b is now Nigra's No 22, p. 149, ' Mal ferito.' The tale which follows this is given p. 148 f.

384 a. There are two good Asturian versions in Pidal, ' Doña Alda,' Nos 46, 47, pp. 181, 183. The editor mentions a copy in the second number of Folk-Lore Betico-Extremeño, much injured by tradition, which is more like the Catalan than the Asturian versions.

43. The Broomfield Hill.

P. 392 b. Sleep-thorns.
Sleep-thorns, or something similar, occur in the West Highland tales. In a story partly reported by Camp-

bell, I, xci, " the sister put gath nimh, a poisonous sting or thorn, into the bed, and the prince was as though he were dead for three days, and he was buried. But Knowledge told the other two dogs what to do, and they scraped up the prince and took out the thorn, and he came alive again and went home." So in "The Widow's Son," Campbell, II, 296 : " On the morrow he went, but the carlin stuck a bior nimh, spike of hurt, in the outside of the door post, and when he came to the church he fell asleep." In another version of The Widow's Son, II, 297, a " big pin " serves as the " spike of hurt." Cf. the needle in Haltrich, Deutsche Volksmärchen aus dem Sachsenlande in Siebenbürgen, 3d ed., p. 141, No 32. (G. L. K.)

393. Italian ballad. Add : Righi, p. 33, No 96 ; Nigra, No 77, p. 393, ' La Bevanda sonnifera,' **A–H ;** Giannini, ' Il Cavaliere ingannato,' p. 157 ; Ferrari, Biblioteca di Lett. pop. italiana, I, 218, ' La bella Brunetta ;' Finamore, in Archivio, I, 89, La Fandell' e lu Cavaljiere (mixed) ; Nerucci, in Archivio, II, 524, ' La Ragazza Fantina ;' Julia, in Archivio, VI, 244, ' La 'nfantina e lu Cavalieri ; ' Rondini, in Archivio, VII, 189.

Ricordi, Canti p. Lombardi, No 9, ' La Moraschina,' gives the first half of the story, with a slight alteration for propriety's sake.

44. The Twa Magicians.

P. 400 a, II, 506 b. **E, F**, partly, in Revue des Traditions populaires, I, 104 f. (**Q** was previously cited as **J.**) **Q.** ' Les Transformations,' Avenay, Marne, Gaston Paris, in Rev. des Trad. pop., I, 98 ; **R**, Haute-Bretagne, Sébillot, the same, p. 100 ; **S**, Le Morvan, Tiersot, p. 102 ; **T**, Tarn-et-Garonne, the same, II, 208. **U.** ' Les Métamorphoses,' Finistère, Rolland, IV, 32, *c*; **V**, environs de Brest, the same, p. 33, *d.* **E** is printed by Rolland, IV, 30, *b.*

Italian. A ballad in Nigra, No 59, p. 329, ' Amore inevitabile.'

401 a. Vuk, I, No 602, is translated in Bowring's Servian Popular Poetry, p. 195.

In a Magyar-Croat ballad the lover advises the maid, who has been chidden by her mother on his account, if her mother repeats the scolding, to turn herself into a fish, then he will be a fisherman, etc. Kurelac, p. 309, XV, 2. (W. W.)

401 b, last two paragraphs.
Other specimens of the first kind (not in Köhler's note to Gonzenbach, II, 214) are :
Luzel, Annuaire de la Société des Traditions populaires, II, 56 ; Baissac, Folk-Lore de l'Île Maurice, p. 88 ff.; Wigström, Sagor ock Äfventyr uppt. i Skåne, p. 37 ; Luzel, Revue des Traditions populaires, I, 287, 288 ; Luzel, Contes pop. de Basse-Bretagne, II, 13, 41 ff., cf. 64–66 ; Vernaleken, Kinder- u. Hausmärchen, No 49, p. 277 ; Bladé, Contes pop. de la Gascogne, II, 26–36 ; Carnoy, Contes populaires picards, Romania, VIII, 227. Cf. also Ortoli, Contes pop. de l'Île de

Corse, pp. 27–29, and Cosquin's notes (which do not cite any of the above-mentioned places), Contes pop. de Lorraine, I, 105 ff.

Other specimens of the second kind:

Luzel, Contes pop. de Basse-Bretagne, II, 92–95, and note ; Haltrich, Deutsche Volksmärchen aus dem Sachsenlande, u. s. w., 3d ed., 1882, No 14, p. 52 f.. (G. L. K.)

402 a, last paragraph. "The pursuit in various forms by the witch lady has an exact counterpart in a story of which I have many versions and which I had intended to give if I had room. It is called ' The Fuller's Son,' ' The Cotter's Son,' and other names, and it bears a strong resemblance to the end of the Norse tale of ' Farmer Weathersky.' " Campbell, Pop. Tales of the West Highlands, IV, 297. (G. L. K.)

46. Captain Wedderburn's Courtship.

P. 415, note †. A version from Scotland has been printed in the Folk-Lore Journal, III, 272, ' I had six lovers over the sea.' (G. L. K.)

417, note †, II, 507 b.

The one stake with no head on it occurs also in Wolfdietrich B. The heathen, whom Wolfdietrich afterwards overcomes at knife-throwing, threatens him thus:

" Sihstu dort an den zinnen fünf hundert houbet stân,
Diu ich mit mînen henden alle verderbet hân ?
Noch stât ein zinne lære an mînem türnlîn :
Dâ muoz dîn werdez houbet ze einem phande sîn."

(St. 595, Jänicke, Deutsches Heldenbuch, III, 256.)

Two cases in Campbell's Pop. T. of the West Highlands. " Many a leech has come, said the porter. There is not a spike on the town without a leech's head but one, and may be it is for thy head that one is." (The Ceabharnach, I, 312.) Conall " saw the very finest castle that ever was seen from the beginning of the universe till the end of eternity, and a great wall at the back of the fortress, and iron spikes within a foot of each other, about and around it ; and a man's head upon every spike but the one spike. Fear struck him and he fell a-shaking. He thought that it was his own head that would go on the headless spike." (The Story of Conall Gulban, III, 202.) In Crestien's Erec et Enide, Erec overcomes a knight in an orchard. There are many stakes crowned with heads, but one stake is empty. Erec is informed that this is for his head, and that it is customary thus to keep a stake waiting for a new-comer, a fresh one being set up as often as a head is taken. Ed. by Bekker in Haupt's Ztschr., X, 520, 521, vv. 5732–66. (G. L. K.)

49. The Twa Brothers.

P. 435. There is a copy in Nimmo, Songs and Ballads of Clydesdale, p. 131, made from D, E, with half a dozen lines for connection.

437 b. It is E (not A) that is translated by Grundtvig ; and D by Afzelius, Grimm, Talvj, Rosa Warrens.

436 f. In one of the older Croat ballads Marko Kraljević and his brother Andrija, who have made booty of three horses, quarrel about the third when they come to dividing, and Marko fells Andrija with a stab. Andrija charges Marko not to tell their mother what took place, but to say that he is not coming home, because he has become enamored of a girl in a foreign country. Bogišić, p. 18, No 6. There is a Magyar-Croat variant of this, in which two brothers returning from war fall out about a girl, and the older (who, by the way, is a married man) stabs the younger. The dying brother wishes the mother to be told that he has staid behind to buy presents for her and his sisters. The mother asks when her son will come home. The elder brother answers, When a crow turns white and a withered maple greens. The (simple) mother gets a crow and bathes it daily in milk, and irrigates the tree with wine ; but in vain. Other Slavic examples of these hopeless eventualities : Little-Russian, Golovatsky, I, 74, No 30, 97, No 7, 164, No 12, 173, No 23, 229, No 59 ; II, 41, No 61, 585, No 18, 592, No 27 ; III, 12, No 9, 136, No 256, 212, No 78 ; Bohemian, Erben, p. 182, No 340 ; Polish, Roger, p. 3, No 2 ; Servian, Vuk, I, No 364, Herzegovine, p. 209, No 176, p. 322, No 332 ; Bulgarian, Verković, No 226 ; Dozon, p. 95 ; Magyar-Croat, Kurelac, p. 11, No 61, p. 130, No 430, p. 156, No 457 (and note), p. 157, No 459, p. 244, No 557. (W. W.)

53. Young Beichan.

P. 454. The modern street or broadside ballad L (see II, 508) is given from singing by Miss Burne, Shropshire Folk-Lore, p. 547.

459 b. The Färöe ballad (of which there are four copies) is printed in Hammershaimb's Færøsk Anthologi, p. 260, No 33, ' Harra Pætur og Elinborg.'

462 a. ' Gerineldo,' also in Pidal, Asturian Romances, p. 90 f.

462 a, b. ' Moran d' Inghilterra,' with a second version, in Nigra, No 42, p. 263.

———◆———

VOL. II.

55. The Carnal and the Crane.

P. 7 f., 510 a. Legend of the Sower. Catalan (with the partridge), Miscelánea Folk-Lórica, 1887, p. 115, No 6.

Moravian, Sušil, p. 19, No 16 ; Little-Russian, Golovatsky, II, 9, No 13. (W. W.)

56. Dives and Lazarus.

P. 10 b. ' Il ricco Epulone,' Nigra, No 159, p. 543, with Jesus and the Madonna for Lazarus.

Little-Russian, Golovatsky, II, 737, No 5; III, 263, No 1, and 267, No 2. Lazarus and the rich man are represented as brothers. (W. W.)

57. Brown Robyn's Confession.

P. 13 b, 5th line. A is not a manuscript of the 'fifteenth' century, but of the date 1590 or 1591. (Note of Mr Axel Olrik.)

59. Sir Aldingar.

Pp. 37–43. The first adventure of the fragmentary romance of Joufrois affords this story. Count Richard of Poitiers has a son Joufrois. The boy begs his father to send him to the English court, that King Henry may knight him. The English king receives him well, but he remains a *vaslet* for some time. The seneschal of the court endeavors to win the queen's *amisté*, but fails. He tells the king that he has seen the queen in bed with a kitchen-boy, and Henry swears that she shall hang or burn. The vaslet Joufrois offers to prove the seneschal a liar, and begs to be knighted for that purpose. Everybody thinks him mad to undertake battle with the seneschal, who is an unmatched man-at-arms : li biaus vaslet estoit enfens. The fight takes place at Winchester. Joufrois' sword is broken, but he picks up a piece of a huge lance and disables his adversary with a blow on the arm. Joufrois then threatens to cut off the felon's head if he does not retract, and as the seneschal prefers death to eating his words, this is done. Joufrois, Altfranzösisches Rittergedicht, ed. Hofmann und Muncker, vv. 91–631, pp. 3–18. (G. L. K.)

60. King Estmere.

Pp. 51, 510 b. Mr Kittredge has noted for me some twenty other cases in metrical romances of knights riding into hall.

Aiol's steed is stabled in the hall, Aiol et Mirabel, ed. Förster, vv. 1758–61, p. 51. So Gawain's horse in the 'Chevalier à l'Espée,' vv. 224–236, Méon, Nouveau Recueil, I, 134. Cf. 'Perceval le Gallois,' ed. Potvin, II, 255 ff., vv. 16803–42. In 'Richars li Biaus,' the hero evidently has his horse with him while at dinner in the hall of the robber-castle: ed. Förster, v. 3396, p. 93; cf. the editor's note, p. 182. In 'Perceval le Gallois,' a knight takes his horse with him into a bedchamber and ties him to a bed-post: ed. Potvin, III, 34, v. 21169 f.. Cf. Elie de Saint Gille, ed. Förster, pp. 377, 379, 380, vv. 2050–55, 2105, 2129–42. (G. L. K.)

61. Sir Cawline.

P. 56 b. Amadas, while watching at the tomb of Ydoine, has a terrific combat with a highly mysterious stranger knight, whom he vanquishes. The stranger then informs Amadas that Ydoine is not really dead, etc., etc. He gives sufficient evidence of his elritch character, and the author clinches the matter by speaking of him as "the maufé" (v. 6709). Amadas et Ydoine, ed. Hippeau, vv. 5465 ff., p. 189 ff.. (G. L. K.)

60. Stanzas 42 ff.. It might have been remarked that this feat of tearing out a lion's heart belongs to King Richard (see Weber's Romances, II, 44), hence, according to the romance, named Cœur de Lion, and that it has also been assigned to an humbler hero, in a well-known broadside ballad, 'The Honour of a London Prentice,' Old Ballads, 1723, I, 199 (where there are two lions for one).

63. Child Waters.

P. 83. **Italian.** 'Ambrogio e Lietta,' Nigra, No 35, p. 201. The Piedmontese ballad, though incomplete, has the rough behavior of the man to the woman, the crossing of the water, the castle and the mother, the stable, and twins brought forth in a manger.

84 b. **Danish.** 'Hr. Peders stalddreng,' Kristensen, Skattegraveren, I, 121, No 441; 'Liden Kirsten som stalddreng,' V, 98, No 645.

'Hr. Grönnevold,' Kristensen, Skattegraveren, VII, 49, No 177, is an imperfect copy of the second sort of Scandinavian ballads.

64. Fair Janet.

P. 103, note. 'La Fidanzata Infedele' is now No 34 of Nigra's collection. See above the addition to No 5, I, 65 b.

65. Lady Maisry.

P. 113 a, last paragraph. Burning, etc. See Amis e Amiloun (the French text), v. 364, p. 134, ed. Kölbing; Elie de St Gille, ed. Förster, vv. 2163–69, p. 381. Amadis de Gaule, Nicolas de Herberay, Anvers, 1573, I, 8 f., book 1, chap. 2, maid or wife; but Venice, 1552, I, 6 b, and Gayangos, Libros de Caballerias, p. 4, wife. (G. L. K.)

113 b. Only certain copies, and those perverted, of Grundtvig Nos 108, 109 have the punishment of burning for simple incontinence. This is rather the penalty for incest: cf. Syv, No 16, = Kristensen, I, No 70, II, No 49, = Grundtvig, No 292, and many other ballads. (Note of Mr Axel Olrik.)

Note §. 'Galanzuca,' 'Galancina,' Pidal, Asturian Romance, Nos 6, 7, pp. 92, 94, belong here. They have much of the story of 'Lady Maisry,' with a happy ending.

66. Lord Ingram and Chiel Wyet.

P. 127 a, 9th line of the second paragraph. A copy of 'Fru Margaretha' in Harald Oluffsons Visbok, Nyare Bidrag, o. s. v., p. 36, No 16, stanzas 21, 22.

127 b, 511 b. In a Breton ballad, Mélusine, III, 350 f., a priest jumps a table, at the cry of his sister, who is in a desperate extremity.

But the greatest achievements in this way are in Slavic ballads. A bride, on learning of her bridegroom's death, jumps over four tables and lights on the fifth, rushes to her chamber and stabs herself: Moravian, Sušil, p. 83. According to a variant, p. 84, note, she jumps over nine. A repentant husband who had projected the death of his wife, on hearing that she is still living, leaps nine tables without touching the glasses on them : Magyar-Croat, Kurelac, p. 184, No 479. (W. W.)

Mr Kittredge has given me many cases from romances.

127 b, note. Sword reduced to a straw: add Nigra, No 113, etc. ' Gerineldo:' add Pidal, Asturian Romances, Nos 3, 4, 5.

67. Glasgerion.

P. 137 b. 'Poter del Canto' is now No 47, p. 284, of Nigra's collection.

68. Young Hunting.

P. 142. A copy in A. Nimmo's Songs and Ballads of Clydesdale, 'Young Hyndford,' p. 155, is made up (with changes) from Scott, Kinloch, Buchan, Motherwell and Herd, **E, J, B, K, F, G**.

143, 512 a. Discovery of drowned bodies. See Revue des Traditions populaires, I, 56; Mélusine, III, 141.

69. Clerk Saunders.

P. 157. There are four copies of the Färöe 'Faðir og dóttir,' and Hammershaimb has printed a second (with but slight variations) in his Færøsk Anthologi: p. 253, No 31.

158. Spanish. Add: 'La Esposa infiel,' Pidal, Asturian Romances, No 33, p. 154.

71. The Bent Sae Brown.

P. 170. Nine versions of 'Jomfruens Brødre' in Kristensen's Skattegraveren, II, 145 ff., Nos 717-23, V, 81 ff., Nos 633, 634.

72. The Clerk's Twa Sons o Owsenford.

Pp. 174, 512. Add to the French ballads one from Carcassonne, first published in a newspaper of that place, Le Bon Sens, August 10, 1878, and reprinted in Mélusine, II, 212. The occurrence which gave rise to the ballad is narrated by Nigra, C. p. del Piemonte, p. 54 f., after Mary Lafon, and the Italian version is No 4 of that collection, 'Gli Scolari di Tolosa.' The ballad is originally French, the scene Toulouse.

73. Lord Thomas and Fair Annet.

P. 179 f. **D.** The Roxburghe copy of 'Lord Thomas and Fair Eleanor,' III, 554, is printed by Mr J. W. Ebsworth in the Ballad Society's edition of the Roxburghe Ballads, VI, 647. (Mr Ebsworth notes that the broadside occurs in the Bagford Ballads, II, 127; Douce, I, 120 v., III, 58 v., IV, 36; Ouvry, II, 38; Jersey, III, 88.) 'The Unfortunate Forrester,' Roxburghe, II, 553, is printed at p. 645 of the same volume. A copy from singing is given (with omissions) in Miss Burne's Shropshire Folk-Lore, 1883–86, p. 545; another, originally from recitation, in Mr G. R. Tomson's Ballads of the North Countrie, 1888, p. 82. Both came, traditionally, from print. Still another, from the singing of a Virginian nurse-maid (helped out by her mother), was communicated by Mr W. H. Babcock to the Folk-Lore Journal, VII, 33, 1889, and may be repeated here, both because it is American and also because of its amusing perversions.

THE BROWN GIRL

1 'O mother, O mother, come read this to me,
        And regulate all as one,
    Whether I shall wed fair Ellinter or no,
        Or fetch you the brown girl home.'

2 'Fair Ellinter she has houses and wealth,
        The brown girl she has none;
    But before I am charged with that blessing,
        Go fetch me the brown girl home.'

3 He dressed himself in skylight green,
        His groomsmen all in red;
    And every town as he rode through
        They took him to be some king.

4 He rode and he rode until he came to fair Ellinter's door;
        He knocked so loud at the ring;
    There was none so ready as fair Ellinter herself
        To rise and let him in.

5 'O what is the news, Lord Thomas?' she said,
        'O what is the news to thee?'
    'I've come to invite you to my wedding,
        And that is bad news to thee.'

6 'God forbid, Lord Thomas,' she said,
        'That any such thing should be!
    For I should have been the bride myself,
        And you should the bridegroom be.

7 'O mother, O mother, come read this to me,
        And regulate all as one,
    Whether I shall go to Lord Thomas' wed,
        Or stay with you at home.'

8 'Here you have one thousand friends,
   Where there you would but one;
So I will invite you, with my blessing,
   To stay with me at home.'

9 But she dressed herself in skylight red,
   Her waiting-maids all in green,
And every town as she rode through
   They took her to be some queen.

10 She rode and she rode till she came to Lord
     Thomas's door;
   She knocked so loud at the ring;
There was none so ready as Lord Thomas himself
   To rise and let her in.

11 He took her by her lily-white hand,
   He led her across the hall;
Sing, 'Here are five and twenty gay maids,
   She is the flower of you all.'

12 He took her by her lily-white hand,
   He led her across the hall,
He sat her down in a big arm-chair,
   And kissed her before them all.

13 The wedding was gotten, the table was set,
. . . .
   The first to sit down was Lord Thomas himself,
   His bride, fair Ellinter, by his side.

14 'Is this your bride, Lord Thomas?' she said;
   'If this is your bride, Lord Thomas, she looks
     most wonderfully dark,
When you could have gotten a fairer
   As ever the sun shone on.'

15 'O don't you despise her,' Lord Thomas said he,
   'O don't you despise her to me;
Yes, I like the end of your little finger
   Better than her whole body.'

16 The brown girl, having a little penknife,
   And being both keen and sharp,
Right between the long and short ribs,
   She pierced poor Ellinter's heart.

17 'O what is the matter, fair Ellinter,' said he,
   'That you look so very dark,
When your cheeks used to have been so red and
     rosy
As ever the sun shined on?'

18 'Are you blind, or don't you see,
   My heart-blood come trickling down to my
     knee?'

$3^{1.2}$. green *and* red *should be interchanged: cf.* 9.
13, 14. *Rearranged.* 15^1. said she.

---

181. Add to the French ballads, 'La Délaissée,' V.
Smith, Romania, VII, 82; Legrand, Romania, X, 386,
No 32; 'La triste Noce,' Thiriat, Mélusine, I, 189; and
to the Italian ballad, Nigra, No 20, p. 139, 'Danze e
Funerali.'

75. Lord Lovel.

P. 205 b. Other copies of 'Den elskedes Død'
('Kjærestens Død'), Kristensen, Skattegraveren, VII,
1, 2, Nos 1, 2; Bergström ock Nordlander, in Nyare
Bidrag, o. s. v., pp. 92, 100; and 'Olof Adelen,' p. 98,
may be added, in which a linden grows from the com-
mon grave, with two boughs which embrace.

Note. With the Scandinavian-German ballads be-
longs 'Greven og lille Lise,' Kristensen, Skattegra-
veren, V, 20, No 14.

206, 512 b. To the southern ballads which have a
partial resemblance may be added: French, Beaure-
paire, p. 52, Combes, Chants p. du Pays castrais, p.
139, Arbaud, I, 117, Victor Smith, Romania, VII, 83,
No. 32; Italian, Nigra, 'La Sposa morta,' No 17, p.
120 ff. (especially **D**).

215. I ought not to have omitted the σήματα by which
Ulysses convinces Penelope, Odyssey, xxiii, 181–208;
to which might be added those which convince Laertes,
xxiv, 328 ff. See also the romance of Don Bueso, Du-
ran, I, lxv:

¿ Qué señas me dabas
   Por ser conocida? et cét.

76. The Lass of Roch Royal.

II, 213. There is a version of this ballad in the Rox-
burghe collection, III, 488, a folio slip without imprint,
dated in the Museum Catalogue 1740. I was not aware
of the existence of this copy till it was printed by Mr
Ebsworth in the Roxburghe Ballads, VI, 609. He puts
the date of issue *circa* 1765. It is here given from the
original. Compare **H**.

THE LASS OF OCRAM

1 I built my love a gallant ship,
   And a ship of Northern fame,
And such a ship as I did build,
   Sure there never was seen.

2 For her sides were of the beaten gold,
   And the doors were of block-tin,
And sure such a ship as I built
   There sure never was seen.

3 And as she was a sailing,
   By herself all alone,
She spied a proud merchant-man,
   Come plowing oer the main.

4 'Thou fairest of all creatures
   Under the heavens,' said she,
'I am the Lass of Ocram,
   Seeking for Lord Gregory.'

5 'If you are the Lass of Ocram,
   As I take you for to be,
You must go to yonder island,
   There Lord Gregory you'll see.'

6 'It rains upon my yellow locks,
   And the dew falls on my skin;
Open the gates, Lord Gregory,
   And let your true-love in!'

7 'If you're the Lass of Ocram,
   As I take you not to be,
You must mention the three tokens
   Which passd between you and me.'

8 'Don't you remember, Lord Gregory,
   One night on my father's hill,
With you I swaft my linen fine?
   It was sore against my will.

9 'For mine was of the Holland fine,
   And yours but Scotch cloth;
For mine cost a guinea a yard,
   And yours but five groats.'

10 'If you are the Lass of Ocram,
    As I think you not to be,
You must mention the second token
    That passd between you and me.'

11 'Don't you remember, Lord Gregory,
    One night in my father's park,
We swaffed our two rings?
    It was all in the dark.

12 'For mine was of the beaten gold,
    And yours was of block-tin;
And mine was true love without,
    And yours all false within.'

13 'If you are the Lass of Ocram,
    As I take you not to be,
You must mention the third token
    Which past between you and me.'

14 'Don't you remember, Lord Gregory,
    One night in my father's hall,
Where you stole my maidenhead?
    Which was the worst of all.'

15 'Begone, you base creature!
    Begone from out of the hall!
Or else in the deep seas
    You and your babe shall fall.'

16 'Then who will shoe my bonny feet?
    And who will close my hands?
And who will lace my waste so small,
    Into a landen span?

17 'And who will comb my yellow locks,
    With a brown berry comb?
And who's to be father of my child
    If Lord Gregory is none?'

18 'Let your brother shoe your bonny feet,
    Let your sister close your hands,
Let your mother lace your waist so small,
    Into a landen span.

19 'Let your father comb your yellow locks,
    With a brown berry comb,
And let God be father of your child,
    For Lord Gregory is none.'

20 'I dreamt a dream, dear mother,
    I could wish to have it read;
I saw the Lass of Ocram
    A floating on the flood.'

21 'Lie still, my dearest son,
    And take thy sweet rest;
It is not half an hour ago,
    The maid passd this place.'

22 'Ah! cursed be you, mother!
    And cursed may you be,
That you did not awake me,
    When the maid passd this way!

23 'I will go down into some silent grove,
    My sad moan for to make;
It is for the Lass of Ocram
    My poor heart now will break.'

(4¹. Perhaps the reading was : The fairest, etc.)

Mr W. H. Babcock has printed a little ballad as
sung in Virginia, in which are two stanzas that be-
long to 'The Lass of Roch Royal:' The Folk-Lore
Journal, VII, 31.

'Come along, come along, my pretty little miss,
   Come along, come along,' said he,
'And seat yourself by me.'

'Neither will I come, and neither sit down,
  For I have not a moment's time;
For I heard that you had a new sweetheart,
  And your heart is no more mine.'

'It never was, and it never shall be,
  And it never was any such a thing;
For yonder she stands, in her own father's garden,
  The garden of the vine,
Mourning for her own true love,
  Just like I 've mourned for mine.'

I laid my head in a little closet-door,
  To hear what my true love had to say,
So that I might know a little of his mind
  Before he went away.

I laid my head on the side of his bed,
  My arms across his breast;
I made him believe, for the fall of the year,
  The sun rose in the west.

'I'm going away, I'm coming back again,
  If it is ten thousand miles;
It's who will shoe your pretty little feet?
  And who will glove your hand?
And who will kiss your red, rosy lips,
  While I'm in a foreign land?'

'My father will shoe my pretty little feet,
  My mother glove my hand,
My babe will kiss my red, rosy lips,
  While you're in a foreign land.'

Mr James Mooney, of the Bureau of Ethnology, obtained two very similar stanzas in the 'Carolina Mountains.'

'O who will shoe your feet, my dear?
  Or who will glove your hands?
Or who will kiss your red rosy cheeks,
  When I'm in the foreign lands?'

'My father will shoe my feet, my dear,
  My mother will glove my hands,
And you may kiss my red rosy cheeks
  When you come from the foreign lands.'

78. The Unquiet Grave.

P. 234.

E

'In Gipsy Tents,' by Francis Hindes Groome, 1880, p. 141, as sung by an old woman.

1 'Cold blows the wind over my true love,
  Cold blows the drops of rain;

I never, never had but one sweet-heart,
  In the green wood he was slain.

2 'But I'll do as much for my true love
  As any young girl can do;
I'll sit and I'll weep by his grave-side
  For a twelvemonth and one day.'

3 When the twelvemonth's end and one day was past,
  This young man he arose:
'What makes you weep by my grave-side
  For twelve months and one day?'

4 'Only one kiss from your lily cold lips,
  One kiss is all I crave;
Only one kiss from your lily cold lips,
  And return back to your grave.'

5 'My lip is cold as the clay, sweet-heart,
  My breath is earthly strong;
If you should have a kiss from my cold lip,
  Your days will not be long.'

6 'Go fetch me a note from the dungeon dark,
  Cold water from a stone;
There I'll sit and weep for my true love
  For a twelvemonth and one day.

7 'Go dig me a grave both long, wide and deep;
  I will lay down in it and take one sleep,
For a twelvemonth and one day;
  I will lay down in it and take a long sleep,
For a twelvemonth and a day.'

F

'Cold blows the wind,' Shropshire Folk-Lore, edited by Charlotte Sophia Burne, 1883–86, p. 542; "sung by Jane Butler, Edgmond, 1870–80."

'Cold blows the wind over my true love,
  Cold blow the drops of rain;
I never, never had but one true love,
  And in Camvĭle he was slain.

'I'll do as much for my true love
  As any young girl may;
I'll sit and weep down by his grave
  For twelve months and one day.'

But when twelve months were come and gone,
  This young man he arose:

'What makes you weep down by my grave?
I can't take my repose.'

'One kiss, one kiss, of your lily-white lips,
One kiss is all I crave ;
One kiss, one kiss, of your lily-white lips,
And return back to your grave.'

'My lips they are as cold as my clay,
My breath is heavy and strong ;
If thou wast to kiss my lily-white lips,
Thy days would not be long.

'O don't you remember the garden-grove
Where we was used to walk ?
Pluck the finest flower of them all,
'T will wither to a stalk.'

'Go fetch me a nut from a dungeon deep,
And water from a stone,
And white milk from a maiden's breast
[That babe bare never none].'

G

From the singing of a wandering minstrel and story-teller
of the parish of Cury, Cornwall. After the last stanza fol-
lowed "a stormy kind of duet between the maiden and her
lover's ghost, who tries to persuade the maid to accompany
him to the world of shadows." Hunt, Popular Romances
of the West of England, First Series, 1865, p. xvi.

1 'Cold blows the wind to-day, sweetheart,
    Cold are the drops of rain ;
  The first truelove that ever I had
    In the green wood he was slain.

2 ''T was down in the garden-green, sweetheart,
    Where you and I did walk ;
  The fairest flower that in the garden grew
    Is witherd to a stalk.

3 'The stalk will bear no leaves, sweetheart,
    The flowers will neer return,
  And since my truelove is dead and gone,
    What can I do but mourn ? '

4 A twelvemonth and a day being gone,
    The spirit rose and spoke :

    .   .   .   .
  .   .   .   .

5 'My body is clay-cold, sweetheart,
    My breath smells heavy and strong,

And if you kiss my lily-white lips
    Your time will not be long.'

235 f. Add: Gaspé, Les anciens Canadiens, Québec,
1877, I, 220 ff.; cited by Sébillot, Annuaire des Tradi-
tions populaires, 1887, p. 38 ff..
236. A 5, etc. So Nigra, 'La Sposa morta,' p. 122,
No 17, D 12 : ' Mia buca morta l'à odur di terra, ch'a
l'era, viva, di roze e fiur.'
Little-Russian tale, Trudy, II, 416, No 122. A
girl who is inconsolable for the death of her mother
is advised to hide herself in the church after vespers
on Thursday of the first week in Lent, and does so.
At midnight the bells ring, and a dead priest performs
the service for a congregation all of whom are dead.
Among them is the girl's godmother, who bids her be-
gone before her mother remarks her. But the mother
has already seen her daughter, and calls out, You here
too ? Weep no more for me. My coffin and my grave
are filled with your tears ; wretched it is to bathe in
them ! (W. W.) After this the mother's behavior is
not quite what we should expect. Cf. the tale in Gaspé,
just cited.

79. The Wife of Usher's Well.

II, 238.

C

'The Widow-Woman,' Shropshire Folk-Lore, edited by
Charlotte Sophia Burne, 1883–86, p. 541 ; "taken down by
Mr Hubert Smith, 24th March, 1883, from the recitation of
an elderly fisherman at Bridgworth, who could neither read
nor write, and had learnt it some forty years before from
his grandmother in Corve Dale."
"The West and South Shropshire folk say *far* for *fair*."

1 There was a widow-woman lived in far Scotland,
    And in far Scotland she did live,
  And all her cry was upon sweet Jesus,
    Sweet Jesus so meek and mild.

2 Then Jesus arose one morning quite soon,
    And arose one morning betime,
  And away he went to far Scotland,
    And to see what the good woman want.

3 And when he came to far Scotland,

    .   .   .   .   .   .

  Crying, What, O what, does the good woman
        want,
    That is calling so much on me ?

4 'It 's you go rise up my three sons,
    Their names, Joe, Peter, and John,
  And put breath in their breast,
    And clothing on their backs,
  And immediately send them to far Scotland,
    That their mother may take some rest.'

5 Then he went and rose up her three sons,
  Their names, Joe, Peter, and John,
And did immediately send them to far Scot-
  land,
  That their mother may take some rest.

6 Then she made up a supper so neat,
  As small, as small, as a yew-tree leaf,
  But never one bit they could eat.

7 Then she made up a bed so soft,
  The softest that ever was seen,
And the widow-woman and her three sons
  They went to bed to sleep.

8 There they lay; about the middle of the night,
  Bespeaks the youngest son:
'The white cock he has crowed once,
  The second has, so has the red.'

9 And then bespeaks the eldest son:
'I think, I think it is high time
  For the wicked to part from their dead.'

10 Then they laid [= led] her along a green road,
  The greenest that ever was seen,
Until they came to some far chaperine,
  Which was builded of lime and sand;
Until they came to some far chaperine,
  Which was builded with lime and stone.

11 And then he opened the door so big,
  And the door so very wide;
Said he to her three sons, Walk in!
  But told her to stay outside.

12 'Go back, go back!' sweet Jesus replied,
  'Go back, go back!' says he;
'For thou hast nine days to repent
  For the wickedness that thou hast done.'

13 Nine days then was past and gone,
  And nine days then was spent,
Sweet Jesus called her once again,
  And took her to heaven with him.

80. Old Robin of Portingale.

P. 240 a. 'Sleep you, wake you.' Add: 'Young
Beichan,' No 53, B 5; Duran, Romancero, I, 488, Nos
742, 743.

240 a, II, 513 a.
The very wicked knight Owen, after coming out of
St Patrick's Purgatory, lay in his orisons fifteen days
and nights before the high altar,

"And suþþe in is bare flech þe holi crois he nom,
And wende to þe holi lond, and holi mon bicom."

Horstmann, Altengl. Legenden, 1875, p. 174, vv. 611–
612; also p. 208, v. 697, and p. 209, v. 658. In a me-
diæval traveller's tale the Abyssinians are said to burn
the cross in their children's foreheads. "Vort wonent
da andere snoide kirsten in deme lande ind die heisch-
ent Ysini; wan man yr kinder douft ind kirsten macht,
dan broet der priester yn eyn cruce vor dat houft."
Ein niederrheinischer Bericht über den Orient, ed.
Röhricht u. Meier, in Zacher's Zeitschrift, XIX, 15.
(G. L. K.)

83. Child Maurice.

P. 272. F.
Mr Macmath has found the edition of 1755, and has
favored me with a copy. Substitute for F. a., p. 263:
Gill Morice, An Ancient Scottish Poem. Second Edi-
tion. Glasgow, Printed and sold by Robert and An-
drew Foulis, 1755. (Small 4°, 15 pages.) The copy
mentioned p. 263 b, note, is a reprint of this or of the
first edition; it has but two variations of reading. The
deviations from the text of 1755 will be put in the list
of things to be corrected in the print.

84. Bonny Barbara Allen.

P. 276. In Miss Burne's Shropshire Folk-Lore, 1883–
86, p. 543, there is a copy, taken from singing, which
I must suppose to be derived ultimately from print.

85. Lady Alice.

P. 279. The following version is printed by Mr G.
R. Tomson in his Ballads of the North Countrie, 1888,
p. 434, from a MS. of Mrs Rider Haggard.

GILES COLLINS AND LADY ANNICE

1 Giles Collins said to his own mother,
  'Mother, come bind up my head,
And send for the parson of our parish,
  For to-morrow I shall be dead.

2 'And if that I be dead,
  As I verily believe I shall,
O bury me not in our churchyard,
  But under Lady Annice's wall.'

3 Lady Annice sat at her bower-window,
  Mending of her night-coif,
When passing she saw as lovely a corpse
  As ever she saw in her life.

4 'Set down, set down, ye six tall men,
  Set down upon the plain,

That I may kiss those clay-cold lips
I neer shall kiss again.

5 'Set down, set down, ye six tall men,
That I may look thereon ;
For to-morrow, before the cock it has crowd,
Giles Collins and I shall be one.

6 'What had you at Giles Collins's burying?
Very good ale and wine?
You shall have the same to-morrow night,
Much about the same time.'

7 Giles Collins died upon the eve,
This fair lady on the morrow ;
Thus may you all now very well know
This couple died for sorrow.

Lt-Col. Prideaux has sent me this copy, from Fly-
Leaves, London, John Miller, 1854, Second Series, p. 98.

GILES COLLINS

1 Lady Annis she sat in her bay-window,
A-mending of her night-coif ;
As she sat, she saw the handsomest corpse
That ever she saw in her life.

2 'Who bear ye there, ye four tall men?
Who bear ye on your shouldyers ? '
'It is the body of Giles Collins,
An old true lovyer of yours.'

3 'Set 'n down, set 'n down,' Lady Annis she
said,
'Set 'n down on the grass so trim ;
Before the clock it strikes twelve this night,
My body shall lie beside him.'

4 Lady Annis then fitted on her night-coif,
Which fitted her wondrous well ;
She then pierced her throat with a sharp-edgd
knife,
As the four pall-bearers can tell.

5 Lady Annis was buried in the east church-yard,
Giles Collins was laid in the west,
And a lily grew out from Giles Collins's grave
Which touched Lady Annis's breast.

6 There blew a cold north-westerly wind,
And cut this lily in twain ;
Which never there was seen before,
And it never will again.

89. Fause Foodrage.

P. 298 a. Add, 'Sönnens hævn,' Kristensen, Skatte-
graveren, IV, 113, No 284 ; a fragment.

90. Jellon Grame.

Pp. 303 b, 513 b. Marvellous growth, etc. Ormr
Stórólfsson very early attained to a great size, and at
seven was a match for the strongest men : Flateyjar-
bok, I, 521, Fornmanna Sögur, III, 205, cited by Bugge
in Paul u. Braune's Beiträge, XII, 58. Wolfdietrich
gains one man's strength every year, and amazes every-
body in his infancy even. Wolfdietrich A, ed. Ame-
lung, sts 31, 38–41, 45, 233, 234, pp. 84, 85, 86, 108.
(Some striking resemblances to Robert le Diable.)
Cf. also Wigalois, ed. Pfeiffer, 36, 2 f., =Benecke,
1226 f. :

In einem jâre wuchs ez mêr
dan ein anderz in zwein tuo.

Elias (afterwards the Knight of the Swan), who is to
avenge his mother, astonishes by his rapid growth the
old hermit who brings him up :

"A! Dieu! dist ly preudons, à qui est cest enfant ?
Il est sy jouènes d'âge et s'a le corps sy grant :
S'il croist sy faitement, ce sera ung gaiant."

Chevalier au Cygne, ed. Reiffenberg, vv. 960–963, I, 45.
"The little Malbrouk grew fast, and at seven years old
he was as tall as a tall man." Webster, basque Le-
gends, 2d ed., p. 78 ; Vinson, Folk-Lore du Pays basque,
p. 81. The Ynca Mayta Ccapac "a few months after
his birth began to talk, and at ten years of age fought
valiantly and defeated his enemies." Markham, Nar-
ratives of the Rites and Laws of the Yncas, Hakluyt
Society, p. 83. A Tête-Rasée infant in four days grows
to the full size of man. Petitot, Traditions Indiennes
du Canada Nord-Ouest, pp. 241–243. (G. L. K.)

91. Fair Mary of Wallington.

P. 310. Danish. Another copy of 'Malfreds Død,'
Kristensen's Skattegraveren, VI, 195, No 804.

93. Lamkin.

P. 320. The negroes of Dumfries, Prince William
County, Virginia, have this ballad, orally transmitted
from the original Scottish settlers of that region, with
the stanza found in F (19) and T (15):

Mr Lammikin, Mr Lammikin,
oh, spare me my life,
And I'll give you my daughter Betsy,
and she shall be your wife.

"They sang it to a monotonous measure." (Mrs Du-
lany.)

94. Young Waters.

P. 343. By the kindness of Mr Macmath, I have now a copy of the original edition.

Young Waters, an Ancient Scottish Poem, never before printed. Glasgow, Printed and sold by Robert and Andrew Foulis, 1755. (Small 4°, 8 pages.) The few differences of reading will be given with corrections to be made in the print.

95. The Maid Freed from the Gallows.

P. 346. Mr Alfred Nutt has communicated to the Folk-Lore Journal, VI, 144, 1888, the outline of a ballad in which, as in some versions of the European continent, the man has the place of the maid. But this may be a modern turn to the story, arising from the disposition to mitigate a tragic tale. The ballad was obtained "from a relative of Dr Birbeck Hill's, in whose family it is traditional. Mother, father, and brethren all refuse him aid, but his sweetheart is kinder, and buys him off." For the burden see C 6, which, as well as B 12, might better have been printed as such.

1 'Hold up, hold up your hands so high !
   Hold up your hands so high !
For I think I see my own mother coming
   Oer yonder stile to me.
Oh the briars, the prickly briars,
   They prick my heart full sore ;
If ever I get free from the gallows-tree,
   I'[ll] never get there any more.

2 'Oh mother hast thou any gold for me,
   Any money to buy me free,
To save my body from the cold clay ground,
   And my head from the gallows-tree ? '

3 'Oh no, I have no gold for thee,
   No money to buy thee free,
For I have come to see thee hanged,
   And hangëd thou shalt be.'

Struppa's text of 'Scibilia Nobili' is repeated in Salomone-Marino's Leggende p. siciliane in Poesia, p. 160, No 29. The editor supplies defects and gives some varying readings from another version, in which Scibilia is the love, not the wife, of a cavalier. — Mango, Calabria, in Archivio, I, 394, No 75 (wife). — 'La Prigioniera,' Giannini, No 25, p. 195, two copies, reduces the story to four or five stanzas. The sequel, No 26, p. 197, is likely to have been originally an independent ballad. It is attached to 'Scibilia Nobili,' but is found separately in Bernoni, XI, No 3, 'La Figlia snaturata,' Finamore, Archivio, I, 212, 'Catarine.'

347 b. 'Frísa vísa' is reprinted by Hammershaimb, Færøsk Anthologi, p. 268, No 34. The editor expressly says that the ballad is used as a children's game, like the English F. So also are Danish A, and a Magyar ballad of like purport, to be mentioned presently.

348 b. **Danish. A,** in Kristensen's Skattegraveren, 'Jomfruens udløsning,' II, 49, No 279, 1884 ; **B,** III, 5, No 3, 1885. From tradition. Both versions agree with the Swedish in all important points, and the language of **B** points to a Swedish derivation.

349 a. Ransom for maid refused by father, mother, brother, sister, and paid by lover: Little-Russian, Golovatsky, I, 50, No 11 ; II, 245, No 7. (W. W.)

349 b, 514 a. Man redeemed by maid when abandoned by his own blood: Little-Russian, Golovatsky, I, 250, No 26 ; Servian, Vuk, III, 547, No 83 ; Magyar-Croat, Kurelac, p. 254, No 61, p. 352, No 96. (W. W.)

In a Slovak ballad in Kollár, Národnie Zpiewanky, II, 13, translated by Herrmann, Ethnologische Mittheilungen, col. 42 f., John, in prison, writes to his father to ransom him ; the father asks how much would have to be paid ; four hundred pieces of gold and as many of silver ; the father replies that he *has not* so much, and his son must perish. An ineffectual letter to mother, brother, sister, follows ; then one to his sweetheart. She brings a long rope, with which he is to let himself down from his dungeon. If the rope proves too short, he is to add his long hair (cf. I, 40 b, line 2, 486 b) ; and if it be still too short, he may light upon her shoulders. John escapes. Nearly the same is the Polish ballad translated in Waldbrühl's Balalaika, which is referred to II, 350 b.

A fragment of a Székler ransom-ballad is found in Arany and Gyulai's collection, III, 42 : Herrmann, as above, col. 49. Another form of love-test is very popular in Hungary, of which Herrmann gives eight versions. In one of these, from a collection made in 1813, Arany and Gyulai, I, 189 (Herrmann's IV), the story is told with the conciseness of the English ballad. A snake has crept into a girl's bosom : she entreats her father to take it out ; he dares not, and sends her to her mother ; the mother has as little devotion and courage as the father, and sends her to her brother ; she is successively passed on to sister-in-law, brother-in-law, sister ; then appeals to her lover, who instantly does the service. This is the kernel, and perhaps all that is original, in versions, I (of Herrmann), col. 34 f., contributed by Kálmány ; II, 36 f., contributed by Szabó ; V, col. 38, Kálmány, Koszorúk az Alföld vad Virágaiból, I, 21, translated into German by Wlislocki, Ungarische Revue, 1884, p. 344 ; VIII, col. 39, Kálmány, Szeged Népe, II, 13. In Herrmann, VI, col. 38, Kálmány, Koszorúk, II, 62 ; VII, col. 38 f., Kálmány, Szeged Népe, II, 12 ; and III, col. 37 (a fragment), young man and maid change parts. In I, III, V (?), VI, VII, the father says he can better do without a daughter (son) than without one of his hands, and the youth (maid) would rather lose one of his (her) hands than his (her) beloved.* In I the snake has been turned to a purse of gold when the maid attempts to take it out; in II, according to a prose and prosaic comment of the reciter, there was no snake, but the girl had put a piece of gold in her bosom, and calls it a yellow adder to experiment upon her family; in VII, again, there is no snake, but a rouleau of gold, and the snake is explained away in like manner in a comment to VIII. Even the transformation in I is to be deprecated; the money in the others is a modern depravation.

A brief ballad of the Transylvania Gipsies, communicated and translated by Wlislocki, Ungarische Revue, 1884, p. 345 f., agrees with the second series of those above. A youth summons mother and sister to take a reptile from his breast; they are afraid; his sweetheart will do it if she dies. A very pretty popular Gipsy tale to the same effect is given by Herrmann, col. 40 f.

A Roumanian ballad, 'Giurgiu,' closely resembling the Magyar I, VII, from Pompiliu Miron's Balade populare române, p. 41, is given in translation by Herrmann, col. 106 ff.; a fragment of another, with parts reversed, col. 213.

A man, to make trial of his blood-relations, begs father, mother, etc., to take out a snake from his breast, and is refused by all. His wife puts in her hand and takes out a pearl necklace, which she receives as her reward: Servian, Vuk, I, No 289, Herzegovine, No 136, Petranović, Serajevo, 1867, p. 191, No 20; Slavonian, Stojanović, No 20. (W. W.)

There are many variations on this theme, of which one more may be specified. A drowning girl given over by her family is saved by her lover: Little-Russian, Golovatsky, II, 80, No 14, 104, No 18, 161, No 15, 726, No 11; Servian, Vuk, I, Nos 290, 291; Bulgarian, Dozon, p. 98, No 61; Polish, Kolberg, Lud, 1857, I, 151, 12ª. Again, man is saved by maid: Little-Russian, Golovatsky, I, 114, No 28; Waclaw z Oleska, p. 226. (W. W.)

96. The Gay Goshawk.

P. 356 a. (1.) (2.) (4.) are now printed in Mélusine, II, 342, III, 1, II, 341. (15.) (16.) 'La Fille dans la Tour,' Victor Smith, Chansons du Velay et du Forez, Romania, VII, 76, 78. (17.) Bladé, Poésies p. rec. dans l'Armagnac, etc., p. 23, 'La Prisonnière.'

There is an Italian form of 'Belle Isambourg' in Nigra, No 45, p. 277, ' Amor costante.'

356 b. For other forms of 'Les trois Capitaines,' see, French, Puymaigre, I, 131, 134 and note; Tiersot, in Revue des Traditions populaires, III, 501, 502 ; Rolland, III, 58 ff., a, b, d; Italian, Marcoaldi, p. 162, 'La Fuga e il Pentimento;' Nigra, No 53, p. 309, 'L'Onore salvato.'

* The "white hand" in the Slovenian ballad, II, 350, is hard to explain unless there is a mixture of a prison-ballad and a snake-ballad.

357 b, second paragraph.

On messenger-birds, see Nigra, p. 339 f., and note.

A girl feigns death simply to avoid a disagreeable suitor. Proof by fire, etc. ; cf. **C** 23 f., **D** 7 f., **E** 27 f., **F** 1–3, **G** 36–38. Servian. (1.) Mara, promised to the Herzog Stephen, and wishing for good reasons to escape him, pretends death. Stephen is incredulous; puts live coals into her bosom, then a snake; she does not flinch. He then tickles her face with his beard; she does not stir. Stephen is convinced and retires; Mara springs from the bier. Her mother asks her what had given her most trouble. She had not minded the coals or the snake, but could hardly keep from laughing when tickled with the beard. Vuk, I, 551, No 727. (2.) The suitor tests the case by thrusting his hands into the girl's bosom, fire, snake. The first is the worst. Vuk, Herzegovine, No 133. (3.) The same probation, with the same verdict (in this case the girl loves another), Petranović, Srpske n. pjesme, Serajevo, 1867, No 362. Cf. Rajković, p. 176, No 211. — Bulgarian. Proofs by snow and ice laid on the heart; a snake. She stands both. Miladinof, No 68, cf. No 468. In the same, No 660, the girl holds out under ice and snake, but when kissed between the eyes wakes up. — Bohemian, Erben, p. 485, No 20, 'The Turk duped,' and Moravian, Sušil, No 128, the tests are lacking. (W. W.)

Three physicians from Salerno pour melted lead in the hands of Fenice, who is apparently dead. (She has taken a drug which makes her unconscious for a certain time. Her object is to escape from her husband to her lover, Cligés.) The lead has no effect in rousing Fenice. Crestien de Troies, Cligés, ed. Förster, vv. 6000–6009, pp. 246, 247. Förster cites Solomon and Moroif (Salman und Morolf, st. 133, ed. F. Vogt, Die deutschen Dichtungen v. Salomon und Markolf, I, 27, *molten gold*), and other parallels. Einleitung, pp. xix–xx. Cf. Revue de Traditions pop., II, 519. (G. L. K.)

100. Willie o Winsbury.

P. 398. There is a 'Lord Thomas of Wynnesbury' in the Murison MS., p. 17, which was derived from recitation in Aberdeenshire, but it seems to me to have had its origin in the stalls, resembling **I**, which is of that source.

101. Willie o Douglas Dale.

Pp. 407, 409, **A** 14², **B** 12², 'An lions gaed to their dens,' 'And the lions took the hill.' "Lions we have had verie manie in the north parts of Scotland, and those with maines of no less force than they of Mauritania are sometimes reported to be; but how and when they were destroied as yet I doo not read:" Holinshed, I, 379.

102. Willie and Earl Richard's Daughter.

P. 412 b. **A** is translated by Anastasius Grün, Robin Hood, p. 57; Doenniges, p. 166; Knortz, L. u. R. Alt-englands, No 18; Loève-Veimars, p. 252.

105. The Bailiff's Daughter of Islington.

II, 426 b, 428. The tune of 105 b is, I have a good old woman at home: of **f**, I have a good old wife at home.

Italian. 'La Prova,' Nigra, No 54, p. 314, **A–D**. 'Il Ritorno,' Giannini, p. 154.

106. The Famous Flower of Serving-Men.

P. 428. The Roxburghe copy, III, 762, Aldermary Church-Yard, is in the Ballad Society's edition, VI, 567. The Euing copy, printed for John Andrews, is signed L. P., for Laurence Price: Mr J. W. Ebsworth, at p. 570.

109. Tom Potts.

P. 441 b. **B. b.** Ritson's copy was "compared with another impression, for the same partners, without date."

I have failed to mention, but am now reminded by Mr Macmath, that the ballad of 'Jamie o Lee' is given, under the title 'James Hatelie,' by Robert Chambers in the Romantic Scottish Ballads, their Epoch and Authorship, 1859, p. 37, Lord Phenix appearing as simple Fenwick.

112. The Baffled Knight.

P. 480 b. Spanish **C**, 'El Caballero burlado,' is now printed in full in Pidal, Asturian Romances, No 34, p. 156.

481 b. Add : 'La Marchande d'Oranges' in Rolland, V, 10. (Say Rolland, I, 258.)

Tears. Add : Rolland, II, 29, *e, g, h*.

Varieties. There may be added : Mélusine I, 483 = Revue des Traditions pop., III, 634 f.; Romania, X, 379 f., No 18; Bladé, Poésies p. de la Gascogne, II, 208.

482 a. **Italian.** Nigra, No 71, p. 375, 'Occasione mancata,' **A–F.** See also 'La Monacella salvata,' No 72, p. 381, and 'Il Galante burlato,' No 75, p. 388.

482 b. The ballad, it seems, is by *Madame* Favart: see Rolland, II, 33, *k*. Add : *l, ib.*, p. 34, and Poésies pop. de la France, MS., III, 493.

483 b. Danish **A** is translated by Prior, III, 182, No 126.

113. The Great Silkie of Sule Skerry.

P. 494.

"On the west coast of Ireland the fishermen are loth to kill the seals, which once abounded in some localities, owing to a popular superstition that they

enshrined 'the souls of thim that were drowned at the flood.' They were supposed to possess the power of casting aside their external skins and disporting themselves in human form on the sea-shore. If a mortal contrived to become possessed of one of these outer coverings belonging to a female, he might claim her and keep her as his bride." Charles Hardwick, Traditions, Superstitions, and Folk-Lore, chiefly Lancashire and the North of England, p. 231. (G. L. K.)

506 a, last paragraph but one. So in Douns Lioð, Strengleikar, ed. Kayser and Unger, p. 52 ff. (G. L. K.)

VOL. III.

116. Adam Bell, etc.

P. 17 b. I have omitted to mention the Norwegian ballad 'Hemingjen aa Harald kungen' in Bugge's Gamle Norske Folkeviser, No 1, p. 1.

44. 'A Robynhode,' etc.

In the Convocation Books of the Corporation of Wells, Somerset, vol. ii, "under the 13th Henry 7, Nicholas Trappe being master, there is the following curious entry, relative, apparently, to a play of Robin Hood, exhibitions of dancing girls, and church ales, provided for at the public expense.

"'Et insuper in eadem Convocatione omnes et singuli burgenses unanimi assensu ad tunc et ibidem dederunt Magistro Nicolao Trappe potestatem generalem ad inquirendum in quorum manibus pecuniæ ecclesiæ ac communitatis Welliæ sunt injuste detentæ ; videlicet, provenientes ante hoc tempus de Robynhode, puellis tripudiantibus, communi cervisia ecclesiæ, et hujusmodi. Atque de bonis et pecuniis dictæ communitati qualitercunque detentis, et in quorumcunque manibus existentibus. Et desuper, eorum nomina scribere qui habent hujusmodi bona, cum summis, etc.'" H. T. Riley in the First Report of the Historical MSS Commission, 1874, Appendix, p. 107.

The passage in the Wells Convocation Records is perhaps illustrated by an entry in the Churchwardens' Accounts of the Parish of Kingston-upon-Thames, cited by Ritson, Robin Hood, 2d ed., I, cxviii, from Lysons, Environs of London, 1792, I, 228 :

"16 Hen. 8. Rec^d at the church-ale and Robynhode all things deducted   3 10 6."

With this may be compared the following :

"Anno MDLXVI, or 9 of Eliz., payde for setting up Robin Hoodes bower ,   0 18 "

(Churchwardens' Accompts of St. Helen's [at Abingdon, Berks], Archæologia, I, 18). This latter entry is loosely cited by Ritson, I, cxiv, 2d ed., as dating from 1556. Ibidem may be found his opinion as to R. H.'s bower (n. *). Hampson, Medii Ævi Kalendarium, I,

265, quotes this entry, also with the wrong year. He has no doubt about the Bower: "An arbour, called Robin Hood's Bower, was erected in the church-yard, and here maidens stood gathering contributions." I, 283. (All the above by G. L. K.)

117. A Gest of Robyn Hode.

P. 46 b, note. The Sloane MS. cited by Ritson as No 715 is No 780 (which is bound up with 715) and is "paper, early xviith century:" Ward, Catalogue of Romances, etc., I, 517. This correction is also to be made at p. 121 b, note; pp. 129 a, 173 b, 175 b.

51 b, sts 62–66.

The late Miss Hamilton McKie, New Galloway, told me this story:

A sturdy beggar, or luscan, came to a farm-house among the hills and asked quarters for the night. The gudewife, before entrusting him with the bedclothes in which to sleep in one of the outhouses, required a pledge or security for their return. He said he had none to offer but his Maker, and got his night's lodging. In the morning he walked off with the bedclothes, but, becoming bewildered in a mist, he wandered about the whole day, and in the evening, seeing the light of a house, made towards it and knocked at the door. A woman opened it and said, "Your Cautioner has proved gude!" He had come back to the same house.

Mactaggart gives the story in his Gallovidian Encyclopedia, p. 325, but without the trait of the security. (W. Macmath.)

147. Robin Hood's Golden Prize.

P. 210. The signature to a, L. P., is for Laurence Price: Ebsworth, Roxburghe Ballads, VI, 64.

150. Robin Hood and Maid Marian.

P. 218 (and 43–46).

Mr H. L. D. Ward, in his invaluable Catalogue of Romances, etc., while treating of Fulk Fitz-Warine, has made the following important remarks concerning the literary history of Maid Marian (p. 506 f.).

"There were three Matildas who were popularly supposed to have been persecuted by King John. The most historical of these was Matilda de Braose. She was imprisoned, with her son and her son's wife, in 1210, some (Matthew Paris and others) say at Windsor, but another chronicler says at Corfe Castle (see a volume published by the Soc. de l'Hist. de France in 1840), and they were all starved to death. The second was Fulk's wife Mahaud, who was the widow of Theobald Walter. The third was the daughter of Robert Fitz-Walter. The only authority that can be quoted for the story of the third Matilda is the Chronicle of Dunmow, of which one copy of the 16th century remains, in the Cotton MS., Cleopatra, C. iii. (ff. 281–7), but which

was probably begun by Nicholas de Brumfeld, a canon of Dunmow in the latter part of the 13th century. It is there stated that, when Robert Fitz-Walter fled to France in 1213, his daughter took refuge in Dunmow Priory, where John, after a vain attempt at seduction, poisoned her. Now all these three Matildas may be said to appear in the two plays known as *The Downfall* and *The Death of Robert Earle of Huntington*, by Anthony Munday and Henry Chettle, which are first mentioned in Henslowe's *Diary* in February and November, 1598. Two of them indeed appear in their own names, Matilda de Braose (or Bruce) and Matilda Fitz-Walter; and the one is starved at Windsor and the other is poisoned at Dunmow in the second play. But in the first play Matilda Fitz-Walter escapes the solicitations of John by joining her newly-married husband in Sherwood, where they are called Robin Hood and Maid Marian. This is clearly owing to a combination of the second and third Matildas. It may have been effected by the course of tradition, or it may have been the arbitrary work of a single author. But if the romance of Fulk Fitz-Warin had been known to either Munday or Chettle, other portions of it would almost certainly have appeared in plays or novels or ballads. Now Munday introduces the piece as a rehearsal, conducted by John Skelton the poet, who himself plays Friar Tuck, with a view to performing it before Henry VIII. And it is not at all unlikely that it was really founded upon a May-day pageant devised by Skelton, but not important enough to be specified in the list of his works in his *Garlande of Laurell*. We know that Skelton did write Interludes, of which one still remains, *Magnyfycence*: and Anthony Wood tells us that at Diss in Norfolk, where Skelton was rector, he was 'esteemed more fit for the stage than the pew or pulpit.' Thus there was no man more likely than Skelton to devise a new Robin Hood pageant for his old pupil, Henry VIII. And again, there was no man more likely to celebrate the story of Matilda Fitz-Walter, for the patron of his living was Robert Lord Fitz-Walter, who was himself a Ratcliffe, but who had inherited the lordship of Diss through his grandmother, the last of the old Fitz-Walters.* But whether Skelton may have read the then accessible poem about Fulk, afterwards described by Leland, or whether either he or Munday may have received the story in its composite form, it is pretty evident that the two reputed objects of King John's desire, Matilda Walter and Matilda Fitz-Walter, have become blended together into the Maid Marian of the play."

155. Sir Hugh, or, The Jew's Daughter.

P. 235 a. Bells ringing of themselves (in ballads).

---

* "The earldom of Huntingdon was vacant from about 1487 to 1529, and, as the Fitz-Walters were lineally descended from the daughter of the first Simon de St Liz, Earl of Huntingdon, this may have suggested to Skelton the idea of giving that title to the husband of Matilda Fitz-Walter."

Pidal, Asturian Romances, 'Il Penitente,' Nos 1, 2, pp. 82, 84; Nigra, 'Sant' Alessio,' No 148, A, B, p. 538 ff., and see p. 541.

161. The Battle of Otterburn.

P. 294. St George our Lady's knight.

A nemnede sein Gorge our leuedi kniʒt:

Sir Beues of Hamtoun, ed. Kölbing, v. 2817, p. 129 ; Maitland Club ed., v. 2640. (G. L. K., who also gave me the case in Roister Doister.)

" Now holy St George, myne only avower,
   In whom I trust for my protection,
O very Chevalier of the stourished Flower,
   By whose Hands thy Sword and Shield hast wone,
Be mediator, that she may to her Sone
   Cause me to hear Rex splendens songen on hye,
   Before the Trinitye, when that I shall dye.''

Poem on the Willoughbies of Eresby, in the form of a prayer to St George put into the mouth of one of the Willoughby family, Dugdale, Baronage of England, 1676, II, 85, 86. Dugdale does not date the MS. The male line of the Willoughbies became extinct in 1525.

(3. flourished?   4. thou thy?) (G. L. K.)

169. Johnie Armstrong.

P. 371 f. **B a, b** are signed T. R., the initials of a purveyor or editor of ballads for the popular press. **B a** of ' Robin Hood and the Butcher,' No 122, and **a** of ' Robin Hood and the Beggar,' I, No 133, bear the same signature : see pp. 116, 156 of this volume. No such rhymster as T. R. shows himself to be in these two last pieces could have made ' Johnie Armstrong,' one of the best ballads in English.

178. Captain Car, or, Edom o Gordon.

P. 423. " The Donean Tourist," by Alexander Laing, Aberdeen, 1828, p. 100, has a very bad copy, extended to fifty-nine stanzas.

182. The Laird o Logie.

P. 449. ' Young Logie ' is among the ballads taken down by Mrs Murison in Aberdeenshire, p. 88 of the collection. The copy is imperfect, and extremely corrupted. Lady Margaret is the daughter of the king (who is not called by that name), but is confused with her mother, who counterfeits her consort's han-write and steals his right-han glove, as is done in **D**. Three ships at the pier of Leith, and three again at Queen's Ferry.

184. The Lads of Wamphray.

P. 458. Mr Macmath has pointed out to me a case in Pitcairn's Criminal Trials, I, 397 f., in which "Jok Johnstoun, callit the Galzeart, Jok J., bruþer to Wille of Kirkhill,'' with a Grahame, a couple of Armstrangs, and their accomplices, are accused of the theft of twelve score sheep from James Johnstoune, in February, 1557. We can make no inference as to the relation of Jok the Galliard to the Galliard of our ballad. There were generations of Jocks and Wills in these families, and the sobriquet of The Galliard, as Pitcairn has remarked, " was very prevalent.'' He cites a " Gilbert Ellote, callit Gib the Galzart,'' III, 441, under the date 1618.

To be Corrected in the Print.

I, 7 b, last line but three of text. *Read* Fordringer.
    71 a, 33². tell thee, ed. 1802 ; tell to thee, ed. 1833.
    132 b, 7². *Read* Lord John.
    159 a, 3¹·². to your, in the MS.
    186 a, Notes to **A b**. *Add* 2². slung at.
    256 a, 1⁴. *Read* Machey *for* May-hay.
    274 b, note ‡. *Read* Romania IX.
    356 b, **D c** 1³. *Read* O go not.
    400 a, **I**. *Read* II, 360.
    469 a, 22³. *Read* your *for* yonr.
    482 a, **D** 16, 17, 5th line. *Read* Hine.
    489 a, between 67 a and 84 b. *Insert* 6. Willie's
        Lady.
    503 a. The title of **I** is ' Hynd Horn.'
    504 b, between 226 a and 231. *Insert* 21. The Maid
        and the Palmer.
II, 70 a, 18⁴. Fall, ed. 1802 ; fell, ed. 1833.
    104 a, 19¹·². *Read* pat.
    129 a, 11¹. *Read* ' O here I am ' the boy says.
    135 a, **A. a.** 11¹. *Drop.*
    176 b, 11³. *Read* Gae.
    179 b, note to **B** 7². *Drop.*
    192 a, 7⁴. *Read* maun. 8². *Read* Ye'r seer.
        9². *Drop* the brackets.
    193 a, 20⁴. *Read* ye never gat.
        22². *Drop* the brackets. 25². *Read* dreams.
    193 b, 28¹. *Read* Ge (= Gae) *for* Ye.
    226 a, 229 a, ' Sweet William's Ghost,' **A**. *Read*
        1750 *for* 1763.
    239 a, **B** 3¹. *Read* O she.
    272 f. *Read (according to the text of* 1755): 2¹. will I.
        7⁴. gar thy. 10². to thy. 18³. maun cum.
        22¹. *Note* : " perhaps fetchie '' nurse.
        23⁴. hes he. 26¹. sits. 26³. means a' those folks.
        26⁴. mother she.
        27¹. And when he cam to gude grene wod.
        27³. first saw. 27⁴. Kemeing down.
        28². Than, *misprint for* That. 34⁴. they lay.
        35⁴. hip was. 39². ill deed.
    275 b. *Read, v.* 17, You see his heid upon my. v. 20,
        that did, *apparently a misprint for* that thocht.

The only variations in the other copy are: 26³, these *for* those; thocht *for* did, in v. 20 of p. 275 b.

276 a. **A. a.** *Read* 1750 *for* 1763 *twice.*

276 b, 4th line of the preface. *Read* Annandale.

13th line of the preface. *Read* our old.

2¹. *Read* man (ed. 1750).

310 a, third paragraph, line seven. *Read* authenticatable.

343. *Read* (ed. 1755): 2³. And there.

3³. And mantel.

12¹. I have. (*Drop* the notes to 3³, 5¹.)

348 b, **G, H.** *Read* Reifferscheid.

352 b, **D** 5⁴. MS. has And free.

378 a, last line. *Read* Andrew Small.

381 b, 20³. *Read* Scotch.

393 a, 14². *Read* shook.

405 b, notes. 16 belongs to **I** and should be on p. 406.

437 b, translations. *Read* **E** is translated by Grundtvig, etc.; **D** by Afzelius, etc.

462 a, 26⁴. *Read* sned *for* sued.

478, first line after the title. *Read* 56 b *for* 27 b.

481 b, third paragraph, sixth line. *Read,* 27.

500, **20**, first line. *Read* **O** *for* **M**. English **N, O** should be **O, P.**

502 b, **34**, first line. *Read* Decurtins *for* Decurtius.

506 b, **44**, 400 a. *Drop* **Q**, etc. . Note to 401, *drop* Revue des Traditions, etc. .

513 a, seventh line from bottom. *Read* quam.

III, 6 a, 12¹. *Read* Braidisbauks.

11, **M.** *Say:* Reminiscences by Thomas Carlyle, II, 171, 1881, Froude's Life of Carlyle, II, 416, 1882. In line 2, *read,* O busk and go with me, me.

46 b, line 9. *Read* S. S. *for* S. G.

95 b, note †. *Say:* Jock o the Side, **B** 13, 14, **C** 10, III, 480, 482.

(The following are mostly trivial variations from the spelling of the text.)

I, 71 b, 51¹. Oh, ed. 1802; O, ed. 1833.

80 b, 14¹. *Read* f[e]ast.

132 a, 5¹. *Read* father[s].

133 a, **M.** *Read* Deer.

137 b, **S** 4². *Read* cam.

256 b, 3². *Read* O. 4². *Read* rocked.

302 a, **B**¹,². *Read* Whare.

321 b, 7⁴. *Read* doun.

325 a, 3³. *Read* Heavn. 6². *Read* danton.

331 a, **C** 2⁴. *Read* thrie. **D** 2³. *Read* micht.

441 a, 1⁶. *Read* warsell. 4³. *Read* bloody.

468 a, 4¹. *Read* stock. 10². *Read* saftly.

b 13². MS. has bone. 16³. *Read* Beachen.

481 a, 31². *Read* dazled.

500 a, 10⁴. *Read* down.

508 a, 7⁴. *Read* by.

II, 32 a, **P** 1⁴. *Read* aboon.

70 a, 19⁴. *Read* cheik. 20². *Read* smil'd.

b, 30⁴. *Read* tine.

90 b, 26¹. *Read* won, *twice.*

108 a, 2⁴. *Read* die. b, 11³. *Read* mony.

130 a, 3³. *Read* Gil. 4³. *Read* Jill.

131 a, 17³. *Read* han. b, 19³. *Read* ain.

152 a, 4³, 5¹. *Read* grene.

153 b, 22³. *Read* grene.

161 a, 7¹, 8¹. *Read* tane.

192 a, 5⁴. *Read* An. 7³. *Read* askin.

193 b, 26¹. *Read* bour.

240 a, note. *Read* Madden.

272 f. *Read* (ed. 1755): 1¹. Gill Morice. 5². said. 6³. red. 8³, 16³, 17³, 24³, 26¹, 36³. guid grene wod. 9², 18². slive. 10², 15². Tho. 11¹. micht. 11². near. 11², 20². coud. 12³. I's. 13³. whar he. 14². woud. 15³. stracht. 17⁴. Even. 21⁴. welcom. 21⁴, 39⁴. me. 22². lie. 22⁴. she. 23². he. 24⁴. with. 26¹. Gill. 26². whistld. 26⁴. tarrys. 27², 36². miekle. 27². cair. 28². well. 29⁴, 31¹, 31⁴, 33³, 34¹. heid. 30³. bodie. 33⁴. town. 34⁴. there. 35³. ance. 37¹. credle. 39². die.

275 a, last line but three. *Read* Wi, pearce.

L. l. but one, naithing, heid. Last line, coud.

b, v. 3. day[s]. 7. been. 8. me.

15. teirs, wensom. 18. bluid. 22. comly.

25. driry.

321 b, note ‡. *Read* Balcanqual.

331 b, 3¹. *Read* nurice.

343. *Read* (ed. 1755): 1⁴. favord. 5¹. spack. 6³. bot. 7³. bin. 9¹. coud. 9⁴, 14⁴. die.

352 b, 3³. *Read* pown.

363 b, 11¹. *Read* ladie's.

364 a, 20¹. *Read* ladye 's.

389 a, 8³. *Read* You'r.

390 b, 29². *Read* hir. 5¹. *Read* bouer.

391 a, 12¹. *Read* Whan.

396 a, 1². *Read* blithe.

404 b, 9¹. *Read* Whan.

473 b, 17³. *Read* mony.

475 a, 11³. *Read* down, *twice.*

478. *Read :* 1². on *for* an. 4¹. sir. 6². do. 14¹. a[t] London. 15¹. medans. 17¹. leyne.

483, 1³. *Read* wel. 6⁴. *Read* beene.

III, 2 a, note, line 5. *Read* Bennet.

5 a, **D** 5². *Read* Lincolm. b, 10¹. *Read* there.

8 b, 24¹. *Read* betide.

253 b, **R,** v. 3. *Read* dochter.

A CATALOG OF SELECTED
DOVER BOOKS
IN ALL FIELDS OF INTEREST

A CATALOG OF SELECTED DOVER
BOOKS IN ALL FIELDS OF INTEREST

CONCERNING THE SPIRITUAL IN ART, Wassily Kandinsky. Pioneering work by father of abstract art. Thoughts on color theory, nature of art. Analysis of earlier masters. 12 illustrations. 80pp. of text. 5⅜ x 8½. 0-486-23411-8

CELTIC ART: The Methods of Construction, George Bain. Simple geometric techniques for making Celtic interlacements, spirals, Kells-type initials, animals, humans, etc. Over 500 illustrations. 160pp. 9 x 12. (Available in U.S. only.) 0-486-22923-8

AN ATLAS OF ANATOMY FOR ARTISTS, Fritz Schider. Most thorough reference work on art anatomy in the world. Hundreds of illustrations, including selections from works by Vesalius, Leonardo, Goya, Ingres, Michelangelo, others. 593 illustrations. 192pp. 7⅞ x 10¼. 0-486-20241-0

CELTIC HAND STROKE-BY-STROKE (Irish Half-Uncial from "The Book of Kells"): An Arthur Baker Calligraphy Manual, Arthur Baker. Complete guide to creating each letter of the alphabet in distinctive Celtic manner. Covers hand position, strokes, pens, inks, paper, more. Illustrated. 48pp. 8¼ x 11. 0-486-24336-2

EASY ORIGAMI, John Montroll. Charming collection of 32 projects (hat, cup, pelican, piano, swan, many more) specially designed for the novice origami hobbyist. Clearly illustrated easy-to-follow instructions insure that even beginning papercrafters will achieve successful results. 48pp. 8¼ x 11. 0-486-27298-2

BLOOMINGDALE'S ILLUSTRATED 1886 CATALOG: Fashions, Dry Goods and Housewares, Bloomingdale Brothers. Famed merchants' extremely rare catalog depicting about 1,700 products: clothing, housewares, firearms, dry goods, jewelry, more. Invaluable for dating, identifying vintage items. Also, copyright-free graphics for artists, designers. Co-published with Henry Ford Museum & Greenfield Village. 160pp. 8¼ x 11. 0-486-25780-0

THE ART OF WORLDLY WISDOM, Baltasar Gracian. "Think with the few and speak with the many," "Friends are a second existence," and "Be able to forget" are among this 1637 volume's 300 pithy maxims. A perfect source of mental and spiritual refreshment, it can be opened at random and appreciated either in brief or at length. 128pp. 5⅜ x 8½. 0-486-44034-6

JOHNSON'S DICTIONARY: A Modern Selection, Samuel Johnson (E. L. McAdam and George Milne, eds.). This modern version reduces the original 1755 edition's 2,300 pages of definitions and literary examples to a more manageable length, retaining the verbal pleasure and historical curiosity of the original. 480pp. 5⁵⁄₁₆ x 8¼. 0-486-44089-3

ADVENTURES OF HUCKLEBERRY FINN, Mark Twain, Illustrated by E. W. Kemble. A work of eternal richness and complexity, a source of ongoing critical debate, and a literary landmark, Twain's 1885 masterpiece about a barefoot boy's journey of self-discovery has enthralled readers around the world. This handsome clothbound reproduction of the first edition features all 174 of the original black-and-white illustrations. 368pp. 5⅜ x 8½. 0-486-44322-1

HOW TO DO BEADWORK, Mary White. Fundamental book on craft from simple projects to five-bead chains and woven works. 106 illustrations. 142pp. 5⅜ x 8. 0-486-20697-1

THE 1912 AND 1915 GUSTAV STICKLEY FURNITURE CATALOGS, Gustav Stickley. With over 200 detailed illustrations and descriptions, these two catalogs are essential reading and reference materials and identification guides for Stickley furniture. Captions cite materials, dimensions and prices. 112pp. 6½ x 9¼. 0-486-26676-1

EARLY AMERICAN LOCOMOTIVES, John H. White, Jr. Finest locomotive engravings from early 19th century: historical (1804–74), main-line (after 1870), special, foreign, etc. 147 plates. 142pp. 11⅜ x 8¼. 0-486-22772-3

LITTLE BOOK OF EARLY AMERICAN CRAFTS AND TRADES, Peter Stockham (ed.). 1807 children's book explains crafts and trades: baker, hatter, cooper, potter, and many others. 23 copperplate illustrations. 140pp. 4⅝ x 6. 0-486-23336-7

VICTORIAN FASHIONS AND COSTUMES FROM HARPER'S BAZAR, 1867–1898, Stella Blum (ed.). Day costumes, evening wear, sports clothes, shoes, hats, other accessories in over 1,000 detailed engravings. 320pp. 9⅜ x 12¼. 0-486-22990-4

THE LONG ISLAND RAIL ROAD IN EARLY PHOTOGRAPHS, Ron Ziel. Over 220 rare photos, informative text document origin (1844) and development of rail service on Long Island. Vintage views of early trains, locomotives, stations, passengers, crews, much more. Captions. 8⅞ x 11¾. 0-486-26301-0

VOYAGE OF THE LIBERDADE, Joshua Slocum. Great 19th-century mariner's thrilling, first-hand account of the wreck of his ship off South America, the 35-foot boat he built from the wreckage, and its remarkable voyage home. 128pp. 5⅜ x 8½. 0-486-40022-0

TEN BOOKS ON ARCHITECTURE, Vitruvius. The most important book ever written on architecture. Early Roman aesthetics, technology, classical orders, site selection, all other aspects. Morgan translation. 331pp. 5⅜ x 8½. 0-486-20645-9

THE HUMAN FIGURE IN MOTION, Eadweard Muybridge. More than 4,500 stopped-action photos, in action series, showing undraped men, women, children jumping, lying down, throwing, sitting, wrestling, carrying, etc. 390pp. 7⅞ x 10⅝. 0-486-20204-6 Clothbd.

TREES OF THE EASTERN AND CENTRAL UNITED STATES AND CANADA, William M. Harlow. Best one-volume guide to 140 trees. Full descriptions, woodlore, range, etc. Over 600 illustrations. Handy size. 288pp. 4½ x 6⅜. 0-486-20395-6

GROWING AND USING HERBS AND SPICES, Milo Miloradovich. Versatile handbook provides all the information needed for cultivation and use of all the herbs and spices available in North America. 4 illustrations. Index. Glossary. 236pp. 5⅜ x 8½. 0-486-25058-X

BIG BOOK OF MAZES AND LABYRINTHS, Walter Shepherd. 50 mazes and labyrinths in all–classical, solid, ripple, and more–in one great volume. Perfect inexpensive puzzler for clever youngsters. Full solutions. 112pp. 8⅛ x 11. 0-486-22951-3

PIANO TUNING, J. Cree Fischer. Clearest, best book for beginner, amateur. Simple repairs, raising dropped notes, tuning by easy method of flattened fifths. No previous skills needed. 4 illustrations. 201pp. 5⅜ x 8½. 0-486-23267-0

HINTS TO SINGERS, Lillian Nordica. Selecting the right teacher, developing confidence, overcoming stage fright, and many other important skills receive thoughtful discussion in this indispensible guide, written by a world-famous diva of four decades' experience. 96pp. 5 3/8 x 8 1/2. 0-486-40094-8

THE COMPLETE NONSENSE OF EDWARD LEAR, Edward Lear. All nonsense limericks, zany alphabets, Owl and Pussycat, songs, nonsense botany, etc., illustrated by Lear. Total of 320pp. 5 3/8 x 8 1/2. (Available in U.S. only.) 0-486-20167-8

VICTORIAN PARLOUR POETRY: An Annotated Anthology, Michael R. Turner. 117 gems by Longfellow, Tennyson, Browning, many lesser-known poets. "The Village Blacksmith," "Curfew Must Not Ring Tonight," "Only a Baby Small," dozens more, often difficult to find elsewhere. Index of poets, titles, first lines. xxiii + 325pp. 5 5/8 x 8 1/4. 0-486-27044-0

DUBLINERS, James Joyce. Fifteen stories offer vivid, tightly focused observations of the lives of Dublin's poorer classes. At least one, "The Dead," is considered a masterpiece. Reprinted complete and unabridged from standard edition. 160pp. 5 3/16 x 8 1/4. 0-486-26870-5

GREAT WEIRD TALES: 14 Stories by Lovecraft, Blackwood, Machen and Others, S. T. Joshi (ed.). 14 spellbinding tales, including "The Sin Eater," by Fiona McLeod, "The Eye Above the Mantel," by Frank Belknap Long, as well as renowned works by R. H. Barlow, Lord Dunsany, Arthur Machen, W. C. Morrow and eight other masters of the genre. 256pp. 5 3/8 x 8 1/2. (Available in U.S. only.) 0-486-40436-6

THE BOOK OF THE SACRED MAGIC OF ABRAMELIN THE MAGE, translated by S. MacGregor Mathers. Medieval manuscript of ceremonial magic. Basic document in Aleister Crowley, Golden Dawn groups. 268pp. 5 3/8 x 8 1/2. 0-486-23211-5

THE BATTLES THAT CHANGED HISTORY, Fletcher Pratt. Eminent historian profiles 16 crucial conflicts, ancient to modern, that changed the course of civilization. 352pp. 5 3/8 x 8 1/2. 0-486-41129-X

NEW RUSSIAN-ENGLISH AND ENGLISH-RUSSIAN DICTIONARY, M. A. O'Brien. This is a remarkably handy Russian dictionary, containing a surprising amount of information, including over 70,000 entries. 366pp. 4 1/2 x 6 1/8. 0-486-20208-9

NEW YORK IN THE FORTIES, Andreas Feininger. 162 brilliant photographs by the well-known photographer, formerly with *Life* magazine. Commuters, shoppers, Times Square at night, much else from city at its peak. Captions by John von Hartz. 181pp. 9 1/4 x 10 3/4. 0-486-23585-8

INDIAN SIGN LANGUAGE, William Tomkins. Over 525 signs developed by Sioux and other tribes. Written instructions and diagrams. Also 290 pictographs. 111pp. 6 1/8 x 9 1/4. 0-486-22029-X

ANATOMY: A Complete Guide for Artists, Joseph Sheppard. A master of figure drawing shows artists how to render human anatomy convincingly. Over 460 illustrations. 224pp. 8 3/8 x 11 1/4. 0-486-27279-6

MEDIEVAL CALLIGRAPHY: Its History and Technique, Marc Drogin. Spirited history, comprehensive instruction manual covers 13 styles (ca. 4th century through 15th). Excellent photographs; directions for duplicating medieval techniques with modern tools. 224pp. 8 3/8 x 11 1/4. 0-486-26142-5

DRIED FLOWERS: How to Prepare Them, Sarah Whitlock and Martha Rankin. Complete instructions on how to use silica gel, meal and borax, perlite aggregate, sand and borax, glycerine and water to create attractive permanent flower arrangements. 12 illustrations. 32pp. 5⅜ x 8½. 0-486-21802-3

EASY-TO-MAKE BIRD FEEDERS FOR WOODWORKERS, Scott D. Campbell. Detailed, simple-to-use guide for designing, constructing, caring for and using feeders. Text, illustrations for 12 classic and contemporary designs. 96pp. 5⅜ x 8½. 0-486-25847-5

THE COMPLETE BOOK OF BIRDHOUSE CONSTRUCTION FOR WOODWORKERS, Scott D. Campbell. Detailed instructions, illustrations, tables. Also data on bird habitat and instinct patterns. Bibliography. 3 tables. 63 illustrations in 15 figures. 48pp. 5¼ x 8½. 0-486-24407-5

SCOTTISH WONDER TALES FROM MYTH AND LEGEND, Donald A. Mackenzie. 16 lively tales tell of giants rumbling down mountainsides, of a magic wand that turns stone pillars into warriors, of gods and goddesses, evil hags, powerful forces and more. 240pp. 5⅜ x 8½. 0-486-29677-6

THE HISTORY OF UNDERCLOTHES, C. Willett Cunnington and Phyllis Cunnington. Fascinating, well-documented survey covering six centuries of English undergarments, enhanced with over 100 illustrations: 12th-century laced-up bodice, footed long drawers (1795), 19th-century bustles, 19th-century corsets for men, Victorian "bust improvers," much more. 272pp. 5⅝ x 8¼. 0-486-27124-2

ARTS AND CRAFTS FURNITURE: The Complete Brooks Catalog of 1912, Brooks Manufacturing Co. Photos and detailed descriptions of more than 150 now very collectible furniture designs from the Arts and Crafts movement depict davenports, settees, buffets, desks, tables, chairs, bedsteads, dressers and more, all built of solid, quarter-sawed oak. Invaluable for students and enthusiasts of antiques, Americana and the decorative arts. 80pp. 6½ x 9¼. 0-486-27471-3

WILBUR AND ORVILLE: A Biography of the Wright Brothers, Fred Howard. Definitive, crisply written study tells the full story of the brothers' lives and work. A vividly written biography, unparalleled in scope and color, that also captures the spirit of an extraordinary era. 560pp. 6⅛ x 9¼. 0-486-40297-5

THE ARTS OF THE SAILOR: Knotting, Splicing and Ropework, Hervey Garrett Smith. Indispensable shipboard reference covers tools, basic knots and useful hitches; handsewing and canvas work, more. Over 100 illustrations. Delightful reading for sea lovers. 256pp. 5⅜ x 8½. 0-486-26440-8

FRANK LLOYD WRIGHT'S FALLINGWATER: The House and Its History, Second, Revised Edition, Donald Hoffmann. A total revision–both in text and illustrations–of the standard document on Fallingwater, the boldest, most personal architectural statement of Wright's mature years, updated with valuable new material from the recently opened Frank Lloyd Wright Archives. "Fascinating"–*The New York Times.* 116 illustrations. 128pp. 9¼ x 10¾. 0-486-27430-6

PHOTOGRAPHIC SKETCHBOOK OF THE CIVIL WAR, Alexander Gardner. 100 photos taken on field during the Civil War. Famous shots of Manassas Harper's Ferry, Lincoln, Richmond, slave pens, etc. 244pp. 10⅝ x 8¼. 0-486-22731-6

FIVE ACRES AND INDEPENDENCE, Maurice G. Kains. Great back-to-the-land classic explains basics of self-sufficient farming. The one book to get. 95 illustrations. 397pp. 5⅜ x 8½. 0-486-20974-1

CATALOG OF DOVER BOOKS

A MODERN HERBAL, Margaret Grieve. Much the fullest, most exact, most useful compilation of herbal material. Gigantic alphabetical encyclopedia, from aconite to zedoary, gives botanical information, medical properties, folklore, economic uses, much else. Indispensable to serious reader. 161 illustrations. 888pp. 6½ x 9¼. 2-vol. set. (Available in U.S. only.) Vol. I: 0-486-22798-7 Vol. II: 0-486-22799-5

HIDDEN TREASURE MAZE BOOK, Dave Phillips. Solve 34 challenging mazes accompanied by heroic tales of adventure. Evil dragons, people-eating plants, blood-thirsty giants, many more dangerous adversaries lurk at every twist and turn. 34 mazes, stories, solutions. 48pp. 8¼ x 11. 0-486-24566-7

LETTERS OF W. A. MOZART, Wolfgang A. Mozart. Remarkable letters show bawdy wit, humor, imagination, musical insights, contemporary musical world; includes some letters from Leopold Mozart. 276pp. 5⅜ x 8½. 0-486-22859-2

BASIC PRINCIPLES OF CLASSICAL BALLET, Agrippina Vaganova. Great Russian theoretician, teacher explains methods for teaching classical ballet. 118 illustrations. 175pp. 5⅜ x 8½. 0-486-22036-2

THE JUMPING FROG, Mark Twain. Revenge edition. The original story of The Celebrated Jumping Frog of Calaveras County, a hapless French translation, and Twain's hilarious "retranslation" from the French. 12 illustrations. 66pp. 5⅜ x 8½. 0-486-22686-7

BEST REMEMBERED POEMS, Martin Gardner (ed.). The 126 poems in this superb collection of 19th- and 20th-century British and American verse range from Shelley's "To a Skylark" to the impassioned "Renascence" of Edna St. Vincent Millay and to Edward Lear's whimsical "The Owl and the Pussycat." 224pp. 5⅜ x 8½. 0-486-27165-X

COMPLETE SONNETS, William Shakespeare. Over 150 exquisite poems deal with love, friendship, the tyranny of time, beauty's evanescence, death and other themes in language of remarkable power, precision and beauty. Glossary of archaic terms. 80pp. 5 3/16 x 8¼. 0-486-26686-9

HISTORIC HOMES OF THE AMERICAN PRESIDENTS, Second, Revised Edition, Irvin Haas. A traveler's guide to American Presidential homes, most open to the public, depicting and describing homes occupied by every American President from George Washington to George Bush. With visiting hours, admission charges, travel routes. 175 photographs. Index. 160pp. 8¼ x 11. 0-486-26751-2

THE WIT AND HUMOR OF OSCAR WILDE, Alvin Redman (ed.). More than 1,000 ripostes, paradoxes, wisecracks: Work is the curse of the drinking classes; I can resist everything except temptation; etc. 258pp. 5⅜ x 8½. 0-486-20602-5

SHAKESPEARE LEXICON AND QUOTATION DICTIONARY, Alexander Schmidt. Full definitions, locations, shades of meaning in every word in plays and poems. More than 50,000 exact quotations. 1,485pp. 6½ x 9¼. 2-vol. set. Vol. 1: 0-486-22726-X Vol. 2: 0-486-22727-8

SELECTED POEMS, Emily Dickinson. Over 100 best-known, best-loved poems by one of America's foremost poets, reprinted from authoritative early editions. No comparable edition at this price. Index of first lines. 64pp. 5 3/16 x 8¼. 0-486-26466-1

THE INSIDIOUS DR. FU-MANCHU, Sax Rohmer. The first of the popular mystery series introduces a pair of English detectives to their archnemesis, the diabolical Dr. Fu-Manchu. Flavorful atmosphere, fast-paced action, and colorful characters enliven this classic of the genre. 208pp. 5 3/16 x 8¼. 0-486-29898-1

THE MALLEUS MALEFICARUM OF KRAMER AND SPRENGER, translated by Montague Summers. Full text of most important witchhunter's "bible," used by both Catholics and Protestants. 278pp. 6⅝ x 10. 0-486-22802-9

SPANISH STORIES/CUENTOS ESPAÑOLES: A Dual-Language Book, Angel Flores (ed.). Unique format offers 13 great stories in Spanish by Cervantes, Borges, others. Faithful English translations on facing pages. 352pp. 5⅜ x 8½. 0-486-25399-6

GARDEN CITY, LONG ISLAND, IN EARLY PHOTOGRAPHS, 1869–1919, Mildred H. Smith. Handsome treasury of 118 vintage pictures, accompanied by carefully researched captions, document the Garden City Hotel fire (1899), the Vanderbilt Cup Race (1908), the first airmail flight departing from the Nassau Boulevard Aerodrome (1911), and much more. 96pp. 8⅞ x 11¾. 0-486-40669-5

OLD QUEENS, N.Y., IN EARLY PHOTOGRAPHS, Vincent F. Seyfried and William Asadorian. Over 160 rare photographs of Maspeth, Jamaica, Jackson Heights, and other areas. Vintage views of DeWitt Clinton mansion, 1939 World's Fair and more. Captions. 192pp. 8⅞ x 11. 0-486-26358-4

CAPTURED BY THE INDIANS: 15 Firsthand Accounts, 1750-1870, Frederick Drimmer. Astounding true historical accounts of grisly torture, bloody conflicts, relentless pursuits, miraculous escapes and more, by people who lived to tell the tale. 384pp. 5⅜ x 8½. 0-486-24901-8

THE WORLD'S GREAT SPEECHES (Fourth Enlarged Edition), Lewis Copeland, Lawrence W. Lamm, and Stephen J. McKenna. Nearly 300 speeches provide public speakers with a wealth of updated quotes and inspiration–from Pericles' funeral oration and William Jennings Bryan's "Cross of Gold Speech" to Malcolm X's powerful words on the Black Revolution and Earl of Spenser's tribute to his sister, Diana, Princess of Wales. 944pp. 5⅜ x 8⅜. 0-486-40903-1

THE BOOK OF THE SWORD, Sir Richard F. Burton. Great Victorian scholar/adventurer's eloquent, erudite history of the "queen of weapons"–from prehistory to early Roman Empire. Evolution and development of early swords, variations (sabre, broadsword, cutlass, scimitar, etc.), much more. 336pp. 6⅛ x 9¼. 0-486-25434-8

AUTOBIOGRAPHY: The Story of My Experiments with Truth, Mohandas K. Gandhi. Boyhood, legal studies, purification, the growth of the Satyagraha (nonviolent protest) movement. Critical, inspiring work of the man responsible for the freedom of India. 480pp. 5⅜ x 8½. (Available in U.S. only.) 0-486-24593-4

CELTIC MYTHS AND LEGENDS, T. W. Rolleston. Masterful retelling of Irish and Welsh stories and tales. Cuchulain, King Arthur, Deirdre, the Grail, many more. First paperback edition. 58 full-page illustrations. 512pp. 5⅜ x 8½. 0-486-26507-2

THE PRINCIPLES OF PSYCHOLOGY, William James. Famous long course complete, unabridged. Stream of thought, time perception, memory, experimental methods; great work decades ahead of its time. 94 figures. 1,391pp. 5⅜ x 8½. 2-vol. set. Vol. I: 0-486-20381-6 Vol. II: 0-486-20382-4

THE WORLD AS WILL AND REPRESENTATION, Arthur Schopenhauer. Definitive English translation of Schopenhauer's life work, correcting more than 1,000 errors, omissions in earlier translations. Translated by E. F. J. Payne. Total of 1,269pp. 5⅜ x 8½. 2-vol. set. Vol. 1: 0-486-21761-2 Vol. 2: 0-486-21762-0

MAGIC AND MYSTERY IN TIBET, Madame Alexandra David-Neel. Experiences among lamas, magicians, sages, sorcerers, Bonpa wizards. A true psychic discovery. 32 illustrations. 321pp. 5⅜ x 8½. (Available in U.S. only.) 0-486-22682-4

THE EGYPTIAN BOOK OF THE DEAD, E. A. Wallis Budge. Complete reproduction of Ani's papyrus, finest ever found. Full hieroglyphic text, interlinear transliteration, word-for-word translation, smooth translation. 533pp. 6½ x 9¼. 0-486-21866-X

HISTORIC COSTUME IN PICTURES, Braun & Schneider. Over 1,450 costumed figures in clearly detailed engravings–from dawn of civilization to end of 19th century. Captions. Many folk costumes. 256pp. 8⅜ x 11¾. 0-486-23150-X

MATHEMATICS FOR THE NONMATHEMATICIAN, Morris Kline. Detailed, college-level treatment of mathematics in cultural and historical context, with numerous exercises. Recommended Reading Lists. Tables. Numerous figures. 641pp. 5⅜ x 8½. 0-486-24823-2

PROBABILISTIC METHODS IN THE THEORY OF STRUCTURES, Isaac Elishakoff. Well-written introduction covers the elements of the theory of probability from two or more random variables, the reliability of such multivariable structures, the theory of random function, Monte Carlo methods of treating problems incapable of exact solution, and more. Examples. 502pp. 5⅜ x 8½. 0-486-40691-1

THE RIME OF THE ANCIENT MARINER, Gustave Doré, S. T. Coleridge. Doré's finest work; 34 plates capture moods, subtleties of poem. Flawless full-size reproductions printed on facing pages with authoritative text of poem. "Beautiful. Simply beautiful."–*Publisher's Weekly*. 77pp. 9¼ x 12. 0-486-22305-1

SCULPTURE: Principles and Practice, Louis Slobodkin. Step-by-step approach to clay, plaster, metals, stone; classical and modern. 253 drawings, photos. 255pp. 8⅛ x 11. 0-486-22960-2

THE INFLUENCE OF SEA POWER UPON HISTORY, 1660–1783, A. T. Mahan. Influential classic of naval history and tactics still used as text in war colleges. First paperback edition. 4 maps. 24 battle plans. 640pp. 5⅜ x 8½. 0-486-25509-3

THE STORY OF THE TITANIC AS TOLD BY ITS SURVIVORS, Jack Winocour (ed.). What it was really like. Panic, despair, shocking inefficiency, and a little heroism. More thrilling than any fictional account. 26 illustrations. 320pp. 5⅜ x 8½. 0-486-20610-6

ONE TWO THREE . . . INFINITY: Facts and Speculations of Science, George Gamow. Great physicist's fascinating, readable overview of contemporary science: number theory, relativity, fourth dimension, entropy, genes, atomic structure, much more. 128 illustrations. Index. 352pp. 5⅜ x 8½. 0-486-25664-2

DALÍ ON MODERN ART: The Cuckolds of Antiquated Modern Art, Salvador Dalí. Influential painter skewers modern art and its practitioners. Outrageous evaluations of Picasso, Cézanne, Turner, more. 15 renderings of paintings discussed. 44 calligraphic decorations by Dalí. 96pp. 5⅜ x 8½. (Available in U.S. only.) 0-486-29220-7

ANTIQUE PLAYING CARDS: A Pictorial History, Henry René D'Allemagne. Over 900 elaborate, decorative images from rare playing cards (14th–20th centuries): Bacchus, death, dancing dogs, hunting scenes, royal coats of arms, players cheating, much more. 96pp. 9¼ x 12¼. 0-486-29265-7

CATALOG OF DOVER BOOKS

LIGHT AND SHADE: A Classic Approach to Three-Dimensional Drawing, Mrs. Mary P. Merrifield. Handy reference clearly demonstrates principles of light and shade by revealing effects of common daylight, sunshine, and candle or artificial light on geometrical solids. 13 plates. 64pp. 5⅜ x 8½. 0-486-44143-1

ASTROLOGY AND ASTRONOMY: A Pictorial Archive of Signs and Symbols, Ernst and Johanna Lehner. Treasure trove of stories, lore, and myth, accompanied by more than 300 rare illustrations of planets, the Milky Way, signs of the zodiac, comets, meteors, and other astronomical phenomena. 192pp. 8⅜ x 11. 0-486-43981-X

JEWELRY MAKING: Techniques for Metal, Tim McCreight. Easy-to-follow instructions and carefully executed illustrations describe tools and techniques, use of gems and enamels, wire inlay, casting, and other topics. 72 line illustrations and diagrams. 176pp. 8¼ x 10⅞. 0-486-44043-5

MAKING BIRDHOUSES: Easy and Advanced Projects, Gladstone Califf. Easy-to-follow instructions include diagrams for everything from a one-room house for bluebirds to a forty-two-room structure for purple martins. 56 plates; 4 figures. 80pp. 8¾ x 6⅜. 0-486-44183-0

LITTLE BOOK OF LOG CABINS: How to Build and Furnish Them, William S. Wicks. Handy how-to manual, with instructions and illustrations for building cabins in the Adirondack style, fireplaces, stairways, furniture, beamed ceilings, and more. 102 line drawings. 96pp. 8¾ x 6⅜. 0-486-44259-4

THE SEASONS OF AMERICA PAST, Eric Sloane. From "sugaring time" and strawberry picking to Indian summer and fall harvest, a whole year's activities described in charming prose and enhanced with 79 of the author's own illustrations. 160pp. 8¼ x 11. 0-486-44220-9

THE METROPOLIS OF TOMORROW, Hugh Ferriss. Generous, prophetic vision of the metropolis of the future, as perceived in 1929. Powerful illustrations of towering structures, wide avenues, and rooftop parks–all features in many of today's modern cities. 59 illustrations. 144pp. 8¼ x 11. 0-486-43727-2

THE PATH TO ROME, Hilaire Belloc. This 1902 memoir abounds in lively vignettes from a vanished time, recounting a pilgrimage on foot across the Alps and Apennines in order to "see all Europe which the Christian Faith has saved." 77 of the author's original line drawings complement his sparkling prose. 272pp. 5⅜ x 8½. 0-486-44001-X

THE HISTORY OF RASSELAS: Prince of Abissinia, Samuel Johnson. Distinguished English writer attacks eighteenth-century optimism and man's unrealistic estimates of what life has to offer. 112pp. 5⅜ x 8½. 0-486-44094-X

A VOYAGE TO ARCTURUS, David Lindsay. A brilliant flight of pure fancy, where wild creatures crowd the fantastic landscape and demented torturers dominate victims with their bizarre mental powers. 272pp. 5⅜ x 8½. 0-486-44198-9

Paperbound unless otherwise indicated. Available at your book dealer, online at **www.doverpublications.com**, or by writing to Dept. GI, Dover Publications, Inc., 31 East 2nd Street, Mineola, NY 11501. For current price information or for free catalogs (please indicate field of interest), write to Dover Publications or log on to **www.doverpublications.com** and see every Dover book in print. Dover publishes more than 500 books each year on science, elementary and advanced mathematics, biology, music, art, literary history, social sciences, and other areas.